Sales Force Management

The Irwin/McGraw-Hill Series in Marketing

Sales Force Management

Sixth Edition

Gilbert A. Churchill, Jr.
Graduate School of Business, University of Wisconsin

Neil M. Ford
Graduate School of Business, University of Wisconsin

Orville C. Walker, Jr.
College of Business Administration, University of Minnesota

Mark W. Johnston
Crummer Graduate School of Business, Rollins College

John F. Tanner, Jr.
Hankamer School of Business, Baylor University

Boston   Burr Ridge, IL   Dubuque, IA   Madison, WI   New York   San Francisco   St. Louis
Bangkok   Bogotá   Caracas   Lisbon   London   Madrid
Mexico City   Milan   New Delhi   Seoul   Singapore   Sydney   Taipei   Toronto

McGraw-Hill Higher Education

A Division of The **McGraw-Hill** Companies

SALES FORCE MANAGEMENT

This book is printed on acid-free paper.

2 3 4 5 6 7 8 9 0 KGP/KGP 9 0 9 8 7 6 5 4 3 2 1 0

ISBN 0-07-027555-6

Vice President/Editor-in-chief: *Michael W. Junior*
Publisher: *David Kendric Brake*
Sponsoring editor: *Rick Adams*
Senior developmental editor: *Nancy Barbour*
Senior marketing manager: *Colleen J. Suljic*
Project manager: *Jim Labeots*
Production supervisor: *Michael R. McCormick*
Designer: *Jennifer McQueen Hollingsworth*
Cover illustration: *© Rob Colvin/SIS*
Photo research coordinator: *Sharon Miller*
Supplement coordinator: *Matt Perry*
Compositor: *ElectraGraphics, Inc.*
Typeface: *10/12 Times Roman*
Printer: *Quebecor Printing Book Group/Kingsport*

Library of Congress Cataloging-in-Publication Data

Sales force management / Gilbert A. Churchill . . . [et al.]. —6th ed.
    p.   cm.
   Includes index.
   ISBN 0-07-027555-6
   1. Sales management.   I. Churchill, Gilbert A.
 HF5438.4.S2267   2000
 658.8′101—dc21   99–15440

www.mhhe.com

Preface

Whoever said that "all good things must come to an end" was wrong. Sometimes, good things get even better. That is the way we feel about the sixth edition of this textbook.

Almost twenty years after the first edition was published the three original authors are focusing more of their efforts on other endeavors: academic administration and the pleasures of semiretirement, among others. But far from coming to an end, the book has gotten better, primarily due to the addition of two dynamic and talented co-authors—Mark Johnston and Jeff Tanner. While the sixth edition retains the organizational structure and the conceptual and empirical rigor that distinguished the earlier editions, our new colleagues have brought fresh ideas and energy to the project. Some topics have been condensed, others more fully integrated, and many others enhanced with the addition of new material reflecting the recent impact of new technology, globalization, and burgeoning customer relationships and alliances on the sales force and its management. The result is an intellectually rigorous but more concise, timely, and reader friendly book.

WHY WE WROTE THIS BOOK

For the first 70 years of this century, the practice of sales management resembled the practice of medicine by tribal witch doctors. Sales managers had to rely on large doses of folklore, tradition, intuition, and personal experience in deciding how to motivate and direct the performance of their sales forces. Few firms did any research to better understand the motives and behaviors of their own salespeople. And sales managers got little information or guidance from marketing academicians. There was scant published theory and even less empirical research concerning the variables that influence one salesperson to perform better than another.

Fortunately, the situation began to change about 30 years ago. Since the early 1970s, an increasing volume of relatively sophisticated and informative research has focused on understanding why salespeople behave as they do and identifying factors critical to their performance. Today, many issues of the academic marketing journals contain at least one article of direct relevance to sales management; and one such journal is entirely dedicated to theory and research in sales management and personal selling. The sales manager who is familiar with this growing body of research has an advantage in planning and directing the sales force's behavior toward desired ends and in evaluating the results produced.

Although the body of theory and research relevant for improving sales management practice grew dramatically throughout the 1970s, students of sales management had no single source to turn to for a detailed summary and analysis of that research and its implications. The textbooks of the time either failed to keep pace with the advancing knowledge or dealt with the emerging find- ings in a piecemeal fashion. Thus, our primary purpose in writing the first edition of this text in 1981 was to offer students a thorough, up-to-date, and integrated overview of the accumulated theory and research evidence relevant to sales management.

We realized, though, that simply providing a compendium of theories and research findings would not only be deadly dull, but it would also do little to help students understand how a sales manager might perform his or her job most effectively. A second purpose for writing this book, then, was to emphasize the link between the determinants of sales performance on the one hand and the actions that sales managers can take to direct, influence, and control that performance on the other. We wanted to showcase the most recent practices and techniques employed by managers in the "real world."

THE STRUCTURE OF THIS BOOK

We developed a framework that views the spectrum of sales managers' activities as focusing on three interrelated, sequential processes, each of which influences the various determinants of salesperson performance:

1. **The formulation of a strategic sales program.** This involves organizing and planning the company's overall personal selling efforts and integrating these efforts with the other elements of the firm's marketing strategy.

2. **The implementation of the sales program.** This includes selecting appropriate sales personnel and designing and implementing policies and procedures that will direct their efforts toward the desired objectives.

3. **The evaluation and control of sales force performance.** This involves developing procedures for monitoring and evaluating sales force performance so adjustments can be made to either the sales program or its implementation when performance is unsatisfactory.

The structure of this book reflects this framework. The first chapter introduces the subject with an overview of the duties and responsibilities of sales managers and how their activities relate to these three processes. Chapter 1 also discusses the attractiveness of sales careers and some of the factors that will impact the management of sales forces in the twenty-first century.

The rest of the book is divided into three sections corresponding to the three processes described above:

- **Part I—Chapters 2 through 7**—looks at the major decisions involved in designing a strategic sales program. This section examines the fit between the external environment, the firm's marketing strategy, and its strategic sales program. It also deals with the formulation of account management policies, ways of organizing the sales force, and methods for estimating demand, setting quotas, and designing sales territories.

- **Part II—Chapters 8 through 13**—addresses issues involved in implementing the sales program. An overview of the determinants of sales performance is presented and the salesperson's role perceptions and motivations are discussed. Part II then examines decisions involving the recruitment and selection of sales personnel, sales training, and the design of compensation and incentive programs.

- **Part III—Chapters 14 through 16**—discusses techniques for monitoring and controlling sales force behavior and performance. It examines various approaches for conducting a sales analysis, cost analysis, and behavioral analysis.

INTENDED AUDIENCE FOR THIS BOOK

This book is designed for use in an introductory course in sales management at either the advanced undergraduate or graduate level. It is also designed to complement a variety of teaching approaches. Instructors who primarily emphasize the lecture-discussion approach will find ample material for either a one-quarter or a one-semester course in the chapters and end-of-chapter discussion questions. For those who prefer case-oriented instruction, we have included 32 cases. These cases can be found at the end of the three sections since they primarily emphasize issues discussed in a particular section. However, the last five cases in Part III are more encompassing. They contain a variety of marketing and sales management issues.

FEATURES OF THE SIXTH EDITION

Those who have used the earlier editions of this text should find the sixth edition quite familiar. We have adhered to the admonition "if it ain't broke, don't fix it." But while we have preserved the basic organization and other features of the book that have proved popular and useful in the past, we have also made many changes and additions to incorporate recent advances in sales management research and practice and to make it an even more effective aid to learning.

First, all chapters have been subjected to thorough scrutiny and rewrite. There has been a major updating of examples, and the discussion in some chapters has been expanded and in others it has been streamlined, always with the intention of making it as clear as possible. Specifically, Chapter 6 combines and integrates material on the related topics of demand estimation and quota setting that was scattered over two chapters in the previous edition. Similarly, Chapter 8 integrates material on salespersons' behavior, role perceptions, and satisfaction that had been contained in two separate chapters in the fifth edition. The end result of the various modifications is a text that has fewer chapters, 16 instead of 18, and that still maintains continuity across all chapters.

Opening Profile

Each chapter begins with an opening profile of a company and its sales management strategy. Each profile was carefully developed for this book in order to illustrate the practice of sales management relative to the material of that particular chapter. All profiles are original to this edition, and some include personal interviews and material that cannot be found anywhere else. Students enjoy these profiles as a foreshadowing of what is to come; professors can find these useful as running examples for lectures and class exercises.

Learning Objectives

Each chapter also now has learning objectives at the beginning, just after the opening profile. These objectives are written using active language so that students understand what is expected of them when the chapter is completed. Professors can use these to guide class discussions and when developing tests so that students can get the most out of their reading.

Ethical Issues, Managing Sales Relationships, and The Global Sales Force

There are other features that have been added to improve the book. Three new boxes appear throughout the text: Ethical Issues, Managing Sales Relationships, and The Global Sales Force. Like the opening profiles, each of these features is designed to illustrate material presented in the chapter, but in regard to a particular context. Professors who integrate these features into lectures and class exercises will find students more able to apply the concepts of the chapter and more involved in the class.

Using the Web

As you'll notice, each opening profile concludes with the appropriate web address where students can go for more information about the company or companies profiled. Further, each chapter also has an **Internet Exercise,** many of which take advantage of the opening profile material. Faculty may find these exercises are most useful as mini-cases for class discussion or as launch pads for student research into the companies and topics. Our feedback from students is that they enjoy incorporating the Web into their work, so these exercises are a way of bringing focus to activities that students enjoy.

For faculty, there is also a Web site (*http://www.mhhe.com/business/marketing/salesmgmt*) built around the book. Here you can communicate with other users and the authors, share teaching ideas and resources, and stay current with the art of teaching the science of sales management.

Experiential Exercises

Each chapter also has an experiential exercise that directs students to conduct active learning activities on their own. Some of the best ideas for these exercises come from users of the text, so please keep us informed as to what you have your students doing.

Discussion Questions

Each chapter also ends with discussion questions. These are either application questions with some limited data or thought-provoking questions that require students to reflect on the material they have just read. As such, these questions make for great discussion starters in class, as well as reviews for exams.

Cases

Finally, there has also been a major revision of the cases. Almost one-fifth of the cases are new. Of the new cases, one introduces students to the subject of activity-based analysis of selling and administrative expenses. Two cases require students to evaluate the effectiveness of key account management programs. Further, several of the earlier cases have been revised and updated. Nine of the cases are now available on computer disc. The computerized cases have been reworked so students can perform more sophisticated analyses using Excel.

Video

The video offerings with this edition have been expanded greatly. We've searched carefully among our business contacts for video that could support the book, and believe we've put together one of the best video packages available for a sales management book. Several new segments, such as the "Day in the Life of a 3M Salesperson," are truly outstanding and worthy of academic Oscars!

PowerPoint Slides

Many faculty prefer using PowerPoint to support their in-class activities. With this edition, you can use PowerPoint to print or display the transparencies.

ACKNOWLEDGMENTS

A book like this is never the work of a small group of authors; rather, there are many people and institutions whose contributions need to be acknowledged. We wish to thank the many scholars and sales managers who have labored so diligently over the last 30 years to move the study of sales management out of the dark ages and into the mainstream of marketing thought. We would also like to acknowledge the special contributions of the Marketing Science Institute, which supported much of the research that underlies our expanding knowledge of effective sales management practices. That support helped produce the critical mass of effort necessary to move the study of the topic forward.

Jerome A. Colletti, president of the Alexander Group and co-author of **Compensating New Sales Roles: How to Design Rewards That Work in Today's Selling Environment,** has contributed to this book in many ways. We particularly thank him for permitting us to use materials from his firm's seminars and publications on sales compensation and incentive programs.

Janet Christopher typed the major part of the **Instructor's Manual,** and her willingness to operate under tight deadlines and the quality of her output are sincerely appreciated. Finally, we wish to thank our families, and each of their many members, for their encouragement and support while this book was being written. It is with love we dedicate it to them.

Gilbert A. Churchill, Jr.
Neil M. Ford
Orville C. Walker, Jr.
Mark W. Johnston
John F. Tanner, Jr.

Brief Contents

Contents

Chapter ✗4 2/3
Organizing the Sales Force   **94**

Chapter ✗5
Demand Estimation and Sales Quotas   **129**

Chapter 5
Sales Territories **172**

Part II   Implementation of the Sales Program   277

Chapter ~~8~~ 6
Salesperson Performance: Behavior, Role Perceptions, and Satisfaction   **278**

Chapter 13

Designing Compensation and Incentive Programs   **410**

Part III   Evaluation and Control of the Sales Program   **509**

Sales Force Management

I An Overview of Sales Management

GE CAPITAL SERVICES: FIND MORE, WIN MORE, KEEP MORE

GE Capital Services (or GEC) has grown revenues at an amazing rate of over 16 percent over the last few years to about $33 billion, almost 40 percent of GE's total revenue. You may know GE for its dishwashers and light bulbs, but GEC is one of the fastest-growing parts of GE, representing 28 different businesses involved in leasing railroad cars, airplanes, manufacturing equipment, and other forms of equipment as well as providing other commercial and consumer financial services. Led by the dynamic Gary Wendt, the company developed an analytic approach to the business that culminated in the Find More, Win More, Keep More (FWK) strategy.

Find More means finding new segments to serve and new customers in existing segments. GE Railcar, a division of GEC that leases railroad cars, has increased its sales staff by over 40 percent in order to increase the company's penetration in key transportation markets. In order to Win More, the company needed experts in both finance and the specific markets, such as grain transportation and chemical transportation. New reps had to demonstrate knowledge of a particular segment, experience in transportation, and strong financial skills. And to Keep More, the company added account managers to grow revenue with larger accounts.

Achieving such impressive sales targets has meant paying attention to detail and doing business the way the customer wants. GE Railcar had salespeople involved in the writing of new standard contracts, for example, writing the contracts so that customers could understand them without having to send them to the legal department. This simple change meant faster decisions could be made, so it was possible to meet customers' delivery needs.

Training was another important component of the FWK program. By the end of 1998, every GEC salesperson will have completed formal FWK training, including segments that salespeople access over the Internet or via CD-ROMs. The training program is so impressive that Jack Welch, CEO of GE, has encouraged other divisions to adopt similar programs, citing the GE Capital program as a best practice.

FWK is not just a U.S.-based program, however. GEC has instituted this strategy with its 14,000 salespeople worldwide. To handle the growth that success brings, GEC plans to increase that number to 20,000 by the year 2000. As Jack Wendt says, "There's only one way to succeed in business, and that is to sell."

Visit GE Capital at its Web site: *www.gecapital.*

Source: Geoffrey Brewer, "Selling an Intangible," *Sales & Marketing Management* (January 1998), pp. 52–58; Erika Rasmussen, "GE Capital," *Sales & Marketing Management* (July 1998), pp. 34–37; "New Sales Contract Cuts the Legalese," *What's New, www.gerailcar.com* (September 30, 1997); "New Account Managers Increase Sales Coverage," *What's New, www.gerailcar.com* (September 30, 1997).

LEARNING OBJECTIVES

Sales management is one of the most important elements in many companies' success. Not only is sales the most expensive component of the marketing mix for most companies, it is the firm's most direct link to the customer. While Thoreau may have believed that the world will beat a path to the door of the company with the best mousetrap, the world needs someone to show how that mousetrap is better—and that role usually belongs to the salesperson. Otherwise, that sale may never occur. Therefore, the management of the sales force is one of the most important executive responsibilities.

After reading this chapter, you should be able to:

• Present a general overview of the sales management process.

• Discuss the components of a strategic sales program.

• Give an overview of the implementation process of a strategic sales program.

• Understand the basic elements of evaluation and control.

• Discuss the key trends that will affect sales management into the 21st century.

SALES IN THE MARKET-ORIENTED FIRM

If asked to describe marketing, many people may list activities that describe only selling. And even though some companies call salespeople *marketing representatives*, selling and marketing are not synonymous. As students of marketing know, marketing involves creating products and services that satisfy customer needs, pricing those products and services to meet the customer's budget and make a profit for the firm, placing those products and services so that the customer can access them, and promoting the products and services so that the customer is aware of where they are and what they do. To some degree, the trend toward calling salespeople marketing representatives is an accurate portrayal because some salespeople identify customer needs, tailor products and services to meet those needs, negotiate price, and so forth. But personal selling is defined as the interpersonal communication process of identifying and satisfying customer needs to the long-term benefit of both parties.[1] As you can see, personal selling is a part of marketing.

The marketing concept states that the key to business success is to identify and satisfy customer needs. Companies that have adopted the marketing concept as a philosophy or way of doing business are considered *market-oriented companies.* In a market-oriented company, salespeople play a very important role because they not only identify customer needs and satisfy those needs through the sale of a product or service, they must also represent the customer to various areas within the company. Companies that can adapt quickly to meet changing customer requirements will be successful—it is the responsibility of the sales force to see that those changing requirements are communicated to the right people so that the company can change.

So selling is important, not only because of the company's immediate need to generate revenue through the sale of products and services, nor only because sales is the largest marketing expense, but also because the future of the company depends on salespeople who can, as GE Capital puts it, find more, win more, and keep more through carrying the voice of the customer throughout the firm. Managing the selling function is one of the most important management functions in any firm, not just because selling is so important, but also because managing selling is unique. Were it not unique, a separate course would not be necessary. But as the rest of this chapter illustrates, there are many decisions unique to selling that must be made by sales executives.

WHAT IS INVOLVED IN SALES MANAGEMENT

The GE Capital example illustrates several key points about sales and sales management. First, companies today realize that sales is an indispensable component of an effective marketing strategy. Top management acknowledges the critical role of personal selling in building customer relationships and customers have come to rely on the problem-solving capabilities of a well-trained sales force. As a result, sales management has become an exciting and challenging career opportunity.

Second, managing a sales force is a dynamic process. Sales management programs must be formulated to respond effectively to a firm's environmental circumstances, and they must be consistent with the organization's marketing strategies. At the same time, however, good sales management policies and practices are essential for the successful implementation of a firm's competitive and marketing strategies. To help understand the scope of the sales management task we can define sales management as all activities, processes, and decisions involved in managing the sales function in an organization. Based on this definition, it is easy to understand how GE Capital's focus on selling, as demonstrated in the FWK program, would not have been as successful without the adoption of appropriate policies concerning the organization, recruiting, training, compensation, and control of the sales force.

GE Capital's approach to marketing and, more specifically, to selling illustrates the benefits of effective sales force management. However, managing a sales force well involves understanding the complexity of selling activities as well as the decisions involved in managing those activities. The purpose of this book is to provide you with an understanding of the sales function in marketing and the entire organization. In addition, the book examines the activities and decisions that make up an effective sales management program.

The Selling Process

Many people have misconceptions about the selling process, the activities carried out by salespeople, and the personal characteristics necessary for a successful sales career. To complicate matters even more, various selling jobs can involve very different tasks and require different skills and abilities. Consider GE Capital's 28 different divisions, each with its own sales force and its own markets. Selling skills and requirements can vary greatly among the different businesses due to the different buying processes and needs in the various markets. Even so, opportunities for selling multiple services across divisions to the same buyers have been growing, causing GEC salespeople to develop superior teams of salespeople and other GEC personnel to develop greater knowledge of each customer's market and competitive situation as well as to enhance their technical marketing skills necessary to collect and interpret large amounts of data related to the various industries in which they sell.

To reduce misconceptions about personal selling, and to establish a solid foundation of knowledge for our subsequent discussion of sales force management, Chapter 2 examines sales relationships in more detail. It begins with a discussion of relationship marketing, a new strategic focus that emphasizes building and managing relationships with vital customers. This strategic focus is called relationship selling and directs the sales force to build long-term strategic relationships with key customers in order to facilitate and influence purchase decisions. Successfully building strategic relationships involves understanding how organizational buyers make purchase decisions. The chapter then explores the variety of activities, tasks, and decisions involved in different types of selling jobs and situations, including career issues and opportunities.

Sales Management Processes

The effective management of a company's sales force involves three interrelated sets of decisions or processes.

1. *The formulation of a strategic sales program.* The strategic sales program should consider the environmental factors faced by the firm. Sales executives organize and plan the company's overall personal selling efforts and integrate these with the other elements of the firm's marketing strategy.

2. *The implementation of the sales program.* The implementation phase involves selecting appropriate sales personnel and designing and implementing policies and procedures that will direct their efforts toward the desired objectives.

3. *The evaluation and control of sales force performance.* The evaluation phase involves developing methods for monitoring and evaluating sales force performance. Evaluation facilitates adjusting the sale program or the way it is implemented when performance is unsatisfactory.

The specific activities involved in these three processes, along with the variables that influence those activities, are summarized in the model of sales management in Exhibit 1.1. While this book explores the components of this model in detail, here we will introduce the variables and sales management activities involved in each of the three processes.

FORMULATING THE STRATEGIC SALES PROGRAM

The activities and influences involved in formulating a company's strategic sales program are shown in Exhibit 1.2. The design of a sales program requires five major sets of decisions.

1. How can the personal selling effort be best adapted to the company's environment and integrated with the other elements of the firm's marketing strategy? In addition, how does personal selling fit into a strategy of adding value to the relationship between the company and the customer (relationship marketing)?

2. How can various types of potential customers best be approached, persuaded, and serviced? In other words, what account management polices should be adopted?

3. How should the sales function be organized to call on and manage various types of customers as efficiently and effectively as possible? How are teams created to handle specific customer issues? Who should be on those teams?

4. What level of performance can each member of the sales force be expected to attain during the next planning period? Sales executives are involved in forecasting demand and setting quotas and budgets.

5. In view of the firm's account management policies and demand forecasts, how should the sales force be deployed? How should sales territories be defined? What is the best way for each salesperson's time to be allocated within a territory?

The policies and plans involved in such a program must take into account the influences and constraints imposed by the external environment. The demands of potential customers and the actions of competitors are two obvious environmental factors. For example, customers' desire for increased contact with salespeople and competitors who enlarged their sales forces challenged GE Capital not only to rethink its competitive marketing strategies but also to reengineer its sales force.

In addition to customers and competitors, other environmental factors such as energy shortages, technical advances, government regulations, and social concerns can affect a company's sales policies and plans. For instance, a furniture manufacturer told its sales-

Exhibit 1.1 An Overview of Sales Management

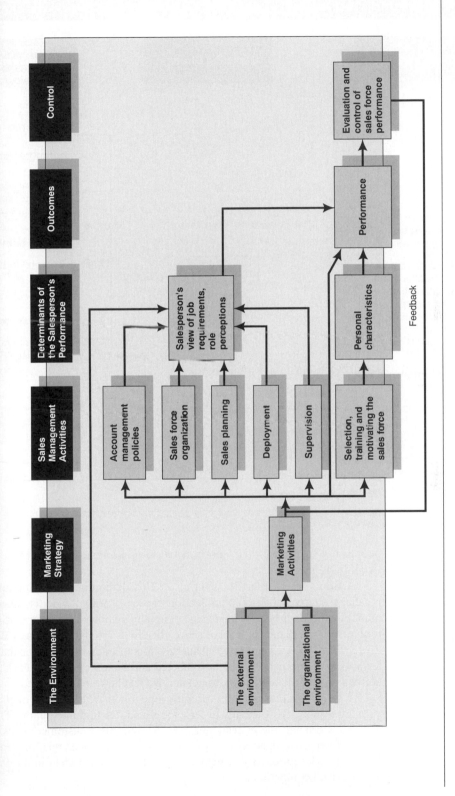

| The Environment | Marketing Strategy | Sales Management Activities | Determinants of the Salesperson's Performance | Outcomes | Control |

The external environment

The organizational environment

Marketing Activities

Account management policies

Sales force organization

Sales planning

Deployment

Supervision

Selection, training and motivating the sales force

Salesperson's view of job requirements, role perceptions

Personal characteristics

Performance

Evaluation and control of sales force performance

Feedback

Exhibit 1.2   Activities and Influences Involved in Formulating a Strategic Sales Program

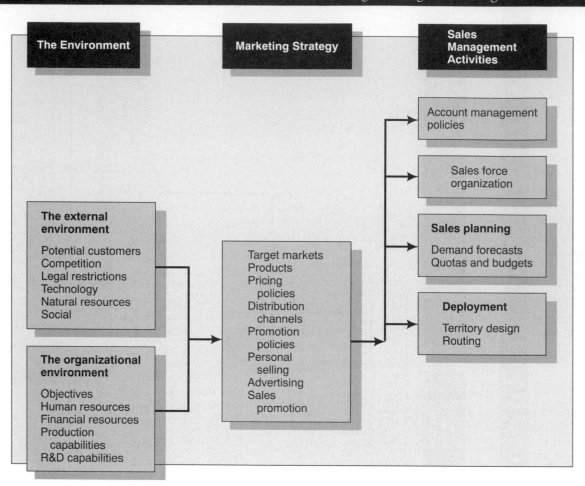

people not to exceed their quotas because a shortage of labor prevented the company from filling more orders.

A firm's internal environment also helps determine sales programs. Human and financial resources, the firm's production capacity, and its expertise in research and development can either help or hinder the company's ability to pursue particular types of customers or to expand its market share. In GE Capital's case, the FWK program (Find More, Win More, Keep More) meant developing internal databases that modeled how often various customers should be contacted and then kept track of each salesperson's sales activity so that the optimal customer service levels were maintained.

A sales program must be carefully integrated with the rest of the firm's marketing strategy. Again, GE Capital's experience illustrates this integration. The firm's salespeople play a crucial role in designing services that meet customer needs. And the information and expertise those sales reps bring to their customer relationships add value to GE Capital's older products that helps them hold onto customers in the face of threats from lower-priced competitors.

Personal selling is only one promotional tool, and promotion is only one element of a marketing strategy. Management must decide what promotional objectives need to be accomplished in view of the firm's product line, price policies, and distribution network. Decisions must then be made concerning what combination of promotional tools—personal selling, media advertising, and sales promotion—can accomplish those objectives most efficiently and effectively. Finally, account management policies and sales plans must be devised that spell out the firm's personal selling objectives, and appropriate organizational and deployment policies must be developed for accomplishing those objectives. Underlying these decisions are two fundamental goals: (1) enhancing value to the customer and (2) building a relationship with the customer rather than focusing on "selling" something.

For example, Planters (a division of Nabisco) targeted sports fans with Super Bowl and March Madness promotions, with Mr. Peanut appearing at a number of sports events. These promotions were tied in with significant television advertising, co-branding with other Nabisco products and co-marketing with partners such as Coca-Cola. Additionally, the company is introducing a new line of Planters Trail Mix products that were the result of feedback from supermarket and wholesale customers. To make these new product launches and promotions work, the company developed account-specific merchandising programs. Salespeople work directly with a single account (such as HEB grocery stores in San Antonio, Texas) to develop merchandising and store-sponsored advertising and promotion specific to the local market. Salespeople also have to make sure enough products are available when Planters runs special national promotions such as the All-Star Baseball promotion involving Cal Ripken, Jr. To make sure there are enough jars of peanuts in stores in July, salespeople have to convince buyers as early as March that the campaign will be successful. Otherwise, those customers will miss out on sales when they run out of Planters peanuts. Sales plays a key role, but is one of many important elements in the overall Planters marketing mix.[2]

IMPLEMENTING THE SALES PROGRAM

As with any kind of management, implementing a sales program involves motivating and directing the behavior of other people—the members of the sales force. To be effective, the sales manager must understand why the people in his or her sales force behave the way they do. Then policies and procedures can be designed to direct that behavior toward the desired objectives.

The model of the activities involved in implementing a sales program shown in Exhibit 1.3 suggests that five factors influence a sales rep's job behavior and performance.

1. *Environmental variables.* Regardless of how highly motivated or competent salespeople are, their ability to achieve a particular level of job performance is influenced—and sometimes constrained—by environmental factors. The ability to reach a given sales volume, for instance, can be affected by such things as the market demand for the products being sold, the number and aggressiveness of competitors, and the health of the economy. Similarly, other elements of a firm's marketing mix, such as the quality of its products and the effectiveness of its advertising, can influence a salesperson's ability to reach a high level of sales performance.

2. *Role perceptions.* To perform adequately, a salesperson must understand what the job entails and how it is supposed to be performed. The activities and behaviors associated with a particular job are defined largely by the expectations and demands

Exhibit 1.3   Activities Involved in Implementing a Sales Program

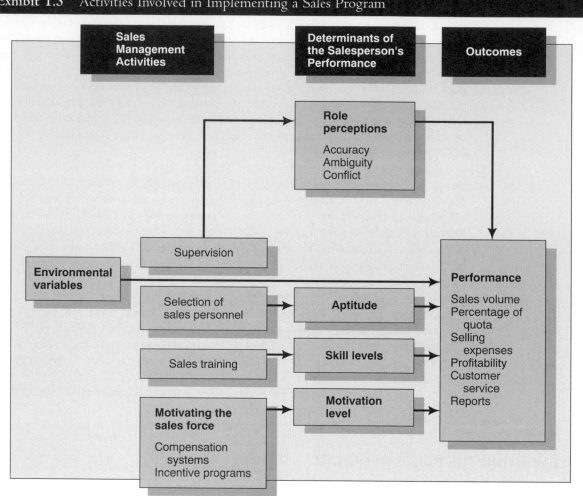

of other people, both inside and outside the organization. Thus, a salesperson's job (or role) is defined by the expectations and desires of the customers, sales manager, other company executives, and family members. The salesperson's ability to do the job well is partly determined by how clearly the sales rep understands those role expectations Also, the salesperson may sometimes face conflicting demands, as when a customer wants a lower price but company management refuses to negotiate. The salesperson's ability to resolve such conflicts helps determine success or failure on the job.

3. *Aptitude.* A salesperson's ability to perform the activities of the job is also influenced by the individual's personal characteristics such as personality traits, intelligence, and analytical ability. No matter how hard they try, some people are never successful at selling because they do not have the aptitude for the job. Of course, different kinds of sales jobs involve different tasks and activities, so a person with certain characteristics may be unsuited for one selling job but tremendously successful at another one.

4. *Skill levels.* Even when salespeople have the aptitude to do their jobs and an understanding of what they are expected to do, they must have the skills necessary to carry out the required tasks. For instance, a salesperson must have a thorough knowledge of the product and how it works, how to make an effective sales presentation, and other sales skills. In addition, the skill set necessary to be successful has changed over time as a result of the emphasis on customer relationship building.

5. *Motivation level.* A salesperson cannot achieve a high level of job performance unless motivated to expend the necessary effort. A person's motivation is determined by the kind of rewards expected for achieving a given level of performance—such as more pay or a promotion—and by the perceived attractiveness of those anticipated rewards. In today's team selling sales environment, developing effective rewards systems is especially difficult because of the combined efforts of many more people in maintaining the customer relationship.

A sales manager can use several policies and procedures to influence the aptitude, skill levels, role perceptions, and motivation of the sales force. Implementing a sales program involves designing those policies and procedures so that the job behavior and performance of each salesperson are shaped and directed toward the specified objectives and performance levels.

The sales manager must decide what kinds of aptitude are required for the firm's salespeople to do the kind of selling involved and to reach the program's objectives. Recruiting techniques and selection criteria can then be developed to ensure that salespeople with the required abilities are hired.

A salesperson's selling skills improve with practice and experiences. In most cases, though, it is inefficient to let the salesperson simply gain skills through on-the-job experience. Good customers might be lost as the result of mistakes by unskilled sales personnel. Consequently, many firms have a formal training program to give new recruits some of the necessary knowledge and skills before they are expected to pull their own weight in the field. And with the increasing rapid changes in technology, global competition, and customer needs occurring in many industries, training is often an ongoing process necessary to upgrade a sales force's knowledge and skills on a regular basis. The sales manager must determine what kinds of selling skills are necessary for the success of the firm's marketing strategy and sales program. The manager can then design training programs that develop those skills as effectively as possible.

Even after completing a training program, salespeople may run into unusual situations where they face conflicting demands or are uncertain about what to do. Supervisory policies and procedures are needed so salespeople can obtain advice and assistance from management with no undue restrictions on their freedom to develop innovative approaches to customers' problems.

Finally, a salesperson's motivation to expend effort on the job is largely a function of the amount and desirability of the rewards expected for a given job performance. The sales manager should determine what rewards are most attractive to the sales force and design compensation and incentive programs that will generate a high level of motivation. Compensation programs involve monetary rewards. Incentive programs can also include a variety of nonfinancial rewards, such as recognition programs, promotions to better territories or to management positions, or opportunities for personal development. Minolta Business Systems, for example, offers salespeople who sell 150 percent of their annual quota a trip to exciting locations such as Monte Carlo.

In the market-oriented firm, salespeople work as part of cross-functional teams. At NCR, for example, the salesperson is the captain of a team involving representatives from manufacturing, marketing, finance, and other areas of the firm. Allegiance, one of the largest medical supply manufacturers and distributors, also uses a team concept with representatives from each product area assisting the salesperson. With the advent of team selling, it has become more difficult to evaluate individual performance and, as a result, to determine appropriate rewards.

EVALUATION AND CONTROL OF THE SALES PROGRAM

For a salesperson to be appropriately rewarded for job performance, that performance must first be measured and evaluated. GE Capital's compensation plan, for example, provides salespeople with salary and incentives based on achievement of specific goals, including total sales volume, sales with new accounts, and customer satisfaction. At a minimum, the firm must monitor and record each sales rep's performance on each of those dimensions to know how big a salary increase and how much incentive compensation the person deserves.

From a sales manager's view, it is equally important to monitor the aggregate performance of the sales force to evaluate and control the firm's strategic sales program and the way it is implemented. Although total sales force performance is particularly important when new programs or policies are instituted, even a successful program should be carefully monitored. Changes in economic conditions, customers' needs, competitors' actions, or other parts of the firm's marketing mix can cause successful programs and policies to suddenly become inappropriate and ineffective. Thus overall performance should be measured frequently and compared with the planned performance levels specified in the sales program so that any deviations can be quickly identified. Then timely changes in the strategic programs or in specific implementation policies and procedures can be made.

A company might utilize three major approaches in evaluating and controlling the sales force to monitor sales program performance.

1. *Sales analysis.* Sales volume can be monitored for each salesperson. In addition, sales figures are often broken down by geographic district, by each product in the line, and by different types of customers. Sales results can then be compared with the quotas and forecasts specified in the firm's sales plans.

2. *Cost analysis.* The costs of various selling functions can be monitored. These might also be examined across individual salespeople, districts, products, and customer types. When combined with the data from sales analysis, this procedure allows a firm to judge the profitability of various products and customer types. However, cost analysis presents some difficult technical questions concerning how certain costs—such as administrative salaries and overhead—should be allocated among salespeople or products.

3. *Behavioral analysis.* A salesperson's ability to achieve a certain sales volume is sometimes constrained by factors beyond the rep's control, such as competition or economic conditions. Therefore, some managers believe it is necessary to evaluate the actual behavior of salespeople as well as their ultimate performance in terms of sale volume. A number of techniques attempt to measure and evaluate various aspects of a salesperson job behavior, including self-rating scales, supervisor ratings, fields observations, and surveys of customer satisfaction.

Although sales analysis is the most common method of control, a growing number of firms use a combination of all three methods to identify shortcomings in the design

Exhibit 1.4   Activities and Influences Involved in Formulating a Strategic Sales Program

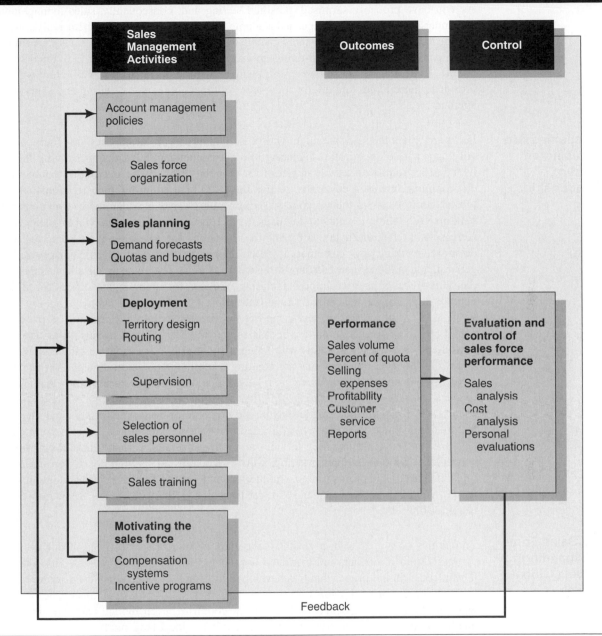

or implementation of their sales programs and to help decide on appropriate changes. For example, 3M's Electronics division measures salesperson performance on 12 different dimensions, which include sales performance, cost control, activities, and knowledge and personal development. Scores for each dimension are then fed into a model to determine an overall performance rating that is used to determine raises and promotions. Exhibit 1.4 illustrates the activities that relate to performance evaluation and control.

SALES MANAGEMENT IN THE 21ST CENTURY

As you have probably surmised, personal selling and, consequently, sales management are undergoing dramatic change. Salespeople and those who manage them realize these changes affect every aspect of sales management from the way the way sales department is structured to the selection, training, motivation, and compensation of individual salespeople. In the course of the book these changes will be discussed in detail. Now we will introduce these topics and briefly address their impact on personal selling and sales management.

Companies Are Focusing on Building Relationships

For many years the sales paradigm was presented as a series of transactions, each one involving separate organizations entering into an independent transaction involving the delivery of a product or service in return for compensation. In today's highly competitive environment, however, customers realize there are benefits in building relationships between themselves and their suppliers. For example, Xerox has identified fewer than 500 vendors with whom it wants to do business; in 1989, there were 5,000 vendors supplying Xerox. As a result of buyers narrowing their vendor pool, salespeople are being asked to do more, working with customers to solve their problems, improve efficiencies, and, in general, add value to their customers' business. More and more companies have salespeople with offices in their customers' facilities. Kinko's, for example, has offices for all key vendors at its corporate headquarters in California.

Providing this level of service is expensive, however, and it cannot be provided equally to all customers across the board. As a result, sales managers must prioritize their customers, creating partnerships with some while seeking to maximize efficiencies with others. In essence, organizations are creating a multilayered sales strategy that seeks to create unique and even more strategic relationships with the best customers while streamlining a transaction-based relationship with others demanding less service. Shell Oil, for example, found that some smaller buyers did not want or have time for personal visits by salespeople. When the company reallocated personal sales efforts to larger accounts and began using only telemarketing to call on smaller accounts, it found that all customers, even those assigned to telemarketing, were more satisfied. Selling costs were reduced, sales increased, and profits soared. Another example of the challenge of managing a sales force involved in such a complex set of relationships is illustrated in the "Managing Sales Relationships" box.

The Sales Force Is Expanding to Serve a Global Market

Companies now operate in a global marketplace. Products are designed in one country, manufactured in another, and marketed around the world. For example, Xerox recently introduced a digital printer that was developed by Xerox engineers in New York and England, in conjunction with software partners in Israel, California, and Japan. The product was simultaneously launched in 26 different countries, even though each one required that the online help and instructions were coded in the local language!

In some cases, competitors in one part of the world are partners in another. Global suppliers have increased the importance of vendor relationships not only around the country but around the world. The internationalization of business was, for many years, considered a process of big multinational corporations. However, in today's global society even small domestic companies are doing business in international markets as a result of independent distributor relationships, trade shows, and the ability of the Internet to generate awareness and interest literally anywhere in the world. As illustrated in the "Managing the Global Sales Force" box, companies have found no universal solution to the challenges raised by selling globally.

What's With-it?

"She kept saying she wanted something 'with-it,'" says Alan Wester, vice president of sales for the Freeman Exhibit Company in Dallas, Texas, a company that builds trade show exhibits. "She'd say something like, 'We don't want the Jetsons, we want high-tech but not metal, *with it,* you know? A *with-it* type of exhibit, not some ole fogey thing, a *with-it thing.*' If we hadn't had the design director there to talk over what she meant by *with-it,* I don't think we'd have gotten that business."

In Alan's business, custom exhibits are designed and presented to potential clients who select from among the offerings of several companies. "The salesperson has to fully understand the customer's requirements and then be able to communicate those requirements to the designer. Then, once a preliminary design is created, the account coordinator determines what it costs us to build the exhibit and puts the price on it. Then we make the presentation to the client and hopefully they choose our proposal." After the client orders the exhibit, production takes over and actually builds it.

"The best reps are those that have strong relationships with design, production, and the account coordination staff," claims Wester. "By creating a team to serve the customer, and involving the customer with the team during the decision process, we are able to get the customer to buy-in incrementally. So when the designer shows some preliminary sketches to the buyer, he can check to see if those designs are *with-it.*"

Alan believes that "In the organizations that do this (build teams between sales and the rest of the firm) the best, they nurture those teams. People have the information to manage activities, but creating the environment for productive relationships is a vital component. It won't happen without someone saying this is valuable and nurturing those relationships. And it has to be done via example, actually participating, not dominating or telling, but doing."

Source: Barton A. Weitz, Stephen B. Castleberry, and John F. Tanner Jr., *Selling: Building Partnerships*, 3d ed. (New York: Irwin/McGraw–Hill, 1998), p. 497.

This global focus is driven by a number of factors. As noted earlier, the ability to communicate anywhere in the world with relative ease has opened new markets. Potential customers worldwide can call, fax, or e-mail questions or orders easily. Even more significant is the realization that, for many companies, significant growth opportunities lie outside domestic markets. This is especially true in the United States as companies as diverse as DuPont and Coca-Cola acknowledge that most of their growth and consequently much of their investment over the next few years will be outside the United States. Finally, many companies have become more international because their customers are global. For example, Acadia Corporation, a supplier of equipment to the automobile industry, moved into international markets at the request of its largest customers, the Big 3 automakers in the United States.

All of these changes have led to dramatic transformations in the focus of personal selling and the way people manage the sales force. Diversity in the sales force has created new challenges for sales managers. In addition, there is a need to understand a wide range of environmental differences (cultural, legal, behavioral) in the selling process. Indeed, a number of companies require managers to spend time overseas because they believe it is important for the individual to learn an international perspective.

Sales Effectiveness Is Being Enhanced through Technology

Broadly speaking, technology has had a profound affect on almost every facet of personal selling. Laptop computers make it easy to have huge databases or complete customer records at the fingertips of the salesperson, cellular phones make it possible to communicate with the salesperson almost continuously, and VCRs and other video equipment enhance training and provide an excellent tool for conveying information. Now, the Internet

Is It Really Different?

A man's feet should be planted in his country, but his eyes should survey the world. — George Santayana

The basic concepts of selling (identifying customer needs and adding value) are universal. However, selling outside a company's home market introduces a number of demands that, in turn, affect every aspect of managing a global force. From recruiting through training, compensation, and motivation, the global sales manager must be able to adjust his or her skills to match the demands of the local environment. Further complicating the process is the lack of consistency across markets. No one global sales management "template" exists. Sales managers must evaluate and manage each market based on the local conditions. For example, in Asia individuals respond positively to direct supervision, while in Latin and South America that same management style will be received negatively by local salespeople.

Recruiting

A fundamental question for companies expanding internationally is "Who should we hire?" A good case can be made for two basic choices. First, hire local nationals and train them to become salespeople. Many countries require companies to hire locals. Local nationals in sales positions increase credibility when calling on local customers. However, training costs are generally significantly higher and managing local nationals can be more difficult when compared to other options. The second option is to bring in expatriates as salespeople. International duty is often considered a good training ground for moving up in the organization,

and expatriates are well versed in the company and product, and they generally have a greater sense of loyalty than would a new local employee. The basic drawback to this approach is the high cost of maintaining expatriates in the country. Cost-of-living adjustments, stress on family relationships, and a host of other issues limit the long-term viability of using expatriates in the sales force.

Training

Training in global markets can be expensive. Adequate local training facilities are often difficult to find and use. As a result, companies seek out local universities and other educational facilities (engineering institutes, for example) to provide not only the location but the staff. Additional costs are incurred when product experts, engineers, and other specialists are brought in to train local salespeople.

Compensation

A number of questions surround the compensation and reward structure in a global sales force. Cost of living varies a great deal around the world and many countries do not enjoy the relatively low rates of inflation found in the United States. In addition, compared to the United States, total compensation structures can be low (as in the Czech Republic) or high (as in Switzerland). Finally, reward systems that are quite effective in the United States may have little positive impact in other parts of the world. For example, in low-wage areas such as Latin America, incentives such as gifts or trips are not as effective as cash bonuses.

Source: Erika Rasmussen, "Can Your Reps Sell Overseas?" *Sales & Marketing Management* (February 1998), p. 110; John S. Hill and Richard R. Hill, "Organizing the Overseas Sales Force: How Multinationals Do It," *Journal of Personal Selling and Sales Management* (Spring 1990), pp. 57–66.

seeks to take the interaction between customer and company to a new level, creating the ability to remain in touch with the customer (update information, handle questions, deal with complaints) in a way that has not been possible in the past. Companies are still learning how to incorporate this kind of technology into the business and, more specifically, into personal selling.

At the cutting edge of the technology is the Internet. Its ability to inform, persuade, and enhance the personal selling component will make it a critical part of sales management learning in the 21st century. Cisco Systems, the leading manufacturer of Internet equipment, created an extensive Web site (*www.cisco.com*) to help service customers. The effect was an immediate jump in sales. The Web site has become an important sales tool as account managers work with customers to help them see the benefits of ordering online.

The Internet is emerging as a significant tool for the salesperson. As a result, we have integrated the Internet throughout the text. Specifically, we have included Web sites for companies discussed in introductory scenarios, cases, and examples in the text. In addition, we have created a Web site for you to browse with up-to-date information about personal selling and sales management.

But technology is not just about the Internet. Electronic data interchange (EDI) systems in manufacturing and efficient consumer response (ECR) systems in retailing enable companies to tie their computers directly to their customers. When a customer's computer recognizes a low inventory, it can generate an order directly to the vendor's computer, which then schedules the product for delivery (and in some cases even schedules the product for manufacturing). Thus, order and delivery systems have become just-in-time delivery systems.

Sales Managers Are Becoming Leaders and Not Just Managers

In today's sales environment traditional work relationships are being questioned and often replaced with new ones. Nowhere is this more prevalent than in the relationship between salesperson and sales manager. In the traditional top-down bureaucratic style, managers were the supervisors responsible for administering the sales force. Conversely, they were held directly accountable for the actions of their salespeople. Words like *control* and *manage* were used to describe their activities.

The highly dynamic and competitive environment of the 21st century demands a more responsive, flexible approach to sales management. Sales forces are becoming less hierarchical with fewer layers of management while more responsibility is being given to the salesperson. Leaders like Jack Wendt of GE Capital are emerging as the exemplars of today's successful sales manager. Effective sales management is now more often defined by how good a leader you are than how good a manager. Examples of a leadership approach include (1) communicating with salespeople rather than controlling them, (2) becoming a cheerleader and coach instead of a supervisor or boss, and (3) empowering them to make decisions rather than directing them. Clearly, being an effective leader requires new and different skills from the traditional manager role.

Doing Business Ethically

Characterizing sales as trending toward more ethical behavior may be unfair to the many ethical salespeople of the past. But it is true that ethical selling practices are becoming more important. For example, the U.S. government has developed Federal Sentencing Guidelines that are designed to punish firms that allow salespeople (and other employees) to engage in unethical behavior. Penalties are reduced for firms that have required ethics training and have adopted other policies that encourage ethical behavior.

Even without encouragement from the government, the increasingly long-term nature of business relationships requires higher ethical standards than earlier relationships did. There may be a sucker born every minute, but if you want to be in the business of selling to auto manufacturers, for example, you can't sucker too many customers and hope to stay in business. In the "Ethical Issues" feature the IBM situation described illustrates the ethical pressures that face professional sales management.

WHY SALESPEOPLE SELL: THE ATTRACTIVENESS OF SALES CAREERS

The complexity and competitiveness of most industrial sales jobs make successful performance a daunting challenge for even the most well-managed sales force. This challenges sales managers to recruit and select the best qualified salespeople, train and supervise

Do Buyers Have to Be Ethical?

Salespeople, rightly or wrongly, have a reputation for doing whatever it takes to make a sale, even if it takes something unethical. Yet, where does the pressure to act unethically come from?

Some salespeople say it comes from buyers themselves. As Memo Diriker, marketing professor at Salisbury State College, reports, "[Salespeople] are being asked very boldly [by their customers], 'What's in it for me?'" Clients ask vendors to pay for trips for the buyer and spouse to attend trade shows; other buyers are more direct, asking for cash kickbacks.

Yet the penalties for being caught acting unethically are higher than ever. Recently, the Federal government enacted the Uniform Sentencing Guidelines that spell out the penalties for companies that engage in unethical behavior. Prudential Insurance Company of America, for example, had to pay $5 million when its reps used customers' cash value of policies to buy them new policies without telling the customers.

Another source of pressure is the company that demands more and more sales. Caught in the middle is the sales manager, who somehow has to deliver those higher sales yet keep the sales force operating ethically. As one manager said, "You're the one that's always squarely in the middle."

In spite of the pressure, a recent survey of managers reported that 85 percent believe salespeople to act with the same or greater integrity than they did five years ago. And many reps believe ethical selling to be good business. Rich Shih-Hseih, an IBM rep in Chicago, was faced with a demand from a customer for 500 PCs to be shipped in under two months. Shih-Hsieh told the buyer that IBM couldn't meet those delivery requirements, but one of the competitors made the commitment and got the order. As Shih-Hsieh expected, the competitor couldn't deliver either. "Now the purchasing agent really respects me and this situation strengthened our relationship. He knows that I'm going to be straight with him."

Sources: Barton A. Weitz, "Good Ethics Is Good Business," in *Selling: Building Partnerships,* 3d ed., Barton A. Weitz, Stephen B. Castleberry, and John F. Tanner Jr. (New York: Irwin/McGraw–Hill, 1998); Michele Marchetti, "Whatever It Takes," *Sales & Marketing Management* (December 1997), pp. 29–38.

them well, keep them highly motivated, and focus their efforts with appropriate sales strategies and account management policies. Unfortunately, the problem of recruiting talented new salespeople is made even thornier for many firms—particularly those that seek recruits with undergraduate degrees or MBAs—by the fact that many college students hold somewhat negative attitudes toward selling as a potential career.

For most industrial salespeople, it is precisely the complexity and challenge of their jobs that motivate them and make them satisfied with their choice of careers. A number of satisfaction surveys over the years have found high levels of job satisfaction among industrial salespeople across a broad cross-section of firms and industries. While these surveys did find some areas of dissatisfaction, that unhappiness tended to focus on the policies and actions of the salesperson's firm or sales manager, not on the nature of the job itself.[3]

Why are so many industrial salespeople so satisfied with their jobs? Different analysts have offered a variety of answers to this question. Some attractive aspects of selling careers most commonly mentioned by these authors—as well as by salespeople themselves—include (1) freedom of action and opportunities for personal initiative, (2) a variety of challenging activities, (3) financial rewards, (4) favorable working conditions, and (5) good opportunities for career development and advancement.[4]

A common complaint among workers in many professions is that they are too closely supervised. They complain about superiors "breathing down their necks" and about rules and standard operating procedures that constrain their freedom to do their jobs as they see fit. Salespeople, on the other hand, spend most of their time in the field calling on customers where there is no one to supervise their every move. They are relatively free to organize their own time and to get the job done in their own way as long as they show satisfactory results.

The freedom of a selling career appeals to people who value their independence, who are confident that they can cope with most situations that they will encounter, and who like to show some personal initiative in deciding how to get their job done. However, this freedom brings responsibilities and pressures. Salespeople are responsible for their territory. Although no one closely supervises the salesperson's behavior, management usually keeps close tabs on the results of that behavior: sales volume, quota attainment, expenses, and the like. To be successful, then, salespeople must be able to manage themselves, to organize time wisely, and to make the right decisions about how to do the job.

People soon become bored doing routine tasks. Consequently, many companies have instituted job enrichment programs to expand the variety and challenge in their employees' jobs. Boredom is seldom a problem among industrial salespeople, however. Each potential customer has different needs and problems for the salesperson to solve. Those problems are often anything but trivial, and a salesperson must display insight, creativity, and analytical skill to close a sale. For example, a six-person selling team from IBM spent four years studying patient care and handling procedures in a large hospital before designing and selling a data processing system that fit the hospital's needs.

Many analysts expect this kind of creative problem solving to become even more common in the future. New technologies—like telemarketing and electronic reordering systems—are making what was a primary function of the salesperson, order taking, almost obsolete. As a result, the salesperson of the future will be "more of a trainer, a technical adviser, and consultant as opposed to an order-taker."[5]

To make the job even more interesting, the marketplace is constantly changing. Salespeople must frequently adjust their sales presentations and other activities to shifts in economic and competitive conditions.

For many people in the selling profession, variety and challenge are the most rewarding aspects of their jobs. In one study, industrial salespeople rated the "sense of accomplishment" and the "opportunities for personal growth" provided by their jobs second only to financial compensation as the most attractive rewards they received.[6]

Selling can be a very lucrative profession. More important, the growth of a salesperson's earnings—particularly earnings of someone receiving a large proportion of incentive pay—is determined largely by performance, and often there are no arbitrary limits placed on the maximum amount a salesperson can earn. Consequently, a sales rep's compensation can grow faster and reach higher levels than that of personnel in other departments at comparable levels in an organization.

Exhibit 1.5 shows the average total compensation earned by industrial salespeople working for small and medium-sized businesses in different industries. It also illustrates how compensation varies between average versus outstanding performers. Of course, new college graduates will start out significantly below the top, but the opportunity is there.

Although salespeople are sometimes reluctant to give up their high-paying jobs to move into managerial positions, most firms recognize the importance of good managerial talent and reward it appropriately, particularly as a person reaches the top executive levels of the sales organization. Total compensation of over $250,000 a year is not unheard of for national sales managers or vice presidents of sales in large firms.

According to the stereotype, salespeople travel extensively, live on big expense accounts, spend much of their time entertaining potential clients, and consequently have lit-

Exhibit 1.5 Median Compensation for Average and Top Salespeople in Small and Medium-Sized Businesses

Industry	Average Performer	Top Performer
Basic materials	$ 80,000	$157,000
Heavy equipment & transportation	97,000	150,000
Electrical and electronics	92,000	172,000
Nondurable goods	120,000	186,000
Fabricated metal and wood products	91,000	127,000
Technological services	133,000	276,000
Business services	96,000	210,000
High technology products	111,000	177,000

Source: "1999 Officer Compensation Reports for Small and Medium-Sized Businesses" (New York: Panel Publishers and The Segal Co.).

tle time for home and family life. Again, this is not an accurate description of the working conditions encountered by most salespeople.

Some selling jobs require extensive travel, but most salespeople can sleep at home every night. Indeed, with the increasing use of computer networks, e-mail, video conferencing, and the like, many sales reps work out of their homes and seldom even travel to their companies' offices.[7]

As we shall see, a major determinant of the size of sales territories is the density of potential customers. In many lines of trade, customers are sufficiently concentrated that firms must define relatively small territories to gain adequate customer contact. Also, smaller territories are the trend in many industries as firms attempt to provide better customer service. For instance, sales reps who serve as major account managers or members of national account teams may spend most of their time with a single customer.

Many businesspeople feel that, before an executive can do an effective job of managing, he or she must "know the territory." What better way is there to learn about a company's customers, products, and competitive strengths and weaknesses than to spend time in the field calling on customers and meeting the competition face to face? For this reason, many companies require managerial trainees to spend time in the sales force in preparation for executive positions in marketing or other functional departments.

The knowledge to be gained through sales experience is also enhanced by formal training programs. As indicated in Exhibit 1.6, such training is typically extensive and involves months of effort (and thousands of dollars in expense) for each trainee. Note, too, that firms in some service industries have longer training programs, on average, than firms in many manufacturing industries. This is because some service organizations, such as those selling insurance or financial services, have relatively complicated product lines that require their salespeople to absorb a substantial body of knowledge. In many high-tech industries—such as computers or plastics—manufacturers also have relatively extensive and costly training programs. Such programs can last up to two years and involve expenditures as high as $100,000 per trainee before a new recruit is prepared to become a productive member of the marketing team.

Exhibit 1.6   Length of Sales Training for New Hires by Industry

Industry Group	Average Training Period (months)	Industry Group	Average Training Period (months)
Agriculture	10.7	Insurance	5.3
Business services	3.2	Machinery	3.4
Chemicals	5.2	Manufacturing	4.4
Communications	3.0	Office equipment	3.0
Construction	6.0	Paper/allied products	4.5
Electronic components	2.0	Primary metal products	3.0
Electronics	3.4	Printing/publishing	6.0
Fabricated metals	4.3	Rubber/plastics	4.0
Food products	3.6	Wholesale (consumer)	4.6
Instruments	3.7	Wholesale (industrial)	3.9
Average (all respondents)	**3.9**		

Note: Industry groups reflect categories selected and reported by Dartnell Corporation.

Source: Dartnell Corporation, *28th Survey of Sales Force Compensation* © 1994, Dartnell Corporation.

Given the wealth of knowledge about a firm's customers, competitors, and products—and the experience at building effective relationships—that a sales job can provide, it is not surprising that more corporation presidents come from sales and marketing backgrounds than from any other functional area.[8] Of course, many managerial opportunities are available to successful salespeople at lower levels of the corporate hierarchy as well, most obviously in sales management and marketing management. A recent survey of human resource managers found that sales professionals are among the most sought-after employees.[9]

Promoting top salespeople into management can sometimes cause problems. Successful selling often requires different personal skills and abilities than does successful management. There is no guarantee that a good salesperson will also be a good sales manager. Also, successful salespeople have been known to refuse promotion to managerial positions—because they enjoy selling, or they can make more money in sales than in management, or both. Finally, recent trends toward corporate downsizing, flatter organizational structures, and cross-functional account teams are changing the number and nature of managerial opportunities available for successful salespeople. The sales manager of the future is more likely to be a coach or team leader rather than an authority figure isolated in the upper reaches of a corporate hierarchy.[10] We will explore these ongoing changes in the nature of the sales manager's job in more detail in Chapter 5.

While there are still many career advancement opportunities available to the successful salesperson, the fact is that not all sales recruits turn out to be successful. Some are fired, others quit and seek different careers, and some simply languish on the lower rungs of the sales hierarchy. Not everyone has the characteristics and abilities necessary for success in selling, which raises the question, "What personal characteristics and abilities are related to successful sales performance?" This question is somewhat difficult to answer because different types of sales jobs require different personal skills and attributes. We will examine this question in detail in Chapter 11 when we discuss the criteria for selecting sales recruits with the potential to be successful salespeople.

SUMMARY

Sales management programs and activities do not exist in a vacuum. Thus, as was illustrated by the GE Capital example, effective sales management programs must be designed to respond to a firm's environmental circumstances, and they must be consistent with the objectives and content of the business's competitive and market strategies. Sales management also plays a crucial role in implementing those higher-level strategies. Good sales management policies and practices are essential ingredients for ensuring the success for firm's competitive and market strategies.

Effective management requires a solid understanding of the activities one is trying to manage. Unfortunately, many people have misconceptions about the selling process, the activities carried out by sales-people, and the personal characteristics necessary for a successful career in professional sales. In part, these misconceptions arise because different types of selling jobs involve different kinds of tasks and require different skills and abilities from the people who do them.

Sales management involves three interrelated processes: (1) the formulation of a strategic sales program, (2) the implementation of the sales program, and (3) the evaluation and control of sales force performance. It is the purpose of this book to describe the variables and sales management activities involved in each of these processes. Each major section of the book elaborates one process: Part I, the formulation of the sales program, Part II the implementation, and Part III, evaluation and control.

DISCUSSION QUESTIONS

1. Will the Internet replace the need for salespeople? In what situations is the Internet most likely to replace salespeople? What characteristics of a situation would make the Internet least likely to replace field salespeople?

2. A number of organizations that did not consider marketing part of their business activities in the past have found the need to begin to market their services. Nowhere is this more prevalent than in the nonprofit community. While not "selling" a product or service, public service organizations such as the Red Cross have developmental officers who market the organization in the community. How might you "sell" a public service organization in the community? What would be your goals and how would you accomplish them?

3. Salespeople are also called *sales representatives*. Define the term *representative*. Whom does the salesperson represent? Why is it important to recognize the different groups that salespeople represent? How does this recognition of who is represented influence sales management?

4. What do you think the differences would be in the selling process for the following products and services?

   • Selling Planter's Peanuts to your grocer.
   • Selling Planter's Peanuts to Southwest Airlines to be given to their customers.
   • Selling telecommunications equipment costing $500,000 to $1 million to the U.S. government.
   • Selling telecommunications equipment costing $500,000 to $1 million to GE Capital.
   • Selling GE Capital's leasing services to Burlington Northern transportation company so it can lease more railcars.

5. Describe the typical salesperson as illustrated in movies, books, and television shows. Why does that image exist as the stereotypical salesperson? How can selling ethically provide a company with a competitive advantage? Whose responsibility is it to see that a company's code of ethics is carried out?

EXPERIENTIAL APPLICATION

1. Identify a friend or associate who has a purchasing role for his or her organization. It could be your family physician or someone with whom you work. Ask this person to describe the best salesperson who sells to him or her on a regular basis. Then ask what percentage of average salespeople meet each descriptor (like how many are professional, courteous, or responsive). Your result could look like a table, with the descriptors of the best salesperson in the first column, and then a percentage for each descriptor in the next column. Repeat the exercise, but substitute the worst salesperson and generate a new list of descriptors. What does this exercise tell you about the challenges and opportunities in sales management?

INTERNET EXERCISES

1. Visit the GE Capital home page (*www.gecapital*) and go to one of the divisions' home pages. Each one has a "Who We Are" or "What We Do" page. Visit one of the commercial divisions (with businesses as its customers) and work your way through that site. Summarize what the company does and the role the sales force plays in accomplishing the company's objectives. You may need to search several before you can find one with enough information, but you should be able to identify the types of companies that the division's salespeople visit, the characteristics of the salesperson (such as what the company looks for when it hires new ones), and an indication of how well the division is doing.

2. Visit the Sales Management Resource Corporation's home page at *smrcareer.com*. This company specializes in finding sales executives and sales managers for companies to hire. Once at its home page, go to a listing of positions currently available (*smrcareer.com/positions/*) and select a vice president of sales position. What are the requirements? What does the person do? Then select a sales manager position and answer those questions. Summarize your paper with a comparison and contrast of the two positions.

2

The Strategic Roles of Selling and Sales Management

EDWARD JONES: SERVING INDIVIDUAL INVESTERS

Edward Jones & Co. is not your typical financial services provider. Unlike Merrill Lynch, Paine Webber, and other firms, Jones has built a business based on the individual investor. And unlike those other companies, Jones brokers find new customers by going door to door, joining community organizations, and getting to know their neighbors on a personal basis. For decades, Jones has grown to become the 34th largest brokerage house (the largest in terms of number of offices) by opening single-broker offices in places like Lebanon, Indiana, and Orrville, Ohio, and then forming personal relationships with the people of those towns. Forming these personal relationships is critical to the sales strategy of Edward Jones. While Jones got its start in small communities, now Jones is taking this relationship strategy to large cities like Seattle and Atlanta and the Dallas–Fort Worth area.

For example, Jeff Pope (Jones' broker in Denison, Texas) was called by one of his clients shortly after she lost her husband. It was time to buy a new car, and she wanted Pope to go with her to the car dealership and help her buy that car. Pope said, "That's when I feel most successful. My client trusted me enough to turn to me as a friend in that situation."

One difference in the Jones sales strategy is apparent right away. Rather than find new ac-

counts by telephone prospecting, each new broker with Jones begins by knocking on a least 1,000 doors. Then he or she can open an office, instead of joining an existing office with 30 other brokers. These single-broker offices let Jones brokers create those personal relationships that are so critical to their sales strategy.

Without strong core values, though, Jones could not maintain its relationship-based business strategy. As entrepreneurs running their own office, Jones brokers have incredible freedom. At the same time, however, those core values are strictly enforced. For example, Jones does not believe in switching clients in and out of different funds in order to make a commission. Should a Jones broker switch an account from one fund to a similar fund, there had better be a good reason. Management guru Peter Drucker sees Jones as "a confederation of highly autonomous entrepreneurial units bound together by a highly centralized core of values of services."

Because Jones brokers can't grow revenue by switching funds around, they have to continually prospect for new clients. Jones broker George Engle of Tryon, North Carolina, says he acts like the owner. "I decide when I run a newspaper ad, I decide what I'll sell, and I decide whether Fridays are casual days in my office." With this entrepreneurial spirit, Jones has captured the Main Street market.

How did Jones develop a strategy of capturing small town communities with single-broker offices? At the beginning, it wasn't a strategy, it was just what Edward Jones, Jr., son of the company founder, liked to do. Against his father's advice, he forsook the large cities and went after the small towns where he liked the people and enjoyed serving them.

Edward Jones managing principal John Bachmann (the CEO) is taking Jones one step further. He sees those same types of investors residing in Canada, Great Britain, and other countries as well as in large cities like New York. The strategy is the same: Find a community and join it. It is just that the community may be suburban rather than rural. Bachmann expects them to begin by knocking on people's doors, getting to know them and their families, and building relationships. Bachmann's goal is to nearly triple the number of brokers to 10,000 by the year 2004, in part by developing relationships with colleges whose students have the kinds of values and dreams that match the Jones culture.

Another key element in the Bachmann growth plan is technology. For Jones brokers to be connected to the corporate office, Bachmann installed the largest satellite network in the industry. Clients and brokers can attend seminars on the network, seminars that could be about investing one day and how to improve a golf swing the next. What is interesting about the Jones technology imperative is that it supports the local broker so that clients can be better served.

At first glance, Jones appears to be changing radically, from small towns to urban centers. The basic core value of serving individual investors through strong personal relationships built in community, though, remains. As Mike Dooseck of Marion, Ohio, says, "I learned a long time ago that if I did what was best for the client, I'll get by and my business will continue to grow."

Visit Edward Jones at its Web site, *jonesopportunity.com*.

Source: Jeff Pope, personal correspondence, 1998; John Bachmann, "The History of Edward Jones," presentation made at Baylor University, September 19, 1998; Rebecca McReynolds, "Ed Jones, America's Community Banker," *US Banker* (September 1997), pp. 58–61; Richard Teitelbaum, "The Wal-Mart of Wall Street," *Fortune* (October 13, 1997), pp. 128–34.

LEARNING OBJECTIVES

To fully understand the increasingly important roles that sales can play in the organization, it is necessary to understand market planning, marketing and the learning organization, and marketing strategy. These factors of planning and strategy shape the sales force and influence the nature of the sales manager's role. After reading this chapter, you should be able to:

- Define market planning.
- Discuss the sales force's role in organizational learning and market orientation.
- Identify the process of developing a strategy.
- Define the strategic choices among relationship types, as well as the situational characteristics influencing choice.
- Discuss the differences in sales roles across relationship types and the importance of customer service in market-oriented firms.

MARKETING PLANNING

Planning is deciding what to do in the present to achieve what is desired in the future. Planning requires decisions concerning the firm's goals and objectives for the future and the actions that should be taken to accomplish them.

Planning involves an analysis of where the organization is and how it got there and a projection of where the organization will end up if it continues to move in the same direction. Given such an analysis, the company can compare where it wants to be with where it is likely to be. Management can then formulate a strategy for moving closer to what is desired. Thus, a strategy is a statement of the fundamental pattern of present and planned objectives, resource deployments, and interactions with markets, competitors, and other environmental factors that indicate how an organization intends to survive and prosper over time.[1]

A strategy provides a broad blueprint to guide the firm's efforts; however, more detailed programs, or tactics, must be developed to spell out how resources are to be allocated and what actions are to be taken, by whom, and when. To use a football analogy, the overall game plan formulated by the coaching staff is a strategy. It is a broad statement of what the team should do to win the game, given its strengths and weaknesses and those of the opponent. One such strategy might be to keep the ball on the ground and run at the tackles. The specific plays designed and practiced by the team are the tactics. Although the quarterback's selection of plays should be guided by the game plan, the tactics used must be adapted to the specific situations encountered during the game, such as an occasional pass to keep the defense honest.

In today's changing environment, planning is crucial to the success of the enterprise. Yet, because things change rapidly, some managers argue planning is a waste of time. They say changing conditions may force management to revise its plan or scrap it in favor of a new one. Others point to highly successful firms that reached success without a clearly stated plan. But without a clearly stated plan, the firm may overreact to short-lived disruptions in the environment; such erratic changes in direction can cause confusion among both employees and customers. What companies are discovering is that learning is key to successful planning, for learning provides companies with the insight necessary to nimbly react to changing conditions.

First, we will discuss two necessary philosophies for effective planning: organizational learning and market orientation. As you read about these concepts, you will also see how sales management plays a key role in the implementation of organizational learning and market orientation. Second, we will present various types of organizational strategies that reflect differences in corporate resources and objectives. Third, you will discover alternatives to selling in order to identify when personal selling is an effective strategic choice.

ORGANIZATIONAL LEARNING AND MARKET ORIENTATION

Organizational learning is an important element in the continued success of any organization, and a market orientation is the principal cultural foundation for successful learning. A learning organization is one that consistently creates and refines its capabilities by connecting new information and skills to customer requirements. Customer requirements are one of the known requisites for success that have been identified by the firm; thus, the market-oriented firm is able to generate customer requirements that are then part of the learning process.

For example, Stork (a Dutch manufacturer of ships, machinery, and industrial coatings) suffered a sharp downfall in profits over a five-year period. The company had been dedicated to developing technology; a shift to dedication to clients was the first step in the turnaround. The company wasn't revitalized until it learned how to identify customer needs and to share those needs (known requisites) throughout the organization.[2] This is an example of how a market orientation is critical for successful learning.

At the most basic level, organizational learning is the process of developing new knowledge, particularly knowledge that has the potential to influence behavior.[3] Management hopes that learning facilitates behavior change that leads to better performance, but some learning takes place for which there is no immediate obvious benefit. Scientific discoveries are like this; sometimes the benefits are not known for generations. At other times, the benefit is more immediate. For example, GE marketers learned that products could be managed using portfolios similar to financial portfolios. The outcomes included the development of a portfolio method of product management that you may have seen in other marketing courses, as well as overall performance improvement in GE's sales and earnings.

Learning Types

Everyone, including organizations, has theories of how the world operates. Theories are based on assumptions and beliefs, but also limit what new beliefs can be created. **Single-loop learning,** or adaptive learning, is learning that occurs within a set of constraints, or **learning boundaries** created by one's assumptions and beliefs. For example, consider the theories held about what causes night and day when people assumed the world was flat. It would be impossible to think of the earth spinning on an axis and night as a shadow if the world was assumed or believed to be flat. Any learning that took place within the assumption of a flat earth only enabled someone to adapt to changes *within* the boundaries of that assumption, and is illustrated in Exhibit 2.1. In a marketing process situation, adaptive learning involves change within a system but the system is defined by the individual's or organization's learning boundaries.

Generative, or double-loop, learning is the creation of knowledge that occurs through changing assumptions and beliefs. Generative learning requires that the firm build new theories of how things work; generative learning occurs when we change our theories as to *why* systems are effective. Going back to our earlier example concerning causes of night and day, if we just change our belief that the earth is the center of the universe and consider that perhaps the sun is, then we cannot explain night and day within the constraint of a flat, stationary earth. We must also reconsider whether the earth is flat and stationary. Both boundaries, as illustrated in Exhibit 2.1, are called into question.

An example of learning boundaries was presented by Ted Leavitt in the classic article, "Marketing Myopia."[4] In that article, he illustrated that railroads lost their competitiveness because they failed to see other modes of transportation as competition. Instead, they focused on being better railroads rather than better forms of transportation. Seeing competition only as other railroads is a learning boundary; railroads have since broken through that boundary and are now intermodal carriers.

Generative learning is difficult; suspending one's assumptions is hard because assumptions are not always easy to identify and are also difficult to distinguish from fact. For example, humans saw light and dark every 24 hours and believed the sun to move because that is what they saw. Tracing that conclusion back to the assumption that the earth is flat requires several steps in logic that seem obvious to us now. More difficult is tracing back assumptions about how a market operates and distinguishing between what has been observed about that market and what was assumed.

Marketing often creates learning boundaries. For example, IBM was married to the mainframe computer market. Enamored with its own hardware, it failed to realize that it was software that people wanted because software represents the applications of the computer. IBM's failure to recognize that change is an example of "tyranny of the served market" or being so focused on one traditional market that the organization is blind to unconventional business opportunities.[5] What usually happens in situations where a company is a captive of its market is that another company takes its place by capturing the unconven-

Exhibit 2.1   Types of Learning

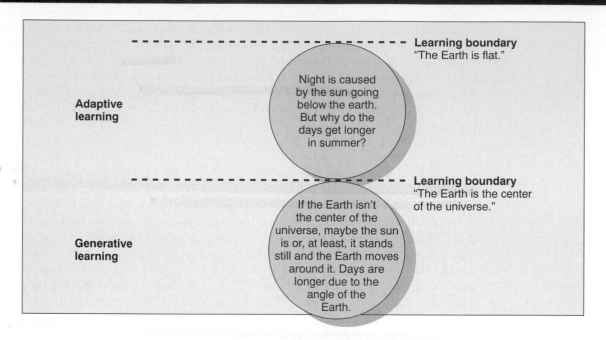

Source: Robert Dwyer and John Tanner Jr., *Business Marketing* (New York: Irwin/McGraw–Hill, 1999), p. 187.

tional opportunity. Hence, the advance of Microsoft, a software company. Who knew what customers wanted? One would expect salespeople to know, but learning boundaries can inhibit their understanding.

Organizational Learning and Competitive Advantage

Many executives have said that the only truly sustainable competitive advantage is to be able to learn faster than the competition. A company that creates a truly innovative product can expect competition in 9 to 15 months, on average. The advantage gained from being first in the market can only be sustained if the company continues to learn and stays ahead of the competition. For example, Lotus was once the dominant spreadsheet software company but did not maintain its early-market advantage because it could not learn how to integrate its software with other applications as quickly as Microsoft did.

Note that this does not mean that all organizational learning is good. Organizations can learn the wrong things, such as concluding that the initial high sales of a new product were due to its features, rather than its availability and low relative price. As soon as even lower priced models become available, that new product will fail.[6]

Further, companies can get caught in competency traps, which are a form of learning boundary. A competency trap is any skill or technology that a company sticks with due to comfort with the familiar, in spite of evidence that better alternatives may exist. For example, Apple's reluctance to embrace the DOS environment has doomed Apple to being a niche player in the computer market. In this case, Apple's operating system may be superior but the better alternative would be one that should lead to greater sales. (We could also make the case that the market has been caught in a competency trap represented by the DOS operating system, at least until the advent of Windows.)

Exhibit 2.2	How Marketing Learns	
Information Acquisition	**Information Dissemination**	**Shared Interpretation**
Marketing research	To	Through
Sales and service feedback	Marketing management	Brainstorming
Environmental scanning	Senior management	Planning
Competitive intelligence	Manufacturing	Other processes
Other learning tools	Engineering and R&D	
	Finance	

Source: Robert Dwyer and John Tanner Jr., *Business Marketing* (New York: Irwin/ McGraw–Hill, 1999), p.190.

Since learning is key to creating competitive advantage and since bad learning can have serious negative consequences, it behooves all managers to study learning processes and tools. Perhaps, though, it is more important for marketing managers to understand organizational learning methods since known requisites are derived from customer requirements.

How Marketing Learns

Organizational learning is comprised of three processes: information acquisition, information dissemination, and shared interpretation, as seen in Exhibit 2.2. Marketing's role in acquiring information, via marketing research, feedback from the sales force, and other methods, is an important element in the acquisition of vital information for the rest of the firm. That information is then disseminated through interpersonal communication and reports created as a function of internal partnerships. Together, as internal partners create a shared interpretation of the information (decide what it means for the organization), they can create an effective strategy to take advantage of what has been learned.

A market orientation has been defined as superior skills of understanding and satisfying customers.[7] When a firm has a market orientation, it is more likely to be financially successful and superior in many areas of performance, such as product development.[8]

A market orientation is the principal *cultural* foundation of the learning organization.[9] By cultural foundation, we mean that a market orientation must exist in the culture of the organization, and that such an orientation should be part of the values and norms of the organization. A company needs a market orientation in order to learn *successfully*. Recall the discussion of Stork, the Dutch company that had to develop an orientation toward customers and away from technology before it could learn the proper set of requisites. Another illustration can be seen in One Company–One World, as Seagate has struggled to maintain a single corporate culture in a worldwide sales force.

At the same time, a market orientation is an outcome of successful organizational learning. The orientation is reinforced when the voice of the customer is carried to every part of the firm and becomes a driving force in daily operational decisions.

How Market Orientation Impacts Performance

Market-driven companies, or those with a strong market orientation, are superior in two important ways. First, market-driven companies do a better job of market sensing, or anticipating market requirements ahead of the competition. Market sensing is the gathering of information from the market. The sales force should be one important avenue of market sensing, but other avenues include observing competitors' and customers' actions at trade shows, marketing research, and monitoring customer complaints.

One Company—One World

The challenge of creating a market-oriented company with a shared set of values is tough enough when all employees are from the same basic culture. When a company goes global, however, creating a corporate culture includes having to integrate world cultures. Seagate Technology may be based in California, but 6 percent of the company's $8.5 billion in sales are made in Germany. Sales offices and plants are can be found in Australia, Korea, and, most recently, Malaysia.

Part of the job of creating one culture falls on the shoulders of the company's trainers, especially sales trainers. Disk drives are component parts, and salespeople can easily default to lowering prices and trying to sell the drives as commodities. Seagate's premium price is justifiable on the basis of the value the company delivers, but Roger Liston, sales trainer for Seagate, found sales reps in Australia were making friends but not making sales. In Asia, he discovered reps were uncomfortable with what they perceived to be inappropriate American selling methods. In both cases, Liston had to first learn the country's culture before he could adapt the corporate culture. After he learned the local culture, he was able to adapt Seagate's selling strategy, changing the sales method to fit local requirements.

Seagate's culture challenges extend to all parts of the corporation, as plants are being added in Asia and other continents. Making the challenge even greater is the company's acquisition binge. Recently, the company purchased several other companies in related businesses, companies that already had global operations. While the future looks bright for the industry, whether Seagate can successfully integrate all of these cultures into one corporate culture remains to be seen.

Source: Robert Dwyer and John F. Tanner Jr., *Business Marketing: Connecting Strategy, Relationships, and Learning* (New York: Irwin/McGraw–Hill, 1999), p. 201.

Similarly, the second important difference is that market-driven companies are able to develop stronger relationships with their customers and their channels of distribution. Stronger relationships include more direct lines of communication; instead of all communication going between a purchasing agent and a salesperson, interaction among engineers, for example, in all three firms (customer, manufacturer, and supplier) can occur. Stronger relationships can result in greater attention to the customer throughout the firm.

Neither important skill (market sensing and relationship building) can develop, however, without the presence of adequate spanning processes, or processes that link internal processes with the customer. Sales management is an important link in the spanning process, as sales managers must represent the sales force and customers to others in the company. For example, salespeople are often the first in the company to run into a new competitor. It takes the sales manager, however, to make sure that those responsible for pricing or product development are aware of the method by which the new competitor is attacking the market. Exhibit 2.3 illustrates the relationship of internal processes with spanning processes to link with customer requirements. In this exhibit, internal processes such as financial management are shown to link with spanning processes, such as order fulfillment, which then impact customer-linking processes or other external processes. For internal processes to contribute to the value delivered by the value chain, there must be adequate spanning processes.

Internal Partnering to Create a Market Orientation

Yet internal and external processes are often in conflict, as different sets of objectives are sought. Sales management wants every potential customer to buy, for example, while credit wants only creditworthy accounts. Internal partnering is one spanning process that, when done well, can result in managing such conflict so that it has a positive effect on the firm. Internal partnering, or creating partnering relationships with other functional areas

Exhibit 2.3 Classifying Capabilities

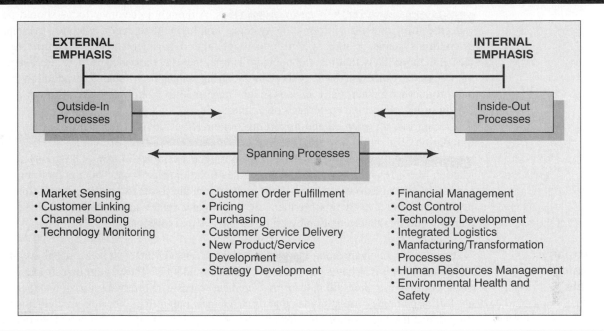

EXTERNAL EMPHASIS

INTERNAL EMPHASIS

Outside-In Processes

Inside-Out Processes

Spanning Processes

- Market Sensing
- Customer Linking
- Channel Bonding
- Technology Monitoring

- Customer Order Fulfillment
- Pricing
- Purchasing
- Customer Service Delivery
- New Product/Service Development
- Strategy Development

- Financial Management
- Cost Control
- Technology Development
- Integrated Logistics
- Manfacturing/Transformation Processes
- Human Resources Management
- Environmental Health and Safety

Source: George S. Day, "Capabilities of Market-Driven Organizations," *Journal of Marketing* 58 (October 1994), pp. 37–52. Reprinted by permission of the American Marketing Association.

(customers and suppliers within the firm), can also serve to carry market requirements to those managers in charge of internal processes, like credit approval. Internal partnering is a spanning process that creates a framework or environment for other spanning processes, such as postsale service, new product development, or market penetration and development processes. The result is a market orientation throughout the firm and not just in the sales force.

Internal partnering carries the voice of the customer

Ron Williams, national accounts director for Champion Products, is a salesperson. The only thing is, he has built many internal partnerships because he often sells for the *customer.* "I find myself selling the needs of the customer to senior management, manufacturing, customer service, or marketing every day," he says. One might think that members of those departments would just do what Ron says because it is in the best interest of the customer. Those managers, however, may have performance evaluation systems that conflict with what the customer needs. "For example, we may normally build a product a certain way. If the customer wants a slight modification, then I have to convince manufacturing and do that early enough that they can schedule the special production without driving their costs way up."[10] Ron works well with manufacturing and other areas of the firm because he has developed internal partnerships with the people in those areas.

In such situations, Ron is the voice of the customer. Other parts of the marketing department also take on the voice of the customer; for example, when new products are being developed, marketing research may have the responsibility of speaking for the customer. If that voice isn't heard, then the product may be built to suit only the company's needs.

The customer's voice must be carried to many parts of the firm—internal partnering is one mechanism for carrying that voice. Recognize, though, that *it is the sales manager's responsibility* to build these partnerships. Although a customer focus should pervade the firm, rarely do information systems, employment selection systems, personnel evaluation systems, or other systems encourage other departments to take the initiative. In fact, it is more likely that just the opposite is true, that there are incentives to not listen to the customer. For example, it costs manufacturing managers to change production from one product to another, yet a sales manager may need to be able to offer different products in order to meet the customer's objectives.

Being market-oriented and a learning organization requires that a firm have a solid foundation of identity. A solid foundation of identity is a clear understanding of what the company is and is striving to be. One of the strongest examples is a small company called Malden Mills, featured in the "Managing Sales Relationships" box. There is too much information available to try to learn it all, just as there are too many potential opportunities in the marketplace to try to serve them all. A company creates an identity that helps focus learning and market orientation by first creating a sound mission.

Company Mission and Goals

A statement of an organization's mission attempts to answer the most basic questions about its reason for being. What is our business? What should it be? These seem like simple questions, but they are often difficult for management to answer. Too many mission statements are full of platitudes and attributes that everyone has, rather than focusing on elements that truly define the organization. To illustrate the problem, one group of managers from over 20 companies identified *the same mission statement* as being that of their own company![11]

Many organizations define their missions too narrowly by focusing on the production of a particular product or service. As technology and customer needs change, specific products and services become obsolete, and firms that define their mission in narrow terms can become obsolete as well. There are few streetcar companies today, for instance, but many organizations are attempting to satisfy the need for urban mass transit through a variety of other means.

The most appropriate way for a firm to define its mission is in terms of the broad human needs it will try to satisfy. Volkswagen might define its mission as providing economical private transportation, while Walt Disney Co. describes its mission as providing family entertainment.

When an organization's mission is defined in terms of satisfying a need, it becomes easier to identify attractive marketing opportunities. When an oil company defines its mission as satisfying people's energy needs, it is then clear that the company should be exploring a variety of energy sources, such as solar power, in addition to locating new sources of petroleum. Similarly, a clearly defined mission helps management evaluate available opportunities and avoid those that are inconsistent with the firm's purpose.

SBU strategy

In organizations with multiple divisions or strategic business units, each SBU is likely to have its own objectives and a distinct strategy for accomplishing them. As mentioned earlier, the keystone of a business-level strategy is a decision about how the business will compete in its industry to achieve a sustainable competitive advantage. Although an SBU may contain a number of different products or brands, its competitive strategy will influence and constrain the marketing objectives, strategies, and functional programs—including the activities of the sales force—appropriate for each of those products.

Several authors have developed classification schemes that identify a few common, or "generic," strategies pursued by business units across a variety of industries. The best

Standing Outside the Fire

Following a fire that burned his textile mill to the ground, Aaron Feuerstein stepped into a firestorm of controversy by pledging to rebuild, and pledging to pay his employees while the mill was rebuilt, even though they would not be producing any fabric. But employees weren't the only ones thrown into panic worrying about lost income. As Malden Mills manufactures textiles used to make jackets and coats for companies like Recreation Equipment, L.L.Bean, and Land's End, one of the first concerns had to be what to tell customers. And as Robert Himmel, director of sales and marketing, said, "We didn't have a manual that read, 'When your mill burns down, this is what you should do.'"

In the days following the fire, Malden split the customer base into two groups: those that had to be serviced immediately and those that could alter their production schedule or receive fabric from another company until Malden could service again. The company also moved undamaged equipment into a warehouse so that some production could begin. But even with that, J. Crew, a major account, was told that its original shipment schedule could not be met. As Diane Chang (J. Crew's senior vice president) noted, "That's where I think they did an outstanding job, in terms of telling us what they could and could not do from a timing standpoint."

Since then, Malden's commitment to its employees and its customers has paid huge dividends. Production is now double for Polartec, one of Malden's primary product lines, with quality ratings higher than ever before. Stronger employee relationships mean better-quality products, which in turn strengthens relationships with customers. Customer retention is a world-class 95 percent, and revenues have grown at superior rates. Malden has come through the fire stronger than ever before.

Sources: Thomas Teal, "Not a Fool, Not a Saint," *Fortune,* text edition, November 11, 1996, *www.fortune/1996/961111/fea.html;* Shelley Donald Coolidge, "Corporate Decency Prevails at Malden Mills," *www.ncl.org/anr/stories/malden.htm.* reprinted from *The Christian Science Monitor,* March 28, 1996; Michele Marchetti, "Rising from the Ashes," Sales & *Marketing Management* (August, 1996), pp. 30–31.

known of these schemes is the one developed by Michael Porter. He defined three basic competitive strategies: Low Cost, Differentiation, and Niche.[12] Another popular typology of competitive strategies was developed by Miles and Snow. They classified strategies according to the emphasis placed on growth through new product and market development, and they labeled the resulting categories Prospector, Defender, and Analyzer strategies.[13] Brief definitions of these six generic business strategies are provided in Exhibit 2.4.

For an SBU to effectively implement its competitive strategy, the marketing strategies and functional programs for each of its products should be tailored to the requirements of that strategy. For example, when the North American PC division of Compaq shifted from a differentiation strategy focused on offering technically superior products to a more price-oriented, low-cost competitive strategy, it also changed its marketing strategy, its product offerings, its distribution channels, its advertising appeals, and the role and structure of its sales force. Some specific implications of different competitive strategies for a business's sales programs and activities are also summarized in Exhibit 2.4.[14]

Once a business has decided how it will compete in order to gain a sustainable advantage over other firms, it must then decide where to compete: what specific product markets or market segments it will target. This decision involves assessing the available market opportunities.

Market opportunity analysis

In the broadest sense, a market opportunity exists whenever some human need is unsatisfied. However, an unsatisfied need represents a viable and attractive opportunity for a firm only if

Exhibit 2.4   Generic Business Strategies and Their Implications for the Sales Force

Porter's Typology	Sales Force Implications
Low-Cost Supplier Aggressive construction of efficient-scale facilities, vigorous pursuit of cost reductions from experience, tight cost and overhead control, usually associated with high relative market share.	Servicing large current customers, pursuing large prospects, minimizing costs, selling on the basis of price, and usually assuming significant order-taking responsibilities.
Differentiation Creation of something perceived industrywide as being unique. Provides insulation against competitive rivalry because of brand loyalty and resulting lower sensitivity to price.	Selling nonprice benefits, generating orders, providing high quality of customer service and responsiveness, possibly significant amount of prospecting if high growth industry, selecting customers based on low price sensitivity. Usually requires a high-quality sales force.
Niche Service of a particular target market, with each functional policy developed with this target market in mind. Although market share in the industry might be low, the firm dominates a segment within the industry.	To become experts in the operations and opportunities associated with the target market. Focusing customer attention on nonprice benefits and allocating selling time to the target market.

Miles and Snow's Typology	Sales Force Implications
Prospector Attempt to pioneer in product market development. Offer a frequently changing product line and be willing to sacrifice short-term profits to gain a long-term stronghold in their markets.	Primary focus is on sales volume growth. Territory management emphasizes customer penetration and prospecting.
Defender Offer a limited, stable product line to a predictable market. Markets are generally in the late growth or early maturity phase of the product life cycle. Emphasis is on being the low-cost producer through high volume.	Maintain the current customer base. Very little prospecting for new customers is involved. Customer service is emphasized along with greater account penetration.
Analyzer Choose high-growth markets while holding onto substantial mature markets. Analyzers are an intermediate type of firm. They make fewer and slower product market changes than prospectors, but are less committed to stability and efficiency than defenders.	Must balance multiple roles: servicing existing customers, prospecting for new customers, uncovering new applications, holding onto distribution of mature products, and supporting campaigns for new products.

Source: Adapted from William L. Cron and Michael Levy, "Sales Management Performance Evaluation: A Residual Income Perspective," *Journal of Personal Selling and Sales Management* (August 1987), p. 58.

1. The opportunity is consistent with the mission and objectives of the firm.
2. There are enough potential customers for the needed product or service so the total potential sales volume is, or will be, substantial.
3. The firm has the necessary resources and expertise to capture an adequate share of the total market.

Evaluating market opportunities involves first evaluating the environmental factors affecting the market and estimating the total market potential for a good or service. Next, the firm must evaluate its capabilities and strengths compared with those of competitors to estimate the share of the total market potential it can reasonably hope to secure. Later, after a specific marketing strategy has been determined, the firm can develop sales forecasts of the actual sales volume it expects to attain over a specified time.

These estimates of total market potential, company sales potential, and sales forecasts are critical to the firm's sales plans. They provide the basis for defining sales territories, deploying salespeople, and setting sales quotas. Methods for analyzing market opportunities and generating sales forecasts are examined in more detail later in this book.

Market opportunities usually do not involve every consumer or organizational buyer in the marketplace. Market opportunities should be defined—and marketing strategies developed—for specific target markets, which usually consist of only one or a few customer segments with relatively homogeneous preferences and characteristics.

Generate strategies

Strategy generation is a creative task. Typically, several strategies will achieve the same objective. For example, a computer firm interested in increasing its market share might (1) attempt to leapfrog its competitors by introducing a technically superior new generation of computers, (2) attempt to become the low-cost producer and compete aggressively on price, as Compaq has done in recent years, or (3) appeal to customers by developing more convenient distribution channels, as Dell Computer did when it started offering PCs via the Internet.

The key at this stage is to be as creative as possible. The idea is not to evaluate strategies but to generate them. Listing some far-out strategies is not only acceptable at this stage, it is desirable. Later stages in the process will reduce this original list to a more reasonable set; however, generating as many ideas as possible to begin with will ensure that the better strategies are entertained when evaluating alternatives. Even the most sophisticated evaluation procedure cannot select the optimal strategy if no one has thought of it.

Select strategies

The criteria used to select the most promising marketing strategy should be directly related to the objectives to be accomplished. For example, if the major marketing objective is to increase market share, then those strategies likely to yield high share increases should be scrutinized. Typically, however, a business will have several marketing objectives, and the strategy that is best for one might be detrimental in achieving another. Thus, the best overall strategy may not be the best for any single objective.

Program marketing mix

As mentioned, a marketing program reflects a particular allocation of financial and human resources. The decision involves three questions: (1) How much is going to be spent on the total marketing effort? (2) How is that expenditure going to be allocated among the elements of the marketing mix? (3) How are the dollars and effort allocated to an element going to be divided among the possible activities? This is where the formation of the firm's strategic sales program enters the planning picture; it is one part of the firm's communications program.

Review and revision

Those in charge of the functional areas of the business are typically charged with generating plans for the functions they supervise. This raises the possibility that the marketing plan prepared by a product manager may be incompatible with the business unit's financial or production plans. For example, the cash flows generated by projected product sales might be insufficient or provide too low a return on capital to produce the product. The various functional plans, therefore, must be reviewed and integrated into a cohesive whole at the business-unit and corporate level.

Audit and adjust

Today's volatile environment makes planning crucial and also necessitates periodic evaluations of these plans. As competitors adjust their strategies and other environmental conditions change, it may be necessary to revise the firm's plans and programs.

When goals and objectives have been spelled out in specific and measurable terms during the planning process, controlling the marketing plan is rather straightforward. It involves periodic comparisons of actual results with the sales volume, market share, expense budgets, and other objectives specified in the plan. When the results deviate from planned levels, management can attempt to find out why and, if necessary, take corrective action. This could involve adjusting specific elements of the marketing mix, adopting a new marketing strategy, or possibly reevaluating market opportunities.

The sales manager, as we have seen, plays a major role in this evaluation and control process since the manager is responsible for evaluating the results of the sales program. Part III of this book is devoted to a discussion of this control and adjustment process.

THE ROLE OF PERSONAL SELLING IN A FIRM'S MARKETING STRATEGY

As mentioned earlier, a number of choices face strategic planners, choices that include the type of strategy à la Porter or Miles and Snow. Another choice facing strategic marketing planners is the type of relationship desired with the market or segments of the market. The nature of the sales force and its role in carrying out a firm's marketing strategy depend on the type of relationship with the market desired by the organization. Other factors, such as the cost to serve a market, also affect the role of the sales force, as we will discuss.

The Relationships Role

Most people think of relationships as the bonds that exist between people, and that definition works in many social instances. In business, though, it is more helpful to recognize that relationships occur along a continuum that can be defined by the types of transactions between a buyer and seller. There are three basic relationship types along this continuum: market exchanges, functional relationships, and strategic partnerships. Exhibit 2.5 summarizes the characteristics of each of these relationship types.

Market exchanges

At one end of the continuum are market exchanges, or one-shot transactions that occur between a buyer and seller without much thought of future interaction. For example, consider a gasoline purchase. Most people purchase gasoline where it is convenient when they are low on gas. They don't buy gasoline at the same place time after time because they like the clerk and want to do business with that store. Yet, over time, it is possible that a large percentage of purchases are made at the same gas station. These purchases still represent market exchanges because it is the location of the station that drives the purchase—it is on the way to work or closest to the house and so on.

Do salespeople have a role in market exchanges? Consider Florida Furniture Industries (FFI), a manufacturer of bedroom furniture headquartered in Palatka, Florida. This company buys poplar logs by the railroad car load. There is no difference in the quality of

Exhibit 2.5   Types of Relationships between Buyers and Sellers

Characteristics of the Relationship	Type of Relationship		
	Market Exchange	Functional Relationship	Strategic Partnerships
Time horizon	Short term	Long term	Long term
Concern for other party	Low	Medium	High
Trust	Low	High	High
Investment in relationship	Low Medium	HIGH	
Nature of relationship	Conflict, bargaining	Cooperation	Collaboration
Risk in relationship	Low	Medium	High
Potential benefits	Low	Medium	High

Source: Barton Weitz, Stephen Castleberry, and John Tanner, *Selling: Building Partnerships,* 3rd ed. (New York: Irwin/McGraw–Hill, 1998), p. 36.

various suppliers' logs. The company shops around each time more logs are needed, and salespeople will call if an opportunity for a good deal arises or if they believe it is about time for FFI to order. These are market exchanges, and salespeople are needed to make sure that their company is among the group shopped by FFI. Further, the salespeople can create selling opportunities by creatively taking advantage of market conditions to offer lower prices or better terms or by simply calling at the right time.

From the examples, it may be obvious that several characteristics of a market can influence the use of a market exchange relationship strategy. Characteristics such as lack of product differentiation, competition on price, and similar factors can make a market exchange strategy appropriate.

Functional relationships

As we move along the continuum, functional relationships reflect the middle area. Functional relationships are long-term relationships between buyer and seller based upon close personal friendships. These personal relationships create a climate of cooperation, with open and honest communication.

When functional relationships are appropriate, the salesperson's relationship with the buyer is critical. Examples include financial planning (where the broker becomes a trusted confidant of the client) and contract manufacturing, an industry where salespeople develop strong relationships with product designers so that the sellers' components are included in new products.

Functional relationships can be appropriate when that level of personal trust is required to manage the business relationship and when the salesperson can be seen to have special expertise that provides competitive advantage. In these situations, it is in the buyer's best interest to seek a functional relationship. Functional relationships can grow for other reasons that are not strategic.

One danger of functional relationships for the selling organization becomes reality when one party leaves. If the buyer changes jobs, even within the buying organization, a new functional relationship must be created. Similarly, if the salesperson leaves, the relationship is at risk, particularly if the salesperson goes to a competing company. In some industries, it is quite common for salespeople to take their accounts with them—these are industries characterized by functional relationships.

Strategic partnerships

At the far end of the continuum from market exchanges are strategic partnerships. Strategic partnerships are long-term relationships in which the partners make significant investments to improve profitability of both companies and jointly achieve strategic objectives. In a true strategic partnership, the relationship is between two organizations and reflects a wide range of personal relationships between members of the two organizations. Thus, the relationship is no longer salesperson-centered.

The salesperson still plays an important role, however. For example, FFI has a strong relationship with Rooms To Go, the fastest-growing furniture retailer. This relationship requires direct communication with production, product designers, and others, but the salesperson is responsible for making sure that the relationship remains strong. Salespeople are both relationship managers and general managers, because they are responsible for ensuring the mutual profitability that arises out of the relationship. As relationship managers, they work directly with the buyer to co-develop joint strategic programs and to strengthen the relationship. As general managers, they work within their own organization to see that the strategic programs are carried out.

Strategic partnerships cannot be created with every customer, nor should they be. Strategic partnerships should only be created with customers who are large and can make the investments needed worthwhile; with customers who are innovative and can provide technology that other customers cannot; or with customers who provide access to markets better than any other customer. For example, Procter & Gamble and Wal-Mart share a strategic partnership. Wal-Mart teaches P&G logistics methods that enable P&G to be more profitable with all customers. Wal-Mart benefits from P&G's market knowledge and marketing technology. Through this knowledge and technology, Wal-Mart is able to co-develop new markets and new products with P&G so that both companies can capitalize on market opportunities.

Wallace, a global commercial printing company that specializes in labels, has a strategic partnership with American Airlines. Five Wallace salespeople have offices at American's headquarters in Dallas. The American account is one of the top Wallace accounts, in part because the companies co-developed a baggage-tagging system that enables American to track and know the location of virtually every bag. This ability to co-develop new technology is an example of why a company selects another as a strategic partner.

Other Factors Affecting the Sales Force's Relationship Role

The sales force, then, plays a role in accomplishing a relationship strategy. A sales force, however, is just one element in a complete marketing communications mix. Other elements, such as advertising, direct response, and electronic media, can also be used as part of a relationship strategy. The choice of such elements can influence the role of the sales force. The factors that affect the actual role of the sales force include the cost to serve a market segment at the desired service level for the realized market value.

Each account has a desired service level. A small account for Wallace would not want a Wallace representative permanently on site. Nor would it make sense for Wallace because the realized market value, or profit, of that account would be too low. The challenge for sales managers is balancing the customer's desired service level with the appropriate cost to serve so that a profit is made.

For example, Shell Oil's Tire, Battery, and Accessory (TBA) division had a field sales force that called on all independent Shell Oil dealers. While individual salespeople may have developed specific territory management strategies, the company had no strategy for which accounts should get more calls and which customers should be visited less. Dealer satisfaction ratings were poor, and profitability was marginal. The company examined their database of dealers and split the dealers into four segments: very large, large, medium, and small. Then, in dialog with dealers, Shell realized that each segment had a different desired level of service. The very large accounts needed to be visited by field salespeople about every other week. Large accounts needed a visit once a month, while medium accounts rarely needed a visit. A telephone call was all these buyers had time for. Small accounts didn't want to see a salesperson.

In response to this information, the company devised a plan where the field salespeople only called on very large and large accounts. A telemarketing sales staff was created to telemarket to large and medium accounts, sending field salespeople to medium accounts only when there was a problem that couldn't be resolved over the phone. Small accounts received only direct mail, although they could call a telemarketer assigned to their account when needed. After only a few months, total revenue was up significantly, sales costs declined dramatically, profit grew at a much higher rate, and dealer satisfaction ratings doubled. Shell Oil had developed a system that balanced the cost to serve with the desired level of service, enhancing profit.

The Role of Personal Selling in the Marketing Communications Mix

The Shell Oil example illustrates some of the advantages personal selling offers when planning the marketing communications mix. In the Shell situation, field sales was used only in larger accounts and telephone sales in smaller accounts. Since the salesperson communicates with only one potential customer at a time, the rep can tailor the message to fit the needs and interests of that specific customer. This tailoring of the message was an important requisite for larger accounts not needed in smaller accounts. In addition, communication flows in both directions during a sales call. The sales representative receives immediate feedback from the customer in the form of questions, objections, and nonverbal communication such as yawns and shrugs. Thus, the representative often knows immediately when a particular sales approach is not working and then can try a different tack.

The advantages of personal selling as a marketing communications tool stem largely from its face-to-face communication with a potential customer. Personal sales messages are often more persuasive than advertising or publicity in the mass media. Another advantage of face-to-face contact in personal selling is that the sales representative can communicate a larger amount of complex information than can be transmitted with other promotional tools. The salesperson can demonstrate the product or use visual aids. And since the salesperson is likely to call on the same client many times, the rep can devote a great deal of time to learning about that client's problems and needs, and to educating the client about the advantages of appropriate products or services. The long-term contact in personal selling is particularly important when the product or service can be customized to fit the needs of an individual customer—as is often the case in functional and strategic relationships—or when the terms of sale are open to negotiation.

The primary disadvantage of personal selling is that a sales rep can communicate with only a small number of potential customers. Consequently, personal selling is much more costly per person reached than the other promotional tools. An advertisement in *Reader's Digest* costs only about a penny per reader, but some estimate the cost of an average industrial sales call at more than $500.[15]

In other words, personal selling should play a substantial role in the firm's marketing mix only when the communications tasks involved are performed better by face-to-face selling than any other method. Such communications tasks include the following:

1. Transmitting large amounts of complex information about the firm's products or policies.

Exhibit 2.6   Factors Influencing the Role of Personal Selling in a Firm's Marketing Strategy

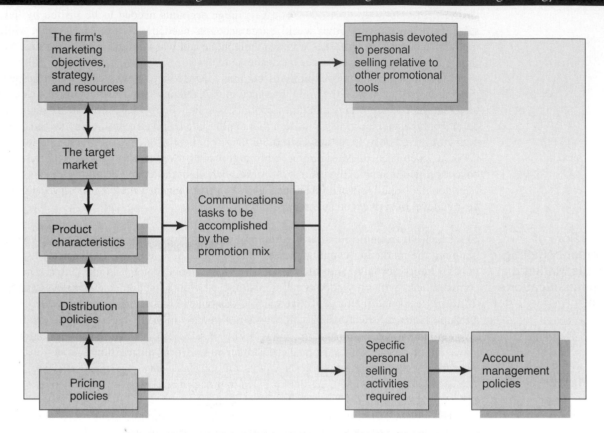

2. Adapting product offerings and/or promotional appeals to the unique needs and interests of specific customers.

3. Convincing customers that the firm's products or services are better on at least some dimensions than similar offerings of competitors.

As Exhibit 2.6 indicates, the communications tasks actually faced by a business—and the appropriate amount of personal selling effort to be used in the marketing strategy—depend on the business's objectives, marketing strategy, and resources; the number and kind of customers in its target market; and the nature of the other elements of its marketing mix.

Company Resources, Objectives, and Marketing Strategy

Although the costs per person reached are high for personal selling, a successful personal selling effort may require a smaller total financial outlay than either an advertising or a sales promotion campaign. One major advertising agency refuses to represent consumer goods manufacturers unless they are willing to spend at least $5 million annually on their advertising campaigns. The agency believes an effective national advertising campaign cannot be undertaken for less. The high costs involved in extensive advertising and sales promotion efforts limit their use by smaller firms. Such firms must often rely on personal selling—perhaps supplemented with less expensive advertising or other forms of communication such as the Internet or trade shows—as their primary promotional tool.

If the firm's objective is to expand distribution by persuading more wholesalers or retailers to carry the product, then a strong personal selling effort and perhaps a trade promotion program are indicated. The highly persuasive nature of personal selling also makes it an appropriate tool when the objective is to take market share away from established competitors, especially if the product is a relatively complex industrial or consumer durable good. Finally, if the objective is simply to maintain the market share of a well-established product, "reminder" advertising should play the primary role in the promotional mix.

Characteristics of the Target Market

Because various marketing communications tools differ greatly in their costs per person reached, the number of potential customers in the firm's target market, their size, and their geographic distribution influence the communications mix. For example, in order to justify the higher costs, personal selling is most often emphasized when the target market contains relatively few customers, the average customer is likely to place a relatively large order, and customers are clustered close together. Firms that sell to industrial markets with few potential customers, and those that distribute their products through a small number of wholesale intermediaries, commonly rely on personal selling as their primary promotional tool. Firms that sell to large, geographically dispersed, consumer markets place primary emphasis on the more cost-efficient advertising and sales promotion methods.

Product Characteristics

Most marketing textbooks suggest that the promotional mixes for industrial products concentrate heavily on personal selling; those for consumer durable goods utilize a combination of personal selling and advertising; and producers of consumer nondurable goods rely most heavily on advertising and sales promotion. The reason is that industrial goods and consumer durables tend to be more complex than nondurable, so potential buyers need more information to make a purchase decision. Also, industrial goods can often be designed or modified to meet the needs of individual customers, and consumer durables (as well as complex services, such as financial or insurance services) often present the buyer with a range of options.

These generalizations are largely supported by the information in Exhibit 2.7, which shows personal selling costs as a percentage of sales across a variety of industries. Note that sales force expenses account for a much larger proportion of total revenue in industrial products and service industries (e.g., construction, chemicals, electronic components, electronics) than in consumer nondurable industries, such as food and recreation.

But these generalizations should be viewed with caution. Industrial goods producers usually stress personal selling, but they might also do extensive advertising and public relations to build awareness of the company and its products so the sales force can gain access to potential customers more easily.[16] Similarly, although a consumer goods producer like Nabisco might spend large sums on media advertising and sales promotion, it is also likely to field a sales force to call on retailers and build reseller support in its distribution channels.

To make matters even more complicated, new technologies—such as the World Wide Web—are blurring the distinctions among the various promotional tools. A company's Web site can (1) communicate large amounts of product information, (2) generate leads for the firm's field sales force to follow up, or (3) allow interested customers to bypass face-to-face contact with a salesperson and order the firm's products electronically.[17] Some contact management software programs, such as GoldMine, can then transfer lead information into the contact database, making it easy for salespeople to follow up.

Exhibit 2.7   Sales Force Costs across Selected Industries

Industry Group	Sales Force Costs as a Percentage of Total Sales	Industry Group	Sales Force Costs as a Percentage of Total Sales
Agriculture	13.8%	Instruments	9.3%
Amusement/recreation services	2.3	Machinery	3.9
Chemicals	14.3	Manufacturing	6.8
Communications	9.0	Office equipment	3.3
Construction	6.8	Paper/allied products	1.5
Electronic components	19.0	Primary metal products	4.1
Electronics	21.0	Printing/publishing	10.8
Fabricated metals	2.7	Rubber/plastics	7.7
Food products	3.4	Wholesale (consumer)	7.4
Average	**6.2%**		

Note: Industry groups reflect categories selected and reported by Dartnell Corporation. The overall average has been calculated based on data from all industries studied.

Source: Dartnell Corporation, *28th Survey of Sales Force Compensation* © 1994; Dartnell Corporation, p. 117.

Distribution Policies

As mentioned, personal selling is often necessary to build reseller support and develop adequate distribution for a product, regardless of whether it is a consumer good or industrial good. The importance of the sales force's role in building a distribution channel is influenced by the firm's strategy for inducing resellers to buy its product. When a firm follows a **pull strategy,** it attempts to build strong customer demand for its brand. This encourages wholesalers and retailers to carry the product to satisfy their customers and reap the resulting sales and profits. A strong advertising program is a key to such a strategy.

When a firm uses a **push strategy** to build reseller support, it offers direct inducements to potential wholesalers and retailers to encourage them to stock the product. When consumers see the product in the store, it is hoped that they will like it and buy it. A wide range of inducements can be offered to resellers, including the development of "just-in-time" reorder and delivery programs—or logistical alliances—that help resellers reduce their investments in inventory and improve inventory turnover, "efficient customer response" or "category management" programs to help resellers improve their sales volumes and margins on the firm's products, price promotions, volume discounts, contests for the reseller's salespeople, training programs, cooperative advertising programs, and point-of-purchase promotional materials.

The manufacturer's sales force plays a principal role in implementing a push strategy. The sales force must explain the advantages of carrying and promoting the supplier's products to prospective channel members, persuade them to stock and aggressively merchandise those products, and maintain cooperative relationships with the firm's channel partners over time.[18]

Pricing Policies

A firm's pricing policies can also influence the composition of its promotion mix. "Big-ticket" items, both industrial goods and consumer durables, typically require substantial amounts of personal selling. Such expensive products are often technically or aesthetically sophisticated, and customers perceive substantial risk in purchasing them. There-

---

Exhibit 2.8 Marketing Strategy Characteristics and the Relative Importance of Personal Selling as a Promotional Tool

Advertising relatively important		Personal selling relatively important
Large	← Number of customers →	Small
Low	← Buyers' information needs →	High
Small	← Size and importance of purchase →	Large
Little	← Postpurchase service required →	Much
Low	← Product complexity →	High
Pull	← Distribution strategy →	Push
Preset	← Pricing policy →	Negotiated
Many	← Resources available for promotion →	Few

Source: Adapted from David W. Cravens, *Strategic Marketing* (New York: Irwin/McGraw-Hill, 2000), p. 363.

fore, potential buyers usually want the kind of detailed information and advice they can get only from a salesperson before making their decisions.

Also, personal selling is essential in marketing products or services where the ultimate selling price is open to negotiation. Price negotiations can occur only when there is face-to-face contact between a salesperson and a potential buyer. Although negotiated pricing policies are most commonly found among marketers of industrial goods and services, they are also followed in the sale of some consumer durables, such as automobiles.

The importance of personal selling relative to other promotional tools depends on various characteristics of the marketing strategy, including the size and nature of the target market, the complexity and service requirements of the product, and the other elements of the marketing mix. The impact of these factors on the relative importance of personal selling is summarized in Exhibit 2.8.

Computerized Ordering and Customer Alliances

To further strengthen relationships with major customers after an initial sale has been made, firms are forming logistical alliances with those customers involving the development of joint information and reorder systems. For instance, Procter & Gamble has formed alliances with major supermarket chains, such as Kroger, to develop a restocking system called efficient consumer response (ECR). Sales information from Kroger's checkout scanners is sent directly to P&G's computers, which figure out automatically when to replenish each product and schedule deliveries direct to each store. This paperless exchange minimizes mistakes and billbacks, minimizes inventory, decreases out-of-stocks, and improves cash flow.[19]

IMPROVING POSTSALE CUSTOMER SERVICE AND LOYALTY

As Exhibit 2.9 indicates, maintaining the loyalty of major current customers can be crucial for improving a business's profitability as its markets mature, and is therefore an important element of any sales strategy. Recall, though, that this chapter began by discussing the importance of a market orientation and the role of customer requirements in determining corporate success. Maintaining customer loyalty is one outcome of a market orientation. The exhibit shows that loyal customers, those with whom a functional or strategic relationship is shared, become more profitable over time. The firm not only avoids the high costs associated with acquiring a new customer, but it typically benefits because loyal customers (a) tend to concentrate their purchases, thus leading to larger volumes and lower selling and distribution costs, (b) provide positive word-of-mouth and customer referrals, and (c) may be willing to pay premium prices for the value they receive.[20]

Periodic measurement of customer satisfaction is important, then, because a dissatisfied customer is unlikely to remain loyal to a company over time. Unfortunately, however, the corollary is not always true: Customers who describe themselves as satisfied are not necessarily loyal. Indeed, one author estimates that 60 to 80 percent of customer defectors in most businesses said they were "satisfied" or "very satisfied" on the last customer survey before their defection.[21] In the interim, perhaps, competitors improved their offerings, the customer's requirements changed, or other environmental factors shifted. The point is that businesses that measure customer satisfaction should be commended—but urged not to stop there. Satisfaction measures need to be supplemented with examinations of customer behavior, such as measures of the annual retention rate, frequency of purchases, and the percentage of a customer's total purchases captured by the firm.

Most important, defecting customers should be studied in detail to discover why the firm failed to provide sufficient value to retain their loyalty. Such failures often provide

---

Exhibit 2.9   Sources of Increased Profit from Loyal Customers

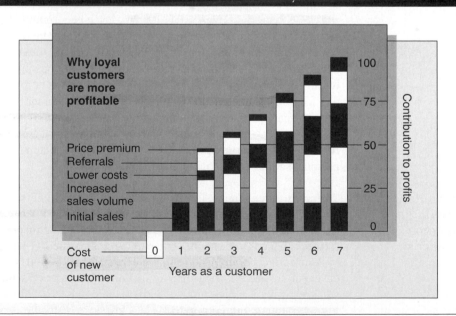

Source: Rahul Jacob, "Why Some Customers Are More Equal than Others," *Fortune* (September 19, 1994), p. 220.

more valuable information than satisfaction measures because they stand out as a clear, understandable message telling the organization exactly where improvements are needed.

While computerized reorder systems have reduced the routine "order-taking" activities performed by many salespeople, they are playing an increasingly important role in maintaining the satisfaction and loyalty of major customers over time. Thus, major account management policies often emphasize activities to be performed by the salesperson after a sale is made. These activities typically include such routine servicing as expediting credit approval and delivery. They can also include more extensive service where the salesperson acts as the customer's representative to the selling company and attempts to ensure that the company is adequately meeting the needs of the buyer.

Because major account management requires that a salesperson devote almost constant attention to the needs of a single customer, firms that use this approach typically have two separate sales forces: one that calls on smaller customers and one that is a force of account managers who devote all their time to one or a few major accounts.

Major Account Teams

Some national accounts are so large and important that a firm may assign a team of representatives (consisting of people from various functional departments of the company) to a single customer. The sales team may include representatives from different levels in the company's management hierarchy, too. Each deals with purchase influencers and decision makers at corresponding levels in the customer's organization. In other words, implementing a major account management program can have important implications for the way a firm organizes its sales force. These and other organizational considerations involved in strategic sales planning are examined in Chapter 5.

SUMMARY

Planning is deciding what to do in the present to achieve what is desired in the future. The planning process begins with a statement of the company's mission and goals. Marketing goals that result from these corporate goals are best achieved through a marketing plan. Organizational learning is a critical component of strategic planning, and requires as a cultural foundation that the company adopt a market orientation. This orientation enables the firm to identify customer requirements and other known requisites more readily. However, learning boundaries can develop restricting the organization to adaptive, rather than generative, learning.

The marketing plan logically includes (1) the assessment of market opportunities available and an estimation of the resources necessary to capture an adequate share of the market, (2) the generation of possible strategies, (3) the selection of a strategy that best achieves the stated objectives, and (4) the programming of the marketing mix or allocation of resources to the marketing effort, including the sales function. The plans prepared by each functional area need to be reviewed and integrated at the corporate level. This may entail some revision to make them

compatible. Once adopted, the plans must be continually monitored and adjusted as conditions warrant.

The advantages of personal selling as a promotional tool stem largely from the fact that it involves face-to-face communication with a potential customer. For many products and in many industries, advertising is viewed as more effective than personal selling in creating awareness and in reinforcing already held opinions. Personal selling is viewed as the more effective in changing opinions and behaviors. The role personal selling should play in the firm's marketing strategy is logically a function of (1) company resources and objectives, (2) characteristics of the target market, (3) product characteristics, (4) distribution policies, and (5) pricing policies.

The company's view of the purchasing process and the roles played by the members of a prospect's buying center affect the account management policies it adopts. Many firms have explicit policies on what salespeople are to do at each stage in the buying process.

In response to the growing importance of major accounts—those very large customers that represent a disproportionate share of the firm's total sales volume—many firms are also developing explicit policies regarding how such customers should be handled. Often these policies dictate that salespeople should perform functions for the customer's organization that make them more valuable to the customer. These functions might involve designing complete systems, which include components not manufactured by the representative's employer, or assisting in the installation of such systems. Sometimes the salesperson is told to act as the customer's representative to make sure the customer's needs are satisfied.

DISCUSSION QUESTIONS

1. Relationship marketing has led to some strange situations. The headline in a *Wall Street Journal* article (January 13, 1995, pp. Al, A6) reads, "Some companies let suppliers work on site and even place orders." The article notes,

   > Vendor sales representatives have desks next to the factory floor. Their badges let them roam wherever they choose, attend production-status meetings, stop by the research lab, and click computers onto sales forecasts. Then, they can write a sales order for which the company is billed.

   What are the advantages of such close buyer–seller relationships as described by the quotation? What are the disadvantages? How could a potential supplier who is not part of this relationship gain access and become a supplier?

2. The chapter discusses various typologies useful for classifying the competitive strategies of strategic business units (SBUs). Using the Miles and Snow typology, how would the marketing strategies and tactics of a prospector SBU vary from those adopted by a defender SBU? Which would be the best option for a prospector SBU? A sales force that sells only for the prospector SBU? Or a sales force that is shared with a defender SBU that sells products for both SBUs? What are the relevant issues to consider?

3. In spite of the strong Wall Street market of the last few years, economic ups and downs occur frequently, particularly within industries. Downturns usually lead to broad, sweeping corporate edicts to become "lean and mean" or "tighten your belts" by eliminating all fat. Such a "wartime" mentality has led firms such as Xerox, IBM, Kodak, Coca-Cola, Heinz, and Wrangler Jeans to reduce "too rich" programs. Carried to the extreme, such cutbacks can hinder an organization's ability to rebound when the economy improves. How can a corporation become "lean and mean," and what symptoms would indicate that cutbacks have gone too far? Relate these cutting efforts to strategy—what is it about strategy and planning that makes such cutbacks necessary? How can organizational learning be affected by such cutbacks?

4. Strategic partnerships require direct peer-to-peer communication, including from senior executive in the buying firm to the selling company's senior executive. What are the advantages of having top corporate officers, presidents in some cases, becoming involved in direct sales activities? What are the disadvantages? What types of challenges does such direct involvement present to the salesperson?

5. How does industry experience become a learning boundary? What other types of learning boundaries can you think of, and how do these boundaries become created?

EXPERIENTIAL APPLICATION

Reflect upon one of your favorite places to shop or eat. List the elements that cause you to go back to that store or restaurant over and over. What type of relationship would you say you have with that establishment? Visit the establishment and ask to speak to the manager. Ask the manager who is the best supplier to that store or restaurant, and why. Compare the manager's answers with yours—are there similar factors that contribute to a favorite relationship? What type of relationship does the manager have with that supplier?

INTERNET EXERCISE

Open the Edward Jones site (*edwardjones.com*) and go to the page that describes the Investment Representative position for new college graduates. Evaluate the site relative to the material presented at the beginning of the chapter. Do you see any inconsistencies between what they tell prospec-

tive salespeople and the culture described at the start of the chapter? How do you see the culture supported by what they tell prospective salespeople? Be as specific as possible in supporting your conclusions.

SUGGESTED READINGS

Colletti, Jerome A., and Lawrence B. Chonko, "Change Management Initiatives: Moving Sales Organizations from Obsolescence to High Performance," *Journal of Personal Selling & Sales Management* 17 (Spring 1997), pp. 1–30.

Cravens, David, "The Changing Role of the Sales Force," *Marketing Management* 3 (1995), pp. 48–57.

Han, Sang-Lin, David T. Wilson, and Shirish P. Dant, "Buyer–Supplier Relationships Today," *Industrial Marketing Management* 22 (1993), pp. 331–38.

Keep, William, Stanley Hollander, and Roger Dickinson, "Forces Impinging on Long-Term Business Relationships: An Historical Perspective," *Journal of Marketing* 62 (April 1998), pp. 31–45.

Lambe, Jay, and Robert Spekman, "National Account Management: Large Account Selling or Buyer–Supplier Alliance?" *Journal of Personal Selling & Sales Management* 17 (Fall 1997), pp. 61–74.

Reichheld, Frederick F., "Loyalty and the Renaissance of Marketing." *Marketing Management* 2 (1994), pp. 10–21.

Sungupta, Sanjit, Robert Krapfel, and Michael Pusateri, "Switching Costs in Key Account Relationships," *Journal of Personal Selling & Sales Management* 17 (Fall 1997), pp. 9–16.

Walker, Orville C., Jr., Harper W. Boyd, Jr., and Jean-Claude Larréché. *Marketing Strategy: Planning and Implementation,* 2d ed. Burr Ridge, IL: Richard D. Irwin, 1996, chapters 1 and 2.

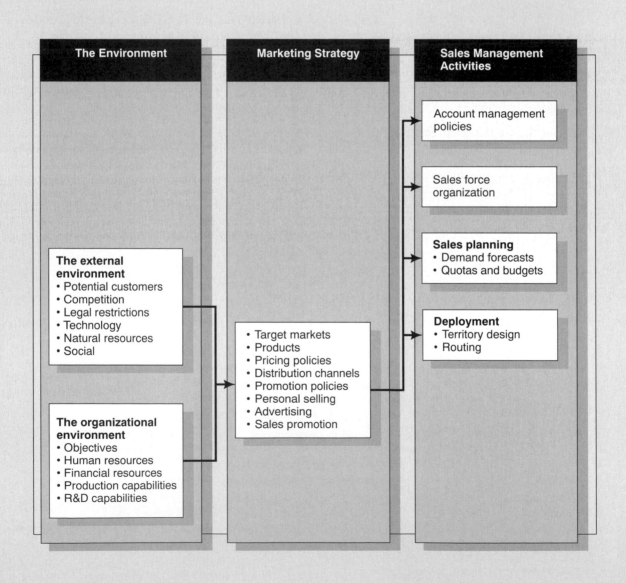

The Environment

Marketing Strategy

Sales Management Activities

Account management policies

Sales force organization

Sales planning
• Demand forecasts
• Quotas and budgets

Deployment
• Territory design
• Routing

The external environment
• Potential customers
• Competition
• Legal restrictions
• Technology
• Natural resources
• Social

The organizational environment
• Objectives
• Human resources
• Financial resources
• Production capabilities
• R&D capabilities

• Target markets
• Products
• Pricing policies
• Distribution channels
• Promotion policies
• Personal selling
• Advertising
• Sales promotion

Part I

Formulation of a Strategic Sales Program

Part I examines the decisions and activities involved in formulating a strategic sales program. First, sales managers must understand their buyers, so Chapter 3 examines how the process of buying and the process of selling intertwine. Chapter 4 then explores how factors in a firm's external and internal environments influence and constrain marketing and sales strategies. Chapter 5 examines alternative ways of organizing the sales force. Chapter 6 discusses the conduct of a market opportunity analysis and forecasting methods which are then used to determine sales quotas. Chapter 7 examines deployment decisions, decisions which also require the use of sound forecasts. These decisions include the design of sales territories, the determination of the number of people needed to adequately cover the market, and methods of allocating effort within territories.

3 The Process of Buying and Selling

WALLACE'S FIVE-YEAR SALE

When asked how long it took to get the business, Harry Murphy sat back and laughed. "From start to finish, the sale took 18 months. But frankly, it took us over a decade to get the business." The business he's talking about is American Airlines' luggage tag business. Wallace, Murphy's company, is now American's sole vendor for baggage tags, or bagtags as they're called.

Wallace is an integrated supply and total print management company. The company produces and distributes business forms, labels, direct response or direct mail pieces, commercial printing products, and office supplies.

"Back in the eighties, we targeted several vertical markets, of which transportation and distribution was one," notes Murphy. Accounts in that market included American Airlines as well as UPS, FedEx, United Airlines, and others. The industry was targeted because it was beginning to consider automation through the use of barcoding. Wallace's considerable experience in barcoding in retailing positioned the company to capture a large portion of the barcoding business in transportation.

When American became serious about automating the baggage-handling process, Murphy and the account manager built a team that included product development people, sales management, and production. In addition, they had to work with other suppliers. As Murphy says, "We had to involve other companies from a technology standpoint: conveyers, printers, scanners, and we did the consumables."

The purchase decision wound through a series of steps. American had to not only buy the bagtags but all of the technology that made the labels work. Further, a standardization committee had to make sure the bagtags would stay on bags even when a flight went from 100+° desert conditions to snowy winter climes. But in the end, the biggest cost justifier was the revenue that American could enjoy from improved service and the elimination of the cost of lost business due to lost baggage.

"So from the time American began seriously looking at automating their luggage handling to when we won the business, it was 18 months. But we had actually targeted them earlier, and earned the right to compete for that business by proving we could serve their needs with earlier, smaller sales." Three years after winning the bagtag sale, American chose Wallace as a single vendor for many printing applications. Wallace now handles so much of American's printing needs that a team of Wallace specialists have offices at American's headquarters.

As Murphy notes, "It has taken us from a product-based business within the relationship to a business-to-business service, even though there is a product. It [the product] is just a commodity, but the service is not. We are selling distribution, functionality, and administration. This is what has really positioned us, and the model has been adapted to over 350 companies across the country." Visit Wallace at its Web site: *www.wallace. com.*

LEARNING OBJECTIVES

In many respects, the relationship between buyer and seller is a kind of a *pais de deux,* or ballet for two. To understand only one dancer is to have an incomplete understanding of the dance. To fully understand the selling process requires some knowledge of the buying process, for what salespeople do is determined by their expectations of and reactions to what buyers do. Therefore, after reading this chapter, you should be able to:

- Identify the participants of the buying center.
- Outline the steps of the buying process.
- Discuss types of sales jobs.
- Match the steps of the selling process to types of jobs and the buying process.
- Discuss the different sales activities across the steps of the relationship.

AN OVERVIEW OF SELLING AND BUYING PROCESSES

Harry Murphy's experience in selling print management services to American Airlines illustrates some important points about the selling process, particularly as it applies to the sale of complex products or services to organizational customers. First, it can take a long time and a lot of effort before the final sale is made. Although there is constant pressure on both customers and suppliers to shorten the selling cycle, companies that sell capital equipment, high tech gear, or other complicated or high-priced goods and services often must work months or years to win an order. Consequently, selling such products and services involves many relationship-building activities in addition to simply making a sales presentation and writing up a contract. The salesperson must first gather information about (1) the prospective customer's operations to determine whether there is a need for the products or services he or she has to offer and (2) the concerns of various personnel within the customer organization who might influence the final purchase. Then, many low-key sales calls may be necessary to educate the various purchase influencers about the seller's offerings and to establish credibility within the customer's organization. Even after a sale is made, the rep—or other members of an account management team—may have a lot of work to do supervising the installation of the product, training the customer's personnel to use it, and providing other postsale services to ensure the customer will be satisfied and to increase the chances for future sales. A later section of this chapter provides a more detailed examination of this wide variety of activities involved in the selling process and the various roles those activities can play in establishing and maintaining successful relationships with customers.

Not every sale requires the extensive amount of effort and patience that Murphy's team expended in the pursuit of American. Different sales jobs can involve different kinds and numbers of activities, depending on the complexity of the product or service being sold, the nature of the firm's relationship with a particular customer, the role of personal selling within the firm's overall marketing strategy, and a variety of other factors. For that reason, we will also examine how the importance of different selling activities varies across different types of sales jobs and situations.

Harry Murphy's boisterous celebration dance back in the Wallace office upon learning of the contract suggests that—from his perspective, at least—winning the American contract made his great expenditure of time and effort seem worthwhile. But the thrill of victory is not the only kind of satisfaction that good salespeople get from their jobs. A sales career offers a number of attractive attributes and rewards. Managers should understand what attracts good salespeople to their jobs, what rewards motivate them, and what career paths they aspire to follow, so a firm can develop effective selection criteria, incentive programs, and promotion policies. Consequently, the last section of this chapter explores a number of attributes associated with sales jobs, and some of the rewards and career opportunities available to successful salespeople.

In order to truly understand the selling process, why successful salespeople do what they do, and how to most effectively manage their efforts, however, it is useful to first understand how customers make purchase decisions. After all, marketing strategies, sales programs, and the efforts of individual sales reps should all be aimed at influencing and facilitating those decisions. Therefore, the next section sets the stage for our discussion of sales activities and strategies by examining how the buying process works and what members of a customer organization are likely to influence that process at various stages.

THE ORGANIZATIONAL BUYING PROCESS

Many topics in this book are appropriate to all kinds of selling; however, the primary emphasis is on commercial or industrial selling. Therefore, we focus on the buying process in which organizations—both industrial users and intermediaries—engage.[1]

In order to automate the luggage-handling aspect of American's operations, a wide variety of people had to participate, including computer analysts, customer service representatives, procurement personnel, and others. These participants in the buying process can be grouped into seven categories: initiators, users, influencers, gatekeepers, buyers, deciders, and controllers.[2]

Initiators

Initiators are the people who perceive a problem or opportunity that may require the purchase of a new product or service and thereby start the buying process. The initiator can be almost anyone at any level in the firm. Complaints from production workers about outmoded and inefficient equipment, for instance, might trigger the purchase of new machinery. Or the decision to replace manufacturing equipment might be initiated through top management's strategic planning deliberations.

Users

The people in the organization who must use or work with the product or service often influence the purchase decision. For example, drill-press operators might request that the purchasing agent buy drills from a particular supplier because they stay sharp longer and reduce downtime in the plant. Users often volunteer to initiate a purchase, so it is possible that the same people may play more than one role.

Influencers

Influencers provide information for evaluating alternative products and suppliers, and they often play a major role in determining the specifications and criteria to use in making the purchase decision. They are usually technical experts from various departments and can include users.

Gatekeepers

Gatekeepers control the flow of information to other people involved in the purchasing process. They include the organization's purchasing agent and suppliers' salespeople. Gatekeepers influence a purchase by controlling the kind and amount of information that reaches the other decision makers. There are two types of gatekeepers: screens (like secretaries who can decide whose telephone call is put through to the executive) and filters (such as the purchasing agent who gathers proposals from three different companies and decides what to tell others in the buying center about each company). The purchasing agent filters information, choosing to pass along some, but not all, information in order to influence the decision.

Buyers

The buyer is the person who actually contacts the selling organization and places the order. In most organizations, buyers have the authority to negotiate purchases. In some cases, they are given wide discretion. In other instances, they are constrained by technical specifications and other contract requirements determined by technical experts and top administrators.

Deciders

The decider is the person with the final authority to make a purchase decision. Sometimes buyers have this authority, but often it is retained by higher executives in the organization. When a company buys a large computer installation, for instance, the final decision is likely to be made by the chief executive or a top management committee.

Controllers

The person who determines the budget for the purchase is the controller. Sometimes the budget is set independently of the purchase; for example, a regional office of Expedex may have a budget for office equipment set by corporate headquarters at the start of the fiscal year. Then, if the copier needs to be replaced, the cost would have to fit in that budget. At other times, the controller may be a product designer who is trying to keep the cost of the new product within a certain budget.

All the people who participate in buying a particular product or service can be referred to as a buying center. Estimates of the number of people in the buying center for a typical purchase range from 3 to 12. Different members of the buying center may participate—and exert different amounts of influence—at different stages in the decision process.[3] For example, people from engineering and R&D often exert the greatest influence on the development of specifications and criteria that a new product must meet, while the purchasing manager often has more influence when it comes time to choose among alternative suppliers. The makeup and size of the buying center varies with the amount of risk perceived by the firm when buying a particular product. The buying center tends to be smaller—and the relative influence of the purchasing manager greater—when reordering products the firm has purchased in the past than when buying something for the first time or buying something that is seen as risky.[4] Risk is a function of the complexity of the product and situation, the relative importance of the purchase, time pressure to make a decision, and the degree of uncertainty about the product's efficacy.

One recent study reported that almost half of all communication during a purchase occurs within groups of several people, and most of those groups are interdepartmental. The same study also found that less than one-third of communications about the purchase involve someone from outside the buying company, which means that any given salesperson has little opportunity to persuade, relative to the amount of communication that occurs within the organization. Therefore, making the most of those opportunities to persuade is important.[5]

Sales Planning Implications

Since different employees of a customer's organization may be active at different stages of the purchase process, an important part of sales planning involves trying to determine who the salesperson should contact, when each contact should be made, and what kinds of information and appeals each participant is likely to find most useful and persuasive. Unfortunately, the answers to such questions are likely to be different for each potential customer, making information gained from past experience with an organization—and from customer surveys or other market research—useful for planning individual sales calls.

In many cases, however, the roles played by various members of the buying center are sufficiently consistent across similar types of firms that a company can establish policies to guide its salespeople. For example, a study of 140 commercial construction companies found that in smaller firms (defined as those with annual sales volumes under $25 million), presidents and vice presidents exert significantly more influence at all stages in the decision process than purchasing agents or construction engineers, while the situation is reversed in large firms, reflecting increasing job specialization and decentralization of purchasing in bigger companies.[6] A firm selling to this industry might adopt a policy of encouraging its salespeople to seek appointments with the top executives when calling on smaller customers, but to initiate contacts through the purchasing department in larger organizations.

Similarly, customers' buying centers are likely to involve a wider variety of participants when they are considering the purchase of a technically complex, expensive product—such as a computer system—than when the purchase involves a simpler or less costly product.[7] Consequently, firms that sell technically complex capital equipment sometimes organize their salespeople into sales teams or utilize multilevel selling, with different salespeople calling on different members of the customer's buying center to reach as many decision participants as possible and to give each participant the kinds of information that person will find most relevant. These team approaches to selling are examined in more detail in Chapter 5.

When a firm develops policies or organizational structures to guide its salespeople in dealing with customers' buying centers, however, managers must periodically review their assumptions about the roles and influence of the participants. For instance, for years, Eastman Kodak's strategy for selling X-ray film to hospitals was to sell through lab technicians. The company was slow to notice that as more and more hospitals struggled to control costs, this decision was becoming increasingly centralized and professional administrators were exerting more influence. As its sales declined, Kodak finally grasped the change in buying practices and hurriedly changed its sales strategy.

We have seen that different members of a buying center may exert influence at different stages in the decision process. This raises the question of what stages are involved. One widely recognized framework identifies seven steps that organizational buyers take in making purchase decisions: (1) anticipation or recognition of a problem or need, (2) determination and description of the characteristics and the quantity of the needed item, (3) search for and qualification of potential suppliers, (4) acquisition and analysis of proposals or bids, (5) evaluation of proposals and selection of suppliers, (6) selection of an order routine, and (7) performance evaluation and feedback.[8]

Anticipation or Recognition of a Problem or Need

Most organizational purchases are motivated by the requirements of the firm's production processes, merchandise inventory, or day-to-day operations. Consequently, a firm's demand for goods and services is derived demand. Its needs are derived from its customers' demand for the goods or services it produces or markets. For example, the demand for bagtags is derived from the demand for air travel. This characteristic of derived demand

Exhibit 3.1	Volatility of Derived Demand				
Time Period	Demand for Salt	Machines Needed to Handle Demand	Worn-Out Machines	Machines Available	New Purchases
1	100%	50			
2	95	47	10	40	7
3	105	52	7	40	12
4	100	50	12	40	10

At the beginning of Period 1, 50 machines are required based on forecast of sales. At the end of the year, 10 are worn out but 7 are purchased because only 47 are needed. Over year 2, 7 machines wear out, but 52 are needed so 10 are purchased.

Source: Robert Dwyer and John Tanner, *Business Marketing* (New York: Irwin/McGraw–Hill, 1999), p. 21.

can make organizational markets quite volatile, because a small change in the market can result in a large (relatively speaking) change in the organization's sales, as Exhibit 3.1 shows. In this illustration of sales for a salt processing machine, a 5 percent reduction in salt demand can result in a 30 percent decrease in equipment sales, followed by a 50 percent increase if salt demand increases only 10 percent. When demand changes rapidly, the organization's requirements for goods and services can change dramatically due to the volatility of derived demand.

Many different situations can lead someone to recognize a need for a particular product or service. In some cases, need recognition may be almost automatic, as when a computerized inventory control system reports that the stock of an item has fallen below the reorder level. In other cases, a need may arise when someone identifies a better way of operating. New needs might also evolve when the focus of the firm's operations changes, as when top management decides to make a new product line. In all these situations, needs may be recognized—and the purchasing process may be initiated—by a variety of people in the organization, including users, technical personnel, top management, or purchasing managers.

Determination and Description of the Characteristics and Quantity of the Needed Item

The kinds and quantities of goods and services to be purchased are usually dictated by the demand for the firm's outputs and by the requirements of its production process and operations. Consequently, the criteria used in specifying the needed materials and equipment must usually be technically precise. Similarly, the quantities needed must be carefully considered to avoid excessive inventories or downtime caused by lack of needed materials. For these reasons, a variety of technical experts, as well as the people who will use the materials or equipment, are commonly involved in this stage of the decision process.

It is not enough for the using department and the technical experts to develop a detailed set of specifications for the needed item, however. They must also communicate a clear and precise description of what is needed, how much is needed, and when it is needed to other members of the buying center and to potential suppliers.

Search for and Qualification of Potential Suppliers

Once the organization has clearly defined the kind of item needed, a search for potential suppliers begins. If the item has been purchased before, this search may be limited to one or a few suppliers that have performed satisfactorily in the past, particularly strategic partners. From the seller's perspective, one advantage of strategic partnerships is that partners get the first opportunity to bid on new products, and often this step of searching for potential suppliers is skipped. For example, when Xerox developed the DocuColor digital imaging system, three vendors participated in the design process. Their products were designed into the new product. If the purchase involves a new item, or if the item is complex and expensive (again, if the product represents a risky decision), organizational buyers often search for several potential suppliers to ensure they can select the one with the best product and most favorable terms.[9]

Acquisition of Proposals or Bids

After potential suppliers are identified, the buyer may request specific proposals or bids from each. When the item is a frequently purchased, standardized, or technically simple product (e.g., nails or copier paper), this process may not be very extensive. The buyer might simply consult several suppliers' catalogs or make a few phone calls. For more complicated and expensive goods and services, lengthy and detailed sales presentations and written proposals may be requested from each potential vendor.

Evaluation of Offerings and Selection of Suppliers

During this stage of the purchasing process, various members of the buying center examine the acceptability of the various proposals and potential suppliers. Also, the buying organization and one or more potential vendors may negotiate about prices, credit terms, and delivery schedules. Ultimately, one or more suppliers are selected, and purchase agreements are signed.

The people in the buying organization's purchasing department usually evaluate offerings and select the supplier. Technical and administrative personnel may also play a role in supplier selection, however, especially when the purchase is complex and costly.

What criteria do members of the buying center use in selecting a supplier? Because organizational buying is largely a rational decision-making process, we would expect "rational" criteria to be considered most important—such as the quality of the product, the price, and the service offered by the supplier. However, social and emotional factors can also influence this decision.

The relative importance of different supplier selection criteria, though, varies across organizations and the types of products or services being purchased. For example, product quality tends to be more important in the purchase of technically complex products, while price and customer service are relatively more important for more standardized, nontechnical items such as concrete.[10] Criteria and the process can also vary across countries, as illustrated in the "Global Sales Force" box, "Buying Equipment in Transitional Economies."

One review suggests that the relative importance of selection criteria has changed over time. In recent years, quality and service considerations have begun to dominate price considerations.[11] Companies such as Rockwell International have learned that quality and service have implications for the total cost of owning a product. After an analysis of Rockwell's quality review process, the company learned that it costs Rockwell over $250 just to correct an invoice or return an unsatisfactory part. To reduce such costs, Rockwell grades the quality and service performance of each vendor annually, rewarding higher-scoring vendors with more business.

Selection of an Order Routine

Until the purchased item is delivered, it is of no use to the organization. Consequently, after an order has been placed with a supplier, the purchasing department often tries to match the delivery of the goods with the company's need for the product. Other internal activities also must occur when the order is delivered. The goods must be received, inspected, paid for, and entered in the firm's inventory records. These activities represent some of the hidden costs alluded to earlier that Rockwell and others have identified. Reducing these costs through computerized order routines is just one way some strategic partners are trying to reduce their buyers' costs.

Buying Equipment in Transitional Economies

In Eastern Europe, dramatic changes continue to occur. Countries used to a centrally planned economy have transitioned to a free economy and must now learn to compete on a free-market basis. In Africa, changes have been just as dramatic, although not always political. African countries must also face global competition, as they develop their industrialized base.

Being a member of the global marketplace means buying equipment from global vendors. How have these transitions influenced buying practices in those two parts of the world?

In the Czech Republic, past formal relationships have been broken or disrupted. Users, who once had no say in the purchase, now have greater control, cutting the time involved and leaving a number of past key participants in advisory roles. What was once a highly bureaucratized process with many stages and lengthy deliberations is now straightforward and problem/solution focused. Still, many buyers are uncertain as to how to handle their newfound power in the marketplace.

Nigerian equipment purchasing is more developed. Nigerian companies are more likely to continuously search for new suppliers, keeping registers of potential suppliers. Nigerian buyers are also less likely to rely on references and more on their own judgment, wanting to see demonstrations, visit with sales engineers, and evaluate technical specs closely. Recognizing their global opportunities, these buyers constantly scan the environment for better sources of equipment.

Source: E.D. Barngboye, "Equipment Buying in Nigeria," *Industrial Marketing Management* 21 (1992), pp. 181–85; Johan Roos, Ellen Veie, and Lawrence S. Welch, "A Case Study of Equipment Purchasing in Czechoslovakia," *Industrial Marketing Management* 21 (1992), pp. 257–63.

Performance Evaluation and Feedback

When the goods have been delivered, evaluation begins. This evaluation focuses on both the product and the supplier. The goods are inspected to determine whether they meet the specifications described in the purchase agreement. Later, users judge whether the purchased item performs according to expectations. Similarly, the supplier's performance can be evaluated on such criteria as promptness of delivery, quality of the product, and service after the sale, as Rockwell and others do. In many organizations, this evaluation is a formal process, involving written reports from the user department and other persons involved in the purchase. The information is kept by the purchasing department for use in evaluating proposals and selecting suppliers the next time a similar purchase is made.

Repeat Purchase Behavior

The steps just described apply only to "new-task" purchases, where a customer is buying a relatively complex and expensive product or service for the first time (e.g., a custom-built office building or a new computer system). At the other extreme is the "straight rebuy," where a customer is reordering an item it has purchased many times (e.g., office supplies, bulk chemicals). Such repeat purchases tend to be much more routine than the new-task situation.

Straight rebuys are often carried out by members of the purchasing department with little influence from other employees, and many of the steps just described (involved with searching for and evaluating alternative suppliers) are dropped. Instead, the buyer chooses from those suppliers on an "approved" list, giving weight to the company's past satisfaction with those suppliers and their products.

From the seller's viewpoint, being an "in" or approved supplier can provide a significant competitive advantage, and policies and procedures should be developed to help maintain and enhance such favored positions with current customers. As we shall see later, many firms have developed "key account management" programs to help preserve the long-term satisfaction of their largest customers.

Also, suppliers are offering new technologies—such as computerized reordering systems—and forming alliances with their customers to help them make their reordering processes more efficient while simultaneously increasing the likelihood they will continue to reorder from the same supplier. For instance, Wal-Mart sends daily sales figures from its stores to the 3M Company so 3M can automatically make and ship appropriate assortments of its products to Wal-Mart's stores on an as-needed basis. This system is called an Efficient Consumer Response (ECR) system and is similar to the Electronic Data Interchange (EDI) ordering systems that Baxter Hospital Supply pioneered with its customers.

For potential suppliers not on a buyer's approved list, the strategic selling problem is more difficult. An "out" supplier's objective must be to move the customer away from the automatic reordering procedures of a straight rebuy toward the more extensive evaluation processes of a "modified rebuy" purchase decision—where the buyer is interested in modifying the product specifications, prices, or other terms it has been receiving from existing suppliers and is willing to consider dealing with new suppliers.

Since the need to consider a change in suppliers can be identified by a variety of members of a firm's buying center, an out supplier might urge its salespeople to bypass the customer's purchasing department and call directly on users or technical personnel and try to convince them the firm's products offer advantages on some important dimension—such as technical design, quality, performance, or financial criteria—over the products they are currently using. Finding someone to play the role of initiator can be difficult, but is possible if latent dissatisfaction exists.

SELLING ACTIVITIES

Given the complexity of the purchasing process in many organizations, it is not surprising that the sales reps who work for Harry Murphy of Wallace spend a large portion of their time collecting information about potential customers, planning, coordinating the activities of other functional departments, and servicing existing customers, in addition to making sales calls. It is difficult to specify the full range of activities in which salespeople engage because they can vary greatly across companies and types of sales jobs. However, in one extensive study, a sample of 1,393 salespeople from 51 firms rated 120 possible activities on a seven-point scale according to how frequently they performed each activity during a typical month. These responses were examined with the statistical technique of factor analysis to identify the underlying dimensions or categories of salesperson behavior represented by the various activities. Ten different dimensions—or job factors—were identified.[12] These are shown in Exhibit 3.2, along with some of the specific activities involved in each dimension.

One obvious conclusion from the study is that a salesperson's job often involves a wide variety of activities beyond simply calling on customers, making sales presentations, and taking orders. While the first two factors in Exhibit 3.2 are directly related to selling and order taking, factors 3 and 5 focus on activities involved in servicing customers after a sale is made. Similarly, factors 4, 6, and 7 incorporate a variety of administrative duties, including such things as collecting and communicating information about customers to sales and marketing executives in the company, attending periodic training sessions, and helping to recruit and develop new sales reps. Finally, some salespeople also expend a good deal of effort helping to build distribution channels and maintain reseller support (factor 10).

The increasing number of nonselling and administrative activities means that many salespeople spend only a small portion of their time actually selling. For example, the re-

Exhibit 3.2   Job Factors and Selected Activities Associated with Each

1. **Selling function**
   Plan selling activities
   Search out leads
   Call potential accounts
   Identify decision makers
   Prepare sales presentation
   Make sales presentation
   Overcome objections
   Introduce new products
   Call new accounts
2. **Working with others**
   Write up orders
   Expedite orders
   Handle back orders
   Handle shipping problems
   Find lost orders
3. **Servicing the product**
   Learn about the product
   Test equipment
   Supervise installation
   Train customers
   Supervise repairs
   Perform maintenance
4. **Managing information**
   Provide technical information
   Receive feedback
   Provide feedback
   Check with superiors
5. **Servicing the account**

   Stock shelves
   Set up displays
   Take inventory for client
   Handle local advertising
6. **Attending conferences and meetings**
   Attend sales conferences
   Attend regional sales meetings
   Work at client conferences
   Set up product exhibitions
   Attend periodic training sessions
7. **Training and recruiting**
   Recruit new sales reps
   Train new salespeople
   Travel with trainees
8. **Entertaining**
   Entertain clients with golf and so forth
   Take clients to dinner
   Take clients out for drink
   Take clients out to lunch
   Throw parties for clients
9. **Traveling**
   Travel out of town
   Spend nights on the road
   Travel in town
10. **Distribution**
   Establish good relations with distributors
   Sell to distributors
   Handle credit
   Collect past due accounts

Source: Adapted from William C. Moncrief III, "Selling Activity and Sales Position Taxonomies for Industrial Sales-forces," *Journal of Marketing Research* (August 1986), pp. 266–67, published by the American Marketing Association. Reprinted by permission of the American Marketing Association.

sults of a survey of salespeople in a variety of industries are diagrammed in Exhibit 3.3. The survey found that, on average, sales reps devote less than half their time to direct contact with customers, either selling or servicing.[13] In firms that sell complicated or customized products or service systems to large customers, the proportion of selling time can be even lower.

The increasing involvement of sales reps in nonselling activities is one major reason why the average cost of a sales call has risen dramatically in recent years. While the cost of a sales call was estimated to be about 0 at the end of the 1970s, that cost increased as much as fivefold over the next 15 years. One survey of Fortune 1,000 firms estimated the cost of an average sales call to be more than $500 in 1995.[14] And to make matters worse, respondents in another survey reported that an average of three calls was necessary to close a sale with an existing account, and seven calls were required to win a sale from a new customer. This suggests that selling expenses average as much as $3,500 per sale to new accounts.[15]

Exhibit 3.3   How Salespeople Spend Their Time

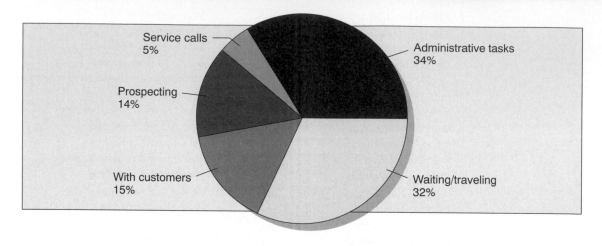

Source: Fenemore Group, as reported in *Sales & Marketing Management* (March 1998), p. 96

This rapid escalation of selling costs helps explain why the search for new ways to improve sales force efficiency has become increasingly urgent in recent years. Using new technologies, reallocating sales effort to customer retention, and purifying the sales job by eliminating nonselling tasks are some of the strategies companies have used to reduce selling costs and increase sales force efficiency.

Not every salesperson engages in all of the activities listed in Exhibit 3.3. Nor does every rep devote the same amount of time and effort to the same kinds of activities. The many different kinds of selling jobs involve widely different tasks and responsibilities, require different kinds of training and skills, and offer varying levels of compensation and opportunities for personal satisfaction and advancement.

Retail Selling versus Industrial Selling

Most salespeople are employed in various kinds of **retail selling.** These jobs involve selling goods and services to ultimate consumers for their own personal use, such as door-to-door salespeople, insurance agents, real estate brokers, and retail store clerks do. A much larger volume of sales, however, is accounted for by **industrial selling**—the sale of goods and services at the wholesale level. Industrial selling involves three types of customers:

1. *Sales to resellers* as when a clothing manufacturer's sales rep sells merchandise to a retail store, which resells the goods to its customers.
2. *Sales to business users* as when manufacturer X sells materials or parts to manufacturer Y, which uses them to produce another product, or when a Xerox salesperson sells a law firm a copier to be used in conducting the firm's business.
3. *Sales to institutions* as when an IBM salesperson sells a computer to a hospital or a government agency.

In many ways, the activities involved in both retail and industrial selling, and in managing the two types of sales forces, are very similar. Success in either type of selling requires interpersonal and communications skills, solid knowledge of the products being sold, an ability to discover the customer's needs and problems, and the creativity necessary to show the customer how a particular product or service can help satisfy those needs and problems. Similarly, managers must recruit and train appropriate people for both types of sales jobs, provide them with objectives consistent with the firm's overall marketing or merchandising program, supervise them, motivate them, and evaluate their performance.

Retail and industrial selling also differ in some important ways. Many of the goods and services sold by industrial salespeople are more expensive and technically complex than those in retailing. Similarly, industrial customers tend to be larger and to engage in extensive decision-making processes involving many people. Consequently, the activities and skills involved in selling to industrial buyers are often quite different from those in retail selling. Furthermore, the decisions made in effectively managing an industrial sales force are broader than those required for a retail sales force. Consequently, although many topics in this book apply to the management of both types of salespeople (selection and training), others apply only to the management of industrial salespeople (sales territory design).

Types of Industrial Sales Jobs

Even within the broad area of industrial selling, there are many different kinds of jobs requiring different skills. Various authors have described more than 100 ways in which industrial sales jobs might be classified.[16] One of the most commonly used, and useful, classifications of selling jobs was developed by Derek Newton.[17] Because his job categories have been the subject of some empirical research, we will refer to this scheme occasionally. It identifies four types of industrial selling found across a variety of industries:

1. *Trade selling.* The sales force's primary responsibility is to increase business from current and potential customers by providing them with merchandising and promotional assistance. The "trade" are resellers such as retailers or distributors. A Procter & Gamble salesperson selling soap and laundry products to chain-store personnel is an example of trade selling.

2. *Missionary selling.* The sales force's primary job is to increase business from current and potential customers by providing them with product information and other personal selling assistance. Missionary salespeople often do not take orders from customers directly but persuade customers to buy their firm's product from distributors or other wholesale suppliers. Examples include representatives of brewers, who call on bar owners and encourage them to order a particular brand of beer from the local distributor, and medical "detailers," who call on doctors as representatives of pharmaceutical manufacturers.

3. *Technical selling.* The sales force's primary responsibility is to increase business from presently identified customers and potential customers by providing them with technical and engineering information and assistance. Sales engineers for machine-tool and computer manufacturers are examples of people engaged in technical selling.

4. *New business selling.* The salesperson's primary responsibility is to identify and obtain business from new customers.

Each type of sales job involves somewhat different activities and requires different skills and training. Therefore, although most of this book focuses on managing industrial selling in general, from time to time special attention will be paid to unique problems encountered in managing people in these specific types of sales jobs.

While a variety of analytical and administrative duties may be important parts of a sales rep's job, the primary focus of most sales jobs is on direct interaction with customers or potential customers. A number of observers have suggested conceptual schemes

Exhibit 3.4   Stages of the Selling Process

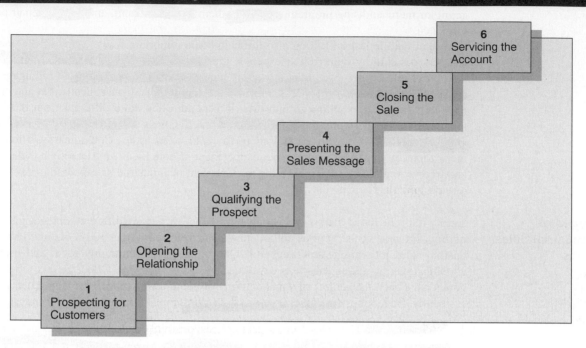

Source: Robert Dwyer and John Tanner, *Business Marketing* (New York: Irwin/McGraw–Hill, 1999), p. 187.

that outline various stages in the selling process and indicate the kinds of activities occurring at each stage.[18] The essence of most of these schemes can be summarized by viewing the selling process as consisting of the six stages diagrammed in Exhibit 3.4: (1) prospecting for customers, (2) opening the relationship, (3) qualifying the prospect, (4) presenting the sales message, (5) closing the sale, and (6) servicing the account.

Although the selling process involves only a few distinct steps, the specific activities involved at each step—and the way those activities are carried out—can vary greatly depending on the type of sales position, such as missionary versus trade salesperson, as well as depending on the relationship strategy. Consequently, a firm's strategic sales plan should incorporate account management policies to guide each salesperson and ensure that all selling efforts are consistent with the firm's marketing and relationship strategy. We will examine the rationale and content of account management policies in more detail in Chapter 5. The following discussion of the stages in the selling process also mentions some of the more common account management policies used to direct sales representatives.

Prospecting for Customers

In many types of selling, prospecting for new customers is critical. It can also be one of the most disheartening aspects of selling, especially for beginning salespeople. Prospecting efforts are often met with rejection, and immediate payoffs are usually minimal. Nevertheless, the ability to uncover potential new customers often separates the successful from the unsuccessful salesperson.

In some consumer goods businesses, prospecting for new customers simply involves cold canvassing—going from house to house knocking on doors. In most cases, though, the target market is more narrowly defined, and the salesperson must identify prospects within that target segment. Salespeople use a variety of information sources to identify relevant prospects, including trade association and industry directories, telephone directories, other salespeople, other customers, suppliers, nonsales employees of the firm, and social and professional contacts.

Telemarketing is used by many firms to find prospects. Outbound telemarketing involves calling potential customers at their home or office, to either make a sale or to make an appointment for a field representative. In-bound telemarketing, where prospective customers call an 800 or 888 number for more information, is also used to identify and qualify prospects. When prospects call for more information about a product or service, an operator attempts to determine the extent of interest and whether the prospect meets the company's qualification for new customers. If so, information about the caller is passed on to the appropriate salesperson or regional office.

The Internet is also proving a useful technology for generating leads to potential new customers. While an increasing number of firms are soliciting orders directly via a home page on the Internet, many—particularly those selling relatively complex goods or services—use their Internet sites primarily to provide technical product information to customers or potential customers. These firms can have their salespeople follow up technical inquiries from potential new accounts with a more traditional sales call.[19]

A firm's account management policies should address how much emphasis salespeople should give to prospecting for new customers versus prospecting and servicing existing accounts. The appropriate policy for a firm depends on the relationship strategy selected, the nature of its product, and the firm's customers. If the firm's strategy is transactional, if the product is in the introductory stage of its life cycle, if it is an infrequently purchased durable good, or if the typical customer does not require much service after the sale, sales reps should devote substantial time to prospecting for new customers. This is the case in industries such as insurance and residential construction. Such firms may design their compensation systems to reward their salespeople more heavily for making sales to new customers than for servicing old ones, as we shall see in Chapter 15.

A company that desires strategic partnerships will assign a specific salesperson to each account, such as the Wallace reps who work at American Airlines' corporate headquarters. These reps service the American account and prospect for new business within only American. Firms with large market shares or those that sell frequently purchased nondurable products or products that require substantial service after the sale to guarantee customer satisfaction should adopt a policy that encourages sales reps to devote most of their efforts to servicing existing customers. Food manufacturers that sell products to retail supermarkets and firms that produce component parts and supplies for other manufacturers fall into this category. Some very large customers may require so much servicing that a sales rep is assigned to do nothing but cater to that customer's needs. In such circumstances, firms have specialized their sales positions so that some representatives service only existing accounts, while others spend all their time prospecting for and opening relationships with new customers.

Opening the Relationship

In the initial approach to a prospective customer, the sales representative should try to accomplish two things: (1) determine who within the organization is likely to have the greatest influence and/or authority to initiate the purchase process and who will ultimately purchase the product and (2) generate enough interest within the firm to obtain the information needed to qualify the prospect as a worthwhile potential customer. An organizational buying center often consists of individuals who play different roles in making the purchase decision. Thus, it is important for the salesperson to identify the key decision makers, their desires, and their relative influence.

Selling organizations can formulate policies to guide sales reps in approaching prospective customers. When the firm's product is inexpensive and routinely purchased, salespeople might be instructed to deal entirely with the purchasing department. For more technically complex and expensive products, the sales representative might be urged to identify and seek appointments with influencers and decision makers in various functional departments and at several managerial levels. When the purchase decision is likely to be very complex, involving many people within the customer's organization, the seller might adopt a policy of multilevel or team selling.

Qualifying the Prospect

Before salespeople attempt to set up an appointment for a major sales presentation or spend much time trying to establish a relationship with a prospective account, they should first determine whether the prospect qualifies as a worthwhile potential customer. If the account does not qualify, the sales rep can spend the time better elsewhere.

Qualification is difficult for some salespeople. It requires them to put aside their eternal optimism and make an objective, realistic judgment about the probability of making a profitable sale, as Wallace's Harry Murphy did before deciding to spend two years pursuing the American Airlines account. As one authority points out, the qualification process involves finding the answers to three important questions:

1. Does the prospect have a need for my product or service?
2. Can I make the people responsible for buying so aware of that need that I can make a sale?
3. Will the sale be profitable to my company?[20]

To answer such questions, the sales representative must learn about the prospect's operations, the kinds of products it makes, its customers, its competitors, and the likely future demand for its products. Information also must be obtained concerning who the customer's present suppliers are and whether there are any special relationships with those firms that would make it difficult for the prospect to change suppliers. Finally, the financial health and the credit rating of the prospect should be checked.

Because so many different kinds of information are needed, nonselling departments within the company—such as the credit and collections department—often are involved in the qualification process when large purchases are made. Often, however, credit departments do not get involved until after the prospect has agreed to buy and filled out a credit application. In these situations, company policies should be formulated to guide the salesperson's judgment concerning whether a specific prospect qualifies as a customer. These policies might spell out minimum acceptable standards for such things as the prospect's annual dollar value of purchases in the product category or credit rating. Similarly, some firms specify a minimum order size to avoid dealing with very small customers and to improve the efficiency of their order-processing and shipping operations.

Presenting the Sales Message

The presentation is the core of the selling process. The salesperson transmits information about a product or service and attempts to persuade the prospect to become a customer. Making good presentations is a critical aspect of the sales job. Unfortunately, many salespeople do not perform this activity very well. Past studies have discovered that 40 percent of purchasing agents perceive the presentations they witness are less than good. In a recent survey of about 70 purchasing executives, the following five presentation-related complaints were among the top 10 complaints the managers had about the salespeople with whom they deal:

- Running down competitors.
- Being too aggressive or abrasive.
- Having inadequate knowledge of competitors' products or services.
- Having inadequate knowledge of our business or organization.
- Delivering poor presentations.[21]

One decision that must be made in preparing for an effective sales presentation concerns how many members of the buying firm should attend. Since more than one person is typically involved in making a purchase decision, should a sales presentation be given to all of them as a group? The answer depends on whether the members of the buying center have divergent attitudes and concerns, and whether those concerns can all be addressed effectively in a single presentation. If not, scheduling a series of one-to-one presentations with different members of the buying group might be more effective.

In many cases, the best way to convince prospects of a product's advantage is to demonstrate it. This is particularly true if the product is technically complex. Two rules should be followed in preparing an effective product demonstration. First, the demonstration should be carefully rehearsed to reduce the possibility of even a minor malfunction. Second, the demonstration should be designed to give members of the buying center hands-on experience with the product. For example, Xerox's salespeople learn about their clients' office operations so they can demonstrate their products actually doing the tasks they would do after they are purchased.

Different firms have widely varying policies concerning how sales presentations should be organized, what selling points should be stressed, and how forcefully the presentation should be made. Encyclopedia companies commonly train their door-to-door salespeople to deliver the same memorized, forceful presentation to every prospect. A person selling computer systems may be trained in very low-key selling, in which the salesperson primarily acts as a source of technical information and advice and does little "pushing" of the company's particular computers.

A firm's policy on sales presentations should be consistent with its other policies for managing accounts. To formulate intelligent sales presentation policies, a sales manager must know about alternative presentation methods and their relative advantages and limitations. Unfortunately, the space limitations of this chapter make it difficult to present a lengthy discussion of such issues. The interested student is urged to examine the appendix at the end of the chapter where a variety of sales presentation methods are discussed and evaluated in more detail.

Closing the Sale

Closing refers to obtaining a final agreement to purchase. All the salesperson's efforts are wasted unless the client "signs on the dotted line"; yet this is where many salespeople fail. It is natural to delay making purchase decisions. But as the time it takes the salesperson to close the sale increases, the profit to be made from the sale goes down, and the risk of losing the sale increases. Consequently, the salesperson's task is to speed up the final decision. Often, this can best be done by simply asking for an order. "May I write that order up for you?" and "When do you want it delivered?" are common closings. Another closing tactic is to ask the client to choose among two alternative decisions, such as, "Will that be cash or charge?" or "Did you want the blue one or the red one?" In industrial buying and selling, professional purchasing agents and other decision makers have had extensive training in buying and selling techniques and can identify manipulative closing techniques, so care should be used in selecting a natural way to ask for the sale.

Servicing the Account

The salesperson's job is not finished when the sale is made. Many kinds of service and assistance must be provided to customers after a sale to ensure their satisfaction and repeat business. This is another area in which some salespeople do not perform well. One consultant estimates that when a customer stops buying from a company, about 60 percent of the time it's because the customer thinks the seller's salespeople developed an indifferent attitude after the product was delivered.[22] The salesperson should follow up each sale to make sure there are no problems with delivery schedules, quality of goods, or customer billing. In addition, the salesperson—or members of a sales team—often supervise the installation of equipment, train the customer's employees in its use, and ensure proper maintenance in order to reduce problems that may lead to customer dissatisfaction.

This kind of postsale service can pay great dividends for both the salesperson and the firm.[23] For one thing, satisfied customers are likely to be repeat purchasers. Also, good service can lead to the sale of other related products and services. For instance, in many capital equipment lines, service contracts—along with supplies and replacement parts—account for greater dollar sales revenue and higher profit margins than the original equipment. However, sometimes the pressure for service can lead to problems, as illustrated in the "Ethical Issues" box, "Do Buyers Have to Be Ethical?"

A firm's relationship strategy should also dictate what type of postsale or ongoing service should occur. Earlier in this chapter, we examined how buyers make purchases in order to recognize the relationship between buying activities and selling activities. It is also important to understand how relationships form in order to understand the different selling activities throughout the relationship.

RELATIONSHIP FORMATION AND SELLING

Simply selecting a partnering strategy does not result in partnerships; salespeople still have to perform the necessary steps to create the right relationship. Relationships between organizations that result in strategic partnerships generally go through four stages: awareness, exploration, expansion, and commitment. The focus here is on the last three because these are the steps that distinguish transactional exchanges from strategic partnerships.

Exploration

In the exploration stage, each side tries to determine the potential value of the relationship. As time goes on, the relationship becomes defined through the development of expectations for each party and results of individual transactions or interactions. For example, the buyer begins by evaluating the timeliness of follow-ups to requests for information or makes a purchase and tests the seller's product and service. At the same time, trust and personal relationships develop.

A strong exploration stage is important for the relationship to flourish over time. When the buyer tries the product for the first time, that customer is excited about receiving the benefits of the product as promised by the salesperson. A poor initial experience is extremely difficult to overcome. Beginning the relationship properly requires the salesperson to set the proper expectations, monitor order processing and delivery, ensure proper use of the product, and assist in servicing the customer.

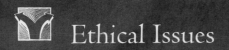
Do Buyers Have to Be Ethical?

In general, people expect salespeople to do whatever it takes to make the sale. But sometimes, that pressure to do something "extra" comes from the buyer. Currently, the International Olympics Committee is investigating a scandal that involves inappropriate demands for gifts from decision makers in order for Salt Lake City to receive the Olympic Games. Texas prison officials investigated a security fence purchase after several death-row killers escaped; did gifts play a role in a poor decision? Don't buyers have to adhere to the same ethical standards as sellers?

In general, they do. Laws regarding bribery and fraud apply equally to buyers as well as sellers. But in the high-pressure arena of selling, salespeople aren't likely to squeal on a customer who just signed a big sale. And the losers aren't likely to know, or be able to prove, why they lost the sale.

Gifts of some type are accepted by an estimated 97 percent of all buyers. Some companies, though, are cracking down on buyers. IBM has a long-standing policy of accepting no gifts, not even a cup of coffee. Yet, IBM does offer promotional products, like clocks and other merchandise, with the IBM logo as gifts to its clients. These gifts are not large enough to sway a sale, but IBM's dilemma is an example of the challenge facing buyers and sellers. How much is enough, without being too much?

Set proper expectations

Many business people try "to underpromise and overdeliver," a catchphrase to encourage salespeople not to promise more than they can deliver, but also to remind salespeople to try to deliver more than was promised in order to pleasantly surprise the buyer. Overpromising can get the initial sale, but a dissatisfied customer not only will not buy again, but also will tell many others to avoid that salesperson.

Monitor order processing and delivery

The first expectation the buyer has is that the product will be delivered on time and ready to use. A common temptation is to quote a short delivery time in order to win the sale, even when the rep knows that delivery time can't be met. Giving in to such temptations causes trouble with the customer and with those responsible for the shipping function. Neither will be happy with the salesperson who makes such promises. On the other hand, the salesperson should monitor the order processing and delivery processes to make sure that nothing goes wrong.

Ensure proper use

Some buyers may know how to operate the basic features of a product, but if the product is not operating at maximum efficiency, the customer is losing value. Many firms have staffed a customer service department or tasked their technical support group with training customers, but it is still the salesperson's responsibility to make sure that the customer is getting full value. For example, Minolta copier salespeople train operators of new copiers so that they can learn and take advantage of all of the features of their new copier.

Assist in servicing

Not all quiet customers are happy. Recent research indicates that users may be dissatisfied long before decision makers are aware of it.[24] Salespeople can learn of such problems by working closely with their company's technical or customer support personnel. Then they can address similar situations in other accounts before the problems grow into complaints.

Complaints can arise at any stage of the partnership, but when complaints arise during the exploration stage, the salesperson has the opportunity to prove commitment to the account. When customers sense that commitment, either through the handling of a complaint or through other forms of special attention, they may be ready to move into the expansion stage.

Expansion

The expansion stage of the relationship process is marked by the opportunity to sell new products or increase the share of the account's business. Trust is developing, allowing the salesperson to focus on identifying additional needs and recommending solutions. Several strategies, including generating repeat sales, cross-selling, and full-line selling, can be used to expand business with current accounts.

Generating repeat sales

In some situations, the most appropriate strategy is to generate repeat orders, particularly for supply items and other operating needs. Generating repeat sales requires recognizing buying cycles and being present at buying time. One technique Harry Murphy's sales team has used to grow sales with American Airlines is to understand the company's usage needs and to time sales calls for when American wants and needs to see the salesperson.

Upgrading

Upgrading is convincing the buyer to use a higher-quality product or newer product, and is similar to generating repeat sales. The buyer selects the upgrade because it meets needs better or more efficiently than did the old product.

Upgrading is crucial to high tech companies. Dell, for example, sells computers to John Deere. When new processors or other technology become available, Dell seeks to upgrade Deere. If Deere's needs are not better met by the new technology, Dell's competitive advantage may disappear and Deere could simply seek the lowest bidder of commonly available products.

Full-line selling

Selling the entire line of associated products is called full-line selling. Many companies try to get their foot in the door with any sale in order to prove their company's worth as a supplier. The hope is that the buyer will want to purchase the full line after trying the company out. Full-line selling is not the same as full-line forcing, a practice used when a company has one top-selling product that it sells through distributors. Full-line forcing occurs when the company forces distributors to carry the full line in order to be able to sell the top seller. Full-line selling is a sales strategy that involves leveraging the relationship in order to sell the entire line of products. Full-line forcing is a questionable sales tactic, one that has gotten Microsoft into trouble by bundling its web browser with its operating system; full-line selling is a legitimate method of strengthening the relationship.

Cross-selling

Cross-selling is similar to full-line selling but reflects selling products that may not be related. For example, Wallace began by selling business forms and then crossed to bagtags. Cross-selling works best when the salesperson can leverage the relationship with the buyer. Trust in the salesperson and the selling organization already exists; therefore, the sale should not be as difficult if the proper needs exist.

Exhibit 3.5 Preferred Supplier Criteria for Suppliers to Bethlehem Steel

- *Capability:* The purchasing team examines manufacturing, shipping, and administrative capabilities. Because Bethlehem requires significant monitoring by suppliers, even paperwork is scrutinized.
- *Organization:* Are employees dedicated? Is the company flexible or bureaucratic? Can it change as we change?
- *Financial health:* Bethlehem reviews audited financial statements to determine if the supplier is managed well.
- *Culture:* Does the corporate culture fit with ours? Do we want the same things and do we work in similar ways? Can we get along?
- *Willingness to commit:* Suppliers must be willing to commit the resources necessary to serve the account. For many suppliers, this means a full-time representative on Bethlehem's site.
- *Ethics:* Is the supplier trustworthy?

Source: Adapted from Jean Graham, "A Simple Idea Saves $8 Million a Year," *Purchasing* (May 21, 1992), pp. 47–49.

If the buying center changes greatly, cross-selling becomes more like the initial sale. For example, if Wallace also had postage equipment, that equipment may be purchased by an entirely different set of people. For those buyers, Wallace has no reputation or relationship, so the expansion of the relationship to a strategic partnership is more challenging.

Commitment

When the buyer–seller relationship has reached the commitment stage, there is a stated or implied pledge to continue the relationship. Formally, this pledge may begin with the seller being designated a preferred supplier, which is the same as being the in-supplier mentioned earlier. While **preferred supplier** status may mean different things in different companies, in general it means that the supplier is assured a large percentage of the buyer's business and will get the first opportunity to earn any new business.[25] For example, at Motorola, only preferred suppliers are eligible to bid on new programs. Thus, *preferred supplier* is a buyer's term for *partner.*

To become a preferred supplier for Bethlehem Steel, a supplier must pass several criteria (including a willingness to commit to the relationship) listed in Exhibit 3.5. Research finds that many buyers examine the suppliers on criteria similar to those used by Bethlehem Steel, including corporate culture. Corporate culture isn't managed by the salesperson, but when there is a match, the salesperson can utilize appropriate selling strategies to lead the customer to the commitment stage.

Securing commitment

Commitment in a partnership should permeate both organizations, supported by a market-oriented culture. Commitment comes from both organizations, and the salesperson must secure commitment not only from the customer, but also from the rest of his or her own company. Senior management must be convinced of the benefits of partnering with the account so that the appropriate investments will be made. Additionally, the salesperson has to see that others in the organization are empowered to serve the needs of this customer. For example, if American Airlines has a problem with Wallace's billing process, the Wallace billing representative should work directly with American's Accounts Payable person to resolve the issue and design a more appropriate process. For other accounts, the billing department would probably be unwilling to make changes to the process.

Selling activities vary depending on the type of sales job, the firm's relationship strategy, and the stage of the relationship. One element, though, that is common is that a competitive advantage can be gained by matching the selling process to how customers want to buy. Few people exclaim to their friends, "Look at the car I was sold!" Rather they say, "Look at the car I bought!" Recognizing how buyers want to buy and creating a selling process that enhances that decision process is an important method of gaining competitive advantage.

SUMMARY

Many people can be involved in an organizational buying decision, and their roles are those of initiator, user, influencer, gatekeeper, buyer, and decider. The stages in the buying process can include the following:

1. Anticipation or recognition of a problem or need.

2. Determination and description of the characteristics and quantity of the needed item.

3. Search for and qualification of potential buyers.

4. Acquisition of proposals or bids.

5. Evaluation of offerings and selection of suppliers.

6. Selection of an order routine.

7. Performance evaluation and feedback.

| Appendix |
| **A** |

Alternative Selling Techniques

Many of the issues sales managers must deal with—including the development of account management policies, the choice of selection criteria for hiring new salespeople, and the design of effective training programs—require an understanding of alternative selling techniques and their advantages and limitations. There are probably as many variations in the way sales presentations are made as there are salespeople. But most selling techniques conform to one of four broad philosophical orientations toward dealing with customers: (1) the stimulus-response approach, (2) the mental-states approach, (3) the need-satisfaction approach, and (4) the problem-solution approach.[26]

Stimulus-response approach

The stimulus-response approach to selling is based on the notion that every sensory stimulus produces a response. Sales recruits thus learn what to say (the stimulus) and what buyers are likely to say in most circumstances (the response). In a well-planned stimulus-response model, most of the unfavorable

buying responses are known. This allows the company the opportunity to train representatives to respond appropriately. If the prospect responds, "I can't afford to buy this product now," the sales representative has memorized not one but several responses to overcome this objection. One answer might be, "Well, we have an excellent financing program that you should be able to afford. Let me explain it to you." The emphasis in training is thus on the standardized sales presentation, the likely responses by customers, and the possible rejoinders to overcome their objections.

There are some advantages to this approach. A well-developed "canned" sales presentation ensures that the salesperson will give a smooth, complete talk that covers all the important selling points in a logical order. The stimulus-response approach also enables a firm to hire inexperienced salespeople and get them ready for the field with only minimal training.

The stimulus-response approach has some major disadvantages that limit its appropriateness for many types of personal selling. It ignores differences in the needs and interests of different customers. Since customers differ, they will not all respond in the same way to a canned sales talk. Also, when salespeople memorize their presentations, they cannot adjust them to the feedback provided by the customer, particularly when the customer's response is not one for which the representative has been trained. One story about such problems involves a pot-and-pan salesperson who insisted on going through the entire memorized presentation even though the couple had already decided to buy the product.

Salespeople can be allowed some freedom to adjust their canned presentation to the specific demands of a given selling situation. One way is to provide the salesperson with a standardized presentation printed on flip charts or slides but then instruct the individual to add comments where necessary. NCH, a company that supplies maintenance items to factory and industrial maintenance departments, uses simple standardized demonstrations to illustrate the effectiveness of various products.

Due to its rigidity, the stimulus-response approach is seldom employed in the sale of complex industrial goods where buyers' needs and product applications are likely to vary from one customer to the next. Its primary application today is when a relatively simple, standardized product is being sold to large numbers of potential customers who are likely to respond favorably to a standardized appeal, as in selling encyclopedias and other consumer goods door to door.

Sales presentations are much more effective when management provides salespeople with guidelines to help organize their approach than when presentations are entirely unstructured. The mental-states approach is one means for providing such organization.

Mental-states approach

This sales approach is based on the idea that a buyer's mind passes through several successive stages before deciding to make a purchase. It is based on the AIDA theory of persuasion, which stresses that promotional messages must attract the prospect's attention, gain interest, create desire, and stimulate action to complete a sale successfully.

Firms that use the mental-states approach emphasize the use of a selling "formula" in designing a presentation that organizes selling points to coincide with the buyer's movement through the stages of attention, interest, desire, and action. One major advantage of this approach over a strictly memorized presentation is that the salesperson can tailor the sales pitch to each individual prospect. Most companies that use the men-

tal-states approach have found that salespeople can be trained to control the direction of a sales interview by carefully observing the responses of the prospect. They then modify the presentation to stress those points most relevant to the prospect's current state of mind.

As with the stimulus-response approach, one disadvantage of a selling formula aimed at moving a prospect through successive mental states is that it is a salesperson-oriented rather than a customer-oriented method. In an effort to move the prospect from one mental state to the next, the salesperson tends to dominate the interview, and the customer may have little chance to participate. Little attention is paid to variations in needs or circumstances among customers. Companies that use this approach tend to emphasize the sales presentation itself at the expense of those steps in the selling process that precede and follow the presentation.

Perhaps the most serious difficulty with the mental-states approach, however, is that there is no general agreement among psychologists that mental states exist in the minds of potential buyers or that all buyers proceed through the same states in the same sequence. Even if such states do exist, however, it can be difficult to train the salespeople to figure out which state a prospect is in at the moment. It is also hard to know when to leave the selling points related to one mental state and move on to the next.

Need-satisfaction approach

Compared with the previous two selling strategies, the need-satisfaction approach is much more compatible with the modern marketing philosophy that emphasizes the customers to be served rather than the product to be sold. Under this approach, the customer's needs are the starting point in making a sale. The salesperson's task is to identify the prospect's needs, make the prospect aware of that need, and then convince the prospect that the rep's product or service will satisfy that need better than any other alternative.

Firms that utilize this approach emphasize the importance of the early stages in the selling process, such as opening the relationship and qualifying the prospect. The salesperson must become familiar with the prospect's business, industry, and even customers and competitors to tailor a sales presentation to the prospect's unique needs and concerns.

One major advantage of the need-satisfaction approach is that it is customer-oriented and flexible. Proponents contend it provides the basis for a friendly buyer-seller relationship with two-way communication. Because the salesperson concentrates on discovering each prospect's needs and developing presentations that demonstrate how the product can satisfy those needs, this approach helps to minimize sales resistance. Over time, salespeople may become a trusted source of information, and their advice and counsel may be sought and accepted by the customer.

The advantages of the need-satisfaction approach outweigh the disadvantages in most selling situations. But the approach does have some practical limitations. It demands highly qualified sales personnel who have an excellent understanding of their potential customers. They must have the training and experience to adjust their selling methods to the needs and concerns of each individual prospect.[27]

Also, this approach requires a lot of time for the salesperson to become familiar with the prospect. Consequently, it is an expensive method, and it should be used only when the value of the potential sale justifies the expense. Finally, firms are likely to adopt this philosophy only when their overall business philosophy is customer-oriented rather than product-oriented. Thus, the need-satisfaction approach is more common in the sale of consumer durables than in the sale of industrial goods. This is gradually changing, however, as more industrial goods producers embrace a customer-oriented philosophy of marketing.

Problem-solution approach

The problem-solution theory of selling is a logical extension of the need-satisfaction approach. Both are customer-oriented approaches where the sales rep focuses on the prospect's individual needs. Under the problem-solution method, however, the salesperson goes one step further to help the prospect identify several alternative solutions, analyze their advantages and disadvantages, and select the best solution. The salesperson deemphasizes the product offering and concentrates on providing expert advice to the prospect much like a true business consultant. The problem-solving approach may lead a sales representative to suggest that a prospect buy a competitor's product, for example. The primary objective is to form long-term relationships with customers in which the sales rep is seen as a trusted source of technical information and advice.

As with the need-satisfaction approach, the problem-solution method requires extremely competent, well-trained, and experienced sales representatives. It also requires that the salesperson spend a great deal of time with each prospect. Consequently, it is a very expensive selling method.[28] However, this approach is the foundation for the development of long-term relationships that are most likely to produce satisfied and loyal customers over time.

DISCUSSION QUESTIONS

1. The team selling concept is not new, but in the 1990s the idea has become very popular. Companies are creating cross-functional teams composed of representatives from several functions whose primary purpose is to better meet customer needs. Customers, as well, are forming cross-functional teams who interact with the supplier teams. What are the implications of cross-functional teams on the activities of the sales force? What problems will management encounter when using teams?

2. The organizational buying center varies as a function of size of the company and product or service being purchased. How does size of the company influence the composition of the buying center? How would the composition of the buying center differ for each of the following products?

   a. Purchasing a new computer.
   b. Purchasing a new copying machine.
   c. Selecting a different public accounting firm.
   d. Selecting a new textbook for an industrial marketing course.
   e. Choosing a different source for industrial oils and lubricants.
   f. Purchasing a new cardiology machine.
   g. Choosing a marketing research firm.

3. Sales transactions, especially those made to industrial customers, have been known to last as long as several years. In one situation, a sales rep called on one customer for eight years just to get on the approved supplier list. Two years later, the sales rep received the first order. What implications does this situation have on compensation, motivation, and maintaining morale?

4. Just-in-time purchasing procedures have been widely adopted by most major firms. An example comes from Permatech, a subsidiary of ALCOA. ALCOA, using a special product produced by Permatech, ships molten aluminum to Briggs & Stratton to be poured immediately into engine molds. What are the implications of just-in-time purchasing procedures on selling and sales management activities?

5. Over the past 15 years, two major events have changed how purchasing agents view their jobs. Inflation has pushed purchasing costs upward, resulting in companies paying close attention to profits. In addition, the evolution and proliferation of computers have allowed companies to better understand manufacturing costs and determine which parts and components they should be making or buying. How have these changes affected the relationship between purchasing agents and the sales reps calling on them?

6. When a firm, such as Wallace, adopts the major account management approach for dealing with its largest customers, it typically assigns only one or a few customers to a national account manager or team. This involves substantial selling costs per account. How can such costs be justified? What is the rationale for the major account management approach? Under what conditions is it justified?

EXPERIENTIAL APPLICATION

Gather in groups of 8 to 10 (you can use other students from the class, but if not, meet with business majors—even better, marketing majors) and discuss career options. Does anyone in the group have sales experience, and if so, was it good experience? If no one has sales experience, do anyone's parents have selling experience? How do you and your peers view selling and sales management as a career? Through the career services office on campus or through a personnel agency, find a recruiter for sales positions. What are the career options in that organization? What would attract someone to that position?

INTERNET EXERCISES

1. Open the AT&T home page (*www.att.com*) and click on the business services line. This should take you to a page that offers an option *success stories*. Click on this and then go to one of the success stories. Each story will tend to focus on one person. Discuss how this person made the decision to go with AT&T, relative to the steps of the decision process discussed in the chapter. Be specific and include any salesperson involvement.

2. Open *jobtrak.com/jobs* or *marketingjobs.com* and find two jobs that interest you. Visit the companies' home pages and summarize what aspects of those jobs and the industries interest you, based on what you learned from the home pages.

SUGGESTED READINGS

Bristor, Julia, "Influence Strategies in Organizational Buying: The Importance of Connections to the Right People in the Right Places," *Journal of Business to Business Marketing* 1, no. 1 (1993), pp. 63–98.

Bunn, Michele D., "Information Search in Industrial Purchase Decisions," *Journal of Business to Business Marketing* 1, no. 2 (1993), pp. 67–102.

Dawes, Phillip, Don Y. Lee, and Grahame R. Dowling, "Information Control and Influence in Emergent Buying Centers," *Journal of Marketing* 62, no. 3 (1998), pp. 55–68.

Dholakia, Ruby Roy, Jean L. Johnson, Albert J. Della Bitta, and Nikhilesh Dholakia, "Decision-Making Time in Organizational Buying Behavior: An Investigation of Its Antecedents," *Journal of the Academy of Marketing Science* 21 (Fall 1993), pp. 281–92.

Gummeson, Evert, "Implementation Requires a Relationship Marketing Paradigm," *Journal of the Academy of Marketing Science* 26 (Summer 1998), pp. 242–49.

Han, Sang-Lin, David Wilson, and Shirish Dant, "Buyer–Seller Relationships Today," *Industrial Marketing Management* 22, no. 4 (1993), pp. 331–38.

Harmon, Harry A., Craig A. Conrad, and Gene Brown, "Industrial Buyer Behavior: Toward an Understanding,"' *Journal of Marketing Management* 7 (Spring/Summer 1997), pp. 101–14.

Jennings, Richard G., and Richard E. Plank, "When the Purchasing Agent Is a Committee," *Industrial Marketing Management* 24 (1995), pp. 411–19.

Johnston, Wesley J., and Jeffrey E. Lewin, "Organizational Buying Behavior: Toward an Integrative Framework," *Journal of Business Research* 35 (1996), pp. 1–15.

Joshi, Ashwin, and Stephen J. Arnold, "How Relational Norms Affect Compliance in Industrial Buying," *Journal of Business Research* 41 (1998), pp. 105–14.

Kalwani, Manohar U., and Narakesari Naryandas, "Long-Term Manufacturer–Supplier Relationships: Do They Pay Off for Supplier Firms?" *Journal of Marketing* 59 (January 1995), pp. 1–16.

Katrichis, Jerome M., "Exploring Departmental Level Interaction Patterns in Organizational Purchasing Decisions," *Industrial Marketing Management* 27 (1998), pp. 135–46.

Moon, Mark A., and Susan Forquer Gupta, "Examining the Formation of Selling Centers: A Conceptual Framework," *Journal of Personal Selling & Sales Management* (Spring 1997), pp. 31–41.

Trent, Robert J., and Robert M. Monckza, "Effective Cross-Functional Sourcing Teams: Critical Success Factors," *International Journal of Purchasing and Materials Management* (November 1994), pp. 3–11.

Wilson, Elizabeth J., and Richard P. Vlosky, "Partnering Relationship Activities: Building Theory from Case Study Research," *Journal of Business Research* 31 (May 1997), pp. 59–64.

Wilson, Elizabeth J., and Arch G. Woodside, "The Relative Importance of Choice Criteria in Organizational Buying: Implications for Adaptive Selling," *Journal of Business to Business Marketing* 2, no. 1 (1995), pp. 33–58.

4

Environmental Influences on Sales Programs and Performance

HEWLETT-PACKARD'S CHANGE IN STRATEGY

For more than a decade, firms in the computer industry have faced more change in their external environment than companies in most other industries. Rapid technological advancements, continual improvements in product performance, the entry of many competitive upstarts, and increased price competition have forced competitors to stay quick on their feet in order to remain successful. By the late 1980s, however, Hewlett–Packard—one of the industry's early innovators—was having trouble keeping up.

HP's corporate management addressed the problem aggressively by completely restructuring the company. The firm was split up into a number of autonomous divisions that could draw on the resources of the corporate parent but have the independence to operate in an entrepreneurial fashion. The goal was to keep each division closer to the customer by giving it sales and marketing responsibility.

A Change in Marketing Strategy for HP's Computer Systems Organization

One of the new divisions HP created in its reorganization was the Computer Systems Organization (CSO). This $7 billion division is responsible for commercial computer equipment ranging from low-end desktop workstations to powerful client-server systems. To meet changing market needs, the division migrated to more open systems and fewer proprietary products. However, marketing the new product designs required new marketing and sales strategies. As Richard Justice, the director of CSO's sales and marketing operations, points out, with open systems, "Hardware would no longer be the main discussion point. 'Can you solve my business problem?' would become the main discussion point." Consequently, the division shifted its strategy from selling computer "boxes" on the basis of their physical performance and relative price to one of creating value for customers by helping to design system solutions to their business problems, even if the best solution might involve some system components or software made by HP's competitors.

New Sales Programs to Implement a New Marketing Strategy

In order to implement its new marketing strategy effectively, each division had to make some major adjustments in its sales organization and programs. To be capable of designing good systems solutions to customers' problems, HP's salespeople had to gain expert knowledge about those customers' businesses and the problems they faced. To help its salespeople accumulate such expertise, HP shifted away from its geographical organization structure (where each salesperson called on accounts from a variety of different industries within a territory) to a structure where each salesperson concentrates on businesses within a specific industry. For example, CSO sales rep Nancy Ewart says, "I was across the board, but now I focus only on banks. That enables me to speak to higher levels of management and build myself into a trusted advisor."

That strategy of serving only banks or some other industry worked only so well. Salespeople still specialized in specific products and couldn't sell the full HP line of products, ranging from computers to ink-jet printers. As the company realized, the same customer needed the full range of products. Manual Diaz, vice president of HP enterprise (large global) accounts worldwide, says, "We've found that all of our customers like to have access to all of our products." The company now has salespeople who specialize in an industry but work with a team of product specialists so that they can sell the full product line. For large global accounts, the company created a new position, the client business manager (CBM), who handles only one account.

"Salespeople who are promoted to client business manager blend the skills of successful salespeople with those of successful consultants and sales managers," says Diaz. HP has 4,000 CBMs calling on top corporate clients and coordinating teams of products specialists, support people, and consultants. In addition to the usual measures of revenue and unit sales, now profitability and customer satisfaction are key elements in determining the compensation for a CBM.

The moving and shaking aren't over. A more recent reorganization resulted in only six divisions. But while it sounds like HP is a company in trouble, these changes simply reflect the increasing flux of environmental factors that drive any company's strategy. HP's flexibility and ability to re-create itself in response to market changes have sales growing at an annual rate of about 20 percent and market share growing in a number of key industry segments.

Visit HP at its Web site: *www.hp.com.*

Sources: Geoffrey Brewer, "Hewlett–Packard," *Sales & Marketing Management* (October 1997), p. 58; Daniel S. Levine, "Justice Served," *Sales & Marketing Management* (May 1995), pp. 53–61; Jim Louderback, "HP Divisions Are Getting Leaner and Meaner," *PC Week* (July 21, 1997), p. 165.

LEARNING OBJECTIVES

Environmental factors influence sales strategy in many ways: by influencing how customers buy, via the nature of strategic goals set by the company, and through the actual sales strategy set by sales management. In this chapter, you will learn more about how external factors constrain sales strategies and plans. After reading this chapter, you should be able to:

- Illustrate the environmental factors that influence marketing and sales plans.
- Discuss the differences between ethical and legal issues, as well as enumerate ethical issues faced by salespeople and sales managers.
- Describe the Federal Sentencing Guidelines' due diligence process.
- Outline the potential impact the natural environment has on a sales firm.
- Explain the influence of technology on sales plans.

ENVIRONMENTAL FACTORS, MARKETING PLANS, AND THE SALES PROGRAM

Hewlett–Packard's experiences illustrate three important points about how factors in the environment influence marketing and sales management decisions and programs.

1. To be successful, a firm's marketing plans must be adapted to the influences and constraints imposed by both the external and internal corporate environments. As those environments change, appropriate adjustments must be made in the firm's marketing strategy.

   Rapid technological and competitive changes in Hewlett–Packard's external environment forced the firm to respond by restructuring itself in order to give more autonomy and flexibility to its various divisions or strategic business units (SBUs). Similarly, the emergence of the new RISC chip technology spurred the CSO division to revamp its marketing strategy and start designing and selling open systems solutions rather than proprietary hardware. Then, internal organizational changes within HP—including the creation of sales teams that gave the account manager full product line responsibility—facilitated the company's ability to effectively implement its new strategy without having to endure a lengthy review and approval process.

2. A firm's sales program is only one part of an integrated marketing strategy. As changes are made in other parts of the marketing strategy, the sales program must be adjusted if it is to remain effective.

   The CSO division's new marketing strategy would have been difficult to implement effectively within the confines of its old geographical sales force structure. In order to sell open system solutions to customers' problems, CSO's sales reps had to develop a more in-depth understanding of individual customers and the specific problems they face. Thus, major changes in the division's sales policies and programs—such as the switch to an industry-focused organization structure where each sales rep specializes in a single industry, as well as increased sales training to improve the reps' knowledge of target industries—were crucial prerequisites for the ultimate success of the division's new marketing approach. But customers' needs for all of HP's product lines led to another shift, from single-line salespeople to a sales team managed by an account manager.

3. Regardless of how well conceived a sales program is or how well it is integrated into a firm's overall marketing strategy, its implementation depends on the willingness and ability of individual members of the sales force to carry out its policies and procedures. Factors in the external and corporate environments can directly influence a salesperson's actions in the field and the rep's ability to achieve the desired level of performance. Ewart, and salespeople like her, embraced the change that gave them single-industry territories for they were able to leverage knowledge about one customer when calling on another. When the company reorganized and gave each rep full product line responsibility, the move worked in part because Ewart and other salespeople wanted to serve each customer with a full line of products.

   On the other hand, although HP swiftly instituted its sales organization and program changes over a two-month period, it still met with resistance from some people who were used to selling in the old way or saw themselves losing power over their regional fiefdoms. Consequently, some personnel changes and adjustments to the division's compensation and incentive systems were necessary to win the enthusiastic support of the division's reps.

Each of the preceding relationships may seem self-evident, but all must be carefully considered when planning a firm's marketing strategy and sales program. Recall that Chapter 2 introduced the role of the sales force in a company's marketing strategy and how that role changes depending on the type of relationship strategy being implemented. The remainder of this chapter explores factors in both the external and internal corporate environments that influence development of effective marketing strategies and sales plans. We also discuss how environmental factors can constrain the ability of individual salespeople to implement a sales program effectively. In Chapter 5, the discussion of sales strategy continues with the development of a sales force structure.

IMPACT OF THE ENVIRONMENT ON MARKETING AND SALES PLANNING

Exhibit 4.1 shows that environmental factors affect every level of strategy, the overall firm's strategy, as well as lower-level strategies such as marketing and sales. Thus, marketing or sales managers must carefully consider the influences and constraints imposed by environmental factors beyond their control when developing strategic plans for a product or service. Internal and external environmental factors influence marketing strategies and programs in four basic ways.

1. Environmental forces can constrain the organization's ability to pursue certain marketing strategies or activities. An example is when the government declares the sale of a product to be illegal or when a well-entrenched competitor makes it unattractive for the firm to enter a new market.

2. Environmental variables, and changes in those variables over time, help determine

Exhibit 4.1   Components of the External Environment

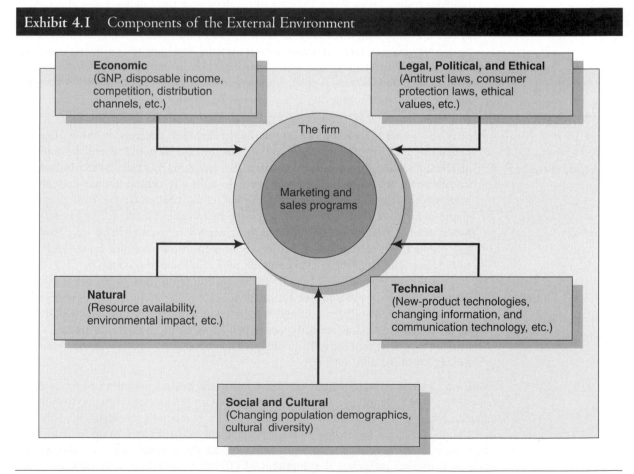

the ultimate success or failure of marketing strategies. The rapid growth in the number of women in the labor force in recent years, for instance, helped ensure the success of Stouffer's Lean Cuisine, ConAgra's Healthy Choice, and other quality brands of convenient frozen entrees.

3. Changes in the environment can create new marketing opportunities for an organization, as when a new technology allows development of new products. The emergence of electronic commerce software, for instance, enabled Hewlett–Packard to develop solutions to problems such as security, design, and flow of data over the Internet, some of the more important challenges that customers face. As one customer said, "There is a lot of value in companies like HP offering to help customers put up electronic commerce sites."

4. Environmental variables are affected and changed by marketing activities, as when new products and promotional programs help to change lifestyles and social values. In view of the increased activity by consumer groups, environmentalists, and other public interest groups and agencies, marketers today must consider how proposed programs will affect the environment as well as how the environment will affect the programs.

Consequently, one of the most important—but increasingly difficult—parts of a marketing manager's job is to monitor the environment, predict how it might change, and develop marketing strategies and plans suited to environmental conditions. Because it is one part of the overall marketing plan, the strategic sales program must be adapted to the environmental circumstances faced by the firm as a whole. Specific environmental factors to be considered when developing marketing plans in general, and strategic sales programs in particular, are examined next.

THE EXTERNAL ENVIRONMENT

Factors in the external environment are beyond the control of the individual manager; however, companies do try to influence external conditions through political lobbying, public relations campaigns, and the like. But for the most part, the marketing or sales manager must take the environment as it exists and adapt strategies to fit it. As indicated in Exhibit 4.1, variables in the external environment that affect marketing and sales programs can be grouped into five broad categories: (1) economic, (2) social and cultural, (3) legal, political, and ethical, (4) natural, and (5) technical.

Markets consist of people. As the demographic, educational, and other characteristics of the population change, market opportunities change. This also affects opportunities in industrial markets, since an organization's demand for goods and services is derived from the demand for its own products. Further, economic systems are becoming more open, meaning that there is ever-increasing competition from global companies. Social and cultural factors can impact the way a company competes globally, which will then influence how the company competes locally.

Legal, political, and ethical factors also influence sales strategies. In China, for example, selling direct to consumers has been banned because it doesn't mesh well with the Communist philosophy. So companies like Mary Kay and Amway have to find other methods of distributing products.

Nature influences demand for many products. Of course, natural disasters such as tornadoes and floods can influence demand for building products and the like. But unseasonable weather can damage or enhance sales, depending on the type of product. La Niña (the winter version of El Niño) caused an increase in snow for the Northwest, leading cities to boost their orders for road salt. Even a rainy Friday after Thanksgiving can negatively impact sales for those companies that rely on the Christmas season.

Technology also influences sales strategies. Of course, the impact of technology is obvious with companies like Hewlett–Packard. But in the mundane world of propane sales, Blue Rhino is one company that has used technology to capture significant market share. By improving the processes of filling and storing tanks, the company has begun to dominate a market that was largely populated by small, independent dealers. In one *King of the Hill* episode, Hank Hill's propane company has to reduce its work force due to the loss in sales at the local Mega Mart. While the *King of the Hill* plot may seem made-up, that is exactly what Blue Rhino has done. Blue Rhino dominates by distributing through the country's largest and fastest-growing retailers (Wal-Mart, Home Depot, and Lowes), a distribution strategy made possible by better technology.

The Economic Environment

People and organizations cannot buy goods and services unless they have the money. The total potential demand for a product within a given country depends on that country's economic conditions—the amount of growth, the unemployment rate, and the level of inflation. These factors must be considered when analyzing market opportunities and developing sales forecasts. Keep in mind, though, that global economic conditions also influence many firms' ability to earn a profit. Companies as diverse as DuPont, Intel, Coca-Cola, and Merrill Lynch were affected by the Asian economic crisis because they generate much of their profit in foreign countries.

A second aspect of the economic environment is the existing distribution structure in an industry. This includes the number, types, and availability of wholesalers, retailers, and other intermediaries a firm might use to distribute its product. Much of a firm's personal selling effort may be directed to trying to persuade such intermediaries to stock and provide marketing support for the company's products.

Understanding competitors

Another critical economic variable is the amount of competition in the firm's industry—both the number of competing firms and their relative strengths in the marketplace. Ideally, a company's marketing and sales programs should be designed to gain a differential advantage over competitors. For example, rather than trying to compete with the low prices of foreign competitors—such as Komatsu—Caterpillar has been successful in the heavy construction equipment business by providing superior product quality and excellent service, while charging prices as much as 10 to 20 percent higher than its competitors.

Salespeople go head to head with competitors on a daily basis; as a result, the sales force is often the first to observe changes in competitive strategy and activity. One of the critical issues is getting information from the sales force to strategic planners so that the company can act on those observations. Reports that detail competitive activity, such as analyses of lost sales, can summarize competitive activity for sales and marketing management.

Salespeople are particularly important when exploring market opportunities in other countries. Given the added risks involved when selling in a foreign country, accurate and timely market information may be more important than in domestic marketing. In many cases, foreign salespeople are the only link the company has to the customer. Companies with international sales forces survey their salespeople, with either formal written surveys or informal telephone surveys, in order to assess foreign markets.[1]

Salespeople also have to use competitive information. The problem seems to lie in determining what is important and useful information, rather than simply gathering data. As Frank

Ruotolo, president of the Futures Group, put it, "This means salespeople end up with reams of data that they don't know what to do with." One fiber optics company learned what to do, though. It created a team of four people to analyze competitive data and then report relevant information to the field. In one situation, they learned that a competitor was offering the same products to different customers for different prices. One customer was about to sign a deal at a price much higher than it needed to be. With information from the competitive intelligence team, the salesperson was able to write a proposal that more precisely met the buyer's needs for less money. According to the VP of marketing for the firm, "when the customer signed, he said how impressed he was with our knowledge of the market."[2]

The Ethical and Social–Cultural Environment

The values of a society also affect marketing and sales programs in a variety of ways. Social values set standards for ethical behavior. Ethics is more than simply a matter of complying with the laws and regulations we will discuss in this section. A particular action may be legal but not ethical. For instance, when a salesperson makes extreme, unsubstantiated statements such as "Our product runs rings around Brand X," the rep may be engaging in legal puffery to make a sale, but many salespeople (and their customers) view such little white lies as unethical.

Ethics is concerned with the development of moral standards by which actions and situations can be judged. It focuses on those actions that may result in actual or potential harm of some kind (e.g., economic, mental, physical) to an individual, group, or organization. Thus, ethics is more proactive than the law. Ethical standards attempt to anticipate and avoid social problems, whereas most laws and regulations emerge only after the negative consequences of an action become apparent.[3]

Two sets of ethical dilemmas are of particular concern to sales managers. The first set is embedded in the manager's dealings with the salespeople. Ethical issues involved in relationships between a sales manager and the sales force include such things as fairness and equal treatment of all social groups in hiring and promotion, respect for the individual in supervisory practices and training programs, and fairness and integrity in the design of sales territories, assignment of quotas, and determination of compensation and incentive rewards. Ethical issues pervade nearly all aspects of sales force management. Consequently, we will revisit the topic of ethics regularly throughout the book.

The second set of ethical issues arises from the interactions between salespeople and their customers. These issues only indirectly involve the sales manager because the manager cannot always directly observe or control the actions of every member of the sales force. But managers have a responsibility to establish standards of ethical behavior for their subordinates, communicate them clearly, and enforce them vigorously. Consequently, the remainder of this section focuses on the ethical issues salespeople face in their dealings with customers and on the actions managers can take to help salespeople resolve such issues appropriately. For more on the issue of ethics and customers, see the "Ethical Issues" box, Giving Gifts—Ethically.

The consequences of unethical selling practices

One might ask why a manager should be responsible for providing moral guidance to subordinates. One might even question whether setting and enforcing standards of ethical conduct for the sales force infringes on the freedom of its individual members and their right to make their own moral choices. While such questions may be legitimate topics for philosophical debate, there is a compelling and practical organizational reason for a firm to impose ethical standards to guide employees' dealings with customers. Unethical selling practices make buyers reluctant to deal with a supplier and are likely to result in the loss of sales and profits over time.

Giving Gifts—Ethically

Does gift giving influence sales and customer satisfaction? One study concluded that even small gifts influence customer satisfaction. In an experiment, Richard Beltramini of Wayne State University sent a plain thank-you letter to some buyers, the letter plus a $20 silver desk set to another group of buyers, and the letter plus a $40 gold desk set to a third group of buyers. Then, he sent a questionnaire measuring satisfaction and intentions to purchase again. The silver-gift group had a 33 percent higher satisfaction rate than the no-gift group, but more importantly the silver group was 33 percent more likely to buy again, and the gold group was twice that, or 66 percent more likely to buy again!

If gift giving influences intentions to purchase, can it be ethical or does gift giving create unfair competitive advantages for the giver? Many companies think so; in fact, more than half of all U.S. companies have en-acted policies against accepting gifts or entertainment from suppliers. IBM buyers, for example, can't even accept a cup of coffee from a supplier. Some guidelines for gift giving include

- Check your motives. Are you trying to foster a mutually beneficial long-term relationship or obligate or pay off a customer for an order?
- Make sure the customer views the gift as a symbol of appreciation and respect. Never give customers the impression that you are attempting to buy their business with a gift.
- Make sure the gift does not violate your company's policies or those of your buyer's company.
- The safest gifts are promotional products, those with the company's or salesperson's name or logo imprinted.

Source: Barton A. Weitz, Stephen B. Castleberry, and John F. Tanner Jr., *Selling: Building Partnerships,* 3d ed. (New York: Irwin/McGraw–Hill, 1998), p. 6; Dawn Myers, "You Get What You Give, so Make It Good," *Promotional Products Business* (June 1998), pp. 105–11.

Exhibit 4.2 reports the findings of a classic survey of 135 purchasing managers from a variety of industries. The first column of numbers in the exhibit indicates how the respondents perceived the ethicality of a variety of selling behaviors. The next column shows the correlation between the perceived ethicality of a given selling behavior and the purchasing manager's intention to purchase from a supplier. In all but one instance, the more unethical a salesperson's behavior was perceived to be, the lower the buyer's intention to purchase from the firm employing that salesperson.[4]

The findings presented in Exhibit 4.3 and those from similar studies suggest that ethical behavior by salespeople can help develop norms of cooperation and trust between a firm and its customers and thereby improve customer loyalty and sales volume.[5] As firms strive to become more market-oriented and target improved customer satisfaction as a marketing objective, the promotion of high ethical standards among members of the sales force is likely to become an even more important component of marketing strategy.

Pressures leading to unethical behavior

Not all customers or competing suppliers adhere to the same ethical standards. As a result, salespeople sometimes feel pressure to engage in actions that are inconsistent with what they believe to be right—in terms of either personal values or formal company standards. Such pressures arise because the sales reps, or sometimes their managers, believe a questionable action is necessary to close a sale or maintain parity with the competition. This point was illustrated by a survey of 59 top sales executives concerning commercial bribery—attempts to influence a potential customer by giving gifts or kickbacks. While nearly two-thirds of the executives considered bribes unethical and did not want to pay them, 88 percent also felt that not paying bribes might put their firms at a competitive disadvantage.

Exhibit 4.2 The Impact of Unethical Selling Behavior on Buyers' Intentions to Purchase from a Supplier

Salesperson Behavior	Perceived Ethicality of the Behavior*	Correlation between Perceived Ethicality and Intention to Purchase from the Supplier†
Gifts to Current Customers		
1. Gives purchaser who was one of best customers a gift worth $50 at Christmas	1.87	.53†
2. Gives one of best customers a $25 Christmas gift	2.26	.65†
3. Buys lunch for a purchasing agent	3.77	.25†
4. Gives very good customer a present worth $10 at Christmas	2.77	.55†
5. Provides entertainment for purchasing agent such as tickets to sporting events	2.63	.55†
Putting Own Interest First		
1. Quotes higher than normal price for product during temporary shortage situation	1.75	.52†
2. Lets it be known he has information about a competitor if purchasing agent is interested	1.90	.61†
3. Hints if order is placed, price might be lower on next order, when it is not so	1.29	.22
4. Only stresses positive aspects of product, omitting possible problem purchasing agent's firm might have with it	1.97	.43†
5. Grants price concession to purchasing agent of company in which he owns stock	1.80	.64†
6. Attempts to sell product to purchasing agent that has little or no value to buyer's company	2.06	.40†
7. Uses "back-door" selling instead of going through purchasing department	1.67	.44†
Gifts to Prospects		
1. Gives purchaser who had done business before a Christmas present worth $10	2.13	.54†
2. Gives purchaser who had not bought from purchaser's firm a Christmas gift worth $25	1.72	.61†
3. A $50 Christmas gift is sent to purchaser who has been called on but has not placed order	1.63	.41†
Pressure or Coercion		
1. In reciprocal buying situation, salesperson hints that unless order is forthcoming, prospect's sales to firm might suffer	1.61	.50†
2. Attempts to use economic power of firm to obtain concessions from the buyer	1.99	.57†
3. Attempts to get purchasing agent to reveal competitor's bid in low-bid buying situation	1.64	.36†
4. Exaggerates how quickly order will be delivered to get sale	1.68	.51†
Preferential Treatment		
1. In shortage situation allocates product shipments to purchasing agent he personally likes	1.91	.67†
2. Grants concessions to purchasing manager depending on how much he likes manager	2.24	.55†
3. Gives preferential treatment to customers who are also good suppliers	2.97	.68†

* 5 = very ethical; 1 = very unethical.

† Significant at 0.01 level.

Source: Adapted from I.F. Trawick, J.E. Swan, G.W. McGee, and D.R. Rink, "Influence of Buyer Ethics and Salesperson Behavior on Intention to Choose a Supplier," *Journal of the Academy of Marketing Science* (Winter 1990), p. 10. Copyright © 1990 *The Journal of the Academy of Marketing Science.*

Exhibit 4.3   Selected Antitrust and Consumer Protection Laws Relevant to Formulating Sales Programs and Policies

Antitrust Provisions

Conspiracies among competing firms to *control their prices,* or to *allocate markets* among themselves, are *per se* illegal under the Sherman Act.

The Robinson-Patman Act prohibits a firm and its representatives from *discriminating in the prices or services* offered to competing customers. The major purpose of this law is to protect smaller customers from being placed at a competitive disadvantage by "key account" programs or price promotions that offer special incentives to larger buyers. However, the law does allow a marketer to grant discounts to larger buyers based on savings in the costs of manufacturing or distributing the product. Thus, some quantity discounts are legal.

Tying agreements, where a seller forces a buyer to purchase one product to gain the right to purchase another, are illegal under the Clayton and Sherman Acts. A computer manufacturer, for example, cannot force a customer to agree to buy cards, paper, and other supplies needed to run a computer as a precondition for buying the computer itself.

Reciprocal dealing arrangements, the "I'll buy from you if you buy from me" type of agreements, are illegal where the effect is to injure competition. Such arrangements do tend to be anticompetitive because large companies—which are large buyers as well as large suppliers—tend to have an advantage over smaller firms.

The Federal Trade Commission Act prohibits *"unfair methods of competition"* in general. Thus, deceptive product claims, interfering with the actions of a competitor's sales representative, and other unfair acts are illegal.

Consumer Protection Provisions

The Fair Packaging and Labeling Act makes *unfair or deceptive packaging* or labeling of certain consumer commodities illegal.

The Truth-in-Lending Act requires *full disclosure of all finance charges* on consumer credit agreements.

State "cooling-off" laws allow consumers to cancel contracts signed with door-to-door sellers within a limited number of days after agreeing to such contracts.

The Federal Trade Commission requires that door-to-door salespeople who work for companies engaged in interstate commerce clearly announce their purpose when making calls on potential customers.

Many cities and towns have so-called Green River Ordinances, which require all door-to-door salespeople to obtain a license.

Such attitudes help explain why the U.S. Chamber of Commerce estimates that of the annual $40 billion in white-collar crime, $7 billion takes the form of bribes and kickbacks.[6] Uncertainty about what to do in such situations—often due to a lack of direction from management—may lead to job stress, poor sales performance, and unhappy customers.

The value of formal ethical policies

Many selling situations involving ethical issues are not addressed by management directives, and many sales personnel want more explicit guidelines to help them resolve such issues. Management can help salespeople avoid the stress and inconsistent performance associated with ethical dilemmas by developing written policies that address problem situations. In 1990, more than 90 percent of the Fortune 1,000 companies had formal codes of ethical conduct, up from 75 percent in 1985.[7] Unfortunately, some of those formal codes are overly broad and fail to provide clear guidance for salespeople in specific situations. And many smaller firms still have no formal guidelines.

The important thing, however, is not just to have a formal policy but to have one that is helpful to the sales force. Such policies should provide clear guidelines for decision making and action so that employees facing similar situations will handle them in a way consistent with the organization's goals. Also, the firm's marketing and sales goals should be set with ethical conduct in mind. "Corporations must go beyond merely educating their employees and look at the motivations that cause a person to make a wrong choice," says Lori Tansey, director of advisory services for the Ethics Resource Center in Washington, D.C. "Setting unrealistic quotas is a perfect example. This situation, probably more than any other, leads to problems."[8]

To further reduce uncertainty, policies must be clearly communicated to both sales personnel and customers. Periodic review sessions, perhaps involving the company's legal staff, can help salespeople remember the policies and can provide an opportunity to discuss any new or unusual situations that might arise. Such communication can be particularly important for newer employees, both because they are likely to have less experience in dealing with ethical dilemmas and because recent studies indicate employees aged 21 to 40 are likely to be significantly more permissive in their ethical attitudes than their older colleagues.[9]

The most effective way for management to influence the ethical performance of their salespeople, however, is to lead by example. Formal policies do not have much impact when top management gives lip service to one set of standards while practicing another. This problem was evident in the comments of a purchasing manager in another study of business ethics: "Our management doesn't want my buyers influenced by the very things they're telling our sales force to do to make sales."[10] Sales managers who expect ethical behavior from their employees should apply high ethical standards to their own actions and decisions.

The Legal–Political Environment

Many of the changes in society's values are eventually reflected in new laws and government regulations—that is where the social–cultural–ethical environment intersects the legal–political environment. Throughout this century, the number of laws regulating the conduct of business—including personal selling—has increased dramatically at all levels of government. Two broad categories of laws are particularly relevant to sales programs: (1) antitrust laws and (2) consumer protection legislation. In addition, the Federal Sentencing Guidelines (FSG) provide companies guidance in setting policies in order to reduce the likelihood of criminal conduct.

The antitrust laws are aimed primarily at preserving and enhancing competition among firms in an industry. They restrict marketing practices that would tend to reduce competition and give one firm a monopoly through unfair competition. Antitrust law provisions of great relevance to sales management are outlined in Exhibit 4.3.

The restrictions on anticompetitive behavior spelled out in the antitrust laws apply to firms selling goods or services to intermediaries, business users, or ultimate consumers. When a firm sells to consumer markets, however, it faces additional restrictions imposed by federal, state, and local consumer protection laws. These laws are aimed more directly at protecting consumer welfare by setting standards of quality and safety. They also require that consumers be provided with accurate information to use in making purchase decisions. Since personal selling is one means of providing consumers with information, many laws requiring full disclosure and prohibiting deceptive or misleading information have a direct impact on selling activities.

Misrepresentation of a company's product by a salesperson can have both ethical and legal consequences, whether the salesperson is dealing with consumers or organizational customers. Many salespeople are unaware that they assume legal obligations every time they approach a customer. By making certain statements, they can embroil their companies in a lawsuit and ruin the very business relationship they are trying to establish. But recent court cases around the United States have held firms liable for multimillion-dollar judgments for misrepresentation or breach of warranty due to statements made by their salespeople, particularly when the sale involved big-ticket, high tech products or services.

One other type of legislation has a direct effect on sales managers as they attempt to implement their sales programs: the equal employment opportunity laws. It is unlawful to discriminate against a person in either hiring or promotion because of race, religion, nationality, sex, or age. For this reason, certain types of aptitude tests are illegal if they are culturally or sexually biased or if they are not valid predictors of a person's job performance. The legal aspects of recruiting and selecting sales representatives, as well as other issues related to the increasing cultural diversity of the labor force, are examined in Chapter 11.

The Federal Sentencing Guidelines (FSG) not only provide judges with guidelines on sentencing companies found guilty of Class A misdemeanors or felonies, but also outline specific steps that companies can take to show that they've made every effort to conduct business in a legal manner. Federal Sentencing Guidelines are most often applied to companies found guilty of price fixing or fraud.[11] If a company can provide evidence of due diligence in preventing misconduct, fines can be reduced. Exhibit 4.4 lists the seven steps for a program to be considered duly diligent.

The Natural Environment

The natural environment is an important consideration in the development of marketing and sales plans. The natural environment is the source of all the raw materials and energy resources needed to make, package, promote, and distribute a product. Over the past 15 years, firms in many industries—such as steel, aluminum, plastics, and synthetic fibers—

Exhibit 4.4   Federal Sentencing Guidelines Requirements for Due Diligence

1. The organization must have established compliance standards and procedures to be followed by its employees and other agents that are reasonably capable of reducing the prospect of criminal conduct.

2. Specific individual(s) among high-level personnel of the organization must have been assigned overall responsibility to oversee compliance with such standards and procedures.

3. The organization must have used due care not to delegate substantial discretionary authority to individuals whom the organization knew, or should have known through the exercise of due diligence, had a propensity to engage in illegal activities.

4. The organization must have taken steps to communicate effectively its standards and procedures to all employees and other agents—for example, by requiring participation in training programs or by disseminating publications that explain in a practical manner what is required.

5. The organization must have taken reasonable steps to achieve compliance with its standards—for example, by utilizing monitoring and auditing systems reasonably designed to detect criminal conduct by its employees and other agents and by having in place and publicizing a reporting system whereby employees and other agents could report criminal conduct by others within the organization without fear of retribution.

6. The standards must have been consistently enforced through appropriate disciplinary mechanisms, including, as appropriate, discipline of individuals responsible for the failure to detect an offense. Adequate discipline of individuals responsible for an offense is a necessary component of enforcement; however, the form of discipline that will be appropriate will be case-specific.

7. After an offense has been detected, the organization must have taken all reasonable steps to respond appropriately to the offense and to prevent further similar offenses—including any necessary modifications to its program to prevent and detect violations of law.

have encountered resource or energy shortages that have forced them to limit sales of their products. One might assume that sales representatives could take life easy under such circumstances, letting customers come to them for badly needed goods. But the sales force often has to work harder during product shortages, and well-formulated account management policies become even more crucial for the firm's success.

During such periods, the sales force is often required to help administer rationing programs, which allocate scarce supplies according to each customer's purchase history. Since shortages are usually temporary, though, sellers have to be sensitive to their customers' problems so they will not lose customers when the shortage is over. Consequently, account management policies must treat all customers fairly, minimize conflict, and maintain the firm's competitive position for the future.

Growing social concern about the possible negative impacts of products and production processes on the natural environment also has important implications for marketing and sales programs. This is increasingly true for firms that sell to organizations as well as for manufacturers of consumer goods. For instance, countries in the European Economic Community have passed legislation requiring manufacturers to take back—and either reuse or recycle—materials used in packaging and shipping their products.

The Technical Environment

The most obvious impact of the technical environment on marketing is in providing opportunities for product development. Technical advances have been occurring at a rapidly increasing rate, and new products are accounting for an increasing percentage of total sales in many industries. In some divisions of the 3M Company, for example, more than half of current sales volume is generated by products that were not in existence five years ago. Most analysts believe the importance of new products and services to the marketing success of many firms will continue to accelerate.[12]

Rapid development of new products requires adjusting a firm's sales programs. New sales plans must be formulated, the sales representatives must be retrained, and, in some cases, new reps must be hired.

Advancing technology also affects sales management in more direct ways. Improvements in transportation, communications, and data processing are changing the way sales territories are defined, sales reps are deployed, and sales performance is evaluated and controlled in many companies. New communications technologies—together with the escalating costs of a traditional field sales call—are changing how the personal selling function is carried out.

The satchel full of samples is giving way to the laptop computer; and telemarketing, teleconferencing, and computerized reordering are replacing the face-to-face sales call in a growing number of situations. Consequently, the nature of many sales jobs—and the role of the sales manager in supervising the sales force—has changed dramatically in recent years. We will explore the impact of these new technologies and the conditions under which they are most likely to improve sales efficiency and effectiveness in greater detail throughout the text.[13]

Keeping a close watch on—and attempting to forecast changes in—the external environment as a basis for formulating marketing and sales plans is easier said than done. There are many examples of well-executed marketing and sales programs that came to grief because one or more elements of the environment changed unexpectedly.

A classic example is the *Encyclopaedia Britannica*. First published 225 years ago in Edinburgh, Scotland, Britannica's sales peaked at $650 million, with profits of $40 million, in 1990. During the early 1990s, competitors entered the market with CD-ROM encyclopedia packages at prices ranging from $99 to $395. Britannica's management failed to foresee or to respond to this threat by either adopting the new technology or altering the firm's traditional direct selling strategy. Instead, the company continued to sell only hardbound sets of encyclopedias priced at $1,500 through its 2,300-person direct sales force. By 1994, seven million U.S. households had purchased CD-ROM encyclopedias, Britannica had reduced its sales force by more than half, its sales had declined drastically, and the firm was in financial trouble.[14]

Part of the reason for such failures to predict changes in the environment is that many corporations do not use sophisticated techniques for environmental scanning and forecasting. A study involving 48 organizations found that business corporations tend to be less sophisticated in their approach to environmental analysis than either consulting firms or government agencies. Environmental scanning and forecasting within business firms occur primarily in response to current crises rather than in an attempt to identify future threats and opportunities.[15]

A study of 149 Fortune 500 firms also revealed that many firms do not pay adequate attention to major factors in their external environment. The study asked top marketing executives how much consideration their firms gave to a variety of external and internal environmental factors in developing strategic marketing plans. As you can see from the results reported in Exhibit 4.5, the vast majority of respondents give frequent consideration to trends affecting their customers, competitors, and technology. But less than half the respondents reported giving frequent consideration to such environmental influences as government controls, political trends, or suppliers.[16]

THE ORGANIZATIONAL ENVIRONMENT

The policies, resources, and talents of the organization also make up a very important part of the marketer's environment. Marketing and sales managers may have some influence over organizational factors due to their participation in making policy and planning decisions; however, in the short run, marketing and sales programs must be designed to fit within organizational limitations. Once again, the variables in the organizational environment can be grouped into five broad categories: (1) goals, objectives, and culture, (2) personnel, (3) financial resources, (4) production capabilities, and (5) research and development capabilities.

Goals, Objectives, and Culture

Formulating marketing plans—and the sales programs that are part of those plans—begins with top management's specification of a company mission and objectives for each functional area within the firm. As the company mission and objectives change, marketing and sales programs must be adjusted.

In some firms, a well-defined mission together with a successful corporate history and top management's values and beliefs leads to development of a strong corporate culture. Such cultures shape the attitudes and actions of employees and help determine the kinds of plans, policies, and procedures managers can implement.

Eastman Chemical Company, winner of a Malcolm Baldrige National Quality Award, provides a good example of how a company's culture and values, competitive strategy, and marketing and sales programs can influence one another. The firm's 10 divisions market a wide variety of specialty chemicals to some 7,000 customers worldwide through a single sales force. What ties the whole operation together are top management's commitment to being responsive to customer needs and a strategy of differentiating the firm from its competitors on the basis of superior customer service. In addition to several other mechanisms for obtaining information about customer needs and satisfaction levels, Eastman administers a satisfaction survey keyed to different customer groups on an 18-

| Exhibit 4.5 | Frequency of Consideration Given to Environmental Factors in Developing Strategic Marketing Plans (N = 149 firms) |

Factor	Frequency of Consideration (Percentage of Respondents)		
	Frequent	Occasional	Seldom/ Never
External Environment			
Competition for customers	90%	5%	5%
Implementing new technology	80	16	4
Update technology	75	20	5
Final customers	72	12	16
Distributors as customers	59	14	27
Government controls/inflation	50	36	28
Raw material supplier	44	26	14
Competition for distributor	35	25	40
Public/political attitudes	34	26	40
Internal Organization Environment			
Organization goals and objectives	78	20	2
Nature of products/services	68	27	5
Existing managerial skills	50	35	15
Employee Involvement and commitment	48	34	18
Interdepartmental dependency	45	35	20
Interdepartmental procedures	45	40	15
Manpower availability	40	40	20
Different technological characteristics	40	16	44
Education and technological skills	40	35	25
Interdepartmental conflicts	28	30	42

Source: Joel E. Ross and Ronnie Silverblatt, "Developing the Strategic Plan," *Industrial Marketing Management* 16 (1987), pp. 103–8. Reprinted by permission of the publisher. Copyright 1987 by Elsevier Science Publishing Co., Inc.

month cycle. The survey covers 25 different performance items and is printed in nine languages. Customer satisfaction is measured on dimensions such as on-time and correct delivery, product quality, pricing practices, and sharing of market information. Responsibility for each dimension is assigned to the function(s) within the company that can take direct action to improve any problems on that dimension. The entire survey is managed by the sales force, and salespeople discuss the results with each customer, indicating actions being taken by the company to overcome any problems.[17]

Personnel

The number of people in the organization, together with their skills and abilities, constrains marketing strategies and sales programs. In view of the difficulties involved in recruiting highly qualified people for sales positions and the often lengthy training programs needed to teach new sales reps necessary skills, it is often difficult to expand a sales force rapidly to take advantage of new products or growing markets. In some cases, however, it may be possible for a firm to compensate for a lack of knowledgeable

Is Technology Building Relationships?

Among the environmental forces that shape the nature of selling is technology, and more specifically, the Internet. The U.S. government expects over $300 billion in business-to-business sales to take place online by 2003. Some companies have even established home pages specifically for customers so that they can place orders. But are buyers buying into the new technology? And can the Internet help to build relationships?

Research suggests that as buyers begin to use technology to place orders, the number of suppliers decreases, which can look like stronger relationships arising. But if Grainger's experience is any indication, the answer is no. Grainger, though, is not taking no for an answer.

So far, only 1 percent of the company's customer base has signed up for a Web account. The company,

a $4.1 billion industrial supplies manufacturer and distributor, faces challenges in getting both customers and salespeople to support the idea. With internal marketing to convince salespeople and direct mail and telemarketing to convince customers, Grainger has bet big bucks on building online ordering. Lower costs, better service, and stronger relationships are all reasons why Grainger believes that the Web will work.

Even so, it may take a new generation of buyers before relationships will truly enable online ordering. As Donald Bielinski, Grainger group president, says, "The longest it is going to take is the amount of time it will take my 12-year-old to enter the work force. There's no way he'll enter the work force without using these types of systems" (Frook, p. 48).

Source: John Evan Frook, "Grainger's Buy-in Plan," *Business Marketing* (November 1998), pp. 1, 48; Carol Krol, "DMA: B-to-B E-Commerce Rising," *Business Marketing* (November 1998), p. 12; Rodney Stump and Ven Sriram, "Employing Information Technology in Purchasing," *Industrial Marketing Management* 26 (March 1997), pp. 127–36.

employees by utilizing outside agencies or specialists on a fee-for-service or commission basis, such as agent intermediaries. For example, many companies use distributors when entering new markets, particularly foreign markets, because entering the market can be accomplished so much more quickly by utilizing preexisting sales forces.

Financial Resources

An organization's financial strength influences many aspects of its marketing programs. It can constrain the firm's ability to develop new products as well as the size of its promotional budget and sales force. Companies sometimes must take drastic measures, such as merging with a larger firm, to obtain the financial resources necessary to realize their full potential in the marketplace. For example, ConAgra was recently able to purchase Plantation Foods, a turkey processor, because Plantation Foods did not have the resources to develop new products and new markets as fast as management felt it should. By merging with ConAgra, the company was able to take advantage of the financial resources of a multibillion-dollar company many times the size of Plantation.

Production Capabilities

The organization's production capacity, the technology and equipment available in its plants, and even the location of its production facilities can influence its marketing and sales programs. A company may be prevented from expanding its product line or moving into new geographic areas because it does not have the capacity to serve increased demand or because transportation costs make the product's price uncompetitive. Florida Furniture Industries (FFI) manufactures bedroom furniture in three plants in south Georgia and north Florida. Because furniture is bulky, it is expensive to ship, which has limited FFI's market to Texas east to the coast and about as far north as Virginia.

Research and Development Capabilities

An organization's technical and engineering expertise is a major factor in determining whether it will be an industry leader or follower in product development. Excellence in engineering and design can also serve as a major promotional appeal in a firm's marketing and sales programs, as it was for Hewlett–Packard's new line of UNIX client-servers. But as the experience of Blue Rhino shows, a firm can find ways to satisfy customer needs and compete effectively even when it competes in a low tech industry.

Some companies are investing heavily in technology, particularly technology that can support marketing and sales objectives. In the "Managing Sales Relationships" box we examine one firm's commitment to the Web.

Because all of the preceding organizational factors influence a firm's ability to implement a given marketing strategy effectively, all should be considered by managers when developing marketing and sales plans and programs. Unfortunately—as the survey results in Exhibit 4.5 indicate—this is not always the case. Although most firms pay frequent attention to defining specific objectives and specifying the kinds of products and services they will offer, less than half pay the same kind of attention to their personnel or technical capabilities. The danger is that such firms may develop marketing programs that look good on paper but are difficult to implement successfully.[18]

SUMMARY

The environmental factors that can severely affect a marketing plan can be grouped into the two broad categories of external and organizational environments. The external environment includes the (1) economic, (2) social, cultural, and ethical, (3) legal–political, (4) natural, and (5) technical environments. The organizational environment includes the firm's (1) goals and objectives, (2) personnel, (3) financial resources, (4) production capabilities, and (5) research and development capabilities.

The values of society set standards for ethical behavior. Ethics is concerned with the development of moral standards by which actions and situations can be judged. It focuses on those actions that may result in actual or potential harm of some kind (e.g., economic, mental, physical) to an individual, group, or organization. Thus, ethics is more proactive than the law, and behaving ethically sometimes means going beyond mere adherence to the law.

Two sets of ethical dilemmas are of particular concern to sales managers. The first set is embedded in the manager's dealings with salespeople. Ethical issues pervade nearly all aspects of the management of a sales force, and such problems will be discussed throughout this text.

The second set of ethical issues arises from the interactions between individual salespeople and their customers. Sales managers must establish standards of ethical behavior for their subordinates, communicate them clearly, and enforce them vigorously. There is mounting evidence that unethical selling practices make buyers reluctant to deal with a supplier and are likely to result in the loss of sales and profits over time.

As part of the firm's marketing program, the company's personal selling program must also be adapted to the external and organizational environments. Some important organizational variables that can cause differences in performance among salespeople are (1) regional variations in the expenditure of money and effort on other elements of the firm's marketing and promotion mix, (2) variations in the firm's experience in different territories, and (3) regional variations in sales management practices—particularly in the number of sales personnel supervised by field sales managers. External factors that can vary from one region to another include (1) intensity of competition, (2) total market potential, (3) concentration of potential sales—the proportion of customers who are relatively large purchasers—and (4) geographic dispersion of customers.

Appendix
A

Approaches to Ethics

Two philosophical traditions are commonly used as bases for evaluating the ethics of a given action: deontology and teleology.[1] Unfortunately, these two approaches can lead to conflicting choices when determining whether a given action is ethical or unethical.

Deontology

Deontological ethics focuses on the welfare of the individual and emphasizes means and intentions for justifying an act. Deontologists believe that features of the act itself make it right or wrong. Deontological thinking rests on two fundamental principles: the rights principle and the justice principle. The rights principle focuses on two criteria for judging an action: (1) universality, which means every act should be based on principles on which everyone could act, and (2) reversibility, which means every act should be based on reasons that the actor would be willing to have all others use, even as a basis for how they treat the actor.

The rights principle is the philosophical source of specific, generally acknowledged rights in society, such as the "right to know." With its emphasis on the notion that every individual has the right to be treated in ways that ensure the person's dignity, respect, and autonomy, the deontological model is sometimes referred to as the rights or entitlements model.

The justice principle reflects three categories of justice: (1) distributive, whereby resources are distributed according to some evaluation of just desserts, (2) retributive, whereby the wrongdoer is punished proportionally to the wrongdoing, provided it was committed knowingly and freely, and (3) compensatory, whereby the injured party is restored to his or her original position. An example of the justice principle applied to a sales situation would be a firm offering a rebate to a customer to compensate for missing a delivery schedule promised by its sales representative.

Teleology

The most well known branch of teleological ethics is utilitarianism, which focuses on society as the unit of analysis and stresses the consequences of an act in evaluating its ethical status rather than the intentions behind it. The utilitarian model emphasizes the consequences an action may have on all those directly or indirectly affected by it. The utilitarian perspective holds that the correct action is the one that promotes "the greatest good for the greatest number."

Utilitarianism requires that a social cost–benefit analysis be conducted for the contemplated action. All benefits and costs to all persons affected by the particular act need to be considered to the degree possible and summarized as the net of all benefits minus all costs. If the net result is positive, the act is morally acceptable; if the net result is negative, the act is not.

To assess the net benefits of an action, however, the manager must be able to answer the following questions.

- What are the viable courses of action available?
- What are the alternatives?
- What are the harms and benefits associated with the course of action available?
- Can these harms and benefits be measured? Can they be compared?
- How long will these harms and benefits last?
- When will these harms and benefits begin?
- Who is directly harmed? Who is indirectly harmed?
- Who is directly benefited? Who is indirectly benefited?
- What are the social and/or economic costs attached to each alternative course of action?
- Which alternatives will most likely yield the greatest net benefit to all individuals affected by the decision? Or, if no alternative yields a net benefit, which one will lead to the least overall harm?

Conflicts between the Two Perspectives

Suppose a firm charges higher prices to loyal customers for whom it is the sole supplier than it does to other organizations where it must compete with other suppliers. Is such an action ethical? The deontological view, with its emphasis on fairness and justice for the individual, would suggest it is not. But the utilitarian or teleological perspective, with its focus on the greatest good for the greatest number, might conclude such a practice is ethical if the higher wages and increased returns to shareholders enabled by the action more than offset the economic harm done to a few customers.

The preceding illustration not only demonstrates how different ethical traditions can lead to different standards, but it also exposes a potential problem inherent in the utilitarian perspective. When a firm bases its ethical standards solely on utilitarian analysis, individuals (either persons or firms) or small groups may suffer major harm because their costs are averaged with small gains to a large number of other people with the result that the net benefit of the act appears positive.

Partly because of this potential problem, some analysts argue utilitarianism is appropriate only for very general planning where no specific harm to individuals is expected, and marketing activities having a foreseeable and potentially serious impact on individuals should be regulated by deontological reasoning.[2] Given that customers are identifiable individuals or organizations and that the effects of most questionable sales practices on them can be anticipated, these analysts would argue that the criteria of universality and

reversibility provide a better basis for formulating ethical standards for the sales force than a broad cost–benefit analysis.

Neither framework can provide precise or mechanistic answers to ethical questions. In a utilitarian analysis, for instance, one must wrestle with the difficult problem of quantifying costs and benefits, while in a deontological analysis, one needs to judge the seriousness of a right's infringement. What constitutes ethical conduct in the eyes of a firm's managers and employees—or in the eyes of the selling profession as a whole—will ultimately be a matter of consensus. But such consensus can be reached only if individual salespeople and sales managers think about ethical issues and exchange views.

---

[1] For more detailed discussions of the differences between the two perspectives, see Robert A. Cooke, *Ethics in Business: A Perspective* (Chicago: Arthur Andersen & Co., 1988); O. C. Ferrell and Larry G. Gresham, "A Contingency Framework for Understanding Ethical Decision Making in Marketing," *Journal of Marketing* (Summer 1985), pp. 87–96; Shelby D. Hunt and Scott Vitell, "A General Theory of Marketing Ethics," *Journal of Macromarketing* (Spring 1986), pp. 5–16; and Donald P. Robin and R. Eric Reidenbach, "Social Responsibility, Ethics, and Marketing Strategy: Closing the Gap between Concept and Application," *Journal of Marketing* (January 1987), pp. 44–58. For a decision-making approach for ethics in marketing, see Lawrence B. Chonko, *Ethical Decision Making in Marketing* (Thousand Oaks, CA: Sage Publications, 1995).

[2] Robin and Reidenbach, "Social Responsibility, Ethics, and Marketing Strategy."

DISCUSSION QUESTIONS

1. The following appeared in the *Wisconsin State Journal,* November 17, 1995, p. 8B: "Merrill Lynch & Co. is offering brokers trips to London or laptop computers in a new competition involving sales of international stocks and bonds. . . . Brokers win the London trip, laptop, or a $1,000 credit to their business expense account in one of two ways: if the value of their clients' international investment rises in market value beyond certain targets, or if the brokers sell a variety of international mutual funds, stocks, bonds, or insurance products to exceed the promotion's goals." What does this say about Merrill's relationship strategy? How would you implement such a competition if you were a Merrill Lynch broker?

2. Kelly Noland, sales manager of Keystone Financial, had just completed her review of sales expenses and

was concerned about the limited expenses incurred by one of Keystone's financial consultants. In particular, she noted that Martin Gregory did not follow Keystone's gift-giving guidelines. When asked about this, Martin replied, "I know I can give gifts and that my expenses will be covered. But I don't like this. It smacks of bribery, and besides, I don't think it helps one bit." Kelly Noland felt differently and wondered if Martin's less-than-spectacular sales results might be improved if he followed Keystone's recommendations. What is the role of gift giving in business relations?

3. Jon Baker was flabbergasted. Collette Lamour, purchasing agent for Colonial Enterprises, indicated to Jon what she thought might be a nice gift. She opened a gift catalog to a page displaying fur coats and circled one she thought would look great on her. She said, "In case

you were wondering what kind of gift to get me, here's an idea." Jon saw the $3,000 price and knew this represented a small part of the 600,000 annual sales made to Colonial. In addition to the dilemma of gift giving on such a large scale, Jon faced another problem. He was opposed to the fur industry's practice. What should Jon do in this situation? What would you do?

4. The chapter illustrates how environmental changes can alter a firm's marketing program and cites three important points. Using these points, what changes have occurred over the past 10 years in how AT&T competes in the market today? What changes have occurred in the public accounting industry? In the legal industry?

5. Karen Coenen (sales rep for Midway Corporation, manufacturer of electronic instruments) has been told

to pad her expense account. She has been told everyone else does it, so she should too. She thinks that since everyone else is doing it, she might as well go along with the group. Do you approve, somewhat approve, somewhat disapprove, or disapprove? If you were confronted with this situation, would you pad your account?

6. Changes in the technological environment have the potential to significantly affect the activities of the sales force. Automation can offer the sales force a competitive advantage—if the sales force is motivated to use computers and other technological methods that are part of automation. What steps should management adopt to ensure that the sales force buys into the company's automation system?

EXPERIENTIAL APPLICATION

Scan the headlines of a major metropolitan newspaper and identify five news stories that reflect different environmental dimensions. Each news story should be about a factor, trend, or event that will influence a business like HP. Write a paragraph for each news story that reflects how you think each story will influence HP. Use the article headline as the headline for each paragraph.

INTERNET EXERCISES

1. Visit the Hewlett–Packard Web site, *HP.com.* As we write this, there is a very interesting section on HP and the Euro (the currency of the European Common Market). Through your research on the Web site and additional reading, evaluate the impact of the Euro on HP relative to each of the environmental areas identified in Exhibit 4.1. In your analysis, consider (1) what had to change in each area for the Euro to be adopted successfully and (2) how that adoption impacts HP.

2. Hit the Grainger home page after you read the "Managing Sales Relationships" box in this chapter. Assess the home page in terms of its ability to draw new customers and encourage current customers to order. First, make a list of dimensions that you think are important; for example, what features should the home page have? Then grade Grainger on each dimension, justifying your decision. Keep in mind that current customers with a Web account will have access to pages that you cannot see. Still, your evaluation should reflect what you think both noncustomers and current customers would think.

SUGGESTED READINGS

Anderson, Rolph, "Personal Selling and Sales Management in the New Millenium," *Journal of Personal Selling & Sales Management* (Fall 1996), pp. 17–32.

Chonko, Lawrence B., *Ethical Decision Making in Marketing.* Thousand Oaks, CA: Sage Publications, 1995.

Chonko, Lawrence B., John F. Tanner Jr., and William A. Weeks, "Ethics in Salesperson Decision Making: A Synthesis of Research Approaches and an Extension of the Scenario Method," *Journal of Personal Selling & Sales Management* (Winter 1996), pp. 35–52.

Cravens, David W., "The Changing Role of the Sales Force," *Marketing Management* (Fall 1995), pp. 48–57.

Kahn, Kenneth, and John Mentzer, "Marketing's Integration with Other Departments," *Journal of Business Research* 42 (May 1998), pp. 53–62.

Leuthesser, Lance, "Supplier Relational Behavior: An Empirical Assessment," *Industrial Marketing Management* 26 (May 1997), pp. 245–54.

Rallapalli, Kumar, Scott J. Vitell, and James Barnes, "The Influence of Norms on Ethical Judgments and Intentions: A Study of Marketing Professionals," *Journal of Business Research* 43 (1998), pp. 157–68.

Walker, Orville C., Jr., Harper W. Boyd, Jr., and Jean-Claude Larréché, *Marketing Strategy: Planning and Implementation,* 2d ed. Burr Ridge, IL: Richard D. Irwin, 1996, chapters 4 and 12.

5 Organizing the Sales Effort

IBM ORGANIZES FOR THE FUTURE

In the highly competitive and dynamic world of technology, companies are constantly forced to restructure themselves to meet the demands of the marketplace. IBM is no exception. As it seeks out new market opportunities, IBM must create new organizational structures within its sales departments. Lou Gerstner, IBM's take-charge CEO, has implemented widespread changes in the way IBM markets its products and services. As Gerstner notes, "IBM is more than big—it's big and fast." IBM speaks of the relationship between IBM and its distributors as a *team*.

The Need for a New Organizational Structure

IBM built its image and its sales by focusing on big business. Big corporate computing was synonymous with IBM representatives in navy blue suits and crisp white shirts. The company has come to realize, however, that small business in America represents a huge market that, for the most part, IBM has failed to capture. Despite its size, $78 billion in 1997, IBM has not aggressively sought out "smaller" businesses with fewer than 1,000 employees. For many years IBM has managed to grow on the basis of its penetration in the IT departments of big businesses around the world. However, growth in small and medium-sized business has led IBM to reassess its market strategies. Specifically, small businesses are responsible for 50 percent of the U.S. GNP and are growing at 11 percent annually. Moreover, small and medium-sized businesses spent $305 billion worldwide on information technology in 1997, a number big enough to get the attention of IBM. However, attacking this market requires IBM to redirect its resources and restructure itself to successfully reach these businesses.

Issues Remain That Are Difficult to Change

Two key issues have led IBM to reevaluate its structure as it relates to the small-business market. First is the nature of the relationship between IBM and the small business market. A key to IBM's success has been its sales force. Companies came to rely on the IBM representative. Unfortunately, the size and diversity of the small business market severely restricts that kind of one-on-one relationship. Worldwide, IBM has built relationships with over 45,000 "business partners" (independent distributors, value-added resellers, system integrators, and software vendors). These partners supplement and enhance their 3,400 field sales force dedicated to small businesses around the world. However, IBM's own sales force and its business partners do not always communicate effectively with one another. It is not uncommon for IBM salespeople as well as business partner representatives to call on the same client, which serves to confuse them.

A second issue is the way IBM is viewed by

many small businesses. While it has been viewed historically as a welcome partner in big corporate IT departments, smaller businesses have found IBM less responsive to their needs. As one IT consultant to small businesses noted, "My small customers don't feel comfortable with IBM. . . . You can't get someone on the phone." Even IBM executives acknowledge a perceptual problem with small businesses. Thomas Smith Jr., IBM's general manager for North American Small and Medium Businesses, stated, "I would never argue with anyone about our current reputation—it took us 80 years to build it."

IBM Creates Hybrid Marketing

As delineated by Ned Lautenbach, senior vice president and group executive, IBM has embarked on a strategy that employs a divergent mix of sales approaches to attack the small and medium-sized markets. This strategy incorporates the venerable IBM sales force with its business partners and telemarketing to reach this huge market more efficiently but, more importantly, more effectively. The heart of the strategy is based on those 20 percent of the small-business customers that drive 70 percent of the dollars spent. Those customers still receive one-on-one attention from IBM's sales force. Sales people are responsible for effectively managing the relationship with those businesses and are organized by industry. However, rather than act alone, they are learning to work with their distributors and resellers to present a more coordinated and effective message to the customer. In addi-

tion, they have learned to use and work with a strong telemarketing group, which enhances the work of the field sales force.

IBM has created a host of services and products designed specifically for their business partners. For example, SystemXtra is a set of related IBM services that are offered by their business partners to their own customers. These services include network management, warranty upgrades, and training as well as flexible financing options. Phil Reifenberg (strategic business unit manager at Pride Technologies in Cincinnati, Ohio) stated it this way: SystemXtra offers "competitive advantage over the direct model, enabling us to provide a complete solution incorporating hardware, software, services, and support in a single deliverable."

IBM Succeeds When the Team Succeeds

IBM has come to realize, as have many companies, that it needs to do a better job of working with its business partners. In addition, IBM's sales force has also learned to work more closely with and coordinate with the in-house IBM telemarketing people. This kind of teamwork has impacted every element of IBM's small-business sales force, from they way they manage information inside the company to the way they are compensated and, finally, to the way they interact with their customers.

Visit IBM at *www.IBM.com*.

Source: This example is based largely on material found in Geoffrey Brewer, "Lou Gerstner Has His Hands Full," *Sales & Marketing Management* (May 1998), pp. 36–41, and the IBM Web site (Business Partners area).

LEARNING OBJECTIVES

Organizing the sales force is one of the most important decisions made by sales management. It has a significant impact on every aspect of the salesperson's performance. Changes in the way selling is done, the increasing importance of effectively managing customer relationships, and the need to assimilate new technologies in the selling function have led to fundamental changes in the organization of sales forces for the next century.

After reading this chapter, you should be able to:

- Identify the different organizational structures of a sales force.

- Understand the complex relationship between the sales force and key national accounts.

- Discuss the unique issues associated with organizing an international sales force.

- Define the major decisions faced by a sales manager in organizing the sales force.

THE INCREASING IMPORTANCE OF SALES ORGANIZATION DECISIONS

Organizing the activities and management of the sales force is a major part of strategic sales planning. Until recently, however, the kind of organizational restructuring undertaken by IBM was not common among either industrial or consumer goods marketers. Once a firm had an organizational structure in place, its managers tended to take it for granted—at least until performance problems became apparent. But in recent years, increasing rates of change in markets, technology, and competition have forced managers to pay closer attention to their sales organizations and to be more proactive in restructuring those organizations when necessary.[1]

As demonstrated in the opening scenario with IBM, strategic market planning is closely linked with how the organization is structured and how it interacts with its customers. This chapter stresses the importance of designing an appropriate organizational framework for the sales force as an integral part of a firm's strategic sales plan and examines issues involved in developing such a framework. It begins with a discussion of the purposes of organization—the things a good organizational plan should accomplish. Next, issues related to the horizontal organization of the sales effort are explored. Horizontal organization is concerned with how specific selling activities are divided among various members of the sales force. Finally, the vertical structuring of the sales organization is discussed. Vertical structuring refers to organizing a firm's sales managers and their activities rather than the personnel in the sales force. An understanding of these issues should provide greater appreciation for the crucial role organizational decisions play in developing an effective strategic sales program.

PURPOSES OF SALES ORGANIZATION

An organizational structure is simply an arrangement of activities involving a group of people. The goal in designing an organization is to divide and coordinate activities so the group can accomplish its common objectives better by acting as a group than by acting as individuals. The starting point in organizing a sales force is determining the goals or objectives to be accomplished; these are specified in the firm's overall marketing plan. The selling activities necessary to accomplish the firm's marketing objectives must then be divided and allocated to members of the sales force so the objectives can be achieved with as little duplication of effort as possible. An organizational structure should serve the following purposes:

1. Activities should be divided and arranged in such a way that the firm can benefit from the *specialization of labor.*

2. The organizational structures should provide for *stability and continuity* in the firm's selling efforts.

3. The structure should provide for the *coordination* of the various activities assigned to different persons in the sales force and different departments in the firm.

Division and Specialization of Labor

Two centuries ago, Adam Smith pointed out that dividing any function into its component activities and assigning each activity to a specialist can increase the efficiency with which almost anything is performed. Division and specialization of labor increase productivity because each specialist can concentrate efforts and become more proficient at the assigned task. Also, management can assign individuals only to those activities for which they have aptitude.

In some cases, the personal selling function is so simple and straightforward a firm could gain few if any benefits by applying the principles of division and specialization of labor to its sales force. Salespeople in such companies are expected to carry out all the activities necessary to sell all the products in the company's line to all types of customers within their territories. But in many firms, the selling function is sufficiently complicated that dividing the necessary selling activities can increase efficiency and effectiveness. Different activities are assigned to various specialists, creating two or more specialized sales forces. IBM has found that partnering with specialists such as resellers and distributors can enhance the effectiveness of their own sales force.

Management must decide the best way to divide the required selling activities to gain the maximum benefits of specialization within the sales force. Should independent agent intermediaries be used to perform some or all of the firm's selling efforts? Should selling activities be organized by product, by customer type, or by selling function (for example, prospecting for new accounts versus servicing old customers)? As discussed later in this chapter, each basis for horizontally structuring the sales organization has its own advantages and disadvantages. Which one is best depends on the firm's objectives, target market, product line, and other internal and external factors.

Division and specialization of labor can benefit managerial functions as well as selling functions. Some firms use a simple "line" form of vertical organization in which the chain of command runs from the chief sales executive down through levels of subordinates. Each subordinate is responsible to only one person on the next higher level, and each is expected to perform all the necessary sales management activities relevant to his or her own level.

The most common form of vertical organization structure—especially in medium- and large-size firms—is the "line and staff" organization. In this form, several sales management activities—such as personnel selection, training, and distributor relations—are assigned to separate staff specialists. This kind of specialization, however, raises some questions concerning organizational design, such as

1. What specific functions should be assigned to staff executives.

2. How can staff activities be integrated with those of line sales managers, and should those activities be performed in-house or outsourced to independent contractors, such as personnel agencies and training firms?

These questions are examined further later in this chapter.

Stability and Continuity of Organizational Performance

Although many companies use division and specialization of labor in designing their sales organizations, they sometimes ignore a related caveat concerning good organizational design: Organize activities, not people. In other words, activities should be assigned to positions within the sales organization without regard to the talents or preferences of current employees.

Once an ideal organizational structure has been designed, people can be trained or, if need be, recruited to fill positions within the structure. Over time, those in lower positions should be given the experience and training necessary to enable them to move into higher positions. In athletic terms, the organization should build depth at all positions. This provides stability and continuity of performance for the organization. The same activities are carried out at the same positions within the firm even if specific individuals are promoted or leave.

Coordination and Integration

The advantages of the division and specialization of labor are clear, but specialization also causes a problem for managers. When activities are divided and performed by different individuals, those activities must be coordinated and integrated so all efforts are directed at accomplishing the same objective. The more an organization's tasks are divided among specialists, the more difficult integrating those tasks becomes. The problem is even worse when outside agents—such as manufacturers' representatives—are used, because the manager has no formal authority over them and cannot always control their actions.

Sales managers must be concerned about the coordination and integration of the efforts of their salespeople in three ways. First, the activities of the sales force must be integrated with the needs and concerns of customers. Second, the firm's selling activities must be coordinated with those of other departments, such as production, product development, logistics, and finance. Finally, if the firm divides its selling tasks among specialized units within the sales force, all those tasks must be integrated.

Consequently, the primary function of the vertical structure of a firm's sales organization is to ensure these three kinds of integration. Questions of vertical organization—such as how many levels of sales management the firm should have, the appropriate span of control for each sales executive, and the most effective use of staff specialists—should be examined with an eye toward effective integration of the firm's overall selling efforts.

HORIZONTAL STRUCTURE OF THE SALES FORCE

There is no best way to divide selling activities among members of the sales force. The best sales organization varies with the objectives, strategies, and tasks of the firm. Furthermore, as the firm's environment, objectives, or marketing strategy changes, its sales force may have to be reorganized. There are several key questions in this discussion such as

1. Should the company employ its own salespeople, or should some or all of its selling efforts be contracted to outside agents—such as manufacturer's representatives?

2. How many different sales forces should the company have, and how should they be arranged?

3. Should separate sales representatives be assigned to different products, types of customers, or sales functions?

4. Who should be responsible for selling to major national accounts?

5. How should firms organize their sales and marketing efforts when they enter foreign markets and become global competitors?

There are four common bases used for structuring the sales effort, and each has unique advantages that make it appropriate for a firm under certain circumstances. The first issue to be decided is whether the firm should hire its own salespeople or use outside agents. When a company sales force is used, alternative approaches include (1) geographic organization, (2) organization by type of product, (3) organization by type of customer, and (4) organization by selling function.

A Company Sales Force or Independent Agents?

This book focuses primarily on issues associated with managing an internal company sales force, where all of the salespeople and their managers are employees of the firm. In many cases, though, the use of independent agents instead of company salespeople is an important option.

Exhibit 5.1 summarizes the results of a survey of over 200 firms. Nearly one-third of the respondents reported using manufacturers' representatives (one type of intermediary) to contact customers. A larger percentage of industrial goods producers use agents (37 percent) than consumer goods firms (19 percent). The use of agents varies even more widely across different industries. While less than 5 percent of grocery products are sold through manufacturers' reps, for example, nearly half of all electrical goods are distributed through such intermediaries.

Notice, too, that the percentages in Exhibit 5.1 add up to far more than 100 percent. Some respondents use more than one method to contact customers. It is not unusual, for instance, for a firm to use both company salespeople and independent agents.[2] IBM, from the chapter introduction, uses both its highly trained sales force as well as a network of business partners around the world to help market its products and services. In such cases, firms usually rely on agents to cover geographic areas with relatively few customers or low sales potential—territories that may not justify the cost of a full-time company salesperson.

However, the use of intermediaries may not grow as fast in the future as other forms of customer contact. As indicated in Exhibit 5.2, a survey of 56 large firms across a variety of industries suggests that the most prevalent organizational changes in the 1990s have involved an increasing emphasis on specialized company salespeople, such as national account managers, and other efforts aimed at improving customer service and adding value to firms' offerings. Nearly half of the respondents also reported a shift to telemarketing for covering their smaller customers. Also, as discussed in earlier chapters, many firms are forming logistical alliances involving the development of computerized information and reordering systems to service their larger customers. On the other hand, only 23 percent of survey respondents reported an increased reliance on agents or distributors.[3]

Types of agents

The two most common types of intermediaries a manufacturer might use to perform the selling function are manufacturers' representatives and selling (or sales) agents. **Manufacturers' representatives** are intermediaries who sell part of the output of their principals—the manufacturers they represent—on an extended contract basis. They take neither ownership nor physical possession of the goods they sell, but concentrate instead on the selling function. They are compensated solely by commissions.

Reps have no authority to modify their principals' instructions concerning the prices, terms of sale, and so forth to be offered to potential buyers. Manufacturers' reps cover a specific and limited territory and specialize in a limited range of products, although they commonly represent several related but noncompeting product lines from different manufacturers.

These characteristics give reps the advantages of having (1) many established contacts with potential customers in their territories, (2) familiarity with the technical nature and applications of the types of products in which they specialize, (3) the ability to keep expenses low by spreading fixed costs over the products of several different manufacturers, and (4) the appearance as a totally variable cost item on their principals' income statements,

Exhibit 5.1   Customer Contact Methods Used by Manufacturers (N = 214)

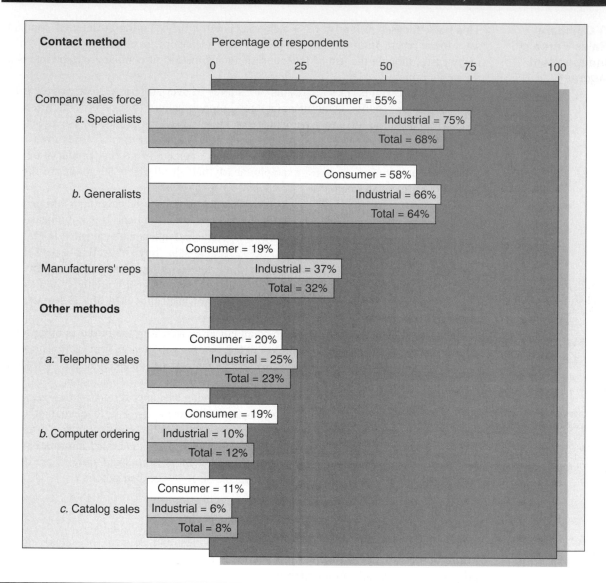

Source: Howard Sutton, *Rethinking the Company's Selling and Distribution Channels* (New York: The Conference Board, 1986), p. 2. See also Jerome A. Colletti and Gary S. Tubridy, eds., *Reinventing the Sales Organization* (Scottsdale, AZ: The Alexander Group, Inc., 1993).

since the reps' commissions vary directly with the amount of goods sold. Increasingly, companies have looked to help reps become more effective. Newton Manufacturing (a distributor of promotional products) created a new position, customer service agent, whose occupants expedite orders generated by its 1,000 manufacturers' agents around the country.

Selling agents are also intermediaries who do not take title or possession of the goods they sell and are compensated solely by commissions from their principals. They differ from reps, however, in that they usually handle the entire output of a principal (operating as the entire sales force for the manufacturer rather than as a representative in

Exhibit 5.2   Four Most Prevalent Changes in Sales Organizations

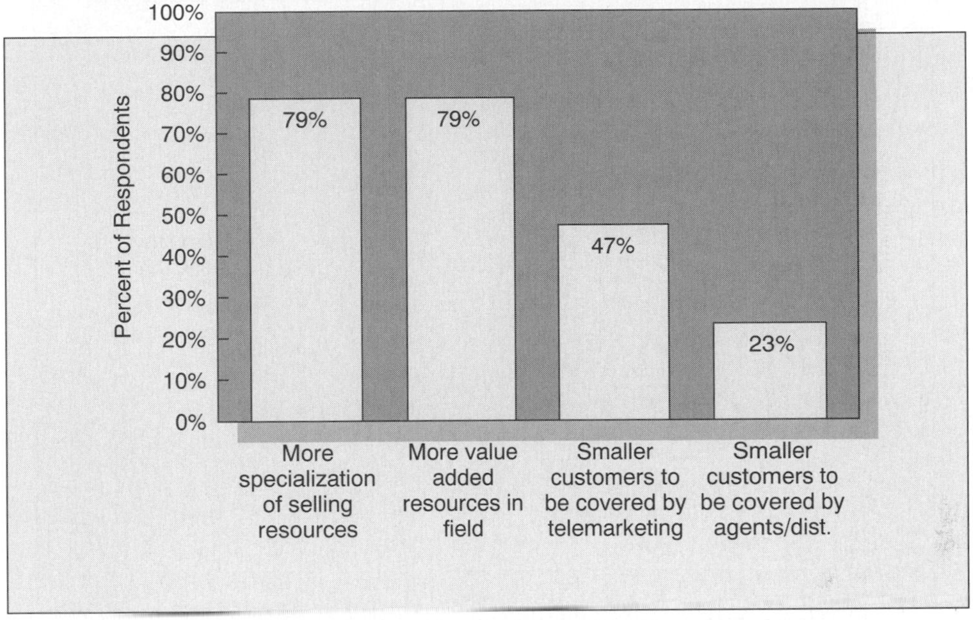

Source: Jerome A. Colletti and Gary S. Tubridy, eds., *Reinventing the Sales Organization* (Scottsdale, AZ: The Alexander Group, Inc., 1993), p. 2.

a single, specified territory). Selling agents are usually granted broader authority by their principals to modify prices and terms of sale, and they actively shape the manufacturer's promotional and sales programs.

Deciding when outside agents are appropriate

The decision about whether to use independent agents or a company sales force to cover a particular product or market involves a variety of considerations and trade-offs. In general, though, the two most important sets of factors for a manager to consider are (1) economic criteria and (2) control and strategic criteria.[4]

Economic criteria.   In a given selling situation, a company sales force and independent agents are likely to produce different levels of costs and sales volume. A first step in deciding which form of sales organization to use is to estimate and compare the costs of the two alternatives. A simplified example of such a cost comparison is illustrated in Exhibit 5.3.

The fixed costs of using external agents are lower than those of using a company sales force because there is usually less administrative overhead and agents do not receive a salary or reimbursement for field selling expenses. But costs of using agents tend to rise faster as sales volume increases because agents usually receive larger commissions than company salespeople. Consequently, there is a break-even level of sales volume (Vb in Exhibit 5.3) below which the costs of external agents are lower but above which a company sales force becomes more efficient. This helps explain why agents tend to be used by smaller firms or by larger firms in their smaller territories where sales volume is too low to warrant a company sales force.

Exhibit 5.3   Cost Comparison between a Company Sales Force and Independent Agents

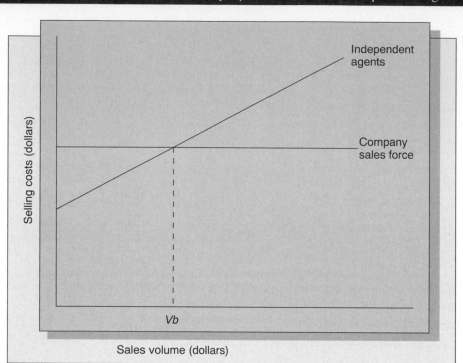

Low fixed costs also make agents attractive when a firm is moving into new territories or product lines where success is uncertain. Since the agent does not get paid unless sales are made, the costs of failure are minimized.

The other side of the economic equation is sales volume. The critical question is whether company salespeople are likely to produce a higher volume of total sales than agents in a given situation. Most sales and marketing managers believe they will because company salespeople concentrate entirely on the firm's products, they may be better trained, they may be more aggressive since their future depends on the company's success, and customers often prefer to deal directly with a supplier. On the other hand, agents' contacts and experience in an industry can make them more effective than company salespeople—particularly when the company is new or is moving into a new geographic area or product line.

Control and strategic criteria.   Regardless of which organizational form produces the greatest sales in the short run, many managers argue that an internal sales force is preferable to agents in the long run due to the difficulty of controlling agents and getting them to conform to their principals' strategic objectives. Agents are seen as independent actors who can be expected to pursue their own short-run objectives. This makes them reluctant to engage in activities with a long-run strategic payoff to their principal, such as cultivating new accounts or small customers with growth potential, performing service and support activities, or promoting new products. Some research supports this argument, suggesting manufacturers' representatives are more dissatisfied with close supervision and attempts to control their behavior than are company salespeople.[5]

Managers can control a company sales force in many different ways—through the selection, training, and supervision of personnel; establishment of operating procedures and policies; formal evaluation and reward mechanisms; and ultimately transferring or firing salespeople whose performance is not satisfactory.

Independent agents can also be replaced if their performance falls below the manufacturer's expectations. But in many cases, it is difficult for the manufacturer to tell whether an agent's poor performance is due to lack of effort or to factors beyond the agent's control, such as difficult competitive or market conditions. While company salespeople can be monitored on a regular basis, it is usually more difficult and costly—and sometimes impossible—to monitor the behavior of independent agents.[6] Finally, switching costs (such as contractual restrictions on termination) or customer loyalty to the agent may make it difficult for a manufacturer to replace an agent with its own salespeople.[7]

Transaction costs. Even when a manufacturer decides a poor-performing agent should be replaced, it may be difficult to find an acceptable replacement. This is particularly likely when an intermediary must invest in specialized (or transaction-specific) assets, such as extensive product training or specialized capital equipment, to sell the manufacturer's product or service effectively. It might take a new manufacturer's rep months to learn enough about a technically complex product and its applications to do an effective selling job. The difficulty of finding acceptable replacements for poor-performing agents under such circumstances makes it even harder for the manufacturer to control those agents.

The theory of **transaction cost analysis (TCA)** states that when substantial transaction-specific assets are necessary to sell a manufacturer's product, the costs of using and administering independent agents (i.e., the manufacturer's transaction costs) are likely to be higher than the costs of hiring and managing a company sales force. This is because TCA assumes independent agents will pursue their own self-interests—even at the expense of the manufacturer they represent—when they think they can get away with it. For instance, they might provide only cursory postsale service or expend too little effort calling on smaller accounts because they are unlikely to earn big commissions from such activities. Because agents are most likely to be able to get away with such behaviors when it is difficult for the manufacturer to monitor or replace them, the transaction cost of using agents under such circumstances is likely to be high.[8]

Recently, however, analysts have questioned TCA's assumption that independent agents will always put their own short-term interests ahead of those of the manufacturer when they can avoid getting caught and replaced. These analysts argue that when both manufacturer and agent believe their relationship can be mutually beneficial for years, norms of trust and cooperation can develop.[9]

Strategic flexibility. Another important strategic issue to consider when deciding whether to use agents or company salespeople is flexibility. Generally, a vertically integrated distribution system incorporating a company sales force is the most difficult to alter quickly. Specialized agent intermediaries can often be added or dismissed at short notice, especially if no specialized assets are needed to sell the manufacturer's product and the firm does not have to sign long-term contracts to gain agents' support.

Firms facing uncertain and rapidly changing competitive or market environments or those in industries characterized by shifting technology and short product life cycles are often best advised to rely on independent agents to preserve the flexibility of their distribution channels.[10] This is a major reason firms in the highly volatile toy industry extensively use manufacturers' representatives.

Most marketing executives argue it is best to use agents in volatile environments, to represent a small company, or for territories with low sales potential where the benefits from scale economies outweigh the difficulties of motivating and controlling the agent's behavior. It is usually preferable to switch to direct salespeople as soon as a company or territory can support the higher fixed costs or when specialized knowledge or other assets are required to do an effective selling job.

Geographic Organization

The simplest and most common method of organizing a company sales force is to assign individual salespeople to separate geographic territories. In this kind of organization, each salesperson is responsible for performing all the activities necessary to sell all the products in the company's line to all potential customers in the territory. A geographic sales organization is illustrated in Exhibit 5.4.

The geographic sales organization has several strengths. Most important, it tends to have the lowest cost. Because there is only one salesperson in each territory and territories tend to be smaller than they are under other forms of organization, travel time and expenses are minimized. Also, fewer managerial levels are required for coordination. Thus, sales administration and overhead expenses are kept relatively low.

The simplicity of a geographic organizational structure leads to another advantage involving the firm's relationships with its customers. Because only one salesperson calls on each customer, there is seldom any confusion about (1) who is responsible for what or (2) to whom the customer should talk when problems arise.

The major disadvantage of a geographic sales organization is that it does not provide any benefits of the division and specialization of labor. Each salesperson is expected to be a jack-of-all-trades. Each must sell all the firm's products to all types of customers and perform all the selling functions.

Also, this organizational structure provides the individual salesperson with freedom to make decisions concerning which selling functions to perform, what products to emphasize, and on which customers to concentrate. Unfortunately, salespeople are likely to expend most of this effort on the functions they perform best and on the products and customers they perceive to be most rewarding, whether or not such effort is consistent with management's objectives and account management policies.

Management can try to direct the efforts of salespeople through close supervision, well-designed compensation and evaluation plans, and clearly defined statements of policy, but the basic problem remains. Since each salesperson is expected to perform a full range of selling functions, the sales rep—rather than management—can control the way that selling effort is allocated across products, customers, and selling tasks.

Although a geographic approach to sales organization has its limitations, its basic simplicity and low cost make it very popular among smaller firms, particularly those with limited uncomplicated product lines. Also, while it is unusual for larger organizations to rely exclusively on geographic organization, they do commonly use it in conjunction with other organizational forms. For example, a firm may have two separate sales forces for different products in its line, but each sales force is likely to be organized geographically.

Product Organization

Some companies have separate sales forces for each product or product category in their line, as shown in Exhibit 5.5. The 3M Company, for example, has more than 50 divisions manufacturing a diverse assortment of products ranging from Scotch tape to abrasives to medical equipment, and many of those divisions have their own separate sales force. You can investigate 3M further by going to its Web site at *www.3m.com.*

The primary advantage of organizing the sales force by product is that individual salespeople can develop familiarity with the technical attributes, applications, and the

Exhibit 5.4   Geographic Sales Organization

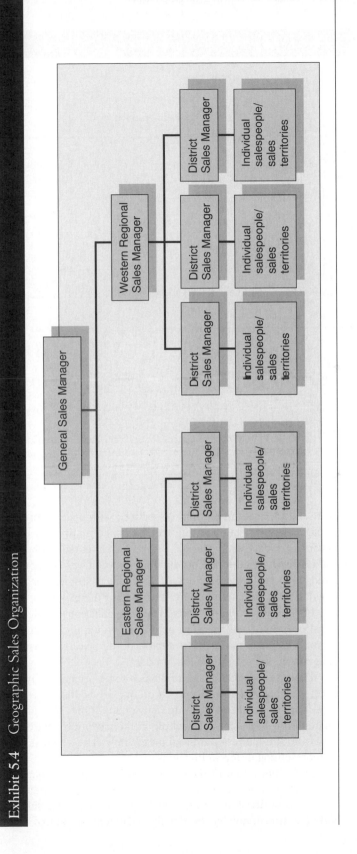

Exhibit 5.5   Sales Force Organized by Product Type

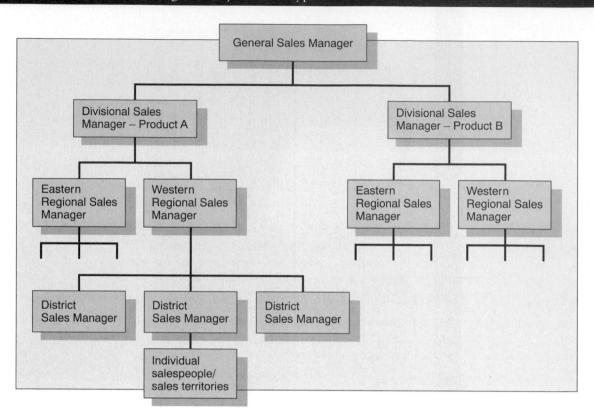

most effective selling methods associated with a single product or related products. Also, when the firm's manufacturing facilities are organized by product type—as when separate factories produce each product—a product-oriented organization can lead to closer cooperation between sales and production. This can be very beneficial when the product is tailored to fit the specifications of different customers or when production and delivery schedules are critical in gaining and keeping a customer.

Finally, a product-oriented sales organization enables sales management to control the allocation of selling effort across the various products in the company's line. If management decides more effort should be devoted to a particular product, it can simply assign more salespeople to that product.

The major disadvantage of a sales force organized by product type is duplication of effort. Salespeople from different product divisions are assigned to the same geographic areas and may call on the same customers. One 3M salesperson, for instance, reports encountering six other salespeople in the reception area of a large Belgian manufacturer while waiting to see a purchasing executive. The seven salespeople discovered they were all representing different divisions of 3M.

Such duplication leads to higher selling expenses than would be the case with a simple geographic organization. It also creates a need for greater coordination across the various product divisions, which, in turn, requires more sales management personnel and higher administrative costs. Finally, such duplication can cause confusion and frustration among the firm's customers when they must deal with two or more representatives from the same supplier.

Since the major advantage of a product-oriented organization is that it allows salespeople to develop specialized knowledge of one or a few products, this form of organization is most commonly used by firms with large and diverse product lines. It is also used by manufacturers of highly technical products that require different kinds of technical expertise or different selling methods. That is the primary reason a firm like 3M, with many different product lines based on widely differing technologies, continues to organize its sales force by product despite the cost disadvantages.

Organization by Customers or Markets

It has become increasingly popular for firms to organize their sales forces by customer type, as IBM did when it created separate sales teams to call on small and large business customers and building contractors. Another example, discussed in Chapter 4, is provided by Hewlett–Packard's Computer Systems Organization (CSO). Recall that in a recent reorganization aimed at making the division more responsive to the increasingly fragmented and specialized market for client servers, CSO created separate sales groups to focus on specific markets, such as retailing and financial services.[11] This kind of customer-oriented sales organization is shown in Exhibit 5.6.

Organizing a sales force by customer type is a natural extension of the "marketing concept" and a strategy of market segmentation. When salespeople specialize in calling on a particular type of customer, they gain a better understanding of such customers' needs and requirements. They can also be trained to use different selling approaches for different markets and to implement specialized marketing and promotional programs.

A related advantage of customer specialization is that as salespeople become familiar with their customers' specific businesses and needs, they are more likely to discover ideas

Exhibit 5.6   Sales Forces Organized by Customer Type

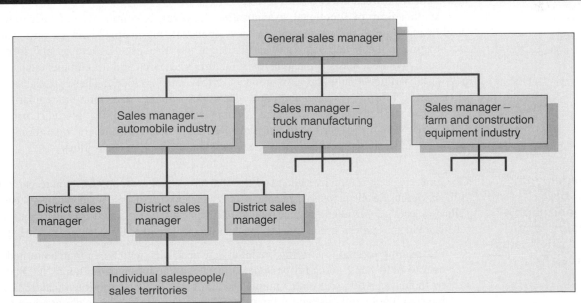

for new products and marketing approaches that will appeal to those customers. This can be a definite advantage in rapidly changing, highly competitive markets. Finally, this organizational structure allows marketing managers to control the allocation of selling effort to different markets by varying the sizes of the specialized sales forces.

The disadvantages of a customer-oriented sales organization are much the same as those of a product-oriented structure. Having different salespeople calling on different types of customers in the same territory can lead to higher selling expenses and administrative costs. Also, when customer firms have different departments or divisions operating in different industries, two or more salespeople may call on the same customer. This can cause confusion and frustration among customers.

Many firms must believe the advantages of a customer-oriented sales organization outweigh its limitations because it is growing in popularity as an organizational approach. This is particularly true for firms with products that have widely different applications in different markets or firms that must use different approaches when selling to different types of customers, as when a company sells to the government as well as to private industry. Also, specialization by customer type is a useful form of organization when a firm's marketing objectives include the penetration of previously untapped markets.

Organization by Selling Function

Different kinds of selling tasks often require different abilities and skills on the part of the salesperson. Thus, it may be logical under some circumstances to organize the sales force so different salespeople specialize in performing different selling functions. One such functional organization is to have one sales force specialize in prospecting for and developing new accounts, while a second force maintains and services old customers.

Such functional specialization can be difficult to implement, however. Since a firm is likely to assign its most competent, experienced, and "flashiest" salespeople to the new-accounts sales force, new customers might object to being turned over from the salesperson who won their patronage to a maintenance salesperson with a personality better suited to mundane tasks. It also can be difficult for management to coordinate the development and maintenance functions because there are likely to be feelings of rivalry and jealousy between the two sales forces.

Another form of functional specialization, however, is commonly and successfully used by many industrial product firms: "developmental salespeople" who are responsible for assisting in the development and early sales of new products. Developmental specialists usually conduct market research, assist the firm's research and development and engineering departments, and sell new products as they are developed. These specialists are often part of a firm's research and development department rather than the regular sales force. Such specialists can help ensure development of successful new products, particularly when they are experienced and knowledgeable about customers' operations and needs as well as about their own firm's technical and production capabilities.

Telemarketing and the Organization of "Inside" and "Outside" Sales Forces

One form of specialization by selling function that has gained great popularity in recent years is the use of inside telephone salespeople and outside field salespeople to accomplish separate selling objectives. Obviously, not all selling functions can be performed over the phone, but telemarketing has proven useful for carrying out selected activities, including the following:

- Prospecting for and qualifying potential new accounts, which can then be turned over to field salespeople for personal contact. This function can often be facilitated by including a toll-free phone number in all of the firm's promotional materials so interested potential customers can call to obtain more information about advertised products or services.

- Servicing existing accounts quickly when unexpected problems arise, such as through the use of technical-assistance hotlines.

- Seeking repeat purchases from existing accounts that cannot be covered efficiently in person, such as small or marginal customers and those in remote geographic locations.

- Gaining quicker communication of newsworthy developments, like the introduction of new or improved products or special sales programs.[12]

The popularity of telemarketing to supplement the activities of the field sales force is growing for two reasons: (1) customers like it and (2) it can increase the productivity of a firm's sales efforts. From the customers' view, the increased centralization of purchasing together with growing numbers of product alternatives and potential suppliers in many industries have increased demands on the time of purchasing agents and other members of organizations' buying centers. Consequently, they like sales contacts over the phone—particularly for routine purposes, such as soliciting reorders or relaying information about special sales programs and price promotions—because they take less time than personal sales calls.

According to a study of trends in the wholesale-distribution industry conducted by Arthur Andersen & Co. (*www.arthurandersen.com*), customers say personal contact with a salesperson is becoming less important to them than contact with a capable inside sales force. The study predicts that eventually half of the average wholesale distributor's sales force will be inside while the role of the outside salesperson will shift toward greater emphasis on promotion and customer instruction and service.[13]

From the seller's viewpoint, a combination of inside and outside salespeople—together with an appropriate mix of other media, such as targeted advertising, direct mail, toll-free phone lines, and a home page on the Internet—offers a way of improving the overall efficiency of the sales force.[14] Moving some salespeople inside and using them in conjunction with other promotional efforts allows the firm to lower the cost of routine sales activities substantially. At the same time, it enables the more expensive outside sales force to concentrate on activities with the highest potential long-term payout, such as new-account generation and the servicing of major customers. The efficiency of telemarketing makes it particularly useful for implementing an account management policy that directs different amounts of effort toward classifications of customers based on differences in size or potential. In the past, some firms prohibited sales forces from calling on very small customers—or told them to visit such accounts infrequently—because their purchase volume was not large enough to cover the cost of a sales call and still contribute to profit. But an inside sales force can call on such customers regularly with much lower costs. As noted at the beginning of the chapter, IBM has been able to reach new customers (small businesses) by expanding their inside sales force to reach businesses that would not normally have been contacted by IBM.

As we discuss later in this book, however, implementing two or more specialized sales forces—as in the case of inside and outside salespeople—can cause additional problems for sales managers. Since each specialized sales force focuses on different types of selling activities, separate policies and procedures are often required. For example, some authorities suggest that an effective telemarketing program requires the development of standardized "scripts" for the salesperson to follow, even though their counterparts in the field might have much more flexibility to tailor their presentations to the needs of individual customers. Such differences in policies and procedures may require recruitment of different types of salespeople for the two sales forces and development of different training and compensation programs.[15]

ORGANIZING TO SERVICE NATIONAL AND KEY ACCOUNTS

Regardless of how their sales forces are organized, many firms are developing new organizational approaches to deliver the customer service necessary to attract and maintain large and important customers—their national or key accounts. Robert J. Hershock (corporate vice president, marketing, 3M) said this about 3M's sales approach: "Today, the sales representative needs to be a business manager who is responsible for key accounts. He or she must be able to customize products, and services, knowledgeable about key account strategies and objectives and capable of building and implementing key account business plans."[16] As discussed in Chapter 4, the increasing technical complexity of products, industrial concentration, and the trend toward centralized purchasing make a few major accounts critical to the marketing success of many firms in both industrial and consumer goods industries. Moreover, in the ever-increasing global marketplace, national accounts often become global accounts demanding a high degree of coordination with their suppliers. A recent survey confirmed that on average, 50 percent of a firm's sales volume is accounted for by only 10 percent of its customers.[17] The importance of major accounts is increasing as large multinational firms seek to coordinate their purchasing across subsidiaries operating in many different countries.[18] On the customer side, Xerox announced it was cutting its list of suppliers by 90 percent. Such trends suggest that companies are looking at developing fewer but more substantial relationships with a limited set of suppliers.[19]

To provide the kinds of service demanded by such key customers, many firms adopt a selling philosophy of major account management. This stresses the dual goals of making sales and developing long-term relationships with major customers. Firms believe national account management policies will improve coordination of selling activities and communications with key customers. This should enable the seller to capture a larger share of the purchases made by those customers and to improve profitability.[20] There are benefits inside the firm as well. Everyone in the organization works a little harder when they know the customer is significant and has a long-term relationship with the firm.

When a firm decides to implement a national account program, a major question is who in the organization should be responsible for the functions of national account management. Some firms have no special organizational arrangements for handling their major customers; they rely on members of their regular sales force to sell to national and key accounts. This requires no additional administrative or selling expense.

The disadvantage is that major accounts often require more detailed and sophisticated treatment than smaller customers. Consequently, servicing major accounts may require more experience, expertise, and organizational authority than the average salesperson possesses. Also, if the sales force is compensated largely by commission, there can be difficult questions about which salesperson should get the commissions for sales to national accounts when one person calls on a customer's headquarters while others service its stores or plants in various territories.

In view of these difficulties, many firms have adopted special organizational arrangements for the major account management function. These arrangements include (1) assigning key accounts to top sales executives, (2) creating a separate corporate division, and (3) creating a separate sales force to handle major accounts.[21]

Assigning key accounts to sales executives

The use of sales or marketing executives to call on the firm's national or key accounts is a common practice, especially among smaller firms that do not have the resources to support a separate division or sales force. It is also common when the firm has relatively few major accounts to be serviced. In addition to the relatively low cost of the approach, it has the advantage of having important customers serviced by people who are high enough in the organizational hierarchy to make—or at least to influence—decisions concerning the allocation of production capacity, inventory levels, and prices. Consequently, they can provide flexible and responsive service.

One problem with this approach is that the managers who are given key account responsibilities sometimes develop a warped view of their firm's marketing objectives. They sometimes allocate too much of the firm's resources to their own accounts to the detriment of smaller, but still profitable, customers. In other words, such managers sometimes become obsessed with getting all the business they can from their large customers without paying sufficient attention to the sales, operating, or profit impact.

Another problem is that assigning important selling tasks to managers takes time away from their management activities. This can hinder the coordination and effectiveness of the firm's overall selling and marketing efforts.

A separate key account division

Some firms create a separate corporate division for dealing with major accounts. For example, some apparel companies have separate divisions for making and selling private-label clothing to large general-merchandise chains, such as Sears, Montgomery Ward, and J.C. Penney. This approach allows for close integration of manufacturing, logistics, marketing, and sales activities. This can be important when one or a few major customers account for such a large proportion of the firm's total sales volume that variations in their purchases have a major impact on the firm's production schedules, inventories, and allocation of resources.

The major disadvantages of this approach are the duplication of effort and the additional expense involved in creating an entire manufacturing and marketing organization for only one or a few customers. It is also risky because the success or failure of the entire division is dependent on the whims of one or a few customers.

A separate sales force for major accounts

Rather than creating an entire separate division to deal with major customers, it is more common for companies to create a separate national or key account sales force. As indicated in Exhibit 5.7, there are four common ways to organize such separate sales forces. In nearly one-quarter of the cases reported in a survey, the national account sales operation was treated as a separate functional area on a par with the firm's marketing and sales department and reported directly to the president or general manager.

More commonly, the national account force and the regular sales force are treated as equal headquarters units reporting to a single sales or marketing executive who is responsible for coordinating their efforts. The most popular organizational approach, though, is to treat major account executives as equal to regional managers in the regular sales force and have both groups report to the top sales executive.

In some companies, account managers perform all necessary selling activities themselves, including in-store or in-plant servicing of the account. In others, account managers coordinate an entire selling team of assistants who work on the account. In still other situations, the national account manager calls on the customer's headquarters, while field salespeople from the regular sales force service the customer's facilities in their territories.

Under this arrangement, if the field salespeople are compensated by commission, they are usually given some portion—perhaps half—of their normal commission of sales made to a national account's local stores or plants. However, this arrangement can cause bookkeeping problems. When an order is shipped to a central distribution point and then dis-

Exhibit 5.7 Four Ways to Organize National Account Sales Forces and the Percentage of Survey Respondents Using Each Approach

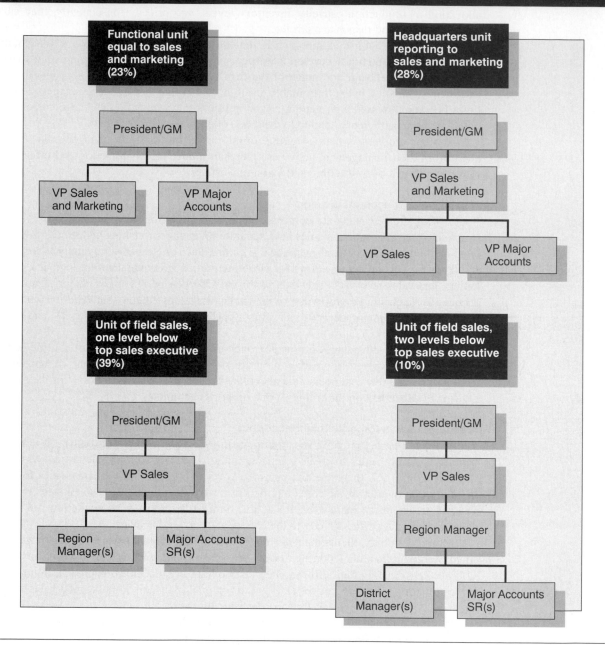

Source: Adapted from Jerome A. Colletti and Gary S. Tubridy, "Effective Major Account Sales Management," *Journal of Personal Selling and Sales Management* (August 1987), p. 4.

tributed by the customer to its plants or stores in several different sales territories, it can be difficult to determine how much of the sale should be credited to each field salesperson.

Regardless of how it is organized, a separate sales force has several advantages in dealing with key accounts. By concentrating on only one or a few major customers, the account manager can become very familiar with each customer's problems and needs and can devote the time necessary to provide a high level of service to each customer. Also, the firm can select its most competent and experienced salespeople to become members of the national account sales force, thus ensuring that important customers receive expert sales attention.

Finally, a separate national account sales force provides an internal benefit to the selling company. Because only the most competent salespeople are typically assigned to national accounts, such an assignment is often viewed as a desirable promotion. Thus, promotion to the national accounts sales force can be used to motivate and reward top salespeople who are either not suited for or not interested in moving into sales management.

In addition to the problem of allocating national account sales to individual members of the field sales force, using a separate sales force for major accounts suffers from many of the other disadvantages associated with organizing sales efforts by customer type. The most troubling problems concern the duplication of effort within the sales organization and the resulting higher selling and administrative expenses.

Team Selling

The relationship between customer and sales organization is complex. Today salespeople are asked to demonstrate a stronger knowledge of the customer's businesses than ever before as well as provide a more consistent and beneficial interface with the customer—in other words, better service. One way companies deal with these demands is to assign specialists inside the firm to individual customers—team selling. There are a number of benefits of allocating more individuals, each with a unique talent, to each customer. First, questions can be answered faster, which reduces the need for the "I will get back to you on that" response to customer inquiries. Second, people with similar interests can speak directly with one another. A technical question from the customer's engineering department can be answered by another engineer in the supplier's support sales team.

The key is identifying a team selling structure that meets the needs of customers. For example, a common structure would make the account manager responsible for working with the entire team selling to and servicing major customers. Often, such major account teams include representatives from a number of functional departments within the firm, such as R&D, operations, and finance. Given that major customers' buying centers often consist of people from different functional areas with different viewpoints and concerns, those concerns can often be most effectively addressed by a team of experts from equivalent functional departments in the selling firm, or even from different divisions within the company. Recently, companies have begun to look at the existence of "selling centers" which bring together individuals from around the organization (marketing, customer service, sales, engineering, and others) to help the salesperson do his or her job more effectively. Just as customers have buying centers, the selling organization needs to work together to present a unified, well-coordinated effort to the customer.[22] In an increasing number of companies, sales teams maintain offices in the customer's facilities. Lear, a leading manufacturer of OEM parts to the automotive industry, maintains sales offices on the premises of each of its 13 major customers (many of the major automotive firms around the world). Pat Burke, VP of sales and business development for Lear, puts it this way: "We try to put a system in place that creates continuous contact with the customers."[23]

At Dun & Bradstreet, for example, George Martin, D&B's executive vice president for U.S. sales, was charged with changing the sales approach of the firm's credit, collections, and marketing business units. Martin established sales teams composed of sales representatives from each of the three units, which up to then operated separately. Each team also had several ad hoc members from other functional departments in the firm who could be brought in on individual calls when their specific expertise was needed. The teams' initial mission was to concentrate on D&B's top 50 accounts, meet with top executives in those firms, identify their needs, and develop effective solutions. In the first year of the program, D&B's sales teams uncovered $200 million in sales opportunities for the three divisions, half of which Martin believes would not have been identified under the old selling approach. Consequently, the firm's teams have been expanded to service D&B's top 200 accounts.[24] Learn more about Dun & Bradstreet by visiting their Web site at *www.dnb.com.*

One disadvantage of the team selling approach is its high cost in time and personnel. In an attempt to improve efficiency, therefore, some companies have opened special sites for team sales meetings, such as the "executive briefing center" run by Xerox in the Dallas Infomart.

Team selling can also present some coordination, motivation, and compensation problems. To encourage and reward team members for working together, for instance, Dun & Bradstreet splits all sales commissions equally across the salespeople on each team. And when a team exceeds its sales goals with an account, a bonus pool is set up to reward the ad hoc team members. The team's sales reps then decide who should receive what percentage of the pool.[25] Team selling is most appropriate for the very largest customers, where the potential purchase represents enough dollars and involves enough functions to justify the high costs. Although team selling is usually used to win new accounts, it is sometimes also used with lower-level personnel for maintenance selling. Production schedulers, expeditors, and shipping personnel may join the sales team to keep an existing account satisfied.[26]

Multilevel Selling

Multilevel selling is a variation of team selling. In multilevel selling, the sales team consists of personnel from various managerial levels who call on their counterparts in the buying organization. Thus, the account manager might call on the customer's purchasing department while the selling firm's vice president of finance calls on the buyer's financial vice president. Sometimes this involves setting up a permanent team to coordinate activities with the customer. Often, however, this is an ad hoc arrangement where individuals at different levels are responsible for maintaining a key relationship with the customer but not as part of an established team.

This approach represents proper organizational etiquette—each member of the selling team calls on a person with corresponding status and authority. Also, it is useful for higher-level executives to participate in opening a relationship with a major new prospect, since they have the authority to make concessions and establish policies necessary to win and maintain that prospect as a customer.

Co-Marketing Alliances

In some high tech industries, such as computers and telecommunications, customers buy systems made up of components manufactured by two or more different suppliers. In some cases, suppliers rely on independent intermediaries—such as value-added resellers (VARs)—to combine their components with those from other suppliers to create a system to meet the needs of a particular end user. Increasingly, however, individual suppliers are forming alliances and developing joint marketing and sales programs to sell integrated systems directly to the ultimate customer. For example, sales teams from MCI Communications, IBM, and Rohm recently made a joint presentation to a large cement manufacturer that was setting up a data-application network. MCI provided the communications network, IBM dealt with the necessary computer hardware and software, and Rohm provided the switching equipment.[27]

In some cases even competitors develop marketing alliances to maximize their resources. Recently, Parke-Davis created a new drug, Lipitor, which offered significant advantages over anything else in the market. However, the firm lacked the sales force necessary to market the drug effectively. The company partnered with Pfizer, a company with a powerful sales force, to create a joint effort managed by a team of individuals from both companies. Salespeople from both companies work together to maximize the sales of Lipitor in a given territory.[28]

Logistical Alliances and Computerized Ordering

Another recent technological change under way in many industries is the formation of logistical alliances involving the development of computerized information and ordering systems. Such systems enable customers to place an order directly—and often automatically—via a dedicated telephone or satellite link to a supplier's computer. As mentioned in Chapter 4, for example, firms like Procter & Gamble and 3M have formed alliances with major supermarket chains and mass merchandisers—such as Wal-Mart—to develop automatic restocking systems. Sales information from the retailer's checkout scanners is sent directly to the supplier's computers, which figure out automatically when to replenish each product and schedule deliveries direct to each of the retailer's stores. Such paperless exchanges reduce mistakes and billbacks, minimize inventory levels, decrease out-of-stocks, and improve cash flow.

As we saw in Exhibit 5.1, 12 percent of the firms in one survey already use computerized systems to contact at least some of their customers, and the adoption of such systems is growing rapidly. Although to date such systems have been most widely adopted by manufacturers of relatively standardized consumer products, many industrial goods manufacturers are also developing computerized reordering systems. This is particularly true for firms that customize their products to a customer's order. By having orders sent directly to its computer, the supplier can quickly organize production schedules, speed up the production process, and minimize finished goods inventories.[29]

From the customer's point of view, computerized ordering is more convenient, flexible, and less time consuming than placing orders through a salesperson. From the supplier's perspective, linking major customers to a dedicated reorder system can help "tie" those customers to the firm and increase the proportion of purchases they make from a single source.[30] Cisco Systems, a leading producer of Internet working equipment, created a Web site so customers could track their order more efficiently as well as reorder commonly replaced items. The results have been dramatic, as sales from the Web site were in excess of $75 million in the first year.

One question that is yet to be answered is how computerized reorder systems might change the role of the sales force. Will salespeople become largely redundant, or will being freed from the more routine order-taking activities enable firms to refocus personal selling efforts on more complex communications, problem solving, and customer servicing tasks? When Cisco introduced its Web site so customers could track and order more efficiently, salespeople were concerned it would have a negative effect on their interaction with customers. The reality was much different. Salespeople are able to devote more time to actually selling products rather than reordering or tracking existing orders.

ORGANIZING TO SERVICE GLOBAL MARKETS

As firms expand their marketing and sales efforts into other countries, they face a critical decision concerning how to organize their selling efforts across national boundaries. While globalization obviously adds complexity to a firm's organizational design, the

Building a Global Sales-Driven Company

How important is the right organizational structure in sales management? Ask Haliburton, a $9 billion oil service company, which restructured its entire organization to place a greater emphasis on the sales function. The results are impressive, a 50 percent increase in sales since 1995 and 20 percent in 1997 alone.

Prior to the restructuring, salespeople reported to executives in the operations department. While these people were technically competent, they did not have a great deal of sales expertise or a detailed knowledge of customer relationships. In 1995 CEO (and former Secretary of Defense) Dick Cheney restructured the company, taking sales out of the operations department and placing it at the same level as operations. Now, top executives in both operations and sales report to the president. The changes led to immediate results. As noted by Gary Moore, business development manager for North America and the Gulf of Mexico, "Now sales and operations people focus on their specific areas of responsibility. We're much better organized to serve the customer."

In the past the sales force was organized geographically. The restructuring led to the creation of global account managers whose task is to coordinate people and resources for Haliburton's top 60 accounts around the world. These account managers work with the 450-person sales force to maximize the relationship with the company's top accounts. Angle Smith, vice president of business development for the Western Hemisphere, talks about this realignment: "We wanted to build a sales force that's aligned with our clients, and we wanted to generate new business from them, instead of just servicing existing business. Our customer base isn't focused on Houston. . . . They have global operations, and expect the same service and consistency in Thailand as they get in Louisiana."

These changes have led competitors to reassess their sales force structure that is still largely based on geographic areas. A consultant in the oil business, Scott Setrakian of Mercer management consulting, noted that "Haliburton has been innovative at developing new relationships with customers and extending relationships with existing customers." The changes at Haliburton are similar to changes in many corporations as they seek to maximize resources and maintain effective relationships with their customers.

Source: Geoffrey Brewer, "Top of the Charts: Haliburton," *Sales & Marketing Management* (July 1998), p. 41.

---

basic questions to be answered are the same as those faced in domestic markets. First, should the firm rely on independent agents to represent its interests in a foreign market or hire its own company salespeople? If the firm decides to establish its own subsidiary or sales office with a dedicated company sales force in a foreign country, a second question arises concerning the appropriate horizontal structure for that sales force. Should it be organized geographically, by product line, by type of customer, or in some other way?

A survey of 14 large multinational corporations (MNCs) examined their sales organization practices across 135 subsidiaries located in 45 countries.[31] As Exhibit 5.8 indicates, about 25 percent of the MNCs' subsidiaries use independent agents, either alone or in combination with company salespeople. This is a somewhat lower percentage than found in the U.S. domestic market, where about one-third of all firms use manufacturers' reps (see Exhibit 5.1). Note, however, that agents are used somewhat more frequently in developing markets than in more developed countries and in markets where the firm's sales volume is relatively small. Both of these findings are consistent with our earlier discussion of the conditions under which firms are most likely to use independent reps.

Industry factors are also related to the use of agents versus company salespeople. Firms selling complex, high tech products, such as computers and pharmaceuticals, are significantly more likely to rely solely on their own salespeople than firms in other industrial or consumer goods industries. This finding is also consistent with our earlier discus-

Exhibit 5.8 Type of Sales Organization: Analyses by Industry, Level of Market Development, Region, Sales Level, and Sales Force Size

	Own Sales Force	Sales Force and Independent Sales Organization
Industry		
General consumer goods	15	9
Pharmaceutical	54	7
Industrial goods	19	14
EDP	13	2
Level of Market Development		
Developed market	58	14
Developing market	39	14
Region		
Canada, Australia, and New Zealand	11	3
Central, South America	16	4
Europe	44	10
Africa	9	1
Far East, Southeast Asia	17	10
Sales Level		
Less than $25 million	62	22
Over $25 million	37	10
Sales Force Size		
Under 50 persons	66	18
Over 50 persons	35	12

Source: John S. Hill and Richard R. Still, "Organizing the Overseas Sales Force: How Multinationals Do It," *Journal of Personal Selling and Sales Management* (Spring 1990), p. 61.

sion. The higher levels of product knowledge and postsale service (transaction-specific assets) required to sell such high tech products make it relatively more desirable for firms to employ their own salespeople. By doing so, they can maintain better control over the marketing and sales efforts devoted to their products and reduce their transaction costs.

Slightly more than half (51.5 percent) of the surveyed MNCs' subsidiaries report using simple geographic territories to organize their selling efforts within a given country. The rest use more specialized organizational structures, with different salespeople assigned to specific products and/or customer types. As you might expect from our earlier discussion, subsidiaries are most likely to employ specialized structures when they are selling relatively complex products (e.g., pharmaceuticals), when their product lines are broad, when they are operating in highly developed markets, and when their sales volumes are relatively large.

While globalization makes the organization of the sales force more complicated, firms tend to resolve organizational issues in international markets in largely the same way as they do in the United States. The situational and strategic factors that influence firms' organizational decisions appear to be similar in both types of markets, and those factors seem to affect organizational choices in similar ways both at home and abroad. It is clear that companies are creating new structures to follow their customers around the world. FedEx, for example, created a hybrid system sending 100 "international development executives" to work with their U.S. sales force to expand international sales of its American-based companies.[32]

VERTICAL STRUCTURE OF THE SALES ORGANIZATION

The beginning of this chapter stressed that the sales organization must be structured vertically as well as horizontally. The vertical organizational structure defines clearly what managerial positions have the authority for carrying out specific sales management activities. This vertical structure also provides for the effective integration and coordination of selling efforts throughout the firm. Other vertical organization issues include

1. How is the sales manager's role changing as the result of computerized information and communication systems, increased use of national account and team structures, downsizing, and other structural changes?

2. How many levels of sales management are appropriate? What span of control is best?

3. Should sales-related functions—such as order entry, credit, or repair and maintenance—be integrated into the sales organization? If so, at what level?

4. What management functions should each sales manager perform? Should staff specialists be hired to perform certain functions? To what level of management should such specialists report?

5. How can the activities of specialized sales forces, staff specialists, and related departments be integrated and coordinated?

The Integration of Sales and Marketing

One vertical organization issue that affects both the authority and the autonomy of sales managers is whether the sales function should be integrated within a firm's marketing department or be organized as a separate unit. While good coordination of sales and marketing activities is important for a firm to service its customers and compete effectively, observation indicates that many organizations do not assign responsibility for all their marketing activities to a single unit. Some treat sales as a separate function. Some also have separate advertising or corporate communications departments. And some assign responsibility for selected marketing activities to other departments, as when R&D is responsible for overseeing new product development.

A survey of 668 U.S. corporations indicates that only about one-third have totally integrated marketing organizations where a single department has responsibility for a full range of marketing activities.[33] In two-thirds of the firms, other departments—such as R&D or customer services—have responsibility for at least one major marketing function. On the other hand, the vast majority of respondents indicate that they do integrate most marketing activities, including sales, within a single marketing organization. Only 20 percent of the responding firms report having a separate sales department, while more than three-quarters incorporate sales within their marketing organization.

Number of Management Levels and Span of Control

Two questions that must be answered in designing an effective vertical structure for a sales organization are (1) how many levels of sales managers should there be and (2) how many people should each manager supervise (span of control)? These questions are related. For a given number of salespeople, the greater the span of control, the fewer the levels of management, and the fewer the managers needed.

There are major differences of opinion about the best policy concerning span of control and the number of vertical levels for a sales organization. Some managers think they have greater control and attain greater responsiveness when the sales force has a "flat" organization with few management levels. They argue that few levels between the top sales executive and the field salespeople facilitate communication and more direct control. But some managers argue that such flat organizations actually limit communication and control because they necessitate large spans of control.

The flat organization with large spans of control has lower administrative costs because of the relatively small number of managers involved. Others argue, however, that such cost savings are an illusion because the lower quantity and quality of management can lead to less effectiveness and productivity.

In view of these disagreements, it is difficult to generalize about the most appropriate number of management levels and span of control for a specific organization. However, managers have a few guidelines to follow. The span of control should be smaller and the number of levels of management should be larger when (1) the sales task is complex, (2) the profit impact of each salesperson's performance is high, and (3) the salespeople in the organization are well paid and professional. In other words, the more difficult and important the sales job, the greater the management support and supervision that should be provided to the members of the sales force.

In general, industry practice is consistent with this generalization. As Exhibit 5.9 indicates, industries characterized by relatively technically complex or customized products or services, such as electronics components, instruments, or banking, have smaller average spans of control than industries whose products are more standardized or commoditylike, such as chemicals or utilities.

Another general rule is that the span of control should usually be smaller at higher levels in the sales organization because top-level managers should have more time for analysis and decision making. Also, the people who report to them typically have more complicated jobs and require more organizational support and communications than persons in lower-level jobs.

In addition to deciding how many subordinates sales managers should supervise, another question is how much authority each manager should be given in managing subordinates. Where should the authority to hire, fire, and evaluate field salespeople be located within the organization? In some sales organizations, first-level field or district sales managers have the authority to hire their own salespeople. In other organizations, the authority to hire and fire is located at higher management levels.

As a general rule of organization, the more important a decision is for the success of a firm, the higher the level of management that should make that decision. In firms that hire many low-paid salespeople who perform relatively routine selling tasks and have only a small impact on the firm's overall profit performance, hiring and evaluation authority is usually given to first-level sales managers. Firms that have professional salespeople who perform complex selling tasks and have a major profit impact usually place the authority to hire and fire at higher levels. This is particularly true when the sales force is viewed as a training ground for future sales or marketing managers.

Exhibit 5.9   Average Spans of Control for Field Sales Managers in Selected Industries

Industry	Average Span of Control (Number of Salespeople per Manager)
Agriculture, forestry, and fishing	6.6
Apparel	8.0
Banking	6.6
Business services	6.8
Chemicals	14.9
Construction	6.7
Electronic components	5.2
Food products	8.2
Health services	8.3
Household appliances	12.0
Instruments	5.3
Machinery	6.8
Primary metals	10.9
Printing and publishing	11.2
Transportation equipment	4.4
Utilities	11.3
Overall average	8.2*

*Average for all 38 industries studied by the Dartnell survey.

Source: Christien P. Heide, *Dartnell's 28th Sales Force Compensation Survey, 1994–95* (Chicago, Ill.: The Dartnell Corporation, 1994), p. 175.

Selling responsibilities

In addition to their supervisory and policy-making roles, many sales managers—particularly those at the field or district level—continue to be actively involved in selling activities. Since many sales managers are promoted to their positions only after proving to be competent and effective salespeople, their employers are often reluctant to lose the benefit of their selling skills. Consequently, sales managers are often allowed to continue servicing at least a few of their largest customers after they join the ranks of management.

Some firms rely on their sales managers for selling and servicing key accounts. Sales managers often prefer this kind of arrangement. They are reluctant to give up the opportunities for commissions and direct contact with the marketplace that they gain by being actively involved in selling. On average, sales managers continue to devote nearly one-third of their time to sales activities, as indicated in Exhibit 5.10.

The danger is that sales managers sometimes spend too much time selling and not enough time managing their subordinates. Consequently, some firms limit the amount of actual selling in which managers can engage. This is particularly true in large firms where coordinating and supervising a vast sales force require a great deal of attention by management personnel.

Exhibit 5.10   How Sales Managers Spend Their Time

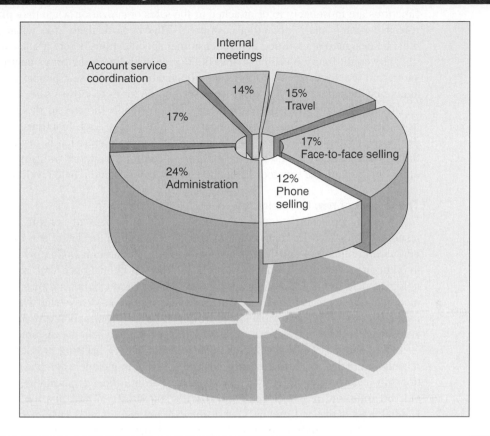

Source: William A. O'Connell and William Keenan, Jr., "The Shape of Things to Come," *Sales & Marketing Management* (January 1990), p. 39.

Sales-related functions

Many firms face markets that demand high levels of service. Firms that sell capital equipment, for instance, must provide their customers with installation and maintenance service; fashion manufacturers must provide rapid order processing and delivery; and firms that sell electronic components must offer special product design and engineering services. These services must be integrated with the rest of the firm's marketing and selling activities for the company to compete effectively.[34]

The question from an organizational viewpoint, though, is whether sales managers should be given the authority to control such sales-related functions. The answer depends on the function and the characteristics and needs of the firm's customers. Order processing and expediting are the least visible but most important sales-related functions. In some firms, persons responsible for order processing report to top-level sales management, whereas in other firms they report to operations management, perhaps as part of an inventory control or data processing department. Usually, the more important rapid order processing and delivery are for keeping customers satisfied, the more appropriate it is for sales management to have authority over this function.

Repair and engineering services tend to be responsible to the sales organization in some firms and to the manufacturing or operations department in others. Again, such functions are most likely to be attached to the sales organization when they play a critical role in winning and maintaining customers. This is particularly true when the product must be designed or modified to meet customer specifications before a sale can be made.

The credit function is almost always the responsibility of the firm's controller or treasurer, and it seldom reports to the sales organization because salespeople and their managers may be tempted to be too generous with credit terms to close a sale.

In firms where sales-related functions do not report directly to the sales organizations, team selling is often a useful means of coordinating such functions—at least when dealing with major customers where the cost of such an approach is justified. Although the account manager has no formal authority to control the actions of team members from other departments, he can coordinate the team's activities at the field level.

The impact of new technologies

Many of the preceding conclusions about appropriate spans of control and managerial responsibilities for sales managers are subject to change in the future due to the impact of new communications and information processing technologies. Companies realize that maximizing sales effort requires that each salesperson be equipped with an array of technologies. The use of technologies has evolved from productivity enhancer (time management and contact management software, proposal generators) to systems that increase profitable sales growth. These tools integrate a great deal of information (pricing, order status, and inventory availability) for the salesperson in real time to help the customer on site.

Heidelberg USA (the U.S. subsidiary of Heidelberg printing presses in Germany) recently upgraded its computer hardware and software to include a complete customer relationship management system which assimilated "front office" applications (customer contact information, proposal generation) with "back office" information (order status). Heidelberg's active and mobile sales force can now access vital customer information at their customers' offices using a laptop. Bruce Mabel, manager of marketing information systems for Heidelberg, puts it this way: "We stay competitive by staying in touch with customers, manufacturers, and employees. [This system] is an integrated part of our business process and is absolutely fundamental to our enterprisewide customer management system."

Clearly technology is changing the salesperson's job and the role of the sales manager. It is no longer a luxury but a necessity in sales. As Exhibit 5.11 suggests, a variety of different technologies are used to help enhance the salesperson's activities. Probably the most common technology used in selling today is the cellular telephone, but computers are now an integral part of the selling process in almost every company.

The experiences of firms like Heidelberg USA suggest that sales managers of the future will need a different set of skills and abilities than the manager of the past. This chapter's "Managing Sales Relationships" box identifies some of these key skills for the sales manager of the future.

Staff support and outsourcing

Many large sales organizations utilize some staff personnel in addition to their line sales managers. Staff executives are responsible for a limited range of specific activities, but they do not have the broad operating responsibility or authority of line managers. Staff executives commonly perform tasks requiring specialized knowledge or abilities that the average sales manager does not have the time to develop. They may also help collect and analyze information that line managers need for decision making. Thus, the most common functions performed by staff specialists in a sales organization are recruitment, train-

Exhibit 5.11 Technology in the Sales Force

What technologies do salespeople use?

	Percentage	
Technology	1997	1998
Telephones	85%	81%
Cellular phones	72	71
Notebook computer	51	51
Desktop PC	40	44
Pager/beeper	29	27
Projector	5	24
LCD panels	4	2
Palmtop computers	3	2

What technologies do sales managers believe is most important to them in their job?

Technology	Percentage
Notebook computer	40%
Cellular phone	33
E-mail	20
Internet access	7

And how often do sales managers log onto the World Wide Web in the course of a typical workday?

• Twice or more	38%
• Once	35
• Never	27

Companies are learning to maximize use of the Internet in selling
Percentage of companies that use the Web principally for:

• Marketing	76%
• Generating leads	42
• Building brands	34
• Customer service	32
• Content publishing	17
• Direct selling	14

Source: "Plug and Play," Sales and Marketing Management (November 1998).

ing, and sales analysis. A typical line and staff sales organization is diagrammed in Exhibit 5.12.

The creative use of staff specialists can enable a sales force to function with fewer managers because of the benefits of specialization and division of labor. It can also improve the effectiveness of the sales organization while cutting costs. In addition, staff positions can be used as a training ground for future top-level sales managers.

What Sales Managers Can Do to Save Their Jobs

What new skills will sales managers need to develop to ensure themselves of a role in the future of their organization—whether as a sales manager or as an evolutionary variation on today's sales manager? Sales managers and consultants suggest these skills:

- *Build your book of business.* "The more you know about customers, the closer your relationship with them, the more valuable you will be to your present company and any future employer. That applies to both salespeople and sales managers."—James Challenger, Challenger, Grey & Christmas

- *Learn to work in teams.* "In the traditional environment, sales managers didn't really sell, they just managed individual salespeople working toward a revenue goal. Now it's a team sell, and the sales manager must ask: 'How do I take the collective resources of these salespeople, take their collective knowledge—about products, services, industry, and everything they know about the customer—and turn it around to support the customer in a truly effective way'."—Mary Ann Maniace, Business Process Design Inc.

- *Learn to treat salespeople as equals.* "To earn salespeople's respect you have to treat them with respect.

You have to be saying, 'Let's work together. What do we need, and what does each of us need to do, to get the job done'?"—Art Wise, sales manager, U.S. Chamber of Commerce

- *Learn marketing skills.* "The sales manager needs to become more astute about how to use direct marketing, telemarketing, and seminars. Don't wait for headquarters to come out with a seminar program or direct mail for lead generation. Study up. Learn how to do it yourself."—Joe Petrone, author of *Building the High-Performance Sales Team*

- *Learn new people-driving skills.* "If all you are is a talking catalog, then you're not necessary. The new sales manager needs to be able to provide salespeople with the skills they need to marshall resources, meet customer expectations, and identify potential business opportunities."—Dennis McCarthy, Paradigm Group

- *Be a consultant.* "Salespeople can read. They don't need to be told that their numbers aren't where they should be. The question sales managers need to be asking is 'Why is this happening, and what can we do about it?'"—Dennis Koczara, IDS Financial Services

Source: William Keenan, Jr., "The Demise of the Sales Manager," *Sales & Marketing Management* (October 1994), p. 72.

On the other hand, staff positions are justified only when the sales organization is large enough so staff specialists have enough work to keep them busy. Increasingly, however, even the largest firms are questioning whether in-house staff specialists are really justified. A growing number of firms are outsourcing some staff functions through the use of specialized suppliers, such as recruiting and personnel testing services and training firms. The rationale for this trend is similar to the argument discussed earlier concerning the use of company salespeople versus independent agents. Activities that do not rely directly on the firm's core competencies (i.e., that do not require specialized or transaction-specific assets) can often be performed more effectively and efficiently by outside specialists on a contractual basis.[35]

SOME ADDITIONAL QUESTIONS

Although many issues concerning the strategic organization of the sales force have been examined, some related questions have yet to be explored. How many salespeople should a firm hire? How should these people be deployed? How should sales territories be defined? What quota, if any, should be assigned to each sales territory?

Exhibit 5.12 Line and Staff Sales Organization

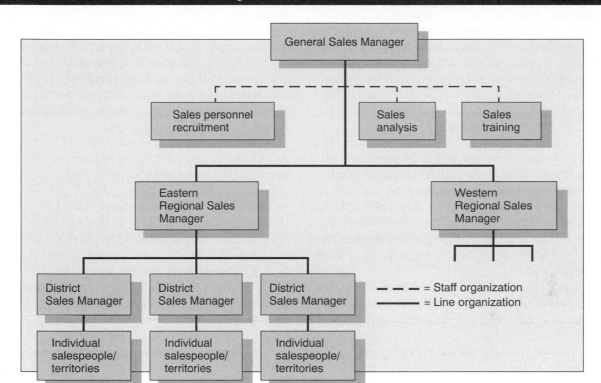

The answers to these questions depend on the markets to be served, the potential sales volume in those markets, and the selling effort necessary to capture a desired share of that potential volume. In Chapter 6, methods of market analysis and sales forecasting are discussed before the questions of sales force size, deployment, and quotas are brought up again in Chapters 6 and 7.

SUMMARY

This chapter examined important issues regarding the organization of the sales force. It looked at the benefits a good organizational plan can provide and at the major issues involved in deciding on the horizontal and vertical organizations of the sales effort.

A good organizational plan should satisfy three criteria. First, it should allow the firm to realize the benefits that can be derived from the division and specialization of labor. Second, it should provide for stability and continuity in the firm's selling efforts. This can best be accomplished by organizing activities and not people. Third, it should produce effective coordination of the various activities assigned to different persons in the sales force and different departments in the firm.

Questions of horizontal organization revolve around how specific selling activities are to be divided among members of the sales force. The first issue to be resolved is whether to use company employees to perform the sales function or to rely on outside manufacturers' representatives or sales agents. The cost of using outside agents is usually lower than that of a company sales force at relatively low sales volumes. However, most executives believe company employees will generate greater levels of sales and they are easier to control than agents.

When a firm employs its own sales force, four types of horizontal organization are commonly found, structured according to (1) geography, (2) type of product, (3) type of customer, and (4) selling function. Geographic organization is the simplest and most common. It possesses the advantages of low cost and clear identification of which salesperson is responsible for each customer. Its primary disadvantage is that it does not provide the firm with any benefits from division and specialization of labor.

Specializing the sales force along product lines allows salespeople to develop great familiarity with the technical attributes, applications, and most effective methods of selling those products. This can be advantageous when products are technically complex or when the firm's manufacturing facilities are also organized by product type. The major disadvantage associated with organization by product type is duplication of effort.

Organizing the sales force by type of customer or market serviced allows salespeople to understand the needs and requirements of the various types of customers better. Salespeople are more likely to discover ideas for new products and marketing approaches that will appeal to those customers. However, this scheme also produces duplication of effort, which tends to increase selling and administrative expenses.

A selling function organizational philosophy holds that people should be allowed to do what they do best. Thus, it makes sense to have, say, one sales force specializing in prospecting for and developing new accounts while another maintains and services old customers. These arrangements are often difficult to implement because of coordination problems.

In addition to deciding on a basic structure, a firm needs to specify how it intends to service national and key accounts in its horizontal organizational plans. Three arrangements are most commonly found: (1) assigning key accounts to top sales executives, (2) creating a separate corporate division, and (3) creating a separate major accounts sales force.

Two key questions must be addressed in deciding on an effective vertical structure of the sales organization: (1) How many levels of sales managers should there be? (2) How many people should each manager supervise? The answers are related; for a given number of salespeople, greater spans of control produce fewer levels of management. Although it is difficult to unequivocally state the optimal span of control for a firm, it is true generally that the span of control should be smaller in those firms where (1) the sales task is complex, (2) the profit impact of each salesperson's performance is high, and (3) the salespeople in the organization are well paid and professional.

Another question that must be addressed in designing the vertical structure of the sales organization is how much authority should be given each manager in the sales management hierarchy, particularly with respect to hiring, firing, and evaluating subordinates. As a general rule, the more important such decisions are to the firm, the higher the level of management that should make such decisions.

DISCUSSION QUESTIONS

1. In its publication *Reinventing the Sales Organization,* The Conference Board offers the insights of a number of leading marketing professionals. One of these individuals, Robert J. Hershock (corporate vice president, marketing, at 3M), states, "You have to go beyond what your customer says to what is really needed. And what is really needed is added value."

2. Intronics Corporation, a manufacturer of electronic circuit boards, reaches the market through the services of 75 manufacturers' agencies. Most of the agencies average two sales agents who call on Intronics's customers. The agents represent seven to eight other manufacturers that produce noncompetitive products. Intronics wants to eliminate the agents and develop its own company sales force. How many salespeople will Intronics have to hire? What issues affect how many salespeople are needed?

3. IBM, Haliburton, and a number of other companies have reorganized to better serve their largest customers. How might a global company reorganize itself to maximize effectiveness with its most important customers? As senior sales management, how would you define "most important" customer (by current sales, future potential sales, or some other criteria)?

4. The chapter mentions the theory of transaction cost analysis. What role does transaction cost analysis play in the decision to use a company sales force rather than independent manufacturers' agents?

5. Telemarketing has resulted in the development of inside sales forces. Some companies assign sales trainees to the inside or telephone sales force as part of the training program. Other companies view the two positions as separate. What functions would an inside (telephone) sales force perform? How would these functions differ from those performed by the external sales force? How would compensation plans differ if they differ at all?

6. LaMarche's Enterprise manufactures both technical and nontechnical products. Its sales forces are organized in the same manner. The technical sales force has 175 people, and the nontechnical group numbers 128. To what extent would such a division affect the following?

   a. Recruiting.
   b. Sales training.
   c. Compensation.
   d. Supervision.
   e. Span of control.

EXPERIENTIAL APPLICATION

The total quality management (TQM) process uses certain terms such as *continuous improvement, employee involvement and empowerment, quality assurance,* and *customer satisfaction.* Visit a company's Web site, review its most recent annual reports, read recent articles about the company, or even interview key marketing executives and identify how the TQM process has affected the sales organization. Hint: To what extent are measures of customer satisfaction used to reward the sales force?

INTERNET EXERCISE

1. Go to the IBM Web site (*www.ibm.com*) and click on "Partner Info." Go to the section on success stories and examine how the relationship of IBM and its business partners has led to successful relationships with customers. Discuss how IBM develops a synergy between its business partners and existing sales force.

SUGGESTED READINGS

Sales and Marketing Organizational Structures

Anderson, Erin, and Barton Weitz, "Make or Buy Decisions: Vertical Integration and Marketing Productivity," *Sloan Management Review* (Spring 1986), pp. 1–19.

Conlin, Joseph, "Teaming Up," *Sales & Marketing Management* (October 1993), pp. 98–104.

Sellers, Patricia, "How to Remake Your Sales Force," *Fortune* (May 4, 1992), pp. 96–102.

Tull, Donald S., Bruce E. Cooley, Mark R. Philips, Jr., and Harry S. Watkins, "The Organization of Marketing Activities of American Manufacturers." Report #91–126. Cambridge, MA: The Marketing Science Institute, October 1991.

Telemarketing and Integrated Direct Marketing Programs

Moncrief, William C., Charles W. Lamb, Jr., and Terry Dielman, "Developing Telemarketing Support Systems," *Journal of Personal Selling and Sales Management* (August 1986), pp. 43–49.

Roman, Ernan, "Integrated Direct Marketing: Managing the Mix," *Sales & Marketing Management* (May 1991), pp. 83–87.

National or Key Account Selling

Cauthern, Cynthia R., "Moving Technical Support into the Sales Loop," *Sales & Marketing Management* (August 1990), pp. 58–61.

Colletti, Jerome A., and Gary S. Tubridy, "Effective Major Account Sales Management," *Journal of Personal Selling and Sales Management* (August 1987), pp. 1–10.

Fuller, Joseph B., James O'Conor, and Richard Rawlinson, "Tailored Logistics: The Next Advantage," *Harvard Business Review* (May–June 1993), pp. 87–98.

Hodgdon, Bill, "How Do You Win a National Account? One Business Result Produced at a Time!" *Journal of the National Account Management Association* (Summer 1998), pp. 6–13.

Jacob, Rahul, "Why Some Customers Are More Equal than Others," *Fortune* (September 19, 1994), pp. 215–24.

Pardo, Catherine, "Key Account Management in the Business to Business Field: The Key Account's Point of View," *Journal of Personal Selling and Sales Management* (Fall 1997), pp. 17–26.

Sengupta, Sangit, Robert E. Krapfel, and Michael A. Pusateri, "Switching Costs in Key Account Relationships," *Journal of Personal Selling and Sales Management* (Fall 1997), pp. 9–16.

Sharma, Arun, "Who Prefers Key Account Management Programs? An Investigation of Business Buying Behavior and Buying Firm Characteristics," *Journal of Personal Selling and Sales Management* (Fall 1997), pp. 27–39.

Global Sales Organization

Hill, John S., and Arthur Allaway, "How U.S.-Based Companies Manage Sales in Foreign Countries," *Industrial Marketing Management* 27 (1993), pp. 7–16.

Hill, John S., and Richard R. Still, "Organizing the Overseas Sales Force: How Multinationals Do It," *Journal of Personal Selling and Sales Management* (Spring 1990), pp. 57–66.

Napolitano, Lisa, "Keys to Success in Global Customer Management," *The Journal of the National Account Management Association* (Summer 1998), pp. 1–5.

Demand Estimation and Sales Quotas

UNDERSTANDING THE FUTURE

Accurately estimating demand is critical to making decisions about how many and what kind of products to manufacture. The farm equipment industry has enjoyed a long period of success. Case, Deere & Company, New Holland NV, and others have witnessed one of the longest periods of growth in their industry. Industry sales in 1998 were up 14 percent over 1997. However, despite this period of success, industry observers and insiders are not optimistic about the future. It is imperative that companies make production decisions based on future demand, *not* on current success. Deere & Company, for example, announced that it would cut production for 1999 despite posting one of its best years on record.

In projecting future demand, a number of factors must be taken into consideration. For example, farm equipment manufacturers must consider commodity prices (the price of corn, grain, etc.). Over the last several years these prices have remained at their lowest since the 1980s. When farmers can't get good prices for the products they grow, they buy less farm equipment. A second factor is that over a long period of growth, buyers will "catch up" with their purchases. Farm equipment companies such as Deere &

Company have noted that aging equipment has been replaced with newer, better machinery, lowering demand for new equipment. A third factor is the economic recession in Asia. Forty percent of U.S. grain exports go to Asia, but because of the economic problems in that part of the world, it cannot afford to buy U.S. grain. Demand has dropped off and farmers have less money for new equipment purchases. Finally, in global markets where demand for farm equipment is strong (Eastern Europe and Russia) there is not sufficient financing in place to pay for the equipment. As noted by one manufacturer, "If they had enough money, we wouldn't have enough capacity."

As a result, while current sales are strong, future trends suggest a weakening of demand. Most notably, global forces are affecting demand for farm equipment. Given the heavy investment required to carry this kind of heavy equipment in inventory, manufacturers have no choice but to scale back their production estimates for the next several years. Agco's CEO summed it up thusly: "There is a recession coming in this industry and we're going to prepare for it."

Source: Carl Quintanilla, "Farm Equipment Makers Brace for Softer Ground Ahead," *The Wall Street Journal,* August 24, 1998. p. B4.

LEARNING OBJECTIVES

One of the most important functions in strategic market planning is the process of determining demand and translating demand into goals and objectives for the sales force. In this chapter you will learn the methods by which companies estimate market demand and the process by which specific sales quotas are created for the individual salesperson. After reading this chapter, you should be able to:

- Discuss the differences between market potential, market demand, sales potential, sales forecast, and sales quota.

- Understand the various methods by which companies estimate market demand.

- Outline the process of setting a sales quota.

- Explain the various kinds of quotas used in sales management.

As the introductory scenario suggests, inaccurate demand estimation can be costly. That is why companies like Deere and others focus a great deal of effort on getting the most accurate demand forecasts possible. While the example of the farm equipment manufacturers applies to only one industry, other examples abound. For example, when Apple Computer introduced its low-cost I-Mac personal computers, it limited production capabilities, triggering shortages, which caused some of its dealers to switch to other PC makers. IBM did the same with its Aptiva line of home PCs, which caused it to miss out on $100 million worth of business.[1]

As these examples at the beginning of the chapter suggest, firms not only need to identify market opportunities but they also need to produce accurate estimates of demand for the products or services that result from this activity. The identification of market opportunities fundamentally affects how firms plan, staff, and operate.

There seems to be confusion over the terms used to describe a firm's marketing opportunities. This chapter reviews the main terms and discusses the interrelationships among these concepts. Next the chapter explores the various ways to estimate demand. Finally the chapter completes the circle of sales management planning by discussing how market potential is translated into specific salesperson goals commonly known as sales quotas. As a result, the chapter begins with a very broad assessment of the market (market potential) and concludes with how that is translated in specific goals and objectives for individual salespeople and territories (sales quotas).

CLARIFICATION OF TERMS

Market opportunity analysis requires an understanding of the differences in the notions of market potential, sales potential, sales forecast, and sales quota.

Market potential is an estimate of the possible sales of a commodity, a group of commodities, or a service for an entire industry in a market during a stated period under ideal conditions. Note several things about this definition. First, market potential is defined for a particular market during a specified time period. The market refers to a specific customer group in a specific geographic area. Thus the statement

> The market potential for portable air compressors (commodity) to the construction industry (specific consumer group) in the Chicago metropolitan area (specific geographic area) in 2002 (specific time period) is 10,000 units or $10 million (maximum sales).

is a complete specification of market potential. The omission of any of the items would make the statement incomplete.

Sales potential refers to the portion of the market potential that a particular firm can reasonably expect to achieve. Market potential represents the maximum possible sales for all sellers of the good or service under ideal conditions, while sales potential reflects the maximum possible sales for an individual firm.

The **sales forecast** is an estimate of the dollar or unit sales for a specified future period under a proposed marketing plan or program. The forecast may be for a specified item of merchandise or for an entire line. It may be for a market as a whole or for any portion of it. Note that a sales forecast specifies the commodity, customer group, geographic area, and time period and includes a specific marketing plan as an essential element. If the proposed plan is changed, predicted sales are also expected to change.

Forecast sales are typically less than the company's sales potential. The firm may not have sufficient production capacity to realize its full potential, or its distribution network may not be sufficiently developed, or its financial resources may be limited. Likewise, forecast sales for an industry are typically less than the industry's market potential.

Sales quotas are sales goals assigned to a marketing unit for use in managing sales efforts. The marketing unit in question might be an individual salesperson, a sales territory, a branch office, a region, a dealer or distributor, or a district, just to name a few possibilities. Each salesperson in each sales territory might be assigned a sales volume goal for the next year. Sales quotas are typically a key measurement used to evaluate the personal selling effort. They apply to specific periods and can be specified in great detail—for example, sales of a particular item to a specified customer by sales rep J. Jones in June.

The sales quota is not the sales forecast or the estimate of the potential for the territory. Sales potential reflects what the company could sell in the territory under ideal conditions. Yet conditions are rarely ideal. The territories may not have been designed optimally, or differences in individual salesperson characteristics (age, ability, experience) may lead to less than (or greater than) expected results. Nor is the sales quota equal to the sales forecast for the territory. The sales forecast is the best estimate of what the company can sell with a particular planned level of marketing effort. It is an aggregate estimate that may or may not be broken down by product line, customer, or territory. The ideal forecast is one that is perfectly accurate because that facilitates planning. Thus, while a firm would not want to reward salespeople for exceeding their forecasts, it would want to reward them for exceeding their quotas.

The distinctions among *market potential, sales potential,* and *sales forecasts* are captured in Exhibit 6.1. Historical sales are shown because they often play a key role in determining the sales forecast. Note that an industry forecast is often developed before a company forecast is generated. The industry forecast presumes a specific level of marketing effort by all the forms that serve the industry. As the company's marketing plan becomes more effective, realized sales and then forecast sales should come closer to sales potential. The same occurs for industry sales and market potential, as the marketing efforts of the competitors become more effective.

Exhibit 6.2 shows the relationship between *potentials, forecasts,* and *quotas.* Typically the process begins with an assessment of the economic environment. Sometimes this is simply an implicit assessment of the immediate future. Is the outlook bright or gloomy? Then, given an initial estimate of industry potential and the company's competitive position, the firm's sales potential can be estimated. This in turn leads to an initial sales forecast, often based on the presumption that the marketing effort will be similar to what it was last year. The initial forecast is then compared with objectives established for the proposed marketing effort. If the marketing program is expected to achieve the objectives, both the program and the sales forecast are adopted. That is rare, however. Usually it is necessary to redesign the marketing program and then revise the sales forecast—often several times.

Exhibit 6.1   Relation among Market and Sales Potentials and Sales Forecast

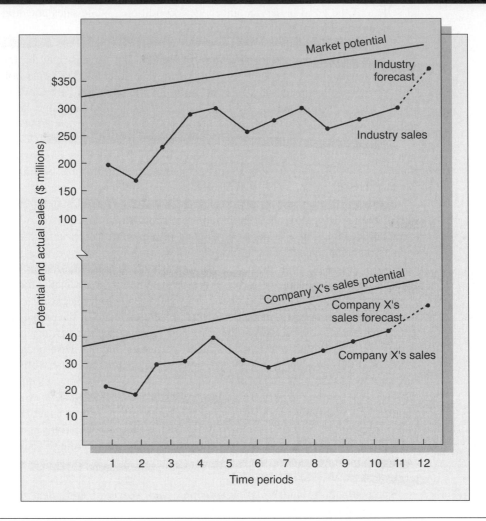

Source: Adapted from Douglas J. Dalrymple and Leonard J. Parsons, *Marketing Management: Strategy and Cases,* 5th ed. (New York: John Wiley & Sons, 1990), p. 234. Used by permission.

The objectives may also need revising; but eventually the process should produce agreement between the forecast or expected sales and the objectives. The sales forecast is then used as a key input in setting individual sales quotas (goals). In addition, it also serves as a basic piece of information in establishing budgets for the various functional areas. Note that the sales forecast presumes a specific marketing program. This is the key to understanding some of the advantages and disadvantages of the various sales forecasting methods discussed later in the chapter.

ESTIMATION OF DEMAND

Potential and forecast are distinct concepts, but they become blurred when estimates of demand are developed. The techniques used to estimate demand differ in their em-

Exhibit 6.2   Market Potential, Sales Potential, and Sales Forecasting Process

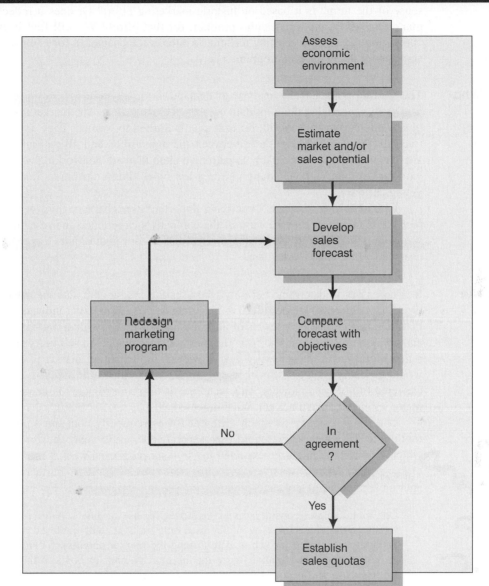

phasis on the proposed marketing effort. For example, some techniques neglect the level of marketing effort and concentrate on the maximum amount of the commodity that might be demanded from an industry or company. Estimates produced with this emphasis are closer to being market or sales potential estimates than they are sales forecasts.

Other techniques give great weight to the marketing effort planned for the period and are sales forecasts in the true sense of the word. Still other techniques use historic sales as a basis for future demand estimates. They rely on the implicit assumption that marketing effort in the future period will be similar to what it was in the past.

The key thing to note from a user's perspective is where on the spectrum one is operating. Is the projection based on near ideal conditions so it represents *potential* in the true sense of the term? Is it based on historic marketing effort? Or does it reflect a level of marketing effort and a particular program for that effort? We will find it useful when comparing the sales forecasting techniques later in the chapter to focus on what they presume about the marketing program.

Determine Who Uses the Product or Service

The starting point for any analysis of demand is to determine who uses or will use the product by specifying the important characteristics of users. The market for figure salons like Women's Workout World, for example, is limited to women. They do not equally attract all women; however, those between the ages of 18 and 40 patronize them more. Working women are more likely to patronize them than are nonworking women, and nonworking women without young children are more likely customers than women with young children.

For established products, specifying important user characteristics or factors that affect use is relatively easy because of the company's experience and research. New products may rely on an analogy with similar products—or might require a survey of potential users or even a small market test.

Determine the Rate of Use

It is necessary to determine not only who uses the product but also the rate at which the product is likely to be consumed. A manufacturer of riding lawn mowers might specify that its potential market consists of all households with more than one-third acre of yard and an income of at least $50,000. The firm could not expect to sell every such household a new riding lawn mower every year, however. In estimating market potential, the firm would probably want to estimate new demand and replacement demand, considering the expected life of lawn mowers. This technique is used to estimate the market potential for major appliances and other consumer durables.

The usage estimate is much different for a frequently consumed product such as toothpaste, of which a household uses several tubes each year, and for soft drinks, of which a household might be expected to use a six-pack each week. Both users and rates of usage must be determined to derive the estimates of demand. Furthermore, the manager must understand the basis on which the demand estimate rests. For example,

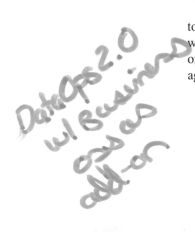

> One manufacturer considered making stoves for use on boats. A brief analysis clearly indicated that these stoves would be used only on boats with enclosed cabins. The market analyst assigned the job of determining the market potential for these stoves came up with a rather substantial figure for the total number of boats in the United States. With such a sizable market potential, the manufacturer went into production. When sales results were disappointing, an investigation showed that the figure for the number of boats included everything from an eight-foot, flat-bottom rowboat to sea-going yachts.[2]

Determine Who Buys the Product or Service

The analysis of demand might also consider who buys the product. This is particularly important when the purchaser is different from the user. While the number of users and their likely rate of use will determine the total potential for the product, buyers and their motivations for buying will affect how much of that potential is likely to be realized. Thus, although an individual firm might choose to direct a major portion of its promotional efforts to buyers, it might also channel a portion of that effort to users. For example, software manufacturers often address part of their advertising effort to purchasing agents as well as potential users of the software.

Determine the Market Motivations for Purchase

A final factor to consider when analyzing demand is market motivations. Why do customers buy the product? What might influence prospective customers to buy it? Some products have naturally induced causes of sales. For example, when people first set up a household, they typically buy major appliances and furniture. Some manufacturers of these products use the marriage rate as a basis for estimating the size of their markets. Similarly, a manufacturer of baby furniture may base its entire market analysis on birthrates. Likewise, a manufacturer of office furniture might base its estimate of demand on the number of new businesses formed in the firm's market area. Or the firm might use the number of new businesses as an indicator of new demand and use other indicators to estimate replacement demand. For example, manufacturers of pumps for the pulp and paper industry often break the demand for pumps into three components—(1) exchange demand, (2) demand for minor investments, and (3) demand for major investments—and develop separate prediction equations for each of the components using different factors as input.

IMPORTANCE OF THE SALES FORECAST

The sales forecast is one of the most important pieces of data used by management and lies at the heart of most companies' planning efforts. Top management uses the sales forecast to allocate resources among functional areas and to control the operations of the firm. Finance uses it to project cash flows, to decide on capital appropriations, and to establish operating budgets. Production uses it to determine quantities and schedules and to control inventories. Human resources uses it to plan personnel requirements and also as an input in collective bargaining. Purchasing uses it to plan the company's overall materials requirements and also the schedule for their arrival. Marketing uses it to plan marketing and sales programs and to allocate resources among the various marketing activities. The importance of accurate sales forecasts is exacerbated as companies coordinate their efforts on a global scale. The "Global Sales Force" box highlights how Lexmark has dealt with this issue.

The sales forecast is also of fundamental importance in planning and evaluating the personal selling effort. Sales managers use it for setting sales quotas, as input to the compensation plan, and in evaluating the field sales force, among other things. The sales manager thus should be familiar with the techniques used to develop sales forecasts. The subjective and objective methods discussed in this chapter are listed in Exhibit 6.3.[3]

Each method has advantages and disadvantages (which are summarized in Exhibit 6.4), and the decision of which to use will not always be clear.[4] In a typical company, the decision will more than likely depend on its level of technical sophistication and the existence of historic sales data. It will also likely depend on the use to which the forecast will be put. A forecasting system designed to estimate production scheduling and inventory requirements may rely on a completely different set of procedures than one designed to plan marketing strategy. One guide a manager might find useful when choosing a forecasting method is what other companies have done.

USERS' EXPECTATIONS

The **users' expectations method** of forecasting sales is also known as the **buyers' intentions method** because it relies on answers from customers regarding their expected consumption or purchases of the product. The customers may be surveyed in person, over the telephone, by mail, or via computer. Oklahoma Gas and Electric (OG&E) wanted to

Coordinating Worldwide Production from Worldwide Forecasts

Lexmark International Group, Inc., a leading manufacturer of printers, must coordinate information regarding product manufacturing and distribution for customers in 100 countries from four distribution centers strategically placed around the world. The company has spent over $30 million in recent years to help it manage the process of demand estimation and production more efficiently and effectively.

To help Lexmark estimate demand as accurately as possible, it employs a great deal of information. First it uses historical data which it combines with market information from its worldwide sales force. The sales force is asked to provide market estimates and projections based on customer input. The company also attempts to determine market potential by conducting analyses of competitors and basic research into the

PC market. By bringing together information from a variety of sources, it is hoped that a clear picture of the demand for Lexmark printers will develop which, in turn, can lead to an accurate assessment of production schedules. Given the lead time from suppliers as well as the time in the production facility to manufacture the product, the cost of a mistake in time and resources can be large.

The goal of this process as stated by Norm Galloway, chief information officer of Lexmark, is "meeting those requested delivery dates, consistently." Demand estimation is critical for Lexmark so it can plan production runs and meet the demands of customers who will buy a competitor's product if a Lexmark printer is not available when they want it.

Source: Rochell Garner, "Everlasting Love," *Sales & Marketing Management* (1996), pp. 84–86.

Exhibit 6.3 Classification of Sales Forecasting Methods

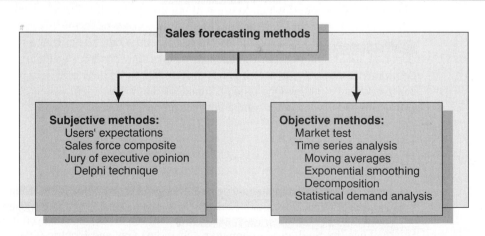

Exhibit 6.4   Summary of Advantages and Disadvantages of Various Sales Forecasting Techniques

Sales Forecasting Method	Advantages	Disadvantages
User expectations	1. Forecast estimates obtained directly from buyers 2. Projected product usage information can be greatly detailed 3. Insights gathered aid in the planning of marketing strategy 4. Useful for new-product forecasting	1. Potential customers must be few and well defined 2. Does not work well for consumer goods 3. Depends on the accuracy of user's estimates 4. Expensive, time-consuming, labor intensive
Sales force composite	1. Involves the people (sales personnel) who will be held responsible for the results 2. Is fairly accurate 3. Aids in controlling and directing the sales effort 4. Forecast is available for individual sales territories	1. Estimators (sales personnel) have a vested interest and therefore may be biased 2. Elaborate schemes sometimes necessary to counteract bias 3. If estimates are biased, process to correct the data can be expensive
Jury of executive opinion	1. Easily done, very quick 2. Does not require elaborate statistics 3. Utilizes "collective wisdom" of the top people 4. Useful for new or innovative products	1. Produces aggregate forecasts 2. Expensive 3. Disperses responsibility for the forecast 4. Group dynamics operate
Delphi technique	1. Minimizes effects of group dynamics 2. Can utilize statistical information	1. Can be expensive and time-consuming
Market test	1. Provides ultimate test of consumers' reactions to the product 2. Allows the assessment of the effectiveness of the total marketing program 3. Useful for new and innovative products	1. Lets competitors know what firm is doing 2. Invites competitive reaction 3. Expensive and time-consuming to set up 4. Often takes a long time to accurately assess level of initial and repeat demand
Time series analysis	1. Utilizes historical data 2. Objective, inexpensive	1. Not useful for new or innovative products 2. Factors for trend, cyclical, seasonal, or product life-cycle phase must be accurately assessed and included 3. Technical skill and good judgment required 4. Final forecast difficult to break down into individual territory estimates 5. Ignores planned marketing effort
Statistical demand analysis	1. Great intuitive appeal 2. Requires quantification of assumptions underlying the estimates 3. Allows management to check results 4. Uncovers hidden factors affecting sales 5. Method is objective	1. Factors affecting sales must remain constant and be accurately identified to produce an accurate estimate 2. Requires technical skill and expertise 3. Some managers reluctant to use method due to its sophistication

how and when to introduce new products (in a list of more than 15 new products and services) to its customers. OG&E used an old research methodology (focus groups) with new technology (Rapid Analysis Measurement System or RAM) to help make those decisions. Using a wireless interactive device held by each participant, the company was able to get instant feedback on which products were well received by its customers. As a result of getting feedback on the users' expectations, OG&E changed its marketing strategy, using a much more targeted approach.[5]

The respondents in a user expectations survey do not necessarily have to be the ultimate consumers. Rather, the firm may find it advantageous to secure the reactions of wholesalers and retailers that serve the channel. For example, Persoft, Inc., a Madison, Wisconsin-based software publisher, typically talks with dealers when trying to gauge demand for its new software packages.[6] The surveys generally are conducted with the ultimate customers, however. Boeing Company, for example, contacts major airlines about their purchase plans for new aircraft when planning its production requirements.

The users' expectations method of forecasting sales may provide estimates closer to market or sales potential than to sales forecasts. In reality, user groups would have difficulty anticipating the industry's or a particular firm's marketing efforts. Rather, the user estimates reflect their anticipated needs. From the sellers' standpoint, they provide a measure of the opportunities available among a particular segment of users.

SALES FORCE COMPOSITE

The sales force composite method of forecasting sales is so named because the initial input is the opinion of each member of the field sales staff. Each person states how much he or she expects to sell during the forecast period. These estimates are typically adjusted at various levels of sales management. They are likely to be checked, discussed, and possibly changed by the branch manager and on up the sales organization chart until the figures are finally accepted at corporate headquarters.

Ex-Cell-O Corporation relies on the sales force composite method of sales forecasting. Ex-Cell-O manufactures a variety of industrial items, including machinery, precision parts and assemblies, aerospace and electronic parts, and expendable tools and accessories. The company manufactures machine tools that range in price from a few thousand dollars to a half-million dollars or more. The products are sold by the machine tool group's own sales force, which consists of approximately 50 salespeople and 100 independent distributors. Each salesperson and distributor is required to forecast the outstanding proposals that he or she expects will be converted into orders during each of the upcoming five quarters. The process is repeated every three months. The regional manager reviews the forecasts with the individual salesperson or distributor and secures agreement on any necessary adjustments. When the manager is satisfied that all of the individual forecasts in the region are as realistic as can be, the manager forwards them to the marketing staff at group headquarters, where they are once again reviewed and sometimes adjusted through phone conversations between marketing management and the regional manager submitting the forecast.[7]

JURY OF EXECUTIVE OPINION

The jury of executive or expert opinion method informally or formally polls the top executives of the company for their assessment of sales possibilities. The separate assessments are combined into a sales forecast for the company. Sometimes this is done by simply averaging the individual judgments; but other times disparate views are resolved through group discussion. The initial views may reflect no more than the executive's hunch about what is going to happen, or the opinion may be based on considerable factual material, sometimes even an initial forecast prepared by other means.

For example, each group product manager at Rubbermaid's Home Products Division prepares 30-, 60-, and 90-day as well as annual forecasts for each item for which he or

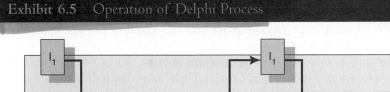

Exhibit 6.5   Operation of Delphi Process

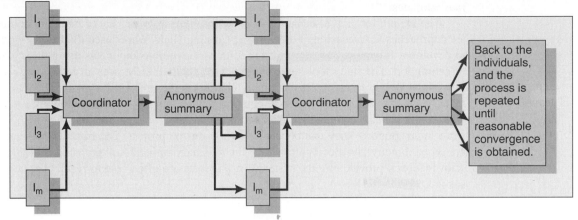

she is responsible. Two upper-level managers provide the managers with the best possible forecasting tools and information to make their forecasts as accurate as possible. Rubbermaid also uses a high-level operating committee to prepare a similar forecast. The separate forecasts are subsequently reconciled using several statistical criteria.[8] For more on Rubbermaid, visit its Web site at *www.rubbermaid.com.*

DELPHI TECHNIQUE

One increasingly popular method for controlling group dynamics to produce a more accurate forecast is the Delphi technique. Delphi uses repeated measurement and controlled feedback instead of direct confrontation and debate among the experts preparing the forecast.[9] Exhibit 6.5 depicts how the method operates. Each individual prepares a forecast using whatever facts, figures, and general knowledge of the environment he or she has available. Then, the forecasts are collected, and an anonymous summary is prepared by the person supervising the process. The summary is distributed to each person who participated in the initial phase. Typically, the summary lists each forecast figure, the average (median), and some summary measure of the spread of the estimates. Often, those whose initial estimates fell outside the midrange of responses are asked to express their reasons for these extreme positions. These explanations are then incorporated in the summary. The participants study the summary and submit a revised forecast. The process is then repeated. There will typically be a number of these iterations. The method is based on the following two premises:

1. The range of responses will decrease, and the estimates will converge with repeated measurements.

2. The total group response or median will move successively toward the "correct" or "true" answer.

Forcing those whose forecasts lie at the extreme ends of the distribution to justify their estimates means that "informed" experts have greater opportunity to influence the final forecast. Those who might have a deviant opinion, but with good reason, can defend that position, rather than giving in to group pressure or a strong-willed superior. Those who feel strongly about their estimates tend to like Delphi because of the anonymity it provides. Since their forecasts are not necessarily revised, this can help produce more accurate estimates.

The Delphi technique seems to be an increasingly popular way of handling committee approaches to forecasting. For example, Corning Glass Works used the Delphi method to develop a 10-year market forecast for certain electronic components using three waves of estimation. The study took nine months to complete.[10] IBM uses an interesting variation of the Delphi technique that virtually eliminates the time lag between ballots to estimate "how ripe" a market is for new equipment the company is considering introducing. The Delphi panel is composed of IBM experts with diverse backgrounds who are isolated from interruption so they can concentrate fully on the project. The panelists' judgments are typed directly into a computer where the summary statistics are prepared. With the instant feedback provided by the system, the panelists are often able to reach near consensus in a few hours.[11]

MARKET TEST

The typical market test involves placing the product in several "representative" cities to see how well it performs and then projecting that experience to the United States as a whole. Often this is done for a new product or an improved version of an old product.

Many firms consider the test market to be the final gauge of consumer acceptance of a new product and ultimate measure of market potential. A. C. Nielsen data, for example, indicate roughly three out of four products that have been test marketed succeed while four out of five that have not been test marketed fail. On the other hand, test markets are costly to administer and are more conducive to testing of consumer products than industrial products. In addition, the time involved in conducting a test market can be considerable. Finally, because a product is being test marketed it receives more attention in the test market than it can ever receive on a national scale, giving an unrealistic picture of the product's potential. All in all, it can be a highly successful sales forecasting technique but one that should not be used unless and until all the positives and negatives have been evaluated by management.

TIME SERIES ANALYSIS

Time series approaches to sales forecasting rely on the analysis of historical data to develop a prediction for the future. The sophistication of these analyses can vary widely. At one extreme, the forecaster might simply forecast next year's sales to be equal to this year's sales. Such a forecast might be reasonably accurate for a mature industry that is experiencing little growth. If there is growth, however, the forecaster might allow for it by predicting the same percentage increase for next year that the company experienced this year. Still further along the spectrum, the forecaster might attempt to break historical sales into basic components by isolating that portion due to trend, cyclical, seasonal, and irregular influences. The trend, cyclical, and seasonal components could all be forecast separately and then combined to produce the aggregate forecast. There are a number of time series approaches to sales forecasting, but only the moving average, exponential smoothing, and decomposition methods are discussed here.[12]

Exhibit 6.6 Annual and Forecast Sales for a Manufacturer of Pens and Pencils

| | | Forecast Sales | |
| | | --- | --- |
Year	Actual Sales	Two-Year Moving Average	Four-Year Moving Average
1987	4,200		
1988	4,410		
1989	4,322	4,305	
1990	4,106	4,366	
1991	4,311	4,214	4,260
1992	4,742	4,209	4,287
1993	4,837	4,527	4,370
1994	5,030	4,790	4,499
1995	4,779	4,934	4,730
1996	4,970	4,905	4,847
1997	5,716	4,875	4,904
1998	6,116	5,343	5,128
1999	5,932	5,916	5,395
2000	5,576	6,024	5,684
2001	5,465	5,754	5,835
2002		5,520	5,772

Moving Averages

The method of moving averages is conceptually quite simple. Consider the forecast that next year's sales will be equal to this year's sales. Such a forecast might be subject to large error if there is much fluctuation in sales from one year to the next. To allow for such randomness, we might consider using some kind of average of recent values. For example, we might average the last two years' sales, the last three years' sales, the last five years' sales, or any number of other periods. The forecast would simply be the average that resulted. The number of observations included in the average is typically determined by trial and error. Differing numbers of periods are tried and the number of periods that produces the most accurate forecasts of the trial data is used to develop the forecast model. Once determined, it remains constant. The term *moving average* is used because a new average is computed and used as a forecast as each new observation becomes available.

Exhibit 6.6 presents 16 years of historical sales data for a manufacturer of pens and pencils and also the resulting forecasts for a number of years using two-year and four-year moving averages. Exhibit 6.7 displays the results graphically. The entry 4,305 for 1989, under the two-year moving average method, for example, is the average of the sales of 4,200 units in 1987 and 4,410 units in 1988. Similarly, the forecast of 5,520 units in 2002 represents the average of the number of units sold in 2000 and 2001. The forecast of 5,772 units in 2002 under the four-year moving average method, on the other hand, represents the average number of units sold during the four-year period 1998–2001. It takes more data to begin forecasting with four-year than with two-year moving averages. This is important when starting to forecast sales for a new product.

Observe also the impact of the number of periods on the fluctuations in the forecast series. The larger the number of observations included, the greater is the smoothing of the forecasts. Thus, whereas the range of forecast values is 1,815 (6,024–4,209) with the two-

Exhibit 6.7   Actual and Forecast Sales Using Moving Averages

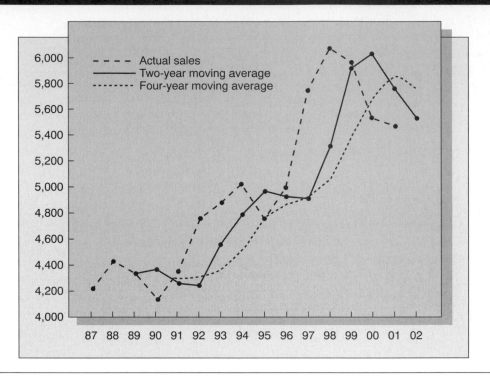

year moving average, it is only 1,575 (5,835–4,260) with the four-year moving average—a difference of 240 units. When we desire a smoother value because we think there is little change in the underlying pattern and we are observing mainly random fluctuations, we should use many periods to determine the moving average. Conversely, when we think the series is changing rapidly or when there is little randomness in sales, we would use fewer periods to compute the moving average so the forecast can react more quickly to the changes that are occurring.

Exponential Smoothing

The method of moving averages gives equal weight to each of the last n values in forecasting the next value. Thus, when $n = 4$ (the four-year moving average is being used), equal weight is given to each of the last four years' sales in predicting the sales for next year. No weight is given to any sales five or more years previous. The forecasting equation, in other words, is

$$\hat{X}_{t+1} = \frac{X_t + X_{t-1} + X_{t-2} + X_{t-3}}{n}$$

$$= \frac{X_t + X_{t-1} + X_{t-2} + X_{t-n+1}}{n}$$

$\hat{X}_{t+1}$ = forecast value for next year or next period
X_t = actual sales that resulted in year or period t.

Exponential smoothing is a type of moving average. However, instead of weighting all observations equally in generating the forecast, exponential smoothing weights the most recent observations heaviest, for good reason. The most recent observations contain

Exhibit 6.8 Annual Sales and Forecast Sales Using Exponential Smoothing and Various Values for the Smoothing Constant α

Year	Actual Sales	Forecast Sales		
		$\alpha = 0.2$	$\alpha = 0.5$	$\alpha = 0.8$
1987	4,200			
1988	4,410	4,200	4,200	4,200
1989	4,322	4,242	4,305	4,368
1990	4,106	4,258	4,314	4,332
1991	4,311	4,228	4,210	4,151
1992	4,742	4,244	4,260	4,279
1993	4,837	4,343	4,501	4,649
1994	5,030	4,441	4,669	4,800
1995	4,779	4,559	4,849	4,984
1996	4,970	4,603	4,814	4,820
1997	5,716	4,676	4,892	4,940
1998	6,116	4,883	5,304	5,561
1999	5,932	4,129	5,710	6,005
2000	5,576	5,289	5,821	5,947
2001	5,465	5,346	5,699	5,650
2002		5,370	5,583	5,502

the most information about what is likely to happen in the future, and they should logically be given more weight. The general form of the exponential smoothing model is

$$\hat{X}_{t-1} = \alpha X_{t} + (1 - \alpha)\hat{X}_{t}$$

where the caret again indicates a forecast value, and an X without a caret indicates an actual value. The exponential smoothing model thus suggests next year's sales will be equal to this year's sales, X_t, times the constant, α, plus the forecast value of this year's sales, $\hat{X}_t$, times the constant $(1 - \alpha)$. It can be shown by successive substitution that the second term in this equation implicitly recognizes older values, thereby overcoming a second limitation of the moving average method, which ignores all those values more than n periods old.

The key decision affecting the use of exponential smoothing is the choice of α, which is known as the smoothing constant, and which is constrained to be between 0 and 1. High values of α give great weight to recent observations and little weight to distant sales; low values of α, on the other hand, give more weight to older observations. If sales change slowly, low values of α work fine. When sales experience rapid changes and fluctuations, however, high values of α should be used so that the forecast series responds to these changes quickly. The value of α is normally determined empirically; various values of α are tried, and the one that produces the smallest forecast error when applied to the historical series is adopted. Exhibits 6.8 and 6.9 show what happens to forecast values when α is set at 0.2, 0.5, and 0.8. Note two things. First, when the forecast is initialized, the first forecast value is simply set equal to the prior year's actual sales.[13] Second, note the impact of α on the speed with which forecast sales respond to changes in actual sales.

Decomposition

The decomposition method of sales forecasting is typically applied to monthly or quarterly data where a seasonal pattern is evident and the manager wishes to forecast sales not only for the year but also for each period in the year. For example, Coleman Cable Systems of Chicago, a manufacturer of wire and cable products, analyzes sales by quarter

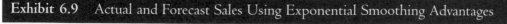

Exhibit 6.9   Actual and Forecast Sales Using Exponential Smoothing Advantages

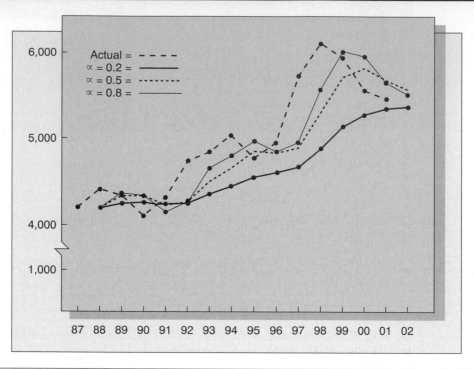

to determine what portion of the sales changes represents an overall, fundamental change in demand and what portion is due to seasonal aberrations. The decomposition method attempts to isolate four separate portions of a time series: the trend, cyclical, seasonal, and random factors.

- The trend reflects the long-run changes experienced in the series when the cyclical, seasonal, and irregular components are removed. It is typically assumed to be a straight line.

- The cyclical factor is not always present because it reflects the waves in a series when the seasonal and irregular components are removed. These ups and downs typically occur over a long period—perhaps two to five years. Some products experience little cyclical fluctuation (canned peas), whereas others experience a great deal (housing starts).

- The seasonal factor reflects the annual fluctuation in the series due to the natural seasons. The seasonal factor normally repeats itself each year, although the exact pattern of sales may be different from year to year.

- The random factor is what is left after the influence of the trend, cyclical, and seasonal factors is removed.

Exhibit 6.10 shows the calculation of a simple seasonal index based on five years of sales history. The data suggest definite seasonal and trend components in the series. The fourth quarter of every year is always the best quarter; the first quarter is the worst. At the same time, sales each year are higher than they were the year previous. One could calculate a seasonal index for each year by simply dividing quarterly sales by the yearly aver-

Exhibit 6.10   Calculation of a Seasonal Index

Year	Quarter 1	Quarter 2	Quarter 3	Quarter 4	Total	Quarter Average
1996	82.8	105.8	119.6	151.8	460.0	115.0
1997	93.1	117.6	122.5	156.9	490.1	122.5
1998	92.0	122.4	132.6	163.2	510.2	127.6
1999	95.3	129.0	151.3	185.0	560.6	140.2
2000	120.1	138.1	162.2	180.2	600.6	150.2
5-year average	96.7	122.6	137.6	167.4	524.3	131.1
Seasonal index*	73.8	93.5	105.0	127.7		

*The seasonal index equals the quarterly average divided by the overall quarterly average times 100; for the first quarter, for example, the seasonal index equals (96.7 ÷ 131.1) × 100 = 73.8.

age per quarter. It is much more typical, though, to base the calculation of the seasonal index on several years of data to smooth out the random fluctuations that occur by quarter.

The exhibit shows five years of sales history. To calculate the index, first determine the average sales for each quarter for the five years. For example, the average sales for the first quarter over the five-year period were 96.7. Then divide these numbers by the average sales per quarter for the entire period, namely 131.1, to give the seasonal index for each quarter.

The calculations suggest the seasonal indexes for the first and fourth quarters, for example, are 73.8 and 127.7. This means sales in the first quarter are typically 26.2 percent less, and those in the fourth quarter are 27.7 percent more than normal because of seasonal factors. A manager should not be upset, therefore, if the company experiences a 40 percent drop in sales from, say, 200 units in the fourth quarter of last year to 120 units in the first quarter this year. That is natural because of the seasonal pattern to the business.

Rather, the appropriate way to interpret the figures is to deseasonalize them—by dividing the actual sales figures by the appropriate seasonal index. The deseasonalized fourth quarter sales are 200 ÷ 127.7 × 100 = 156.6 while the deseasonalized first quarter sales are 120 ÷ 73.8 × 100 = 162.6. The deseasonalized sales per quarter times four gives the expected yearly sales if sales were to continue at the same rate. While the first inclination was to suggest that the company's sales performance was worse in the first quarter than it was in the prior fourth quarter, the first quarter, in fact, was better. After accounting for the normal seasonal fluctuations in sales by comparing the deseasonalized values, the results suggest that sales in the first quarter were actually up.

In using the decomposition method, the analyst typically first determines the seasonal pattern and removes its impact to identify the trend. Then the cyclical factor is estimated. After the three components are isolated, the forecast is developed by applying each factor in turn to the historical data.[14]

STATISTICAL DEMAND ANALYSIS

Time series analysis attempts to determine the relationship between sales and time as the basis of the forecast for the future. Statistical demand analysis attempts to determine the

Exhibit 6.11   Use of Regression Analysis to Forecast Demand of Natural Gas by Household

$$Y_t = 74{,}111X_1 + 752X_2 + 251X_3 + 30X_4 + 41{,}942X_5 - 136{,}747X_6$$

$$R^2 = .99$$

where

Y_t = monthly reported deliveries of natural gas to residential customers in 1,000s of cubic feet

X_1 = index of changes in total personal income in constant dollars received by gas customers and changes in the number of gas customers

X_2 = heating degree days weighted by gas residential space-heating customers

X_3 = cooling degree days weighted by population

X_4 = household wealth in constant dollars

X_5 = price index of natural gas in constant dollars

X_6 = seasonal shift in residential gas demand for the one-month period from mid-December to mid-January

Source: John H. Herbert and Erik Kreil, "Specifying and Evaluating Aggregate Monthly Natural Gas Demand by Households," *Applied Economics* 21 (October 1989), pp. 1369–81.

relationship between sales and the important factors affecting sales to forecast the future. Typically, regression analysis is used to estimate the relationship. The emphasis is not to isolate all factors that affect sales but simply to identify those that have the most dramatic impact and then to estimate the magnitude of the impact. For example, Exhibit 6.11 illustrates the use of regression analysis to estimate U.S. monthly demand of natural gas by household. Note that the predictor variables were successful in accounting for variations in demand by household; they explained 99 percent of the variation, as indicated by R^2.

Sometimes firms attempt to relate their sales to one or more aggregate indicators of economic activity. For example, a major durable goods manufacturer found the following equation adequately accounted for its factory-to-distributor parts sales:

$$S_t = \$2{,}032{,}243 + 11{,}595X_t$$

where

S_t = parts sales
X_t = composite index of six economic indicators published in *Business Conditions Digest.*

This simple forecast equation accounted for almost half the dramatic variations in sales of parts.[15]

CHOOSING A FORECASTING METHOD

The sales manager faced with a forecasting problem has a dilemma: Which forecasting method should be used and how accurate is the forecast likely to be? The dilemma is particularly acute when several methods are tried and the forecasts don't agree, a common happening, as the "Managing Sales Relationships" box suggests.

Reconciling Inconsistent Forecasts

May Building Systems manufactures self-storage or miniwarehouse buildings. The buildings are sold primarily to those who rent space to individual households for storage, typically on a month-to-month basis. May's management has found that its business tends to lag behind the general economy. Its sales tend to decline after the country has gone into recession and recover after the economy has improved. Management has also determined that sales correlate closely with commercial construction and other lagging series of the general economy.

The company, in using statistical demand analysis, found that the number of construction contracts awarded for industrial building was the best predictor variable for warehouse sales 10 months in advance.

Using current information on this series found in *Business Conditions Digest,* the company has developed a one-year sales forecast for its self-storage buildings that it hopes to use in preparing budgets. However, management is concerned that the statistical demand-based forecast does not agree with the forecasts prepared using both sales force composite and jury of executive opinion. It is 25 percent higher than the forecast prepared by the salespeople using the sales force composite and 18 percent higher than the sales forecast by a panel of company executives.

Which system should management use when developing its budget plans and budgets? How should it reconcile the differences?

Exhibit 6.12	Various Sales Forecasting Methods Used by U.S. Firms (in percent)		
Forecasting Method	**Firms That Use Regularly**	**Firms That Use Occasionally**	**Firms That No Longer Use**
Subjective Methods			
Users' expectations			
Intention to buy survey	16%	10%	19%
Industry survey	15	21	18
Sales force composite	45	17	13
Jury of executive opinion	37	22	8
Objective Methods			
Time series analysis			
Naive	31	21	9
Moving average	21	10	16
Exponential smoothing	11	12	19
Statistical demand analysis			
Simple regression	6	13	20
Multiple regression	12	9	21

Source: Developed from the data in Douglas J. Dalrymple, "Sales Forecasting Practices: Results from a United States Survey," *International Journal of Forecasting* 3, nos. 2–4 (1987), pp. 379–91. The percentages are based on the 134 firms that responded to the survey.

What Companies Use

Exhibit 6.12 summarizes the results of a survey of U.S. firms. While there is not perfect agreement between the categories used in the survey and the classification used to frame our discussion, the empirical evidence suggests there is heavier reliance on the subjective methods versus the quantitative, objective methods. The sales force composite method and jury of executive opinion seem particularly popular. Both of these findings mirror the situation that existed 15 years previously.[16]

One might wonder why the situation did not change much in 15 years in light of the greater sophistication of the quantitative techniques, managers' increased exposure to them, and the advances in computer technology that have made these techniques more readily available. Part of the answer seems to lie in the benefits to be gained from involving line people in the forecasting process.

> The process of forecasting is stimulating to the committeemen [the company's forecasting committee] who participate. It forces them to think ahead, to evaluate opportunities for improving performance, and to mesh plans in a coordinated way. *These things are more important than the accuracy of the figures that emerge from the process.* [emphasis added][17]

These sentiments were shared by a vice president of an equipment company, who stated, "We do not want to substitute a procedure which may be more accurate but would reduce the present in-depth involvement of the line and staff personnel."[18]

Accuracy

Another consideration in the choice of forecasting technique is the accuracy of the approach. A number of studies have attempted to assess forecast accuracy using the various techniques. Some studies have been conducted within individual companies; others have used selected data series to which the various forecasting techniques have been systematically applied. One of the most extensive comparisons involved 1,001 time series from a variety of sources in which each series was forecast with each of 24 extrapolation methods. The general conclusion was that the method used made little difference with respect to forecast accuracy.[19] Similarly, comparisons of forecast accuracy of objective versus subjective methods gave no clear conclusion as to which method is superior. Some of the comparisons seem to favor the quantitative methods,[20] but others found that the subjective methods produce more accurate forecasts.[21]

In general, the various forecast comparisons suggest that no method is likely to be superior under all conditions. Rather, a number of factors are likely to impact the superiority of any particular technique, including the stability of the data series, the time horizon, the degree of structure imposed on the process, the degree to which computers were used, and deseasonalization of the data, which is perhaps the most important factor affecting forecast accuracy.[22]

The various forecast comparisons do suggest several important conclusions that are helpful when choosing a forecasting method. First, a technique that works well for one series may not work on another. Managers need to be flexible in their approach, although the quantitative approaches seem to do best when the forecast is short-term, frequent, low-level, and easy to correct, and where the database is rich with observations and not subject to major changes. The subjective methods, on the other hand, seem to work best when the forecast is long-term, infrequent, and hard to correct, and where the database is skimpy but forecast errors are likely to cause large losses. Thus, the choice of technique should depend partially on the use of the forecast and the consequences if it is in error.

A second major conclusion from the forecast comparisons is that more accurate forecasts can be generated by combining forecasts developed from different techniques than can be generated by searching for the one "best" technique. Accordingly, the literature has recently switched emphasis from identifying the optimal method of forecasting across all situations toward better ways of combining forecasts developed by different schemes. Invariably, this seems to improve overall forecast accuracy.[23]

A third important conclusion is that forecast accuracy can be overemphasized. Forecasts are not always wrong; more often than not, they can be reasonably accurate. And that is what makes them so dangerous. They are usually constructed on the assumption that tomorrow's world will be much like today's. They often work because the world does not always change. But sooner or later forecasts will fail when they are needed most, in anticipating major shifts in the business environment that make whole strategies obsolete.[24]

To cope with the revolutionary changes that can especially affect the business and to better understand the critical sensitivities of the business, firms are increasingly turning to scenario planning when developing sales forecasts. Scenario planning involves asking those preparing the forecast a series of "what-if" questions, where the "what-ifs" reflect different environmental changes that could occur. Some very unlikely changes are considered along with more probable events. The key idea is "not so much to have one scenario that 'gets it right' as to have a set of scenarios that illuminate the major forces driving the system, their interrelationships, and the critical uncertainties."[25]

DEVELOPING TERRITORY ESTIMATES

Not only must firms develop global estimates of demand, but most also develop territory-by-territory estimates. Territory estimates recognize the condition that the potential for any product may not be uniform by area. Awareness of the differences in territory demand allows the firm to do a better job in designing marketing strategy. For example, S. C. Johnson became "concerned that its dominant share of the household insecticide market had plateaued just above 40 percent . . . Johnson figured out where and when different bugs were about to start biting, stinging, and otherwise making people's lives miserable. The company promoted cockroach zappers in roach capitals such as Houston and New York and flea sprays in flea-bitten cities such as Tampa and Birmingham." This approach increased the company's share of the overall $450 million market for insecticides by some five percentage points.[26] Territory estimates of demand are particularly important to the sales manager who must deal with a geographically dispersed sales force. Territory demand estimates allow for effective planning, directing, and controlling of salespeople in that the estimates affect the following:

1. The design of sales territories.
2. The procedures used to identify potential customers.
3. The establishment of sales quotas.
4. Compensation levels and the mix of components in the firm's sales compensation scheme.
5. The evaluation of salespeople's performance.

In subsequent chapters, particularly in the chapters on territory design, quotas, and motivation and the three chapters on evaluation and control, we will see how territory demand estimates allow sales managers to more effectively manage their salespeople. For the moment, however, simply accept the fact that good territory demand estimates are a key ingredient to effective sales management.

This begs the question, of course, of how territory estimates can be derived. Some of the sales forecasting schemes provide them naturally. A survey of users or salespeople provides detailed estimates of demand, often by product by customer. These estimates can easily be combined into larger aggregates to produce demand estimates by product by territory. Similarly, the use of the sales history for a particular product in a particular territory in, say, a time series approach produces a forecast with the desired geographic detail. Some other forecasting schemes—such as the jury of executive opinion—produce only aggregate forecasts, which then must be broken down by appropriate geographical boundaries. Statistical demand analysis also typically produces aggregate estimates that have to be apportioned to areas.

The use of market factors or market indexes is the basic way aggregate estimates of demand are broken out by territory. A market factor is a feature or characteristic in a market that is related to the demand for the product. For example, the number of households in an area is one market factor influencing the demand for microwave ovens. A **market index** is a mathematical expression that combines two or more market factors into a numerical index. For instance, the market for microwave ovens might also be affected by income levels and whether both spouses work. Thus, when assessing the likely demand for microwave ovens in a particular geographic area, we might wish to combine the number of households and the income level in the area and the proportion of households with both spouses working. Typically this would be done by forming a linear combination of the factors where the weights assigned each factor would reflect their expected relative importance in affecting demand for microwave ovens. The amount of total demand apportioned to the territory would reflect the relative size of the index versus the national total. Typically, this means treating the national total as 100 percent and assessing the portion of it that lies within the geographic boundaries being considered.[27]

Industrial Goods

Territory demand estimates for industrial goods are typically developed by relating sales to some common denominator. The common denominator or market factor might be the number of total employees, number of production employees, value added by manufacturing process, value of materials consumed, value of products shipped, or expenditures for new plant and equipment. Say the ratio of sales per employee is developed for each of several identifiable markets. By then looking at the number of employees in a particular geographic area within each of those identifiable markets, one can estimate the total demand for the product within the area.

The identifiable markets are usually defined using Standard Industrial Classification (SIC) codes, a system developed by the U.S. Bureau of the Census for organizing the reporting of business information, such as employment, value added in manufacturing, capital expenditures, and total sales. Each major industry in the United States is assigned a two-digit number, indicating the group to which it belongs. The types of businesses making up each industry are further identified by additional digits. Exhibit 6.13 displays a partial breakdown of the construction industry.

Consider a firm that wants to estimate the demand for its portable air compressors (those typically used on construction sites to power pavement breakers and other equipment) in Kent County, Rhode Island. A priori, sales of portable air compressors are logically related to the number of employees working in the industry, and the number of employees is a direct indicator of the amount of construction activity in the area. At the same time, sales per employee would not be the same across the three major SIC construction categories shown in Exhibit 6.13. Firms in road building (SIC 16) have much greater need for portable air compressors than firms in building construction (SIC 15), which in turn have greater need than special contractors (SIC 17). Suppose the historical evidence suggests dollar sales of portable air compressors per employee are $90, $28, and $13 for the SIC codes 16, 15, and 17, respectively. By knowing the number of construction em-

Exhibit 6.13   Partial Breakdown of Standard Industrial Classification Codes

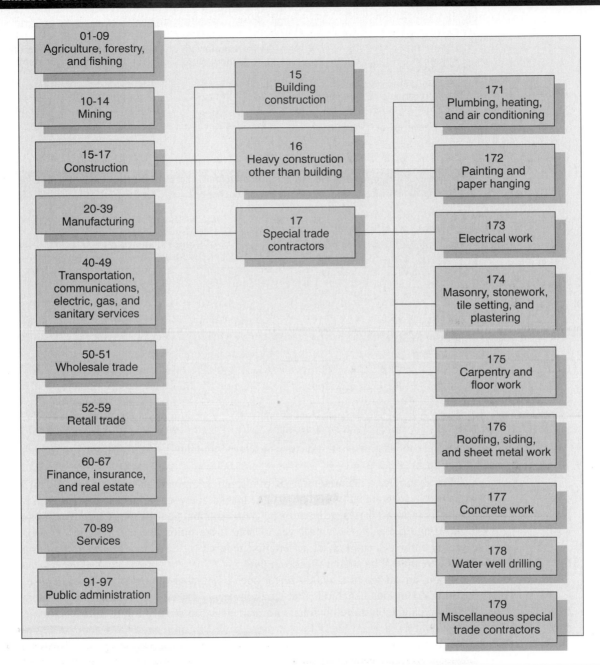

ployees of each type, one can estimate total market demand for portable air compressors in Kent County, Rhode Island. Exhibit 6.14 illustrates the calculations. By considering its competitive position in the Kent market, the firm could develop estimates for sales of its own brand. Alternatively, the firm could use total market demand to assess how well it is doing in the Kent market and could plan its marketing strategy accordingly.

Exhibit 6.14 Estimation of Market Demand for Portable Air Compressors by the Construction Industry in Kent County, Rhode Island

Industry	Number of Employees	Sales per Employee	Estimated Demand
15—Building construction	551	$28	$15,428
16—Construction other than building	172	90	15,480
17—Special trade contractor	1,128	13	14,664

Exhibit 6.15 Use of Various Plumbing Supplies in Commercial Construction

Product Group	Dollar Usage per 1,000 Square Feet of Nonresidential Construction
1	$ 2.40
2	9.30
3	4.60
4	.40
5	9.00
6	1.50
7	3.60
8	1.40
9	.40
10	.40
11	1.60
Total for all product groups	$34.60

For example, a manufacturer of plumbing equipment categorized its 47 different types of products into 11 product groups. It then analyzed published construction award data to determine the usage pattern by item. Exhibit 6.15 displays the overall product group usage factors for a typical year. Using these ratios, the company developed sales potential estimates and market penetration indexes for each area in which it sold, and it devised its marketing strategy accordingly.[28]

A big advantage of a market factor such as number of employees or square feet for breaking down total demand is that territory demand is derived objectively. The assumptions and calculations are obvious, and managers can readily follow the development of the estimates. They are likely to feel more confident with something they totally understand. Furthermore, the assumptions can be varied in systematic ways, and the impact on estimated demand can be calculated. For example, the portable air compressor estimates might allow for the fact that the size of a firm affects potential by taking into account the number of firms of different sizes in Kent County. Thus, the method allows the calculation of not only area potentials but also customer potentials if the firm wishes to push the calculations that far. The methods require that data are available in the necessary detail. This is a primary reason firms selling to industrial consumers base their calculations on SIC codes, since the Bureau of the Census publishes a great deal of detailed area data by SIC code.[29]

Exhibit 6.16 Basic Components and BPI for the Atlanta, Georgia, Area

	Atlanta	Fulton County	Atlanta Metro Area	Total United States
Total effective buying income ($000)	6,731,382	14,515,289	61,320,569	4,161,512,384
Percentage of U.S.	(.1617)	(.3488)	(1.4735)	(100.0)
Total population (000)	402.6	725.8	3582.2	267,540.6
Percentage of U.S.	(.1505)	(.2713)	(1.3389)	(100.0)
Total retail sales ($000)	3,727,587	8,300,257	37,638,467	2,465,147,126
Percentage of U.S.	(.1512)	(.3367)	(1.5268)	(100.0)
Buying Power Index $(5I + 2P + 3R)/10$	.1563	.3297	1.4626	

Source: "1997 Survey of Buying Power," *Sales & Marketing Management* (August 30, 1997), pp. C-78 and C-79, © 1997 by Bell Communications, Inc.

Consumer Goods

We have seen that firms selling to industrial consumers rely most heavily on identifiable market segments using SIC codes when estimating territory demand. Sellers of consumer goods, however, are more apt to rely on aggregate conditions in each territory. Sometimes this will be a single variable or market factor like the number of households, population, or perhaps the level of income in the area. In other instances, the firm attempts to relate demand to several variables combined in a systematic way. The demand for washing machines, for example, has been shown through regression analysis to be a function of (1) the level of consumers' stock of washing machines, (2) the number of wired dwelling units, (3) disposable personal income, (4) net credit, and (5) the price index for house furnishings. Since these statistics are published by area, a firm can use the regression equation to estimate demand by area.

Many firms are willing to expend the effort necessary to develop an expression for the relationship between total demand for the product and several variables that are logically related to its sales. Many other firms, however, are content to base their estimates of territory demand on one of the standard multiple-factor indexes that have been developed.

One of the most popular standard indexes is the buying power index (BPI), which is generated and published by *Sales & Marketing Management* magazine. The index considers income, population, and retail sales. These are weighted by the factors 5, 2, and 3, respectively, to generate a single number for a geographic region. This number is used to estimate the share of total market demand in the area. More specifically, the BPI for an area can be calculated using the formula

$$BPI = \frac{5I + 2P + 3R}{10}$$

where I is the percentage of disposable personal income in the area, P is the percentage of U.S. population, and R is the percentage of total retail sales.

Exhibit 6.16 shows the basic statistics and the BPI for the Atlanta, Georgia, area. Statistics are provided for the city, the county in which it is located, and the total metropolitan area. These statistics, as well as some category details such as how retail sales break out by store group, are published each year in *Sales & Market Management*'s "Survey of Buying Power." Firms using the BPI would concentrate their analysis on the total percentage of the BPI found in the territory in question. The Atlanta metropolitan area, for example, has a BPI of $1.4626 - [(1.4735 \times 5) + (1.3389 \times 2) + (1.5268 \times 3)]/10$. This means that slightly more than 1 percent of the total potential for the product could be expected to be within the Atlanta metropolitan area. If the total demand for furniture polish, for example, was anticipated to be $400 million, the BPI suggests the demand within the Atlanta metropolitan area would be $5,850,400 (400,000,000 × .014626).

As one might expect, the BPI is not especially useful for estimating territory potentials for industrial products. Nor is it especially useful for infrequently purchased, high-priced consumer goods. It is very popular, though, when estimating territory potential for frequently purchased, low-priced convenience goods. One strategy for a firm selling consumer goods is to determine empirically if the BPI correlates with industry sales by area. A firm is fortunate when it does because the BPI index is convenient—it is updated annually and is available by small geographic area. If the index does not correlate well with sales of the product, then the firm is probably better off (1) using a single market factor or (2) developing its own index using factors logically related to sales and some a priori or empirically determined weights regarding their relative importance, rather than blindly using the BPI to develop territory demand estimates.

SALES QUOTAS

The last major element in sales management planning is establishing goals for each sales representative. As discussed earlier in the chapter, goals assigned to salespeople are called quotas. Quotas are one of the most valuable devices sales managers have for planning the field selling effort, and they are indispensable for evaluating the effectiveness of that effort. They help managers plan the amount of sales and profit that will be available at the end of the planning period and anticipate the activities of the sales team. Quotas are also often used to motivate salespeople, and as such must be reasonable. Volume quotas are typically set to a level that is less than the sales potential in the territory and equal to or slightly above the sales forecast for the territory, although they also can be set less than the sales forecast if conditions warrant.

Sales quotas apply to specific periods and may be expressed in dollars or physical units. Thus, management can specify quarterly, annual, and longer-term quotas for each of the company's field representatives in both dollars and physical units. It might even specify these goals for individual products and customers. The product quotas can be varied systematically to reflect the profitability of different items in the line, and customer quotas can be varied to reflect the relative desirability of serving particular accounts.

The full set of quota assignments is called the quota plan.[30] The full specification of the quota plan requires decisions about the types of quotas that will be used, the relative importance of each, and the target levels for each salesperson or other marketing unit.

Purposes of Quotas

Quotas facilitate the planning and control of the field selling effort in a number of ways. One useful way of viewing the benefits is by assessing their contribution in (1) providing incentives for sales representatives, (2) evaluating salespeople's performance, and (3) controlling salespeople's efforts.

Provide incentives for salespeople

Quotas serve as incentives for sales in several ways. At an elementary level, they are an objective to be secured and a challenge to be met. For example, the definite objective of selling $200,000 worth of product X this year is more motivation to most salespeople than the indefinite charge to go out and do better. It seems one can always do better, but what standard is a reasonable goal? How hard should one push product X in relation to other products in the line? Sales quotas provide an answer to these questions. As one source put it, "Without a standard of measurement, a football team cannot tell whether it made a first down, golfers cannot tell whether they shot par, and sales reps cannot be certain their performance is satisfactory."[31] Evidence suggests most sales personnel are "quota achievers" rather than "dollar maximizers," and salespeople's motivation tends to decline when they have easily attainable goals.

Quotas also influence salespeople's incentive through sales contests. A key notion underlying such contests is that those who perform "best" will receive the contest prizes. Unfortunately, not all salespeople have the same opportunity to win unless some allowance is made for differences in sales abilities and in territorial potential and work load. These differences exist despite the company's best efforts to the contrary. Thus, the company needs to design the sales contest so that all sales reps have a chance to win. Sales quotas provide a common denominator by which territory and personal differences can be neutralized, so all sales representatives have a relatively equal chance.

Quotas can also create incentive via their key role in the compensation systems of most firms. More will be said about compensation in later chapters, but it should be noted here that many firms use a commission or bonus plan, sometimes in conjunction with their base salary plan. In such schemes, salespeople are paid in direct proportion to what they sell (commission plan), or they receive some percentage increment for sales in excess of target sales (bonus plan). Typically, such plans are tied directly to sales quotas. Even when salespeople are compensated with salary only, quotas can provide incentive when salary raises are tied to quota attainment in the previous year.

Evaluate sales performance

Quotas provide a quantitative standard against which the performance of individual sales representatives or other marketing units can be evaluated. They allow management to pinpoint the marketing units that are performing above average and those that are experiencing difficulty. They can be used relatively easily and lend themselves to management by exception.

Salespeople who miss their quotas by some appreciable amount, either above or below, can be singled out for more intensive investigation. Perhaps salespeople who perform far above quota are doing something especially right from which all salespeople might profit. Alternatively, perhaps others are having difficulty selling one type of product or to one type of customer.[32] There may be something the company can do to assist them. Maybe they are facing some intense competition from a regional competitor that is not being experienced elsewhere. Perhaps the firm needs to assume a more aggressive price posture in the region or to increase its advertising effort to neutralize the competitor's impact. Quotas localize spots that need more intensive investigation; this would be hard to do without these quantitative standards.

Control sales efforts

Quotas can be used not only to evaluate salespeople's performance but also to evaluate and control their efforts. As part of their job, salespeople are expected to engage in specific activities. Although the activities and the time devoted to them vary by company and industry, typical ones include calling on new accounts, collecting past-due accounts, and planning and developing sales presentations. Activity quotas allow the company to monitor whether sales reps are engaging in these activities to the extent desired. If they are not, corrective action can be taken early rather than waiting for these small activity problems to become large sales and profit problems.

Can Quotas Be Discriminatory?

Mary Mestousis, the sales manager for Custom Design Office Furniture, was wondering what she should do. She had just completed analyzing the annual performance of each of the 12 sales reps she supervised. While 8 of the 12 had made their quotas, 4 had not.

Mestousis was troubled because three of the four had not made their quotas last year either. At that time, she had met with each salesperson. They had discussed each person's performance in detail, going over the territory account by account for the larger accounts. All three salespeople had argued that their quotas were unrealistic.

Mestousis had reviewed her calculations. She had used the same criteria and indexes for potential in establishing all quotas. She was confident they had been determined correctly, but she knew she was going to hear the same arguments this year.

She was undecided as to what she should do when she met with each sales representative to go over the most recent performances. One option would be to let the three go. That would be consistent with how she had historically handled things when a salesperson had not made quota in two successive years. She was concerned though that such an action could lead to a discrimination suit being filed against her and the company because two of the reps in question were women and one was black. That represented two-thirds of all of the female reps in the company and the only black salesperson.

After deliberating, Mestousis decided not to let any of them go. Rather, she would meet with them again and discuss the situations, just like last year.

Do you

Approve _____

Somewhat approve _____

Somewhat disapprove _____

Disapprove _____

of Mary Mestousis's decision?

Problems with Quotas

There are many advantages to using quotas, but there are also some problems. For one thing, they sometimes prove to be a difficult comparative yardstick. See the "Ethical Issues" box for one example of the types of problems they can cause. Many sales are the result of several people. One salesperson may call on corporate headquarters and another on the plant where the equipment will be installed. Both may play important but different roles in securing the order. In such cases, it is hard to decide what share of the total sale should be allocated to each salesperson; thus, it is hard to decide how well the salesperson did in relation to quota. It is equally troublesome when a salesperson's influence is relatively minor in obtaining a sale. Finally, quotas can be costly to establish, particularly if they are to be done well.

Characteristics of a Good Quota Plan

For a quota to be effective, the quotas must be (1) attainable, (2) easy to understand, and (3) complete.

Quota level

There is a great deal of controversy regarding the level at which quotas should be set. Some argue that quotas should be set high so they can be achieved only with extraordinary effort. Although most salespeople may not reach their quotas, the argument is that they are spurred to greater effort than they would have expended in the absence of such a "carrot." Although perhaps intuitively appealing, high quotas can cause problems. They create irritation among salespeople. They can also cause salespeople and others in the organization to engage in undesirable behaviors to make their quotas. One of the main reasons cited for Sears' public relations nightmare with its auto centers several years ago was its unrealistic sales quotas, which caused employees to sell customers services they didn't need. Unrealistic sales quotas also caused its major-appliance and Allstate Insurance salespeople to engage in similar undesirable behaviors.[33] Similarly, unrealistic sales quotas at Dun & Bradstreet Corporation set off a chain of events, including lawsuits, that has hurt D&B for much of the past decade.[34]

The use of very high carrot quotas seems to be the exception rather than the rule. The prevailing philosophy is that quotas should be realistic. They should represent attainable goals that can be achieved with normal or reasonable, not Herculean, efforts. That seems to motivate most salespeople best.

To take advantage of the small percentage of salespeople who might be challenged more by high carrot quotas, firms can consider two-tier quota systems. For example, Ramtek Corporation, a pioneer in the color computer graphics business, devised a two-level quota system. Level 1 quotas are based on realistically attainable revenue targets. Level 2 quotas are set higher, and salespeople can secure considerably higher bonuses for meeting them. Ramtek allows salespeople to pick the level by which they want to be measured. However, those picking the higher level (about one in five) need to get their sales manager's approval so they do not take on more than they can handle and get discouraged.[35]

Quota complexity

Quotas should be not only realistic but also easy to understand. Complex quota plans may cause suspicion and mistrust among sales representatives and thereby discourage rather than motivate them. It helps when salespeople can be shown exactly how their quotas were derived. They are much more likely to accept quotas that are related to market potential when they can see the assumptions used in translating the potential estimate into sales goals.

Quotas should also be easy to understand definitionally. If a salesperson's quota is 50 calls on new accounts within a quarter, it is important for the representative to be told exactly what customers qualify as new accounts. Does a call on a customer who has not placed an order within the past year qualify as a new-account call? How about a company that has not placed an order within the past three years but before that was a steady customer? What about a call this quarter on an account that placed its first small order the previous quarter? Does the call qualify if an account makes only a partial payment? To avoid conflicts, the sales manager and all sales personnel must understand the quota and the conditions.

Quota items

A third desirable feature of a quota plan is that it is complete. It should cover the many criteria on which sales reps are to be judged. Thus, if all sales representatives are supposed to engage in new-account development, it is important to specify how much. Otherwise that activity will likely be neglected while the salesperson pursues volume and profit goals. Similarly, volume and profit goals should be adjusted to allow for the time the representative has to spend identifying and soliciting new accounts.

Carlisle Tire and Rubber, for example, develops quotas for each salesperson using both bottom-up and top-down sales forecasts as a basis. The bottom-up sales forecast requires each district manager to make a detailed, account-by-account analysis, which is the basis for establishing account sales objectives with specific plans and strategies for their achievement. The top-down forecast is prepared at the same time by the product management group, and any differences in the two forecasts are reconciled by the national sales manager, who then negotiates a final quota with each district manager in line with the company total. Salespeople receive 80 percent of their bonuses for achieving their sales

Exhibit 6.17   Quota-Setting Process

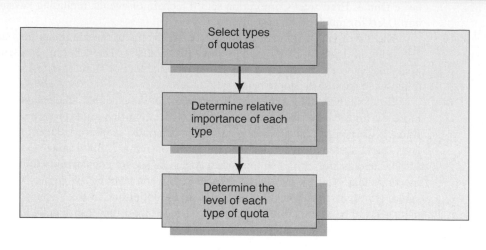

Source: Adapted from Thomas R. Wotruba, *Sales Management: Planning, Accomplishment, and Evaluation* (New York: Holt, Rinehart & Winston, 1971), p. 201.

volume quotas. "The remaining 20 percent can be earned through the completion of various nonsales quotas. These nonsales quotas are not standard but tailored to each district manager to encourage specific growth."[36]

THE QUOTA-SETTING PROCESS

Quota setting actually involves the three-step process shown in Exhibit 6.17.[37] First, the sales manager or someone else must decide on the types of quotas the firm will use. Next, the person must determine the relative importance of each type of quota. Finally, the sales manager needs to determine specific quota levels.

Select Types of Quotas

There are three basic types of quotas: (1) those emphasizing sales or some aspect of sales volume, (2) those that focus on the activities in which sales representatives are supposed to engage, and (3) those that examine financial criteria such as gross margin or contribution to overhead. Sales volume quotas are the most popular.[38] All types seemed to be used more by large firms than small firms (see Exhibit 6.18).

Sales volume

The popularity of quotas that emphasize dollar sales or some other aspect of sales volume is understandable. They can be related directly to market potential and thereby be made more credible. They are easily understood by those who must achieve them. They are consistent with what most salespeople envision their jobs to be—that is, to sell. Furthermore, they are consistent with the old adage, "Someone must sell something before the other functions of business can be brought to bear." The production, finance, and personnel functions depend on a certain amount of the product being sold. Sales volume quotas can be expressed in dollars, physical units, or points.

Exhibit 6.18 Firms That "Extensively Use" the Various Types of Quotas

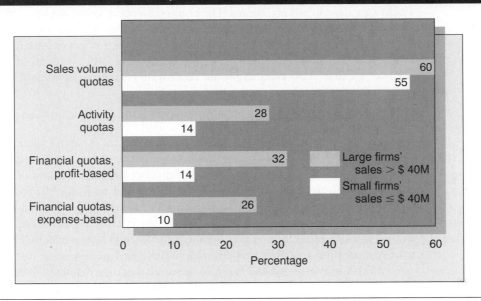

Source: Developed from Alan J. Dubinsky and Thomas E. Barry, "A Survey of Sales Management Practices," *Industrial Marketing Management* 11 (April 1982), pp. 133–41. For discussion of the factors considered when developing quotas, see David J. Good and Robert W. Stone, "How Sales Quotas Are Developed," *Industrial Marketing Management* 20 (February 1991), pp. 51–55.

Dollar quotas

Dollars provide a common measure for all products. This helps to reduce communication problems when each sales representative handles a variety of products. In such instances, establishing physical volume quotas for each product for each sales rep can be very complex.

Dollar volume quotas permit a more direct analysis of salespeople's expenses in relation to quota than other types of quotas. The ratio of expenses to sales for each salesperson can be calculated directly, and salespeople can be compared in terms of these expense ratios. Dollar volume quotas are also advantageous when sales reps have some discretion over price. Sales managers can see immediately whether they are using the discretion wisely or whether they are cutting prices so drastically that it cuts into profits. To accomplish the same kinds of analyses with physical volume quotas, it would be necessary to estimate the total dollars of targeted sales by assuming some average price per sale.

Physical volume quotas

Physical volume quotas express a salesperson's goals in some physical unit of measurement such as number of specific items, weight in pounds or tons, or some volume measure such as gallons.

Physical volume quotas are especially attractive when sales representatives handle only a few products. Thus, a sales quota for a salesperson who works for a chemical manufacturer might be expressed as so many gallons of toluene, whereas that for a cement manufacturer might be expressed as so many pounds of cement, and that for a steel sales rep as so many tons of carbon steel and so many tons of stainless.

Physical volume quotas are also attractive when prices fluctuate widely because of cyclical and competitive factors. In a price-intensive, competitive market, it may not be unusual for a normal $100 drum of chemicals to sell for $75. Whereas before the salesperson might have had to sell 500 barrels to reach the quota of $50,000, the sales rep would now have to sell 667 drums. The change, however, could not be controlled personally by the representative. Dollar quotas in such situations can demoralize salespeople.

Physical volume quotas are also attractive when unit prices are high. A dollar quota of $2 million, for example, might be psychologically overwhelming to a salesperson, whereas a quota of 20 units might not seem nearly so imposing even though each unit sells for $100,000.

Point quotas

Point quotas are another variation of sales volume quotas. A certain number of points are given for each dollar or unit sale of particular products. For example, each $100 of sales of product X might be worth three points; of product Y, two points; and of product Z, one point. Alternatively, each ton of steel tubing sold might be worth five points, while each ton of bar stock might be worth only two points. The total sales quota for the salesperson is expressed as the total number of points he or she is expected to achieve. The point system is typically used when a firm wants to emphasize certain products in the line. Those that are more profitable, for example, might be assigned more points.

Porter–Cable Machine Company, for instance, once used dollar volume quotas exclusively. On analysis, however, management found that sales personnel often attained most of their quotas through selling only one or two easy-to-sell products. Management initiated a program whereby Porter–Cable products were put into eight different categories according to their relative profitability. Then, individual point volume quotas were set for each product category, and bonus points were awarded for sales over quota in each category. Sales personnel were required to meet all the point volume quotas before becoming eligible for any bonus points. Furthermore, in appraising performance, management regarded a 150 percent total point volume attainment with four points as poorer than a 120 percent point volume attainment with five bonus points. This quota system led to the selling of a considerably more profitable mixture of products.[39]

Point quotas can also be used to promote selective emphases. New products might receive more points than old ones to encourage sales representatives to push them. A given dollar of sales to new accounts might be worth more points than the same level of sales to more established accounts. Point quota systems allow sales managers to design quota systems that promote certain desired goals; yet, point quotas can be easily understood by salespeople.

Activity

Activity quotas attempt to recognize the investment nature of a salesperson's efforts. For example, the letter to a prospect, the product demonstration, and the arrangement of a display may not produce an immediate sale. On the other hand, they may influence a future sale. If the quota system emphasizes only sales, however, salespeople may be inclined to neglect these activities. Left unchecked, sales volume quotas can become an obsession with salespeople and can result in a breakdown in control of other activities. Activity quotas provide such a counterbalance.

Activity quotas are directly related to factors that sales representatives can actually control. As David Fields, vice president of sales for Zellerbach, a distributor of paper products, says, "[Salespeople] can't do sales. [They] do activities that generate sales."[40] Although salespeople may be able to influence sales volume, they cannot control it. Economic conditions and competitive behavior may thwart the salesperson's best efforts. Yet salespeople can control the number of new accounts they call on, the number of ser-

Exhibit 6.19   Common Types of Activity Quotas

Number of
1. Calls on new accounts.
2. Letters to potential customers.
3. Proposals submitted.
4. Field demonstrations arranged.
5. Service calls made.
6. Equipment installations supervised.
7. Displays arranged.
8. Dealer sales meetings held.
9. Meetings and conventions attended.
10. Past-due accounts collected.

vice calls they make, the call reports they complete, and so on. Thus, it is reasonable to judge their performance on these activities. Furthermore, if these activities are important to the success of the company, it is reasonable to judge salespeople on whether their performance meets or exceeds these criteria.

Some common types of activity quotas are listed in Exhibit 6.19. Measuring a salesperson's efforts in each activity takes much effort. The number of proposals a salesperson develops or the number of demonstrations he or she arranges is not recorded in the normal accounting cycle. This information has to be developed by requiring salespeople to complete activity reports. This increases paperwork and represents time away from the sales reps' primary activity of face-to-face selling. Furthermore, since sales representatives complete the activity report themselves, there is opportunity for sloppiness and misrepresentation unless this function is closely supervised. The activity report reflects only the amount of effort expended on various activities; that the salesperson called on 20 new accounts in the period says nothing about the quality of these calls. They may have represented nothing more than a salesperson spending five ineffective, or perhaps even detrimental, minutes with a new customer.

All of these problems are reduced when a sales volume measure is used for quotas. The normal accounting cycle reveals the figures necessary to compare performance with the established standard. The amount of sales produced, although not perfect, is a somewhat direct measure of the quality of the effort expended on the client. A sales volume quota decreases the amount of paperwork necessary and increases the amount of time sales representatives have available for selling.

Financial

Financial quotas make salespeople conscious of the cost and profile implications of what they sell. Being human, sales representatives left to their own devices often take the easy way out. They emphasize products that are easiest to sell or concentrate on customers with whom they feel most comfortable. Unfortunately, these products may be costly to produce and have a lower-than-average return. Similarly, the customers with whom the representative feels comfortable may not purchase much and may be less profitable than other potential accounts. Financial quotas attempt to make salespeople aware of these conditions so that they direct their efforts to more profitable products and customers.

Financial quotas are often stated in terms of direct selling expenses, gross margin, or net profit. They are most applicable when the firm's market penetration approaches saturation levels. In such instances, it is hard to increase sales or market share, and an emphasis on selling efficiency and cost control becomes a logical mechanism for increasing profit.

Expense quotas

A key to improving profits is to control the field selling expenses incurred in generating a given level of sales. Expense quotas are typically stated as a certain percentage of sales, although they are sometimes expressed in absolute dollar amounts.

Although expense quotas force sales representatives to recognize the costs of what they are doing and to be aware of their responsibilities for controlling expenses, they can also have dysfunctional effects. They may cause salespeople to do other than what they should because they are worried about expenses. Instead of calling four times in a quarter, for example, the salesperson may call only twice because he or she believes the chances for purchase are low. Thus, he or she loses the opportunity to secure a big equipment purchase. Field sales expenses, on the other hand, contribute substantially to the difference in profitability of firms in the same industry, and their control is important.

Gross margin quotas

Gross margin quotas are useful when there are significant differences in gross margins by product, since they can be set so salespeople concentrate on items with higher returns. Unfortunately, gross margin quotas are somewhat difficult to administer. Some firms simply do not wish to disclose production cost information to sales representatives. Even among those that do, it is hard for salespeople to tell how they are doing with respect to their own gross margin quotas at any given time, and thus the quotas do not produce the desired motivation effects.

Margin information is typically not provided in the normal accounting cycle by a unit of analysis so small as a salesperson. At the same time, the same objective can be accomplished with a well-designed point quota system. Products that bear higher gross margins can simply carry more points. Point quota systems are much easier for salespeople to understand and thereby make it easier for them to monitor their progress.

Net profit quotas

Some managers believe net profit quotas are the ultimate because they emphasize what the selling effort should be—profitable sales volume and not sales volume for its own sake. Net profit quotas are tied directly to a major goal of top management. Also, net profit quotas can be superior to gross margin quotas when products with high gross margins require extensive effort and thereby produce higher field selling expenses and lower net profit.

Net profit quotas also have some disadvantages. First, they are harder than the other types for salespeople to understand, making it difficult for them to monitor their progress. The net profit they produce depends on the product mix they sell, the margins on these products, and the expenses they incur. At any given time, it is difficult for sales representatives to determine how they are doing. This can prove frustrating and stifle motivation.

Second, net profit quota schemes are difficult to administer. Again, the information required to operate them—net profit produced by a given salesperson in a given period—is not produced in the normal accounting cycle in most firms. It can be acquired, but it is typically very expensive to do so.

Finally, the profit a salesperson produces is affected by many factors beyond his or her control—competitive reaction, economic conditions, and the firm's willingness to ne-

Exhibit 6.20 Performance Evaluation with Multiple Quotas

Salesperson/Quota Basis	Quota	Actual	Percentage of Quota	Weight	Percentage of Quota × Weight
Leslie Curtain:					
Sales volume	$150,000	$150,000	100.0%	3	300.0%
New account calls	22	20	91.0	1	91.0
Gross margin	$ 50,000	$ 40,000	80.0	2	160.0
Average			90.3		91.8
David Michael:					
Sales volume	$200,000	$180,000	90.0	3	270.0
New account calls	20	24	120.0	1	120.0
Gross margin	$ 66,000	$ 70,000	106.1	2	212.2
Average			105.4		100.4
Carol Suchomel:					
Sales volume	$170,000	$160,000	94.0	3	282.0
New account calls	18	21	117.0	1	117.0
Gross margin	$ 56,000	$ 60,000	107.1	2	214.2
Average			106.0		102.2

gotiate on price, for example. Some would argue that it is unreasonable to hold the individual salesperson responsible for all these external influences.

Determine Relative Importance of Each Type

As the preceding discussion indicates, each main type of quota system has advantages and disadvantages. In some situations, the firm may believe the advantages of one scheme outweigh the disadvantages and so may use it without even considering other options. Although quota schemes with a single basis can work well in relatively stable situations, they can prove disastrous in dynamic environments. For example, a sales volume quota may work well for an established product with an established market. That same scheme, however, can lead to an overconcentration of calls on existing accounts and the neglect of new accounts with new products for which new uses are being discovered. In such instances, the sales manager may want to use a combination of criteria that produces the best balance of goals for each salesperson. Furthermore, the conditions from territory to territory and from customer to customer may be different, and the sales manager might wish to reflect such differences in the quota plan. A key question that must be addressed is how the various quotas should be combined to produce a single criterion by which performance can be evaluated.

The problem is illustrated in Exhibit 6.20. The example assumes there are three criteria, one of each of the three main types, on which each salesperson should be evaluated. Note that each sales rep performed best with respect to a single criterion. Thus, if sales volume quota attainment was emphasized, Curtain would be considered the top salesperson. She is the only one who made her sales volume quota. On the other hand, if the activity measure, number of new account calls, was emphasized, Michael would be rated best. Suchomel would be rated best if the emphasis was on the financial measure, gross margin. The example illustrates Finagle's rule of management, which holds "that if you look long enough, you can find a ratio which makes any performer look good—or bad."[41] Rather than simply "looking hard enough" and becoming confused as to who truly performed best, management needs some objective mechanism for determining which representatives satisfied their quota responsibilities.

Simple average

One way is simply to average the ratios reflecting percentage of quota achieved. Suchomel performed best using the simple average; her performance was 106.0 percent of quota, while Michael's was 105.4 percent, and Curtain's was 90.3 percent.

One problem with the simple average is that it weights all three performance criteria equally when they might not be equally important to the firm. While the firm may want to emphasize the number of new-account calls a salesperson makes by including it in the quota system, for example, it may not want to place as much emphasis on this activity as it does on actual sales volume produced by the salesperson.

Weighted average

In situations where the firm may want to give unequal emphasis to the different quota bases, a linear combination can provide a useful summary measure of each representative's overall performance. A linear combination is a weighted average of the results on the individual dimensions, where the weights reflect the importance of each component to management. In the example in Exhibit 6.20, a weight of 3 was assigned to sales volume (SV), a weight of 2 to gross margin (GM), and a weight of 1 to new account calls (C). Thus, the weighted average for overall performance (OP) is

$$OP = \frac{3SV + 1C + 2GM}{6}$$

The sum is divided by the sum of the weights, 6, to reduce the weighted combination to a basis of 100. To use the weighted criterion, Suchomel performed best and Curtain worst. Michael was almost right on target, with an aggregate index of 100.4 versus a 100.0 if he had simply met quota.

Although the weights 3, 2, and 1 were used in the example, other weights could be used. The weights should reflect the importance of performance on each component. The weights can be determined in a number of ways. They might simply be set by the sales manager using his or her own best judgment. They might reflect the collective opinion of a group of top managers, or they might be based on some objective analysis of the importance of each component to the firm's long-run goals. One attractive feature of the linear combination as a measure of overall performance versus quota is that it allows differential weights to reflect unique territory or customer differences. Another advantage is that it can be easily explained to salespeople.

Determine the Level of Each Type

The final stage in determining the quota plan assigned to each marketing unit is to decide the level for each type of quota. In establishing these levels, the sales manager must balance a number of factors, including the potential available in the territory, the impact of the quota level on the salesperson's motivation, the long-term objectives of the company, and the impact on short-term profitability. When discussing quota levels, it is useful to separate sales volume, activity, and financial quotas.

Sales volume quotas

As mentioned, sales volume quotas are the most commonly used. Unfortunately, some firms do not use them very intelligently.

Using historical sales.   Some firms, for example, simply set sales volume quotas on the basis of past sales. Each marketing unit is exhorted to "beat last year's sales." Sometimes the standard is the average of sales in the territory over some past time period—five years, for example. Sometimes the admonition is expressed more concretely. If the company's sales forecast suggests a 7 percent sales increase this year, each marketing unit is assigned a quota 7 percent higher than last year's or the average of the past five years' sales.

The most attractive feature of this quota-setting scheme is that it is easy to administer. One does not have to engage in an extensive analysis to determine what the quotas should be. This makes it inexpensive to use. Also, salespeople readily understand it.

Unfortunately, such schemes forgo many potential advantages of using sales volume quotas. For one thing, such quotas ignore current conditions. A territory may be rapidly growing, and the influx of new potential customers could justify a much larger increase than the 7 percent established by the overall company's sales forecast. Alternatively, the territory might be so intensely competitive or depressed that any increase in the assigned sales quota is not justified.

A quota based solely on past sales ignores territory potentials and provides a poor yardstick for evaluating individual sales reps. Two salespeople, for example, might each have generated $300,000 in sales last year. It clearly makes a difference in what one can expect from each of them this year if the market potential in one territory is $500,000 while that in the other is $1 million. The firm may be forgoing tremendous market opportunities simply because it is unaware of them.

A quota based solely on past years' sales can also demoralize salespeople and cause undesirable behaviors. For example, a salesperson who has realized quota for one year may be tempted to delay placing orders secured at the end of the year until the new accounting cycle begins. This accomplishes two things: It makes his or her quota for the next year lower, and it gives him or her a start on satisfying that quota.

Although sales quotas should not be based solely on sales in prior years, historic sales should be considered when quotas are established. Historic sales provide some indication of how competitive a firm is within a territory. By comparing historic sales with potential sales, one can localize trouble spots and determine the problem and what action should be taken.

Using territory potential.   Territory potentials provide a useful start for establishing quotas for territory sales volume. However, the firm should not adhere strictly to a formula relating quota to potential, but it should attempt to reflect the special situations within each territory. For example, Haworth, Inc., an office equipment marketer, develops its territory quotas by explicitly considering its three biggest customer industries in each local market. When developing quotas for its Boston, New York, Philadelphia, and Washington, D.C., offices, for instance, it takes special note of what is happening to the insurance industry because the Northeast is such a hotbed of insurance.[42]

Determining how to set territory quotas that reflect the special situations within each territory is often difficult. On one hand, the sales representative who serves the territory should be involved in setting the territory quota, because he or she should have the most intimate knowledge of the conditions in the territory. On the other hand, since the representative will be affected by the quota established, he or she may not be impartial. One might expect sales representatives to understate potential to generate lower, easier-to-reach quotas.

Some firms have resolved the problem of potential bias when salespeople are used to help set their own quotas by tying their compensation into the process. For example, IBM of Brazil established a system that considers territory potential differences and company objectives for the territory. It also encourages good forecasts by rewarding sales representatives according to how close their actual results are to the company's objectives. The system rewards good planning because it simultaneously incorporates the company objectives (O), a salesperson's forecast (F), and the results the salesperson actually achieves (A) in a compensation grid. Exhibit 6.21 describes how the system works. The system seems to work best when the salespeople possess more information about their own prospects than central office personnel and when significant costs are linked to under- and overfulfillment of sales forecasts.[43]

Activity quotas

The levels for activity quotas are most likely to be set according to the territory conditions. They require a detailed analysis of the work required to cover the territory effectively. Activity quotas are affected by the size of the territory and by the number of accounts and prospects the salesperson is expected to call on. The size of the representative's customers can also make a difference, as can their purchasing patterns. These factors affect the number of times the salesperson needs to call on them in the period, the number of service calls or calls to demonstrate the use of the firm's equipment he or she must make, and so on.

The inputs for activity quotas can come from at least three sources: (1) discussions between the sales representative serving the territory and the sales manager, (2) the salesperson's reports, and (3) marketing research.

The sales manager and territory salesperson can use past experience as a basis for determining what activities are necessary to cover the territory effectively. Such a discussion typically revolves around key accounts and what needs to be done to serve them better. It may mean more frequent calls or fewer calls. The specification for a potential account might be simply to bid on three equipment installations during the next year. These assessments are then combined with estimates of other activities—for example, traveling—to determine the total activity level in the territory, from which a judgment can be made as to whether that level is reasonable. If not, some modification is warranted.

The iterative process ceases when reasonable activity levels have been determined. They must be reasonable in the sense of being consistent with the objectives of the firm for the territory and with the time available from the salesperson.

Sometimes activity quotas can be established from salespeople's reports. Suppose, for example, one main duty of field representatives is erecting displays in retail outlets. An analysis of historic call reports can often indicate how long it takes to set up a display on average and for various sizes of displays. Suppose further that different sizes of accounts typically receive differently sized displays. It is then relatively easy to determine the number of displays and the time required to erect them by analyzing the number of accounts of each class size in the salesperson's territory.

The firm might also rely on marketing research to determine activity level quotas. The firm might systematically vary the number of calls per account to determine the optimal number to be made on each account in any time period. Alternatively, it might study past bid behavior to establish rules as to when the firm should bid on some equipment request.

Financial quotas

The levels of financial quotas are typically set to reflect the financial goals of the firm. For example, a firm may want a particular net profit or gross margin on all sales in a territory. Suppose the potential for a representative is basically concentrated on two products—one with a gross margin of 30 percent and one with a gross margin of 40 percent. The sales manager could shift the relative attention given to one versus the other by assigning a gross margin goal of 37 percent. The salesperson would then have to sell a greater proportion of the products with 40 percent margin to achieve that goal than if the goal were 34 percent.

Exhibit 6.21   Systems Used by IBM of Brazil to Reduce Salesperson Bias When Helping to Set Own Quotas

After receiving his objective, *O,* a salesman must turn in his forecast, *F; F* divided by *O* determines the column in which the salesman's bonus percentage will fall. For instance, the 1.0 column represents a forecast equal to the quota, the 0.5 column means the forecast is half the objective, and the 1.5 column indicates a forecast 50 percent larger than the objective. The letter *A* stands for actual sales results. Thus, *A* divided by *O* and multiplied by 100 is the percentage of the objective achieved by the salesperson; 100 percent means full achievement of the company's objective, not of the salesperson's forecast.

Now let us see how it works. John sells photographic equipment. His quota is 500 cameras. Let us assume that John fully agrees to his quota and turns in a 500-units forecast. (On the grid, *F/O* equals 1.0.) If John sells 500 cameras, he makes 100 percent of his objective and is entitled to 120 percent of his bonus. In other words, he gets a 20 percent premium for his good planning capability. How much that represents in dollars depends on John's personal value, namely, his experience, time with the company, and merit.

If John sells 750 cameras, which is 150 percent of his objective, he is entitled to 150 percent of his bonus; the more he sells, the more he earns. But now John realizes that if his forecast had been 750 instead of 500 units (1.5 on the grid), then he would have received 180 percent of his bonus instead of 150 percent. Bad planning on his part has deprived him of a good chunk of money. If John had sold 250 units, half of his objective, he would have earned just 30 percent of his incentive. Here again, John sees

that it would have been better to have forecasted 250 instead of 500, for his earnings would have been 60 percent.

In other words, the best earnings lie in the diagonal that goes down from left to right in the grid. For a given result, *A,* the more precise John's forecast is, the higher his earnings. But John will always earn most if his forecast is perfect.

After being introduced to the grid, John goes back to study his territory. This time he does not want to return a faulty forecast—his earnings are at stake. He may still complain that the objective set up by his manager is too high—there is no solution to that—but for the first time he can enhance his earnings through a good work plan. If he comes in with a low forecast, he may damage his earnings in exchange for safety. On the other hand, a high forecast may plunge him into trouble if his sales are too low. John understands that he must be precise. This is exactly what his manager is waiting for.

From that moment on, John becomes committed to the number he forecasts. The grid tells him his sales should be equal to or higher than the forecast in order for his earnings to increase. Soon, John sees that because of the new interactive approach, the headquarters staff begins to really understand the market and sets sales objectives that approach his own forecast. Total accuracy will never happen, but for practical purposes the three main objectives of the system—sales volume, payment for performance, and good field information for planning—will be brought about.

F/O (Forecast Divided by Objectives)

		0	0.5	1.0	1.5	2.0	2.5	3.0	3.5	4.0	4.5	5.0
A/O × 100	0	—	—	—	—	—	—	—	—	—	—	—
(actual results	50	30	60	30	—	—	—	—	—	—	—	—
divided by	100	60	90	120	90	60	30	—	—	—	—	—
objective, then	150	90	120	150	180	150	120	90	60	30	—	—
multiplied	200	120	150	180	210	240	210	180	150	120	90	60
by 100)	250	150	180	210	240	270	300	270	240	210	180	150
	300	180	210	240	270	300	330	360	330	300	270	240
	350	210	240	270	300	330	360	390	420	390	360	330
	400	240	270	300	330	360	390	420	450	480	450	420
	450	270	300	330	360	390	420	450	480	510	540	510
	500	300	330	360	390	420	450	480	510	540	570	600

Calculation of grid numbers:
   If *F* equal to *A,* then $OFA = 120 \times FO$
   If *F* smaller than *A,* then $OFA = 60 \times (AF)/O$
   If *F* bigger than *A,* then $OFA = 60 \times (3AF)/O$

A field selling expense quota may be based on last year's ratio of field selling expenses to sales. The sales manager might analyze these ratios across territories and establish a target for the territory given the potential in the territory. Although it is tempting to use the historic average across territories as the target, the unique conditions of the territory should be considered. Perhaps the field selling expense target should be less than the average because of the geographic concentration of customers. Perhaps it should be higher than average because of the intense competition in the territory. Perhaps the accounts require more entertaining at first-class restaurants and social events if the firm is going to have any chance of remaining competitive.

SUMMARY

This chapter reviewed the analysis of market opportunity, a pivotal ingredient in the design of marketing plans in general and sales plans in particular. Market opportunity analysis involved (1) estimation of market potential or the expected sales of a commodity by the entire industry serving the market during a stated period, (2) estimation of sales potential or the share likely to be realized by the company, and (3) preparation of the sales forecast or the estimate of sales for a specified future period under an assumed marketing plan. The difference between potential estimates and forecasts is that potential estimates reflect maximum demand under ideal conditions, while a forecast reflects a specific marketing plan. Thus, potential reflects opportunities while a forecast reflects expectations. Finally, the chapter examined the last major element in sales management planning—establishing sales quotas. A sales quota is the sales goal assigned to a marketing unit in a specified period.

The notions of potential and forecast are conceptually distinct, but they become blurred when estimates of demand are actually developed as the various techniques available for estimating demand treat the proposed marketing effort differently. Although all are called sales forecasting methods, some ignore the marketing plan when estimates are developed, while others incorporate the proposed effort directly.

The main methods for preparing sales forecasts are users' expectations, sales force composite, jury of executive opinion, market test, time series analysis, and statistical demand analysis. The users' expectations method is also known as the buyers' intentions method because it relies on answers from customers regarding their expected consumption or purchases of the product. The sales force composite method requires estimates of expected sales from each member of the sales force. These estimates are typically discussed, revised, and then pooled to form estimates for other levels of the sales organization hierarchy—for example, salesperson, branch, region, district, and overall. The jury of executive or expert opinion polls top executives of the company for their assessment of sales possibilities for the coming period. The forecast may be developed using face-to-face discussion or through anonymous interaction using Delphi procedures, in which each person in the group submits a forecast to the group coordinator. The coordinator prepares a summary of these estimates, which is distributed to all those who submit forecasts. They then have the opportunity to revise their estimates. The process continues until a reasonable consensus is reached. The market test is a controlled experiment in which the product is placed in several representative cities where its performance is monitored; the results are then projected to the area in which the firm operates. Time series analysis relies on the analysis of historical sales data to isolate the underlying pattern and the use of that pattern to predict the future. Statistical demand analysis rests on determining the relationship between sales and the important factors affecting sales. That relationship is then used to forecast the future.

Evidence indicates that the subjective methods (particularly the jury of executive opinion and the sales force composite) are currently used more than the quantitative techniques (time series and statistical demand analysis). The evidence also indicates that no method is superior under all conditions and that greater forecast accuracy can be achieved by systematically combining forecasts developed by different schemes.

It is quite common to divide the total estimate of demand among the geographic areas the company serves. Typically this is done using a market factor or a market index. A market factor is a feature or characteristic in a market that is related to the demand for the product. An often-used market factor for estimating territory demand for industrial goods, for example, is the number of employees in each of several industries (denoted by their SIC codes) the company serves. A market index is a mathematical expression that combines two or more market factors into a numerical index. The buying power index, for example, which combines income, population, and retail sales in an area into a single number, is often used to estimate territory potentials for frequently purchased, low-priced consumer goods.

Sales quotas may be expressed in the aggregate or broken down by customers and products. The full set of quota assignments is called the quota plan. Sales quotas are used to motivate salespeople, evaluate their performance, and control their efforts. For a quota plan to produce its potential benefits, the quotas must be attainable with normal effort, easy to understand, and complete.

Setting quotas involves a three-step process. First, the sales manager must decide on the types of quotas the firm will use. This choice entails determining whether the firm will use quotas that emphasize (1)

sales or some aspect of sales volume, (2) the activities in which salespeople are supposed to engage, or (3) financial criteria such as gross margin or contribution to overhead. These are known as sales volume, activity, and financial quotas, respectively. Typically, firms use some combination of these quotas rather than relying exclusively on one type because each has advantages and disadvantages.

The second step in the process involves specifying the relative importance of each type of quota. Then most firms seek some mechanism for combining the individual quotas into a single summary measure that serves as the standard for each representative's performance. Often a linear combination or weighted average is used in which the weights reflect the importance of each component to management. The final step in determining the quotas assigned to each marketing unit is to determine the level at which each type of quota is to be set. In establishing these levels, the sales manager must balance a number of factors, including the potential available in the territory, the impact of the quota level on the salesperson's motivation, the long-term objectives of the company, and the impact on short-term profitability.

DISCUSSION QUESTIONS

1. A common problem faced by those responsible for making sales forecasts is "selling" the predictions to others such as the vice presidents of marketing, production, and human resources, and to the CEO or the CFO. These parties hesitate to use forecasts that can have major implications, especially if they are wrong, on their functional area. What can those responsible for sales forecasting do to sell their results to management? What forecasting guidelines should be followed to improve the predictions?

2. A survey of local business firms to determine how they forecast sales will produce a variety of answers. Some will claim they do not use any formal techniques to forecast sales. You know they must be using some approach, no matter how loosely defined. How do you know the business firm is making a sales forecast? What are the implications of not making a sales forecast?

3. For the following products, indicate what factor(s) you would use to estimate market potential:

   a. Yoplait yogurt
   b. Rolex watches

   c. IBM Aptiva personal computers
   d. Power riding lawnmowers
   e. Ektelon racquetball racquets
   f. Nicole Miller designer ties
   g. SWATCH watches
   h. Tylenol
   i. Mary Kay cosmetics

4. To estimate market potential for the garden tractor division of the M–F Implement Co., Mark Haynes, the statistician, estimated the following relationship using multiple regression analyses:

$$Y = a + b_1X_1 + b_2X_2 + b_3X_3 + b_4X_4$$

where
Y = unit sales of U.S. garden tractors
X_1 = number of single-family homes
X_2 = disposable personal income
X_3 = index of food prices
X_4 = family size.

Using data for 1992–99, $R^2 = 65$ was obtained. Should this method be used to predict market potential?

5. A new cake mix is to be introduced by Miracle Foods. To develop territory potentials, a corollary index has been proposed. The index contains several factors, such as income, population, and retail food sales. Can you justify these factors? Does it make sense to use retail food sales, which means cake sales are a function of food sales?

6. Once a quarter, every six months, or annually, each salesperson should estimate the buying potential of each account for each major product or product line. Such a request usually causes the sales force to panic. What goals are likely to be achieved by having the sales force participate in sales forecasting?

EXPERIENTIAL APPLICATIONS

1. Select two companies that are in different businesses. For example, pick a firm that provides services and another that manufactures products. Interview the appropriate executives in each business and determine how they forecast sales. Compare and contrast your findings from each business.

2. Select a company that is publicly traded on the stock market. Using annual reports or computer databases, develop a forecasting model for predicting the company's total sales. Eliminate the last year of sales from your database and make a forecast for that period. For example, if your database includes sales for 1998, eliminate the 1998 data to determine how well your forecasting model predicts sales for 1999. Discuss the predictive power of your model. Does it accurately predict sales? Why?

INTERNET EXERCISES

1. You are the leading economist for one of the leading airlines. It is your job to estimate demand for business travelers over the next 12 months. Go the Web site of the U.S. Bureau of the Census (*www.census.gov*). Click on the icon marked Current Economic Indicators. What information found in this area could be helpful for you in estimating the number of business travelers? Search through the rest of the Bureau of the Census Web site. What other information is available that could be useful in your job?

APPLICATION QUESTIONS

A1. The Crystal Pure Bottled Water Company has experienced explosive growth in recent years, unlike the steady trend in earlier years. What would you suggest as a forecasting technique using the following sales data?

Year	Sales	Year	Sales
1983	$2,843	1991	$10,054
1984	3,523	1992	11,256
1985	4,507	1993	16,074
1986	5,576	1994	19,831
1987	6,462	1995	28,764
1988	7,115	1996	34,093
1989	7,928	1997	39,420
1990	9,371	1998	47,325

A2. The Flambeau Corporation manufactures plastic parts for a variety of customers. Past attempts at sales forecasting have not met with success. Sales patterns display considerable fluctuations. Using the following data, develop a sales forecast for the first quarter of 2000.

	1995	1996	1997	1998	1999
Quarter 1	202	367	576	520	607
Quarter 2	75	158	278	295	309
Quarter 3	157	287	353	326	437
Quarter 4	476	659	901	1007	988

A3. The APCO Division manufactures electric motors used by the parent company, a manufacturer of small household appliances. To plan production for 2000, the sales manager must develop a forecast for one of the models.

The following data reflect monthly sales of the product using the particular model. What does the database reveal?

Month	1996	1997	1998	1999
January	68.3	88.9	104.9	156.9
February	107.1	97.9	155.8	228.4
March	107.3	128.9	172.1	308.7
April	69.7	113.8	180.8	198.1
May	78.5	114.2	192.9	281.0
June	127.7	78.0	246.4	272.8
July	151.1	151.3	245.3	225.5
August	187.7	133.5	227.9	194.2
September	157.9	159.7	224.2	348.0
October	142.2	201.8	209.4	308.7
November	141.1	115.9	245.4	315.7
December	142.7	134.5	314.7	306.0

A4. RapidStream, manufacturer of aerodynamic mobile homes, wants to test two different moving average approaches: a three-month versus a five-month approach. Which method provides the more accurate forecast?

Month	1995	1996	1997	1998	1999
January	15.9	13.9	18.2	20.0	18.6
February	17.4	17.3	19.7	22.2	10.7
March	21.6	22.1	25.4	25.6	24.0
April	24.1	22.3	25.1	25.8	26.2
May	22.9	21.9	26.9	29.0	28.0
June	23.1	23.7	29.5	27.8	25.1
July	21.8	19.5	23.4	24.6	24.3
August	22.4	22.3	30.2	30.0	27.7
September	21.6	21.3	28.1	24.4	24.5
October	20.3	20.4	26.9	27.7	27.7
November	15.7	18.9	23.5	21.9	20.9
December	14.2	16.0	18.8	16.6	16.9

A5. The management of the Farnsworth Corporation, specialists in automobile detailing, wants to expand the number of franchises, currently 10, into new market areas. Management strongly believes sales are related to household income and population over 25 years. Sales for the 10 metropolitan areas along with associated household income and population over 25 years are:

Area	Farnsworth Sales (FS)	Household Income ($000) (HI)	Population over 25 (000) (PO)
1	$185,792	$23,406	133.17
2	85,643	19,215	110.86
3	97,101	20,374	68.04
4	100,249	16,107	99.59
5	527,817	23,432	289.52
6	403,916	19,426	339.98
7	78,283	18,742	89.53
8	188,756	18,553	155.78
9	329,531	21,953	248.95
10	91,944	16,358	102.13

a. Calculate estimates for the Farnsworth sales model

$$FS = b_0 + b_1(HI) + b_2(PO).$$

b. Farnsworth is considering establishing a franchise in a new location that has a population over 25 of 128.07 and household income of $23,175. Approximately how much sales can Farnsworth expect?

A6. The number of orders received at Grainger Wholesale for the last four months is presented below:

Month	Number of Orders Received
March	19
April	31
May	27
June	29

Forecast the number of orders for July using simple exponential smoothing with a smoothing constant of 0.1. (You have to assume April's forecast was 21.)

SUGGESTED READINGS

Darmon, Rene Y., "Selecting Appropriate Sales Quota Plan Structures and Quota-Setting Procedures," *The Journal of Personal Selling and Sales Management* (Winter 1997), pp. 1–16.

Dubinsky, Alan J., and Thomas E. Barry. "A Survey of Sales Management Practices," *Industrial Marketing Management* 11 (April 1982), pp. 133–41.

Georgoff, David M., and Robert Murdick, "Manager's Guide to Forecasting," *Harvard Business Review* 64 (January–February 1986), pp. 110–20.

Good, David J., and Robert W. Stone. "How Sales Quotas Are Developed," *Industrial Marketing Management* 20 (February 1991), pp. 51–55.

Makridakis, Spyros, *Handbook of Forecasting: A Manager's Guide,* 2d ed. New York: John Wiley & Sons, 1987.

7 Sales Territories

SAFEGUARDING THE BUSINESS . . . ANALYZING YOUR SALES TERRITORIES

In the highly competitive sales environment of the 21st century the need to monitor and evaluate sales territories has never been more important. Ralph Rothfelder, president of Mapping Analytics, a consulting firm, suggests that sales managers should evaluate their territories at least annually and recommends two to four times a year. "[Sales managers] ought to look at how the territories are performing. Is [performance] because of the reasons they expect." An ongoing process of territory analysis can prevent problems and identify new opportunities.

Edward Hu, senior territory manager for AT&T's consumer direct sales organization in the Northeast/Atlantic region, manages 100 salespeople divided into sales teams in New York City. He makes it a point to review the territories under his control four times a year. He notes, "Sales organizations are very numbers oriented. If you can't achieve your goals in a territory, you need to change." Hu believes that evaluating territories on a regular basis enables him to spot a potential problem before it affects yearly targeted goals.

Assisting Hu in his territory analysis is AT&T's huge database that provides a plethora of information on each territory including the number of current and former AT&T customers in each ZIP code. Hu indicates that kind of information is extremely important to his salespeople. "That's crucial information that helps us assign territories because we all have sales quotas and budgets that we have to meet."

So what if an analysis reveals territory realignment is required? Rothfelder advises that the first step in territory analysis is ascertaining each territory's potential. He notes, "If you have a salesperson who breaks quota every year but isn't even tapping the territory's potential that's when you go and evaluate territories." Of course, the opposite could also be true. A salesperson may not be meeting quota goals even if an assessment of the territory's potential indicates he/she is getting the maximum business from that territory.

Matching a salesperson to a territory is a critical part of the process. All territories, like salespeople, are not created the same. While it is important to maximize the geographic efficiency of each territory, it is equally important to maximize the fit of each salesperson to each territory.

Source: "Protecting Your Turf," *Sales and Marketing Management* (September 1997), p. 90. Visit AT&T at its Web site, *www.att.com.*

LEARNING OBJECTIVES

Designing individual sales territories is a critical task for the sales manager because it can have a significant influence on sales, profitability, and even customer satisfaction. When territories are effective and efficiently created and managed the results can be impressive. Territory design is a complicated process made up of a number of important decisions. The changing sales environment has created new challenges as sales managers seek to maximize the size of the territory (by customer, geography, or some other characteristic) while at the same time providing adequate customer coverage and attention.

After reading this chapter, you should be able to:

- Understand the importance of sales territories.
- Determine the optimal sales force size.
- Understand the sales territory design process.

As the introductory scenario suggests, the number of salespeople and the design of the individual sales territories can have important sales and profit implications for firms. Poorly designed territories can increase the cost of doing business and produce other negative consequences. These impacts are reviewed in the first part of this chapter. The remainder of the chapter looks at how a sales manager can determine how many sales territories the firm needs and what each territory should be like.

THE NEED FOR SALES TERRITORIES

A sales territory is a group of present and potential customers assigned to a salesperson, branch, dealer, or distributor for a given period. The key word in this definition is *customers.* "Good" sales territories are made up of customers who have money to spend and the willingness to spend it.

While the key to sales territory design is customers, geographical boundaries determine territories in many firms. The salesperson might be assigned the state of Pennsylvania or the city of Philadelphia because geographically defined territories yield certain advantages, as we will discuss. There are exceptions, though, when firms are unlikely to realize advantages from geographic territories.

When the firm is small or just getting started, for example, management can plan and control the sales operation without using territories. As a firm grows and its markets expand geographically, the advantages of geographically defined sales territories become clearer.

Sometimes firms forgo geographic territories when their products are highly technical and sophisticated, choosing instead to rely on product specialists. Rather than using salespeople who might not be able to answer the customer's technical questions, the firm uses technical specialists who have the necessary expertise. The disadvantage of this scheme is that several field salespeople might call on the same account. An alternative is to have a single salesperson responsible for the account, and the salesperson can call in home-office technical specialists when needed.

Sales territories also are not geographically specified when personal relationships and friendships have a bearing on the sale, such as with the sale of securities or real estate. It would be dysfunctional to tell a customer that he or she had to deal with a salesperson other than the one the customer knew and liked.

Other than these exceptions, geographically defined sales territories are the norm in most companies, and sales territory design is one of the most critical decisions for sales managers. The design of sales territories can affect sales force morale, the firm's ability to serve the market, and the firm's ability to evaluate and control the selling effort.

Sales Force Morale

A salesperson's territory can dramatically influence the individual's interest and morale. While companies must adequately cover their accounts, salespeople must also have the opportunity to earn an adequate living. Obviously, a salesperson's territory can have great influence on his or her success. Few salespeople will be content with what they consider to be inferior assignments while their colleagues can make more money with less effort because of superior territories. In short, unequal sales territories are a prime cause of poor morale.

Just as poor sales territory design can hurt morale, good territory design can improve it. There are advantages for salespeople who have their own territories; in some ways, they are in business for themselves. Since they have responsibility for the accounts in their district, they can take pride in what their customers buy and how their customers are served.

Clearly defined territories lead to clarified responsibilities. Sales reps can more readily appreciate the goals assigned them and can better visualize the effort necessary to achieve those goals. Delineating responsibilities by territories can reduce conflicts among salespeople over who is responsible for a given account and who is entitled to the commission from the sales to a particular customer. If disputes arise, as they always do when customers transact business in more than one territory, they can be more amicably settled when sales territories are clearly defined. Many firms have very standard divisions; for example, half the commission goes to the sales representative serving the account's national office and half goes to the representative serving the plant to which the merchandise is shipped. Salespeople understand these ground rules. Although the home office may have no influence on a particular sale, it may be very important in another. Thus, salespeople can appreciate the necessity and desirability of such division of compensation.

Market Coverage

Soundly designed sales territories can improve how the market is served. For example, the Variable Annuity Life Insurance Company was able to realize savings of $8.8 million by redesigning its sales territories.[1]

It is much easier to pinpoint customers and prospects and to determine who should call on them and how often when the market is geographically divided than when the market is considered a large aggregate of potential accounts. Salespeople who are restricted to a geographic area are more likely to get more out of that territory than when they can roam at will. Instead of simply skimming the cream off the top, they are more likely to develop small accounts that have the potential to become important accounts. When sales territories are designed to force such effort, salespeople cannot meet their performance goals calling on only "easy accounts."

Customer service can also be improved with properly designed sales territories. Because sales reps call on the accounts in their territory on a regular basis, they can develop in-depth understanding of their customers' problems and needs. They can better anticipate products that will help the customer. They also understand the account better and learn who is involved in the purchasing decision. This helps the representative sell more effectively and service the account better, thereby producing greater long-term customer satisfaction.

Good territory design allows better integration of the personal selling effort with other elements in the marketing program, particularly the communications program. In territories that have little potential, the manager may emphasize advertising and supplement that with a telephone sales program; he or she may place only minimal emphasis on personal visits by field representatives. In a territory that has good potential and a concentration of customers, the manager may forgo the telephone-call program, relying instead on personal sales calls while committing fewer dollars to advertising. Before launching a new product, salespeople may be instructed to call on distributors and dealers and to supply them with sufficient point-of-purchase display materials and other marketing aids. Sales representatives could also help to ensure that intermediaries have adequate inventories of the product and they know how the product operates and should be serviced.

Evaluation and Control

Effective territory design can improve management's evaluation and control of field selling. Geographically defined sales territories allow sales and cost data to be collected and analyzed by geographic area. This permits area comparisons—an important benefit because the strength of the competition often varies by area. One can compare market shares across areas in total and by product; thus, companies can more accurately pinpoint competitive strengths and weaknesses. In one metropolitan area, the company may be doing poorly because of a dominant distributor that handles a competitor's product. The remedy might involve committing more resources to assist the distributor handling the firm's product. In a territory where the problem is awareness of the company and its products, the remedy could be different.

Managers can also evaluate the sales force better with geographically defined sales territories. Salespeople can be compared with respect to their sales versus potential, and those who may need training can be spotted. The problem may be knowing how to sell to a particular type of account, or it may be linked to less than satisfactory sales of a product. In any case, a more effective cure can be formulated when the exact nature of the problem can be pinpointed.

The experience of Bindicator, a supplier of instruments that measure the levels of wheat, cement, plastic pellets, and numerous other raw materials in the bins of process industries, illustrates a benefit of area comparisons. When Bindicator found its sales were off sharply, the company attempted to determine the extent of the problem by developing marketing potential estimates by territory for the first time in its history. It then compared its sales to potential and looked at the number of sales leads by territory. Bindicator found that smaller territories received a higher proportion of sales leads than larger territories and that two of its highest potential areas were being starved for sales leads generated by national advertising. The company consequently revised its advertising schedule, and sales more than doubled in one of the starved high-potential areas and increased substantially in the other.[2]

Cost-control advantages also accrue to the firm with defined sales territories. Again, comparing sales representatives in terms of number of calls they make, their travel and other expenses, and proportion of time spent in face-to-face customer contact versus other related selling activities can provide important insights into doing the job more efficiently. Slight, incremental differences can have important profit implications for the firm. In 1990, the median cost of an industrial sales call was $250.54, while the number of calls per day was approximately four.[3] Furthermore, industrial salespeople spend only 39 percent of their typical 9-hour, 32-minute workday, or 3.72 hours, in face-to-face selling,[4] with the remainder spent driving to interviews, waiting for interviews, making service calls, attending meetings, and making reports. If one considers face-to-face time as the real "productive" time of the salesperson, the average industrial sales representative's productive time costs its firm $269 per hour (4 calls/day × $250.54/call × 1 day ÷ 3.72 hours)—comparable to that of a $538,000-a-year executive. Of course, some of this other time is also productive time—for example, planning a sales presentation.

As Automation Increases, So Does the Need for Technology Training to Improve Sales Force Productivity

Nearly two-thirds of salespeople now use a laptop computer and nearly 70 percent have access to a desktop PC. The question is no longer whether a salesperson is using technology but how well. Sales managers are realizing that simply putting the technology in the hands of the right people does not help in the field unless they are trained to use it properly. The problem has been that as new technology is adopted, it is put into the field without proper training.

A recent survey indicated that, on average, companies spend over four days (roughly one week) each year training their sales force in how to use the technology available to them. The most common form of training media is in-class instruction by technology professionals (72 percent use instructor-led classes). Over a third of companies are using videos to support those efforts. Michael Tucker, a partner with Booz–Allen Hamilton's IT group, puts it this way: "[Corporate America] is filled with train wrecks of companies that have failed to recognize the difficulty of designing and rolling out automation for the field sales force."

As new technology is assimilated into field sales forces, the need to establish support for those technologies (e.g., expanded phone lines for modem access) as well as training will increase. Sales managers have come to see the benefits of technology but are learning that the technology is only as good as the people who are using it.

Source: "Plug and Play," *Sales & Marketing Management*, "State of Sales & Marketing Technology, Special Issue (December 1998), pp. 64–67.

Reducing the unproductive portions through more effective coverage of accounts and more efficient routing within territories can achieve substantial cost economies. Small incremental cost improvements for each salesperson for a firm that employs 50 to 100 or more representatives can significantly boost profits. For example, one small grocery products firm, "with only 34 salespeople, estimated savings of $250,000 from changes in the allocation of sales calls to existing grocery products accounts."[5] One way firms are helping their salespeople cover their accounts more effectively and improve their productivity is by equipping them with laptop computers. However, the "Managing Sales Relationships" box notes that while many companies now consider the laptop, as well as other technologies, an essential part of field sales, there is an ever increasing need for salespeople to be properly trained to maximize the use of that technology.

SALES FORCE SIZE

Salespeople are among the most productive assets of a company; they are also among the most expensive. Determining the optimal number to employ presents several fundamental dilemmas. On the one hand, increasing the number of salespeople will increase sales; on the other hand, it will also increase costs. Achieving the optimal balance between these considerations, although difficult, is vitally important.

The optimal number of territories depends on the design of the individual territories. Different assignments to salespeople and even different call patterns can produce different sales levels. Of course, the number of calls the sales force must make directly affects the number of salespeople the firm needs. In sum, the number of sales territories and the design of individual territories must be looked at as interrelated decisions whose outcomes affect each other.

The decisions need to be made jointly and not sequentially. Deployment models are available that simultaneously consider the three interrelated decisions of (1) sales force size or the number of territories, (2) design of the individual territories, and (3) allocation of the total selling effort to accounts. Use of these deployment models is promising, as Exhibit 7.1 suggests. At the same time, it is useful for discussion purposes to separate the issues so as to throw the underlying considerations into bolder relief. Consequently, the subsequent discussion first addresses the issue of sales force size and then the issue of sales territory design. However, the size of the sales force may need to be revised as a result of the sales territory design.[6]

There are several techniques for determining the size of the field sales force. Three of the more popular are the (1) breakdown, (2) work load, and (3) incremental methods.

Breakdown Method

The breakdown method is conceptually one of the simplest. An average salesperson is treated as a salesperson unit, and each salesperson unit is assumed to possess the same productivity potential. To determine the size of the sales force needed, divide total forecasted sales for the company by the sales likely to be produced by each individual. Mathematically,

$$N = \frac{S}{P}$$

where

N = number of sales personnel needed.
S = forecasted sales volume.
P = estimated productivity of one salesperson unit.

Exhibit 7.1   Some Company Experiences Redeploying Sales Force across Geographic Areas or Accounts

Type of Product	Redeployment Basis	Consequence
Medical X-ray film	Redeployment of salespeople across sales districts	$131,000 increase in gross profits
Advertising	Redeployment of selling effort and reassignment of salespeople to accounts	17–21 percent profit increase
Appliances	Redeployment of selling effort across trading areas	$830,000 sales increase
Airline travel and cargo	Redeployment of selling effort to accounts	8.1 percent sales increase
Consumer products	Reduction in sales force size and redeployment of selling effort to accounts	Current sales levels maintained with nearly 50 percent reduction in selling effort
Consumer products	Redeployment of salespeople across regions and distribution channels	7 percent sales increase
Grocery products	Redeployment of selling effort to accounts	8–30 percent sales improvement
Transportation services	Reduction in sales force size and redeployment of selling effort	Current sales levels maintained with 10–20 percent reduction in sales force size

Source: Adapted from Raymond W. LaForge, David W. Cravens, and Clifford E. Young, "Using Contingency Analysis to Select Selling Effort Allocation Methods," *Journal of Personal Selling and Sales Management* 6 (August 1986), p. 23. The original table also lists the sources in which each of the experiences was reported.

Thus, a firm that had forecast sales of $5 million and in which each salesperson unit could be expected to sell $250,000 would need 20 salespeople. Although conceptually simple, the breakdown method is not without its problems. For one thing, it uses reverse logic. It treats sales force size as a consequence of sales. Yet the logical causation is in the opposite direction. As discussed in Chapter 6, the level of sales expected should depend on the level of the marketing effort. The number of salespeople in the field is an important part of that marketing effort—in some companies, the most important part. Determining the number of sales representatives to cover the market in a given year should logically precede forecasting final sales.

A second problem with the breakdown method is that it depends on the estimate of productivity per salesperson. The firm can compute the average of what each salesperson sold, say, in the previous year. However, such averages can obscure important facts. They fail to account for different ability levels of salespeople, differing potentials in the markets they service, and different levels of competition in sales territories. Perhaps the "most productive" salesperson had lower sales than average because the market area had below-average potential and intense competitive pressure. The technique fails to allow for such differences.

Also, this simple expression of the formula does not allow for turnover in the sales force. New salespeople are usually not as productive as those who have been on the job for several years. The formula can be modified to allow for sales force turnover, but it loses some of its simplicity and conceptual appeal.

One alternative for smoothing out person-to-person differences in productivity due to ability, market potential, and experience differences is to use industry-average productivity estimates in the formula. Unfortunately, an industry-average productivity estimate tends to ignore the market position of the firm trying to determine the best size of its sales force.

Finally, a key shortcoming of the breakdown method is that it does not allow for profitability. It treats sales as the end in itself rather than as the means to an end. The number of salespeople is determined as a function of the level of forecast sales, not as a determinant of targeted profit.

Work Load Method

The basic premise underlying the work load approach (or, as it is sometimes called, the buildup method) is that all sales personnel should shoulder an equal amount of work. Management estimates the work required to serve the entire market. The total work calculation is treated as a function of the number of accounts, how often each should be called on, and for how long. This estimate is then divided by the amount of work an individual salesperson should be able to handle, and the result is the total number of salespeople required.[7] More specifically, the method consists of the six steps shown in Exhibit 7.2.

1. **Classify all the firm's customers into categories.** Often the classification is based on the level of sales to each customer. The ABC Rule of Account Classification holds that the first 15 percent of a firm's customers will account for 65 percent of the firm's sales, the next 20 percent will yield 20 percent, and the last 65 percent will produce only 15 percent.[8] The top group is categorized as A accounts, the middle group as B accounts, and the bottom group as C accounts.

   Classification could be based on other criteria also. One firm, for example, rates each customer by the prospect's type of business, credit rating, and product line.[9] Fansteel, a maker of milling cutters and other machine tool products, considers each account's sales potential and need for technical advice in forming its classification of A, B, and C accounts, which determines the mix of its sales force and its distribution

Exhibit 7.2 Steps to Determine Sales Force Size by the Work Load Method

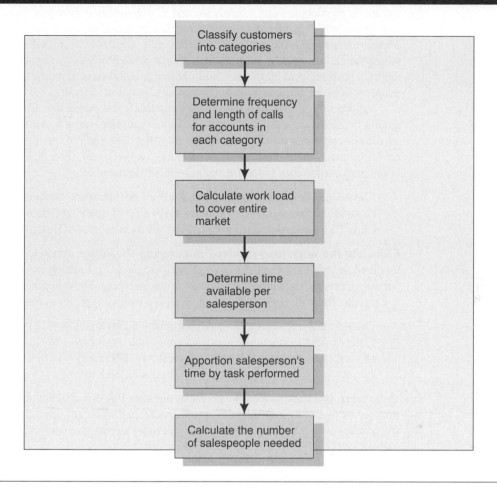

when selling the account. General Telephone of Florida classifies present customers by their potential for additional services using revenue per employee in each SIC code. Marion/Merrell Dow classifies accounts strictly by sales potential. It considers the top 20 percent of physicians on whom its salespeople call A accounts and the other 80 percent B accounts. All noncustomers or physicians with low sales potential are considered C accounts.

Any classification system should reflect the different amounts of selling effort required to service the different classes of accounts and consequently the attractiveness of each class of accounts to the firm. Suppose, for example, the firm had 1,030 accounts that could be classified into three basic types or classes, as follows:

Type A: Large or very attractive—200.
Type B: Medium or moderately attractive—350.
Type C: Small, but attractive—480.

2. **Determine the frequency with which each type of account should be called upon and the desired length of each call.** These inputs can be generated in several ways.

They can be based directly on the judgments of management. For example, management at Marion/Merrell Dow wants its salespeople to call on A physicians every two weeks, B physicians every six weeks, and C physicians only when there is nothing else to do, which is rare. The inputs can also be based on the judgments of experienced salespeople. Alternatively, the firm may conduct controlled experiments in which the frequency of contact and the length of each contact are systematically varied to determine what is optimal. Still another possibility is to analyze historical data using appropriate statistical methods such as regression analysis.

Suppose the firm, using one of these methods, estimates that Class A accounts should be called on every two weeks, Class B accounts once a month, and Class C accounts every other month. It also estimates that the length of the typical call should be 60 minutes, 30 minutes, and 20 minutes, respectively. The number of contact hours per year for each type of account is thus calculated as

Class A: 26 times/year × 60 minutes/call = 1,560 minutes, or 26 hours.
Class B: 12 times/year × 30 minutes/call = 360 minutes, or 6 hours.
Class C: 6 times/year × 20 minutes/call = 120 minutes, or 2 hours.

3. **Calculate the work load involved in covering the entire market.** The total work involved in covering each class of account is given by multiplying the number of such accounts by the number of contact hours per year. These products are summed to estimate the work entailed in covering all the various types of accounts:

Class A: 200 accounts × 26 hours/account = 5,200 hours
Class B: 350 accounts × 6 hours/account = 2,100 hours
Class C: 480 accounts × 2 hours/account =   960 hours
                                 Total = 8,260 hours.

4. **Determine the time available per salesperson.** For this calculation, estimate the number of hours the typical salesperson works per week and then multiply that by the number of weeks the representative will work during the year. Suppose the typical workweek is 40 hours and the average salesperson can be expected to work 48 weeks during the year, after allowing for vacation time, sickness, and other emergencies. This suggests the average representative has 1,920 hours available per year—that is,

40 hours/week × 48 weeks/year = 1,920 hours/year.

5. **Apportion the salesperson's time by task performed.** Unfortunately, not all the salesperson's time is consumed in face-to-face customer contact. Much of it is devoted to nonselling activities such as making reports, attending meetings, and making service calls. Another major portion is spent traveling. Suppose a time study of salespeople's effort suggested the following division:

Selling   40 percent =   768 hours/year
Nonselling   30 percent =   576 hours/year
Traveling   30 percent =   576 hours/year
            100 percent = 1,920 hours/year.

6. **Calculate the number of salespeople needed.** The number of salespeople the firm will need can now be readily determined by dividing the total number of hours needed to serve the entire market by the number of hours available per salesperson for selling—that is, by the calculation

$$\frac{8,260 \text{ hours}}{768 \text{ hours/salesperson}} = 10.75 \text{ or } 11 \text{ salespeople.}$$

The work load or buildup method is a common way to determine sales force size. It has several attractive features. It is easy to understand, and it explicitly recognizes that different types of accounts should be called on with different frequencies. The inputs are readily available or can be secured without much trouble.

Unfortunately, it also possesses some weaknesses. It does not allow for differences in sales response among accounts that receive the same sales effort. Two Class A accounts might respond differently to sales effort. One may be content with the products and services of the firm and continue to order even if the salesperson does not call every two weeks. Another, which does most of its business with a competitor, may willingly switch some of its orders if it receives more frequent contact. Also, the method does not explicitly consider the profitability of the call frequencies. It does not take into account such factors as the cost of servicing and the gross margins on the product mix purchased by the account.[10]

Finally, the method assumes that all salespeople use their time with equal efficiency—for example, that each will have 768 hours available for face-to-face selling. This is simply not true. Some are better able to plan their calls to generate more direct selling time; those in smaller geographic territories can spend less time traveling and more time selling. Some more than others simply make good use of the selling time they have available; the quality of time invested in a sales call is at least as important as the quantity of time spent. Yet the buildup method does not explicitly consider this dimension. The work load method to determine sales force size is popular though.

Incremental Method

The basic premise underlying the incremental method of determining sales force size is that sales representatives should be added as long as the incremental profit produced by their addition exceeds the incremental costs.[11] The method recognizes that there will be decreasing returns associated with the addition of salespeople. Thus, while one more salesperson might produce $300,000, two more might produce only $550,000 in new sales. The incremental sales produced by the first salesperson is $300,000, while that for the second salesperson is $250,000. Suppose the addition of a third salesperson could be expected to produce $225,000 in new sales and a fourth, $200,000. Adding all four would increase sales by $975,000. Suppose further that the company's profit margin was 20 percent, and placing another salesperson in the field cost $50,000 on average.

Exhibit 7.3 summarizes the situation. The analysis suggests that two salespeople should be added. At that point, the incremental profit from the additional salespeople equals the incremental cost. Adding more than two salespeople would cause profits to go down, as is seen by subtracting column (6) "total additional cost" from column (4) "total additional profit."

The incremental approach to determining sales force size is conceptually correct. Also, it is consistent with the empirical evidence that decreasing returns can be expected with additional salespeople. Decreasing returns can also be expected with other territory design features such as the number of buyers per salesperson, the number of calls the salesperson makes on an account, and the actual time the representative spends in face-to-face contact.[12]

The disadvantage of the incremental approach is that it is the most difficult of the three to implement. While the cost of an additional salesperson can be estimated with reasonable accuracy, estimating the likely profit is difficult. It depends on the additional revenue the salesperson is expected to produce, and that depends on how the territories are restructured, who is assigned to each territory, and how effective they might be. To com-

Exhibit 7.3   Illustration of Incremental Approach

Number of Additional Salespeople (1)	Total Additional Revenue (2)	Incremental Revenue Due to Additional Salesperson (3)	Total Additional Profit* (4)	Incremental Profit Due to Additional Salesperson (5)	Total Additional Cost (6)	Incremental Cost Due to Additional Salesperson (7)
1	$300,000	$300,000	$ 60,000	$60,000	$ 50,000	$50,000
2	550,000	250,000	110,000	50,000	100,000	50,000
3	775,000	225,000	155,000	44,500	150,000	50,000
4	975,000	200,000	195,000	40,000	200,000	50,000

*Based on assumption of 20 percent profit margin.

pound things further, the profitability of the new arrangement also depends on the mix of products generating the sales increase and how profitable each is to the company.

SALES TERRITORY DESIGN

After the number of sales territories has been determined, the sales manager can address territory design questions. The general issues involved and the process to follow are shown in Exhibit 7.4. The sales manager strives for the ideal of making all territories equal with respect to the amount of sales potential they contain and the amount of work it takes a salesperson to cover them effectively. When territories are equal in potential, it is easier to evaluate each representative's performance and to compare salespeople. Equal work loads tend to improve sales force morale and diminish disputes between management and the sales force. While considering these questions, the sales manager should take into account the impact on market response of particular territory structures and call frequencies. Obviously, it is difficult, if not impossible, to achieve an optimal balance with respect to all these factors. The sales manager should constantly strive for the proper balance, however.

Select Basic Control Unit

The basic control unit is the most elemental geographic area used to form sales territories—county or city, for example. As a general rule, small geographic control units are preferable to large ones. With large units, areas with low potential may be hidden by their inclusion in areas with high potential, and vice versa. This makes it difficult to pinpoint geographic potential, which is a primary reason for forming geographically defined sales territories in the first place. Also, small control units make it easier to adjust sales territories when conditions warrant. It is much easier to reassign the accounts in a particular county from one salesperson to another, for example, than it is to reassign all the accounts in a state. Some commonly used basic control units are states, trading areas, counties, cities or metropolitan statistical areas (MSAs), and ZIP code areas.

States

Although it has become less popular, some companies still use states as basic control units. There are some advantages in doing so. State boundaries are clearly defined and thus are simple and inexpensive to use. A good deal of statistical data are accumulated by state, which makes it easy to analyze territory potential.

Exhibit 7.4 Stages in Territory Design

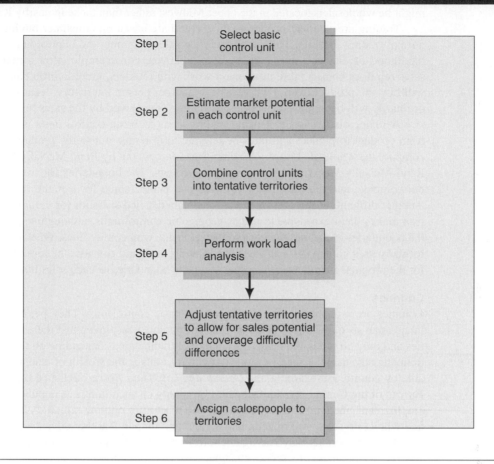

Step 1 — Select basic control unit

Step 2 — Estimate market potential in each control unit

Step 3 — Combine control units into tentative territories

Step 4 — Perform work load analysis

Step 5 — Adjust tentative territories to allow for sales potential and coverage difficulty differences

Step 6 — Assign salespeople to territories

One primary weakness of using states as control units is that buying habits do not reflect state boundaries. The state represents a political rather than an economic division of the national market. Consumption patterns in Gary, Indiana, for example, may have more in common with those in Chicago than with those in other parts of Indiana. Also, the size of states makes it difficult to pinpoint problem areas. A problem in Ohio may be localized in Cincinnati, but it is hard to determine that if the only figures available are for Ohio as a whole. States also contain great variations in market potential; the potential in New York City alone, for example, might be greater than the combined potential of all the Rocky Mountain states.

State units are sometimes used by firms that do not have the sophistication or staff to use counties or smaller geographic units—for example, firms at the early stages of territory design. States are also used by firms that cover a national market with only a few sales representatives, particularly when they can specify potential accounts by name (e.g., a firm selling dryers to paper mills).

Trading areas

Trading areas are made up of a principal city and the surrounding dependent area. A trading area is an economic unit that ignores political and other noneconomic boundaries. Trading areas recognize that consumers who live in New Jersey, for example, may prefer to shop in New York City rather than locally. The trading area for a food processor in western Iowa might be wholesalers located in the upper Midwest rather than those in nearby Kansas.

Trading areas reflect economic factors and are based on consumer buying habits and normal trading patterns. Thus, they facilitate sales planning and control and diminish the likelihood of disputes among sales representatives. For example, after a manufacturer's sales rep does considerable missionary work with retailers, there is little danger that they will buy the product from a wholesaler in another person's territory because the retailers ordinarily will be in the same wholesale trading area served by the sales rep.

A major disadvantage of using trading areas as basic control units is that they vary from product to product and must be referred to in terms of specific products. To see this, compare the wholesale Grocery Trading Area Map put out by Rand McNally (check out the Rand McNally Web site at: *www.randmcnally.com.* The boundaries for two products may not coincide, and this can prove awkward and cumbersome for a multiproduct company. Another difficulty is that it is often hard to obtain detailed statistics for trading areas. This in turn makes them expensive to use as geographic control units, although some firms adjust the boundaries of the trading areas so they coincide with county lines. Whether or not a firm formally uses trading areas as basic control units, it should consider the logical trading areas for the products it produces when specifying the boundaries of each sales territory.

Counties

Counties are probably the most widely used basic control unit. They permit a more fine-tuned analysis of the market than do states or trading areas, given that there are 3,133 counties and only 50 states and a varying number of trading areas depending on the product. One dramatic advantage of using counties as control units is the wealth of statistical data available by county. For example, the *County and City Data Book,* published biennially by the Bureau of the Census, provides statistics by county on such things as population, education, employment, income, housing, banking, manufacturing output, capital expenditures, retail and wholesale sales, and mineral and agricultural output. Another advantage of counties is that their size permits easy reassignment from one sales territory to another. Thus, sales territories can be altered to reflect changing economic conditions without major upheaval in basic service. Furthermore, potentials do not have to be recalculated before doing so.

The most serious drawback to using counties as basic control units is that for some purposes they are still too large. Los Angeles County or Cook County (Chicago), for example, may require several sales representatives. In such cases, it is necessary to divide these counties into even smaller basic control units.

Cities and metropolitan statistical areas (MSAs)

Historically, when most of the market potential was within city boundaries, the city was a good basic control unit. Cities are rarely satisfactory anymore, however. For many products, the area surrounding a city now contains as much or more potential than the central city. Consequently, many firms that formerly used cities now employ broader classification systems to help them identify and organize their territories. Developed by the Census Bureau, the most basic control unit is called an MSA (metropolitan statistical area).

MSAs, which replace the former standard metropolitical statistical area (SMSA) designation,[13] are integrated economic and social units with a large population nucleus. An area can qualify as an MSA in either of two ways:

1. If it contains a city of at least 50,000 people.
2. If it includes a census-defined urbanized area of 50,000, with a total metropolitan population of at least 100,000 people (75,000 in New England).

An MSA includes the county containing the central city and any counties having close social and economic ties to the central county. MSAs always include entire counties, except in New England.

Any area that qualifies as an MSA and also has a population of one million or more can be recognized as a CMSA (consolidated metropolitan statistical area). Key elements to consider in classifying a CMSA include (1) the ability to identify separate component areas within the composite area using statistical criteria specified in the standards and (2) whether there is local opinion to support the component areas. Component areas are recognized as PMSAs (primary metropolitan statistical areas). As of June 30, 1998, there were 256 MSAs plus 18 CMSAs comprising 73 PMSAs. Exhibit 7.5 ranks the 25 largest population centers in the United States in order of size. The concentration of economic activity matches the concentration of people.

The heavy concentration of population, income, and retail sales in the MSAs explains why many firms are content to concentrate their field selling efforts on MSAs. Some assign all their field representatives to such large areas. Such a strategy minimizes

Exhibit 7.5 Twenty-Five Largest CMSA/MSAs in Decreasing Order of Size

Rank	Area	Estimated 1996 Population (In 000s)
1	New York–northern New Jersey–Long Island, NY–NJ–CT–PA (CMSA)	19,938.5
2	Los Angeles–Riverside–Orange County, CA (CMSA)	15,495.2
3	Chicago, IL–Gary, IN–Kenosha, WI (CMSA)	8,599.8
4	Washington, DC–Baltimore, MD–VA–WV (CMSA)	7,164.5
5	San Francisco–Oakland–San Jose, CA (CMSA)	6,605.4
6	Philadelphia–Wilmington–Atlantic City, PA–NJ–DE–MD (CMSA)	5,973.4
7	Boston–Worcester–Lawrence, MA–NH–ME–CT (CMSA)	5,563.5
8	Detroit–Ann Arbor–Flint, MI (CMSA)	5,284.2
9	Dallas–Fort Worth, TX (CMSA)	4,574.6
10	Houston–Galveston–Brazoria, TX (CMSA)	4,253.4
11	Atlanta, GA (MSA)	3,541.2
12	Miami–Fort Lauderdale, FL (CMSA)	3,514.4
13	Seattle–Tacoma–Bremerton, WA (CMSA)	3,320.8
14	Cleveland–Akron, OH (CMSA)	2,913.4
15	Minneapolis–St. Paul, MN (MSA)	2,765.1
16	Phoenix, AZ (MSA)	2,746.7
17	San Diego, CA (MSA)	2,655.4
18	St. Louis, MO–IL (MSA)	2,548.2
19	Pittsburgh, PA (MSA)	2,379.4
20	Denver–Boulder–Greeley, CO (CMSA)	2,227.5
21	Tampa–St. Petersburg–Clearwater, FL (MSA)	2,199.2
22	Portland–Salem, OR–WA (CMSA)	2,078.5
23	Cincinnati–Hamilton, OH–KY–IN (CMSA)	1,920.9
24	Kansas City, MO–KS (MSA)	1,690.3
25	Milwaukee–Racine, WI (CMSA)	1,642.6

Source: "MSA Web Page," U.S. Bureau of the Census Web site (1998).

Exhibit 7.6   Map of Metropolitan Statistical Areas

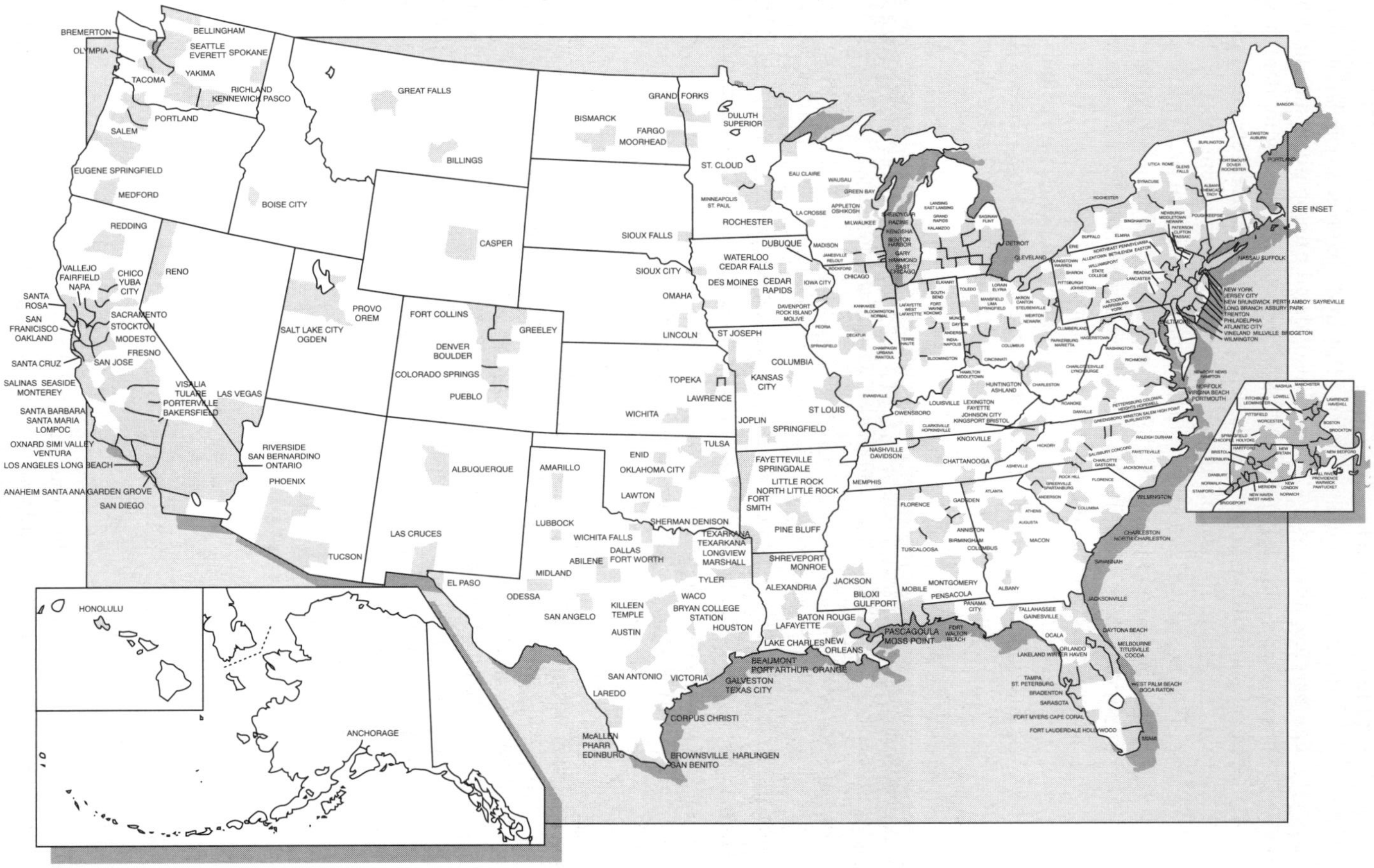

travel time and expense because of the geographic concentration of MSAs (see Exhibit 7.6—Map of Metropolitan Statistical Areas). For the most up-to-date census information visit their Web site at *www.census.gov.*

ZIP code areas

Some firms, for which city or MSA boundaries are too large, use ZIP code areas as basic control units. The U.S. Postal Service has defined more than 36,000 five-digit ZIP code areas.

An advantage of ZIP code areas is that they are relatively homogeneous with respect to basic socioeconomic data. Whereas residents within an MSA might display great heterogeneity, those within a ZIP code area are likely to be relatively similar in age, income, education, and so forth and to even display similar consumption patterns. While the Bureau of the Census typically does not publish data by ZIP code area, it does provide data from the census and surveys of population and housing to individual companies on computer tape or optical disk. An industry has developed to tabulate such data by arbitrary geographic boundaries. The "geodemographers," as they are typically called, combine census data with their own survey data or data they gather from administrative records, such as motor vehicle registrations or credit transactions, to produce customized products for their clients.

A typical product involves the cluster analysis of census-produced data to produce homogeneous groups that describe the American population. For example, Claritas (the first firm to do this and still one of the leaders in the industry) used over 500 demographic variables in its PRIZM (Potential Ratings for Zip Markets) system when classifying residential neighborhoods. This system breaks the 25,000 neighborhood areas in the United States into 40 types based on consumer behavior and lifestyle. Each of the types has a name that theoretically describes the type of people living there, such as Urban Gold Coast, Shotguns and Pickups, Pools and Patios, and so on. Claritas and the other suppliers will do a customized analysis for whatever geographic boundaries a client specifics. Alternatively, a client can send a tape listing the ZIP code addresses of some customer database, and the geodemographer will attach the cluster codes. For a great deal more information about PRIZM visit the Claritas Web site at *www.claritas.com.*

One of industrial marketers' major sources of market data, Dun's Market Identifiers (DMI), contains ZIP code information. DMI is a special name given by Dun & Bradstreet to its marketing information service. DMI is a roster of U.S. and Canadian firms updated monthly so that the record of each company is accurate and current. Exhibit 7.7 is an example of a card record that is available on each industrial establishment—an establishment being a single physical location such as a manufacturing plant or a nonmanufacturing headquarters address. The information is also available as computer records. The ability to locate establishments by geographic area can greatly facilitate estimating market potential in planning territory design.

One disadvantage of using ZIP code areas as basic control units is that the boundaries change over time. However, with the new computerized geographic information systems (GIS), that is less of a problem than it used to be in that the boundaries can easily be reconfigured.[14]

Estimate Market Potential   Step 2 in territory design involves estimating market potential in each basic control unit. This is done using one of the schemes suggested in Chapter 6. If a relationship can be established between sales of the product in question and some other variable or variables, for example, this relationship can be applied to each basic control unit. Data must be available for each of the variables for the small geographic area, though. Sometimes the potential within each basic control unit is estimated by considering the likely demand

Exhibit 7.7   DMI Sales Prospecting Record

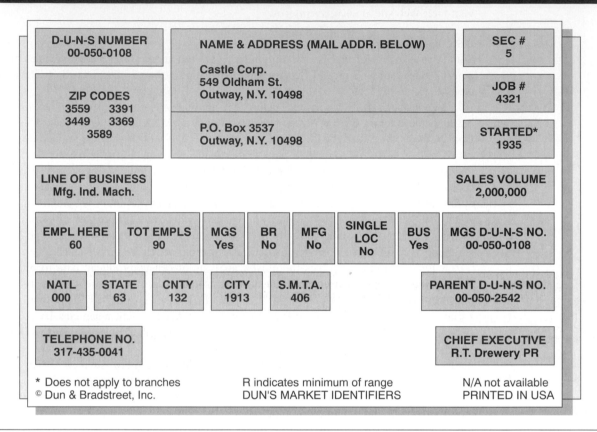

D-U-N-S NUMBER 00-050-0108	**NAME & ADDRESS (MAIL ADDR. BELOW)** Castle Corp. 549 Oldham St. Outway, N.Y. 10498	**SEC #** 5
ZIP CODES 3559 3391 3449 3369 3589		**JOB #** 4321
	P.O. Box 3537 Outway, N.Y. 10498	**STARTED*** 1935
LINE OF BUSINESS Mfg. Ind. Mach.		**SALES VOLUME** 2,000,000

EMPL HERE 60	TOT EMPLS 90	MGS Yes	BR No	MFG No	SINGLE LOC No	BUS Yes	MGS D-U-N-S NO. 00-050-0108

NATL 000	STATE 63	CNTY 132	CITY 1913	S.M.T.A. 406		PARENT D-U-N-S NO. 00-050-2542

TELEPHONE NO. 317-435-0041		CHIEF EXECUTIVE R.T. Drewery PR

* Does not apply to branches   R indicates minimum of range   N/A not available
© Dun & Bradstreet, Inc.   DUN'S MARKET IDENTIFIERS   PRINTED IN USA

Source: Reprinted with permission from Dun's Market Identifiers, © Dun & Bradstreet, Inc.

from each customer and prospect in the control unit. This works much better for industrial goods manufacturers than it does for consumer goods producers. The consumers of industrial goods are typically fewer in number and more easily identified—for example, using Dun's Market Identifiers. Furthermore, each typically buys much more product than is true with consumer goods. This makes it worthwhile to identify at least the larger ones by name, to estimate the likely demand from each, and to add up these individual estimates to produce an estimate for the territory as a whole.

Form Tentative Territories

Step 3 in territory design involves combining contiguous basic control units into larger geographic aggregates. Adjoining units are combined to prevent salespeople from having to crisscross paths while skipping over geographic areas covered by another representative. The basic emphasis at this stage is to make the tentative territories as equal as possible in market potential. Each territory should provide an opportunity for the same standard of living for sales representatives. Differences in work load or sales potential (the share of total market potential a company expects to achieve) because of different levels of competitive activity are not taken into account at this stage. It is also presumed that all sales representatives have relatively equal abilities. All these assumptions are relaxed at subsequent stages of the territory planning process. The attempt at this stage is simply to develop an approximation of the final territory alignment. The total number of territories defined equals the number of territories the firm has previously determined it needs. If the firm has not made such a calculation, it needs to do so now.

Perform Work Load Analysis

Once tentative initial boundaries have been established for all sales territories, it is necessary to determine how much work is required to cover each. Ideally, firms like to form sales territories that are equal in both potential and work load. Although Step 3 should produce territories roughly equal in potential, the territories will probably be decidedly unequal with respect to the amount of work necessary to cover them adequately. In Step 4, the analyst tries to estimate the amount of work involved in covering each.

Example account analysis

Typically, the work load analysis considers each customer (most assuredly, the larger ones) in the territory. The analysis is often conducted in two stages. First, the sales potential for each customer and prospect in the territory is estimated. This step is often called an account analysis. The sales potential estimate derived from the account analysis is then used to decide how often each account should be called on and for how long. The total effort required to cover the territory can be determined by considering the number of accounts, the number of calls to be made on each, the duration of each call, and the estimated amount of nonselling and travel time.

Exhibit 7.8 contains an account analysis for a small sample of accounts in a single territory. Note several things in the table. First, the analysis is carried out customer by customer. Although the firm may not want to do this for every customer in the territory, it would for the potentially larger ones. Second, the potentials in the "Potential by Product" columns are market potentials. Thus, they represent the expected sales of each product to the customer for the entire industry for the period in question. While the analysis here is broken out by product, it is sometimes simply computed in the aggregate. Third, the "Estimated Share" columns show the firm's competitive positions with each customer. The firm is particularly entrenched with respect to product Y to Pelton Industries in that it expects to get a 40 percent share, but it has a reasonable share of sales of all three products to

Exhibit 7.8 Sample Account Analysis

Account Name	Potential by Product			Estimated Share			Sales Potential			Total	Classi-fication
	X	Y	Z	X	Y	Z	X	Y	Z		
Ballard Manufacturing	$200,000	$140,000	$300,000	0.15	0.30	0.10	$ 30,000	$ 42,000	$ 30,000	$ 102,000	C
Pelton Industries	420,000	310,000	100,000	0.20	0.40	0.10	84,000	124,000	10,000	218,000	B
The Blattner Company	650,000	180,000	480,000	0.20	0.30	0.25	130,000	54,000	120,000	304,000	A

Classification	Number of Accounts
A	20
B	60
C	150

Source: Adapted from Raymond W. La Forge, David W. Cravens, and Clifford E. Young, "Using Contingency Analysis to Select Selling Effort Allocation Methods," *Journal of Personal Selling and Sales Management* 6 (August 1986), p. 23. The original table also lists the sources in which each of the experiences was reported.

all three customers. The multiplication of market potential by product by the firm's estimated share produces an estimate of the firm's sales potential for each product for each customer. The sum of sales potentials by product is the total sales potential of the account.

In the example, the firm uses sales potential by account to classify accounts. Accounts with potential sales greater than $300,000 are classified as A accounts, those with expected sales of $200,000 to $300,000 as B accounts, and those whose potential is less than $200,000 as C accounts. Thus, the Blattner Company is classified as an A account, Pelton Industries as a B account, and Ballard Manufacturing as a C account. The table also indicates that applying a similar analysis to all accounts indicates the firm has 20 A accounts, 60 B accounts, and 150 C accounts.

Criteria for classifying accounts

Total sales potential is one criterion used to classify accounts into categories dictating the frequency and length of sales calls. A number of other criteria have been suggested as well for determining the attractiveness of an individual account to the firm. The key is to identify those factors likely to affect the productivity of the sales call. Some of these other factors include competitive pressures for the account, the prestige of the account, how many products the firm produces that the account buys, and the number and level of buying influences within the account.[15] The factors that affect the productivity of an individual sales call are likely to change from firm to firm.

Determining account call rates

Once the specific factors affecting the productivity of a sales call have been isolated, they can be treated in various ways. One way is to use the ABC Rule of Account Classification discussed earlier in the chapter and illustrated in Exhibit 7.8.

Another way is to employ a variation of the matrix concept of strategic planning, which suggests that accounts, like strategic business units or markets, can be divided along two dimensions reflecting the overall opportunity they represent and the firm's abilities to capitalize on those opportunities. In the case of accounts, the division should reflect (1) the attractiveness of the account to the firm and (2) the likely difficulties to be encountered in managing the account.[16] The accounts are then sorted into either a four- or nine-cell strategic planning matrix. For example, Exhibit 7.9 uses the criteria of account potential and the firm's competitive advantage or disadvantage with the account to classify accounts into four cells. It would use different call frequencies in each cell. The heaviest call rates in the sample matrix depicted in Exhibit 7.9 would be on accounts in cells 1, 2, and possibly 3, depending on the firm's abilities to overcome its competitive disadvantages. The lowest planned call rates would be on accounts in cell 4.

Determining call frequencies account by account

Accounts do not have to be divided into classes and call frequencies set at the same level for all accounts in the class. Rather, the firm might want to determine the work load in each tentative territory on an account-by-account basis. There are several ways of doing this. The firm can rate each account on each factor deemed critical to the success of the sales call effort and then develop a sales effort allocation index for each account.[17] The sales effort allocation index is formed by multiplying each rating score by its factor importance weight, summing over all factors, and then dividing by the sum of the importance weights. The resulting sales effort allocation index reflects the relative amount of sales call effort that should be allocated to the account in comparison to other accounts—the larger the index, the greater the number of planned calls on the account.

Still another scheme is to estimate the likely sales to be realized from each account

Exhibit 7.9   Account Planning Matrix

	Strong	Weak
High	**Opportunity** Account offers good opportunity. It has high potential and sales organization has a differential advantage in serving it. **Strategy** Commit high levels of sales resources to take advantage of the opportunity. 1	**Opportunity** Account may represent a good opportunity. Sales organization needs to overcome its competitive disadvantage and strengthen its position to capitalize on the opportunity. **Strategy** Either direct a high level of sales resources to improve position and to take advantage of the opportunity or shift resources to other accounts. 2
Low	**Opportunity** Account offers stable opportunity since sales organization has differential advantage in serving it. **Strategy** Allocate moderate level of sales resources to maintain current advantage. 3	**Opportunity** Account offers little opportunity. Its potential is small and the sales organization is at a competitive disadvantage in serving it. **Strategy** Devote minimal level of resources to the account or consider abandoning the account altogether. 4

Account Potential (vertical axis: High / Low)

Competitive Strength (horizontal axis: Strong / Weak)

Source: Adapted from Raymond La Forge and David W. Cravens, "Steps in Selling Effort Deployment," *Industrial Marketing Management* 11 (1982). pp. 83–94; Renato Fiocca. "Account Portfolio Analysis for Strategy Development," *Industrial Marketing Management* 11 (1982). pp. 53–62; and Raymond La Forge, David W. Cravens, and Clifford E. Young, "Improving Salesforce Productivity," *Business Horizons* 28 (September–October 1985), pp. 50–51.

as a function of the number of calls on the account. The actual sales response function is the key in determining the optimal number of sales calls to be made on any account and the work load in each tentative territory. A typical sales response function is shown in Exhibit 7.10. The figure shows that there are first increasing, then diminishing, and finally decreasing returns to the number of sales calls. The increasing returns are realized at low levels of sales force effort. The account, never having been contacted previously or only on rare occasions, responds positively and places orders with the salesperson as the number of salesperson calls increases. At first, the rise in sales is swift but then begins to flatten as the number of sales calls is increased. Decreasing returns set in when the number of calls becomes excessive, and the salesperson becomes a nuisance to the account. In the hypothetical example in Exhibit 7.10, this occurs when the salesperson calls on the ac-

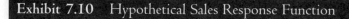

Exhibit 7.10   Hypothetical Sales Response Function

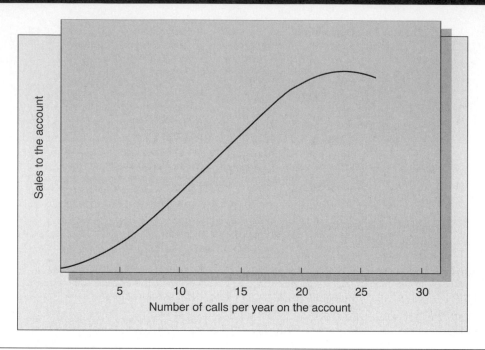

count more than twice a month. The costs associated with calling on the account are directly proportional to the number of calls. The firm must balance sales/cost issues to determine the optimal call level on each account, taking into consideration the sales response functions of all the accounts in the territory.

There are two popular ways of estimating the function relating sales to the number of calls on an account: empirical-based methods and judgment-based methods.[18] The former use regression analysis to estimate the function relating historical sales in each territory to an a priori set of predictors likely to affect sales, including the number of calls. The function so determined represents the line of average sales relationship across all planning and control units.[19]

The judgment-based approaches require that someone in the sales organization, typically the salesperson serving the account but sometimes the sales manager, estimate the sales-per-sales-call function so that the optimal number of calls to be made on each account can be determined. One of the original, but still popular, judgment-based approaches relies on the interactive computer program CALLPLAN, in which the response function for each account is generated from the salesperson's own inputs.[20] The program operates in the following way. The salesperson assigned to the territory is asked what sales will result from each current customer and prospect in the following situations:

- No calls are made.
- One-half the present calls are made.
- The present level of calls is continued.
- Fifty percent more calls are scheduled.
- A saturation level of calls is made.

The salesperson is also asked the probabilities that prospects will be converted into customers with different call frequencies. CALLPLAN then fits curves to these data points and prints out the expected sales for all feasible call frequencies and the optimal number of calls and the length of each call to be made on each client and prospect during an average effort period. In one experiment designed to test CALLPLAN, 20 representatives from United Airlines were matched and then one from each pair was randomly assigned to one of two groups. The 10 control group salespeople were asked to manually estimate their optimal call frequency on each account. The 10 experimental group salespeople were asked their inputs via the CALLPLAN interactive system, and their optimal call levels were determined by the program. Both groups then called on their accounts at these predetermined levels during the experiment. "After six months, the average CALLPLAN salesperson had sales 8.1 percent higher than his matched counterpart."[21] CALLPLAN seems best suited to repetitive selling situations where the amount of time spent with an account is an important factor in the amount of sales generated.

Determine total work load
When the account analysis is complete, a work load analysis can be performed for each territory. The procedure parallels that discussed previously for determining the size of the sales force using the work load method. The total amount of face-to-face contact is computed by multiplying the frequency with which each type of account should be called on by the number of such accounts. The products are then summed. This figure is combined with estimates of the nonselling and travel time necessary to cover the territory to determine the total amount of work involved in covering that territory.[22] A similar set of calculations is made for each tentative territory.

Adjust Tentative Territories

Step 5 in territory planning adjusts the boundaries of the tentative territories established in Step 3 to compensate for the differences in work load found in Step 4. It is likely, for example, that Washington, Oregon, Montana, Idaho, Wyoming, and Utah together might contain the same sales potential as Ohio. Since considerably less travel time would be necessary to cover the Ohio territory, the work load in the two territories would be far from equal and adjustments will need to be made.

While attempting to balance potentials and work loads across territories, the analyst must keep in mind that the sale potential per account is not fixed. It is likely to vary with the number of calls made. While computer call allocation models like CALLPLAN consider this, it is not taken into account when, for example, the firm uses the ABC Rule of Account Classification and relies exclusively on historic sales when making account classifications. Clearly there is reciprocal causation between account attractiveness and account effort.

Account attractiveness affects how hard the account should be worked. At the same time, the number of calls and length of the calls affect the sales likely to be realized from the account. Yet, this reciprocal causation is only implicitly recognized in some schemes used to determine work loads for territories. The firm needs a mechanism for balancing potentials and work loads when adjusting the initial territories if it is not using a computer model.

There are several ways to accomplish this balance. One way is to formally estimate the function that relates sales in a territory to the potential and work load in the territory, using regression-based or judgment-based methods discussed previously. An alternative is to use the subjective judgment of executives to decide on all changes in call frequency to achieve some specific objective. For example, a Midwestern wholesaler of farm machinery used this approach: It classified all accounts into three categories (A, B, and C) according to potential. It then changed the frequency with which salespeople called on farm equipment dealers and almost doubled sales per territory within three years.[23] Another subjective method restructures the tentative territories so that each territory involves relatively equal amounts of work, since the tentative areas already reflect equal amounts of potential, and continues adjusting by trial and error until the proper balance is achieved.

Whether an analytical, objective-and-task, or trial-and-error approach is taken, some realignment of the tentative territories should be expected, and those involved should allow for this when planning territories. Because of the many ways sales territories can be altered, firms increasingly are using computers to investigate potential realignments. For example, Exhibit 7.11 describes how companies like Professional Detailing Network use computer software, specifically TerrAlign, to reconfigure sales territories.

Exhibit 7.11   Technology in Sales Management Using Computer Software to Realign Sales Territories

The Need for Speed

Divvying up sales territories is a monumental, headache-filled job for most companies. Steve Baumhover (director of information services at Professional Detailing Network, a contract pharmaceutical sales organization in the Northeast), needs to be able to realign his sales force quickly and effectively. When new or existing clients call, they want new salespeople in the field immediately. This requires Baumhover to be constantly reevaluating and reconfiguring the company's sales force.

"Around here things happen quickly. Our clients decide that they can't cover the market themselves and they're going to have us do it, and all of a sudden they want us to add another 100 sales reps." This has precipitated the use of computer mapping software to help him create sales territories. He notes that when you have to build new sales forces in a hurry, using computer software enables you to "get really far along and [you] can work from there, rather than just starting from scratch. That cuts days of work." The bottom line is that in companies large and small, sales managers are realizing that computer software can be a critical tool in maximizing the configuration of sales territories.

Benefits of the Computer System

Several companies dominate the geographic information systems (GIS) business. TerrAlign, a family of software products from Metron, Inc., uses a mapping format to help users develop, administer, and adjust sales territories. Other major players include Environmental Systems Research Institute (ESRI), which focuses on government and educational users, and MapInfo, whose clients include AT&T, UPS, and Exxon. The benefits of using such mapping software are substantial. Pfizer realized a 10 to 15 percent reduction in travel time expenses and an amazing ROI of 2,000 percent after incorporating Metron's TerrAlign. The cost of this software is high. A one-time purchase of TerrAlign is $2,000 while one year of full customer support and consulting can run more than $100,000.

Using the System with Salespeople

Uses for this software have expanded as technology has improved and needs of sales managers have been better defined. For example, current products such as TerrAlign have the ability to model how well a salesperson will do when he or she enters a new territory. Based on a salesperson's prior performance, it is possible to build a model that estimates his or her success in a new or reconfigured territory. In addition, and even more importantly, the software can be used to establish performance standards for individual salespeople. Using data from the territory and its potential, sales managers can model sales goals for individual territories and salespeople. While the initial costs can be high, these products offer managers desktop computer solutions to the complexity of territory design and a host of other sales management issues. Moreover, as more companies enter the market, the cost of mapping software goes down, making it affordable for more companies.

Source: "Take a Right and . . . ," *Sales and Marketing Management* (September 1997), pp. 91–96. Check out these Web sites for more information: *www.mapinfo.com* (MapInfo's Web site for MapInfo) and *www.terralign.com* (Metron's Web site for TerrAlign).

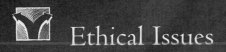

Assigning Salespeople to Sales Territories

As assistant to the vice president of sales, David was in a quandary. His boss had just handed him the job of developing tentative sales territory assignments for the college recruits who had just completed the company's training program. The company's philosophy was to assign each new rep to the smaller trade accounts in the area. Reps who performed exceptionally well in serving the small, independent outlets in the area could be expected to be promoted to better territories—territories that meant calling on regional headquarters offices of large, national accounts. These offices typically ordered for all the stores in the area and thus placed much larger orders.

Reps were evaluated on the basis of the sales potential of each account. The company used square foot per outlet as its yardstick to assess potential. It had previously established that was a good measure of the size and volume of the account. It had also established some historic standards as to the average amount of each client's potential it could be reasonably expected to secure. Those salespeople who consistently beat the standard could expect early promotions.

In making the assignments, David was trying to balance what he thought to be the honest interests of the sales reps and the company. At the same time, he was trying to be sensitive to discrimination issues. He believed that by assigning the black sales reps to those areas in which the greatest proportion of the outlets were managed by black managers and Hispanic reps to those areas that had the largest concentration of Hispanic owners, he could maximize their chances for early promotion. The reps might feel more comfortable in operating in these territories, and he was also familiar with empirical evidence that indicated salesperson–customer similarity can affect the likelihood of a sale and its size. If his thinking was correct, assigning salespeople on this basis would also improve company performance, thereby enhancing his own position. He did not want to be charged with racial discrimination though.

Do you approve or disapprove of David's thinking to assign salespeople to territories based primarily on racial considerations?

Source: Barton A. Weitz, Stephen B. Castleberry, and John F. Tanner Jr., *Selling: Building Partnerships,* 3d ed. (New York: Irwin/McGraw–Hill, 1998) p. 61; Dawn Myers, "You Get What You Give, So Make It Good," *Promotional Products Business* (June 1998), pp. 105–11.

Assign Salespeople to Territories

After territory boundaries are established, the analyst can determine which salesperson should be assigned to which territory. Up to now, it has generally been assumed there are no differences in abilities among salespersons or in the effectiveness of different salespeople with different accounts or different products.[24] Such differences do arise, however. All salespeople do not have the same ability, nor are they equally effective with the same customers or products. At this stage in territory planning, the analyst should consider such differences and should attempt to assign each salesperson to the territory where his or her relative contribution to profit is the highest.

Unfortunately, the ideal cannot always be met. It would be too disruptive to an established sales force with established sales territories to change practically all account coverage. As the "Ethical Issues" box indicates, changing territory assignments can upset salespeople. If the firm is operating without assigned sales territories, then the realignment might be closer to the ideal. The firm with established territories typically must be content to change assignments on a more limited basis.

One way of allowing for differences in general ability among salespeople is by rating each representative's ability using an index form. The best salespeople may be rated 1.0, for example, and all other salespeople rated relative to them. One such relative scheme is to consider that a salesperson with a rating of 0.8 could secure 80 percent of the business in the territory that a representative with a rating of 1.0 could obtain. One can then systematically vary the assignments of salespeople to territories to determine which assignment maximizes the company's return.

The actual assignment of salespeople to sales territories also incorporates personal considerations. The firm may not want to change salesperson call assignments for particular accounts because of the potential for lost business. It may not want to reduce sales force size even if the analysis suggests it should because of morale problems associated with downsizing. Even increasing sales force size can be disruptive. More salespeople mean more sales territories, which means redrawing existing boundaries. In sum, sales managers will want to reflect people considerations when they redraw territory boundaries. They will want to minimize disruptions to existing personal relationships between salespeople and customers.

SUMMARY

This chapter reviewed the important sales management planning decisions involving the number of sales territories needed and the process that can be used to decide on the design of each. A sales territory represents a group of present and potential customers assigned to a salesperson, branch, dealer, or distributor for a given time. Although territories are often defined by their geographic boundaries, the key distinguishing component is customers. Good territory design can positively influence sales force morale and the firm's ability to serve the market and to evaluate the selling effort, whereas poorly designed territories can have the opposite effect.

The administrative decisions regarding the number of sales territories or the size of the sales force, the design of the individual territories themselves, and the allocation of the total selling effort to accounts are closely intertwined. For purposes of understanding, though, it is useful to treat the issues of sales force size before addressing the other issues.

The three primary methods for determining how many territories there should be are the breakdown, work load, and incremental methods. The breakdown method relies on an estimate of what an average salesperson could be expected to sell; the number of sales-person required is then determined by dividing forecasted sales by this average. The work load method rests on the premise that all sales personnel should shoulder an equal amount of work. Management estimates the total amount of work required to serve the market, taking into account the number of customers, how often each should be called on, and for how long. This estimate is then divided by the amount of work an individual salesperson should be able to handle to determine the total number of salespeople required. The basic premise underlying the incremental method of determining the sales force size is that sales representatives should be added so long as the incremental profit produced by their addition exceeds the incremental cost. While conceptually correct, this is the most difficult method to implement.

Once the number of territories is determined, the sales manager can design the individual territories. The general process he or she might be expected to follow is (1) select the basic control unit, (2) estimate market potential in each control unit, (3) combine control units into tentative territories, (4) perform a work load analysis for each territory, (5) adjust tentative territories to allow for sales potential and coverage difficulty differences, and (6) assign salespeople to territories.

DISCUSSION QUESTIONS

1. In spite of careful planning, companies occasionally face the problems that arise when one or more territories collapse. In one case, a company had recently introduced an innovative compensation plan. Territories do collapse and sales representatives and managers realize that quotas are not going to be reached. What can cause a territory to collapse? How should a company compensate sales reps after their territories collapse, even though the sales reps are not at fault?

2. Most sales managers hesitate to modify sales territories unless supported by compelling reasons. Likewise, sales managers are reluctant to make major changes in the sales compensation package. On the other hand, reassigning salespeople from one territory

to another is fairly common and often reflects a form of promotion. One expert contends that if a company's sales force knows the territory too well, then it's time to reassign territories. Why would a company reassign all or most of the territories? What are the advantages and disadvantages of this approach?

3.   Many sales managers dislike changing either territories or compensation plans unless it is absolutely necessary. Why is this so? What evidence does a sales manager need to determine if a territory change is needed?

4.   Some companies have developed computer models, such as CALLPLAN, for determining the call patterns to be used by their sales personnel. Determining call patterns (routing plans) is very much like deciding how you would visit the 10 largest cities in your state while traveling the least amount of miles or time. In what situations would computer-determined call patterns be appropriate? Have you ever had a job where routing plans were applicable?

5.   Chapter 7 describes the process to follow to develop territories. After territories have been developed, changes may occur that indicate that the territories need to be realigned. What changes can you identify that indicate the need for realignment? How would you go about the process of realigning territories? How would you implement the changes?

EXPERIENTIAL APPLICATION

You have been hired as a sales representative by Interconics, Inc., and assigned to the Texas territory. The customers are located in the following cities: Dallas, Houston, San Antonio, and Austin. Using the Internet to gather information about each of the cities in the territory, prepare a routing plan that will minimize the number of driving miles. As a starting point, consider referencing the book John P. Norback and Robert F. Love, "Geometric Approaches to Solving the Traveling Salesman Problem," *Management Science* 23 (July 1977), pp. 1,208–33.

INTERNET EXERCISE

Visit the Web site for the companies discussed in Exhibit 7.11 (MapInfo is *www.mapinfo.com* and Metron is *www.terralign.com*). As a sales manager, how could you use this information to help you design the most efficient and effective sales territory? What other information might be useful? Consider visiting the Web site for Claritas (*www.claritas.com*). How could you build that information into the mapping software offered by MapInfo and Metron?

SUGGESTED READINGS

Berger, Melanie, "Take a Right at the Light," *Sales & Marketing Management* (September 1997), pp. 91–96.

La Forge, Raymond W., and David W. Cravens, "Empirical and Judgment-Based Sales Force Decision Models: A Comparative Analysis," *Decision Sciences* 16 (Spring 1985), pp. 177–95.

La Forge, Raymond W., David W. Cravens, and Clifford E. Young, "Improving Salesforce Productivity," *Business Horizons* 28 (September–October 1985), pp. 50–59.

La Forge, Raymond W., David W. Cravens, and Clifford E. Young, "Using Contingency Analysis to Select Selling Effort Allocation Methods," *Journal of Personal Selling and Sales Management* 6 (August 1986), pp. 19–28.

Schlon, Charles C., *The Complete Guide to Sales Territory Planning & Management.* Chicago: Dartnell Corp., 1990.

Comprehensive Cases for Part I

Case 1–1

The Valley Winery*

Pat Waller, recently hired as sales manager of the San Francisco region's chain division, was lamenting the problems he inherited. Despite favorable sales results for the San Francisco region, turnover was so severe Waller could not understand how sales increased during the past several years. He was surprised to learn the average sales rep had been with the San Francisco division of Valley Winery for only seven months and sales force turnover neared 100 percent a year. In fact, only one sales rep had more than two years' experience. Waller had heard that high turnover was a problem nationwide but did not expect such high figures for San Francisco.

Waller supervises two area managers, who in turn direct nine district managers. District managers supervise 5 to 6 sales reps, of which there are 50 in the San Francisco division. Approximately 50 new sales reps are hired each year, but the sales force size remains relatively constant. Waller knew the increased competitiveness in the market would make it more difficult to continue to obtain future sales increases. The excessive turnover problem would command immediate attention.

The Company

The Valley Winery, founded in 1933 in Napa, California, is the largest domestic producer of wine in the United States. Started with only a $7,500 investment at the end of Prohibition, it has become the leading producer of low-priced, consistent-quality wines. Favorite brands include Santo Rey and Valley premium table wines, Astral sparkling wines, Valley brandy, and most recently the Cool Valley line of wine coolers. As is true with most other wineries, Valley produces a low-grade, fortified sherry known in the streets as "sneaky pete." This product appeals to a small market niche and receives virtually no marketing support. The Valley name does not even appear on the label, a practice followed by other wineries as well. Brand names for this low-end product include Snake-Eye, 20/20, and Acey-Deucy. Valley also bottles a line of pop wines, which have never achieved high sales. Brands in the pop line are California Dream and Mile-High. The Valley Winery sells over 40 percent of all wine produced in the United States each year.

The Valley Winery is also one of this nation's largest privately held companies. As such, it is not required to disclose any financial information. However, according to financial analysts who specialize in the wine and distilled spirits industry, 1998 sales were believed to have exceeded $1.5 billion. Of the various producers of wine and distilled spirits, the Valley Winery is believed to be the best managed and most innovative.

Valley's phenomenal growth and success can be traced to two broad factors. As already stated, it produces wines of consistently high quality at relatively low prices. Second, Valley's sales force, using a push strategy, is considered by many to be the most ag-

---

*Jeffrey J. Ertel, MBA–Marketing, University of Wisconsin–Madison, assisted in preparing this case. Copyright © 1998 Neil M. Ford.

gressive and innovative in the industry. As the manager of a San Francisco liquor store states, "Turn your back on a Valley sales rep, and your store becomes a Valley warehouse." Heading up the sales force is Carl Roman, whose passion for detail and success is well known.

Valley Winery distributes nationwide through liquor and beer distributors located in metropolitan areas. Valley owns roughly 50 percent of these distributors, mostly those that are larger and more profitable. Valley's field representatives call on noncompany liquor and beer wholesalers across the country. Valley uses a major account system with reps calling on the headquarters of large chain stores.

The organization of the San Francisco division is typical, especially in those market areas where Valley owns the distributor. There are three sales groups. The first group calls on liquor stores and bars. Career-type salespeople dominate this group and most are older. These sales reps are paid a straight commission of 6 percent on sales. Almost all, 95 percent, are male. The second group calls on restaurants, resorts, hotels, and motels. This predominantly female sales group is paid a straight salary ($19,500 to $23,500) plus a company car. The third group is the chain division. This group, 99 percent male, receives a straight salary plus car and a year-end bonus. Their salary ranged from $22,000 to $27,000. The chain group is considered the major source of future sales managers.

The San Francisco chain division sales organization has experienced numerous changes. Early in 1994, the company had a wine division and a wine cooler division. Exhibit 1 illustrates this organization. Early in 1995, Carl Roman revamped the structure and created a product line division reflecting premium and vintage products. Within the Premium Division were the Valley wines, the aperitif wines, and the Astral sparkling wines. The Vintage Division carried the Estate wines, Santo Rey wines, the Cool Valley line of wine coolers, and the Valley brandy. Exhibit 2 shows this organization. Less than six months later, Carl Roman introduced yet another modification reflecting the importance of key customers, which were classified as major accounts. Exhibit 3 illustrates this change. Sales reps calling on major accounts represented the entire Valley line of wines and distilled spirits. The San Francisco division is responsible for sales to all of the major grocery headquarters, such as Safeway, Lucky, and Alpha Beta.

Forward integration decisions are a function of how well the independent distributor covers the market and the size of the market potential. Carl Roman had been very concerned with the chain store sales performance in the San Francisco area for some time. The previous distributor assigned 15 sales reps to call on the chain outlets and had resisted Valley's pleas to increase the sales force to 30 to 35 reps. After Valley Winery bought out the San Francisco distributor, sales of Valley Wines increased dramatically, primarily due to the increased number of sales reps calling on chain stores—from 15 up to 50. None of the 15 reps who worked for the previous owner was retained after Valley purchased the distributorship.

The buying process for these major chain accounts is fairly standard. Each sales rep is personally responsible for a specific number of stores taken from all major grocery chains. Thus, a sales rep will call on Safeway, Lucky, and Alpha Beta stores. The total number of outlets constitutes the sales rep's territory.

The sales rep is responsible for reaching monthly display quotas on each line of products. For instance, one month the representative is responsible for displaying 50 cases of Santo Rey wine in 1.5- and 4.0-liter sizes. The next month the rep may have a display quota of 50 cases of Santo Rey in 3.0-liter sizes. This pattern repeats itself throughout the year. Exhibit 4 illustrates monthly quota patterns for different display results by sales rep and the extent of the turnover problem.

Exhibit 1   San Francisco Division: Chain Store Division Organizational Chart (May 1994)

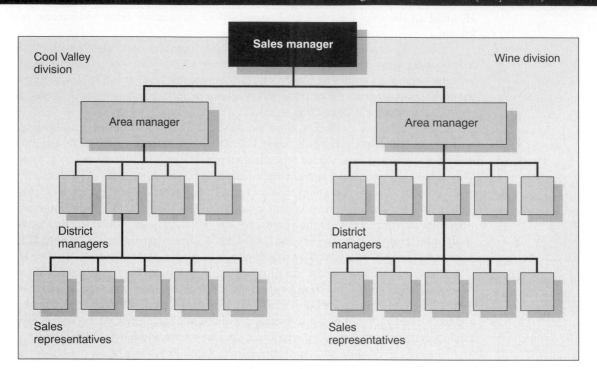

Sales reps call on either the store manager or the wine clerk, using preprepared sales sheets. The store manager or wine clerk must then order the beverages from the chain's warehouse, where all wines and distilled spirits are stored. The sales rep is responsible for all merchandising, service, and anything else related to Valley Winery that is needed in the chain outlet.

Rumors are abundant about the aggressiveness displayed by sales reps in the wine and liquor industry, especially Valley sales reps, who have been accused of relocating competitive displays and products to obtain the best space for Valley wines. Sales reps from other wineries dislike the "competitive spirit" shown by Valley reps, who have also been accused of such tactics as spraying hair spray on competitive displays and bottles so that they will gather dust and so discourage sales. Other so-called tricks of the trade have sales reps dumping bags of ice into the cardboard boxes supporting the display so they will collapse after the ice melts. Occasionally, bottles and even cases are "accidentally" broken by sales reps from competitive producers.

Waller's concern about the turnover problem led to a series of conclusions. First, recruiting and training costs approached $20,000 per year per representative. Waller knew that with less turnover, Valley Winery and the San Francisco division profitability would improve. Second, Waller believed sales would improve. The $20,000 figure does not include opportunity costs associated with lost sales resulting from not having accounts called on. And these costs do not include the time it would take for a new rep to adequately develop rapport with the accounts. Considering all these factors, Waller felt confident that decreasing turnover would improve sales and company profits. On the other hand, Waller knew Carl Roman was pleased with the division's improving performance.

Exhibit 2 San Francisco Division: Chain Store Division Organizational Chart (January 1995)

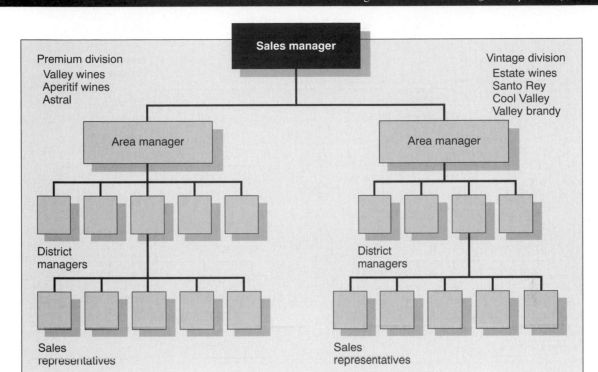

Pat Waller decided at least to investigate the situation. As a start, Waller examined two possible sources to see if they were the crux of the problem. These included the recruiting and hiring process and the nature of the position. To research the recruiting and hiring process, Waller contacted the personnel office. To learn about the nature of the position, Waller traveled with a number of the sales reps.

Mike Wehner, personnel manager for the San Francisco division, was responsible for hiring all personnel for the division, including warehouse workers, truck drivers, office personnel, and the sales force. Wehner used a variety of methods to attract sales candidates. Recruiting college graduates from a number of area universities was common. This generally resulted in 10 to 15 new sales reps a year. Open newspaper advertisements usually produced 10 hires per year. The use of six local employment agencies, with fees of approximately $2,000 per hired individual, resulted in 15 to 20 new reps per year. Last, any employee recommending a friend or an acquaintance who was subsequently hired received a $200 finder's fee. This practice typically cost the company $2,000 per year. Wehner claims not to recruit personnel from competitors or customers. Wehner said he thought those hired through employment agencies were the most successful, but he was not positive.

The hiring process generally followed a similar pattern. The selected applicant completes a simple application form and is then interviewed by Wehner or his assistant for approximately 30 minutes. During that time, if the candidate seems motivated and enthusiastic, and asks for the sales job, the applicant is asked back for additional interviews.

Exhibit 3   San Francisco Division: Chain Store Division Organizational Chart (June 1995)

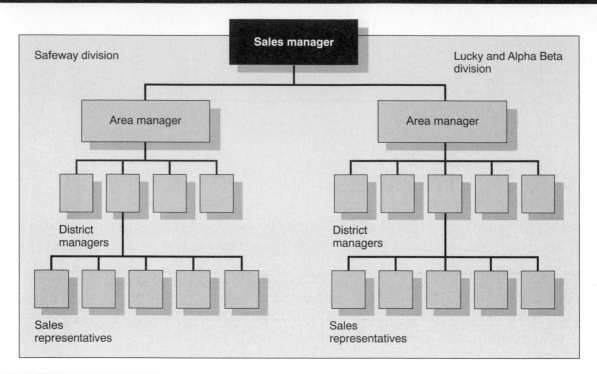

The candidate then interviews with the distributorship's top manager for no more than 10 minutes. The San Francisco distributor is owned by Valley, and the new sales rep works for the distributor. Valley can reassign the sales rep to wholly owned distributors. All sales reps interact with the area distributor and often participate in training programs with the distributor's other two sales groups. Waller learned the distributor's top manager regards youth and physical characteristics as the most important traits an applicant should have to pass this stage.

The next step involves an interview with Waller's predecessor, John Ruppert, who was promoted to a home office assignment as a major account manager. The recruit is then whisked off to spend a day in the field with an experienced sales rep. Waller questioned whether this day in the field, during which the recruit is "wined and dined," is an accurate representation of the job. If all of these hurdles are passed, the applicant is then offered the job.

Pat Waller's work with the sales reps provided useful information. Waller traveled with two sales reps and discovered many new things about the sales job. Before being promoted to the sales manager position for the San Francisco division, Waller had moved through the ranks, starting as a sales rep in the Seattle division. As a sales rep, Waller served primarily in a missionary capacity, calling on liquor stores and taverns. Waller then advanced to district manager for the Seattle division. Next, Waller moved to the Phoenix division, where he served as area manager before accepting a home office assignment as a product manager assistant. This itinerary was typical for a person selected to move into

Exhibit 4   Cases on Display: Quota versus Actual Results by Sales Representative

Product: Cool Valley
Store: Safeway 711

Month	J	F	M	A	M	J	J	A	S	O	N	D	J	F	M	A	M	J	J	A	S
Quota	40	15	40	75	75	100	125	125	75	25	25	40	40	0	50	75	100	110	125	125	115
Mike Fisk	28	15	32	50	0	0	(terminated)														
Tom Rhea							22	45	39	25	30	27	0	45	62	94	94	96	100	120	70

Product: Santo Rey
Store: Lucky 42

Month	J	F	M	A	M	J	J	A	S	O	N	D	J	F	M	A	M	J	J	A	S
Quota	30	0	75	0	75	0	60	0	80	0	90	0	30	0	75	0	75	0	60	0	80
Stan Smith	0	0	12	0	50	0	60	(terminated)													
John Mahorn								0	21	0	28	(terminated)									
Steve Anderson												0	18	42	0	0	(terminated)				
Neil Johnson																	50	0	50	0	85

Product: Valley Wines
Store: Alpha Beta 572

Month	J	F	M	A	M	J	J	A	S	O	N	D	J	F	M	A	M	J	J	A	S
Quota	50	0	60	0	75	0	50	0	80	0	90	0	50	0	60	0	75	0	50	0	80
Paul Barling	30	0	27	0	60	0	45	0	45	0	50	0	(terminated)								
Mark Boringer													33	0	45	0	50	0	50	0	75

sales management, except that most sales managers are promoted from the chain store sales force. Waller's new assignment represented his first exposure to major account management.

On September 8, 1999, Waller traveled with Marv Flanigan, a nine-month veteran. Although scheduled to meet at 7 A.M., Marv was late, stating his hour-long drive was delayed by a terrible accident. Flanigan said the latest territory change created a longer commute for him. Since he was late, they started to work immediately, forgoing the customary cup of coffee Waller intended to buy as a warm-up tactic to learn about Flanigan's plans for the day. Waller and Flanigan spent nearly the entire morning at an Alpha Beta store (#561) building a 50-case display for Valley wines, resetting the cold box, and servicing the shelves. After a 15-minute presentation to the wine clerk, Flanigan and Waller left for the next call. When Waller congratulated Flanigan on the 50-case display, Flanigan quipped, "Thanks, but unfortunately it's not enough to make quota. Nobody, but *nobody*, ever makes quota. That's 25 cases short, and that store is one of my best accounts. And did you see my Santo Rey quota—90 cases—no way!"

During their afternoon together, Waller observed a very aggressive sales promotion that Flanigan presented to a wine clerk at a Safeway store (#724). Afterward, Waller questioned the tenuous sales figures Flanigan quoted to the wine buyer. He responded by claiming, "John [division's previous sales manager] and Rick [Marv's current area manager] told me to stretch the sales estimates." Continuing, he revealed, "They said it's the only way to make my numbers. Rick even told me to pump up the numbers on the recap I send to Napa."

Pumping up the numbers meant a sales rep would claim a 50-case display had been installed when the store manager or wine clerk would only order a 25- to 30-case display.

The display would only look like a 50-case display; center boxes in the display would be empty.

On September 23, 1999, Waller worked with Bill Murphy. Murphy, a six-month veteran, arrived grumbling. He said his district manager called him at 10:30 the night before complaining about the condition of Safeway #507. After 30 minutes of specific instructions and other messages, Murphy had agreed to visit the store early that morning to correct the deficiencies. He mentioned that he received calls at night from his district manager about two to three times a week, often to check his progress on winery directives. These usually occurred, he claimed, during the hour or two he spent on preparation each night.

During lunch, Murphy discussed his desire to move into management. He said, "Although district managers are often considered to be no more than baby sitters for the new reps, I really think that I can do a great job. The pay doesn't even bother me. [District managers received $3,000 to $4,000 more.] I mean, with all the cases I've sold, if I were paid on commission, I'd already be rich. I think I can really train those new reps just as the manual says."

At this point, Waller thought he was starting to get a good sense of the situation.

Case 1–2

Omega Medical Products, Inc.*

Omega Medical Products (OMP), located in Denver, Colorado, is one of the top manufacturers of life-support medical equipment and surgical pharmaceuticals. In fiscal year 1998, OMP recorded sales of $380 million (see Exhibit 1). Over the past three years, sales have increased at an annual rate of 18 percent. The company currently employs 175 sales reps, including a separate sales force of 40 that handles the company's anesthesia line exclusively. As the result of a recent staff organization, a decision was made to realign the sales and marketing department to better meet the future goals of the company.

Five years ago, Omega's president retired, and the top position was filled by the executive vice president, Christopher John. Subsequently, several other major changes occurred in the executive staff hierarchy. The most important were elimination of the executive vice president position and creation of the position of vice president, marketing and sales. Reporting to the new vice president would be the current vice president of international sales; the general manager of medical equipment marketing; the general manager of distribution, customer services and gases; the director of market research and strategic planning; the director of communications; and the marketing manager of architectural products (see Exhibit 2).

The vice president of marketing and sales, destined to be one of the most powerful positions at OMP, was filled by Earl Callahan. Callahan had previously held the top marketing job in a firm that manufactured medical products unrelated to those sold by Omega. Filling this position with an outsider generated noticeable discontent among several executives who had been considered top contenders. Soon after he began to work, Callahan was pressured by John to have a revised sales organization chart completed before Omega's new fiscal year, beginning July 1. After reviewing Omega's current organization charts, sales figures, and marketing plans for new products, Callahan realized there were several major problems.

Marketing Activities

Omega's marketing function was divided into four product areas. The patient care group consisted of anesthesia equipment and disposables, nursing equipment, and infant care supplies. The anesthesia equipment and disposables line accounted for the greater dollar volume with 1998 sales of almost $100 million. With new products as the primary growth factor in the portable patient monitoring area, sales were expected to be $191 million by 2000. Product prices ranged from a few cents for disposables to several thousand dollars for equipment.

The respiratory therapy line accounted for $66 million in sales in 1998. The line had

---

*Bonnie J. Queram, MBA–Marketing, University of Wisconsin–Madison, assisted in preparing this case. Copyright © 1998 Neil M. Ford.

Exhibit I 1998 Sales ($000)		
Patient care		$139,045
Anesthesia equipment	$66,165	
Anesthesia disposables	33,742	
Nursing products	22,638	
Infant care	16,500	
Respiratory therapy		66,690
Architectural products		59,367
Anesthesia (gases)		82,591
Other (government, OEM, service, military)		32,424
Total		$380,117

experienced only slight growth over the last few years but was expected to generate $97 million by 2002 with the introduction of one major new critical care ventilator, priced as high as $35,000 with all accessories. The prime market for this do-everything machine was the small- to medium-size hospital. Although Omega was the leader in the anesthesia field, it did not enjoy the same position in respiratory care. Because of several major failures with new products during the past 10 to 15 years, the Omega name was still associated by many therapists with inferior quality, poor product design, and inadequate service.

The architectural product line, composed of pipelines and gas outlets, had sales of $59 million in 1998 while the anesthesia line (gases), sold by a separate sales organization, accounted for $82 million. The major product was a liquid that, when converted to gas, was used to anesthetize patients for surgery.

Sales Activities

The general sales force, consisting of 135 representatives in the United States and Canada reporting to 16 district managers and six regional vice presidents (see Exhibit 3), were expected to call on four major departments in each hospital: operating room, recovery room, emergency room, and nursery. Additionally, they were expected to keep in contact with purchasing and, if one existed, with the biomedical engineering department. The latter, usually present only in larger hospitals, was often responsible for reviewing and testing potential new equipment. Biomedical engineers were becoming instrumental in the purchase of sophisticated electronic monitoring devices.

Also, the sales force was expected to sell bulk oxygen and nitrous oxide as well as Omega's architectural product line equipment to new hospitals or those being remodeled. This required that sales reps work closely with architects and construction contractors, usually a very time-consuming endeavor, ranging from several months to over one year.

The anesthesia sales force called on the anesthesia staff exclusively. Close and frequent contact was necessary in most cases. The members of the sales force, all with chemical backgrounds, were expected to keep abreast of technological developments in the field. Some sales reps were formerly anesthetists.

Although Omega's products covered a variety of medical applications and necessitated sales calls to many different departments, the general line sales force had handled the lines very well. Callahan thought one primary reason they had done so well was that the majority of Omega's products were not particularly complicated and the sales force could be adequately trained by product managers when new products were introduced. Additionally, although Omega sold several thousand items, which realistically is too much for a sales rep to handle effectively, Callahan knew many products sold with little or no

Exhibit 2 Current Organization Chart

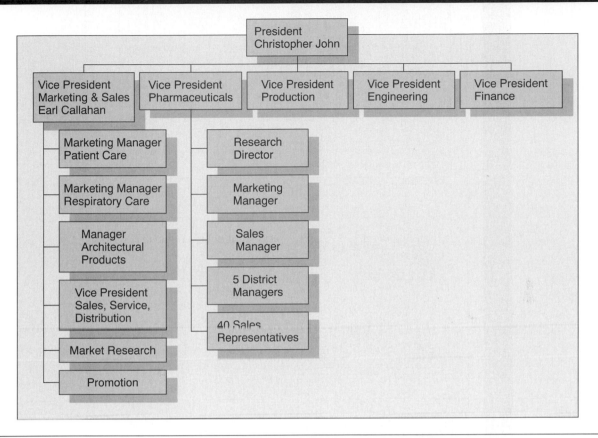

sales effort because of the Omega name and strong dealer network. Most dealers handled low-cost, easy-to-sell products, although some of the very large dealers sold high-priced equipment.

Callahan believed, however, that this would not continue because many products planned for market introduction in the next five years were state-of-the-art electronic monitoring equipment. Most of these products were in the anesthesia line. Omega's lack of experience in the medical electronics field would require an intensive sales effort to enter the market profitably, as there were several formidable competitors.

Unfortunately, as many as half of Omega's sales reps did not have the training or experience to sell these kinds of products. In view of the need to deal with hospital biomedical engineers on a very technical level, in the long run, Callahan surmised, it would be better to use only sales personnel experienced in selling electronic equipment rather than attempt to train the entire force. Besides, he knew from personal conversations that no more than 10 percent of the representatives had any interest in learning about or selling the new equipment. Thus, he wondered about augmenting the sales force with specialists who would be able to provide technical assistance to sell portable patient monitoring equipment. But since there were already general line and anesthesia sales representatives calling on hospital personnel, he did not want a third party calling on the same personnel. Callahan thought this would be more confusing than advantageous.

Exhibit 3 Current Sales Organization Chart

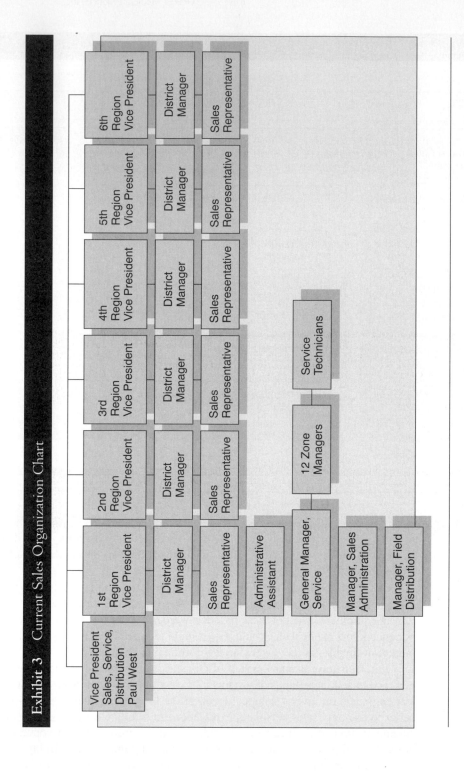

Other Information

For the past year, the marketing manager of respiratory care, Bill Griese, had been attempting to convince Callahan that despite the line's history, real growth potential existed in respiratory therapy. He wanted the company to spend more time and money pursuing this market. Griese had also indicated that to sell and service the products adequately— particularly the new critical care ventilator—the line should be handled by a separate sales force. He argued that because most of Omega's products were in the anesthesia field, the representatives were spending a disproportionate amount of sales time in that area. Thus, Omega's relatively poor sales and image in respiratory therapy were perpetuated.

Callahan knew that Jeff Hardy, marketing manager for patient care, would lobby for a separate sales group for anesthesia products since that line represents one quarter of the company's sales. Apparently this request had been made several times over the past five years. One proposal had included plans for the anesthesia (gases) sales force to handle the anesthesia equipment also because both were sold to the same department. Another proposal had called for a separate anesthesia equipment force altogether.

Callahan thought drugs and equipment required substantially different sales techniques and one force could not adequately handle both. But he also had reservations about two different representatives calling on the same customer, as was currently the case. On the other hand, a separate anesthesia equipment force would result in substantially more sales time spent on respiratory products by the general line sales force.

Anesthesia Sales Organization

About 10 years before, Omega's chemical research department had discovered a revolutionary new drug (a gas) to anesthetize patients safely for surgery. After two years of testing for the Food and Drug Administration, the drug was approved and successfully introduced to the marketplace. It is currently used on 60 percent of all surgical patients, and it continues to capture market share. The drug has a very high gross margin, and in 1998, it had profits of $35 million on sales of $83 million. Its patent runs through 2002.

To develop the surgical drug market fully and lead the marketing and sales activities, a vice president position was created at the time of the discovery of the new drug. Ronald Hagen was hired for this position. He put together a separate sales organization with 40 persons by 1997. Most of the sales reps were hired away from pharmaceutical companies and thus demanded and were paid salaries and commissions somewhat above those paid to Omega's general line sales force (see Exhibit 4).

Hagen is very proud of his organization, believing his sales representatives are a cut above the general line organization. Consequently, he wants no part of any plans to join the two forces. Besides, other new drugs are scheduled for introduction in the 1998–99 period and will provide the drug sales group with a sufficient product load for several years.

General Line Sales Organization

The general line sales organization, reporting to Paul West, consisted of 135 representatives, 16 district managers, and six regional vice presidents. The service department, also under West, consisted of 172 technicians reporting to 16 zone managers. Also reporting to West were the managers of sales administration, the manager of field distribution, and an administrative assistant.

West was initially upset about the apparent demotion of his position as a result of the reorganization; he had reported directly to John before Callahan was hired. Knowing that further reorganization was imminent, West believed he would ultimately lose control of the

Exhibit 4	Sales Compensation Plans	
	General Line Representatives	**Anesthesia Representatives**
Base salary	$3,500–$3,850	$3,650–$4,100
Commission on sales up to quota (percent)	1%	1%
Commission on sales over quota (percent)	2–5%	2–5%
1997 salary range	$46,200–$57,800	$51,800–$64,750
Average salary	$50,100	$54,000

service and distribution areas. Although this would narrow his responsibilities somewhat, West was not concerned. Because of the need to update both the service organization and the distribution organization to handle the new portable patient care monitoring products, those areas had been commanding a disproportionate amount of his time for the past few months. West would prefer to hire a general manager for service and distribution and have that new individual, reporting to him, handle most of the responsibility in those two crucial areas. He intended to propose this to Callahan.

In the meantime, West was most interested in studying the sales force reorganization and conveying his ideas to Callahan. West had always been interested in developing a separate sales force for anesthesia equipment and disposables. He thought there was sufficient sales volume to support it, and customers would be receptive to the extra attention and service. When selling this equipment, the rep would call on the anesthesia staff, a group typically more difficult to deal with and more technically oriented than personnel from other hospital departments. Often the sale also involved the hospital's biomedical engineers, which was not true of Omega's other products. A separate force could be more intensely trained, thus ensuring better customer service.

West also believed a strong case could be made for putting architectural products under the mandate of a small but specialized sales force. General line sales reps tended to ignore architectural products because their sales consumed too much time and involved contact with nonhospital personnel.

If a separate anesthesia equipment force were developed, the remaining general line would be left with nursing, infant care, respiratory therapy, and architectural products. This seemed reasonable because many of these products were sold in the same hospital departments even though they were categorized in different product lines. West also thought the dealers should be encouraged to handle more low-cost products, giving the general line sales force more time for other products.

The real problem with splitting out the anesthesia products, West thought, was that each group would remain responsible for the new portable patient monitoring equipment. West further believed that since each force would be responsible for a smaller number of the new products, they could be sufficiently trained to do this work. Since most of the new portable monitoring equipment was in the anesthesia area, this group would be selected from those with the most training and experience with electronics products. Additionally, West thought there was a strong case to be made for having "monitoring specialists" in both sales groups. These persons would handle all the products of their groups but would emphasize the new equipment and would be available for dual sales calls with their colleagues who were not so well versed in the items.

At a recent convention, West briefly discussed his ideas with Tom Reinke, the western regional vice president and one of West's closest friends. Reinke had, at one time, worked for a company that manufactured sterilization equipment for hospitals. Following the development of a new, very sophisticated unit, it had divided the sales organization into two groups. One handled the existing line, and the other group specialized in the new equipment. Reinke indicated the sales force division proved disastrous, leading to duplicate sales calls, customer confusion, and increased expenses. He thought the same would occur with West's monitoring specialists. He recommended that Omega hire more technically qualified personnel for the general line sales force. West left the convention somewhat less enthusiastic about his sales force proposal.

Case 1–3

Barro Stickney, Inc.*

Introduction

With four people and sales of $5.5 million, Barro Stickney, Inc. (BSI), had become a successful and profitable manufacturers' representative firm. It enjoyed a reputation for outstanding sales results and friendly, thorough service to both its customers and principals. In addition, BSI was considered a great place to work. The office was comfortable and the atmosphere relaxed but professional. All members of the group had come to value the close, friendly working relationships that had grown with the organization.

Success had brought with it increased profits as well as the inevitable decision regarding further growth. Recent requests from two principals, Franklin Key Electronics and R. D. Ocean, had forced BSI to focus its attention on the question of expansion. It was not to be an easy decision, for expansion offered both risk and opportunity.

Company Background

John Barro and Bill Stickney had established their small manufacturers' representative agency, Barro Stickney, Inc., 10 years before. Both men were close friends who left different manufacturers' representative firms to join as partners in their own "rep" agency. The two worked very well together, and their talents complemented each other.

John Barro was energetic and gregarious. He enjoyed meeting new people and taking on new challenges. It was mainly through John's efforts that many of BSI's eight principals had signed on with BSI. Even after producing $1.75 million in sales this past year, John still made an effort to contribute much of his free time to community organizations in addition to perfecting his golf score.

Bill Stickney liked to think of himself as someone a person could count on. He was thoughtful and thorough. He liked to figure how things could get done, and how they could be better. Much of the administrative work of the agency, such as resource allocation and territory assignments, was handled by Bill. In addition to his contribution of $1.5 million to total company sales, Bill also had a Boy Scout troop and was interested in gourmet cooking. In fact, he often prepared specialties to share with his fellow workers.

A few years later, as the business grew, J. Todd Smith (J.T.) joined as an additional salesperson. J.T. had worked for a nationally known corporation, and he brought his experience dealing with large customers with him. He and his family loved the Harrisburg area, and J.T. was very happy when he was asked to join BSI just as his firm was ready to transfer him to Chicago. John and Bill had worked with J.T. in connection with a hospital fund-raising project, and they were impressed with his tenacity and enthusiasm. Because

*This case was prepared by Tony Langan, B. Jane Stewart, and Lawrence M. Stratton, Jr., under the supervision of Professor Erin Anderson of the Wharton School, University of Pennsylvania. The writing of the case was sponsored by the Manufacturers' Representatives Educational Research Foundation. The cooperation of the Mid-Atlantic Chapter of the Electronic Representatives Association (ERA) is greatly appreciated.

he had produced sales of over $2 million this past year, J.T. was now considered eligible to buy a partnership share of BSI.

Soon after J.T. joined BSI, Elizabeth Lee, a school friend of John's older sister, was hired as office manager. She was cheerful and put as much effort into her work as she did coaching the local swim team. The three salespeople knew they could rely on her to keep track of orders and schedules, and she was very helpful when customers and principals called with requests or problems.

Most principals in the industry assigned their reps exclusive territories, and BSI's ranged over the Pennsylvania, New Jersey, and Delaware area. The partners purchased a small house and converted it into their present office located in Camp Hill, a suburb of Harrisburg, the state capitol of Pennsylvania. The converted home contributed to the familylike atmosphere and attitude that was promoted and prevalent throughout the agency.

Over the years, in addition to local interests, BSI and its people had made an effort to participate in and support the efforts of the Electronics Representative Association (ERA). A wall of the company library was covered with awards and letters of appreciation. BSI had made many friends and important contacts through the organization. Just last year, BSI received a recommendation from Chuck Goodman, a Chicago manufacturers' rep who knew a principal in need of representation in the Philadelphia area. The principal's line worked well with BSI's existing portfolio, and customer response had been quite favorable. BSI planned to continue active participation in the ERA.

Each week, BSI held a 5 o'clock meeting in the office library where all members of the company shared their experiences of the week. It was a time when new ideas were encouraged and everyone was brought up to date. For example, many customer problems were solved here, and principals' and members' suggestions were discussed. An established agenda enabled members to prepare. Most meetings took about 60 to 90 minutes, with emphasis placed on group consensus. It was during this group meeting that BSI would discuss the future of the company.

Opportunities for Expansion

R. D. Ocean was BSI's largest principal, and it accounted for 32 percent of BSI's revenues. Ocean had just promoted James Innve as new sales manager, and he felt an additional salesperson was needed for BSI to achieve the new sales projections. Innve expressed the opinion that BSI's large commission checks justified the additional effort, and he further commented that J.T.'s expensive new car was proof that BSI could afford it.

BSI was not sure an additional salesperson was necessary, but it did not want to lose the goodwill of R. D. Ocean or its business. Also, while it was customary for all principals to meet and tacitly approve new representatives, BSI wanted to be very sure that any new salesperson would fit into the close-knit BSI organization.

Franklin Key Electronics was BSI's initial principal and had remained a consistent contributor of approximately 15 percent of BSI's revenues. BSI felt its customer base was well suited to the Franklin line, and it had worked hard to establish the Franklin Key name with these customers. As a consequence, BSI now considered Franklin Key relatively easy to sell.

A few days previously, Mark Heil, Franklin's representative from Virginia, perished when his private plane crashed, leaving Franklin Key without representation in its D.C./Virginia territory. Franklin did not want to jeopardize its sales of over $800,000 and was desperate to replace Heil before its customers found other sources. Franklin offered the territory to BSI and was anxious to hear the decision within one week.

BSI was not familiar with the territory, but it did understand that there were many military accounts. This meant there was a potential for sizable orders, although a different and

Exhibit I   Return versus Difficulty in Selling

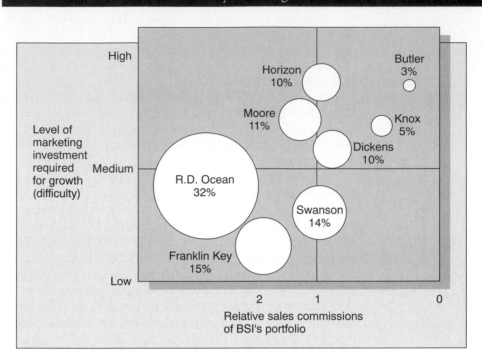

specialized sales approach would be required. Military customers are known to have their own unique approach to purchase decisions.

Because of the distance and the size of the territory, serious consideration was needed as to whether a branch office would be necessary. A branch office would mean less interaction with and a greater independence from the main BSI office. None of the current BSI members seemed eager to move there, but it might be possible to hire someone who was familiar with the territory. There was, of course, always the risk that any successful salesperson might leave and start his or her own rep firm.

In addition to possibilities of expanding its territory and its sales force, BSI also wanted to consider whether it should increase or maintain its number of principals. BSI's established customer base and its valued reputation put it in a strong position to approach potential principals. If, however, BSI had too many principals, it might not be able to offer them all the attention and service they might require.

Preparation for the Meeting

Each member received an agenda and supporting data for the upcoming meeting asking them to consider the issue of expansion. They would be asked whether BSI should or should not expand its territory, its sales force, and/or its number of principals. In preparation, they were each asked to take a good hard look at the current BSI portfolio and to consider all possibilities for growth, including the effect any changes would have on the company's profits, its reputation, and its work environment.

Exhibit 2 Barro Stickney, Inc., Estimation of Cost of Additional Sales Representative

Compensation Costs for New Sales Representative

Depending on the new sales representative's level of experience, BSI would pay a base salary of $15,000–$25,000 with the following bonus schedule:

0% firm's commission revenue up to $500,000 in sales

20% firm's commission revenue for the first $.5 million in sales over $500,000

25% firm's commission revenue for the next $.5 million in sales

30% firm's commission for the next $.5 million in sales

40% firm's commission sales above $2 million

Estimate of Support Costs[1] for New Representative[2]

Search applicant pool, psychological testing, hiring, training,[3] flying final choice to principals for approval[4]	$28,000
Automobile expenses, telephone costs, business cards, entertainment promotion	22,000
Insurance, payroll taxes (social security, unemployment compensation)	16,000
Total expenses	$66,000

Incremental Expenses for New Territory

Transportation (additional mileage from Camp Hill to Virginia)	2,000
Office equipment and rent (same regardless of headquarters' location)	4,000
Cost of hiring office manager[5]	18,000
Total incremental expenses	$24,000

[1]Rounded to the nearest thousand.

[2]In current territory.

[3]Excludes the lost revenue from selling instead of engaging in this activity (opportunity cost).

[4]Although rep agencies are not legally required to show prospective employees to principals, it is generally held to be good business practice.

[5]Discretionary.

Exhibit 3 Barro Stickney, Inc., Statement of Revenue: Total Revenue 1998, $5.5 million

Principal	Estimated Market Saturation	Product Type	Sales/ Commission Rate	Share of BSI's Portfolio	Commission Revenue
R. D. Ocean	High	Components	5 %	32%	$96,756
Franklin Key	High	Components	5	15	45,354
Butler	Low	Technical/computer	12	3	9,070
Dickens	Low	Components	5	10	30,236
Horizon	Medium	Components	5.5	10	30,237
Swanson	High	Components	5.25	14	42,331
Moore	Medium	Consumer/electronics	5.25	11	33,260
Knox	Low	Technical/communications	8.5	5	15,118

It was an ambitious agenda, one that would determine the future of the company. It would take even more time than usual to discuss everything and reach consensus. Consequently, this week's meeting was set to occur over the weekend at Bill Stickney's vacation lodge in the Poconos starting with a gourmet dinner served at 7 P.M. sharp.

Before the meeting, Bill Stickney examined the sources of BSI's revenue and the firm's income for the previous year. He also estimated the future prospects for each of

Exhibit 4   Barro Stickney, Inc., Statement of Income (for the year ending December 31, 1998)

Revenue	
Commission income	$302,362
Expenses	
Salaries for sales and bonuses (includes Barro Stickney)	130,250
Office manager's salary	20,000
Total nonpersonnel expenses[1]	128,279
Total expenses	$278,529
New Income[2]	**$23,833 (7.9% of revenue)**

[1]Includes travel, advertising, taxes, office supplies, retirement, automobile expenses, communications, office equipment, and miscellaneous expenses.

[2]Currently held in negotiable certificates of deposits in a Harrisburg bank.

BSI's lines, considering each line's market potential and BSI's level of saturation in each market. Finally, he estimated the costs of hiring a new employee both in the current sales territory and in the Washington/Virginia area. Immediately before the meeting, Elizabeth finished compiling Bill's data into four exhibits.

Exhibit 1 evaluates the amount of sales effort (difficulty in selling) necessary to achieve a certain percentage of sales in BSI's portfolio (return). Difficulty in selling is measured by the level of marketing investment required for growth. Stickney's estimate is shown on the vertical axis. Return for this investment is measured by the relative sales commissions as a percent of BSI's portfolio shown on the horizontal axis. If BSI's time were evenly divided among its eight principals, each would receive 12.5 percent of the agency's time. The X axis shows each principal's time allocation as a proportion of 12.5 percent, the "par" time allocation. The area of each ellipse reflects each principal's share of BSI's commission revenue.

Bill Stickney presented the following additional comments as a result of his research:

1. Swanson's products are being replaced by the competition's computerized electronic equipment, a product category the firm has ignored. As a result, the company is losing its once prominent market position.

2. Although small amounts of effort are required to promote Ocean's product line to customers in the current sales territory, Ocean is extremely demanding of both BSI and other manufacturers' representative firms.

3. According to a seminar at the last ERA meeting, the maximum safe proportion of a rep firm's commissions from a single principal should be 25 to 30 percent. Also, at the meeting, one speaker indicated that if a firm commands 80 percent of a market, it should focus on another product or expand its territory rather than attempt to obtain the remainder of the market.

4. The revenue for investment for the manufacturers' representative firm comes from one or more of several sources. These sources include reduced forthcoming commission income, retained previous income, and borrowed money from a financial institution. Most successful firms expand their sales force or sales territory when they experience income growth and use of the investment as a tax write-off.

Case 1–4

Mediquip S.A.*

On December 18, Kurt Thaldorf, a sales engineer for the German sales subsidiary of Mediquip, S.A., was informed by Lohmann University Hospital in Stuttgart that it had decided to place an order with Sigma, a Dutch competitor, for a CT scanner. The hospital's decision came as disappointing news to Thaldorf, who had worked for nearly eight months on the account. The order, if obtained, would have meant a sale of DM 2,370,000 for the sales engineer.[1] He was convinced that Mediquip's CT scanner was technologically superior to Sigma's and, overall, a better product.

Thaldorf began a review of his call reports in order to better understand the factors that had led to Lohmann University Hospital's decision. He wanted to apply the lessons from this experience to future sales situations.

Background

At the time, the computer tomography (CT) scanner was a relatively recent product in the field of diagnostic imaging. This medical device, used for diagnostic purposes, allowed examination of cross sections of the human body through display of images. CT scanners combined sophisticated X-ray equipment with a computer to collect the necessary data and translate them into visual images.

When computer tomography was first introduced in the late 1960s, radiologists had hailed it as a major technological breakthrough. Commenting on the advantages of CT scanners, a product specialist with Mediquip said, "The end product looks very much like an X-ray image. The only difference is that with scanners you can see sections of the body that were never seen before on a screen—like the pancreas. A radiologist, for example, can diagnose cancer of the pancreas in less than two weeks after it develops. This was not possible before CT scanners."

Mediquip was a subsidiary of Technologie Universelle, a French conglomerate. The company's product line included, in addition to CT scanners, X-ray, ultrasonic, and nuclear diagnostic equipment. Mediquip enjoyed a worldwide reputation for advanced technology and competent after-sales service.

"Our competitors are mostly from other European countries," commented Mediquip's Sales Director for Europe. "In some markets they have been there longer than we have, and

---

*This case was prepared by Professor Kamran Kashani as a basis for class discussion rather than to illustrate either effective or ineffective handling of a business situation. All names and financial data have been disguised. Copyright © 1998 by **IMD**—International Institute for Management Development, Lausanne, Switzerland. Not to be used or reproduced without written permission directly from **IMD**.

[1]For the purposes of this case, use the following exchange rates for the Deutschmark (DM): DM1.00 = SFr0.85, $0.60, Ecu 0.50, £0.35.

they know the decision-makers better than we do. But we are learning fast." Sigma, the subsidiary of a diversified Dutch company under the same name, was the company's most serious competitor. Other major contenders in the CT scanner market were FNC, Eldora, Magna, and Piper.

Mediquip executives estimated the European market for CT scanners to be around 200 units per year. They pointed out that prices ranged from DM 1.5 to DM 3.0 million per unit. The company's CT scanner sold in the upper end of the price range. "Our equipment is at least two years ahead of our most advanced competition," explained a sales executive. "And our price reflects this technological superiority."

Mediquip's sales organization in Europe included eight country sales subsidiaries, each headed by a managing director. Within each country, sales engineers reported to regional sales managers who, in turn, reported to the managing director. Product specialists provided technical support to the sales force in each country.

Buyers of CT Scanners

A sales executive at Mediquip described the buyers of CT scanners as follows:

> Most of our sales are to what we call the public sector, health agencies that are either government-owned or belong to non-profit support organizations such as universities and philanthropic institutions. They are the sort of buyers that buy through formal tenders and have to budget their purchases at least one year in advance. Once the budget is allocated, it must then be spent before the end of the year. Only a minor share of our CT scanner sales goes to the private sector, profit-oriented organizations such as private hospitals or private radiologists.
>
> Of the two markets, the public sector is much more complex. Typically, there are at least four groups that get involved in the purchase decision: radiologists, physicists, administrators and people from the supporting agency—usually the ones who approve the budget for purchasing a CT scanner.
>
> Radiologists are the ones who use the equipment. They are doctors whose diagnostic services are sought by other doctors in the hospital or clinic. Patients remember their doctors, but not the radiologists. They never receive flowers from the patients! A CT scanner could really enhance their professional image among their colleagues.
>
> Physicists are the scientists in residence. They write the technical specifications which competing CT scanners must meet; they should know the state of the art in X-ray technology. Their primary concern is the patient's safety.
>
> The administrators are, well, administrators. They have the financial responsibility for their organizations. They are concerned with the cost of CT scanners, but also with what revenues they can generate. The administrators are extremely wary of purchasing an expensive technological toy that will become obsolete in a few years.
>
> The people from the supporting agency are usually not directly involved with decisions as to which product to purchase. But, since they must approve the expenditures, they do play an indirect role. Their influence is mostly felt by the administrators.
>
> The interplay among the four groups, as you can imagine, is rather complex. The power of each group in relationship to the others varies from organization to organization. The administrator, for example, is the top decision-maker in certain hospitals. In others, he is only a buyer. One of the key tasks of our sales engineers is to define for each potential account the relative power of the players. Only then can they set priorities and formulate selling strategies.

The European sales organization at Mediquip had recently started using a series of forms designed to help sales engineers in their account analysis and strategy formulation. (A sample of the forms, called Account Management Analysis, is reproduced in Exhibit 1.)

Exhibit I   Mediquip S.A.–Account Management Analysis Forms (condensed version)

Key Account:_____

ACCOUNT MANAGEMENT ANALYSIS

The enclosed forms are designed to facilitate your management of:

1   A key sales account
2   The *Mediquip* resources that can be applied to this key account

Completing the enclosed forms, you will:

• Identify installed equipment, and planned or potential new equipment
• Analyze purchase decision process and influence patterns, including:
  – Identify and prioritize all major sources of influence
  – Project probable sequence of events and timing of decision process
  – Assess position/interest of each major influence source
  – Identify major competition and probable strategies
  – Identify needed information/support
• Establish an account development strategy, including:
  – Select key contacts
  – Establish strategy and tactics for each key contact, identify appropriate *Mediquip* personnel
  – Assess plans for the most effective use of local team and headquarters resources

KEY ACCOUNT DATA

☐ Original (Date:_____)   Account No.:_____   Type of Institute:_____

☐ Revision (Date:_____)   Sales Specialist:_____   Bed Size:_____

Country/Region/District:_____   Telephone:_____

1. CUSTOMER (HOSPITAL, CLINIC, PRIVATE INSTITUTE)

Name:_____

Street Address:_____

City, State:_____

2. DECISION MAKERS – IMPORTANT CONTACTS

INDIVIDUALS	NAME	SPECIALTY	REMARKS
Medical Staff			
Administration			
Local Government			
State Government			

(continued)

Exhibit 1 *(continued)*

3. INSTALLED EQUIPMENT

TYPE	DESCRIPTION	SUPPLIED BY	INSTALLATION DATE	YEAR TO REPLACE	VALUE OF POTENTIAL ORDER
X-ray Nuclear Ultrasound RTP CT					

4. PLANNED NEW EQUIPMENT

TYPE	QUOTE		% CHANCE	EST. ORDER DATE		EST. DELIVERY		QUOTED PRICE
	NO.	DATE		1980	1981	1980	1981	

5. COMPETITION

COMPANY/PRODUCT	STRATEGY/ TACTICS	% CHANCE	STRENGTH	WEAKNESS

6. SALES PLAN   Product: _____   Quote No: _____   Quoted Price: _____

KEY ISSUES	*Mediquip's* PLAN	SUPPORT NEEDED FROM:	DATE OF FOLLOW-UP/REMARKS

7. ACTIONS – IN SUPPORT OF PLAN

SPECIFIC ACTION	RESPONSIBILITY	DUE DATES			RESULTS/REMARKS
		ORIGINAL	REVISED	COMPLETED	

8. ORDER STATUS REPORT

REVISION DATE	ACCOUNT NAME AND LOCATION	ISSUES/COMPETITIVE STRATEGY	ACTIONS/ STRATEGY	RESPON- SIBILITY	% CHANCE	EXPECTED ORDER TIMING	WIN/LOSE

Lohmann University Hospital

Lohmann University Hospital (LUH) was a large general hospital serving Stuttgart, a city of one million residents. The hospital was part of the university's medical school. The university was a leading teaching center and enjoyed an excellent reputation. LUH's radiology department had a wide range of X-ray equipment from a number of European manufacturers, including Sigma and FNC. The radiology department had five staff members, headed by a senior and nationally known radiologist, Professor Steinborn.

Thaldorf's sales activities

From the records he had kept of his sales calls, Thaldorf reviewed the events for the period between May 5, when he learned of LUH's interest in purchasing a CT scanner, and December 18, when he was informed that Mediquip had lost the order.

May 5

Office received a call from a Professor Steinborn from Lohmann University Hospital regarding a CT scanner. I was assigned to make the call on the professor. Looked through our files to find out if we had sold anything to the hospital before. We had not. Made an appointment to see the professor on May 9.

May 9

Called on Professor Steinborn, who informed me of a recent decision by university directors to set aside funds next year for the purchase of the hospital's first CT scanner. The professor wanted to know what we had to offer. Described the general features of our CT system. Gave him some brochures. Asked a few questions which led me to believe other companies had come to see him before I did. Told me to check with Dr. Rufer, the hospital's physicist, regarding the specs. Made an appointment to see him again ten days later. Called on Dr. Rufer, who was not there. His secretary gave me a lengthy document on the scanner specs.

May 10

Read the specs last night. Looked like they had been copied straight from somebody's technical manual. Showed them to our Product Specialist, who confirmed my own hunch that our system met and exceeded the specs. Made an appointment to see Dr. Rufer next week.

May 15

Called on Dr. Rufer. Told him about our system's features and the fact that we met all the specs set down on the document. He did not seem particularly impressed. Left him with technical documents about our system.

May 19

Called on Professor Steinborn. He had read the material I had left with him. Seemed rather pleased with the features. Asked about our upgrading scheme. Told him we would undertake to upgrade the system as new features became available. Explained that Mediquip, unlike other systems, can be made to accommodate the latest technology, with no risk of obsolescence for a long time. This impressed him. Also answered his questions regarding image manipulation, image processing speed and our service capability. Just before I left, he inquired about our price. Told him I would have an informative quote for him at our next meeting. Made an appointment to see him on June 23 after he returned from his vacation. Told me to get in touch with Carl Hartmann, the hospital's general director in the interim.

June 1

Called on Hartmann. It was difficult to get an appointment with him. Told him about our interest in supplying his hospital with our CT scanner which met all the specs as defined by Dr. Rufer. Also informed him of our excellent service capability. He wanted to know which other hospitals in the country had purchased our system. Told him I would provide him with a list of buyers within a few days. He asked about the price. Gave him an informative quote of DM 2,850,000—a price my boss and I had determined after my visit to Professor Steinborn. He shook his head saying, "Other scanners are cheaper by a wide margin." I explained that our price reflected the fact that the latest technology was already built into our scanner. Also mentioned that the price differential was an investment that could pay for itself several times over through faster speed of operation. He was noncommittal. Before my leaving his office, he instructed me not to talk to anybody else about the price. Asked him specifically if that included Professor Steinborn. He said it did. Left him with a lot of material about our system.

June 3

Went to Hartmann's office with a list of three hospitals similar in size to LUH that had installed our system. He was out. Left it with his secretary, who recognized me. Learned from her that at least two other firms, Sigma and FNC, were competing for the order. She also volunteered the information that "prices are so different, Mr. Hartmann is confused." She added that the final decision will be made by a committee made up of Hartmann, Professor Steinborn and one other person whom she could not recall.

June 20

Called on Dr. Rufer. Asked him if he had read the material about our system. He had, but did not have much to say. I repeated some of the key operational advantages our product enjoyed over those produced by others, including Sigma and FNC. Left him some more technical documents.

On the way out, stopped by Hartmann's office. His secretary told me that we had received favorable comments from the hospitals using our system.

June 23

Professor Steinborn was flabbergasted to hear that I could not discuss our price with him. Told him about the hospital administration's instructions to that effect. He could not believe this, especially when Sigma had already given him their quote of DM 2,100,000. When he calmed down, he wanted to know if we were going to be at least competitive with the others. Told him our system was more advanced than Sigma's. Promised him we would do our best to come up with an attractive offer. Then we talked about his vacation and sailing experience in the Aegean Sea. He said he loved the Greek food.

July 15

Called to see if Hartmann had returned from his vacation. He had. While checking his calendar, his secretary told me that our system seemed to be the "radiologists' choice," but that Hartmann had not yet made up his mind.

July 30

Visited Hartmann accompanied by the regional manager. Hartmann seemed to have a fixation about the price. He said, "All the companies claim they have the latest technology."

So he could not understand why our offer was "so much above the rest." He concluded that only a "very attractive price" could tip the balance in our favor. After repeating the operational advantages our system enjoyed over others, including those produced by Sigma and FNC, my boss indicated that we were willing to lower our price to DM 2,610,000 if the equipment were ordered before the end of the current year. Hartmann said he would consider the offer and seek "objective" expert opinion. He also said a decision would be made before Christmas.

August 14
Called on Professor Steinborn, who was too busy to see me for more than ten minutes. He wanted to know if we had lowered our price since the last meeting with him. I said we had. He shook his head and said with a laugh, "Maybe that was not your best offer." He then wanted to know how fast we could make deliveries. Told him within six months. He did not say anything.

September 2
The regional manager and I discussed the desirability of inviting one or more people from the LUH to visit the Mediquip headquarters operations near Paris. The three-day trip would give the participants a chance to see the scope of the facilities and become better acquainted with CT scanner applications. This idea was finally rejected as inappropriate.

September 3
Dropped in to see Hartmann. He was busy but had time to ask for a formal "final offer" from us by October 1. On the way out, his secretary told me there had been "a lot of heated discussions" about which scanner seemed best suited for the hospital. She would not say more.

September 25
The question of price was raised in a meeting with the regional manager and the managing director. I had recommended a sizable cut in our price to win the order. The regional manager seemed to agree with me, but the managing director was reluctant. His concern was that too big a drop in price looked "unhealthy." They finally agreed to a final offer of DM 2,370,000.

Made an appointment to see Hartmann later that week.

September 29
Took our offer of DM 2,370,000 in a sealed envelope to Hartmann. He did not open it, but he said he hoped the scanner question would soon be resolved to the "satisfaction of all concerned." Asked him how the decision was going to be made. He evaded the question but said he would notify us as soon as a decision was reached. Left his office feeling that our price had a good chance of being accepted.

October 20
Called on Professor Steinborn. He had nothing to tell me except that "the CT scanner is the last thing I want to talk about." Felt he was unhappy with the way things were going.

Tried to make an appointment with Hartmann in November, but he was too busy.

November 5
Called on Hartmann, who told me that a decision would probably not be reached before next month. He indicated that our price was "within the range," but that all the competing

systems were being evaluated to see which seemed most appropriate for the hospital. He repeated that he would call us when a decision was reached.

December 18
Received a brief letter from Hartmann thanking Mediquip for participating in the bid for the CT scanner, along with the announcement that LUH had decided to place the order with Sigma.

Case 1–5

Persoft, Inc.*

Pat Alea, Persoft's director of marketing, faced two difficult decisions. The first concerned the outlook for Persoft's new software package, IZE. An information management package launched last year, IZE represents a radically different program compared to Persoft's other software programs. Forecasting 1989 sales for IZE will be difficult since Pat does not have a database available to use time series methods.

The second problem related to Persoft's more mature products—for example, the SmarTerm terminal emulation and communications software. For these products, Persoft combines statistical and qualitative techniques, including analyses of past sales data and a bottom-up approach based on the sales force and contact with customers. Even for the more mature products, Pat Alea hopes to improve the accuracy of their forecasts.

The Company

Persoft, Inc., was formed late in 1982 almost by accident when John Swenson, cofounder, noticed a void in the marketplace. Microcomputers had just begun to multiply in the business community, and Swenson saw a need to design software to emulate the terminals that communicated with the bigger and faster minicomputers made by Digital Equipment Corporation and Data General Corporation. The result of Swenson's efforts was a highly popular series of products called SmarTerm.

Swenson started Persoft on $4,000 and two IBM PCs, all out of his basement. Today, Persoft operates out of a 26,000-square-foot building and employs 85 people. Sales for its first fiscal year, 1983, were $169,000. In 1987, sales reached $4.6 million and rose to $5.9 million in 1988, although 1988 sales were $1.1 million under projections. Projected sales for 1989 of $12 to $15 million have been revised downward to exceed $7 million. These revisions reflect changing market conditions and difficulty in forecasting sales of IZE.

The Products

Until the introduction of IZE, Persoft's major product was a series of software packages produced under the SmarTerm name. Company literature describes the product:

> SmarTerm: a family of powerful, flexible, easy-to-use terminal emulation products. With SmarTerm, you can link your PC to powerful minicomputer and mainframe systems—and do everything on your PC that you can do on an expensive and cumbersome dedicated hardware terminal. SmarTerm is offered by Persoft, the leader in terminal emulation software.

---

*This case is based on information obtained from *Venture,* December 1988; *State Journal,* January 10, 1989; *Newsweek,* December 14, 1987; and Persoft company literature and personnel. Names and unit sales data have been changed. Copyright © 1996 Neil M. Ford.

IZE® provides the user with four major environments in which to work. Most of IZE's functions are available for groups of texts in outlines and the workspace, as well as for individual texts.

1. Word processing allows the user to create texts within IZE or to manipulate information that has been imported into IZE. It contains such features as block copy, delete, and print, as well as on-screen page breaks and "search and replace" operations.

2. The workspace allows the user to quickly work with and switch between texts in memory without making new search requests. Texts remain in memory until they are released. The workspace is similar to a desktop with a number of different documents and folders on it.

Operations such as cutting and pasting between texts are fast and easy using the workspace.

3. Outlines provide a summary of all information requested by the user. A new outline is generated each time the user makes a search request. It always reflects the nature of the request and the current contents of the textbase. It is based on an analysis of the frequency of all the keywords in all texts that meet the initial search criteria. Groups within an outline can be expanded to deeper and deeper levels of detail.

4. Guidelines are custom-made forms that allow the user to control the shape of outlines. These are important if the user wants the outline to be different than the one that IZE would provide automatically.

Persoft's newest entry in the software market is IZE, a $445 program that achieved critical acclaim in trade publications. The new program is part of a new generation of text-based office management programs. IZE can pull together research reports and search volumes of text, using a powerful and sophisticated word search rather than a complicated pathway, dictated by the program, that a user must learn. Early reviews have been enthusiastic. According to one reviewer, "text-based programs on PCs are so new that no one can predict their potential market size with any accuracy." The *Newsweek* article describes IZE as another way to "take arms against a sea of data. It builds ingeniously detailed indexes." A Chicago attorney "uses IZE to help associates pinpoint thousands of paragraphs from contracts, giving them a guide for their own work." A computer consultant says the program reminds him of "computers in science fiction, which figure out what you mean when you ask them a simple question." Despite these glowing reviews, Swenson and Alea are aware that the history of software is littered with good ideas that never caught on, a situation they hope to avoid.

The excerpt at the top of the page, taken from Persoft's promotional literature, describes the capabilities of IZE.

Swenson and Alea acknowledge that it may take a year for text-based programs to catch on and establish a market. Persoft is not alone in the market and faces competition from Apple's HyperCard, which is given away with each new Macintosh to get around having to explain it, and Lotus's Agenda, which sells for $400. These new programs have been referred to as *software Erector sets.*

To help market its new product, Persoft obtained $2 million financing from a venture capital firm, Frontenac, of which $750,000 to $1 million will be used to help launch IZE.

The Marketing Program

Persoft's software programs are available nationwide and overseas. About 13,000 value-added resellers (VARS), value-added dealers (VADS), and computer specialty stores (CSS) such as ComputerLand, ValCom, and Inacomp carry Persoft products. These re-

Exhibit I   Monthly Unit Sales of SmarTerm 1985–88

Month/Year	Unit Sales	Month/Year	Unit Sales
January 1985	206	March	172
February	245	April	210
March	185	May	205
April	169	June	244
May	162	July	218
June	177	August	182
July	207	September	206
August	216	October	211
September	193	November	273
October	230	December	248
November	212	January 1988	262
December	192	February	258
January 1986	162	March	233
February	189	April	255
March	244	May	303
April	209	June	282
May	207	July	291
June	211	August	280
July	210	September	255
August	173	October	312
September	194	November	296
October	234	December	307
November	156	January 1989	281
December	206	February	308
January 1987	188	March	280
February	162	April	345

sellers receive Persoft software from a distributor (SoftSell) that provides other programs and peripherals.

Persoft employs five salespeople who call on major value-added resellers and major end-user customers and prospects. In addition, the sales force works with Persoft's wholesaler and its sales force. Persoft provides backup support for all of its software programs. Currently, the sales force directs its efforts on the new IZE product to calling on end-users. The sales force is responsible for obtaining information from SoftSell and key resellers as to the identity of end-users. Current users of IZE are asked to identify other potential end-users as well.

Persoft management wanted IZE to be the dBase III of information management. This line of reasoning influenced the pricing of IZE, which was set at $445.

Pat Alea faced two problems. The first concerned development of a new forecasting procedure for one of the SmarTerm software packages. She had not been satisfied with previous results and wanted to learn if an improved technique would be feasible. Sales data by units for the last three years are in Exhibit 1. Exhibit 2 shows actual versus forecast sales of the SmarTerm product line. As illustrated, the accuracy of the forecasting

Exhibit 2   Actual versus Forecast SmarTerm Sales

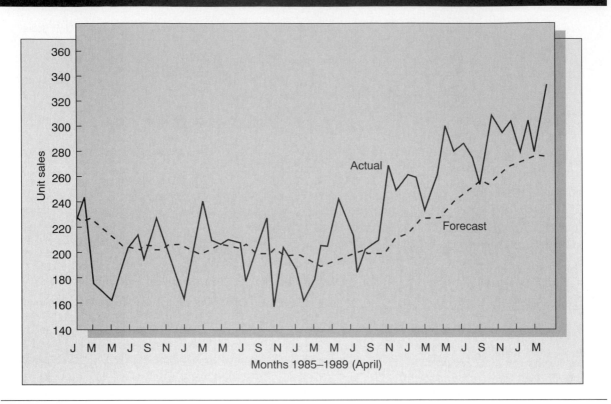

method has diminished rather markedly since late 1987. Forecasts are made using simple exponential smoothing at the beginning of the year. Because of accuracy problems, Persoft has had production problems meeting demand. Recently, revised forecasts on a quarterly basis have been necessary to help overcome the problem. Alea has relied on qualitative methods to make the revised forecasts.

Her second problem constituted a major challenge: estimating the market potential and resulting sales forecast for IZE. She knew the sales forecast would be a critical factor in determining the feasibility of the marketing plan. Moreover, since IZE was so revolutionary, she knew it would be questionable to rely on past sales growth patterns experienced with the SmarTerm line as an indicator of future sales of IZE.

Delaware Paint and Plate Glass Industries, Inc.*

The Strategic Forecasting and Planning Committee had just completed its review of the company's activities for all of its divisions for the last 33 years. The committee was reasonably pleased with its ability to prepare forecasts of sales, recognizing how important forecasts are to division heads for planning cash flows, production scheduling, personnel planning, budgeting, inventory control, purchasing, and other purposes. However, the committee was perplexed by problems that had been experienced in the Glass Division.

The Glass Division has confronted rather uncertain times due mainly to fluctuations in the economic environment. As a result, inventories are bloated, and the division is operating at less than 60 percent of capacity. Karl Backes, president of the Glass Division, is concerned about these problems and has assigned to his forecasting and planning group the responsibility for reviewing past forecasting procedures and for developing new methods that offer greater accuracy. Heading up the forecasting and planning group is Jackie Vandenberg. Although Jackie was transferred recently from another division, she has managed to impress her peers in the Glass Division with her knowledge of the industry and of the various methods available for forecasting. Her first activity involved a careful review of past methods and results. It was very apparent that the division's forecasting procedures needed revamping in order to be more useful to the numerous departments relying on the forecasts for their own planning and scheduling activities.

The Company

Delaware Paint and Plate Glass incorporated in Delaware in 1895. Delaware P&PG wholly owns a variety of companies, which have been integrated into four basic business segments. In addition, Delaware P&PG has entered several joint ventures with other corporations in such areas as oil and gas exploration, iodine production, and ethylene glycol production.

The company is concentrated in four basic business segments: glass, chemicals, coatings and resins, and fiberglass. The diversity of Delaware's markets helped to soften the effects of the economic downturn that started in 1980. Major markets are transportation and construction, which are served in varying degrees by the business's four segments. Other industrial and agricultural markets are served by the basic business lines. Foreign markets comprise the same basic categories as the domestic mix.

Domestic sales in 1980 were divided about equally among Delaware's major markets: transportation, primarily automotive; residential and commercial construction, including

---

building and remodeling; chemical processing and refining; and other industrial and agricultural areas.

The previous slump in the automobile industry had had a substantial impact on the glass and fiberglass business segments. Manufacture of original equipment glass parts was affected by the decline in U.S. car production, falling to one of the lowest levels in recent years. Sales of fiberglass products declined due to poor economic conditions and, as a result, affected the recreational vehicle and pleasure boat markets. The low level of domestic auto production also affected Delaware's factory-applied automotive finishes business. The company's leading position in several areas of technology, which provided superior products, helped offset some of this effect. The recent reversal of this trend improved Delaware's sales, but automobile production declined again in 1986.

Delaware's strong position in the aircraft market remained fairly stable. Sales were strong for windshields and other transparencies for business aviation and military aircraft. The company also provides coatings for specialty ballistics glazing.

In 1982, housing starts were at their lowest level in 35 years and had an adverse effect on Delaware P&PG's insulating glass units, as well as fiberglass products for such items as bathtubs and shower enclosures. However, in 1983, housing starts increased by almost 60 percent, and the use of fiberglass roofing products and shingles increased dramatically in 1984. Housing starts declined 8 percent from 1987 to 1988.

In contrast to the depressed residential construction market, commercial construction continued strong in the early '80s. Demand grew for Delaware's energy-efficient architectural glass products.

Because of weak economic conditions, demand for most of Delaware's chemical products were down. Sales of farm fertilizers declined along with most of their industrial chemicals. However, demand was strong for the company's line of chemicals used in the oil- and gas-exploration markets.

The Glass Division

Delaware P&PG is one of the nation's largest producers of flat glass, manufacturing about one-third of total domestic industry output. The company's major markets are automotive original equipment, automotive replacement, residential construction, commercial construction, and aircraft transparencies. Delaware also supplies the furniture industry and other markets. Most glass products are sold to other manufacturing and construction companies, although some are sold directly to independent distributors and to consumers through Delaware's franchised distribution centers.

The Forecasting and Planning Group

In addition to Jackie Vandenberg, the group was composed of Clair Voyance, sales analyst; Gregg O. Strander, national sales manager; and Scott Wilson, production planning. The group could rely on a staff statistical group that reported to corporate headquarters for technical assistance, if needed.

Specifically, the group was expected not only to come up with an overall sales forecast of division sales but also to break down this forecast by market, product, quarter, and major account. Its first task concerned the development of a sales forecast for the glass division.

Some differences over what methods to use arose within the group. Gregg felt that the group should rely on the sales force composite method, arguing that the end result would be more receptive to the sales force because of their involvement in its preparation. Scott, on the other hand, felt that sales force input should be minimal since they have little impact on OEM contracts. These contracts are determined at the top. Clair felt that regardless of method used, it is mandatory that the group be able to provide forecasts for each major market. Then, by adding up the forecasts, a total estimate of dollar sales for the division would result.

Despite these differences, Jackie felt that the group would be able to work together without any major problems. She was aware that numerous techniques existed for making forecasts and was pondering which would be most appropriate. Believing that simplicity is an advantage, she hoped the group would not allow the process to become overly complicated. For example, she knew that trend analysis, using either simple regression analysis or exponential smoothing, would be easier than more complicated methods.

At their first meeting, she initiated the discussion by asking the group to identify factors that they thought would have a significant effect on glass sales. Gregg's immediate response was that sales were dependent on efforts of the sales force. Although the rest of the group agreed, Jackie pointed out that external variables were desired for purposes of developing a sales forecasting model. To illustrate, she suggested that some national economic variables would be appropriate, such as gross national product, personal income, per capita income, employment, and so on. Clair suggested variables that would closely reflect activities in the division's major markets, such as automobile production, automobile repair, and construction. Scott pointed out that construction is too broad and that this variable needs to be separated into types of construction, such as residential, nonresidential, and nonbusiness. Housing starts would be useful as well. Jackie suggested accident rates as a proxy for automobile repair. Buildings are remodeled and repaired, and some index reflecting this might be useful. In addition, since weather causes various kinds of damage, some measure of weather, such as the incidence of tornadoes, could be of value.

Realizing that the group was headed in the right direction, Jackie suggested that they attempt to use these variables and then examine the results for their forecasting effectiveness. She proposed that regression analysis be used at first along with trend analysis over time and exponential smoothing. She felt that multiple methods were more effective than trying to rely on a single approach.

Collecting data for the suggested variables was relatively simple. Exhibit 1 contains information for division sales and for per capita income, auto production, housing starts, accidents, residential construction, nonresidential construction, nonbuilding construction, and tornadoes. In case these variables were not useful, Jackie instructed the group to be prepared to discuss the addition of extra variables. This, she hoped, would not be necessary, since more variables violated her principles of parsimony.

Before scheduling another meeting with her group, she met with Karl Backes to discuss progress. He was pleased with her efforts and expressed confidence that the group's results would be useful in helping to improve some of the Glass Division's problems. Karl mentioned other factors the group may want to consider. For example, Karl suggested the following data series and/or sources: *Business Conditions Digest, Standard & Poor's Index of Stock Prices, The Conference Board's Index of Help-Wanted Advertising, The Federal Reserve Board's Index of Industrial Production,* and several of the indexes from *Forbes* and *Business Week.* He indicated these sources have been useful as predictors of sales for other Delaware P&PG divisions.

Exhibit 1 Statistical Series for Delaware Paint and Plate Glass Industries, Inc. (1965–1997)

Year	Plate Glass Sales (millions)	Automobile Production Units (thousands)	New Housing Units Started (thousands)	Per Capita Personal Income (dollars)	Motor Vehicle Accidents (millions)	Residential Construction (billions)	Nonresidential Construction (billions)	Nonbuilding Construction (billions)	Tornadoes (units)
1965	897	9,306	1,510	$2,773	13.2	$21.2	$17.2	$10.8	899
1966	942	8,598	1,196	2,987	13.6	17.8	19.4	12.9	570
1967	943	7,437	1,322	3,167	13.7	21.2	20.1	13.2	912
1968	1,044	8,822	1,545	3,433	14.6	24.8	22.5	14.4	661
1969	1,147	8,224	1,500	2,705	15.5	25.6	25.9	16.7	604
1970	1,094	6,547	1,434	4,056	16.0	24.8	24.6	19.0	649
1971	1,238	8,585	2,052	4,305	15.9	31.3	26.7	20.7	888
1972	1,396	8,824	2,357	4,676	16.3	42.4	29.8	21.3	741
1973	1,513	9,658	2,045	5,198	16.6	45.7	31.4	22.1	1,102
1974	1,744	7,331	1,338	5,657	15.6	33.6	33.2	27.0	947
1975	1,887	6,713	1,160	6,081	16.5	31.3	31.6	29.8	920
1976	2,255	8,500	1,538	6,655	16.8	44.2	30.0	35.9	835
1977	2,506	9,201	1,987	7,297	17.6	62.0	35.1	42.6	852
1978	2,794	9,165	2,020	8,141	18.3	74.9	45.0	39.9	788
1979	3,092	8,419	1,745	9,036	18.1	74.6	50.2	43.7	852
1980	3,158	6,376	1,292	9,916	17.9	63.7	52.5	32.2	866
1981	3,354	5,049	1,084	10,952	18.0	60.2	60.1	33.2	783
1982	3,296	5,073	1,062	11,485	18.4	59.2	59.5	37.4	1,046
1983	3,682	6,781	1,703	12,088	18.3	93.6	62.2	37.8	931
1984	4,242	7,773	1,750	13,114	18.8	101.4	74.4	35.5	907
1985	4,346	8,185	1,742	13,895	19.3	106.8	83.2	40.5	684
1986	4,687	7,829	1,805	14,592	17.7	122.9	83.8	42.0	784
1987	5,182	7,099	1,620	15,483	20.8	121.1	91.0	45.9	656
1988	5,617	7,111	1,488	16,497	n/a	120.9	86.8	45.5	702
1989	5,734	6,825	1,376	17,706	12.8	116.2	106.1	49.0	856
1990	6,021	6,078	1,193	18,699	11.5	100.9	95.3	49.7	1,133
1991	5,673	5,439	1,014	19,196	11.3	94.5	86.3	50.2	1,132
1992	5,814	5,663	1,200	20,660	10.0	110.6	87.1	58.9	1,303
1993	5,754	5,981	1,288	21,288	6.1	123.9	88.3	61.6	1,173
1994	6,331	6,614	1,457	22,104	6.5	133.6	101.0	64.0	1,082
1995	7,058	6,351	1,354	23,233	6.6	127.9	113.6	64.8	1,235
1996	7,218	na	1,477	24,294	na	146.2	119.1	na	na
1997	7,379	na	na	na	na	na	na	na	na

Statistical Abstract of the United States; 1997, 117th ed. (Washington, DC: U.S. Bureau of the Census, 1997).

Case 1–7

In-Sink-Erator Division*

In July 1998, John Hammond, operations research manager, was reviewing market projections derived from the In-Sink-Erator Division's industry forecasting models. It was clear that In-Sink-Erator's (ISE) forecasting methods needed modification given the discrepancies between forecasted values and actual values. In-Sink-Erator is the leading producer of food waste disposers, producing more than 75 percent of the disposers sold in America.

The In-Sink-Erator Division's forecasting procedures begin with predictions of industry demand for such segments as new housing starts, replacement demand, first-time installation, and U.S. exports. The Association of Home Appliance Manufacturers provides member companies, which include ISE, with industry shipment data for a broad range of home appliances, including food waste disposers, commonly known as garbage disposers. The operations research function also collects information from a variety of other external and internal sources.

Company History

The multimillion-dollar In-Sink-Erator Company and a major industry began in 1927 when John W. Hammes, a Racine, Wisconsin, architect, created the world's first garbage disposer. This first garbage disposer was not much to look at, but it did the job, as Exhibit 1 illustrates.

In 1938, Hammes founded In-Sink-Erator Manufacturing Company. Fifty disposers were made and sold that first year. Early growth was hampered by the reluctance of municipal officials to approve the appliance's installation. Various studies pointed out that disposers reduce the incidence of vermin and insects in a home environment and reduce the cost of garbage collection and processing. This led many municipal officials to pass ordinances recommending or requiring the use of household food disposers in all new construction.

During the 1950s, industry disposer sales grew dramatically. In-Sink-Erator had to share the market with competitors that included some of the nation's largest home appliance manufacturers. In-Sink-Erator's market share ranked only third in disposer production at one time in the 1950s.

By 1960, the disposer industry was selling more than 750,000 disposers a year. To meet this tremendous increase in demand, ISE designed and built a 114,300-square-foot manufacturing facility. This facility is the world's largest of its kind devoted exclusively

---

*This case was made possible through the cooperation of John R. Yerwiel, director–financial analysis, of the In-Sink-Erator Division. It was prepared by Professor Neil M. Ford, School of Business, University of Wisconsin–Madison, as a basis for class discussion and is not designed to illustrate effective or ineffective handling of an administrative situation. Certain names and data have been disguised. Copyright © 1999 Neil M. Ford.

Exhibit 1   In-Sink-Erator

It all started with a great idea, a pair of tin snips and a soldering iron!

The multimillion-dollar In-Sink-Erator Company and a major industry began very simply overnight back in 1927 when founder John W. Hammes, a Racine, Wisconsin architect, watched his wife grab the garbage and carry it outside to the garbage can.

He felt that there had to be a better way and struck upon an idea. Armed with ingenuity, determination, a soldering iron and a pair of tin snips, he worked in his basement that night to create the world's first garbage disposer.

Not much to look at. But it did the job.

A food shredder in the sink drain.

The operating principle of Hammes' shredder was basically simple: put a power source and grinding mechanism in the kitchen sink drain to shred waste into particles small enough to be easily carried away by drain water into the regular sewerage lines. Hammes correctly assumed that at treatment plants, as well as in septic tanks, those tiny food particles would be broken down along with the regular sewage.

Here was a highly practical, workable idea for helping homeowners eliminate a disagreeable and time-consuming task. Yet it took Hammes eleven long years of constant refining and testing to develop a disposer that would do the job quickly and conveniently.

World's first garbage disposer. Created by In-Sink-Erator founder John W. Hammes in 1927 in his basement workshop.

---

to the production of garbage disposers. By 1966, expansion increased facilities to 242,900 square feet.

In 1968, In-Sink-Erator was acquired by the Emerson Electric Company. Emerson provided new capital and management disciplines that created a solid base for additional growth of the new division. Within five years, the division almost doubled its sales volume and nearly doubled it again by 1975.

After the acquisition by Emerson, ISE expanded its product line to include trash compactors, hot water dispensers, dishwashers (discontinued in 1995), point-of-use water heating systems, and disposer adaptor rings, which permit the installation of an In-Sink-Erator model to replace competitive brands.

By 1974, ISE had regained its position as the leading producer of garbage disposers with 33 percent of the industry, which had grown to over 2.5 million units annually. Today, more than 75 percent of all food waste disposers sold in America are manufactured by In-Sink-Erator in an industry that sells an average of 4 million garbage disposers a year. In-Sink-Erator also manufactures disposers under private-label arrangements for

Whirlpool, Sears/Kenmore, KitchenAid, Maytag, Magic Chef, Jennair, Ace, True Value, and other private-label brands. ISE warrants its disposers for five years and backs the warranties with 2,500 independent service agencies. Other disposer manufacturers have similar long-term warranty programs. Disposers have an estimated average life of nine years.

Although the In-Sink-Erator Division leads the industry in the production of food disposers, it competes with three other manufacturers. The largest is Anaheim Manufacturing of Anaheim, California, which merged with Waste King in 1994 and has a combined market share of approximately 17 percent. Anaheim is followed by Watertown Manufacturing of Watertown, Wisconsin, which sells to General Electric, with approximately 4 percent and Sinkguard, a relatively new competitor, manufacturing product on the Chinese mainland. Anaheim's acquisition of WasteKing was poorly executed and they failed to achieve the economies of scale anticipated from the merger. The Chinese imports are struggling. They entered the market with inferior quality and the plumbing trade has been reluctant to incur the high labor cost of installing defective products. The disposer industry has grown approximately one million units during the past five years, 1994–1998. Housing starts have been stable, but replacement and increased saturation are driving the growth. Disposer growth is also being supported by stable interest rates. The sale of existing homes has increased dramatically and has supported the remodel/replacement market.

Market Distribution and Saturation

Although ISE's primary marketing commitment has traditionally been through the plumbing wholesaler to the plumbing-heating-cooling contractor, as well as the emerging growth of new "do-it-yourself" homecenters such as Home Depot, Builders Square, and Lowe's, industry consolidations continue to accelerate. Home Depot and Lowe's are dominating the retail channel. Plumbing wholesalers are also either consolidating or joining buying groups for additional leverage.

Appliance market saturation rates for refrigerators, clothes washers, garbage disposers, and dishwashers vary considerably. The saturation rate for refrigerators is almost 100 percent, but slightly less than half of households have dishwashers. Disposers are found in 52 percent of households, although regional saturation rates differ substantially. Few major cities restrict garbage disposers. Historically, New York City restricted garbage disposers; this policy changed in early 1998. However, with only 8,000 housing starts per year, market growth will be slow. Estimates show only 14 percent saturation in New York, whereas disposers are commonly accepted in California. Exhibit 2 illustrates regional saturation estimates based on data provided by the Association of Home Appliance Manufacturers.

Exhibit 3 shows U.S. appliance saturation rates for fiscal years 1960 to the present with ISE-derived estimates for disposers to fiscal year 1995. The division's fiscal year begins October 1.

Division Forecasting Approach

The marketing of food disposers has three segments—new housing, existing houses (involving both replacement and first-time installation), and exports.

To study the new housing market, the operations research department uses government statistics and estimates from the F. W. Dodge National Information Services Division. Exhibit 4 presents new housing starts by fiscal year from 1976 to 1998 and an inclusion rate that reflects the number of new houses with garbage disposers. As Exhibit 4 shows, the inclusion rate rose steadily from 70 percent in 1981 to 82 percent in 1990. The decline in inclusion rate since 1990 reflects a decline in housing in Southern California.

Exhibit 2   Regional Disposer Saturation Estimates

Region	Percent Saturation
New England	45
Middle Atlantic	22
East North Central	52
West North Central	57
South Atlantic	45
East South Central	25
West South Central	53
Mountain	85
Pacific	73
Total	52

Sources: Association of Home Appliance Manufacturers and ISE estimates.

Exhibit 3   Appliance Market Saturation Rates (Fiscal year 1960 to fiscal year 1993)

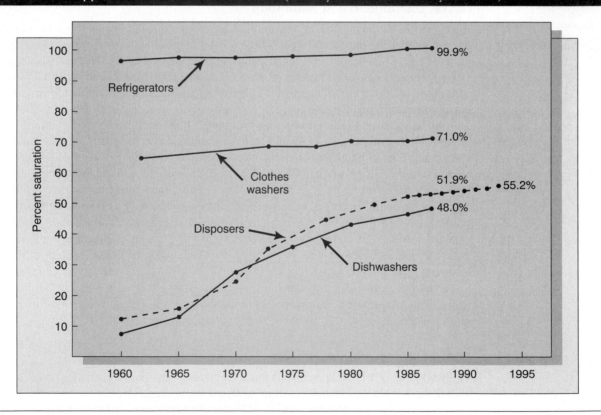

Source: Disposers—ISE Estimates. Other Products—*Appliance,* October 1987.

Exhibit 4   Estimated Sales of New Housing Disposers (1973–1998)

Year	Housing Starts[1] (000)	Inclusion[2] Rate Percent	New Housing[2] Disposers (000)
1973	2,239		
1974	1,487		
1975	1,080		
1976	1,448	70%	
1977	1,866	70	
1978	2,010	70	1,407
1979	1,835	70	1,285
1980	1,316	70	921
1981	1,254	70	878
1982	962	75	722
1983	1,594	75	1,196
1984	1,791	75	1,343
1985	1,693	75	1,270
1986	1,840	78.3	1,441
1987	1,678	81.8	1,373
1988	1,481	77.1	1,142
1989	1,436	76.6	1,100
1990	1,282	82.1	1,053
1991	1,000	74.6	746
1992	1,169	74.0	865
1993	1,234	73.4	906
1994	1,437	74.0	1,063
1995	1,375	76.5	1,052
1996	1,468	76.5	1,123
1997	1,452	76.5	1,111
1998	1,508	76.5	1,154

Sources: [1]U.S. Bureau of the Census, Construction Reports, series C20.
[2]Association of Home Appliance Manufacturers.

Installation of garbage disposers in existing houses has been a difficult segment to manage. Demand in this segment is twofold: replacement of existing food disposers and first-time installation. Hammond and his associates are confident the majority of households with a disposer will replace it with a new one. Their estimates range from 80 to 90 percent. But it is difficult to forecast when disposers will wear out. First-time installation costs average $80 plus costs for electrical work, and replacement costs average $40. The lower replacement costs reflect ISE's 75 percent market share. With 75 percent of the market, chances are that the consumer will be replacing an ISE disposer, and fittings are standard.

Manufacturers report total sales to the association monthly. The association reports the combined results for the industry, and In-Sink-Erator estimates its replacement and first-time installations from survey cards returned by purchasers.

Exhibit 5 presents factory shipments for garbage disposers from 1973 to 1998 and first-time installation sales from 1982 to 1998. The association also provides monthly in-

Exhibit 5   Total Industry Shipments and Estimated First-Time Installation Sales in Existing Houses (000)

Year	First-Time Installation	Total Industry Shipment
1973		2,929
1974		2,741
1975		2,077
1976		2,456
1977		2,814
1978		3,281
1979		3,359
1980		2,953
1981		3,265
1982	319	2,690
1983	344	3,411
1984	318	4,006
1985	299	4,146
1986	302	4,182
1987	351	4,440
1988	388	4,210
1989	394	4,380
1990	383	4,358
1991	375	3,946
1992	402	4,098
1993	393	4,290
1994	414	4,560
1995	461	4,801
1996	477	4,842
1997	479	4,962
1998	486	5,180

Source: Association of Home Appliance Manufacturers.

dustry shipments of food disposers, as shown in Exhibit 6. Hammond and his associates were considering new databases that would help increase the accuracy of ISE's forecasts. Exhibit 7 shows expenditures for maintenance and improvements, and repair.

With this database, John Hammond and his associates faced the problem of developing industry forecasts for the new housing market, the replacement and first-time installation market in existing houses, and the U.S. export market. In addition, industry forecasts would have to reflect regional variations.

Exhibit 6 Monthly Industry Shipments, October 1986–June 1999

Month	Industry Shipments	Month	Industry Shipments	Month	Industry Shipments
October 1986	364,134	October 1989	387,246	October 1992	312,409
November	334,372	November	380,778	November	279,484
December	303,354	December	342,841	December	338,305
January	384,685	January	391,193	January	349,214
February	339,917	February	380,296	February	293,581
March	345,431	March	413,600	March	349,800
April	300,503	April	334,729	April	298,487
May	317,943	May	335,776	May	303,630
June	410,142	June	331,337	June	415,866
July	296,311	July	285,379	July	310,798
August	363,881	August	362,772	August	388,928
September	421,049	September	434,261	September	457,810
October 1987	404,347	October 1990	425,729	October 1993	330,772
November	346,772	November	369,105	November	294,881
December	337,978	December	298,599	December	401,440
January	449,258	January	361,961	January	342,055
February	367,239	February	359,840	February	333,250
March	364,870	March	394,330	March	428,370
April	352,019	April	296,681	April	320,283
May	347,386	May	346,918	May	273,045
June	357,003	June	430,554	June	423,801
July	343,500	July	306,464	July	308,850
August	357,795	August	348,293	August	327,068
September	411,635	September	419,348	September	506,185
October 1988	436,938	October 1991	346,690	October 1994	302,457
November	324,408	November	265,003	November	345,192
December	325,706	December	262,028	December	405,265
January	361,279	January	361,902	January	375,399
February	360,084	February	308,781	February	323,688
March	361,530	March	362,450	March	439,868
April	301,620	April	281,621	April	304,211
May	323,580	May	306,507	May	353,658
June	335,694	June	360,286	June	459,017
July	345,172	July	294,058	July	324,754
August	353,593	August	355,285	August	445,353
September	369,214	September	440,544	September	481,138
					(continued)

Source: Association of Home Appliance Manufacturers.

Exhibit 6   Monthly Industry Shipments, October 1995–June 1999 (concluded)

Month	Industry Shipments	Month	Industry Shipments	Month	Industry Shipments
October 1995	385,765	January	373,199	April	390,018
November	365,438	February	354,858	May	390,135
December	411,632	March	467,807	June	469,518
January	387,596	April	348,180	July	373,283
February	380,772	May	387,424	August	437,817
March	417,610	June	487,722	September	434,951
April	338,684	July	347,867	October 1998	486,256
May	381,624	August	465,169	November	398,352
June	481,906	September	464,111	December	481,736
July	291,499	October 1997	428,116	January	436,347
August	439,581	November	386,381	February	418,920
September	519,167	December	410,864	March	512,367
October 1996	350,352	January	383,703	April	361,255
November	447,061	February	406,681	May	407,427
December	348,299	March	450,288	June	492,749

Source: Association of Home Appliance Manufacturers.

Exhibit 7   Expenditures for Maintenance and Improvements and Repair, 1975–1995

Year	Expenditures for Maintenance and Improvements and Repair (millions)
1975	$ 25,239
1976	29,034
1977	31,280
1978	37,461
1979	42,231
1980	46,338
1981	46,351
1982	45,291
1983	49,295
1984	69,784
1985	80,267
1986	91,274
1987	94,082
1988	101,117
1989	100,891
1990	106,773
1991	97,528
1992	103,734
1993	108,305
1994	115,030
1995	111,683

Source: U.S. Bureau of the Census, Current Construction Reports, Series C50.

Case 1–8

Wilkinson Sword USA*

Norman R. Proulx, president, and Ronald E. Mineo, vice president of sales for Wilkinson Sword USA, were faced with a decision of strategic importance. They had to decide whether or not Wilkinson Sword USA should establish its own sales force in 1985. In the past, the company had used manufacturers' representatives, brokers, and/or the sales forces of other companies to represent its line of razors and blades in the United States. If they decided to form a company sales force for Wilkinson Sword USA, they would reverse a policy that had existed for 30 years dating back to the creation of the U.S. arm of the London-based Wilkinson Sword Ltd.

Wet-Shave Market

The shaving market is broadly divided into two segments: the dry-shave (electric) market and the wet-shave (razor) market. The wet-shave market accounts for the majority of sales volume. In the United States it is variously estimated at $450 to $500 million annually, at manufacturers' prices. The Gillette Company is recognized as the worldwide leader in the production and marketing of razors and blades. It is estimated that 6 out of 10 U.S. men and women who shave use Gillette products.

Four other companies are major competitors in the wet-shave market: Schick, American Safety Razor, Wilkinson Sword USA, and Bic (leader in the disposable-razor segment). These four competitors, coupled with private (store) brands, capture the great majority of the wet-shave market.

Distribution

Razors and blades are sold primarily through supermarkets, drugstores, and mass (discount) merchandisers. Although the dollar volume sold through each type of retail outlet varies over time, it is estimated that supermarkets account for 45 percent, drugstores for 30 percent, and mass merchandisers for 25 percent of razor and blade sales. Catalog and department stores also account for a small percentage of razor and blade sales in any given year.

Advertising and sales

Advertising and consumer promotions play an important role in the marketing of razors and blades. For example, in 1983 Gillette was reported to have spent $205 million in advertising all company products. A sizable percentage was presumably earmarked for razors and blades, since these products account for almost 80 percent of Gillette's total sales. Consumer promotions typically take the form of premium offers, coupons, cents-off deals, and on-package premiums such as a free razor with a cartridge of blades.

---

*This case was prepared by Professor Roger A. Kerin, Edwin L. Cox School of Business, Southern Methodist University, Dallas, TX. Copyright © 1996 Roger A. Kerin.

Similarly, personal selling is important in the marketing of razors and blades. Salespeople typically call on retail buyers responsible for purchasing items for the health and beauty aid sections of supermarkets, drugstores, and mass-merchandise stores. Salespeople introduce new products and special promotions and generally work with buyers to gain shelf space and adequate display for their products. They also assist with joint advertising programs. Industry practice indicates that salespeople call on retail buyers an average of 10 times per year, with an average sales call lasting three hours including travel and waiting time. Industry standards suggest that a salesperson spends an average of 190 eight-hour days selling per year. In addition, some firms, like Gillette, employ retail merchandisers who make sure that store displays are adequately stocked. Firms differ in terms of how the selling function is performed. Gillette, American Safety Razor, Bic, and Schick have their own company sales forces, whereas Wilkinson Sword USA relies on manufacturers' agents, brokers, and the sales forces of other companies.

Technological innovation and product development

Technological innovation plays an instrumental role in the marketing of razors and blades. According to Dr. J. F. Sackman, research chief at Wilkinson Sword's Technical Center in London, "The objective is closeness without pain." Accordingly, product development is an ongoing process that involves studying hair growth and razor and blade technology. This research has shown that there are approximately 310 hairs per square inch on a man's face, that 15,000 hairs are cut during an average shave, and that facial hair grows at a rate of 0.4 millimeter per day. Cutting this hair without pulling under-the-skin hair roots and damaging nerve fibers has been the purpose of razor and blade product development since the first blade was produced.

Each advance in product technology has rewarded its investor. For example, Wilkinson Sword developed the first safety razor in 1898 and revolutionized the shaving industry. Gillette developed the Super Blue Blade (which significantly reduced the force necessary to cut facial hair) in 1958, the Techmatic shaving system in 1966, and Trac II and Atra razors in the 1970s. Each technological advance improved Gillette's sales volume and market share. Bic introduced the first disposable razor in 1975, an innovation that literally changed the face of the wet-shave industry.

The Company

Wilkinson Sword Ltd. traces its origins back to 1772, when it was a major producer of guns and bayonets. The company began manufacturing cavalry swords in 1820. At the close of the 19th century, Wilkinson Sword's production of cavalry swords was between 30,000 and 60,000 units annually.

The company produced its first straight-edged razor in 1890 and the first safety razor in 1898. In 1956 the company introduced its Teflon-coated Wilkinson Sword Blade. Consumer response to this innovation was phenomenal. The company's market share in Great Britain increased from 20 percent in 1962 to 45 percent in 1966. During the same period, Wilkinson Sword's market share increased from 3 percent to 15 percent in the United States.

Wilkinson Sword U.S. operations

Wilkinson Sword's competitive position in the United States through the late 1960s and mid-1970s was continually buffeted by product innovation and aggressive marketing efforts on the part of Gillette, American Safety Razor, Schick, and Bic. Nevertheless,

Wilkinson's market share in the United States remained at a respectable level throughout the 1970s. By the end of 1984, however, Wilkinson Sword's market share for razors and blades had fallen to less than 1 percent. Actual sales were about $4 million at manufacturers' prices. Industry observers cited three factors that contributed to Wilkinson Sword's decline in market share. First, Wilkinson Sword elected to stop advertising in the United States in 1974 and focus advertising and promotional efforts on European markets. This practice was scheduled to change in 1985, with a plan to invest heavily in advertising and sales promotion for Wilkinson Sword products. Second, Wilkinson Sword's product innovation had not kept pace with that of its United States-based competitors. Recent development efforts, however, had resulted in several new products, which were to be introduced in 1985. A third factor was the lack of a company sales force. In the late 1960s and early 1970s, Wilkinson Sword's product line was sold by the sales force of Colgate–Palmolive, a large *Fortune* 500 manufacturer and marketer of personal care products. Wilkinson Sword parted with Colgate–Palmolive in the mid-1970s. In its place, Wilkinson Sword used manufacturers' agents to call on and service drugstores and brokers for supermarkets. According to industry sources, the commissions paid to manufacturers' agents and brokers amounted to about 10 percent of sales at manufacturers' prices.

Acquisition by Allegheny International

In late 1980, Wilkinson Sword was acquired by Allegheny International Holdings, Inc., a wholly owned subsidiary of Allegheny International, a Pittsburgh-based conglomerate. Allegheny International also owned or had major equity positions in such well-known consumer product firms as Scripto, Inc., and Sunbeam Appliance Company. Scripto, Inc., was engaged in the production and marketing of writing instruments and components and the marketing of disposable lighters. Sunbeam Appliance Company manufactured and marketed a broad line of portable electric products, including hair dryers, curling irons, and electric razors.

In the early 1980s, Wilkinson Sword's sales, marketing, and administrative functions in the United States were integrated with those of Scripto, Inc., but this action failed to arrest the decline in Wilkinson Sword's market share in the United States. Then, in 1984, Allegheny International sold Scripto, Inc., to Tokai Seiki Company Ltd., a Japanese lighter manufacturer. This action left Wilkinson Sword without the sales, marketing, and administrative support that had been provided by Scripto.

At the time of Scripto's acquisition by Tokai Seiki, Norman R. Proulx was vice president and general manager of Scripto, Inc. When it became apparent that Proulx was not going to stay with Scripto, top management at Allegheny International offered him the presidency of Wilkinson Sword USA. Proulx accepted, and he asked Ronald E. Mineo, who had been vice president of sales for Scripto, to serve in that same capacity at Wilkinson Sword USA.

Sales Force Decision

One of the major issues facing Norman Proulx and Ronald Mineo was whether Wilkinson Sword USA should change its sales program in the United States. Wilkinson Sword USA had historically relied on manufacturers' agents, brokers, or the sales forces of other companies to represent its product line in the United States. To recruit, train, organize, and manage its own sales force would be a major undertaking. For example, the cost of recruiting and training one salesperson was as high as $20,000 in 1985. The decision also had a time dimension to it. For a fee, the Scripto sales force would continue to represent Wilkinson Sword USA for two months following the acquisition. After that, Wilkinson

Sword USA would assume responsibility for its sales and marketing function. Furthermore, if Wilkinson Sword USA elected to recruit its own sales force, these salespeople would also represent the company's line of cutlery products. Like razors and blades, this product line had been sold by manufacturers' agents and brokers. Cutlery product sales in the United States were about $3.3 million at manufacturers' prices.[1]

If Proulx and Mineo decided to form a Wilkinson Sword USA sales force, then a sales plan would be necessary. This plan would have to include the policies and procedures for recruiting, training, organizing, and managing a sales force. The first step in the decision process was account identification. Mineo identified 25 key accounts from among the supermarkets, drugstores, and mass merchandisers that carried razors and blades. Key accounts represented very large customers whose accounts could be managed from Wilkinson Sword's Atlanta headquarters. Four hundred additional accounts were identified that could be serviced by a sales force.

An experienced salesperson's salary plus expenses would be about $42,000 per year. The sales organization would include two key-account managers to handle the 25 key accounts. A key-account manager's salary plus expenses would be about $40,000 per year. In addition, salespeople and key-account managers would be paid a commission of 5 percent of sales.

Alternatively, Proulx and Mineo could contract with manufacturers' agents, brokers, or another company's sales force to represent the Wilkinson Sword USA product line in return for a commission or fee. This approach would be consistent with past policies.

---

[1]For analysis purposes, the commissions paid to salespeople or agents and the channels are the same for cutlery sales as for razors and blades.

Case 1–9

Kildonnen Textiles*

In early 1992, the Kildonnen Textile Company was faced with a diminished market share in the face of a highly competitive market where a recession had resulted in slumping demand. The management of the company wished to ensure that the selling division was capable of dealing with the situation. Therefore, they conducted a careful examination of the organization and personnel of the division. In particular, they wished to discover the effectiveness of the organizational structure which had been introduced into the division during 1989. They felt that the plan had been in operation for a long enough period of time to allow a fair evaluation of it.

The Kildonnen Company was a large manufacturer which produced and sold over 300 kinds of textiles. The head office of the company was situated in Montreal and salespeople from this office called on customers in the province of Quebec and the Maritimes. The remainder of Canada was divided into four sales territories with offices located in Toronto, Winnipeg, Edmonton, and Vancouver. (See Exhibit 1.)

The population of Canada was concentrated in the southern areas of the country and 80 percent lived within 200 miles of the U.S. border. Textile manufacturing was centered in the southern areas of Quebec, south-central Ontario, and Winnipeg, Manitoba. As well, major industrial customers were located in southern Quebec and south-central Ontario, particularly in the "Golden Horseshoe" stretching from Hamilton to Oshawa. The fashion industry had been traditionally centered in Montreal, Quebec, but Toronto, Ontario, had recently become more important as the locus of Canadian fashion design and production. (See Exhibit 2 for a map of Canada.)

Although the seven mills which the company owned and operated were scattered among several small towns in Quebec, they were all located within a relatively short distance of Montreal. The manager of manufacturing, who was in charge of the overall operations of the various mills, resided in Montreal and traveled from one mill to another as circumstances demanded. A production manager was in charge of each mill.

Three principal processes—spinning, weaving, and converting—were carried out at the mills. In six of these mills, raw cotton and manufactured fibers (nylon, polyester, etc.) were spun into different kinds of yarn and yarn was woven into various kinds and widths

IVEY

*This case was originally prepared by Professor Donald H. Thain and revised by John O'Sullivan under the supervision of Professor C. B. Johnston solely to provide material for class discussion. The authors do not intend to illustrate either effective or ineffective handling of a managerial situation. The authors may have disguised certain names and other identifying information to protect confidentiality.

Exhibit I   Number of Salespeople

	1988	1989	1990	1991	1992
Quebec–Maritimes					
Salespeople	26	27	19	19	21
Inside salespeople	—	—	4	10	10
House accounts S.p.	—	—	2	2	—
Toronto–United States					
Salespeople	13	19	15	16	15
Inside salespeople	—	—	4	4	5
Winnipeg					
Salespeople	3	4	4	3	3
Inside salespeople	—	—	—	—	1
Edmonton					
Salespeople	1	2	2	1	2
Vancouver					
Salespeople	1	1	1	1	1
Total:					
Salespeople	44	53	41	40	42
Inside salespeople	—	—	8	14	16
House accounts S.p.	—	—	2	2	—

Exhibit 2   Map of Canada

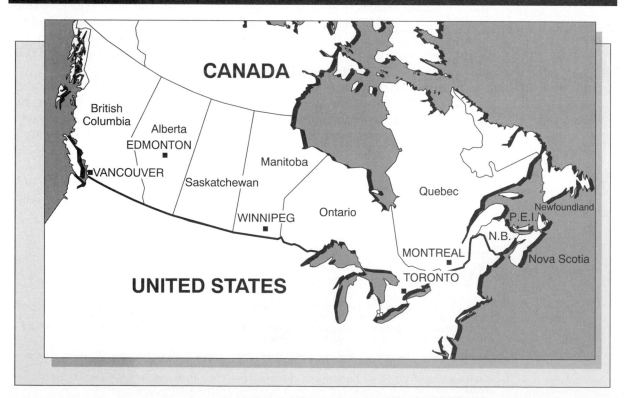

of grey cloth. The remaining plant specialized in converting operations which included bleaching, printing, dyeing, and finishing of grey cloth.

The products of these different processes fell into broad groups which were classified as (1) yarns, (2) industrial fabrics, (3) household fabrics, and (4) apparel fabrics. Approximately 25 percent of the sales of the company were made up of different kinds of yarns, while the remaining 75 percent were made up of the various kinds of industrial, household, and apparel fabrics.

The yarn that was produced by the mills was sold to various kinds of users. Altogether, there were between 25 and 30 different trade groups which bought yarn. The largest of these are knitters. The remainder included weavers of narrow fabrics such as ribbons and tape and manufacturers of wire coverings and thread-wrapping twines.

Ms. Dawson, the manager of market research, described the market for yarns as one which was constantly changing. She noted, for example, that "feed bags used to be sewn with cotton thread. They then discovered rayon was better and used that. Now, they are using nylon. Soon, they may begin to use monofilament. We have to be constantly alert to keep up with the changes in demand. The uses of yarn are becoming more diversified all the time."

Some of the fabrics produced by the mill were sold to a variety of manufacturers. Among the industrial users of grey cloth were manufacturers of coated abrasives and bags. Automobile and rubber industries were also large buyers of this type of cloth. The general sales manager described the kind of selling problem faced by the company when dealing with buyers of industrial fabrics by referring specifically to the tire manufacturers. He said,

> A tire company may come to me today and say they want a certain amount of nylon tire cord. I then go ahead and lay out plans to get it for them. By next Friday, they may call and say they have changed their minds and are going to make 20 percent of their tires of nylon cord instead of 15 percent as they had planned. So we change our plans. Later they say they are going to make only 10 percent of the tires out of nylon cord, and so we change again.

This business is like that all the time. Another typical example is the automobile manufacturers. They are now using much less woven and more nonwoven materials. We have to be prepared for these developments and we try to develop our products so that they satisfy the changing demands of the user. This requires constant redesign so that our products suit the new conditions of the market. At the same time, of course, we keep a lookout for new markets.

The products of the converting plant had many end uses, and consequently the customers to whom they were sold varied greatly. For example, a large portion of the dyed and printed fabrics were sold to the garment industry, which included manufacturers of dresses, sportswear, and suit-linings for men. In addition, wholesalers and retailers were large customers for these fabrics. Manufacturers of work clothing and draperies were also buyers.

The general sales manager also emphasized the aspect of change which characterized the market for apparel fabrics. He pointed out: "We may think blue is going to be the popular color for a certain kind of fabric and that it will really sell. Suddenly, we discover that blue is not as popular as we predicted and some other color, such as green, has taken the lead. If we had ordered a large volume of blue earlier, we may have to change our emphasis and have more green produced than we originally planned. If we do not, we have to be prepared to take a loss on some of the blue that has been produced."

A large percentage of the grey cloth which was used for household products was bleached, while the remainder was dyed. After it had been processed in one of these ways, it was used by the company for the manufacture of sheets, pillowcases, bedspreads, and towels. These were sold to retailers, wholesalers, mail order houses, and institutions such as hospitals and hotels.

During the 1980s, the company produced and sold white and colored cotton and cotton-blend sheets and pillowcases of good quality in a variety of sizes. Some towels were in white, but these made up a small portion of the total volume of household products.

Between 1950 and 1979, the Kildonnen Company had been very successful. The boom years of the 1960s and 1970s had been good for the industry in general, and for Kildonnen in particular. Despite a few economic downturns, sales and profits had risen in almost every one of those years. The recession of 1981, however, was devastating. The Canadian economy performed more poorly than the OECD average, and the textile industry performance was worse than the Canadian average. The Kildonnen Company did somewhat better than most textile manufacturers because it was a large supplier to government institutions such as hospitals and the military. Nevertheless, it was a painful experience for the company as several of its long-standing customers went out of business.

The industry began a recovery in the summer of 1984. During this period, many companies spent heavily to improve equipment and increase efficiency. It was widely felt that an increased level of investment was needed to fight off imports.

The years 1986–89 were characterized by strongly growing demand and profits. With Kildonnen working at nearly 100 percent of capacity, the selling organization merely booked orders and was faced with little actual selling. Kildonnen's expertise in industrial cloth and yarns made its products superior to many others on the market, and the company was never able to keep up with demand, despite several capacity expansions. The introduction of the Free Trade Agreement (FTA) with the United States in January 1989 meant that the Canadian industry had to compete with larger and sometimes lower-cost U.S. producers. In 1989, many Canadian firms moved swiftly into exporting to the United States. Their massive equipment investments in the '80s made them quite competitive with the U.S. giants. Kildonnen also moved into exporting textiles to the United States, although with capacity utilization dropping across the industry because of a recession in Canada, there was surprisingly little activity among the sales managers to develop American customers.

The Kildonnen Company had other problems as well. Mr. Carmichael, who had been with the company since its inception and had been general sales manager and director, died suddenly in 1983. He knew all of the salespeople very well and was the unquestioned leader of the group. One executive remarked: "What Mr. Carmichael said—went!"

Because of a series of unexpected events, there were to be four different persons in this post within the next six years:

Mr. Moore, the first of these executives, was appointed in 1983. He had been a senior salesperson for 15 years before he became the assistant general sales manager in 1979. At the time of his appointment as general sales manager and director of the company, he was 65 years of age. One executive later remarked: "Mr. Moore was one of the finest men I ever knew, but he let his heart rule his head. He was far too kind and hated to hurt anyone's feelings." Mr. Moore was forced to retire because of health problems in December 1987.

Mr. Burton, the assistant general sales manager, took over in January 1988. He and his wife were tragically killed in an automobile crash that July.

Mr. Jewel then took over. In 1985, he was appointed sales manager of apparel fabrics, and in 1988, he took over the position of assistant general sales manager. Mr. Jewel resigned in February 1989 to become the president of a smaller competitor.

As it had in the past, the company offered the position to Mr. Forrester, the assistant general sales manager. Mr. Forrester was 60, and had gained all of his experience with the company in the yarn division.

Exhibit 3 Organization of Selling Division—1989

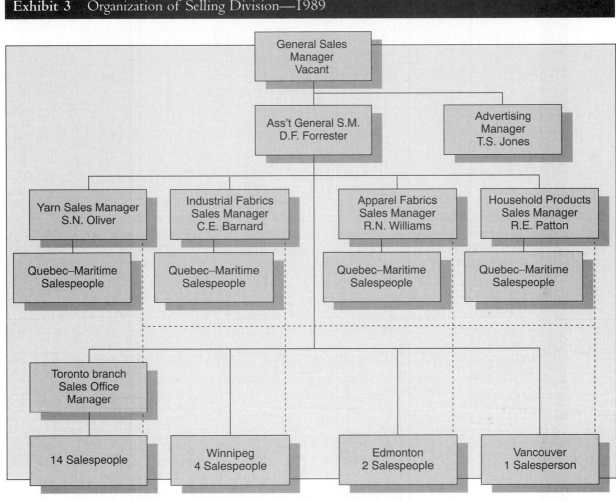

During 1988, the company began to see a decline in its market share. U.S. sales had not been as high as hoped, a recession was widely expected, and there was evidence that the government would lower tariffs for imported textiles. If this transpired, Kildonnen was likely to find itself at a price disadvantage due to its relative lack of investment in modernizing its older equipment. The management became concerned that the lack of continuity in the sales division had made it less responsive to changes in the market and hired consultants to make recommendations about restructuring.

The consultants recommended dividing the division into two main groups: selling and merchandising. Under this system, product specialization was discontinued to some extent. Now, instead of four major product groups of salesmen, there were only two—yarn and fabrics. In the East, salespeople specialized in one or the other; in the West, as in the past, salespeople carried all the products. The merchandising functions, however, were still divided among the four major product groups of the company. The U.S. market was to become the responsibility of the Toronto sales office. (See Exhibits 3 and 4 for the old structure and the new structure respectively.)

Exhibit 4 Sales Organization Recommended by Consultants

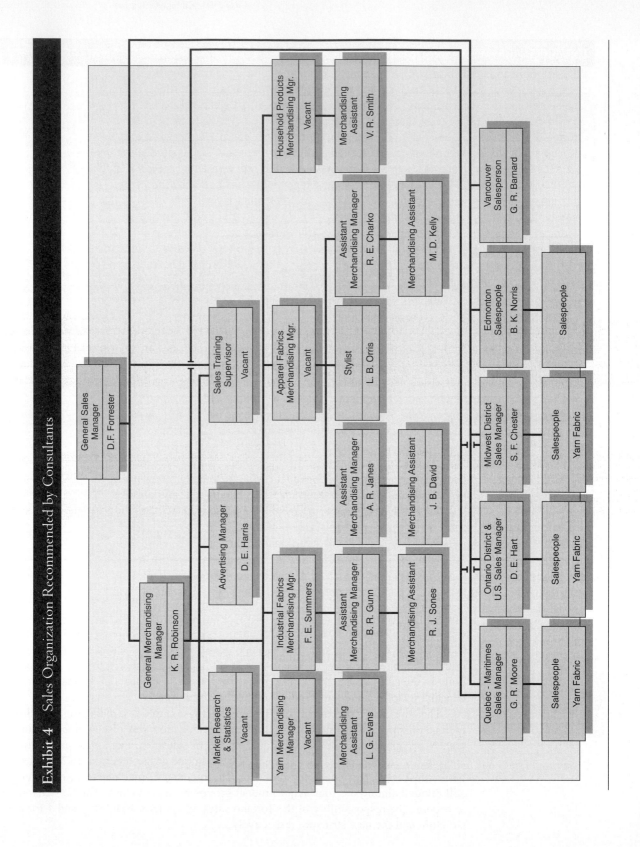

Several new positions were created by the suggested reorganization. These appeared mostly in the merchandising division and included a general merchandising manager and four product group merchandising managers who were to be in charge of yarns, industrial fabrics, household products, and apparel fabrics. As well, some junior management positions were eliminated. A new information system would improve productivity and flexibility. The new plan also included the introduction of a formal technique to achieve coordination in the division. A merchandising committee was set up which was to meet once a week. The members of this committee included the general merchandising manager who was the chair, the merchandising managers, the advertising manager, and the market research manager. After the directors studied the plan, they decided to introduce it into the selling division.

The new structure required a reorganization of personnel within the division. Mr. Forrester, however, retained his position as general sales manager. His responsibilities included the supervision and direction of all salespersons in the field. He did not have direct contact with all the salespersons. Only those in British Columbia and Alberta reported directly to him. In the Quebec, Maritimes, Toronto, Midwest, and U.S. territories, district sales managers were placed in charge of the selling operations. These managers reported directly to Mr. Forrester and were responsible for relaying his instructions to the salespersons. In addition, they were also responsible to the general merchandising manager and were required to relay the instructions of the merchandising division to the salespersons.

The position of sales manager in the individual product groups had been done away with under the new organizational setup. The persons who had held these positions were transferred. Two of these had a long history with the company:

Mr. Barnard, the sales manager of industrial fabrics, had been appointed to this position in 1985. He had been with the company since 1953 and had spent 20 years in sales before he took over as a sales manager. He had a very agreeable and hearty manner which customers enjoyed. One of the top executives of the company described him in the following manner: "He was the old-time salesman type who was a good dinner and golf companion and that sort of thing. He was very popular with the trade. He did not have to sell too hard during the prosperous years of the mid-1980s." With the reorganization he was transferred to British Columbia as the company's sales representative in that territory.

Mr. Patton, the sales manager of household products, had received his appointment to this position in 1988. From 1970 to 1986, he had been a sales rep for the company. At the time of the reorganization, he was transferred to the position of sales rep for household products in the Quebec-Maritimes area. He was later described by a top executive as "a man who had not been tested in the 1980s."

In the merchandising division of the new structure, one of the consultants, Mr. Robinson, was appointed to the position of general merchandising manager. He was 39 years of age and had spent 10 years as a manager in the sales and advertising divisions of a computer software company before he joined the management consulting firm in 1986. He had been in charge of the study of the Kildonnen Company.

Mr. Summers, who was 37 years of age, was made merchandising manager of industrial fabrics. From 1970 to 1984, he had worked in various clerical and inside selling positions within the selling division. In 1984, he was made a sales rep, and in 1988, he was appointed assistant sales manager of industrial fabrics. His assistant merchandising manager was Ms. Gunn, who was 32 years old and had spent 10 years in the production planning department of the company. She had been manager of this department from 1988 to 1989.

In the apparel fabrics department, two assistant merchandising managers were given the responsibility of carrying on until a merchandising manager was appointed. Mr.

Perkins had been the assistant sales manager in the department before the reorganization, while Ms. Anderson had been a salesperson. Both were 37 years of age.

In the yarn and household products departments, merchandising assistants were left with the responsibility of carrying on until managers could be found. Both were approximately 40 years of age and both had been salespersons before their appointments to the merchandising division.

To fill the managerial position in the market research and advertising departments, the company brought in two persons. Ms. Dawson, who was put in charge of market research and statistics, had been one of the members of the consulting team. Ms. Harris, who became the advertising manager, was a new member of the division and replaced the previous manager of this department.

The introduction of the plan was accompanied by several other changes. The consultants presented the personnel in the division with a large book of procedures in which specific lines of communication were outlined. Careful instructions were provided for the handling of many of the routine jobs that salespersons and managers had to carry out. In particular, traditional methods of keeping track of the weekly sales routes and expenses of the salespeople were replaced by new and greatly detailed forms and procedures. To alleviate the extra burden these changes imposed and to improve efficiency, custom software was ordered for the new information system.

The expected recession began to appear during 1989. Some of the sales staff at the Kildonnen Company felt that it would not be a severe recession, while others were more pessimistic. Also in 1989, the government directed the Canadian International Trade Tribunal to study the implications of lowering most-favored-nation tariffs unilaterally, but as of 1992, the recommendations of the Tribunal to lower the tariffs had not yet been acted upon. Export activity in the Canadian industry picked up dramatically during this period. Some of Kildonnen's competitors were selling as much as 50 percent of their production to the United States by 1991. Kildonnen's export performance was disappointing, but while the boom of the 1980s lasted, this was of no great concern to the sales division. Indeed, no one in the Toronto office was assigned to the U.S. market full-time and so little was done to develop customers there.

The recession was well under way by mid-1990. Kildonnen's business dropped by over 30 percent in the next 12 months. While other companies used their new-found export markets to cushion the blow, Kildonnen could not. Their haphazard pursuit of the U.S. market had left them with few export customers. In addition, the 1980s had seen the emergence of imported textiles, as well as finished apparel. The Canadian apparel industry found that the FTA was less restrictive than anticipated and the industry was able to utilize many cheaper foreign fabrics for apparel fabrication. The high Canadian dollar exacerbated this situation, and Kildonnen found itself with a rapidly declining share of the declining converted textile market.

One executive said: "The sales organization went overnight from pampered favorites to people trying to sell a surplus commodity. The psychological effect was dramatic. We had gone to a tremendous amount of effort to restructure for the inevitable recession, and when it came, we found that we still couldn't cope."

By the beginning of 1991, sales of the Kildonnen Company were dropping quickly. It was at this time that the management of the company increased its efforts to strengthen and stabilize the selling division. They had been looking for some time for able and experienced people to fill the vacancies in the merchandising division. Early in 1991, they decided that they had found the people that they wanted. They announced the appointments of Ms. Lovette and Mr. Young to the respective positions of merchandising managers of apparel fabrics and household products. Both were around 40 years of age and had extensive experience selling and merchandising textile fabrics in the New York area.

Also, to strengthen the division, they moved Mr. Summers from his position of merchandising manager of industrial fabrics and made him merchandising manager of yarns. Until that time Mr. Forrester, who had extensive experience in yarn selling and merchandising, had been attempting to work closely with Mr. Evans, the merchandising assistant in the yarn division. It was felt that the demands of Mr. Forrester's job as general sales manager were too heavy to enable him to continue in this manner.

To fill the vacancy in industrial fabrics which was created by this move, the management appointed Ms. Gunn to the position of merchandising manager. She was given this position because it was felt that she had gained the experience necessary while she was assistant merchandising manager to Mr. Summers.

Although these appointments eased the staffing situation within the selling division, management was still not completely satisfied that all had been done that needed to be done. Therefore, they closely watched the operation of the division as a whole.

As the competition became more intense, many complaints and dissatisfactions began to emerge among the salespeople. They resented the detailed expense accounts and sales route plans which they were required to fill out. They did not see the necessity of these and consequently found them very irksome. To make matters worse, the custom software that was to automate these tasks was still not fully in place and the salespeople had to spend extra time doing them by hand. Also, the consultants were very unpopular with the sales group. One sales rep stated: "The consultants asked us to take the intelligence and aptitude tests so that they could discover the qualities that make a good textile salesperson. We soon realized, however, that they were interpreting the results of the test against a very rigid standard which they had in their own minds. Promotions and transfers were made on the basis of the tests. Experience and selling records made little or no difference."

Mr. Barnard and Mr. Patton agreed with this criticism. They both felt that the consultants misevaluated the tests. They besieged Mr. Forrester who, like themselves, was a long-time member of the organization, with requests for a change. One of the executives observed that "Mr. Forrester spent a great deal of time listening to their complaints and getting involved in their troubles."

The organizational setup devised by the consultants was also criticized. Mr. Moore, who had been promoted from a salesperson to the position of district sales manager of the Quebec–Maritime area, complained that it was almost impossible for him to handle all the details of his job. In addition to supervising the salespeople and their activities, he had to relay to them the instructions which he received from the sales and merchandising people at head office. The situation was further complicated by the semifunctional computer system that was supposed to expedite these communications. He remarked: "Both the salespeople and myself were confused most of the time. The fact that the fabrics salespeople were carrying all the fabrics lines did not help the situation."

Salespersons who wished to give special service to their customers found that they were unable to do this satisfactorily. Requests for information and product adjustments which were sent to head office did not receive the kind of attention that the salespeople felt they should have. One salesperson remarked: "Every request from us created a major event at head office. They had extended meetings and consultations throughout the selling division. Consequently, by the time any action was taken, it was usually too late and often not adequate."

Customers began to complain also. They were not satisfied with the results of their requests to the company and were irritated and confused by the fact that these requests often resulted in visits from salespeople, merchandisers, and the district sales manager.

Both Ms. Lovette and Mr. Young, the new merchandising managers, encountered difficulties during their attempts to carry out their jobs at head office. During the first six months after their arrival in Montreal, they spent their time in building up a new line of products. However, they both discovered that their requests for changes in the production of products were not acted upon as quickly as they wished. Many delays occurred before any final decisions were made as to the type of products that the production people would or could make. Ms. Lovette felt that the detailed procedures which she had to follow when making her requests were the main cause of these delays, while Mr. Young suspected that the production people had not adjusted to the new market conditions and therefore attempted to operate as they had during the 1980s. The production department, meanwhile, had closed several plants and was unwilling to reopen any to produce new products until the recession ended.

In addition, Mr. Young was dissatisfied with the promotion and selling activities which the selling group devoted to his new lines. Despite all his efforts to improve the products, the sales household products continued to decline. His complaints to the general manager brought forth little or no response.

The management discovered, also, that the formal machinery for coordination which had been incorporated into the new organizational structure had not proved effective. The manager of market research described the sequence of events in the following words:

> You see, the committee never did anything. No one was expected to express an opinion about the problems at hand and no one did. People spent most of the time complaining about the computer system.
>
> I remember one meeting in 1990 in which the entire time was spent reading a report on the fact that the company had over 3,000 clients. Mr. Robinson upbraided the meeting for the fact that only a few hundred of these had been entered into the company database by the salespeople. It was necessary for these entries to be made so that the computer system could track the salespeople's progress. He ordered the selling group to get busy and make these entries. During the period of high demand which had existed, it was impossible for the salespeople to do this.
>
> At another meeting, Mr. Summers suggested that the division might function more effectively if the salespeople were grouped according to products and not according to geographic location. Mr. Robinson replied, "You mean you think my organization chart is wrong?"
>
> Gradually, people started coming late to these meetings and finally they didn't show up at all.

In December 1991, Mr. Forrester, the general sales manager, took an early retirement. Shortly after this time, Mr. Robinson also left to establish his own consulting company. The management appointed Mr. Shaw to the position of general sales manager of the selling division. They also made him a director of the company. In this way, they felt that they had placed him in a position which would enable him to take whatever steps he felt to be necessary to deal with the situation which they had found within the selling division. They had a great deal of confidence in Mr. Shaw because he had been president of a subsidiary of the Kildonnen Company and had been connected with the textile industry during all of his career.

Case 1–10

BT: Telephone Account Management*

"So what would you do in my place, Michael?" asked the regional sales manager.

Michael Tarte-Booth, sales development manager at BT (formerly British Telecom), listened over a pub lunch as his colleague, John Lambert, described the situation. It concerned a small business customer whose telecommunication needs were handled by BT's telephone account management (TAM) programme. Tarte-Booth was very familiar with TAM, having been involved with the programme from its early days.

The customer in question had grown in size and, with the addition of a sixth line, now qualified for personal contact with an account executive. But when informed of what BT viewed as an upgrade in account handling service, the customer demurred, asking to remain with TAM. Said Lambert:

> They wrote us a letter—I've got it here in my briefcase. It was polite but very firm. They don't want to shift from TAM. But now the field sales people are raising hell, claiming these folks as their own. This situation challenges the whole basis of our account management structure for different sizes of business customer.

British Telecommunications

The United Kingdom (UK) was the first European country to depart from the traditional PTT (post, telegraph, telephone) model under which postal and telecommunication services were administered by the same government agency. After being transformed from a government department into a public corporation in 1969, the postal and telecommunications businesses were split apart in 1981. Post Office Telephones became British Telecom. Under the conservative government of prime minister Margaret Thatcher, numerous public corporations such as British Airways and British Gas were privatized.

Soon the government announced its intention to privatize BT and sell up to 51% of the corporation to the public. In November 1984, more than two million people, including 222,000 BT employees, applied for the one billion shares available. A total of ƒ3.9 billion was raised.[1]

---

*This case was prepared by Professor Christopher H. Lovelock and Research Associate Martin Bless as a basis for class discussion rather than to illustrate either effective or ineffective handling of a business situation. Certain data have been disguised. The names John Lambert, Helen Dewhurst and Green & Meakin are also disguised. Copyright © 1998 by **IMD**—International Institute for Management Development (IMD), Lausanne, Switzerland. All rights reserved. Not to be used or reproduced without permission directly from **IMD**.

[1]The value of the pound sterling (£) varied widely against other currencies during the 1980s. Typical exchange rates in 1991 were: £1.00 = ECU 1.40 = US$1.70 = Sƒr 2.50. A second sale of government shares in BT took place in 1991.

As the sole licensing authority for telecommunication operators, the government took the view that competition and choice between operators would be beneficial to customers. In 1984 it awarded a license to provide domestic services to Mercury Communications, owned by Cable & Wireless (a recently privatized operator of international telecommunication services).

The Government provided breathing space to BT and Mercury by making clear its intention not to license any further fixed network operators for seven years. Separate licenses were awarded to four operators of mobile telecommunication services, including BT and Mercury. To ensure that BT did not abuse its initial virtual monopoly position of fixed network services, an Office of Telecommunications (Oftel) was established to protect the interest of customers. Oftel was widely empowered to oversee and regulate the business conduct and pricing policies of both BT and Mercury. Among other things, it prohibited access by BT marketing personnel to information on customer billing records.

Privatization and the introduction of domestic competition forced a refocussing of BT's activities. Between 1984 and 1991, the company went through two major reorganizations. The second, termed Project Sovereign, was one of the most ambitious attempts to date by a British company to reform its organization, management and culture. These reforms were meant to prepare BT for three challenges. First, the industry's traditional structure—national monopoly operators supplied by national manufacturers—was breaking down throughout the world. Regulatory barriers to international competition were expected to crumble, gradually in some countries, faster in the UK. Second, as companies internationalized, they might prefer to deal with a single telecommunications company worldwide. Providers of telecommunications services would have to tailor their products less to neatly defined geographic markets and more to groups of customers, who could be located globally. And third, more intense international competition and the growing costs of the technology race would lead to concentration of the industry. One manager commented:

> Many people welcomed the changes because of the greater freedom they offered us to respond to evolving market needs and to take advantage of new technologies. But, an equally large group continued to think and act like civil servants, as though we were still a government department. A third group were fence sitters who took a "wait and see" attitude, but were willing to be converted.

During the 1980s, telecommunications had made tremendous technological strides. For many corporate users, data communications became as important as voice communications. The use of fax machines and electronic mail exploded. BT invested heavily in modernization, unconstrained by the public sector borrowing requirements that the government had imposed before privatization. Coaxial copper cables were replaced by fibre optic cables which offered much greater capacity and better signal quality. New electronic exchanges with digital switches not only operated faster and more accurately but also enabled BT to offer a host of extra services such as automatic call forwarding.

In April 1991, the company changed its trading name from British Telecom to BT and adopted a new motto "Putting customers first." The new organization was structured around three customer-centred divisions: Business Communications, Personal Communications, and Special Businesses (including mobile and operator services). Each would deal directly with customers for sales and services, while being supported by other divisions that either managed BT's products and services, operated a worldwide networking capability, or provided development and procurement services. The 31 districts were abolished and only five regions remained of the original geographical structure.

Current situation

With 1990–91 revenues of £13.15 billion, BT was Britain's second-largest company (after British Petroleum plc). Reflecting the growth in both domestic and international markets, plus significant cost cutting efforts, BT's pre-tax operating profit in fiscal 1991 rose to £3.08 billion.

BT operated a technologically advanced network, boasting the highest proportion of optical fibre in its system of any major telecommunications operator. The long distance digital network was complete, while more than three quarters of all customers in the UK were connected to modern electronic exchanges (a few percentage points behind France, which had the highest share of digitalized exchanges of any major country). Further modernization continued at a rapid pace. Britain and Spain remained the only European nations to have privatized their telecommunication services, but a number of others were expected to follow in 1992–93. BT had also invested heavily in international ventures.

Domestically, BT retained a 94% market share. However, Mercury had adopted a strategy of penetrating the business market, starting with the largest customers—which might have thousands of lines. It was not uncommon for big customers to split their telecommunications business between BT and Mercury. At the consumer level, Mercury's presence was minimal except for pay telephones in busy locations—such as city centres and airports. Exhibit 1 shows the breakdown of the market by type of subscriber and number of lines.

Since Mercury had built its network from nothing, it could offer customers state-of-the-art technology and had pioneered a number of service innovations, which BT was seeking to match. But Mercury's network was still geographically limited, being focused on connecting London to Britain's business centres. Broader penetration required connecting customers to its network via BT's local lines, which often still used conventional technology. Mercury planned to spend £500 million annually during the three years 1992–94 to extend its network and boost its share of the domestic market. It already had 15% of the UK's international traffic and a greater share of private networks. The American telecommunications giant, AT&T (described as the 800-pound gorilla of the industry), was rumoured to be eager to invest in Mercury's future.

Additional network competition was expected to come from British Rail Telecom and from a joint venture between US Sprint and British Waterways (which planned to lay cable along the bottom of its canal network). Local competition was seen as coming from cable television operators, many of whom were affiliated with American regional phone companies, and from operators of mobile (cellular) services.

Creating a Pilot Telemarketing Operation

"You are the most difficult people in the world to buy from!" was how a customer described BT to Anna Thomson soon after she joined the marketing department of the newly created Thameswey district in 1985. Her colleagues quickly came to recognize Thomson's energy, drive, and enthusiasm for seeking out innovative approaches. Although recruited as network marketing manager, her responsibilities were soon extended to marketing BT's products and services, and she became district marketing operations manager.

Thomson's prior experience had been in the electricity industry, marketing network usage. In her new position, she demonstrated the value of selling customer premises equipment (CPE) as a means of generating network revenues rather than as an end in itself. She adopted an integrated approach to marketing both networks and CPE as complementary products. Thomson remarked that "inevitably the selling of the one would lead to the selling of the other." She emphasized that network sales were far more profitable than CPE sales, but traditionally BT had found it difficult to sell the more intangible product.

| Exhibit I | BT's Exchange Connections in Service by Type of Subscriber, 1980–1990, United Kingdom | | |

Year (at 31 March)	Total Exchange Connection (000s)	Residential Subscription (000s)	Business Subscribers (000s)
1980	17,353	13,937	3,416
1981	18,174	14,671	3,503
1982	18,727	15,159	3,568
1983	19,186	15,546	3,640
1984	19,812	16,044	3,768
1985	20,528	16,596	3,932
1986	21,261	17,120	4,141
1987	21,908	17,549	4,359
1988	22,857	18,145	4,712
1989	23,946	18,737	5,209
1990	25,013	19,281	5,732

Source: British Telecom plc.

While analyzing customer relationships at BT, Thomson singled out small business customers as a neglected market.

> The crux of the whole thing is that effective use of modern telecommunications products and services can make a real difference to the development of any small business today. Use of mobile communication tools, the choice of the right fax machine, installation of a switch that can grow easily and cost effectively to cover extra lines, the use of toll-free numbers and a wide range of datacomms services—all these things help a small business to be flexible as it reorganizes to meet its own customers' changing needs.
>
> The right telecom choices at the right time can enable a small business to offer new services (like out-of-hours customer service with call redirect), cut operating costs, and steal a march on their competitors. But, small business owners don't have time to research this all alone and so either miss opportunities altogether or make the wrong choices.

In her view, BT had not devoted enough time and energy to building the type of relationships that created loyalty. The only contact BT generally had with these customers was when they called with a problem or a bill was sent out. Typically, BT sales staff were only talking to small business customers once every three to five years, except when the customer initiated contact. Thomson warned that if nothing changed, BT was liable to lose these customers to competition.

Further analysis revealed that some 750,000 inquiries from customers of all types had not been followed up the previous year. The existing sales process, which was almost entirely focussed upon reactive responses to inbound customer calls, was obviously not working. Large accounts (served by field-based account managers) and those that screamed for attention were catered to at the cost of ignoring a huge market of smaller accounts. What was needed, argued Thomson, were telephone-based reps (representatives) to look after smaller business accounts.

Recognizing that the most sophisticated applications of telemarketing strategy were to be found in the USA, Thomson convinced headquarters to retain a leading American consultant, Rudy Oetting, to advise on conducting a pilot test in the Thameswey district. This district extended west and south of London, beyond Heathrow airport, along the M3 and

M4 motorway corridors. It contained many vibrant business communities, including a significant number of small high-technology firms. The consultant recommended that BT recruit and train telephone-based sales representatives to sell proactively into exactly that market.

Telephone account management

A variety of terms were used to describe the use of the telephone as a marketing tool. *Telesales* was often used to describe use of the telephone by salespeople as a communication channel through which prospects could be contacted and a single sales transaction consummated. *Telemarketing* was a broader umbrella term for all types of marketing-related telephone usage. *Telephone account management* was defined as proactive contact through the telephone channel to customers who required a continuing personal relationship—but not necessarily face-to-face contact—with skilled sales representatives who could function as communication consultants to small businesses.

Rudy Oetting described such people as bright, aggressive account managers who had been trained to listen carefully to customer needs and ask structured, probing questions about each business and its communication activities. The goal was to build a database of information on each customer which would enable managers to farm a territory systematically without ever leaving the office. In some cases, Oetting declared, they would work jointly with field sales; sometimes they called the shots for the field force, and in other instances, they were the *only* salesforce.

Thomson recognized the potential of such an approach for BT, using its own channel—the telephone—to contact the company's small business customers. She did not accept the traditional view that British business culture would not respond positively to telephone sales contact, being confident it would work well provided the process was oriented towards uncovering and meeting customer needs. But she saw that the approach would have to be nonthreatening and employ well-trained representatives who operated on a much higher level than conventional sales support or customer service personnel. As the concept took shape, Thomson coined the term *telemanaging,* which she defined as:

> Managing the customer primarily through the medium of the telephone, using all the sales, marketing systems and management disciplines of account management.

The TAM concept

The term *TAM* came to be used at BT as an acronym for both telephone account management and a telephone account manager. The latter would be a carefully selected salesperson trained to handle a wide portfolio of products and services, working with up to 1,000 assigned accounts entirely by telephone. TAMs would be trained to develop specific objectives for each call. During the call, they were expected to update their knowledge of the customer's situation and needs, check whether any problems needed solving, advise on products and services, take orders, and plan a specific date for the next call. The basic goals would be to ensure that the accounts continued buying from BT rather than the competition, and to develop accounts by selling additional products and services. Said Thomson:

> The job of TAMs is to understand the business objectives and organization of their customers and to help their customers make the right investment decisions at the right time—so that we *and* they become increasing successful. It's a partnership based on trust, which has to be earned through proven good advice over time. BT believes that this is the way you become a customer's preferred supplier. The basic goal is to continually build and refresh knowledge of the account base, and be the first to address or even anticipate communications needs. This is true relationship marketing but effected within a volume mar-

Exhibit 2   Sample Voice and Data Services Offered by BT, 1992

Voice Services

CityDirect provides direct connections between London and the USA offering call facilities such as abbreviated dialling and security safeguards.

SpeechLines is a service for intra-company speech connection.

LinkLine is an automatic freefone service which allows business to offer their customers a free enquiry and ordering facility.

CallStream is a service for information providers who sell stored voice or data information via the normal telephone line.

Network services offers call facilities such as call diversion, call barring, call waiting, last number redial, abbreviated dialling and conference call.

Voicecom International provides a 24-hour network of voice mailboxes to send, receive or forward messages from any telephone in the world.

Data Services

Datel is a data transmission service available internationally to over 100 countries.

KeyLine provides analogue private circuits for data transmission using modems.

Leaseline offers analogue circuits that enable subscribers to transport voice, facsimile, data and telegraph messages nationally and internationally.

KiloStream and MegaStream provide digital, private circuits between centres at high operating speeds.

PSS is a nationwide public data network using packet switching techniques.

MultiStream enhances access to the public network at local call rates for the business community.

Data Direct is a high speed public data service to the USA and Japan.

Prestel is BT's public Videotex service.

SatStream is a satellite service for business communication with North America and Europe.

Telecom Gold is an electronic mail service with over 250,000 mailboxes in 17 countries.

Integrated Services Digital Network (ISDN) allows customers to transmit voice, data, text or image information at high speeds and assured quality without dedicated private circuits.

Source: British Telecom plc.

ket because the TAM goes through this process a thousandfold. We use our own core product—the telephone—to do the job, because it allows us to manage and market efficiently to hundreds of thousands of customers. You could say we practise what we preach!

Each TAM would endeavour to develop a relationship based on trust. The customer call would remain the focal point throughout the contact cycle. Whether an order was taken or not, the TAM would establish when the next call was to take place and put it on the calendar. All the information collected would be fed into each customer's electronic file.

Thomson emphasized that the value of an account to BT was much more than just line rental charges and fees for network usage. The company also sold a wide range of telecommunications equipment (ranging from individual handsets to private branch exchanges), installation and maintenance, and an array of value-added services (refer to Exhibit 2 for examples).

When face-to-face contact with the customer was needed, the field sales staff would work together with the TAM. The ultimate responsibility for managing an account, however, would remain with the TAM. Thomson saw teamwork as an essential part of the process. One TAM later described the relationship as follows:

It works on the basis of whoever can close the sale, should close the sale. This means that we have to work as a team; you cannot have a "them and us syndrome." If the TAM is in contact with a customer who wants somebody to pay a visit, the field representative can go out with a better understanding. And if, after the visit, it's clear that the sales representative cannot sign the customer up there and then, he or she will pass the case back to the TAM to monitor it. The priniciple is that if I achieve, we both achieve.

Michael Tarte-Booth

To assist her in implementing the TAM concept, Thomson hired Michael Tarte-Booth, a man with experience in telemarketing on both sides of the Atlantic. Thomson later insisted that although the vision was hers, nothing would have happened in the field without her colleague's determination to get it right, day after day. His original career had nothing to do with telecommunications. As he observed, "How I fell into telephone marketing is pure chance."

After obtaining his undergraduate degree from a British university, Tarte-Booth obtained a master's degree in geography from the University of Minnesota. Then he went to work in Minneapolis for the American Heart Association, a major nonprofit organization. They needed someone with demographic expertise to analyze census data and pinpoint those geographic locations (down to specific street blocks) where their best potential lay for recruiting volunteer fund-raisers. Tarte-Booth also inherited responsibility for the association's telemarketing operation. He developed the use of the telephone as a primary contact for volunteer recruitment or direct solicitation of donations. One objective was to ensure that the volunteer callers should use their precious phone hours wisely by contacting only the better prospects. The potential power of this marriage between database marketing and the phone as a delivery channel was demonstrated when revenues increased by over 60% during the first year and 90% in the second.

On returning to Britain, Tarte-Booth was hired by a manufacturer of business systems to set up its telemarketing operation. The company was running a large direct field salesforce, but had neglected its customer base for paper-based products, and had disposed of its customer records for this market. The firm's telephone contact strategy was limited to proactive cold calls by sales representatives to new prospects. Thereafter, the channel strategy was simply inbound, waiting for customers to come back by phone or mail with repeat orders. Tarte-Booth's job was to set up a team that would revitalize the business:

> The goal was to re-create the database by acquisition and integration of lists from numerous different sources so that we knew, after telephone contact, who the customers were and who the prospects were. Our initial objective was to derive sales principally through referrals out to the salesforce. But, we had to start out by qualifying our prospects and calling all the names on our list. The response was impressive.

Other groups within the sales organization recognized the value of this activity. Within two years, the company was also targeting other vertical markets in the hospitality, leisure, and car retail and after-sales industries. Said Tarte-Booth:

> The programme diversified into new markets and more sophisticated applications. We had truly graduated to an account management operation with a primary focus on repeat purchase. Historically, customers had made repeat purchases roughly once every three years, now they were making them every three months! The whole thing about account management is getting to know and anticipate customers' needs by amalgamating the power of the database, the information you glean from customers, and the immediacy of contact by telephone. We found that customers liked the cloak of invisibility provided by the telephone contact. It gives them greater perceived control. Ultimately, they can drop the neutron bomb and hang up.

Inauguration of the TAM pilot

After three months' preparation, the new pilot programme was inaugurated in November 1986. Almost immediately, BT found that customers demanded a continuing dialogue focussed on an understanding of their needs, as opposed to a tactical contact aiming to sell them "the flavour of the month." Customers were also motivated by continuity of contact, wanting to deal with a specific person on a regular basis. They would spend up to 20 minutes disclosing information about their business and needs; but having invested that amount of time, they expected the relationship to be perpetuated.

Thomson's primary mission was to tackle the strategic and political issues related to getting TAM accepted within BT and to develop an overall "Integrated Channel Strategy" to show how all the sales, service and marketing channels (including TAM) should interrelate for BT's objectives to be met. The success of the pilot attracted growing attention. Over the course of the first year, Thameswey achieved a tenfold increase in account coverage and a threefold increase in customer purchasing levels among the pilot customers. These results were achieved at a lower ratio of cost to sales revenues than could have been obtained with face-to-face contact. It also left the field salesforce with more time to talk to larger customers, and enabled them to achieve the high level of consultancy needed in that sector. Tarte-Booth observed:

> The project succeeded strategically because of senior management sponsorship and the interest that Anna generated in the programme. It was driven through centrally and had very high visibility within the organization.

National Implementation

Anna Thomson and Michael Tarte-Booth kept in sight the ultimate aim of national implementation. Achieving that goal required careful documentation of the whole process. Other districts would have to be convinced rather than coerced to adopt TAM. In 1987, Thomson left the district to become national telemarketing manager. She saw her role as selling the concept of telemarketing to senior BT managers. Monthly steering committee meetings were held to discuss the progress of the pilot and make tactical changes. Progress reports, detailing success in achieving evolutionary benchmarks, were widely circulated.

As Tarte-Booth recalled, Thomson did not try to convince the corporation that TAM was the "greatest thing since sliced bread." Instead, he pointed out:

> We allowed it to prove itself and concentrated on keeping colleagues around the country advised of progress through workshops and seminars. As a result, other districts came of their own accord to inquire about possible implementation. As soon as a district showed serious interest, we followed up with more information in order to gain a commitment. With district autonomy and the fact that TAM was to be implemented on a voluntary basis, the soft sales approach was critical.

In early 1988, Tarte-Booth was appointed national implementation manager. He found that districts whose customer base was dispersed over a wide territory were quick to recognize TAM's value. During 1988, six districts established teams to focus on the small business market. A central development programme was created to train the trainers, build the necessary support structure, and develop the database software for TAM. That programme provided implementation expertise through a "franchise" package which demanded adherence to the proven methods established in the pilot in exchange for implementation assistance.

By early 1989, districts fell into three distinct categories. In the vanguard were six districts that had already established teams. The second group, described as "the soft underbelly of resistance," was interested but wanted to wait until TAM had proved itself elsewhere. Some sales managers were reluctant to embrace TAM, which was perceived as threatening since it involved a reappraisal of their approach to customers and a reorganization of field sales responsibilities. Strong resistance came from a third group of districts, principally in London and the South East. This hard core was located in the region that not only had the highest customer density but also faced the greatest competitive threat.

Following the Project Sovereign reorganization, the districts were abolished and field sales territories expanded, thus increasing field reps' travel times. Exhibit 3 shows the reorganized sales structure, in which first Thomson and later Tarte-Booth held the position of manager of sales development, operating at the same level as the five regional sales managers.

Training

Tarte-Booth emphasized that "the TAM programme is not about creaming the market. It's about building loyalty and defending against future competition." Given the complexity of the task demanded of a TAM, considerable effort was placed on recruiting the right people. The initial interview with candidates was conducted by telephone, followed by written tests and face-to-face interviews, and concluding with psychometric profiling of each candidate prior to final selection. Recruitment was followed by intensive training. BT built three special training schools to develop a consistent approach to customer care.

Training covered attitudes, as well as skills, ranging from how not to sound like a robot when using a call guide (recommended dialogue) to how to gather and enter relevant information about customers. Training also included hands-on experience with the equipment that TAMs would be selling. Over a 12-month period, a future TAM would follow five training modules interlinked with live frontline experience at his or her home base. The five modules collectively lasted for 13 weeks. Said Tarte-Booth:

> The training programme is designed to be holistic and so embraces the skills, the techniques, the methods, the tools, and the product knowledge integral to the future TAM's job. Their understanding is tested by rigorous role-playiing and coaching sessions. The entire account team is trained together, so all members emerge with a clear understanding of how their jobs interrelate. Before returning to their home units, each team converts theory into practice by making live customer calls from the training centre.

Future Plans

By early 1992, BT operated 25 TAM call centres around the UK. Total staffing, including TAMs, TOMs (TAM operations managers) and support personnel, exceeded 450 persons. The annual cost of a TAM was around £41,000, of which 50% was salary (in comparison, field account managers cost £40,000–£60,000 a year, of which about 65% was salary). Anna Thomson had been promoted to a new position, where her task was to develop a global customer service strategy for BT as the company began to expand into a worldwide organization. In this context, TAM was just one part of the jigsaw.

With TAM catering for small business accounts having two to five lines each, Tarte-Booth now turned his attention to other categories of business. His objective was to apply comprehensive account management to the entire customer base, integrating field and phone account management to address the needs of any type of customer. He saw BT's accounts as grouped into slices across a pyramid, with national accounts at the apex and single-line customers at the base. Exhibit 4 documents the number of accounts in each group and representative average annual revenues per account.

In three regions, BT was piloting TAM for medium-sized business customers with 6 to 15 lines. Since these customers required an expanded portfolio of products and services,

Exhibit 3

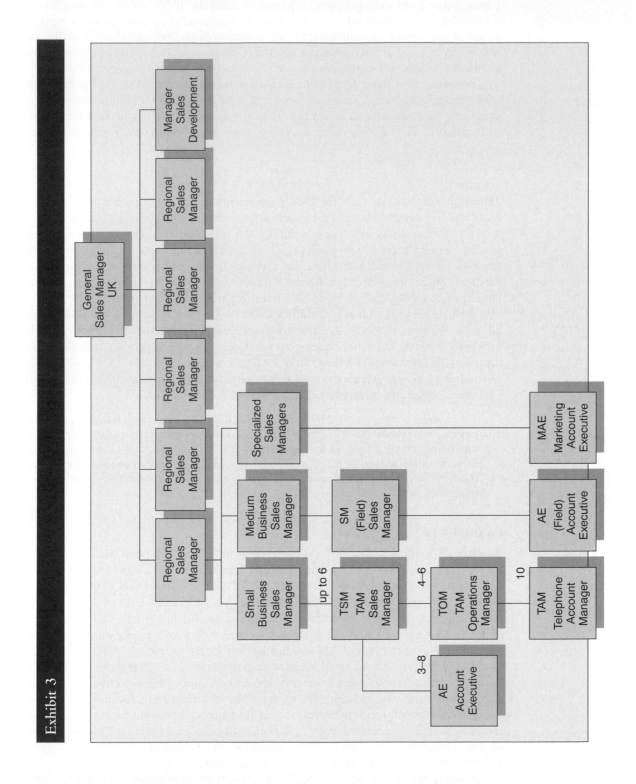

Exhibit 4   Profile of the Account Management Pyramid at BT

Group	No. of Accounts	No. of Lines per Account	Annual Revenue per Line (Range)	Representative Account Data Annual Revenue from Sales or Rental of Customer Premises Equipment	Annual Revenue from Value Added Network (Range)
National accounts	300	100+	£1,000–3,000	£100,000	£200,000–500,000,000
Key regional accounts	3,000	15+	1,000–2,000	3,000	25,000–200,000
Medium business accounts	200,000	6–15	900–1,500	500	5,400–22,500
Small business accounts	650,000	2–5	600–900	200	1,200–4,500
Very small business accounts	800,000	1	200–600	100	400

Source: British Telecom plc.

the new programme was more complex than the small business TAM. Bigger customers tended to have a more sophisticated approach to decision making. This process had to be reflected in the call guides, the systems, and the training. Tarte-Booth described the new programme as follows:

> It's an evolution of TAM and premised on the same channel structure. As such, it shares much of the methodology established for the small business programme, but has evolved to fit the needs of a new market segment.

Further up the pyramid were the key regional accounts, those with more than 15 lines. These customers would continue to be managed on a face-to-face basis through a field salesforce channel. Account managers and specialist executives were in the field to support them, backed by proactive and reactive telephone support. At the top of the pyramid were national accounts—large and lucrative customers with sophisticated communication needs, often international in nature.

Very small business customers with a single line, such as the consultant who worked from home or the small retail establishment, remained an untapped market. BT had experimentally incorporated the top 10% of this group in TAM but quickly learned that the use of TAMs was not a cost effective proposition. The cost of TAMs was viewed by some as prohibitively expensive for very small business (VSB) customers. Tarte-Booth contended that "it's inappropriate to think of TAM in purely cost substitution terms, since BT's objectives are market coverage resulting in account protection and development."

His proposed solution was to test the use of direct mail, designed to generate inbound calls to a VSB account management team. Catalogues of telephone equipment and services useful to very small businesses would be mailed to large numbers of prospects. The goal would be to stimulate the purchase of upgraded telephone products and services. As these single-line customers grew and acquired second lines, they could migrate up the account management pyramid.

Looking ahead, Tarte-Booth envisaged the desirability of creating a more flexible account management structure:

> Developing and implementing account management structures is a fundamentally different task from salesforce management, and the two may well conflict. They also require dif-

ferent skills. What we need is a range of account management options based on different channel configurations. TAM is just one channel within the sales structure at BT. We need a totally integrated and flexible structure for customers, in which their changing needs and preferences will be consistently catered for, whether their need for products and services grows, stabilizes, or shrinks.

The Case of Green & Meakin Ltd.

Green & Meakin Ltd. was a manufacturer of aircraft parts. When the TAM programme was first initiated, the firm had three lines and was assigned to Helen Dewhurst, who had exclusive responsibility for its account. As their TAM, she kept in touch with the company on a regular basis and followed through on all its requests, be it for a single socket, a new piece of telecommunications equipment or an additional line. Feedback from the two partners who owned the firm was very positive. They were pleased, they said, with the prompt and efficient way in which Dewhurst handled their business needs. Their experiences with BT prior to the introduction of TAM had been far from satisfactory: hours had been wasted chasing up requests passed from one person who didn't know or couldn't help to another who often proved to be no better.

As the company grew, so did Green & Meakin's use of telecommunication services. One December day, a sixth line was installed. Unknown to the firm, this additional line automatically set in motion the upgrading process. Dewhurst compiled a file on the company which was handed up to the new team. She then contacted Green & Meakin to inform the company that in future it would be handled by a field account executive, reflecting the growing size and importance of the Green & Meakin account. But the partners were unhappy. One of them called Dewhurst to state that the firm liked the service she had provided and did not view reassigning their account to a new account group as a useful move. Dewhurst responded that unfortunately, this was company policy, but added that she was sure they would receive excellent service in the future. When the senior partner still expressed dissatisfaction with the proposed move, she suggested that he call her supervisor, the TAM operations manager. Meeting a similar response from this individual and in turn from her superior, the TAM sales manager, the senior partner wrote to John Lambert, the regional sales manager, to complain (Exhibit 5).

The letter

"Ah, here it is!" exclaimed Lambert, pulling a sheet of paper from his briefcase. "Read it for yourself, Michael."

Michael Tarte-Booth unfolded the letter and quickly read it through. It was firm, and to the point. "This is dated ten days ago," he said. "What's happened in the meantime, John?"

"Well, I simply made copies and sent one each with a covering memo to the relevant TAM operations manager and the sales manager, and told them to sort it out. Neither could agree on a course of action because both claimed Green & Meakin as their own. So they passed the buck back up to their superiors."

"And then?" queried Tarte-Booth.

"Same problem!" responded Lambert, gloomily. "Neither of those two folks could agree, either. So yesterday it landed neatly back on my desk like a boomerang. What do you suggest I do?"

The waitress came, cleared away their plates and brought them coffee, which gave Tarte-Booth a moment's breathing space to think. "This could well happen again in the future," he said finally, sipping his coffee. "We can't spend all our time deciding when to make exceptions to the rules. I've been working on a plan to restructure the whole account

Exhibit 5   Letter to BT from Green & Meakin, Ltd.

Green & Meakin, Ltd
582 Thamesview Centre
Reading, Berkshire

Mr. John Lambert

7 January 1992

Regional Sales Manager
BT Southwest Region

Dear Mr. Lambert,

I am writing to you to express my concern over a proposed change in our account coverage status with BT. For the past four years, we have received excellent service through our telephone account manager, Helen Dewhurst. Recently, she informed us that due to our acquisition of a sixth line, we were scheduled to be "upgraded" in the New Year to a field-based account manager who would make personal visits to us at our offices.

My partner, Jim Meakin, and I phoned Helen (using the new speakerphone we recently acquired from BT) to tell her that we were very happy with the service she provided and did not wish to change to a new account manager. But she told us that the decision was company policy and not hers to change.

Subsequently, I called her superior, Ms. Anderson, and got a similar response. Next, the field sales manager called to introduce himself and the account manager who would be taking over from Helen. Jim took the call and said we didn't want to change, but we got the same story about "company policy." We had a similar response when we called the small business manager and the medium business sales manager, respectively. They don't seem to get the point that we are happy being served by Helen over the telephone.

So now I'm writing to you and appealing to your common sense rather than to company rulebooks. I know it's your internal policy to reassign customers when they reach a certain size (and we're flattered that you now consider us a "medium-sized company"). But the fact is, we don't need someone to keep coming out to visit us all the time, unless it's to install new equipment or undertake maintenance—which is a technician's job in any case. We feel strongly we're better off remaining with Helen.

We thank you for your consideration and look forward to your response.

Yours sincerely,

/s/ W. F. F. GREEN, Partner

management function at BT. Let me get back with a draft proposal to you in a few days, and I'll tell you then what I think we should do about Green & Meakin, too."

Tarte-Booth swallowed the rest of his coffee, put down the cup and stood up. "Be in touch with you on Tuesday, John. Thanks for lunch. You did say you were paying, didn't you?"

Case 1–11

Stubblefield Appliances*

Stubblefield Appliances
Serving Our Customers Around the World Since 1947
Internal Memorandum

To: G.A. Johanssen
             Sales Manager for Northern European Operations
From: J. Galbraith
             Vice President of Sales
Date: March 5, 1999
Regarding: Temporary Redeployment of Sales Personnel to Newly Designated Territories

Recent dramatic political changes in former Communist bloc countries have created significant opportunities for companies such as ours. The opening of Eastern Germany and the accelerated unification effort underway there, combined with a number of other political and economic realignments in the former U.S.S.R. have opened a strategic window for first mover companies.

I will be meeting with other senior management officers and the Board of Directors at the upcoming global company meetings in Boston in April. In preparation for those meetings I am developing recommendations for exploiting this strategic window. At present I am considering a proposal that would select 15 sales representatives from your division and reassign them for a period of 12 months to newly designed territories in the former Soviet bloc (an additional 17 sales representatives are being selected from the Southern European Division for placement in other newly created territories). During that 12-month time period, additional sales representatives would be hired and trained. At the 8-month point in their training, they would be deployed to the field to join the current sales representatives, and at the one-year mark they would take over the territory, allowing the original 15 representatives to return to their previous assignments. During their absence, the remaining field staff would assume responsibility for their accounts. It is at this point in the planning stage that I would like your analysis and input.

On the accompanying pages are data from our M.I.S. department concerning sales levels, territory staffing, and related information for each of the territory offices in the Northern European division as well as selected forecast data for the new territories. Please make your recommendations and describe your rationale related to each of the following issues and questions:

1.   From which territory(s) should the 15 sales representatives be drawn?
2.   How should the selected sales representatives be deployed among the designated territories?
3.   What do you see as the potential benefits and problems associated with the plan of a 12-month redeployment using current sales force personnel?
4.   Are there any additional resources needed or alterations to our sales force compensation program that the plan may necessitate?
5.   If you have a better plan, what is it?

---

*Professor Michael Luthy of Drake University prepared this case as the basis for class discussion rather than to illustrate either effective or ineffective handling of a sales force management situation. Certain data have been disguised and/or developed specifically for this case.

Stubblefield Appliances
Northern European Operations Division
Report Alpha/DT—12-month period ending 2/28/1999
printed 3/3/1999—2:05:47 A.M. G.M.T.

Territory Designation	Territory Office	Territory in Square Miles	General Population	Number of Salespeople	Local Currency	Sales in U.S. Dollars
Belgium	Brussels	11,781	10,100,000	3	Belgian franc	$ 977,552
Denmark	Copenhagen	16,331	5,200,000	2	Krone	857,419
Finland	Helsinki	130,119	5,100,000	4	Markka	1,235,588
Iceland	Reykjavik	39,709	300,000	1	M.N. krona	246,988
Luxembourg	Luxembourg	999	400,000	1	Luxembourg franc	328,911
Netherlands	Amsterdam	16,041	15,400,000	6	Guilder	3,498,913
Norway	Oslo	125,049	4,300,000	4	Krone	1,463,215
Sweden	Stockholm	173,800	8,800,000	9	Krona	4,298,713
United Kingdom	London	94,247	58,400,000	39	Pound sterling	25,548,914
West Germany	Bonn	96,010	63,200,000	43	Deutsche mark	27,229,741

Annual Hours by Territory

Territory Code	Territory Office	Face-to-Face Selling	Phone Selling	Travel	Administration	Other Nonselling	Vacation
Belgium	Brussels	2,850	900	1,050	1,125	825	270
Denmark	Copenhagen	1,750	600	850	750	550	180
Finland	Helsinki	3,250	1,200	1,950	1,500	1,100	360
Iceland	Reykjavik	788	300	513	375	275	90
Luxembourg	Luxembourg	1,075	300	225	375	275	90
Netherlands	Amsterdam	5,775	1,800	2,025	2,250	1,650	540
Norway	Oslo	3,250	1,200	1,950	1,500	1,100	360
Sweden	Stockholm	7,538	2,700	4,163	3,375	2,475	810
United Kingdom	London	38,025	11,700	12,675	14,625	10,725	3,510
West Germany	Bonn	42,463	12,900	13,438	16,125	11,825	3,870

Territory Code	Territory Office	Large Accounts (5 Calls per Quarter)		Medium Accounts (3 Calls per Quarter)		Small Accounts (2 Calls per Quarter)	
		Number	Average Call Duration	Number	Average Call Duration	Number	Average Call Duration
Belgium	Brussels	29	150 min.	46	90 min.	95	45 min.
Denmark	Copenhagen	17	150 min.	32	90 min.	54	45 min.
Finland	Helsinki	35	150 min.	58	90 min.	76	45 min.
Iceland	Reykjavik	6	150 min.	17	90 min.	30	45 min.
Luxembourg	Luxembourg	9	150 min.	26	90 min.	26	45 min.
Netherlands	Amsterdam	44	150 min.	125	90 min.	221	45 min.
Norway	Oslo	35	150 min.	66	90 min.	52	45 min.
Sweden	Stockholm	75	150 min.	132	90 min.	235	45 min.
United Kingdom	London	375	150 min.	688	90 min.	1,148	45 min.
West Germany	Bonn	425	150 min.	766	90 min.	1,237	45 min.

Stubblefield Appliances
Northern European Operations Division
Report Alpha/DT—12-month period ending 2/28/1999
printed 3/3/1999—2:05:47 A.M. G.M.T.

Notes to report:

1. Sales representatives work a typical 50-week year of approximately 45 hours per week.

2. For analysis purposes, dollar amounts, time assessments, and so on, do not include territory managers. These individuals' activities and performance are evaluated under other criteria and with other systems.

3. Sales of Stubblefield products are not subject to seasonal and cyclical variations.

4. Vacation hours taken by sales representatives are sufficiently spread out to have no significant effect on the maintenance of existing accounts.

Stubblefield Appliances
Special Report—Forecast Data for New Territories Assigned to Northern European Division
printed 3/3/1999—2:08:10 A.M. G.M.T.

Territory Designation	Territory Office	Territory in Square Miles	General Population	Local Currency
Belarus	Minsk	80,200	10,300,000	Belarusian ruble
East Germany	Berlin	41,767	16,300,000	Deutsche mark
Estonia	Tallinn	18,370	1,500,000	Kroon
Latvia	Riga	25,400	2,500,000	Lats
Lithuania	Vilnius	25,174	3,700,000	Litas
Poland	Warsaw	120,727	38,600,000	Zloty
Ukraine	Kiev	233,000	51,500,000	Karbovanets

Forecast Annual Hours by Territory

Territory Code	Territory Office	Face-to-Face Selling	Phone Selling	Travel	Administration	Other Nonselling	Vacation
Belarus	Minsk	Unknown	20% of average	Average	Average	200% of average	None
East Germany	Berlin	Unknown	100% of average	Average	Average	125% of average	None
Estonia	Tallinn	Unknown	20% of average	Average	Average	200% of average	None
Latvia	Riga	Unknown	25% of average	Average	Average	175% of average	None
Lithuania	Vilnius	Unknown	25% of average	Average	Average	150% of average	None
Poland	Warsaw	Unknown	100% of average	Average	Average	125% of average	None
Ukraine	Kiev	Unknown	50% of average	Average	Average	150% of average	None

Notes to report:

1. Due to the influx of new sales representatives, no vacations will be granted until after the initial 12-month period is concluded.

2. Percentages of average values are pegged to appropriate averages given geographic business location characteristics, infrastructure, and other relevant considerations.

Case 1–12

Springfield Interiors, Inc.*

In November 1998, Springfield Interiors, Inc., merged with S&O, Inc., a manufacturer of upholstered furniture for living and family rooms. The merger was not planned in a conventional sense. Art Robinson's father-in-law died suddenly in early August 1998, leaving his daughter with controlling interest in S&O. The merger proceeded smoothly, since the two firms were located on adjacent properties and the general consensus was that the two firms would maintain as much autonomy as was economically justified. Moreover, the upholstery line filled a gap in the Springfield product mix, even though it would retain its own identity and brand names.

The only real issue that continued to plague Robinson was merging the selling effort. Springfield had its own sales force, but S&O relied on sales agents to represent it. The question was straightforward, in his opinion: "Do we give the upholstery line of chairs and sofas to our sales force, or do we continue using the sales agents?" Andy Norem, Springfield's Vice President of Sales, said the line should be given to his sales group; Kristina Ekstrom, National Sales Manager at S&O, said the upholstery line should remain with her sales agents.

S&O, Inc.

S&O, Inc., is a small privately owned manufacturer of upholstered furniture for use in living and family rooms. The firm is more than 75 years old. The company uses some of the finest fabrics and frame construction in the industry, according to trade sources. Net sales in 1998 were $5 million. Total estimated industry sales of 1,100 upholstered furniture manufacturers in 1998 were $5.6 billion. Company sales had increased 7 percent annually over the past five years, and company executives believed this growth rate would continue for the foreseeable future.

S&O employed 15 sales agents to represent its products. These sales agents also represented several manufacturers of noncompeting furniture and home furnishings. Often a sales agent found it necessary to deal with several buyers in a store in order to represent all the lines carried. On a typical sales call, a sales agent first visited buyers to discuss new lines, in addition to any promotions being offered by manufacturers. New orders were sought where and when it was appropriate. The sales agent then visited the selling floor to check displays, inspect furniture, and inform salespeople about furniture styles and construction. S&O paid an agent commission of 5 percent of net company sales for these services. Ekstrom thought sales agents spent 10 to 15 percent of their in-store time on S&O products.

The company did not attempt to influence the type of retailers that agents contacted, although it was implicit in the agency agreement that agents would not sell to discount

---

*This case was prepared by Professor Roger Kerin, of the Edwin L. Cox School of Business, Southern Methodist University, Dallas, TX. Copyright © by Roger A. Kerin. No part of this case may be reproduced without written permission from the copyright holder.

houses. Sales records indicated that agents were calling on specialty furniture and department stores. An estimated 1,000 retail accounts were called on in 1998. All agents had established relationships with their retail accounts and worked closely with them.

Springfield Interiors, Inc.

Springfield Interiors, Inc., is a manufacturer of medium- to high-priced wood bedroom, living room, and dining room furniture. Net sales in 1998 were $75 million; before-tax profit was $3.7 million. Total estimated industry sales of wood furniture in 1998 were $10 billion at manufacturers' prices. Projected sales for 1999 were $10.3 billion.

The company employed 10 full-time sales representatives, who called on 1,000 retail accounts in 1998. These individuals performed the same function as sales agents but were paid a salary plus a small commission. In 1998, the average Springfield sales representative received an annual salary of $70,000 (plus expenses) and a commission of 0.5 percent on net company sales. Total sales administration costs were $130,000.

Springfield's salespeople were highly regarded in the industry. They were known particularly for their knowledge of wood furniture and willingness to work with buyers and retail sales personnel. Despite these advantages, Robinson knew that all retail accounts did not carry the complete Springfield furniture line. He had therefore instructed Norem to "push the group a little harder." At present, sales representatives were making 10 sales calls per week, with the average sales call running three hours. Salespeople's remaining time was accounted for by administrative activities and travel. Robinson recommended that the call frequency be increased to seven calls per account per year, which was consistent with what he thought was the industry norm.

Merging the Sales Efforts

Through separate meetings with Norem and Ekstrom, Robinson was able to piece together a variety of data and perspectives on the question of merging the sales efforts. These meetings also made it clear that Norem and Ekstrom differed dramatically in their views.

Andy Norem had no doubts about assigning the line to the Springfield sales force. Among the reasons he gave for this view were the following. First, Springfield had developed one of the most well-respected, professional sales forces in the industry. The representatives could easily learn the fabric jargon, and they already knew personally many of the buyers who were responsible for upholstered furniture. Second, selling the S&O line would require only about 15 percent of present sales call time. Thus, he thought that the new line would not be a major burden. Third, more control over sales efforts was possible. Norem noted that Art Robinson's father had created the sales group 30 years earlier because of the commitment it engendered and the service "only our own people are able and willing to give." Moreover, the company salespeople have the Springfield "look" and presentation style, which is instilled in every one of them. Fourth, Norem said that it wouldn't look right if both representatives and agents called on the same stores and buyers. He noted that Springfield and S&O overlapped on all their accounts. He said, "We'd be paying a commission on sales to these accounts when we would have gotten them anyway. The difference in commission percentages would not be good for morale."

Kristina Ekstrom advocated keeping sales agents for the S&O line. Her arguments were as follows. First, all sales agents had established contacts and were highly regarded by store buyers, and most had represented the line in a professional manner for many years. She, too, had a good working relationship with all 15 agents. Second, sales agents represented little, if any, cost beyond commissions. Ekstrom noted, "Agents get paid when we get paid." Third, sales agents were committed to the S&O line: "The agents earn a part of their living representing us. They have to service retail accounts to get the repeat business." Fourth, sales agents were calling on buyers not contacted by the Springfield sales force. Ekstrom noted, "If we let Springfield people handle the line, we might lose these accounts, have to hire more sales personnel, or take away 25 percent of the present selling time given to Springfield product lines."

As Robinson reflected on the meetings, he felt that a broader perspective was necessary beyond the views expressed by Norem and Ekstrom. One factor was profitability. Existing Springfield furniture lines typically had gross margins that were 5 percent higher than those for S&O upholstered lines. Another factor was the "us and them" references apparent in the meetings with Norem and Ekstrom. Would merging the sales effort overcome this, or would it cause more problems? The idea of increasing the sales force to incorporate the S&O line did not sit well with him. Adding new salespeople would require restructuring of sales territories, involve potential loss of commissions by existing salespeople, and be "a big headache." Finally, there was the subtle issue of Ekstrom's future. Esktrom, who was 50 years old, had worked for S&O for 25 years and was a family friend and godmother to Robinson's youngest child. If the S&O line was represented by the Springfield sales force, Ekstrom's position would be eliminated.

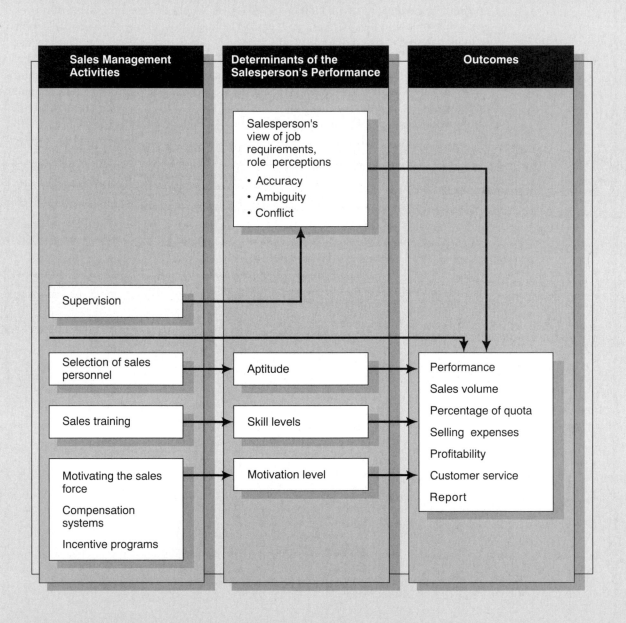

Part II

Implementation of the Sales Program

Chapter 1 suggested that sales management involves three interrelated processes: (1) formulation of a strategic sales program, (2) implementation of the sales program, and (3) evaluation and control of sales force performance. Part I of the book concentrated on the first of these processes.

Part II concentrates on the second. It explores the policies and procedures involved in implementing a firm's sales program. Chapter 8 provides a model that incorporates the main factors that affect a salesperson's performance and job behavior. In addition, it focuses on role perceptions, which are a key element in the model. Role perceptions are the demands salespeople receive from their customers, managers, and families. Finally, the chapter discusses how supervisory policies can help them deal with ambiguous and conflicting demands. Chapter 9 concentrates on motivation and its critical role in sales management. Chapter 10 examines the personal characteristics related to sales aptitude and the ways in which recruiting and selection procedures can be designed to build a sales force with the abilities needed to carry out the required selling tasks and activities. Sales force recruitment and selection are investigated in Chapter 11, while the objectives of sales training and a variety of training techniques are examined in Chapter 12. Finally, Chapter 13 concludes Part II of the text by examining how rewards can be incorporated into effective sales compensation and incentive programs. The first three chapters focus on explaining the complex process of salesperson performance and behavior. The last three implement that understanding in sales management practice.

8

Salesperson Performance: Behavior, Role Perceptions, and Satisfaction

TURNING LOAFERS INTO STARS

Tom Murphy, divisional sales director for Sprint Communications, had called his regional managers together for an important set of sales meetings. Late one evening his regional and key sales representatives began to openly complain that their salaries were not competitive with other companies. Murphy, known for his candor, stood up and announced to the entire group they if they believed they were worth more outside the company, then they should consider leaving Sprint. As one individual who was there said, "He treated us like adults, and in most big companies you don't get treated like adults."

With a reputation as a turnaround artist inside Sprint, Murphy was given the task of "turning around" the multimedia sales division, which is responsible for business-to-business sales of voice mail systems, fax services, and prepaid phone cards. The division had failed to meet sales targets the three years prior to Murphy's arrival. In the three years since his takeover sales have increased 350 percent to over $180 million.

Using the Right Tools to Achieve High Performance

The key to the turnaround was a complete restructuring of the rewards system. Prior to his arrival the highest reward level (President's Club) could be achieved after reaching only 81 percent of quota. The *top* performer in the division was at 100 percent of quota! Murphy quickly changed the rules, requiring sales representatives to reach 110 percent of quota to become a member of the President's Club. In addition, he sought to create more of a team spirit by introducing humor and a little lightheartedness to the meetings (for example, sumo wrestling).

To help him overhaul the compensation program, a team of managers and sales reps was brought together and told to put together a plan. Murphy feels that this was an important element in the success of the revised program, "It's important to involve reps in the process." The new program rewarded high performers (a rep reaching 110 percent of quota would be compensated at 120 percent) while penalizing low performers (a rep reaching only 90 percent of quota was compensated at 80 percent).

One other thing Murphy did to help motivate the sales force was to post monthly sales figures and to report those figures to senior management. One of the reps working for the division commented on the procedure, saying, "It did help motivate us. It felt good, not just from a monetary perspective, but to feel like you're profitably contributing to the organization."

Understanding the how and why of salesperson performance is key to successfully managing a sales force. Beginning with this chapter and continuing throughout Part II, the book will focus on this important element of sales management. Managers like Tom Murphy understand that getting the maximum performance out of each sales representative requires an understanding of salesperson performance and the tools available to managers that will enable each salesperson to reach his or her full sales potential.

Source: "Meet Sprint's Turnaround Artist," *Sales & Marketing Management* (January 1998), p. 79 and the Sprint Web site, at *www.sprint.com*.

LEARNING OBJECTIVES

How a salesperson performs is the result of a complex interaction of many factors. Many of those factors are the result of an individual's personal characteristics, motivation, and perceptions of the job. It is vital that sales managers have a clear understanding of salesperson performance so that he or she can maximize the performance potential of the salespeople in the organization. This chapter will present a model of salesperson performance and lay the groundwork for the information in Chapters 9 through 13. In addition, this chapter focuses on one of the key elements in the model—the salesperson's role perceptions.

After reading this chapter, you should be able to:

- Understand the model of salesperson performance.
- Identify the various components that make up the model.
- Discuss the role perception process.
- Understand why the role of salesperson is susceptible to role issues.
- Discuss how role conflict, role ambiguity, and role accuracy influence a salesperson's role perceptions.

As the introductory scenario suggests, a number of factors can affect a salesperson's performance. When sales managers implement sales programs, they must motivate and direct the behavior of sales representatives toward the company's goals. Sales managers, therefore, must understand why people in the sales force behave the way they do. This chapter offers a model to understand sales force behavior. The model highlights the links between a salesperson's performance and the determinants of that performance. In addition, the chapter examines one of the key elements of the model, a salesperson's role perceptions. Put simply, salespeople operate in a unique environment where the nature of the roles is changing. The second part of the chapter will delineate how a salesperson's role perceptions affect his or her performance. Complete understanding of the model should develop as you study the remainder of this section, which discusses the basic components of the model in detail.

UNDERSTANDING SALESPERSON PERFORMANCE— WHY IS IT IMPORTANT FOR SALES MANAGEMENT?

Understanding the model of salesperson performance—as discussed over the next several chapters and presented in Exhibit 8.1—is extremely important to the sales manager. As mentioned in Chapter 1, sales management involves three interrelated processes:

1. The formulation of a strategic sales program.

2.   The implementation of the sales program.

3.   The evaluation and control of sales force performance.

Almost everything the sales manager does can influence sales performance. For example, the way the sales manager organizes and deploys the sales force can affect salespeople's perceptions of the job. How the manager selects salespeople and the kind of training they receive can affect the aptitude and skill of sales personnel. The compensation program and the way it is administered can influence motivation levels and overall sales performance. The model offers the sales manager a tool for visualizing the effects of his or her activities and for appreciating the interrelated roles of the options under his or her command. This chapter outlines the model and highlights the various components. In addition, it discusses a critical component of the model—the role component—and delineates the evidence supporting its effects and the influences on it. The remaining chapters in this section elaborate on the components. Chapter 9 examines the complexity of motivation and its relationship to rewards. Chapter 10 focuses on aptitude and necessary skills. Chapter 11 discusses the selection process and its implications for effective sales management. Chapter 12 delves into sales training programs; these directly affect skill levels but can also influence the role component. Finally, Chapter 13 examines the design of compensation systems. These key elements under the sales manager's control can profoundly affect the motivation level of the sales force.

THE MODEL

The literature on industrial and organizational psychology suggests a worker's job performance is a function of five basic factors: (1) role perceptions, (2) aptitude, (3) skill level, (4) motivation, and (5) personal, organizational, and environmental variables.[1] Exhibit 8.1 presents an overall model of a salesperson's performance that includes these factors as primary determinants.

Although not pictured in the model, there is substantial interaction among the determinants. Much of the published literature, for example, holds that the various factors combine and interact to influence performance. The rationale is that if a worker is deficient in any of these factors, the individual could be expected to perform poorly. If the salesperson had native ability and the motivation to perform but lacked understanding of how the job should be done, for example, he or she could be expected to perform at a low level. Similarly, if the salesperson had the ability and accurately perceived how the job should be performed but lacked motivation, the representative is likely to perform poorly.

The empirical research is somewhat equivocal about just how the factors interact, but it is fairly certain that the determinants are not independent. There are substantial interaction effects among and between them. Although we know little about the form or the magnitude of those interactions, we need to recognize that they do exist.

The Role Perceptions Component

While discussed in much greater detail later in the chapter, the role attached to the position of salesperson in any firm represents the set of activities or behaviors to be performed by any person occupying that position. This role is defined largely through the expectations, demands, and pressures communicated to the salesperson by his or her role partners. These partners include persons both outside and within the individual's firm who have a vested interest in how the salesperson performs the job—top management, the individual's supervisor, customers, and family members. The salesperson's **perceptions** of these expectations strongly influence the individual's definition of his or her role in the company and behavior on the job.

Exhibit 8.1   Model of the Determinants of a Salesperson's Performance

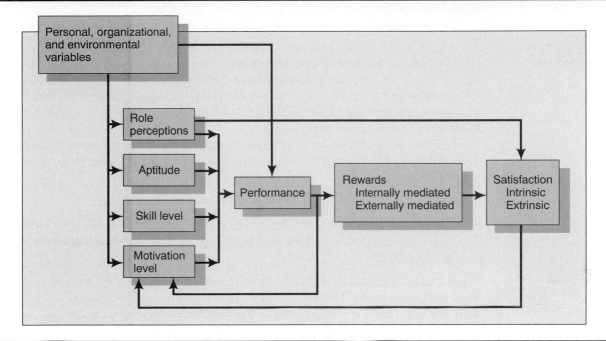

The role perceptions component of the model has three dimensions: role accuracy, perceived role conflict, and perceived role ambiguity. The term **role accuracy** refers to the degree to which the salesperson's perceptions of his or her role partners' demands—particularly company superiors—are accurate. Does what salespeople think their superiors want them to do on the job correspond to their actual expectations and demands?

Perceived role conflict arises when a salesperson believes the role demands of two or more of his or her role partners are incompatible. Thus, he or she cannot possibly satisfy them all at the same time. A salesperson suffers from perceptions of conflict, for example, when a customer demands a delivery schedule or credit terms the sales rep believes will be unacceptable to company superiors.

Perceived role ambiguity occurs when salespeople believe they do not have the information necessary to perform the job adequately. The salespeople may be uncertain about what some role partners expect of them in certain situations, how they should satisfy those expectations, or how their performance will be evaluated and rewarded.

The model indicates the three role perception variables have psychological consequences for the individual salesperson. They can produce dissatisfaction with the job. They can also affect the salesperson's motivation.[2] All these effects can increase turnover within the sales force and hurt performance. However, roles stress (role conflict and role ambiguity) does not necessarily always imply a negative job outcome (i.e., increased turnover). Indeed, research suggests that a certain degree of role conflict and ambiguity enables salespeople to make creative decisions that can be beneficial to the customer and the organization.

Industrial salespeople are particularly vulnerable to role inaccuracy, conflict, and ambiguity. Several personal and organizational variables can affect people's role perceptions.

Fortunately, many of these variables can be controlled or influenced by sales management policies and methods, thus allowing the sales manager to influence the performance of individual salespeople.[3]

The Aptitude Component

The overall model of sales performance in Exhibit 8.1 treats the sales aptitude of an individual largely as a constraint on the person's ability to perform the sales job. This assumes there is an adequate understanding of the role to be performed, motivation, and learned skills and an absence of other constraints. In other words, two people with equal motivation, role perceptions, and skills might perform at very different levels because one has more aptitude or ability than the other.

Aptitude and its impact on sales performance have received much research attention. Sales ability has been thought to be a function of such personal and psychological characteristics as the following:

1. *Physical factors* such as age, height, sex, and physical attractiveness.
2. *Aptitude factors* such as verbal intelligence, mathematical ability, and sales expertise.
3. *Personality characteristics* such as empathy, ego strength, sociability, aggressiveness, and dominance.

Many studies have found statistically significant relationships between the aptitude variables and performance. However, the broad measures of aptitude by themselves have not been able to explain a very large proportion of the variation in sales performance.[4]

Broad measures of aptitude may not predict sales performance for several reasons. Consider first the motivation component of the overall model. Motivation refers to the salesperson's desire to expend effort on specific sales tasks such as calling on new accounts or preparing sales presentations. This effort should lead to improved performance on one or more dimensions. The link between the effort a salesperson expends on any task and the resulting performance is affected by that salesperson's ability to carry out the task successfully.

In other words, the concept of sales ability or aptitude is very task-specific. Therefore, the appropriate definition of aptitude, and the appropriate measures of the construct, may vary greatly from industry to industry, firm to firm, and product line to product line. It depends on what specific tasks must be performed and what performance dimensions are considered important. Broad measures of aptitude may fail to capture the task-specific nature of the construct.

Second, aptitude may affect performance in more ways than by simply moderating an individual's ability to do the job. It may also affect the salesperson's motivation to perform. It seems, for example, that the salesperson's perceived ability to perform a task and general self-confidence influence the individual's perceptions of whether increased effort will lead to improved performance. Furthermore, salespeople's intelligence and feelings as to whether they largely control their own destiny or whether this destiny is largely controlled by outside forces (internal versus external locus of control) affect whether the representatives believe improved performance will lead to improvement in the rewards they desire. Thus, the salesperson's intelligence and perceptions of his or her own ability as a salesperson may strongly influence the individual's motivation to expend effort on various aspects of the job. All this suggests that objective measures of sales aptitude may be insufficient by themselves. Predictions of sales performance could be improved by including measures of perceived aptitude as well. The role of sales aptitude in salesperson performance as well as methods by which sales managers ascertain an individual's sales aptitude are discussed in Chapter 10.

The Skill Level Component

Role perceptions determine how well the salesperson knows what must be done in performing a job, and aptitude determines whether the person has the necessary native abilities. Skill levels refer to the individual's learned proficiency at performing the necessary tasks[5] and include such learned abilities as interpersonal skills, leadership, technical knowledge, and presentation skills. The relative importance of each of these skills, and the necessity of having other skills, depends on the selling situation. Different kinds of skills are needed for different types of selling tasks. Aptitude and skill levels are thus related constructs. Aptitude consists of relatively enduring personal abilities, while skills are proficiency levels that can change rapidly with learning and experience.

The salesperson's past selling experience and the extensiveness and content of the firm's sales training programs influence skill level. While American companies spend large amounts of money on sales training, there is almost no published research concerning the effects of these training programs on salespeople's skills, behavior, and performance.

There are a number of articles on training in the sales literature, but they are typically how-to-do-it or experiential pieces. Few studies have evaluated the psychological or behavioral effects of alternative training methods.

The Motivation Component

Over the years, motivation has meant various, and often inconsistent, things in the literature, although some recent consensus seems to be emerging. For our purposes, motivation is viewed as the amount of effort the salesperson desires to expend on each activity or task associated with the job. These activities include calling on existing and potential new accounts, developing and delivering sales presentations, and filling out orders and reports.

The salesperson's motivation to expend effort on any task seems to be a function of the person's (1) expectancies and (2) valences for performance. Expectancies are the salesperson's estimates of the probability that expending effort on a specific task will lead to improved performance on some specific dimension. For example, will increasing the number of calls made on potential new accounts lead to increased sales? Valences for performance are the salesperson's perceptions of the desirability of attaining improved performance on some dimension or dimensions. For example, does the salesperson find increased sales attractive?

A salesperson's valence for performance on a specific dimension, in turn, seems to be a function of the salesperson's (1) instrumentalities and (2) valences for rewards. Instrumentalities are the salesperson's estimates of the probability that improved performance on that dimension will lead to increased attainment of particular rewards. For example, will increased sales lead to increased compensation? Valences for rewards are the salesperson's perceptions of the desirability of receiving increased rewards as a result of improved performance. Does the salesperson, say, find an increase in the compensation level attractive?

A salesperson's expectancy, instrumentality, and valence perceptions can all affect the person's willingness to expend effort on a specific task or to engage in specific behaviors. Sales managers constantly try to find the right mix of motivation elements to direct salespeople in specific directions. The problem is particularly difficult because rewards that motivate one salesperson may not motivate another. Moreover, what motivated a person at one stage in his or her career may not motivate the rep during some other period, as the "Managing Sales Relationships," box indicates.

The salesperson's expectancy, instrumentality, and valence perceptions are not directly under the sales manager's control. But they can be influenced by things the sales manager does, such as how he or she supervises the salesperson or rewards the individual.[6] Since the salesperson's motivation strongly influences performance, the sales manager must be sensitive to how various factors exert their impact. These issues are explored more fully in the next chapter.

What to Do about the Great Salesperson Who Is No Longer So Great

Dave Parrett, sales manager for Ace Chemicals, was wrestling with the issue of how to get Kay Powers back on track. Kay had been with the company 20 years. Historically, she had been one of the company's top salespeople, although her performance had fallen off during the past three to five years.

That concerned Dave because Kay called on some of the largest accounts Ace served. She had earned each of those assignments. When she joined Ace Chemicals, Kay had turned heads with her performance. She had secured business in companies the firm had never previously served. Customers were extremely pleased with the service she provided. Ace received more unsolicited compliments on how she serviced her accounts than on any other salesperson. Her call reports indicated she made more calls in a week than almost any other salesperson with the company, and her sales showed it. She regularly exceeded the quotas she was assigned.

All this seemed to change in the last couple of years. She had developed very few accounts in that time.

Complaints from customers, while not the highest in the sales force, had shown a marked increase during the same time period. Kay seemed to start later and quit earlier than she had historically. She made fewer calls on average in a week than most of the other salespeople. She barely met her quota in three of the last five years and fell short of it once. Yet she was still a good enough salesperson that her income with salary and commissions exceeded six figures every year.

At the same time senior management had a big push on inside the company to increase productivity. Parrett also had several younger salespeople who were eager to move into larger, more demanding accounts. As he contemplated the future, he considered several options:

- Attempt to discern the reasons why Kay's performance had deteriorated and offer training and assistance to help improve her performance.
- Fire Kay and bring in new salespeople.
- What do you suggest?

The Personal, Organizational, and Environmental Variable Component

The sales performance model in Exhibit 8.1 suggests that personal, organizational, and environmental variables influence sales performance in two ways: (1) by directly facilitating or constraining performance and (2) by influencing and interacting with the other performance determinants, such as role perceptions and motivation.

Part I described how these variables can influence sales performance directly. The discussion of the organization of the sales force and the design of sales territories reviewed much of the evidence and logic supporting the relationship between performance and organizational factors. These factors include company advertising expenditures, the firm's current market share, and the degree of sales force supervision. There is a relationship between performance and environmental factors like territory potential, concentration of customers, the salesperson's workload, and the intensity of competition. The direct impact of the personal, organizational, and environmental variables on performance is thus rather clear.

Unfortunately, there has been less empirical work investigating the interactions among personal, organizational, and environmental variables and other determinants of performance. As discussed, studies have had modest success identifying personal characteristics associated with sales aptitude and relating them to variations in sales performance.

A few studies have found significant relationships between personal and organizational variables—such as job experience, closeness of supervision, performance feedback, influence in determining standards, and span of control—and the amount of role conflict and ambiguity perceived by salespeople. Other studies related personal characteristics to variations in motivation by showing that salespeople's desires for different job-related rewards (e.g., pay, promotion) differ with such demographic characteristics as age, educa-

What Does It Take to Succeed Globally?

The global salesperson will have to possess many skills in order to maximize his or her performance potential. He or she will have to be an excellent communicator who posseses cultural sensitivity. Moving among cultures has been and will continue to be part of the global salesperson's job description. Increasingly companies require global salespeople to possess business expertise beyond the product and relationships skills of the domestic salesperson. For example, in managing customers worldwide, global sales representatives will need to have the financial skills to manage a customer's "assets" around the world. Relationship marketing has led to global alliances between suppliers and their customers, making salespeople responsible for managing huge investments for their company.

Team building and team selling are an integral part of managing worldwide accounts. Performance expectations will be based in no small part on the ability of the individual salesperson to work with counterparts around the world. Coordination, communication, and the ability to work with a team spread around the world will be essential. For example, Ford requires its suppliers to have "one voice." The company wants a seamless relationship with its suppliers. This requires Ford suppliers to develop a high level of coordination inside their own organizations.

Finally, salespeople will need to be "technology friendly." As the relationship between supplier and customer becomes more complex, the exchange of information between organizations will grow. The ability to understand and incorporate technology into the selling relationship will become a major component of maintaining customer satisfaction. Bottom line, the global salesperson needs all the requisite skills of any successful salesperson . . . only more so.

Source: Doug Bosse, "What Does the Future Hold?" *Journal of the National Account Management Association* (Fall 1998), pp. 1, 14–15.

tion, family size, career stage, or organizational climate.[7] Overall, though, many questions concerning the effects of personal, organizational, and environmental variables on the other determinants of sales performance remain unanswered. An important question in recent years has been the effect of global sales responsibilities on individual salesperson performance. For example, are there unique issues faced by salespeople as they move into new international markets that impact their individual performance? The "Global Sales Force" box discusses this issue.

REWARDS

The performance model in Exhibit 8.1 indicates that the salesperson's job performance affects the rewards the representative receives. The relationship between performance and rewards is very complex, however. For one thing, a firm may choose to evaluate and reward different dimensions of sales performance. A company might evaluate its salespeople on total sales volume, quota attainment, selling expenses, profitability of sales, new accounts generated, services provided to customers, performance of administrative duties, or some combination of these. Different firms are likely to use different dimensions. Even firms that use the same performance criteria are likely to have different relative emphases.

A company can also bestow a variety of rewards for any given level of performance. The model distinguishes between two broad types of rewards—extrinsic and intrinsic. **Extrinsic rewards** are those controlled and bestowed by people other than the salesperson, such as managers or customers. These include such things as pay, financial incentives, security, recognition, and promotion—rewards that are generally related to low-order human needs. **Intrinsic rewards** are those that salespeople primarily attain for themselves. They include such things as feelings of accomplishment, personal growth, and self-worth—all of which relate to high-order human needs.

As the model in Exhibit 8.1 suggests, salespeople's perceptions of rewards they will receive in return for various types of job performance, together with the value they place on those rewards, strongly influence their motivation to perform.

SATISFACTION

The **job satisfaction** of salespeople refers to all the characteristics of the job that representatives find rewarding, fulfilling, and satisfying, or frustrating and unsatisfying. As Exhibit 8.2 indicates, there seem to be seven different dimensions to sales job satisfaction: (1) the job itself, (2) fellow workers, (3) supervision, (4) company policies and support, (5) pay, (6) promotion and advancement opportunities, and (7) customers. Salespeople's total satisfaction with their jobs is a reflection of their satisfaction with each of these elements.[8]

As Exhibit 8.1 suggests, the rewards received by a salesperson have a major impact on the individual's satisfaction with the job and the total work environment. The seven dimensions of satisfaction can be grouped, like rewards, into two major components—intrinsic and extrinsic. Extrinsic satisfaction is associated with the extrinsic rewards bestowed on the salesperson, such as satisfaction with pay, company policies and support, supervision, fellow workers, chances for promotion, and customers. Intrinsic satisfaction is related to the intrinsic rewards the salesperson obtains from the job, such as satisfaction with the work itself and with the opportunities it provides for personal growth and accomplishment.

The amount of satisfaction salespeople obtain from their jobs is also influenced by their role perceptions.[9] Salespeople who perceive much conflict in the demands placed on them tend to be less satisfied than those who do not. So do those who experience great uncertainty in what is expected from them on the job.

Finally, a salesperson's job satisfaction is likely to affect the individual's motivation to perform, as suggested by the feedback loop in Exhibit 8.1. The relationship between satisfaction and motivation is, however, neither simple nor well understood. It is explored more fully in the next chapter.

As noted previously, the salesperson's role perceptions play a critical role in their overall performance. In the remainder of the chapter we will explore this variable in the model. First, the concept of role and the process that defines the salesperson's role will be discussed. Second, we examine the unique aspects of the salesperson's role that make it susceptible to conflicts, ambiguities, and inaccurate perceptions. Next, we focus on three critical components of role perceptions: role conflict, ambiguity, and accuracy. Finally, we discuss some common demands salespeople receive and the consequences and causes of the conflict and ambiguity they feel.

THE SALESPERSON'S ROLE PERCEPTIONS

Why Are Role Perceptions So Important to the Sales Manager?

The role component of the model has important implications for sales managers. Role perceptions affect salesperson performance in many ways. For example, feelings of ambiguity, conflict, and inaccurate role perceptions can cause psychological stress and job-related anxiety for salespeople. These, in turn, can lead to lowered performance.

Exhibit 8.2 Components of Job Satisfaction and Sample Items

Component	Number of Items	Sample Items
The job	12	My work is challenging. My job is often dull and monotonous. My work gives me a sense of accomplishment. My job is exciting.
Fellow workers	12	The people I work with get along well together. My fellow workers are selfish. My fellow workers are intelligent. My fellow workers are responsible.
Supervision	16	My sales manager is tactful. My sales manager really tries to get our ideas about things. My sales manager doesn't seem to try too hard to get our problems across to management. My sales manager sees that we have the things we need to do our jobs.
Company policies and support	21	Compared with other companies, employee benefits here are good. Sometimes when I learn of management's plans, I wonder if they know the territory situation at all. The company's sales training is not carried out in a well-planned program. The company is highly aggressive in its sales promotional efforts. Management is progressive.
Pay	11	My pay is high in comparison with what others get for similar work in other companies. My pay doesn't give me much incentive to increase my sales. My selling ability largely determines my earnings in this company. My income provides for luxuries.
Promotion and advancement	8	My opportunities for advancement are limited. Promotion here is based on ability. I have a good chance for promotion. Regular promotions are the rule in this company.
Customers	15	My customers are fair. My customers blame me for problems over which I have no control. My customers respect my judgment. I seldom know who really makes the purchase decisions in the companies I call on.

Fortunately, there are things the sales manager can do to minimize the negative consequences associated with role perceptions. The kind of salespeople that are hired, the way they are trained, the incentives used to motivate them, the criteria used to evaluate them, and the way they are supervised can all affect perceptions of role. These factors can also determine whether these perceptions are ambiguous, in conflict, or inaccurate. That is why the role component of the salesperson performance model was discussed first. Its early discussion allows a fuller appreciation of the significance of the sales manager's primary duties, which were outlined in Chapter 1 and discussed more fully in subsequent chapters.

Another strategy sales managers can follow is to help the organizations' salespeople deal better with the stress they do feel by introducing them to effective stress management techniques. These might include relaxation training such as through transcendental meditation, training in coping and social skills, physical fitness programs, or other programs to enhance salespeople's stress management skills.

What makes understanding and managing role perceptions even more complicated is that not all the consequences of role ambiguity, role conflict, and role accuracy are negative. Creating sales positions that eliminate ambiguity and conflict can reduce the "challenge" for a salesperson and actually limit long-term performance. The task for the sales manager is creating an environment that will stimulate and motivate the salesperson while reducing or at least minimizing the negative effects of role stress that are a natural part of selling.

THE SALESPERSON'S ROLE

Every employee within the firm occupies a position to which a role is attached. This role represents the activities and behaviors that are to be performed by any person who occupies that position. The salesperson's role is defined through a three-step process.[10]

Stage 1: Role Partners Communicate Expectations

First, expectations and demands concerning how the salesperson should behave, together with pressures to conform, are communicated to the salesperson by members of that person's role set. The salesperson's role set consists of people with a vested interest in how the representative performs the job. These people include the individual's immediate superior, other executives in the firm, purchasing agents and other members of customers' organizations, and the salesperson's family. They all try to influence the person's behavior, either formally through organizational policies, operating procedures, training programs, and the like, or informally through social pressures, rewards, and sanctions.

Stage 2: Salespeople Develop Perceptions

The second part of the role definition process involves the perceived role. This is salespeople's perceptions of the expectations and demands communicated to them by their role-set members. Salespeople perform according to what they think the role-set members expect, even though their perceptions of those expectations may not be accurate. To really understand why salespeople perform the way they do, it is necessary to understand what salespeople think the members of the role set expect.

At this stage of the role definition process, three factors can wreak havoc with a salesperson's job performance and mental well-being. As Exhibit 8.3 suggests, the salesperson may suffer from perceptions of role ambiguity, role conflict, or role inaccuracy.

Perceived role ambiguity occurs when representatives do not think they have the necessary information to perform the job adequately. They feel uncertain about how to do a specific task, what the members of the role set expect in a particular situation, or how their performance is evaluated by members of the role set.

Perceived role conflict exists when a salesperson believes the role demands of two or more members of the role set are incompatible. A customer, for example, may demand unusually liberal credit terms or delivery schedules that are unacceptable to the salesperson's superiors. The representative's perception that it is not possible to simultaneously satisfy all members of the role set creates conflicting role forces and psychological conflict within the salesperson.

Perceived role inaccuracy arises when the salesperson's perceptions of the role partners' demands are inaccurate. Does the salesperson's idea about what the role partners

Exhibit 8.3 Sales Perceptions of the Job

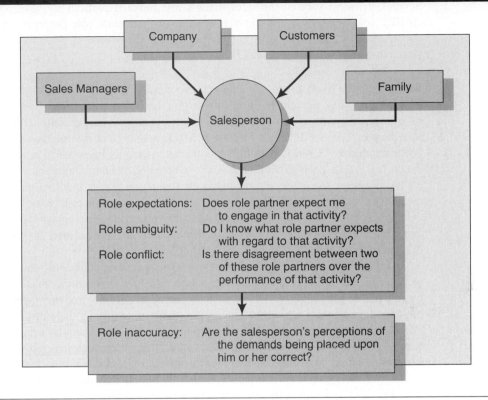

desire correspond to their actual expectations? Role inaccuracy differs from role ambiguity in that, with role inaccuracy, the salesperson feels fairly certain about what should be done—except that the sales rep is wrong. It differs from role conflict in that the salesperson does not see any inconsistencies in that it is unrealized. The representative does not know that the perceptions held are inaccurate.

Stage 3: Salespeople Convert Perceptions into Behaviors

The final step in the role definition process involves the salesperson's conversion of these role perceptions into actual behavior. Both the salesperson's job behavior and psychological well-being can be affected if there are perceptions of role ambiguity or conflict or if these perceptions are inaccurate. There is a good deal of evidence, for example, that high levels of both perceived ambiguity and conflict are directly related to high mental anxiety and tension and low job satisfaction. Also, the salesperson's feelings of uncertainty and conflict and the actions taken to resolve them can have a strong impact on ultimate job performance.[11] At a minimum, the salesperson's performance is less likely to be consistent with management's expectations and desires when the representative is uncertain about what those expectations are, or believes that the customers or family hold conflicting expectations, or has inaccurate perceptions of those expectations.

SUSCEPTIBILITY OF THE SALESPERSON'S ROLE

Several characteristics of the salesperson's role make it particularly susceptible to role conflict, role ambiguity, and the development of inaccurate role perceptions: (1) It is at the boundary of the firm. (2) The salesperson's performance affects the occupants of a large number of other positions. (3) It is an innovative role.

Boundary Position

Salespeople are likely to experience more role conflict than most other organization members because they occupy positions at the boundaries of their firms. Some members of each salesperson's role set—the customers—are in external organizations. As a result, the salesperson receives demands from organizations that have diverse goals, policies, and problems. Since each role partner wants the salesperson's behavior to be consistent with the partner's own goals, their demands are diverse and often incompatible.

A customer, for example, might request that a product be modified to suit her or his company's specific needs. The representative's company, however, may balk at making the modification because of additional design and production costs.[12] The salesperson gets caught in the middle. To satisfy the demands of one role partner, the rep must ignore or attempt to change the demands of the other.

Another problem that arises from the salesperson's boundary position is that the role partners in one organization often don't appreciate the expectations and demands made by role partners in another. A customer, for example, may not know company policies or the constraints under which the salesperson must operate. Or the sales rep's superiors may formulate company policies without understanding the particular needs of some customers. Even a role partner who is aware of another's demands may not understand the reasoning behind them and consider them arbitrary or illegitimate.

A boundary position also increases the likelihood that the salesperson will experience role ambiguity or form inaccurate perceptions. Contact with many of the salesperson's role partners, though regular, is probably infrequent and often brief. Under such conditions, it is easy for the salesperson to feel uncertain about what the customers really expect in delivery, service, or credit or how they really feel about how well the representative services the account. Furthermore, the salesperson's perceptions with respect to these issues may be inaccurate.

Large Role Set

The salespeople's role set includes many diverse individuals. The representative may sell to hundreds of customers, and each expects his or her own particular needs and requirements to be satisfied. In addition, people within the firm rely on the rep to execute company policies in dealings with customers and for the ultimate success of the firm's revenue-producing efforts. The specific design-performance criteria a product is supposed to satisfy, and the delivery and credit terms the salesperson quotes, can directly influence people in the engineering, production, and credit departments, for example. All these people may hold definite beliefs about how the salesperson should perform the job, and they will all pressure the individual to conform to their expectations.

Salespeople for a Fortune 500 subsidiary that manufactured automotive components, for example, were once caught up in such disagreement. Engineering wanted sales to emphasize the technical consistencies in the product line as a prelude to redesigning the line to make it simpler and more consistent. At the same time, marketing wanted sales to downplay the consistencies to maintain some technical mystique, which marketing believed was needed for product differentiation.[13]

The large number of people from diverse departments and organizations who depend on the salesperson increases the probability that at least some role demands will be in-

To Give or Not to Give

Due to increasing reports of unethical behavior on the part of its sales force, top management of a manufacturing firm recently held a meeting to denounce some of the alleged practices. Frank Harris has been a salesman for the company for several years. His recent performance has been less than what both he and the company had hoped. Frank believes his future with the company rests on his performance in the next few months. Frank has the opportunity of landing a large customer account, provided he presents certain expensive gifts to the purchaser. This is one of the practices that was just condemned by the firm. However, Frank believes this large sale will secure his job, so he provides the gifts, charging them against his expense account disguised as other expenses.

Do you approve? Somewhat approve? Somewhat disapprove? Disapprove?

compatible. It also increases the probability that the salesperson's perceptions of some demands will be inaccurate and that the rep will be uncertain about others.

Innovative Role

The salesperson's role is frequently innovative in that the rep is often called on to produce new solutions to nonroutine problems. This is particularly true when the salesperson is selling highly technical products or engineered systems designed to the customer's specifications. Even the salesperson who sells standardized products must display some creativity in matching the company's offerings to the customer's particular needs. With potential new accounts, this is an extremely difficult, but critical, task. The "Ethical Issues" box indicates another way in which salespeople can be caught in the middle between the demands of their customers and the expectations of their employers.

Occupants of innovative roles tend to experience more conflict than other organization members because they must have flexibility to perform their roles well. Such people must have the authority to develop and carry out innovative solutions. This need for flexibility often brings the salesperson into conflict with the standard operating procedures of the firm and the expectations of the organization members who want to maintain the status quo. The production manager, for example, may frown on orders for nonstandard products because of their adverse effects on production costs and schedules, although marketing, and particularly the salespeople, might desire flexible production schedules and the ability to sell custom-designed products.

Occupants of innovative roles also tend to experience more role ambiguity and inaccurate role perceptions than occupants of noninnovative roles because they frequently face unusual situations where they have no standard procedures or past experience to guide them. Consequently, they are often uncertain about how their role partners expect them to proceed. The perceptions they do have are more likely to be inaccurate because of the nonroutine nature of the task. The flexibility that is needed to fulfill an innovative role can consequently have unforeseen, negative consequences.

A salesman of a major manufacturer of heating, ventilating, and air conditioning equipment was recently embarrassed during a sales demonstration. Since the product was higher priced than the competition, the salesman decided to prove that there would be less labor costs for installation. On the field demonstration day, engineering sent the prototype with a last-minute design change without notifying the salesman. The alteration made the product similar to the competition. Thus, the customer was indifferent during the sales installation demonstration, and more importantly, because of the last-minute engineering change, there was no labor advantage. Besides experiencing a demeaning demonstration, the salesman lost the potential sale.[14]

ROLE CONFLICT AND AMBIGUITY

In discussing the causes and consequences of the various role perceptions, it is useful to separate the concepts of role conflict and role ambiguity, on the one hand, and inaccurate role perceptions, on the other. This section concentrates on role conflict and role ambiguity, and the next section emphasizes role accuracy.

Common Expectations and Key Areas of Conflict and Ambiguity

Different sales jobs require different tasks and place different demands on salespeople. The person selling dresses to a woman's fashion store may be most concerned with follow-up service to make sure the reorders for styles, colors, or sizes arrive in time for the current selling season. The rep selling pumps to a refinery may have to be most concerned with making sure the equipment can handle the load, chemicals, and other harsh conditions to which it will be subjected. Thus, it is next to impossible to develop one set of expectations common to all sales jobs. Even firms within the same industry often place different demands on their salespeople. Nevertheless, the empirical evidence prompts several major conclusions:[15]

1. Different role partners emphasize different types of expectations. Salespeople see some role partners as being concerned with what they do—company superiors focus on the functional aspects of the job such as handling back charges and adjustments, expediting orders, and supervising installations. Others are more concerned with how they do it—family members are concerned about the salesperson's hours of work and personal relations with customers.
2. Perceived role expectations are consistent among salespeople. A large proportion of sales representatives are consistent in their perceptions of what their company superiors and sales managers expect of them. The major area where sales representatives do not perceive similar role expectations involves the demands of family members. These demands are much more likely to differ from one salesperson to the next than are the expectations of customers or company superiors. This suggests that no matter what the company expects in hours of work, relations with customers, travel, and the like, a substantial number of its salespeople are likely to be in conflict with the expectations of their families. That is becoming an increasingly serious problem for today's workers, as the "Ethical Issues" box (8.2) indicates.
3. Most industrial salespeople do not seem uncertain about what they are expected to do or how their performance is being evaluated. However, a substantial proportion are plagued by ambiguity concerning some aspects of their job and some role partners. Sales reps say they are particularly uncertain about company policies, how their performance is being evaluated by company superiors, and what their sales managers expect. In comparison, very few are uncertain about the expectations or evaluations of customers or family members. This suggests customers and family members communicate their role expectations more effectively than company superiors do. Perhaps this is not surprising since a representative faces customers and family members almost daily, whereas company policies are communicated through infrequent sales meetings, written memos, and other less effective means.
4. Most salespeople perceive conflicts between some company policies or expectations

The Impact When Job, Family Collide

Companies demand much of their salespeople and management. Travel and entertaining are part of the sales environment. The challenge of balancing home and work demands has never been greater. It is not surprising then to learn that work–family conflicts take a greater toll on the family than on an employee's job performance, research shows.

Employers are increasingly worried about productivity problems among workers with conflicting job and family responsibilities. But recent research by the Families and Work Institute, a nonprofit research and planning group, shows the family also bears a heavy burden. The institute found that more than 25 percent of 1,000 headquarters employees of a Fortune 1,000 corporation said they refused overtime because of their families. More than 10 percent said they refused promotions; 24 percent, travel; and 10 percent, relocations.

Though these are serious problems for employers, families are paying an even higher price, says Ellen Galinsky, co-president of the institute. More than 60 percent of those surveyed said their jobs robbed them of adequate energy and time to do things with their families. More than 80 percent said they were only sometimes, rarely, or never able to completely fulfill their personal responsibilities.

The findings, which echo those of similar studies by the institute, have major implications, Ms. Galinsky says. Other studies show that "when parents have demanding and hectic jobs and report [the effects] spilling over on the family, you can see the repercussions" in the quality of family life and the way children develop cognitively and socially.

and their customers' demands. Customers are usually seen as demanding more functions performed by the salesperson, more services, more honesty, more liberal use of the expense account, and so forth. Sales managers and other company executives are seen as demanding that the salesperson hold down selling expenses and customer concessions. Most salespeople believe that their company superiors and customers expect them to travel, work flexible hours, and be available to customers in the evenings and on weekends. Unfortunately, most representatives believe these expectations conflict with the desires of their families. Although job–family conflicts are not unique to salespeople, their pervasiveness in the sales force should be recognized as a major influence on job satisfaction and performance.

Consequences of Conflict and Ambiguity

Most people experience some occasional role conflict and ambiguity. In small doses, role conflict and ambiguity may be good for the individual and the organization. When there are no disagreements and no uncertainty associated with a role, people can become so comfortable in the position that they constantly strive to preserve the status quo. Some role stress, therefore, can lead to useful adaptation and change. In sum, there is a level of hostility below which conflict and ambiguity may be benign but above which they will be malign. Excessive role stress can have dysfunctional consequences, both psychological and behavioral, for the individual and the organization, as Exhibit 8.4 indicates. Consider first the psychological consequences.

Psychological consequences

When a salesperson perceives that role partners have conflicting expectations about how the job should be performed, the salesperson becomes the "person in the middle." How

Exhibit 8.4   Causes and Consequences of a Salespersons Job Perceptions

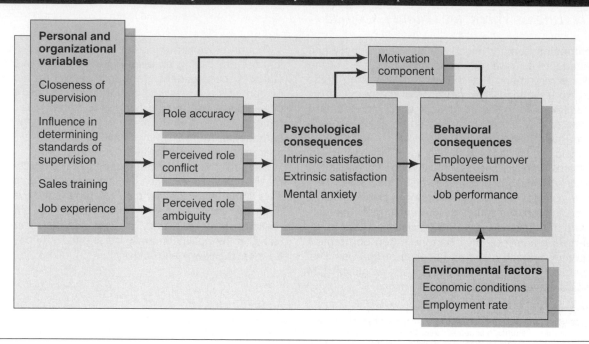

can the rep satisfy the demands of one role partner without incurring the wrath or disappointment of others? This situation can produce psychological conflict, which is uncomfortable for the individual and can produce various kinds of emotional turmoil. Job tensions increase, and the salesperson tends to worry more about conditions and events at work than usual. The salesperson's overall feelings of anxiety increase, and the rep is likely to become less satisfied with role partners, the company, and the job.[16]

Perceived role ambiguity can have similar negative consequences. When salespeople feel they lack the information necessary to perform the job adequately, when they don't know what role partners expect of them, or when they are uncertain about their ability to perform, they likely lose confidence in their ability to perform the sales role successfully. Salespeople tend to worry a great deal about whether they are doing the right thing and about how role partners will react to their performance. Representatives may also lose confidence in role partners and blame them for failing to communicate their expectations and evaluations adequately. Like conflict, then, perceived role ambiguity is likely to increase a salesperson's mental anxiety and decrease job satisfaction.[17]

Although both conflict and ambiguity affect job satisfaction negatively, they affect it somewhat differently. Perceived role conflict primarily affects extrinsic job satisfaction, but has little or no effect on the intrinsic satisfactions salespeople derive from the job. Salespeople's ability to obtain extrinsic rewards, such as more pay, a promotion, praise, and recognition, is influenced by role partners. Therefore, conflicts among the expectations and demands of those role partners not only make it more difficult for salespeople to satisfy their demands but also jeopardize the reps' ability to earn desired extrinsic rewards. On the other hand, such conflicts may not restrain their ability to obtain intrinsic satisfactions from the job. Even when two or more role partners cannot agree on how reps should perform, salespeople may still gain a sense of accomplishment from working or improving personal abilities.

Unlike perceived conflict, ambiguity has a negative impact on the intrinsic components of salespeople's job satisfaction as well as the extrinsic components.[18] When salespeople are uncertain about how they should be doing the job, whether they are doing it right, and how others are evaluating their performance, they are likely to lose self-confidence, and their self-esteem suffers. Ambiguity, therefore, reduces the ability to obtain intrinsic rewards and satisfactions from the job. Similarly, if salespeople are uncertain about how role partners are evaluating their performance, they become uncertain about their chances for promotion or pay increases. Finally, salespeople are likely to be dissatisfied with role partners who fail to make clear their expectations and evaluations, thus causing emotional discomfort in the sales force.

Behavioral consequences

Perceived role conflict and ambiguity can produce dysfunctional behavior consequences among the sales force. It is naive to think that a happy worker is invariably a productive worker, but evidence collected from a variety of occupations suggests that a worker's satisfaction influences job behavior. For instance, a negative relationship consistently appears between job satisfaction and absenteeism and employee turnover. Low satisfaction is also related to turnover among salespeople, although the relationship is moderated by economic conditions and the availability of alternative jobs.[19]

Another relationship that appears in studies of other occupations is a positive correlation between satisfaction and performance, although there is controversy over the nature of the relationship. Some theorists argue that high satisfaction leads to good performance; others argue that good performance makes workers more satisfied with their jobs. The available sales management literature seems to suggest a salesperson's job satisfaction is directly related to performance on the job and that conflict and ambiguity are negatively related to sales performance.[20] Role ambiguity and role conflict even affect whether sales managers and salespeople agree on how well the salesperson is doing the job.[21]

Causes of Conflict and Ambiguity

Given that conflict and ambiguity produce dysfunctional psychological and behavioral consequences for salespeople, the next question is: Can sales management do anything to hold conflicts and ambiguities at a manageable level or help the salesperson to deal with them when they occur? Evidence suggests that experienced salespeople perceive less conflict than less-experienced representatives.[22] Perhaps this is because salespeople who experience a great deal of conflict become dissatisfied and quit, whereas those who stay on the job do not perceive much conflict.

On the other hand, sales reps may learn with experience how to deal with conflict. They may learn that demands that initially appear to be in conflict may turn out to be compatible. They may learn how to resolve or cope with conflicts so they are no longer so stressful. Finally, they may build up psychological defense mechanisms to screen out conflicts and ease the tension. If these hypotheses are correct, perhaps sales training programs can prepare new salespeople to deal with the conflicts they will encounter on the job. Training, after all, attempts to compress the learning and experience curve into a shorter time period.

Perceived role conflict also seems to be affected by how closely salespeople are supervised. When their sales managers structure and define their roles, salespeople seem to experience more conflict. Perhaps close supervision decreases flexibility in dealing with the diverse role expectations with which salespeople must contend. Another way to reduce role conflict, then, would be to give salespeople a greater voice in what they do and how they do it.

There also seem to be things management can do to reduce role ambiguity. It too depends on experience, and thus sales training should help salespeople cope with it. Perhaps more important, it also depends on the manager's supervisory style. Less ambiguity is experienced when salespeople are closely supervised and have some influence over the standards used to control and evaluate their performance.[23] Closely supervised salespeople are more aware of the expectations and demands of their supervisors, and inconsistent behaviors can be more quickly brought to their attention.

Similarly, salespeople who have an input in determining the standards by which they are evaluated are more familiar with these standards, which tends to reduce role ambiguity. One direct way of affecting the closeness with which salespeople feel supervised is by altering the sales manager's span of control by changing the number of people the sales manager directly supervises. An increase in the span of control tends to increase salespeople's perceived role ambiguity. Reducing it tends to allow closer supervision, which tends to make job-related issues clearer to salespeople.[24]

Close supervision can thus be a two-edged sword. While it can reduce ambiguity, supervision that is too close can increase a salesperson's role conflict and job dissatisfaction when the rep no longer feels there is enough latitude to deal effectively with the customer or enough creativity to service the account. The problem is particularly acute when sales managers use coercion and threats to direct the salespeople under them.[25] Sales managers must walk a very fine line in how closely and by what means they supervise the people under them.

ROLE ACCURACY

The role component of the model contains three variables: role conflict, role ambiguity, and role accuracy. It is convenient to highlight role accuracy for separate discussion for two reasons. First, role accuracy can be viewed both generally and from the standpoint of specific linkages. When it is viewed generally, its impact and antecedents are similar to those for role conflict and ambiguity. But additional insight is gained by looking at role accuracy with respect to specific linkages. Second, role accuracy specifically influences the motivation component of the model and to understand role accuracy, it is necessary to assess its impact on the salesperson's motivation to perform.[26]

Nature of Role Accuracy

A salesperson has accurate role perceptions when he or she correctly understands what role partners expect when performing the job. Role inaccuracy can be either general or linkage-specific. General role inaccuracy involves such considerations as whether salespeople correctly think they can negotiate on price, promise shorter delivery times than normal, and handle back charges and adjustments for customers. General role inaccuracy can occur on almost any job dimension that also gives rise to role ambiguity and conflict. Its antecedents and consequences are also similar.

Linkage role inaccuracy arises when the salesperson incorrectly perceives the relationships between the activities and performance dimensions, or between the performance dimensions and the rewards. In terms of the model in Exhibit 8.1, linkage role inaccuracy relates to the motivational component and, more particularly, to the expectancy and instrumentality estimates. For example, a salesperson who does not accurately perceive how making more calls leads to more sales has linkage role inaccuracy with respect to this expectancy, or activity–performance, linkage. If the rep does not accurately perceive the relationship between more sales and a promotion, the person has linkage role inaccuracy with respect to this instrumentality, or performance–reward, linkage.

There is great potential for linkage role inaccuracy among salespeople because all

Exhibit 8.5 Common Activities, Performance Criteria, and Rewards for Industrial Salespeople

Activities*

1. Selling: plan selling activities, search out leads, identify person in authority, select products for calls, prepare sales presentations, call on accounts, make sales presentations, overcome objections.
2. Working with orders: correct orders, expedite orders, handle back orders, handle shipment problems.
3. Servicing the product: supervise installation, test equipment, train customers to use product, teach safety instructions, order accessories, perform maintenance.
4. Information management: receive feedback from clients, provide feedback to superiors, provide technical information, read trade publications.
5. Servicing the account: set up point-of-purchase displays, assist with inventory control, stock shelves, handle local advertising.
6. Conferences/meetings: attend sales conferences, attend regional sales meetings, set up exhibitions and trade shows, work client conferences, attend training sessions, fill out questionnaires.
7. Training/recruiting: look for new sales representatives, train new representatives, travel with trainees, help company management plan selling activities.
8. Entertaining: take clients to lunch, drink with clients, have dinner with clients, party with clients, go golfing or fishing or play tennis with clients.
9. Out-of-town traveling: travel out of town, spend night on road.
10. Working with distributors: establish relations with distributors, sell to distributors, extend credit, collect past-due accounts.

Performance Criteria

1. Total sales volume and volume increase over last year.
2. Degree of quota attainment.
3. Selling expenses and their decrease versus last year.
4. Profitability of sales and their increase over last year.
5. New accounts generated.
6. Improvement in performance of administrative duties.
7. Improvement in service provided customers.

Rewards

1. Pay
   a. Increased take-home pay.
   b. Increased bonuses and other financial incentives.
2. Promotion
   a. Higher-level job.
   b. Better territory.
3. Nonfinancial incentives (contests, travel, prizes, etc.)
4. Special recognitions (clubs, awards, etc.).
5. Job security.
6. Feeling of self-fulfillment.
7. Feeling of worthwhile accomplishment.
8. Opportunity for personal growth and development.
9. Opportunity for independent thought and action.

*The list of activities in which salespeople commonly engage is developed from the articles by William C. Moncrief, "Selling Activity and Sales Position Taxonomies for Industrial Salesforces," *Journal of Marketing Research* 23 (August 1986), pp. 261–70, and William C. Moncrief, "Ten Key Activities of Industrial Salespeople," *Industrial Marketing Management* 15 (November 1986), pp. 309–17.

three components—activities, performance dimensions, and rewards—are multidimensional. There are consequently a great many linkages, which increases the chances a salesperson will have inaccurate perceptions about at least some of them. Some common activities in which salespeople are expected to engage, the criteria used to evaluate their performance, and the rewards typically used to motivate them are listed in Exhibit 8.5.[27] Not all salespeople in every firm are expected to engage in all these activities, nor are they evaluated on each performance dimension. Neither do all firms provide the same rewards to the same degree. This makes it very difficult to discuss linkage inaccuracy in a way that is useful to sales managers in general. One has to get down to the level of the individual firm and the linkages operating there to discuss the concept.

One commonly emphasized salesperson activity is new-account calls. Similarly, the number of new accounts generated is often used to evaluate how salespeople performed. Despite this, it is not unusual to find that salespeople do not spend enough time calling on new accounts, even when they recognize there are many such opportunities in their territories and know their sales managers want them to spend more time on such accounts. One study that investigated the question using reasonably large samples of salespeople and sales managers (over 400 of each) found (1) salespeople fail to see the payoff to themselves in new-account development and (2) they did not know what it takes to perform these activities successfully.[28] Further,

> [t]he difference in priorities between sales representatives and sales managers appears to start very early in the sales planning process. At the very basic step of classifying accounts, 80 percent of sales managers state that this should be done on the basis of potential volumes, whereas only 54 percent of sales representatives indicate that they do so. The other 46 percent, if they classify their accounts at all, prefer to utilize other factors such as historic volumes or geography.[29]

Clearly, the sales managers in the study did not effectively communicate the linkages between activities and performance and performance and rewards to the sales force. Yet the accuracy of a salesperson's expectancy and instrumentality estimates, as well as their magnitude, can influence performance and consequently have important implications for sales managers.

SUMMARY

This chapter, the first on implementing the sales program, sought to present a model for understanding the performance of salespeople. In addition, the chapter examined the first component of the model, specifically the salesperson's role perceptions.

The model suggests that a salesperson's performance is a function of five basic factors: (1) role perceptions, (2) aptitude, (3) skill level, (4) motivation, and (5) personal, organizational, and environmental variables. There is substantial interaction among the components. A salesperson who is deficient with respect to any one could be expected to perform poorly.

The *role perceptions* of the salesperson are defined largely through the expectations, demands, and pressures communicated by his or her role partners.

Role partners are people both within and outside the company who are affected by the way the salesperson performs the job. The role of salesperson is defined through a three-step process: (1) Expectations and demands concerning how the salesperson should behave in various situations, together with pressures to conform, are communicated to the salesperson by members of the individual's role set. (2) The salesperson perceives these expectations and demands that are communicated by members of the role set. (3) The salesperson converts these perceptions into actual behavior.

The three major variables in the role perception component are role accuracy, perceived role ambiguity, and perceived role conflict. *Role accuracy* refers to the degree to which the salesperson's perceptions of his or her role partners' demands are accurate. *Perceived role ambiguity* occurs when the salesperson does not believe he or she has the information to perform the job adequately. *Perceived role conflict* arises when a salesperson believes that the demands of two or more of his or her role partners are incompatible.

The role of salesperson is particularly susceptible to feelings of ambiguity and conflict and to forming inaccurate perceptions. There are three reasons for this: (1) It is at the boundary of the firm, (2) the salesperson's relevant role set includes many other people both within and outside the firm, and (3) the position of sales rep often requires a good deal of innovativeness.

Important managerial consequences are associated with salespeople experiencing feelings of ambiguity or conflict or having inaccurate perceptions. Such feelings can cause psychological stress, produce low satisfaction, and lead to poorer performance. Fortunately, the sales manager can affect these consequences through decisions on the type of salespeople that are hired, the way they are trained, the incentives used to motivate them, the criteria used to evaluate them, and the way they are supervised and controlled.

Aptitude refers to the salesperson's native ability to do the job and includes such things as physical factors, mental abilities, and personality characteristics. Aptitude is a constraint on the person's ability to perform the sales job given an adequate understanding of the role to be performed, motivation, and learned skills and the absence of other constraints.

Skill level refers to the person's learned proficiency at performing the necessary tasks. It is different from aptitude. Whereas aptitude consists of relatively enduring personal abilities, skills are proficiency levels that can change rapidly with learning and experience.

Motivation refers to the effort the salesperson desires to expend on each activity or task associated with the job. These include calling on potential new accounts, developing sales presentations, and the like. The motivation to expend effort on any particular task depends on (1) expectancy—the salesperson's estimate of the probability that expending effort on the task will lead to improved performance on some dimension—and (2) valence for performance—the salesperson's perception of the desirability of improving performance on that dimension. The valence for performance on any dimension is, in turn, a function of (1) instrumentality—the salesperson's estimate of the probability that improved performance on that dimension will lead to increased attainment of particular rewards—and (2) valence for rewards—the salesperson's perception of the desirability of receiving increased rewards as a result of improved performance.

The personal, organizational, and environmental variables influence sales performance in two ways: (1) by directly facilitating or constraining performance and (2) by influencing and interacting with other performance determinants, such as role perceptions and motivation.

The performance of the salesperson affects the rewards the individual receives. There are two basic types of rewards: extrinsic rewards, which are controlled and bestowed by people other than the salesperson, and intrinsic rewards, which are those that people primarily attain for themselves.

The rewards received by a salesperson have a major impact on the individual's satisfaction with the job and the total work environment. Satisfaction can also be of two types. Intrinsic satisfaction is related to the intrinsic rewards the salesperson obtains from the job, such as satisfaction with the work and the opportunities it provides for personal growth and sense of accomplishment. Extrinsic satisfaction is associated with the extrinsic rewards bestowed on the salesperson, such as pay, chances for promotion, and supervisory and company policies.

DISCUSSION QUESTIONS

1. A sales rep's past and present performances will affect how that person feels about future performance. In fact, after experiencing several failures, many new salespeople quit their sales job within a few months because they assume that selling is not for them. What role can a sales manager play in such situations?

2. The president of Part-I-Tyme, manufacturer of salty snack foods, was dismayed over the dismal sales results reported for the first six months. A new product, a deluxe cookie, had been taste tested and consumers' responses were very positive. Part-I-Tyme's sales force consists of over 5,000 truck driver distributors who had

developed excellent reputations with their customers. Part-I-Tyme's president was convinced that the existing sales force of 5,000 enthusiastically supported the new product line. It was obvious that something was wrong. How would you determine the nature of the problem? Can you use the model of salesperson performance in this situation?

3. Although many aptitude tests exist, their ability to predict sales performance has been weak. How do you account for this?

4. Frequently, sales managers use contests and recognition rewards to motivate the sales force. If sales managers understand salesperson performance, then why is it necessary to employ these additional techniques?

5. "I want sales representatives who can stand on their own. Once a representative has been through training and shows how to apply this knowledge, it shouldn't be necessary for me to constantly tell them how they are doing. The stars always shine; it's the other sales representatives that need my attention." Comment on this statement. Do you agree or disagree?

6. A sales representative for the Railroad Equipment Corporation is faced with a demand from an important customer that is in direct conflict with company policies. The customer wants several product modifications with no change in price. What can the sales rep do to handle this conflict?

7. Sales reps for the Ansul Company, a manufacturer of fire prevention systems for industrial applications, have been told they will now have to sell small fire extinguishers to the retail market. What role problems are likely to occur?

8. Maria Gomez-Simpson, a customer service rep with MAR–JON Associates, spends considerable time traveling to various customer offices. As a result, she often arrives home late. Maria asked her manager if she could rearrange her Thursday work schedule to allow her to attend an evening class at a local college. Which of the following statements best reflects how to manage the conflict created by Maria's request?

   a. "Since we're talking about only one night, go ahead, sign up for the course, and we'll work out the details."
   b. "We need to discuss this first to see if there is some way you can be back most of the Thursdays in time for your course and still get the job done as well."
   c. "We know that you get home late on certain days, but it is part of the job. Maybe you can take the course some other time."

EXPERIENTIAL APPLICATIONS

Select a small sample of salespeople composed of both sexes and different age brackets (young and old salespeople). Interview the salespeople to determine what selling activities (described in Exhibit 8.5) they feel will lead to more sales or a promotion. Do these terms apply to the responses provided by the salespeople? Are there any differences based on sex or age of the sales rep?

INTERNET EXERCISE

Visit the Web sites of five leading marketing organizations such as IBM (*www.ibm.com*) or Hewlett–Packard (*www.hewlett-packard.com*) and examine how leading marketing organizations describe the job of salesperson. Specifically, what is the "role" of the salesperson in the selling process? Whom do they report to? Where will the salesperson have his or her office (at the company, at home, or at the customers' offices)?

SUGGESTED READINGS

Brown, Steven P., William Cron, and John W. Slocum, Jr., "Effects of Goal Directed Emotions on Salesperson Volitions, Behavior, and Performance: A Longitudinal Study," *Journal of Marketing* (January 1997), pp. 39–50.

Challagalla, Goutam N., and Tasaddug A. Servani, "Dimensions and Types of Supervisory Control: Effects of Salesperson Performance and Satisfaction," *Journal of Marketing* (January 1996), pp. 89–105.

DeCarlo, Thomas E., R. Kenneth Teas, and James C. McElroy, "Salesperson Performance Attribution Process and the Formation of Expectancy Estimates," *The Journal of Personal Selling and Sales Management* (Summer 1997), pp. 1–17.

Ford, Neil M., Orville C. Walker, Jr., and Gilbert A. Churchill, Jr., "Expectation-Specific Measures of the Intersender Conflict and Role Ambiguity Experienced by Industrial Salesmen," *Journal of Business Research* 3 (April 1975), pp. 95–112.

MacKenzie, Scott B., Philip M Podsakoff, and Michael Ahearne, "Some Possible Antecedents and Consequences of In-Role and Extra-Role Salesperson Performance," *Journal of Marketing* (July 1998), pp. 87–98.

Moncrief, William C., "Selling Activity and Sales Position Taxonomies for Industrial Salesforces," *Journal of Marketing Research* 23 (August 1986), pp. 261–76.

Rhoads, Gary K., Jagdip Singh, and Phillips W. Goodell, "The Multiple Dimensions of Role Ambiguity and Their Impact upon Psychological and Behavioral Outcomes of Industrial Salespeople," *Journal of Personal Selling and Sales Management* 14 (Summer 1994), pp. 1–24.

Plank, Richard E., and David A. Reid, "The Mediating Role of Sales Behaviors: An Alternative Perspective of Sales Performance and Effectiveness," *Journal of Personal Selling and Sales Management* 14 (Summer 1994), pp. 43–56.

Sager, Jeffrey, "A Structural Model Depicting Salespeople's Job Stress," *Journal of the Academy of Marketing Science* 22 (Winter 1994), pp. 74–84.

Singh, Jagdip, "Boundary Role Ambiguity: Facets, Determinants, and Impacts," *Journal of Marketing* 57 (April 1993), pp. 11–31.

Walker, Orville, C., Jr., Gilbert A. Churchill, Jr., and Neil M. Ford, "Motivation and Performance in Industrial Selling: Present Knowledge and Needed Research," *Journal of Marketing Research* 14 (May 1977), pp. 156–68.

Walker, Orville C., Jr., Gilbert A. Churchill, Jr., and Neil M. Ford, "Organizational Determinants of the Role Conflict and Ambiguity Experienced by Industrial Salesmen," *Journal of Marketing* 39 (January 1975), pp. 32–39.

Walker, Orville C., Jr., Gilbert A. Churchill, Jr., and Neil M. Ford, "Where Do We Go from Here? Selected Conceptual and Empirical Issues concerning the Motivation and Performance of the Industrial Salesforce," in *Critical Issues in Sales Management: State of the Art and Future Research Needs*, ed. Gerald Albaum and Gilbert A. Churchill, Jr. (Eugene: University of Oregon, 1979), pp. 10–75.

9 Salesperson Performance: Motivating the Sales Force

MOTIVATING THE INDIVIDUAL AND MOTIVATING THE TEAM ARE NOT THE SAME THING

Incentives and cash can motivate individuals, but there are also right and wrong ways to motivate salespeople. John Jack (vice president of BI Performance Services, a performance enhancement consulting company) puts it this way: "People tend to think a sales incentive is some kind of magic pill that's going to fix everything. But it doesn't work that way. The first step toward having a motivated sales staff is hiring people who love to sell." Simply put, motivating salespeople is a complex process that begins with hiring the right kind of individuals and then finding the right tools to motivate them properly. Chapter 10 examines the personal characteristics that managers need to be aware of in making the hiring selection. However, hiring people who want to sell is only a part of the motivation equation.

Lantech Inc., a Kentucky-based manufacturer of packaging machinery, has long used incentives to motivate its sales force. The company sought various methods to motivate the sales force in its four operating divisions. There was an understanding that it was important to motivate individuals to reach sales goals, but the question was how to do that. After much trial and error a pay-for-performance system was instituted across the company that awarded separate bonuses for each division.

Once it was implemented, however, Pat Lancaster, chairman of Lantech, began to notice a problem. He did not realize how interrelated the operating divisions all were in the selling process. As a result, a great deal of internal fighting began to occur as each division considered the other three to be competitors rather than part of the same team. Lancaster put it this way: "Our divisions are so interdependent that it was often difficult to sort out which division was entitled to claim profits." Customers were not receiving the attention they needed because the divisions were working against one another.

Lantech struggled with a divisional incentive program for 10 years. Mr. Lancaster wanted to find a way of motivating each division, but over time it became apparent that customers were not being adequately taken care of under the current incentive system. The result was that Lancaster abandoned the pay-for-performance divisional incentive system and replaced it with a plan that rewards all salespeople cash bonuses based on the success of the entire company. Lantech, however, still believes it is important to reward individuals for outstanding performance. As a result, the company offers travel awards for top salespeople. However, rather than focus on cash awards, the incentives offered to salespeople are viewed as recognition for individuals. This dual system, which focuses on company goals and individual recognition, has been much more successful for Lantech than its previous system.

Factors That Affect Motivation

On the surface, the incentive compensation system that Mr. Lancaster developed to motivate the Lantech sales force seems quite simple, straightforward, and appropriate. But the system failed because it did not consider the need for the operating divisions to work together or, put another way, the "team" aspect of sales. A successful motivational program works well when it takes into account a variety of underlying factors including (1) market conditions, product characteristics, and the nature of the sales task to be accomplished, (2) related management policies and programs within the company (e.g., the decision to combine sales reps and systems engineers in teams), and (3) the different personal characteristics of the people to be motivated.

Source: Vincent Alonzo, "Recognition? Who Needs It?" *Sales & Marketing Management* (February 1997), pp. 26–28, and the Lantech Web site at *www.lantech.com.*

LEARNING OBJECTIVES

Salespeople operate in a highly dynamic, stressful environment outside of the company. As we have already seen in Chapter 8, there are many factors that influence the salesperson's ability to perform. One of the most critical factors is motivation. It is very important that sales managers understand the process of motivation and be able to apply it to each individual in the sales force in such a manner so as to maximize his or her performance potential.

After reading this chapter you should be able to:

- Understand the process of motivation.
- Discuss the effect of personal characteristics on salesperson motivation.
- Understand how an individual's career stage influences motivation.
- Discuss the effect of environmental factors on motivation.
- Discuss the effect of factors inside the company on motivation.

Unfortunately, many firms unlike Lantech are not successful in designing compensation systems or incentive programs that are appropriate for the marketing challenges they face and the kinds of people they employ. Consequently, their salespeople are either undermotivated or stimulated to expend too much time and effort on the wrong tasks and activities. In either case, sales effectiveness and productivity suffer.

In view of the complicated nature of motivation and its critical role in sales management, the rest of this chapter as well as Chapter 13 (on compensation) are devoted to the subject. This chapter examines what is known about motivation as a psychological process and how a person's motivation to perform a given job is affected by environmental, organizational, and personal variables. Chapter 13 discusses compensation plans and incentive programs sales managers use to stimulate and direct salespeople's efforts.

THE PSYCHOLOGICAL PROCESS OF MOTIVATION

Most industrial and organizational psychologists view motivation as a general label referring to an individual's choice to (1) initiate action on a certain task, (2) expend a certain amount of effort on that task, and (3) persist in expending effort over a period of time.[1] For our purposes, **motivation** is viewed as the amount of effort the salesperson desires to

Exhibit 9.1   The Psychological Determinants of Motivation

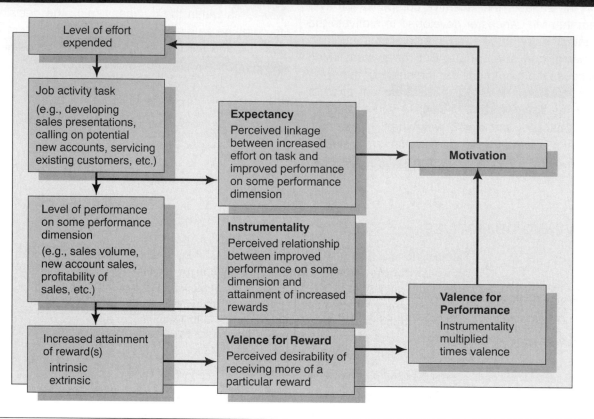

expend on each activity or task associated with the job. This may include calling on potential new accounts, developing sales presentations, and filling out reports. The psychological process involved in determining how much effort a salesperson will want to expend and some variables that influence the process are shown in Exhibit 9.1.

The conceptual framework outlined in Exhibit 9.1 is based on a view of motivation known as expectancy theory. A number of other theories of motivation exist,[2] and many of them are useful for explaining at least a part of the motivation process. However, expectancy theory incorporates and ties together (at least implicitly) important aspects of many of those theories, it has been the subject of much empirical research in sales management, and it also provides a useful framework for guiding the many decisions managers must make when designing effective motivational programs for a sales force. Consequently, the remainder of this discussion focuses primarily on expectancy theory, although several other theories are mentioned later when we examine how personal characteristics affect the motivation of different individuals.

Major Components of the Model

The model in Exhibit 9.1 suggests the effort expended by a salesperson on each task associated with the job will lead to some level of achievement on one or more dimensions of job performance. These dimensions include total sales volume, profitability of sales, and new accounts generated. It is assumed the salesperson's performance on some of these dimensions will be evaluated by superiors and rewarded with one or more rewards. These might be externally mediated rewards, like a promotion, or internally mediated rewards, such as feelings of accomplishment or personal growth. A salesperson's motivation to expend effort on a given task is determined by three sets of perceptions: (1) expectancies— the perceived linkages between expending more effort on a particular task and achieving improved performance—(2) instrumentalities—the perceived relationship between improved performance and the attainment of increased rewards—and (3) valence for rewards—the perceived attractiveness of the various rewards the salesperson might receive.

Expectancies— Perceived Link between Effort and Performance

Expectancies are the salesperson's perceptions of the link between job effort and performance. Specifically, an expectancy is the person's estimate of the probability that expending effort on some task will lead to improved performance on a dimension. The following statement illustrates an expectancy perception: "If I increase my calls on potential new accounts by 10 percent [effort], then there is a 50 percent chance [expectancy] that my volume of new account sales will increase by 10 percent during the next six months [performance level]." Key questions that arise from a salesperson's expectancies and their implications for sales managers are identified in Exhibit 9.2.

When attempting to motivate salespeople, sales managers should be concerned with two aspects of their subordinates' expectancy perceptions: magnitude and accuracy. The magnitude of a salesperson's expectancy perceptions indicates the degree to which that person believes expending effort on job activities will influence ultimate job performance. Other things being equal, the larger a salesperson's expectancy perceptions, the more willing the sales rep is to devote effort to the job in hopes of bettering performance.

Accuracy of expectancies

The *accuracy* of a salesperson's expectancy perceptions refers to how clearly the rep understands the relationship between effort expended on a task and the resulting achievement on some performance dimension. When salespeople's expectancies are inaccurate, they are likely to misallocate job efforts. They spend too much time and energy on activities that have little impact on performance and not enough on activities with a greater impact. Consequently, some authorities refer to attempts to improve the accuracy of expectancy estimates as "trying to get salespeople to work smarter rather than harder."[3]

Working smarter requires that the salesperson have an accurate understanding of what activities are most critical—and therefore should receive the greatest effort—for concluding a sale. Of course, a single activity might be carried out in a number of ways. For instance, a salesperson might employ any of several different sales techniques or strategies when making a sales presentation. Therefore, working smarter also requires an ability to adapt the techniques used to the needs and preferences of a given buyer. Motivating a salesperson to expend more effort on inappropriate activities or approaches can worsen performance and lead to great frustration within the sales force.

Unfortunately it is possible for a salesperson to misjudge the true relationship between the effort expended on a particular task and resulting performance. When this happens, the salesperson misallocates efforts. The rep spends too much time and energy on activities that have relatively little impact on performance and not enough on activities with greater impact.

Most industrial psychology literature concerning work expectancies assumes that a worker's immediate superior, by virtue of greater knowledge and experience, will more accurately perceive the linkages between effort and performance in the worker's job than the worker will. If this is also true in the selling profession, then inaccurate expectancy perceptions in the sales force can be improved through closer contact between salespeople and their supervisors. Expanded sales training programs, closer day-to-day supervi-

Exhibit 9.2   Important Questions and Management Implications
of Salespeople's Expectancy Estimates

Question	Management Implications
Accuracy of Expectancy Estimates	
• Are salespeople's views of the linkage between activities and performance outcomes consistent with those of sales managers?	• If substantial variation exists, salespeople may devote too much effort to activities considered unimportant by management, and vice versa. This might indicate a need for the following: —More extensive/explicit sales training. —Closer supervision. —Evaluation of salesperson's effort and time allocation as well as performance.
• Are there large variations in expectancy perceptions between high performers and low performers in the sales force?	• If high-performing salespeople hold reasonably consistent views concerning which activities are most important in producing good performance, those views might be used as a model for sales training/professional development programs.
Magnitude of Expectancy Estimates	

• All other things equal, the higher the salesperson's expectancy estimates, the greater the individual's motivation to expend effort.
—Do personal characteristics of salespeople influence the size of their expectancies?
    Overall self-esteem?
    Perceived competence?
    Mental ability? (Intelligence?)
    Previous sales experience?
	• If such relationships are found, they may suggest additional criteria for recruitment/selection.

—Do perceptions of uncertainty or constraints in the environment (e.g., materials shortages, recession, etc.) reduce salespeople's expectancy estimates?	• During periods of economic uncertainty, management may have to change performance criteria, evaluation methods, and/or compensation systems to maintain desired levels of effort from the sales force (e.g., lower quotas, reward servicing rather than selling activities).

sion of the sales force, and periodic review of each salesperson's time and effort allocation by the supervisor might improve the accuracy of expectancy estimates.

Salespeople often complain that their supervisors have an unrealistic view of conditions in the field. In addition, they do not realize what it takes to make a sale.[4] If these complaints are valid, managers' perceptions of the linkages between effort and performance may not be appropriate criteria for judging the accuracy of salespeople's expectancies. It may be better to use the expectancy estimates of the highest performing salesperson in the company as a model for sales training and supervision.

Magnitude of expectancies

The magnitude of a salesperson's expectancy estimates reflects the rep's perceptions of his or her ability to control or influence his or her own job performance.

Several individual characteristics are likely to affect these expectancies. Some psy-

Exhibit 9.3   Factors Influencing the Motivation Process

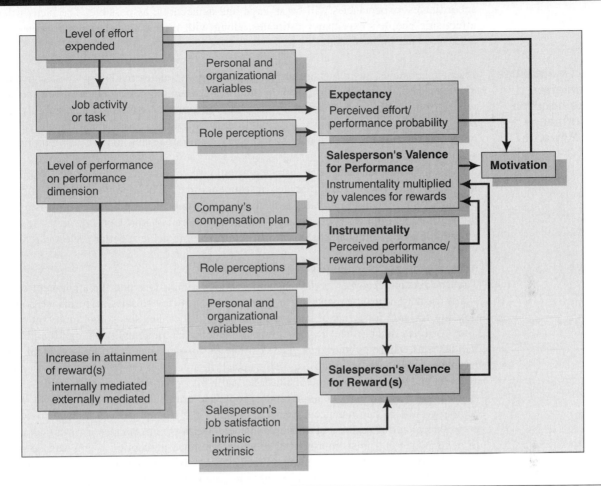

chologists suggest that a worker's overall level of self-esteem and perceived ability to perform necessary tasks are positively related to the magnitude of the person's expectancy estimates.[5] Similarly, the salesperson's general intelligence and previous sales experience may influence the individual's perceived ability to improve performance through personal efforts. If these relationships are also true for salespeople, the characteristics may be useful supplementary criteria for the recruitment and selection of salespeople.

Environmental characteristics also influence a salesperson's perceptions of the linkages between effort and performance. How the rep perceives general economic conditions, territory potential, the strength of competition, restrictions on product availability, and so forth are all likely to affect his thoughts on how much sales performance can be improved by simply increasing efforts. The greater the environmental constraints a salesperson sees as restricting performance, the lower the rep's expectancy estimates will be. Therefore, managers may find it desirable to change performance criteria and/or evaluation methods during periods of economic uncertainty to maintain desired levels of effort from the sales force.

As Exhibit 9.3 indicates, personal and organizational characteristics affect the magnitude and accuracy of salespeople's expectancy perceptions. Managers must consider these factors when deciding on supervisory policies, compensation, and incentive plans so their subordinates' expectancies will be as large and as accurate as possible. The factors that affect salespeople's expectancy estimates, along with their managerial implications, are discussed later in this chapter.

Instrumentalities —Perceived Links between Performance and Rewards

Like expectancies, instrumentalities are probability estimates made by the salesperson. They are the individual's perceptions of the link between job performance and various rewards. Specifically, an instrumentality is a salesperson's estimate of the probability that an improvement in performance on some dimension will lead to a specific increase in a particular reward. The reward may be more pay, winning a sales contest, or promotion to a better territory.

As with expectancies, sales managers should be concerned with both the magnitude and the accuracy of their subordinates' instrumentalities. When the magnitude of a salesperson's instrumentality estimates is relatively large, the sales rep believes there is a high probability that improved performance will lead to more rewards. Consequently, the sales rep will be more willing to expend the effort necessary to achieve better performance.

Accuracy of instrumentalities

The true linkages between performance on various dimensions and the attainment of rewards are determined by management practices and policies on sales performance evaluation and rewards for levels of performance.[6] Exhibit 9.4 identifies some important questions for sales management regarding a salesperson's instrumentality estimates and their implications. These policies and practices may be misperceived by the salesperson. The rep may concentrate on improving performance in areas that are less important to management and ultimately become disillusioned with his or her ability to attain rewards.

Thus, it is important to compare salespeople's instrumentality perceptions with stated company policies and management perceptions of the true or desired linkages between performance and rewards. If salespeople misperceive how performance is rewarded in the firm, management must improve the accuracy of those perceptions. This can be done through closer supervision and more direct feedback about evaluation and the determination of rewards. Sometimes, however, its salespeople may inaccurately perceive a firm's evaluation and reward policies. They may devote too much attention to activities or objectives that are relatively unimportant to management, and they may ultimately become disillusioned with their inability to attain desired rewards. In the Lantech sales force, for instance, each of the operating divisions viewed the others as competitors rather than members of the same team to receive the cash bonuses.

Magnitude of instrumentalities

One variable that has a notable impact on the magnitude of a salesperson's instrumentality estimates is the firm's compensation plan. A salesperson compensated largely or entirely by commission is likely to perceive a greater probability of attaining more pay by improving performance on the dimensions directly related to total sales volume (increase in total sales dollars or percentage of quota). On the other hand, the salaried salesperson is more likely to perceive a greater probability of receiving increased pay for improving performance on dimensions not directly related to short-term sales volume (new-account generation, reduction of selling expenses, or performance of administrative duties).

The salesperson may also be rewarded with promotion, recognition, and feelings of accomplishment. The rep may value these other rewards more highly than an increase in pay. In any case, the company's compensation plan is unlikely to affect the rep's percep-

Exhibit 9.4 Important Questions and Management Implications
of Salespeople's Instrumentality Estimates

Question	Management Implications
Accuracy of Instrumentality Estimates	
• Are salespeople's views of the linkage between performance on various dimensions and the rewards they will receive consistent with those of sales managers?	• If substantial variation exists, salespeople may concentrate on aspects of performance considered relatively unimportant by management, and vice versa. This might indicate the need for the following: —More extensive/explicit sales training. —Closer supervision. —More direct feedback to salespeople concerning how performance is evaluated and how rewards are determined.
Magnitude of Instrumentality Estimates	
• How are salespeople's instrumentality estimates influenced by their compensation system (salary versus commission)? —Do salespeople on commission have higher instrumentality estimates for performance dimensions related to short-term sales volume? —Do salaried salespeople have higher instrumentalities for performance dimensions not directly related to short-term sales volume?	• If such relationships are found, managers should select the type of compensation plan that maximizes instrumentality estimates for those performance dimensions considered most crucial.
• Do personal characteristics of salespeople influence the size of their instrumentality estimates? —Feelings of internal control? —Mental ability? —Sales experience?	• If such relationships are found, they may suggest additional criteria for recruitment/selection.

tions of the linkages between performance and these nonfinancial rewards. Therefore, a compensation plan by itself is inadequate for explaining differences in motivation among salespeople.

The salesperson's personal characteristics may also influence the magnitude of instrumentality estimates. One such characteristic is the individual's perception of whether the rep controls life's events or whether these events are determined by external forces beyond the individual's control. Specifically, the greater the degree to which a salesperson believes he has internal control over his life, the more likely the rep is to feel that an improvement in performance will result in the attainment of rewards. Similarly, some evidence in industrial psychology suggests a worker's intelligence is positively related to the individual's instrumentality estimates. Once again, if such relationships hold true for industrial salespeople, these personal characteristics may be useful criteria for the recruitment and selection of salespeople.

Besides the firm's compensation policies, other organizational factors and the personal characteristics of the salespeople can influence both the magnitude and the accuracy of their instrumentality estimates. These factors and their managerial implications are explored in a later section of this chapter and in Chapter 13.

Valence for Rewards

Valences are salespeople's perceptions of the desirability of receiving increased amounts of the rewards they might attain as a result of improved performance. One question about valences that has always interested sales managers is whether there are consistent preferences among salespeople for specific kinds of rewards. Are some rewards consistently valued more highly than others?

Historically, many sales managers and most authors of books and articles on motivating salespeople have assumed monetary rewards are the most highly valued and motivating rewards. They believe recognition and other psychological rewards are less valued and spur additional sales effort only under certain circumstances. However, only a few recent studies have empirically tested whether salespeople typically have higher valences for more pay than for other rewards. Thus, the assumption that they do has been based largely on the perceptions of sales managers rather than on any evidence obtained from salespeople themselves.

Surveys conducted among employees in other occupations often find that increased pay is not always the most highly desired reward. For example, one psychologist reviewed 43 surveys of nonsales workers in which the importance of more pay was rated relative to other rewards. Pay was ranked most important in only 25 percent of these studies, and its average importance across all studies was third.[7]

At least one author takes an even more extreme view of financial rewards. He argues that linking pay or other financial incentives to performance can have a negative effect on employees' motivation over time.[8] In his view, when pay is tied to performance, employees become less interested in what they are doing and more interested in simply capturing the reward. Intrinsic motivation is eaten away by extrinsic motivators like commissions and incentive contests, and employee creativity and quality of work may suffer as a result.

In light of these contradictory arguments and research results, is the conventional wisdom that salespeople desire money more than other rewards wrong? Or do salespeople simply desire different rewards than workers in other kinds of jobs, as Lancaster determined when he realized the need to design a different incentive compensation system for the Lantech salespeople? Several studies focused on industrial salespeople generally support the conventional view. Their findings suggest that on average, salespeople place a higher value on receiving more pay than any other reward, including intrinsic rewards like feelings of accomplishment or opportunities for personal growth.[9]

But increased pay is not always seen as the most attractive reward by all salespeople in all companies. For instance, one study of two large firms found that while pay was by far the most attractive reward for salespeople in Company A, it ranked only third behind intrinsic rewards such as opportunities for personal development in Company B.[10]

Why did the salespeople in one company value a pay increase more than those in the other? One plausible answer is that the average total compensation received by salespeople in Company B was about $5,000 higher than that of salespeople in A at the time of the study. Also, the proportion of salespeople reaching quota and qualifying for bonuses in Company A in the year preceding the study had declined sharply due to quota increases of as much as 25 percent over the year before. No such changes had occurred in Company B. It is possible, then, that the salespeople in Company A had a higher valence for more pay because they were less satisfied with the financial compensation they were receiving.

No universal statements can be made about what kinds of rewards are most desired by salespeople and most effective for motivating them. Salespeople's valences for rewards are likely to be influenced by their satisfaction with the rewards they are currently receiving. Their satisfaction with current rewards, in turn, is influenced by their personal characteristics and by the compensation policies and management practices of their firm.

CAN THE MOTIVATION MODEL PREDICT SALESPERSON EFFORT AND PERFORMANCE?

Several studies have tested the ability of motivation models such as the ones outlined in Exhibits 9.1 and 9.3 to predict the amount of effort workers will expend on various job activities. The findings support the validity of such expectancy models of motivation, explaining as much as 25 percent of the variation in effort among workers.[11]

The salesperson model of performance discussed previously suggests motivation is only one determinant of job performance. Thus, it seems inappropriate to use only motivation to predict differences in job performance among workers. Nevertheless, several studies have attempted to do just that, and with surprising success. Some studies have found that predictions of workers' motivation to expend effort can explain as much as 40 percent of the variation in their overall job performance.[12]

It is nice to know that models like Exhibit 9.1 are valid descriptions of the psychological processes that determine a salesperson's motivation. However, there is a question of even greater relevance to sales managers as they struggle to design effective compensation and incentive programs. The question is how the three determinants of motivation—expectancy perceptions, instrumentality perceptions, and valences for rewards—are affected by (1) differences in the personal characteristics of individuals, (2) environmental conditions, and (3) the organization's policies and procedures. Therefore, the impact of each of these variables on the determinants of motivation is now examined in greater detail.

THE IMPACT OF A SALESPERSON'S PERSONAL CHARACTERISTICS ON MOTIVATION

When placed in the same job with the same compensation and incentive programs, different salespeople are likely to be motivated to expend widely differing amounts of effort. People with different personal characteristics have divergent perceptions of the links between effort and performance (expectancies) and between performance and rewards (instrumentalities). They are also likely to have different valences for the rewards they might obtain through improved job performance. The personal characteristics that affect motivation include (1) the individual's satisfaction with current rewards, (2) demographic variables, (3) job experience, and (4) psychological variables—particularly the salesperson's personality traits and attributions about why performance has been good or bad. The impacts of each of these sets of variables on salespeople's expectancies, instrumentalities, and valences are examined next.

Also, as we will see later, many of these personal characteristics change and interact with one another as a salesperson moves through various career stages. For instance, when people begin their first sales job, they are likely to be relatively young and have few family responsibilities, little job experience, and low task-specific self-esteem. Later in their careers, those salespeople will be older and have more family obligations, more experience, and more self-esteem. As a result, their valences for various rewards and their expectancy and instrumentality estimates are all likely to change as their careers progress. Consequently, a later section of this chapter examines how salespeople's motivation is likely to change during their careers, and addresses some managerial implications of such changes.

Satisfaction

Is it possible to pay a salesperson too much? After a salesperson reaches a certain satisfactory level of compensation, does the sales rep lose interest in working to obtain still more money? Does the attainment of nonfinancial rewards similarly affect the salesperson's desire to earn more of those rewards? The basic issues underlying these questions is whether a salesperson's satisfaction with current rewards has any impact on the valence for more of those rewards or on the desire for different kinds of rewards.

The relationship between satisfaction and the valence for rewards is different for rewards that satisfy lower-order needs (e.g., pay and job security) than for those that satisfy higher-order needs (e.g., promotions, recognition, opportunities for personal growth, self-fulfillment). Maslow's theory of a need hierarchy,[13] Herzberg's theory of motivation,[14] and Alderfer's "existence, relatedness, and growth theory"[15] all suggest that lower-order rewards are valued most highly by workers currently dissatisfied with their attainment of those rewards. In other words, the more dissatisfied a salesperson is with current pay, job security, and other rewards related to lower-order needs, the higher the valence attached to increases in those rewards. In contrast, as salespeople become more satisfied with their attainment of lower-order rewards, the value of further increases in those rewards declines.

The theories of Maslow, Herzberg, and Alderfer further suggest that high-order rewards are not valued highly by salespeople until they are relatively satisfied with their low-order rewards. The greater the salesperson's satisfaction with low-order rewards, the higher the valence of increased attainment of high-order rewards.

Perhaps the most controversial aspect of Maslow's and Alderfer's theories is the proposition that high-order rewards have increasing marginal utility. The more satisfied a salesperson is with the high-order rewards received from the job, the higher the value the sales rep places on further increases in those rewards.

Research in industrial psychology provides at least partial support for these suggested relationships between satisfaction and the valence of low-order and high-order rewards. Some of the evidence is equivocal, though, and some propositions—particularly the idea that high-order rewards have increasing marginal utility—have not been tested adequately.

Several studies of valence for rewards conducted among salespeople also provide partial—though mixed—support for the preceding hypotheses. In general, these studies show that salespeople who are relatively satisfied with their current income (a lower-order reward) have lower valences for more pay than those who are less satisfied. Most of these studies also suggest salespeople who are relatively satisfied with their current attainment of higher-order rewards, such as recognition and personal growth, tend to have higher valences for more of those rewards than those who are less satisfied. However, the evidence is mixed concerning whether salespeople who are relatively satisfied with their lower-order rewards have significantly higher valences for higher-order rewards than those who are less satisfied, as the theories would predict.[16]

Demographic Characteristics

Demographic characteristics, such as age, family size, and education, also affect a salesperson's valence for rewards. At least part of the reason for this is that people with different characteristics tend to attain different levels of rewards and are therefore likely to have different levels of satisfaction with their current rewards. Although there is only limited empirical evidence regarding salespeople, some conclusions can be drawn from studies in other occupations.[17] These conclusions are summarized in Exhibit 9.5.

Generally, older, more experienced salespeople obtain higher levels of low-order rewards (e.g., higher pay, a better territory) than newer members of the sales force. Thus, it could be expected that more experienced salespeople are more satisfied with their lower-order rewards. Consequently, they also should have lower valences for lower-order rewards and higher valences for higher-order rewards than younger and less experienced salespeople.

Exhibit 9.5 The Influence of Demographic Characteristics on Valence
for Rewards

Demographic Variable	Valence for Higher-Order Rewards	Valence for Lower-Order Rewards
Age	+	−
Family size		+
Education	+	

A salesperson's satisfaction with the current level of lower-order rewards may also be influenced by the demands and responsibilities the sales rep must satisfy with those rewards. The salesperson with a large family to support, for instance, is less likely to be satisfied with a given level of financial compensation than the single salesperson. Consequently, the more family members a salesperson must support, the higher the valence for more lower-order rewards.

Finally, individuals with more formal education are more likely to desire opportunities for personal growth, career advancement, and self-fulfillment than those with less education. Consequently, highly educated salespeople are likely to have higher valences for higher-order rewards.

Job Experience

As people gain experience on a job, they are likely to gain a clearer idea of how expending effort on particular tasks affects performance. Experienced salespeople are also more likely to understand how their superiors evaluate performance and how particular types of performance are rewarded in the company than their inexperienced counterparts. Consequently, a positive relationship is likely between the years a salesperson has spent on the job and the accuracy of the rep's expectancy and instrumentality perceptions.

In addition, the magnitude of a salesperson's expectancy perceptions may be affected by experience. As they gain experience, salespeople have opportunities to sharpen their selling skills; and they gain confidence in their ability to perform successfully. As a result, experienced salespeople are likely to have larger expectancy estimates than inexperienced ones.[18]

Psychological Traits

An individual's motivation also seems to be affected by psychological traits. Various traits can influence the magnitude and accuracy of a person's expectancy and instrumentality estimates, as well as valences for various rewards, as summarized in Exhibit 9.6. People with strong achievement needs are likely to have higher valences for such higher-order rewards as recognition, personal growth, and feeling of accomplishment. This is particularly true when they see their jobs as being relatively difficult to perform successfully.[19]

The degree to which individuals believe they have internal control over the events in their lives or whether those events are determined by external forces beyond their control also affects their motivation. Specifically, the greater the degree to which salespeople believe they have internal control over events, the more likely they are to think they can improve their performance by expending more effort. They also believe improved performance will be appropriately rewarded. Therefore, salespeople with high "internal locus of control" are likely to have relatively high expectancy and instrumentality estimates.[20]

There is some evidence that intelligence is positively related to feelings of internal

Exhibit 9.6   The Influence of Psychological Traits on the Determinants of Motivation

Personality Trait	Motivational Variables					
	Expectancies		Instrumentalities		Valences	
	Magnitude	Accuracy	Magnitude	Accuracy	Higher Order	Lower Order
High need achievement					+	
Internal locus of control	+		+			
Verbal intelligence	+	+	+	+		
General self-esteem	+				+	
Task-specific self-esteem	+				+	

control.[21] Therefore, more intelligent salespeople may have higher expectancy and instrumentality perceptions than those less intelligent. Those with higher levels of intelligence—particularly verbal intelligence—are more likely to understand their jobs and their companies' reward policies quickly and accurately. Thus, their instrumentality and expectancy estimates are likely to be more accurate.

Finally, a worker's general feeling of self-esteem and perceived competence and ability to perform job activities (task-specific self-esteem) are both positively related to the magnitude of expectancy estimates.[22] Since such people believe they have the talents and abilities to be successful, they are likely to see a strong relationship between effort expended and good performance. Also, people with high levels of self-esteem are especially likely to attach importance to, and receive satisfaction from, good performance. Consequently, such people probably have higher valences for the higher-order, intrinsic rewards attained from successful job performance, although the lone study to examine the impact of self-esteem on salespeople's reward valences failed to support this proposition.[23]

Performance Attributions

People try to identify and understand the causes of major events and outcomes in their lives. A given individual might attribute the cause of a particular event—such as good sales performance last quarter—to the following:

1. **Stable internal factors** that are unlikely to change much in the near future, such as personal skills and abilities.

2, **Unstable internal factors** that may vary from time to time, such as the amount of effort expended or mood at the time.

3 **Stable external factors,** such as the nature of the task or the competitive situation in a particular territory.

4. **Unstable external factors** that might change next time, such as assistance from an unusually aggressive advertising campaign or good luck.

The nature of a salesperson's recent job performance, together with the kind of causes to which the rep attributes that performance, can affect the individual's expectancy estimates concerning the likelihood that increased effort will lead to improved performance in the future.[24] Various attributions' likely effects on the magnitude of a salesperson's expectancy estimates are summarized in Exhibit 9.7.

As Exhibit 9.7 indicates, expectancy estimates are likely to increase if recent suc-

Exhibit 9.7 The Influence of Performance Attributions on the Magnitude of a Salesperson's Expectancy Estimates

Performance Attribution	Impact on Magnitude of Salesperson's Expectancy Estimates
Good Performance Attributed to:	
Stable internal cause	+
Unstable internal cause	+
Stable external cause	+
Unstable external cause	0
Poor Performance Attributed to:	
Stable internal cause	−
Unstable internal cause	+
Stable external cause	−
Unstable external cause	0

cessful sales performance is attributed to either stable or unstable internal causes or to stable external causes. For instance, salespeople are likely to attach even higher expectancies to future performance where they take credit for past success, as the result of either superior skill (stable internal cause) or personal effort (unstable internal cause). Salespeople's expectancies are also likely to increase where past success is attributed to a perception that the task is relatively easy (stable external cause). However, if past successful performance is attributed to an unstable external cause that could change in the next performance period—such as good luck—there is no basis for salespeople to revise their expectancy estimates in any systematic way.

Suppose a salesperson performed poorly last quarter. Exhibit 9.7 indicates the impact of that poor performance on the individual's expectancy estimates is influenced by the causal attributions the person makes. If the salesperson attributes poor past performance to stable causes that cannot be changed in the foreseeable future, such as low ability (stable internal cause) or a difficult competitive environment (stable external cause), the sales rep's expectancy estimates are likely to be lower. However, if the poor performance is attributed to an unstable internal cause—such as not expending sufficient effort to be successful—the person's expectancies may actually increase. The person may believe performance can be improved simply by changing the internal factor that caused the problem last time—by expending more effort or by improving selling skills.

Management Implications

The relationships between salespeople's personal characteristics and motivation levels have two broad implications for sales managers. First, they suggest people with certain characteristics are likely to understand their jobs and their companies' policies especially well. They also should perceive higher expectancy and instrumentality links. Such people should be easier to train and be motivated to expend greater effort and achieve better performance. Therefore, as researchers and managers gain a better understanding of these relationships, it may be possible to develop improved selection criteria for hiring salespeople who are easy to train and motivate.

More important, some personal characteristics are related to the kinds of rewards salespeople are likely to value and find motivating. This suggests sales managers should examine

Exhibit 9.8   Sales Career Path

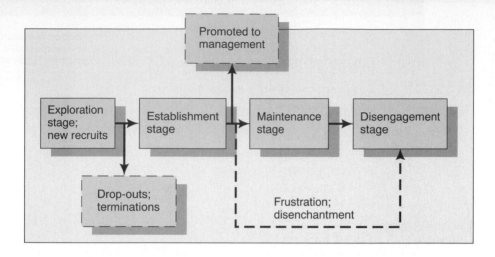

the characteristics of their salespeople and attempt to determine their relative valences for various rewards when designing compensation and incentive programs. Also, as the demographic characteristics of a sales force change, the manager should be aware that salespeople's satisfaction with rewards and their valences for future rewards may also change.

CAREER STAGES AND SALESPERSON MOTIVATION

The previous discussion of the personal factors affecting motivation also suggests that salespeople's expectancy estimates and reward valences are likely to change as they move through different stages in their careers. As a person grows older and gains experience, demographic characteristics and financial obligations change, skills and confidence tend to improve, and the rewards the salesperson receives—as well as satisfaction with those rewards—are likely to change. We have seen that all of these factors can affect an individual's expectancies and reward valences.

Career Stages

Research has identified four stages through which salespeople go during their careers: exploration, establishment, maintenance, and disengagement.[25] Typical paths of progression through these four career stages are diagrammed in Exhibit 9.8. The individual concerns, challenges, and needs associated with each career stage—together with their implications for motivating a salesperson at that stage—are summarized in Exhibit 9.9 and discussed next.

Exploration stage

People in the earliest stage of their careers (typically individuals in their 20s) are often unsure about whether selling is the most appropriate occupation for them to pursue and whether they can be successful salespeople. To make matters worse, underdeveloped skills and a lack of knowledge about their roles tend to make people at this early stage among the poorest performers in the sales force. Consequently, people in the exploratory stage tend to have low psychological involvement with their job and low job satisfaction.

Exhibit 9.9	Characteristics of Different Stages in a Salesperson's Career			
	Exploration	**Establishment**	**Maintenance**	**Disengagement**
Career concerns	Finding an appropriate occupational field	Successfully establishing a career in a certain occupation	Holding on to what has been achieved Reassessing career, with possible redirection	Completing one's career
Developmental tasks	Learning the skills required to do the job well Becoming a contributing member of an organization	Using skills to produce results Adjusting to working with greater autonomy Developing creativity and innovativeness	Developing broader view of work and organization Maintaining a high performance level	Establishing a stronger self-identity outside of work Maintaining an acceptable performance level
Personal challenges	Must establish a good initial professional self-concept	Producing superior results on the job in order to be promoted Balancing the conflicting demands of career and family	Maintaining motivation though possible rewards have changed Facing concerns about aging and disappointment over what one has accomplished Maintaining motivation and productivity	Acceptance of career accomplishments Adjusting self-image
Psychosocial needs	Support Peer acceptance Challenging position	Achievement Esteem Autonomy Competition	Reduced competitiveness Security Helping younger colleagues	Detachment from organization and organizational life
Impact on motivation	Low expectancy and instrumentality perceptions High valences for higher-order rewards, such as personal growth and recognition Supportive supervision is critical	Highest expectancy and instrumentality perceptions High valences for pay, but highest valences for promotion and recognition Must avoid generating unrealistic expectations	Instrumentality and valence for promotion fall Valences for recognition and respect remain high Highest valences for increased pay	Lowest instrumentality perceptions and valences for both higher-order and lower-order rewards Still desires respect, but that is unlikely to motivate additional effort

Source: Adapted from William L. Cron, "Industrial Salesperson Development: A Career Stages Perspective," *Journal of Marketing* (Fall 1984), p. 40; and William L. Cron, Alan J. Dubinsky, and Ronald E. Michaels, "The Influence of Career Stages on Components of Salesperson Motivation," *Journal of Marketing* (January 1988), pp. 78–92.

As Exhibit 9.8 indicates, this can cause some people to become discouraged and quit and others to be terminated if their performance does not improve.

Because salespeople in the exploratory career stage are uncertain about their own skills and the requirements of their new jobs, they tend to have the lowest expectancy and instrumentality perceptions in a firm's sales force. They have little confidence that expending more effort will lead to better performance or that improved performance will produce increased rewards. But they do have relatively high valences for high-order rewards, particularly for personal growth and recognition. They need reassurance that they are making progress and that they will eventually be successful in their new career. Consequently, good training programs, supportive supervision, and much recognition and encouragement are useful for motivating and improving the performance of salespeople at this formative stage of their careers.

Establishment stage

Those in the establishment stage—usually in their late 20s or early 30s—have settled on an occupation and desire to build it into a successful career. Thus, the major concerns of salespeople at this stage involve improving their skills and their sales performance. As they gain confidence, these people's expectancy and instrumentality perceptions reach their highest level. People at this stage believe they will be successful if they devote sufficient effort to the job and their success will be rewarded.

Because people at this career stage are often making other important commitments in their lives—such as buying homes, marrying, and having children—their valences for increased financial rewards tend to be relatively high. However, their strong desire to be successful—and in many cases the desire to move into management—makes their valences for promotion higher at this stage than at any other. They also have very high valences for recognition and other indications that their superiors approve of their performance and perhaps consider them worthy of promotion.

However, the strong desire for promotion at this stage can have negative consequences. As shown in Exhibit 9.8, some successful people may win promotions into sales or marketing management, but many others will not, at least not as soon as they hoped. Some of these individuals may become so frustrated by what they consider to be slow progress that they quit for jobs in other companies that promise faster advancement or they move prematurely into a "disengagement" stage. To help prevent this, managers should guard against building unrealistic expectations concerning the likelihood and speed of future promotions among their establishment-stage salespeople.

Maintenance stage

This stage normally begins in a salesperson's late 30s or early 40s. The individual's primary concern at this stage is with retaining the present position, status, and performance level within the sales force, all of which are likely to be quite high. For this reason, people in the maintenance stage continue to have high valences for rewards that reflect high status and good performance, such as formal recognition and the respect of their peers and superiors.

By this stage, though, both the opportunity and desire for promotion diminish. Consequently, instrumentality estimates and valences concerning promotion fall to lower levels. But salespeople at this stage often have the highest valences for increased pay and financial incentives of anyone in the sales force. Even though such people are among the highest paid salespeople, they tend to want more money due to both increased financial obligations (e.g., children getting ready for college, large mortgages) and a desire for a symbol of success in lieu of promotion.

Disengagement stage

At some point, everyone must begin to prepare for retirement and the possible loss of self-identity that can accompany separation from one's job. This usually begins to happen when people reach their late 50s or early 60s. During this disengagement stage, people psychologically withdraw from their job, often seeking to maintain just an "acceptable" level of performance with a minimum amount of effort in order to spend more time developing inter-

Exhibit 9.10   How Extensive Is Plateauing?

Age Group (Years)	Mean Percentage of the Sales Force That Is Plateaued
20–29.9	2.3%
30–39.9	9.8
40–49.9	22.5
50–59.9	20.0
60 and over	14.9
Total sample	17.5%

Source: Robin T. Peterson, "Beyond the Plateau," *Sales & Marketing Management* (July 1993), p. 80.

ests outside of work. As a result, such people have little interest in attaining more high-order rewards—such as recognition, personal development, or a promotion—from their jobs.

Because they tend to have fewer financial obligations at this stage, they are also relatively satisfied with their low-order rewards and have low valences for attaining more pay or other financial incentives. Not surprisingly, then, salespeople at this career stage have average performance levels lower than any others except new recruits in the exploratory stage. And their low valences for either high- or low-order rewards make it difficult to motivate them.

What is most disconcerting about disengagement, however, is that it does not occur only among salespeople at the end of their careers. As mentioned earlier, long before they approach retirement age, people may become bored with their jobs and frustrated by a failure to win promotion. Such people may psychologically withdraw from their jobs rather than search for a new position or occupation. They are commonly referred to as plateaued salespeople—people who have stopped developing, stopped improving, and often stopped showing an interest.

The Problem of the Plateaued Salesperson

Plateauing, or early disengagement, is not an isolated phenomenon among salespeople. As shown in Exhibit 9.10, a survey of sales managers in 340 firms suggests an average of about 17.5 percent of a firm's sales force can be expected to have reached a plateau, and in some companies the percentage is even higher.[26] While this study suggests that most plateaued salespeople are in their 40s or 50s, respondents reported that some salespeople reach a plateau while still in their 20s or 30s.

Causes of plateauing

Exhibit 9.11 shows managers' perceptions of the relative importance of various causes of plateauing among salespeople. These rankings are broken down according to whether the sales force consists of a majority of men or women and according to the type of compensation plan employed (e.g., salary only, commission only). Overall, these managerial perceptions are consistent with what was mentioned earlier. The primary causes of early disengagement are the boredom and frustration that arise when a relatively young person is kept in the same job too long and sees little likelihood of a promotion or other expansion in job responsibilities in the near future. Among the top-ranked causes of plateauing are a lack of a clear career path, boredom, and a failure to manage the person effectively. Note, too, that these factors are viewed as important regardless of the gender of the sales force or the compensation system used.

Exhibit 9.11   Manager's Rankings of the Causes of Plateauing among Salespeople

	Overall	Mostly Men	Mostly Women	Salary Only	Salary plus Bonus	Salary plus Commission	Salary Commission Bonus	Commission Only
No clear career path	1	1	2	1	2	1	3	4
Not managed adequately	2	2	4	3	1	3	4	1
Bored	3	3	3	2	4	4	2	5
Burned out	4	5	1	5	3	5	1	2
Economic needs met	5	4	7	6	5	2	6	3
Discouraged with company	6	6	5	4	6	6	5	6
Overlooked for promotion	7	7	6	7	7	7	7	8
Lack of ability	8	8	9	8	10	8	8	7
Avoiding risk of management job	9	9	10	10	8	9	9	9
Reluctance to be transferred	10	10	8	9	9	10	10	10

Note: The numbers in each column indicate how early warning signals and causes of plateauing were ranked by *S&MM* survey respondents overall and by several subgroups. (By "mostly men" or "mostly women" we mean sales forces comprised of at least 60 percent men or 60 percent women.)

Source: Reprinted with permission from William Keenan, Jr., "The Nagging Problem of the Plateaued Salesperson," *Sales & Marketing Management* (March 1989), p. 38. © 1989 by Bill Communications, Inc.

However, the respondents did believe that simple burnout may be a more important cause of plateauing among saleswomen than salesmen, perhaps due to the demands of their multiple roles as mothers and homemakers in addition to those of their jobs. Also, the survey results suggest the opportunity to earn high levels of pay provided by compensation systems made up entirely or substantially of commission payments can exacerbate the plateauing problem. Managers indicate salespeople compensated by commission may more easily earn sufficient pay to meet their economic needs and thereby become less motivated by the chance to earn still higher financial compensation. We explore this issue in more detail in Chapter 13.

Possible solutions

All of this suggests that one way of reducing the plateauing problem in a sales force—and of remotivating salespeople who have reached a plateau—is to develop clearly defined career paths for salespeople who are good performers but are not promoted into management early in their careers. Such "alternative" career paths typically involve promotions to positions within the sales force that involve additional responsibility and more demanding challenges.

For instance, a firm might develop a career path involving frequent promotions to increasingly lucrative and challenging territories or assignments to larger and more sophisticated accounts. For instance, some firms promote high-performing salespeople into national account management positions. Assignments to new product development teams or staff support positions (e.g., director of sales recruiting or training) might also be part of the sales career path. The idea is to provide opportunities for frequent changes in job duties and responsibilities to increase the variety of salespeople's jobs. Simultaneously, those changes can be used as rewards for good performance to motivate the members of the sales force and to show that they are valued employees even though they do not rise to management positions.

To be effective, however, the promotions along the sales career path must be real rather than simply changes in title. They must involve real changes in duties and responsibilities, and they must be offered on the basis of good past performance. Cosmetic promotions—particularly when they are doled out simply on the basis of time in rank—do little to stimulate continued effort among a firm's older salespeople.

Another closely related approach to revitalizing plateaued salespeople is to enrich their current jobs by finding ways to add variety and responsibility without developing a complicated system of hierarchical positions and promotion criteria. This is likely to be a more viable approach in smaller firms, and will probably become more popular as technology allows firms to reduce the number of sales managers and to adopt flatter sales force structures. For example, plateaued salespeople might be asked to devote time to training and mentoring new recruits, to gathering competitive intelligence, or to becoming members of cross-functional account management or product development teams. A number of other suggestions for dealing with disengaged salespeople offered by sales managers are discussed in the "Ethical Issues" box.

THE IMPACT OF ENVIRONMENTAL CONDITIONS ON MOTIVATION

Environmental factors such as variations in territory potential and strength of competition can constrain a salesperson's ability to achieve high levels of performance. Such environmental constraints can cause substantial variations in performance across salespeople. In addition to placing actual constraints on performance, however, environmental conditions can affect salespeople's perceptions of their likelihood of succeeding and thus their willingness to expend effort.

Although management can do little to change the environment faced by its salespeople (with the possible exception of rearranging sales territories), an understanding of how and why salespeople perform differently under varying environmental circumstances is useful to sales managers. Such an understanding provides clues about the compensation methods and management policies that will have the greatest impact on sales performance under specific environmental conditions. The effects of various environmental factors on salespeople's perceptions and motivations are summarized in Exhibit 9.12.

In some industries, the pace of technological change is very rapid, as recent advances in the computer and office machine industries show. Salespeople in such industries must deal with a constant flow of product innovations, modifications, and applications. Salespeople often look with favor on a constantly changing product line because it adds variety to their jobs, and their markets never have a chance to become saturated and stagnant. However, a rapidly changing product line can also cause problems for the salesperson. New products and services may require new selling methods and result in new expectations and demands from role partners. Consequently, an unstable product line may lead to less accurate expectancy estimates among the sales force.

In some firms, salespeople must perform in the face of output constraints, which can result from short supplies of production factors, including shortages of raw materials, plant capacity, or labor. Such constraints can cause severe problems for the salesperson. In one paper-products firm a few years ago, salespeople were penalized for exceeding quotas. In general, salespeople operating in the face of uncertain or limited product supplies are likely to feel relatively powerless to improve their performance or rewards through their own efforts. After all, their ultimate effectiveness is constrained by factors beyond their control. Therefore, their expectancy and instrumentality estimates are likely to be low.

Dealing with the Plateaued Salesperson

Since plateauing or early disengagement is so pervasive among salespeople, finding ways to remotivate such employees represents a thorny issue for nearly every sales manager. The following table shows the percentage of sales managers in a survey of 340 firms who agreed that various potential solutions might be viable ways to rekindle the motivation of plateaued sales personnel. While these solutions vary a great deal, termination was almost universally viewed as a last resort. Plateaued salespeople often have a past history of successful performance, and they are potentially too valuable to simply dismiss without first trying to find creative ways to regenerate their energy and enthusiasm.

Possible Solutions	Percentage of Managers Who Agree
Talk with salesperson about problem	70.9%
Discuss reasons and possible solutions	69.4
Conduct motivation sessions	63.8
Manage, lead, and communicate	63.2
Cut salesperson's responsibilities	61.5
Provide new responsibilities	61.2
Assign to a new territory	57.4
Inform rep on his/her responsibilities	55.9
Provide time off	50.0
Ask to assist new reps	44.7
Use ongoing goal assessment program	42.9
Clear the air and redefine goal	40.6
Assign to a different sales manager	32.6
Use bonus plans	30.9
Have rep come up with solutions	30.9
Provide perks after sales success	27.1
Recognition plans	23.8
Encourage reps to be creative	21.5
Use competent sales managers	18.8
Use training sessions	14.4
Change: new products, prospects, etc.	6.5

Source: Robin T. Peterson, "Beyond the Plateau," *Sales & Marketing Management* (July 1993), p. 82. Also see William Keenan, Jr., "The Nagging Problem of the Plateaued Salesperson," *Sales & Marketing Management* (March 1989), pp. 36–41.

Exhibit 9.12   Influence of Environmental Factors on the Determinants of Motivation

Environmental Factors	Motivational Variables			
	Expectancies		Instrumentalities	
	Magnitude	Accuracy	Magnitude	Accuracy
Stability of product offerings		+		
Output constraints	−		−	
Superiority of competitive position	+			
Territory potential	+			

Exhibit 9.13	Influence of Organizational Variables on the Determinants of Motivation					
	Motivational Variables					
	Expectancies		**Instrumentalities**		**Valences**	
Organizational Variables	**Magnitude**	**Accuracy**	**Magnitude**	**Accuracy**	**Higher Order**	**Lower Order**
Closeness of supervision		+		+		
Span of control		−		−		
Influence over standards				+		
Frequency of communication		+		+		
Opportunity rate					Curvilinear	
Recognition rate					Curvilinear	
Compensation rate						−
Earnings opportunity ratio						+

There are many ways of assessing the strength of a firm's competitive position in the marketplace. One might look at its market share, the quality of its products and services as perceived by customers, or its prices. Regardless of how competitive superiority is defined, though, when salespeople believe they work for a strongly competitive firm, they are more likely to think selling effort will result in successful performance. In other words, the stronger a firm's competitive position, the higher its salespeople's expectancy estimates are likely to be.

Sales territories often have very different potentials for future sales. These potentials are affected by many environmental factors, including economic conditions, competitors' activities, and customer concentrations. Again, though, the salesperson's perception of the unrealized potential of the territory can influence that person's motivation to expend selling effort. Specifically, the greater the perceived potential of a territory, the higher the salesperson's expectancy estimates are likely to be.

THE IMPACT OF ORGANIZATIONAL VARIABLES ON MOTIVATION

Company policies and characteristics can directly facilitate or hinder a salesperson's effectiveness. Such organizational variables may also influence salespeople's performance indirectly, however, by affecting their valences for company rewards and the size and accuracy of their expectancy and instrumentality estimates. These relationships between organizational variables and the determinants of motivation are summarized in Exhibit 9.13.

Supervisory Variables and Leadership

According to one highly regarded theory of leadership, a leader attains good performance from the work unit by increasing subordinates' personal rewards from goal attainment and by making the path to those rewards easier to follow—through instructions and training, by reducing roadblocks and pitfalls, and by increasing the opportunities for personal satisfaction.[27]

This theory suggests that effective leaders tailor their style and approach to the needs of their subordinates and the kinds of tasks they must perform. When the subordinates' task is well defined, routine, and repetitive, the leader should seek ways to increase the intrinsic rewards of the task. This might be accomplished by assigning subordinates a broader range of activities or by giving them more flexibility to perform tasks. When the subordinate's job is complex and ambiguous, that person is likely to be happier and more productive when the leader provides relatively high levels of guidance and structure.[28]

In most occupations, workers perform relatively well defined and routine jobs, and they prefer to be relatively free from supervision. They do not like to feel their superiors "breathing down their necks." Industrial salespeople, however, are different. They occupy a position at the boundary of their companies, dealing with customers and other nonorganization people who may make conflicting demands. Salespeople frequently face new, nonroutine problems. Consequently, evidence shows industrial salespeople are happier when they feel relatively closely supervised, and supportive supervision can increase their expectancy and instrumentality estimates for attaining extrinsic rewards.[29] Closely supervised salespeople can learn more quickly what is expected of them and how they should perform their job. Consequently, such individuals should have more accurate expectancies and instrumentalities than less closely supervised salespeople. But close supervision can increase role conflict since it can reduce flexibility in accommodating and adapting to customers' demands.

Another organization variable related to the closeness of supervision is the firm's first-level sales managers' span of control. The more salespeople each manager must supervise (the larger the span of control), the less closely the manager can supervise each person. Therefore, the impact of span of control on role perceptions and motivation variables should be the opposite of the expected impact of close supervision, although this is changing as the result of new technologies.

Another related supervisory variable is the frequency with which salespeople communicate with their superiors. The greater the frequency of communication, the less role ambiguity salespeople are likely to experience and the more accurate their expectancy and instrumentality estimates should be. Again, however, frequent contact with superiors may increase the individual's feelings of role conflict.

Management by objectives (MBO) is a popular supervisory technique in sales management. Specific procedures vary from firm to firm, but one basic principle of MBO is to give the individual a voice in determining the standards and criteria by which performance will be evaluated and rewarded. Salespeople who believe that they influence such standards are likely to have a clearer understanding of how to perform their jobs and how performance will be rewarded.

Incentive and Compensation Policies

Management policies and programs concerning higher-order rewards, such as recognition and promotion, can influence the desirability of such rewards in the salesperson's mind. For these rewards, there is likely to be a curvilinear relationship between the perceived likelihood of receiving them and the salesperson's valence for them. For example, if a large proportion of the sales force receives some formal recognition each year, salespeople may think such recognition is too common, too easy to obtain, and not worth much. If very few members receive formal recognition, however, salespeople may believe it is not a very attractive or motivating reward simply because the odds of attaining it are so low. The same curvilinear relationship is likely to exist between the proportion of salespeople promoted into management each year (the opportunity rate) and salespeople's valence for promotion.[30]

A company's policies on the kinds and amounts of financial compensation paid to its salespeople are also likely to affect their motivation. As seen, when a person's lower-order needs are satisfied, they become less important and the individual's valence for rewards that satisfy such needs, such as pay and job security, is reduced. This suggests that in firms where the current financial compensation is relatively high, salespeople will be satisfied with their attainment of lower-order rewards. They will have lower valences for more of these rewards than people in firms where compensation is lower.

The Reward Mix and Motivation

Motivating the sales force is big business. Nearly $6.5 billion was spent in 1997 on incentives directed toward salespeople (this included merchandise and travel-related incentives). Another $9.5 billion of incentives was directed toward distributors in the channel of distribution. Nearly half of all distributors/wholesalers use incentive programs to motivate salespeople. Companies in the channel of distribution count on incentives to help motivate their sales forces.

The decision to use incentives is made at the highest levels in many organizations. While sales departments are often involved (65 percent of the time the sales department participates in the decision to implement an incentive program), senior management are the primary drivers. In nearly four out of five companies senior management is involved in the decision to develop incentive programs in the sales force. Further information reveals the following:

What are the most popular types of motivators (ranked in order)?

1. Cash awards
2. Gift certificates
3. Merchandise
4. Discounts or rebates
5. Individual travel
6. Time off from the job
7. Group travel
8. Debit cards

Where do companies purchase the noncash incentives (top five ranked in order)?

1. Direct from manufacturer
2. Local retail store
3. Corporate travel agency
4. Sales promotion agency/ad agency
5. Incentive company

And where are the sources for incentive program award ideas (ranked in order)?

1. Employee feedback
2. Peers (networking)
3. Trade magazines
4. Vendors
5. Trade shows
6. Direct mail
7. Employee surveys
8. Consumer magazines

Source: "The $23 Billion Motivation Machine," *Promo Magazine* (October 1997), pp. R28–R29.

The *range* of financial rewards currently received by members of a sales force also might affect their valences for more financial rewards. If some salespeople receive much more money than the average, many others may feel underpaid and have high valences for more money. The ratio of the total financial compensation of the highest paid salesperson to that of the average in a sales force is the **earnings opportunity ratio.** The higher this ratio is within a company, the higher the average salesperson's valence for pay is likely to be.

Finally, the kind of reward mix offered by the firm is a factor. Reward mix is the relative emphasis placed on salary versus commissions or other incentive pay and nonfinancial rewards. In the opening vignette Lantech experienced the problems associated with not configuring the reward mix properly. By focusing on individual rewards, the company did not maximize the potential of the entire sales force. It is likely to influence the salesperson's instrumentality estimates and help determine which job activities and types of performance will receive the greatest effort from that salesperson. The question from a manager's viewpoint is how to design an effective reward mix for directing the sales force's efforts toward the activities believed to be most important to the overall success of the firm's sales program. The issue of reward mix and motivation is discussed in greater detail in the "Managing Sales Relationships" box. This leads to a discussion of the relative advantages and weaknesses of alternative compensation and incentive programs—the topic of Chapter 13.

SUMMARY

The amount of effort the salesperson desires to expend on each activity or task associated with the job—the individual's motivation—can strongly influence job performance. This chapter reviewed the factors that affect an individual's motivation level. The chapter suggested an individual's motivation to expend effort on any particular task is a function of that person's (1) expectancy, (2) instrumentality, and (3) valence perceptions.

Expectancy refers to the salesperson's estimate of the probability that expending a given amount of effort on some task will lead to improved performance on some dimension. Expectancies have two dimensions that are important to sales managers—magnitude and accuracy. The magnitude of a salesperson's expectancy perceptions indicates the degree to which the individual believes that expending effort on job activities will directly influence job performance. The *accuracy of expectancy perceptions* refers to how clearly the individual understands the relationship between the effort expended on a task and the performance on some specific dimension that is likely to result.

Instrumentalities are the person's perceptions of links between job performance and various rewards.

Specifically, an instrumentality is a salesperson's estimate of the probability that a given improvement in performance on some dimension will lead to a specific increase in the amount of a particular reward. A reward can be more pay, winning a sales contest, or promotion to a better territory. As with expectancies, sales managers need to be concerned with both the magnitude and accuracy of their subordinates' instrumentalities.

The salesperson's valence for a specific reward is the individual's perception of the desirability of receiving increased amounts of that reward. This valence, along with the individual's valence for all other attractive rewards and the person's instrumentality perceptions, determines how attractive it is to perform well on some specific dimension.

Several factors influence salespeople's expectancy, instrumentality, and valence perceptions. Three major forces are (1) the personal characteristics of the individuals in the sales force, (2) the environmental conditions they face, and (3) the company's own policies and procedures. The chapter reviewed some major influences and their likely impacts on each of the three categories.

DISCUSSION QUESTIONS

1. Sales support personnel include customer service reps, account coordinators, sales assistants, and others whose efforts have a critical impact on a sales force's success. The chapter discusses motivation from the perspective of the sales force. How would you apply the concepts discussed in the chapter to sales support personnel? What can a company do to motivate sales support personnel?

2. "What's all this stuff about different pay packages and different incentive plans based on how long a sales rep has been with the company?" demanded the irate sales manager. "Around here, everybody gets the same treat-

ment. We're not offering customized compensation packages." What are the problems associated with motivating sales reps based on their stage in the career cycle?

3. What sales manager has not had the problem of motivating the older sales representative? The once-valuable producer has dried up and is not meeting quotas. He or she is a drag on the rest of the district sales team. What do you do? Fire the sales rep? Baby him or her? What can a sales manager do to turn the older sales rep into a valuable asset?

4. A situation different from the preceding concerns how to motivate the sales representative when money or

merchandise is not the question. When ordinary incentives—commissions, incentives, or cars—no longer work, what can a sales manager do to motivate the successful salesperson?

5. Most sales reps dislike preparing call reports. They think their time could be spent more profitably, such as

in calling on accounts. Using Exhibit 9.3, trace the thought process sales reps go through as they consider applying more effort to the preparation of call reports. Do the same for applying more effort to calling on accounts.

EXPERIENTIAL APPLICATION

The chapter discusses the motivational process. Key elements of this process include valence for performance and valence for rewards. Select a small sample of salespeople from a variety of businesses. Ask each sales rep what performance outcome is number one on their list. Then ask each sales rep which rewards are most important to him or her. Next ask why these outcomes are so important. Is there a clear link between the most important performance outcome and the most important reward? For example, a sales rep may identify making sales quota as the most important performance outcome. Being promoted may be the most important reward. Is there a relationship between making quota and being promoted?

INTERNET EXERCISES

Visit the Web site of *Sales & Marketing Management* (*www.salesandmarketing.com*). Click on SMM Magazine and go to its listing of Best Sales Forces. Read through the list of companies whose sales forces were selected as the best of the year. What factors (rewards, performance-enhancing techniques such as training) are mentioned consistently as critical to success? Note how these factors play a role in the motivation process discussed in this chapter.

SUGGESTED READINGS

Motivation and Valences for Rewards

DeCarlo, Thomas E., R. Kenneth Teas, and James C. McElroy, "Salesperson Performance Attribution Processes and Formation of Expectancy Estimates," *Journal of Personal Selling and Sales Management* (Summer 1997), pp. 1–17.

Ford, Neil M., Orville C. Walker, Jr., and Gilbert A. Churchill, Jr., "Differences in the Attractiveness of Alternative Rewards among Industrial Salespeople: Additional Evidence," *Journal of Business Research* (April 1985), pp. 123–38.

Ingram, Thomas N., and Danny N. Bellenger, "Personal and Organizational Variables: Their Relative Effect on Reward Valences of Industrial Salespeople," *Journal of Marketing Research* (May 1983), pp. 198–205.

Johnson, Wesley J., and Keysuk Kim, "Performance, Attribution, and Expectancy Linkages in Personal Selling," *Journal of Marketing* (October 1994), pp. 68–81.

Sager, Jeffrey K., Junsub Yi, and Charles M. Futrell, "A Model Depicting Salespeople's Perceptions," *Journal of Personal Selling and Sales Management* (Summer 1998), pp. 1–22.

Teas, R. Kenneth, and James C. McElroy, "Causal Attributions and Expectancy Estimates: A Framework for Understanding the Dynamics of Salesforce Motivation," *Journal of Marketing* (January 1986), pp. 75–86.

Weitz, Barton A., Harish Sujan, and Mita Sujan, "Knowledge, Motivation, and Adaptive Behavior: A Framework for Improving Selling Effectiveness," *Journal of Marketing* (October 1986), pp. 174–91.

Leadership and Motivation

DelVecchio, Susan K., "The Quality of Salesperson–Manager Relationship: The Effect of Latitude, Loyalty and Competence," *Journal of Personal Selling and Sales Management* (Winter 1998), pp. 31–48.

Kelley, Bill, "How Much Help Does a Salesperson Need?" *Sales & Marketing Management* (May 1989), pp. 32–34.

Tyagi, Pradeep K., "Relative Importance of Key Job Dimensions and Leadership Behaviors in Motivating Salesperson Work Performance," *Journal of Marketing* (Summer 1985), pp. 76–86.

Career Stages and the Problem of Plateaued Salespeople

Cron, William L., "Industrial Salesperson Development: A Career Stages Perspective," *Journal of Marketing* (Fall 1984), pp. 41–52.

Cron, William L., Alan J. Dubinsky, and Ronald E. Michaels, "The Influence of Career Stages on Components of Salesperson Motivation," *Journal of Marketing* (January 1988), pp. 78–92.

Cron, William L., Ellen F. Jackofsky, and John W. Slocum, Jr., "Job Performance and Attitudes of Disengagement Stage Salespeople Who Are About to Retire," *Journal of Personal Selling and Sales Management* (Spring 1993), pp. 1–13.

Peterson, Robin T., "Beyond the Plateau," *Sales & Marketing Management* (July 1993), pp. 78–82.

10 Personal Characteristics and Sales Aptitude: Criteria for Selecting Salespeople

DHL: DELIVERING SUCCESS AROUND THE WORLD

In the highly competitive package delivery business dominated by UPS and FedEx, DHL has demonstrated an ability to succeed. It has consistently shown double-digit growth and recently sales increased 12.8 percent to over $1 billion. With 59,446 employees, 16,621 vehicles, and 222 aircraft, it services 227 countries. The company maintains a sales force of 380 in the United States and was recently designated as having one of the 25 best sales forces in the country.

Jeff Corbett, senior vice president of sales and marketing in the United States, believes that a key to DHL's success has been the company's sales force. In an effort to increase the effectiveness of the sales force, DHL developed a comprehensive personality profile of its salespeople in 1995. It then revised that profile in 1997. The profile is an important tool in the recruitment and selection process for DHL. Managers in the field develop interview questions that will help determine the extent to which individuals possess the qualities enumerated in a comprehensive person-

ality profile. Among the 12 qualities identified in the profile are leadership, analytical skills, and interpretation as well as business judgment.

One of the keys to the success of the personality profile is that DHL uses the profile not only to recruit new salespeople but to develop its training program. Salespeople match their individual training program with their personality profile. Training focuses on giving salespeople the necessary skills to deal with a variety of people inside their customers' organizations. Financial decision makers (such as the CFO) have different needs than marketing managers. As Corbett notes, "[Our salespeople] are trained to be partners with their customers in offering flexible solutions, resolving problems and negotiating the terms of the business relationship." DHL believes that understanding the key characteristics that lead to success in their business is a critical part of each salesperson's potential for success.

Source: "Best Salesforces of 1998," *Sales & Marketing Management* (July 1998), p. 48; the DHL Web site at *www.dhl.com*.

LEARNING OBJECTIVES

What makes a good salesperson? This question is the focus of this chapter. Perhaps no other question faced by sales managers is more important because it has such a profound effect on every aspect of a manager's job. From recruiting and selecting through to motivating and evaluating a sales force, one of the important questions—if not the most important—is "What makes that person successful (or not successful)?" Sales managers are constantly looking for those characteristics that consistently define success or failure.

At the end of this chapter you should be able to:

- Understand the answer to the question, "Are good salespeople born or made?"
- Define the characteristics of successful salespeople.
- Explain the role of sales aptitude in sales performance.

ARE GOOD SALESPEOPLE BORN OR MADE? THE DETERMINANTS OF SUCCESSFUL SALES PERFORMANCE

Stable, self-sufficient, self-confident, goal-directed, decisive, intellectually curious, accurate—these are personal traits one major personnel testing company says an individual should have to be a successful salesperson. A crucial question, though, is whether the presence or absence of such traits is determined by a person's genetic makeup and early life experiences or whether they can be developed through training, supervision, and experience after the person is hired for a sales position. In other words, are good salespeople born or made?

DHL appears to believe that successful salespeople are both born and made. The firm spends an unusual amount of time and energy developing relationships with colleges and faculty members to help identify promising recruits. And it gathers large amounts of information about potential new hires through interviews, references, and tests to determine which candidates have the traits and characteristics the firm believes are important determinants of future sales success. But DHL also devotes substantial resources to training and supervisory programs aimed at further developing each new salesperson's skills, knowledge, and motivation.

Like the managers at DHL, many sales executives seem to have somewhat ambivalent feelings concerning what it takes to become a successful salesperson. When forced to make an explicit choice, a majority of managers say they believe good salespeople are made rather than born that way. For instance, by a margin of 7 to 1, the 2,000 respondents in a survey of sales and marketing executives said training and supervision are more critical determinants of selling success than the inherent personal characteristics of the individual.[1] But many of those respondents also described men and women they knew as being "a born salesperson." And a minority argued that personal traits were critical determinants of good sales performance. For example, one executive asked, "Can they teach ego, train it into an individual? Can they teach personal drive or persistence that gets the sale? Hardly. The best salespeople acquired what it takes to excel when they were kids . . . Training won't do it. Yet a lot of companies try and waste a lot of money in the process."[2]

Thus, while most managers believe that the things a firm does to train and develop its salespeople are the most critical determinants of their future success, many also believe that a firm cannot make a silk purse out of a sow's ear and that certain basic personal traits—such as a strong ego, self-confidence, decisiveness, and a need for achievement—

are necessary requirements. Is it possible that both sets of factors play crucial roles in shaping a salesperson's performance? A review of past empirical research on this issue can help provide a more definitive answer.

A Review of Past Research

A research technique known as meta-analysis has been used to integrate and evaluate the findings of a large number of past research studies examining relationships between the performance of individual salespeople and a variety of personal and organizational factors that might influence that performance.[3] The review examined more than 400 published and unpublished studies conducted between 1918 and 1983, 116 of which reported some statistical evidence regarding the strength of the relationship between one or more variables and differences in performance. Since most of those studies investigated more than one variable, the review actually summarized 1,653 reported relationships between various individual and organizational characteristics and individual sales performance.

For purposes of analysis, variables were grouped into the six categories shown in Exhibit 10.1. The exhibit also shows the actions a sales manager or top executive might take to influence or control each group of determinant variables. Note that two of the categories—aptitude and personal characteristics—contain enduring personal traits and past experiences of the salesperson. These variables are impossible for the manager to influence or change, except by choosing salespeople with desirable traits. A third category—skill levels—includes personal abilities that can change and improve as the salesperson gains knowledge and experience. Thus, skill variables can be influenced by management through effective training programs and supervision. The remaining three categories of determinant variables—role perceptions, motivation, and organizational characteristics—are also directly influenced by management through such means as supervision, compensation and reward systems, and other company policies and programs.

Exhibit 10.2 shows the number of correlations reported in past studies for each of the six categories and the average correlation (weighted to reflect differences in sample sizes across studies) between the variables in each category and salesperson performance. When the weighted average correlation coefficient is squared, it indicates the percentage of variation in performance across salespeople that can be accounted for or explained, on average, by the variables in each category. Thus, aptitude variables—with a weighted average correlation coefficient of 0.138—explain an average of only about 2 percent of the variation in performance across salespeople.

On the surface, the results reported in Exhibit 10.2 may seem a bit disappointing since no category of variables appears capable of explaining a very large percentage of the variation in salesperson performance. While differences in role perceptions explain a greater share of variance in performance than any other category of variables, they account for an average of only 8.6 percent of that variance. At the other extreme, organizational and environmental factors account for only slightly more than 1 percent of the differences in performance across salespeople.

However, when interpreting these findings, several points should be kept in mind. First, each of the six categories contains a large number of specific variables. The aptitude category, for instance, encompasses many specific personality traits and mental abilities. As we will see later in this chapter, some of the specific variables included in each category explain a larger proportion of the variation in performance across salespeople (and some explain a smaller portion) than does the average reported for the whole category.

Second, different studies have measured the same variable in different ways. Consequently, the low correlations between categories of variables and salesperson performance may be partly due to measurement error. Some studies may have used inaccurate or invalid instruments to measure a given trait or characteristic. As we will see in

Exhibit 10.1   Variables That Cause Differences in Performance across Individual Salespeople and the Actions Management Can Take to Influence Them

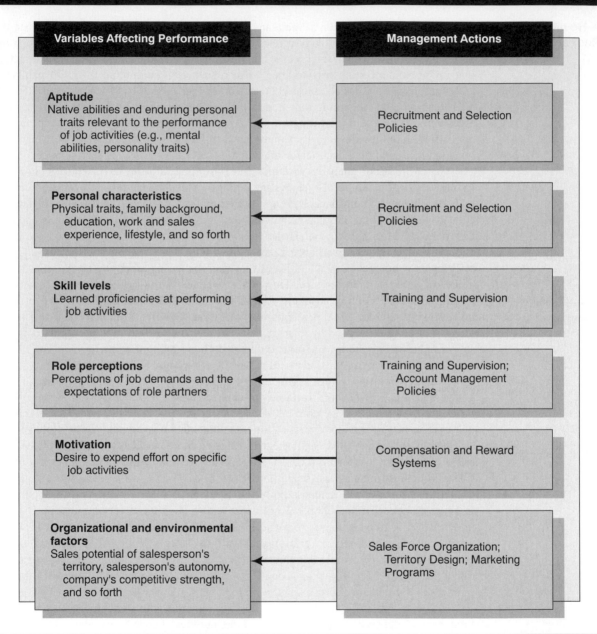

Variables Affecting Performance	Management Actions
Aptitude Native abilities and enduring personal traits relevant to the performance of job activities (e.g., mental abilities, personality traits)	Recruitment and Selection Policies
Personal characteristics Physical traits, family background, education, work and sales experience, lifestyle, and so forth	Recruitment and Selection Policies
Skill levels Learned proficiencies at performing job activities	Training and Supervision
Role perceptions Perceptions of job demands and the expectations of role partners	Training and Supervision; Account Management Policies
Motivation Desire to expend effort on specific job activities	Compensation and Reward Systems
Organizational and environmental factors Sales potential of salesperson's territory, salesperson's autonomy, company's competitive strength, and so forth	Sales Force Organization; Territory Design; Marketing Programs

Chapter 11, much controversy surrounds which measurement methods (e.g., personal interviews versus references versus paper-and-pencil tests) are most appropriate for evaluating whether potential sales recruits possess the specific attributes and abilities a firm is seeking.

Finally, in interpreting the findings, consider that the size of the correlations between each type of determinant variable and sales performance varied widely across studies. One reason for the variation was that different studies examined samples of people en-

Exhibit 10.2 Average Correlations between Types of Determinant Variables and Variations in Salesperson Performance

Variables Affecting Performance	Number of Correlations Reported	Weighted Mean Correlation Coefficient (R)	Percentage of Variance in Performance Explained (R^2)
1. Aptitude	820	.138	.019
2. Personal characteristics	407	.161	.026
3. Skill levels	178	.268	.072
4. Role perceptions	59	.294	.086
5. Motivation	126	.184	.034
6. Organizational/ environmental factors	51	.104	.011

Source: Adapted from Gilbert A. Churchill, Jr., Neil M. Ford, Steven W. Hartley, and Orville C. Walker, Jr., "The Determinants of Salesperson Performance: A Meta-Analysis," *Journal of Marketing Research* (May 1985), p. 107, published by the American Marketing Association.

gaged in different types of sales jobs. The review found that some categories of predictor variables could explain a greater proportion of the variation in performance for salespeople selling certain types of goods or dealing with certain types of customers, but could not explain performance variations as well in other selling situations. For instance, aptitude variables were found to be more positively related to performance for people selling industrial products to organizational customers than for those selling either consumer goods or services.

With these points in mind, one can draw the following conclusions from the meta-analysis of past studies of the determinants of sales performance:

- While all six categories of personal and organizational variables account for some of the variance in performance across salespeople, no single category accounts for more than about 8.5 percent of the variance by itself. This suggests the performance of a given salesperson is a function of a variety of influences, including both personal traits and organizational factors.

- The strengths of the relationships between some categories of variables and sales performance vary according to the type of customer and the kind of product or service being sold. This suggests that different personal traits, aptitudes, and skills are required for success in different kinds of sales jobs.

- On average, factors that sales managers can control or influence—such as role perceptions, skills, and motivation—account for the largest proportion of the variance in performance across salespeople. But enduring personal characteristics—such as aptitude, personal background, and personality traits—are also related to individual differences in performance.

These conclusions suggest that successful salespeople are both born and made. Selecting recruits who have personal traits and abilities appropriate for specific selling tasks is an important determinant of their ultimate sales performance. But while who is hired is important, how those salespeople are managed is even more crucial to their success.

Exhibit 10.3   The Length of Time before a New Salesperson Becomes Productive in Selected Industries (Percentage of respondents, $N = 2,000$)

	Time					
Industry	1 Month	3 Months	6 Months	1 Year	More than 1 Year	Don't Know/ No Answer
Textiles	—	14	45	25	11	4
Glass and building materials	5	23	32	25	9	6
Publishing and printing	9	32	30	17	9	3
Metal manufacturing	5	23	42	16	13	1
Telecommunications	—	31	50	16	2	—
Diversified financial services	8	22	42	12	12	3
Rubber products	7	27	37	24	4	1
Transportation services	6	38	39	10	5	2
Soaps and cosmetics	4	20	46	26	4	—
Electronics	3	18	51	16	11	1

Source: Adapted with permission from Arthur Bragg, "Are Good Salespeople Born or Made?" *Sales & Marketing Management* (September 1988), p. 36. © 1988 by Bill Communications, Inc.

The Costs of Inappropriate Selection Standards

Although personal characteristics may have less influence on a salesperson's long-term performance than do company policies and management actions, firms should pay close attention to hiring the right kinds of people for their sales forces for another reason. People who lack the personal traits and abilities to be truly successful in a given sales job are more likely to become frustrated and to quit—or be fired—before training and experience can turn them into productive employees.

One survey suggests that on average, about 16 percent of a firm's sales force will quit or be terminated in a given year.[4] And the odds that a given salesperson will either quit or be fired during his or her first five years of employment with a firm approach 50–50. This suggests companies are not always successful in identifying and hiring people who have the personal characteristics and abilities to become satisfied and successful salespeople.[5]

Because firms spend much money and time training and supporting new salespeople before they begin to earn their keep, mistakes in recruitment and selection that lead to high early turnover rates can be very costly. Firms with high tech products or broad and complex product lines can spend more than a year and over $100,000 training a new salesperson. Across a broader range of consumer and industrial goods and service industries, firms spend an average of four months and more than $6,000 training each new sales rep.[6] And as the results of the survey shown in Exhibit 10.3 indicate, in most industries, it takes from three months to a year before new sales reps generate enough sales to cover their compensation and expenses.[7] Thus, when a frustrated salesperson quits in the first year or two of employment, the firm can never recoup the costs of recruiting and training that individual.

Because mistakes in recruitment and selection can both be costly in the short term and lead to lower productivity in the long term regardless of how well a firm trains, supervises, and motivates its sales force, many sales managers consider the evaluation and selection of new recruits to be among the most important aspects of their jobs. Thus, the remainder of this chapter examines some of the personal and psychological characteristics related to a person's ability to carry out different types of sales jobs.

CHARACTERISTICS OF SUCCESSFUL SALESPEOPLE

Aptitude and personal characteristics are typically thought to place an upper limit on an individual's ability to perform a given sales job. Two people with equal motivation, role perceptions, and training might perform at different levels because one does not have the personal traits or abilities necessary to do the job as well as the other. The questions to consider are these: What specific personal traits and abilities enable a person to achieve good sales performance? What are the determinants of sales aptitude?

Characteristics Sales Managers Look For

One way to answer these questions is to identify the personal characteristics that sales managers look for when selecting new salespeople. Based on the results of several surveys of sales managers, enthusiasm consistently ranks among the personal attributes they consider most important when deciding whom to hire. Other characteristics considered relatively important are an ability to be well organized, ambition, and the two related attributes of persuasiveness and verbal skill. Although many executives consider previous sales experience to be important in indicating the sales aptitude of new employees, general experience in selling is typically viewed as more relevant than specific product or industry experience.[8]

Surveys asking executives what they look for when hiring new salespeople are instructive, but they do not provide a definitive answer to the question of what personal characteristics make some individuals better salespeople than others. For one thing, the studies cited above reflect only the opinions of American managers concerning what characteristics are related to selling success in the U.S. market. As more firms become global competitors, managers must wrestle with the question of whether different characteristics are related to successful sales performance in different countries. This question is examined further in the "Global Sales Force" box.

Also, manager surveys merely reflect the opinions and perceptions of those sales executives who responded. Although those perceptions may be based on years of practical experience, they can still be inaccurate, biased, or based on knowledge of only a limited range of industries or types of selling jobs.

A more objective way to determine what specific personal characteristics are most strongly related to selling success is to study a large cross section of salespeople. To this end, it would be very useful to examine in more detail the specific variables included in the "aptitude," "skill levels," and "personal characteristics" categories of the meta-analysis of past research that we discussed earlier. Fortunately, a published study does exactly that.[9]

Research Concerning the Personal Characteristics of Successful Salespeople

One limitation of the initial meta-analysis of factors related to differences in sales performance was that the six categories of variables were very broadly defined. Each category contained a large number of more specific items, some of which may be much more strongly related to differences in sales performance than the average for the whole category. Consequently, a second analysis was done after breaking up the broad aptitude, skill levels, and personal characteristics categories into more narrowly defined subcategories of closely related variables.

Are Different Criteria Appropriate for Selecting Salespeople in Different Countries?

As we see in the next chapter, many firms have well-developed and explicit criteria for evaluating potential new salespeople and deciding whom to hire. In some cases, those criteria have been validated by comparing the characteristics of high-performing salespeople within the company to those of reps who have performed less well, quit, or been dismissed.

But when such companies expand their operations into foreign markets—particularly those in developing nations—it is often more difficult to find sales recruits who fit the established criteria. More important, cultural differences can cause some personal traits and characteristics to be more critical for selling success in some countries than in others. Consequently, many global companies have had to adapt their salesperson selection criteria to the cultural and social conditions that prevail in different national markets.

This fact is illustrated by a study of 14 multinational corporations. The study surveyed recruiting practices in 135 of those firms' subsidiaries operating in 45 countries. Table A indicates the percentage of foreign subsidiaries that reported using various salesperson selection criteria. Note that some factors that are unlawful and seldom explicitly used as selection criteria in the United States, such as ethnic and religious background, are used in a large portion of foreign countries. As the ratings shown in Table B indicate, such factors are perceived to be especially important for selecting salespeople in developing markets as compared to the more developed markets of North America and Europe.

Some of the factors Americans deem inappropriate or irrelevant for choosing good salespeople are considered important in other countries are suggested by the following caveats offered by the study's authors concerning sales force recruitment in Malaysia:

- There are definite tensions between the native Malays (55 percent of the population) and the Chinese (33 percent), who dominate large sections of commerce. To correct this, U.S.-style affirmative action laws encourage Malay participation in business.
- Cultural differences are enhanced by religious differences, as Malays are mainly Muslims and Chinese are Buddhists.
- Malay society is highly stratified, and behavior toward individuals depends on the person's background, family, and social position. Malays are not comfortable in situations where social positions have not been defined.

Table A   Salesperson Selection Criteria, Rank-Ordered according to Frequency Mentioned

Criterion	Number of Subsidiaries Using	Percentage
Education	130/135	96.3%
Interview	122/135	90.4
Previous experience	119/135	88.1
Personal appearance	109/135	80.7
References	90/135	66.7
Psychological tests	62/135	45.9
Social class	43/135	31.8
Ethnic background	42/135	31.1
Religious background	34/135	25.2

Table B   Percentage of Subsidiaries Rating Various Salesperson Selection Criteria Important in Developing versus Developed Markets

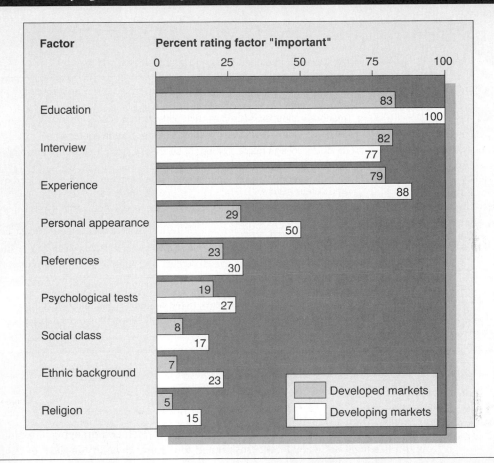

Factor	Percent rating factor "important"	
	Developed markets	Developing markets
Education	83	100
Interview	82	77
Experience	79	88
Personal appearance	29	50
References	23	30
Psychological tests	19	27
Social class	8	17
Ethnic background	7	23
Religion	5	15

Source: John S. Hill and Meg Birdseye, "Salesperson Selection in Multinational Corporations: An Empirical Study," *Journal of Personal Selling and Sales Management* (Summer 1989), pp. 39–47.

First, personal factors related to differences in sales performance were broken down into more precisely defined groupings of (a) physical and behavioral characteristics and (b) psychological traits and abilities. Exhibit 10.4 displays a variety of the physical and behavioral factors that past research studies have examined in trying to explain individual differences in sales performance. The exhibit defines three subcategories of demographic and physical variables, five groups of background and experience factors, and three groups of variables reflecting a person's current status and lifestyle. Such physical and behavioral characteristics are typically measured via subjective or self-report information from résumés, application blanks, or personal interviews. It is important to note, though, that some of the variables reported in Exhibit 10.4 can no longer be legally collected for use in the selection process. For example, potentially discriminatory information about

Exhibit 10.4 Categories of Physical and Behavioral Variables Used as Selection Criteria	
Variable Category	**Definition**
Demographic and physical characteristics	**Classifications based on physical traits of an individual**
Age	
Sex	
Physical appearance	Height, weight, neatness, and general appearance and manner
Background and experience	**Developmental education and work experiences of an individual**
Personal history and family background	Father's/mother's occupation; number of siblings, sibling rank; early family responsibilities; extracurricular and athletic activities
Level of educational attainment	Individual's years of schooling; degrees earned; grade average
Educational content	Individual's college major; number of business/sales courses; executive development programs
Sales experience	Individual's years of sales experience; number and type of sales jobs; promotions and career history
Nonsales work experience	Individual's work history, including military service; length of time in past jobs; past occupation most and least enjoyed
Current status and lifestyle	**Individual's present marital, family, and financial status; leisure activities**
Marital/family status	Individual's current marital status; number and ages of dependents; spouse's occupation
Financial status	Individual's past and current income levels, family income; history of salary increases; assets and liabilities; home ownership; amount of insurance
Activities/lifestyle	Time individual gives to church, clubs, etc.; number of memberships; offices held in organizations; hobbies and interests

Source: Neil M. Ford, Orville C. Walker, Jr., and Gilbert A. Churchill, Jr., "Selecting Successful Salespeople: A Meta-Analysis of Biographical and Psychological Selection Criteria," in *Review of Marketing,* ed. Michael J. Houston (Chicago: American Marketing Association, 1988), pp. 90–131.

such characteristics as age, sex, and race cannot be included on application blanks. These and other legal and social concerns related to cultural diversity in the work force are discussed later in this chapter and in Chapter 11.

A number of variables related to salespeople's psychological traits and abilities are described in Exhibit 10.5. The exhibit defines seven subcategories of personality traits, five groups of other enduring aptitude factors or mental abilities, and five groups of skills. Note that the variables in this exhibit must be measured explicitly during the selection process through the use of formal paper-and-pencil tests or assessment techniques.[10]

Overview of the Findings

As expected, this detailed analysis uncovered specific personal characteristics and traits that can better distinguish between high- and low-performing salespeople—and some that are even worse predictors of performance—than the broad categories of variables examined earlier. Although no single trait could account for a majority of the variance in performance across salespeople, Exhibit 10.6 shows that some personal variables (such as an individual's personal history and family background, current marital and family status, and vocational skills) can account for as much as 20 percent of the variance in selling success. Some traits on which sales managers commonly rely to evaluate new recruits (such as educational attainment, intelligence test scores, or sociability) have proven incapable of accounting for much more than 1 percent of the difference in their subsequent

Exhibit 10.5	Categories of Psychological Traits and Abilities Used as Selection Criteria
Variable Category	**Definition**
Aptitude	**Enduring personal characteristics that determine an individual's overall ability to perform a sales job**
Intelligence	Summary measures of mental abilities; total scores on multifactor intelligence tests
Cognitive abilities	Measures of specific mental processes and abilities, including mental flexibility, ideational fluency, spatial visualization, inductive and logical reasoning, and associative and visual memory
Verbal intelligence	Mental abilities related to the comprehension and manipulation of words; verbal fluency
Math ability	Mental abilities related to the comprehension and manipulation of numbers and quantitative relationships
Sales aptitude	Enduring personal characteristics and abilities thought to be related to the performance of specific sales tasks
Personality	**Enduring personal traits that reflect an individual's consistent reactions to situations encountered in the environment**
Responsibility	The person is dependable, emotionally stable, and punctual, adjusts well to frustration; keeps promises, follows plans
Dominance	The person takes command, exerts leadership, pushes own ideas, wants power versus being submissive; is egotistic
Sociability	The person enjoys social activities and interaction, likes to be around people, is talkative and gregarious, enjoys attention
Self-esteem	The person is confident physically, personally, and careerwise; can stand criticism, claims to have abilities and skills, is confident of success, believes others have a positive attitude toward him/her
Creativity/flexibility	The person is innovative, flexible, ready to entertain new ideas and ways of doing things, individualistic, tolerant of human nature
Need for achievement/intrinsic rewards	The person works hard, likes to do his/her best, seeks success in competition, wants to produce something "great," gains satisfaction from accomplishment and personal development
Need for power/extrinsic rewards	The person is motivated primarily by desires for money or advancement, has strong need for security, desires increased power and authority
Skills	**Learned proficiencies and attitudes necessary for effective performance of specific job tasks; skills can change over time with training and experience**
Vocational skills	Job- and company-specific skills; technical knowledge and vocabulary related to the firm's product line, knowledge of the company and its policies
Sales presentation	Skills related to evaluating customer needs, presentation style, ability to handle objections and close the sale
Interpersonal	Skills related to understanding, persuading, and getting along with other people
General management	Skills related to organizing, directing, and leading other people
Vocational esteem	Degree of liking or preference for the tasks and activities associated with sales jobs

Source: Neil M. Ford, Orville C. Walker, Jr., and Gilbert A. Churchill, Jr., "Selecting Successful Salespeople: A Meta-Analysis of Biographical and Psychological Selection Criteria," in *Review of Marketing,* ed. Michael J. Houston (Chicago: American Marketing Association, 1988), pp. 90–131.

sales performance. Thus, the following sections discuss these widely varying relationships between personal variables and sales performance in depth.

One finding was consistent, however, across both meta-analysis studies. Different types of selling situations appear to require salespeople with different personal traits and abilities. Consequently, the last section of this chapter examines the evidence concerning what personal traits and abilities are best suited to different types of sales jobs.

Exhibit 10.6   The Percentage of Variance in Salesperson Performance Explained by Various Personal Factors

Variables Affecting Performance	Number of Correlations Reported	Percentage of Variance in Performance Explained*
I. Demographic and Physical Characteristics		
Age	61	.011%
Sex	37	.007
Physical appearance	49	.010
II. Background and Experience		
Personal history and family background	29	.209
Educational attainment	40	.002
Educational content	42	.009
Sales experience	28	.028
Nonsales work experience	54	.014
III. Current Status and Lifestyle		
Marital/family status	32	.119
Financial status	31	.061
Activities/lifestyle	38	.017
IV. Aptitude		
Intelligence	38	.014
Cognitive abilities	21	.067
Verbal intelligence	20	.018
Math ability	41	.023
Sales aptitude	58	.037
V. Personality		
Responsibility	42	.040
Dominance	125	.024
Sociability	94	.011
Self-esteem	106	.019
Creativity/flexibility	51	.014
Need for achievement/intrinsic rewards	81	.024
Need for power/extrinsic rewards	25	.018
VI. Skills		
Vocational skills	28	.094
Sales presentation skills	44	.048
Interpersonal skills	43	.022
General management skills	25	.091
Vocational esteem	115	.010

*As determined by R^2, the square of the weighted mean correlation coefficient.

Source: From Neil M. Ford, Orville C. Walker, Jr., and Gilbert A. Churchill, Jr., "Selecting Successful Salespeople: A Meta-Analysis of Biographical and Psychological Criteria," in *Review of Marketing,* ed. Michael J. Houston (Chicago: American Marketing Association, 1988), pp. 90–131.

Demographic and physical variables

The meta-analysis results in Exhibit 10.6 indicate that demographic factors, such as sex and age, and physical attributes, such as height and appearance, account for only about 1 percent or less of the difference in performance across salespeople. The lack of any strong relationships between these variables and sales performance is a very important finding. It has implications for public policy regarding equal employment opportunities for women and minorities, and it refutes the "conventional wisdom" espoused by some sales managers in the past.

Sex and race.   Like many other job categories, industrial selling was predominantly a white male occupation for many decades, and employment opportunities for women and racial minorities were severely limited. The 1980 U.S. Census indicated that while blacks accounted for about 12 percent of the population, only 6 percent of all sales jobs were held by black workers, and the proportion of blacks in more prestigious and rewarding industrial sales positions was even lower. Similarly, women accounted for less than 16 percent of people selling manufactured goods at other than the retail level in 1980.

One major reason for this unequal employment was that many sales managers believed women and racial minorities would not do as well as white men. It was widely believed that some customers would be reluctant to deal with or buy from minority salespeople. Similarly, many sales managers thought women were too emotional and lacking in aggressiveness and self-confidence to be effective salespeople. Some managers thought turnover rates would be higher for women due to marriage and childbirth and women would be less willing to travel and entertain. Consequently, 80 percent of the 180 top sales and marketing executives surveyed by *Sales Management* in the late 1960s admitted they were unwilling to hire women for outside sales positions.[11]

Social changes have improved employment opportunities.   Women and minorities have made some inroads into industrial selling, but their progress has been slow. As Exhibit 10.7 indicates, women accounted for an average of more than 24 percent of sales reps across a sample of industries in 1998, and they held 14 percent of the sales management positions in those industries. Note, however, that women have achieved greater acceptance in some industries, such as communications, publishing, insurance, and business services, than in more traditionally male-dominated industries such as construction, machinery, and primary metals.

While not overwhelming, the positive trends in the employment of women and minorities in recent years have resulted from a variety of social changes, including pressures exerted by the civil rights movement, changing attitudes concerning women's roles, increasing career orientation among women, and legal requirements. The rights of women and minorities to equal employment opportunities in selling, as well as in other occupations, are protected by federal laws. Title VII of the 1964 Civil Rights Act prohibits discrimination in hiring, promotions, and compensation. It covers all private employers of 15 or more persons. The Equal Employment Opportunity Commission administers Title VII. Since 1972, it has had broad enforcement powers. While enforcement policies have fluctuated with political changes in the executive branch of the federal government over the years, the commission's guidelines prohibit withholding jobs or promotions because of either customer preferences for salespeople of a particular race or sex or presumed differences in turnover rates. They also prohibit separate promotional paths or seniority lists. Recently, additional legislation has outlawed discrimination on the basis of age and physical disabilities. These important pieces of employment legislation and their implications for sales force recruitment and hiring decisions are examined in more detail in Chapter 11.[12]

Cultural diversity and changing attitudes.   As firms have hired more minorities and women for sales positions, have the old concerns about the possible shortcomings of such individuals been supported or disproved? Have sales managers' attitudes changed as more women and minorities have been added to their sales forces? Do sex and race have anything to do with a person's sales aptitude and ultimate performance?

Exhibit 10.7   Women in Sales and Sales Management Positions: Percentages by Industry

Industry Group	Percentage of Women Sales Reps	Percentage of Women Sales Managers
Agriculture	4.7%	0.0%
Banks	24.7	23.3
Business services	30.3	21.5
Chemicals	9.1	5.7
Communications	34.7	15.3
Construction	20.0	20.0
Electronic components	10.8	14.2
Electronics	19.6	5.4
Fabricated metals	5.9	10.3
Food products	28.5	43.8
Instruments	10.7	8.2
Insurance	27.4	14.0
Machinery	8.2	3.8
Manufacturing	17.6	6.8
Office equipment	24.1	7.4
Paper/allied products	1.8	12.5
Printing/publishing	38.9	23.2
Rubber/plastics	17.7	20.8
Wholesale (consumer)	19.5	4.8
Average	24.3%	14.3%

Source: Christen P. Heide, *Dartnell's 30th Sales Force Compensation Survey 1998–99* (Chicago: The Dartnell Corporation, 1999), p. 171.

Unfortunately, the existing research relevant to such questions is neither extensive nor conclusive. Few published studies have compared the job performance of minority salespeople with that of whites, or examined sales managers' attitudes or perceptions of minority salespeople. One reason for this lack of empirical evidence is that still relatively few minorities are employed in industrial selling. As a result, race could not be included as one of the demographic variables examined in the meta-analysis reported in Exhibit 10.6. However, many firms have been active and successful in recruiting minorities for their sales forces in recent years.

The experiences of these companies suggest that, given adequate training and solid company support, minority salespeople have no major difficulties gaining access to customers. Also, their job performance is not systematically different from that of the rest of the sales force. Furthermore, in some selling situations minority salespeople have performed better than whites. For example, some food companies, such as Armour, have found that minority salespeople are more effective than white salespeople in calling on retail stores in minority neighborhoods.

Recent demographic trends in the U.S. population indicate our country's labor force is becoming increasingly culturally diverse. As the discussion in the "Ethical Issues" box

The Implications of Increasing Cultural Diversity

The typical salesperson will be a bit more atypical in the years to come, according to a study conducted by Towers Perrin, a New York consulting firm, and the Hudson Institute, an Indianapolis research group. The study examined the reactions of 645 U.S. companies across a variety of industries to emerging work force issues such as the decline in the number of entry-level workers, the aging labor pool, and increasing cultural diversity.

According to the survey respondents, American managers in the next decade will be faced with an older, more culturally diverse work force that will be increasingly difficult to recruit and train. And Frank X. Dowd, a principal in the Stamford, Connecticut, office of Towers Perrin, says these trends will also hold true for sales forces. "Sales managers will no longer be able to find someone that fits the demographics of what they view as their ideal candidate," Dowd says. "They need to start taking a much broader view of who'll be working for them."

Even today, managers are facing an increasingly kaleidoscopic work force. One-fourth of the surveyed companies reported minority employment of 26 percent or more, and this figure is expected to increase substantially by the year 2000 when nearly one in three Americans will be from a minority group. To best respond to this trend, Dowd says sales managers should rethink the criteria they use in selecting new sales candidates. "Traditionally, managers selected their sales force so that it would match the demographics of their customers, with the idea that their similar backgrounds would stimulate interaction. Usually—especially in technical fields—this meant that the sales force would be predominantly white and male." Dowd argues that this rationale has to change. Since the new demographic trends will also affect their customers' work forces and purchasing departments, sales managers who do not anticipate this trend by changing the complexion of their sales forces are likely to find it harder to build close relationships with those customers.

Surprisingly, many firms appear to be slow in responding to these challenges. While 35 percent of the respondents report they are already having difficulty recruiting salespeople, only about one-fourth of the respondents are training supervisors in managing ethnically or culturally mixed groups of employees. A quarter of the companies state they are not at all concerned with cultural diversity in their organizations.

Similarly, more than half the respondents said they were unconcerned about the effects the "gray drain" would have on their sales forces. That lack of concern could have serious consequences as today's baby boomers get closer to retirement and the manpower to replace them isn't available. This blind spot is particularly surprising, says Dowd, given that companies could be taking measures now to ease the problem. For instance, nontraditional work patterns—things like using retirees on a part-time basis—are one answer to an aging work force. Some companies are beginning to get the message. About 30 percent of the study's respondents said they sometimes use retirees as consultants or on special projects. But only 3 percent currently offer retraining programs for older workers or gradual retirement plans to capitalize on older workers' knowledge and skills.

Team selling may also offer at least a partial solution to the problems created by an older and more culturally diverse work force. "Team selling," Dowd says, "reduces the reliance on the sales generalist and allows a company to match the task with available talent. For example, an organization may have a non–U.S.-born employee who is technically superior but who hasn't yet mastered presentation skills. Teaming this person with an outstanding sales type should lead to more productive sales calls."

Source: Jeffery D. Smith, "Radical Changes in Store for Workforce 2000," *Sales & Marketing Management* (November 1990), pp. 122–23.

suggests, these trends will present both challenges and opportunities for sales managers over the next decade.

As for saleswomen, the results in Exhibit 10.6 suggest sex is largely irrelevant for explaining differences in performance across salespeople. There is no evidence of consistent differences in the productivity of men and women in industrial sales. The attitudes of sales managers and industrial buyers toward women sales reps have also become more positive over the years.

While both men and women are seen as sharing the potential for sales success, however, both groups are still often perceived to have unique job requirements and concerns and special strengths that enable them to perform better on different aspects of the sales job. For instance, the etiquette involved in traveling with male colleagues or entertaining male clients can still pose uncertainties for some saleswomen.[13] Similarly, surveys suggest some sales managers and purchasing agents judge salesmen as being better than saleswomen on some dimensions of job performance, such as product knowledge and technical assistance, but perceive saleswomen to be superior on other attributes, including preparation for sales presentations and follow-through.[14]

One should view such generalizations concerning the comparative strengths and weaknesses of salesmen and saleswomen with caution, however. Both the meta-analysis results and other recent research suggest variations in sales performance are probably much greater within each group than between them. For instance, one recent study indicates saleswomen whose selling styles are judged to fit "female" gender stereotypes (e.g., have weak product knowledge, little technical aptitude, and low self-confidence, are un-aggressive and reluctant to "close") perform less well in some kinds of selling situations than saleswomen with more "masculine" styles. As the authors point out, many aspects of these gender-specific perceptions, such as product knowledge and self-confidence, can be modified through appropriate training, supervision, and company and peer support.[15] Thus, there appears to be little that is inherently and unalterably either "male" or "female" about any aspect of good sales performance.

Physical characteristics and customer similarity.   While demographic and physical attributes are not strongly related to sales performance in general, particular characteristics may enable a salesperson to deal more effectively with some types of customers than with others. Consequently, some research studies have taken a "dyadic" approach to try to explain variations in performance among salespeople.

Most of the studies test a very simple hypothesis: Salespeople are more likely to be successful when they are dealing with prospects who are similar to themselves in demographic characteristics, personality traits, and attitudes than when their prospects have characteristics different from their own. We tend to understand, have empathy for, and be attracted to other people more when they are like us. Therefore, a salesperson may be better able to understand a customer's problems and needs, communicate a sales message, and persuade the prospect to make a purchase when the rep has physical characteristics, personality traits, and attitudes similar to those of the prospect.[16]

The implications of this hypothesis seem simple and straightforward: Managers should hire salespeople with demographic and personality characteristics as similar as possible to those of the prospects upon whom they will be calling. However, there are two fundamental problems with this prescription. For one thing, it is often impossible to implement. Because buyers and purchasing agents come in all shapes and sizes and vary widely in characteristics, it can be difficult to match a salesperson's attributes with those of all or even most potential customers. And as we saw in our discussion of the thorny issue of cultural diversity, those customers are likely to become even more diverse in the future.

A second problem is that research has cast doubt on the validity of the similarity hypothesis. For example, one study found that only 2 percent of the variance in the amounts purchased by different customers could be explained by salesperson–customer similarity.[17] In view of such weak research support and the practical problems involved in implementation, choosing salespeople who have characteristics similar to those of their potential customers does not appear to be a viable method of sales force selection.

Background and experience

One of the surprises in the findings presented in Exhibit 10.6 is that personal history and family background variables are among the best predictors of sales success, accounting for an average of about 20 percent of the variance in performance across salespeople. This suggests that information about such things as whether a person held part-time jobs or had substantial family responsibilities as a youngster provides a good indication of likely emotional maturity and motivation. These traits, in turn, are important determinants of sales performance, particularly for young recruits.

Even more surprising, perhaps, is that some of the background factors on which sales managers most commonly rely when evaluating potential recruits—such as the person's educational attainment, course of study, and general work experience—do not show much relationship with sales performance. Even a person's past sales experience—a factor that receives primary emphasis in some firms' recruitment and selection—explains only about 3 percent of the variation in performance across salespeople. Indeed, one study suggests that prior experience with a company—but in nonsales jobs—may be a better predictor of future sales success.[18]

Current status and lifestyle variables

As was the case with personal history and family background, a person's current marital and family status, income level, and financial obligations (e.g., a large mortgage) also appear to reflect emotional maturity and motivation and are relatively good predictors of sales performance. Variables related to marital and family status account for about 12 percent of the variance in performance across salespeople, while those reflecting financial status explain about 5 percent of that variance. As we see later, though, these relationships are much stronger for some kinds of sales jobs than for others.

But the ways in which people spend their time outside of their jobs do not appear to be closely related to their likely performance as salespeople. Lifestyle and activity variables account for less than 2 percent of individual differences in sales performance.

Aptitude variables

Despite the variety of tests of sales aptitude developed specifically for selecting salespeople, such measures explain an average of only about 4 percent of differences in sales performance. Once again, however, the ability of sales aptitude measures to predict performance varies greatly across different types of sales jobs. We explore this in more detail in the next section of this chapter.

Most tests of general mental aptitude or abilities—such as general intelligence tests, measures of verbal ability and fluency, and tests of math ability—are all relatively uncorrelated with sales performance. But a person's ability to think logically and display flexibility in solving problems—an ability measured by tests of cognitive ability—is a relatively good indicator of likely success in selling. Cognitive ability measures explain nearly 7 percent of the variance in performance across salespeople.

Personality variables

More studies have attempted to explain variations in sales performance across salespeople by examining differences in their personality traits than any other personal characteristic. Also, much of the conventional wisdom to which sales managers and consultants have adhered over the years has stressed the importance of such personality traits as self-esteem, sociability, dominance, and a strong need for achievement as determinants of sales success. It is rather disappointing, then, to discover that individual personality traits explain an average of no more than 3 percent of the variation in salespeople's performance. However, some newer personality tests that focus on only a few broad, stable traits—such as extraversion, openness to experience, and conscientiousness—may be more strongly related to sales success.[19]

Skill variables

Vocational skills encompass a salesperson's acquired knowledge and abilities directly related to the company, its products, and customers. Not surprisingly, the more skill a salesperson has, the better the performance is likely to be. Vocational skills account on average for more than 9 percent of the variance in sales performance. It is also no surprise that differences in salespeople's skill at preparing and delivering good sales presentations can explain as much as 5 percent of the differences in their performance.

A more unexpected finding is that general management skills, such as organizational and leadership abilities, account for about 9 percent of the variance in performance across salespeople. Perhaps this shouldn't come as a surprise, though, given that many field salespeople have much freedom to manage their own time and to organize their own efforts within their territories. Also, some salespeople must work closely and coordinate their efforts with a customer's personnel to carry out such tasks as sales engineering, installation of equipment, and training of the customer's employees.

Finally, neither interpersonal skills related to understanding and getting along with people nor the salesperson's vocational esteem—the attitude toward the tasks and activities involved in selling—are strongly related to ultimate sales performance. Both of these findings run counter to the conventional wisdom offered by many authorities.

JOB-SPECIFIC DETERMINANTS OF GOOD SALES PERFORMANCE

Different types of sales jobs require salespeople to perform different tasks and activities under different circumstances. It would seem to make sense, then, to develop task-specific definitions of sales aptitude and ability, since the traits and skills needed to be successful in one type of sales job may be irrelevant to another. As discussed in Chapter 11, this kind of task-specific, or "contingency," approach is the one sales managers should use when determining what traits and abilities to look for in new sales recruits. Unfortunately, little published research is available to guide sales managers in deciding what personal characteristics are most important in enabling salespeople to perform well in specific types of sales jobs. Only two published studies have examined this issue across different types of selling jobs.[20] One was carried out as part of the meta-analysis discussed earlier. The other was a survey of a large sample of firms conducted some years ago. Both studies' findings are examined in the following sections.

Selling Different Types of Products and Services

The meta-analysis of previous research discussed in the preceding section found that the strength of the relationships between some personal characteristics and sales performance varied widely across studies. Some of the variation was because different studies examined samples of salespeople engaged in selling different types of products. Thus, a given trait might bear a strong relationship with performance in studies where the respondents were selling industrial goods to organizational customers, but the same trait might have only a weak relationship to performance in studies focused on people selling consumer goods or services.

Overall, seven of the subcategories of personal characteristics described in Exhibit 10.5 were found to be systematically different in their ability to explain variations in sales performance depending on the types of products being sold. Exhibit 10.8 summarizes these seven categories and the strength of their relationship to performance for different types of products.

Exhibit 10.8   Strength of Relationships between Selected Personal Characteristics and Salesperson Performance When Selling Different Types of Products*

Variables Affecting Performance	Type of Product Being Sold		
	Industrial Goods	Consumer Goods	Services†
Personal history and family background	Weak	Weak	Strong
Marital/family status	Weak	Moderate	Strong
Sales aptitude	Strong	Moderate	Weak
Dominance	Weak	Weak	Moderate
Self-esteem	Strong	Moderate	Moderate
Sales presentation skills	Strong	Moderate	Weak
Interpersonal skills	Moderate	Moderate	Weak

*Strong = the variable on average accounts for more than 9 percent of the variance in performance.

Moderate = the variable on average accounts for 4 to 9 percent of the variance in performance.

Weak = the variable on average accounts for less than 4 percent of the variance in performance.

†The services examined in past studies were primarily financial services sold to individual consumers, such as life insurance, banking, and brokerage services.

Source: Neil M. Ford, Orville C. Walker, Jr., and Gilbert A. Churchill, Jr., "Selecting Successful Salespeople: A Meta-Analysis of Biographical and Psychological Selection Criteria," in *Review of Marketing,* ed. Michael J. Houston (Chicago: American Marketing Association, 1988), pp. 90–131.

The findings in Exhibit 10.8 suggest that for people selling industrial goods to institutional customers, "professional" skills and traits—such as sales aptitude, sales presentation skills, interpersonal skills, and self-esteem—are relatively good predictors of successful performance. But for jobs involving the sale of services, such job-related skills appear to be relatively less important. Traits related to aggressiveness and motivation, such as a dominant personality and family obligations, are better indicators of success in selling services than they are for jobs involving either consumer or industrial goods.

Different Types of Sales Jobs

One survey directly compared the characteristics of successful and unsuccessful salespeople in specific sales jobs across a large number of organizations. In this study, responses were obtained from a sample of 1,029 sales executives in a variety of manufacturing, wholesaling, and service firms. These firms were classified according to the type of selling in which their salespeople were primarily engaged. The four categories of industrial sales jobs were used: (1) trade selling, (2) missionary selling, (3) technical selling, and (4) new business selling. The study then compared personal characteristics of successful and unsuccessful salespeople in each of the four kinds of sales jobs. The results of this survey are summarized in Exhibit 10.9 and discussed here.[21]

Trade selling

The primary responsibility of the trade sales force is to increase the volume of a firm's sales to its customers (usually wholesalers or retailers). It does this by providing them with merchandising and promotional assistance to help them become more effective at selling to their customers. The trade sales force sells through, rather than sells to, its customers. Trade selling is common in many industries, but it predominates in such consumer goods fields as food and apparel and in selling to wholesalers in general.

Exhibit 10.9   Characteristics Related to Sales Performance in Different Types of Sales Jobs

Type of Sales Job	Relatively Important Characteristics	Relatively Less Important Characteristics
Trade selling	Age, maturity, empathy, knowledge of customer and business methods	Aggressiveness, technical ability, product knowledge, persuasiveness
Missionary selling	Youth, high energy and stamina, verbal skill, persuasiveness	Empathy, knowledge of customers, maturity, previous sales experience
Technical selling	Education, product and customer knowledge—usually gained through training, intelligence	Empathy, persuasiveness, aggressiveness, age
New business selling	Experience, age and maturity, aggressiveness, persuasiveness, persistence	Customer knowledge, product knowledge, education, empathy

Products sold through trade selling tend to be well established; thus, a company's personal selling effort is often less important than its advertising and promotion efforts. The exception is when a new item is being introduced and the trade must be persuaded to stock it. Trade salespeople are usually not so highly pressured by management as salespeople in other fields, such as new business selling. However, the trade sales job can become dull and repetitive if it involves nothing but stocking shelves or taking orders, although this problem is becoming less prevalent due to increased use of computerized reordering systems.

Long-term personal relationships are critical for successful trade selling. The salesperson must have empathy and experience to understand customers. Technical competence is less important than getting along well with customers, and aggressiveness is less important than maturity. Consequently, successful trade salespeople tend to be older on the average than successful salespeople in other types of sales jobs.

Missionary selling

The primary responsibility of the missionary salesperson is to provide the firm's direct customers (wholesalers, retailers) with personal selling assistance. This is done by providing product information to indirect customers and persuading then to buy from the firm's direct customers. For example, a brewer's sales rep might call on bar owners and attempt to persuade them to order the company's brand from its local distributor.

Like trade selling, missionary selling is low key and low pressure, but it differs in its primary objective; the missionary force sells for its direct customers, whereas the trade sales force sells through them. This type of selling is common in many industries, particularly foods, pharmaceuticals, chemicals, transportation, and the utilities.

Good coverage of potential indirect customers and the ability to make a succinct, yet persuasive, presentation of product benefits is vitally important in missionary selling. Missionary salespeople tend to be more communicators and persuaders than problem solvers. Consequently, missionary salespeople should be energetic and articulate. They need not be particularly aggressive at closing sales because the people to whom they talk do not buy directly from them.

Also, while it helps to have a pleasing personality, missionary salespeople need not be particularly empathetic to customers because the development of long-term relationships is not so important. The lack of an opportunity to develop satisfying relationships with customers and the lack of intellectually challenging problem-solving activities are often cited as two unattractive aspects of the missionary sales job. In view of this, successful missionary sales forces tend to consist of young people with the energy and stamina to make a lot of calls. After a few years, such people commonly move into other marketing jobs or more challenging types of sales work.

Technical selling

The major job of the technical sales force is to increase the volume of sales to existing customers by providing them with technical advice and assistance. These salespeople sell directly to the firms that use their products. Technical selling is especially important in industries such as chemicals, machinery, and heavy equipment.

Technical selling is much like management consulting in that the ability to identify, analyze, and solve customer problems is vitally important. Technical competence and knowledge of both product and customer are necessary for such salespeople since they need to discover customer problems and then explain the product's benefits for solving the problems. However, too much aggressiveness can undermine the customer's confidence in the objectiveness of the salesperson. Because of the need for technical competence, the successful technical sales force tends to be relatively young, with a high proportion of recent college graduates. To provide product knowledge, successful firms give technical salespeople extensive training and company support.

New business selling

The primary responsibility of the new business sales force is to seek and persuade new customers to buy from the firm for the first time. Persuasiveness, aggressiveness, and persistence are important attributes for success. The greatest difficulty in new business selling is the frequent rejection, and consequent deflation of the ego, that salespeople experience. Young, inexperienced people typically do not perform well in this kind of selling; they are too easily discouraged and their turnover rate is very high. Consequently, successful new business salespeople tend to be older persons with substantial sales experience. They like the challenge and independence from supervision that goes along with "cold canvassing" potential new accounts.

IMPLICATIONS FOR SALES MANAGEMENT

What has this review of the wisdom accumulated through experience and published research taught us about the personal characteristics that are related to sales aptitude and the potential for selling success? For one thing, no general physical characteristics, mental abilities, or personality traits appear to be consistently related to sales aptitude and performance in all companies and selling situations. Also, the evidence suggests it is probably neither wise nor practical for a sales manager to try to select salespeople with characteristics that match those of their potential customers. (The possible exception is in retail selling.) Instead, the most potentially useful approach to defining sales aptitude and evaluating a person's potential is first to determine the kinds of tasks involved in a specific sales job. Then, one can evaluate the relevance of particular characteristics and abilities for enabling a person to carry out those tasks successfully.

Unfortunately, few published studies have either analyzed the tasks and activities unique to particular types of selling or identified the personal traits and abilities important for success in different sales jobs. For the time being, then, sales executives must develop their own specifications concerning what to look for in new sales recruits. Those specifications should be developed after a careful analysis and description of the tasks and activities involved in selling the firm's products to its target market. There should also be an evaluation of the characteristics and qualifications that new salespeople must have to perform those tasks and activities. Therefore, Chapter 11 examines the methods and procedures involved in sales force recruitment and selection. It begins with a discussion of how to carry out a job analysis and develop a list of qualifications to use in evaluating recruits.

SUMMARY

This chapter, the first of two dealing with salesperson selection, sought to review the evidence regarding what personal and psychological characteristics are related to an individual's likely performance as a salesperson. Personal traits and aptitude are typically thought to place an upper limit on an individual's ability to perform a given sales job.

Several sets of personal factors are thought to affect a salesperson's ability to perform, including the following:

1. **Demographic and physical characteristics**—such as age, sex, and physical appearance.

2. **Background and experience factors**—such as a person's personal history and family background, educational attainment, and sales experience.

3. **Current status and lifestyle variables**—including a person's marital and financial status and activities outside of the job.

4. **Aptitude variables**—enduring mental characteristics such as intelligence, cognitive abilities, and sales aptitude.

5. **Personality traits**—including such characteristics as sociability, dominance, and self-esteem.

6. **Skill levels**—learned proficiencies, such as vocational skills (e.g., product knowledge), interpersonal skills, sales presentation skills, and general management skills.

Although a number of reasons can be advanced as to why these factors might be related to sales performance, the available evidence suggests that none is consistently related to performance when examined across industries and job settings.

One of the more persuasive reasons for these inconsistent relationships is that particular characteristics of salespeople enable them to deal more effectively with some kinds of customers than with others. Consequently, some studies have used a dyadic approach to explain variations in performance among salespeople. The basic hypothesis is that salespeople are more likely to be successful when they deal with prospects who are similar to themselves in terms of demographic characteristics, personality traits, and attitudes. The implication of the dyadic perspective for sales managers is that they should hire salespeople with characteristics similar to the customers on whom they will call. But such a strategy can be hard to implement in industrial selling, and it is likely to become even more difficult as both sales recruits and customer organizations become more culturally diverse. Also, the existing research evidence does not consistently support the proposition.

The most important conclusion regarding salespeople selection is that there are many different types of selling jobs. Each type requires the salesperson to perform a variety of different tasks and activities under different circumstances. Consequently, the most useful approach to defining sales aptitude and evaluating a person's potential for future success is, first, to determine the kinds of tasks involved in a specific sales job. Then, one can evaluate the relevance of particular characteristics and abilities for enabling a person to carry out those tasks successfully.

DISCUSSION QUESTIONS

1. Is there any scientific evidence to support the contention that men and women have different selling styles and different levels of selling ability? What is required for evidence to be considered scientific?

2. Mark and Cynthia had just finished a long session that produced a heated discussion concerning hiring people who are overweight. Mark stressed that overweight people are considered lazy, sloppy, and lacking in self-

esteem. He insisted that no sales manager would overlook these features and hire such a person. "What a waste of money since customers don't want to do business with a tubbo," argued Mark.

Cynthia countered with equal conviction, accusing Mark of stereotyping all people who are overweight. She asked Mark if he knew that for some people the problem was genetic and not overindulgence. "Besides," she stressed, "not hiring someone because of their weight just happens to be illegal. "She recited a line from Dickens's *Pickwick Papers*, 'You'll find that as you get wider you'll get wiser. Width and wisdom . . . always grow together.' "

Is it legal not to hire a person because of his or her weight?

3. An article in *Sales & Marketing Management* (July 1988, p. 80) discusses women in sales. William O'Connell, partner in Personnel Corporation of America, discusses the phenomenal increase of women in sales and attributes part of this increase to the more equitable compensation practices that reward people based on quantitative measures of performance (e.g., sales volume). *S&MM* laments that "Women are not enjoying sales success across the board—there is an alarming disparity in their ability to secure sales jobs on an industry basis." O'Connell notes that women are securing jobs where the buyers are predominantly female; and where the buyers are predominantly male, men are hired. What are the dangers of this situation? Will it lead to a "pink ghetto" in sales for women, similar to the situation where blacks and Hispanics are hired to call only on stores in ghetto neighborhoods?

4. Enthusiasm is one of the more important attributes sales executives look for in new salespeople. How would you measure or determine whether an applicant possessed enthusiasm? If an applicant lacks enthusiasm but shows a positive interest in sales, would it be possible to "teach" enthusiasm?

5. The sales manager of a company manufacturing metal castings attempts to hire salespeople based on the personalities of the customers. The sales manager uses the same process when assigning salespeople to customers. In other words, the similarity hypothesis discussed earlier is being applied. Does this process make sense? Does this procedure agree with contingency theory?

6. The following brief appeared in "Selling Is in Their Blood," *Sales & Marketing Management* (February 1987, p. 68): Some Japanese companies now recruit executives based on their blood type. A new theory suggests that basic personality traits can be linked to the four major blood types. People with Type O are said to be born leaders, Type A are deep thinkers, Type B are creative, and Type AB are problem-solvers. Some job ads now state, "Only those with Type A or B should apply." What evidence is needed to establish that blood type should be used to determine hiring preferences?

EXPERIENTIAL APPLICATION

Identify a small sample of companies such as retailers, insurance companies, automobile dealers, manufacturers, and others. Interview managers responsible for recruiting, hiring, and training salespeople and ask them to identify the three most important factors or characteristics that they feel are related to sales performance. Do your results vary across different types of selling positions?

INTERNET EXERCISE

Go to the DHL USA Web site (*www.dhl-usa.com*) and click on human resources. Read about the culture at DHL and consider what personal characteristics would be important for a new sales recruit at the company. How might those characteristics be different from those of a candidate at Compaq computer (*www.compaq.com*)?

SUGGESTED READINGS

Determinants of Sales Performance

Bragg, Arthur, "Are Good Salespeople Born or Made?" *Sales & Marketing Management* (September 1988), pp. 74–78.

Challagalla, Goutam N., and Tasaddug A. Shervani, "Dimensions and Types of Supervisory Control: Effects on Sales Performance and Satisfaction," *Journal of Marketing* (January 1996), pp. 47–60.

Churchill, Gilbert A., Jr., Neil M. Ford, Steven W. Hartley, and Orville C. Walker, Jr., "The Determinants of Salesperson Performance: A Meta-Analysis," *Journal of Marketing Research* (May 1985), pp. 103–18.

Ford, Neil M., Orville C. Walker, Jr., and Gilbert A. Churchill, Jr., "Selecting Successful Salespeople: A Meta-Analysis of Biographical and Psychological Selection Criteria," in *Review of Marketing,* ed. Michael J. Houston. Chicago: American Marketing Association, 1988, pp. 90–131.

Weilbaker, Dan C., "The Identification of Selling Abilities Needed for Missionary Type Sales," *Journal of Personal Selling and Sales Management* (Summer 1990), pp. 45–58.

Women and Cultural Diversity

Arnott, Nancy, "It's a Woman's World," *Sales & Marketing Management* (March 1995), pp. 54–59.

Comer, Lucette B., and Marvin A. Jolson, "Perceptions of Gender Stereotypic Behavior: An Exploratory Study of Women in Selling," *Journal of Personal Selling and Sales Management* (Winter 1991), pp. 43–59.

Comer, Lucette B., J.A.F. Nicholls, and Leslie J. Vermillion, "Diversity in the Sales Force: Problems and Challenges," *Journal of Personal Selling and Sales Management* (Fall 1998), pp. 1–20.

Shepherd, C. David, and James C. Heartfield, "Discrimination Issues in the Selection of Salespeople: A Review and Managerial Suggestions," *Journal of Personal Selling and Sales Management* (Fall 1991), pp. 67–75.

Sigua, Judy A., and Earl D. Honeycutt, Jr., "An Examination of Gender Differences in Selling Behaviors and Job Attitudes," *Industrial Marketing Management* 24 (1995), pp. 45–52.

Smith, Jeffery D., "Radical Changes in Store for Workforce 2000," *Sales & Marketing Management* (November 1990), pp. 122–23.

II Sales Force Recruitment and Selection

INTEL BUILDS A POWERFUL SALES FORCE

Intel, the powerhouse computer chip manufacturer with sales over $21 billion, has played an essential role in redefining computing in the 21st century. With the ability to manufacturer 70 million chips a year (and plans to add even more capacity) Intel dominates the competition. By comparison, Advanced Micro Devices can manufacture only 4 million chips and Cyrix 1.5 million. The industry is characterized by nearly continuous innovation, producing ever more powerful chips at a great deal of price pressure. Advanced Micro Devices routinely prices its chips 25 to 50 percent below Intel, which constrains Intel's ability to hold prices for a very long time even on the latest technology. As a result, Intel continues to be the market leader in R&D spending while at the same time maintaining a very price competitive position in the marketplace.

A key to the success of Intel has been the 1,000-person sales force recently rated as the number three sales force by *Sales & Marketing Management*. Intel has a very "results oriented" approach to conducting its business, which is carried over to the sales force. Ed Bauer, vice president and director of Americas sales and marketing, puts it this way: "I measure success first by results. Intel prides itself on a planning process that sets very aggressive objectives. Next comes confidence in the ability of our sales force to communicate our technology initiatives. Then, all of that is measured in terms of feedback from our customers—are we satisfying the customer?"

Recruiting Intel Reps

A number of factors influence the kind of people Intel recruits to be a part of its highly successful sales team. Not surprisingly, the potential Intel rep needs to be comfortable with technology. He or she needs to be enthusiastic about using technology and, even more importantly, must be able to communicate that excitement to the customer. Bauer takes a long-term strategic perspective in defining key qualifications for an Intel Rep. "The products we sell are fundamentally impacting the way the world conducts business and the way consumers use their free time. So [our salespeople] have to be as enthusiastic about using the technology as they are about communicating it."

Intel often looks for individuals with advanced degrees. Nearly half of the sales force has an MBA or other type of master's degree. Intel believes that a strong educational foundation is critical in its rapidly changing competitive environment. In addition, Intel seeks out new recruits with engineering or computer science backgrounds. The focus is on hiring the best and brightest people capable of communicating the enthusiasm of computing and Intel computer chips.

Training and Motivation

However, Intel does not rely solely on hiring the right kind of people. The sales force is backed up with a strong commitment to continuing education. University-style classroom training consisting of week-long seminars are available to salespeople all year long. Due to the highly innovative nature of Intel products, salespeople must work with clients to help understand how Intel products can be used to help the customers do a better job. Intel believes that providing their salespeople with a wide range of courses (they offer 50 to 100 courses a year) is a critical element in preparing them for successfully dealing with their clients. Kurt Oppenhiemer, regional applications manager at Intel, discusses how important training is at Intel: "There are various degrees of selling. We've been working to go beyond the simple order-taker and really be a business partner to our customers."

Intel also believes that communication plays an important role in training and motivation. The company provides each salesperson with a laptop capable of receiving data in real time from a satellite network. The goal is to enhance the communications with its sales force and, even more importantly, its customers. In-house videoteleconferencing provides an additional communication instrument that sales people and managers use to communicate with each other and is often used for remote training sessions.

Improved Results

No one can argue with Intel's results. The company has consistently reported double-digit growth. It often ends up on any list of best sales forces. Finally, the company has no shortage of applicants. Intel has developed a reputation, much like Microsoft, that encourages the best and brightest to apply. As a result, the pool of applicants is full of highly qualified and motivated individuals wishing to become part of the Intel sales team.

Source: "America's Best Sales Forces," *Sales & Marketing Management* (July 1998), pp. 32–51; Intel Web site, *www.intel.com.*

LEARNING OBJECTIVES

Perhaps more than any other function of the sales manager, successfully recruiting new salespeople into the company is critical to the long-term success of the organization. As markets expand both domestically and internationally, companies continue to seek qualified new candidates to fill sales positions. At the same time talented people in your own organization are being recruited, often by competitors, and leaving for other opportunities. Finally, competition for talented candidates is fierce and the cost of poor recruiting is high (in both direct and indirect costs). For all these reasons, recruiting and selecting salespeople has become a very important part of the sales manager's job. This chapter will outline the process of recruiting new salespeople into the organizations.

At the end of this chapter you should be able to:

- Understand the key issues that drive the recruitment and selection of salespeople.
- Identify who is responsible for the recruitment and selection process.
- Understand a job analysis and how selection criteria are determined.
- Define the sources for new sales recruits.
- Explain the selection procedures.
- Understand the equal opportunity requirements for selecting salespeople.

Exhibit 11.1 The Decision Process for Recruiting and Selecting Salespeople

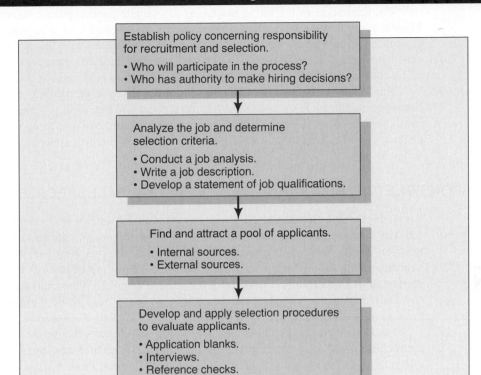

Establish policy concerning responsibility
for recruitment and selection.

• Who will participate in the process?
• Who has authority to make hiring decisions?

Analyze the job and determine
selection criteria.

• Conduct a job analysis.
• Write a job description.
• Develop a statement of job qualifications.

Find and attract a pool of applicants.

• Internal sources.
• External sources.

Develop and apply selection procedures
to evaluate applicants.

• Application blanks.
• Interviews.
• Reference checks.
• Formal tests.

RECRUITMENT AND SELECTION ISSUES

The Intel example illustrates the variety of important issues that must be resolved when recruiting and selecting new salespeople. These issues are diagrammed in Exhibit 11.1.

The first decision to be made concerns who in the company will have the responsibility for hiring new salespeople. While it is common to assign this responsibility to field sales managers, top sales executives or personnel departments play a more active role and bear more of the burden for this important function in some firms.

Regardless of who has the responsibility for recruiting new sales reps, certain procedures should be followed to ensure that the new recruits have the aptitude for the job and the potential to be successful. As discussed in Chapter 10, there do not seem to be any general characteristics that make some people better performers across all types of sales jobs. Therefore, the starting point in the recruitment process should be a thorough analysis of the job to be filled and a description of the qualifications that a new hire should have.

The next step is to find and attract a pool of job applicants with the qualifications for which the firm is looking. The objective, in other words, usually is not to maximize the number of job applicants but to attract a few good applicants. This is because of the high costs involved in attracting and evaluating candidates. For instance, a large industrial services firm estimates that it spent more than $750,000 for want ads, employment agency fees, psychological tests, and the time sales managers spent interviewing and evaluating candidates in order to hire 50 new salespeople. And it cost another $1 million to train those new recruits.

The final stage in the hiring process is to evaluate each applicant through personal history information, interviews, reference checks, and formal tests. The purpose is to determine which applicants have the characteristics and abilities most likely to lead to success. During this stage of the evaluation and selection process, managers must be especially careful not to violate equal employment opportunity laws and regulations.

The remaining sections of this chapter discuss the specific methods and procedures managers might use at each stage of the recruitment and selection process. Although the primary focus is on "how to do it" from a manager's point of view, some material in this chapter should be useful for learning what is expected if you ever apply for a sales job.

WHO IS RESPONSIBLE FOR RECRUITING AND SELECTING SALESPEOPLE?

Several years ago, an MBA student at one of the authors' schools was recruited for a sales job with a major manufacturer of outdoor and garden equipment. She was interviewed extensively and wined and dined, not only by the sales manager, who was her prospective supervisor, but also by higher-level executives in the firm, including the vice president of marketing. All this attention from top-level managers surprised the candidate. "After all," she said, "it's only a sales job. Is it common for so many executives to be involved in recruiting new salespeople?"

The student's question raises the issue of who should have the primary responsibility for recruiting and selecting new salespeople. The way in which a company answers this question typically depends on the size of the sales force and the kind of selling involved. In firms with small sales forces, the top-level sales manager commonly views the recruitment and selection of new people as a primary responsibility. In larger, multilevel sales forces, however, the job of attracting and choosing new recruits is usually too extensive and time-consuming for a single executive. In such firms, authority for recruitment and selection is commonly delegated to lower-level sales managers or staff specialists.

In companies where the sales job is not very difficult or complex, new recruits do not need any special qualifications, and turnover rates in the sales force are high—as in firms that sell consumer goods door to door—first-level sales managers often have sole responsibility for hiring. When a firm must be more selective in choosing new recruits with certain qualifications and abilities, however, a recruiting specialist may assist first-level managers in evaluating new recruits and making hiring decisions. These staff positions are usually filled by sales managers who are being groomed for higher-level executive positions.

In some firms, members of the personnel department—or outside personnel specialists—assist and advise sales managers in hiring new salespeople instead of assigning such duties to a member of the sales management staff. This approach helps reduce duplication of effort and avoids friction between the sales and personnel departments. One disadvantage is that personnel specialists may not be as knowledgeable about the job to be filled and the qualifications necessary as a member of the sales management staff. When the personnel department or outside specialist is involved in sales recruiting and hiring, they usually help attract applicants and aid in evaluating them. The sales manager, however, typically has the final responsibility for deciding whom to hire.

Finally, when the firm sees its sales force as a training ground for sales and marketing managers, either personnel executives or other top-level managers may participate in recruiting to ensure the new hires have management potential. This was the situation in the firm that interviewed our MBA student. Although it wanted to hire her for "just a sales job," company executives saw that job as a stepping stone to management responsibilities.

JOB ANALYSIS AND DETERMINATION OF SELECTION CRITERIA

Research relating salespeople's personal characteristics to sales aptitude and job performance suggests there is no single set of traits and abilities sales managers can use as criteria in deciding what kind of recruits to hire. Different sales jobs require the performance of different activities, and this suggests people with different personality traits and abilities should be hired to fill them. The first activities in the recruitment and selection process thus should be the following:

1. *Conduct a job analysis* to determine what activities, tasks, responsibilities, and environmental influences are involved in the job to be filled.

2. *Write a job description* that details the findings of the job analysis.

3. *Develop a statement of job qualifications* that determines and describes the personal traits and abilities a person should have to perform the tasks and responsibilities involved in the job.

Job Analysis and Description

Most companies—particularly larger ones—have written job descriptions for sales force positions. Unfortunately, often those job descriptions are out of date and do not accurately reflect the current scope and content of the positions. The responsibilities of a given sales job change as the customers, the firm's account management policies, the competition, and other environmental factors change. But firms often do not conduct new analyses and prepare updated descriptions to reflect those changes. Also, firms create new sales positions, and the tasks to be accomplished by people in these jobs may not be spelled out. Consequently, a critical first step in the hiring process is for management to make sure the job to be filled has been analyzed recently and the findings have been written out in great detail. Without such a detailed and up-to-date description, the sales manager will have more difficulty deciding what kind of person is needed. In addition, prospective recruits will not really know for what position they are applying.

Who conducts the analysis and prepares the description?

In some firms, analyzing and describing sales jobs are assigned to someone in sales management. In other firms, the task is assigned to a job analysis specialist, who is either someone from the company's personnel department or an outside consultant. Regardless of who is responsible for analyzing and describing the various selling positions within a company, however, it is important that the person collect information about the job's content from two sources: (1) the current occupants of the job and (2) the sales managers who supervise the people in the job.

Current job occupants should be observed and/or interviewed to determine what they actually do. Sales managers at various levels should be asked what they think the job occupant should be doing in view of the firm's strategic sales program and account management policies. It is not uncommon for the person who analyzes a job to discover the salespeople are doing things of which management is not aware and they are "slacking off" on some activities management believes are important. Such misunderstandings and inaccurate role perceptions illustrate the need for accurate and detailed job descriptions.[1]

Job descriptions written to reflect a consensus between salespeople and their managers concerning what a job should entail can serve several useful functions in addition to guiding the firm's recruiting efforts. They can guide the design of a sales training program that will provide new salespeople with the skills to do their job effectively and that will improve their understanding of how the job should be done. Similarly, detailed job descriptions can serve as standards for evaluating each salesperson's job performance, as discussed in Chapter 16. W.S. Reed (a manufacturer of office products in Michigan) presents a job description to each sales candidate that includes six areas: objectives/goals, leadership, professional development, account responsibility, customer responsibility, and business activity responsibility. Candidates are often asked to sign the job description so that both candidate and company understand and agree on what is expected. While unusual, it is extremely beneficial to the probability of long-term success for the candidate if both the company and potential salesperson know exactly what the expectations are *before* employment.

Content of the job description

Good descriptions of sales jobs typically cover the following dimensions and requirements:

1. *The nature of product(s) or service(s) to be sold.*
2. *The types of customers to be called on,* including the policies concerning the frequency with which calls are to be made and the types of personnel within customer organizations who should be contacted (e.g., buyers, purchasing agents, plant supervisors).
3. *The specific tasks and responsibilities to be carried out,* including planning tasks, research and information collection activities, specific selling tasks, other promotional duties, customer servicing activities, and clerical and reporting duties.
4. *The relationships between the job occupant and other positions within the organization.* To whom does the job occupant report? What are the salesperson's responsibilities to the immediate superior? How and under what circumstances does the salesperson interact with members of other departments, such as production or engineering?
5. *The mental and physical demands of the job,* including the amount of technical knowledge the salesperson should have concerning the company's products, other necessary skills, and the amount of travel involved.
6. *The environmental pressures and constraints that might influence performance of the job,* such as market trends, the strengths and weaknesses of the competition, the company's reputation among customers, and resource and supply problems.

An example of a job description that addresses most of these job dimensions is presented in Exhibit 11.2.

Determining Job Qualifications and Selection Criteria

Determining the qualifications a prospective employee should have to perform a given sales job is the most difficult part of the recruitment and selection process. The sales manager—perhaps with assistance from a manpower planning specialist or a vocational psychologist—should consider the relative importance of all the personal traits and characteristics discussed previously. These include physical attributes, mental abilities and experience, and personality traits.

The problem is that nearly all these characteristics are of at least some importance in choosing new salespeople. No firm, for instance, would actively seek sales recruits who are unintelligent or lacking in self-confidence. It is unlikely that many job candidates will possess high levels of all these desirable characteristics. The task, then, is to decide which traits and abilities are most important in qualifying an individual for a particular job and

Exhibit 11.2   Job Description

JOB TITLE	JOB CODE
SALES REPRESENTATIVE—BUSINESS DIVISION (BD)	

ESTABLISHMENT—DEPARTMENT	DATE
MARKETING BD SALES	

Function

Promotes and consummates the sale of office systems and related equipment, paper, accessories, and other supplies within an assigned geographic territory, for the Business Division.

Major Activities

A. Establishes and maintains close liaison between the company and customers within an assigned geographic territory, for the ultimate purpose of selling Business Division products.

B. Establishes and maintains a working rapport with customers by providing expertise in the analysis of systems problems and the application of BD products and services to the solution of these problems.

C. Provides service to customers by recommending changes in operating procedures, assisting them in planning for office systems applications, recommending equipment purchases and supervising their installation, suggesting methods of quality control, and checking to determine that equipment and systems function properly.

D. Provides accurate and timely information on office products and demonstrates to customers the benefits derived from utilizing these products in his or her business. Keeps customers and prospects updated on new products and office systems.

E. Assists customers in achieving the high-quality capabilities of the company's office products.

F. Prepares a variety of reports and correspondence including data reports on activities, expenses, market acceptance of office products, product problems, market needs, etc.

G. Studies customers' systems needs and formulates written proposals to satisfy these with the general philosophies established by BD. Outlines systems recommendations incorporating products in customer proposals, cites advantages and operating cost reductions resulting from the proposed system.

H. Maintains a thorough familiarity of the products of other manufacturers to deal with questions posed by customers and prospects in daily activities.

I. Participates in and/or originates customer seminars and education programs by instructing customers and their personnel in the capabilities of office systems and the proper application and operation of BD products. Provides information and assistance at trade shows and exhibits to interested persons.

J. Keeps abreast of the new developments and trends in office equipment and systems to be capable of understanding customer needs and to be better prepared to provide workable solutions to customer systems requirements.

K. Handles product complaints and makes recommendations to the marketing center regarding goodwill replacements of products.

L. Advises district, and/or regional, and/or BD management of any information pertinent to BD activities gathered as a result of observations made in the field. Reports include new systems applications, activities of other manufacturers, equipment modifications and improvements, customer needs, etc.

M. Follows up on all sales leads as quickly as possible. Makes new calls on potential customers to stimulate interest in BD products.

N. Plans activities in a manner that provides for adequate territory coverage. Allocates time on the basis of maximum potential yield and/or priorities established by the district sales manager.

Scope of the Position

A. Accountability

   1. Reports to the district sales manager of the marketing center to which assigned. May direct the activities of less experienced sales representatives assigned to assist on a project basis or for training and development purposes.

   2. Responsible for reviewing unusual complex and/or sensitive problems, proposals, or controversial matters with supervision before taking any action. Manages the assigned territory with considerable independence.

(continued)

Exhibit 11.2   Job Description (concluded)

3. The assigned territory is in the middle range in relation to others in the region in overall dollar accountability, and/or customers have complex installations with sophisticated systems and product applications with which the sales representative must be familiar.

4. Responsible for having a thorough knowledge of all BD products and services and is capable of effectively analyzing, from a systems viewpoint, customers' problems and needs in developing new business by demonstrating the capabilities of Business Division products to satisfy these needs.

5. Is capable of independently meeting expected sales goals for all categories of products in the assigned territories.

6. Responsible for submitting knowledgeable reports on emerging trends in the marketplace, market needs, and ideas for new products that demonstrate a thorough understanding of the company's position in the marketplace and the direction it must pursue to maintain and improve this position.

7. Shows increasing expertise and professionalism in customer contracts, diagnosis of customers' needs, analysis of systems, preparation and presentation of proposals for new systems based on sound economic evaluations.

8. Is expected to exhibit maturity and competence in running the assigned territory with a minimum of direction. Has demonstrated the ability of developing large accounts, multiple sales, etc.

B. Innovation
1. Has a thorough understanding of the capabilities of other manufacturers' products and effectively uses this information to serve customers' needs.

2. Demonstrates originality and creativity in solving systems problems and meeting needs of the market.

3. Responsible for consistently aiding customers by disseminating information on new methods, systems, and techniques that are applicable to their operations.

Job Knowledge

A. Has a college degree or the equivalent in applicable training and experience.

B. Requires completion of the basic BD training program.

C. Requires a thorough knowledge of all billing, credit, and distribution procedures, paperwork, and policies and is capable of resolving complex problems in these areas with a minimum of confusion, frustration, and inconvenience for all parties concerned.

D. This level of activity is generally achieved with four years' selling experience, or the equivalent, with the assigned products where the individual is subjected to all types of problems and challenges covering the entire product line.

WRITTEN BY	APPROVED	DATE	APPROVED	DATE

which are less critical. Also, some thought should be given to trade-offs among the qualification criteria. Will a person with a deficiency in one important attribute still be considered acceptable if he or she has outstanding qualities in other areas? For example, will the firm be willing to hire someone with only average verbal ability and persuasiveness if that person has an extremely high degree of ambition and persistence?

Methods for deciding on selection criteria

Decisions about the qualifications that should be looked for in selecting new employees can often be made by simply *examining the job description*. If the job requires extensive travel, for instance, management might look for applicants who are young, have few family responsibilities, and want to travel. Similarly, statements in the job description concerning technical knowledge and skill can help management determine the educational background and previous job experience to look for when selecting hires.

Most larger firms go one step further and *evaluate the personal histories of their existing salespeople* to determine what characteristics differentiate between good and poor performers. As seen in Chapter 10, this analysis seldom produces consistent results across different jobs and different companies. It can produce useful insight, however, when applied to a single type of sales job within a single firm.

Current sales employees might be divided into two groups according to their level of performance on the job—one group of high performers and one group of low performers. The characteristics of the two groups can be compared on the basis of information from job application forms, records of personal interviews, and intelligence, aptitude, and personality test scores. Alternatively, statistical techniques might be used to look for significant correlations between variations in the personal characteristics of current salespeople and variations in their job performance. In either case, management attempts to identify personal attributes that differ significantly between high-performing and low-performing salespeople. The assumption is that there may be a cause-and-effect relationship between such attributes and job performance. If new employees are selected who have attributes similar to those of people who are currently performing the job successfully, they also may be successful.[2]

In addition to improving management's ability to specify relevant criteria in selecting new salespeople, a firm should conduct a personnel history analysis for another compelling reason. Such analyses are necessary to validate the selection criteria the firm is using, as required by government regulations on equal employment opportunity in hiring. This issue is discussed later in this chapter.

Besides comparing the characteristics of good and poor performers in a particular job, management might also try to *analyze the unique characteristics of employees who have failed*—people who either quit or were fired. One consulting firm, the Klein Institute for Aptitude Testing, suggests that the following characteristics are frequently found among salespeople who fail:

1. Instability of residence.
2. Failure in business within the past two years.
3. Unexplained gaps in the person's employment record.
4. Recent divorce or marital problems.
5. Excessive personal indebtedness; for example, bills could not be paid within two years from earnings on the new job.

The firm might attempt to identify such characteristics among its own sales failures by conducting exit interviews with all salespeople who quit or are fired. Although this sounds like a good idea, it seldom works well in practice. Salespeople who quit are often reluctant to discuss the real reasons for leaving a job, and people who are fired are not likely to cooperate in any research that will be of value to their former employer. However, some useful information about ex-salespeople can often be obtained from the application forms and test scores recorded when they were hired. They may also have spoken with the managers who were their supervisors at the time they left the company.

On the basis of these kinds of information, a written statement of job qualifications should be prepared that is specific enough to guide the selection of new salespeople. These qualifications can then be reflected in the forms and tests used in the selection process, such as the interview form in Exhibit 11.3.[3]

RECRUITING APPLICANTS

Some firms do not actively recruit salespeople. They simply choose new employees from applicants who come to them and ask for work. Although this may be a satisfactory policy for a few well-known firms with good products, strong positions in the market, and at-

Exhibit 11.3   Applicant Interview Form

Business Division
Applicant Interview Form

Applicant name: _____   Date: _____

Interview with: Time:

1. _____   _____

2. _____   _____

3. _____   _____

4. _____   _____

Rating:
5—Excellent
4—Above average
3—Average
2—Fair
1—Poor

Directions: Check square that most correctly reflects characteristics applicable to candidate. An outstanding candidate would score 95 to 100.

	1	2	3	4	5
General appearance					
1. Neatness, dress					
2. Business image					
Impressions					
3. Positive mannerisms					
4. Speech, expressions					
5. Outgoing personality					
6. Positive attitude					
Potential sales ability					
7. Persuasive communication					
8. Aggressiveness					
9. Sell and manage large accounts					
10. Make executive calls					
11. Organize and manage a territory					
12. Work with others					
13. Successful prior experience					
14. Potential for career growth					
Maturity					
15. General intelligence, common sense					
16. Self-confidence					
17. Self-motivation, ambition					
18. Composure, stability					
19. Adaptability					
20. Sense of ethics					

General comments: _____
_____

Overall rating (total score): _____

Would you recommend this candidate for the position? _____

Why or why not? _____

tractive compensation policies, today's labor market makes such an approach unworkable for most companies.

Firms that seek well-educated people for industrial sales jobs must compete with many other occupations in attracting such individuals. To make matters worse, people with no selling experience often tend to have negative attitudes toward sales jobs. Also, the kinds of people who do seek employment in sales often do not have the qualifications a firm is looking for, particularly when the job involves relatively sophisticated selling, such as technical or new business sales. Consequently, the company may have to evaluate many applicants to find one qualified person.

This is one area where some firms are "penny-wise but pound-foolish." They attempt to hold down recruiting costs on the assumption that a good training program can convert marginal recruits into solid sales performers. As we saw in the last chapter, however, some of the determinants of sales success, such as aptitude and personal characteristics, are difficult or impossible to change through training or experience. Therefore, spending the money and effort to find well-qualified candidates can be a profitable investment.[4]

In view of the difficulties in attracting qualified people to fill sales positions, a well-planned and effectively implemented recruiting effort is usually a crucial part of the firm's hiring program. The primary objective of the recruiting process should not be to maximize the total number of job applicants. Too many recruits can overload the selection process, forcing the manager to use less thorough screening and evaluation procedures. Besides, numbers do not ensure quality. The focus should not be on how many recruits can be found, but on finding a few good ones.

Therefore, the recruiting process should be designed to be the first step in the selection process. Self-selection by the prospective employees is the most efficient means of selection. The recruiting effort should be implemented in a way that discourages unqualified people from applying. To accomplish this, recruiting communications should point out both the attractive and unattractive aspects of the job to be filled, spell out the qualifications, and state the likely compensation. This will help ensure that only qualified and interested people apply for the job. Also, recruiting efforts should be focused only on sources of potential applicants where fully qualified people are most likely to be found.

Sales managers can go to a number of places to find recruits or leads concerning potential recruits. Internal sources consist of other people already employed in other departments within the firm, while external sources include people in other firms (who are often identified and referred by current members of the sales force), educational institutions, advertisements, and employment agencies.

Each source is likely to produce candidates with somewhat different backgrounds and characteristics. Therefore, while most firms seek recruits from more than one source, a company's recruiting efforts should be concentrated on sources that are most likely to produce the kinds of people needed. A survey of 113 firms found that companies use different sources for finding recruits depending on the type of sales job they are trying to fill. When the job involves missionary or trade selling, firms rely most heavily on a variety of external sources, such as advertisements, employment agencies, and educational institutions. When the job involves technical selling requiring substantial product knowledge and industry experience, firms focus more heavily on employees in other departments within the company and on personal referrals of people working for other firms in the industry.[5] The relative advantages and limitations of each of these sources of new recruits are discussed in more depth in the following sections.

All of the recruiting issues faced by sales managers are magnified as companies expand globally and seek to hire salespeople in new international markets. Cultural differences, language barriers, and legal restrictions create additional concerns about hiring the

Most sales professionals consider it impossible to build long-term success in a new international market without incorporating local talent in the sales function. While it is common for companies to send in trained salespeople to help with key accounts or start up new markets, the long-run success of a company's sales efforts will require hiring local individuals to represent the company on a day-to-day basis.

In preparing to enter a new market, the first step is to conduct market research that will enable management to make an informed decision about a market's potential. Research professionals provide several recommendations. First, study each market thoroughly. Learn as much as you can about the market's potential. In addition, talk with local professionals in the country who know the market. This includes learning about the pool of individuals available to hire once the operation is up and running. Second, don't make assumptions based on preconceived ideas about a market. Companies often make decisions about a market based on old stereotypes and not on facts.

As the operation is starting up, it is critical that companies seek out local talent and begin the recruiting process. Benchmark Hospitality, Inc., which develops and manages conference centers, conference hotels, and resorts, actually allocates a certain number of senior management positions in each new global market to local nationals. They believe having experienced local professionals on the management team saves them money in the long run because fewer mistakes are made as the company enters the market.

Given that the pool of available sales professionals may be relatively small in less developed or emerging markets, this places a great deal of pressure on companies to target local sales professionals. Sources for these individuals may include competitors who already do business in the country or individuals inside the company who were originally from the new market and may wish to return home.

Source: "Are You Smart Enough to Sell Globally?" *Sales & Marketing Management* (July 1998), pp. 53–56.

right people for the sales position. The key is for a company to have done its "homework" and research each new market before making the decision to enter it. For example, in many European countries it is much more difficult to terminate an employee than in the United States. This makes the hiring decision much more difficult. It is important for a company to understand what the legal requirements of hiring new salespeople are before hiring a new salesperson. "The Global Sales Force" discusses how a company can prepare to enter a new global market.

Internal Sources—People within the Company

People in nonsales departments within the firm, such as manufacturing, maintenance, engineering, or the office staff, sometimes have latent sales talent and are a common source of sales recruits. Past surveys suggest more than half of U.S. industrial goods producers hire at least some of their salespeople from other internal departments.

Recruiting current company employees for the sales force has distinct advantages:

1. Company employees have established performance records, and they are more of a known quantity than outsiders.

2. Recruits from inside the firm should require less orientation and training because they are already familiar with the company's products, policies, and operations.

3. Recruiting from within can bolster company morale as employees become aware that

Exhibit 11.4 External Sources of Sales Recruits

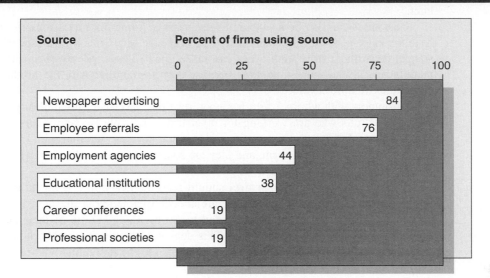

Source: *Recruiting and Selection Procedures,* Personnel Policies Forum Survey No. 146, pp. 7, 9 (May 1988). Copyright 1989 by the Bureau of National Affairs, Inc. Also see Julia Lawlor, "I lighly Classified," *Sales & Marketing Management* (March 1995), p. 84.

opportunities for advancement are available outside of their own departments or divisions.

To facilitate successful internal recruiting, the company's personnel department should always be kept abreast of sales staff needs. Because the personnel staff is familiar with the qualifications of all employees and continuously evaluates their performance, they are in the best position to identify people with the attributes necessary to fill available sales jobs.

Internal recruiting has some limitations. People in nonsales departments seldom have much previous selling experience. Also, internal recruiting can cause some animosity within the firm if supervisors of other departments think their best employees are being pirated by the sales force.

External Sources   Although it is often a good idea to start with internal sources when recruiting new salespeople, there may not be enough qualified internal candidates to meet the human resource needs of a firm's sales force. At this time, the search is expanded to cover external sources. Exhibit 11.4 lists a number of commonly used external sources of sales recruits along with the percentage of firms that use each source.

Referral of people in other firms

In addition to being potential sales employees themselves, company personnel can provide management with leads to potential recruits from outside the firm. Current salespeople are in a good position to provide their superiors with leads to new recruits. They know the requirements of the job, they often have contacts with other salespeople who may be willing to change jobs, and they can do much to help "sell" an available job to potential recruits. Consequently, many sales managers make sure their salespeople are aware of the company's recruiting needs. Some companies offer bonuses as incentives for their salespeople to recruit new prospects. Such referrals from current employees must be handled tactfully so as not to cause hard feelings if the applicant is rejected later.

Customers can also be a source of sales recruits. Sometimes a customer's employees have the kinds of knowledge that make them attractive as prospective salespeople. For instance, department store employees can make good salespeople for the wholesalers or manufacturers who supply the store because they are familiar with the product and the procedures of store buyers.

Customers with whom a firm has good relations may also provide leads concerning potential recruits who are working for other firms, particularly competitors. Purchasing agents know what impresses them in a salesperson, they are familiar with the abilities of the sales reps who call on them, and they are sometimes aware when a sales rep is interested in changing jobs.

The question of whether a firm should recruit salespeople from its competitors, however, is controversial. Such people are knowledgeable about the industry from their experience. They also might be expected to "bring along" some of their current customers when they switch companies. This does not happen frequently, however, since customers are usually more loyal to a supplier than to the individual who represents that supplier.

On the other side of the argument, it is sometimes difficult to get salespeople who have worked for a competing firm to unlearn old practices and to conform to their new employer's account management policies. Also, some managers think recruiting a competitor's personnel is unethical. They believe it is unfair for firm B to recruit actively someone from firm A after A has spent the money to hire and train that person. Such people may be in a position to divulge A's company secrets to B. Consequently, some firms refuse to recruit their competitor's salespeople, although whether such policies are due to high ethical standards, the expense of retraining, or fear of possible retaliation is open to question.

Advertisements

A less selective means of attracting job applicants is to advertise the available position. When a technically qualified or experienced person is needed, an ad might be placed in an industry trade or technical journal. More commonly, advertisements are placed in the personnel or marketplace sections of local newspapers to attract applicants for relatively less demanding sales jobs where special qualifications are not required. A well-written ad can be very effective for attracting applicants. As suggested, however, this is not necessarily a good thing. When a firm's advertisements attract large numbers of applicants who are unqualified or only marginally interested, the firm must engage in costly screening to "separate the wheat from the chaff."[6]

If a firm does use newspaper ads in recruiting, it must decide how much information about the job should be included in its ads. Many sales managers argue that "open" ads, which disclose the firm's name, product to be sold, compensation, and specific job duties, generate a more select pool of high-quality applicants, lower selection costs, and decreased turnover rates than ads without such information. Open ads also avoid any ethical questions concerning possible deception.

However, for less attractive, high-turnover sales jobs—such as door-to-door selling—some sales managers prefer "blind" ads, which carry only minimal information—sometimes only a phone number. These maximize the number of applicants and give the manager an opportunity to explain the attractive features of the job in a personal meeting with the applicant.[7]

Employment agencies

Employment agencies are sometimes used to find recruits, usually for more routine sales jobs such as retail and door-to-door sales. However, some agencies specialize in finding applicants for more demanding sales jobs. Some sales managers have had unsatisfactory experiences with employment agencies. They charge that agencies are sometimes overzealous in attempting to earn their fees, and they tend to send applicants who do not meet the job qualifications. Consequently, many firms turn to employment agencies only as a last resort.

Others argue, however, that when a firm has problems with an employment agency, it is often the fault of the company for not understanding the agency's role and not providing sufficient information about the kinds of recruits it is seeking. When a firm carefully selects an agency with a good reputation, establishes a long-term relationship, and provides detailed descriptions of job qualifications, the agency can perform a valuable service. It locates and screens job applicants and reduces the amount of time and effort the company's sales managers must devote to recruiting.

Educational institutions

College and university placement offices are a common source of recruits for firms that require salespeople with sound mental abilities or technical backgrounds. They are used particularly when the sales job is viewed as a first step toward a career in management. College graduates are often more socially poised than people of the same age without college training, and good grades are at least some evidence the person can think logically, budget time efficiently, and communicate reasonably well.

But college graduates seldom have much selling experience, and they are likely to require more extensive orientation and training in the basics of salesmanship. Also, college-educated sales recruits have a reputation for "job hopping," unless their jobs are challenging and promotions are rapid. One insurance company, for instance, stopped recruiting college graduates when it found that such recruits did not stay with their jobs very long. Such early turnover is sometimes more the fault of the company than of the recruits. When recruiters paint an unrealistic picture of the job demands and rewards of the position to be filled, or when they recruit people who are overqualified for the job, high turnover is often the result.[8]

Junior colleges and vocational schools are another source of sales recruits that has expanded rapidly in recent years. Many such schools have programs explicitly designed to prepare people for selling careers. Thus, firms that recruit the graduates of such programs do not have to contend with the negative attitudes toward selling they sometimes encounter in four-year college graduates. Junior colleges and vocational schools are particularly good sources of recruits for sales jobs that require reasonably well developed mental and communications abilities, but where advanced technical knowledge or a four-year degree is not essential.

SELECTION PROCEDURES

After the qualifications necessary to fill a job have been determined and some applicants have been recruited, the final task is to determine which applicants best meet the qualifications and have the greatest aptitude for the job. To gain the information needed to evaluate each prospective employee, firms typically use some combination of the following selection tools and procedures.[9]

1. Application blanks.

Exhibit 11.5   Predictive Validity of Various Selection Criteria

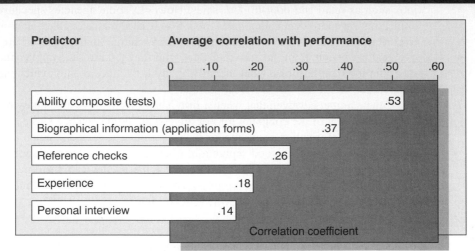

Source: Reprinted from John E. Hunter and R.F. Hunter, "Validity and Utility of Alternative Predictors of Job Performance," *Psychological Bulletin* 96 (1984), pp. 72–98. © 1984 by the American Psychological Association. Reprinted by permission.

2. Personal interviews.

3. Reference checks.

4. Physical examinations.

5. Psychological tests.

    a. Intelligence.

    b. Personality.

    c. Aptitude/skills.

A meta-analysis of past research studies that have examined the use of these selection tools found that—on average across all occupations—composites of psychological test scores have the greatest predictive validity for evaluating a potential employee's future job performance, whereas evaluations based on personal interviews have the lowest. In other words, test scores have the highest correlations with candidates' subsequent performance on the job, with an average correlation coefficient of 0.53. Thus, test scores account for about 28 percent of the variance in subsequent performance across hirees. Ratings based on personal interviews, on the other hand, have an average correlation of only 0.14 with (and account for only about 2 percent of variance in) subsequent performance.[10] These findings are shown in more detail in Exhibit 11.5. A bit surprising, though, is that the frequency with which firms actually use the various selection tools for evaluating potential salespeople is not consistent with the demonstrated validity of those tools. As Exhibit 11.6 indicates, a survey of selection procedures followed by 121 industrial firms suggests personal interviews are almost universally employed while psychological tests are the least-used selection tools. However, large firms are somewhat more thorough in their use of psychological tests—and the development of detailed job descriptions—than smaller firms.

Why do many firms avoid selection tools that appear to be valid predictors of a candidate's future success while relying on tools with less predictive validity? Some of the

Exhibit 11.6 Percentage of Small and Large Firms That "Extensively Use" Various Tools for Selecting Salespeople

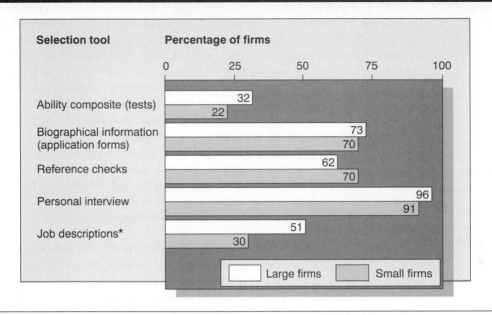

*A statistically significant difference ($p < 0.05$) exists between the percentage of small and large firms that "extensively use" this sales management tool. In this survey, *small* firms were defined as those with annual sales of less than $40 million ($n = 74$), and *large* firms were those with sales of $40 million or more ($r = 47$)

Source: Alan J. Dubinsky and Thomas E. Barry, "A Survey of Sales Management Practices," *Industrial Marketing Management* 11 (1982), p. 136.

practical advantages and limitations of the various tools—and some possible reasons for managers' historical reluctance to use psychological tests—are discussed in the following sections.

Application Blanks

Although professional salespeople often have résumés to submit to prospective employers, many personnel experts believe a standard company application form makes it easier to assess applicants. A well-designed application blank helps ensure that the same information is obtained in the same form from all candidates.

The primary purpose of the application form is to collect information about the recruit's physical characteristics and personal history. Forms typically ask for facts about the candidate's physical condition, family status, education, business experience, military service, participation in social organizations, and outside interests and activities. This information can be reviewed to determine whether the applicant is qualified for the job on such dimensions as education and experience.

A second function of the application form is to help managers prepare for personal interviews with job candidates. Often a recruit's responses to items on the application form raise questions that should be explored during an interview. If the application shows that a person has held several jobs within the past few years, for example, the interviewer should attempt to find out the reasons for these changes. Perhaps the interviewer can determine whether the applicant is a "job hopper" who is unlikely to stay with the company very long. Indeed, a study conducted at one pharmaceutical firm found that common application blank information—such as candidates' tenure in their previous jobs and their amount of sales experience—was able to distinguish salespeople most likely to stay with the hiring company over time from those who were more likely to quit.[11]

Personal Interviews

In addition to probing into the applicant's history, personal interviews enable managers to gain insight into the applicant's mental abilities and personality. An interview provides a manager with the opportunity to assess a candidate's communication skills, intelligence, sociability, aggressiveness, empathy, ambition, and other traits related to the qualifications necessary for the job. Different managers use many different interviewing approaches to accomplish these objectives. These methods of conducting personal interviews, however, can all be classified as either structured or unstructured.

In *structured interviews,* each applicant is asked the same predetermined questions. This approach is particularly good when the interviewer is inexperienced at evaluating candidates. The standard questions help guide the interview and ensure that all factors relevant to the candidate's qualifications are covered. Also, asking the same questions of all candidates makes it easier to compare their strengths and weaknesses. To facilitate such comparisons, many firms use a standard interview evaluation form on which interviewers rate each applicant's response to each question together with their overall impressions of the candidate.

One potential weakness of structured interviews is that the interviewer may rigidly stick to the prepared questions and fail to identify or probe the unique qualities or flaws of each candidate. In practice, though, structured interviews are often not so inflexible as the criticism implies. As a manager gains interviewing experience, he or she often learns to ask additional questions when an applicant's response is inadequate without disturbing the flow of the interview.[12]

At the other end of the spectrum of interviewing techniques is the *unstructured interview.* Such interviews seek to get the applicant talking freely on a variety of subjects. The interviewer asks only a few questions to direct the conversation to topics of interest, such as the applicant's work experiences, career objectives, and outside activities. The rationale for this approach is that significant insights into the applicant's character and motivations can be gained by allowing the applicant to talk freely with a minimum of direction. Also, the interviewer is free to spend more time on topics where the applicant's responses are interesting or unusual.

Successful, unstructured interviewing requires interviewers with experience and interpretive skills. Because there is no predetermined set of questions, there is always a danger that the interviewer will neglect some relevant topics. It is also more difficult to compare the responses of two or more applicants. Consequently, since most firms' sales managers have relatively little experience as interviewers, structured interviews are much more common in selecting new salespeople than unstructured approaches.

Within the interview itself, particularly those that are relatively unstructured, some sales managers use additional techniques to learn as much as possible about the applicant's character and aptitude. One such technique is the *stress interview.* The interviewer puts the applicant under stress in one of many ways, ranging from silence or rudeness on the part of the interviewer to constant, aggressive probing and questioning. The rationale for this technique is that the interviewer may learn how the applicant will respond to and deal with the stress encountered in selling situations.

Another approach is for the interviewer to ask the applicant to sell something. "Hand the prospect a stapler, a pencil, or any other object that's handy and ask him to 'sell' it. . . . A pro should be able to sell anything," says one sales manager. "The one thing he's got to do is to ask for the order. Seven of ten fail to do so."[13]

Techniques like these can be useful to assess a candidate's character and selling

Are Personal Interviews a Valid Tool for Selecting Salespeople?

Personal interviews are both the most commonly used method of selecting salespeople and the one considered most helpful by sales managers. But assessments of the use of evaluations based on personal interviews across a variety of occupations suggest they are disappointing predictors of future job performance. As we have seen, the meta-analysis conducted by Hunter and Hunter found that evaluations based on interviews have a correlation of only 0.14 with candidates' subsequent performance, and an even lower correlation of 0.08 with candidates' future promotion within the firm.

Professor Richard Arvey and his colleagues have a more favorable opinion of the usefulness of interviews when they are used specifically to select new sales personnel. In one study of the use of structured interviews to select retail salespeople, they found a correlation of 0.44 between interviewers' ratings of candidates and their subsequent job performance. Arvey and his colleagues explain this positive result by suggesting that interviews are a more valid selection tool when the job to be filled requires skills and behaviors similar to those that are on display in a personal interview setting, as is often the case with sales jobs. They also indicate that interviews are most useful when several different people interview the candidate and then compare their evaluations, and when at least some of those interviewers have a detailed knowledge of the requirements of the job to be filled (as sales managers typically do concerning sales positions).

These findings suggest that sales managers should play an active role in interviewing prospective salespeople, rather than rely on employment agencies or members of the personnel department to do all the interviewing. They also indicate the manager should employ interviewing techniques that require the candidate to display product and industry knowledge and selling skills—techniques such as asking the candidate to "sell something." When these guidelines are followed, personal interviews may provide as valid an indication of a candidate's future success as any other selection tool.

Source: Richard D. Arvey and J.E. Campion, "The Employment Interview: A Summary and Review of Recent Research," *Personnel Psychology* 35 (1982), pp. 736–65; Richard D. Arvey et al., "Enhanced Interview Validity: A Sight for Sore Eyes," unpublished working paper (Minneapolis: Carlson School of Management, University of Minnesota, 1986); and E. James Randall and Cindy H. Randall, "Review of Salesperson Selection Techniques and Criteria: A Managerial Approach," *International Journal of Research in Marketing* 7 (1990), pp. 81–95.

skills, but they should be used as only one part of the interview. Sometimes sales managers become so obsessed with finding the "one best way" to assess candidates that they allow interviewing gimmicks to get in the way of real communication. After all, another purpose of job interviews is to provide candidates with information about the job and company so they will be interested in taking the job. One real danger with gimmicky interviewing techniques is that the applicant will be "turned off" and lose interest in working for the firm.

Regardless of what kinds of interviewing techniques are used, more managers rely on interviews as a means of evaluating sales candidates than any other selection tool. Yet as we saw earlier, there is some evidence that evaluations based on personal interviews are among the least valid predictors of subsequent job performance. Does this mean many firms are doing a less than optimal job of evaluating and selecting new salespeople? Are there ways to improve the accuracy of impressions gained from interviews? These questions are explored in the "Managing Sales Relationships" box.

Reference Checks

If an applicant passes the face-to-face interview, a reference check is often the next step. Some sales managers question the value of references because "they always say nice things." However, with a little resourcefulness, reference checks can be a valuable selection tool.

Checking references can ensure the accuracy of factual data about the applicant. It is naive to assume that everything a candidate has written on a résumé or application form is true. Facts about previous job experiences and college degrees should be checked. The discovery of false data on a candidate's application raises a question about basic honesty as well as about what the candidate is trying to hide.

References can supply additional information and opinions about a prospect's aptitude and past job performance. Although it is important to respect applicants' requests not to prejudice their position with a current employer, useful information can be obtained from previous employers and supervisors. Even though most applicants try to provide only "good references," a resourceful interviewer can probe beyond a reference's positive biases with questions such as "If you were hiring this individual today, what qualities would you think it most important to develop?" Also, some firms require applicants to supply as many as six or seven references on the theory that it is unlikely so many people will all have strong personal biases in favor of the applicant. Calling a large number of references and probing them in depth can be time-consuming and costly, but it can also produce worthwhile information and protect against making expensive hiring mistakes.[14]

Physical Examinations

One typically does not think of selling as physically demanding, yet sales jobs often require a great deal of stamina and the physical ability to withstand lots of stress. Consequently, even though physical examinations are relatively expensive compared with other selection tools, many sales managers see them as valuable aids for evaluating candidates.

However, managers should be very cautious in requiring medical examinations, including specific tests for such things as drug use or the HIV virus, for prospective employees. Under the Americans with Disabilities Act (discussed in more detail later in this chapter), it is no longer advisable to use a standard physical examination for all positions. If used, the physical exam should focus only on attributes directly related to the requirements of the job to be filled. For example, in many sales positions, conditions such as diabetes or epilepsy would have little or no impact on the candidate's ability to perform. Therefore, questions concerning such conditions should be avoided, and any information collected for emergency situations should be kept confidential. Under the law's guidelines, a physical examination should be performed only after a job offer has been extended. And the job offer cannot be made conditional on the results of the physical exam unless all hirees for a position are subjected to the same physical exam and the results of those exams are treated as confidential medical records.[15]

Tests

A final set of selection tools used by many firms consists of tests aimed at measuring an applicant's mental abilities and personality traits. The most commonly used tests can be grouped into three types: (1) intelligence, (2) aptitude, and (3) personality tests. Within each category, there are a variety of different tests used by different companies.

Intelligence tests

Intelligence tests are useful for determining whether an applicant has sufficient mental ability to perform a job successfully. Sales managers tend to believe these are the most useful of all the tests commonly used in selecting salespeople. General intelligence tests are designed to measure an applicant's overall mental abilities by examining how well the applicant comprehends, reasons, and learns. The Wonderlic Personnel Test is one common general intelligence test. It is popular because it is short; it consists of 50 items and requires only about 12 minutes to complete.

When the job to be filled requires special competence in one or a few areas of mental ability, a specialized intelligence test might be used to evaluate candidates. Tests are available for measuring such things as speed of learning, number facility, memory, logical reasoning, and verbal ability.

Aptitude tests

Aptitude tests are designed to determine whether an applicant has an interest in, or the ability to perform, certain tasks and activities. For example, the Strong Vocational Interest Blank asks respondents to indicate whether they like or dislike a variety of situations and activities. This can determine whether applicants' interests are similar to those of people who are successful in a variety of different occupations, including selling. Other tests measure skills or abilities such as mechanical or mathematical aptitude that might be related to success in particular selling jobs.

One problem with at least some aptitude tests is that instead of measuring a person's native abilities, they measure current level of skill at certain tasks. At least some skills necessary for successful selling can be taught, or improved, through a well-designed training program. Therefore, rejecting applicants because they currently do not have the necessary skills can mean losing people who could be trained to be successful salespeople.

Personality tests

Many general personality tests evaluate an individual on numerous traits. The Edwards Personal Preference Schedule, for instance, measures 17 traits such as sociability, aggressiveness, and independence. Such tests, however, contain many questions, require substantial time to complete, and gather information about some traits that may be irrelevant for evaluating future salespeople. Consequently, more limited personality tests have been developed in recent years that concentrate on only a few traits thought to be directly relevant to a person's future success in sales.[16] The Multiple Personal Inventory, for example, uses a small number of "forced-choice" questions to measure the strength of two personality traits: empathy with other people and ego drive.

Concerns about the use of tests

During the 1950s and early 1960s, tests—particularly general intelligence and sales aptitude tests—were widely used as selection tools for evaluating potential salespeople. A survey conducted by the National Society of Sales Training Executives in 1964 found that 83 percent of its member companies were using tests as part of the salesperson selection process. A follow-up survey in 1975, however, revealed the proportion of companies using tests had fallen to 22 percent, largely due to concerns over the possible legal problems and restrictions posed by civil rights legislation and equal opportunity hiring practices; we discuss these concerns and restrictions shortly. Recently, however, evidence that properly designed and administered tests are among the most valid selection tools has spurred an increase in their popularity; although (as we saw in Exhibit 11.6) they are somewhat more widely used in large firms than in smaller ones.[17]

Despite the empirical evidence, however, many managers continue to be leery of tests, and a majority of firms do not use them as part of their evaluation of sales recruits. There are a number of reasons for these negative attitudes.

For one thing, despite the evidence that tests have relatively high predictive validity on average, some managers continue to doubt that tests are valid for predicting the future success of salespeople in their specific firm. As discussed in Chapter 10, no mental abilities or personality traits have been found to be positively related to performance across a variety of selling jobs in different firms. Thus, specific tests that measure such abilities and traits may be valid for selecting salespeople for some jobs, but invalid for others.

Also, tests for measuring specific abilities and characteristics of applicants do not always produce consistent scores. Some commercially available tests have not been developed according to the most scientific measurement procedures; as a result, their reliability and validity are questionable. Even when a firm believes a particular trait, such as empathy or sociability, is related to job performance, there is still a question about which test should be used to measure that trait.

A related concern, particularly in the case of personality tests, is that some creative and talented people may be rejected simply because their personalities do not conform to the test norms. Many sales jobs require creative people, particularly when those people are being groomed for future management responsibilities. Yet these people seldom fit an average personality profile because the "average" person is not particularly creative.

Another concern about testing involves the possible reactions of the people who are tested. A reasonably intelligent, "test-wise" person can "fudge" the results of many tests by selecting answers the applicant thinks management will want. These answers may not accurately reflect that person's feelings or behavior. Also, many prospective employees view extensive testing as a burden and perhaps an invasion of privacy. Therefore, some managers fear that requiring a large battery of tests may turn off a candidate and reduce the likelihood of accepting a job with the firm.

Finally, a given test may discriminate between people of different races or sexes, and the use of such tests is illegal. Consequently, some firms have abandoned the use of tests rather than risk getting into trouble with the government.

Guidelines for the appropriate use of tests

To avoid, or at least minimize, the preceding testing problems, managers should keep the following guidelines in mind:

1. Test scores should be considered only one input to the selection decision. Managers should not rely on them to do the work of other parts of the selection process—such as interviewing and checking references. Candidates should not be eliminated solely on the basis of test scores.

2. Applicants should be tested only on those abilities and traits that management, on the basis of a thorough job analysis, has determined to be relevant for the specific job. Broad tests that evaluate a large number of traits not relevant to a specific job are probably inappropriate.

3. When possible, tests with built-in "internal consistency checks" should be used. Then the person who analyzes the test results can determine whether the applicant responded honestly or was faking some answers. Many recently designed tests ask similar questions with slightly different wording several times throughout the test. If respondents are answering honestly, they should always give the same response to similar questions.

4. A firm should conduct empirical studies to ensure the tests are valid for predicting an applicant's future performance in the job. This kind of hard evidence of test validity is particularly important in view of the government's equal employment opportunity requirements.

EQUAL EMPLOYMENT OPPORTUNITY REQUIREMENTS IN SELECTING SALESPEOPLE

The number of federal lawsuits alleging workplace discrimination is large and growing.[18] The primary basis for these suits is Title VII of the 1964 Civil Rights Act, which forbids discrimination in employment on the basis of race, sex, religion, color, or national origin. A number of more recent federal laws have extended this protection against job discrimi-

Exhibit 11.7   Legislation Affecting Recruitment and Selection

Legislative Act	Purpose
Civil Rights Act of 1866	Gives blacks the same rights as whites and has since been extended by the courts to include all ethnic groups.
Civil Rights Act of 1964 (Title VII)	Prohibits discrimination in employment based on race, color, religion, national origin, or sex.
Age Discrimination in Employment Act (1967)	Prohibits discrimination against people ages 40 to 70.
Fair Employment Opportunity Act (1972)	Founded the Equal Employment Opportunity Commission to ensure compliance with the Civil Rights Act.
Rehabilitation Act of 1973	Requires affirmative action to hire and promote handicapped persons if the firm employs 50 or more workers and is seeking a federal contract in excess of $50,000.
Vietnam Era Veterans Readjustment Act (1974)	Requires affirmative action to hire Vietnam veterans and disabled veterans of any war by firms holding federal contracts in excess of $10,000.
Americans with Disabilities Act (1990)	Prohibits discrimination based on handicaps or disabilities—either physical or mental. Applied to all employers with 25 or more employees beginning July 26, 1992, and extended to employers with 15 or more workers on July 26, 1994.

nation to include such factors as age and physical and mental disabilities, as summarized in Exhibit 11.7. Consequently, extreme care should be taken to ensure the selection tools a firm uses in hiring salespeople—especially its interviewing and testing procedures—are not biased against any subgroup of the labor force. Exhibit 11.8 offers guidelines concerning the kinds of illegal or sensitive questions managers should avoid when conducting employment interviews or designing application forms.

Requirements for Tests

Section 703(h) of the 1964 Civil Rights Act approves the use of "professionally developed ability tests," provided such tests are not "designed, intended, or used to discriminate because of race, color, religion, sex, or national origin." Suppose, however, an employer innocently uses a test that does discriminate in that a larger proportion of men than women, or a larger percentage of whites than blacks, receive passing scores. Has the employer violated the law? Not necessarily.

In such cases, the employer must prove the test scores are valid predictors of successful performance on the job in question. In other words, it is legal for a firm to hire more men than women for a job if it can be proven that men possess more of some trait or ability that will enable them to do the job better. This requires that the employer have empirical evidence showing a significant relationship between scores on the test and actual job performance. The procedures a firm might use to produce this kind of evidence were described earlier in this chapter when discussing how to determine whether particular job qualifications are valid.[19]

Requirements for Interviews and Application Forms

Because it is illegal to discriminate in hiring on the basis of race, sex, religion, age, and national origin, there is no reason for a firm to ask for such information on its job application forms or during personal interviews. It is wise to avoid all questions in any way related to such factors. Then there will be no question in the applicant's mind about whether the hiring decision was biased or unfair. This is easier said than done, however, because some seemingly innocent questions can be viewed as attempts to gain information that might be used to discriminate against a candidate.

Exhibit 11.8   Illegal or Sensitive Questions That Should Be Eliminated from Employment Applications and Interviews

Nationality and Race

Comments or questions relating to the race, color, national origin, or descent of the applicant—or his or her spouse—must be avoided. Applicants should not be asked to supply a photo of themselves when applying for a job. If proficiency in another language is an important part of the job, the applicant can be asked to demonstrate that proficiency but cannot be asked whether it is his or her native language. Applicants may be asked if they are U.S. citizens, but not whether they—or their parents or spouse—are naturalized or native-born Americans. Applicants who are not citizens may be asked whether they have the legal right to remain and work in the United States.

Religion

Applicants should not be asked about their religious beliefs or whether the company's workweek or the job schedule would interfere with their religious convictions.

Sex and Marital Status

Except for jobs where sex is clearly related to job performance—as in a TV commercial role—the applicant's sex should not enter the hiring discussion. Applicants should not be asked about their marital status, whether or not their spouse works, or even whom the prospective employer should notify in an emergency. A woman should not be asked whether she would like to be addressed as Mrs., Miss, or Ms. Applicants should not be asked any questions about their children, baby-sitting arrangements, contraceptive practices, or planned family size.

Age

Applicants may be asked whether they are minors or age 70 or over, because special laws govern the employment of such people. With those exceptions, however, applicants should not be asked their age or date of birth.

Physical Characteristics, Disabilities, Handicaps, and Health Problems

In view of the recently passed Americans with Disabilities Act, all such questions are best avoided. However, once an employer has described the job to be performed, applicants *can* be asked whether they have any physical or mental condition that would limit their ability to perform the job.

Height and Weight

While not illegal, such questions are sensitive since they may provide a basis for discrimination against females or Americans of Asian or Spanish descent.

Bankruptcy or Garnishments

Both questions are suspect because the bankruptcy code prohibits discrimination against individuals who have filed bankruptcy.

Arrests and Convictions

Questions about past arrests are barred. Applicants can be asked about past convictions, but the employer should include a statement that the nature and circumstances of the conviction will be considered.

Source: Adapted from C. David Shepherd and James C. Heartfield, "Discrimination Issues in the Selection of Salespeople: A Review and Managerial Suggestions," *Journal of Personal Selling and Sales Management* (Fall 1991), p. 71.

SUMMARY

This chapter reviewed the issues that surround the recruitment and selection of new salespeople. The issues discussed ranged from who is responsible for these tasks to the impact of federal legislation barring job discrimination on selection procedures.

Two factors are primary in determining who has the responsibility for recruiting and selecting salespeople: (1) the size of the sales force and (2) the kind of selling involved. In general, the smaller the sales force, the more sophisticated the selling task; and the more the sales force is used as a training ground for

marketing and sales managers, the more likely it is that higher-level people, including the sales manager, will be directly involved in the recruitment and selection effort. To ensure that recruits have the aptitude for the job, it is useful to look at the recruitment and selection procedures as a three-step process. The steps are (1) a job analysis and description, (2) the recruitment of a pool of applicants, and (3) the selection of the best applicants from the available pool.

The job analysis and description phase includes a detailed examination of the job to determine what activities, tasks, responsibilities, and environmental influences are involved. This analysis may be conducted by someone in the sales management ranks or by a job analysis specialist. Regardless of who does it, it is important for that person to prepare a job description that details the findings of the job analysis. Finally, the job description is used to develop a statement of job qualifications, which lists and describes the personal traits and abilities a person should have to perform the tasks and responsibilities involved.

The pool of recruits from which the firm finally selects can be generated from a number of sources, including (1) people within the company, (2) people in other firms, (3) educational institutions, (4) advertisements, and (5) employment agencies. Each source has its own advantages and disadvantages. Some, such as advertisements, typically produce a large pool. The key question the sales manager needs to address is which source or combination of sources is likely to produce the largest pool of good, qualified recruits.

Once the qualifications necessary to fill a job have been determined and applicants have been recruited, the final task is to determine which applicant best meets the qualifications and has the greatest aptitude for the job. To make this determination, firms often use most, and in some cases all, of the following tools and procedures: (1) application blanks, (2) face-to-face interviews, (3) reference checks, (4) physical examinations, and (5) intelligence, aptitude, and personality tests. Although most employers find the interview and then the application blank most helpful, each device seems to perform some functions better than the other alternatives. This may explain why most firms use a combination of selection tools.

Title VII of the 1964 Civil Rights Act forbids discrimination in employment on the basis of race, sex, color, religion, or national origin. A firm must be careful, therefore, about how it uses tests, how it structures its application form, and the questions it asks during personal interviews so as not to be charged with noncompliance with the act. A firm that uses tests, for example, must be able to demonstrate empirically that the attributes measured are related to the salesperson's performance on the job.

DISCUSSION QUESTIONS

1. The sales manager for one of the nation's largest producers of consumer goods has identified eight factors that appear to be positively related to effective performance. The manager of human resources, who is concerned about high turnover rates among the sales force, would like to use this information to improve the company's recruiting and hiring process. The key factors are

   Priority setting
   Initiative and follow-through
   Working effectively with others
   Creativity and innovation
   Thinking and problem solving
   Leadership
   Communication
   Technical mastery

   How could these factors become part of the company's recruiting and hiring process? How would you define these factors and determine if applicants for sales positions possess these factors?

2. The following quote from *Marketing News* (March 2, 1992, p. 14) illustrates an application of computers to the recruiting and selection process:

   It doesn't care who you know, what kind of suit you're wearing, or whether you have a firm handshake. Salespeople looking for a job may soon have to face their toughest interview yet—with a computer.

   What are the advantages of using a software program to conduct preliminary job interviews? What problems is a company that uses computer-aided interviewing likely to encounter?

3. The demanding process of recruiting and selecting new sales reps has led many sales managers to search out faster methods. Beyond the traditional tools described in the chapter, other questionable techniques appear such as graphology, astrology, and numerology. Numerology assumes there is a codified relationship between the conscious and the unconscious. The letters used in one's first and last names, along with their values (e.g., A = 1, H = 8, N = 5), when summed produce a value that indicates the individual's personality. How would you test the predictive validity of numerology?

4. The following quote was taken from *The Wall Street Journal* (August 25, 1988, p. 17):

   Thomas Klobucher is looking for employees with the write stuff.

Before someone is hired at Thomas Interior Systems, Inc., the president of the Elmhurst, Ill., office-furniture company has a handwriting analyst examine the candidate's writing to develop a personality profile.

Mr. Klobucher says he believes that ignoring the results can be costly. He was once so impressed with a sales candidate—the man had a pleasant personality, good recommendations, and an MBA—that he dismissed a handwriting specialist's warning that the candidate was argumentative and defiant. It proved true, and within months of being hired the man was out.

The article also mentions, "Handwriting analysis is quietly spreading through corporate America." What accounts for this trend? What are the implications of this trend? How would you design a study to test the reliability and validity of handwriting analysis as a selection tool? Please prepare your answer in writing, not typed.

5. Two college recruiters were discussing some of the students they had interviewed that day. One female applicant with excellent credentials was described by one interviewer as follows: "She looked too feminine, like she would need someone to take care of her, and she was not all that serious about a sales job with us." When asked to explain her comments, the interviewer said, "Under her jacket she wore a flowery blouse with little flouncy sleeves and a lace collar." The other recruiter countered and asked, "What do a flowery blouse, flouncy sleeves, and a lace collar have to do with performance?" Comment.

6. One potential source of applicants for sales positions is sales representatives who work for competitors. One sales manager indicated, "Pirating sales representatives from other companies makes sense. Let them do the training, then we'll hire them." Is this ethical? Is this legal? Does this practice make good business sense?

EXPERIENTIAL APPLICATION

Seek out the sales manager with a company in your area. Interview him or her to determine the criteria by which that company recruits and selects salespeople. Learn about the screening process. For example, how many interviews must the job candidate undergo before a final decision is made? Who makes the decision? Is it the sales manager?

INTERNET EXERCISE

Recruiting for many different positions including sales representatives has become quite common over the Internet. Go to the Web sites of companies you may be interested in working for after graduation. Review the job descriptions and other relevant information about these sales positions, being careful to note that some of the position announcements may indicate that a sales manager position is open. In addition, some of the ads may carefully avoid using the word *sales* and identify the attributes or characteristics that applicants should possess. How does your analysis compare to the findings presented in Chapters 10 and 11? Based on your analysis, what assumptions are being made concerning what motivates salespeople? Why do companies recruiting salespeople through newspaper ads advertise for sales managers, no experience required, or avoid referring to selling or sales activities?

SUGGESTED READINGS

Bragg, Arthur, "Checking References," *Sales & Marketing Management* (November 1990), pp. 68—71.

Comer, Lucette B., J.A.F. Nicholls, and Leslie J. Vermillion, "Diversity in the Sales Force: Problems and Challenges," *Journal of Personal Selling and Sales Management* (Fall 1998), pp. 1–20.

Farber, Barry, "Start at the Beginning," *Sales & Marketing Management* (March 1996), pp. 24–25.

Gable, Myron, Charles Hollon, and Frank Dangello, "Increasing the Utility of the Application Blank: Relationship between Job Application Information and Subsequent Performance and Turnover of Salespeople,"

Journal of Personal Selling and Sales Management (Summer 1992), pp. 39 55.

Lawlor, Julia, "Highly Classified," *Sales & Marketing Management* (March 1995), pp. 75–85.

Lucas, Allison, "Race Matters," *Sales & Marketing Management* (September 1996), pp. 50–62.

Matthews, Marianne, "If Your Ads Aren't Pulling Top Sales Talent . . . ," *Sales & Marketing Management* (February 1990), pp. 73–79.

Nelson, Richard, "Maybe It's Time to Take Another Look at Tests as a Selection Tool," *Journal of Personal Selling and Sales Management* (August 1987), pp. 33–38.

Randall, E. James, and Cindy H. Randall, "Review of Salesperson Selection Techniques and Criteria: A Managerial Approach," *International Journal of Research in Marketing* 7 (1990), pp. 81–95.

Shepherd, C. David, and James C. Heartfield, "Discrimination Issues in the Selection of Salespeople: A Review and Managerial Suggestions," *Journal of Personal Selling and Sales Management* (Fall 1991), pp. 67–75.

Trumifio, Ginger, "Recruiting Goes High Tech," *Sales & Marketing Management* (April 1995), pp. 42–44.

Voss, Bristol, "Six Steps to Better Hires," *Sales & Marketing Management* (June 1993), pp. 44–48.

I2 Sales Training: Objectives, Techniques, and Evaluation

LUCENT BELIEVES TRAINING IS A CRITICAL PART OF SALES SUCCESS

Lucent Technologies, the technology subsidiary of AT&T spun off in 1996, has demonstrated double-digit sale increases since its inception. Its fastest growing division, Systems for Network Operators, grew at an annual rate of 18 percent. By almost any measure Lucent has a track record of success. Art Medeiros, president of Lucent's Caribbean, Latin America and U.S. South Global Service Providers, cites several reasons why Lucent has enjoyed great success since its creation in 1996. One key is Lucent's focus on locating salespeople close to the customer and hiring individuals who are representative of the customers they call on.

Medeiros also credits a major emphasis on developing and training the Lucent sales force. There is no question that telecommunications is undergoing radical changes around the world. Technology, new emerging markets (such as China, Hungary, and the Czech Republic), and the deregulating of other markets (France, Germany) has created new opportunities and competitive pressures for the companies in the industry. To help their sales force keep up with these changes, Lucent offers a wide range of training and developmental experiences to better prepare its salespeople for the issues and problems of its customers.

There is, as you might expect, a great deal of training on new and existing products and services. However, salespeople are also encouraged to participate in training on a wide range of sales-enhancing skills including strategic selling and cross-functional team selling. A major emphasis in the various training programs is helping each salesperson understand emerging technologies and how they can affect their customers' decisions. As voice, data, and video communication technologies merge, customer needs change rapidly. Lucent salespeople are trained extensively on how to add value to the customer in this highly dynamic environment.

The results of the training are impressive. Its sales force is consistently ranked one of the best in the country. Its focus on providing relevant and continuous training has been a key part of that success.

Source: "Best Sales Forces," *Sales & Marketing Management* (July 1998), p. 48; and the Lucent Technologies website.

Visit Lucent Technologies at its Web site, *www.lucent.com*.

LEARNING OBJECTIVES

Salespeople operate in a highly competitive and dynamic environment. In addition, new salespeople must assimilate a great deal of information to make them effective with customers. A key element in enhancing the success of existing salespeople and preparing new salespeople is training. Companies in the 21st century realize that good training is an essential component of success for the sales force. This chapter will examine the objectives, techniques, and methods of evaluating training in the sales force.

After reading this chapter you should be able to:

- Identify the key issues in sales training for the 21st century.
- Understand the objectives of sales training.
- Discuss the development of sales training programs.
- Understand the training of new sales recruits and experienced salespeople.
- Define the topics covered in a sales training program.
- Understand the various methods for conducting sales training.
- Discuss how to measure the costs and benefits of sales training.

ISSUES IN SALES TRAINING

The subject of sales training usually produces considerable interest among various managers of the company. Sales managers—national, regional, and district—hope that the training will lead to sales reps meeting their quotas. A national accounts manager wants the sales training to provide specific details about certain industries and to teach the sales rep how to develop close relationships with customers—a critical issue, especially with large national accounts. A market manager, such as those at Lucent, will be interested in how much training a sales rep receives in the buying process for communications hardware/software at your local phone company. Product managers, of course, will hope that the reps have been well schooled in product knowledge, specifications, and applications. Even managers who are external to the marketing function, such as human resource managers, will have a stake in the sales training process. Recruiters know that highly regarded sales training programs enhance the firm's ability to recruit and retain salespeople. A few firms have developed such strong sales training programs that participants who complete the program liken the process to having earned a second degree or an MBA.

When determining sales training needs, Frank Cespedes identifies three issues that must be considered:[1]

- Who should be trained? In most organizations, new sales recruits receive a combination of training and orientation to company policies and procedures. But this raises the issues of training for different types of salespeople and, depending upon how market or competitive changes may have altered the nature of sales tasks, training for different stages of the same salesperson's career.
- What should be the primary emphasis in the training program? Sales training can encompass the following: product knowledge, company knowledge, customer knowledge, and/or generic selling skills (e.g., time management or presentation skills). All of these may be important, but the relative importance of each type of training differs depending upon the selling situation, the feasible scope and costs of sales training, and the nature of the company's marketing strategy.
- How should the training process be structured in terms of the following: on-the-job

training and experience versus a formal and more consistent centralized program, field initiatives and participation versus headquarters programs, and in-house training versus outside expertise?

The Lucent example plus those from most other companies and the points raised by Frank Cespedes clearly indicate that sales training is an ongoing process and not likely to be completed in a one-time event. Sales training for new recruits hopes to instill in a relatively short period of time a vast amount of knowledge that has taken skilled sales representatives years and years to acquire. Sales training for experienced salespeople, on the other hand, may be the result of new product offerings, changes in market structure, new technologies, competitive activities, and so on, plus a desire to reinforce and upgrade critical selling skills. Although some sales managers have a narrow view about the objectives of sales training—for example, to increase motivation—others identify a variety of objectives, as the next few paragraphs reveal.

OBJECTIVES OF SALES TRAINING

Although the specific objectives of sales training may vary from firm to firm, there is some agreement on the broad objectives. Sales training is undertaken to increase productivity, improve morale, lower turnover, improve customer relations, and produce better management of time and territory.

Increase Productivity

One objective of sales training is to provide trainees with the necessary skills so their selling performance makes a positive contribution to the firm. In a relatively short time, sales training attempts to teach the skills possessed by the more experienced members of the sales force. The time it takes for a new member of the sales force to achieve satisfactory levels of productivity is thus shortened considerably. The productivity of sales training receives strong support from George Hartmann, vice president of sales for the Commercial Products Division of the Fort Howard Corporation. Sales grew from $300 million in 1981 to $1.5 billion in 1994. When asked to name his proudest accomplishment, Hartmann identifies training, saying, "If I had to point to one single resource that's had the greatest impact, it would be training."[2]

Improve Morale

How does sales training lead to better morale? One objective of sales training is to prepare trainees to perform tasks so their productivity increases as quickly as possible. If sales trainees know what is expected of them, they will be less likely to experience the frustrations that arise from trying to perform a job without adequate preparation. Without sales training, customers may ask questions that sales representatives cannot answer, leading to frustration and lower morale. Evidence indicates salespeople who are uncertain about their job requirements tend to be less satisfied with their jobs. This same evidence shows that reps who are most aware of the job requirements are also more satisfied with their company's sales training activities.

Improving morale should not include extensive use of the so-called high-pitch, high-priced motivational speaker. The "Managing Sales Relationships" box questions the relationship between motivational hype and sales training. Jack Falvey, a sales consultant, dislikes using football players and coaches as part of the sales training program. He sees little similarity between professional selling and professional football.[3]

Lower Turnover

If sales training can lead to improved morale (greater job satisfaction), then this should result in lower turnover. Young, inexperienced salespeople are more likely to get discour-

Motivational Hype and Sales Training: Is There a Relationship?

A large screen rises in front of the hotel meeting room. Just behind it, cloaked beneath yards of black fabric, are 16 slide projectors, a videotape player, a sound system, and a computer system that will digitally drive a multithousand-dollar four minutes of hype.

Silence settles over this chapel of capitalism as a minister of motivation grabs a microphone and, like a Vegas showman, spins his tale, winding his rhythmic rhetoric faster and faster, preaching the salvation of salespeople—motivation. The faces of the converted lean toward him, and their silent refrain fills the room.

We believe! Oh, yes! We believe!

The house lights dim and BAM! The multimedia presentation synchronously beams images of products and company personnel in cadence with crescendoing music driven by a heavy bass.

Hallelujah! That's it! We're saved!

These salespeople are whipped to a frenzy of enthusiasm fortified with an emotional fervor that their company hopes will help them sell.

Do motivational presentations like this have any lasting effect? Do they constitute an entertaining form of sales training? Jack Snader, president of Systema,

Inc., says, "These types of meetings create an illusion of team spirit—a feeling that fades on the second Tuesday after the meeting." Snader compares these motivational pitches to "high school pep rallies: They're momentarily inspiring, but without training for the players, the game is lost."

The same philosophy applies to sales meetings. Rather than spend $12,000 on this form of entertainment, companies would be better off spending the money on sales training. After all, with the cost of a sales call now exceeding $300 in many industries, it becomes imperative that companies address ways to become more efficient.

Management is starting to scrutinize the cost of their sales meetings and ask, "What are we getting out of this?" Snader believes, "National sales meetings will become wonderful opportunities for a large amount of support for the continued development of salespeople." Sales meetings represent an excellent opportunity for refresher training for the entire sales force and should have one goal: to enhance the ability and reputation of the sales force so they can help customers solve real-world problems.

Source: Joseph Conlin, "The Lowdown on Sales Meetings," *Sales & Marketing Management* (May 1990), pp. 111–12.

---

aged and quit as a result of not being better prepared for the task than their experienced counterparts. Turnover can also lead to customer problems, since many customers prefer continuity with sales representatives. A customer who is called on by a sales representative who suddenly quits may transfer business to other suppliers rather than wait for a new representative. Sales training, by leading to lower turnover, alleviates such problems.

Fort Howard's national sales director, Paul Ferrin, feels that the company's strong training program enhances his ability to recruit top-notch salespeople. Hartmann feels that the training program has helped to cut turnover, which dropped by almost 80 percent in 14 years.[4]

Improve Customer Relations

One benefit of sales training that accompanies lower turnover is continuity in customer relationships. Having the same sales representative call on customers on a regular basis promotes customer loyalty, especially when the salesperson can handle customer questions, objections, and complaints. Customers place orders for their own benefits. Inadequately trained salespeople are usually not able to provide these benefits, and customer relations suffer.

Lucent Technologies, as demonstrated at the beginning of the chapter, places a great deal of emphasis on training that enhances customer value. In a highly dynamic environment, such as telecommunications, Lucent realizes that if their salespeople are not trained on the latest technologies, competitors will have an opportunity with their customers to take business away from them.

Manage Time and Territory Better

Time and territory management is a subject in many sales training programs. How much time should be devoted to calls on existing accounts and how much time to calls on potential new accounts? How often should each class of account be called on? What is the most effective way of covering the territory to ensure routes traveled are the most efficient with respect to miles driven and time spent? Many sales training programs provide salespeople with answers to these questions.

The impact of technology on time and territory management has led to improved coverage for Yellow Freight, the Overland Park, Illinois-based trucking company. Yellow Freight went through a reengineering process that produced a sales force automation (SFA) system. Both sales managers and sales reps went through a training program on how to use the new computerized system, including the software and the hardware. Yellow Freight officials claim that salespeople already on the system have increased their face-to-face selling time with customers by 30 percent.[5]

THE DEVELOPMENT OF SALES TRAINING PROGRAMS

Sales training is an important function, as the previous paragraphs indicate. However, there are numerous problems that companies face when trying to implement sales training programs. A survey by Peterson, reviewed by *Training* magazine, asked sales managers to identify the problems they face when trying to introduce sales training programs. The top five obstacles identified by the 297 respondents are the following:

- Top management is not dedicated to sales training.
- Sales training programs are not adequately funded.
- Salespeople are apathetic about sales training.
- Salespeople resent training's intrusion on their time
- Salespeople resist changes suggested by training programs.[6]

This rather negative perspective on sales training should raise an important question. What is management doing that allows some of these problems to occur? In evaluating sales training programs, wouldn't management discover that the cost exceeds the benefits? Two problems exist. First, management too often expects that sales training will be a panacea for all of the company's sales problems. If the sales problems are not resolved, budget-cutting activities often start with the sales training program. Or management fails to understand sales training. Sales training is viewed as a cost of doing business rather than as an investment that pays future dividends. Why are only costs evaluated and not the other half of the operating statement?[7]

The second problem rests within the sales training function: namely, the evaluation of sales training programs. Too many sales training programs are conducted without any thought of measuring the benefits. Evaluation is difficult, but considering the millions of dollars devoted to sales training, it is not unreasonable to expect some attempt to measure the benefits. More is said later about how to evaluate sales training programs.

Many of the problems overlap and can be resolved by adopting a more objective approach. First, sales training often lacks credibility. Programs fail to deliver what they promise and are viewed by many as being a waste of time and money. Second, the level of approach assumes too much: "Trainees already know how to listen or to be enthusiastic, so why spend time on such basic areas?" Or, "Sales veterans already know how to sell, so time is not needed on this subject." Third, once techniques have been taught, it is not necessary to worry about the use of reinforcers or rewards to stimulate sales reps to continue to use them.

Creating Credibility in Sales Training

Many sales trainers believe their programs lack credibility. Budget-cutting efforts are too often directed at existing sales training programs.[8] This may reflect management's feelings that these programs are accomplishing little and are expendable. Sales training programs have to be sold, just like any other product or service. Well-designed programs are easier to sell to management than those put together with little thought.

Analyze needs
The starting point in creating credibility is to analyze the needs of the sales force (see Exhibit 12.1). One way to do this is to travel with sales reps, observing them and asking what they need to know that will help them perform more effectively. (Recent research designed to elicit selling procedures is discussed later in the chapter.) Field sales managers are a useful source of information because they are closest to the sales reps. Interviews with key members of management are productive ways to identify training needs. One expert advocates sending anonymous questionnaires to customers asking, "What do you expect of a salesperson in the industry? How do salespeople disappoint you? Which company in the industry does the best selling job? In what ways are its salespeople better?" Other sources include company records showing turnover data, performance evaluations, and sales and cost analyses. Attitudinal studies conducted with the sales force are useful sources of information. This analysis of needs answers three basic questions: Where in the organization is training needed, what should be the content of the training program, and who needs the training?

Determine objectives
Setting specific, realistic, and measurable objectives adds to the credibility of a sales training program. The objectives may include learning about new products, new techniques, or new procedures. It pays to keep the objectives simple. Management may want a 10 percent sales increase, which then becomes the broad objective of the training program. The specific objective might be to teach sales reps how to call on new accounts, which will help lead to the broad objective. Measurability is critical in sales training. More will be said about this later.

Develop and implement program
At this point, a decision has to be made concerning developing the training program or hiring an outside organization to conduct it. Many companies, both large and small, use outside agencies for sales training. Small companies may farm out most of their training needs. Large companies develop most of their own programs and will use outside agencies to handle specialized needs. Lack of careful investigation of outside suppliers can lead to problems. One sales manager mentioned how embarrassed he was by retaining a company that put on an "entertaining song-and-dance routine" that cost $5,000 but failed to have any lasting effect. Use of outside sources is encouraged if they meet the objectives of the company.

Evaluate and review program
Designing a measurement system is the next step. Here are some questions that need to be asked: What do we want to measure? When do we want to measure? How do we do it?

Exhibit 12.1   Analyzing the Needs of the Sales Force

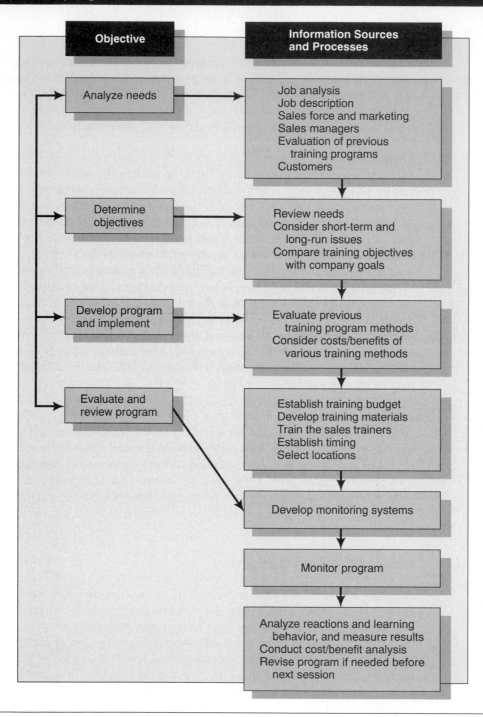

Or, what measuring tools are available? Using tests to measure learning is not difficult; measuring application in the field is difficult. Training a sales rep to demonstrate a product can be evaluated during the training session. But whether the sales rep demonstrates effectively in front of a customer is harder to evaluate. This is why field sales managers are an important link: They can provide follow-up and feedback information on how well the sales rep demonstrates the product. The field sales managers can coach the salesperson on how to demonstrate the product.

Finally, evaluations of sales performance provide additional evidence on the value of training, although such information must be used carefully. Changes in performance, like sales increases, may be due to factors not related to sales training. To claim that they are casts doubts on the sales training efforts.

Larger companies must decide which group to train. Not everyone in the sales force needs training. Certainly, newly hired recruits need training, whether it's on the job at first and then more centralized later or some other arrangement. When procedures or products change, training needs are universal. However, if certain sales reps are having a sales slump, then the training needs to be directed at them and not everybody. To include the entire force may create problems, especially among those not experiencing the sales slump. This latter group may resent being included and let others know as well. When a new training method is being tested, it is wise to use a group that will be receptive. This increases credibility, creating a favorable climate for continuation.

Since measurement is crucial, the sales trainer needs to collect data before training starts. The needs analysis provided relevant information pertaining to program content. For example, if it was observed that some salespeople had difficulty managing their sales calls, then observation by the trainer or the field sales manager after the program should provide data indicating the value of the training. Call reports would be another source of information. Follow-up must continue beyond the initial check since the use of new skills may drop off. If this happens, reinforcement is necessary.

The data collection process should provide sales trainers with information that will justify the program. Top management wants to know if the benefits exceed or equal the costs. Keeping top management informed about the success of training programs contributes to the overall credibility.

Continuous follow-up and evaluation of all sales training efforts is mandatory. Gene Hahne, manager of training for Shell Oil Company, comments, "We used one program for seven years in our company. We used it because nobody evaluated it. Nobody followed up on it. Nobody ever took the time out to go out in the field and ask participants, 'What did you get out of the program?'"[9] In this case, the program had attempted to teach sales reps how to probe for information during a sales call. Although most sales reps identified the subject matter, very few were able to identify the skills that had been taught. The program was not working and probably had been written off as a poor investment by management.

Sales training programs, whether being sold to the sales manager or to top management, must be credible. Management can always find other alternatives for spending resources.

THE TIMING OF SALES TRAINING

Although sales training is a continuous process, exactly when firms accept sales trainees into the formal sales training program varies considerably. A common practice is to have sales trainees work in the field calling on accounts before any formal sales training occurs. It is also common to start with formal training followed by a field assignment. In either case, the length of the formal training program can vary from a few days to more than a year, depending on company needs.

Training of experienced sales personnel varies also. Some companies have annual programs, and others have programs only when the need arises. The length of both types of programs varies from firm to firm. Training of experienced sales personnel may be routine, such as when it is associated with an annual sales convention. It may be nonroutine or remedial and may occur because of problems experienced by one or more members of the sales force. The introduction of new products often leads to sales training.

TRAINING NEW SALES RECRUITS

Most larger companies have programs for training new sales recruits. These programs differ considerably in length and content, however. The differences often reflect variations in company policies, nature of the selling job, and types of products and services. Even within the same industry, sales training programs vary in length, content, and technique.

Although a few companies have no preset time for training sales recruits, most firms have embraced the notion of a fixed period for formal training. The time varies from just a couple of days in the office, followed by actual selling combined with on-the-job coaching, to as long as two or three years of intensive training in a number of fields and skills.

What accounts for this variation? First, training needs vary from firm to firm and even within a firm. For example, one manufacturer of drugs has a seven-week program for new recruits who will sell conventional consumer products. For those recruits destined to sell more technical products, the training lasts two years.

Second, training needs vary because of differences in the needs and aptitudes of the recruits. Experienced recruits have less need for training than inexperienced recruits, although most large firms require everyone to go through some formal training. One industrial firm requires a one-week program for experienced recruits, but inexperienced recruits may require a two- to three-year program.

A final reason for variation in the length of training programs is company philosophy. Some sales managers believe training for new recruits should be concentrated at the beginning of a sales career, but others think it should be spread over a longer time, including a large dose of learning by doing. Exhibit 12.2 illustrates the differences in the length of sales training programs for new hires.

Exhibit 12.3 illustrates how much time and money it takes to train new sales reps. Dartnell provides trend data and reports that the following shifts have taken place:

- Compared with data from two years earlier, smaller companies, those under $5 million in annual sales, are spending approximately almost 50 percent more on sales training per new hire—$5,500 in the current survey compared with $3,688 two years earlier.

- At the same time, the length of training in these smaller companies has increased significantly, from 3.3 months in 1994 to 4.4 months in the current survey.

- The data suggest that smaller companies are placing a great deal more emphasis on training than they were several years ago.

- Companies say they are spending time and money on training experienced salespeople, indicating a strong commitment to a well-trained sales force.

- Large companies, those with more than $5 million in annual sales, reported spending a little less money on training than in the last survey period.[10]

Exhibit 12.2   Length and Cost of Sales Training for New Hires

	Training Period for New Hires (Months)	Cost
Company Size		
Under $5 million	4.4	$5,500.0
$5–$24.9 million	4.2	8,141.1
$25–$99.9 million	3.7	8,090.9
$100–$250 million	1.7	7,400.0
Over $250 million	3.6	7,000.0
Product or Service		
Consumer products	3.4	5,354.2
Consumer services	3.3	4,537.3
Industrial products	4.8	9,893.5
Industrial services	4.8	9,060.5
Office products	3.8	6,269.4
Office services	3.2	6,200.0
Type of Buyer		
Consumers	3.3	4,220.6
Distributors	3.9	7,256.5
Industry	4.3	8,234.2
Retailers	3.2	6,711.0
Overall	**3.9**	**$7,079.8**

Source: *Dartnell's 30th Sales Force Compensation Survey: 1998–1999* (Chicago: Dartnell Corp., 1999), p.143.

TRAINING EXPERIENCED SALES PERSONNEL

After sales trainees are assigned to field positions, they quickly become involved in customer relationships, competitive developments, and other related matters. Over time, their knowledge of competitive developments and market conditions becomes dated. Even their personal selling styles may become stereotyped and less effective. Also, because of changes in company policies and product line, sales representatives require refresher or advanced training programs. Few companies halt training after the trainee has completed the basics. Most managements endorse the view that the need to learn is a never-ending process and even the most successful of their sales representatives can benefit from refresher training. Exhibit 12.3 shows the length, type, and cost of sales training for experienced sales reps. Dartnell's access to trend data produces the following observations:

- Experienced sales reps in this survey are given, on average, 32.5 hours of ongoing training per year at a cost of $4,032 per rep. This compares with 32.2 hours of training at a cost of $3,716 per rep in 1994. Seven years ago, experienced reps received just 27 hours of training per year.

- The fact that experienced reps continue to receive increasing amounts of training reflects a continuing commitment on the part of management to provide ongoing learning opportunities for their senior salespeople.

- The fact that companies are spending, on average, nearly 25 percent more on training

Exhibit 12.3   Length, Type, and Cost of Sales Training for Experienced Reps

| | Hours per Year of Ongoing Training | Type of Training | | |
		Selling Skills (%)	Product (%)	Cost
Company Size				
Under $5 million	30.1	40.7%	60.0%	$3,752
$5–$24.9 million	36.1	44.6	53.3	3,947
$25–$99.9 million	31.0	45.4	47.6	3,902
$100–$250 million	25.2	43.4	56.9	5,365
Over $250 million	38.0	44.2	51.3	4,824
Product or Service				
Consumer products	35.8	44.1	50.1	4,039
Consumer services	33.9	49.3	47.5	3,623
Industrial products	31.6	37.1	58.9	5,149
Industrial services	30.8	41.8	53.9	4,867
Office products	41.8	38.0	59.0	4,261
Office services	33.3	45.2	56.0	3,470
Type of Buyer				
Consumers	36.2	45.3	53.4	3,142
Distributors	35.7	40.2	55.1	4,168
Industry	31.5	43.2	55.2	4,605
Retailers	32.9	43.7	51.9	4,181
Overall	**32.5**	**43.6%**	**54.0%**	**$4,032**

Source: *Dartnell's 30th Sales Force Compensation Survey: 1998–1999* (Chicago: Dartnell Corp., 1999), p.145.

per experienced rep over seven years ago is a further indication that companies continue to be committed to ongoing training.

- From previous editions where the split was roughly equal, companies now are spending an increasing amount of time on product training and less on training in selling skills. This is a new trend that has developed since the previous edition of this survey.

- Based on [these] two previous studies, [Dartnell] conclude[s], "Quite simply, companies realize that training, by and large, is an inexpensive way to protect their investments in their sales forces."[11]

Additional training often occurs when a sales representative is being considered for promotion. In many companies, a promotion is more than moving from sales to district sales manager. A promotion can include being assigned better customers, transferring to a better territory, moving to a staff position, or being promoted to sales management. Whenever salespeople are assigned better customers or better territories, additional sales training acquaints them with their increased responsibilities.

Some large companies try to reduce training time for experienced salespeople by emphasizing initial training. Hercules, Inc., a chemical industry company, provides new sales reps 26 weeks of training during the first year. Formal training programs for experienced sales reps last one week or less.

Many companies decentralize the training for experienced salespeople. Hercules,

Bergen–Brunswig, and Xerox are among many companies that attempt to get training into the field using self-paced training manuals, videos, and computer-based programs.

Training experienced salespeople is viewed as providing insurance for a company's major asset. David Barousse of Bergen–Brunswig notes, "Find me a company without that insurance, that has stopped training its salespeople, and I'll target that market and that company and have its business by year's end."[12]

SALES TRAINING TOPICS

For new sales trainees, the content of sales training tends to remain constant over time. Product or service knowledge subjects appear in the majority of programs. The same can be said about market/industry orientation, company orientation, and selling skills. Beyond these standard topics there exists a vast array of different subjects that range from the logical, such as training sales reps in how to use the company's new computerized procedures, instructing the sales force in how to build relationships, and educating the sales reps in team selling procedures, to some very questionable topics such as training the sales force to modify their sales presentation based on whether the customer is "left-brained" or "right-brained" as well as instructing the sales reps to learn how to read and interpret body language including eye movements.

Product Knowledge

Although product knowledge is one of the most important topics, knowing when and how to discuss the subject in a sales call is probably even more important. More time is typically spent on product knowledge than any other subject, although the time spent varies with the commodity sold.

Companies that produce technical products, such as computer manufacturers, spend more time on this subject than do manufacturers of nontechnical products. One manufacturer of specialized industrial components allocates 90 percent of its sales training program to application engineering and product knowledge for graduate engineers recruited directly from campuses. Producers of personal care products and toiletry preparations spend less time on product knowledge. In the service industry, the complexity of the service influences the amount of time needed to learn the service, such as with various types of insurance.

Product knowledge involves knowing not only how the product is made but also how the product is used and, in some cases, how it should not be used. One producer of machine tools gives newly hired sales engineers extensive in-plant exposure to technical and engineering matters. Before field assignment, they spend time in a customer's plant, where they are taught machine setup and operations under realistic conditions.

Product knowledge is not limited to only those products the sales trainee will eventually sell. Customers often want to know how competitive products compare on price, construction, performance, and compatibility with each other. Customers expect reps to show them how the seller's products can be coordinated with competitive products, such as in a computer installation that involves products made by different manufacturers. One paper products manufacturer that supplies paper towels to industrial firms exposes sales trainees to competitive towel dispensers so they will know which dispensers handle their paper towels.

A major objective in training in product knowledge is to enable a salesperson to provide potential customers with the information needed for rational decision making. Some benefits that accrue to salespeople as they acquire product knowledge include the following:

1. Pride and confidence in product quality.

2. Self-assurance emanating from technical knowledge of product makeup.

3. Communication with customers through the use of the operational vocabulary peculiar to the industry.

4. Understanding of product functioning that allows effective diagnosis of customer problems.[13]

All these benefits contribute to improved salesperson–customer interaction.

Market/Industry Orientation

Sales training in market/industry orientation covers both broad and specific factors. From a broad viewpoint, salespeople need to know how their particular industry fits into the overall economy. Economic fluctuations affect buying behavior, which affects selling techniques. Information about inflationary pressure, for example, may be used to persuade prospective buyers to move their decision dates ahead. If the sales force is involved in forecasting sales and setting quotas, knowledge of the industry and the economy is essential.

From a narrower viewpoint, salespeople must have detailed knowledge about present customers. They need to know their customers' buying policies, patterns, and preferences and the products or services these companies produce. In some cases, sales reps need to be knowledgeable about their customers' customers. This is especially true when sales representatives sell through wholesalers or distributors who often want reps to assist them with their customers' problems. Missionary salespeople are expected to know the needs of both wholesalers and retailers, even though the retailers buy from the wholesalers.

Company Orientation

Sales trainees must be aware of company policies that affect their selling activities. Like all new employees, they need indoctrination in personnel policies on such items as salary structure and company benefits.

Sales representatives can expect customers to request price adjustments, product modifications, faster delivery, and different credit terms. Most companies have policies on such matters arising from legal requirements or industry practices. Too often, however, avoidable delays and possibly lost sales result from inadequate sales training in company policies.

Two practices provide salespeople with knowledge of company policies. The first requires sales trainees to learn about company policies and procedures by working in the home office in various departments, such as credit, order processing, advertising, sales promotion, and shipping. The second approach has the trainee work as a sales correspondent for a time. The trainee processes customer orders, maintains mail and telephone contact with customers, and sometimes serves as the company contact for a group of customers.

Major corporations provide the sales force with sales manuals that cover product line information and company policies. A well-prepared sales manual can give a sales representative a quick answer to a customer's question.

Time and Territory Management

Sales trainees also need assistance in how to manage their time and territories. The survey by Learning International suggests that salespeople perceive this as an important problem.[14]

The familiar 20:80 ratio, where 20 percent of a company's customers account for 80 percent of the business, applies to time and territory management in the reverse direction. It is not unusual to find sales representatives who are skilled in all areas except efficient time management spending 80 percent of their time with customers who account for only 20 percent of sales.

Teaching Ethics

In an industry plagued by deceptive sales practices, The Mutual Life Insurance Company of New York (MONY) is trying to set the standard for ethical selling.

The company requires all its agents and support staff to take an ethics course that is taught by agency managers (who are in turn trained during regional meetings). The sales professionals are given study materials on ethics and take an exam. "If they fail, they have to restudy the material and take the exam again," says Stephen J. Hall, MONY's senior vice president of sales. "I don't think there's one person associated with the sales organization who will not go through this course. We want to make certain that the sales force has a clear understanding of what it means to conduct business in an ethical fashion." The approach appears to be working. Says Peter Patrino, an analyst with Chicago-based credit-rating company Duff & Phelps, "To date, they haven't been hit with the big problems that other players in the insurance industry have faced. That's good news for them."

Source: Geoffrey Brewer, "1995 Best Sales Force Awards," *Sales & Marketing Management* (October 1995), p. 54.

Poor assignment of customers and development of territories contribute to the time management problem. Sales managers need to know how to develop territories to enhance the sales rep's efficiency. Assigning a sales representative too many accounts or a territory that is too large leads to time and territory management problems.

The program for a manufacturer of micrographic equipment and supplies trains salespeople to "plan your work—work your plan." Although some instruction in time management is provided by this company during classroom training, the major responsibility rests with the district sales managers. Effective time management is more likely to be achieved via on-the-job training. Sales representatives turn in their projected activities every two weeks and review their district sales manager's past plans and performance. The district sales manager helps them modify the projected plans for greater efficiency. The desire for more effective time and territory management has led to greater telephone usage and telemarketing sales training courses.

Legal/Ethical Issues

Statements—or, rather, misstatements—made by salespeople have legal and ethical implications. The "Ethical Issues" box describes a company's response to ethical problems.

Lapses in ethical conduct have been known to lead to legal problems. The example in the "Ethical Issues" box stems from problems confronted by major insurance companies that allowed sales representatives to engage in unethical practices, such as selling whole life insurance policies as annuities. In one case, the legal settlement ran into millions of dollars. An article in *Business Week* makes the following point:

> After a year of scandals involving some of the biggest names in life insurance, consumers are finally waking up to churning. This abusive sales practice occurs when agents dupe customers into replacing perfectly good cash-value policies. While agents reap big commissions, switching policies costs consumers more than $6 billion annually, the Consumer Federation of America estimates.[15]

Other Subjects

Recent technological developments have led to a new sales training subject: how to use a personal computer. Many companies now require their sales reps to carry personal computers with them to improve productivity. Salespeople use PCs to plan their call activities,

Automated Training Goal: How to Use This Computer

Dun & Bradstreet has seen the light of sales force automation. It has equipped its nearly 600 salespeople with multimedia laptops and CD-ROM drives, which they use to sell the company's information services to credit, marketing, and purchasing professionals. In fact, many of the actual products from D&B are sold on CD-ROM.

Early in the process of automation the company realized it faced the daunting task of teaching hundreds of people, some of whom had never before operated a laptop computer, to be capable and comfortable with the hardware and software. To that end they commissioned a two-part interactive training program that invites new users to have fun getting to know their computer and walks them through the system's key components.

Developed by Logical Design Solutions in Murray Hill, New Jersey, the first half of the program is designed as a game called Alpine Adventure, in which salespeople are told that they have gone on a hypothetical trip to Europe to ski the Alps, but they must first go on a scavenger hunt to recover lost skis, boots, and poles. As they travel Europe, they are asked questions by various locals. If they answer the questions correctly, they are led to the missing equipment. Upon successful completion of the game, the program prints out a certificate that the salesperson sends to the sales manager, who in turn sends them a ski trophy.

"This technology is very, very new to our sales process and sales culture," says Tom Shea, D&B assistant vice president of business development. "We have a wide range of levels of understanding and comfort,

and wanted something that would make them feel comfortable with the technology."

The game and the tutorials, which can be upgraded via modem, diskette, and soon CD-ROM, do not replace in-person training but provide a refresher course whenever needed. The next logical phase of the project, Shea says, will be to embed sales training into the program as well.

Dun & Bradstreet Salespeople have fun getting to know their computers with Alps Adventures, an electronic board game.

Source: "Training Hits the Road," *Sales & Marketing Management,* June 1995, Part 2, pp. 10–14.

submit orders, send reports, check on inventory and price levels, receive messages, and present product and service demonstrations. In some cases, the sales rep can access the company's decision support system (DSS) to learn what products have been selling in an area or for a specific customer. A few companies have found that the use of PCs allows their salespeople more face-to-face customer contact time. The "Managing Sales Relationships" box describes the computer training used by Dun & Bradstreet as it introduced laptop computers into its sales force.

Sales training topics may be very specific. Price objections are common in sales transactions and sales managers are not pleased if they feel that sales reps offer discounts too quickly. Recently, Johnson Controls Inc., a manufacturer of automated control systems based in Atlanta, instituted a six-month training program to address the issue of price negotiations. Linda DeMars, regional sales manager for Johnson Controls, reports, "What we notice is that our salespeople find it more comfortable, or it looks like the only option, to erode market pricing as opposed to 'bundling' or building value." One solution adopted by Johnson Controls was to provide salespeople with detailed financial information to help them make more profitable decisions.[16]

Many companies, like Caterpillar Inc., spend substantial sums of money each year on trade shows. Increasing cost pressures have forced management to be more concerned about the return from trade shows and other similar expenditures. As a result, Caterpillar Inc. personnel selected to staff trade show exhibits undergo a training program designed to handle a trade show's unique features. Most salespeople selected have the "training and experience to make in-depth presentations in their specialties. But even though they're very good at what they normally do, they are not necessarily skilled at working a trade show. They don't always know how to engage and qualify new prospects, handle big crowds, or weed out the buyers from the 'tire kickers'."[17]

Other subjects addressed in training programs include body language, eye movement, and attempts to determine if the prospect is right-brained or left-brained. One advocate comments, "Customers come in right- and left-brained thinking styles, and understanding their differences and your own brain waves can help you make your next sale." Indicators of left- or right-brained people might be whether or not a customer wears a watch or carries a calculator.[18] Evidence supporting the efficacy of this concept as a sales training subject is not available.

Alan J. Zaremba, in a *Business Marketing* article, notes that analyzing body language has received attention since Julius Fast published *Body Language* in 1970. Zaremba states, "Nonverbal gestures do affect how messages are perceived." He cautions, however, that a harmful assumption about body language is that there is not a "finite and universal meaning for all messages transmitted nonverbally."[19] Training salespeople to observe and interpret a customer's body movements may help improve the sales presentation, but it is a skill that would require extensive training to accomplish. As with any training technique, evaluation of the process is mandatory to measure costs and benefits.

SALES TRAINING METHODS

The most commonly used methods of sales training are on-the-job training (OJT), individual instruction, in-house classes, and external seminars. Exhibit 12.4 summarizes industry preferences. Companies use a variety of techniques, recognizing that different subjects require different methods. Overlap exists within a given method. On-the-job training includes individual instruction (coaching) and in-house classes held at district sales offices. District sales personnel attend external seminars as well.

The Dartnell Corporation provides a review of trends in the use of training methods:

- On-the-job training continues to be the most prevalent method of training salespeople and is used by nearly 84 percent of responding companies. Nearly 82 percent of responding companies said they used this method in 1994, an insignificant change.

- External seminars, used by 71 percent of responding companies, and individual instruction, used by nearly 70 percent of responding companies, are again among the "top three picks" of survey participants.

- As a training method, "home assignments" are least favored and used by just 18 percent of respondents.

- External seminars continue to be a major training tool. In 1990, 59 percent of re-

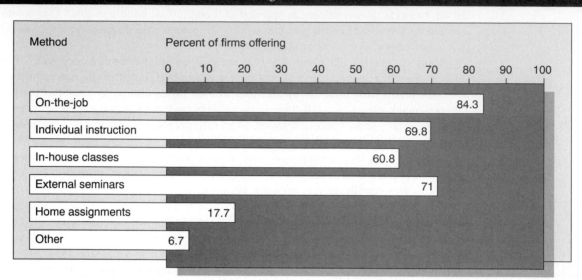

Exhibit 12.4   Methods Used in Sales Training

Method	Percent of firms offering
On-the-job	84.3
Individual instruction	69.8
In-house classes	60.8
External seminars	71
Home assignments	17.7
Other	6.7

Source: *Dartnell's 30th Sales Force Compensation Survey: 1998–1999* (Chicago: Dartnell Corporation, 1999), p. 141.

sponding companies said they used this training method for their salespeople. This percentage increased to 69 percent in 1992 and now stands at 71 percent of responding companies.

- This is a strong indication that companies are now more willing than in the past to seek help from the outside when it comes to solving their training/motivation problems. It also shows more of a willingness on the part of companies to accept differing approaches and points of view when it comes to problem solving.[20]

The techniques of instruction vary, as Exhibit 12.4 shows. The most prevalent forms of instruction are videotapes, lectures, and one-on-one instruction, and companies combine techniques to achieve the best possible balance.

One source of sales training comes from outside suppliers, which use many of the techniques listed in Exhibit 12.5. Exhibit 12.4 and the trend information provided by Dartnell Corp. in Exhibit 12.6 indicate a major shift in the use of external sources for sales training. The use of outside sources is not without some controversy. Jack Falvey, sales consultant, indicates, "The design, development, and sale of training materials is a big business these days." Companies question if they should spend money on outside sales training sources. Falvey's response is, "Only if you have lots of discretionary money to spend and don't know what to do with it."[21]

"Selling," according to Falvey, "is an interactive skill that must be acquired in combination with the knowledge of how both you and your customers do business. It can't be separated out into a generic system that can later be recombined in some way with your business."[22]

Corning, a manufacturer of ceramics, like many other companies established an outsourcing partnership with a company that provides a complete training program for all types and levels of employees. The outsourcing move did not eliminate the training function at Corning. The net effect was to enhance the training capabilities of Corning.[23] The

Exhibit 12.5   Instructional Methods*

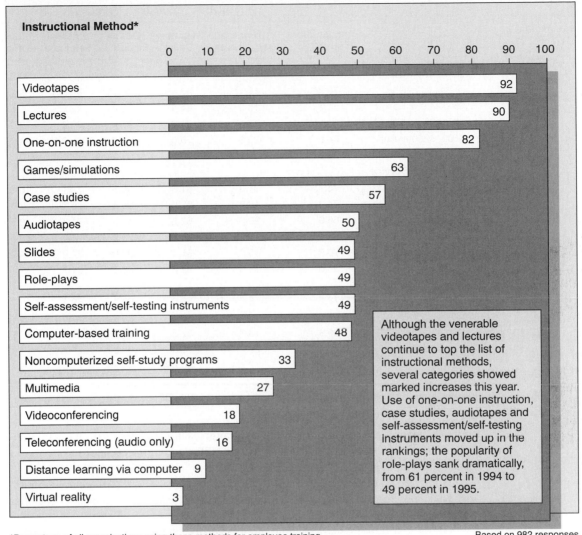

Instructional Method*

Method	Value
Videotapes	92
Lectures	90
One-on-one instruction	82
Games/simulations	63
Case studies	57
Audiotapes	50
Slides	49
Role-plays	49
Self-assessment/self-testing instruments	49
Computer-based training	48
Noncomputerized self-study programs	33
Multimedia	27
Videoconferencing	18
Teleconferencing (audio only)	16
Distance learning via computer	9
Virtual reality	3

Although the venerable videotapes and lectures continue to top the list of instructional methods, several categories showed marked increases this year. Use of one-on-one instruction, case studies, audiotapes and self-assessment/self-testing instruments moved up in the rankings; the popularity of role-plays sank dramatically, from 61 percent in 1994 to 49 percent in 1995.

*Percentage of all organizations using these methods for employee training.   Based on 982 responses.

Source: "Vital Statistics: 1995 Industry Report," *Training* (October 1995), p. 62.

"Managing Sales Relationships" box illustrates a process for companies to use when looking for external training programs.

On-the-Job Training

The mere mention of OJT sometimes scares new sales recruits. The thought of "learning by doing" is psychologically discomforting to many. Often, this is due to their incorrect perceptions of what is involved in OJT. On-the-job training is not a "sink or swim" approach in which the trainee is handed an order book and maybe a sales manual, and told to "go out and sell." OJT should be a carefully planned process in which the new recruit learns by doing and, at the same time, is productively employed. Furthermore, a good OJT program contains established procedures for evaluating and reviewing a sales

Exhibit 12.6   Sales Training Methods

	Percentage of Companies Using					
	Individual Instruction	Home Assignments	In-House Class	On the Job	External Seminars	Other
Company Size						
Under $5 million	72.3%	13.1%	43.1%	78.5%	59.2%	6.2%
$5–$24.9 million	71.2	16.9	64.4	85.0	72.5	8.8
$25–$99.9 million	65.1	17.4	69.8	87.2	80.2	7.0
$100–$250 million	54.2	20.8	75.0	91.7	79.2	4.2
Over $250 million	76.5	38.2	79.4	91.2	79.4	0.0
Product or Service						
Consumer products	75.7	21.3	61.8	89.7	72.1	6.6
Consumer services	74.3	16.9	62.5	85.3	69.1	7.4
Industrial products	66.0	20.0	62.5	83.0	71.5	6.5
Industrial services	66.9	18.2	60.4	79.2	76.0	7.8
Office products	70.9	25.6	65.1	93.0	74.4	4.7
Office services	69.0	19.5	62.8	88.5	71.7	7.1
Type of Buyer						
Consumers	73.6	18.2	56.6	87.4	69.8	6.3
Distributors	69.6	18.7	62.6	85.4	74.9	5.8
Industry	69.7	18.1	62.3	83.2	72.6	7.1
Retailers	72.4	20.0	60.0	91.0	71.7	7.6
Overall	**69.8%**	**17.7%**	**60.8%**	**84.3%**	**71.0%**	**6.7%**

Source: *Dartnell's 30th Sales Force Compensation Survey: 1998–1999* (Chicago: Dartnell Corp., 1999), p. 141.

trainee's progress. Critiques should be held after each OJT sales call and summarized daily. The critiques cover effectiveness, selling skills, communication of information in a persuasive manner, and other criteria.

A key aspect of on-the-job training is the coaching sales trainees receive from trainers, who may be experienced sales personnel, sales managers, or personnel specifically assigned to do sales training.

On-the-job training and coaching often occur together; this is referred to as one-on-one training. Observation is an integral part of the process. One-on-one training should not become "two-on-one" selling, where the objective becomes getting the order, not training the recruit. The sales manager or trainer is supposed to be a coach, not a player, and should stay out of the game no matter what the score. When the manager jumps in and says, "Let me take it from here," the recruit knows training has stopped and two-on-one selling has begun.[24] Some suggestions for making one-on-one training most effective are as follows:

1. Set pre-call objectives with the trainee.
2. Practice actual questions to be used to accomplish objectives (such as informational, directional, and closing).
3. Make the call (with the manager as a nonparticipating observer).
4. Contribute only positive reinforcement and act as a resource only on specific points and only on the request of the trainee.

How to Pick a Training Program

Barry Farber, coauthor of *Breakthrough Selling* and head of Farber Training Systems, Inc., in Florham Park, N.J., says that companies searching for independent trainers should look for five crucial elements:

- Solid, real-world content that the sales force can immediately apply.
- An engaging program that will peak people's interest.
- Interaction between the group and the instructor.
- Measurable goals from the field.
- Follow-through that reinforces the program's skills.

Companies may want to prescribe to the philosophy of Richard Campbell, sales communications/education manager for AT&T's Microelectronics. He judges the content of all training programs on the basis of a simple formula, SWC. It stands for "So what? Who cares?" If he cannot answer those two questions from the point of view of people in the field, the program's content is considered useless.

In the end, there's no magic formula to investing in training, but there is one sure thing: Today salespeople are even more receptive to the new concepts offered in training programs. Chris Heide of The Dartnell Corporation in Chicago says there are two reasons for this:

Competition is much tougher than salespeople have ever experienced.
Some 62 percent of the nation's sales force (up considerably from 10 years ago) is college educated, and salespeople who have higher education are usually more receptive to new ideas.

Source: Joe Conlin, "Training in Turbulent Times," *Sales & Marketing Management* (July 1993), p. 95.

5. Conduct the postcall analysis by letting the sales representative do the majority of the talking.[25]

OJT often involves job rotation—assigning trainees to different departments where they learn about such things as manufacturing, marketing, shipping, credits and collections, and servicing procedures. After on-the-job training, many sales trainees proceed to formal classroom training.

Classroom Training

For most companies, formal classroom training is an indispensable part of sales training, although very few of them rely solely on it. Classroom training has several advantages. First, each trainee receives standard briefings on such subjects as product knowledge, company policies, customer and market characteristics, and selling skills. Second, formal training sessions often save substantial amounts of executive time because executives can meet an entire group of trainees at once. Third, classroom sessions permit the use of audiovisual materials such as movies and videotape. Lectures, presentations, and case discussions can also be programmed into a classroom setting. The opportunity for interaction between sales trainees is a fourth advantage.

Such interaction is beneficial, since reinforcement and ideas for improvement can come from other sales trainees. Interaction is so important that many companies divide sales trainees into teams for case presentations, which results in interaction and forces trainees to become actively involved.

Classroom training also has its disadvantages. It is expensive and time-consuming. It requires recruits to be brought together and facilities, meals, transportation, recreation, and lodging to be provided for them. Sales managers, who are cognizant of these costs and time demands, sometimes attempt to cover too much material in too short a time. This results in less retention of information. Many sessions become mere cram sessions. Sales managers must avoid the natural tendency to add more and more material because the additional exposure is often gained at the expense of retention and opportunity for interaction.

Role playing

A popular technique used in most companies has the trainee act out the part of a sales rep in a simulated buying session. The buyer may be either a sales instructor or another trainee. Role playing is widely used to develop selling skills, but it can also be used to determine whether the trainee can apply knowledge taught via other methods of instruction. Immediately following the role playing session, the trainee's performance is critiqued by the trainee, the trainer, and other trainees.

Role playing where a sales trainee performs in front of others and where that performance is subsequently critiqued can be harsh. One sales training expert compares this approach with the guillotine, pointing out that:

The victims are kept in line and forced to witness the execution of others.

The victims' fates are published and scheduled in advance with much fanfare and an apprehensive countdown.

The method seems to be designed for surgical incisiveness and spectator enjoyment.[26]

Some of these problems disappear if the critique is conducted only in the presence of the sales trainee and then only by the sales instructor. When role playing is handled well, most trainees can still identify their own strengths and weaknesses.

Electronic Training Methods

A recent phenomenon in training methods involves the use of computers. IBM uses interactive video to train redeployed technical people to become salespeople. IBM's program, InfoWindow, combines a personal computer and a laser videodisc that provides an interactive TV. A trainee can practice calls with an on-screen actor whose response is a function of the trainee's approach.[27]

IBM is not the only company that uses such a system. Massachusetts Mutual Life Insurance (Mass Mutual) recently implemented an interactive video (IAV) training method for on-site sales training.[28] Mass Mutual retained Performax (a Westport, Connecticut, developer of electronic training systems) to develop a system. Performax's Simulation System Trainer (SST) combines a PC with a videodisc player and a video camera to simulate for novice salespeople the entire sales process and enables them to practice their selling styles by taping their responses to customer objections. Mass Mutual's new program lets trainees sharpen their skills in their offices before meeting with potential customers. Exhibit 12.7 illustrates an interactive video script.

Even before the development of interactive video training methods, also known as expert systems, electronic training had been introduced to help trainees learn "soft" selling skills.[29] These earlier programs, known as artificial intelligence (AI), include Sales Edge produced by Human Edge Software, Sell Sell Sell from Thoughtware, and more recently SELLSTAR! available from SELL-STAR! ESPRIT Software Technology. These training programs are based on psychological demographic models that require the salesperson to answer a series of questions about the customer and themselves. The programs provide a strategy report based on the psychological profiles of both parties.[30] The Sales Edge's output is a five-to-seven–page report that tells the salesperson what to expect from the customer and the appropriate response needed to make a sale.

Do these programs work? Can they train salespeople to effectively interact with customers? Answers to these questions have not been well documented. As with all methods,

Exhibit 12.7   Example of an Interactive Video Script

A beginning video shot has Mr. X answering your telephone call; then a computer screen will ask you several questions about the content of your call and your evaluation of background information on Mr. X.

For example, when starting your qualifying interview with Mr. X, the computer will prompt:

Will you . . . .

   (*a*) ask him an open question about any changes he may be planning for the future?
   (*b*) ask him a closed question concerning whether or not he'd like to upgrade his equipment?
   (*c*) make a statement about what you see as his needs and match them to your product's features?
   (*d*) introduce yourself and state that you work for Company Y?

If the trainee selected the wrong option, the computer program could remind the trainee of the role model for the sales process.

The interactive video has been designed to respond to the individual style of the trainee. For example, in the meeting after qualifying Mr. X, the computer will show Mr. X greeting you, and then you make a statement that is recorded by the video camera. After the camera has finished recording your response, the computer lets you describe what you did by selecting from the following:

Did you . . . .

   (*a*) describe a need identified during the qualifying telephone call?
   (*b*) make a benefit statement?
   (*c*) make a reference?
   (*d*) describe need and state purpose of the call?
   (*e*) make a reference and state purpose of the call?
   (*f*) state purpose of the call?

The response from Mr. X will depend on the trainee's answer. There are a large number of different combinations of responses, based on the way the trainee handles the call. As a result, one role-play contains many different scenarios.

If the trainee selects option *a*, Mr. X would respond positively if the need had been identified in the qualifying telephone call.

If the need had not been defined, Mr. X would give a negative response.

If the trainee selects option *b*, Mr. X will agree with the benefit statement.

if the trainee selects option *c*, Mr. X will express agreement.

If tho trainee selects option *d*, Mr. X will agree with the need and ask to get right down to business.

if the trainee selects option *e*, Mr. X will express agreement and ask to get right down to business.

If the trainee selects option *f*, Mr. X will ask to get right down to business.

If option *a*, *b*, or *c* is selected, one set of prompts on what the trainee would do next is provided.

If option *d*, *e*, or *f* is selected, another set of prompts on what the trainee would do next is provided.

Source: Warren S. Martin and Ben H. Collins, "Sales Technology Applications: Interactive Video Technology in Sales Training: A Case Study," *Journal of Personal Selling and Sales Management* 11 (Summer 1991), p. 65. Adapted with permission.

be it understanding body language or eye movements, if they help salespeople to be more sensitive to customer differences, then they may make a contribution. The output of these artificial intelligence programs should not be thought of as the "final word on how to handle any customer."[31]

ADAPTIVE SELLING: KNOWING HOW TO SELL

Extensive knowledge about products, customers, competitors, company procedures, plus a myriad of other factual items is a necessary but not sufficient condition for successful sales performance. It is like the quarterback who memorizes all of the plays but doesn't know the right play to call at the right time or like the novice chess player who knows the basic moves but doesn't understand the various patterns that call for specific strategies. The experienced quarterback or master chess player can assess situations and adapt accordingly. Conveying this ability to adapt is what sales training is all about.

Sales training attempts to teach sales trainees in a relatively short period the skills of the more experienced and successful members of the sales force. Weitz, Sujan, and Sujan stress the potential role of salesperson knowledge, especially as it applies to specific selling situations and the appropriate selling responses, and the salesperson's ability to process customer information as key determinants of sales performance.[32]

Leigh and McGraw contend that experienced and effective salespersons have "sophisticated knowledge structures that enable them to categorize selling situations more effectively and efficiently on the basis of similarity to other 'remembered' situations, then apply the activities and behaviors of an appropriate selling approach to each."[33] This knowledge, known as declarative and procedural knowledge, permits an experienced salesperson "to recognize or classify a particular selling situation as an instance of a more general selling category." The salesperson, as a result of interacting with the customer, may determine the buyer is task-oriented rather than relationship-oriented and adopt a task-oriented selling approach.

The potential impact of the adaptive selling concept on sales training is significant. Through sales training, novices can be taught how to classify customers, how to determine which approach would be most effective, and how to apply the selected approach. Novices also need to learn that as relationships change so will selling styles change, as governed by the situation. Adaptive selling is an approach that recognizes differences across customers and differences in the salesperson as well.

Do experienced and successful salespeople possess knowledge structures and can these structures be identified and used as a basis for sales training? Research indicates both questions can be answered with a yes. Exhibit 12.8 identifies the script objectives and activities for an initial sales call derived from a sample of 25 salespeople from a major hospital supply corporation. Note that the most common objective (84 percent) is to gather information about buyer needs.

Leigh and McGraw conclude that the procedural knowledge of experienced and effective salespeople can be identified and subsequently used in sales training. Behavior modeling requires that a sales trainee and an experienced salesperson interact to allow the trainee to observe and practice the methods used by the successful salesperson. Over time, the sales trainee develops a customized approach that represents individual traits to be used according to the situation.

In another study, Szymanski found that successful salespeople were more effective than unsuccessful salespeople at categorizing prospects. Successful salespeople not only were able to rely on fewer customer traits, but they also placed different weights or values on these traits.[34]

Furthermore, Szymanski reveals that the effective sales rep has a definite ordering of attributes according to their discriminating power, unlike the random ordering for the ineffective sales rep. And the effective sales rep has better discriminating power, relying on three attributes for classifying the prospect. The ineffective sales rep faces two problems: The first involves having to rely on more attributes, and the second is the greater risk of incorrectly classifying the prospect.[35] Clearly, training salespeople how to correctly classify prospects is a worthy topic of most sales training programs.

MEASURING THE COSTS AND BENEFITS OF SALES TRAINING

Sales training is a time-consuming and very costly activity. Is all this effort worth the cost? Does sales training produce enough benefits to justify its existence?

Sales training and increased profits have an obscure relationship at best. In the begin-

Exhibit 12.8   Script Objectives for an Initial Sales Call

Initial Sales Call Objectives (*n* = 25)	Percent
1. Gather information about buyer needs, objectives	84
2. Develop personal rapport with the buyer	44
3. Create favorable impression of me as a salesperson	44
4. Communicate positive impression of my company	33
5. Determine who are key decision makers	24
6. Assess sales potential	20
7. Assess the buyer's attitude toward my company	20
8. Lay groundwork for follow-up contact	20
9. Set specific follow-up appointment	20
Interjudge reliability = 0.91	

Source: Reprinted from Thomas W. Leigh and Patrick F. McGraw, "Mapping the Procedural Knowledge of Industrial Sales Personnel: A Script-Theoretic Investigation," *Journal of Marketing* 53 (January 1989), p. 22. Reprinted by the permission of the American Marketing Association.

ning of this chapter, we identified some broad objectives of sales training: improved selling skills, increased productivity, improved morale, lower sales force turnover, better customer relations, and better time and territory management. Unfortunately, pinning down the relationship between sales training and these broad objectives is not easy. Very little research has been done to determine what effect, if any, sales training has on the sales force. Most sales organizations simply assume on blind faith that their sales training programs are successful. After all, if a company has high sales and high profits, why should a sales manager assume sales training is anything but effective?

Sales Training Costs

Business firms spend millions of dollars each year on sales training in hopes of improving overall productivity. Exhibit 12.9 shows direct sales training costs for new hires in 1998. Exhibit 12.9 suggests that only the largest companies can afford to support a full-scale training program, yet all firms need sales training, regardless of size. The statistics suggest that business has a relatively generous attitude toward sales training. It allocates funds for training with minimal regard for the results. Clearly, measuring the benefits of sales training needs some attention.

Is the measurement process that difficult? After all, if sales training is supposed to lead to better productivity, improved morale, and lower turnover, then why not measure the changes in these variables after training has occurred? Some sales managers have done just that. They have assumed, We instituted sales training and shortly afterwards sales increased. Therefore, sales training was the reason. Right? Wrong! Unless appropriate procedures are used to design the research by which the benefits are assessed, it is hard to say what caused the sales increase. Sales may have increased as a result of improved economic conditions, competitive activity, environmental changes, seasonal trends, or other reasons. Consequently, research must be carefully designed to isolate these contaminating effects to identify the benefits directly attributable to training.

Measurement Criteria

Even though intervening variables such as changes in competitive activities make evaluation of sales training programs difficult, some measurement must occur. This raises the question of what characteristics of sales training should be assessed. Exhibit 12.10 illustrates an evaluation options matrix.

Exhibit 12.9   Average Sales Training Costs per New Hire by Industry: 1999

	Products	Services
Consumer	5,354.2	$ 4,537.3
Industrial	9,893.5	9,060.5
Office	6,269.4	6,200.0

Source: *Dartnell's 30th Sales Force Compensation Survey: 1998–99* (Chicago: Dartnell Corp., 1999), pp. 143, 145.

Exhibit 12.10   Evaluation Options Matrix

Evaluation Level: What Is the Question?	Information Required: What Information to Collect?	Method: How to Collect?
Reaction Did participants respond favorably to the program?	Attitudinal	Evaluation Questionnaires Comments Anecdotes Interviews with participants
Learning Did participants learn concepts or skills?	Understanding of concepts, ability to use skills	Before-and-after test
Behavior Did participants change their on-the-job behavior?	On-the-job behavior	Behavior ratings, before and after Critical incident technique Time-series analysis
Results What personal or organizational results occurred?	Changes in sales, productivity, or other performance	Cost–benefit methods

Source: Thomas Atkinson and Theodore L. Higgins, "Evaluation Obstacles and Opportunities," from *A Forum Issues Special Report* (February 1988), p. 22

One could certainly single out one of the criteria shown in Exhibit 12.10 as the measure of effectiveness, but a strong argument can be made that several criteria should be used in assessing the results of any sales training program. Measuring what was learned, for example, seems inappropriate because the obtained knowledge may not produce desired behavior changes. However, it is also inappropriate not to assess sales training programs, because the program might be considered a failure if nothing was learned or if what was learned is inappropriate. The solution rests in properly specifying the objectives and content of the sales training program, the criteria used to evaluate the program, and the proper design of the research so benefits can be unambiguously determined.

Measuring Broad Benefits

Broad benefits of sales training include improved morale and lower turnover. Morale can be partially measured by studies of job satisfaction. This approach is feasible with experienced sales personnel. Suppose, for instance, a company measured job satisfaction as part of a needs analysis and found evidence of problems. A follow-up job satisfaction study after the corrective sales training program would determine if morale changed noticeably.

Measuring reactions and learning is important in sales training for both new and experienced personnel. Most companies measure reactions by asking those attending the training to complete an evaluation form either immediately after the session or several weeks later. Emotions and enthusiasm may be high right after a session, but sales training effectiveness is much more than a "warm feeling."

Measuring what was learned requires tests. To what extent did sales trainees learn the facts, concepts, and techniques included in the training session? Objective examinations are appropriate.

Measuring Specific Benefits

Liking the program and learning something are not enough. Specific measures to examine behavior and results are needed to assess effectiveness. The effectiveness of a sales training program aimed at securing more new customers, for example, can be partially assessed by examining call reports to see whether more new customers are being called on. Results can be measured by tracking new account sales to see whether they have increased. If the specific objective of sales training is to increase the sales of more profitable items, evidence that this has been accomplished provides a partial measure of training effectiveness. Finally, if reducing customer complaints was the objective, then the appropriate specific measure is whether customer complaints decreased.

The measurement of both specific and broad benefits presumes the sales training program is designed to achieve certain goals. The goals should be established before sales training begins. When specific objectives have been determined, the best training program can be developed to achieve these objectives. Most training programs have several objectives. Multiple measurements of the effectiveness of the training program are then a necessary part of evaluating the benefits.

Recent studies reveal that most sales training evaluation measures are simple, consisting primarily of reactions to the program. Meaningful evaluation measures, such as learning, behavior, and results, are used much less frequently.[36] Exhibit 12.11 presents frequency of usage for the different methods of evaluating sales training programs. As can be seen, the weakest or easiest-to-collect measures—staff comments and feedback from supervisors and trainees—are used the most. Bottom-line evaluation (e.g., changes in sales volume) is relatively limited.

Exhibit 12.12 shows how sales managers rank the various measures by both importance and frequency of use. The rankings are inconsistent. The most frequently used measure is course evaluation, but its importance is ninth out of a list of 14. Course evaluation is a reaction measure that fails to reveal learning, behavioral, and results changes associated with the sales training.

Evaluating the benefits of sales training is difficult. One study asked sales managers to identify the most important restrictions against sales training evaluation. The most common restrictions were time and money and difficulty in gathering the data and/or gaining access to data.[37]

RECENT TRENDS IN SALES TRAINING EVALUATION

In recent years there has been a surge of interest in sales training evaluation, especially at levels three and four. Managers are no longer willing to rest on the assumption that sales training must be effective since sales are rising. Managers are now being asked to provide concrete evidence that sales training makes a difference. Evidence based on level one

Exhibit 12.11   Group Ranking of Evaluation Approaches by Frequency

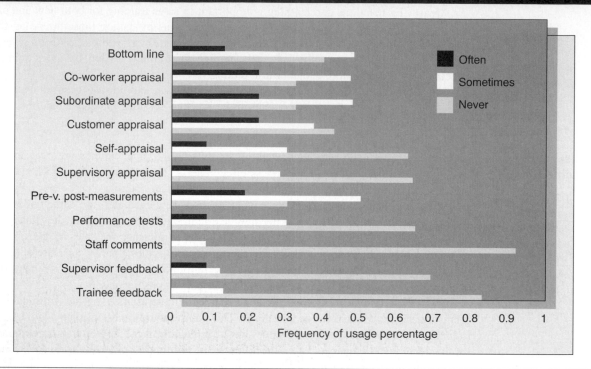

Source: Robert C. Erffmeyer, K. Randall Russ, and Joseph F. Hair, Jr., "Needs Assessment and Evaluation in Sales-Training Programs," *Journal of Personal Selling and Sales Management* 11 (Winter 1991), p. 24.

evaluations, facetiously referred to as smile sheets, or level two evaluations, testing what was learned, is useful but no longer sufficient proof. If sales training is to be viewed as an investment rather than a cost, then managers must be able to document the benefits in order to calculate a return on investment (ROI).

What's behind this movement toward more levels three and four evaluation? According to Beverly Geber, special projects editor of *Training* magazine, "Blame TQM or downsizing or impatient managers. Fact is, trainers are being pressured to evaluate training courses at much deeper levels."[38] Cost-cutting activities at most corporations force training departments and others as well to use money more wisely.

A dilemma facing many sales training managers is that while management wants evidence that supports the value of training, funds needed for evaluation, especially at level four, have not been budgeted. Level four evaluations usually require using a control group, a rare activity in most companies. "In the businesses I've been in, nobody, especially in sales, wants to volunteer to be in the control group," says Mark Faber, research and measurement manager, sales planning, for Microsoft Corporation. "The military has no trouble getting control groups: 'You guys go out with guns and you other guys go out without them.' Nobody in sales wants to go out without guns."[39]

Faber and others have been able to achieve the ends of a control method without actually using control groups. "You can implement training in one site and see a change," suggests Dan Baitch, research project manager for Learning International in Stamford, Connecticut. "Then you implement it in another site and see another change. Meanwhile, nothing is changing in the other sites, so each acts as a control group for the one before it."[40]

Exhibit 12.12 Overall Ranking of Evaluation Measures

Approach	Type	Importance	Frequency
Trainee feedback	Reaction	1	2
Supervisory appraisal	Behavior	2	6
Self-appraisal	Behavior	3	7
Bottom-line measurement	Results	4	9
Customer appraisal	Behavior	5	10
Supervisory feedback	Reaction	6	4
Performance tests	Learning	7	5
Training staff comments	Reaction	8	3
Course evaluations	Reaction	9	1
Subordinate appraisal	Behavior	10	12
Pre- vs. post-training measurements	Learning	11	11
Co-workers appraisal	Behavior	12	13
Knowledge tests	Learning	13	8
Control group	Learning	14	14

Source: Robert C. Erffmeyer, K. Randall Russ, and Joseph F. Hair, Jr., "Needs Assessment and Evaluation in Sales-Training Programs," *Journal of Personal Selling & Sales Management* 11 (Winter 1991), p. 24.

There are problems, of course, in equating sales increases with sales training. There are too many variables that could have had a positive effect on sales: introduction of a new product, failure of a competitor, increase in advertising, or improvement in price competitiveness. Level three evaluations may be sufficient for some managers who contend that sales results will follow changes in behavior. Regardless of the evaluation method employed, sales training managers face increasing demands as to the value of their programs.

SUMMARY

Sales training is a varied and ongoing activity that is time-consuming and expensive. Most companies engage in some type of sales training. In fact, most sales managers feel that sales training is such an important activity that they require it for everybody, regardless of their experience. Some common objectives of sales training are to teach selling skills, increase productivity, improve morale, lower turnover, improve customer relations, and improve time and territory management.

Considerable variability exists in the length of sales training programs. Industry differences account not only for variations in length but also variations in program content. Company policies, the nature of the selling job, and the types of products and services offered also contribute to differences in time spent and on topics covered.

Product knowledge receives the most attention, followed by selling techniques, market/industry orientation, and company orientation. This allocation is the subject of considerable criticism, as described in the chapter.

As a result of various environmental changes, the content and method of sales training has changed. How to use the telephone in selling is a commonly taught subject. Salespeople receive instruction on how to use a microcomputer to better plan their activities. And salespeople are now being trained via personal computers and VCR systems. Companies recognize that their technical people need sales training.

Recent sales training methodology and research provide promising developments. Expert systems allow sales trainees to interact with an actor using a personal computer and a video screen to practice their selling skills. Several companies provide artificial intelligence programs using personal computers that help the sales reps plan their strategies based on customer and sales rep psychological demographics. Research into the existence of declarative and procedural knowledge structures possessed by effective salespeople promises to provide a new source of knowledge needed to train novice sales representatives.

Sales training is very expensive and generally considered beneficial. Accurate measurement of the benefits is difficult. It is hard to isolate the effects produced solely by sales training from those that might have been produced by other factors such as changes in the economy or the nature of competition.

Sales training provides managers with the opportunity to convey their expectations to the sales force. A well-designed training program shows the sales force how to sell. Sales managers can communicate high performance expectations through training and equip the force with the skills needed to reach high performance levels.

DISCUSSION QUESTIONS

1. The response from a few of the sales reps from Marlow Technologies toward the new sales training topic was not encouraging. Geoff Marlow, national sales manager, was dismayed at what he perceived to be a total lack of social graces on the part of the 15-person sales force. To rectify this situation, he retained a consulting firm that specializes in etiquette training to provide a day-long session on the subject. Frank Casey, one of Marlow's sales trainees, was not pleased and said, "What's this? Now we have to go to charm school too! Next thing you know, they'll want to teach us how to dress." Are such topics as etiquette and dress appropriate for sales training? How would you evaluate the effectiveness of this kind of training?

2. The newly assigned sales representative was perplexed about her inability to learn about consumers' needs. She contends her customers are not willing to tell her what problems they are experiencing. After making several joint calls with her, the district sales manager agreed she was not receiving informative responses to her questions. What are the characteristics of good questions? How can sales reps be trained to ask better questions?

3. Various artificial intelligence (AI) programs such as Sales Edge, Sell Sell Sell, and SELLSTAR! promise to help sales representatives adapt their selling style to more effectively match the customer's style. The results are based on the psychological demographics of both parties. What do you see as the advantages and disadvantages of these programs? How would you design a research program to test the effectiveness of these AI programs?

4. Experimental design, a subject taught in most marketing research courses, has had limited application in measuring the benefits of sales training programs. Why is this? How would you design an experiment to measure the benefits of a sales training program?

5. One expert contends that sales training is not at all complicated as some would claim. He predicts that regardless of the advances in communication, resources, technology, and training tools, the basic selling skills that trainers teach salespeople will change very little from those that have been successful during the past 50 years. What will change, according to the expert, is how salespeople are trained to use these skills effectively. Do you agree with this prediction? What advantages does interactive video (IV) offer to sales training?

6. A quote from the April 1987 issue of *Sales & Marketing Management* (p. 76) reads, "Research now identifies that much eye contact between seller and prospect can be a sign of trouble, visible proof that a person is resisting a sales effort or has little or no interest in the offered product." An associate of yours thinks this idea has merit and wants to train the sales force how to read and interpret eye movements. What would you advise?

EXPERIENTIAL APPLICATION

You have been retained by the Admissions Office of your college to develop a recruiting program that will lead to an increase in students who attend your college. One of your recommendations for the Admissions

Office is to hire a number of admission counselors who would visit high schools and attend college fairs to recruit new students. These admission counselors, like sales reps, will have quotas and will need to be trained.

You are to design a recruiting program that includes developing a training program for the admission counselors. Make sure that you design an evaluation method to assess the effectiveness of your training program.

INTERNET EXERCISE

Go to the Lucent Technologies Web site (*www.lucent.com*). Click on the Search icon and type in Training and Sales. You will notice literally thousands of Lucent publications on training. While many of these publications are technical, a number reference the training offered to customers and salespeople. Read through some of the publications and assess the

kind of training Lucent requires its salespeople to have in order to satisfy their customers. In addition, examine the kind of training Lucent offers its customers. You will note a large number of publications and courses available to customers to help them maximize their Lucent products.

SUGGESTED READINGS

Anderson, Rolph, Rajiv Mehta, and James Strong, "An Empirical Investigation of Sales Management Training Programs for Sales Managers," *Journal of Personal Selling and Sales Management* (Summer 1997), pp. 53–66.

Corcoran, Kevin J., Laura K. Petersen, Daniel B. Baitch, and Mark F. Barrett, *High Performance Sales Organizations.* Burr Ridge, IL: Irwin, 1995.

Dubinsky, Alan J., "Sales Training and Education: Some Assumptions about the Effectiveness of Sales Training," *Journal of Personal Selling and Sales Management* (Summer 1996), pp. 67–76.

Fine, Leslie M., and Ellen Bolman Pullins, "Peer Mentoring in the Industrial Sales Force: An Exploratory Investigation of Men and Women in Developmental Relationships," *Journal of Personal Selling and Sales Management* (Fall 1998), pp. 89–104.

Hanan, Mack, *Consultative Selling.* New York: AMA-COM, 1990.

Hise, Richard T., and Edward L. Reid, "Improving the Performance of the Industrial Sales Force in the 1990s," *Industrial Marketing Management* 23 (1994), pp. 273–79.

Honeycutt, Earl D., Jr., John B. Ford, and John F. Tanner, Jr., "Who Trains Salespeople?" *Industrial Marketing Management* 23 (1994), pp. 65–70.

Miller, Robert B., and Stephen E. Heiman, *Successful Large Account Management.* New York: Warner Books, 1991.

Peoples, David A., *Selling to the Top: David Peoples' Executive Selling Skills.* New York: John Wiley & Sons, Inc., 1993.

Rich, Gregory, "Selling and Sales Management in Action: The Constructs of Sales Coaching and Supervisory Feedback, Role Modeling and Trust," *Journal of Personal Selling and Sales Management* (Spring 1998), pp. 53–64.

Russ, Frederick A., Kevin M. McNeilly, James M. Comer, and Theodore B. Light, "Exploring the Impact of Critical Sales Events," *Journal of Personal Selling and Sales Management* (Spring 1998), pp. 19–34.

Young, Jeffrey, "Can Computers Really Boost Sales?" *Forbes ASAP,* August 28, 1995, pp. 85–98.

13 Designing Compensation and Incentive Programs

REWARDING WINNERS AT MERCK

Merck, with sales in excess of $23 billion, is a worldwide leader in health-related and pharmaceutical products. Its sales and profit growth has been consistent over the years. Indeed, the company's revenue jumped 19 percent between 1996 and 1997 alone. Merck's sales force numbers over 2,900 worldwide and has a reputation for being one of the best in the industry. The company has plans for significant growth, adding hundreds of salespeople over the next few years as it anticipates demand for its products to be strong into the 21st century. Its strategy is to focus on new products that add value in the marketplace. This requires a sales force that is highly trained (on the new products) and highly motivated (to convince customers that new products do indeed add value).

As we have seen in earlier chapters, a key to motivation is compensation and reward systems. Merck recognizes this in the development and creation of its reward program. Gerry Gallivan, senior vice president of sales, puts it this way: "Merck keeps good salespeople by rewarding each individual for their performance."

Financial Compensation: The Foundation of the Compensation Plan

The foundation of Merck's reward program combines incentive compensation and salary. Merck's goal is to provide a package that is very competitive in the pharmaceutical industry. The company believes this is critical to attracting and retaining the best salespeople. By combining a small incentive component with a large percentage of fixed salary, the company seeks to motivate the sales force while at the same time encouraging them to provide the customer service that Merck feels is such an important part of its success.

Incentives

While the company provides many incentives to its sales force, a critical motivator, in the minds of management, is the stock option program. Salespeople are offered the opportunity to purchase Merck stock at a price significantly below current market values. Gallivan feels strongly that this is a major component in their total reward package. "We believe Merck's stock option program, which is a component of the total compensation package, plays a role in retaining good salespeople. The program enables sales employees to have a vested interest in the future of the company."

Source: "Best Sales Forces 1998," *Sales & Marketing Management* (July 1998), pp. 32–51, and the Merck Web site, *www.merck.com*.

LEARNING OBJECTIVES

The ability to successfully motivate salespeople is essential to maximizing their performance potential. Compensation and reward systems are the single most important source of motivation for the salesperson. In addition, while financial compensation is at the heart of any compensation program, nonfinancial rewards play a big role in helping motivate salespeople. Understanding the balance between financial and nonfinancial incentives is an important element in a successful reward program. However, the design, implementation, and maintenance of a good compensation program are difficult sales management tasks. This chapter will discuss this process.

After reading this chapter you should be able to:

- Discuss the major issues in the development of a compensation program.

- Understand how to design a compensation and incentive program.

- Determine the elements of job performance to evaluate and reward in a compensation program.

- Determine the most appropriate mix of financial compensation programs.

- Define nonfinancial incentive programs.

SOME MAJOR COMPENSATION AND INCENTIVE ISSUES

Merck's compensation plan illustrates some of the difficult questions involved in designing effective compensation programs. First, which compensation method among the variety available—from straight salary, to a combination of salary and incentive bonuses, to 100 percent commission—is best for motivating specific kinds of selling activities in specific situations? Merck has opted for a combination of salary plus a variety of incentive bonuses, but in some circumstances straight salary or straight commission plans may be more appropriate.

A related issue concerns the proportion of a salesperson's total compensation that should be determined by incentive pay. In Merck's plan, a majority of each rep's compensation is determined by his or her base salary. In some other firms, a much larger portion of a salesperson's pay is determined by bonuses or commissions tied to specific performance dimensions. Which approach is most appropriate?

A final question concerns the appropriate mix of financial and nonfinancial incentives for motivating salespeople. While there are opportunities for some of Merck's top performing salespeople to be promoted to regional manager positions, most of the incentives in its reward program are financial. Many other firms offer a broader mix of both financial and nonfinancial incentives, including formal recognition programs as well as opportunities for advancement. Because salespeople with different personal characteristics have different valences for various kinds of rewards, the ideal motivation program would offer different rewards tailored to the unique needs and characteristics of each salesperson. Such an approach is usually not practical, though, because of the administrative complexities involved. Nevertheless, many firms offer compensation and incentive programs that are flexible enough, and incorporate a sufficient variety of rewards, so that most salespeople are offered at least something they consider worth working for.[1]

This chapter discusses the relative strengths and shortcomings of a variety of financial and nonfinancial incentives. The financial rewards examined include the total level of compensation; forms of incentive pay, such as commissions and bonuses; and short-term incentives, such as sales contests. Among the nonfinancial rewards discussed are programs for personal and career development and recognition programs. The most appropriate conditions for using each type of reward are also examined.

One other crucial question addressed is how to choose among such a diverse variety of rewards and integrate them into one effective compensation and incentive program. To answer this question, it is useful to examine the analytical procedures and decisions involved in designing such a program.

PROCEDURES FOR DESIGNING A COMPENSATION AND INCENTIVE PROGRAM

The many complex issues involved make designing and implementing an effective compensation and incentive program difficult. Many managers wonder whether their company's program is as effective as possible in motivating the kinds and amounts of effort they desire from their sales personnel. Indeed, a recent survey of over 300 salespeople from Fortune 1,000 companies found that less than one-third were "very satisfied" with their firms' compensation plan.[2]

To make matters worse, even well-designed motivational programs can lose their effectiveness over time. The changing nature of the market environment and evolving characteristics of the sales force can cause motivation programs to lose their balance and power of stimulation. As salespeople become satisfied with the rewards offered by a particular plan, for instance, their valences for more of those rewards may decline.

Recognizing such problems, an increasing number of firms frequently review their compensation and incentive policies. Many firms adjust their total compensation levels at least annually, and they are increasingly willing to make more substantial adjustments in their programs when circumstances demand. Some firms have established compensation and incentive committees to regularly monitor sales motivation programs for fairness and effectiveness.

The critical question is this: How should a firm design a new compensation and incentive program? What factors should be considered in designing a program to effectively motivate the sales force to expend effort on activities that are most consistent with the firm's marketing objectives? This question becomes even more complicated as companies seek to develop compensation programs that will be effective with a sales force that operates around the world. The "Global Sales Force" box speaks to how IBM dealt with this problem. Exhibit 13.1 diagrams the analytical processes and decisions involved in designing an integrated and effective sales motivation program. The components of this diagram are examined in more detail in the following sections.

ASSESSING THE FIRM'S SITUATION AND SALES OBJECTIVES

A major purpose of any sales compensation program is to stimulate and influence the sales force to do what management wants, how it wants it done, and within the desired time. Before managers can design a program that accomplishes this purpose, though, they must have a clear idea of what they want the sales force to do.

As a first step in deciding what job activities and performance dimensions a new or improved motivation program should stimulate, a manager should evaluate how salespeople are allocating their time. On what job activities do they focus and how much time do they devote to each? How good are their current outcomes on various dimensions of performance, such as total sales volume, sales to new accounts, or sales of particular items in the line? Much of this information can be obtained from job analyses the firm conducts as

Compensating the World Wide Sales Force

Compensating a worldwide sales force of over 140,000 salespeople is no small task. Just ask Ned Lauterbach, IBM's senior vice president and group executive of worldwide sales and services. Louis Gerstner, CEO of IBM, gave the job of restructuring the compensation program for the entire IBM sales force to him. Bringing together people from around the world, Lauterbach sought to understand the unique compensation and motivation issues faced by salespeople around the world before deciding on a plan.

While there were certainly some issues that were culture-specific, IBM found the basic problems to be surprisingly similar whether the salesperson was in Chicago or Tokyo. First, incentives were structured to reward salespeople for work in their own territory. The result was that they had little or no motivation to service larger customers whose needs extended beyond one salesperson's area of responsibility. The second problem was IBM's corporate philosophy of rewarding everything. Corporate objectives were translated into multiple performance (and subsequent incentive) objectives. It was not uncommon for salespeople to be operating under as many as 20 different performance objectives. The result was that focus on the customer was lost. Salespeople were more interested in getting the next bonus than meeting the needs of the customer. Third, IBM's network of business partners (discussed in Chapter 5) had been badly damaged. Business partners were competing with IBM salespeople in some accounts. The result was that IBM products were competing against IBM products sold by outside business partners.

Lauterbach and his team of compensation specialists worked hard to develop a new compensation program. The plan is designed to meet the needs of IBM corporate objectives but also provides enough latitude for regional directors around the world to motivate people with unique incentives. Total compensation is broken down as follows: benefits; variable pay (based on meeting IBM corporate objectives and distributed annually); incentive compensation based on teamwork (paid monthly), personal contribution (paid quarterly), and sales challenges (paid when they are earned); recognition; and base salary.

IBM is constantly enhancing not only the compensation program itself but also the ability of each salesperson to understand and use the plan. Recently, IBM introduced a new intranet site for its North American sales force. The site enables IBM salespeople to calculate their individual incentive compensation by working through a set of questions. It provides IBM representatives with real-time feedback on their compensation across a wide range of scenarios from best to worst. In addition, it has lowered IBM's costs. Instead of spending $130,000 on printing a new compensation brochure every time there was a change in the compensation program, IBM managers go to the Web site and make the necessary adjustments. The company is now preparing to roll out the site to its sales force around the world.

IBM's problem, designing compensation programs that are appropriate around the world, is faced by a number companies as they seek to maintain customer relationships in a global environment. While each program must be tailored to the individual needs of each company, some general rules apply. These can be summarized as the do's and don'ts of global compensation:

DO

- Involve the salespeople from key countries in creating the compensation program.
- Allow local managers to decide the mix between base and incentive pay.
- Use consistent performance measures (results paid for) and emphasis on each measure.
- Allow local countries flexibility in implementation.
- Use consistent communication and training themes worldwide.

DON'T

- Design the plan centrally and dictate to local counties.
- Create a similar framework for jobs with different responsibilities.
- Require consistency on every performance measure within the incentive plan.
- Assume cultural differences can be managed through the incentive plan.
- Proceed without the support of senior sales executives worldwide.

Source: "Compensation Gamble," *Sales & Marketing Management* (July 1996), pp. 65–69; "Helping Reps Count Every Penny," *Sales & Marketing Management* (July 1998), p. 77.

Exhibit 13.1   Procedures for Designing Compensation and Incentive Programs

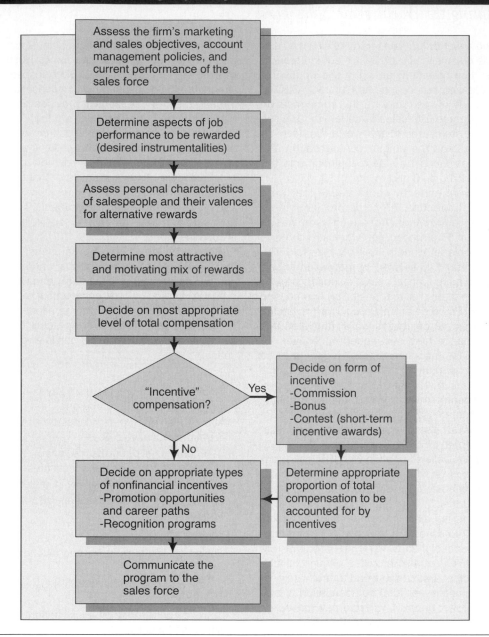

part of its recruitment and selection procedures, as well as from performance evaluations and company records.

This assessment of the sales force's current allocation of effort and levels of performance can then be compared to the firm's marketing and sales objectives, as outlined in the company's marketing plans, strategic sales program, and account management policies. Such comparisons often reveal that some selling activities and dimensions of performance are receiving too much emphasis from the sales force, while others are not receiving enough.

> **Exhibit 13.2** Sales Activities and Performance Outcomes That Might Be Encouraged by Compensation and Incentive Programs
>
> - Sell a greater overall dollar volume.
> - Increase sales of more profitable products.
> - Push new products.
> - Push selected items at designated seasons.
> - Achieve a higher degree of market penetration by products, kinds of customers, or territories.
> - Secure large average orders.
> - Secure new customers.
>
> - Service and maintain existing business.
> - Reduce turnover of customers.
> - Encourage cooperation among members of sales or account management teams.
> - Achieve full-line (balanced) selling.
> - Reduce direct selling costs.
> - Increase the number of calls made.
> - Submit reports and other data promptly.

DETERMINING WHICH ASPECTS OF JOB PERFORMANCE TO REWARD

When the firm's objectives are misaligned with its sales force's allocation of time, the compensation and incentive program can be redesigned to reward desired activities or performance outcomes more strongly, thus motivating the sales reps to redirect their efforts. In terms of the motivation model discussed in Chapter 9, management can increase the instrumentalities of desired activities and performance dimensions by increasing the rewards associated with them.

Exhibit 13.2 lists specific activities and performance dimensions that can be stimulated by a properly designed compensation and incentive program. Of course, managers would like their salespeople to perform well on all of these dimensions.[3] And as we shall see, different components of a compensation program can be designed to reward different activities and achieve multiple objectives.

However, it is a mistake to try to motivate salespeople to do too many things at once. When rewards are tied to numerous different aspects of performance, the salesperson's motivation to improve performance dramatically in any one area is diffused. Also, when rewards are based on many different aspects of performance, the salesperson is more likely to be uncertain about how total performance will be evaluated and about what rewards can be obtained as a result of that performance. In other words, complex compensation and incentive programs may lead to inaccurate instrumentality perceptions by salespeople. Consequently, most authorities recommend that compensation and incentive plans link rewards to only two or three aspects of job performance. They should be linked to those aspects consistent with the firm's highest-priority sales and marketing objectives. Other aspects of the sales force's behavior and performance should be directed and controlled through effective training programs and supervision by field sales managers.

One objective mentioned in Exhibit 13.2—servicing existing customers—deserves special mention. As more firms work to improve their market orientation and adopt the principles of Total Quality Management (TQM), they are beginning to target customer service and satisfaction as important objectives to be rewarded in incentive programs. However, a survey of 450 firms found that only about 10 percent link some portion of sales force compensation to customer satisfaction.[4] One reason for the reluctance of many firms to base rewards on customer satisfaction is the difficulty of measuring changes in satisfaction over time. Also, while there is some evidence that strong satisfaction-based incentives improve customer service by salespeople, some managers worry that such incentives may distract sales reps from the tasks necessary to capture additional sales volume in the short term. To offset this problem, some firms combine customer-satisfaction–based incentives with bonus or commission payments tied to sales quotas or revenue. Unfortunately, such mixed-incentive plans can sometimes cause confusion in the sales force—and even lead to reductions in customer service levels.[5] The bottom line, then, is that rewarding customer service can present some thorny measurement and design issues for the sales manager[6]—issues discussed in more detail in the "Managing Sales Relationships" box.

Assessing Sales Reps' Valences and Determining the Most Attractive Mix of Rewards

All salespeople do not find the same kinds of rewards equally attractive. Salespeople may be more or less satisfied with their current attainment of a given reward, and this causes them to have different valences for more of that reward. Similarly, people's needs for a particular reward vary, depending on their personalities, demographic characteristics, and lifestyles. Consequently, no single reward—including money—is likely to be effective for motivating all of the firm's salespeople. Similarly, a mix of rewards that is effective for motivating a sales force at one time may lose its appeal as the members' personal circumstances and needs change and as new salespeople are hired. In view of this, a wise preliminary step in designing a sales compensation and incentive package is for a firm to determine its salespeople's current valences for various rewards. This could be done with a simple survey in which each salesperson is asked to rate the attractiveness of specific increases of various rewards on a numerical scale, say from zero to 100.[7] Also, one of the techniques specifically aimed at assessing a person's preferences could be used, such as conjoint analysis.[8]

Today, few managers actually carry out such surveys when designing motivation programs because they believe they know their salespeople's needs and desires well enough. Yet, when salespeople's actual valences for rewards have been compared with their managers' perceptions of those valences, the managers' perceptions could be very inaccurate. For example, in one large firm, top sales executives believed their recognition program was an important reward in the eyes of their salespeople. In a subsequent survey of those salespeople's actual valences, it was discovered they rated recognition as the least attractive of seven alternative rewards. Rather than offering rewards that managers think their subordinates find attractive, it may be worth the time and trouble to conduct a study of salespeople's actual valences for rewards before designing a motivation program.

DECIDING ON THE MOST APPROPRIATE MIX OF COMPENSATION

The total amount of compensation a salesperson receives affects satisfaction with pay and with the company, as well as valence for more pay in the future. Thus, the decision about how much total compensation (base pay plus any commissions or bonuses) a salesperson may earn is crucial in designing an effective motivation program. The starting point for making this decision is to determine the gross amount of compensation necessary to attract, retain, and motivate the right type of salespeople. This, in turn, depends on the type of sales job in question, the size of the firm and the sales force, and the sales management policies.

Average compensation varies substantially in different types of sales jobs. In general, more complex and demanding sales jobs, which require salespeople with special qualifications, offer higher pay than more routine sales jobs. To compete for the best talent, a firm should determine how much total compensation other firms in its industry or related ones pay people in similar jobs. Then the firm can decide whether to pay its salespeople an amount that is average in relation to what others are paying or above average. Few

Designing Incentives for Customer Service and Satisfaction

As many markets mature and become more competitive, firms are attaching greater importance to providing excellent service to keep those customers satisfied and loyal and to sustain a competitive advantage. Salespeople often play a crucial role in generating customer satisfaction, particularly in industrial goods and services industries where customers rely on salespeople to act as consultants and problem solvers rather than simply "pushing products," and where post sale services are often important for enabling customers to obtain full value from their purchases.

A recent study points out how companies are evaluating the role of customer input in the evaluation and compensation of salespeople. The Alexander Group reported that 73 percent of the companies they surveyed reported using a formal program to measure customer satisfaction and 58 percent had restructured sales efforts to reflect new priorities with regard to customer satisfaction. Nearly half (47 percent) of the incentive pay plans were directly affected by customer satisfaction. The bottom line is that customer satisfaction is playing an increasingly important role in sales force compensation.

In order to motivate salespeople to focus more effort on providing customer service and satisfaction, many firms are trying to incorporate these performance dimensions as an explicit part of their incentive and compensation programs. But this raises two thorny issues. First, how can a salesperson's performance on customer service and satisfaction dimensions be accurately measured to provide a basis for rewarding that performance? And second, how can customer service performance be rewarded without deflecting the salesperson's efforts from the equally important objective of increasing sales volume?

Measurement

One problem with some attempts to reward salespeople for good customer service is that subjective measures, such as the perceptions of the sales manager, are used to evaluate the salesperson's service performance. Such measures frequently are challenged by the sales force, leading to a lack of trust in the program and low instrumentality estimates.

A variety of more objective measures can be employed to measure both customer service and satisfaction. With respect to customer service, internal measures are most commonly used. These include such things as percentage of on-time deliveries and/or installations, merchandise returns, customer credits, and the number of customer complaints received. For measuring customer satisfaction, companies typically rely on information gained from periodic customer surveys using focus groups, telephone interviews, or mail questionnaires.

Because ongoing customer surveys are expensive, some firms statistically analyze and compare internal measures of customer service with survey-based measures of customer satisfaction. The objective is to identify those internal measures with the strongest relationship to actual customer satisfaction. With this relationship established, service incentives can then be based on internal measures that are both easier to obtain and shown to directly affect customer satisfaction.

Linking Customer Satisfaction and Sales Volume Incentives

Some firms have made the mistake of tying only a small proportion of salespeople's total incentives to performance on customer service or satisfaction dimensions to avoid deflecting too much attention from the pursuit of new customers and increased sales volume. Such an approach is likely to provide little motivation for reps to expend additional effort satisfying customers, and it may signal a lack of management commitment to the program.

A more promising approach is to link incentive rewards for customer satisfaction to the salesperson's overall sales volume performance. This can be done by making the reward for customer satisfaction contingent on the salesperson's sales volume, as illustrated in the following example. Note that the plan establishes bonus awards for various levels of sales quota attainment. Those bonuses are then either increased or decreased by a multiplier determined by a measure of customer satisfaction in the salesperson's territory. Thus, a rep whose sales volume equals 100 percent of quota and who achieves higher than a 96 percent customer satisfaction rating would earn a bonus amounting to $15,000 \times 1.75 = \$26,250$.

(continued)

Sales Quota Attainment		Customer Satisfaction Performance Multiplier	
Percentage of Sales Quota	**Target Award**	**Satisfaction Score**	**Multiplier**
<90%	$10,000	<90%	0.75
91–100	15,000	91–95	1.25
>100	20,000	>96	1.75

Source: Jerome A. Colletti and Linda J. Mahoney, "Should You Pay Your Sales Force for Customer Satisfaction?" *Perspectives in Total Compensation* 2, no. 11 (Scottsdale, AZ: American Compensation Association, November 1991), and "Compensating New Sales Roles," The Alexander Group, April 1998, pp. 2–10.

companies consciously pay below average (although some do so without realizing it) because below-average compensation generally cannot attract the right level of selling talent.

The decision about whether to offer average total pay or premium compensation depends on the size of the firm and its sales force. Large firms with good reputations in their industries and large sales forces (more than 75 or 100 salespeople) generally offer only average or slightly below average compensation. Such firms can attract sales talent because of their reputation in the marketplace and because they are big enough to offer advancement into management. Also, such firms can hire younger people (often just out of school) as sales trainees and put them through an extensive training program. This allows them to pay relatively low gross compensation levels because they do not have to pay a market premium to attract older, more experienced salespeople. Smaller firms often cannot afford extensive training programs. Consequently, they must often offer above-average compensation to attract experienced sales reps from other firms.

Dangers of Paying Too Much

Some firms, regardless of their size or position in their industries, offer their salespeople opportunities to make very large amounts of financial compensation. For example, a survey found that salespeople working for manufacturers with compensation plans based on straight commission commonly earned six-figure incomes, and the highest-paid salesperson in the survey made over a quarter of a million dollars.[9] The rationale for such high incomes is that opportunities for high pay will attract the best talent and motivate members of the sales force to continue working for higher and higher sales volumes. As some managers say, "We don't care how much we pay our salespeople, since their compensation relates to their volume of sales."[10]

Overpaying salespeople relative to what other firms pay for similar jobs and relative to what other employees in the same firm are paid for nonsales jobs can cause major problems, however. For one thing, compensation is usually the largest element of a firm's selling costs. Therefore, overpaying salespeople unnecessarily increases selling costs and reduces profits. Also, it can cause resentment and low morale among the firm's other employees and executives when salespeople earn more money than even top management. It then becomes virtually impossible to promote good salespeople into managerial positions because of the financial sacrifice they would have to make. Finally, it is not clear that offering unlimited opportunities to earn higher pay is always an effective way to motivate continually increasing selling effort. "Need theory," for example, suggests that when salespeople reach a compensation level they consider satisfactory, their valences for still more money are likely to be reduced. One empirical study found that most salespeople tend to work toward a "satisfactory" level of compensation rather than to maximize their pay.[11]

Dangers of Paying Too Little

Overpaying salespeople can cause problems, but it is equally important not to underpay them. Holding down sales compensation may appear to be a convenient way to hold down selling costs and enhance profits, but this is usually not true in the long run. When buying talent in the labor market, a company tends to get what it pays for. If poor salespeople are hired at low pay, poor performance will almost surely result. If good salespeople are hired at low pay, the firm is likely to have high turnover, with higher costs for recruiting and training replacements and lost sales.

The results of a survey of 192 companies in a variety of industries appear to support the wisdom of offering enough compensation to attract good sales talent. The survey found that firms in the top quartile of performance on dimensions such as volume growth and profitability pay their salespeople significantly higher average compensation than firms in the lowest quartile.[12] This raises a question of cause and effect. Do firms perform well because they pay to attract good salespeople, or do they pay better simply because they can afford to? In either case, paying what it takes to attract and keep a competent sales force seems a more likely path to good marketing performance than being overly tightfisted with sales compensation.

FINANCIAL INCENTIVES: CHOOSING THE MOST EFFECTIVE FORM OF FINANCIAL COMPENSATION

In most firms, the total financial compensation paid to salespeople comprises several components, each of which may be designed to achieve different strategic sales and personnel management objectives. These components are listed in Exhibit 13.3, along with the specific objectives appropriate for each.

The foundation of most compensation plans is a package of benefits. These are designed to satisfy the salesperson's basic needs for security. They typically include such things as medical and disability insurance, life insurance, and a pension plan. The types and amount of benefits included in a compensation plan are usually a matter of company policy and apply to all employees. However, the benefit package a firm offers its salespeople should be reasonably comparable to those offered by competitors to avoid being at a disadvantage when recruiting new sales talent.

The core of sales compensation plans consists of a salary or commissions. A **commission** is a payment based on short-term results, usually a salesperson's dollar or unit sales volume. Since there is a direct link between sales volume and the amount of commission received, commission payments are particularly useful for motivating a high level of selling effort.

A **salary** is a fixed sum of money paid at regular intervals. The amount of salary paid to a given salesperson is usually a function of the salesperson's experience, competence, and time on the job, as well as superiors' judgments about the quality of the individual's performance. As we shall see, salary adjustments are useful for rewarding salespeople for performing activities that may not directly result in sales in the short term, such as prospecting for new customers or providing postsale service. They can also help adjust for differences in sales potential across territories.

Many firms that pay their salespeople a salary also offer additional **incentive payments** to encourage good performance. Those incentives may take the form of commissions tied to sales volume or profitability, or bonuses for meeting or exceeding specific

Exhibit 13.3   Components and Objectives of Financial Compensation Plans

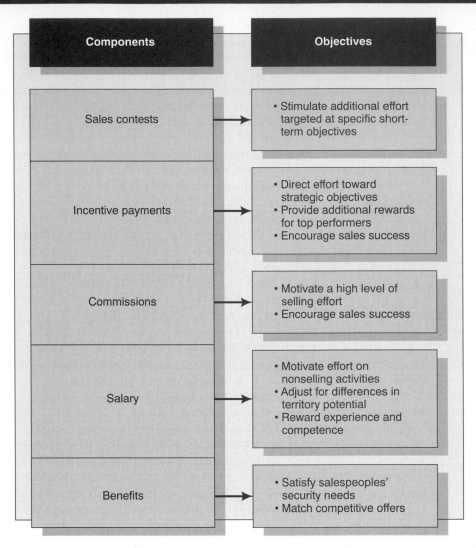

Components	Objectives
Sales contests	• Stimulate additional effort targeted at specific short-term objectives
Incentive payments	• Direct effort toward strategic objectives • Provide additional rewards for top performers • Encourage sales success
Commissions	• Motivate a high level of selling effort • Encourage sales success
Salary	• Motivate effort on nonselling activities • Adjust for differences in territory potential • Reward experience and competence
Benefits	• Satisfy salespeoples' security needs • Match competitive offers

Source: Adapted from *Sales Compensation Concepts and Trends* (New York: The Alexander Group, Inc., 1988), p. 3.

performance targets (e.g., meeting quotas for particular products within the company's line or for particular types of customers). Such incentives are useful for directing salespeople's efforts toward specific strategic objectives during the year, as well as providing additional rewards for the top performers within the sales force.

Finally, many firms conduct **sales contests** to encourage extra effort aimed at specific short-term objectives. For example, a contest might offer additional rewards for salespeople who obtain a specified volume of orders from new customers or who exceed their quotas for a new product during a three-month period. Contest winners might be given additional cash, merchandise, or travel awards.

TYPES OF COMPENSATION PLANS

Commissions, salary, and incentive payments constitute the essential building blocks of most financial compensation plans for sales forces. Thus, while nearly all firms provide benefit packages and many run sales contests from time to time, the three primary methods of compensating salespeople are (1) straight salary, (2) straight commission, and (3) a combination of base salary plus incentive pay in the form of commissions, bonuses, or both. Over the past 35 years, there has been a steady trend away from both straight salary and straight commission plans toward combination plans. Today, combination plans are by far the most common form of compensation, as the survey results in Exhibit 13.4 indicate. The data in Exhibit 13.4 also show that individual bonuses are the most popular form of incentive pay found within combination plans, followed by commissions. Bonuses based on the overall performance of a group of salespeople or a sales team are not very common, although they are growing in popularity. Indeed, a survey of American manufacturers conducted in 1994 found that 13 percent now provide some form of group or team performance rewards.[13]

Straight Salary

Two sets of conditions favor the use of a straight salary compensation plan: (1) when management wishes to motivate salespeople to achieve objectives other than short-run sales volume and (2) when the individual salesperson's impact on sales volume is difficult to measure in a reasonable time.

The primary advantage of a straight salary is that management can require salespeople to spend their time on activities that may not result in immediate sales. Therefore, a salary plan or a plan offering a large proportion of fixed salary is appropriate when the salesperson is expected to perform many account servicing or other nonselling activities. These may include market research, customer problem analysis, stocking, or sales promotion. Straight salary plans are also common in industries where many engineering and design services are required as part of the selling function, such as in the aerospace and other high technology industries.

Straight salary compensation plans are also desirable when it is difficult for management to measure the individual salesperson's actual impact on sales volume or other aspects of performance. Thus, firms tend to pay salaries to their sales force when (1) their salespeople are engaged in missionary selling, as in the pharmaceutical industry, (2) other parts of the marketing program, such as advertising or dealer promotions, are the primary determinants of sales success, as in some consumer packaged goods businesses, or (3) the selling process is complex and involves a team or multilevel selling effort, as in the case of computers.

Straight salary plans provide salespeople with a steady, guaranteed income. Thus, salary compensation plans are often used when the salesperson's ability to generate immediate sales is uncertain, as in the case of new recruits in a field-training program or when a firm is introducing a new product line or opening new territories.

Finally, salary plans are easy for management to compute and administer. They also give management more flexibility. It is easy to reassign salespeople to new territories or product lines because they do not have to worry about how such changes will affect their sales volumes. Also, since salaries are fixed costs, the compensation cost per unit sold is lower at relatively high levels of sales volume.

The major limitation of straight salary compensation is that financial rewards are not tied directly to any specific aspect of job performance. Management should attempt to give bigger salary increases each year to the good performers than those given to the poor ones. However, the amount of those increases and the way performance is

Exhibit 13.4 Percent of Companies Using Three Types of Compensation Plans

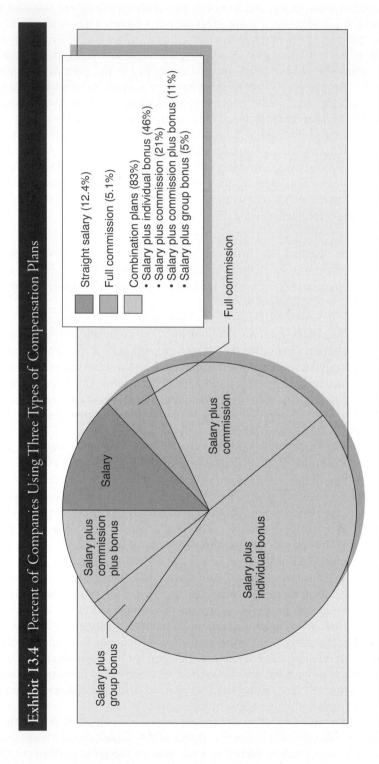

Straight salary (12.4%)

Full commission (5.1%)

Combination plans (83%)
- Salary plus individual bonus (46%)
- Salary plus commission (21%)
- Salary plus commission plus bonus (11%)
- Salary plus group bonus (5%)

Full commission

Salary plus commission

Salary

Salary plus commission plus bonus

Salary plus individual bonus

Salary plus group bonus

Source: *1986/1987 Sales Personnel Report* (New York: The Alexander Group, Inc., 1988).

evaluated are subject to the whims of the manager who makes the decision. Consequently, salespeople are likely to have lower and less accurate instrumentality perceptions about how much more money they are likely to receive as the result of a given increase in sales volume, profitability, or the like. In other words, salaries do not provide any direct financial incentive for improving sales-related aspects of performance. Consequently, salary plans appeal more to security-oriented rather than achievement-oriented salespeople.

Straight Commission

A commission is payment for achieving a given level of performance. Salespeople are paid for results. Usually, commission payments are based on the salesperson's dollar or unit sales volume. However, it is becoming more popular for firms to base commissions on the profitability of sales to motivate the sales force to extend effort on the most profitable products or customers. The most common way is to offer salespeople variable commissions, where relatively high commissions are paid for sales of the most profitable products or sales to the most profitable accounts. Variable commission rates can also be used to direct the sales force's efforts toward other straight sales objectives, such as introduction of a new product line.

Advantages

Direct motivation is the key advantage of a commission compensation plan. There is a direct link between sales performance and the financial compensation the salesperson earns. Consequently, salespeople are strongly motivated to improve their sales productivity to increase their compensation, at least until they reach such high pay that further increases become less attractive. Commission plans also have a built-in element of fairness (if sales territories are properly defined with about equal potential), because good performers are automatically rewarded, whereas poor performers are discouraged from continuing their low productivity.

Commission plans have some advantages from an administrative view. Commissions are usually easy to compute and administer. Also, compensation costs vary directly with sales volume. This is an advantage for firms that are short of working capital because they do not need to worry about paying high wages to the sales force unless it generates high sales revenues.

Limitations

Straight commission compensation plans have some important limitations that have caused many firms to abandon them. Perhaps the most critical weakness is that management has little control over the sales force. When all their financial rewards are tied directly to sales volume, it is difficult to motivate salespeople to engage in account management activities that do not lead directly to short-term sales. Consequently, salespeople on commission are likely to "milk" existing customers rather than work to develop new accounts. They may overstock their customers and neglect service after the sale. Finally, they have little motivation to engage in market analysis and other administrative duties that take time away from actual selling activities.

Straight commission plans also have a disadvantage for many salespeople. Such plans make a salesperson's earnings unstable and hard to predict. When business conditions are poor, turnover rates in the sales force are likely to be high because salespeople find it hard to live on the low earnings produced by poor sales. And agency theory, a conceptual framework developed in economics, suggests such problems are likely to be even more severe when a firm's salespeople are relatively risk averse—that is, when they prefer a predictable future income stream to one that offers uncertain chances to earn either unusually high or unusually low levels of income.[14]

To combat the inherent instability of commission plans, some firms provide their salespeople with a drawing account. Money is advanced to salespeople in months when commissions are low to ensure they will always take home a specified minimum amount of pay. The amount of the salesperson's "draw" in poor months is deducted from earned commissions when sales improve. This gives salespeople some secure salary, and it allows management more control over their activities. A problem arises, however, when a salesperson fails to earn enough commissions to repay the draw. Then the person may quit or be fired, and the company must absorb the loss.[15]

Combination Plans

As indicated by the survey results in Exhibit 13.4, compensation plans that offer a base salary plus some proportion of incentive pay are the most popular. They have many of the advantages but avoid most of the limitations of both straight salary and straight commission plans. The base salary provides the salesperson with a stable income and gives management some capability to reward salespeople for performing customer servicing and administrative tasks that are not directly related to short-term sales. At the same time, the incentive portion of such compensation plans provides direct rewards to motivate the salesperson to expend effort to improve sales volume or profitability.

Combination plans combine a base salary with commissions, bonuses, or both. When salary plus commission is used, the commissions are tied to sales volume or profitability, just as with a straight commission plan. The only difference is that the commissions are smaller in a combination plan than when the salesperson is compensated solely by commission.

A **bonus** is a payment made at the discretion of management for achieving or surpassing some set level of performance. Whereas commissions are typically paid for each sale that is made, a bonus is typically not paid until the salesperson surpasses some level of total sales or other aspect of performance. When the salesperson reaches the minimum level of performance required to earn a bonus, however, the size of the bonus might be determined by the degree to which the sales rep exceeds that minimum. Thus, bonuses are usually additional incentives to motivate salespeople to reach high levels of performance, rather than part of the basic compensation plan.

Attaining quota is often the minimum requirement for a salesperson to earn a bonus. As mentioned in Chapter 6, quotas can be based on sales volume, profitability of sales, or other account-servicing activities. Therefore, bonuses can be offered as a reward for attaining or surpassing a predetermined level of performance on any dimensions for which quotas are set. The use of bonuses as an element in an overall compensation package has been increasing over the last decade. For further discussion of the use of bonuses, refer to the "Managing Sales Relationship" box.

Reader's Digest was faced with declining ad pages and a sales force that had known great success but was becoming unmotivated and less productive. Publisher Greg Coleman decided that the key to turning around the company was to revamp the compensation program using a combination plan that provided a base salary with ample opportunities for incentive income. He took a compensation program that was primarily base salary (90 percent of the old plan was base salary) and added a major incentive component (the new plan offered only 65 percent base salary). In addition, sales representatives were unable to receive any kinds of awards or other bonuses if they did not reach at least 80 percent of their revenue goals. Companies like Reader's Digest are constantly looking for innovative compensation programs to help motivate salespeople while at the same time maintaining the advantages of a fixed-income base salary.

Bonus Pay Plays an Important Role in Compensation Plans

Companies have been expanding their use of bonuses in the overall compensation plan for many sales forces. As noted in Table 1, nearly 72 percent of firms use bonuses either alone or in conjunction with commission pay. Indeed, 37 percent use bonuses as the only form of incentive compensation. Conversely, only 4 percent reported no incentive compensation and a fixed base salary. Incentive compensation is an important element in the vast majority of overall sales force compensation situations.

But how do companies determine bonus payments? Table 2 lists the criteria used to assess bonuses. It also identifies the relative importance of each of the criteria. Not surprisingly, the single most important criterion is "sales relative to quota." Seventy-six percent of the companies reported using this as a criterion in bonus determination, and 69 percent said it was the single most important criterion. However, as the list demonstrates, bonuses (like other incentive compensation plans) can be tailored to reward a number of different goals or criteria. For example, 23 percent of the companies use "control of sales expenses" as a criterion for determining bonuses. While not listed as the most important criterion by any firms, it nevertheless was one factor in assigning bonus compensation. Note also that customer satisfaction was listed by 15 percent of companies surveyed in the study. Bonuses offer companies an opportunity to link salesperson compensation directly with company objectives and goals.

Table 1

Distribution of Incentive Pay Type

Compensation Method	Percentage of Firms Using Method
Bonus pay	37%
Bonus and commission pay	35
Commission only	24
No incentive pay	4

Table 2

Criteria Used to Determine Amount of Bonus Award

Criterion	Percentage of Firms Using Criterion in Bonus Pay	Percentage of Firms Indicating This Was the Most Important Criterion
Sales relative to quota	76%	69%
Division profitability	38	20
Sales from new customers	34	3
New product sales	26	3
Control of sales expenses	23	0
Account retention	16	0
Customer satisfaction	15	0

Source: Joseph Kissan and Manohar U. Kalwani, "The Role of Bonus Pay in Salesforce Compensation Plans," *Industrial Marketing Management* 27 (1998), pp. 147–159.

Other Issues in Designing Combination Plans

Whether base salary is combined with commission payments or bonuses, managers must answer several other questions when designing effective combination compensation plans. These include (1) the appropriate size of the incentive relative to the base salary, (2) whether there should be a ceiling on incentive earnings, (3) when the salesperson should be credited with a sale, (4) whether group incentives should be used and, if so, how they should be allocated across members of a sales team, and (5) how often the salesperson should receive incentive payments.

Relative proportion of incentive pay

What proportion of total compensation should be incentive pay? One of the most common reasons combination plans are not very effective at motivating salespeople is that the incentive portion is too small to generate much interest. After studying the reasons for the success or failure of 180 compensation plans, two researchers concluded that "if the average successful salesman working under a sales incentive plan cannot make at least 25 percent of his gross earnings as incentive pay in the form of bonus or commissions, the plan will never be truly successful."[16]

The 25 percent figure appears to be not only a good rule of thumb but also a reasonably accurate reflection of industry practice. A survey of more than 1,600 organizations conducted by the American Productivity Center found that salespeople on combination compensation plans earned an average of slightly more than 20 percent of their total pay from incentive payments.[17] However, the relative size of such payments varies substantially across different industries (e.g., service firms tend to pay a larger proportion of incentive pay than goods producers) and across different types of plans. For instance, another survey found that plans offering a salary plus bonus based on one or more dimensions of total performance contained incentive pay that averaged only 11 percent of total compensation, while "salary plus commission" plans averaged 33 percent incentive pay.[18]

A manager's decision concerning what proportion of the overall compensation package is represented by incentive pay should be based on the company's objectives and the nature of the selling job. When the firm's primary objectives are directly related to short-term sales (such as increasing sales volume, profitability, or new customers), a large incentive component should be offered. When customer service and other nonsales objectives are deemed more important, the major emphasis should be on the base salary component of the plan. This gives management more control over the sales force's account management activities.

Similarly, when the salesperson's selling skill is the key to sales success, the incentive portion of compensation should be large. However, when the product has been presold through advertising and the salesperson is largely an order taker, or when the salesperson's job involves a large proportion of missionary or customer service work, the incentive component should be relatively small.

Incentive ceilings

Should there be a ceiling or cap on incentive earnings to ensure top salespeople do not earn substantially more money than other employees? This is an issue that is dealt with in very different ways across companies and industries, and for which strong arguments can be made on both sides. Part of the variation in how different firms handle this issue seems to reflect differences in average compensation levels, with firms in relatively low paying industries being more likely to impose caps than those in higher-paying lines of trade. The use of caps also varies by type of compensation plan. Two out of every three firms with "salary plus bonus" plans impose incentive ceilings, while only one-third of firms using "salary plus commission" plans do so.[19]

Arguments in favor of using ceilings include that they ensure top salespeople will not make such high earnings that other employees suffer resentment and low morale. Ceilings also protect against windfalls—such as increased sales due to the introduction of successful new products—where a salesperson's earnings might become very large without corresponding effort. Finally, ceilings make a firm's maximum potential sales compensation expense more predictable and controllable. Capping compensation diminishes the valence of compensation by reducing the earning opportunity ratio discussed in Chapter 9.

A strong argument can be made, however, that such ceilings have a bad effect on motivation and dampen the sales force's enthusiasm. Indeed, 25 percent of the 305 salespeople responding to a recent survey pointed to incentive caps as the one aspect of their firm's compensation plans with which they were most dissatisfied.[20] Also, some salespeople may reach the earnings maximum early in the year and be inclined to take it easy for the rest of the year.

The issue of incentive ceilings has become a growing problem with major accounts. One problem has been compensating the salesperson in a team selling environment. As team selling brings individuals from around the company to help with a customer, the question becomes how much the sales representative should make in a sale that is the result of many individuals inside the company. This problem is exacerbated as the size of each sale grows larger and larger. A second problem occurs as customers move around the world. How much should the sales representative be compensated for a sale in another part of the world even though that salesperson is servicing the customer's headquarters in his or her territory? The solution many companies have chosen is limiting or capping a salesperson's incentive compensation.[21]

Some functions of ceilings can be accomplished without arbitrarily limiting the motivation of the sales force if management pretests any new or revised compensation plan before it is implemented. Managers can do this by applying the plan to the historical sales performance of selected salespeople. Particular attention should be given to the amount of compensation that would have been earned by the best and poorest performers to ensure that the compensation provided by the plan is both fair and reasonable.

When is a sale a sale?

When incentives are based on sales volume or other sales-related aspects of performance, the precise meaning of a sale should be defined to avoid confusion and irritation. Most plans credit a salesperson with a sale when the order is accepted by the company, less any returns and allowances. Occasionally, though, crediting the salesperson with a sale only after the goods have been shipped or payment is received from the customer makes good sense. This is particularly true when the time between receipt of an order and shipment of the goods is long and the company wants its salespeople to maintain close contact with the customer to prevent cancellations and other problems. As a compromise, some plans credit salespeople with half a sale when the order is received and the other half when payment is made.

Team versus individual incentives

The increasing use of sales or cross-functional teams to win new customers and service major accounts raises some important questions about the kinds of incentive to include in a combination compensation plan. Should incentives be tied to the overall performance of the entire team, should separate incentives be keyed to the individual performance of each team member, or both? If both group and individual incentives are used, which should be given the greatest weight? At the beginning of this chapter we saw how Merck uses multiple incentives to reward both the overall sales performance of its sales teams and the individual contributions of the members of each team. Some other possible solutions to the problem of compensating cross-functional sales teams are discussed in the "Managing Sales Relationships" box.

When should the sales rep receive incentive payments?

One survey of over 500 compensation plans found that 21 percent paid salespeople incentive earnings on an annual basis, 3 percent paid semiannually, 24 percent paid quarterly,

Incentives for Sales Teams

Firms that use teams to sell to or service customers typically adopt one of three approaches for tying incentive rewards to a team's performance. As shown in Figure 1, these three approaches are:

1. *Team performance as the sole determinant.* Here all incentive pay is based on achievement of pre-defined team objectives. Incentive rewards may be allocated equally to all team members, or divided among members on the basis of individual contributions to team results.

2. *Team performance as the primary determinant.* These plans include two incentives—a larger one based on team performance and a smaller one based on each member's individual performance. As Figure 1 indicates, the two incentives are sometimes "linked" in such a way that the magnitude of the team's bonus directly influences the size of the individual bonuses each team member can earn. In "unlinked" plans, the two incentive awards are independent of each other.

Figure 2 illustrates both a linked and an unlinked plan. Note first that in both cases the team bonus is tied to how well the team performs relative to its sales goal, and all team members receive an equal incentive amount based on the team's sales volume. However, the sales reps on the team can also earn an individual incentive tied to the amount of new business (contracts) they bring in. This individual incentive encourages the reps to do some prospecting for new accounts in addition to working with other team members in selling to existing customers. Note also that under the linked plan, if the team fails to achieve at least 90 percent of its volume quota and earns no incentive bonus, the individual sales reps on that team will also earn zero individual incentive rewards even if they achieve 100 percent of their new contracts goal (25 percent of zero equals zero). Thus, the linkage feature encourages members to work toward the team objective first. On the other hand, in the unlinked plan, team and individual bonuses are determined separately and simply added together for each individual.

3. *Individual performance as the primary determinant.* These plans also include two incentive components that may be either linked or unlinked. However, they emphasize individual performance by tying larger incentive rewards to individual rather than to team outcomes.

(continued)

Source: Jerome A. Colletti and Mary S. Fiss, *Designing Incentive Plans for Customer Teams* (Scottsdale, AZ: American Compensation Association, 1995).

and 52 percent made monthly payments. In general, plans offering salary plus commission were more likely to involve monthly incentive payments, while salary plus bonus plans more often made incentive payments on a quarterly or annual schedule.[22]

Shorter intervals between performance and the receipt of rewards increase the motivating power of the plan. However, short intervals add to the computation required, increase administrative expenses, and may make the absolute amount of money received by the salespeople appear so small they may not be very impressed with their rewards. Consequently, many authorities argue that quarterly incentive payments are an effective compromise.

Compensation of direct sales people versus manufacturer's representatives

Many organizations use a direct sales force and outside manufacturer's representatives to help sell their products and services. Manufacturer's representatives most often receive a flat commission on everything they sell, but (as we have seen) the compensation of direct

Figure I

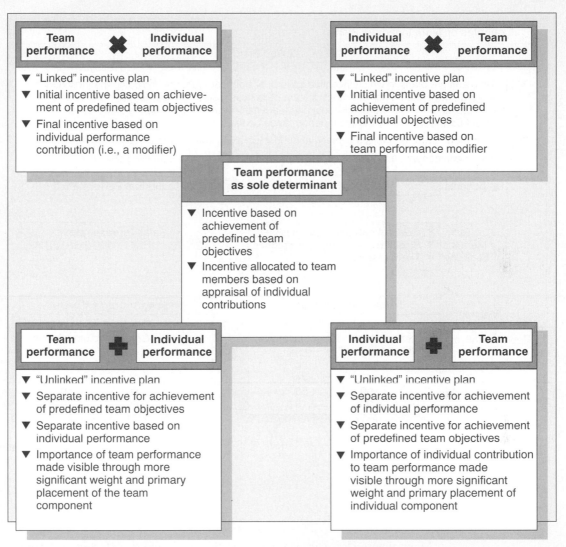

Team performance ✖ **Individual performance**

- ▼ "Linked" incentive plan
- ▼ Initial incentive based on achievement of predefined team objectives
- ▼ Final incentive based on individual performance contribution (i.e., a modifier)

Individual performance ✖ **Team performance**

- ▼ "Linked" incentive plan
- ▼ Initial incentive based on achievement of predefined individual objectives
- ▼ Final incentive based on team performance modifier

Team performance as sole determinant

- ▼ Incentive based on achievement of predefined team objectives
- ▼ Incentive allocated to team members based on appraisal of individual contributions

Team performance ➕ **Individual performance**

- ▼ "Unlinked" incentive plan
- ▼ Separate incentive for achievement of predefined team objectives
- ▼ Separate incentive based on individual performance
- ▼ Importance of team performance made visible through more significant weight and primary placement of the team component

Individual performance ➕ **Team performance**

- ▼ "Unlinked" incentive plan
- ▼ Separate incentive for achievement of individual performance
- ▼ Separate incentive for achievement of predefined team objectives
- ▼ Importance of individual contribution to team performance made visible through more significant weight and primary placement of individual component

(continued)

salespeople can be much more complex. As discussed in Chapter 5, manufacturer's representatives can offer a company several advantages. However, compensation questions do arise between outside manufacturer's representatives and direct salespeople. For example, the salespeople at Polyflex Film and Converting noted that after hitting quota they were eligible to receive an additional $20,000 on the next $1 million sold (depending on years of service and base salary). However, they were also aware that the company's outside manufacturer's representatives would receive $50,000 for the same $1 million sale and they didn't need to hit any sales quotas to receive it.[23] This kind of discrepancy requires companies to address the concerns of their direct sales force.

Figure 2

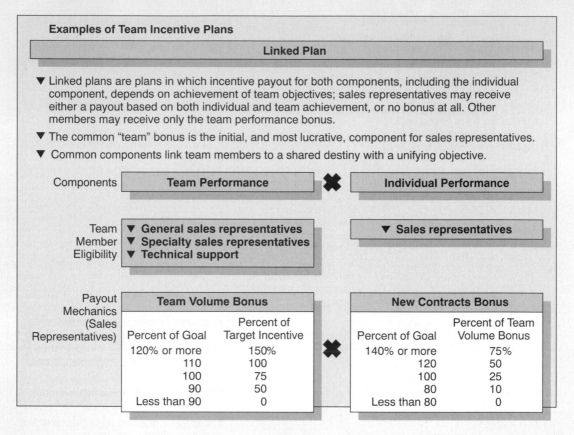

Examples of Team Incentive Plans

Linked Plan

▼ Linked plans are plans in which incentive payout for both components, including the individual component, depends on achievement of team objectives; sales representatives may receive either a payout based on both individual and team achievement, or no bonus at all. Other members may receive only the team performance bonus.

▼ The common "team" bonus is the initial, and most lucrative, component for sales representatives.

▼ Common components link team members to a shared destiny with a unifying objective.

Components: **Team Performance** ✖ **Individual Performance**

Team Member Eligibility:
▼ General sales representatives
▼ Specialty sales representatives
▼ Technical support

▼ Sales representatives

Payout Mechanics (Sales Representatives):

Team Volume Bonus

Percent of Goal	Percent of Target Incentive
120% or more	150%
110	100
100	75
90	50
Less than 90	0

✖

New Contracts Bonus

Percent of Goal	Percent of Team Volume Bonus
140% or more	75%
120	50
100	25
80	10
Less than 80	0

(continued)

Many times sales managers point out that while the manufacturer's representatives receive a higher commission, they must also cover their own expenses. In addition, they are not paid unless they sell product while the direct sales force benefits from a fixed base salary. One benefit is the ability of the company to offer special recognition and other nonfinancial compensation rewards to the direct sales force.

A Summary Overview of Financial Compensation Methods

The preceding discussion indicates combination plans pose more prickly administrative and control problems than either straight salary or straight commission plans. This may be one reason combination plans are more commonly found in larger firms than in smaller ones. Despite such problems, however, the offsetting advantages offered by combination plans make them the most popular method of compensating salespeople. But as we have seen, all three types of plans have some unique advantages and limitations that make each of them particularly well suited for use in certain circumstances. Those advantages, limitations, and uses are summarized in Exhibit 13.5.

Figure 2 (concluded)

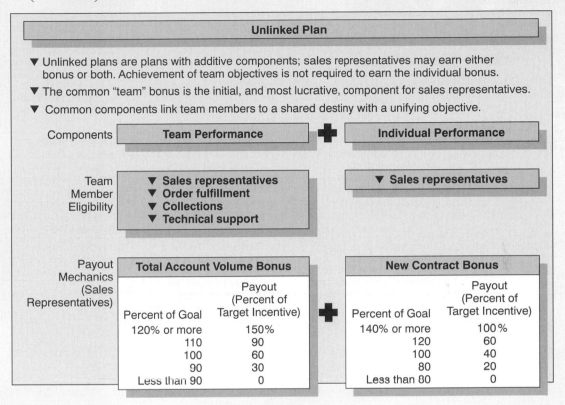

Unlinked Plan

▼ Unlinked plans are plans with additive components; sales representatives may earn either bonus or both. Achievement of team objectives is not required to earn the individual bonus.

▼ The common "team" bonus is the initial, and most lucrative, component for sales representatives.

▼ Common components link team members to a shared destiny with a unifying objective.

Components | **Team Performance** ✚ **Individual Performance**

Team Member Eligibility
- ▼ Sales representatives
- ▼ Order fulfillment
- ▼ Collections
- ▼ Technical support

▼ Sales representatives

Payout Mechanics (Sales Representatives)

Total Account Volume Bonus

Percent of Goal	Payout (Percent of Target Incentive)
120% or more	150%
110	90
100	60
90	30
Less than 90	0

✚

New Contract Bonus

Percent of Goal	Payout (Percent of Target Incentive)
140% or more	100%
120	60
100	40
80	20
Less than 80	0

SALES CONTESTS

Sales contests are short-term incentive programs designed to motivate sales personnel to accomplish specific sales objectives. Although contests should not be considered part of the firm's ongoing compensation plan, they offer sales people the opportunity to gain financial, as well as nonfinancial, rewards. Contest winners often receive prizes in cash or merchandise or travel. Winners also receive nonfinancial rewards in the form of recognition and a sense of accomplishment.

Successful contests require the following:

- Clearly defined, specific objectives.
- An exciting theme.
- Reasonable probability of rewards for all salespeople.
- Attractive rewards.
- Promotion and follow-through.

Contest Objectives

Because contests supplement the firm's compensation program and are designed to motivate extra effort toward some short-term goal, their objectives should be very specific and

431

Exhibit 13.5   Characteristics of Compensation Methods for Sales Personnel

Compensation Method (Frequency of Use)	Especially Useful	Advantages	Disadvantages
Straight salary (10%)	When compensating new sales reps; when firm moves into new sales territories that require developmental work; when sale reps must perform many nonselling activities	Provides sales rep with maximum amount of security; gives sales manager large amount of control over sales reps; is easy to administer; yields more predictable selling expenses	Provides no incentive; necessitates closer supervision of sale reps' activities; during sales declines, selling expenses remain at same level
Straight commission (5%)	When highly aggressive selling is required; when nonselling tasks are minimized; when company cannot closely control sales force activities	Provides maximum amount of incentive; by increasing commission rate, sales managers can encourage reps to sell certain items; selling expenses relate directly to sales resources	Sales reps have little financial security; sales manager has minimum control over sales force; may cause reps to provide inadequate service to smaller accounts; selling costs less predictable
Combination (85%)	When sales territories have relatively similar sales potentials; when firm wishes to provide incentive but still control sales force activities	Provides certain level of financial security; provides some incentive; selling expenses fluctuate with sales revenue; sales manager has some control over reps' nonselling activities	Selling expenses less predictable; may be difficult to administer

clearly defined. What kinds of objectives do firms pursue with contests? The weighted ratings shown in Exhibit 13.6 reflect the frequency with which managers in 254 firms reported that each listed objective was either a primary or secondary purpose of their sales contests. Note that while "stimulate overall sales volume" was the number one objective (i.e., most often a primary contest goal), most of the others are much more specific and narrowly focused (e.g., stimulate specific product sales, introduce new products, acquire new accounts).

The time in which the contest's objectives are to be achieved should be relatively short. This ensures that salespeople will maintain their enthusiasm and effort throughout the contest. But the contest should be long enough to allow all members of the sales force to cover their territories at least once and to have a reasonable chance of generating the performance necessary to win. Therefore, the median duration of sales contests is three months.

Contest Themes

A sales contest should have an exciting theme to help build enthusiasm among the participants and promote the event. The theme should also be designed to stress the contest's objectives and appeal to all participants. Sports themes, such as "a sales superbowl" or "world series," are popular because they provide a competitive atmosphere.

Probability of Winning

There are three popular contest formats. In some contests, salespeople compete with themselves by trying to attain individual quotas. Everyone who reaches or exceeds quota during the contest period wins. A second form requires that all members of the sales force compete with each other. The people who achieve the highest overall performance on

Exhibit 13.6   Managers' Ratings of Sales Contest Objectives

Contest Objective	Weighted Rating
Stimulate overall sales volume	586
Stimulate specific product sales	521
Increase market penetration	479
Introduce new products	463
Acquire new accounts	460
Get balanced sales	422
Emphasize higher-profit products	396
Improve service to accounts	351
Overcome seasonal slump	323
Increase activity in new area	322
Ease unfavorable inventory situation	284
Develop or improve sales skills	254

Source: *Current Practices in Sales Incentives* (New York: The Alexander Group, Inc., 1988), p. 20.

some dimension are the winners, and everyone else loses. A third format organizes the sales force into teams, which compete for group and individual prizes.

The results of the survey conducted by the Alexander Group suggest that the assignment of individual quotas is by far the most popular contest format. Eighty-three percent of responding firms reported using quota-based contests, and only 28 percent evaluated the performance of sale teams rather than that of individuals.[24] This reliance on individual quotas allows firms to design contests that focus salespeople's effort on specific objectives, do not put representatives in low-potential territories at a disadvantage, and do not undermine cooperation in the sales force by forcing salespeople to compete against each other.

Whichever format is used, every member of the sales force should have a reasonable chance of winning an award. If there are to be only one or a few winners, many salespeople may think their chances of coming out on top are remote. Consequently, their instrumentality perceptions of the likelihood of winning are low, and they are not motivated to expend much effort to win. As one sales executive put it, "The percentage of winners you get is very important. If you have only a few winners, the salesmen say, 'See, I told you the goals were unrealistic.' You get much better reaction if you can come in with 40 percent to 50 percent of your men winners."[25] In this respect, contests that provide rewards to everyone who meets quotas during the contest period are desirable. The number of possible winners is not arbitrarily limited, and everyone has a chance for a reward. As the survey results in Exhibit 13.7 indicate, however, the odds of a salesperson being a winner in a majority of sales contests are less than two out of five, with the average percentage of winners falling between 25 and 30 percent.

Types of Rewards

Contest rewards can take the form of cash, merchandise, or travel. All three types of rewards are commonly used, and a company may vary the kinds of rewards offered from contest to contest. In the Alexander Group's survey, for instance, 77 percent of respondents used cash awards in one or more recent contests, 61 percent offered merchandise, and 60 percent gave travel awards.[26]

Whatever form of reward is used, the monetary value must be large enough to be at-

Exhibit 13.7   The Odds of a Salesperson Being a Contest Winner

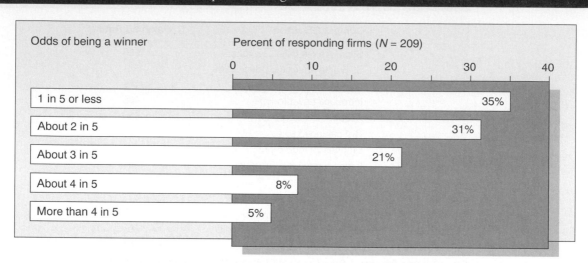

Odds of being a winner   Percent of responding firms (*N* = 209)

Odds of being a winner	Percent
1 in 5 or less	35%
About 2 in 5	31%
About 3 in 5	21%
About 4 in 5	8%
More than 4 in 5	5%

Source: Adapted from *Current Practices in Sales Incentives* (New York: The Alexander Group, Inc., 1988), p. 22.

tractive to the participants, given their level of compensation. A portable TV, for example, may be more attractive where the average salesperson makes $25,000 per year than where the average compensation is $60,000. One authority recommends that contest awards should be worth the equivalent of at least one week's compensation of the average person in the sales force.[27] As Exhibit 13.8 indicates, however, a substantial percentage of sales contests provide rewards with an average monetary value of only $500 or less.

Promotion and Follow-Through

To generate interest and enthusiasm, contests should be launched with fanfare. Firms announce contests at national or regional sales meetings. Follow-up promotion is also necessary to maintain interest throughout the contest period. As the contest proceeds, salespeople should be given frequent feedback concerning their progress so they know how much more they must do to win an award. Finally, winners should be recognized within the company, and prizes should be awarded promptly.

Criticism of Sales Contests

Although many sales managers believe contests are effective for motivating special efforts from salespeople, contests can cause a few potential problems, particularly if they are poorly designed or used.

Some critics argue that contests designed to stimulate sales volume may produce results that are largely illusory, with no lasting improvement in market share. Salespeople may "borrow" sales from before and/or after the contest to increase their volume during the contest. They may hold back orders before the start of the contest and rush orders that would normally not be placed until after the contest. As a result, customers may be overstocked, causing sales volume to fall off for some time after the contest is over.

Contests may also hurt the cohesiveness and morale of the company's salespeople. This is particularly true when plans force individual salespeople to compete with one another for rewards and when the number of rewards is limited.

Finally, some firms tend to use sales contests to "cover up" faulty compensation plans. Sales personnel should not have to be compensated a second time for what they are already being paid to do. Thus, contests should be used only on a short-term basis to mo-

Exhibit 13.8 Average Monetary Value of Sales Contest Prizes

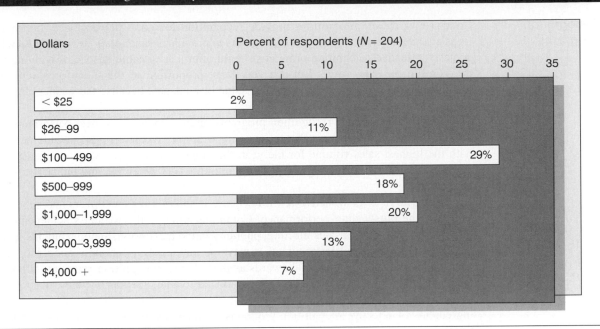

Source: *Current Practices in Sales Incentives* (New York: The Alexander Group, Inc., 1988), p. 25.

tivate special efforts beyond the normal performance expected of the sales force. If a firm conducts frequent contests to maintain an acceptable level of sales performance, it should reexamine its entire compensation and incentive program.[28]

NONFINANCIAL REWARDS

Promotion and Career Paths

Most sales managers consider opportunities for promotion and advancement second only to financial incentives as an effective sales force motivator. This is particularly true for young, well-educated salespeople who tend to view their jobs as stepping-stones to top management. Unfortunately, salespeople's valences for promotion tend to decline in many companies as they get older. As we saw in the last chapter, one likely reason for this is that many firms do not provide many promotion opportunities for salespeople. The common career path is from salesperson to district sales manager to top sales management. Thus, if a person has been with a firm for several years without making it into sales management, the individual may start to believe such a promotion will never happen. Consequently, older salespeople may concentrate solely on financial rewards, or they may lose motivation and not work as hard at their jobs.[29]

To overcome this problem, some firms have instituted two different career paths for salespeople. One leads to management positions for promising candidates, while the other leads to more advanced positions within the sales force. The latter usually involves responsibility for dealing with key accounts or leading sales teams. In this system, even though a salesperson may not make it into management, the rep can still work toward a more prestigious and lucrative position within the sales force. To make advanced sales positions more attractive as promotions, many firms provide people in those positions with additional perquisites ("perks"), including higher compensation, a better automobile, and better office facilities.

Recognition Programs

Contest awards and promotions provide recognition for good performance, but many firms also have separate recognition programs to provide nonmonetary rewards.[30] As with contests, effective recognition programs should offer a reasonable chance of winning for everyone in the sales force. But if a very large proportion of the sales force achieves recognition, the program is likely to lose some of its appeal because the winners feel no special sense of accomplishment.

Consequently, better recognition programs often recognize the best performers for several different performance dimensions. For example, winners might include persons with the highest sales volume for the year, the biggest percentage increase in sales, the biggest dollar increase, the highest penetration of territory potential, and the largest sales per account.

Recognition is an attractive reward because it makes a person's peers and superiors aware of the outstanding performance. Communication of the winner's achievements, through recognition at a sales meeting, publicity in the local press, announcements in the company's internal newsletter, or other ways, is an essential part of a good program. Also, firms typically give special awards as part of their recognition program, although these are often symbolic awards with low monetary value, such as trophies, plaques, or rings. Finally, as Exhibit 13.9 points out, objectivity and good taste are also important ingredients of effective recognition programs, as they are for contests and other incentives.

THE REIMBURSEMENT OF SELLING EXPENSES

As we have seen, firms have become increasingly concerned with finding ways to control and reduce the costs—and increase the efficiency—of their field sales forces. A large portion of those sales force costs are accounted for by salespeople's salaries and financial incentives. But expense items incurred by sales reps in the field—travel, lodging, meals, and entertaining customers—are also substantial. While field selling expenses vary across industries and types of sales jobs, they average nearly $13,000 per salesperson, and in some cases they are much higher.[31]

As mentioned in earlier chapters, the rapid rise in selling costs has caused many sales managers to question the economic viability of having field salespeople make face-to-face calls on smaller customers and to turn to telemarketing and other approaches to reduce the expenses involved in servicing smaller firms. A second response to cost increases has been a search for improved methods of expense control. Many firms have experimented with a variety of expense reimbursement plans. Such plans range from unlimited reimbursement for all "reasonable and allowable" expenses to plans where salespeople must pay all expenses out of their total compensation.

When deciding which form of expense reimbursement to use, sales managers must make trade-offs between tight control aimed at holding down total expenses and the financial well-being—and the subsequent motivation level—of salespeople. Some expense items—such as entertainment expenses, club dues, and the costs of personal services while the salesperson is away from home—can be considered either legitimate business expenses that should be reimbursed by the company or personal expenses that the salesperson should pay. Obviously, company policies and reimbursement plans that treat such costs as business expenses increase the salesperson's total financial compensation but also

Exhibit 13.9 Guidelines for Effective Formal Recognition Programs

Regardless of its size or cost, any recognition program should incorporate the following features, says consultant Dr. Richard Boyatiz of McBer and Co.:

- The program must be strictly performance-based with no room for subjective judgments. If people suspect that it is in any way a personality contest, the program will not work. Says Boyatiz: "It should be clear to anyone looking at the data that, yes, these people won."

- It should be balanced. The program should not be so difficult that only a few can hope to win, or so easy that just about everyone does. In the first case, people will not try; in the second, the program will be meaningless.

- A ceremony should be involved. If rings are casually passed out, or plaques sent through the mail, a lot of the glamour of the program will be lost.

- The program must be in good taste. If not, it will be subject to ridicule and, rather than motivate people, leave them uninspired. No one wants to be part of a recognition program that is condescending or tacky. Says Boyatiz: "The program should make people feel good about being part of the company."

- There must be adequate publicity. In some cases, sales managers do such a poor job of explaining a program or promoting it to their own salespeople that no one seems to understand or care about it. Prominent mention of the program in company publications is the first step to overcoming this handicap.

Source: Bill Kelley, "Recognition Reaps Rewards," *Sales & Marketing Management* (June 1986), p. 104. See also Thomas R. Wotruba, John S. Macfie, and Jerome A. Colletti, "Effective Sales Force Recognition Programs," *Industrial Marketing Management* 20 (1991), pp. 9-15.

increase the firm's total selling costs. The issue of expense control and techniques firms might use to improve their control over selling expenses are discussed in more detail in Chapter 15. Since different reimbursement plans have an impact on the effective financial compensation received by, and the motivation level of, a firm's salespeople, however, some of the relative advantages and limitations of alternative plans and policies are discussed now.

Direct Reimbursement Plans

The most popular type of expense reimbursement plan—employed by about 85 percent of all firms—involves direct and unlimited reimbursement of all "allowable and reasonable" expenses.[32] However, reimbursement under such plans is contingent on the salesperson submitting receipts or detailed records justifying expense claims. So the processing and evaluation of expense claims add to the firm's sales administration costs.

The primary advantage is that such plans give the sales manager some control over both the total magnitude of sales expenses and the kinds of activities in which salespeople will be motivated to engage. If a particular activity, such as entertaining potential new accounts, is thought to be an important ingredient of the firm's account management policies, salespeople can be encouraged to engage in that activity by being informed that all related expenses will be reimbursed. On the other hand, managers can discourage their subordinates from spending time on unimportant tasks by refusing to reimburse expenditures for such activities.

Thus, company policies concerning reimbursable expenses can be a useful tool for motivating and directing sales effort. Some firms report they adjusted their expense reimbursement policies according to the differences in the territories covered or the job activities required of different members of their sales forces.[33] For example, some firms reimburse a broader range and higher levels of expenses for their national account managers than for members of their regular field sales force. The results of a survey of company

Exhibit 13.10   Sales Expenses: For What Do Companies Pay?

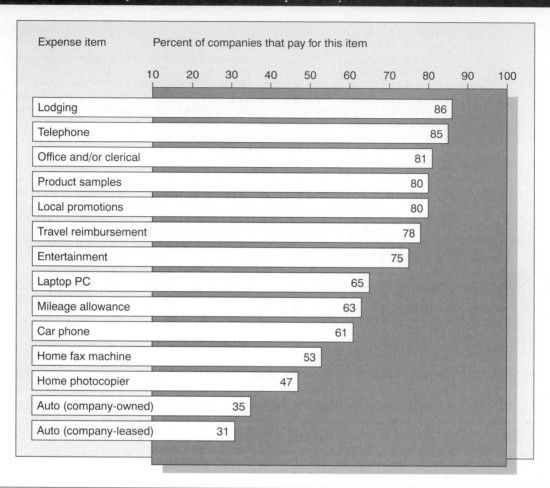

Source: Christen P. Heide, *Dartnell's 30th Sales Force Compensation Survey* (Chicago: The Dartnell Corporation, 1999), p. 121.

reimbursement policies concerning a variety of different expense items are displayed in Exhibit 13.10.

Limited Reimbursement Plans

Some firms limit the total amount of expense reimbursement, either by setting maximum limits for each expense item (e.g., a policy that limits reimbursement for restaurant meals to $40 per person) or by providing each salesperson with a predetermined lump-sum payment to cover total expenses. This approach keeps total selling expenses within planned limits, limits that are often determined by the sales expense budget set at the beginning of the year. In some cases, budgeted expense amounts may vary across members of the sales force, depending on the past or forecasted sales volume or the requirements of the territories.

Unless the budgeted limits are based on an accurate understanding of the costs associated with successful sales performance in each territory, however, these kinds of plans can hurt motivation and sales performance. Individual salespeople may believe their ability to do a good job is constrained by tightfisted company expense reimbursement policies. Rather than pay for necessary activities out of their own pockets, salespeople are likely to avoid or cut back on certain expense activities to keep their costs within their budgets.

No Reimbursement Plans

A variation of the advanced lump-sum plan still found in some firms is a policy of requiring salespeople to cover all of their own expenses. Such plans usually involve paying the salesperson a relatively high total financial compensation to help cover necessary expenses. Such plans are most commonly associated with "straight commission" compensation plans involving high-percentage commissions. The rationale is that salespeople will be motivated to spend both the effort and money necessary to increase sales volume as long as the resulting financial rewards are big enough to be worthwhile.

Since these plans are simply a variation of the limited reimbursement plans discussed previously, they have similar advantages and drawbacks. They help the firm limit sales expenses or—in the case of commission plans—make them a totally variable cost that moves up and down with changes in sales volume. They also sacrifice management control over the motivation and types of activities engaged in by members of the sales force.

SUMMARY

The sales manager concerned with motivating the members of the sales force needs to be concerned with the firm's compensation system. Which rewards do salespeople value? How much of each is optimum? How should the rewards be integrated in a total compensation system? This chapter sought to provide answers to these questions.

The chapter suggested a framework that sales managers can use when designing compensation and incentive programs. The framework includes the following steps: (1) assess the firm's marketing and sales objectives, account management policies, and current performance of the sales force; (2) determine the aspects of job performance that are to be rewarded; (3) assess personal characteristics of salespeople and their valences for alternative rewards; (4) determine the most attractive and motivating mix of rewards; (5) decide on the most appropriate level of total compensation; (6) decide whether incentive compensation is to be used and, if the answer is yes, what kind and proportion of total compensation it should represent; (7) decide on the appropriate types of nonfinancial incentives; and (8) communicate the program to the sales force.

A major purpose of any sales compensation program is to influence the sales force to do what management wants, the way they want it done, and within the desired time. These requirements are largely dictated by the firm's marketing and sales objectives and account management policies. The important first two

steps, then, are to establish the most important objectives for the personal selling effort and to decide which priorities the compensation system should attempt to address.

The success of any compensation system depends on whether those affected by it find the rewards attractive. Thus, the third and fourth steps in the process involve finding out exactly which rewards the company's salespeople value and what combination of rewards they find most attractive. These often vary by salesperson and can be determined by simple surveys or other research methods that assess a person's preferences. Given this determination, the firm is in a position to weight the benefits and costs associated with various combinations of rewards.

The fifth step in the process is determining the total amount of compensation. Here the firm often walks a fine line. If it overpays its salespeople, it incurs increased costs and runs the risk of creating low morale among other employees of the company. If it pays less than its competitors, it generally attracts lower-quality recruits and experiences higher turnover and its attendant costs.

In determining the most effective form of financial compensation, the firm must decide whether it should use (1) straight salary, (2) straight commission, or (3) a combination of base salary and incentive pay such as commissions, bonuses, or both. Most companies today use the combination approach. The base salary provides the salesperson with a stable income while allowing the company to reward its salespeople for performing tasks not directly related to short-term sales. The incentive portion of combination plans provides direct rewards to motivate salespeople to expend effort to improve their sales volume or profitability. To be effective, the incentive pay portion of the combination plan has to be large enough to generate the necessary interest among salespeople. Although the opportunity to earn 25 percent of the base salary in incentive has been suggested as a good rule of thumb, the decision should be based on the company's objectives and the nature of the selling job.

Sales contests are often part of the incentive portion of compensation systems. To be successful, a sales contest needs to have (1) clearly defined, specific objectives, (2) an exciting theme, (3) a reasonable probability of rewards for all salespeople, (4) attractive rewards, and (5) the necessary promotion and follow-through.

Nonfinancial incentives can play an important role in a firm's compensation system. In one survey of sales managers, it was found that they consider opportunities for promotion and advancement to be second only to special recognition as effective sales motivators. Because all salespeople cannot possibly move into sales management positions, some companies have dual career paths to maintain the motivating potential of promotion and advancement. One path leads to positions in the sales management hierarchy, while the other leads to greater responsibility in selling itself, such as a better territory or key account sales. For recognition programs to be effective, the salesperson's peers and superiors must be made aware of the representative's outstanding performance. This can be done through a formal recognition program at a sales meeting, publicity in the local press, announcements in the company's internal newsletter, or other desirable ways.

The last stage in the process is to communicate the compensation program to the sales force. Salespeople need to have a clear understanding of its overall structure and what they have to do to secure the elements in the total package that they find desirable.

DISCUSSION QUESTIONS

1. The use of customer teams is becoming a more widespread practice. The success of these teams depends, in part, on the rewards systems used to motivate and recognize performance. Much of the literature available on compensation does not address the design of incentive programs for customer teams. For example, a large manufacturer of consumer products created customer teams to cover strategically important customers. When these team members were brought together, one of the major challenges was what to do about their incentive pay. Some team members, such as sales reps, were accustomed to receiving commissions, while others, such as customer service reps, were on a straight salary. How would you develop a compensation plan that motivates customer teams? What is the first step that you would take in this situation?

2. The Ruppert Company needed to build market share quickly. To motivate sales growth, Ruppert installed a straight commission compensation plan: The more the sales reps sold, the more they made. This strategy seemed to work; sales volume climbed and the Ruppert Company captured more market share. After two years on this program, sales growth flattened out and Ruppert began to lose market share. Sales reps continued to earn $75,000 to $80,000 on average in commissions through developing and penetrating key accounts in their territories. Studies showed the sales force was not overworked and further territory penetration was clearly possible. What was happening?

3. When OfficeSolutions, software producer, went into business, it needed to establish market share quickly. To accomplish this, it decided to pay the sales force on a commission basis. After two years, however, the company had a large base business and customers began to complain that salespeople were not spending enough time with them on postsale service and problem solving. The salespeople said they did not make any money on problem solving and they would rather spend their time finding new accounts. What's more, salespeople spent little or no time selling the new products on which OfficeSolutions was staking its future. Salespeople said they could sell the old products more easily and earn more money for both themselves and the company. How can the company resolve this issue?

4. The Walker Company was an established company in a medium-growth market with significant competition.

The sales force was paid on a salary-plus-commission plan. Fifty percent of expected earnings were commission. Sales rep Victor managed an established territory and consistently earned the target level of total compensation (base salary plus commission). Sales rep Downey faced a different situation in a low-volume territory with stiff competition; after one year, commission earnings were next to nothing with no relief in sight. Discouraged, Downey left Walker, just like the last four reps in that territory. That territory and others like it would stay underpenetrated. The best the Walker Company could do was to maintain its current market share. How can Walker Company solve this problem?

5. When designing sales compensation plans, it is important to match objectives with the sales environment and at the same time reward appropriately the person who has to meet those objectives. How would you design sales compensation plans to match the following objectives?

   a. Company has a high revenue growth objective in a sales environment characterized by frequent product introductions, "boom" markets, and a loose competitive structure.

   b. Company has a protect-and-grow revenue objective in a sales environment characterized by slow growth, many competitors, and few product introductions; the differentiation is determined by the excellence of the sales force.

   c. Company's objectives are to have an overall revenue growth and balanced product mix sales in an environment with multiple customer markets, many product groups, high-growth and low-growth products, and high and low sales intensity.

   d. Company's objective is to maintain revenue and have new account sales growth (that is, conversion selling by taking customers from the competition); the environment is a moderate-to-slow–growth marketplace.

6. West Virginia Paper, a paper distributor in a mature market, currently earns 18 to 20 percent gross margins. Commissions for salespeople are 20 percent of gross profit. Overall, the plan seems to be in line with the paper distributor's goal of improving profitability. Recently, growth in gross profit has been accompanied by a drop in net profit. The sales manager believes the sales reps are concentrating on small orders, which take less time, rather than large accounts, which have longer sales cycles. The larger accounts have lower service and processing costs. The growth in small orders increases overhead costs faster than the increase in gross profit, and net profit margins drop. West Virginia Paper needs a plan that will maintain its high gross profit and increase net profit as well. The problem facing the company is how to reward sales reps who maintain, or come close to, the desired price and how to motivate sales reps to pursue larger orders.

7. Sales contests, although very popular, raise questions concerning their value. Questions asked include: Don't they simply shift into the contest period sales volume that would have occurred anyway? How can everyone be equally motivated when certain territories have a built-in edge because of customer and market characteristics? Won't the contest backfire if people feel they haven't had a fair chance to win? Will all sales reps participate with equal enthusiasm when there can be only a few winners? How would you handle these objectives?

8. Things are tough at Morgan, Inc. For the last several months, sales reps, who are paid on a commission basis, have barely covered their personal monthly expenses. To help the sales force through these tough times, Morgan executives decided to introduce monthly draws. Sales reps whose commission earnings fall below a specified monthly amount receive a special loan, or draw, against commissions. When sales and commissions improve, the sales reps will repay the cash advance from future earnings. Will this plan help Morgan achieve its sales strategy?

EXPERIENTIAL APPLICATION

Although widely used, sales contests may not produce the desired outcomes. For example, the sales contest may not have any effect on the activities of the sales force. Interview a small sample of sales reps and ask them if they have had any experience with sales contests. If yes, ask each sales rep to define the object of the sales contest and how the contest affected their activities. For example, if the contest's goals were to obtain new accounts, did the sales rep make an attempt to call on more new accounts? Ask the sales reps if their company should have more contests and why or why not.

INTERNET EXERCISE

Visit the Merck (*www.merck.com*) and Johnson & Johnson (*www.johnsonandjohnson.com*) Web sites. Go to the pages marked career opportunities. Investigate the sales positions. What kinds of incentives and compensation packages do they offer? Are they compara- ble? Now, turning to other industries, consider visiting the sites of companies you know such as IBM (*www.ibm.com*) and investigate how compensation packages in the pharmaceutical industry differ from those in other industries.

SUGGESTED READINGS

Design of Compensation and Incentive Programs

Cohen, Andy, "Right on Target," *Sales & Marketing Management* (December 1994), pp. 59–63.

Colletti, Jerome A., and Mary S. Fiss, *Designing Incentive Plans for Customer Teams.* Scottsdale, AZ: American Compensation Association, 1995.

Eisman, Regina, "Justifying Your Incentive Program," *Sales & Marketing Management* (April 1993), pp. 43–52.

Englander, Todd J., "Let Salespeople Design Your Incentive Plan," *Sales & Marketing Management* (September 1991), pp. 155–56.

Fine, Leslie M., and Janice R. Fanke, "Legal Aspects of Salesperson Commission Payments: Implications for the Implementation of Commission Sales Programs," *Journal of Personal Selling and Sales Management* (Winter 1995), pp. 53–68.

John, George, and Barton Weitz, "Salesforce Compensation: An Empirical Investigation of Factors Related to the Use of Salary versus Incentive Compensation," *Journal of Marketing Research* (February 1989), pp. 1–14.

Keenan, William, Jr., "Is Your Pay Plan Putting the Squeeze on Top Performers?" *Sales & Marketing Management* (January 1990), pp. 74–75.

Sharma, Arun, "Customer Satisfaction–Based Incentive Systems: Some Managerial and Salesperson Considerations," *Journal of Personal Selling and Sales Management* (Spring 1997), pp. 61–70.

Sharma, Arun, and Dan Sarel, "The Impact of Customer Satisfaction-Based Incentive Systems on Salespeople's Customer Service Response: An Empirical Study," *Journal of Personal Selling and Sales Management* (Summer 1995), pp. 17–29.

Tice, Thomas E., "Managing Compensation Caps in Key Accounts," *Journal of Personal Selling and Sales Management* (Fall 1997), pp. 41–47.

Contests and Nonfinancial Incentives

Cron, William L., Alan J. Dubinsky, and Ronald E. Michaels, "The Influence of Career Stages on Components of Salesperson Motivation," *Journal of Marketing* (January 1988), pp. 78–92.

Kelley, Bill, "Recognition Reaps Rewards," *Sales & Marketing Management* (June 1986), pp. 102–5.

Moncrief, William C., Sandra H. Hart, and Dan H. Robertson, "Sales Contests: A New Look at an Old Management Tool," *Journal of Personal Selling and Sales Management* (November 1988), pp. 55–61.

Wotruba, Thomas R., John S. Macfie, and Jerome A. Colletti, "Effective Sales Force Recognition Programs," *Industrial Marketing Management* 20 (1991), pp. 9–15.

Comprehensive Cases for Part II

Case 2–1

General Electric Appliances*

Larry Barr had recently been promoted to the position of district sales manager (B.C.) for G.E. Appliances, a division of Canadian Appliance Manufacturing Co. Ltd. (CAMCO). One of his more important duties in that position was the allocation of his district's sales quota among his five salesmen. Barr received his quota for 1999 in October 1998. His immediate task was to determine an equitable allocation of that quota. This was important because the company's incentive pay plan was based on the salesmen's attainment of quota. A portion of Barr's remuneration was also based on the degree to which his sales force met their quotas.

Barr graduated from the University of British Columbia in 1990 with the degree of bachelor of commerce. He was immediately hired as a product manager for a mining equipment manufacturing firm because of his summer job experience with that firm. In 1993, he joined Canadian General Electric (C.G.E.) in Montreal as a product manager for refrigerators. There he was responsible for creating and merchandising a product line, as well as developing product and marketing plans. In January 1996, he was transferred to Coburg, Ontario, as a sales manager for industrial plastics. In September 1997, he became administrative manager (Western Region) and when the position of district sales manager became available, Barr was promoted to it. There his duties included development of sales strategies, supervision of salesmen, and budgeting.

Background

Canadian Appliance Manufacturing Co. Ltd. (CAMCO) was created in 1995 under the joint ownership of Canadian General Electric Ltd. and General Steel Wares Ltd. (G.S.W.). CAMCO then purchased the production facilities of Westinghouse Canada Ltd. Under the purchase agreement, the Westinghouse brand name was transferred to White Consolidated Industries Ltd., where it became White-Westinghouse. Appliances manufactured by CAMCO in the former Westinghouse plant were branded Hotpoint. (See Exhibit 1.)

The G.E., G.S.W., and Hotpoint major appliance plants became divisions of CAMCO. These divisions operated independently and had their own separate management staff, although they were all ultimately accountable to CAMCO management. The divisions competed for sales, although not directly, because they each produced product lines for different price segments.

Competition

Competition in the appliance industry was vigorous. CAMCO was the largest firm in the industry, with approximately 45 percent market share, split between G.E., G.S.W. (Moffatt & McClary brands), and Hotpoint. The following three firms each had 10 to 15 percent market share: Inglis (washers and dryers only), W.C.I. (makers of White-Westinghouse, Kelvinator, and Gibson), and Admiral. These firms also produced appliances under

Exhibit 1   Organization Chart

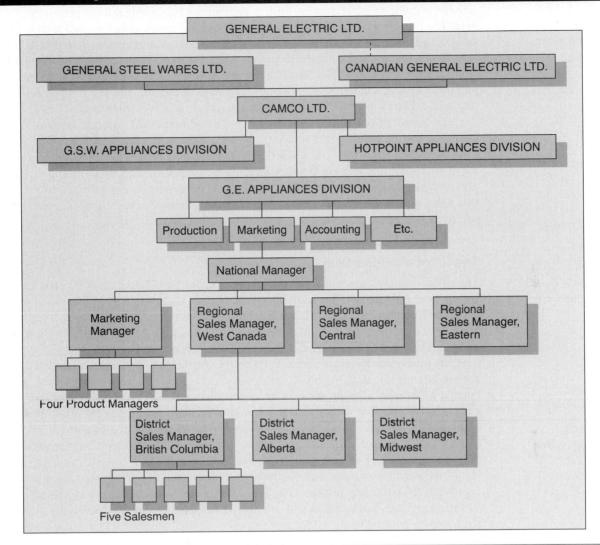

department store brand names such as Viking, Baycrest, and Kenmore, which accounted for an additional 15 percent of the market. The remainder of the market was divided among brands such as Maytag, Roper Dishwasher, Gurney, Tappan, and Danby.

G.E. marketed a full major appliance product line, including refrigerators, ranges, washers, dryers, dishwashers, and television sets. G.E. appliances generally had many features and were priced at the upper end of the price range. Their major competition came from Maytag and Westinghouse.

The Budgeting Process

G.E. Appliances was one of the most advanced firms in the consumer goods industry in terms of sales budgeting. Budgeting received careful analysis at all levels of management.

The budgetary process began in June of each year. The management of G.E. Appliances division assessed the economic outlook, growth trends in the industry, competitive activity, population growth, and so forth to determine a reasonable sales target for the next year. The president of CAMCO received this estimate, checked and revised it as necessary, and submitted it to the president of G.E. Canada. Final authorization rested with G.E. Ltd., which had a definite minimum growth target for the G.E. branch of CAMCO. G.E. Appliances was considered an "invest and grow" division, which meant it was expected to produce a healthy sales growth each year, regardless of the state of the economy. As Barr observed, "This is difficult, but meeting challenges is the job of management."

The approved budget was expressed as a desired percentage increase in sales. Once the figure had been decided, it was not subject to change. The quota was communicated back through G.E. Canada Ltd., CAMCO, and G.E. Appliances, where it was available to the district sales managers in October. Each district was then required to meet an overall growth figure (quota), but each sales territory was not automatically expected to achieve that same growth. Barr was required to assess the situation in each territory, determine where growth potential was highest, and allocate his quota accordingly.

The Sales Incentive Plan

The sales incentive plan was a critical part of General Electric's sales force plan and an important consideration in the quota allocation of Barr. Each salesman had a portion of his earnings dependent on his performance with respect to quota. Also, Barr was awarded a bonus based on the sales performance of his district, making it advantageous to Barr and good for staff morale for all his salesmen to attain their quotas.

The sales force incentive plan was relatively simple. A bonus system is fairly typical for salesmen in any field. With G.E., each salesman agreed to a basic salary figure called "planned earnings." The planned salary varied according to experience, education, past performance, and competitive salaries. A salesman was paid 75 percent of his planned earnings on a guaranteed regular basis. The remaining 25 percent of salary was at risk, dependent on the person's sales record. There was also the possibility of earning substantially more money by selling more than quota (see Exhibit 2).

The bonus was awarded such that total salary (base plus bonus) equaled planned earnings when the quota was just met. The greatest increase in bonus came between 101 and 110 percent of quota. The bonus was paid quarterly on the cumulative total quota. A holdback system ensured that a salesman was never required to pay back previously earned bonus because of a poor quarter. Because of this system, it was critical that each salesman's quota be fair in relation to the other salesmen. Nothing was worse for morale than one person earning large bonuses while the others struggled.

Quota attainment was not the sole basis for evaluating the salesmen. They were required to fulfill a wide range of duties including service, franchising of new dealers, maintaining good relations with dealers, and maintaining a balance of sales among the different product lines. Because the bonus system was based on sales only, Barr had to ensure the salesmen did not neglect their other duties.

A formal salary review was held each year for each salesman. However, Barr preferred to give his salesmen continuous feedback on their performances. Through human relations skills, he hoped to avoid problems that could lead to dismissal of a salesman and loss of sales for the company.

Barr's incentive bonus plan was more complex than the salesmen's. He was awarded a maximum of 75 annual bonus points broken down as follows: market share, 15; total sales performance, 30; sales representative balance, 30. Each point had a specific money

Exhibit 2   Sales Incentive Earnings Schedule: Major Appliances and Home Entertainment Products

Sales Quota Realization (Percent)	Percent of Base Salary Total	Sales Quota Realization (Percent)	Incentive Percent of Base Salary Total
70%	0 %	105%	35.00%
71	0.75	106	37.00
72	1.50	107	39.00
73	2.25	108	41.00
74	3.00	109	43.00
75	3.75	110	45.00
76	4.50	111	46.00
77	5.25	112	47.00
78	6.00	113	48.00
79	6.75	114	49.00
80	7.50	115	50.00
81	8.25	116	51.00
82	9.00	117	52.00
83	9.75	118	53.00
84	10.50	119	54.00
85	11.25	120	55.00
86	12.00	121	56.00
87	12.75	122	57.00
88	13.50	123	58.00
89	14.25	124	59.00
90	15.00	125	60.00
91	16.00	126	61.00
92	17.00	127	62.00
93	18.00	128	63.00
94	19.00	129	64.00
95	20.00	130	65.00
96	21.00	131	66.00
97	22.00	132	67.00
98	23.00	133	68.00
99	24.00	134	69.00
100	25.00	135	70.00
101	27.00	136	71.00
102	29.00	137	72.00
103	31.00	138	73.00
104	33.00	139	74.00
		140	75.00

value. The system ensured that Barr allocate his quota carefully. For instance, if one quota was so difficult that the salesmen sold only 80 percent of it, while the other salesmen exceeded quota, Barr's bonus would be reduced, even if the overall area sales exceeded the quota. (See Appendix, "Development of a Sales Commission Plan.")

Exhibit 3   G.E. Appliances—Sales Territories

Territory Designation	Description
9961 Greater Vancouver (Garth Rizzuto)	Hudson's Bay, Firestone, Kmart, McDonald Supply, plus seven independent dealers
9962 Interior (Dan Seguin)	All customers from Quesnel to Nelson, including contract sales (50 customers)
9963 Coastal (Ken Block)	Eatons, Woodwards, plus Vancouver Island north of Duncan and upper Fraser Valley (east of Clearbrook) (20 customers)
9964 Independent and Northern (Fred Speck)	All independents in lower mainland and South Vancouver Island, plus northern B.C. and Yukon (30 customers)
9967 Contract (Jim Wiste)	Contract sales Vancouver, Victoria. All contract sales outside 9962 (50–60 customers)

Quota Allocation

The total 1999 sales budget for G.E. Appliances division was about $100 million, a 14 percent sales increase over 1996. Barr's share of the $33 million Western Region quota was $13.3 million, also a 14 percent increase over 1996. Barr had two weeks to allocate the quota among his five territories. He needed to consider factors such as historical allocation, economic outlook, dealer changes, personnel changes, untapped potential, new franchises or store openings, and buying group activity (volume purchases by associations of independent dealers).

Sales force

There were five sales territories within B.C. (Exhibit 3). Territories were determined on the basis of number of customers, sales volume of customers, geographic size, and experience of the salesman. Territories were altered periodically to deal with changed circumstances.

One territory was comprised entirely of contract customers. Contract sales were sales in bulk lots to builders and developers who used the appliances in housing units. Because the appliances were not resold at retail, G.E. took a lower profit margin on such sales.

G.E. Appliances recruited M.B.A. graduates for their sales force. They sought bright, educated people who were willing to relocate anywhere in Canada. The company intended that these people would ultimately be promoted to managerial positions. The company also hired experienced career salesmen to get a blend of experience in the sales force. However, the typical salesman was under 30, aggressive, and upwardly mobile. G.E.'s sales training program covered only product knowledge. It was not felt necessary to train recruits in sales techniques.

Allocation procedure

At the time Barr assumed the job of district sales manager, he had a meeting with the former sales manager, Ken Philips. Philips described to Barr the method he had used in the past to allocate the quota. As Barr understood it, the procedure was as follows.

The quota was received in October in the form of a desired percentage sales increase. The first step was to project current sales to the end of the year. This gave a base to which the increase was added for an estimation of the next year's quota.

From this quota, the value of contract sales was allocated. Contract sales were allocated first because the market was considered the easiest to forecast. The amount of contract sales in the sales mix was constrained by the lower profit margin on such sales.

The next step was to make a preliminary allocation by simply adding the budgeted percentage increase to the year-end estimates for each territory. Although this allocation seemed fair on the surface, it did not take into account the differing situations in the territories, or the difficulty of attaining such an increase.

The next step was examination of the sales data compiled by G.E. Weekly sales reports from all regions were fed into a central computer, which compiled them and printed out sales totals by product line for each customer, as well as other information. This information enabled the sales manager to check the reasonableness of his initial allocation through a careful analysis of the growth potential for each customer.

The analysis began with the largest accounts, such as Firestone, Hudson's Bay, and Eatons, which each bought over $1 million in appliances annually. Accounts that size were expected to achieve at least the budgeted growth. The main reason for this was that a shortfall of a few percentage points on such a large account would be difficult to make up elsewhere.

Next, the growth potential for medium-sized accounts was estimated. These accounts included McDonald Supply, Kmart, Federated Cooperative, and buying groups such as Volume Independent Purchasers (V.I.P.). Management expected the majority of sales growth to come from such accounts, which had annual sales of between $150,000 and $1 million.

At that point, about 70 percent of the accounts had been analyzed. The small accounts were estimated last. These had generally lower growth potential but were an important part of the company's distribution system.

Once all the accounts had been analyzed, the growth estimates were summed and the total compared to the budget. Usually, the growth estimates were well below the budget.

The next step was to gather more information. The salesmen were usually consulted to ensure that no potential trouble areas or good opportunities had been overlooked. The manager continued to revise and adjust the figures until the total estimated matched the budget. These projections were then summed by territory and compared to the preliminary territorial allocation.

Frequently, there were substantial differences between the two allocations. Historical allocations were then examined and the manager used his judgment in adjusting the figures until he was satisfied that the allocation was both equitable and attainable. Some factors that were considered at this stage included experience of the salesmen, competitive activities, potential store closures or openings, potential labor disputes in areas, and so forth.

The completed allocation was passed on to the regional sales manager for his approval. The process had usually taken one week or longer by this stage. Once the allocations had been approved, the district sales manager then divided them into sales quotas by product line. Often, the resulting average price did not match the expected mix between higher- and lower-priced units. Therefore, some additional adjusting of figures was necessary. The house account (used for sales to employees of the company) was used as the adjustment factor.

Once this breakdown had been completed, the numbers were printed on a budget sheet and given to the regional sales manager. He forwarded all the sheets for his region to the central computer, which printed out sales numbers for each product line by salesman, by month. These figures were used as the salesmen's quotas for the next year.

Current situation

Barr recognized that he faced a difficult task. He thought he was too new to the job and the area to confidently undertake an account-by-account growth analysis. However, due to his previous experience with sales budgets, he did have some sound general ideas. He also had the records of past allocation and quota attainment (Exhibit 4), as well as the assistance of the regional sales manager, Anthony Foyt.

Barr's first step was to project the current sales figures to end-of-year totals. This task was facilitated because the former manager, Philips, had been making successive projections monthly since June. Barr then made a preliminary quota allocation by adding the budgeted sales increase of 14 percent to each territory's total (Exhibit 5).

Barr then began to assess circumstances that could cause him to alter that allocation. One major problem was the resignation, effective at the end of the year, of one of the company's top salesmen, Ken Block. His territory had traditionally been one of the most difficult, and Barr believed it would be unwise to replace Block with a novice salesman.

Barr considered shifting one of the more experienced salesmen into that area. However, that would have disrupted service in an additional territory, which was undesirable because it took several months for a salesman to build up a good rapport with customers. Barr's decision would affect his quota allocation because a salesman new to a territory could not be expected to immediately sell as well as the incumbent, and a novice salesman would require an even longer period of adaptation.

Barr was also concerned about territory 9961. The territory comprised two large na-

Exhibit 4   Sales Results

Territory	1996 Budget (× 1,000)	Percent of Total Budget	1996 Actual (× 1,000)	1996 Variance from Quota (V%)
9967 (Contract)	$2,440	26.5%	$2,267	(7)%
9961 (Greater Vancouver)	1,790	19.4	1,824	2
9962 (Interior)	1,624	17.7	1,433	(11)
9963 (Coastal)	2,111	23.0	2,364	12
9964 (Ind. dealers)	1,131	12.3	1,176	4
House	84	1.1	235	—
Total	$9,180	100.0%	$9,299	1%

Territory	1997 Budget (× 1,000)	Percent of Total Budget	1997 Actual (× 1,000)	1997 Variance from Quota (V%)
9967 (Contract)	$2,587	26.2%	$2,845	10%
9961 (Greater Vancouver)	2,005	20.3	2,165	8
9962 (Interior)	1,465	14.8	1,450	(1)
9963 (Coastal)	2,405	24.4	2,358	(2)
9964 (Ind. dealers)	1,334	13.5	1,494	12
House	52	0.8	86	—
Total	$9,848	100.0%	$10,398	5%

Exhibit 5 Sales Projections and Quotas, 1998–1999

Projected Sales Results 1998

Territory	Oct. 1998 Year to Date	1998 Projected Total	1998 Budget	Percent of Total Budget	Projected Variance from Quota (V%)
9967	$2,447	$3,002	$2,859	25.0%	5%
9961	2,057	2,545	2,401	21.0	6
9962	1,318	1,623	1,727	15.1	(6)
9963	2,124	2,625	2,734	23.9	(4)
9964	1,394	1,720	1,578	13.8	
House	132	162	139	1.2	—
Total	$9,474	$11,677	$11,438	100.0%	2%

Preliminary Allocation 1999

Territory	1998 Projection	1999 Budget*	Percent of Total Budget
9967	$ 3,002	$ 3,422	25.7%
9961	2,545	2,901	21.8
9962	1,623	1,854	13.9
9963	2,625	2,992	22.5
9964	1,720	1,961	14.7
House	162	185	1.3
Total	$11,677	$13,315	100.0%

*1999 budget = 1998 territory projections + 14% = $13,315.

tional accounts and several major independent dealers. The buying decisions for the national accounts were made at their head offices, where G.E.'s regional salesmen had no control over the decisions. Recently, Barr had heard rumors that one of the national accounts was reviewing its purchase of G.E. Appliances. If it were to delist even some product lines, it would be a major blow to the salesman, Rizzuto, whose potential sales would be greatly reduced. Barr was unsure how to deal with that situation.

Another concern for Barr was the wide variance in buying of some accounts. Woodwards, Eatons, and McDonald Supply had large fluctuations from year to year. Also, Eatons, Hudson's Bay, and Woodwards had plans to open new stores in the Vancouver area sometime during the year. The sales increase to be generated by these events was hard to estimate.

The general economic outlook was poor. The Canadian dollar had fallen to 92 cents U.S. and unemployment was at about 8 percent. The government's anti-inflation program, which was scheduled to end in November 1999, had managed to keep inflation to the 8 percent level, but economists expected higher inflation and increased labor unrest during the postcontrol period.

The economic outlook was not the same in all areas. For instance, the Okanagan (9962) was a very depressed area. Tourism was down and fruit farmers were doing poorly despite good weather and record prices. Vancouver Island was still recovering from a 200 percent increase in ferry fares, while the lower mainland appeared to be in a relatively better position.

In the contract segment, construction had shown an increase over 1997. However, labor unrest was common. There had been a crippling eight-week strike in 1997, and there was a strong possibility of another strike in 1999.

With all of this in mind, Barr was very concerned that he allocate the quota properly because of the bonus system implications. How should he proceed? To help him in his decision, he reviewed a note on development of a sales commission plan that he had obtained while attending a seminar on sales management the previous year (see Appendix below).

Appendix: Development of a Sales Commission Plan

A series of steps are required to establish the foundation on which a sales commission plan can be built. These steps are as follows:

A. Determine specific sales objectives of positions to be included in plan

For a sales commission plan to succeed, it must be designed to encourage the attainment of the business objectives of the component division. Before deciding on the specific measures of performance to be used in the plan, the component should review and define its major objectives. Typical objectives might be:

- Increase sales volume.
- Do an effective balanced selling job in a variety of product lines.
- Improve market share.
- Reduce selling expense to sales ratios.
- Develop new accounts or territories.
- Introduce new products.

Although it is probably neither desirable nor necessary to include all such objectives as specific measures of performance in the plan, they should be kept in mind, at least to the extent that the performance measures chosen for the plan are compatible with and do not work against the overall accomplishment of the component's business objectives.

Also, the relative current importance or ranking of these objectives will provide guidance in selecting the number and type of performance measures to be included in the plan.

B. Determine quantitative performance measures to be used

Although it may be possible to include a number of measures in a particular plan, there is a drawback to using so many as to overly complicate it and fragment the impact of any one measure on the participants. A plan that is difficult to understand will lose a great deal of its motivation force, as well as be costly to administer properly.

For those who currently have a variable sales compensation plan(s) for their salespeople, a good starting point would be to consider the measures used in those plans. Although the measurements used for sales managers need not be identical, they should at least be compatible with those used to determine their salespeople's commissions.

However, keep in mind that a performance measure that may not be appropriate for individual salespeople may be a good one to apply to their manager. Measurements involving attainment of a share of a defined market, balanced selling for a variety of products, and control of district or region expenses might fall into this category.

Listed in Exhibit 6 are a variety of measurements that might be used to emphasize specific sales objectives.

Exhibit 6   Tailoring Commission Plan Measurements to Fit Component Objectives

Objectives	Possible Plan Measurements
1. Increase sales/orders volume	Net sales billed or orders received against quota.
2. Increase sales of particular lines	Sales against product line quotas with weighted sales credits on individual lines.
3. Increase market share	Percent realization (%R) of shares bogey.
4. Do balanced selling job	%R of product line quotas with commissions increasing in proportion to number of lines up to quota.
5. Increase profitability	Margin realized from sales. Vary sales credits to emphasize profitable product lines. Vary sales credit in relation to amount of price discount.
6. Increase dealer sales	Pay distributor *salespeople* or sales manager in relation to realization of sales quotas of assigned dealers.
7. Increase sales calls	%R of targeted calls per district or region.
8. Introduce new product	Additional sales credits on new line for limited period.
9. Control expense	%R of expense to sales or margin ratio. Adjust sales credit in proportion to variance from expense budget.
10. Sales teamwork	Share of incentive based upon group results.

For most components, all or most of these objectives will be desirable to some extent. The point is to select those of greatest importance where it will be possible to establish measures of standard or normal performance for individuals, or at least small groups of individuals working as a team.

If more than one performance measurement is to be used, the relative weighting of each measurement must be determined. If a measure is to be effective, it must carry enough weight to have at least some noticeable effect on the commission earnings of an individual.

As a general guide, it would be unusual for a plan to include more than two or three quantitative measures with a minimum weighting of 15 to 20 percent of planned commissions for any one measurement.

C. Establish commission payment schedule for each performance measure

1. Determine appropriate range of performance for each measurement. The performance range for a measurement defines the percent of standard performance (%R) at which commission earnings start to the point where they reach maximum.

The minimum point of the performance range for a given measurement should be set so that a majority of the participants can earn at least some incentive pay and the maximum set at a point that is possible of attainment by some participants. These points will vary with the type of measure used and the degree of predictability of individual budgets or other forms of measurement. In a period where overall performance is close to standard, 90 to 95 percent of the participants should fall within the performance range.

For the commission plan to be effective, most of the participants should be operating within the performance range most of the time. If a participant is either far below the minimum of this range or has reached the maximum, further improvement will not affect his or her commission earnings, and the plan will be largely inoperative as far as he or she is concerned.

Actual past experience of %R attained by participants is obviously the best indicator of what this range should be for each measure used. Lacking this, it is better to err on the side of having a wider range than one that proves to be too narrow. If some form of group measure is used, the variation from standard performance is likely to be less for the group in total than for individuals within it. For example, the performance range for total district performance would probably be narrower than the range established for individual salespeople within a district.

2. Determine appropriate reward to risk ratio for commission earnings. This refers to the relationship of commission earned at standard performance to maximum commission earnings available under the plan. A plan that pays 10 percent of base salary for normal or standard performance and pays 30 percent as a maximum commission would have a 2 to 1 ratio. In other words, the participant can earn twice as much (20 percent) for above-standard performance as he or she stands to lose for below-standard performance (10 percent).

Reward under a sales commission plan should be related to the effort involved to produce a given result. To adequately encourage above-standard results, the reward to risk ratio should generally be at least 2 to 1. The proper control of incentive plan payments lies in the proper setting of performance standards, not in the setting of a low maximum payment for outstanding results that provides a minimum variation in individual earnings. Generally, a higher percentage of base salary should be paid for each 1%R above 100 percent than has been paid for each 1%R up to 100%R to reflect the relative difficulty involved in producing above-standard results.

Once the performance range and reward to risk ratios have been determined, the schedule of payments for each performance measure can then be calculated. This will show the percentage of the participant's base salary earned for various performance results (%R) from the point at which commissions start to maximum performance. For example, for measurement paying 20 percent of salary for standard performance:

Percent Base Salary Earned		Percent of Sales Quota
1% of base salary for each + 1%R	0%	80% or below
	20%	100% (standard performance)
1.33% of base salary for each + 1%R	60%	130% or above

D. Prepare draft of sales commission plan

After completing the above steps, a draft of a sales commission plan should be prepared using the outline below as a guide.

Keys to effective commission plans

1. Get the understanding and acceptance of the commission plan by the managers who will be involved in carrying it out. They must be convinced of its effectiveness to properly explain and "sell" the plan to the salespeople.

2. In turn, be sure the plan is presented clearly to the salespeople so that they have a good understanding of how the plan will work. We find that good acceptance of a sales commission plan on the part of salespeople correlates closely with how well they understood the plan and its effect on their commission. Salespeople must be convinced that the measurements used are factors they can control by their selling efforts.

3. Be sure the measurements used in the commission plan encourage the salespeople to achieve the marketing goals of your operation. For example, if sales volume is the only performance measure, salespeople will concentrate on producing as much dollar volume as possible by spending most of their time on products with high volume potential. It will be difficult to get them to spend much time on introducing new products with relatively low volume, handling customer complaints, and so on. Even though a good portion of their compensation may still be in salary, you can be sure they will wind up doing the things they feel will maximize their commission earnings.

4. One good solution to maintaining good sales direction is to put at least a portion of the commission earnings in an "incentive pool" to be distributed by the sales manager according to his or her judgment. This "pool" can vary in size according to some qualitative measure of the sales group's performance, but the manager can set individual measurements for each salesperson and reward each person according to how well he or she fulfills the goals.

5. If at all possible, you should test the plan for a period of time, perhaps in one or two sales areas or districts. To make it a real test, you should actually pay commission earnings to the participants, but the potential risk and rewards can be limited. No matter how well a plan has been conceived, not all the potential pitfalls will be apparent until you've actually operated the plan for a period of time. The test period is a relatively painless way to get some experience.

6. Finally, after the plan is in operation, take time to analyze the results. Is the plan accomplishing what you want it to do, both in terms of business results produced and in realistically compensating salespeople for their efforts?

Case 2–2

Adams Brands*

Ken Bannister, Ontario regional manager for Adams Brands, was faced with the decision of which of three candidates he should hire as the key account supervisor for the Ontario region. This salesperson would be responsible for working with eight major accounts in the Toronto area. Mr. Bannister had narrowed the list to the three applicants and began reviewing their files.

The Company

Warner-Lambert Inc., a large diversified U.S. multinational, manufactured and marketed a wide range of health care and consumer products. Warner-Lambert Canada Ltd., the largest subsidiary, had annual sales exceeding $200 million. Over half the Canadian sales were generated by Adams Brands, which focused on the confectionery business. The major product lines carried by Adams were (1) chewing gum with brands such as Chiclets, Dentyne, and Trident, (2) portable breath fresheners, including Certs and Clorets, (3) cough tablets and antacids such as Halls and Rolaids, and (4) several other products including Blue Diamond Almonds and Sparkies Mini-Fruits. In these product categories, Adams Brands was usually the market leader or had a substantial market share.

The division was a stable unit for Warner-Lambert Canada with profits being used for investments throughout the company. Success of the Adams Brands was built on (1) quality products; (2) strong marketing management; (3) sales force efforts on distribution, display, and merchandising; and (4) excellent customer service.

Adams was organized on a regional basis. The Ontario region, which also included the Atlantic provinces, had 46 sales representatives whose responsibilities were to service individual stores. Five district managers coordinated the activities of the sales representatives. Also, three key-accounts supervisors worked with the large retail chains (e.g., supermarkets) in Ontario and the Atlantic area. The key-accounts supervisor in the Toronto area had recently joined one of Adams's major competitors.

The Market

The confectionery industry included six major competitors that manufactured chocolate bars, chewing gum, mints, cough drops, chewy candy, and other products. The 1998 market shares of these six companies and others are provided in Exhibit 1.

In the past few years, total industry sales in the confectionery category had been flat to marginally declining in unit volume. This sales decline was attributed to the changing age distribution of the population (i.e., fewer young people). As consumers got older, their

---

*This case was written by Gordon H. G. McDougall and Douglas Snetsinger. Copyright © by Gordon H. G. McDougall. Adapted with permission.

Exhibit I   Major Competitors in Confectionery Industry

Company	1998 Market Share (Percent)	Major Product Lines	Major Brands
Adams	23	Gum, portable breath fresheners, cough drops	Trident, Chiclets, Dentyne, Certs, Halls
Cadbury/Nielson	22	Chocolate bars	Caramilk, Crunchie, Dairy Milk, Crispy Crunch
Rowntree	15	Chocolate bars	Black Magic, Kit-Kat, Smarties, Turtles
Nabisco/Hershey	14	Gum, chocolate bars, chewy candy	Lowney, Reese's Pieces, Lifesavers
Wrigley's	9	Gum	Hubba Bubba, Extra, Doublemint
Effem Foods Ltd.	9	Chocolate bars, chewy candy	Mars, Snickers, M&Ms, Skittles
Richardson-Vicks	2	Cough drops	Vicks
Others	6		

Source: Company records and industry data.

consumption of confectionery products tended to decline. While unit sales were flat or declining, dollar sales were increasing at a rate of 10 percent per annum as a result of price increases.

In the confectionery business, it was critical to obtain extensive distribution in as many stores as possible and, within each store, to obtain as much prominent shelf space as possible. Most confectionery products were purchased on impulse. One study found that up to 85 percent of chewing gum and 70 percent of chocolate bar purchases were unplanned. While chocolate bars could be viewed as an indirect competitor to gum and mints, they were direct competitors for retail space and were usually merchandised on the same display. Retailers earned similar margins from all confectionery products (25 percent to 36 percent of retail selling price) and often sought the best-selling brands to generate those revenues. Some industry executives believed that catering to the retailers' needs was even more important than understanding the ultimate consumers' needs.

Adams Brands had always provided store display racks for merchandising all confectionery items including competitive products and chocolate bars. The advantage of supplying the displays was that the manufacturer could influence the number of prelabeled slots that contained brand logos and the proportion of the display devoted to various product groups, such as chewing gum versus chocolate bars. The displays were usually customized to the unique requirements of a retailer, such as the height and width of the display.

Recently, a competitor, Effem, had become more competitive in the design and display of merchandising systems. Effem was regarded as an innovator in the industry, in part because of its limited product line and new approach to the retail trade. The company had only eight fast-turnover products in its line. Effem had developed its own sales force, consisting of over 100 part-time merchandising salespeople and eight full-time sales personnel, and focused on the head offices of A accounts. A accounts were large retail chains such as Mac's, Beckers, Loblaws, A & P, Food City, Miracle Food Mart, Kmart, Towers, and Zellers. Other than Adams, Effem was one of a few companies that conducted considerable research on racking systems and merchandising.

The Retail Trade

Within the Adams Brands, over two-thirds of confectionery volume flowed through wholesalers. The remaining balance was split between direct sales and drop shipments to retailers. Wholesalers were necessary because, with over 66,000 outlets in food, drug, and variety stores alone, the sales force could not adequately cover a large proportion of the retailers. The percentage of Adams sales through the various channels is provided in Exhibit 2.

The volume of all consumer packaged goods sold in Canada had increasingly been dominated by fewer and larger retail chains. This increased retail concentration resulted in retailers becoming more influential in trade promotion decisions, including dictating the size, timing, and numbers of allowance, distribution, and co-op advertising events. The new power of the retailers had not yet been fully wielded against the confectionery business. Confectionery lines were some of the most profitable lines for the retailer. Further, the manufacturers were not as reliant on listings from any given retailer as were other food and household product manufacturers.

The increased size of some retail chains also changed the degree of management sophistication at all levels, including the retail buyer—those responsible for deciding what products were carried by the retail stores. At one time, the relationship between manufacturers' sales representatives and retail buyers was largely based on long-term and personal associations. Usually the sales representative had strong social skills, and an important task was to "get along well" with the buyers. Often when the representatives and buyers met to discuss various promotions or listings, part of the conversation dealt with making plans for dinner or going to a hockey game. The sales representative would be the host for these social events.

More recently, a new breed of buyer was emerging in the retail chains. Typically, the new retail managers and buyers had been trained in business schools. They often had prod-

Exhibit 2   Adams Brands Sales by Distribution Channel

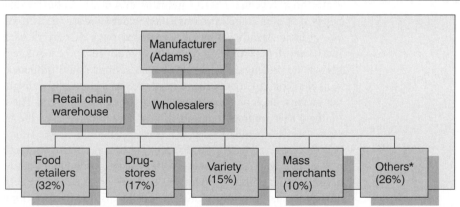

*Consists of a wide variety of locations, including vending machines, restaurants, cafeterias, bowling alleys, and resorts.

uct management experience, relied on analytical skills, and used state-of-the-art, computer-supported planning systems. In some instances, the buyer was now more sophisticated than the sales representative with respect to analytical approaches to display and inventory management. The buyers were frequently requesting detailed plan-o-grams with strong analytical support for expected sales, profits, and inventory turns. The buyer would also at times become the salesperson. After listening to a sales presentation and giving an initial indication of interest, the buyer would attempt to sell space—space on the store floor and space in the weekly advertising supplements. For example, the buyer for Shopper's Drug Mart could offer a dump bin location in every store in the chain for a week. In some instances, both the buyer and the representative had the authority to conclude such a deal at that meeting. At other times, both would have to wait for approval from their respective companies.

The interesting aspect of the key-accounts supervisor's position was that the individual would have to feel comfortable dealing with the "old" and "new" school of retail management. The task for Bannister was to select the right candidate for this position. The salary for the position ranged from $25,000 to $48,200, depending on qualifications and experience. Bannister expected the candidate selected would probably be paid somewhere between $32,000 and $40,000. An expense allowance would also be included in the compensation package.

The Key-Accounts Supervisor

The main responsibility of the key-accounts supervisor was to establish and maintain a close working relationship with the buyers of eight A accounts whose head offices were located in the Toronto area. An important task was to make presentations (15 to 30 minutes in length) to the retail buyers of these key accounts every three to six weeks. At these meetings, promotions or deals for up to five brands would be presented. The supervisor was responsible for all Adams brands. The buyer might have to take the promotions to his buying committee where the final decision would be made. In addition, the supervisor used these meetings to hear from the buyer about any merchandising problems occurring at the store level.

Midyear reviews were undertaken with each account. These reviews, lasting for one hour, were focused on reviewing sales trends and tying them into merchandising programs, listings, service, and new payment terms. Another important and time-consuming responsibility of the key-accounts supervisor was to devise and present plan-o-grams and be involved with the installation of the displays. The supervisor also conducted store checks and spent time on competitive intelligence. Working with the field staff was a further requirement of the position.

Bannister reflected on what he thought were the attributes the ideal candidate would possess. First, the individual should have selling and merchandising experience in the retail business to understand the language and dynamics of the situation. On the merchandising side, the individual would be required to initiate and coordinate the design of customized display systems for individual stores, a task that involved a certain amount of creativity. Second, strong interpersonal skills were needed. The individual had to establish rapport and make effective sales presentations to the buyers. Because of the wide range of buyer sophistication, these skills were particularly important. Bannister made a mental note to recommend that whoever was hired be sent on the professional selling skills course, a one-week program designed to enhance listening, selling, and presentation skills.

Exhibit 3

Lydia Cohen

Personal:	Born 1968; 5'6"; 140 lbs.: single
Education:	B.B.A. (1990), Wilfrid Laurier University; active in Marketing Club and Intramural sports.
Work:	1997–99, Rowntree Mackintosh Canada Inc.—District Manager
	Responsible for sales staff of three in Ottawa and Eastern Ontario region. Establish annual sales plan and ensure that district meets its quota.
	1990–96, Rowntree Mackintosh Canada Inc.—Confectionery Sales Representative
	Responsible for selling a full line of confectionery and grocery products to key accounts in Toronto (1993–94) and Ottawa (1990–94). 1996—Sales Representative of the Year for highest volume growth.
Interests:	Racquet sports
Candidate's comments:	I am interested in working in the Toronto area, and I would look forward to concentrating on the sales task. My best years at Rowntree were in sales in the Toronto region.
Interviewer's comments:	Lydia presents herself very well and has a strong background in confectionery sales. Her record at Rowntree is very good. Rowntree paid for her to take an introductory course in Lotus 1-2-3 in 1996, but she has not had much opportunity to develop her computer skills. She does not seem to be overly ambitious or aggressive. She stated that personal reasons were preeminent in seeking a job in Toronto.

John Fisher

Personal:	Born 1972; 6'3"; 195 lbs.; single
Education:	B.A. (Phys. Ed.) (1997), University of British Columbia
	While at U.B.C. played four years of varsity basketball (team captain in 1995–96). Assistant Coach, Senior Basketball at University Hill High School, 1993–97. Developed and ran a two-week summer basketball camp at U.B.C. for three years. Profits from the camp were donated to the Varsity Basketball Fund.
Work:	1992–98, Jacobs Suchard Canada Inc. (Nabob Foods)
	Six-years' experience (full-time, 1997–98, and five years, 1992–97, part-time during school terms and full-time during summers) in coffee and chocolate distribution and sales; two years on the loading docks, one year driving truck, and three years as a sales representative. Sales tasks included calling on regular customers, order taking, rack jobbing, and customer relations development.
	1998–99, Scavolini (Professional Basketball)
	One year after completing studies at U.B.C., traveled Western Europe and Northern Africa. Travel was financed by playing professional basketball in the Italian First Division.
Candidate's comment:	I feel the combination of educational preparation, work experience, and my demonstrated ability as a team player and leader make me well suited for this job. I am particularly interested in a job, such as sales, which rewards personal initiative.
Interviewer's comments:	A very ambitious and engaging individual with a good record of achievements. Strong management potential is evident, but interest in sales as a career is questionable. Minored in Computer Science at U.B.C. Has a standing offer to return to a sales management position at Nabob.

(continued)

Finally, the candidate should possess analytic skills because many of the sales and performance reports (from both manufacturer and retailer) were or would be computerized. Thus, the individual should feel comfortable working with computers. Bannister hoped he could find a candidate who would be willing to spend a minimum of three years in the job to establish a personal relationship with the buyers.

Ideally, the candidate selected would have a blend of all three skills because of the mix of buyers he or she would contact. Bannister believed it was most likely these characteristics would be found in a business school graduate. He had advertised the job internally (through the company's newsletter) and externally (in the *Toronto Star*). A total of 20 applications were received. After an initial screening, three possible candidates for the position were identified. None were from Warner-Lambert.

Exhibit 3   (concluded)

Barry Moore

Personal: Born 1959; 5'11"; 185 lbs.; married with two children

Education: Business Administration Diploma (1984), Humber College

While at school was active participant in a number of clubs and political organizations. President of the Young Liberals (1983–84).

Work: 1996–99, Barrigans Food Markets—Merchandising Analyst

Developed merchandising plans for a wide variety of product categories. Negotiated merchandising programs and trade deals with manufacturers and brokers. Managed a staff of four.

1993–96, Dominion Stores Ltd.—Assistant Merchandise Manager

Liaison responsibilities between stores and head office merchandise planning. Responsible for execution of merchandising plans for several food categories.

1992, Robin Hood Multifoods, Inc.—Assistant Product Manager

Responsible for the analysis and development of promotion planning for Robin Hood Flour.

1987–92, Nestlé Enterprises Ltd.—Carnation Division Sales Representative

Major responsibilities were developing and maintaining sales and distribution to wholesale and retail accounts.

1984–87, McCain Foods Ltd.—Inventory Analyst

Worked with sales staff and head office planning to ensure the quality and timing of shipments to brokers and stores.

Activities: Board of Directors, Richview Community Club
Board of Directors, Volunteer Centre of Etobicoke
Past President of Etobicoke Big Brothers
Active in United Way
Yachting—C&C34 Canadian Champion

Candidate's comment: It would be a great challenge and joy to work with a progressive industry leader such as Adams Brands.

Interviewer's comments: Very articulate and professionally groomed. Dominated the interview with a variety of anecdotes and humorous stories, some of which were relevant to the job. Likes to read popular books on management, particularly books that champion the bold gut-feel entrepreneur. He would probably earn more money at Adams if hired.

In early August 1999, Bannister and a member of the personnel department then interviewed each of the candidates. After completing the interviews, brief fact sheets were prepared (see Exhibit 3). Bannister reviewed the sheets before making the decision.

Case 2–3

Chips-to-Dip, Inc.*

During the past few months, regional management of the Chips-to-Dip Corporation has noticed an increasing negative attitude prevailing in their sales force. The focus of the complaints centers on the sales force's role in the performance of a recent addition to the Chips-to-Dip product line, Bakers' Choice Cookies.

For more than twenty years, Chips-to-Dip has been a national leader in the sales of salty snacks with market shares that run into the 60s and 70s throughout the country. Until recently, the Chips-to-Dip product line consisted exclusively of potato and corn chips, tortilla chips, cheese puffs and pretzels. Many of the salty snack products have developed over time to include flavor variations and alternative package sizes. Historically, they have faced little competition and have built a reputation for premium quality products sold at premium prices. However, in the past three to five years, several market characteristics have changed, causing Chips-to-Dip management some concern. Their salty-snack line has been challenged by an increasing number of lower-priced salty snack brands entering the market. Store managers, believing that consumers favor lower-priced products, have devoted significant shelf space to these new brands.

In response to these competitive inroads, Chips-to-Dip considered several new products that would be compatible with their present form of distribution. They acquired Bakers' Choice Cookies of Seattle, Washington. Management felt that the new cookie line would be sold to many of the same accounts as the salty snack line. The cookie line was added to the sales reps' existing line. Chips-to-Dip management did not alter either the existing route schedules or the account assignments for their sales reps. As a result, the route sales reps are responsible for selling, delivering and promoting two product lines. The Bakers' Choice line consists of five different types of cookies.

Sales projections for the new line of cookies have not met expectations. In fact, sales have plateaued at less than an optimal level, causing some disillusionment among the sales force. The national sales force numbers in excess of 10,000, and the company prides itself on its ability to provide daily service to its accounts. In fact, Chips' "99.5 percent service level" has been criticized by analysts as being excessive, especially for a commodity product such as salty snacks. The market share results, however, seem to support the feasibility of providing such high levels of service.

During this time, the Chips-to-Dip selling task was straightforward. Given a route in an urban or rural area, the sales reps were to sell to grocery stores, convenience stores, taverns, and gas stations with the goal of achieving the highest possible volume while making the best use of their time. Because they dealt exclusively in salty snacks, the route sales reps ordered from and delivered to only one area of the store. This usually required only one trip to the delivery truck to get the product once the initial sales order was taken.

*The assistance of Patricia Zarnstorff Erickson, General Mills, in the preparation of this case is greatly appreciated.
Copyright © 1999 Neil M. Ford.

In order to provide excellent service, which is Chips-to-Dip's differential advantage, a well-planned distribution system exits in both rural and urban areas. In the rural areas, small warehouses known as "bins" provide the products for one to two sales reps. Shipments arrive on a weekly basis. In urban areas, the facilities are known as "distribution centers" and supply one or more sales districts. Shipments arrive daily and in large quantities.

Many aspects of the route salesperson's job have since changed. First, their job task is larger. Sales reps are now required to not only introduce and sell the cookie line to all of their salty accounts, but, in addition, set up displays and offer samples, discounts and coupons to encourage product trial. However, the salespeople are still expected to continue their excellent sales and service record in the salty snack line. Second, the addition of the Bakers' Choice line has naturally increased the time a salesperson must spend at each account. The existence of two order forms, separate grocery sections, different buyers in the larger stores and the frequent need for two trips from delivery truck to store door require additional time to complete each sales stop. Third, district sales managers require route sales reps to make substantial effort promoting sales of Bakers' Choice Cookies. Reports itemizing sales of cookies and the regular salty line are demanded by management on a daily basis. Frequent conferences between district sales managers and route sales reps are held to discuss sales efforts promoting the Bakers' Choice line. In addition, sales contests and dealer incentives have been used to further motivate the sales force.

When the Bakers' Choice line was added, very little attention was given to its impact on the length of the salesperson's day. Sales routes were not restructured to allow for the extra margin of time needed to properly promote both products. Those salespeople who were able to provide a satisfactory effort selling the cookie line found that their average workday increased by 1 1/2 to 2 1/2 hours.

Jeff Bartz, regional sales manager, believes that the existing financial incentive should be sufficient to motivate the sales reps. According to Jeff: "If my salespeople make an effort to sell Bakers' Choice Cookies, they will realize a substantial gain in their weekly commission." However, with cookie commissions equal to salty snack commissions—both are 10 percent of sales—the salespeople feel differently. As Jim Riley, a route salesman, said: "Why should I lengthen my sales day with a completely new product? It isn't worth hassling with store managers and elbowing for space in the cookie section. For the same 10 percent commission, I would rather spend my time selling the tried-and-true Chips-to-Dip salty snacks."

In an attempt to alleviate the time demands placed on the sales reps as a result of the additional product line, Chips-to-Dip top management created a new position. The company hired people to serve as missionary representatives who were responsible for helping the route people with the introduction of the new product line. They would approach the store managers and attempt to persuade them to adopt the Bakers' Choice line. If the store manager approved, the missionary reps would arrange the shelf displays and monitor cookie sales weekly and monthly. Basically they were to help the sales rep. The success of these people, who became known as "cookie reps," was not known due to the brief time period this approach had been in effect. Three cookie reps were assigned to Bartz's region and worked out of the distribution centers usually located in the metropolitan cities.

Jeff Bartz knew that his eight district sales managers had a serious problem on their hands. Although initial sales of Bakers' Choice had been strong, market enthusiasm over the new cookie line had dropped significantly over the past year. As a result, the sales force was less confident in the future of the cookie line. Serious discussions between certain salespeople about the value of their cookie sales efforts and the quality of the cookie product had erupted over the past four months. Afraid of morale problems which could poten-

Exhibit 1   Chips-to-Dip Route Salesperson Questionnaire

Instructions: Please fill out the following questionnaire
by placing an X on the appropriate line. (Please use numbers
where they apply.)

I. Bakers' Choice Cookies

1. How well do you feel the Bakers' Choice cookie line is selling compared to other brands in your market?

much worse	4	10	15	23	7	—	—	much better

2. Please rate Bakers' Choice cookies against the competitors on the following attributes:

PRICE

much higher	6	22	19	9	2	1	—	much lower

QUALITY

much better	18	11	11	13	4	2	—	much worse

PACKAGING

more appealing	4	17	16	11	3	5	3	less appealing

ADVERTISING SUPPORT

greater support	7	15	11	11	7	6	2	less support

3. Do you feel that the fact that you have to promote two product lines is hurting your effectiveness on either or both lines?

Check the appropriate box:

26	8	8	17
is not hurting either line	is hurting cookie line	is hurting salty line	is hurting both lines

4. Please indicate the percentage of your selling time spent in:

Salty snacks	85 %
Bakers' Choice cookies	15 %
=	100 %

5. Please indicate the percentage of your selling time that should be spent in:

Salty snacks	75 %
Bakers' Choice cookies	25 %
=	100 %

(continued)

tially affect the entire regional sales force, Bartz decided to conduct an attitude survey of the salespeople in his region. A questionnaire was developed and mailed to the 72 route salespeople in Bartz's region. Questionnaires were completed and returned by 59 sales reps for a response rate of 81.9 percent. Exhibit 1 presents the questionnaire and frequencies.

Exhibit 1   Chips-to-Dip Route Salesperson Questionnaire *(continued)*

6. Do you currently use cookie displays?

54	5
Yes	No

7. What type of display equipment do you use most often?

26	cookie hutch	16	shelf signs	4	pole bins
24	stairstep display	11	weekender units	10	knockout displays

8. What effect do the cookie representatives have on your sales?

very helpful	4	9	11	16	7	10	3	very harmful

9. In general, how cooperative are the store managers on your route toward the promotion of Bakers' Choice cookies?

very cooperative	2	3	6	11	14	15	8	very uncooperative

10. Please indicate the type of cookie which you feel tastes the best.

9	18	2	4	26
Sandwich Stacks	Twirl	Fruit Filled	Ho-made	Old-tyme

II. Chips-to-Dip versus the Competition

1. Please rate Chips-to-Dip salty snacks against all competitors' salty snacks on the following attributes:

PRICE

much higher	6	22	19	9	2	1	—	much lower

QUALITY

much better	18	11	11	13	4	2	—	much worse

PACKAGING

more appealing	4	17	16	11	3	5	3	less appealing

ADVERTISING SUPPORT

greater support	7	15	11	11	7	6	2	less support

2. Please indicate your degree of agreement or disagreement with the following statements:

   a. The lower priced salty snacks brands are a threat to your sales.

12	32	6	8	1
strongly agree	agree	neither agree nor disagree	disagree	strongly disagree

Exhibit I   Chips-to-Dip Route Salesperson Questionnaire *(concluded)*

b. The quality of the Chips-to-Dip product compensates for its higher price.

8	30	8	12	1
strongly agree	agree	neither agree or disagree	disagree	strongly disagree

c. The lower-priced competitors produce a product of equal quality to the Chips-to-Dip product.

3	2	12	25	17
strongly agree	agree	neither agree or disagree	disagree	strongly disagree

3. Please indicate your perception of Chips-to-Dip's company image on the following attributes:

GROWTH

very satisfactory	18	25	7	5	2	1	1	very unsatisfactory

QUALITY

very satisfactory	23	28	5	2	—	1	—	very unsatisfactory

MARKET LEADERSHIP

very satisfactory	22	19	12	2	1	1	1	very unsatisfactory

CUSTOMER LOYALTY

very satisfactory	12	17	12	9	6	3	—	very unsatisfactory

4. Your overall perception of Chips-to-Dip as a company:

good	36	16	4	3	—	bad

5. Do you feel that Chips-to-Dip's marketing activities are:

passive	1	4	8	18	28	aggressive

6. Please rate Chips-to-Dip's performance on the following activities:

Scale of 1–5:   1 = poor,   5 = excellent

Activity	1		2		3		4		5	
Product advertising	1	1	2	4	3	6	4	22	5	26
New product introductions	1	4	2	10	3	11	4	21	5	13
Sales support	1	4	2	4	3	18	4	19	5	14
Aggressive pricing	1	7	2	22	3	21	4	7	5	2
Discounts and coupons	1	5	2	5	3	12	4	19	5	18

Case 2–4

Outdoor Sporting Products, Inc.*

The annual sales volume of Outdoor Sporting Products, Inc., for the past six years had ranged between $6.2 million and $6.8 million. Although profits continued to be satisfactory, Mr. Hudson McDonald, president and chief operating officer, was concerned because sales had not increased appreciably from year to year. Consequently, he asked a consultant in New York City and the officers of the company to submit proposals for improving the salesmen's compensation plan, which he believed was the basic weakness in the firm's marketing operations.

Outdoor's factory and warehouse were located in Albany, New York, where the company manufactured and distributed sporting equipment, clothing, and accessories. Mr. McDonald, who managed the company, organized it in 1956 when he envisioned a growing market for sporting goods resulting from the predicted increase in leisure time and the rising levels of income in the United States.

Products of the company, numbering approximately 700 items, were grouped into three lines: (1) fishing supplies, (2) hunting supplies, and (3) accessories. The fishing supplies line, which accounted for approximately 40 percent of the company's annual sales, included nearly every item a fisherman would need such as fishing jackets, vests, caps, rods and reels of all types, lines, flies, lures, landing nets, and creels. Thirty percent of annual sales were in the hunting supplies line, which consisted of hunting clothing of all types including insulated and thermal underwear, safety garments, shell holders, whistles, calls, and gun cases. The accessories line, which made up the balance of the company's annual sales volume, included items such as compasses, cooking kits, lanterns, hunting and fishing knives, hand warmers, and novelty gifts.

While the sales of the hunting and fishing lines were very seasonal, they tended to complement one another. The January–April period accounted for the bulk of the company's annual volume in fishing items, and most sales of hunting supplies were made from May through August. Typically, the company's sales of all products reached their lows for the year during December.

Outdoor's sales volume was $6.37 million in the current year with self-manufactured products accounting for 35 percent of this total. Fifty percent of the company's volume consisted of imported products, which came principally from Japan. Items manufactured by other domestic producers and distributed by Outdoor accounted for the remaining 15 percent of total sales.

---

*Adapted from a case written by Zarrel V. Lambert, Southern Illinois University, Carbondale, and Fred W. Kniffin, University of Connecticut, Stamford. Previously used with permission.

Mr. McDonald reported that wholesale prices to retailers were established by adding a markup of 50 to 100 percent to Outdoor's cost for the item. This rule was followed on self-manufactured products as well as for items purchased from other manufacturers. The resulting average markup across all products was 70 percent on cost.

Outdoor's market area consisted of the New England states, New York, Pennsylvania, Ohio, Michigan, Wisconsin, Indiana, Illinois, Kentucky, Tennessee, West Virginia, Virginia, Maryland, Delaware, and New Jersey. The area over which Outdoor could effectively compete was limited to some extent by shipping costs, since all orders were shipped from the factory and warehouse in Albany.

Outdoor's salesmen sold to approximately 6,000 retail stores in small- and medium-sized cities in its market area. Analysis of sales records showed that the firm's customer coverage was very poor in the large metropolitan areas. Typically, each account was a one- or two-store operation. Mr. McDonald stated that he knew Outdoor's share of the market was very low, perhaps 2 to 3 percent; and for all practical purposes, he felt the company's sales potential was unlimited.

Mr. McDonald believed that with few exceptions, Outdoor's customers had little or no brand preference and in the vast majority of cases they bought hunting and fishing supplies from several suppliers.

It was McDonald's opinion that the pattern of retail distribution for hunting and fishing products had been changing during the past 10 years as a result of the growth of discount stores. He thought that the proportion of retail sales for hunting and fishing supplies made by small- and medium-sized sporting goods outlets had been declining compared to the percent sold by discounters and chain stores. An analysis of company records revealed Outdoor had not developed business among the discounters with the exception of a few small discount stores. Some of Outdoor's executives felt that the lack of business with discounters might have been due in part to the company's pricing policy and in part to the pressures current customers had exerted on company salesmen to keep them from calling on the discounters.

Outdoor's Sales Force

The company's sales force played a major role in its marketing efforts since Outdoor did not use magazine, newspaper, or radio advertising to reach either the retail trade or consumers. One advertising piece that supplemented the work of the salesmen was Outdoor's merchandise catalog. It contained a complete listing of all the company's products and was mailed to all retailers who were either current accounts or prospective accounts. Typically, store buyers used the catalog for reordering.

Most accounts were contacted by a salesman two or three times a year. The salesmen planned their activities so that each store would be called on at the beginning of the fishing season and again before the hunting season. Certain key accounts of some salesmen were contacted more often than two or three times a year.

Management believed that product knowledge was the major ingredient of a successful sales call. Consequently, Mr. McDonald had developed a "selling formula," which each salesman was required to learn before he took over a territory. The "formula" contained five parts: (1) the name and catalog number of each item sold by the company; (2) the sizes and colors in which each item was available; (3) the wholesale price of each item; (4) the suggested retail price of each item; and (5) the primary selling features of each item. After a new salesman had mastered the product knowledge specified by this "formula," he began working in his assigned territory and was usually accompanied by Mr. McDonald for several weeks.

Managing the sales force consumed approximately one-third of Mr. McDonald's efforts. The remaining two-thirds of his time was spent purchasing products for resale and in general administrative duties as the company's chief operating officer.

Mr. McDonald held semiannual sales meetings, had weekly telephone conversations with each salesman, and had mimeographed bulletins containing information on products, prices, and special promotional deals mailed to all salesmen each week. Daily call reports and attendance at the semiannual sales meetings were required of all salesmen. One meeting was held the first week in January to introduce the spring line of fishing supplies. The hunting line was presented at the second meeting, which was scheduled in May. Each of these sales meetings spanned four to five days so the salesmen were able to study the new products being introduced and any changes in sales and company policies. The production manager and comptroller attended these sales meetings to answer questions and to discuss problems the salesmen might have concerning deliveries and credit.

On a predetermined schedule, each salesman telephoned Mr. McDonald every Monday morning to learn of changes in prices, special promotional offers, and delivery schedules of unshipped orders. At this time, the salesman's activities for the week were discussed, and sometimes the salesman was asked by Mr. McDonald to collect past due accounts in his territory. In addition, the salesmen submitted daily call reports, which listed the name of each account contacted and the results of the call. Generally, the salesmen planned their own itineraries in terms of the accounts and prospects that were to be contacted and the amount of time to be spent on each call.

Outdoor's sales force during the current year totaled 11 full-time employees. Their ages ranged from 23 to 67 years, and their tenure with the company ranged from 1 to 10 years. Salesmen, territories, and sales volumes for the previous year and the current year are shown in Exhibit 1.

Compensation of Salesmen

The salesmen were paid straight commissions on their dollar sales volume for the calendar year. The commission rate was 5 percent on the first $300,000, 6 percent on the next $200,000 in volume, and 7 percent on all sales over $500,000 for the year. Each week a salesman could draw all or a portion of his accumulated commissions. Mr. McDonald encouraged the salesmen to draw commissions as they accumulated since he felt the men were motivated to work harder when they had a very small or zero balance in their commission accounts. These accounts were closed at the end of the year, so each salesman began the new year with nothing in his account.

The salesmen provided their own automobiles and paid their traveling expenses, of which all or a portion were reimbursed by per diem. Under the per diem plan, each salesman received $70 per day for Monday through Thursday and $42 for Friday, or a total of $322 for the normal workweek. No per diem was paid for Saturday, but a salesman received an additional $70 if he spent Saturday and Sunday nights in the territory.

In addition to the commission and per diem, a salesman could earn cash awards under two sales incentive plans that were installed two years ago. Under the Annual Sales Increase Awards Plan, a total of $10,400 was paid to the five salesmen having the largest percentage increase in dollar sales volume over the previous year. To be eligible for these awards, a salesman had to show a sales increase over the previous year. These awards were made at the January sales meeting, and the winners were determined by dividing the dollar amount of each salesman's increase by his volume for the previous year with the percentage increases ranked in descending order. The salesmen's earnings under this plan for the current year are shown in Exhibit 2.

Exhibit 1   Salesmen: Age, Years of Service, Territory, and Sales

Salesmen	Age	Years of Service	Territory	Sales Previous Year	Sales Current Year
Allen	45	2	Illinois and Indiana	$ 330,264	$ 329,216
Campbell	62	10	Pennsylvania	1,192,192	1,380,240
Duvall	23	1	New England	—	414,656
Edwards	39	1	Michigan	—	419,416
Gatewood	63	5	West Virginia	358,528	358,552
Hammond	54	2	Virginia	414,936	414,728
Logan	37	1	Kentucky and Tennessee	—	447,720
Mason	57	2	Delaware and Maryland	645,032	825,088
O'Bryan	59	4	Ohio	343,928	372,392
Samuels	42	3	New York and New Jersey	737,024	824,472
Wates	67	5	Wisconsin	370,712	342,200
Salesmen terminated in previous year				1,828,816	—
House account				257,384	244,480
Total				$6,478,816	$6,373,160

Exhibit 2   Salesmen's Earnings and Incentive Awards in the Current Year

Salesmen	Sales Previous Year	Sales Current Year	Annual Sales Increase Awards — Increase in Sales (percent)	Annual Sales Increase Awards — Award	Weekly Sales Increase Awards (total accrued)	Earnings*
Allen	$ 330,264	$ 329,216	(0.3%)	—	$1,012	$30,000†
Campbell	1,192,192	1,380,240	15.8	$3,000 (2nd)	2,244	88,617
Duvall	—	414,656	—	—	—	30,000†
Edwards	—	419,416	—	—	—	30,000†
Gatewood	358,528	358,552	(0.1)	400 (5th)	1,104	18,513
Hammond	414,936	414,728	—	—	420	30,000†
Logan	—	447,720	—	—	—	30,000†
Mason	645,032	825,088	27.9	4,000 (1st)	3,444	49,756
O'Bryan	343,928	372,392	8.3	1,000 (4th)	1,512	19,344
Samuels	737,024	824,472	11.9	2,000 (3rd)	1,300	49,713
Wates	370,712	342,200	(7.7)	—	612	17,532

*Exclusive of incentive awards and per diem.

†Guarantee of $600 per week or $30,000 per year.

Under the second incentive plan, each salesman could win a Weekly Sales Increase Award for each week in which his dollar volume in the current year exceeded his sales for the corresponding week in the previous year. Beginning with an award of $4 for the first week, the amount of the award increased by $4 for each week in which the salesman surpassed his sales for the comparable week in the previous year. If a salesman produced higher sales during each of the 50 weeks in the current year, he received $4 for the 1st week, $8 for the 2nd week, and $200 for the 50th week, or a total of $4,100 for the year. The salesman had to be employed by the company during the previous year to be eligible for these awards. A check for the total amount of the awards accrued during the year was presented to the salesman at the sales meeting held in January. Earnings of the salesmen under this plan for the current year are shown in Exhibit 2.

The company frequently used "spiffs" to promote the sales of special items. The salesman was paid a spiff, which usually was $4, for each order he obtained for the designated items in the promotion.

For the past three years in recruiting salesmen, Mr. McDonald had guaranteed the more qualified applicants a weekly income while they learned the business and developed their respective territories. During the current year, five salesmen, Allen, Duvall, Edwards, Hammond, and Logan, had a guarantee of $600 a week, which they drew against their commissions. If the year's cumulative commissions for any of these salesmen were less than their cumulative weekly drawing accounts, they received no commissions. The commission and drawing accounts were closed on December 31, so each salesman began the new year with a zero balance in each account.

The company did not have a stated or written policy specifying the maximum length of time a salesman could receive a guarantee if his commissions continued to be less than his draw. Mr. McDonald believed the five salesmen who currently had guarantees would quit if these guarantees were withdrawn before their commissions reached $30,000 per year.

Mr. McDonald stated that he was convinced the annual earnings of Outdoor's salesmen had fallen behind earnings for comparable selling positions, particularly in the past six years. As a result, he felt that the company's ability to attract and hold high-caliber professional salesmen was being adversely affected. He strongly expressed the opinion that each salesman should be earning $50,000 annually.

Compensation Plan Proposals

In December of the current year, Mr. McDonald met with his comptroller and production manager, who were the only other executives of the company, and solicited their ideas concerning changes in the company's compensation plan for salesmen.

The comptroller pointed out that the salesmen having guarantees were not producing the sales that had been expected from their territories. He was concerned that the annual commissions earned by four of the five salesmen on guarantees were approximately half or less than their drawing accounts.

Furthermore, according to the comptroller, several of the salesmen who did not have guarantees were producing a relatively low volume of sales year after year. For example, annual sales remained at relatively low levels for Gatewood, O'Bryan, and Wates, who had been working four to five years in their respective territories.

The comptroller proposed that guarantees be reduced to $250 per week plus commissions at the regular rate on all sales. The $250 would not be drawn against commissions as was the case under the existing plan but would be in addition to any commissions earned. In the comptroller's opinion, this plan would motivate the salesmen to increase

Exhibit 3   Comparison of Earnings in Current Year under Existing Guarantee Plan with Earnings

Salesmen	Sales	Existing Plan			Comptroller's Plan		
		Commissions	Guarantee	Earnings	Commissions	Guarantee	Earnings
Allen	$329,216	$16,753	$30,000	$30,000	$16,753	$12,500	$29,253
Duvall	414,656	21,879	30,000	30,000	21,879	12,500	34,379
Edwards	419,416	22,165	30,000	30,000	22,165	12,500	34,665
Hammond	358,552	18,513	30,000	30,000	18,513	12,500	31,013
Logan	447,720	23,863	30,000	30,000	23,863	12,500	36,363

*Exclusive of incentive awards and per diem.

sales rapidly since their incomes would rise directly with their sales. The comptroller presented Exhibit 3, which showed the incomes of the five salesmen having guarantees in the current year as compared with the incomes they would have received under his plan.

From a sample check of recent shipments, the production manager had concluded the salesmen tended to overwork accounts located within a 50-mile radius of their homes. Sales coverage was extremely light in a 60- to 100-mile radius of the salesmen's homes with somewhat better coverage beyond 100 miles. He argued that this pattern of sales coverage seemed to result from a desire by the salesmen to spend most evenings during the week at home with their families.

He proposed that the per diem be increased from $70 to $90 per day for Monday through Thursday, $42 for Friday, and $90 for Sunday if the salesman spent Sunday evening away from his home. He reasoned that the per diem of $90 for Sunday would act as a strong incentive for the salesmen to drive to the perimeters of their territories on Sunday evenings rather than use Monday morning for traveling. Further, he believed the increase in per diem would encourage the salesmen to spend more evenings away from their homes, which would result in a more uniform coverage of the sales territories and an overall increase in sales volume.

The consultant from New York City recommended that the guarantees and per diem be retained on the present basis and proposed that Outdoor adopt what he called a "Ten Percent Self-Improvement Plan." Under the consultant's plan, each salesman would be paid, in addition to the regular commission, a monthly bonus commission of 10 percent on all dollar volume over his sales in the comparable month of the previous year. For example, if a salesman sold $40,000 worth of merchandise in January of the current year and $36,000 in January of the previous year, he would receive a $400 bonus check in February. For salesmen on guarantees, bonuses would be in addition to earnings. The consultant reasoned that the bonus commission would motivate the salesmen, both those with and without guarantees, to increase their sales.

He further recommended the discontinuation of the two sales incentive plans currently in effect. He felt the savings from these plans would nearly cover the costs of his proposal.

Following a discussion of these proposals with the management group, Mr. McDonald was undecided on which proposal to adopt, if any. Further, he wondered if any change in the compensation of salesmen would alleviate all of the present problems.

Case 2–5*

Denver Illini Genetics*

In September 1998, Denver Illini Genetics' marketing director, Mr. Robson, noticed a trend toward fluctuating yearly sales volumes by some of the company's sales representatives. Certain sales representatives had good sales years followed by poor sales years every other year. Their sales growth, as a result, is flat and not anywhere close to DIG's objectives. Robson needed to determine the cause and extent of the problem.

The Company

Denver Illini Genetics (DIG), based in Denver, Colorado, is a young artificial insemination (AI) company with a small share of the total market. Although there are many small firms that provide AI services, such as Tri-State Breeders in Wisconsin, DIG's major competitors are American Breeders Service (ABS), also a Wisconsin firm, who is recognized as the world leader, and Select Sires from Ohio. The major market of both firms is dairy and only a small portion, estimated at less than 10 percent, is in the beef market. Artificial insemination is the artificial introduction of semen into the genital tract of the female animal. This procedure provides several advantages of economic importance to beef and dairy cattle breeders. Of prime benefit is that it allows the breeder the opportunity to take advantage of the superior genetics of certain sires. Second, cattle breeders have used artificial insemination to avoid and prevent recurrence of livestock diseases. With both beef and dairy cattle, artificial insemination has proven itself to be a major factor in improving herd productivity.

Mr. Robson started with the Western Beef Breeders Association when it was organized, eight years ago. A few years ago, Western merged with Illini Breeders, Inc., of Springfield, Illinois. Subsequently, the company was renamed Denver Illini Genetics. DIG "produces" and sells beef semen and sees sizable growth potential in the beef part of the market. DIG's management sees the company's niche in the beef market rather than the dairy cattle market because this is where DIG has technical expertise and the dairy market is dominated by ABS. DIG is aiming for leadership position in the U.S. beef AI industry.

The Sales Force

DIG employs two regional sales managers and fourteen sales representatives. The sales representatives are self-employed, independent contractors. These representatives are responsible for providing:

---

*This case was prepared especially for this text by Regina Downey and Brett Kronholm, MBA's–Marketing, University of Wisconsin–Madison. Copyright © 1998, Neil M. Ford.

1. Insemination service, and

2. Semen sales and refrigerator service to customers who breed their own herds in their designated, exclusive sales areas.

The list of customer services provided by DIG representatives includes the distribution of semen, equipment, and supplies. Utilizing DIG-owned equipment, they deliver semen, liquid nitrogen, refrigerators, and breeding supplies to their customers on regular, precise schedules.

The representatives promote their products and services through on-the-farm sales calls with the aid of DIG-prepared publications, promotional materials, and advertising. Promotional supplies that the representatives can purchase from DIG include car emblems, fabric decals, baseball caps, down vests, etc. In addition, DIG furnishes an annual cooperative advertising package that is designed to help the representatives get the attention of beef breeders. The ads use a theme similar to DIG's national advertising theme. The terms of the cooperative advertising package state:

1. DIG will reimburse you (the representative) for one-half of your local advertising expense up to 2 percent of your 1998 semen purchases.

2. First-year representatives are eligible for reimbursement up to one-half of $125 spent for advertising during that year.

The DIG cooperative advertising program is designed to help cover the cost of advertising in the print and radio media.

The main source and amount of the representatives' income vary considerably between areas and representatives. A major portion is derived through selling DIG products and services, which are all individually commissionable. Payment by the herd owner for insemination service presents the second portion of the representatives' income. Most representatives, about 65 percent, work part time and have farms or part-time jobs elsewhere. A country veterinarian who sells DIG products and services "on the side" is an example of a part-time DIG representative.

DIG compensates its representatives using the commission/discount program shown in Exhibit 1. The company estimates that 65 percent of its total sales are made to the representatives at discounts determined using Plan D. The representatives buy DIG products for their own inventory and sell from this inventory to breeders. The representatives sell the products to the herd owners at suggested list prices. The remaining 35 percent of DIG's total sales are made directly to the herd owners. Direct sales to beef farmers occur primarily with new representatives who, due to financial limitations, are unable to carry enough inventory to meet demand. The representatives receive commissions as stated in Plan D for their assistance in these sales. Average sales volumes are hard to compute due to the full-time/part-time split. For part-time people, annual average sales are $15,000. Full-time people average $65,000. Usually, 90 percent of sales are for semen and 10 percent for products and supplies. For example, Harry Turner, Southern region, had 1996 semen sales of $96,023 and $10,669 sales of products and supplies for a total of $106,692. Turner also provides breeding services and, in a typical year, will breed 3,000 cows at a charge of $5 each.

In addition, the company motivates its representatives with a sales growth incentive program entitled "Beef Bonanza" which has been employed since 1990. Under the plan, an escalating commission (7 to 12 percent) is paid at year-end, based on unit volume growth over the previous year. In 1999, all representatives whose 1999 average dollar sales exceed 105 percent of their 1998 average dollar sales will be eligible for the Beef

Exhibit I Plan D

DENVER ILLINI GENETICS
PRICES AND TERMS
Effective January 1, 1999

F.O.B. Denver, Colorado. Semen may be purchased at the representative discount by paying cash with order. C.O.D. DIG truck using the DIG price list for beef. Or credit can be obtained with prior approval from the district sales manager.

Accelerated Commission Prediscount Program

The prediscounted amount and the commission schedule will be accelerated during the calendar year, based on semen dollar volume of business by the representative both from purchase F.O.B. Denver or DIG Truck and commissionable sales to DIG customers at prevailing DIG list prices. The commission/discount level will be escalated under the following schedule:

Semen Only	$ 0 to	$ 8,000	at 23%
	8,001 to	13,000	at 26%
	13,001 to	20,000	at 30%
	20,001	and up	at 34%

Commissions shall be paid to the representative during the DIG fiscal month following the date of billing the sale. The representative discount will be applied to all purchases at the time of billing the representative account.

Sales discount on all cash purchases made at the truck will be calculated by the route serviceman at 23 precent from the list price. The amount of discount greater than 23 percent will be credited as additional discount to the representative's account at the time of billing because charge purchases will be calculated at the full discount level when billed.

Discount/Commission on Additional Items

A 12 percent commission will be paid on the following items:

Refrigeration equipment
Breeding certificates
Refrigerator rental charges (based on $1.75 per day equals 21 cents per day)

7 percent commission will be paid on supplies sold in representative's area.
A 12 percent discount will be allowed on the purchase price of breeding supplies.

Cooperative Advertising Program Charges

There will be a charge each month to representative's account for the DIG cooperative advertising program based on the following schedule:

Representative Commission/Discount Level	Monthly Fee
23%	$12.00
26	17.00
30	22.00
34	27.00

The representative commission/discount level in effect at year-end (December 31) will be used for the following year for both the monthly fee and eligibility of benefits.

Commissions for Semen, Supplies, and Additional Items Sold on Credit by Representatives

Commission will be paid to representative the DIG fiscal month following the date of billing of the sale. A commission will be granted the representative under these terms even though a credit sale. DIG will charge back the commission to representative against current commissions if the account balance should reach or exceed *120* days past due.

Refrigerator Rental and Nitrogen Service Charge

Refrigerator(s) for representative's own use, $12.00 per month, $17.00 for some special models. All other refrigerators used in sales area are subject to a charge of $1.75 per day.

Exhibit 2

February 9, 1999

TO: All DIG Representatives
FROM: Bob Robson, Marketing Director
RE: Beef Bonanza 1999
cc: Regional Sales Personnel
           Management Staff

With a tremendous finish for the month of December, 1998 will go into the record books as the best year ever for Denver Illini Genetics. As we review 1998 and look to 1999, we:

1. increased our market share,
2. refined our sales-oriented distribution system,
3. have increased our number of beef bulls and programs to provide you with the tools for continued success, and
4. have our total offering of beef bulls priced competitively to provide a very aggressive posture.

Following are the details of the plan:

A. All representatives whose 1999 average dollar sales exceed 105 percent of 1998 average dollar sales will be eligible for Beef Bonanza bonus.
B. An escalating bonus of 7 to 12 percent will be paid at year-end based on unit volume growth over prior year as follows:

Unit Volume Growth over Prior Year	Beef Bonanza Bonus Multiplier
0%	7%
2	8
5	9
7	10
8	11
10 and over	12

Following are some examples of the bonus potential of this program:

EXAMPLES

	Year	Units	Average Price	Retail Sales	1998 Base 105%	+ Increased Sales
A.	1999	4,400	$11.55	$50,820	$46,200	+$4620
	1998	4,000	11.00	44,000		
		+400				

Unit increase = 400/4,000 = 10%
Bonus at 12% (10% unit growth) of $4,620 = $554
Total bonus = $554.00

	Year	Units	Average Price	Retail Sales	1998 Base 105%	+ Increased Sales
B.	1999	4,160	$11.55	$48,048	$46,200	+$1,848
	1998	4,000	11.00	44,000		
		+160				

Unit increase = 160/4,000 = 4%
Bonus at 8% (4% unit growth) of $1,848 = $148
Total bonus = $148.00

	Year	Units	Average Price	Retail Sales	1998 Base 105%	+ Increased Sales
C.	1999	6,400	$13.20	$84,480	$72,072	+$12,408
	1998	5,200	13.20	68,640		
		+1,200				

Unit increase = 1,200/5,200 = 23%
Bonus at 12% (10% and over unit growth) of $12,408 = $1,489
Total Bonus = $1,489.00

	Year	Units	Average Price	Retail Sales	1998 Base 105%	+ Increased Sales
D.	1999	3,840	$13.20	$50,688	$46,200	+$4,488
	1998	4,000	11.00	44,000		
		-160				

Unit decrease = 160/4,000 = −4%
Bonus at 7% (0% unit growth) of $4,488 = $314
Total bonus = $255.00

(continued)

Exhibit 2   *(concluded)*

E.	1999	9,600	$13.20	$126,720	$101,871	+$24,849
	1998	8,400	11.55	97,020		
		+1,200				

Unit increase = 1,200/8,400 = + 14%
Bonus at 12% (+14% unit growth) of $24,849 = $2,982
Total bonus = $2,982

F.	1999	3,360	$ 9.90	$33,264	$36,960	-$3,696
	1998	3,200	11.00	35,200		
		+160				

Unit increase = 160/3,200 = +5%
Bonus at 9% (5% unit growth) of -$3,696 = -$333
Total bonus = 0

In summary, the 1999 Beef Bonanza program revolves around total increased retail sales with an added incentive for increased unit sales but no penalty for decreased units.

Bonanza bonus (Exhibit 2). According to Mr. Robson, "It's a dollars program and no growth still gets you dollars. You can't get dollars for just a dollar's (not unit) increase."

The company's objective is to increase both the number of semen units sold and the average semen unit blend price. This price is the average price paid for all semen units sold. A representative, therefore, can increase his unit blend price by selling the more expensive units of semen. In 1998, semen prices ranged from $6 to $100, with most semen units sold in the $8 to $16 range.

The Problem

As stated, in late 1998, Mr. Robson noticed fluctuations in some representatives' yearly sales totals. "A growing concern is that the current program is being 'worked' and we [DIG] pay for the same growth again and again with the good-year, bad-year syndrome, instead of paying real dollars for real growth." Robson felt that the problem existed in both the Southern and Northern regions (Exhibit 3). Robson suspected that the sales incentive program, Beef Bonanza, was the reason for the fluctuations. The incentive payments are based entirely on the increase over the previous year. This allows a sales representative to manipulate his or her bonus by having a poor sales year and thus establishing a very low unit sales base to improve on. After establishing a low base figure in 1997, for example, the sales representative would not have to increase his or her sales volume very much in 1998 to earn a sizable incentive payment at year's end. The percentage gain in unit volume determines the bonus paid. "With sales reps playing this numbers game," exclaimed Robson, "we don't grow!"

Mr. Robson wondered if the Beef Bonanza bonus program should be changed to deter the sales representatives from channeling their sales efforts in this fluctuating manner. The company's goal of steadily increasing growth could not be realized if this "numbers game-playing" continued. With this in mind, Robson requested suggestions from the regional sales managers on how to motivate the representatives to strive for consistent, yearly sales growth. An actual response memo that he received from Rick Stone, Northern regional sales manager, is shown in Exhibit 4. This program revision suggestion includes a change to:

1. Using a historical best-year base for both units and total retail sales dollars and

2. Awarding a quarterly, instead of yearly, bonus payment.

Exhibit 3   Total Representative Semen Sales, Northern and Southern Regions, 1996–1998

Name/Region	Year	Units	Average Unit Price	Dollar Sales
Northern Region				
Al Dempsey	1996	3,978	10.13	$ 40,297
	1997	6,075	10.78	65,489
	1998	3,715	12.26	45,546
Harry Turner	1996	7,280	13.19	96,023
	1997	7,840	14.09	110,466
	1998	6,473	13.28	85,961
Bill McDowney	1996	4,188	9.68	40,540
	1997	3,763	10.02	37,705
	1998	3,842	10.52	40,418
Jack Rabin	1996	4,765	12.48	59,467
	1997	5,569	14.10	78,523
	1998	6,719	11.42	76,731
Dean Morgan	1996	5,043	11.51	58,045
	1997	6,670	10.26	68,434
	1998	8,787	12.24	107,553
Dan McLaren	1996	242	47.20	11,422
	1997	312	40.35	12,590
	1998	297	36.71	10,903
Jerry Martin	1996	583	13.14	7,661
	1997	515	9.18	4,728
	1998	228	17.09	3,896
Southern Region				
Walt Earl	1996	4,569	13.84	63,235
	1997	3,636	13.78	50,104
	1998	4,073	14.90	60,688
Gene Harms	1996	6,954	14.04	97,634
	1997	6,314	13.40	84,608
	1998	7,501	12.94	97,063
F. G. Brand	1996	4,437	9.88	43,838
	1997	4,146	11.81	48,964
	1998	7,242	12.63	91,466
Mitch Kramer	1996	2,518	12.52	31,525
	1997	2,099	12.66	26,573
	1998	1,683	11.40	19,186
H & M Arnold	1996	4,102	9.72	39,871
	1997	4,191	10.63	44,550
	1998	3,709	9.87	36,608
Don Larson	1996	5,555	11.36	63,105
	1997	6,485	11.03	71,530
	1998	6,798	11.70	79,537
Dave Ipson	1996	5,102	13.46	68,673
	1997	7,268	14.00	101,752
	1998	8,987	12.46	111,978

Source: DIG records.

Stone affirmed, "I support a quarterly bonus system that will allow the Beef Bonanza program to work the entire year rather than encouraging heavy buying to take advantage of accelerated commissions and Beef Bonanza bonuses." However, his suggestion was rejected by Robson, who concluded that it would just provide an incentive for the game-playing representatives to manipulate their sales on a quarterly instead of yearly basis. Also, "Stone's idea ignores the seasonal aspect of beef seman *sales*." It was typical for a DIG representative with annual beef semen sales of $50,000 to sell $35,000 of those sales in the second quarter, due to the inherent seasonality factor.

Exhibit 4   Denver Illini Genetics

October 12, 1998

TO: Bob Robson
FROM: Rick Stone, Northern Regional Sales Manager
SUBJECT: Beef Bonanza Bonus Program

Bob, you asked that I put some of my thoughts on the Beef Bonanza Bonus Program together for you. My feeling on the matter is that we continue a bonus program that pays real dollars for real growth.

Rule 1:   Best year for units and best year for retail sales dollars become the base year. They may be different years.
Rule 2:   A 5% beef bonanza will be paid quarterly on retail sales dollars above $ base with a 10% unit volume growth over unit base. This would apply to the first three quarters. Fourth quarter would apply to year-end.
Rule 3–A: Retail sales $ base is established as follows:
            105% x best retail sales $ = total base $
            Total base $ / 4 = quarterly base $
            (Quarterly base $ x 2 = midyear base $, etc.)
Rule 3–B: Total unit base = previous best-year units. Previous best units / 4 = quarterly base units (Quarterly base units x 2 = midyear base etc.)
Rule 4:   At year-end the final bonus will be calculated and any quarterly bonuses subtracted and the difference paid based on the following:

Unit Volume Growth over Base	Over $ Base Beef Bonanza Bonus Escalation
0%	5%
3%	6%
6%	7%
9%	8%
12%	9%
15% and over	10%

EXAMPLE:

		Units	$	Bonus
1st Quarter	Base	100	1,000	0% x 100 = $0 bonus
	Actual	105	1,100	
	Dev.	5	100	5% = 0% bonus
2nd Quarter	Base	200	2,000	5% x $1,000 = $50 total
	Actual	240	3,000	
	Dev.	40	1,000	20% = 5% bonus
3rd Quarter	Base	300	3,000	0% x 1,000 = $0 bonus
	Actual	300	4,000	
	Dev.	0	1,000	0% = 0% bonus
4th Quarter	Base	400	4,000	No 4th quarter bonus pd
	Actual	600	6,000	but go to year-end.
	Dev.	200	2,000	50% = year-end schedule
Year-end	Base	400	4,000	10% x 2,000 = 200
	Actual	600	6,000	200 - 50 = $150
	Dev.	200	2,000	pay $150 bonus
				Total bonus = $200

Conclusion: This program would eliminate the good-year, bad-year problem and allow the truly progressive, growing representative to be recognized and paid for his efforts.

The effect of good quarters would be eliminated by dividing the base for units and dollars over the entire year.

Representatives who have been working the system will not like such a program.

A quarterly system will allow the program to work the entire year rather than encourage heavy buying to take advantage of accelerated commissions and Beef Bonanza bonuses.

Summary: My description may be rough, but I feel the idea is described.

In January 1999, Robson held a sales meeting with the company's managers to obtain their input on this problem. He explained that some of the representatives had experienced questionable yearly sales fluctuations that were possibly due to the Beef Bonanaz bonus plan and asked for the sales managers' thoughts on this matter. The managers strongly opposed the idea that a serious problem existed. According to Dave Williams, Southern regional sales manager, "Some people perhaps have a good year and then a bad year, and are not purposely playing games. Maybe it's a little unrealistic to think that a person would grow every year for eight years in a row." Robson quickly interjected, "The long-term man does not count on Beef Bonanza because he is not counting on overall growth increases as much as a solidification of his business and holding good value. The man that is starting is the one that we should aim Beef Bonanza at." When questioned about the extent of the problem, Robson admitted, "I don't know how large it is. All I have is a gut feeling. I do know that the representatives are very sensitive about this issue."

The discussion then turned to generation of possible solutions to this problem. Barry Norem, sales analyst, was not enthusiastic about changing the Beef Bonanza program. "Let's say that we do want to put a stop to the good-year, bad-year reps. What about the other reps that had a good year in 98? . . . You're almost damned if you do and damned if you don't." The managers were generally supportive in their comments about Beef Bonanza.

When queried about the program's effectiveness, Robson replied, "Beef Bonanza has served us well. It's been fairly motivational. We want to motivate the rep . . . even if he does play games."

At the meeting, the managers generated these additional ideas for adjusting the Beef Bonanza program:

1. Changing the unit base to the historical best year's base instead of the previous year's base. In opposition, one manager stated, "If we look at 1999 and say it's an unsettled one because of the economy, etc., then it may not be a good time to increase the unit base because it'll probably have a poor psychological effect on a lot of people. . . . A lot more people would be negatively affected psychologically than would be affected financially."

2. Determining the base by averaging the previous two years sales figures. This idea came from Kyle Dean, vice president of finance. Dean felt that this would make it more difficult to work the system.

3. Increasing the unit base increase needed to reach the highest bonus level to 15 percent instead of 10 percent. Andy Marien, research director, said, "This is easy to use and would help solve the problem."

4. Making the dollar base the highest of the last two years. "This would prevent the good-year, bad-year problem," claimed John Ruppert, Kyle Dean's assistant.

   The managers also suggested:

5. Rewarding with gifts or travel instead of, or in addition to, cash. "When you're talking about incentives, you can have monetary incentives, gift incentives, or travel incentives. That's basically what you have to deal with," claimed Dave Williams.

6. Refunding a portion of the sales representative's travel expenses.

7. Awarding national recognition for top performers. Rick Stone noted, "We could publish the sales results in the newsletter throughout the year. You'd be surprised at how much just having their name on a list excites them. They are motivated by this."

8. Attaching incentives to particular breed-specific sales rather than overall sales. For example, "Beef Up Brahman in '99."

A frequently voiced concern of Bob Robson and his managers was the uncertain economic outlook of 1999. "It's very undecided what the economy is going to do to our business," Robson claimed. This uncertainty affected their decision when the roll call vote was taken on how to handle the sales fluctuation problem.

Case 2–6

Oppenheimer Management Corporation*

The national sales manager of Oppenheimer Management Corporation was confident that the sales contest developed to reward stockbrokers and others who sell Oppenheimer's three new mutual funds would be a strong motivator. Oppenheimer Management offers 18 mutual funds to the public and, like other brokerage houses, frequently uses various incentives to motivate the stockbrokers/sales reps to push certain funds. Oppenheimer Management is a unit of Mercantile House Holdings PLC, a British financial services firm. Mercantile sold Oppenheimer & Company, the securities broker and investment bank, in early 1986.

Mercantile House Holdings PLC

Mercantile House Holdings PLC is a holding company involved in wholesale brokerage, money brokerage, fixed-interest brokerage, investment banking and securities trading, fund management, and financial information services. Established in the United Kingdom, Mercantile House has approximately 2,700 employees. Sales in 1986 were £385 million, which produced a profit of £44.5 million. In April 1986, Mercantile sold 82 percent of Oppenheimer & Company, Inc., and Oppenheimer Capital Corp. for $100 million cash plus $50 million in other assets.

Incentives for the New Mutual Funds

The sales awards for the three new mutual funds have attracted considerable attention, At a recent convention in Chicago's McCormick Place exposition center, a red Porsche 944 Turbo was the star attraction. Financial planners, attending the International Association for Financial Planning conventions, heard representatives of Oppenheimer Management promote three new mutual funds with the promise of the sports car to whoever sells the highest amount, exceeding $5 million, and with a minimum of 10 sales. Other cars offered were a Jaguar XJ-S or a Corvette coupe or convertible. Financial planners can win other rewards, as Exhibit 1 illustrates.

Offering sales incentives to financial planners, stockbrokers, insurance agents, and others is not uncommon. What is uncommon, according to some critics, is the size and range of prizes being offered by Oppenheimer.

---

*This case is based on published information found in Robert L. Rose, "Incentives vs. Clients: Which Ones Most Concern Financial Planners?" *The Wall Street Journal,* November 24, 1986, pp. C1, C4; *Wiesenberger Investment Companies Service,* 1986 edition; and *Moody's International Manual,* 1986 edition. Copyright © 1998 Neil M. Ford.

Exhibit I Sales Awards and Requirements

Requirements	Sales Awards
$100,000 and 5 sales	Casio pocket color television, or Cobra cordless telephone, or Simac II Gelataio 800 ice-cream maker
$250,000 and 5 sales	Sony compact disc player, or Canon PC 10 personal copier, or Panasonic microwave convection oven
$500,000 and 10 sales	Sony Video 8 camcorder, or attaché case with $1,000 cash, or Waterford crystal barware
$1 million and 10 sales	Honda scooter, or IBM PC laptop computer, or Sony rear-projection videoscope TV
$3 million and 10 sales	Blackglama mink coat, or IBM Personal Computer XT, or Sony entertainment system
Grand Prize: highest total over $5 million and 10 sales	Porsche 944 Turbo, or Jaguar XJ-S, or Corvette coupe or convertible

Other contests sponsored by brokerage houses and fund developers offer prizes that are just as generous. Trips, for example, are a common incentive. Companies typically will mix business with pleasure. Recently, JMB/Carlyle, a real estate firm, planned a business symposium in Kauai, Hawaii, for top sellers of its real estate partnerships. Winners were to receive five days in an exotic paradise along with an opportunity to expand their business expertise.

Some incentive programs are more modest. First Investors Corporation gave away turkeys for financial planners who sold $5,000 or more of the company's funds prior to a recent Thanksgiving holiday. Investors range from individuals to institutions such as companies that manage pension programs.

To the critics, however, the issue is when does the financial planner start to think more about the Porsche rather than whether the product is right for the consumer. One critic argues that giving a gift, such as a Gucci handbag, will lead brokers to compromise their ethics.

A supporter of the use of incentives claims they are a normal part of any salesperson's job. He sees incentives as part of the American system: if you produce above-average results, your efforts should be rewarded, within reason.

Others contend the issue is serious enough that disclosure laws are needed to inform prospective investors about these noncash incentives. This proposal is viewed as being unrealistic by the president of one financial planning firm, who claims few brokers would announce that another $5,000 in sales is needed to win a trip somewhere.

The president of a real estate partnership firm disputes the effectiveness of such disclosure laws. He notes that such a statement would represent one paragraph out of several thousand in a 250-page prospectus. Oppenheimer Management's prospectus contains a disclosure about the noncash sales incentives available for the three new funds.

Oppenheimer's Experience

The prizes offered by Oppenheimer may be having the hoped-for effect. Sales of the three funds are going well. One of them, the GNMA fund, was number four in sales out of the

Exhibit 2   Oppenheimer Mutual Funds

Name of Fund	Primary Objective*
Oppenheimer A.I.M. Fund	MCG
Oppenheimer Challenger Fund	G
Oppenheimer Directors Fund	G
Oppenheimer Equity Income Fund	I
Oppenheimer Fund	MCG
Oppenheimer Gold & Special Minerals	I
Oppenheimer High Yield Fund	I
Oppenheimer Money Market Fund	I
Oppenheimer N.Y. Tax-Exempt Fund	TF
Oppenheimer Premium Income Fund	I
Oppenheimer Regency Fund	G
Oppenheimer Special Fund	MCG
Oppenheimer Target Fund	G
Oppenheimer Tax-Free Bond Fund	G
Oppenheimer Time Fund	MCG
Oppenheimer U.S. Government Trust	I

*Abbreviations used are MCG—maximum capital gain; G—growth; I—income; S—stability; and TF—tax-free municipal bond.

firm's 18 funds and appears to be headed for the number one position. Exhibit 2 details characteristics of 16 Oppenheimer funds.

Oppenheimer's national sales manager insists that all three funds are timely investments. He seriously doubts, given the environment existing today, that anybody could be hurt.

Case 2–7

WBYL/Z108 Radio Station☆

By the late 1990s, competition in the Gainesville radio market was hot. In a city of about 250,000, nine major radio stations compete for listening audiences and advertising commitments from businesses, local government, and area schools and colleges. Four station competitors sell a combination AM and FM offering, one station sells a simulcast AM/FM offering, and four others sell a single offering (three FM and one AM).

Radio stations in the Gainesville market have developed positioning strategies that focus their efforts on specific target audiences, so program formatting varies by target audience. However, most competing sales representatives find themselves vying for advertising commitments from many of the same sponsors.

WBYL/Z108 Radio

WBYL/Z108 is one of four combination AM/FM competitors in the Gainesville radio market. WBYL-AM is best classified as a sports–news–talk station that features country music. The target audience for WBYL-AM is those over 35. Play-by-play action of both professional and collegiate sports along with several sports talk shows are emphasized. Z108-FM targets 18-to-39–year-olds with its programming focus on Top 40 hits.

Z108-FM held top market share of the Gainesville listening audience until early 1996 when a new competitor entered the market. The new competitor targets the same audience and uses a similar program format. Following a large rating loss, Z108 tightened its programming offering and brought in new disc jockey talent. Z108 also changed program directors and hired a consultant to help direct its efforts. By early 1997, the rating slide was halted and a new, potentially stronger Z108 faced the mid-1990s with enthusiasm.

Similar to other stations, WBYL/Z108 has commission sales representatives. Sales reps are responsible for both selling, on which they make about 15 percent of sales, and collections. Reps lose a portion of their commissions, up to all of it, if payments are 60, 90, or 120 days late. Sales reps at WBYL/Z108 tend to earn slightly more than at other stations, with annual pay ranging from $17,500 to $38,000.

Bill Bennett, sales manager for WBYL/Z108, works with a sales staff of nine commission-only sales reps. He reports to the station manager but is generally left to his own judgment in focusing sales staff efforts and achieving station sales goals. To focus selling activities and provide incentive for extra efforts (or "recharge" the reps, as Bill puts it), sales contests are promoted to the sales team two or three times yearly. Bill is convinced by past contest outcomes that they lead to increased sales.

Ever since new competition hit the Gainesville market, station management had been pressing Bill to reduce account losses and to find ways to bring ad revenues back to pre-

*This case was prepared especially for this text by William H. Murphy, Babson College, Babson Park, MA. Copyright © 1998 Neil M. Ford and William H. Murphy.

1996 levels. To Bill, this meant finding ways to increase the efforts of his sales team. In 1997, Bill decided a sales contest would provide the sales boost management wanted. With the fall/winter season approaching, Bill spent many hours designing the most extensive and what he hoped would be the most successful sales contest to date.

The WBYL/Z108 Sales Football Scoreboard Contest

Bill reflected on past contests and on articles he had read about contest dos and don'ts before deciding on the final format for the contest. Deciding on an exciting theme was easy, especially since WBYL-AM was dedicated to sports. Bill knew he could get station approval for the awards he wanted since increased revenues from the contest would more than offset contest expenses.

When sales reps arrived at the station for their weekly sales meeting in the last week of September, they were greeted with much fanfare. The station was decorated with a Hawaiian look. Sales reps were told a new contest was about to get under way—and the first person to reach contest goals would receive a trip for two to Hawaii! Pictures were taken with reps holding coconuts, posed in front of exotic posters of the winning destination. At the meeting, Bill passed out a detail sheet of his carefully conceived contest (see Exhibit 1).

During the meeting, Bill discussed the contest and asked for questions from the reps. By the meeting's end, everyone seemed to understand the goals and objectives, and everyone was clearly enthusiastic about the awards. Even so, the contest seemed to get off to a slow start. After the first week, two reps were tied for most yardage gained—at one yard each. By the end of the second week, the yardage leader had gained 4.5 yards. At the same time, four reps still had zero yardage. Bill assumed his reps were "getting the feel of the contest" and "soon things would get rolling."

Each week thereafter, Bill provided his sales representatives enthusiastic updates of their standings. He also made regular announcements of specials that would win extra yards. Examples of these updates and specials are shown in Exhibit 2.

After posting "second-quarter" results (results through November as shown in 12/14 memo), Bill was convinced he had hit on a winning contest. Three reps, Jenny, Mike, and Kurt, were in a close race to be first to the 100-yard mark. Bill thought the other reps, though further behind, might be encouraged by the successes of the leaders to push harder for the final two months of the contest.

As with most well-laid plans, the approaching holiday season saw unforeseen delays in getting results tabulated for the "third quarter," due in part to changes in the station computer system and to vacation schedules—including Bill's two weeks away from the station. Postings for the third quarter of the football contest came over a month late, with promises for a rapid posting of final contest results (see Exhibit 3).

As Bill calculated January totals, he realized no sales rep had reached the 100-yard goal. On the positive side, the station would be saving the cost of the award that had been promised for those attaining 100 yards. On the other hand, Bill thought his reps had been working hard on the contest. Rather than jeopardize the credibility of the contest, Bill sent out a closing memo, thanking the reps for their efforts and promising an even more exciting contest in the next month or two.

Behind the Scenes

Bill was right; a trip to Hawaii was appealing to the members of his sales team. What Bill hadn't counted on was the slow start of many of the reps. By the end of the second quarter (12/14 memo), it was clear that no one besides Jenny, Mike, and maybe Kurt had a chance at winning. The rest of the sales team dropped interest in the football contest.

Exhibit I   Details of the WBYL/Z108 Sales Contest

The WBYL/Z108 Sales Football Scoreboard Contest!

Gainesville's newest, most exciting sales contest kicks off today with the grand prize trip for two to . . . where else . . . Hawaii!!! Earn yardage as quickly as you can! Avoid getting penalized! First person to get over the 100 yard goal line wins the trip for two to Hawaii!

1st Quarter—October   2nd Quarter—November

3rd Quarter—December   4th Quarter—January

% Goal Attainment	100%	110%	120%	130%	140%
	Yardage Gained				
Monthly sales goal	4	5	6	7	8
Monthly new business goal	3	4	5	5	6
Monthly sports goal	2	3	3	3	4
Monthly production goal	1	2	2	2	2
26- or 52-week contracts	1				
Highest weekly average	1				
Best-written proposal	1				
Client testimonial letters	.5 (Maximum 5 yards total)				
Showing up at station promotions	.5 (Maximum 5 yards total)				
Sales committee work	1				
Highest % goal entering month	2				

*Please turn in copy of order, contract, or memo to earn yards. You will be provided weekly yardage summaries. Unreported yardage will not be carried into new month.

Specials—Yardage will vary but opportunities for yardage will at times be posted. Example: "I'll give you 2 bonus yards if you sell a Football Saturday available by 5 P.M. today."

	Negative Yards
Missed monthly goal	2
Missed monthly new business goal	2
Missed monthly sports goal	2
Missed monthly production goal	2
Missed sales meeting	1
Late monitor report	1

1st person to reach 100 yards—Wins a trip for two to Hawaii in February including the additional vacation week ($4,000 value).

2nd person to reach 100 yards—Wins a $500 shopping spree to Spruce Mall.

3rd person to reach 100 yards—Wins a $250 shopping spree to Spruce Mall.

All people that go over 100 yards win a $50 dinner for two gift certificate.

Worse yet, several began blaming Bill for intentionally setting their contest goals beyond reach. Ensuing memos from Bill, designed to encourage contest enthusiasm and participation, actually became annoyances to most of the sales team.

Meanwhile the top contenders, Jenny and Mike in particular, began to believe they could win the football contest. During the final month, each increased efforts to try to be the first to reach 100 yards. With less than a month remaining, Mike figured out a scheme, a "slight breaking of the rules" as he later called it, to give himself an edge. Some orders were written in advance of a customer's actually placing the order. Other orders were

---

Exhibit 2   Contest Updates and Specials

To: Sales Reps
From: Bill

Date: 10/9/97

Earn extra yards with Spec production. For the remainder of October we will pay you 0.5 yard, maximum of 5 yards, for all spec production. Please give me a copy of the production order to qualify for yardage!

Think Hawaii!!

To: Sales Reps
From: Bill

Date: 12/14/97

We have summarized all of the contest points for November. After two quarters of play here are the standings!!

Rep	Yardage
Jenny	49.5
Mike	43
Kurt	31
Kaili	19
Toni	9
Ben	6
Tahir	4
Albert	3.5
Connie	3

Don't forget the points you can earn for testimonial letters, volunteer work, and Best Written Proposal each month!!

More bonus point opportunities still to come!

---

padded, with the intention that after the contest date Mike would simply write off portions of the orders as nonpayments. Of course, Mike hadn't counted on several of his customers calling the station to complain about being overbilled. Some of these calls came through when Mike was on the road, resulting in others at the station being faced with irate customers. At the same time, Jenny focused her January contest efforts on asking for favors from customers she had close relationships with. Several of these accounts were willing to "buy a little more than they needed to help me out."

After receiving Bill's final memo, announcing no rep had reached 100 yards, Jenny and Mike were furious. As Mike said privately, "To this day it's affecting me in some way . . . in my relationship with the company . . . in my attitude toward future contests." Ben, one of the reps who dropped out of contest pursuit early on, later commented privately, "You lay this big thing down and do this song and dance and then screw the thing up. What does that tell me about our management?"

Closing Thoughts

Not knowing the behind-the-scenes sentiments of the sales team, Bill analyzed contest outcomes. He was pleased to find that improvements were made in most contest-related objectives, and ad revenues in particular showed gains from October through January. Reporting to his superiors, Bill commented on the effectiveness of the football scoreboard sales contest and enthusiastically mentioned several new contest ideas to further motivate his sales team. Given the apparent success of the football scoreboard sales contest, the station manager continued to give Bill a free hand in developing and running sales contests.

Exhibit 3   Third-Quarter Contest Posting

To: Sales
From: Bill

February 11, 1998

Here is the long-lost update on the Scoreboard contest. The computer switchover has delayed end-of-month figures, thus delaying related new business figures, etc.

Closing figures for January are still to come, and final yardage to be awarded. Here are the standings after 3 out of 4 months.

Jenny	73	yards
Mike	59.5	
Kurt	32	
Kaili	27	
Toni	16	
Ben	13	
Tahir	8.5	
Albert	7	
Connie	5	

Good Luck! (It's almost over!)

Case 2–8

Midwest Business Forms, Inc.*

Sandro Rossi, Midwest Business Forms vice president of marketing, cut right to the point, "We have an excess inventory problem that needs your immediate attention. Our vice president of finance wants to know why our sales force is not doing a better job of selling off the excess inventory of standard forms." Toni Carter, sales director for the firm, defended her sales team. "The inventory problem was not created by the sales force. Our inventory problem is the result of poor sales forecasting," she said. "That may be true," replied Rossi, "but we still have to sell off the inventory and that's the job of the sales force."

On her way back to her office, Carter knew she had to get her salespeople to refocus their efforts on the inventory problem. Even so, she did not like this situation. "Pushing the sales force to solve an inventory problem that they did not create, especially when it would lead to less selling effort for other responsibility areas, could lead to all sorts of problems," she thought. She also considered some recent revelations about the attitudes of her salespeople, furthering her concern about the next steps to take.

Midwest Business Forms, Inc.

Midwest Business Forms, Inc., is a regional printer of a large line of business forms used by companies, institutions, and government agencies. Midwest, located in Des Moines, Iowa, sells business forms throughout the region including North and South Dakota, Minnesota, Wisconsin, Illinois, and Nebraska. Sales are made directly to users by 22 sales representatives who work under sales managers based in either St. Paul or Chicago. Toni Carter directs the sales effort out of the Des Moines headquarters.

At Midwest, a sales rep's compensation consists of 85 percent salary plus 15 percent commission on gross margin for all sales. Most of the business forms are standard and have the customer's name imprinted if needed. In some situations, sales reps help customers design business forms. The average base salary in 1997 was $33,500 and the average commission was $6,700. Midwest's 1997 sales totaled $6,737,000, cost of goods sold averaged 40 percent, and profit before taxes was $942,000.

The inventory problem Rossi voiced was in the company's standard line of legal documents. These were preprinted forms that contain space for imprinting the customer's name and address. The forms meet very specific legal requirements for content and format. Based on 1997 sales of these documents, Midwest has inventory on hand to last well into 2000. Inventory-carrying charges are substantial enough to cause real concern among several Midwest executives. Another concern related to impending changes in legislation that would require changes in the forms, likely rendering all inventory worthless. As one

*William H. Murphy, Babson College, Babson Park, MA, assisted in preparing this case. Copyright © 1998 Neil M. Ford.

Midwest executive said, "We have to get these forms unloaded before the laws change, or they will become candidates for recycling."

Carter had her own concerns. She had recently commissioned an outside consulting agency to conduct a sales force survey. Sitting on her desk were synopses of the survey results, suggesting the sales force's attitudes toward Midwest's compensation program were unfavorable (see Exhibit 1). Carter had thought the sales force was satisfied with the program, yet the findings, which also included the results of surveys to competing sales forces, strongly suggested otherwise.

She was also concerned about another part of the same study. One of the findings suggested the sales force believed they were not being adequately recognized for good performance (see Exhibit 2).

"What do they want?" she wondered. "A pat on the back every time they make a sale?" In any event, Carter now faced a number of problems. She had to find a way to meet the directive to move excess inventory and move it quickly if possible. She was also faced with the awareness that sales force attitudes toward both compensation and recognition issues were unfavorable. She suspected she would have to turn attitudes around in the near future, or the consequences could be severe.

Problem Resolution

Carter read several sales publications to gain additional insight about sales force compensation. As a result of this study, the idea of having a sales contest seemed appealing. Moreover, a sales contest, in addition to providing financial rewards, would provide recognition for contest winners. Carter's attention turned to publications and articles dealing specifically with sales contests. Eventually, she developed a sales contest proposal for Rossi to approve.

The proposed sales contest would involve all the sales force and their spouses as well. To increase spouse awareness and interest, contest details would be mailed directly to the sales representatives' homes. The contest would last three months, beginning in April 1998. Cash prizes would be awarded monthly and a grand prize awarded at the end of the contest.

Exhibit I   Pay Component of Job Attitude Index*

	Midwest Mean	Mean across All Companies
1. My pay is high in comparison with what others get for similar work in other companies . . .	2.41	2.51
2. My pay doesn't give me much incentive to increase my sales	2.24	3.59
3. My pay is low in comparison with what others get for similar work in other companies . . .	3.10	2.91
4. In my opinion the pay here is lower than in other companies	3.22	2.97
5. My income provides for luxuries	2.66	2.91
6. My selling ability largely determines my earnings in this company	2.15	3.25
7. I'm paid fairly compared with other employees in this company	3.32	3.38
8. My income is adequate for normal expenses	3.78	3.49
9. I am very much underpaid for the work that I do	3.71	3.43
10. I can barely live on my income	4.12	3.78

*Sales representatives responded to the question, "To what extent do you agree with each of the followng statements?" A 5-point response set was used, anchored with "strongly disagree" (1) and "strongly agree" (5).

Exhibit 2	Company Policy and Management Support Component of Job Attitude Index*	Midwest Mean	Mean across All Companies
1.	Management keeps us in the dark about things we ought to know	2.78	2.79
2.	Our sales goals are set by the higher-ups without considering market conditions	2.73	3.15
3.	Management really knows its job	3.34	2.88
4.	This company operates efficiently and smoothly	2.73	2.46
5.	Our home office isn't always cooperative in servicing our customers	3.22	2.65
6.	I'm satisified with the way employee benefits here are handled	3.97	3.26
7.	Sometimes when I learn of management's plans, I wonder if they knew the territory situation at all	2.66	2.57
8.	I have confidence in the fairness and honesty of management	3.10	3.29
9.	Management here is really interested in the welfare of employees	3.39	3.25
10.	I feel that the company is highly aggressive in its sales promotion efforts	2.61	2.42
11.	Sales representatives in this company receive good support from the home office	2.63	3.09
12.	Management here sees to it that there is cooperation between departments	2.85	2.71
13.	There isn't enough training for sales representatives who have been on the job for a while	2.90	2.65
14.	Management ignores our suggestions and complaints	3.12	3.07
15.	Management fails to give clear-cut orders and instructions	3.17	3.08
16.	Formal recognition programs compare favorably with those of other companies	2.34	None
17.	There are not enough formal recognition programs in this company	2.61	None
18.	I do not get enough formal recognition for the work I do	2.76	None
19.	Formal recognition programs in this company are attractive	2.12	None
20.	I am satisfied with the way our formal recognition programs are administered	2.39	None
21.	Recognition awards are based on ability	2.44	None
22.	Recognition awards are given in an arbitrary manner	2.97	None

*The higher the score, the more the sales representatives are satisfied. This applies to both positive and negative items, since the negative items are reverse scored. The range is from 1 to 5.

Sales reps responded to the question "To what extent do you agree with each of the following statements?" A 5-point response set was used, anchored with "strongly disagree" (1) and "strongly agree" (5).

Monthly winners would be the three sales reps who achieved the highest percentage increase in sales compared with their sales for the same months the previous year. Monthly winners would receive cash awards of $1,000, $800, or $600. The grand prize of $2,000 would be awarded to the sales rep obtaining the highest average increase for all three months in 1998 (April, May, and June), compared to the same three-month period in 1997.

In addition to the cash prizes, merchandise points would be awarded each month to sales reps whose sales for the month exceeded sales for the same month in 1997. Each percentage point over the previous year would be worth $10 of merchandise points. Thus, if a sales representative's sales for April 1998 exceeded April 1997 sales by 18 percent, then $180 of merchandise points would be earned. Carter also proposed that four prize points be awarded for each case of the standardized legal documents sold during the contest. Each case carried a suggested retail price of $80. Merchandise points could be cashed in immediately by selecting items from a prize catalog or saved to be "built up" over the three months.

The prize catalog would contain pictures of merchandise and the points needed to obtain the various items. Carter proposed using a firm specializing in sales contests to design the catalog. The firm, Starr Enterprizes, Inc., would also handle distribution of the merchandise prizes. Midwest would be billed for the retail price of the merchandise. Starr Enterprizes considered the retail markup as its fee.

The final aspect of the sales contest was the opportunity for a member of the sales force to win a merchandise grand prize. In addition to the cash awards and the merchandise opportunities, each point earned during the contest also earned a chance to win a home entertainment center, valued at $1,500. The drawing would occur at a dinner dance, at which time all cash prize winners would be recognized and the cash awards presented.

Toni Carter presented the contest proposal to Sandro Rossi for approval.

Case 2–9

California Credit Life Insurance Group*

Diane Flanagan, vice president of human resources at California Credit Life Insurance Group (CCLI), had just returned to her office after a lengthy conversation with Kevin Stark, vice president of sales. Flanagan and Stark had spent many hours reviewing the results of several reports that described the problems and opportunities experienced by women in sales.

The reports came from a variety of sources and were based on one-on-one discussions between women and men in sales and another person such as a reporter or a human resource manager. In some cases, the information resulted from focus group interviews. Flanagan and Stark hoped to gain a comprehensive understanding of the environment faced by women in sales.

Toward the end of their meeting, Flanagan received a rather urgent telephone call from Shelley Ryan, a lawyer from CCLI's legal staff. Ryan was calling to inform Flanagan that Suzette Renoldi, a sales rep in the southeastern region, had just filed a sexual discrimination suit against James Bradford, CCLI area sales manager from the southeastern region. Ryan called to Flanagan's attention that this was not the first complaint of sexual discrimination involving Bradford. Flanagan was aware of this and, in addition, knew of another situation that could have led to sexual harassment charges being brought against Bradford. The person involved, Ilse Riebolt, declined to pursue the matter for a variety of reasons. Diane Flanagan had been unable to assure Ilse Riebolt that bringing charges would be very reasonable, based on the description of the events. After an excellent start with CCLI, Riebolt quit in 1991 and took a position with a competitor.

California Credit Life prided itself on being an equal opportunity employer and wanted to avoid any adverse publicity. Flanagan was very concerned about the veracity and implications of the suit. On the other hand, she was not interested in any attempts to cover up the situation if the charges were true.

According to company policy and advice provided by Shelly Ryan, the first action to be taken should be a thorough investigation of the charges and of all available data. Ryan urged Flanagan to gather the necessary information as quickly and as quietly as possible.

Initially, Flanagan determined she would need a vast amount of information. CCLI's computerized decision support system (DSS) would be a source of much of the needed data. The DSS contained such files as sales performance, quotas, expenses, salaries, and commissions for all of CCLI's sales reps across the country. The DSS contained the data

---

for the numerous studies conducted by Human Resources on such subjects as job satisfaction, role conflict, role ambiguity, supervisory style, and numerous other subjects.

The Company

California Credit Life Insurance Group was incorporated in Los Angeles in 1955. CCLI's initial product line included all types of life insurance. Since its inception, CCLI has expanded its product line to include all types of insurance such as health, automobile, professional liability, pension and retirement programs, commercial packages, and related financial services.

In 1988, CCLI decided to open an office in the southeastern area of the United States as soon as all staffing and physical details could be resolved. The southeastern region became a reality in 1992, with James Bradford selected to be area sales manager. Bradford had been a sales rep in the Dallas region and had been selected for the new position based on his excellent sales performance and his strong interpersonal skills. Shortly after Bradford accepted the position, it became apparent to Diane Flanagan that Bradford did not wholeheartedly support CCLI's position concerning equal opportunity. In fact, it became necessary to instruct Bradford that one-third of his sales force would be female, a figure in line with CCLI's experience in its other regional offices.

California Credit Life Insurance has 15 regional offices and 230 sales representatives. Area sales managers typically supervise 15 people, a large number but manageable given the nature of the selling job. The sales reps work independently and do not need day-to-day supervision or contact with their area sales manager. CCLI requires two performance evaluations each year. Area sales managers have hiring authority and can set base salaries with approval from CCLI. Promotional opportunities are limited, and turnover among the area sales managers has been very low.

Area sales managers can recognize excellent performance by increasing the base salary and modifying a sales rep's territory to cover better accounts. Sales reps receive a 3 percent commission on sales in addition to their base salaries. Yearly bonuses are distributed by the area sales manager based on a sales rep's performance. Records indicated Bradford's bonus allocation did not reflect sales volume and seemed to be determined by taking the total bonus award and dividing it by 15. This process added an average of $1,750 to each sales rep's income.

The Suzette Renoldi Matter

Renoldi joined CCLI in 1992 after graduating with a business degree from the University of South Carolina. Her initial performance was strong, and she made quota each year except for the last two years. Quotas are set by the area sales manager based on guidelines handed down from Kevin Stark, vice president of sales, and negotiations between the area sales manager and each sales representative.

Diane Flanagan contacted Shelly Ryan to determine what was behind Renoldi's legal action against CCLI and Bradford. Ryan informed her that she had not seen the actual complaint but knew that Renoldi had asked for territory changes so that her sales opportunities would be greater, a request that Bradford denied. Bradford allegedly told Renoldi that her unwillingness to entertain clients, especially males, was the reason her sales had fallen off and not because of a lack of sales potential. Renoldi refuted this accusation and claims Bradford's territory assignment was discriminatory from the start. Flanagan knew she would need to see the complete complaint and personally discuss the situation with both Renoldi and Bradford. Meanwhile, Flanagan started compiling as much information as possible from company sources.

Exhibit I   Total Sales and Sales to Quota, 1992–1998*

	1992 Total Sales	Percent to Quota	1993 Total Sales	Percent to Quota	1994 Total Sales	Percent to Quota
Suzette Renoldi	$228,800	101.4	$247,104	102.1	$261,930	101.4
Stuart Pletz	215,600	97.3	219,912	99.4	230,908	99.9
Alvin Polard	100,000	96.7	101,000	97.2	103,020	100.0
Ted Hervington	350,000	100.3	346,500	95.4	343,035	99.6
Tim Hart	264,900	99.8	270,198	100.4	275,602	100.9
Brett Moore	234,000	98.9	231,660	96.7	231,660	99.0
Shari Swaggert	375,000	105.3	397,500	103.5	413,400	102.6
Mark Hoffton	189,000	101.2	192,780	100.6	198,563	101.1
Bob Pizzano	250,100	100.1	257,603	101.0	265,331	101.8
Felicia Abler	289,650	100.8	309,926	104.5	325,422	103.2
Kathy Levenhagen	190,000	103.8	209,000	106.2	223,630	103.5
Jeff Birdest	195,640	95.4	205,422	100.4	211,585	102.9
Larry Green	320,000	99.6	326,400	99.7	336,192	102.4
Chris Brackett	296,430	101.3	311,252	102.4	326,815	103.6
Ilse Rieboldt	287,500	102.4	296,125	105.3	T	
Mike Peck					100,412	102.3
Jeff Martin						
Cliff Arlen						
Kim Babler						(continued)

*Terminations are noted by T.

The first documents received by Flanagan revealed sales volumes for each sales representative (Exhibit 1), expense account data (Exhibit 2), number of performance evaluations (Exhibit 3), and base salaries (Exhibit 4). Her office conducts various personnel studies, and she had available the summary results of a recent job satisfaction survey for the entire company. She requested a breakout based on region and sex, knowing that the small number of women in the southeastern region posed a statistical problem. Exhibit 5 presents job satisfaction scores for the sales representatives by sex for the southeastern region and the entire company. Flanagan was somewhat pleased with the results for the entire company but disappointed with the southeastern region's showing. At this juncture, Flanagan decided to summarize some of the studies she and Stark had been reviewing.

The first study, conducted by HBRS (a research company), was based on a series of focus group interviews with women sales reps from a variety of selling positions. HBRS also conducted focus group sessions with men. No attempt was made to conduct sessions with both men and women since it was believed this would limit discussion. Flanagan read the following verbatim comments:

Karen R.   *(computer sales): I really enjoy the challenge of selling high-priced, high-tech computers. It feels great to help somebody solve a problem. But I still get questions from my friends when I tell them about my travel demands.*

Margaret McC.   *(medical equipment sales): I don't mind the travel, but at times it is all lumped together. Making child care agreements can be a hassle.*

Exhibit I   *(concluded)*

1995 Total Sales	Percent to Quota	1996 Total Sales	Percent to Quota	1997 Total Sales	Percent to Quota	1998 Total Sales	Percent to Quota
$267,169	102.3	$264,340	101.1	$282,844	99.6	$288,500	98.5
242,453	101.1	245,442	101.6	262,623	98.4	288,885	100.2
106,111	100.3	107,500	100.6	115,025	100.3	124,227	100.6
T							
281,114	100.8	282,445	101.2	302,216	102.0	326,395	102.7
232,818	98.1	T					
417,534	102.1	410,890	99.8	T			
204,520	100.8	204,800	100.7	219,136	100.1	230,093	100.4
273,291	101.2	275,364	101.6	294,639	102.1	318,210	102.0
326,724	103.4	322,745	101.9	345,337	102.9	348,790	98.7
230,339	103.9	225,990	102.1	241,809	100.1	265,990	99.0
217,932	101.6	218,500	101.7	233,795	101.4	252,110	101.7
347,959	102.3	348,660	102.0	373,066	103.1	414,103	102.5
339,887	103.0	342,110	103.4	366,057	104.1	406,323	103.8
253,117	101.6	241,553	99.1	281,313	101.8	305,014	102.4
213,419	99.1	235,017	100.2	279,106	101.2	312,844	102.8
		185,442	97.1	214,877	99.3	264,651	98.1
				204,913	98.4	278,228	100.2

Sherry W.   *(office equipment sales): This travel thing is bad news at my house. My husband becomes aloof the minute I mention that I have to be gone overnight. He's still aloof after I return. I know he wants me to quit and get a job with no travel.*

Martha W.   *(cosmetics sales): I don't have a husband to contend with, but with my travel schedule I don't have much of a social life either. My biggest problem was deciding what to pack and lost luggage. I'm supposed to carry a sample case that weighs 35 pounds plus a garment bag and my briefcase.*

Deirdre B.   *(insurance sales): I rarely travel outside of the city. My major headache is the guy who thinks that I should be home sewing and cooking or, if I have to work, in the typing pool.*

Karen R.   *(computer sales): I've made quota every year for the last five years only to confront men who say I'm lucky. One guy told me that I make more sales because customers want to see what a female sales rep looks like; then when I'm making my presentation, I rely on my feminine wiles to make the sale.*

Cherie I.   *(aluminum sales): I've had the credibility problem too. One purchasing agent informed me that my predecessor stood 6 feet 2 inches, weighed 195 pounds, and had a beard. I was really flustered with that comment and even more so when he asked me if I was busy in the evening. No doubt he wanted to explain the intricacies of aluminum to me.*

Laura W.   *(advertising sales): Being hassled comes with the territory. And I don't have to leave the office either. But I've adapted. I either play naive and ignore the comments, or I told one fellow laughingly that he could do better than me. But I do get tired of the hassle.*

Exhibit 2   Expense Account Data, 1992-1998*

	1992	1993	1994	1995	1996	1997	1998
Suzette Renoldi	$1,800	$1,875	$1,820	$1,830	$1,790	$1,933	$1,905
Stuart Pletz	1,100	1,367	1,450	1,690	1,855	2,078	2,210
Alvin Polard	1,250	1,462	1,667	1,723	1,775	1,988	1,995
Ted Hervington	1,790	1,890	1,993	T			
Tim Hart	2,000	2,134	2,177	2,189	2,950	3,304	3,380
Brett Moore	2,500	2,578	2,673	2,774	T		
Shari Swaggert	1,540	1,603	1,615	1,672	1,715	T	
Mark Hoffton	1,778	1,800	1,829	1,950	2,059	2,306	2,384
Bob Pizzano	1,892	1,966	1,998	2,150	2,331	2,611	2,673
Felicia Abler	1,224	1,250	1,282	1,354	1,332	1,439	1,461
Kathy Levenhagen	1,452	1,466	1,562	1,432	1,455	1,571	1,543
Jeff Birdest	1,970	1,980	2,155	2,245	2,778	3,111	3,260
Larry Green	2,145	2,256	2,347	2,355	2,679	3,000	3,114
Chris Brackett	2,234	2,457	2,679	2,789	2,887	3,233	3,211
Ilse Rieboldt	1,234	1,423	T				
Mike Peck			1,131	2,046	2,811	2,270	2,413
Jeff Martin				1,548	2,060	2,316	2,385
Cliff Arlen					1,440	2,119	2,376
Kim Babler						1,804	2,223

*Terminations are noted by T.

Candace S.   *(commercial lending): The surprises never end. My first attempt at customer entertaining was a shocker. The customer said he would join me for dinner if he could bring his wife along. I was dumbfounded. Do I take both and report the expenses? I did, but business talk was very limited. I got the account, but it was weird.*

Laura W.   *(advertising sales): Entertaining has been a problem with me too, especially when it comes to paying the check. Some men must feel threatened by this.*

Brenda S.   *(building supply sales): Remember when we were girls? The boys wouldn't let us join their stupid clubs. Not much has changed, has it? Now it's the country club where decisions are made. And, damn it, don't tell me that I have to take up golf. I may get good and win. I remember my boss's reaction when I clobbered him in tennis.*

Roseann S.   *(textbook sales): Speaking of bosses, my manager's evaluation of my performance is an embarrassment. He is absolutely unable to criticize my performance. Most reviews have been late too.*

Karla H.   *(software programs): This is my second sales job. My first put me into a "pioneer" situation, industrial equipment. To succeed with that company you had to be a "superwoman" and become "one of the guys." I was told that I could not succeed without experience. What a catch-22! I can't get experience without succeeding.*

Peggy T.   *(chemical sales): You know, I've experienced a lot. This is my 10th year with _____. And I've been hassled, rejected, had to cancel a sales call due to a sick child, but I wouldn't trade it for anything. Your sales manager is really key. Mine treats me the same as he treats everybody else, but he does recognize that there are gender differences.*

The male commentators had this to say:

Bill M.   *(computer sales): Well, I can tell you this much. When the first women showed up,*

Exhibit 3 Number of Performance Evaluations 1992-1998*

	1992		1993		1994		1995		1996		1997		1998	
	1st	2nd	1st	2nd	1st	2nd	1st	2nd	1st	2nd	1st	2nd	1st	2nd
Suzette Renoldi	Y	—	Y	Y	Y	Y	Y	Y	—	Y	Y	—	Y	Y
Stuart Pletz	Y	Y	Y	Y	Y	Y	Y	Y	Y	Y	Y	Y	Y	Y
Alvin Polard	Y	Y	Y	Y	Y	—	Y	Y	Y	Y	Y	Y	Y	Y
Ted Hervington	Y	Y	Y	Y	Y	Y	T							
Ted Hart	Y	Y	—	Y	Y	Y	Y	Y	Y	Y	Y	Y	Y	Y
Brett Moore	Y	Y	Y	Y	Y	Y	Y	Y	T					
Shari Swaggert	Y	Y	Y	Y	Y	Y	Y	Y	—	Y	T			
Mark Hoffton	Y	Y	Y	Y	Y	Y	Y	Y	Y	Y	Y	—	Y	Y
Bob Pizzano	Y	Y	Y	Y	Y	Y	Y	Y	Y	Y	Y	Y	Y	Y
Felicia Abler	Y	Y	—	Y	Y	Y	Y	Y	Y	Y	—	Y	—	Y
Kathy Levenhagen	Y	—	Y	Y	—	Y	Y	Y	—	Y	Y	Y	—	Y
Jeff Birdest	Y	—	Y	Y	Y	Y	Y	Y	Y	Y	Y	Y	Y	Y
Larry Green	Y	Y	Y	Y	Y	Y	Y	Y	Y	Y	Y	Y	Y	Y
Chris Brackett	Y	Y	Y	—	Y	Y	Y	Y	Y	—	Y	Y	—	Y
Ilse Rieboldt	Y	Y	—	Y	T									
Mike Peck						Y	Y	Y	Y	Y	Y	Y	Y	Y
Jeff Martin							Y	Y	Y	Y	Y	Y	Y	Y
Cliff Arlen										Y	Y	Y	Y	Y
Kim Babler											Y	—		Y

*Terminations are noted by T.

I was really surprised. Not that women cannot sell computers, after all many of my customers are women and most of them are really sharp, but we weren't informed that a woman had been hired.

Joe M.   (machine tool sales): Yeah, I was surprised too. But this "little thing" wanted to set the pace. You know, be the first woman ever to sell heavy-duty machinery costing $250,000 and up. She just didn't look the part, flowery dresses, heels, perfume. One of her customers called my boss and asked him to send a man the next time.

Frank C.   (office furniture sales): We have several women in my district. Like everybody else, some are super, some are average. I think that it has been a good move. We are now selling accounts that we were unable to sell before. And our national sales manager had us attend several company training sessions on how to integrate women into the sales force.

John R.   (tractor sales): I know this is going to sound strange, but I don't like it. A woman's place is in the home, not out selling and taking up space that some man could occupy. They have no business selling tractors!

Mike R.   (pharmaceutical sales): Talk about problems. We now have the token gal on our sales force. You should have seen the other reps when she was introduced at a sales meeting. You would have thought that she was the first gal these guys had ever seen. But I just about lost it when she comes up to me one day and asks if I would help her carry some boxes to her car. "Carry them yourself" is what I should have said.

Paul T.   (building materials sales): The thing that bugs me is the equal rights stuff, or should I say unequal rights. I'd like to see what happens if I call the boss or a customer and

Exhibit 4　Base Salaries for All Sales Reps in the SE Region, 1992-1998*

	1992	1993	1994	1995	1996	1997	1998
Suzette Renoldi	$25,000	$27,600	$29,200	$29,200	$29,250	$29,300	$30,750
Stuart Pletz	25,000	27,300	28,900	29,150	29,860	30,580	32,750
Alvin Polard	25,000	28,930	29,600	29,990	30,650	31,320	33,850
Ted Hervington	25,000	26,000	26,700	T			
Tim Hart	25,000	25,780	26,750	26,890	26,900	27,000	29,700
Brett Moore	25,000	25,900	26,200	26,750	T		
Shari Swaggert	25,000	29,000	29,500	29,750	29,800	T	
Mark Hoffton	25,000	26,200	27,150	27,450	27,900	28,500	30,500
Bob Pizzano	25,000	27,100	28,450	28,600	28,770	28,900	31,300
Felicia Abler	25,000	28,750	29,200	29,450	29,500	29,750	31,500
Kathy Levenhagen	25,000	28,450	28,750	28,950	29,340	29,750	31,500
Jeff Birdest	25,000	25,700	26,500	27,800	29,100	31,000	33,750
Larry Green	25,000	25,900	28,000	28,750	30,100	31,500	34,000
Chris Brackett	25,000	27,000	27,800	28,900	29,900	31,000	33,750
Ilse Rieboldt	25,000	26,200	T				
Mike Peck			26,000	27,500	28,300	28,750	30,000
Jeff Martin				26,500	27,500	28,250	29,500
Cliff Arlen					27,000	27,500	28,250
Kim Babler						27,250	28,000

*Terminations are noted by T.

tell them I can't keep an appointment because my baby sitter is sick. Not only that, Susan just got back from maternity leave—something I'll never get—and I had to cover her accounts while she was gone.

Mack H.　(stockbroker): I don't want to play "Can You Top This," but we have a similar situation. Karen comes back off of maternity leave (this was her second child) and then decides that full-time is too much for her. She asks (and gets it too) to work only from Tuesday to Thursday. And she still gets full benefits but at a reduced salary.

Calvin H.　(chemical sales): We have a few women in the sales force, and the problems have been minimal, sort of what you would expect with any change. Management handled it well. They even had discussions with the sales force about how to call on customers who are women. Our purchasing agents, production engineers—they're all men—have had sessions on how to deal with women sales reps.

Brad M.　(food product sales): Well, with women in my group we've had the usual mess. Office romance, you know. He was married—was, that is—and now he's divorced, and she is working for another company. I think she was fired, but nobody will admit it.

Bob R.　(aluminum sales): Yeah, I can identify with that. It almost caused a divorce in my house. I was expected to travel with Beth and show her the ropes. Well, my wife wanted to know what "ropes" I was going to show her. All I had to do was mention that I was going to travel with Beth, and things went to hell. It's OK now, but it was shaky for a while.

Todd B.　(commercial lending sales): I've made joint calls with Katherine, and I've learned a lot. I thought I knew all the answers, but watching Kate interact with customers has been

Exhibit 5   Job Satisfaction Summary, 1998*

	Southeastern Region			Total Company		
	Male	**Female**	**Total**	**Male**	**Female**	**Total**
1. Job	54.06	45.13	52.16	53.84	50.19	53.61
2. Fellow workers	58.35	49.63	55.82	57.98	51.11	57.39
3. Supervisor	59.91	41.24	57.33	54.13	48.54	51.43
4. Company policy and management support	61.58	52.28	60.17	58.91	53.28	56.46
5. Pay	49.31	52.39	50.07	49.88	51.65	49.92
6. Promotion and advancement	59.41	48.37	57.30	58.28	49.87	57.06
7. Customer	53.70	48.44	51.19	54.07	48.56	52.09
Total	59.47	48.14	59.12	58.19	50.23	57.48

*All scores are standardized at a mean of 50. The higher the score, the more sales representatives are satisfied.

a real treat. She's good and really has a knack for finding out customer needs. My own sales have increased as a result, I'm sure.

Flanagan finished her review of the HBRS report and thought that most of the comments reinforced what she suspected were the major problems confronting women in sales. Other reports she reviewed supported the findings of the HBRS report. She wondered if she could get the remaining women in the southeastern region to discuss their feelings, attitudes, and problems with her or with a neutral third party. She knew the legal proceedings might prevent her from contacting the women. Shelley Ryan, CCLI's legal staff, suggested she could bring in several women from different regions for a focus group or one-on-one sessions. Ryan told her to bring in some men too since their perceptions will be valuable. Flanagan decided to adopt this strategy. After all, regardless of the outcome of the Renoldi case, CCLI should learn as much as possible about the subject to avoid future incidents.

Flanagan decided to retain a research firm to conduct the focus group interviews with samples of women and men sales reps. Six groups of 10 sales reps each participated in the project. The sessions lasted approximately two hours. Dana Moore and Bill Carson moderated the focus groups and reported to Flanagan that they felt very positive about the process and the results. The report was accompanied with videotapes so Flanagan could see and hear the proceedings. To remain objective, Flanagan did not review the tapes and asked Moore and Carson to prepare their verbatim comments without identifying the respondent.

Flanagan reviewed the report hoping to find some insight as to how CCLI might avoid future problems such as the one existing in the southeastern region. Many of the comments coincided with those from the HBRS report, although a few provided additional insight concerning the problem in the southeastern region. Flanagan read with great interest the following verbatim comments from the women:

Sales rep #1:   *Basically, I like my job a lot. But it has taken me much time to get to that point. And it's been my doing, all the way, especially with the limited support that I get from my manager.*

Sales rep #2:   *Speaking of support, some of the guys I work with view me as a threat to their* *precious power structure. One guy told me that I should be home making soup and not taking up space that a man could fill.*

Sales rep #3:   *I can relate to that. My manager at my last sales job was the only woman district sales manager in the company. She was told that she should not take credit for work done by the men who worked for her.*

Sales rep #4:   *It's not just how I relate to my manager but the whole support issue. I don't feel like I'm part of the company. Why just the other day, a customer asked about a new policy that he knew about but nobody told me about. I asked one of the men in our office, and he knew.*

Sales rep #5:   *I had a similar situation just the other day, and I don't like having to say, "I don't know the answer, but I'll find out for you." But I knew that the customer expected an answer then, not later.*

Sales rep #6:   *I'd like to think that if I needed an answer my manager would be the logical source. But in my office I ask one of the other women.*

Sales rep #4:   *I really question the ability of the higher-ups to tell me what's going on. It would be great to have a mentor or someone that I could rely on for the straight scoop.*

Sales rep #7:   *Hey, I don't want to seem odd, but my manager is really supportive. I told him about my problem taking a customer to dinner and getting into the hassle about who pays the bill. The customer just would not let a woman buy him dinner. My manager said I should join the Capital Club and take customers there where the bill doesn't come to the table. It works like a charm.*

Sales rep #8:   *I've had a similar experience. A customer, a good one, sent me a bottle of Passion perfume and a cashmere sweater. I was dumbfounded and asked my manager what to do, since I didn't recall hearing anything about receiving gifts during our training program. He gave me several suggestions, and I decided which one to try. It worked, and I still have the account.*

Sales rep #9:   *My manager is pretty supportive. But he can't eliminate the hassling that goes on with some customers. Do the purchasing agents and others with CCLI treat women sales reps the same?*

Sales rep #10:   *I'd really like a chance to move into sales management. That's why I got into sales to begin with. Now, all I have to do is figure out what it takes to get promoted. It's a big mystery at CCLI. And if something doesn't happen soon, I'll go elsewhere.*

Sales rep #11:   *This whole performance evaluation process is a joke. My manager is usually late, and on top of it the review is so general and vague that I have no idea what I'm supposed to do to better myself. And our annual bonuses show no relation to contribution. We all get the same bonus.*

The comments from the men did not add anything to her understanding of CCLI's problems. They were very similar to those provided by HBRS, plus they duplicated many of the comments made by the women concerning performance evaluations and promotion policies.

The report suggested to Diane Flanagan that CCLI has much work ahead if it is going to avoid problems similar to those in the southeastern region. Although names were not given in the report, Flanagan thought she could associate many of the comments with James Bradford, CCLI's problem sales manager. She did not learn anything from the focus groups that would help with the legal proceedings in the Suzette Renoldi matter. But, for certain, she wanted to change things to avoid future problems.

The Well-Paid Receptionist*

Harvey Finley did a quick double take when he caught a glimpse of the figure representing Ms. Brannen's salary on the year-end printout. A hurried call to payroll confirmed it. Yes, his receptionist had been paid $127,614.21 for her services last year. As he sat in stunned silence, he had the sudden realization that since his firm was doing so well this year, she would earn at least 10 to 15 percent more money during the current fiscal year. This was a shock, indeed.

With a second call to payroll, Harvey found out that Ms. Brannen's salary had been approximately $112,000 the year before last and $100,000 the year before that. She had been well paid for some time, he concluded.

Background

Harvey began his career as a service technician for a major manufacturer of copy machines. He received rather extensive technical training, but his duties were limited to performing routine, on-site maintenance and service for customers. After a year's experience as a service technician, he asked for and received a promotion to sales representative. In this capacity, he established many favorable contacts in the business community of Troupville and the surrounding towns. He began to think seriously about capitalizing on his success by opening his own business.

Then, seven years ago, he decided to take the plunge and start his own firm. He was tired of selling for someone else. When he mentioned his plan to his friends, they all expressed serious doubts; Troupville, a city of approximately 35,000 people located in the deep South, had just begun to recover from a severe recession. The painful memories of the layoffs, bankruptcies, and plummeting real estate values were too recent and vivid to be forgotten.

Undeterred by the skeptics, Harvey was optimistic that Troupville's slow recovery would soon become a boom. Even though his firm would certainly have to be started on a shoestring, Harvey thought his sales experience and technical competence would enable him to survive what was sure to be a difficult beginning. He was nervous but excited when he signed the lease on the first little building. A lifelong dream was either about to be realized or dashed forever. Troupville Business Systems was born.

While he had managed to borrow, rent, lease, or subcontract for almost everything that was absolutely necessary, he did need one employee immediately. Of course, he hoped the business would expand rapidly and that he would soon have a complete and

*By Roland B. Cousins, of La Grange College. Management cooperated in the field research for this case, which was written solely for the purpose of stimulating student discussion. All individuals and incidents are real, but names and data have been disguised at the request of the organization. Copyright © 1992 by the *Case Research Journal* and Roland B. Cousins.

competent staff. But until he could be sure that some revenue would be generated, he thought he could get by with one person who would be a combination receptionist/secretary and general assistant.

The typical salary for such a position in the area was about $14,000 per year; for Harvey, this was a major expense. Nevertheless, he placed what he thought was a well-worded ad in the "Help Wanted" section of the local newspaper. There were five applicants, four of whom just did not seem quite right for the position he envisioned. The fifth applicant, Ms. Cathy Brannen, was absolutely captivating.

Ms. Brannen was a 27-year-old divorcée with one small child. Her résumé showed that she had graduated from a two-year office administration program at a state university. She had worked for only two employers following graduation, one for five years and the most recent for two years. Since returning to her hometown of Troupville two months ago, following her divorce, she had not been able to find suitable employment.

From the moment she sat down for the interview, Harvey and Ms. Brannen seemed to be on exactly the same wavelength. She was very articulate, obviously quite bright, and, most important, very enthusiastic about assisting with the start-up of the new venture. She seemed to be exactly the sort of person Harvey had envisioned when he first began to think seriously about taking the big plunge. He resisted the temptation to offer her the job on the spot, but ended the hour-long interview by telling her that he would check her references and contact her again very soon.

Telephone calls to her two former employers convinced Harvey that he had actually underestimated Ms. Brannen's suitability for the position. Each one said without equivocation that she was the best employee he had ever had in any position. Both former employers concluded the conversation by saying they would rehire her in a minute if she were still available. The only bit of disturbing information gleaned from these two calls was the fact that her annual salary had risen to $15,900 in her last job. Although Harvey thought that the cost of living was probably a bit higher in Houston, where she had last worked, he wasn't sure she would react favorably to the $14,000 offer he was planning to make. However, he was determined that, somehow, Cathy Brannen would be his first employee.

Ms. Brannen seemed quite pleased when Harvey telephoned her at home that same evening. She said she would be delighted to meet him at the office the next morning to discuss the position more fully.

Cathy Brannen was obviously very enthusiastic about the job as outlined in the meeting. She asked all of the right questions, responded quickly and articulately to every query posed to her, and seemed ready to accept the position even before the offer was extended. When Harvey finally got around to mentioning the salary, there was a slight change in Cathy's eager expression. She stiffened. Since Harvey realized that salary might be a problem, he decided to offer Cathy an incentive of sorts in addition to the $14,000 annual salary. He told her that he realized his salary offer was lower than the amount she had earned on her last job. And, he told her, he understood that a definite disadvantage of working for a new firm was the complete absence of financial security. Although he was extremely reluctant to guarantee a larger salary because of his own uncertainty regarding the future, he offered her a sales override in the amount of 2 percent of sales. He explained that she would largely determine the success or failure of the firm. She needed to represent the firm in the finest possible manner to potential customers who telephoned and to those who walked in the front door. For this reason, the sales override seemed to be an appropriate addition to her straight salary. It would provide her with incentive to take an active interest in the firm.

Cathy accepted the offer immediately. Even though she was expecting a salary offer of $16,000, she hoped the sales override might make up the difference. "Who knows," she thought, "2 percent of sales may amount to big money someday." It did not, however, seem very likely at the time.

Troupville Business Systems began as a very small distributor of copy machines. The original business plan was just to sell copy machines and provide routine, on-site service. More extensive on-site service and repairs requiring that a machine be removed from a customer's premises were to be provided by a regional distributor located in a major city approximately 100 miles from Troupville.

Troupville Business Systems did well from the start. Several important changes were made in the services the firm offered during the first year. Harvey soon found that there was a greater demand for the leasing of copy machines, particularly the large expensive models which he originally planned to sell. He also soon discovered that his customers wanted to be able to contract directly with his firm for all of their service needs. Merely guaranteeing that he could get the machines serviced was not sufficient in the eyes of potential customers. In attempting to accommodate the market, he developed a complete service facility and began to offer leasing options on all models. These changes in the business all occurred during the first year. Growth during that year was steady but not spectacular. While sales continued to grow steadily the second year, it was early in the third year that Harvey made what turned out to be his best decision. He entered the computer business.

Harvey had purchased a personal computer soon after Troupville Business Systems was founded. The machine and its capabilities fascinated him, although he knew virtually nothing about computers. He was soon a member of a local users club, was subscribing to all the magazines, and was taking evening computer courses at the local university—in short, he became a computer buff. Harvey recognized the business potential of the rapidly growing computer market, but he did not believe that his original business was sufficiently stable to introduce a new product line just yet.

During his third year of operations, he decided the time was right to enter the computer business. He added to his product line a number of personal computers popular with small businesses in the area. This key decision caused a virtual explosion in the growth of his firm. Several key positions were added, including that of comptroller. By the fourth year of operations, computers produced by several other manufacturers had been added to Harvey's product line, and he had developed the capability of providing complete service for all products carried. His computer enterprise was not limited to business customers, because he quickly developed a significant walk-in retail trade. Rapid growth continued unabated.

During the first seven years of the company's existence, Cathy Brannen had proven truly indispensable. Her performance exceeded Harvey's highest expectations. Although her official position remained that of secretary/receptionist, she took it upon herself to learn about each new product or service. During the early years, Harvey often thought that she did a better job than he did whenever a potential customer called in his absence. Even after he acquired a qualified sales staff, Harvey had no concerns when Cathy had to field questions from a potential customer because a regular salesperson was not available. The customer never realized that the professional young lady capably handling all inquiries was "only" the receptionist.

Cathy began performing fewer sales functions because of the increased number of professional salespersons, but her secretarial duties expanded tremendously. She was still Harvey's secretary, and she continued to answer virtually every telephone call coming into the business. Since her office was in an open area, she still was the first to greet many visitors.

Cathy took a word processing course at a local business school shortly after joining the firm. As she began working with Harvey's first personal computer, she, too, developed into a computer aficionado and became the best computer operator in the firm.

The Current Situation

Harvey was shaken by the realization that Cathy Brannen had been paid over $127,000 last year. As he wondered what, if anything, should be done about her earnings, he began to reflect on the previous seven years.

Success had come almost overnight. It seemed as though Troupville Business Systems could do no wrong. The workforce had grown at a rate of approximately 15 percent per year since the third year of operations. Seventeen people were now employed by the firm. While Harvey did acknowledge that some of this success was due to being in the right place at the right time, he also had reason to be proud of the choices he had made. Time had proven that all of his major decisions had been correct. He also could not over-estimate Cathy's contribution to the success of the firm. Yes, certainly, one of the most important days in the life of the firm was the day when Cathy responded to his ad in the newspaper.

Success had brought with it ever-increasing demands on his time. He had never worked so hard, but the rewards were certainly forthcoming. First there was the new Jaguar, then the new home on Country Club Drive, the vacation home on the coast, the European trips. . . . Yes, success was wonderful.

During these years Cathy too, had prospered. Harvey had not thought much about it, but he did remember making a joking comment the first day she drove her new Mercedes to work. He also remembered commenting on her mink coat at the company banquet last December. Cathy had been dazzling.

Now that Harvey realized what he was paying Cathy, he was greatly disturbed. She was making over twice as much money as anyone else in the firm with the exception of himself. The best salesman had earned an amount in the low sixties last year. His top managers were paid salaries ranging from the high forties to the mid-fifties. The average salary in the area for executive secretaries was now probably between $22,000 and $25,000 per year. A good receptionist could be hired for under $20,000, and yet Cathy had been paid $127,614.21 last year. The sales override had certainly enabled Cathy to share in the firm's success. Yes, indeed.

As Harvey thought more and more about the situation, he kept returning to the same conclusion. He felt something had to be done about her compensation. It was just too far out of line with other salaries in the firm. Although Harvey was drawing over $200,000 per year in salary and had built an equity in the business of more than $1 million, these facts did not seem relevant as he pondered what to do. It seemed likely that a number of other employees did know about Cathy's compensation level. Harvey wondered why no one ever mentioned it. Even the comptroller never mentioned Cathy's compensation. This did seem quite odd to Harvey, as the comptroller, Frank Bain, knew that Harvey did not even attempt to keep up with the financial details. He relied on Frank to bring important matters to his attention.

With no idea of how to approach this problem, Harvey decided to begin by making a list of alternatives. He got out a piece of paper and, as he stared at the blank lines, overheard Cathy's cheerful exchange with a customer in the next room.

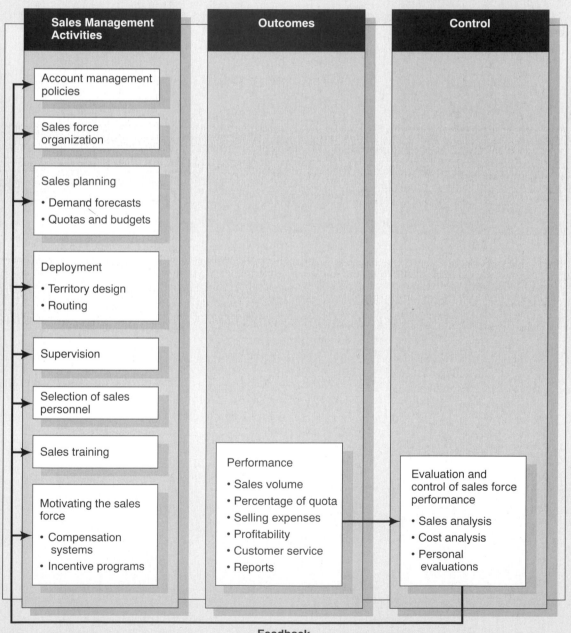

Sales Management Activities	Outcomes	Control
Account management policies		
Sales force organization		
Sales planning • Demand forecasts • Quotas and budgets		
Deployment • Territory design • Routing		
Supervision		
Selection of sales personnel		
Sales training		
Motivating the sales force • Compensation systems • Incentive programs	Performance • Sales volume • Percentage of quota • Selling expenses • Profitability • Customer service • Reports	Evaluation and control of sales force performance • Sales analysis • Cost analysis • Personal evaluations

Feedback

Part III

Evaluation and Control of the Sales Program

Three activities are central to the basic process by which sales or any other managers operate: planning, implementing, and evaluating and controlling. Part III explores the policies and procedures involved in evaluating and controlling a firm's sales program. Chapter 14 discusses audits, information systems, and sales analysis, three primary mechanisms of evaluation. Chapter 15 discusses cost analysis, which focuses on the profitability of the personal selling effort in general and specific salespeople in particular. Chapter 16 looks at other measures for assessing the performance of sales people, both objective and subjective.

$I4$ Sales Analysis

ARE ALL SALES WORTH THE SAME? THE CHALLENGE AT RUSH PETERBILT

On May 1, 1998, the United Autoworkers Union walked out on Peterbilt. The strike severely limits but hasn't halted Peterbilt's ability to build trucks. As a result, Rush Peterbilt, the largest dealer for Peterbilt trucks, has had some interesting sales management challenges.

Consider these factors: Low interest rates and high availability of funds make trucks easier to buy, so demand has soared. Union Pacific Railroad can't solve incredible bottlenecks, causing many companies to shift from rail transportation to trucking, also raising demand for trucks. And two manufacturers, Freightliner and Mac, have partnership agreements with major carriers, which locks up their production. Volvo's production is locked up for another 12 months in large purchases, so no one can pick up any slack caused by the strike at Peterbilt.

As a result, selling trucks has never been easier. The challenge is deciding which ones to build. In the Rush Peterbilt Houston office, for example, the branch manager turns in an order for 180 trucks every month, and hopes to get 112. Each one of those 180 has to be prioritized, from 1 to 180, and the plant builds as many as it can.

Several factors go into the prioritization. The first 80 trucks per month go to the largest customer, who has a standing order. The other 32 that get built come from an inventory of 800 sales. Since reps work on straight commission paid when the truck is delivered to the customer, sometimes a truck will be built just so a rep can get paid. Otherwise, the biggest priority is gross profit, followed by customer size and length of relationship. Gross profit is determined not only by the price at which the truck is sold, but also how it is furnished, and whether the rep was also able to sell a full-service maintenance agreement.

These management challenges are unusual, to be sure. No one wants a strike, particularly when demand is so high. But by carefully managing what is built, the company is still able to hit gross profit objectives.

Visit Rush Peterbilt at its Web site, *www.Rushtruckcenters.com.*

LEARNING OBJECTIVES

The three steps of planning, implementing, and controlling are the basic processes by which managers operate. In sales management, planning involves such problems as organizational structure, territory design, and establishment of sales quotas. Implementing includes selecting, training, and motivating sales representatives. All these topics have been treated in this book. Now we turn to evaluating and controlling the field selling effort.

After reading this chapter, you should be able to:

- Illustrate the control process.
- Discuss the nature of sales and marketing audits, and tell how they interrelate.
- Demonstrate the difference between simple and comparative sales analyses.
- Complete a hierarchical sales analysis.

Evaluation and control are vital parts of the management process. As the opening scenario suggests, management needs feedback on the effectiveness of its plans and the quality of their execution to operate more effectively; otherwise it is easy to lose sight of the firm's objectives and how to achieve them. A firm with no effective evaluation and control programs can easily end up under full power and no direction, consuming resources to no effective end, much like a ship that has lost its bearing because of a broken compass.

NATURE OF CONTROL

The key role played by evaluation and control in the management process is depicted in the feedback-control loop of Exhibit 14.1. Company goals initiate the process by serving as the targets that guide the formulation of plans. Once designed, the plans need to be implemented to become part of the daily operations. The firm then needs to collect and organize information about its operations so it can compare these data with its goals to determine how well it is doing. This evaluation and comparison provide the control for the enterprise. They allow the assessment of where the firm is now versus where it wants to go so corrective action may be taken.

The situation again parallels that of a ship at sea: By knowing where the ship is now compared with its target destination, the captain can adjust the course to arrive at the destination. It is not impossible for the ship to arrive there without such evaluation. By simply wandering about aimlessly, it may eventually get there by a stroke of good luck. Similarly, the firm may eventually get where it wants to go without proper evaluation and control procedures. But it is much more likely to get there faster and at less cost if it can assess where it is now and compare that with where it wants to go so the appropriate corrective action can be taken, as the opening scenario indicates.

Marketing Audit

The most thorough mechanism for evaluating the marketing effort is a marketing audit. A marketing audit is a complete, systematic, objective evaluation of the total marketing effort of a firm. Marketing audits examine the firm's goals, policies, organization, methods and procedures, and personnel. They also assess the firm's current position and its strengths and weaknesses so a new course can be plotted if necessary.

The two basic types of marketing audits are vertical and horizontal. The horizontal audit is often referred to as a marketing mix audit in that it examines all the elements that go into the marketing mix. It emphasizes the relative importance of the various elements

Exhibit 14.1   Basic Management Control Process

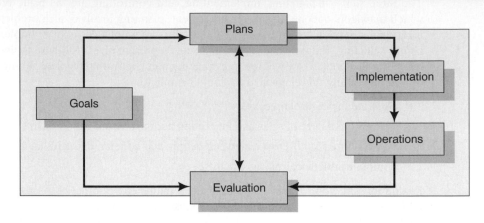

and the mix between them. In contrast, the vertical audit singles out selected elements of the marketing operation and subjects them to thorough study and evaluation.

The horizontal audit is a systems-level audit in which the focus is more on the relationship among marketing activities than on any one activity. Certain activities may be isolated for more detailed investigation through the horizontal audit, but that is not its main purpose; that is the purpose of the vertical audit. The vertical audit is a complete, objective, systematic analysis of one part of the total marketing effort—for example, the personal selling effort. The term *sales management audit* refers to the vertical audit associated with the sales manager's responsibilities.[1]

Although this book emphasizes sales management audits, all functional audits within the firm must be coordinated so their timing and scope coincide. Suppose, for example, a sales management audit indicated the sales force is encountering unusual difficulty selling one major product line. Information on the advertising effort and its effectiveness must also be available by product line. If the advertising audit analyzes the function only by geographical area and not product line, the available information would not be sufficient to diagnose the reason for the sales problems. A similar problem arises if the two functional audits do not correspond in their timing.

The relation between the vertical sales management audit and the horizontal marketing audit can be discerned by looking at some of the issues addressed under each.

The initial step in a horizontal marketing audit is to secure a clear statement of the company's goals and mission. As we discussed in Chapter 2, goals and mission statements are often difficult to craft, and many times, goals are not necessarily as readily available as the mission statement. Even if goals have been stated by corporate executives, the goals may not be useful because they are too vague. The goal "to achieve a high rate of sales" is too nebulous to be of value. A marketing audit often uncovers executives operating with different goals and imprecise targets.

The goals for the personal selling effort must be coordinated with those of the firm. The sales management audit attempts to specify goals for the personal selling function and the role personal selling is to play in the total marketing effort of the firm. It also includes a statement of short-run objectives. Two examples are (1) increase the number of salespeople in the southeastern territory by two in the next two years and (2) increase the frequency with which sales reps contact type A accounts by 10 percent within the next year.

The next audit step is to examine how well the firm's current policies coincide with its goals. Policies can grow obsolete in dynamic economies. For example, Moore Business Forms found that it had developed a set of policies that resulted in incorrect invoices. Each policy, by itself, was a good policy under the conditions it was created, but as time changed and systems grew more complex, the policies could not work.[2]

Policies about personal selling might also need revision. Thus, if the firm's policy of promoting from within the sales force prevents it from filling an area manager's position with the type of person needed for that territory, the policy may need changing. Similarly, a policy of frequent assignment changes (even if to bigger and better territories) that produce excessive turnover in the sales force would be questioned.

Any policy made obsolete by a changing external environment should be revised. For example, after analyzing its sales figures, Welded Tube Co. of America decided to reduce the number of small orders it processed. It did so by redirecting orders for its patented Kleen Kote Tube products to distributors instead of handling them itself.[3]

The sales management audit similarly might suggest a change in salespeople's compensation scheme or the criteria used in hiring new reps. The important thing is that the spectrum of sales management policies be systematically evaluated and those that need to be changed be identified. For example, such an audit at Edward Jones (a financial services firm) resulted in an increased emphasis on hiring from college campuses.

The marketing audit looks at the organization of the company as a whole and the marketing department in particular. Auditors seek to determine whether the organization is optimal in terms of the company's resources and talent. Recall Hewlett–Packard's experience in changing to a vertical market by product structure, then combining all products under one account manager.

The sales management audit focuses on the organization of the sales force. Is it large enough? Is it organized optimally given the firm's current situation? Take, for example, Bantam Doubleday Dell, which comprises the U.S. publishing operations of Bertelsmann AG of Germany. After an organizational audit, it decided to reorganize into four sales forces organized according to how its books are distributed (e.g., retail, wholesale), rather than two sales forces, one for Bantam hardcover and paperback titles and Dell paperbacks and another handling Doubleday and Delacorte hardcovers.[4] "The Global Sales Force" describes how IBM reorganized its European operations to take better advantage of the changes occurring there with unification.

Methods and procedures are the tactical means by which the firm's policies are carried out. Perhaps the policies are good, but their implementation is inadequate. The marketing audit would attempt to assess the quality of execution of each marketing activity. Have new products been properly test marketed? Have distribution channels evolved to reflect changing consumption patterns? Have pricing policies been adhered to?

The sales management audit attempts to assess how well those activities that directly influence the personal selling function have been carried out. It looks at such issues as how well recent recruits have been trained, how quickly customer orders have been processed, whether salespeople have been given accurate and prompt feedback on their sales and costs, and whether customer requests have been promptly satisfied.

The marketing audit does not stop with a review of the goals, policies, organization, and procedures used to carry out the marketing function. It also examines the people involved to determine how well they are performing.

The sales management audit is similar. Most of its attention, however, is directed at individual salespeople and at branch, district, regional, and other area managers. In such audits, determining where people are now versus where they should be if the personal selling effort were on target is emphasized. Three of the more productive and partly over-

Reorganization of IBM's European Operations

The planning and implementation of IBM's European operations began a decade before the introduction of the euro, or common European currency, but was driven by the unification of the European market. Taking more than six years to complete, the blueprint called for increased centralization in some respects, and decentralization in others. Further, African and Mid-East operations were combined into the European division. Internal operations such as warehousing and in-house computing were centralized to save money. Several computing facilities were closed and merged with the primary office in Paris.

But external affairs, including sales operations, were decentralized so that decisions can be made close to the customer. Better decisions can be made faster locally than in a centralized headquarters. To accomplish this decentralization, many managers were moved from the Paris headquarters to various local offices. Local evaluation of sales performance can strengthen weaker offices, as root causes of problems can be identified, and local competitors can be accounted for. Conversely, best practices can be more quickly identified and copied.

Some countries, such as Romania, have only had an IBM presence for a very short time. Economies in these formerly Communist countries are still developing and require different management competencies than in well-established countries such as Great Britain. Local offices with local management can adapt strategies to serve customers in those developing economies more effectively.

While it is difficult to know how successful such a massive reorganization has been, the European/Mid-East/African operations are growing at a rate over 15 percent and now account for over $32 billion (U.S. operations are just over $40 billion). These strong performance figures indicate better than industry performance, suggesting that, at least on the sales side, the new structure is paying off.

Source: Richard L. Hudson, "IBM Again Revamps European Sector: It Seeks to Find Proper Mix as Market Grows Tougher," *The Wall Street Journal,* April 22, 1991; *www.ibm.com, www.roibm.com,* and *IBM Annual Report* (1998).

lapping programs for making such assessments are sales analysis, cost and profitability analysis, and individual performance evaluation.

Not all firms use all three, though many are moving in that direction. Sales analysis is the most common, and cost analysis is the least used. The remainder of this chapter concentrates on sales analysis; Chapter 15 focuses on cost and profitability analysis; and Chapter 16 examines performance evaluation of individual salespeople using ratios and subjective supervisor ratings.

ELEMENTS OF A SALES ANALYSIS

A sales analysis involves gathering, classifying, comparing, and studying company sales data. It may "simply involve the comparison of total company sales in two different time periods. Or it may entail subjecting thousands of component sales (or sales-related) figures to a variety of comparisons—among themselves, with external data, and with like figures for earlier periods of time."[5]

A major benefit of even the most elementary sales analysis is in highlighting those products, customers, orders, or territories in which the firm's sales are concentrated. A heavy concentration is so common that some have labeled the general phenomenon the 80:20 principle.[6] This means it is not at all unusual to find 80 percent of the customers or products accounting for only 20 percent of total sales. Conversely, the remaining 20 percent of the customers or products account for 80 percent of the total sales volume. The same phenomenon applies to orders and territories; only a small percentage of the total number of orders or a few of the firm's many territories account for the great percentage of its sales. The 80:20 principle describes the general situation, although the exact concentration ratio varies by company. In a study conducted over 30 years ago to assess the magnitude of the concentration ratio, 200 questionnaires were mailed to companies listed in the American Institute of Management's *Manual of Excellent Managements.* The companies were asked to rank their products, orders, customers, salespeople, and sales territories according to sales volume and to indicate the percentage of sales generated by the top third of each. Of those contacted, 80 responded. While the results did not yield an 80:20 ratio, they did suggest a heavy concentration. For example, the percentages of sales accounted for by each of the top one-third items in each category were as follows:[7]

Products	72 percent
Orders	73 percent
Customers	74 percent
Salespeople	59 percent
Sales territories	62 percent

Contrast those findings with a statement made by a FedEx marketing manager who said that his company's commercial account profits came from the top 1 percent of their customers. That is a highly concentrated ratio.

To produce these overall percentages, some individual companies had to have concentration ratios much higher than these averages. There are some other interesting examples in this regard. One manufacturer found that 78 percent of his customers produced only slightly more than 2 percent of his sales volume. In another business, 48 percent of the orders accounted for only 5 percent of the sales. In yet another case, 76 percent of the number of products manufactured accounted for only 3 percent of the sales volume. In another business, 59 percent of the sales reps' calls were made on accounts from which only 12 percent of the sales were obtained.

In a wholesale grocery firm, more than 50 percent of the total number of customers brought in less than 2 percent of the total sales volume. Similarly, 40 percent of the total number of items carried in stock accounted for less than 2 percent of the total sales volume.[8]

The most cursory sales analysis should reveal such concentrations. The Mosinee Paper Company, for example, almost dropped one of its products because of its dismal sales performance. Then an elementary sales analysis found that only a single sales rep was selling the specific grade of industrial paper. On further investigation, Mosinee discovered how the buyers "were using the paper—an application that had been known only to the one salesman and his customers. This information enabled management to educate its other salespeople as to the potential market for the paper and sales rose substantially."[9]

Key Decisions in a Sales Analysis

Those wishing to undertake a sales analysis must decide (1) the type of evaluation system, (2) the sources of information, and (3) the sales breakdowns that will be used. Exhibit 14.2 gives an overview of the nature of these decisions.

The type of evaluation system determines how the sales analysis will be conducted. Will it be a simple sales analysis or a comparative analysis? When it is to be a comparative analysis, two additional questions arise: (1) What is to be the base for the comparison? (2) What type of reporting and control system is to be used?

In a simple sales analysis, the facts are listed and not measured against any standard. In a comparative analysis or, as it is sometimes called, a performance analysis, compar-

Exhibit 14.2   Some Key Decisions When Conducting a Sales Analysis

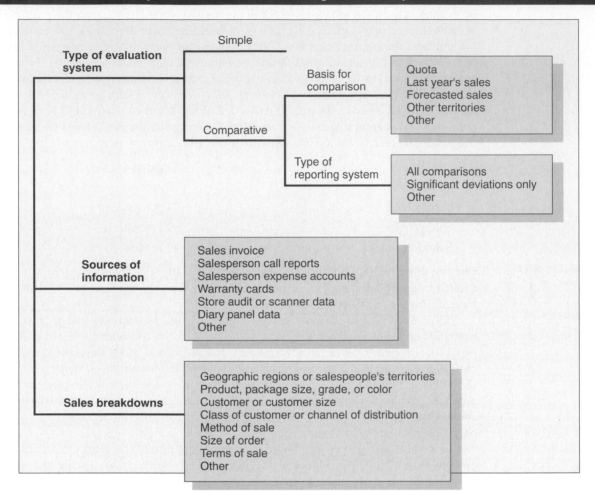

isons are made. Consider, for example, the data in Exhibit 14.3. A simple sales analysis would be restricted to the facts in column (1). These figures suggest Dawson sold the most and Barrington the least. A performance analysis would attempt to go beyond the mere listing of sales to determine where they are greatest and poorest; it would try to make comparisons against some "standard." In Exhibit 14.3, the standard is the quota for each salesman, and column (3) provides a performance index for each. This performance index is calculated as the ratio of actual sales to sales quota (PI = S/Q × 100). It suggests Dawson was not the "best" in 2000, but rather Bendt was; and in fact, Dawson realized the smallest percentage of total potential as judged by quota.

Base for Comparison

The comparison with quota is only one type of comparison that can be made. Quota is one of the most common standards because it is very useful, particularly when quotas have been specified well. Specifying quotas well is a big if, however. Quotas can be a real problem—as we saw in Chapter 8—when they are done poorly and perhaps even when they are done well. Consequently, some firms resort to other bases of comparison for a

Exhibit 14.3 Differences between Simple Sales Analysis and Comparative Analysis

Sales Representative	(1) 2000 Sales ($000)	(2) 2000 Quota ($000)	(3) Performance Index
Duane Barrington	$760.9	$700	108.7
John Bendt	793.5	690	115.0
James Dawson	859.2	895	96.0
George Richardson	837.0	775	108.0
Walter Keyes	780.3	765	102.0

sales analysis. These include this year's sales versus last year's sales or the average of a number of prior years' sales; this year's sales versus forecasted sales; sales in one territory versus sales in another, either absolutely or in relation to the ratios in prior years; and the percentage change in sales from one territory to another, as compared with last year.

Such comparisons are certainly better than simply viewing raw sales figures, but they are not generally as productive as a "true" performance analysis. In the latter, variations from planned performance are highlighted, and the reasons for such exceptions are isolated.

Type of Reporting System

The other major question that arises in a comparative sales analysis is the type of reporting and control system to be used. For example, if one relevant comparison is to be sales as a percentage of quota, this statistic would be provided for each salesperson, branch, district, region, customer, product, and every other unit by which sales are to be analyzed. The problem with this is that it can inundate the sales manager with information. To aid the sales manager, the reports can focus on exceptions, or significant deviations from the norm or from budget. Sales managers can then concentrate on the exceptions while having the full profile of comparisons for assessing the significance of what happened.

A second class of major decisions that must be made with respect to sales analysis is what information is to serve as input to the system and how the basic source documents are to be processed. To address this question, the firm first needs to determine the types of comparisons to be made. A comparison with sales in other territories will require fewer documents than a comparison against market potential or quota or against the average sales in the territory for the last five years. The firm also needs to decide the extent to which preparing the sales report should be integrated with preparing other types of reports. These may include inventory or production reports or sales reports for other company units such as other divisions.

Generally, the one most productive source document is the sales invoice. From this, the following information can usually be extracted:

- Customer name and location.
- Product(s) or service(s) sold.
- Volume and dollar amount of the transaction.
- Salesperson (or agent) responsible for the sale.
- End use of product sold.
- Location of customer facility where product is to be shipped and/or used.

- Customer's industry, class of trade, and/or channel of distribution.
- Terms of sale and applicable discount.
- Freight paid and/or to be collected.
- Shipment point for the order.
- Transportation used in shipment.[10]

Other documents provide more specialized output. Some of the more important of these are listed in Exhibit 14.4. Most companies are likely to use only two or three of these sources of sales information in addition to the sales invoice, primarily because computer systems are not in place that automate and link those functions.

Software that does link bid estimation, order entry, shipping, billing systems, and other work processes is called enterprise software. Trilogy's Sales Suite is an example of enterprise software that links a number of sales-related functions. For example, Boeing uses the software to price out airplanes. Each airline and private customer who buys a jet will fit out each jet differently. As a result, the salesperson's proposal has to account for each different item in order to derive a price. Plus, commission has to be paid on the sale, parts have to be ordered for manufacturing, delivery has to be schedule—and the enterprise software helps manage all of these functions.

From a sales evaluation perspective, enterprise software collects and distributes data that sales managers can use to evaluate the sales force. As was mentioned, much of the data that is needed for sales analysis comes from the invoice; when enterprise software is used, the data listed earlier can be extracted automatically. Further, the software can then model that data to provide the sales executive with a sales analysis by product line, territory, or other unit.

The third major decision management must confront when designing a sales analysis is which variables will serve as points of aggregation. Without such categories, the firm would be forced to analyze every transaction in isolation or would need to look at sales in the aggregate. The latter is not particularly informative, and the former is almost impossible. The most common and instructive procedure is to assemble and tabulate sales by some appropriate groupings, such as these:

- Geographic regions such as states, counties, regions, or salespeople's territories.
- Product, package size, grade, or color.
- Customer or customer size.
- Market, including class of customer, end use, or channel of distribution.
- Method of sale, including mail, telephone, or direct salespeople.
- Size of order.
- Financial arrangement such as cash or charge.

The classes of information a company may use depends on such things as its size, the diversity of its product line, the geographic extent of its sales area, the number of markets and customers it serves, and the level of management for which the information is to be supplied. The firms with a product management form of organization, for example, would be interested in sales by product groups. These managers might focus on territory-by-territory sales of their products. The sales manager and regional managers might be much more interested in territory and customer analyses and only secondarily interested in the territory sales broken out by product.

These breakdowns are not necessarily mutually exclusive in that the manager has to choose a breakdown by region or product or customer. Rather, sales analyses are most

Exhibit 14.4 Other Sources of Information for Evaluating Salespeople

Cash register receipts

Type (cash or credit) and dollar amount of transaction by department by salesperson

Salesperson's call reports

Customers and prospects called on (company and individual seen; planned or unplanned calls)
Products discussed
Orders obtained
Customers' product needs and usage
Other significant information about customers
Distribution of salespeople's time among customer calls, travel, and office work
Sales-related activities: meetings, conventions, etc.

Salespeople's expense accounts

Expenses by day by item (hotel, meals, travel, etc.)

Individual customer (and prospect) records

Name and location and customer number
Number of calls by company salesperson (agents)
Sales by company (in dollars and/or units by product or service by location of customer facility)
Customer's industry, class of trade, and/or trade channel
Estimated total annual usage of each product or service sold by the company
Estimated annual purchases from the company of each such product or service
Location (in terms of company sales territory)

Financial records

Sales revenue (by products, geographic markets, customers, class of trade, unit of sales organization, etc.)
Direct sales expenses (similarly classified)
Overhead sales costs (similarly classified)
Profits (similarly classified)

Credit memos

Returns and allowances

Warranty cards

Indirect measures of dealer sales
Customer service

Exhibit 14.5   Sales Reports in a Consumer Food Products Company

Report Name	Purpose	Report Access*
Region	To provide sales information in units and dollars for each sales office or center in the region as well as a regional total	Appropriate regional manager
Sales office or center	To provide sales information in units and dollars for each district manager assigned to a sales office	Appropriate sales office or center manager
District	To provide sales information in units and dollars for each account supervisor and retail salesperson reporting to the district manager	Appropriate district manager
Salesperson summary	To provide sales information in units and dollars for each customer on whom the salesperson calls	Appropriate salesperson
Salesperson customer/product	To provide sales information in units and dollars for each customer on whom the salesperson calls	Appropriate salesperson
Salesperson/ product	To provide sales information in units and dollars for each product that the salesperson sells	Appropriate salesperson
Region/product	To provide sales information in units and dollars for each product sold within the region. Similar reports would be available by sales office and by district.	Appropriate regional manager
Region/customer class	To provide sales information in units and dollars for each class of customer located in the region. Similar reports would be available by sales office and by district.	Appropriate regional manager

*To understand the report access, it is useful to know that salespeople were assigned accounts in sales districts. Salespeople were assigned one or, at most, a couple of large accounts and were responsible for all the grocery stores, regardless of geography, affiliated with these large accounts, or they were assigned a geographic territory and were responsible for all of the stores within that territory. All sales districts were assigned to sales offices or sales centers. The centers were, in turn, organized into regions.

productive when they are done hierarchically, in the sense that one breakdown is carried out within another category. The categories are treated simultaneously instead of separately. For example, the analysis may end up showing that customer XYZ in the western region purchased so many units each of products A, B, C, and D; this illustrates a territory, customer, and product hierarchical breakdown.

The advantage of hierarchical breakdowns is illustrated later. For now, you should know that the typical sales analysis results not in a single report but in a family of reports, each reflecting a different level of aggregation, tailored to the person receiving it. Exhibit 14.5, for example, shows the types of sales reports used in a consumer food products company for which one of the authors served as consultant.

A Hierarchical Sales Analysis

To illustrate some relevant comparisons and the process used in conducting a sales analysis, consider the data in Exhibit 14.6. The figures apply to a national manufacturer of small kitchen appliances, though the actual number, as well as the identity of the company, has been disguised. The Kitchenware Company previously determined its sales are highly correlated with population, income, and the general level of retail sales. Thus, it

Exhibit 14.6	Sales and Sales Quotas for Kitchenware Company				
Region	BPI (percentage of U.S.)	Sales Quota ($ millions)	Sales ($ millions)	Difference ($ millions)	Performance Index (*PI* = *S/Q* × 100)
New England	5.8193%	$ 24.44	$ 25.03	$ 0.59	102.4
Middle Atlantic	18.3856	77.22	78.19	0.97	101.3
East North-Central	20.1419	84.60	79.48	−5.12	94.0
West North-Central	7.3982	31.07	30.51	−0.56	98.2
South Atlantic	14.7525	61.96	64.07	2.11	103.4
East South-Central	5.2571	22.08	23.20	1.12	105.1
West South-Central	9.2022	38.65	38.42	−0.23	99.4
Mountain	4.2819	17.98	17.73	−0.25	98.6
Pacific	14.7613	62.00	64.60	2.60	104.2
Total United States	100.0000%	$420.00	$421.23	$ 1.23	100.3

has determined market potential by region using the corollary index method. More particularly, it has used the Buying Power Index (BPI) published by *Sales & Marketing Management* to determine each region's market potential and has then multiplied these potentials by the company's expected market share to generate the regional quotas in Exhibit 14.6. The "Managing Sales Relationship" box illustrates how smart use of sales data can strengthen relationships and help one evaluate performance.

Note that although the annual quota was $420 million, total sales in all regions were $421.23 million. Not only has the total company met quota, but also so have most of the regions. The performance index, the ratio of sales to quota, is greater than 100 for five regions. Four regions fell short of their targets, but three of those came very close. Only the east north-central region fell short by more than 2 percent, but it still had the highest absolute dollar value of sales of any of the major regions. Many sales managers might be tempted from this to assume all is well. At the most, they might send a letter to the manager of the east north-central region, urging her to push the salespeople in the region to do better. Fortunately, the sales manager for Kitchenware did neither. Rather he simply interrogated the information system to generate the sales breakdown for the east north-central region, shown in Exhibit 14.7. The state quotas were determined by multiplying the BPI total U.S. percentages for each state by the $420 million total forecasted sales. In many cases, the firm might wish to convert each percentage to a percentage of the region, rather than of the United States as a whole. Thus, the percentage for Illinois would be (6.0037 ÷ 20.1419) × 100 = 29.8; this percentage would then be applied to the $8.60 million quota for the region to get the quota for Illinois. Although the result is the same, this second alternative provides a clearer picture of the concentration of demand in the region; the benefit holds particularly when one works with smaller and smaller units of analysis.

Exhibit 14.7 shows a problem with sales throughout the region. Only the sales representatives in Indiana exceeded quota, and then only slightly. Note that the deviations about quota are larger than they were in Exhibit 14.6. This generally happens as one moves to smaller units of analysis. With larger aggregates—for example, regions versus states—the statistician's law of large numbers seems to apply in that the pluses and minuses about quota tend to balance each other; thus, the performance indexes in the larger analysis tend to be closer to 100. A smaller deviation from quota should initiate further

Electronic Data Interchange and Relationships

In the retail business, barcoding and scanning have changed the nature of sales data in many ways. For example, electronic data interchange (EDI) means that retailers know at the time something is purchased that more needs to be ordered. Quick response systems, or computer systems used by their suppliers, then schedule the replacement items for delivery and ensure that products flow continuously through the retail locations. Such systems minimize costs and help improve profits for both companies.

More importantly, however, sales executives can now track how minute changes in price at the retailer's shelf, in-store promotion, and other factors impact sales. For example, Martin Newman Shoes tracks sales at its 14 stores by using computerized cash registers. Brown Shoe, Martin Newman's primary vendor, can use the computerized ordering system to track the effectiveness of sales promotions in the various Martin Newman stores. With this information, the Brown salesperson can help each Martin Newman store manager plan sales promotions and merchandise products more effectively. By helping each manager do a more effective job, the Brown salesperson keeps other vendors out of his biggest account.

Similarly, Mott's USA uses FastTrack sales automation software, TIPS promotion expense software, and data from IRI (a third-party supplier of grocery sales data) on market share for Mott's apple juice to show how well Mott's products have sold. Mott's salespeople can show buyers how Mott's has done in their store compared to competitors, how well sales promotions have worked, and other vital information that helps Mott's build stronger relationships with each buyer.

Sources: Michael Levy and Barton Weitz, *Retailing,* 2d ed. (Burr Ridge, IL: Irwin, 1995), p. 248; Scott Corriveau, "Mott's USA Empowers Brokers," *Sales and Marketing Strategies & News* (June–July 1996), p. 24.

Exhibit 14.7 Sales Breakdown for East North-Central Region

State	BPI (percentage of U.S.)	Sales Quota ($ millions)	Sales ($ millions)	Difference ($ millions)	Performance Index ($PI = S/Q \times 100$)
Illinois	6.0037%	$25.22	$24.30	$-0.92	96.4
Indiana	2.4103	10.12	10.24	0.12	101.2
Michigan	4.6401	19.49	17.77	-1.72	91.2
Ohio	4.9764	20.90	20.43	-0.47	97.8
Wisconsin	2.1114	8.87	6.74	-2.13	76.0
Total region	20.1419%	$84.60	$79.48	$-5.12	94.0

investigation when the analysis is based on large aggregates (regions) rather than on small ones (salespeople). Although there is some negative deviation in actual sales from standard in Exhibit 14.7 among four of the five states, the deviation in Wisconsin is most pronounced. Only 76 percent of the quota was realized here.

Again, it would be very easy for a sales manager to take impulsive action. Instead of getting on a plane to Wisconsin, having the east north-central regional manager call the Wisconsin district manager, or calling himself, the Kitchenware general sales manager looked at the tabulation of sales by sales representatives in the Wisconsin district. The eight areas into which the state is divided are shown in Exhibit 14.8 and the results of the tabulation are shown in Exhibit 14.9. Sales are below quota in all sales areas in the state.

Exhibit 14.8 Sales Territories in Wisconsin

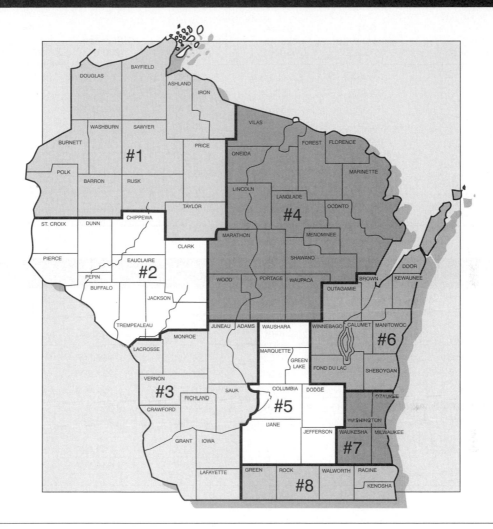

This suggests there may be something fundamentally wrong. Perhaps economic conditions are poor and unemployment is high; perhaps competition is more intense than in other areas; or there may be a problem with sales force morale and motivation. Although there are many plausible explanations for the sales manager to check, the core problem seems to be Hutchins. If he had done as well as the other sales reps in the state, sales for the district would have been much closer to target. The problem is particularly acute because Hutchins has the prime Milwaukee market as his sales territory. Before taking action about Hutchins, the sales manager wanted more information. Consequently, he requested the tabulation of Hutchins's sales by product, shown in Exhibit 14.10. Hutchins is below quota on the entire product line; however, he seems to be having the most problem with coffee makers and blenders/mixers/food processors.

Is the problem Hutchins or these products? A further analysis of sales of these products by customer indicated the problem was concentrated among large department store buyers. Furthermore, the problem was not unique to Hutchins but was common to all reps

Exhibit 14.9   Sales by Representative in the Wisconsin District

Area Representative	BPI (percentage of U.S.)	Sales Quota ($000)	Sales ($000)	Difference ($000)	Performance Index ($PI = S/Q \times 100$)
1. T. Tate	0.0953%	$ 400.2	$ 392.6	$ −7.6	98.1
2. T. Bir	0.1332	559.4	501.0	−58.4	89.6
3. C. Holzem	0.1325	556.5	512.4	−44.1	92.1
4. A. Elliott	0.2021	848.8	768.7	−80.1	90.6
5. P. Martin	0.2596	1,090.3	969.3	−121.0	88.9
6. J. Campbell	0.3384	1,421.3	1,340.3	−81.0	94.3
7. L. Hutchins	0.6975	2,929.5	1,285.0	−1,644.5	43.9
8. B. Lessner	0.2528	1,061.8	970.5	−91.3	91.4
Total Wisconsin	2.1114%	$8,867.8	$6,739.8	$−2,128.0	76.0

Exhibit 14.10   Hutchins's Sales by Product

Product	Sales Quota	Sales	Difference	Performance Index ($PI = S/Q \times 100$)
Can openers/knife sharpeners	$ 212,000	$ 124,500	$ −87,500	58.7
Toasters	468,000	237,000	−231,000	50.6
Coffee makers	627,000	176,000	−451,000	28.1
Blenders/mixers/food processors	604,000	159,200	−444,800	26.4
Griddles/electric fry pans	573,000	340,000	−233,000	59.3
Other—electric carving knives/popcorn makers/hot trays, etc.	445,500	248,300	−197,200	55.7
Total	$2,929,500	$1,285,000	$−1,644,500	43.9

in the east and west north-central regions. A major competitor had been attempting to improve its position in the north-central region through a combination of heavy advertising and purchase rebate offers on these products. This problem had been obscured in other sales territories because sales of other products had compensated for lost sales in coffee makers and blenders/mixers/food processors. Hutchins's sales of other products did not make up the deficit. The problem was compounded by an economic slowdown in the metal-working industry, a big employer in the Milwaukee area.

The problem then is not Hutchins. Rather, it is the special competitive situation in the north-central region. This situation would not have come to light without the sales analysis. One important principle illustrated by the preceding example is that aggregate figures can be deceiving and small, visible problems are often symptoms of large, unseen problems. The phenomenon has been linked to an iceberg. Only about 10 percent of an iceberg's mass is above the water level. The other 90 percent is below the surface, and not always directly below it either. The submerged portion can be very dangerous to ships. So it is with much marketing and business data.

The typical business engages in many varied activities and collects large volumes of data to support these activities. Thus, it is very common for difficulties or problems in one area to be submerged. On the surface, all appears calm and peaceful, but more careful analyses may reveal submerged problems with jagged edges that can "sink the business" if they are not attended to properly. Those analyzing the information that is collected need to be especially wary that the summaries they produce by aggregating and averaging data do not hide more than they reveal.

The iceberg principle is pervasive. The 80:20 rule or concentration ratio discussed earlier is one manifestation of it. Often, the concentration of sales within certain territories, products, or customers hides specific weaknesses. More than one company has shown satisfactory total sales, but when the total was subdivided by territories, customers, and products, serious weaknesses were uncovered.

The preceding example also shows the difference between a simple sales analysis and a comparative sales analysis, as well as the advantages of the latter. The simple sales analysis would have focused on the sales data in Exhibit 14.6; it would not have examined the differences from quota, but simply the raw figures. It probably would not have generated any detailed investigation of the east north-central region because sales there were higher than in any other region. The comparison with quota, however, emphasized that the potential in this region was also greater than in any other and the firm was failing to get its share. The comparative analysis triggered the more intensive investigation and isolated the primary reason for the sales shortfall. The execution of the process depended on having sales quotas available on a very small basis. They had to be available by customer, by product, and by salesperson or the problem would never have come to light.

Quotas are sometimes difficult to generate on such a small basis. In the Kitchenware Company, it was possible because detailed geographic statistics on the BPI were available. In situations where other data should be used, they need to be available by small geographic area. That is one reason the sales planning and sales evaluation questions are so intertwined. One must keep in mind the questions of evaluation and the comparisons needed when designing sales territories and sales quotas.

Another concept the example illustrates is the principle of "isolate and explode," in which the most significant discrepancies between actual and standard are identified, or isolated, and then examined in detail, or exploded. The detail this explosion reveals is then analyzed, the most significant discrepancies are again isolated, and these are exploded. The process continues until the "real" problems are isolated. Thus, in the Kitchenware example, the following were all isolated and exploded in turn: the east north-central region, the Wisconsin district, Hutchins's sales by product, and Hutchins's product sales by customer.

An alternative would have been to have masses of data available to the sales manager initially. For example, the information system could have supplied the sales manager with the detailed tabulations of sales by each salesperson of each product to each customer in the beginning. More than likely, such a tabulation would go unused because of its size and the time it would take to decipher its contents. The isolate-and-explode principle makes the task manageable. The sales manager can quickly localize trouble spots by focusing on the most substantial exceptions from standard and then home in more efficiently on an effective cure.

The principle can also be used to isolate exceptional performances for the clues they might provide to what the firm is doing right. Investigating why the east south-central region was 5.1 percent over quota when the entire company was only 0.3 percent over quota might suggest effective competitive strategies.

The isolate-and-explode principle assumes the company's information system can provide sales data hierarchically. In Kitchenware, the sales manager could secure data

Exhibit 14.11   Hierarchical Sales Analyses Possible in Kitchenware Company

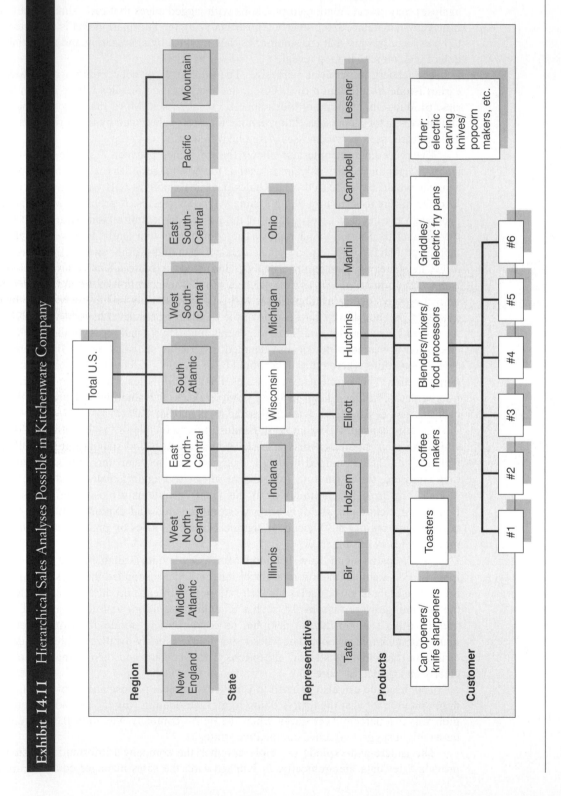

broken out by customer, by product, by sales rep, by district, and by region (see Exhibit 14.11). The breakdowns resemble a tree: Total U.S. sales are the trunk, regions are the main limbs, districts the next branches, and so on. Further, all combinations of these branches are possible. For example, it is possible to do a study by product and territory, or by customer and product. These alternate types of analysis can also be productive, as can simple one-way categorizing of sales data. The simple tabulation of sales by product, for example, is very useful in showing a firm's product line strengths. Similarly, the simple tabulation of sales by major classes of customers is often informative about the company's market strengths.

Keep in mind that these analyses are diagnostics, not decision rules. They do not tell the manager what to do, but only offer clues as to causes of problems. And sales analyses are only part of the story. Sales managers might want to consider other factors when evaluating salespeople. That is why cost and other analyses also play a role in the evaluation of salespeople.

SUMMARY

This chapter is the first of three to discuss management evaluation and control of the field selling effort. The most thorough evaluation mechanism is a marketing audit, which is a complete, systematic, objective evaluation of the total marketing effort of the firm. The sales management audit is an example of a vertical audit because it is the detailed analysis of one part of the total marketing effort. The sales management audit should examine objectives, policies, organization, methods, and procedures used in managing the personal selling function, as well as assess how individual personnel are performing.

A sales analysis can be one of the more revealing inputs in a performance appraisal. A sales analysis involves gathering, classifying, comparing, and studying company sales data. The study may simply involve the comparison of total company sales in two time periods, or it may subject thousands of component sales figures to a variety of comparisons. One real benefit of a sales analysis is in highlighting the concentration ratio, or the 80:20 principle, for products, customers, and the like.

Those wishing to make a sales analysis must decide at least three things. First, the sales manager must decide the type of control system to be used. Will it involve simple or comparative sales analyses? Will it

be one that provides all relevant comparisons, or one that reports only significant exceptions, or some combination of these schemes? Second, the source documents must be pinpointed or designed. The sales invoice is typically one of the most useful source documents, so great care must go into its design. Third, the sales manager must decide which variables are to serve as points of aggregation—for example, geographic regions, products, or salespeople. Most likely, the manager will want the input records to be maintained disaggregatively, so hierarchical sales analyses can be conducted. A hierarchical sales analysis involves the investigation of sales by several components when the components are considered simultaneously.

One productive way to conduct a sales analysis is via the principle of isolate and explode, in which the most significant discrepancies between actual and standard are isolated and then exploded. The detail this explosion reveals is then analyzed, the most significant discrepancies are noted, and these are exploded. A rather common output of an isolate-and-explode analysis is to find that small, barely visible problems are often underlying symptoms of large, invisible problems, much like an iceberg; thus, the phenomenon has been referred to as the iceberg principle.

DISCUSSION QUESTIONS

1. In the typical case, management by exception leads to a close examination of below-par situations. Only sales

representatives who are not meeting objectives, products that are not selling according to expectations, and customers who are not buying products as predicted are carefully reviewed to determine corrective action. What arguments can be advanced for conducting a close examination of the opposite, above-par situations?

2. The use of scanner data collected at the time of checkout in supermarkets has increased dramatically in sales analysis. One company has recruited families nationwide to participate in a panel study. When a shopper enters the checkout lane, he or she gives the clerk a plastic card that is passed over the scanner. All items purchased that are scanned are recorded in the shopper's diary. Oscar Mayer, a Wisconsin-based producer of meat, turkey, and seafood, has used different advertising campaigns in several markets to determine which ad campaign was most effective. How else could Oscar Mayer and other companies use scanner data? Of what value would scanner data be to sales reps? To food retailers? What are other industries that could benefit from the same type of data?

3. The Recall Computer Co. has six territories, each represented by one sales rep. After extensive planning, the company determines that each territory would be expected to achieve the following percentages of total company sales for 2001:

Territory 1	27%	Territory 4	12%
Territory 2	15	Territory 5	20
Territory 3	18	Territory 6	8

These figures are used as the standard for comparing each sales representative's actual 2001 sales. The company projected sales for 2001 of $18,500,000. Determine which sales representative's territory had the best performance, by using the performance index, if the actual sales for 2001 in each territory were $5,425,000, $3,205,000, $3,710,000, $2,400,000, $3,900,000, and $2,000,000, respectively.

4. The use of enterprise software and networked contact management software by managers has been viewed as an invasion of privacy by some salespeople. According to one critic, "Sales information is transmitted immediately, and I don't have a chance to explain any strange variations." Another commented, "This is like 'Big Brother' watching me. Before, my sales manager couldn't care less; now he's on my back constantly." Comment. Are these views justifiable?

5. The Amjoy Corporation has developed a series of ratios to evaluate regional, district, and individual perfor-

mance. Upper and lower control limits permit quick identification of significant deviations. The accompanying chart shows the sales-expense–to–sales ratio for Barbara Smith. What does this chart reveal? What action, if any, should Barbara's district sales manager take?

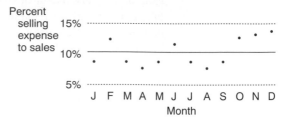

6. In planning a sales analysis system, one must consider that information needs vary from district sales manager to regional sales manager to national sales manager. Give specific examples of how information needs vary among individuals.

7. On the basis of a marketing audit, Crosby Chemical, a manufacturer of industrial cleaning compounds and solvents, decided to develop market potentials for each of its sales territories, both domestic and international, and to use these potentials to develop quotas, which would be used to assess each salesperson's performance. The first year's results are in, and Andrea Parrett has complained loudly and continuously to her manager Irma Pelton about her most recent performance evaluation. Parrett produced a 16 percent sales increase in her Venezuelan territory, but was given a below-average performance evaluation using the company's new criterion of sales versus quota. Pelton explained to Parrett that the company used the same criteria—number of establishments and number of employees—to establish the market potential for its products in Venezuela that it had used for other territories. Parrett countered that those criteria were inappropriate in Venezuela. Not only was there less manufacturing equipment per person in Venezuela, and thus less cleanup per employee, but also users of the cleaning compounds were more likely to reuse them in Venezuela than in other countries where single use and disposal were the norms. What would you recommend Pelton do, particularly given the fact that Parrett had been considered one of the company's top young salespeople?

EXPERIENTIAL APPLICATION

Divide into groups of three. Using the material found in the chapter exhibits and in the following tables, each person in the group should take on a salesperson role. (One of the group will be Hutchins, another person will be Tate, and the third will be Holzem.) Role-play a meeting with each rep to discuss performance. Each member of the group will take turns being the sales manager, and the extra person will observe, using the table below. (Note, each person should individually determine the performance index for Tate and Holzem.)

Person	Role Play 1	Role Play 2	Role Play 3
1	Hutchins	Sales Manager	Observer
2	Observer	Tate	Sales Manager
3	Sales Manager	Observer	Holzem

Now assess performance by product. (For Hutchins, use Exhibit 14.10.)

	Tate		Holzem	
Product	**Quota**	**Sales**	**Quota**	**Sales**
Can openers/ knife sharpeners	29,000	40,300	40,000	52,300
Toasters	64,000	77,800	89,000	103,500
Coffee makers	86,000	57,000	119,000	57,000
Blenders/mixers/ food processors	82,000	46,900	114,600	50,100
Griddles/electric fry pans	80,000	101,000	111,300	153,000
Other	59,200	69,600	82,600	96,500
Total	400,200	392,600	556,500	512,400

INTERNET EXERCISE

Open the Rush Truck Centers home page (*rushtruckcenters.com*) and click on *Trucks*. This will take you to a page where you can search for used trucks in its inventory to purchase. Put in a year (98 will do) and hit search. What you will see is page after page describing the trucks. Note all of the different features they list. Each of these features represents a different price and profit. Create a grid using that information to show how a sales manager could develop a performance analysis for Rush salespeople. What other analyses or performance measures might a manager want to use?

SUGGESTED READINGS

Challagalla, Goutam, and Tasadduq A. Shervanti, "A Measurement Model of the Dimensions and Types of Output and Behavior Control: An Empirical Test in a Salesforce Context," *Journal of Business Research* 39 (July 1997), pp. 159–72.

Cravens, David W., Raymond LaForge, Gregory M. Pickett, and Clifford E. Young, "Incorporating a Quality Improvement Perspective into Measures of Salesperson Performance," *Journal of Personal Selling and Sales Management* 13 (Winter 1993), pp. 1–14.

Jaworski, Bernard, Vlasis Stathakopoulos, and Shanker Krishan, "Control Combinations in Marketing: Conceptual Framework and Empirical Evidence," *Journal of Marketing* 57 (January 1993), pp. 57–69.

Kaplan, Robert S., "Devising a Balanced Scorecard Matched to Business Strategy," *Planning Review* (September–October 1994), pp. 15–19, 48.

Kaplan, Robert S., and David P. Norton, "Putting the Balanced Scorecard to Work," *Harvard Business Review,* (September–October 1993), pp. 134–42.

Kaplan, Robert S., and David P. Norton, "Using the Balanced Scorecard as a Strategic Management System," *Harvard Business Review* (September–October 1993), pp. 75–85.

Reed, Richard, David J. Lemak, and Joseph C. Montgomery, "Beyond Process: TQM Content and Firm Performance," *Academy of Management Review* 21, no. 1 (1996), pp. 173–202.

Rothe, James T., Michael G. Harvey, and Candice Jackson, "The Marketing Audit: Five Decades Later," *Journal of Marketing Theory and Practice* 5 (Summer 1997), pp. 1–16.

15 Cost Analysis

ANALYZING COSTS FOR PROFITABLE SALES

Seymour Barker is the director of the buying group for Whirlpool's Kitchenaid and Major Appliance Division in Benton Harbor, Michigan. His job is to develop national group sales programs, the programs that Whirlpool salespeople offer to certain types of retailers.

Barker recently had the challenge of creating a sales program for small appliance stores and chains, a group that is being driven out of business by the larger, national chains. Yet, Barker was tasked with figuring out a way to increase sales through these types of stores. "Since the businesses in this particular group were actually losing share, I knew that would pose a stumbling block to negotiating a volume increase for us. If you push too hard, you run the risk of losing the customer because they feel they cannot commit to the terms of the program that you want them to sign up for. In the end, I had to discuss the issue with our VP and get him to realize that we were dealing with shrinking opportunities in that channel."

One of the challenges in putting such programs together is determining a price which allows both the retailer and Whirlpool to make money. When salespeople call on these smaller retailers, there are two costs involved: the actual dollars spent in terms of salesperson salary and travel expenses, plus the opportunity cost of the salesperson's time that could have been spent on larger retailers. Barker, and other sales managers like him, must have the right cost information to know whether continuing to serve such channels is profitable and what price to charge.

"The deal I finally concluded . . . was one where we agreed that this customer group could receive the benefits of the merchandising program if they were able to maintain their market share, which satisfied both customers and management. I really enjoy selling and the opportunity it gives me to develop creative solutions to problems while working with an infinite set of resources."

Source: Barton A. Weitz, Stephen B. Castleberry, and John F. Tanner, Jr., *Selling: Building Partnerships,* 3d ed.(New York: Irwin/McGraw–Hill, 1998), pp. 84–86.

Visit Whirlpool at its Web site, *www.whirlpool.com.*

LEARNING OBJECTIVES

Many students of sales and marketing like to focus on the revenue side. They migrate to sales positions because making things happen is a function of creating business. But costs are important, too, and managing costs carefully is often the difference between a thriving business and one that struggles to exist.

After completing this chapter, you should be able to:

- Select the appropriate cost allocation method for various sales management situations.

- Describe how such methods would be implemented.

- Discuss the importance of return on assets managed (ROAM) and be able to calculate ROAM.

- Apply financial cost analysis to sales management situations in order to make decisions.

Not too long ago, a company (which asked to remain nameless) set a goal for a particular product of selling 100,000 units. It dropped two products that were similar and increased sales for the preferred product from 70,000 units to three times the goal, or 300,000 units. The sales force had their best year ever, making more money per rep than ever before. Yet, every unit they sold cost an average $2.00 in losses.[1] How could this happen?

Over a half-million dollars was lost because information concerning performance wasn't gathered and shared on a timely basis. Costs were higher than expected, prices were lower than expected as more buyers took advantage of quantity discounts, and, worse, the information didn't reach decision makers in time.

Cost analysis is complementary to sales analysis in the management of the personal selling effort. While sales analysis focuses on the results achieved, cost analysis looks at the costs incurred in producing those results and whether the returns justify the expenditures. As the opening scenario suggests, sales increases do not always produce profit increases. To determine whether the returns justify the expenditures, it is necessary to gather, classify, compare, and study marketing cost data, which is the essence of marketing cost analysis. (See how one salesperson uses cost analysis to prove to his customers that he saves them money in "Managing Sales Relationships.")

Marketing cost analysis can help identify opportunities for increasing the effectiveness of marketing expenditures. Sales are achieved at some cost, and marketing productivity focuses on the sales or profit output per unit of marketing effort input. Unfortunately, it is often difficult for a firm to know what the output/input relationships are without detailed analyses.

Most firms today produce multiple products, which they sell in multiple markets. For each product and market, the mix of marketing elements differs. Only by analyzing specific relationships among these products and markets can the firm hope to identify situations where marketing input should be increased or altered, where it should remain at historic levels, and where it should be decreased. These insights are simply not produced by the information that flows from normal accounting operations. Similarly, to deploy the firm's salespeople most effectively, the sales manager needs to appreciate the output/input relationships by product, territory, customer, channel of distribution, and so on. Marketing cost analysis estimates these relationships.

COST ANALYSIS DEVELOPMENT

Sales management has been somewhat slower to adopt cost analysis (or, as it is sometimes called, profitability analysis) than sales analysis for managing the sales function.

Proving Contribution to Customers

Costs are important for all companies to manage. That's why Tim Pavlovich, sales representative for Carlton–Bates, creates contribution reports for his major accounts. "In my major accounts, I work with people at all levels. Sometimes, the senior executives are not fully aware of what Carlton–Bates has been able to do for them." Keeping everyone in the account aware of what Carlton–Bates has done, particularly in the area of saving the company money, is a real challenge but crucial in order to develop partnerships.

Carlton–Bates (C–B) is an electronics parts distributor. Headquartered in Little Rock, Arkansas, it has offices all over the country. Pavlovich began working for C–B right out of college and has enjoyed substantial success. But the job has not been without its challenges.

"I worked on a tooling solution with the head of the maintenance department in one account, and he submitted my solution to purchasing but forgot to specify me as the vendor," recalled Pavlovich. As a result, C–B didn't get that business. "Now, every time I see someone, I let purchasing know what I'm doing."

Pavlovich then used the contribution report to gain access to the president of the company. "The report is an introduction and a work-in-progress list, too," says Pavlovich. The report details how C–B delivers, stocks, provides engineering support, offers special pricing, and preassembles products for the customer. All of these activities save the customer money, which Pavlovich details. "Most higher execs will not see sales reps but after they see this, they are excited. The cost savings *are* important!"

Pavlovich believes these contribution reports are a critical element in building partnerships. He notes that he "tried starting at the bottom of the chain and working up, but things seem to mover quicker top-down." Documenting and proving cost savings gives him the access to the top that he needs.

The empirical evidence indicates that if they do it at all, firms are most likely to conduct profitability analyses for products, and are less likely to do it for customers. Only about half of all companies do it for any one of these bases, and less than a third analyze profits by all four bases of products, territories, salespeople, and customers.[2]

One apparent reason for this neglect seems to be that most accounting systems are still not designed to meet the needs of marketing management, in that they were originally designed to report the aggregate effects of a firm's operations to its creditors and stockholders. They were subsequently modified to provide a better handle on the production operations of the firm, so most accounting systems are currently oriented toward external reporting and production cost analysis. This orientation is unfortunate because a company can realize many benefits from carefully conducted marketing cost and profitability analyses.

Not all accounting systems, however, are suited to the types of cost and profitability analysis needed by sales executives. Accounting systems measure financial performance: costs and revenue. For a sales manager, the key is to understand how costs are allocated so that the true profitability of any particular area, product, or market can be determined. Any accounting system can take the direct cost of supplies and components and add those together to come up with the cost of a product. The challenge is adding into the cost of that product costs for management, office supplies, warehousing, and so forth. There are three approaches to cost allocation: full costing, contribution analysis, and activity-based costing (ABC). Choice of a costing approach is very important to sales managers; territories have been mistakenly cut, for example, because the accounting information used by managers didn't allocate costs appropriately.

Full Cost versus Contribution Margin

The more popular and traditional methods of accounting are the full-cost (or, as it is sometimes called, net profit) approach and the contribution margin approach. The argument over which should be used has generated controversy through the years.[3] To appreciate the controversy fully, it is helpful to understand the differences between direct and indirect costs and specific and general expenses.

A direct cost can be specifically identified with a product or a function.[4] The cost is incurred because the product or function exists or is contemplated. If the product or function were eliminated, the cost would also disappear. An example is inventory carrying costs for a product.

An indirect cost is a shared cost because it is tied to several functions or products. Even if one of the products or functions were eliminated, the cost would not be. Rather, the share of the cost previously borne by the product or function that was eliminated would shift to the remaining products or functions. An example of an indirect cost is the travel expenses of a salesperson selling a multiple product line. Even if one product the rep sells is eliminated, the travel cost would not be.

The profit and loss or net income statement typically distinguishes between costs and expenses. The term *costs* is often restricted to the materials, labor, power, rent, and so on used in making the product. The cost of goods sold on the following conceptual net income statement reflects these costs.

Sales

Less: Cost of goods sold
_____
        Gross margin

Less: General administrative and selling expenses
_____
        Profit or net income before taxes

The expenses reflect the other costs incurred in operating the business, such as the cost of advertising and of maintaining branches. Expenses cannot be tied nearly as well as costs to specific products, since they are general expenses associated with doing business. In marketing cost analysis, the distinction between costs and expenses is not nearly so clear, and the terms are often used interchangeably.

Just like costs, expenses can be classified into two broad categories: specific and general expenses. A specific expense is just like a direct cost—it can be identified with a specific product or function. The expense would be eliminated if the product or function were eliminated. If the product were eliminated, for example, the specific expense of the product manager's salary need not be incurred.

A general expense is like an indirect cost—it cannot be identified directly with a specific object of profit measurement such as a territory, salesperson, or product. Thus, the expense would not be eliminated if the specific object were eliminated. An example is the sales manager's salary when the object of measurement is a product in a multiple-product company. The elimination of the product would not eliminate this salary.

A particular cost or expense may be direct for some measurement purposes and indirect for others. The object of the measurement determines how the cost should be treated.

If this is a product line, costs directly associated with the manufacture and sales of the product line are direct. All other costs in the business are indirect. If the object of measurement shifts to a sales territory, some of the costs of product-line measurement, which were direct, will remain direct costs now associated with the territory; some will become indirect; and others that were indirect will become direct. For example:[5]

	Object of Measurement	
Cost	Product	Territory
Sales promotion display	Direct	Direct
Sales rep compensation	Indirect	Direct
Product-line manager's salary	Direct	Indirect
Corporate president's salary	Indirect	Indirect

As mentioned, there is controversy about whether one should use a full-cost or contribution margin approach in marketing cost analysis. Proponents of the full-cost or net profit approach argue that all costs should be assigned and somehow accounted for in determining the profitability of any segment (e.g., territory, product, salesperson) of the business.

Under this approach, each unit bears not only its own direct costs that can be traced to it, but also a share of the company's cost of doing business, referred to as indirect costs. Full-costing advocates argue that many of the indirect costs can be assigned to the unit being costed on the basis of a demonstrable cost relationship. If a strong relationship does not exist, the cost must be prorated on as reasonable a basis as possible. Under the full-costing approach, a net income for each marketing segment can be determined by matching the segment's revenue with its direct and its share of indirect costs.[6]

Contribution margin advocates argue, on the other hand, that it is misleading to allocate costs arbitrarily. They suggest that only those costs that can be specifically identified with the segment of the business should be deducted from the revenue produced by the segment to determine how well the segment is doing. Any excess of revenues over these costs contributes to the common costs of the business and thereby to profits. The contribution margin approach does not distinguish where the costs are incurred, but rather simply whether they are variable or fixed. Thus, the difference between sales and all variable costs, whether they originate in manufacturing, selling, or some administrative function, are subtracted from revenues or sales to produce the contribution margin of the segment.

The net profit approach does attempt to determine where the costs were incurred. The difference in perspectives is highlighted in Exhibit 15.1. Not only is segment net income derived differently in the two approaches, but also advocates of the contribution margin approach do not even focus on net income when evaluating the profitability of a segment of the business. Rather, they focus on the contribution produced by the segment after subtracting the costs directly traceable to it from its sales.

The contribution margin advocates are winning the controversy. Although the early emphasis in accounting for distribution costs was on full-cost allocation,[7] the recent emphasis is on the contribution margin approach.[8] The contribution margin approach has unmistakable logic. If the costs associated with the segment are not removed with the elimination of the segment, why should they be arbitrarily allocated? That just confuses things and provides a blurred, distorted picture for management decision making. The costs still have to be borne after the segment is eliminated, but they must be borne by other segments of the business. Such allocation can simply tax the ability of these other segments to remain profitable. Exhibits 15.2 and 15.3 illustrate this phenomenon.

The example involves a department store with three main departments. The administrative expenses in Exhibit 15.2 are all fixed costs; they were allocated to departments on the basis of the total percentage of sales accounted for by each department. This is a common allocation basis about which more will be said later. Those who embrace the full-cost approach would argue that Department 1 should be eliminated because of the net loss of $12,500 it is producing.

Exhibit 15.1 Differences in Perspective between Full-Cost and Contribution Margin Approaches to Marketing Cost Analysis

Full-Cost Approach		Contribution Margin Approach	
	Sales		Sales
Less:	Cost of goods sold	Less:	Variable manufacturing costs
Equal:	Gross margin	Less:	Other variable costs directly traceable to the segment
		Equal:	Contribution margin
Less:	Operating expenses (including the segment's allocated share of company administration and general expenses)	Less:	Fixed costs directly traceable to products Fixed costs directly traceable to the market segment
Equal:	Segment net income	Equal:	Segment net income

Exhibit 15.2 Profit and Loss Statement by Departments Using a Full-Cost Approach

	Totals	Department 1	Department 2	Department 3
Sales	$500,000	$250,000	$150,000	$100,000
Cost of goods sold	400,000	225,000	125,000	50,000
Gross margin	100,000	25,000	25,000	50,000
Other expenses:				
Selling expenses	25,000	12,500	7,500	5,000
Administrative expenses	50,000	25,000	15,000	10,000
Total other expenses	75,000	37,500	22,500	15,000
Net profit (loss)	25,000	(12,500)	2,500	35,000

Exhibit 15.3 Profit and Loss Statement if Department 1 Were Eliminated

	Total	Department 2	Department 3
Sales	$250,000	$150,000	$100,000
Cost of goods sold	175,000	125,000	50,000
Gross margin	75,000	25,000	50,000
Other expenses:			
Selling expenses	12,500	7,500	5,000
Administrative expenses	50,000	30,000	20,000
Total other expenses	62,500	37,500	25,000
Net profit (loss)	12,500	(12,500)	25,000

Exhibit 15.4   Contribution Margin by Departments

	Totals	Department 1	Department 2	Department 3
Sales	$500,000	$250,000	$150,000	$100,000
Variable costs:				
Cost of goods sold	400,000	225,000	125,000	50,000
Selling expenses	25,000	12,500	7,500	5,000
Total variable costs	425,000	237,500	132,500	55,000
Contribution margin	75,000	12,500	17,500	45,000
Fixed costs:				
Administrative expenses	50,000			
Net profit	25,000			

Note what would happen if this were pursued. First, the sales of the department would be lost, but $12,500 of selling expenses would also be eliminated. However, the $25,000 of fixed costs must now be borne by the other departments. Allocating these costs on the basis of percentage of sales suggests that Department 2 is unprofitable (see Exhibit 15.3). If one used the same argument as before, it too should be considered for elimination. Then the $50,000 of administrative expenses would be borne entirely by Department 3, making Department 3 (the entire store) unprofitable. That would suggest the store be closed, meaning management would close a profitable store simply because one department displayed a small dollar loss—a loss that could be attributed to an arbitrary allocation of fixed costs. Department 1, in fact, makes a positive contribution to profits, as the contribution margin statement in Exhibit 15.4 shows.

A contribution margin versus a full-cost profitability analysis is also supported by the recognition that most marketing phenomena are highly interrelated. For example, the demand for one product in a multiproduct company is often influenced by the availability of others, while the absence of a product may cause the sale of another product to decline. The entire product line may be greater than the sum of its parts in terms of sales and profits. The same argument applies to other elements of the marketing mix. They have interdependent effects. The contribution margin approach implicitly recognizes this synergy through its emphasis on the contribution of each segment or part.

In sum, allocations of indirect costs for segment performance evaluation are generally inappropriate. That is, any measure of segment performance that includes allocated shares of indirect costs includes factors that do not really reflect performance in the segment as a separate entity. Hence, indirect cost allocations should not be made if the purpose is to measure true performance.

ABC Accounting   Activity-based costing (ABC) allocates fixed costs to products or other units (such as a sales office) according to the activity that creates or drives the cost. For example, suppose a sales office is responsible for selling two products and has only one team of salespeople selling both products. Each product represents 50 percent of the office's sales. The important activity in this situation would be the number of sales calls per product. If digital wamometers (DW) take three sales calls to close and tricometers take 2 sales calls to close, then the total calls to close two sales (one of each product) is five. The DW is allocated 60 percent of the office's costs because it is more difficult to sell, and the tricometer gets 40 percent. Contribution or full-cost approaches would allocate 50 percent of fixed

	Digital Wamometer			Tricometer
Sales	$545			$545
Less variable costs[1]	320			335
Contribution margin	$225			$210
		Contribution Method		
Less fixed mfg. costs[2]	85	50	50	15
Less fixed selling costs[3]	30	25	25	20
Income using ABC	$110			$185
Income using contribution		$150	$135	

Exhibit 15.5 Comparison of Contribution and ABC Methods

[1] Includes commission paid to salespeople as well as direct manufacturing and shipping costs.
[2] Total fixed mfg. costs = $100 but allocated based on complexity of setup and other activities in mfg. process in ABC.
[3] Total fixed selling costs (administrative overhead and sales office expenses) = $50, but allocated on the basis of digital wamometer requiring six calls to every four for the tricometer using ABC.

Source: Robert A. Dwyer and John F. Tanner, Jr., *Business Marketing: Connecting Strategy Relationships and Learning* (New York: McGraw–Hill, 1999).

costs to each product on the basis of sales volume. Note the difference in income in Exhibit 15.5; would management decisions be the same using ABC versus the contribution approach?

PROCEDURE

The general procedure followed in conducting a cost or profitability analysis first involves specifying the purpose for which the cost study is being done. Knowing the purpose helps to determine the functional cost centers. The next step is to spread the natural account costs to these functional cost centers. Then the functional costs are allocated to appropriate segments using some reasonable basis. Finally, the allocated costs are summed, and the contribution of the segment is determined. Incidentally, the term *segment* is used here to mean a portion of the business, not in the normal sense of market segment.

The process is shown in Exhibit 15.6. Although the diagram is simple, its execution is difficult. Hard decisions about what costs or expenses are to be treated as fixed, semi-fixed, or variable and how various costs should be allocated to segments must be made.

As mentioned, the first step in a marketing profitability analysis is to determine the purpose for which it is being done. Is it designed to investigate the profitability of the various products in the line? Or is it designed to determine the profitability of sales branches, customers, or individual salespersons? The decision is essential because the treatment of the various costs and expenses depends on the purpose.

Ideally, the firm would want to break all its costs or revenues into small building blocks or modules. These elements would be as small as possible and yet still be meaningful.[9] Such a breakdown allows the firm to aggregate these building blocks as needed to produce profitability analyses for various segments of the business. An example of a basic building block or module of cost is a regional sales manager's salary, which is a general expense when the profitability of various product lines is at issue. But that same sales manager's salary is a specific expense and needs to be considered when determining the contribution to profit of the region.

Thus, good profitability analyses require that the various costs be partitioned into di-

Exhibit 15.6   Steps in Conducting a Marketing Profitability Analysis

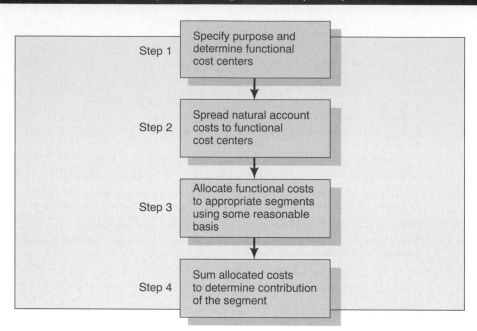

Step 1 — Specify purpose and determine functional cost centers

Step 2 — Spread natural account costs to functional cost centers

Step 3 — Allocate functional costs to appropriate segments using some reasonable basis

Step 4 — Sum allocated costs to determine contribution of the segment

rect and indirect expenses so the proper aggregations can be made. What is properly treated as direct and what should be treated as indirect or general depend on the study's purpose. Sales managers typically are most concerned with the profitability of various regions, branches, salespeople, and customers; they are only remotely concerned with the profitability of various products. Thus, a salesperson's salary is more likely to be treated as a direct than an indirect expense, whereas a product manager's salary is likely indirect, when the profitability of regions, branches, salespeople, and customers is at issue. Investigation of the profitability of the product line requires just the opposite treatment, which again illustrates the importance of specifying the purpose of the study.

In the second step of a profitability analysis, natural account costs need to be spread to the functional cost centers. Natural accounts are the categories of cost used in the normal accounting cycle. These costs include such things as salaries, wages, rent, heat, light, taxes, auto expenses, raw materials, and office supplies. They are called natural accounts because they bear the name of their expense categories.

Natural accounts are not the only way of classifying costs. In manufacturing cost accounting, for example, costs are often reclassified according to the purpose for which they were incurred. Thus, production wages might be broken into the cost categories of forging, turning, grinding, milling, polishing, and assembling. These categories are functional account categories because they recognize the function performed, which is the purpose for incurring the cost.

Marketing cost analysis has a similar orientation. It recognizes that marketing costs are incurred for some purpose, and it recognizes general selling and administrative expenses according to their purposes or functions. As Edmund D. McCarry stated so elegantly years ago, "The term *function* should be defined so as to meet the purpose for

Exhibit 15.7 Major Functional Accounts That Are Useful in Marketing Cost Analysis

- Direct selling
- Advertising and sales promotion
- Product and package design
- Technical product services
- Sales discounts and allowances
- Credit extension
- Warranty costs
- Marketing research

- Warehousing and handling
- Inventory
- Packaging, shipping, and delivery
- Order processing
- Customer service
- Billing and recording of accounts receivable
- Returned merchandise

which it is used. The function of the heart is not simply to beat, which is its activity, but rather to supply the body with a continuous flow of blood."[10]

The salaries paid in a branch office, for example, could go to perform such functions as direct selling, advertising, order processing, and extending credit. A functional cost analysis would involve spreading the total salaries paid in the office to these various functions. Exhibit 15.7 lists the major functional accounts that are useful in marketing cost analyses.

As Exhibit 15.6 indicates, the third step in conducting a cost or profitability analysis is to allocate the functional costs to the various segments of the business. One needs to recognize immediately that the bases for allocation are not fixed. Rather, they depend on the discretion of the decision maker and what he or she feels are "reasonable" bases.

One basis often used is to divide the expenses according to volume attained, which is in line with traditional cost accounting. Thus, if a regional sales manager was responsible for six branch offices, and one office produced 25 percent of the sales in the region, it would be charged with one-fourth of the sale manager's salary and expenses. This method is often used because of its simplicity.[11]

Allocating costs by sales volume is an erroneous method, however, in that it fails to recognize the purpose for which the regional sales manager's costs were incurred, which is the reason for a functional cost analysis. Maybe the branch was troublesome to manage and consumed 50 percent of the manager's time. In this case, it should bear half his salary. Alternatively, it may have run smoothly. The manager rarely had to get involved with the branch activities, so it consumed only 10 percent of his time and effort. In this case, only one-tenth of the regional sales manager's salary should be charged against the branch in determining its profit contribution. As Horngren, the eminent cost accountant, stated years ago, "The costs of efforts are independent of the results actually obtained, in the sense that the costs are programmed by management, not determined by sales. Moreover, the allocation of costs on the basis of dollar sales entails circular reasoning."[12] Thus, the trend is toward activity-based cost allocations.

The causal relationships used can, and most likely will, be different for different questions. Exhibit 15.8 shows some common bases for allocating functional costs to product groups, account size classes, and sales territories. The "Ethical Issues" feature (T&E: Travel & Entertainment or Trickery & Exploitation?) shows how important appropriate breakdowns can be deleted to manage salespeople's activities.

The fourth step in the process is to sum the costs allocated to the segment. Costs for which there is no direct causal relationship remain unallocated in determining the contribution of the segment. A comparison of the contributions of like segments then indicates the remedial action that might be taken, if any.

Exhibit 15.8   Functional Cost Groups and Bases of Allocation

Functional Cost Group	Basis of Allocation		
	To Product Groups	To Account Size Classes	To Sales Territories
1. Selling—Direct Costs: Personal calls by salespeople and supervisors on accounts and prospects. Sales salaries, incentive compensation, travel, and other expenses	Selling time devoted to each product, as shown by special sales call reports or other special studies	Number of sales calls times average time per call, as shown by special sales call reports or other special studies	Direct
2. Selling—Indirect Costs: Field supervision, field sales office expense, sales administration expenses, sales personnel training, sales management. Market research, new product development, sales statistics, tabulating services, sales accounting	In proportion to direct selling time, or time records by project	In proportion to direct selling time, or time records by project	Equal charge for each sales rep
3. Advertising: Media costs such as TV, radio, billboards, newspaper, magazine. Advertising production costs; advertising department salaries	Direct, or analysis of space and time by media, other costs in proportion to media costs	Equal charge to each account, or number of ultimate consumers and prospects in each account's trading area	Direct, or analysis of media circulation records
4. Sales Promotion: Consumer promotions such as coupons, patches, premiums. Trade promotions such as price allowances, point-of-purchase displays, cooperative advertising	Direct, or analysis of source records	Direct, or analysis of source records	Direct, or analysis of source records
5. Transportation: Railroad, truck, barge, etc., payments to carriers for delivery of finished goods from plants to warehouses and from warehouses to customers. Traffic department costs	Applicable rates times tonnages	Analysis of sampling of bills of lading	Applicable rates times tonnages
6. Storage and Shipping: Storage of finished goods inventories in warehouses. Rent (or equivalent costs), public warehouse charges, fire insurance and taxes on finished goods inventories, etc. Physical handling, assembling, and loading out	Warehouse space occupied by average inventory. Number of shipping units	Number of shipping units	Number of shipping units

(continued)

| Exhibit 15.8 *(concluded)* | | | |

| | **Basis of Allocation** | | |
Functional Cost Group	**To Product Groups**	**To Account Size Classes**	**To Sales Territories**
of rail cars, trucks, barges for shipping finished products from warehouses and mills to customers. Labor, equipment, space, and material costs.			
7. **Order Processing:** Checking and processing of orders from customers to mills for prices, weights and carload accumulation, shipping dates, coordination with production planning, transmittal to mills, etc. Pricing department. Preparation of customer invoices. Freight accounting. Credit and collection. Handling cash receipts. Provision for bad debts. Salary, supplies, space, and equipment costs (teletypes, flexowriters, etc.)	Number of order lines	Number of order lines	Number of order lines

THE PROCESS ILLUSTRATED

To illustrate the process of conducting a cost or profitability analysis, consider the situation encountered by the Baitinger Bicycle Company, in Exhibit 15.9, which was faced with a loss in its St. Louis branch of more than $160,000.[13] Suppose the sales manager is interested in further analyzing the branch to see whether the loss can be traced to particular sales reps or customers, much as the discrepancy between sales and quota was localized in Chapter 14.

The sales manager has completed the first step in a cost analysis—the manager has decided the purpose of the analysis is to isolate the profit contributions of the various sales representatives in the branch. The next thing the manager must do is spread the general selling and administrative expenses incurred by the branch in the profit and loss statement to the various functional accounts. To keep the example simple, the costs incurred in manufacturing will not be separated, although a more sophisticated contribution margin analysis would reflect such differences. Rather, the cost of goods sold is assumed to be a fixed charge to the St. Louis branch, meaning the manager needs to concentrate on spreading only the selling and administrative expenses of functional cost groups.

Exhibit 15.10 lists the functional cost categories across the top and the natural account categories along the side. The individual entries indicate how a total natural cost is apportioned according to purpose. Note that the sum of all the functional costs in a row equals the natural cost for that row; that is, all natural costs are accounted for in the spread.

The details in the division of costs depend on the operation of the branch. In this case, the branch in the previous year paid $309,000 in salaries. They were distributed in

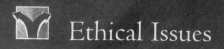

T&E: Travel & Entertainment or Trickery & Exploitation?

According to a survey conducted by *Sales & Marketing Management* magazine, 27 percent of sales managers have caught an employee cheating on an expense report. One manager remembers a salesperson who claimed to be entertaining clients at a restaurant called the Country Squire—until the company president discovered that it was a men's clothing store.

Typically, entertaining expenses include lunch, dinner, drinks, sporting events, and leisure activities. In many cultures, such as Mexico, lunch is an important time to build personal relationships, not a time to do business, as U.S. salespeople tend to think. The problem for managers is to know what is a legitimate business expense and to allow salespeople to spend the right amount. Spend too little, and the account may be lost. Spend too much, and the sale may be unprofitable.

And there's always the question of the type of entertainment. In one survey of male salespeople, nearly half reported taking a customer to a topless bar. Only 25 percent said they would rather lose a customer than go to a topless bar, and 35 percent said their company doesn't allow that kind of activity. And while no lawsuits have been filed yet with the EEOC citing topless bars as a source of sexual harassment, most women sales professionals believe such bars give male salespeople an unfair advantage.

As one salesperson says, "There's nothing wrong with entertaining the customer. Yet, when a customer cares less about the quality of your product than your readiness to treat him to an evening of simulated sex, it probably doesn't bode well for business in the long run." And managing those types of expenses is just one challenge in the T&E category.

Source: David Finn and William Moncrief, "Salesforce Entertainment Activities," *Industrial Marketing Management* (October 1990), pp. 69–73; Sarah Lorge, "T&E: Trickery & Exploitation?" *Sales & Marketing Management* (December 1997), p. 34; Rob Zieger, "Sex, Sales, & Stereotypes," *Sales & Marketing Management* (July 1995), pp. 48–51.

Exhibit 15.9 Example Profit and Loss Statement

Profit and Loss Statement for
BAITINGER BICYCLE COMPANY
St. Louis Office

Sales		$4,963,500
Cost of goods sold		4,061,000
Gross margin		902,500
Selling and administrative expenses:		
Salaries	$309,000	
Commissions	49,635	
Advertising	254,000	
Postage and office supplies	980	
Packaging materials	60,840	
Transportation charges	182,520	
Travel expenses	76,000	
Rent	130,000	
Total selling and administrative expenses		1,062,975
Net profit (loss)		$ (160,475)

Exhibit 15.10 Allocation of Natural Accounts to Functional Accounts

Natural Accounts		Functional Accounts				
		Direct Selling	Advertising	Warehousing and Shipping	Order Processing and Billing	Transportation
Salaries	$ 309,000	$257,000		$ 24,000	$28,000	
Commissions	49,635	49,635				
Advertising	254,000		$254,000			
Postage and supplies	980				980	
Packaging materials	60,840			60,840		
Transportation charges	182,520					$182,520
Travel expenses	76,000	76,000				
Rent	130,000	28,000		95,000	7,000	
	$1,062,975	$410,635	$254,000	$179,840	$35,980	$182,520

the following way: branch manager—$78,000; four salespeople—$179,000; warehouse clerk—$24,000; and a clerical person handling order processing and billing—$28,000. The salaries of the branch manager and salespeople are charged against direct selling expenses because that is the purpose for which they were incurred.

Similarly, the office and warehouse clerk salaries are charged against their main functions. The functional account direct selling is also charged with the commissions earned by the four representatives; in addition to their base salaries, all salespeople were paid a commission equal to 1 percent of sales. Advertising charges reflect both a natural account cost and a functional account cost. Advertising charges are typically maintained in a separate category in the normal accounting cycle, and their name speaks to their purpose. The same is true of transportation charges.

The postage and supplies the office consumed were used to support the order processing and billing functions, and thus they are assigned to this category. Similarly, packaging material costs are assigned to warehousing and shipping because that is the function for which they are used. Travel expenses reflect the food, lodging, and other expenses incurred by the sales representatives in carrying out their main function of selling; thus, these costs are so assigned.

Perhaps the one natural account cost that requires the most explanation is rent. The company was paying $70 per square foot for office space and $20 per square foot for warehouse space. These costs are spread to the functional accounts in proportion to the space used by each activity. More particularly, the order processing and selling functions used 100 of the 500 square feet of office space the company rented; the salespeople and sales manager used the remainder. The $95,000 assignment of rent to warehousing and shipping costs reflects the 4,750 square feet of warehouse space the company rented at $20 per square foot.

To assess the profit contribution of each salesperson, it is necessary to allocate all "relevant" functional costs to salespeople. Costs that bear some causal relationship to the level of activity should be allocated; these include salaries, commissions, and travel expenses. Conversely, costs that are not affected by the level of activity are not allocated. Office rent is an example. Even if one salesperson were fired, this cost would not change; thus, it should not be allocated.

Exhibit 15.11 provides much of the data on which the allocations to generate the profitability analysis by salesperson in Exhibit 15.12 are based. Exhibit 15.12 lists the gross margin by salesperson. From this, all direct expenses are subtracted to derive the contribution to profit by salesperson. Let us consider each expense category.

Direct Selling

The salary and commission items need little explanation; they reflect what each representative is paid and the 1 percent commission each earned on what was sold. Travel expenses per sales rep were determined by dividing total travel expenses by the number of calls to generate the cost per call, or $190. Branch accounting records allowed the identification of travel expenses by sales representative. Contact management software, such as GoldMine (see *GoldMinesw.com*) enables sales managers and salespeople to track their sales calls by type (such as new account calls, cold calls, customer calls), so sales managers can use the software to track the time they spend with field salespeople. This cost is not allocated in the example because this information was not available, and in its absence, there is not reasonable cause-and-effect basis for making the allocation.

Advertising

Panel A of Exhibit 15.11 lists the amount spent on advertising for each product. When these amounts are divided by the number of units sold, the following advertising charges per unit are generated:

$$A—\$120,000 \div 6,450 \text{ units} = \$18.60/\text{unit}$$
$$B—\$\ 80,000 \div 10,060 \text{ units} = \$\ 7.95/\text{unit}$$
$$C—\$\ 54,000 \div 13,910 \text{ units} = \$\ 3.88/\text{unit}$$

The advertising expenses borne by each salesperson are determined by multiplying these per-unit advertising charges by the number of bicycles of each model that each rep sold.

The number of units of the product sold is a very common basis for allocating advertising expenses. Two other common bases are the number of prospects secured and the number of sales transactions. The decision to allocate advertising expenses on the basis of the number of units sold is controversial. While the per-unit-of-product-sold approach is popular, it is not hard to develop an argument against it. One could argue, for example, that advertising expenses are fixed for a period, and since they are fixed costs, productive salespeople should not have to assume a larger advertising burden than unproductive salespeople. One could also argue that the per-unit approach treats advertising as a consequence of sales, rather than as a cause, and therefore the scheme violates the control principle alluded to earlier that one should search for factors that control the functional cost.

While both of these arguments have merit, we will use the per-unit-of-product basis for allocating advertising expenses below for three reasons: (1) the per-unit approach is one of the most popular; (2) there is no clearly preferred alternative in the literature; (3) the example is designed to illustrate the cost analysis process, not to provide the last word on all possible nuances. Yet, you should be aware that the decision as to how to allocate advertising expenses or any of the expense categories can change the fundamental conclusions one draws about the profitability of a particular segment.

Warehousing and Shipping

The profitability analysis by sales representatives does not include an allocation for the warehouseperson's salary because that salary would continue regardless of what any sales rep sold. Rather, all that is allocated to the salespeople are the packaging costs per unit, which amounted to $2 per bicycle.

Order Processing

The office clerk's salary is not allocated to salespeople because there is no causal link between an individual representative's sales and that salary. The office rent charged to this

Exhibit 15.11 Basic Data Used for Allocations

A. Information by Product

Products	Selling Price per Unit	Cost per Unit	Gross Margin per Unit	Number Sold in Period	Sales in Period	Advertising Expenditures
A	$230	$180	$50	6,450	$1,483,500	$120,000
B	180	150	30	10,060	1,810,800	80,000
C	120	100	20	13,910	1,669,200	54,000
				30,420	$4,963,500	$254,000

B. Information by Salesperson

Salesperson	Number of Sales Calls	Number of Orders	Number of Units Sold A	B	C	Total
Nicholls	75	50	1,400	2,210	3,410	7,020
Pogue	125	65	1,725	2,725	3,515	7,965
Vilwock	100	50	1,711	2,609	3,506	7,826
Tucker	100	80	1,614	2,516	3,479	7,609
	400	245	6,450	10,060	13,910	30,420

Exhibit 15.12 Profitability Analysis by Salesperson

	Total	Nicholls	Pogue	Vilwock	Tucker
Sales					
Product A	$1,483,500	$ 322,000	$ 396,750	$ 393,530	$ 371,220
Product B	1,810,800	397,800	490,500	469,620	452,880
Product C	1,669,200	409,200	421,800	420,720	417,480
Total Sales	4,963,500	1,129,000	1,309,050	1,283,870	1,241,580
Cost of Goods Sold					
Product A	1,161,000	252,000	310,500	307,980	290,520
Product B	1,509,000	331,500	408,750	391,350	377,400
Product C	1,391,000	341,000	351,500	350,600	347,900
Total COGS	4,061,000	924,500	1,070,750	1,049,930	1,015,820
Gross Margin	902,500	204,500	238,300	233,940	225,760
Expenses					
Direct selling:					
Salary	179,000	40,000	45,000	46,000	48,000
Commissions	49,635	11,290	13,091	12,839	12,416
Travel	76,000	14,250	23,750	19,000	19,000
Advertising:					
Product A	120,000	26,047	32,093	31,833	30,028
Product B	80,000	17,575	21,670	20,748	20,008
Product C	54,000	13,238	13,646	13,611	13,506
Warehousing and shipping	60,840	14,040	15,930	15,652	15,218
Order processing	980	200	260	200	320
Transportation	182,520	42,120	47,790	46,956	45,654
Total Expenses	802,975	178,759	213,229	206,837	204,149
Contribution to Profit (Loss)	$ 99,525	$ 25,741	$ 25,071	$ 27,103	$ 21,611

Exhibit 15.13   Activities of Tucker Broken Down by Account

Customers of Tucker	Number of Sales Calls	Number of Orders	Number of Units Purchased			
			A	B	C	Total
Allen	50	35	807	1,258	1,567	3,632
Brown	25	20	645	880	1,043	2,568
Cooper	25	25	162	378	869	1,409
Total	100	80	1,614	2,516	3,479	7,609

activity is similarly not allocated. The order processing costs that are allocated are the direct expenses for postage and supplies. Order processing costs are most directly linked to the number of orders, which produces an allocation of $4 per order.

Transportation

Transportation charges amounted to $6 per bike. These are charged against the individual sales representatives according to the number of bicycles each sold. When all these expenses are aggregated and subtracted from gross margin, it is found that each representative is contributing to profits. Such a result poses a dilemma for the company sales manager. The branch is not profitable, but each salesperson in the branch is contributing to profits. Admittedly, the sales reps may not be making a large enough contribution. If there were a profit standard for each salesperson, performance could be compared to the standard. This example demonstrates the difference between a performance analysis in which a standard of comparison is established beforehand and a straight cost and profitability analysis.

The company sales manager could compare the contributions to profit of the representatives in the St. Louis branch with those of other sales representatives by doing a similar analysis for other branches. If the St. Louis salespeople were found to be low, it might indicate the payroll in the St. Louis branch was too high for the number of bicycles sold. The sales manager might then consider removing one or more reps from the territory. Alternatively, the manager might consider increasing the number of calls or changing the salary/commission mixture in the salespeople's compensation package. Still other strategies would be to close the warehouse associated with the branch or to close the branch. The profit implications of each strategy would be different. They could be calculated, however, if the company maintains sales and cost records by small units. Conversely, when basic records are aggregated into larger totals and are stored that way in the company's accounting system, such isolate and explode analyses are precluded.

Suppose the sales manager felt that for strategic reasons, she did not wish to close the branch or the warehouse. Rather, she wished to consider reassigning one representative in the branch to another office and territory. Since there are typically significant company costs and personal disruptions to the rep in such a switch, the sales manager did not take these reassignments lightly. Suppose, therefore, she wanted to ascertain the profitability of each account to the salesperson and the company.

Exhibit 15.13 and Exhibit 15.14 contain, respectively, the activity levels of Tucker, the "worst"-performing representative in terms of the analysis contained in Exhibit 15.12, broken down by account and the resulting profit contribution of each account based on the same allocation criteria used previously. The analysis illustrates the operation of the iceberg principle.

Although Tucker overall contributes to profit, one account is generating a loss. The loss can be traced to the number of bicycles ordered by Cooper. While Cooper orders

	Total	Allen	Brown	Cooper
Sales				
Product A	$ 371,220	$185,610	$148,350	$ 37,260
Product B	452,880	226,440	158,400	68,040
Product C	417,480	188,040	125,160	104,280
Total Sales	1,214,580	600,090	431,910	209,580
Cost of Goods Sold				
Product A	290,520	145,260	116,100	29,160
Product B	377,400	188,700	132,000	56,700
Product C	347,900	156,700	104,300	86,900
Total COGS	1,015,820	490,660	352,400	172,760
Gross Margin	225,760	109,430	79,510	36,820
Expenses				
Direct selling:				
Salary	48,000	24,000	12,000	12,000
Commissions	12,416	6,001	4,319	2,096
Travel	19,000	9,500	4,750	4,750
Advertising:				
Product A	30,028	15,014	12,000	3,014
Product B	20,008	10,004	6,998	3,006
Product C	13,506	6,083	4,049	3,374
Warehousing and shipping	15,218	7,264	5,136	2,818
Order processing	320	140	80	100
Transportation	45,654	21,792	15,408	8,454
Total Expenses	204,149	99,798	64,740	39,611
Contribution to Profit (Loss)	$ 21,611	$ 9,632	$ 14,770	$ (2,791)

Exhibit 15.14   Profitability Analysis for Tucker Broken Down by Customer

every time Tucker calls, the average order size is very low. Less frequent calls might be the answer; fewer calls might produce the same net sales but reduce Tucker's travel expenses charged to Cooper. The analysis also reveals that although Allen purchased the most bikes, Brown was the most profitable account Tucker had. Again, these insights would be impossible to generate if Baitinger Bicycle Company did not use modularized marketing cost analyses.

The profitability analyses by marketing segment do not tell the sales manager of Baitinger Bicycle Company or any other manager what to do. They do, however, provide managers with some basic information for making intelligent choices.

Prospects and Problems

The preceding example, while basic, reveals both the promise and some of the problems associated with marketing cost analysis. The real benefit is the opportunity it provides managers to isolate segments of the business that are most profitable as well as those that generate losses. This information allows those involved to improve their planning and control of the firm's activities. When combined with proper sales analysis techniques discussed in Chapter 14, it provides sales managers with a formidable analytical weapon for managing the personal selling function.

The example also illustrates the problems associated with the technique. Sales analysis requires that data be available in the proper detail. Some data can be costly to generate and expensive to maintain, but enterprise software and contact management software can lower the cost. Furthermore, the technique requires a sophisticated information system, such as enterprise software. The system must be able to select and aggregate only those inputs appropriate to the segment of the business being analyzed. As the example indicates, there is often a question as to which costs should be allocated and what bases should be used to allocate these costs. The most appropriate allocation bases can generate spirited discussion among those involved. Allocations cannot be taken lightly because they ultimately affect the profitability of a segment; at the same time, however, there are usually no perfect answers as to how costs should be allocated. Thus, setting up a good marketing cost system can take a good deal of expensive executive time.

The benefits increasingly seem to be higher than the costs, if the literature on the subject is a reliable barometer. Not only has more been written on the subject of late, but the literature also describes an increasing number of companies that have profited from implementing market cost analysis.[14]

Return on Assets Managed

Sales and cost analyses provide the sales manager with two important financial techniques for controlling the personal selling function. The first measures the results achieved and the second the cost of producing those results. The important financial ingredient left out of those analyses is the assets needed to produce those results. At a minimum, the company will be committing working capital in the form of accounts receivable and inventories to support the sales function.[15] The return produced on the assets used in each segment of the business provides sales managers with a useful variation of more traditional cost analysis procedures for evaluating and controlling various elements of the personal selling function.

The formula for return on assets managed (ROAM) reflects both the contribution margin associated with a given level of sales and asset turnover.[16] More particularly, it is as follows:

ROAM = Contribution as a percentage of sales × Asset turnover rate

The formula indicates that the return to a segment of the business can be improved either by increasing the profit margin on sales or by maintaining the same profit margin and increasing the asset turnover rate. The formula can then be used to evaluate segments or to select the best alternative from strategies being considered.

Think of, for example, the use of the concept to evaluate the performance of two sales branches. Exhibit 15.15 contains the basic financial data. Note that Branch A sold more than Branch B and the gross margin on these sales was higher, both in total and as a percentage of sales, because of the mix of products. Furthermore, the contribution to total company profits was higher for Branch A than for Branch B, and earnings as a percentage of sales were 10.0 percent in Branch A and only 6.3 percent in Branch B. By all these standards, Branch A performed better.

These criteria, however, ignore the assets needed to produce these results. When the investment in assets, which in the example consists of accounts receivable and inventories for each branch, is also considered, the picture changes. Branch B required a smaller commitment of the firm's capital. Consequently, Branch B was able to effect an asset turnover twice as large as Branch A, so the return on investment was higher in Branch B than in Branch A.

While the basic ROAM formula can be used to provide useful management information, the managerial insights it affords can be magnified by breaking the basic formula down by its components. The first component—contribution as a percentage of sales— equals the ratio of net contribution divided by sales. The second component—the asset turnover rate—equals sales divided by the assets needed to produce those sales. Each of these second-level components could be expanded. One could, for example, break down

Exhibit 15.15   Analysis of Return on Assets Managed

	Branch A	Branch B
Sales	$2,500,000	$1,500,000
Cost of Goods Sold	2,000,000	1,275,000
Gross Margin	500,000 (20%)	225,000 (15%)
Less variable branch expenses:		
Salaries	155,000	80,000
Commissions	25,000	10,000
Office expenses	30,000	20,000
Travel and entertainment	40,000	20,000
	250,000	130,000
Branch contribution to profit	250,000	95,000
Branch investments:		
Accounts receivable	500,000	150,000
Inventories	750,000	225,000
	1,250,000	375,000
Earnings as a percentage of sales	10.0%	6.3%
Turnover	2.0	4.0
Branch percent return on assets managed	20.0%	25.2%

the sales component by product or salesperson and could similarly break down the assets to assess the impact of each product or salesperson on profitability. Alternatively, one might choose to explode into its detailed elements only one of the second-level components of net contributions, sales, and assets. Exploding one or more of the components of the equation allows management to trace the impact of a number of "what if" scenarios.

Exhibit 15.16, for example, diagrams the return on assets model, with the asset component exploded. Each of the boxes applies to the segment of the business being analyzed. Previously, we saw, for example, that Branch B produced a higher ROAM than Branch A. With the exploded model, management can quickly explore what might be done to bring the returns into line. Exhibit 15.15 indicates, for example, that the amount invested in receivables and inventories as a percentage of sales varies across the two branches and that, in particular:

	Branch A	Branch B
Receivables as a percentage of sales	$\dfrac{500,000}{2,500,000} = 20\%$	$\dfrac{150,000}{1,500,000} = 10\%$
Inventories as a percentage of sales	$\dfrac{750,000}{2,500,000} = 30\%$	$\dfrac{225,000}{1,500,000} = 15\%$

Management might logically ask what would happen to ROAM in Branch A if receivables or inventories as a percentage of sales or both were reduced to the levels existing in Branch B. Exhibit 15.17 traces the implication of what a reduction in accounts receivables to 10 percent of sales (to $250,000) in Branch A through better billing and follow-up procedures might do for its profitability. The example, which assumes no lost sales because of these billing efforts, demonstrates the returns could be brought directly in line with this one change. Management could just as easily assess the profit implications of, say, 5, 10, and 15 percent declines in sales to determine how sensitive the branch returns might be to a change in the billing procedures.

In sum, assets managed adds another important dimension to the financial control

Exhibit 15.16   Expanded Return on Assets Managed (ROAM) Model

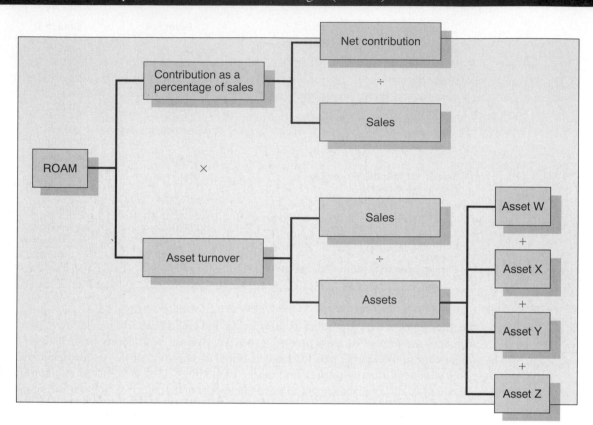

picture. The investment required for a venture needs to be recognized because long-run profits can be maximized only if the optimal level of investment in each asset is achieved. As Alfred P. Sloan, who was chief executive officer for 23 years at General Motors, comments in his book, *My Years with General Motors,* "No other financial principle with which I am acquainted serves better than rate of return as an objective aid to business judgment."[17]

The point was made earlier that marketers have been slower to embrace cost analysis than sales analysis. The evidence indicates they have been even slower to adopt ROAM. Exhibit 15.18, for example, summarizes the results of a survey among 146 industrial manufacturers in SIC codes 20–39 regarding their use of sales, cost, and ROAM analysis in managing the marketing function in general and the personal selling function in particular. SIC (Standardized Industrial Classification) codes, now being replaced by NAICS (North American Industrial Classification System), are used to classify the type of business of each company in North America. While most of these firms engaged in sales analysis by customer, salesperson, or geographic area, only about one-third of them engaged in profitability analysis by these segments, and only one-tenth investigated the returns they realized on the assets devoted to these segments.

Clearly, despite their compelling intuitive appeal, cost or profitability analysis and asset return analysis have a way to go before they match the popularity of sales analysis in managing the personal selling function.

Exhibit 15.17 Impact of a Reduction in Accounts Receivable to $250,000 in Branch A

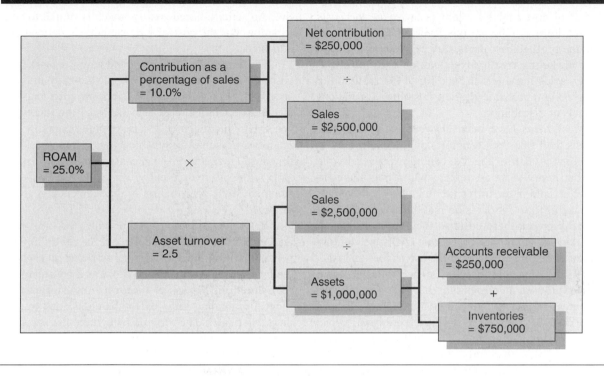

Exhibit 15.18 Popularity of Sales, Cost, and Asset Return Analysis by Segment

	Segment			
Description	**Product**	**Customers**	**Salesperson**	**Geographic Area**
Sales analysis:				
Sales volume (units or dollars)	92	91	87	92
Sales volume (versus quota or objective)	54	48	75	70
Cost analysis:				
Expenses	40	18	53	38
Contribution to profit (sales less direct costs)	75	41	32	26
Net profit (sales less direct costs less allocated indirect costs)	57	24	19	12
Return on assets	29	10	10	7

Source: Developed from information provided in Donald W. Jackson, Jr., Lonnie L. Ostrom, and Kenneth R. Evans, "Measures Used to Evaluate Industrial Marketing Activities," *Industrial Marketing Management* 11 (October 1982), pp. 269–74.

SUMMARY

Marketing cost analysis attempts to isolate the costs incurred in producing various levels of sales to determine the profitability of sales by segment of the business. Marketing cost analysis can be used to advantage by sales managers to investigate the profitability of regions, branches, territories, customers, or various channels of distribution.

Most firms have been slower to embrace cost analysis than sales analysis for studying their marketing activities. Part of this lag can be explained by the fact that many costs associated with doing business are not entered in the firm's accounting system in their most useful form for decision making. Thus, it is necessary to rework these costs so they are more useful. The adoption of activity-based cost (ABC) accounting systems is helping to increase the use of cost analysis.

A marketing cost analysis can be conducted using either a full-cost, a contribution margin, or an activity-based cost approach. The full-cost approach allocates all the costs of doing business, even fixed costs, to one of the operating segments. The contribution margin approach holds that only those costs that can be specifically identified with the segment of the business should be deducted from the revenue produced by the segment. The contribution margin approach is more logically defensible from a decision-making perspec-

tive. An activity-based cost approach is similar to contribution, but the cost of each activity is defined and allocated.

There are four steps in conducting a marketing cost analysis. First, the purpose of the study must be specified. Second, the natural account costs must be spread to functional cost centers. Next, the functional costs must be allocated to appropriate operating segments using some reasonable bases. Here one looks for those factors that bear a cause-and-effect relationship with the cost. Finally, the allocated costs are summed so the contribution of the segment can be determined.

Return on assets managed provides the sales manager with still another financial tool for controlling the personal selling function. Return on assets managed is the product of contribution to profit as a percentage of sales multiplied by asset turnover. Asset turnover is found by dividing sales by the assets needed to produce those sales. The formula recognizes that the sales manager has only limited assets with which to work. He can maximize the profits produced by the personal selling function only if each asset is put to its highest and best use. Return on assets managed is currently less popular than either sales or cost analysis in managing the personal selling function.

DISCUSSION QUESTIONS

1. "Our costs are out of control," claimed Rosemary Harper, chief financial officer of Broadway United. "In particular, I am really concerned about the level of marketing costs, especially for the sales force." With a 235-person sales force, Broadway sells computer hardware and software packages to financial institutions. Harper supports the recommendations of a sales consulting firm to reduce the sales force by 50 percent and to hire a third sales force consisting of manufacturer's agents who would be paid on a straight commission basis. The reduction in the sales force would mean that 10 district sales managers would lose their jobs. The sales training manager position would be eliminated as well since manufacturer's agents do not need training according to the sales consultant. Harper intended to keep only the best sales reps and eliminate the others in the 50 percent reduction process. "Those experienced sales reps

    that remain with Broadway will not need enough training to justify keeping Broadway's training department," noted Harper. What are the advantages and disadvantages of the sales consultant's proposal? Is it possible for a company to cut costs too far?

2. Advertising has a synergistic effect. For example, in the Baitinger Bicycle Company case, the $254,000 advertising expenditure for product A had a positive impact on products B and C and on the company as well. Besides, dollars spent in one period have a carryover effect to future periods. What recommendations would you make to handle these situations?

3. The Rite-Way Corporation, a manufacturer of a line of writing instruments, has completed a ROAM analysis for all products. The deluxe model in its line of fountain pens sells for 5.50 but produces a ROAM of 8.3

percent, well below the 23.5 percent average for the other products. Management believes rising raw material costs, such as gold and silver prices, are beyond Rite-Way's control. Should Rite-Way drop its deluxe product? Should Rite-Way eliminate commissions paid to sales representatives for deluxe sales?

4. The sales manager of Branch A (Exhibit 15.15) was dismayed with the results. The 20 percent ROAM for the branch was below expectations. The sales manager's response was "OK, they want better results, then we'll increase sales by at least 10 percent. But we'll have to cut prices by 5 percent to do this." Will this benefit Branch A?

5. Accounts receivable are too high for Branch A in Exhibit 15.15. One sales analyst recommends giving credit and collection responsibilities to the sales force. Sales reps would be provided with delinquency objectives aimed at reducing accounts receivables by 20 percent. Those meeting their objectives would earn an additional 1 percent of sales for commission. Will this work? Another analyst contends that since the sales force has no training in credits and collections, accounts receivable should be excluded from ROAM calculations. Do you agree? What would happen to Branch A's ROAM if accounts receivable were excluded?

6. Given the following profit and loss statement for the XYZ Company, allocate the natural accounts to the functional accounts:

XYZ Company
Profit and Loss Statement
1996

Sales		$1,676,000
Cost of goods sold		1,003,000
Gross margin		$ 673,000
Selling and administrative expenses:		
Salaries:		
Salespeople	120,000	
Sales manager	30,000	
Office personnel	38,000	
Warehouse personnel	30,000	
Commissions	16,760	
Advertising	93,800	
Postage	450	
Supplies:		
Office	200	
Warehouse	500	
Packaging	30,000	
Transportation	80,290	
Travel expenses	40,000	
Rent:		
Sales	15,000	
Warehouse	35,000	
Order processing	10,000	
Heat and electricity:		
Sales	7,000	
Warehouse	18,000	
Order processing	5,000	
Total selling and administrative expenses:		570,000
Net profit (loss)		$ 103,000

7.　Nancy Troyer, the sales manager for InterCraft, a manufacturer and distributor of picture frames and supplies, was in the midst of a heavy discussion with representatives from the company's accounting department. The discussion revolved around the new cost system the accounting department was developing so the sales function could be managed more effectively. The topic at the moment was how each salesperson's automobile expenses should be allocated, given that salespeople were handling eight product lines and selling to three different types of outlets—office supply stores, book stores, and arts and crafts specialty supply outlets. The situation was complicated further because sales reps were also expected to prospect for new accounts and attend trade shows in their own and contiguous territories.

How would you recommend the costs be allocated if Troyer wanted to determine the profitability of each salesperson? Each product line? Each customer?

EXPERIENTIAL APPLICATION

1.　Use the following information to determine for the company and for each sales representative:

　　　Market share

　　　Account penetration

　　　Contribution margin

　　　Sales calls per active account

　　　Selling expenses ratio

What problems do your results identify? What additional information or calculations are needed to fully understand the situation?

APPLICATION QUESTIONS

A1. You are given the following information on two salespeople:

Sales-person	Number of Calls	Number of Orders	Units Sold	Total Sales	Cost of Goods Sold
A	200	250	15,000	$750,000	$600,000
B	295	230	18,000	900,000	720,000

Salesperson A earns a $22,000 salary compared to $23,000 for salesperson B. Both earn 1 percent commission. Advertising costs $3 per unit. Shipping expenses are $2 per unit. Order processing costs total $1 per order. Travel expenses amount to $0.50 per call. Your task is to calculate the contribution to profit (loss) made by each salesperson.

A2. As the sales manager of the M.N.O. Company, you are trying to evaluate the performance of two districts. You have decided to look at how each district has managed its assets employed in the selling function. From the following information, determine each district's ROAM.

	District 1		District 2
Sales		$800,000	$500,000
Cost of goods sold		624,000	390,000
Gross margin		176,000	110,000
Variable district expenses:			
Salaries	$49,600		$31,000
Commissions	8,000		5,000
Office expenses	9,600		6,000
Travel	12,800		8,000
Total expenses		80,000	50,000
Net profit (loss)		96,000	60,000
District investment in assets:			
Accounts receivable		120,000	45,000
Inventories		200,000	80,000
Earnings as a percent of sales		.12	.12
Turnover		2.5	4.0

A3. Sylvie Faivre, sales analyst for the Bouvre Cheese Company located in Lyons, France, had completed her analysis of one of the southern districts. The district was a candidate for consolidation since management believed sales were not as expected. Sylvie suggested she should first determine the district's return on assets managed before any decisions were made concerning territory modification. The following provides the data needed to calculate ROAM for the district:

Sales	Fr4,500,000
Cost of goods sold	4,000,000
Gross margin	500,000
Less variable branch expenses:	
Salaries	175,000
Commissions	30,000
Office expenses	35,000
Travel and entertainment	55,000
	295,000

District contribution to profit	205,000
District investments:	
Accounts receivable	750,000
Inventories	900,000
	Fr1,650,000

Determine the ROAM for the district. What would happen if inventories were reduced by 20 percent? How much would sales have to increase to obtain the company average ROAM of 25 percent? Bouvre management believes salaries are too high and is considering a 15 percent reduction. Assuming no impact on sales, how would this affect district ROAM?

INTERNET EXERCISE

Many trade associations collect data from their members so that the members can compare themselves to the rest of the industry. One such association is the Hospitality Sales and Marketing Association, which is the trade association for the travel and tourism industry. Visit its home page (*http://www.hsmai.org*) to get a feel for the industry. Then click over to *http://www.hsmai.org/3_resources/3b_publications.htm,* where you should find descriptions of two publications of the results of such surveys. Call or visit with a sales manager or general manager of a local hotel (call someone at a business hotel, like a Hilton or Marriott, in a downtown location), or a sales manager at your local Convention and Visitors Bureau or a large travel agency. Ask the sales manager what type of cost information she would find helpful, if she is a member of the HSMA, and if so, does she use either or both of the publications. If she doesn't, describe the publications to the manager and discuss how important such information might be. The purposes of this exercise are to expose you to sources of information that can be helpful in managing costs, and to help you consider the difference between "nice to have" and "have to have" information. In your write-up, give examples of what the manager believes is essential and what would be nice to have (but is not essential).

SUGGESTED READINGS

Challagalla, Goutam N., and Tasadduq A. Shervani, "Dimensions and Types of Supervisory Control: Effects on Salesperson Performance and Satisfaction," *Journal of Marketing* 60 (January 1996), pp. 89–105.

Rothe, James T., Michael G. Harvey, and Candice Jackson, "The Marketing Audit: Five Decades Later," *Journal of Marketing Theory & Practice* 5 (Summer 1997), pp. 1–16.

16 Behavior and Other Performance Analyses

MEASURING PERFORMANCE—CHECKING FOR FIT

Northwestern Mutual (The Quiet Company ©) is usually listed among the annual winners of *Sales & Marketing Management*'s best sales forces competition, and also makes the annual list of best companies to work for published by *Fortune*. Being one of the top sales forces is quite an honor, as it requires high marks of satisfaction from customers. Likewise, being a best place to work means that few people leave, and those who stay like being there. When put together, these two honors mean that Northwestern has found a way to measure the softer parts of performance, for both customers and salespeople are highly satisfied.

Al Angell, who leads a sales office in Dallas, has been an innovator in finding ways to measure and motivate. For example, he surveyed his sales staff as to who in the company they believed were the best all-time salespeople. Then he created a chart that showed the top three's performances in various stages of their careers. When he meets with each of his salespeople individually, he is able to compare where they are now with where their heroes were at the same career stage. It's kind of like comparing how many home runs Mark McGwire hit in his first three years to Babe Ruth's first-three-years tally—if you want to be the next Mark McGwire or Babe Ruth, Angell can tell you how you stand.

He also knows how many sales calls a rep should be making and what type of calls those should be (whether with current accounts talking about new services or working to gain new accounts) and how those numbers should vary based on the agent's tenure and desired performance levels.

Northwestern Mutual begins building its top-rated sales force through internships—internships that have been rated as the best in the country, in any industry (by *Princeton Review*). These internships give college students the opportunity to act as real agents, which means that they are introduced early to the concepts of measuring the behaviors and activities that drive performance. Many internships turn into permanent positions. Jennifer Lee, however, was one intern who did not pursue a permanent position. While she appreciated the real and complete look at what being a Northwestern agent is and does, she also found out that it didn't fit her—and that's good for both parties. Finding out while still in college that the behaviors and activities of a job weren't meant for her saved both parties a lot of time.

By keeping close tabs on behaviors and activities, Northwestern Mutual is able to guide its salespeople to success, while maintaining the highest customer satisfaction ratings possible. That's why the Quiet Company has so much noise made about it in the rankings.

Visit Northwestern Mutual at its Web site, *www.northwesternmutual.com*.

LEARNING OBJECTIVES

David Fields, vice president of sales for Zellerbach, says, "You can't do *sales*. You do activities that lead to sales." The previous two chapters have examined sales performance in terms of what has been sold and at what cost. This chapter considers the activities that lead to sales and how to evaluate salespeople and their activities.

After reading this chapter, you should be able to:

- Describe the concept of sales processes and how that relates to performance measurement.

- List sales activities that should be measured and describe how these measurements are used to assess salesperson performance.

- Evaluate salesperson performance using combinations of activity and sales performance measures.

- Discuss the implications of salesperson performance for sales activities on policies and decisions of sales managers.

Sales and cost analysis are two very important techniques sales managers can use to assess the overall personal selling effort. They help to measure whether the selling effort is on target with respect to the goals established for this portion of the marketing mix and also provide strong clues of where and how it can be improved.

Although these techniques also provide valuable input for evaluating individual salespeople, relying on them exclusively can produce a distorted picture of what an individual sales rep accomplished. Measures of salesperson sales or profits ignore the goodwill the rep may have generated for the company, the efforts to develop new accounts that offer long-term profit potential, the information brought back from the field, and so on. Recognizing this, most firms supplement sales and cost analyses with other evaluations of how individual salespeople are doing, as the scenario suggests. These firms recognize that what gets measured, gets managed.

This chapter reviews other evaluation measures. The chapter first highlights why they are necessary. It discusses some supplemental objective measures for evaluation and then some subjective or qualitative measures.

PERFORMANCE VERSUS EFFECTIVENESS

Part II of this book was concerned with understanding the individual salesperson. The model used to structure that discussion suggested a sales representative's performance was a function of five factors: the individual's (1) role perceptions, (2) aptitude, (3) skill level, (4) motivation level, and (5) personal, organizational, and environmental variables that influence performance. Exhibit 16.1 depicts a slightly modified form of that model. The main change is the distinction among behavior, performance, and effectiveness.[1] While role perceptions, aptitude, skill level, and motivation level were previously pictured as being directly linked to performance, now they are directly linked to behavior. The modified model is useful for understanding the role of sales and cost analyses in salespeople's evaluation as well as why other measures for evaluating representatives are necessary.

Behavior refers to what representatives do—that is, the tasks on which they expend effort while working. These tasks might include calling on customers, writing orders, preparing sales presentations, developing formal equipment proposals, and the like.

Performance is behavior evaluated in terms of its contributions to the goals of the organization. Performance, in other words, has a normative element reflecting whether a

Exhibit 16.1 Sales Behavior, Performance, and Effectiveness

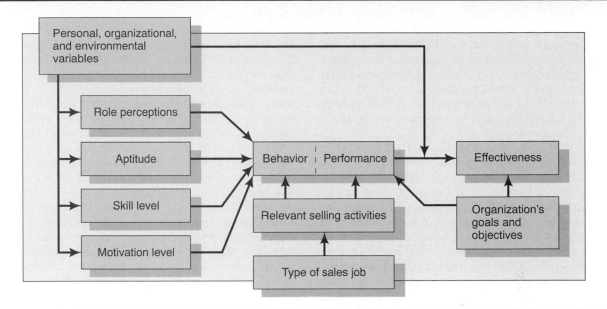

Source: Orville C. Walker, Jr., Gilbert A. Churchill, Jr., and Neil M. Ford, "Where Do We Go from Here? Selected Conceptual and Empirical Issues Concerning the Motivation and Performance of the Industrial Salesforce," in *Critical Issues in Sales Management: State-of-the-Art and Future Research Needs,* ed. Gerald Albaum and Gilbert A. Churchill, Jr. (Eugene: College of Business Administration, University of Oregon, 1979), p. 36.

salesperson's behavior is "good" or "bad" in light of the organization's goals and objectives. Note that behavior and performance are both influenced by relevant sales activities. These in turn depend on the types of sales jobs in question.

Exhibit 16.1 also distinguishes between performance and effectiveness. By definition, effectiveness refers to some summary index of organizational outcomes for which an individual is at least partly responsible, such as sales volume, market share, or profitability of sales. The crucial distinction between performance and effectiveness is that the latter does not refer to behavior directly; rather it is a function of additional factors not under the individual salesperson's control. These include top management policies, the sales potential of a territory, and the actions of competitors.

In terms of Exhibit 16.1, sales and cost analyses produce effectiveness measures; that is, the results are partially determined by the performance of the sales reps. However, differences between two salespersons' "performances" are not solely determined in this way. There may be differences in the potential in their territories or in the physical makeup of the territories and consequently in what it takes to service them. There may be differences in the level of company support by territory or the competitive conditions within each. When such differences exist, is it reasonable to say that one salesperson did better than another because his sales, market share, or contribution to profit was higher?

It is generally agreed that salespeople should be judged solely on those phases of sales performance over which they exercise control, and should not be held responsible for results beyond their control. If a company's method of measuring salespeople's performance is to result in valid comparisons, serious consideration must be given to such factors in developing yardsticks for objective or subjective evaluation.[2] Furthermore, such measurements can be used for terminating salespeople, a situation that calls for objectivity, as can be seen in the "Ethical Issues" box.

When All Else Fails—Terminating a Sales Representative

As distasteful as it is, terminating a sales representative for poor performance is sometimes unavoidable. Although the objective of a sales performance evaluation is to reward effective performance and to modify behavior to lead to future improvement, termination may be the best solution for both parties if corrective actions have been exhausted.

The right to fire an employee has long been an accepted prerogative of employers. However, terminating a salesperson can be expensive if done incorrectly.

You are vice president of sales. You consider your top salesperson an SOB, but because he's your best producer you've put up with him for 10 years. One morning his arrogance and rudeness are too much. You fire him on the spot. Two years later you're in court defending your action in a wrongful discharge suit filed by the salesperson. You have to agree that the salesperson's job performance was excellent. When asked why you fired him, you say his boorishness and obnoxious manner became too much to handle. While the salesperson's behavior didn't affect his own performance, it was disruptive and upsetting to the sales support staff.

The jury finds in favor of the salesperson and then awards him $200,000 for lost wages and benefits and even more in punitive damages.

This scenario would not have occurred a quarter of a century ago. Today, however, the nation's courts are jammed with "wrongful termination suits charging everything from broken promises, invasion of privacy, violation of public policy, and, in Montana and California, a failure of good faith and fair dealing" (Murphy, p. 26). One legal expert contends that even with a carefully documented case involving termination, a lawsuit may still occur. However, companies can reduce the risk.

The first step is to maintain extensive documentation, starting with employee manuals that describe in detail all relevant company policies and procedures. Current job descriptions for each sales position are mandatory, and salespeople must be familiar with the manual's contents and be advised of any changes. Performance reviews should be routine, occur when scheduled, and bear the signatures of both the sales representative and the sales manager(s). During a performance review management must effectively communicate its expectations and identify what actions will be taken when goals are met or not met. Evidence of failure to communicate is obvious when the sales representative, upon being terminated, states, "I didn't know I was supposed to do that. I didn't know anything was wrong." One consultant identifies weak communications as the primary cause of many terminations.

Another source of the problem stems from the performance evaluation process. Sales managers would much rather conduct a positive evaluation than a negative one. Some managers will even delay a negative evaluation, hoping the problem will go away or the sales rep will quit. Another equally undesirable outcome occurs when the manager, trying to avoid a confrontation, rates the sales rep as "average" when "inadequate" would be more appropriate. If termination eventually does result, a lawsuit would not be surprising given the lack of documentation justifying the action.

What can sales managers do to prevent being sued by a dissatisfied or dismissed sales representative? Nothing. But they can make these lawsuits difficult to win by following some simple legal guidelines. The idea is to create documentation in advance that will prove the salesperson was not treated unfairly. Some tips from lawyers:

- Spell out job duties in writing before hiring someone.
- Conduct reviews at least once a year, preferably more often.
- Fill out a standard form, the same for all sales representatives, that uses specific measurements of objective criteria.
- Fill out this form honestly. Employers are asking for trouble if they allow salespeople to think their performances are satisfactory if they're not.
- Address both a salesperson's strengths and weaknesses.
- Develop with a sales representative a plan of action and specific goals for the coming months.
- Both the sales manager and salesperson should sign and date the evaluation after the meeting.
- If the meeting is a sensitive one, a third party should be present.

(continued)

- Never make reference to a legally protected class of which the salesperson is a member (such as a racial, religious, gender, or age group).

- Be direct. Do not use words like *layoff* that indicate that the employee may be able to return.
- Prepare a written account of the meeting, and have the employee sign it.

Source: Joseph Gelb, "Avoiding Lawsuits from Former Employees," originally printed in *Small Business Advisor Newsletter*, 1996, *www.smartbiz.com/sbs/arts/sba24.htm;* Liz Murphy, "The Art of Firing Smarter," *Sales & Marketing Management* (February 1988), pp. 36–40; Minda Zetlin, "Up for Review," *Sales & Marketing Management* (December 1994), pp. 82–86.

One could argue that a careful specification of performance standards by territory should eliminate inequities across territories. For example, percentage of quota attained should be an acceptable measure of performance because quotas supposedly consider variations in environmental factors across territories. Admittedly, a comparison of salespeople with respect to percentage of quota attained is a better measure of their performance than is a comparison that simply looks at each representative's level of absolute sales or market share, assuming the quotas were done well. Assuming that quotas are done well is a big if, however; sometimes they are not. In some instances, they are arbitrary and are not necessarily based on an objective assessment of all the factors that facilitate or constrain a salesperson's ability to make a sale.

Even when quotas are done well, the measure "percentage of quota attained" still omits much with respect to a salesperson's performance. For one thing, it ignores the profitability of sales. Sales reps can be compared with respect to profitability, or the return they produce on the assets under their control, as shown in Chapter 15. Nevertheless, determining the appropriate standards of profitability for each territory is even more difficult than establishing quotas that accurately consider the many factors that affect the level of sales a representative should be able to produce in a territory.

Even if good sales and profit standards could be developed, the problem of salespeople's evaluation would not be solved because neither measure incorporates activities that may have no short-term payout but still have substantial consequences to the firm in the long run. These include the time devoted to developing a potential large account, to building long-term territorial goodwill for the company, or to developing detailed understanding of the capabilities of the firm's products. That is why many firms supplement sales and cost analyses with other measures that more directly reflect each sales rep's performance.

The other measures firms use to evaluate salespeople fall into two broad categories: (1) objective measures and (2) subjective measures.[3] The objective measures reflect other statistics the manager can gather from the firm's internal data. These measures are best used when they reflect the sales process. The subjective measures rely on personal evaluations by someone in the organization, typically the salesperson's immediate supervisor, of how individual salespeople are doing.

OBJECTIVE MEASURES

The objective measures that firms use to supplement traditional sales and cost analyses fall into the three subcategories of output measures, input measures, and ratios of output and/or input measures. Exhibit 16.2 summarizes the more common output and input measures, and Exhibit 16.3 displays some of the more commonly used ratios. Next the rationales for why these measures are used are discussed briefly.

Exhibit 16.2   Common Output and Input Factors Used to Evaluate Salespeople

Output Factors	Input Factors
Orders	Calls
Number of orders	Number of calls
Average size of orders	Number of planned calls
Number of canceled orders	Number of unplanned calls
Accounts	Time and time utilization
Number of active accounts	Days worked
Number of new accounts	Calls per day (call rate)
Number of lost accounts	Selling time versus nonselling time
Number of overdue accounts	Expenses
Number of prospective accounts	Total
	By type
	As a percentage of sales
	As a percentage of quota
	Nonselling activities
	Letters written to prospects
	Telephone calls to prospects
	Number of formal proposals developed
	Advertising displays set up
	Number of meetings held with distributors/dealers
	Number of training sessions held with distributor/dealer personnel
	Number of calls on distributor/dealer customers
	Number of service calls made
	Number of overdue accounts collected

The use of outputs, inputs, and ratios to measure salesperson performance is a recognition of the nature of the selling process. As the Fields quote at the start of the chapter illustrates, sales are the output of a process, a process that involves a number of identifiable and repeatable steps, critical points, and decisions. This process is often referred to in the field as a sales funnel or pipeline. The most common model of the sales funnel is a four-step process that begins with leads, then suspects, prospects, and finally customers. A lead is simply a name and method of contact (physical address, phone, e-mail, etc.) of someone who might be interested. A suspect is a lead who has agreed to see the salesperson. As these definitions indicate, every customer was once a lead and a suspect, but not all leads become suspects. Hence, like a funnel, the process begins very wide at the top and leads to a few customers at the bottom. Exhibit 16.4 illustrates the sales funnel for Stewart Label.

Some sales processes, such as that experienced by Harry Murphy when selling to American Airlines, can take years. But all sales processes can be characterized by decisions made by the buyer. That first decision, to see a salesperson, qualifies the buyer as a suspect. Once the needs have been identified and the buyer agrees that something should be purchased, the buyer is now a prospect. But the buyer hasn't yet committed to buying the salesperson's solution; a competitor's alternative could still be chosen. Additional activities, such as demonstrating a solution or presenting a proposal, must still be done before the buyer is ready to purchase. So, like leads, all prospects were once suspects, but not all suspects become prospects. Nor do all prospects become customers.

Within each step of the process, salespeople engage in activities with the buyer. The

Exhibit 16.3 Common Ratios Used to Evaluate Salespeople

Expense Ratios

- Sales expense ratio $= \dfrac{\text{Expenses}}{\text{Sales}}$

- Cost per call ratio $= \dfrac{\text{Total costs}}{\text{Number of calls}}$

Account Development and Servicing Ratios

- Account penetration ratio $= \dfrac{\text{Accounts sold}}{\text{Total accounts available}}$

- New account conversion ratio $= \dfrac{\text{Number of new accounts}}{\text{Total number of accounts}}$

- Lost account ratio $= \dfrac{\text{Prior accounts not sold}}{\text{Total number of accounts}}$

- Sales per account ratio $= \dfrac{\text{Sales dollar volume}}{\text{Total number of accounts}}$

- Average order size ratio $= \dfrac{\text{Sales dollar volume}}{\text{Total number of orders}}$

- Order cancellation ratio $= \dfrac{\text{Number of canceled orders}}{\text{Total number of orders}}$

Call Activity and/or Productivity

- Calls per day ratio $= \dfrac{\text{Number of calls}}{\text{Number of days worked}}$

- Calls per account ratio $= \dfrac{\text{Number of calls}}{\text{Number of accounts}}$

- Planned call ratio $= \dfrac{\text{Number of planned calls}}{\text{Total number of calls}}$

- Order per call (hit) ratio $= \dfrac{\text{Number of orders}}{\text{Total number of calls}}$

manager can measure those activities and compare the activities with results for each stage. By examining behaviors and outcomes, managers can pinpoint areas of improvement for each salesperson, or identify changes that should be made in the sales strategy so that it is aligned with how buyers want to buy. First, we will start with outputs and work back to the start of the funnel.

Orders

The number of orders each salesperson secures is often used to assess the rep's ability to make sales presentations since it reflects the individual's ability to close. Not only must the timing of the close be right, but also the salesperson must have adequately moved the buyer through the prior stages of the buying process via the sales presentation if the close is going to be successful.[4]

Although the number of orders a salesperson secures is important, the average size of those orders is equally so. Having many orders may mean the orders are small and may indicate the person is spending too much time calling on small, type C accounts and not enough time calling on large, type A accounts.

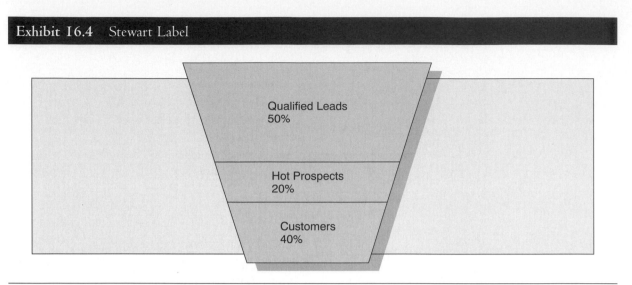

Exhibit 16.4   Stewart Label

Qualified Leads
50%

Hot Prospects
20%

Customers
40%

Half of Stewart Label's leads are qualified as prospects, but only 20% of those qualified prospects become "hot" prospects, or people ready to buy. Salespeople for Stewart are then able to close about 40% of hot prospects.

Still another measure of a salesperson's presentation effectiveness is the number of canceled orders. A salesperson who loses a large proportion of total orders to subsequent cancellation may be using high-pressure tactics in sales presentations.

Accounts

The various account measures provide a perspective on the equity of territorial assignments and also on how the salesperson is handling the territory. One popular measure focuses on the number of active accounts in the salesperson's customer portfolio. Various definitions of active account are used. It may be any customer that has placed an order in the past six months or in the past year. A salesperson's performance in one year may be compared to performance in past years by contrasting the number of active accounts. Closely related to this yardstick is a measure that tracks the number of new accounts a salesperson develops in a given time. Some companies even establish new-prospect quotas by salespeople that allow a ready comparison of performance to standard.

While not as popular as the number of new accounts, the number of lost accounts can be a revealing statistic, since it indicates how successfully the salesperson is satisfying the ongoing needs of the established accounts in the territory. Still other account measures by which salespeople can be compared are the number of overdue accounts, which might indicate the salesperson is not following company procedures in screening accounts for their creditworthiness, and the number of prospective accounts, which assesses the salesperson's ability in identifying potential target customers.

Many objective measures of performance evaluation focus on the efforts sales representatives expend rather than the results of those efforts. There are at least two good reasons for this. First, efforts or desirable behaviors are much more controllable than results. If a rep's sales fall short of quota, the problem may lie with the person, the quota, or a change in the environment. If the number of calls a salesperson makes falls short of the target, however, the problem lies much more directly with the individual.[5] Second, in many selling situations, there is a time lag between inputs and outputs. A particularly large sale may be the result of several years of efforts.

Recall the sale Harry Murphy and his team made for Wallace at American Airlines. During the time that American was considering bagtags, they were buying other Wallace products, so there was some revenue against which the costs of developing bagtags could be offset. But in such situations, it seems more reasonable to conclude that performance was good during all three years, rather than it was bad in all years except the one in which the order was finally placed. Sales representatives' efforts are measured in a number of ways.

Calls

The number of current customer and/or prospect calls is often used to decide whether a salesperson is covering the territory in accord with the company's plan. As discussed previously, the number of calls on each of the various classes of accounts (e.g., suspects, prospects, customers) is an important factor in the design of territories. Thus, such information should also be used to evaluate the salesperson assigned to the territory. After all, sales calls are a resource with finite supply. They represent a resource that is time-sensitive in that the time available to make them evaporates if it is not used.[6] The number of calls typically can be determined from a salesperson's call reports.

Contact management software, like GoldMine, automates the call report process. In a record established for each account, the salesperson can input information about each call. This information can be summarized by the software for a report to be e-mailed to the sales manager. Or, if the software resides on a network, the sales manager can access the information directly. These features minimize the time spent preparing paperwork and help salespeople maximize their time in front of buyers.

Time and Time Utilization

The number of days worked and the calls per day (or call rate) are routinely used by many companies to assess salespeople's efforts since the product of the two quantities provides a direct measure of the extent of customer contact. If the amount of customer contact by a salesperson is low, one can look separately at the components to see where the problem lies. Perhaps the salesperson has not been working enough because of sickness, extenuating circumstances, or just plain laziness—a situation that would show up in the number of days worked. Alternatively, perhaps the salesperson's total time input was satisfactory, but the salesperson was not using that time wisely and, consequently, had a low call rate.

Comparing salespeople's division of time between sales calls, traveling, and office work offers a useful perspective. For the most part, the firm would want salespeople to maximize the time in face-to-face customer contact at the expense of the other two factors. The company would want representatives particularly to minimize unproductive travel time. Such analyses require detailed input on how each person is spending time and they can be expensive. Some companies, however, routinely conduct such analyses because the benefits are deemed to outweigh the costs.

Expenses

The objective inputs discussed so far for evaluating salespeople focus mainly on the extent of the salespeople's effort. Another key emphasis when evaluating them is the cost of those efforts. Many firms keep records detailing the total expenses incurred by each salesperson. Some break these expenses down by type, such as automobile expenses, lodging expenses, entertainment expenses, and so on. They might look at these expenses in total and/or as a percentage of sales or quotas by salesperson and use these expense ratios to evaluate salespeople.

NONSELLING ACTIVITIES

In addition to assessing the direct contact of salespeople with customers, some firms monitor indirect contact. They use indexes such as the number of letters written, the number of telephone calls made, and the number of formal proposals developed.

In many industries, the sales rep's duties go beyond what might be considered a normal selling emphasis. For example, companies who sell to retailers may ask salespeople to monitor and stock shelves, create displays, help retailers advertise, and handle a number of other nonselling duties. In such instances, firms often try to monitor the extent of these duties, using such indexes as the number of promotion or advertising displays set up, the number of dealer meetings and the number of training sessions for distributor personnel held, the number of calls the salesperson made on dealer customers, the number of service calls made, the number of customer complaints received, and the number of overdue accounts collected. Some of this information can be gathered from sales call reports. The rest of it, such as the number of customer complaints, requires monitoring other correspondence.

There are also other ways to secure feedback. Consider, for example, the lengths to which one company went to assess sales force feedback. The company had always emphasized to its sales force the importance of feedback and prided itself on the amount it secured. Nevertheless, to quantify the amount of information it actually did get, the firm decided to conduct an experiment. Two other firms agreed to supply new products that were strategically placed with customers who would mention to the firm's salespeople that these were superior competitive products. The salespeople's feedback about the new competitive products was then carefully monitored. You can appreciate the firm's dismay when it found that this information was transmitted back to management less than 20 percent of the time.[7]

The focus on outputs rather than sales volume can reveal how salespeople are performing. So can analysis of their efforts. Additional insights can also be gathered by combining the various outputs and/or inputs in selected ways, typically in the form of ratios.[8] Exhibit 16.3, for example, lists some of the ratios commonly used to evaluate salespeople.

Expense Ratios

The sales–expense ratio combines both salespeople's inputs and the results produced by those inputs in a single number. Salespeople can affect this ratio either by making sales or by controlling expenses. The ratio can also be used to analyze salesperson expenses by type. Thus, a sales/transportation-expense ratio that is much higher for one salesperson than others might indicate the salesperson is covering his or her territory inefficiently. One does need to recognize territorial differences when comparing these ratios, though; the salesperson who has the out-of-line ratio may simply have a larger, more geographically dispersed sales territory to cover.

The cost-per-call ratio expresses the costs of supporting each salesperson in the field as a function of the number of calls the salesperson makes. The ratio can be evaluated using total costs or the costs can be broken down by elements, and ratios such as expenses per call and travel costs per call can be computed. Not only are these ratios useful for comparing salespeople from the same firm, but they can also be compared to those of other companies in the same industry to assess how efficient the firm's personal selling effort is. Such data can be available from trade or professional associations, and there are companies such as Dartnell that also gather expense data and ratios for sales managers to use.

Account Development and Servicing Ratios

A number of ratios concern accounts and orders that reflect on how well salespeople are capturing the potential business that exists in their territories. The account penetration ratio, for example, measures the percentage of accounts in the territory from which the salesperson secures orders. It provides a direct measure of whether the salesperson is simply skimming the cream of the business or is working the territory systematically and hard.

The new account conversion ratio similarly measures the salesperson's ability to convert prospects to customers; a similar ratio can be calculated for the number of suspects converted to prospects. The lost account ratio measures how well the salesperson keeps prior accounts as active customers and reflects on how well the representative is serving the established accounts in the territory.

The sales per account ratio indicates the salesperson's success per account on average. A low ratio could indicate the salesperson is spending too much time calling on small, unprofitable accounts and not enough time calling on larger ones. One could also look at the sales per account ratios by class of account, which can reveal the strengths and weaknesses of each salesperson. A salesperson who has a low sales per account ratio for class A accounts might need help in learning how to sell when there are multiple buying influences, for example.

The average order size ratio can also reveal the salesperson's call patterns. A very low average size might suggest the calls are too frequent and the salesperson's productivity could be improved by spacing them more. The order cancellation ratio reflects on the salesperson's method of selling; a very high ratio could mean the salesperson is using high-pressure tactics to secure orders, rather than satisfactorily handling customer concerns.

A key measurement in some types of businesses, particularly those that provide supplies and raw materials, is account share, or the percentage of the account's business that the salesperson gets. Many buyers will split their business among a number of vendors, believing (often erroneously) that they get better service and lower prices when sellers have to compete for the business. In industries where such buying practices are prevalent, the number of accounts is less important than the share of each account. As account share increases, economies of scale increase, which raises the profit of the account. Similarly, the measure is an indication of the strength of the relationship with the account. Measuring relationship strength is a challenge, as you can see in the "Managing Sales Relationships" box.

Call Activity and/or Productivity Ratios

The call activity ratios measure the effort and planning salespeople put into their customer call activities and the successes they derive from it. The measures might be used to compare salesperson activities in total—such as when using calls per day or when using calls per total number of accounts, or by type of account. The planned call ratio could be used to assess if the salesperson is systematically planning territory coverage or whether the representative is working the territory without an overall game plan. The orders per call ratio bears directly on the question of whether the salesperson's calls on average are productive. This ratio is sometimes called the hit ratio or batting average, since it captures the number of successes (hits or orders) in relation to the number of at-bats (calls).

As Exhibits 16.2, 16.3, and the above discussion indicate, there are many objective outputs, inputs, and ratios by which salespeople can be compared. As you probably sense, many of the measures are somewhat redundant; they provide overlapping information on salespeople's behavior and successes. A number of other ratios could be developed by combining the various outputs, inputs, or ratios in various ways. One combination that is often used to evaluate salespeople, for example, is the equation

How Do You Measure a Relationship?

How do you measure the strength of a relationship? In a research study of the commercial printing business, account share was found to be a strong predictor of profit performance—the higher the account share, the better the profit picture. Account share is the percentage of business given to one supplier.

But account share is really just one outcome of a strong relationship and reflects a long history of activity by the salesperson. When account share was low but the relationship was strengthened, how would a manager know that the rep was on the right track?

Another study suggests that the answer lies with asking the customer directly. The authors of the study recommended that four dimensions be covered in a customer evaluation: the salesperson's trustworthiness, technical knowledge, product knowledge, and availability. These dimensions were found to be related to the customer's evaluation of the company, meaning that strong salespeople lead to strong evaluations of the company. But interestingly, while the customers' evaluations of salespeople were correlated with performance evaluations conducted by the sales manager, the correlations weren't particularly strong. In other words, sales managers and customers don't always agree.

A recent lawsuit illustrates this problem. A relatively inexperienced rep located a prospect with the potential of a million sale. She was teamed up with a senior person and asked to share the commission 50:50 (commission was 10 percent). She sued for the full commission (the company did get the sale). While they settled out of court, the case hinged on the strength of the relationship she had built with the account versus her manager's estimation of her ability to close the sale. What might the customer have said if asked to testify?

Sources: Douglas M. Lambert, Arun Sharma, and Michael Levy, "What Information Can Relationship Marketers Obtain from Customer Evaluations of Salespeople?" *Industrial Marketing Management* 26 (March 1997), pp. 177–88; Adel El-Ansary, *Winning Customers, Building Accounts: Some Do It Better than Others* (Jacksonville, FL: Paper and Plastics Education and Research Foundation, 1994).

$$\text{Sales} = \text{Days worked} \times \frac{\text{Calls}}{\text{Days worked}} \times \frac{\text{Orders}}{\text{Calls}} \times \frac{\text{Sales}}{\text{Orders}}$$

or

$$\text{Sales} = \frac{\text{Days}}{\text{worked}} \times \frac{\text{Call}}{\text{rate}} \times \frac{\text{Batting}}{\text{average}} \times \frac{\text{Average}}{\text{order size}}$$

The equation highlights nicely what the salesperson can do to increase sales. The representative can increase (1) the number of days worked, (2) the calls made per day, (3) success in securing an order on a given call, and (4) the size of those orders. Thus, the equation can be used to isolate how an individual salesperson's performance could be improved. Such an equation, though, focuses on the results of the salesperson's efforts and ignores the cost of these efforts. Similarly, many of the other measures that have been reviewed and could be combined via similar equations would probably ignore one or more elements of salesperson success.

There are two essential points to this discussion. First, just as sales and cost analyses have advantages and disadvantages, so do all of these other objective measures of performance. Rather than reliance on only one or two of the measures to assess performance, the methods are more productively used in combination. Second, and more important, all of the indexes are an aid to judgment, not a substitute for it. For example, the United States Army Recruiting Command (the part of the Army that sells young people on joining) once overrelied on conversion ratios. Orders were issued that calls of certain types had to be increased by a high percentage. The problem was that while the calls could be increased, quality could not be maintained. Performance not only did not increase but actually went down as morale declined. The comparisons the indexes allow should be the beginning, not the conclusion, of any analysis aimed at assessing how well individual salespeople or the entire sales force are doing.

SUBJECTIVE MEASURES

A useful conceptual distinction exists between the objective measures of effort and performance discussed in the preceding section and the subjective measures discussed here. Quantitative measures of effort focus on what salespeople do, whereas qualitative measures reflect how well they do what they are doing. This subtle difference in what is being measured creates some marked differences in the way the measurements are made.

In many ways, it is more difficult to assess the quality than the quantity of a salesperson's efforts. The quantity measures can require a detailed analysis of salespeople's call reports, an extensive time and duty analysis, or even some experimentation. Once the process is set up, though, it can be conducted with little bias and inconsistency. Not so with quality assessments. Even with a well-designed process that is firmly in place, there is substantial room for bias. Such schemes must invariably rely on the personal judgment of the individual or individuals charged with evaluation. Typically, these judgments are secured by having the appraiser rate the salesperson on each of a number of attributes using some kind of rating scale.

The attributes most commonly evaluated using merit rating forms are these:

1. Sales results—volume performance, sales to new accounts and selling the full product line.
2. Job knowledge—knowledge of company policies, prices, and products.
3. Management of territory—planning of activities and calls, controlling expenses, and handling reports and records.
4. Customer and company relations—standing with customers, associates, and company.
5. Personal characteristics—initiative, personal appearance, personality, resourcefulness, and so on.

The emphasis given to each varies by company. The emphasis also seems to depend on the purpose for which the evaluation is being used. For example, sales performance measures seem to be more important in termination and compensation decisions, whereas product knowledge and customer relations seem to be more important in transfer and promotion decisions.[9]

Exhibit 16.5 shows the rating scale used by the Testor Corporation. This sales personnel inventory is completed for every Testor salesperson every six months. These evaluations supplement the computer-generated reports of sales of each product to each customer to provide an overall evaluation of a salesperson's performance. The Testor inventory form is better than many of those in use because it contains anchors or verbal descriptors for the various points on the scale. Furthermore, it provides room for verbal comments, which enhance understanding of the ratings supplied. The form contains a section where needed improvements and corrective action can be detailed. All in all, the form should help salespeople understand their weaknesses and improve performance.

Exhibit 16.5   Sales Personnel Inventory, Used by the Testor Corporation

SALES PERSONNEL INVENTORY

Employer's Name _____   Territory _____

Position Title _____   Date _____

INSTRUCTIONS (Read Carefully)
1. Base your judgment on the previous six-month period and not upon isolated incidents alone.
2. Place a check in the block which most nearly expressess your judgment on each factor.
3. For those employees who are rated at either extreme of the scale on any factor—for example, outstanding, deficient, limited—please enter a brief explanation for the rating in the appropriate space below the factor.
4. Make your rating an accurate description of the person rated.

FACTORS TO BE CONSIDERED AND RATED:

1. **Knowledge of Work** (includes knowledge of product, knowledge of customer's business)

☐	☐	☐	☐	☐
Does not have sufficient knowledge of products and application to represent Company effectively.	Has mastered minimum knowledge. Needs further training.	Has average amount of knowledge needed to handle job satisfactorily.	Is above average in knowledge needed to handle job satisfactorily.	Is thoroughly acquainted with our products and technical problems involved in this application.

Comments _____

_____

2. **Degree of Acceptance by Customers**

☐	☐	☐	☐	☐
Not acceptable to most customers. Cannot gain entry to their offices.	Manages to see customers but not generally liked.	Has satisfactory relationship with most customers.	Is on very good terms and is accepted by virtually all customers.	Enjoys excellent personal relationship with virtually all customers.

Comments _____

_____

3. **Amount of Effort Devoted to Acquiring Business**

☐	☐	☐	☐	☐
Exceptional in the amount of time and effort put forth in selling.	Devotes constant effort in developing business.	Devotes intermittent effort in acquiring moderate amount of business.	Exerts only minimum amount of time and effort.	Unsatisfactory. Does not put forth sufficient effort to produce business.

Comments _____

_____

(continued)

Exhibit 16.5 *(continued)*

4. **Ability to Acquire Business**	☐ Is able to acquire business under the most difficult situations.	☐ Does a good job under most circumstances.	☐ Manages to acquire good percentage of customer's business if initial resistance is not too strong.	☐ Able to acquire enough business to maintain only a minimum sales averagee	☐ Rarely able to acquire business except in a seller's markett
	Comments _____				

5. **Amount of Service Given to Customers**	☐ Rarely services his accounts once a sale is made.	☐ Gives only minimum service at all times.	☐ Services accounts with regularity but does not do any more than he is called on to do.	☐ Gives very good service to all customers.	☐ Goes out of his way to give outstanding service within scope of Company policy.
	Comments _____				

6. **Dependability— Amount of Supervision Needed**	☐ Always thoroughly abreast of problems in his territory, even under most difficult conditions. Rises to emergencies and assumes leadership without being requested to do so.	☐ Consistently reliable under normal conditions. Does special as well as regular assignments promptly. Little or no supervision required.	☐ Performs with reasonable promptness under normal supervision.	☐ Effort occasionally lags. Requires moro than normal supervision.	☐ Requires close supervision in all phases of job.
	Comments _____				

7. **Attitude toward Company— Support Given to Company Policies**	☐ Does not support Company policy— blames Company for factors that affect his	☐ Gives only passive support to Company policy—does not act as member of a team.	☐ Goes along with Company policies on most occasions.	☐ Adopts and supports Company viewpoint in all transactions.	☐ Gives unwavering support to Company and Company policies to customers even though

(continued)

Exhibit 16.5   *(continued)*

	customers unfavorably.				he personally may not agree with them.

Comments _____

8. **Judgment**	☐	☐	☐	☐	☐
	Analyses and conclusions subject to frequent error and are often based on bias. Decisions require careful review by supervisor.	Judgments usually sound on routine, simple matters but cannot be relied on when any degree of complexity is involved.	Capable of careful analyzing of day-to-day problems involving some complexity and rendering sound decisions. Decision rarely influenced by prejudice or personal bias.	Decisions can be accepted without question except when problems of extreme complexity are involved. Little or no personal bias enters into judgment.	Possesses unusal comprehension and analytical ability. Complete reliance may be placed on all judgments irrespective of degree of complexity. Decisions and judgments are completely free of personal bias or prejudice.

Comments _____

9. **Resourcefulness**	☐	☐	☐	☐	☐
	Work is consistently characterized by marked originality, alertness, initiative, and imagination. Can be relied on to develop new ideas and techniques in solving the most difficult problems.	Frequently develops new ideas of merit. Handling of emergencies is generally characterized by sound decisive action.	Meets new situations in satisfactory manner. Occasionally develops original ideas, methods, and techniques.	Follows closely previously learned methods and procedures. Slow to adapt to changes. Tends to become confused in new situations.	Requires frequent reinstruction. Has failed to demonstrate initiative or imagination in solving problems.

Comments _____

To be more effective on present job, this employee should:

1. Be given additional instruction on _____

_____

(continued)

Exhibit 16.5 *(concluded)*

2. Be given additional experience such as _____

_____

3. Study such subjects as _____

_____

4. Change attitude as follows: _____

_____

5. There is nothing more that I can do for this employee because _____

_____

6. Remarks _____

_____

_____

The worst type of merit rating forms simply list the attributes of interest along one side of the form and the evaluation adjectives along the other. Exhibit 16.6, which is a recast version of the Testor inventory, illustrates such a form. The form can be completed very easily; the evaluator simply checks the adjective that most clearly describes the salesperson's performance on that attribute. While such forms are common, they work very poorly in practice.

Some common problems with performance appraisal systems that rely on merit rating forms, particularly those using the simple checklist type, include the following:[10]

1. *Lack of an outcome focus.* The most useful type of performance appraisal highlights areas of improvement and the actions that must be taken to effect such improvements. For this to occur, the key behaviors in accomplishing the tasks assigned must be identified. Unfortunately, many companies have not taken this step. Rather, they have simply identified attributes thought to be related to performance, but they have not attempted to assess systematically whether the attributes are key. One type of performance appraisal called BARS (behavioral anchored rating scale) overcomes this weakness. A BARS system attempts to identify behaviors that are more or less effective with respect to the goals established for the person. We will say more about BARS shortly.

2. *Ill-defined personality traits.* Many merit rating forms contain personality factors as attributes. In the case of salespeople, these attributes might include such things as initiative and resourcefulness. Although these attributes are intuitively appealing, their actual relationship to performance is open to question.[11]

3. *Halo effect.* A halo effect is a common phenomenon in the use of any rating form. It refers to the fact that the rating assigned to one characteristic significantly influences the ratings assigned to all others. One experiment that investigated the phenomenon among sales managers found that their overall evaluations could be predicted quite well from their rating of the salesperson on the single performance dimension they felt to be the most important.[12] Different branch or regional managers might have different feelings about what is most important, compounding the problem.

Exhibit 16.6 Modified Version of Testor Personnel Inventory

	Poor	Fair	Satisfactory	Good	Outstanding
Knowledge of work	☐	☐	☐	☐	☐
Degree of acceptance by customers	☐	☐	☐	☐	☐
Amount of effort devoted to acquiring business	☐	☐	☐	☐	☐
Ability to acquire business	☐	☐	☐	☐	☐
Amount of service given to customers	☐	☐	☐	☐	☐
Dependability—amount of supervision needed	☐	☐	☐	☐	☐
Attitude toward company—support given to company policies	☐	☐	☐	☐	☐
Judgment	☐	☐	☐	☐	☐
Resourcefulness	☐	☐	☐	☐	☐

4. *Leniency or harshness.* Some sales managers rate at the extremes. Some are very lenient and rate every salesperson as good or outstanding on every attribute, whereas others do just the opposite. This behavior is often a function of their own personalities and their perceptions of what is outstanding performance. There may be no fundamental differences in the way the salespeople under each of the managers are performing. The use of different definitions of performance can seriously undermine the whole performance, appraisal system.

5. *Central tendency.* Some managers err in the opposite direction in that they never, or very rarely, rate people at the ends of the scale. Rather, they use middle-of-the-road or play-it-safe ratings. One learns very little from such ratings about differences in performance, and such ratings can be particularly troublesome when used as the basis of termination decisions.

6. *Interpersonal bias.* Interpersonal refers to the fact that our perceptions of others and the social acceptability of their behaviors are influenced by how much we like or dislike them personally. Many sales managers' evaluations of sales reps are similarly affected. Furthermore, research suggests a salesperson can use personal influence strategies on the manager to bias evaluations upward.

7. *Organizational uses influence.* Performance ratings are often affected by the use to which they will be put. If promotions and monetary payments hinge on the ratings, there is often a tendency for leniency on the part of the manager who values the friendship and support of subordinates who press for higher ratings. It is not difficult to imagine the dilemma of a district sales manager if other district sales teams received consistently higher compensation increments and more promotions than his or her sales group. On the other hand, when appraisals are used for the development of subordinates, managers tend to more freely pinpoint weaknesses and focus on what is wrong and how it can be improved.[13]

To guard against the distortions introduced in the performance appraisal system by such occurrences, many firms issue admonitions to those completing the forms. Some common instructions issued with such forms are the following:

1. Read the definitions of each trait thoroughly and carefully before rating.

2. Guard against the common tendency to overrate.

3.   Do not let personal like or dislike influence your rating. Be as objective as possible.

4.   Do not permit your evaluation of one factor to influence your evaluation of another.

5.   Base your rating on the observed performance of the salesperson, not on potential abilities.

6.   Never rate an employee on several instances of good or poor work, but rather on general success or failure over the whole period.

7.   Have sound reasons for your ratings.[14]

These admonitions probably help, particularly when the evaluator must supply the reasons for ratings. They do not resolve the question of attributes used for the evaluation in the first place, however. A recent emphasis in performance appraisal directed at this question is BARS, which stands for behaviorally anchored rating scale.

A BARS system attempts to concentrate on the behaviors and performance criteria that can be controlled by the individual. The system focuses on the fact that a number of factors affect any employee's performance. However, some of these factors are more critical to job success than are others, and the key to evaluating people is to focus on these "critical success factors" (CSFs). Many investigations have found through extensive field studies that three critical behaviors had a direct impact on the selling success of representatives: (1) identifying needs and opportunities, (2) probing for information, and (3) handling objections.[15] Implementing a BARS system for evaluating salespeople requires identifying the behaviors that are key to their performance. Also, the subsequent evaluation of a salesperson's performance must be conducted by rating these key behaviors using the appropriate descriptions.

The whole process is implemented in the following way.[16] First, the key behaviors with respect to performance are identified using critical incidents. Critical incidents are occurrences that are critical or vital to performance. To use the critical incident technique, those involved could be asked to identify some particularly outstanding examples of good or bad performance and to detail the reasons why.[17] The performances identified are then reduced to a smaller number of performance dimensions by those working on the BARS development.

Next, the group of critical incidents is presented to a group of sales personnel who are asked to assign each critical incident to an appropriate dimension. An incident is typically kept in if 60 percent or more of the group assigns it to the same dimension as did the instrument development group. The sales personnel group is also asked to rate the behavior described in the critical incident on a 7- or 10-point scale with respect to how effectively or ineffectively it represents performance on the dimension. Incidents that generate good agreement in ratings, typically measured by the standard deviation, are considered for the final scale. The particular incidents chosen are determined by their location along the scale, as measured by the means. Typically, the final scale has six to eight anchors. An example of a BARS scale that resulted from such a process for the attribute "promptness in meeting deadlines" is shown in Exhibit 16.7.

The advantage of a BARS system is that it requires appropriate personnel to consider in detail the components of a salesperson's job performance. They must also define anchors for those performance criteria in specific behavioral terms. In terms of the model of Exhibit 16.1, a BARS system tends to emphasize behavior and performance rather than effectiveness. Perhaps that is what a system appraising the performance of salespeople should emphasize, particularly when effectiveness is already assessed through sales and cost analyses.

BARS systems are not without their limitations, though.[18] For one thing, the job-

Exhibit 16.7   A BARS Scale with Behavioral Anchors for the Attribute "Promptness in Meeting Deadlines"

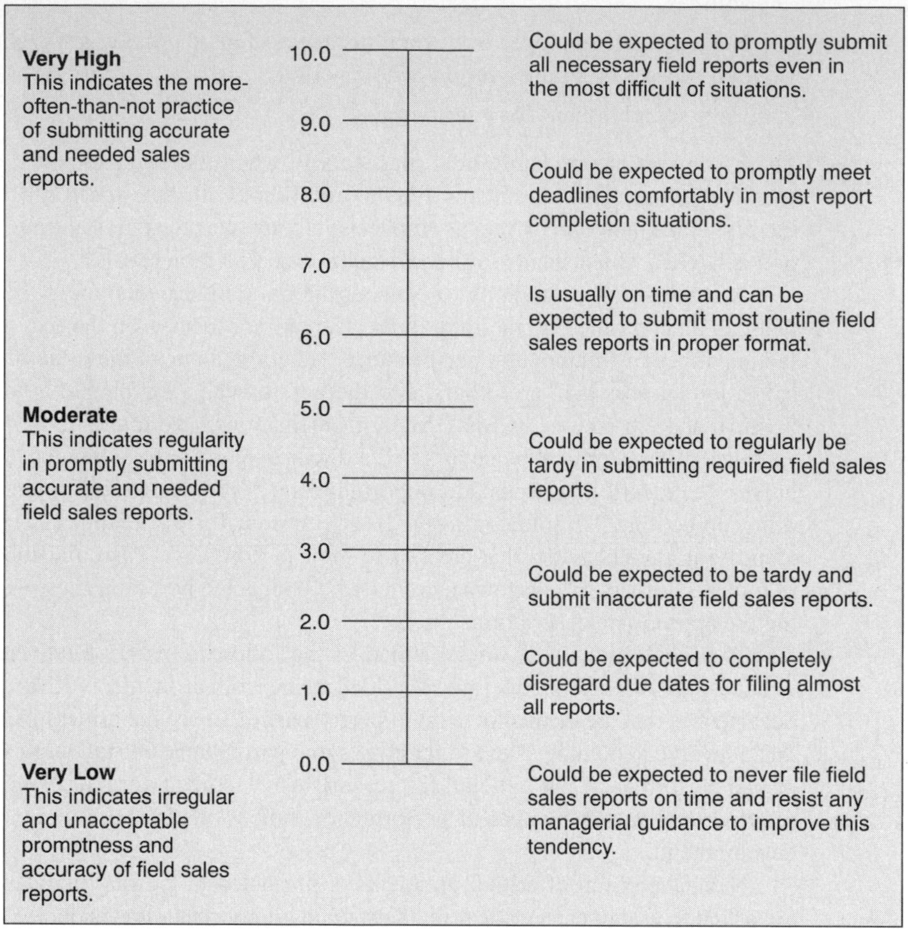

Very High
This indicates the more-often-than-not practice of submitting accurate and needed sales reports.

10.0 — Could be expected to promptly submit all necessary field reports even in the most difficult of situations.

9.0 —

8.0 — Could be expected to promptly meet deadlines comfortably in most report completion situations.

7.0 —

6.0 — Is usually on time and can be expected to submit most routine field sales reports in proper format.

5.0 —

Moderate
This indicates regularity in promptly submitting accurate and needed field sales reports.

4.0 — Could be expected to regularly be tardy in submitting required field sales reports.

3.0 —

2.0 — Could be expected to be tardy and submit inaccurate field sales reports.

1.0 — Could be expected to completely disregard due dates for filing almost all reports.

Very Low
This indicates irregular and unacceptable promptness and accuracy of field sales reports.

0.0 — Could be expected to never file field sales reports on time and resist any managerial guidance to improve this tendency.

Source: Reprinted from A. Benton Cocanougher and John M. Ivancevich, "'BARS' Performance Rating for Sales Personnel," *Journal of Marketing* 42 (June 1978), p. 92. Reprinted by permission of the American Marketing Association.

specific nature of the scales they produce suggests they are most effective in evaluating salespeople performing very similar functions. They might be effective in comparing one national account rep to another national account rep or two territory representatives against each other, but they could suffer major shortcomings if used to compare a national account representative against a territory salesperson, because of differences in their responsibilities. They also can be relatively costly to develop since they require a good deal of time from a number of people.

SUMMARY

Although sales and cost analyses are two important tools in sales management control and evaluation of

individual representatives, they do have problems. A main difficulty in using them is that they measure effectiveness rather than performance. The distinction between these notions is important. Performance is directly related to salesperson behavior. Behavior refers to what the representatives do or the tasks on which they expend effort. Performance is behavior evaluated in terms of its contributions to the organization. It focuses on whether the number of calls a salesperson made or the number of proposals the representative developed are good or bad, above expectations or below. Effectiveness includes additional factors not under the individual salesperson's control, such as the potential within the territory and the actions of competitors. Many firms supplement their sales and cost analyses with other measures that assess salesperson performance more directly.

These other measures can be either objective or subjective, and either group can be used to assess inputs or outputs. The objective measures reflect other statistics the manager can gather from the firm's internal data. Some of the most common objective output measures focus on orders or accounts such as the number of orders, the number of canceled orders, the number of active accounts, the number of new accounts, and the number of lost accounts.

The more common objective input measures emphasize calls, time and time utilization, expenses, and nonselling activities. Typical ones from each category would be the number of calls, the number of days worked, the salesperson's total expenses, and the number of service calls made. The input for these objective measures often comes from salespeople's call reports or from time and duty analyses. The data can also be secured from other operating systems within the firm or can emanate from special research investigations.

Many firms combine the various outputs and/or inputs to form ratios, based on their company's sales process and other factors. The three most common types are expense ratios, account development and servicing ratios, and call activity and/or productivity ratios.

The various measures are most productively used in combination. They are an aid to judgment, not a substitute for it. The comparisons that the indexes allow should be the beginning and not the end of any analysis aimed at assessing how well the personal selling effort is going and how individual salespeople are doing.

Some common performance attributes assessed using subjective measures are job knowledge, management of the territory, customer and company relations, and personal characteristics. Also included are other aspects of sales such as whether the person sold the full product line.

The subjective assessments are typically made using some type of merit rating form in which the evaluator checks the amount of each of a number of predetermined attributes of the salesperson. A severe problem with merit rating forms is their lack of an outcome focus; that is, they often contain many attributes not critical or vital to performance. To get at the more essential attributes, a number of firms are turning to BARS (behaviorally anchored rating scales). The BARS procedure emphasizes the isolation of behaviors most critical to performing the duties assigned. Subsequent evaluations are carried out with respect to these critical behaviors.

DISCUSSION QUESTIONS

1. Kevin Harrison, sales rep for Allied Steel Distributors, had an appointment with his sales manager to discuss his first year's sales performance. Kevin knew that the meeting would not go well. One of Allied's major accounts had changed suppliers due to problems with Kevin. The purchasing agent claimed that personality differences were so serious that future business with Allied was not possible. Kevin knew that these so-called personality differences involved his unwillingness to entertain in the same style as the previous sales rep. The previous sales rep frequently took the purchasing agent and others to a local topless bar for lunch. The rep told Kevin that this was expected and that if he wanted to keep the business, it was necessary; besides, tickets to the professional basketball games didn't count anymore. What are the short- and long-range implications of this type of customer entertaining? What would you do in a similar situation?

2. A large corporation notices an irregular decrease in the sales of a particular representative. The sales rep, normally in very high standing among other salespeople and quotas, has of late failed to achieve her own quota. What can be done by the corporation to determine whether the slump in the sales curve is the responsibility of the representative or due to things beyond her control?

3. Given the following information from evaluations of the performance of different sales representatives, what possible deductions could be made about the sales reps not achieving quota?

   a. Representative 1: Achieved target goals for sales calls, telephone calls, and new accounts; customer relations good; no noticeable deficiencies in any areas.

   b. Representative 2: Completed substantially fewer sales calls than target; telephone calls high in number, but primarily with one firm. Time management analysis shows the sales representative to be spending a disproportionately large amount of time with one firm. New accounts are low; all other areas good to outstanding.

   c. Representative 3: Number of sales calls low, below target; telephone calls, letters, proposals all very low and below target; evaluation shows poor time utilization, very high amount of service-related activities in sales representative's log; customer relations extremely positive, high amount of feedback on product function produced lately.

4. Is sales "just a numbers game," as one sales manager states? She believes that all you have to do is make the right number of calls of the right type, and the odds will work in your favor. Make 10 calls, get one sale. So to get two sales, make 20 calls. Will this work? Why or why not?

5. Jackie Hitchcock, recently promoted to district sales manager, faced a new problem she wasn't sure how to resolve. The district's top sales rep is also the district's number one headache. Barton Coombs traditionally leads the company in sales but also leads the company in problems. He has broken every rule, bent every policy, deviated from guidelines, and been less than truthful. Jackie knew Barton had never done anything illegal or unethical, but she was worried that something could happen. Other problems with Barton include not preparing call reports on time, failing to show up at trade shows, and not attending sales training programs.

   How should Jackie handle this problem? How does a sales manager manage a maverick sales rep?

EXPERIENTIAL APPLICATIONS

1. Bill Smith has just finished performing a cost analysis on his district. The results show that while two salespeople have reached their planned sales goal, two other salespeople have missed their planned sales goals (see Table 1). To gain insight into what is happening in his district, Bill has decided to do a ratio analysis. He used the information shown in Table 2 to complete the ratio analysis. Compute the following ratios for each salesperson:

Table 1

| | Sales Representative | | | |
	1	2	3	4
Planned sales	$575,000	$650,000	$640,000	$650,000
Actual sales	550,000	650,000	640,000	620,000
Cost of sales	445,000	530,000	520,000	500,000
Gross margin	105,000	120,000	120,000	120,000
Expenses:				
Salaries	20,000	22,000	21,000	23,000
Commissions	5,500	6,500	6,400	6,200
Travel	7,000	10,000	9,500	9,500
Advertising	27,000	28,000	31,000	31,000
Warehouse	7,000	8,000	8,000	7,600
Order processing	100	140	100	160
Transportation	21,000	24,000	24,000	23,000
Total expenses	87,600	98,640	100,000	100,460
Net profit (loss)	$ 17,400	$ 21,360	$ 20,000	$ 19,540

Table 2

	Sales Representative			
	1	2	3	4
Number of calls	90	125	100	100
Number of orders	50	70	50	80
Number of accounts in territory	250	260	240	275
Number of accounts sold	40	70	70	75
Number of new accounts	3	7	6	7
Number of days worked	20	20	20	20

a. Sales expense ratio.

b. Account penetration ratio.

c. New account conversion ratio.

d. Average order size ratio.

e. Calls per day ratio.

f. Orders per call ratio.

2. Use the information contained in the following table to evaluate Marsha Jackson's sales performance. What conclusions do you reach? What are your recommendations?

**Marsha Jackson
District: New Orleans**

	1997	1998	1999	2000
1. Sales class I	339,125	339,288	361,800	352,554
2. Quota class I	354,730	368,791	411,136	419,707
3. Sales class II	529,000	588,528	742,226	752,946
4. Quota class II	439,360	481,216	550,204	575,646
5. Gross margin–class I	67,825	67,858	72,360	70,511
6. Gross margin–class II	52,900	58,853	74,223	75,295
7. Sales expenses	12,750	13,875	14,500	16,500
8. Number of calls	1,685	1,710	1,690	1,670
9. Number of orders	1,011	1,060	1,115	1,119
10. Average number of customers	330	334	338	344
11. Average number of potential customers	577	573	564	562
12. Number of new customers	18	19	20	25
13. Number of lost customers	13	15	16	19
14. Number of days worked	241	246	245	248

INTERNET EXERCISE

Visit the Northwestern Mutual home page and scan through the awards it has won. Then look at information concerning the sales position (*northwesternmutual.com/sales/*). Knowing what you are able to learn about Northwestern from the home page and the insurance industry, what types of behavioral measures of performance do you expect to find at this company? Specifically cite quotes from the home page to support your position. Then open a home page of any other featured company in the text (chose one of the companies profiled at the start of a chapter) and again, using quotes from the home pages to support your conclusions, compare and contrast that company's expected measurement system with the Northwestern Mutual system.

SUGGESTED READINGS

DeCarlo, Thomas, Kenneth Teas, and James McElroy, "Salesperson Performance Attribution Processes and the Formation of Expectancy Estimates," *Journal of Personal Selling and Sales Management* 17 (Summer 1997), pp. 1–18.

Dion, Paul A., Debbie Easterling, and Raj Javalgi, "Women in the Business-to-Business Salesforce: Some Differences in Performance Factors," *Industrial Marketing Management* 26 (1997), pp. 447–58.

Hill, John S., and Arthur W. Allaway, "How U.S.-Based Companies Manage Sales in Foreign Countries," *Industrial Marketing Management* 22 (February 1993), pp. 7–16.

Jobber, David, Graham J. Hooley, and David Shipley, "Organizational Size and Salesforce Evaluation Practices," *Journal of Personal Selling and Sales Management* 13 (Spring 1993), pp. 37–48.

Mackenzie, Scott B., Philip M. Podsakoff, and Michael Ahearne, "Some Possible Antecedents and Consequences of In-Role and Extra-Role Salesperson Performance," *Journal of Marketing* 62 (July 1998), pp. 87–98.

Paun, Dorothy, "A Study of 'Best' versus 'Average' Buyer–Seller Relationships," *Journal of Business Research* 39 (May 1997), pp. 13–22.

Rich, Gregory, "The Constructs of Coaching: Supervisory Feedback, Role Modeling, and Trust," *Journal of Personal Selling and Sales Management* 18 (Winter 1998), pp. 53–64.

Weinrauch, J. Donald, Marilyn Stevens, and Rodney Carlson, "Training Requirements for Professional Certification of Manufacturer's Representatives," *Industrial Marketing Management* 26 (1997), pp. 509–18.

Comprehensive Cases
for Part III

Case 3–1

Supersonic Stereo, Inc.*

"At this rate, I'll be looking for a new job," thought Bob Basler, sales manager of Supersonic's Atlanta district. "Our sales are stagnant, and what's worse, our profits are down." Sales and profit results for the last five years did not measure up to objectives established for the Atlanta district (see Exhibit 1). Basler knew that soon he would be hearing from Pete Lockhart, Supersonic's national sales manager, and the same question would be asked: "When are you going to turn the Atlanta district around?"

Basler was faced with another problem that added to his worries. One of his sales representatives, Charlie Lyons, was very upset and was threatening to quit unless he received a substantial salary increase. Lyons thought that since he led the district in sales volume, he should be amply rewarded. "I have to find out what's happening in the Atlanta district before I go and make recommendations for salary increases," Basler thought. "Besides, if I make such a recommendation, Pete will think that I have taken leave of my senses. He will not approve any salary increases for anybody as long as the Atlanta district's performance is so weak."

Supersonic Stereo is one of the country's leading manufacturers of stereo equipment. Since its formation in 1962, Supersonic has experienced rapid growth based largely on its reputation for high-quality stereo products. Prices were competitive, although some dealers engaged in discounting. Supersonic distributed its stereo equipment on a selective basis. Only those dealers who could provide strong marketing support and reliable servicing were selected by Supersonic. Dealers were supported by Supersonic's national advertising campaign. Advertising averaged 5 percent of sales, somewhat more than other stereo manufacturers spent for this item.

Supersonic's sales force was compensated with salary plus commission of 6 percent based on gross margin. Gross margin was used to discourage sales reps from cutting prices. Accounts were assigned to sales representatives based on size. New sales reps were usually assigned a number of small accounts. As they progressed, they were assigned larger accounts. The more experienced sales representatives were assigned the larger, more desirable accounts. In some cases, a sales rep would have only three or four accounts, each averaging $250,000 a year.

The average base salary for the sales force reached $26,500 in 1998 and commissions averaged $9,500. Total average sales force compensation was $36,000 in 1998. Travel expenses were paid by Supersonic. The total package was considered by one executive to be too plush. This executive, Stella Jordan, thought not enough was expected from the sales force. "I know of one sales representative who calls on three accounts and in 1997 earned $38,563," she stated at a recent meeting. "If we want to improve our profits, then we need to either reduce our base salaries or cut back our commission rate."

Exhibit 1   Total Sales and Profits for the Atlanta District, 1994–1998

	1994	1995	1996	1997	1998
Total sales	$2,641,081	$2,445,120	$2,610,029	$2,514,113	$2,638,340
Net profit	13,873	14,050	15,381	16,511	14,383

Exhibit 2   Profit and Loss Statement, Atlanta District, 1998

Sales		$2,638,340
Cost of goods sold		2,014,485
Gross margin		$ 623,855
Expenses:		
Salaries	$177,000	
Commissions	37,431	
Advertising	131,915	
Packaging	43,642	
Warehousing and transportation	76,374	
Travel expenses	59,340	
Order processing	770	
Rent	83,000	
Total expenses		609,472
Net profit (before taxes)		$ 14,383

Jordan's suggestion was not favorably received by Basler, who believed such a move would have a disastrous effect on sales force motivation. Jordan countered by pointing out that motivation must be lacking since the Atlanta district's performance is so poor. "If salaries or commissions cannot be reduced, at least let's not raise them," she suggested. "Maybe we should consider raising quotas and not pay commissions until sales representatives exceed their quotas. Or," she continued. "maybe a management by objectives approach should be developed."

Basler knew that Jordan's comments demanded a response. He also knew she was talking about Charlie Lyons when she mentioned a sales rep with three accounts earning $38,563. Basler suggested he should be allowed time to do a complete cost analysis by sales representative before adopting any corrective action. Jordan agreed and offered her assistance. Salaries for the others were as follows: Sand, $24,500; Gallo, $27,500; and Parks, $26,000.

Basler's first activity was to identify available information for his district. He was able to secure a profit and loss statement for the Atlanta district (see Exhibit 2). Jordan suggested that since Basler was interested in sales force profitability, his next step should be to allocate the natural accounts in Exhibit 2 to their appropriate functional accounts. Exhibit 3 shows the results of this step.

"If we are going to do an analysis by sales representative, we need much more information," Jordan indicated. To help in this regard, she compiled product sales data (see Exhibit 4).

Basler provided data for each sales representative, showing number of sales calls, number of orders, and unit sales by product line (see Exhibit 5). The next step would be to compile the data to develop a profitability analysis by sales representative.

The problem with Charlie Lyons is still there, mused Basler. He wants more money,

Exhibit 3   Allocation of Natural Accounts to Functional Accounts, Atlanta District

Natural Accounts		Selling Direct Costs	Selling Indirect Costs	Advertising	Order Processing	Warehouse and Transportation	Packaging
					Functional Accounts		
Salaries	$177,000	$106,500	$47,500		$12,000		$11,000
Commissions	37,431	37,431					
Advertising	131,915			$131,915			
Packaging	43,642						43,642
Warehousing and transportation	76,374					$76,374	
Travel expenses	59,340	57,340	2,000				
Order processing	770				770		
Rent	83,000		18,500		4,500	40,000	20,000
Total expenses	$609,472	$201,271	$68,000	$131,915	$17,270	$116,374	$74,642

Exhibit 4   Product Line Sales and Costs

Product	Selling Price per Unit	Cost per Unit	Gross Margin per Unit	Number Sold in Period	Sales in Period	Advertising Expenditures	Packaging
Receivers	$250	$212	$38	3,151	$ 787,750	$ 40,000	$ 6,302
CD Players	85	64	21	12,079	1,026,715	50,000	24,158
Speakers	125	87	38	6,591	823,875	40,000	13,182
				21,821	$2,638,340	$130,000	$43,642

and Stella Jordan thinks he is overpaid and underworked. Since Charlie Lyons is something of a focal point, we ought to do a profitability analysis for each of his customers. Basler's next step was to compile data by customer. Exhibit 6 presents customer data for each of Lyons's three accounts.

Preparing guidelines for allocating costs to sales representatives and customers was Basler's next task. On the basis of his review of several distribution cost and analysis textbooks and further conversations with Stella Jordan, Basler developed the following guidelines:

Functional Cost Item	Basis of Allocation
Direct selling	Number of calls × average time spent with each customer
Commissions	6 percent of gross margin
Travel	Total travel costs by number of calls; this figure is then multiplied by individual salesperson calls or customer calls.
Advertising	5 percent of sales dollars
Packaging	Number of units × $2
Warehousing and transportation	Number of units × $3.50
Order processing	Number of orders × $2.75

Exhibit 5   Sales Calls, Orders, and Units Sold by Salesperson

Salesperson	Sales Calls	Orders	Number of Units Sold			
			Receivers	CD Players	Speakers	Total
Paul Sand	85	60	668	2,652	1,534	4,854
Diane Gallo	105	85	823	3,270	1,582	5,675
Kathy Parks	110	60	816	3,131	1,578	5,525
Charlie Lyons	170	75	844	3,026	1,897	5,767
	470	280	3,151	12,079	6,591	21,821

Exhibit 6   Customer Activity Analysis for Charlie Lyons

Customers of Charlie Lyons	Sales Calls	Average Time Spent on Each Call (minutes)	Orders	Number of Units Purchased			
				Receivers	CD Players	Speakers	Total
American TV	65	55	40	422	1,513	854	2,789
Appliance Mart	55	45	15	337	1,058	569	1,964
Audio Emporium	50	45	20	85	455	474	1,014
	170	48	75	844	3,026	1,897	5,767

Basler's next step is developing the necessary accounting statement, which will permit a detailed analysis of each sales rep's profitability. From there he will proceed to a customer profitability analysis for Charlie Lyons's customers.

Case 3–2

National Telecommunications Corporation*

After two years as an account executive in southern Illinois for National Telecommunications, Dan Peters was well on his way to developing a rewarding and challenging career. Although the majority of his experience was in consumer sales, he quickly adapted to a more sophisticated selling environment. He enjoyed the challenge the work offered and discovered that his selling skills were perfectly matched for longer selling cycles and extended customer relations. After five months, he was a consistent top performer within the division, and his monthly sales were steadily increasing.

His second year with National was highlighted by sales to two major accounts that would generate substantial revenue for the company and earnings for himself. Dan invested in a new car and considered starting a family, something he was hesitant to do before going to work for National. The beginning of his third year was accompanied by a serious change at National on a corporate level. Top management perceived the company's sales performance to be substandard, and personnel at even the highest levels were either reassigned or terminated.

Several divisions also began to experience delays in customer service due to equipment failure and only marginal backup and repair. Dan was frustrated by the lack of management and company support he was receiving in the field to serve major accounts and their changing demands.

To deal with his major customer's problems, Dan had to spend an increasing amount of time away from his primary selling duties, including the signing of new accounts. Since his monthly quota was based on originating new business, he was unable to reach quota several times. Although his immediate supervisor showed little concern, Dan received a strong written warning concerning his performance.

With upper management threatening termination, Dan became confused as to what his actual responsibilities should include and how he could be expected to actively sell and service accounts at the same time. Dan also thought upper management failed to consider the service disadvantage National had in eastern Illinois. The company's major competitor, AT&T, possessed superior equipment and reliability. This hindered Dan's sales performance.

Company Background

National Telecommunications originated in 1963 when communications expert John Gross formed National Microwave, Inc. The company under Gross's guidance implemented a microwave link between St. Louis and Kansas City to assist trucking firms op-

*This case was prepared especially for this text by Dale Humphrey, MBA, University of Wisconsin–Madison, under the supervision of Professor Neil M. Ford, University of Wisconsin–Madison. Copyright © 1998 Neil M. Ford.

erating between the two cities. After five years of successful operation, Gross and long-time friend Roger Deane, current National chairman, decided to expand operations by moving headquarters to Kansas City and renaming the company National Communications of America, Inc. Deane, who then owned a substantial portion of the company, agreed to buy Gross's share and pursue other opportunities for expansion.

The early 70s for National were a period of difficult change dictated by legislation governing telecommunications. National and others relied on the government to provide opportunities for expansion. In the wake of Federal Communications Commission approvals for a national network, National Telecommunications Corporation was born. National placed itself against industry giant AT&T, which, in conjunction with local Bell operating companies, controlled the vast majority of required interconnects. AT&T used this advantage to discourage and even prevent major competition from entering several markets. The result was 10 years of legal maneuvering between National and AT&T over equipment rights.

Gradually, AT&T lost its complete hold on interconnects and services after several major lawsuits went in National's favor. In 1982, National became a *Fortune* 500 company and acquired several regionally based communication firms. From 1983 to 1985, legal actions against AT&T by National and others culminated when the government initiated the breakup of AT&T into separate entities. National was then able to develop its own operating system in conjunction with the Bell system.

Following the breakup, National extended its national network and service base. The introduction of National Mail and COMMNET established the company as an innovator in business communication technology and service. In 1992, National purchased Vericom Global Communications, an established market leader in international telex and data transfer services. At the close of 1993, National registered its most profitable year with annual revenue reaching a historic high of $6.4 billion. In 1995, National's market share reached 12 percent, slowly penetrating AT&T's dominant position (see Exhibit 1).

Exhibit 1   National 1995 Market Share

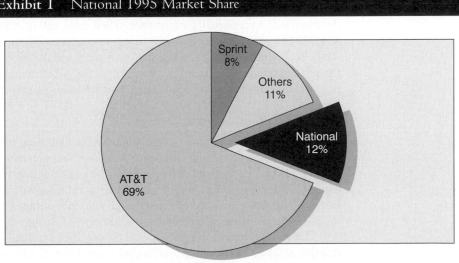

Today, national is truly an international company, providing services in over 10 countries. The company's $6.9 billion network is comprised of systems owned and operated by National and 60 independently operated regional networks. In addition to basic phone line service, National provides over 50 customer service options to the consumer and business markets. Using aggressive advertising, National has directly confronted AT&T, creating a telecommunications war between the two companies. AT&T is now defending its dominant market share as National continues to invest in new equipment and regional networks.

National's Sales Organization

National's selling efforts are directed at consumer and business markets. The consumer market is serviced by the company's media-based promotion efforts and telemarketing division. The advertising campaigns of National and AT&T resemble the "cola war" being waged by Pepsi and Coke. National promotes a cost advantage while AT&T counters with claims of superior customer service. Advertising is direct and openly critical of the other's product. National's telemarketing division contacts consumers directly to promote the company's long-distance service and other products.

National's primary selling effort is carried out by the company's general business sales force. Comprised of over 5,000 sales representatives (account executives) and six levels of management, the general business sales organization is the largest and most profitable division of National. Exhibit 2 outlines the sales organization with detail on the Midwest division.

The other sales divisions are the West, Southwest, Pacific, Mid-Atlantic, Southeast, Northeast, and International. The vertical composition of the Midwest division is reflective of the other national divisions. Many states with larger markets are much larger horizontally to balance the lower-level manager's span of control.

State and area sales managers (ASMs) are typically former account executives with the company. Major account representatives (MARs) are responsible for a number of larger National business customers and report directly to regional sales directors. Their compensation is on an 80/20 plan with a base salary averaging $26,000 to $32,000 plus a 20 percent commission base on customer billing. Account executives are divided into two classes: AE1 and AE2.

AE2s have typically been with the company over five years or are former AE1s who demonstrated exceptional performance. Their base salary ranges between $20,000 and $24,000 per year plus commissions based on customer billing schedules. AE1s have typically been with the company less than five years and do not have previous experience in the telecommunications industry. Base salary for AE1s ranges from $18,000 to $22,000 per year in addition to a rolling average commission schedule.

Account Executive Work Analysis

Dan Peters's first six months with National were dedicated primarily to training. He attended various seminars and company workshops that presented operating policies, product knowledge, specialized selling tactics, and information on the telecommunications market. Following several weeks of on-the-job training with another account executive, Dan was officially assigned as an AE1 with National–Illinois. His assigned territory consisted of eastern Illinois, including a portion of the Chicago market.

The product he was assigned to sell is actually a service—custom-designed communication systems. The term *systems* includes any form of wire or optical transmission utilizing existing telephone networks. The complexity of the system varied in proportion to

Exhibit 2   National Sales Organization

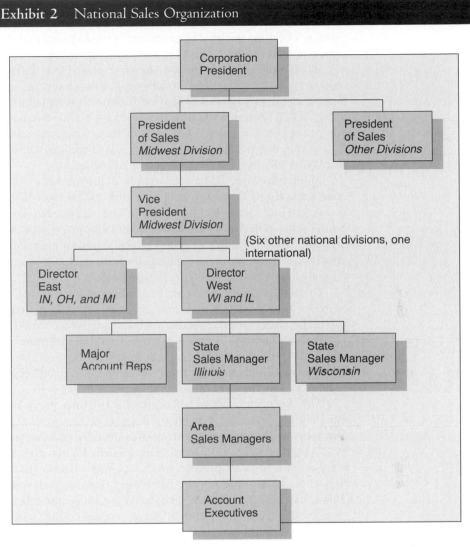

the type and size of the business for which it was being designed. For example, a company relying on telemarketing would demand a more complex and customer-driven long-distance service than a small business operating in a local market.

Dan was responsible for assessing the long-distance needs of such customers and presenting National systems and services that fulfilled these needs. As discussed earlier, the entrenchment of AT&T and the Bell companies presented Dan with one primary task: offer services that were more flexible, reliable, and cost-effective than those offered by AT&T and Bell. Since the vast majority of prospective customers used AT&T services, Dan was presenting many with a competing service for the first time. For prospecting purposes, Dan was expected to generate his own calling schedule based on company listings of firms not currently using National services. The listings are distributed to each AE based on territory. Each AE is required to compile weekly reports that contain the number of calls made (in person or on the phone) and the number of presentations made during a week. The reports are used to monitor AE activity and provide a written summary for the meeting of calling quotas. The quotas are set at 25 phone calls per day to prospective customers and 10 person-to-person appointments per week.

In addition to activity quotas, AEs are expected to reach monthly dollar quotas based on new customer billing. The monthly long-distance revenue a new account will generate is estimated from past billing behavior. If Dan was attempting to sign a customer currently using AT&T, he would examine that company's long-distance usage and then present a competing estimate based on that information. This same estimate was then credited to Dan during the month the new account was signed to National. The quota for AE1s is $4,000 per month and $5,000 per month for AE2s.

Monthly revenue figures are straight dollar amounts, and the actual number of accounts making up the total is not considered critical. Dan could sign 10 smaller accounts that would bill over $4,000 per month or one account that would reach the same level of billing activity. Such a system does not discipline an AE who is able to sign only one large account, although calling schedules (activity quotas) must still be attained. Levels in excess of selling quotas are not candidates for bonuses or incentives. The AR is rewarded through a commission structure discussed next.

Dan's total compensation included a base salary plus two types of commissions. The base or primary commissions are calculated from the billing activity of each account signed by the AE while working for National. Thus, the AE would earn income on a month-to-month basis from the entire account base retained by that AE. Dan, for example, would receive monthly reports that would outline each account to which he sold National services and the long-distance charges the account accumulated during the month. Exhibit 3 illustrates a commission statement for Dan.

The statement is totaled and combined with three previous months to arrive at a four-month billing statement. Commissions are set at 22 percent of the average billing over the four months. Commission payments are generally paid one month after the fourth statement is closed. The AE then receives account listings for the final month and a summary sheet displaying previous totals and commissions based on the average. In addition to these commissions, the AE is paid on what National calls "retention revenue." This is based on the percentage of the AE's signed accounts that are still using National services. Payments are calculated from a schedule that initiates payment at a level of 90 percent. Percentages go up to 1,000 percent and commissions range from $16 to $320 per month.

Dan was extremely satisfied with the working conditions and compensation structure at National. He consistently met both his activity and selling quotas from month to month and received a base salary raise at the start of his second year. Unfortunately, his satisfaction with work and his superiors began to change drastically during his third year.

Dan Peters's Difficulties

During the spring of 1994, Dan was concentrating on developing a proposal for two large potential accounts located in his portion of the Chicago sales territory. Due to the size of the accounts and the complexity of their communication needs, Dan spent many hours outside of work analyzing their current long-distance usage and the National services he would propose for replacement. He also worked with technicians from National to provide accurate estimates on hardware requirements and installation times. After making several appointments with the key decision makers in each company, he was confident of securing a sale with at least one of the firms.

Exhibit 3

NATIONAL TELECOMMUNICATIONS
Commission Calculation Statement
Employee SSN: 355-34-4947

Office: 71334200 East Illinois
SALES REPRESENTATIVE: Peters, Daniel
SEPTEMBER ACTIVITY: TYPE/STATUS: AE AE/ACTV

| | | | | Commissionable Revenue | |
| | | Total Account | Account | | |
Account Name	Inst Date	Revenue	History Peak	New Growth	Retention
Assigned Accounts:					
The Illinois Press	940605	15.39	13.29	2.10	13.29
Veterans Affairs	921227	109.74	163.05	0.00	109.74
Plastics Inc.	930616	111.84	141.39	0.00	111.84
Illinois Press	930920	2251.01	1594.35	0.00	2251.04
Illinois Physicians	940515	3102.11	394.31	2707.80	394.31
Illinois Physicians	940227	2012.24	6773.18	0.00	2012.24
Illinois Power & Li	921003	157.86	196.84	0.00	157.86
Illinois Power & Li	930808	83.59	100.77	0.00	83.69
Illinois Power & Li	930808	59.53	67.88	0.00	59.53
Illinois Power & Li	930808	157.88	179.27	0.00	157.88
Illinois Power & Li	930808	47.77	79.38	0.00	47.77
Illinois Power & Li	930320	20.99	43.24	0.00	20.99
Illinois Power & Li	930613	35.64	100.70	0.00	35.64
Illinois Power & Li	930712	31.87	52.81	0.00	31.87
Illinoic Powor & Li	930523	104.42	121.45	0.00	104.42
Illinois Power & Li	930411	10.91	33.32	0.00	10.91
Illinois Power & Li	921025	850.43	1097.07	0.00	850.43
Illinois Power & Li	930821	20.97	26.41	0.00	20.97
Illinois Power & Li	930320	29.10	53.24	0.00	29.10
Illinois Power & Li	940824	0.73	0.00	0.00	0.73
Illinois Power & Li	940814	2.29	0.00	2.29	0.00
Illinois Power & Li	930620	97.04	124.32	0.00	97.04
Illinois Power & Li	940718	20.81	9.37	11.44	9.37
IPS	940515	54778.39	40996.29	13783.10	40996.29
Assigned Account Totals:		103704.82		16744.18	86873.81
Total Month's Activity:		103704.82		16744.18	86873.81

Exhibit 4

To: D. R. Peters
CC: Karen Sullivan
CC: Jim Sanders
CC: Diane Robinson
CC: Mark Hanusa
SUBJECT: Congratulations!

Your position as a contender for CIC 100 is outstanding given the top quality of NTC's sales reps! Keep up the great work and you'll be among the first recipients to achieve this new and exclusive distinction. Mark your calendars for Tahiti, May 15–19, 1996!

After nearly two months of negotiations, Dan closed sales with both of the firms. Combined, the two companies would bill an estimated $70,000 in long-distance charges, nearly exceeding Dan's entire account base. The accounts would provide healthy monthly commissions and would put Dan among the top 15 National AEs in the country. His position also put him in contention for a major company sales award that was given to the top 100 representatives in the country (see Exhibit 4).

Dan did not have much time to enjoy his success or compliments from upper management. Following installation, his two major accounts began to experience serious equipment failures. He was constantly at their offices trying to remedy the problems and repair deteriorating relations with his customers. Dan's selling time did not permit such extensive post-sale responsibilities. Following a sale, major technical issues were to be handed over to National-Service, not the AE. In Dan's case, National was slow to react and Dan was pinned down in his customers' offices listening to their concerns and trying to assure them the system merely had to be "broken in."

Most of the technical problems were due to an unexpected degree of incompatibility between National's internal equipment and Illinois Bell's regional network. As Dan explained, "National has experienced problems developing its own regional network here (Chicago), and it has handicapped National's larger installation projects." After a month of inconsistent service, Dan's accounts were moving beyond frustration. One of the accounts refused to pay a National bill and was immediately disconnected.

Dan was voicing his concerns, but his immediate manager only would urge him to continue servicing the accounts to the best of his abilities. During this period, Dan was off his selling quota two months in a row because of the difficulties experienced by his major accounts. Dan's office took little action until the regional office pressured his manager for an explanation of Dan's performance. Dan was shocked when his manager presented him with a written warning (see Exhibit 5).

Dan's explanation went seemingly unheard as he said, "What was I to do? I couldn't possibly make quota while trying to satisfy my largest customers. They were ready to go back to AT&T and I was simply trying to make up for my company's dismal reliability." Dan became increasingly frustrated, especially after receiving memos congratulating him for his two largest sales.

Dan learned one month after receiving his written warning that National was dealing with problems at the highest levels of the company. Several division presidents were reassigned, and two decided to leave National for employment at AT&T. The reason was twofold: inconsistent sales in several regions and companywide growth far below fore-

Exhibit 5

NTC Telecommunications Corporation
NTC Midwest
6300 Exclusive Drive
Suite 333
Champaign, IL 63909
217 304 2222
800 423 6125
FAX 217 304 3333

August 6, 1995

To: Daniel R. Peters
From: Karen Sullivan
Subject: Disciplinary Action/Written Warning

Dan,

As we discussed today, your sales performance as Account Executive has been substandard. The issue discussed pertained to a lack of sales activity. Both reported sales and UCS revenues have been below divisional and corporate standards. Weekly activity and monthly sales funnel are very weak and require immediate attention.

This is your Official Written Warning, which means we (you and I) must bring your abilities in these areas up to speed. You have my commitment to help you develop the skills required to increase sales activity.

If your performance has not met minimum and acceptable levels, there will be additional disciplinary action taken which may include termination.

I have discussed this with my manager, Karen Sullivan, and agree to work diligently to increase my abilities in the areas described above.

_____   _____
Daniel R. Peters
Account Executive I
NTC Midwest Division

_____
Karen Sullivan
Manager I
NTC Midwest Division

KS/bh

---

casted levels. Dan could only relate it to his own experience by stating, "I knew after signing those accounts that National still had network problems in several regions, including eastern Illinois. This damaged the company's reputation and hindered the selling effort. The company was making a big mistake by pointing the finger at the salespeople and not themselves."

Nearly two months after receiving his written warning, Dan got the feeling that his area office was falling apart. Two AEs in the office quit after receiving similar warnings, and his area manager was noticeably concerned about his own future. Dan continued to have problems in the field, but his two largest accounts initiated billing, handing him the largest paycheck of his career. He was also pleased after receiving the national and divisional sales rankings (see Exhibit 6).

Unfortunately, Dan did not get the chance to have his place "in the sun." One week after receiving the rankings, the state sales manager requested his immediate resignation due to his "inconsistent month-to-month performance." Dan was not surprised. He had spent two months trying to deal with his customers and the company, and he got caught in the middle. His area sales manager was not there to help him because she was busy fighting for her own job. Dan put the situation into perspective by stating, "I performed well at National; my sales record proved it. Near the end it was clear everyone was looking out for themselves and not dealing with the real problem. I was labeled as the problem and paid for it with my job."

Exhibit 6

Command: Fri, Sep 28, 1995 10:12 AM CST
Date: Sally Hickman/NTC Midwestern Region
From:

To: Karen Sullivan/NTC Midwestern Region

Subject: CIC REP RESULTS—AUGUST BILLING

The CIC rep rankings through August Billing were distributed via Fax Broadcast to each office on Wednesday, September 26th. The ranking report is based on National performance listing the top 75 reps in the country qualifying for CIC 100, followed then by all reps performing at 125% or better based on their Revenue Goal qualifying for CIC.

The Midwest Division has 59 CIC contenders as of August Billing! Congratulations to each of those fortunate reps that are vying for positions "In the Sun"! It is not too late to turn up the heat and reserve a lounge chair by the pool in Tahiti or Florida! The rules are such that each rep is in competition with his/her own abilities. Perform at 125% or better and a reservation for a "Place in the Sun" is guaranteed!!!

The following highlights our top performers as of August UCS Billing:

CIC 100 Contenders:

CIC Rank	Div Rank	Name	Rep Type	Branch Name	YTD Rev	% of Goal
3	1	Kevin Hugh	AE2	Chicago North	$240,693	401%
6	2	Collin Cherney	AE2	Chicago North	160,569	378
15	3	Belle Starr	AE2	Wisconsin	107,407	275
16	4	Theodore Spinks	AE1	Michigan East	87,363	273
19	5	Tulula Sentry	AE2	NE Ohio	106,028	272
21	6	Sandy Tyson	MAR	Chicago North	319,341	266
34	7	Brenda Hasse	AE2	Chicago Downtown	147,036	245
36	8	Mark Anderson	AE1	Columbus	76,693	230
39	9	Teddy Johannes	AE1	SW Illinois	73,693	230
42	10	Jonlee Devlin	AE2	Wisconsin	95,579	225
55	11	Mary Birdwhistle	AE2	Chicago North	122,074	203
57	12	Marge Kenton	AE1	SW Ohio	64,895	203
58	13	Dan Peters	AE1	Eastern Illinois	64,762	202
70	14	Roberta Prancer	AE2	Michigan West	88,221	192
73	15	Stephen Willey	AE2	Chicago North	94,399	191
74	16	Michael Dubois	AE1	Chicago Downtown	60,725	190
75	17	Danielle Morrison	AE1	Wisconsin	60,581	189

Case 3–3

Country Roads, Inc.*

Camille Berggren had just completed a review of a staff report covering the various problems facing the telemarketing program at Country Roads, Inc.—a large, multimillion-dollar direct marketing organization that sells merchandise throughout North America. Although attractive catalogs that contain mail order forms are mailed to customers 13 times a year, approximately 60 percent of Country Roads's sales are made by customers calling the 800 number to place an order.

The telemarketing division was the subject of the staff report. A special committee had been convened to review morale problems and to make recommendations. The relatively high turnover among Country Roads's telemarketing specialists (personal shopping representatives—PSRs) was of considerable concern not only to Camille but also to her superiors. Despite the fact that PSRs were paid a straight salary plus a year-end bonus (unlike conventional telemarketing compensation programs that usually pay a straight commission), morale and turnover problems were serious enough to warrant the special committee's assignment.

The Company

Country Roads, Inc., established in 1971, is located in Burlington, Vermont. Since its inception, Country Roads has experienced rapid growth in catalog sales. The catalogs contain mostly clothing, but other unique items are also available. Country Roads prides itself on high-quality merchandise at reasonable prices. In addition, Country Roads set a trend in the fast-growing catalog mail order business by following a customer complete satisfaction policy. Customers can receive a full refund with no questions asked if they are not completely satisfied with their purchases. Company executives believe this policy has been instrumental in helping Country Roads enjoy unprecedented growth in the direct marketing business. Not only have sales increased dramatically, but employee growth has also been significant.

Country Roads, Inc., provides 24-hour telephone service, hiring people mostly from the Burlington, Vermont, area. Most of the telemarketing reps are full-time, although about one-fifth of the PSRs are part-time employees. About two-thirds are women. Average compensation including year-end bonuses is $15,000. Turnover among this group in recent years has averaged 60 percent. Company executives realize this is low in comparison with turnover rates experienced by other direct marketing companies, but they think the 60 percent rate will cause future problems. In fact, one study recommends that Country Roads, Inc., consider establishing telemarketing operations at other locations away from the Burlington, Vermont, area. The study supported this recommendation by point-

*Katherine Cheney assisted in preparing this case. Copyright © 1998 Neil M. Ford.

ing out that unless the turnover problem was resolved, Country Roads would find it difficult to hire more personal shopping representatives from the Burlington area.

The Staff Report

Mike Peck, chairman of the committee, initiated the project by conducting one-on-one interviews with a sample of personal shopping representatives. Interviews were conducted with the PSRs' supervisors and with others at Country Roads, Inc., as well. Mike then held a series of four focus group interviews with 36 of the PSRs. Following these interviews, the committee, with the assistance of Country Roads's personnel manager, administered a series of questionnaires that measured such variables as job satisfaction, role ambiguity, role conflict, and organizational climate. The personnel manager provided a report for the committee to review.

The following comments are based on the information the committee collected:

1.   The personal shopping representatives are reasonably satisfied with pay, the nature of the job, their fellow workers, company policies and benefits, and their customers.

2.   The PSRs are dissatisfied with promotion, supervision, and company support.

3.   Role conflict was a problem, especially between the PSRs' supervisors and their customers. Little conflict existed between customers and Country Roads, Inc., and between their supervisors and Country Roads, Inc.

4.   PSRs perceive role ambiguity, especially as it affects promotions and supervision.

5.   The one-on-one and focus group interviews were not too productive. The committee thought PSRs did not trust the process, afraid that their comments would reach the wrong people. Despite these reservations, the committee did learn that PSRs were not pleased with their supervisors. One PSR, leaving Country Roads, indicated the performance evaluation system was a joke, but she did not care to elaborate for fear that her cohorts who were still there might suffer. Another PSR indicated that getting promoted was a mysterious process.

The committee suspected that the dissatisfaction with company support was related to supervision and promotion problems. Finally, the committee recommended that Country Roads, Inc., review the performance evaluation process and the promotion procedure.

Camille Berggren met with Mike Peck to discuss the staff report his committee had prepared. She was particularly concerned about the criticism of Country Roads's performance evaluation procedure, a relatively recent creation implemented on September 4, 1994. Considerable effort had gone into developing the new system. Mike indicated that maybe the system was fine but the implementation was at fault. He informed Camille that one of his committee members recommended that Country Roads consider using behaviorally anchored rating scales to improve the performance evaluation process. Due to time constraints, this idea was not investigated. Anyway, Mike suggested the process sounded too complicated for Country Roads's supervisors to use.

Next, Camille obtained a copy of the evaluation system implemented in 1994 (see Exhibit 1). She believed the current program's objectives were meaningful (1) to help develop good performance and (2) to project Country Roads's image of friendliness and service. Fulfilling these objectives was certainly important for Country Roads, Inc., as they would be for any firm. However, Camille thought it would be difficult to measure performance in either of these categories without more specific objectives or intermediate goals.

Using reading materials provided by Country Roads's personnel manager, Camille

Exhibit I

Country Roads, Inc.
Burlington, Vermont

To: Customer Sales
From: Supervisors
Date: September 4, 1994
Subject: Country Roads's philosophy

Country Roads's philosophy is based on friendliness and service to our customers. It is extremely important that this Country Roads image be projected.

To help develop good performance and ensure that a positive Country Roads image is being projected, we are going to formalize performance observation.

The attached information will explain the program.

KF/rsp
Attachment

P.S. PSR is the abbreviation for Personal Sales Representative.

---

formulated objectives of performance appraisal procedures. The traditional function of a performance appraisal system is threefold:

1. To provide adequate feedback to employees about their performance.

2. To serve as a basis for modifying behavior to initiate more effective, desirable working habits.

3. To provide data to managers for purposes of sales and cost analysis and promotion.

These goals are simply a more detailed derivation of Country Roads's purposes. For instance, good performance can be developed only when employees first receive proper feedback about their performance and then modify their behavior accordingly. Further, if data are compiled during the procedure, it is possible to ensure that the proper image is being portrayed by rewarding those PSRs with good ratings and working with those who have less than acceptable scores. If these objectives were utilized as intermediate goals, the long-term purpose would be easier to measure and obtain.

In her review of Country Roads's performance evaluation system, Camille noted the following points:

1. The program offers performance observation guidelines the supervisor should follow when monitoring PSRs.

2. The program names eight specific points on which PSRs will be rated; these points take into account most of the performance observation guidelines.

3. Directions are given for the supervisor to follow when filling out the monitoring form.

4. The monitoring form lists attributes on the left-hand side of the form, and leaves space for the evaluation marks; E and N, respectively, stand for *effective* and *noneffective*.

Although Camille felt that the system had been put together in a hurry, she thought it was better than no system, which was pretty much the situation before the 1994 procedure. If implementation was difficult, then a review of actual performance evaluations should reveal any problems. Next, Camille asked for a sample of completed evaluation forms from Country Roads's personnel function.

Before she had received the completed evaluation forms, Camille discussed the situation with Peter Bylow, Country Roads's public relations director, to determine if any image studies had been conducted. Bylow assured her that Country Roads had a sound image based on company surveys and other sources. In their discussion, Bylow mentioned customer shopping studies that had been conducted at his former place of employment, a bank in Boston. He indicated that tellers, personal bankers, and other bank employees with public contact were observed frequently and evaluated on their customer relations skills, sales skills, and technical skills. These observations were prepared by a consulting firm that had hired people to conduct actual transactions, both in person and by telephone. Results of the shopping studies were to be part of the performance evaluation process, but Bylow indicated that this idea was dropped due to lack of acceptance on the part of the supervisors. Bylow indicated the telephone approach might be suitable for Country Roads, Inc. Camille was intrigued with the approach and wondered if it might be appropriate. She liked the idea of the three broad areas of evaluation—customer relations skills, sales skills, and technical skills. Acceptance by the supervisors, however, might be a problem.

Finally, the sample of completed evaluation forms arrived on Camille's desk. She hoped they would provide further insight into Country Roads's morale and turnover problems. She knew her boss was waiting for recommendations on how to resolve the problem.

Customer Sales Performance Observation Guidelines

The following items and their definitions should be used as the criteria for assessing the effectiveness of customer contacts. Each item contains a variety of descriptive definitions based on the type of contact.

Greeting: Was the greeting prompt, cordial, courteous, and friendly? Did the PSR give the impression that he/she was ready to serve the customer? Did the greeting follow the prescribed script?

Overcoming objections: Did the PSR counter negative comments made by the customers? Were positive questions and statements used? Were alternate positive suggestions provided by the operator?

Understand the customer: Did the PSR effectively listen to the customer to avoid unnecessary repetition of conversations? Did the PSR provide correct information? Was there an even exchange of information, thus avoiding a confrontation and an unsatisfied customer?

Voice quality: Did the PSR's conversation contain proper voice inflection or did it appear to be harsh, indifferent, or monotonous?

Ask for the business: Did the PSR suggest alternate merchandise on out-of-stock items? If an item was on back order, did the PSR handle the back-order information in a positive manner? Did the PSR listen to the customer and suggest additional merchandise if the opening was given?

Customer responsiveness: Did the PSR project interest, enthusiasm, friendliness, and courtesy toward the customer? Did the PSR's tone of voice and infection indicate a positive interaction with the customer, the company, and other

Observation Dates _____

Employee Name _____

Annual Review Due _____

Supervisor _____

Employment Status _____

Subjects of Evaluation:

Greeting _____

Pleasantries _____

Complete Information Volunteered _____

Understand Customer _____

Overcome Customer Objections _____

Read CRT—Use System _____

Telephone Techniques _____

Closing _____

_____

_____

Comments _____

_____

_____

_____

_____

_____

_____

_____

E = Effective   N = Noneffective

Employee Signature _____ Date _____

CRI: 9/4/94

Observation Dates ___ 4/18 4/29 5/3 5/18 7/11 8/15 9/3 11/14

Employee Name ___ DEIRDRE BURNS

Annual Review Due ___ 9/1/96

Supervisor ___ DANA MOORE

Employment Status ___ PSR - II SECOND SHIFT

Subjects of Evaluation:	4/18	4/29	5/3	5/18	7/11	8/15	9/3	11/14
Greeting	E	E	N	E	E	N	N	N
Pleasantries	E	E	N	E	E	N	N	N
Complete Information Volunteered	E	E	N	E	E	N	N	N
Understand Customer	E	E	E	E	E	E	E	N
Overcome Customer Objections	E	E	N	E	E	N	N	N
Read CRT—Use System	E	E	E	E	E	E	N	N
Telephone Techniques	E	E	N	E	E	N	N	N
Closing	E	E	N	E	E	N	N	N

Comments ___ 4/18 GOOD PERFORMANCE 4/29 SOLID

RESULTS 5/3 NEEDS TO GET BACK ON

TRACK 5/18 MUCH BETTER 7/11 EXCELLENT

8/15 DEIRDRE IS INCONSISTENT AND

MUST TRY HARDER 9/3 POOR TREND —

SHE IS NOT TRYING 11/14 PLACED HER

ON 60 DAYS PROBATION

E = Effective   N = Noneffective

Employee Signature _Deirdre Burns_ ___ Date _12/15/96_

CRI: 9/4/94

Observation Dates ___ *3/11 3/26 4/3 4/12 5/15 6/10(1) 6/10(2) 6/10(3)* ___

Employee Name ___ *Jack Murray* ___

Annual Review Due ___ *6/12/96* ___

Supervisor ___ *Jayne Perrin* ___

Employment Status ___ *PSR III Third Shift* ___

Subjects of Evaluation:	3/11	3/26	4/3	4/12	5/15	6/10(1)	6/10(2)	6/10(3)
Greeting	E	E	E	E	E	N	N	N
Pleasantries	E	E	E	E	E	N	N	N
Complete Information Volunteered	E	E	E	E	E	E	E	E
Understand Customer	E	E	E	E	E	E	E	E
Overcome Customer Objections	E	E	E	E	E	N	N	N
Read CRT—Use System	E	E	E	E	E	E	E	E
Telephone Techniques	E	E	E	E	E	N	N	N
Closing	E	E	E	E	E	N	N	N

Comments ___ *Jack's excellent performance changed directions. He needs to figure out how to get back on track.* ___

E = Effective   N = Noneffective

Employee Signature *Jack Murray* ___ Date ___ *6/15/96* ___

CRI: 9/4/94

Observation Dates ___ 7/1 7/3 8/5 8/16 8/17 10/1 10/5 10/15 ___

Employee Name ___ Lisa Daniel ___

Annual Review Due ___ 10/17/96 ___

Supervisor ___ John Ruppert ___

Employment Status ___ PSR - I First Shift ___

Subjects of Evaluation:

	7/1	7/3	8/5	8/16	8/17	10/1	10/5	10/15
Greeting	E	E	E	E	N	E	E	E
Pleasantries	E	E	E	E	N	E	E	E
Complete Information Volunteered	E	E	E	E	N	E	E	E
Understand Customer	N	N	E	E	N	E	E	E
Overcome Customer Objections	N	N	N	N	N	E	E	E
Read CRT—Use System	E	E	E	E	N	E	E	E
Telephone Techniques	E	E	E	E	N	E	E	E
Closing	E	E	E	E	N	E	E	E

Comments ___ Lisa has had problems overcoming objections
and needs to practice. Her poor performance on
8/17 is not significant. She had a bad day.

E = Effective   N = Noneffective

Employee Signature *Lisa Daniel* ___ Date ___ 11/1/96 ___

CRI: 9/4/94

Observation Dates ___ 9/1 10/3 11/7 12/18 3/23 5/16 7/1 8/5 ___

Employee Name ___ GRETCHEN NELSON ___

Annual Review Due ___ 8/17/96 ___

Supervisor ___ MARY CABLE ___

Employment Status ___ PSR - 1 FIRST SHIFT ___

Subjects of Evaluation: 9/1 10/3 11/7 12/18 3/23 5/16   7/1 8/5

Greeting _____ E | E | E | E | E | E | E | E

Pleasantries _____ E | E | E | E | E | E | E | E

Complete Information Volunteered ___ E | E | E | E | E | E | E | E

Understand Customer _____ E | E | E | E | E | E | E | E

Overcome Customer Objections _____ N | N | N | N | N | N | N | N

Read CRT—Use System _____ E | E | E | E | E | E | E | E

Telephone Techniques _____ E | E | E | E | E | E | E | E

Closing _____ N | N | N | N | N | N | N | N

_____

_____

Comments ___ GRETCHEN NEEDS TO LEARN HOW TO

_____ HANDLE OBJECTIONS. HER CLOSING

_____ TECHNIQUE IS NOT EFFECTIVE AND SHE

_____ IS LOSING SALES. I PLACED HER ON

_____ 90 DAYS PROBATION. _____

_____

_____

E = Effective   N = Noneffective

Employee Signature _Gretchen Nelson_____ Date _9/1/96_____

CRI: 9/4/94

Observation Dates   *6/12 7/18 10/8 10/9 1/17(1) 1/17(2) 4/12(1) 4/12(2)*

Employee Name   *Nancy Luther*

Annual Review Due   *4/12/96*

Supervisor   *Pam Benjamin*

Employment Status   *PSR - I Third Shift*

Subjects of Evaluation:	6/12	7/18	10/8	10/9	1/17(1)	1/17(2)	4/12(1)	4/12(2)
Greeting	E	E	N	E	N	N	E	E
Pleasantries	E	E	N	E	N	N	E	E
Complete Information Volunteered	E	E	N	N	N	N	E	E
Understand Customer	E	E	N	N	N	N	E	E
Overcome Customer Objections	E	N	N	N	N	N	E	E
Read CRT—Use System	E	E	N	E	N	N	E	E
Telephone Techniques	E	E	N	E	N	N	E	E
Closing	E	N	N	N	N	N	E	E

Comments   *Nancy needs to improve if she hopes to be promoted to PSR-II.*

E = Effective   N = Noneffective

Employee Signature   *Nancy Luther*   Date   *4/12/96*

CRI: 9/4/94

employees? Did the PSR appear to be complacent or was a positive friendly feeling projected to the customer? Did the PSR project the Country Roads's image of service to the customer? Did the PSR maintain control of the conversation? Was a sincere desire to serve the customer projected and were the PSR's efforts directed immediately toward answering the customer's questions or resolving a problem, if any? Did the PSR quickly understand the customer's problem? Did he/she understand the steps necessary to solve the problem?

Shipping procedures: Are shipping procedures understood by the PSR? Was the "bill-to" information taken correctly? Was the customer asked if he/she wanted to ship to another address?

Closing: Was the order number given in an appropriate manner? Did the PSR use a suitable expression of appreciation in closing, such as "Thank you for calling Country Roads" or "Thank you and have a pleasant day/evening"?

Returns/refunds: Was proper information provided to the customer regarding return of merchandise and/or refunds?

Credit: Was the proper procedure followed for credit card number and billing address? Was proper information provided the customer concerning his/her account?

Courtesy: Did the PSR use courtesy phrases such as please and thank you when appropriate during the contact? Did the PSR excuse himself or herself if it was necessary to put the customer on hold to check a reference? Upon return to the telephone, did the PSR thank the customer for waiting? In short, did the PSR provide the customer with positive recognition throughout the contact?

Work habits—on-line system: Does the PSR know how to use the system to take full advantage of its efficiencies, thus providing customer service? Is the information on the screen used effectively to answer customers' inquiries? Are problems with the system reported to management?

Work habits—forms: Are all forms completed as required? Are the forms legible and are they completed quickly or at a time that avoids customer inconvenience?

Control of the conversation: Was the conversation controlled in a positive and effective manner? Did the PSR acknowledge customer comments and move effectively back to business?

Use of time: Is the PSR utilizing time efficiently during a contact while maintaining a friendly and courteous attitude? Is the PSR minimizing unavailable time during contacts? Is time used effectively between calls?

Appearance—personal: Does the PSR dress in an appropriate manner? Did the PSR chew gum during a contact?

Appearance—work area: Did the PSR check the position for material and forms necessary to properly service customers over the telephone, thus avoiding interruptions while on the telephone? Did the PSR maintain the position so that it appeared clean, orderly, and businesslike? Did the PSR report equipment out of service (i.e., desk, telephone, or chair)?

Adjustment—inquiry handling: Did the PSR handle shipment inquiries in the proper manner? Did the PSR provide correct information for general inquiry calls— avoiding inconvenience to our customers? Were proper adjustment procedures followed?

Monitoring Observation

Greeting: Was the greeting prompt, cordial, courteous, and friendly? Did the PSR give the impression that he/she was ready to serve the customer?

Pleasantries: Did the agent use courtesy phrases such as *please* and *thank you* when appropriate during the contact? Did the PSR excuse himself or herself if it was necessary to leave the telephone to check on something? Upon returning to the telephone, did the PSR thank the customer for waiting?

Complete information volunteered: Was proper information provided to the customer regarding return of merchandise and/or refunds? Did the PSR offer alternative merchandise for out-of-stock items? Did PSR offer information on back-order dates and shipping info?

Understand customer: Did the PSR provide correct information? Did the PSR listen to the customer to avoid unnecessary repetition of conversations?

Overcome customer objections: Did the PSR counter negative comments made by the customer? Were positive questions and statements used by the PSR?

Read CRT—use system fully: Does the PSR know how to use the system to take full advantage of helping the customer? Are problems with the system reported to the supervisor or lead?

Telephone techniques: Are irritating mannerisms (i.e., heavy breathing, gum chewing) avoided when speaking on the telephone? Is the headset adjusted properly? When dialing out for another extension, does the PSR allow sufficient rings or ring too long before hanging up if no answer?

Closing: Did the PSR acknowledge any expression of appreciation for the customer? Did the PSR use a suitable expression of appreciation in closing, such as *thank you for calling Country Roads and have a pleasant day or evening?*

1. Date of observation period.
2. Personal sales rep to be observed.
3. Supervisor, lead, trainer performing the observation.
4. Employment status.
5. Enter an *E* for effective contact or an *N* for a noneffective contact.
6. Record subjective comments and reference each item of noncompliance. Note all positive aspects of an employee's performance.
7. Personal sales rep's signature acknowledging review of the observation.

Case 3–4

Hanover–Bates Chemical Corporation*

James Sprague, newly appointed northeast district sales manager for the Hanover–Bates Chemical Corporation, leaned back in his chair as the door to his office slammed shut. "Great beginnings," he thought. "Three days in my new job and the district's most experienced sales representative is threatening to quit."

On the previous night, Sprague, Hank Carver (the district's most experienced sales representative), and John Follet, another senior member of the district sales staff, had met for dinner at Sprague's suggestion. During dinner he had mentioned that one of his top priorities would be to conduct a sales and profit analysis of the district's business in order to identify opportunities to improve the district's profit performance. He had stated that he was confident that the analysis would indicate opportunities to reallocate district sales efforts in a manner that would increase profits. As Sprague had indicated during the conversation, "My experience in analyzing district sales performance data for the national sales manager has convinced me that any district's allocation of sales effort to products and customer categories can be improved." Both Carver and Follet had nodded as Sprague discussed his plans.

Carver was waiting when Sprague arrived at the district sales office this morning. It soon became apparent that Carver was very upset by what he perceived as Sprague's criticism of how he and the other district sales representatives were doing their jobs—and, more particularly, of how they were allocating their time in terms of customers and products. As he concluded his heated comments, Carver said:

> This company has made it darned clear that 34 years of experience don't count for anything . . . and now someone with not much more than two years of selling experience and two years of pushing paper for the national sales manager at corporate headquarters tells me I'm not doing my job . . . Maybe it's time for me to look for a new job . . . and since Trumbull Chemical [Hanover–Bates's major competitor] is hiring, maybe that's where I should start looking . . . and I'm not the only one who feels this way.

As Sprague reflected on the scene that had just occurred, he wondered what he should do. It had been made clear to him when he had been promoted to manager of the northeast sales district that one of his top priorities should be improvement of the district's profit performance. As the national sales manager had said, "The northeast sales district may rank third in dollar sales, but it's our worst district in terms of profit performance."

Prior to assuming his new position, Sprague had assembled the data presented in Ex-

---

*This case was prepared by Professor Robert E. Witt, of the University of Texas–Arlington, as a basis for class discussion and is not designed to illustrate effective or ineffective handling of an administrative situation.

hibits 1 through 6 to assist him in analyzing the district sales and profits. The data had been compiled from records maintained in the national sales manager's office. Although he believed the data would provide a sound basis for a preliminary analysis of district sales and profit performance, Sprague had recognized that additional data would probably have to be collected when he arrived in the northeast district (District 3).

In response to the national sales manager's comment about the northeast district's poor performance, Sprague had been particularly interested in how the district had performed on its gross profit quota. He knew that district gross profit quotas were assigned in a manner that took into account variation in price competition. Thus, he felt that poor performance in the gross profit quota area reflected misallocated sales efforts either in terms of customers or in terms of the mix of product line items sold. To provide himself with a frame of reference, he had also requested data on the north-central sales district (District 7). This district is generally considered to be one of the best, if not the best, in the company. Furthermore, the north-central district sales manager, who is only three years older than Sprague, is highly regarded by the national sales manager.

The Company and the Industry

The Hanover–Bates Chemical Corporation is a leading producer of processing chemicals for the chemical plating industry. The company's products are produced in four plants, located in Los Angeles, Houston, Chicago, and Newark, New Jersey. The company's production process is, in essence, a mixing operation. Chemicals purchased from a broad range of suppliers are mixed according to a variety of user-based formulas. Company sales in 1996 had reached a new high of $23.89 million, up from $21.98 million in 1995. Net pre-tax profit in 1996 had been $3.822 million, up from $3.169 million in 1995. Hanover–Bates has a strong balance sheet, and the company enjoys a favorable price–earnings ratio on its stock, which trades on the OTC (over-the-counter) market.

Although Hanover–Bates does not produce commodity-type chemicals (such as sulfuric acid), industry customers tend to perceive minimal quality differences among the products produced by Hanover–Bates and its competitors. Given the customers' perception of a lack of variation in product quality and the industrywide practice of limiting advertising expenditures, field sales efforts are of major importance in the marketing programs of all firms in the industry.

Hanover–Bates's market consists of several thousand job-shop and captive (in-house) plating operations. Chemical platers process a wide variety of materials including industrial fasteners (for example, screws, rivets, bolts, and washers), industrial components (for example, clamps, casings, and couplings), and miscellaneous items (for example, umbrella frames, eyelets, and decorative items). The chemical plating process involves the electrolytic application of metallic coatings such as zinc, cadmium, nickel, and brass. The degree of plating precision required varies substantially, with some work being primarily decorative, some involving relatively loose standards (for example, 0.0002 zinc, which means that anything over two ten-thousandths of an inch of plate is acceptable), and some involving relatively precise standards (for example, 0.0003–0.0004 zinc).

Regardless of the degree of plating precision involved, quality control is of critical concern to all chemical platers. Extensive variation in the condition of materials received for plating requires a high level of service from the firms supplying chemicals to platers. This service is normally provided by the sales representatives of the firm(s) supplying the plater with processing chemicals.

Hanover–Bates and the majority of the firms in its industry produce the same line of basic processing chemicals for the chemical plating industry. The line consists of a

Exhibit 1   Hanover–Bates Chemical Corporation: Summary Income Statements, 1992–1996

	1992	1993	1994	1995	1996
Sales	$19,890,000	$21,710,000	$19,060,000	$21,980,000	$23,890,000
Production expenses	11,934,000	13,497,000	12,198,000	13,612,000	14,563,000
Gross profit	7,956,000	8,213,000	6,862,000	8,368,000	9,327,000
Administrative expenses	2,606,000	2,887,000	2,792,000	2,925,000	3,106,000
Selling expenses	2,024,000	2,241,000	2,134,000	2,274,000	2,399,000
Pretax profit	3,326,000	3,085,000	1,936,000	3,169,000	3,822,000
Taxes	1,512,000	1,388,000	790,000	1,426,000	1,718,000
Net profit	$ 1,814,000	$ 1,697,000	$ 1,146,000	$ 1,743,000	$ 2,104,000

Exhibit 2   District Sales Quota and Gross Profit Quota Performance, 1996

District	Number of Sales Reps	Sales Quota	Sales—Actual	Gross Profit Quota[a]	Gross Profit—Actual
1	7	$ 3,880,000	$ 3,906,000	$1,552,000	$1,589,000
2	6	3,750,000	3,740,000	1,500,000	1,529,000
3	6	3,650,000	3,406,000	1,460,000	1,239,000
4	6	3,370,000	3,318,000	1,348,000	1,295,000
5	5	3,300,000	3,210,000	1,320,000	1,186,000
6	5	3,130,000	3,205,000	1,252,000	1,179,000
7	5	2,720,000	3,105,000	1,088,000	1,310,000
		$23,800,000	$23,890,000	$9,520,000	$9,327,000

[a]District gross profit quotas were developed by the national sales manager in consultation with the district managers and took into account price competition in the respective districts.

trisodium phosphate cleaner (SPX); anesic aldahyde brightening agents for zinc plating (ZBX), cadmium plating (CBX), and nickel plating (NBX); a protective post-plating chromate dip (CHX); and a protective burnishing compound (BUX). The company's product line is detailed as follows:

Product	Container Size	List Price	Gross Margin
SPX	400-lb. drum	$ 80	$28
ZBX	50-lb. drum	76	34
CBX	50-lb. drum	76	34
NBX	50-lb. drum	80	35
CHX	100-lb. drum	220	90
BUX	400-lb. drum	120	44

Company Sales Organization

Hanover–Bates's sales organization consists of 40 sales representatives operating in seven sales districts. Most sales representatives had formerly worked for a Hanover–Bates customer, and none were college-educated. Sales representatives' salaries range from $22,000

Exhibit 3   District Selling Expenses, 1996

District	Sales Rep. Salaries[a]	Sales Commission	Sales Rep. Expenses	District Office	District Manager Salary	District Manager Expenses	Sales Support	Total Selling Expenses
1	$177,100	$19,426	$56,280	$21,150	$33,500	$11,460	$69,500	$ 388,416
2	143,220	18,700	50,760	21,312	34,000	12,034	71,320	351,346
3	157,380	17,030	54,436	22,123	35,000[b]	12,382	70,010	368,529
4	150,480	16,590	49,104	22,004	32,500	11,005	66,470	348,153
5	125,950	16,050	42,720	21,115	33,000	11,123	76,600	326,558
6	124,850	16,265	41,520	20,992	33,500	11,428	67,100	315,655
7	114,850	17,530	44,700	22,485	31,500	11,643	58,750	300,258
								$2,398,915

[a]Includes cost of fringe benefit program, which was 10 percent of base salary.
[b]Salary of James Sprague's predecessor.

Exhibit 4   District Contribution to Corporate Administrative Expense and Profit, 1996

District	Sales	Gross Profit	Selling Expenses	Contribution to Administrative Expense and Profit
1	$ 3,906,000	$1,589,000	$ 388,416	$1,200,544
2	3,740,000	1,529,000	351,346	1,177,654
3	3,406,000	1,239,000	368,529	870,471
4	3,318,000	1,295,000	348,153	946,847
5	3,210,000	1,186,000	326,558	859,442
6	3,205,000	1,179,000	315,376	863,624
7	3,105,000	1,310,000	300,258	1,009,742
	$23,890,000	$9,327,000	$2,398,636	$6,928,324

to $30,000, with fringe benefit costs amounting to an additional 10 percent of salary. In addition to their salaries, Hanover-Bates's sales representatives receive commissions of 0.5 percent of their dollar sales volume on all sales up to their sales quotas. The commission on sales in excess of quota is 1 percent. District sales manager salaries range from $31,500 to $35,000. Sales managers are also eligible for a bonus based on district sales performance.

In 1994 the national sales manager of Hanover–Bates had developed a sales program based on selling the full line of Hanover–Bates products. He believed that if the sales representatives could successfully carry out his program, the following benefits would accrue to Hanover–Bates and its customers:

1. Sales volume per account would be greater, and selling costs as a percentage of sales would decrease.

2. A Hanover–Bates sales representative could justify spending more time with an ac-

Exhibit 5 Northeast (#3) and North-Central (#7) District Sales and Gross Profit Performance by Account Category, 1996

District	(A)	(B)	(C)	Total
Sales by Account Category				
Northeast	$915,000	$1,681,000	$810,000	$3,406,000
North-central	751,000	1,702,000	652,000	3,105,000
Gross Profit by Account Category				
Northeast	$356,000	$623,000	$260,000	$1,239,000
North-central	330,000	725,000	255,000	1,310,000

Exhibit 6 Potential Accounts, Active Accounts, and Account Call Coverage: Northeast and North-Central Districts, 1996

District	Potential Accounts			Active Accounts			Account Coverage (Total Calls)		
	(A)	(B)	(C)	(A)	(B)	(C)	(A)	(B)	(C)
Northeast	90	381	635	53	210	313	1,297	3,051	2,118
North-central	60	286	499	42	182	218	1,030	2,618	1,299

count, thus becoming more knowledgeable about the account's business and becoming better able to provide technical assistance and identify selling opportunities.

3. Full-line sales would strengthen Hanover–Bates's competitive position by reducing the likelihood of account loss to other chemical-plating suppliers (a problem that existed in multiple-supplier situations).

The national sales manager's 1994 sales program had also included the following account call-frequency guidelines:

A accounts (major accounts generating $12,000 or more in yearly sales)—two calls per month

B accounts (medium-sized accounts generating $6,000–$11,999 in yearly sales)—one call per month

C accounts (small accounts generating less than $6,000 yearly in sales)—one call every two months

The account call–frequency guidelines were developed by the national sales manager after discussions with the district managers. The national sales manager had been concerned about the optimal allocation of sales effort to accounts and felt that the guidelines would increase the efficiency of the company's sales force, although not all of the district sales managers agreed with this conclusion.

It was common knowledge in Hanover–Bates's corporate sales office that Sprague's predecessor as northeast district sales manager had not been one of the company's better district sales managers. His attitude toward the sales plans and programs of the national sales manager had been one of reluctant compliance rather than acceptance and support. However, when the national sales manager succeeded in persuading Sprague's predecessor to take early retirement, no replacement was readily available.

Carver, who most of the sales representatives had assumed would get the district manager job, had been passed over in part because he would be 65 in three years. The national sales manager had not wanted to face the same replacement problem again in three years and also had wanted someone in the position who would be more likely to be responsive to the company's sales plans and policies. The appointment of Sprague as district manager had caused considerable talk, not only in the district but also at corporate headquarters. In fact, the national sales manager had warned Sprague that "a lot of people are expecting you to fall on your face . . . they don't think you have the experience to handle the job, in particular, and to manage and motivate a group of sales representatives, most of whom are considerably older and more experienced than you." The general sales manager had concluded by saying, "I think you can handle the job, Jim . . . I think you can manage those sales reps and improve the district's profit performance . . . and I'm depending on you to do both."

Case 3–5

Kanthal (A)*

Carl-Erik Ridderstråle, president of Kanthal, was describing his motivation for developing a system to measure customer profitability.

> Before, when we got an order from a big, important customer, we didn't ask questions. We were glad to get the business. But a small company, competing around the world, has to concentrate its sales and marketing resources. We needed an account management system if we were to achieve our strategy for higher growth and profitability. An account management system as part of the Kanthal 90 Strategy will enable us to get sales managers to accept responsibility for promoting high-margin products to high-profit customers.

History

Kanthal, the largest of six divisions in the Kanthal–Hoganas group of Sweden, was headquartered in Hallstahammar, a town of 17,000 persons about 150 km. northwest of Stockholm. The company's history can be traced back to an ironworks founded in the 17th century to exploit the water power available from the stream running through the town. Kanthal specialized in the production and sales of electrical resistance heating elements. "We work for a warmer world" was its motto.

Kanthal had about 10,000 customers and 15,000 items that it produced. Sales during 1985 through 1987 had been level at about SEK 850 million.[1] Export sales, outside of Sweden, accounted for 95% of the total. Summary statistics for the past two years appear in Exhibit 1.

Kanthal consisted of three divisions:

> Kanthal Heating Technology supplied manufacturers of electrical appliances and heating systems with wire that generated heat through electrical resistance. Products included heating wire and ribbon, foil elements, machinery and precision wire. Kanthal's 25% market share made it a world leader in supplying heating alloys. Sales growth was sluggish in Europe and the United States but rapid growth was occurring in the Far East and Latin America.

> Kanthal Furnace Products produced a wide range of heating elements for electric industrial furnaces. Its 40% market share gave it a dominant position in the large markets of the United States, Japan, West Germany, and the United Kingdom. A new

*Professor Robert S. Kaplan prepared this case as the basis for class discussion rather than to illustrate either effective or ineffective handling of an administrative situation.

[1]In 1988, the Swedish kronor (SEK) was worth about US$0.16.

Exhibit I	Summary of Operations		
		1986	**1987**
	Invoiced sales (MSEK)	839	849
	Profit after financial items	87	107
	Return on capital	20%	21%
	Number of employees	1,606	1,591

product, Kanthal Super, was generating substantial growth because of its substantially improved performance over conventional materials, including longer service life, lower service costs, and higher operating temperatures.

Kanthal Bimetals was one of the few companies in the world with fully integrated manufacturing of thermo-bimetals for temperature control devices used in the manufacture of thermostats, circuit breakers, and household appliances.

Kanthal's manufacturing facilities were located in Hallstahammar, Brazil, the United Kingdom, West Germany, the United States, and Italy.

Kanthal 90

Ridderstråle, upon becoming president in 1985, saw the need for a strategic plan for Kanthal.

> The company had been successful in the past. We needed to use this base of experience to influence the future. We had to have a consolidated view to ensure that we did not sub-optimize in narrow markets or with a narrow functional view. Resources were to be allocated so that we could increase profits while maintaining a return on employed capital in excess of 20%.

The Kanthal 90 plan specified overall profit objectives by division, by product line, and by market. Currently, however, salespersons were compensated mostly on gross sales volume. Higher commissions were being paid for selling obviously higher-margin products, such as Super, and higher bonuses were being awarded for achieving sales targets in the high-margin products. But Ridderstråle wanted to achieve the additional growth planned under Kanthal 90 without adding sales and administrative resources to handle the increased volume anticipated.

> We needed to know where in the organization the resources could be taken from and redeployed into more profitable uses. We did not want to eliminate resources in a steady-state environment. We wanted to reallocate people to generate future growth.
>
> With our historically good profitability, and lacking any current or imminent crisis, we could not realistically consider laying off people at the Hallstahammar plant. But we wanted to be able to redeploy people so that they could earn more profit for us; to move people from corporate staff to divisions, from the parent company to operating subsidiaries, and from staff functions into sales, R&D, and production. Ideally, if we could transform an accounting clerk at Hallstahammar into a salesman of Kanthal-Super in Japan, we could generate a substantial profit increase.

Exhibit 2 shows the distribution of Kanthal's incurred costs. The existing cost system treated most sales, marketing, and administrative costs as a percentage of sales revenue. Therefore, customers whose selling price exceeded the standard full cost of manufacturing plus the percentage mark-up for general, selling, and administrative expenses appeared to be profitable, while a customer order whose selling price was below standard

Exhibit 2   Cost Structure

Cost Component	Percentage
Materials	23
Production salaries and wages	19
Variable processing costs	5
Fixed processing costs	16
Subcontracted services	3
Selling and administrative	34
Total costs	100

manufacturing cost plus the percentage mark-up appeared unprofitable. Ridderstråle knew, however, that individual customers made quite different demands on Kanthal's administrative and sales staff.

Low profit customers place high demands on technical and commercial service. They buy low-margin products in small orders. Frequently they order nonstandard products that have to be specially produced for them. And we have to supply special selling discounts in order to get the business.

High profit customers buy high-margin, standard products in larger orders. They make no demands for technical or commercial service, and accurately forecast for us their annual demands.

He felt that a new system was needed to determine how much profit was earned each time a customer placed a particular order. The system should attempt to measure the costs that individual customer orders place on the production, sales, and administrative resources of the company. The goal was to find both "hidden profit" orders, those whose demands on the company were quite low, and the "hidden loss" orders, those customer orders that under the existing system looked profitable but which in fact demanded a disproportionate share of the company's resources to fulfill.

Ridderstråle pointed out the weaknesses with the present method of profitability measurement.

We distribute resources equally across all products and customers. We do not measure individual customer's profitability or the real costs of individual orders. In this environment, our sales and marketing efforts emphasize volume, more than profits. In the future, we want Kanthal to handle significantly increased sales volume without any corresponding increase in support resources, and to gain the share in our most profitable products.

Our current method of calculating product costs may show two customers to be equally profitable on a gross margin basis. But there could be hidden profits and hidden costs associated with these customers that we are not seeing (see Exhibit 3). If we could get more accurate information about our own manufacturing cost structure, as well as the costs of supplying individual customers and orders, we could direct our resources to customers with hidden profits, and reduce our efforts to customers with the hidden losses. We might end up with the same market share, so that our competitors would not even see this shift in our strategy, but our profitability would be much higher. To execute such a strategy, however, we need better information about the profitability of each order, each product, and each customer.

The biggest barrier we have to overcome is the notion that production overhead, selling, and administrative costs are "fixed." The definition of strategy is to recognize that all

Exhibit 3   Hidden Profit and Hidden Cost Customers

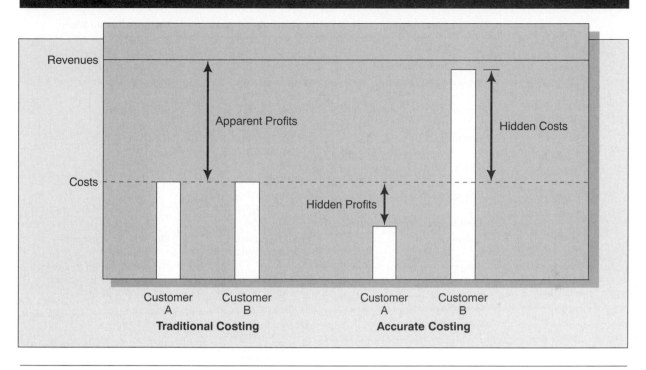

costs are variable. Our sales people must learn how to deploy resources to their most profitable use.

The New Account Management System

Per O. Ehrling, Financial Manager of Kanthal, worked with SAM, a Swedish management advisory group, to develop a system to analyze production, sales, and administrative costs at the Hallstahammar facility. Over a period of several months, finance managers and the consultants conducted extensive interviews with all department heads and key personnel. The interviews were designed to elicit information about the nature of the activities being performed by support department personnel and the events that triggered the demands for these organizational activities. Ehrling described the philosophy of the new approach:

> In our previous system, indirect costs were either manufacturing costs that were allocated to products based on direct labor, or they were Selling & Administrative Costs, that were treated as period expenses and were unanalyzed. This treatment may have been correct 100 years ago when we had one bookkeeper for every 10 blacksmiths, but today we have eight bookkeepers for every three blacksmiths. This means that most of our costs today are indirect and our previous system didn't know how to allocate them.
>
> We wanted to move away from our traditional financial accounting categories. We found that most of our organizational costs could be classified either as Order-related or Volume Costs. Actually, we did investigate three additional cost drivers—product range, technical support, and new products. But the total costs assigned to these three categories ended up being less than 5% of total costs so we eliminated them.

Exhibit 4   Order and Volume Costs

Type of Personnel	Order-Related Work	Volume-Related Work
Production		
Stock Replenishment	None	All Activities
Production Planning	Order Planning Order Follow-up	Inventory Management
Operators	Set-up Start-up Expense	Direct Hours
Foremen	Order Planning Order Support	Machine Problems
Stock	Order Input Order Output	Order Handling
Transportation	Order Planning Order Handling	
Selling and Administrative		
Management	Offer Discussion Offer Negotiation	General Management
Sales	Offer Work Order Negotiation Delivery Follow-up	Sales—Unrelated to Orders General Public Relations Sales Management
Secretarial	Offer Typing	
Administration	Order Booking Order Adjustment Invoice Typing Customer Ledger Supervision	Accounting

Using the interview information, the project team determined how much of the expenses of each support department related to the volume of sales and production and how much related to handling individual production and sales orders (see Exhibit 4). The **manufacturing volume** costs, in addition to material, direct labor, and variable overhead, also included the costs of production orders to replenish inventory stocks. Only 20% of Kanthal's products were stocked in inventory, but these products represented 80% of sales orders so the cost of continually replenishing these products was assumed to be related to the volume of production. **Manufacturing order** costs therefore included only the cost set-up and other activities that were triggered when a customer ordered a product not normally stocked. Manufacturing order costs were calculated separately for each major product group. The **sales order** costs represented the selling & administrative costs that could be traced to processing an individual customer's order. The S&A costs that remained after subtracting sales order costs were treated as **sales volume** costs and were allocated proportionately to the **manufacturing volume** costs.

For example, the Sales Department activities (see Exhibit 4) relating to preparing a bid for an order, negotiating with the customer about the order, and following-up with the customer after the order was delivered were classified as "order-related." All remaining activities, such as public relations and sales management, that could not be traced to individual orders were classified as "volume-related."

Follow-up interviews were conducted to corroborate the split of effort in each department between volume- and order-related activities. Sample calculations are shown in Exhibit 5.

Exhibit 5 Sample Calculation of Order and Volume Costs: By Product Group

Step 1. Calculate Selling & Administrative (S&A) Order Costs

Total Selling & Administrative Order Costs:		SEK2,000,000
Total number of orders	2,000	
Stocked products	1,500	
Non-stocked products	500	
S&A order costs per order		SEK 1,000

Step 2. Calculate Manufacturing Order Cost for Non-stocked Products

Total Manufacturing Order Costs		SEK1,000,000
(for non-stocked products)		
Number of orders for non-stocked products		500
Manufacturing order costs per non-stocked order		SEK 2,000

Step 3. Calculate Allocation Factor for S&A Volume Costs

Compute Total Manufacturing and S&A Costs:		SEK7,000,000
Subtract Order Costs:		
Non-stocked products:	1,000,000	
Selling and Administrative Order Costs:	2,000,000	3,000,000
Total Volume Costs:		SEK4,000,000
Manufacturing Volume Costs of Goods Sold (CGS)	3,200,000	
Selling & Administrative Volume-Related Costs	800,000	
S&A Volume Allocation Factor: S&A Volume Costs/Mfg. Volume CGS (800/3,200)		25%

Step 4. Calculate Operating Profit on Individual Orders for Non-stocked Product

Sales Value		SEK 10,000
Less: Volume Costs: Manufacutring Cost of Goods Sold (@ 40% of Sales Value)		4,000
Volume Costs: Selling & Administrative (@ 25% of Mfg. CGS)		1,000
Margin on Volume-related Costs		5,000
Less: Mfg. Order Cost for Non-stocked Product		2,000
Selling & Administrative Order Cost		1,000
Operating Profit for Order		SEK 2,000

Bo Martin Tell, controller of the Furnace Products Division, recalled the amount of tedious work required to collect all the numbers.

It took almost a year to develop a system to collect the data in the proper form. Even in production, we had problems identifying the costs that related to stocked and non-stocked orders.

Initial Output from the Account Management System

Exhibit 6 shows a profitability report for a sample of individual orders from Swedish customers. Profit margins on these individual orders ranged from −179% to +65%. Previously, almost all of these orders would have appeared profitable. Similar reports were prepared to show total profitability by customer, by product group, or by all the orders received from customers in a country. For example, Exhibit 7 shows, for a given product group—Finished Wire N—the sales volume and profitability of a sample of Swedish customers.

Leif Rick, general manager of Heating Technology, remembered the initial reactions to the account management reports:

The study was a real eye-opener. We saw how the traditional cost accounting system had been unable to truly report costs and profits by market, product, and customer.

At first, the new approach seemed strange. We had to explain it three or four times before people started to understand and accept it. People did not want to believe that order

Exhibit 6   Customer Order Analysis

Standard order cost: SEK572
Manufacturing order cost for non-stocked products: **Foil Elements: SEK1508**
Finished Wire: SEK2340

Country Customer	Order Lines	Invoiced Value (SEK)	Volume Cost (SEK)	Order Cost (SEK)	Non-Stocked (SEK)	Operating Profit (SEK)	Profit Margin
Sweden							
S001	1	1,210	543	572	0	95	8%
S002	3	46,184	10,080	1,716	4,524	29,864	65
S003	8	51,102	50,567	4,576	12,064	(16,105)	−32
S004	9	98,880	60,785	5,148	13,572	19,375	20
S005	1	3,150	1,557	572	2,340	(1,319)	−42
S006	5	24,104	14,889	2,860	4,680	1,675	7
S007	2	4,860	2,657	1,144	4,680	(3,621)	−75
S008	1	2,705	1,194	572	0	939	35
S009	1	518	233	572	0	(287)	−55
S010	8	67,958	51,953	4,576	12,064	(635)	−1
S011	2	4,105	1,471	1,144	0	1,490	36
S012	8	87,865	57,581	4,576	12,064	13,644	16
S013	1	1,274	641	572	2,340	(2,279)	−179
S014	2	1,813	784	1,144	0	(115)	−6
S015	2	37,060	15,974	1,144	3,016	16,926	46
S016	2	6,500	6,432	1,144	3,016	(4,092)	−63

Note: All financial data reported in Swedish kroner (SEK).

costs could be so high; that order costs had to be treated as an explicit cost of selling. Most surprising was finding that customers thought to be very profitable were actually break-even or even loss customers. Salesmen initially thought the approach was part of a master plan to get rid of small customers. But people who have been working with the system now are convinced of its value and are beginning to take sensible actions based on the information.

Exhibit 8 shows the profits from Swedish customers, ranked by customer profitability. The results surprised even Ridderstråle. Only 40% of Kanthal's Swedish customers were profitable and these generated 250% of realized profits. In fact the most profitable 5% of the customers generated 150% of the country's profits. The least profitable 10% of customers lost 120% of the profits (see cumulative profitability chart in Exhibit 9).

Even more surprising, two of the most unprofitable customers turned out to be among the top three in total sales volume. These two customers had gone to just-in-time (JIT) delivery for its suppliers. They had pushed inventory back onto Kanthal, which had not recognized the new demands being placed on its production and order-handling processes by the JIT approach. Moreover, further investigation revealed that one of these customers was using Kanthal as a back-up supplier, to handle small special orders of a low-priced item when its main supplier could not deliver. Because of the size and prestige of the two customers, Kanthal people had always welcomed and encouraged their orders. Ridderstråle now realized how expensive it had become to satisfy them.

The immediate problem was to devise a strategy for the large number of nonprofitable customers, particularly the very high volume ones. Corporate management had started a series of meetings with the general and sales managers of the operating divisions in Sweden to discuss how to handle these customers.

Exhibit 7   Finished Wire N Customer List

Customer #	Invoiced Sales (SEK)	Volume Costs (SEK)	Order Cost (SEK)	Non-Stocked Cost (SEK)	Operating Profit (SEK)	Profit Margin
33507	3,969	1,440	750	0	1,779	45%
33508	4,165	1,692	750	2,150	(427)	–10
33509	601	139	750	2,150	(2,438)	–406
33510	13,655	6.014	750	2,150	4,741	35
33511	2,088	350	750	2,150	(1,162)	–56
33512	1,742	637	750	0	355	20
33513	4,177	932	750	2,150	345	8
33514	7,361	3,314	750	0	3,477	47
33515	1,045	318	750	0	(23)	–2
33516	429,205	198,277	9,000	0	221,928	52
33517	31,696	13,128	3,750	0	14,818	47
33518	159,612	58,036	2,250	6,450	92,876	58
33519	48,648	17,872	9,750	12,900	8,126	17
33520	5,012	1,119	750	2,150	993	20
33521	4,933	2,170	1,500	4,300	(3,037)	–62
33522	17,277	7,278	1,500	0	8,499	49
33523	134	120	1,500	4,300	(5,786)	–4,318
33524	1,825	523	1,500	0	(198)	–11
33525	13,874	4,914	3,750	6,450	(1,240)	–9
33526	3,762	1,452	750	0	1,560	41
33527	64,875	18,559	3,750	8,600	33,966	52
33528	13,052	5,542	3,000	6,450	(1,940)	–15
33529	39,175	12,683	3,750	8,600	14,142	36
33530	383	87	750	0	(454)	–119
33531	6,962	1,865	750	2,150	2,197	32
33532	1,072	314	1,500	0	(742)	–69
33533	14,050	6,333	1,500	2,150	4,067	29
33534	820	244	750	0	(174)	–21
33535	809	181	750	2,150	(2,272)	–281
33536	1,366	316	750	2,150	(1,850)	–135
33537	155,793	65,718	21,750	49,450	18,875	12
33538	7,593	2,772	2,250	2,150	421	6
Total	1,060,731	434,159	84,000	131,150	411,422	39%

Note: All financial data reported in Swedish kroner (SEK).

Also, while the account management system had been developed for the Swedish operating divisions, some overseas divisions remained skeptical about the value of the exercise. The account management system was seen as yet another intrusion of the headquarters staff into their operations. Ridderstråle knew he faced an uphill battle gaining acceptance for the account management system around the world.

Exhibit 8   Customer Profitability: Ranked from Most to Least Profitable Customers

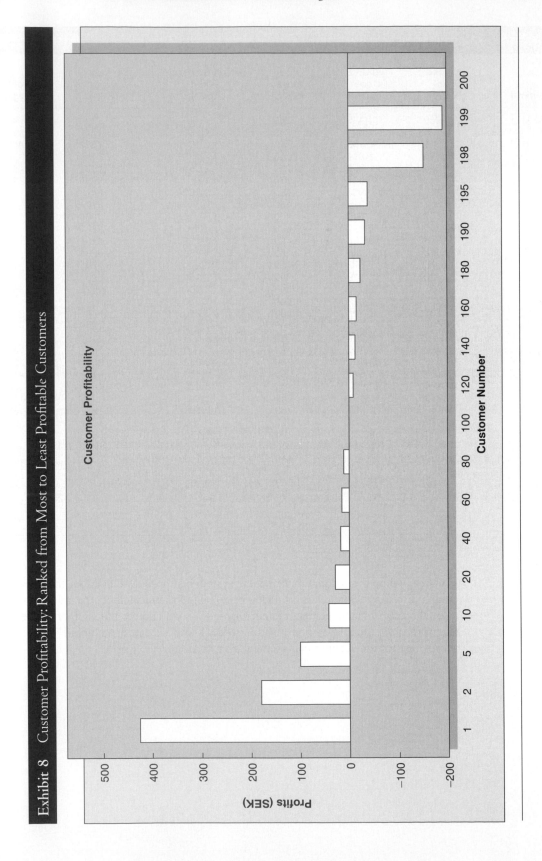

Exhibit 9   Cumulative Profitability by Customers

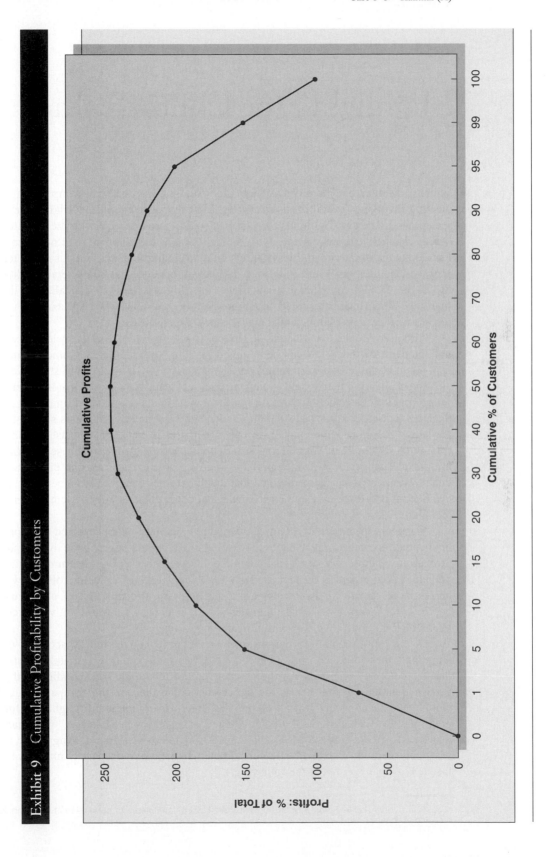

Cumulative Profits

Profits: % of Total

Cumulative % of Customers

Case 3–6

Highlights for Children, Inc.*

Elmer C. Meider, president of Highlights for Children, Inc., had just completed a lengthy meeting involving several of his managers. Each manager had been assigned the task of recommending ways Highlights for Children could more effectively utilize the three marketing channels currently being used. Meider thought the company had not been taking full advantage of the capabilities of direct mail, telemarketing, and direct sales in terms of prospecting, lead distribution, current and new product sales, and overall profitability. Moreover, Meider contends that Highlights for Children needs to capitalize on the continuity of direct mail, the rapid follow-up possible via telemarketing, and the value of face-to-face customer contact available through direct sales.

Although Meider knew he had the authority to eliminate the direct sales force operation, he believed this would not be in the best interests of Highlights. Rumors were abundant about possible legal restrictions on telemarketing programs. Several states were considering legislation that would greatly restrict when telephone calls could be made for sales purposes. One such law would limit telephone calls to specified times and no later than 7 P.M. Meider knew such a limit would sharply curtail Highlights's successful telemarketing program. Moreover, the threat of increases in postal rates caused Meider concern about the future of Highlights's successful direct mail program. These possible environmental changes provided support for Meider's position to keep the direct sales arm intact. Company experience revealed that the direct sales force was in a better position to learn about and resolve customer problems and concerns than either telemarketing or direct mail.

Managers from each of the three distribution methods had been asked to prepare recommendations concerning changes they would implement to improve the overall sales and profitability picture. Meider's task would be to review the various recommendations and prepare a final report to present to Garry C. Myers III, chief executive officer, who was present at the meeting. Also present at the meeting were Richard H. Bell, chairman of the board; Lynn Wearsch, national rep. sales service manager; Chuck Rout, vice president–telemarketing; and Gayle Ruwe, mail marketing manager.

Of the various recommendations, the one that provoked the most discussion was that Highlights for Children rely exclusively on telemarketing and direct mail distribution and that the company eliminate the direct sales force. Richard Bell, responding to this suggestion, pointed out that it was the direct sales force that got the company started and would keep the company going well into the future. He commented, "Highlights for Children might as well close its doors if the direct sales force is eliminated." One manager's response to Bell's defense of the direct sales force consisted of referring to the relative sales contributions from each source and how telemarketing and direct mail have grown faster. This manager noted the following:

Telemarketing and direct sales are in a competitive position from a lead utilization stand-point. Profitability is greatly enhanced when leads are sent directly to telemarketing rather than to the direct sales force. Sure, representatives can sell a bigger package and a longer-term subscription than the other marketing arms, but the reps rely solely on company-generated leads and are not using referrals generated from customers, nor are they doing any local prospecting. The resources assigned to the direct sales force could be more profitably used by telemarketing and direct mail. Our opportunity costs, or losses, have been rising as a result of sending leads to the direct sales group. They cannot handle all of the leads, and by the time telemarketing receives them they are stale and of little value.

Bell agreed in part with these observations but was quick to note that the size of the direct sales force had dropped from an all-time high of 750 to the current level of 265 independent sales reps, which includes 65 area managers. "We need to be more effective recruiting new sales reps. Just doubling the direct sales force would produce significant benefits," noted Bell. After this interchange, Garry Myers suggested that Meider would consider all proposals and attempt to arrive at a recommendation that would combine the best of everything.

The Company

General information

Begun in 1946 as a children's publication, Highlights for Children, Inc., has become a multidivisional company, selling not only magazines but also textbooks, newsletters, criterion-referenced tests, and other materials. The consumers include children, parents, and teachers.

The mission statement of Highlights for Children, Inc., states:

> Highlights for Children, Inc.'s mission is to create, publish, produce, or distribute on a profitable basis quality products and services uniquely designed for the educational development of children, their parents and teachers, and others with specific educational needs.

Each of the current divisions or subsidiaries operates within these guidelines.

Highlights emphasizes the fair and courteous treatment of its customers. Promotional offers are closely reviewed to ensure prospective customers are not being misled. Highlights is committed to maintaining a "pure" image in the marketplace in terms of marketing efforts as well as quality of its product.

Highlights for Children magazine is circulated to approximately 2 million subscribers. It is marketed through direct selling (via independent contractors), telephone marketing, and direct mail. Parents, teachers, doctors, and gift donors are targeted by the different marketing arms. In addition, Highlights sells various educational products that have been promoted through the introductory-offer school programs.

History

Dr. Garry C. Myers, Jr., and Caroline C. Myers founded Highlights for Children, Inc., in 1946 in Honesdale, Pennsylvania. Based on the belief that learning must begin early to fully develop a child's learning ability, the magazine was geared to challenge children's creative thinking and abilities. Today, the editorial offices are still in Honesdale, although the corporate headquarters are in Columbus, Ohio, and the magazine is printed in Nashville, Tennessee.

At the time Highlights for Children, Inc., was founded, magazines were sold almost exclusively by door-to-door salesmen. *Highlights for Children* followed suit. Today, Highlights continues to use direct selling in conjunction with telephone marketing and direct mail to market the magazine.

In 1955, Myers hit on the idea of putting *Highlights for Children* in doctors' offices with lead cards. At about the same time, his wife came up with the introductory-offer program to be marketed to parents through the schools. This was the beginning of marketing *Highlights for Children* by mail. Both programs met with immediate and resounding success.

Magazine content

Highlights for Children targets and services a diverse age group from 2 to 12. The material in the magazine ranges from easy to advanced. This conforms to the philosophy of challenging children: Rather than having material graded and directed to a particular age child, children are allowed to work at their own rate and are "encouraged" to achieve and understand more.

The tag line of *Highlights for Children* is "Fun with a Purpose" (see Exhibit 1). The *purpose* of the magazine is to educate and instruct, not merely entertain. The magazine is positioned as supplemental material to be used in the home, rather than in the classroom.

Highlights for Children likes to maintain the image of an educational magazine. No cut-outs or mark-ups are included in the magazine content, enhancing the idea of *lasting* quality. There is no paid advertising in *Highlights for Children,* which is in line with the educational image. Throughout the years, advertising has been considered at various times. Management continues to believe the magazine is more salable as an educational supplement without advertising. Highlights also believes children are already subjected to more than enough advertising pressure through other sources, much of which is resented by parents and teachers. Recently, President Elmer Meider raised the advertising issue and suggested that advertising revenues might be a way to improve *Highlights*'s profit performance.

The Marketing Program

Highlights for Children, Inc., uses three different marketing arms to sell its products: direct selling, telephone marketing, and mail marketing. Each type is discussed in the following sections. Exhibit 2 shows the current organization.

Direct selling

The direct selling organization has two kinds of representatives: the school representatives and regular representatives. Almost all reps receive company-generated leads; however, school reps make most of their sales from self-generated "school drop" leads.

School representatives

Reps make their initial presentation to a school principal or superintendent. The object of the presentation is to gain permission to leave sample copies of *Highlights for Children* in grades K–4. If the school agrees to participate, a sample copy, along with a lead card, is sent home with each child. The child is instructed to return the card to the school if the parents are interested in ordering *Highlights*. Reps then pick up the lead cards from the schools. A school rep usually visits a particular school once every two to three years. Currently *Highlights for Children* has about 70 school reps.

Exhibit I

Regular reps

Regular reps contact the following company-generated leads:

1. *Parent inquiries (PI)* and *doctor inquiries (DI)*. These people have not had a subscription but have sent in a card indicating interest.

2. *Introductory-offer renewals (IO)*. These people have been sold the six-month introductory offer through the school and are now up for renewal.

3. *Regular renewals (RR)*. These people have had a regular subscription (11 issues or more) and are up for renewal.

4. *Donor renewals (DR)*. These people have given a gift subscription (11 issues or more) and are up for renewal.

A rep has a set amount of time to work the leads (depending on the type). At the end of that time period, the lead automatically goes to either phone or mail for follow-up. Reps send back the leads marked "no contact" or "no sale" once they have been worked, so the other departments can follow up quickly.

Reps call on parents at home. The increasing number of women working and higher gasoline prices have made the rep's job more difficult over the years. When reps do find

Exhibit 2   Highlights for Children, Inc., Organization Chart

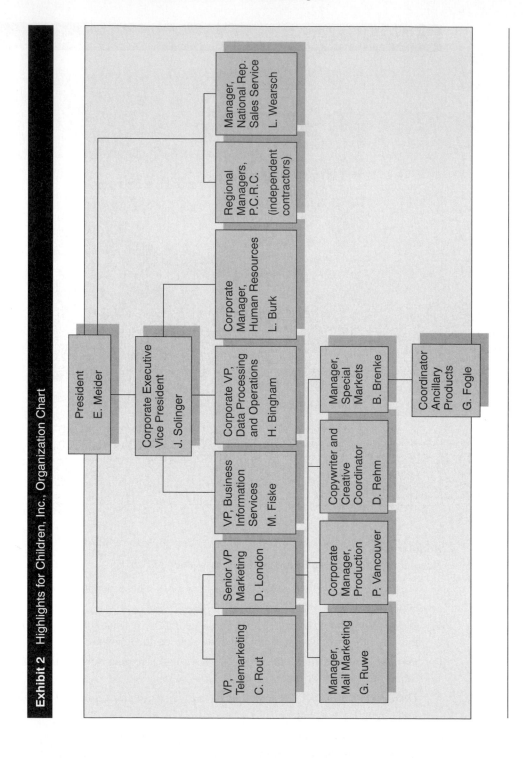

someone at home, their presentation hits mainly on what *Highlights for Children* is, how to use it, and its educational value. The rep can sell, on average, a 2.8-year term subscription.

There is a management structure in the regular rep program. Not all reps are under a manager; none reports directly to the home office. Managers receive an override on all area sales (personal and representative's sales).

The current rep structure is composed of about 265 active reps, of which about 65 are managers. The Columbus, Ohio office has seven employees who are assigned to the direct-selling arm. Reps are independent contractors and as such are not paid a salary, but rather they earn a commission on their sales. Their commission is calculated by commission level times sales units. Units are determined by term sold: (five-year subscription = 1.4 units; three-year subscription = 1.0 unit; two-year subscription = 0.7 unit; and one-year subscription = 0.3 unit). *Highlights for Children* subscription rates are $49.95 for 33 issues (three years) and $79.95 for 55 issues (five years). For example, the commission for a three-year subscription is $24.97 (1.0 unit = .50; $49.95 × .50 = $24.97).

Telephone marketing

Started over 10 years ago in response to the energy crisis and the possibility of the greatly reduced mobility of the representative selling arm, telephone marketing has grown and flourished from a staff of 3 to 190 telemarketing reps, all paid on a commission basis. Telemarketing commissions are about one-half (23 percent) of direct sales commissions. Commissions are not paid for sales that are canceled or never paid by the customers. These reps are located in Columbus along with 25 staff employees.

Telemarketing receives basically three types of leads: parent and doctor inquiries, introductory-offer renewals, and regular renewals. Telemarketing reps have a specified time period in which to contact and sell their leads before they go to mail marketing for followup. They attempt to contact leads, all types, 10 times before giving up. In one day's time, they can make up to four attempts. On average, telemarketing sells a 2.3-year term.

Mail marketing

The mail marketing department consists of three primary areas: creative, production/analysis, and list rental. Currently, 10 employees work in the mail marketing department. Major responsibilities, in addition to list rental, include acquiring *new customers* (through efforts such as the Christmas mailing and school teacher introductory-offer mailing), acquiring *new leads* (through the doctors' offices, doctor inquiries, and parent inquiries mailings), and converting leads (these leads may be new or renewals) to customers (typically after regular reps and/or phone reps have tried to convert). All activities are conducted through direct mail.

More specifically, all promotion packages (to acquire either a lead or a customer), space ads, package inserts, billing stuffers, preprinted computer forms, and so forth are created and produced through the efforts of this department. The actual mail production (merge/purge, lettershop, etc.) is also coordinated here. Finally, the results are analyzed here as well.

Christmas program

The Christmas program is a multimedia effort to acquire one-year subscriptions targeting a donor. The mail program consists of over 5 million names, mailed from mid-September to mid-October.

Additionally, the Christmas program includes card inserts in the October, November, and December issues of *Highlights for Children* magazine, statement stuffers, approximately 2 million package inserts in outside packages (*Drawing Board, Current,* etc.) and space ads (*The Wall Street Journal, New York Times, Christian Science Monitor,* etc.).

Introductory-offer program

A mailing is made to teachers who hand out "take-home" slips on which the parents can subscribe. The subscription offer to the parents is for six months of *Highlights for Children,* an "introductory offer."

Parent inquiry/doctor inquiry program

Several times a year, *Highlights for Children* purchases doctor lists for an outside mailing to produce doctor inquiries. General practitioners, pediatricians, dentists, any doctors who have children, and/or parents visiting their offices and waiting rooms are targeted. Doctors who subscribe are especially valuable because they provide a vehicle to reach parents, and the primary purpose of the doctor mailing is to eventually reach parents. Highlights for Children can send the magazine, complete with parent inquiry cards, into a doctor subscriber's office on a *monthly* basis, potentially reaching many parents.

Marketing Arm Effectiveness

Background information revealed that mail marketing produced the most revenue for seven years. In 1983, telemarketing surpassed direct marketing in terms of revenue. Exhibit 3 shows sales by marketing arm from 1976 through 1985. Order-per-lead ratios by marketing arm are as follows:

Telemarketing: over 30 percent.

Direct sales: over 20 percent.

Mail: over 5 percent.

Normally, order-per-lead ratios are higher for direct sales. In fact, for a given number of leads, say 50, the direct sales group will produce more orders than the telemarketing group. However, since the reps are asking for more leads than they can possibly handle, many end up wasted and are not viable by the time they are received by telemarketing and direct mail.

The decline in the number of independent contractors has been of some concern for several years. Various programs have been initiated over the years to increase the number of reps. These programs have not met with much success, as evidenced by the size of the direct sales force. Selling low-ticket items, however, limits how much a regular rep can earn. About one-half of the regular reps work part time. Earnings range from as low as $1,000 a year for some reps to as high as six figures for those reps who are managers. Managers earn overrides on the sales of those reps they have recruited into the sales organization, a common practice in direct selling programs. Exhibit 4 is typical of the literature used by Highlights to recruit new reps.

Meider and others are aware that this is a problem that others in direct selling have faced. Giants in the direct selling industry such as Avon, Tupperware, Mary Kay, Amway, and so forth have all confronted this problem and have adopted various techniques to alleviate the negative impact that fewer reps have had on sales. A major contributing factor has been the dramatic increase in the number of working mothers.

The ability of people in direct selling to earn a reasonable level of income has been inhibited due to these trends. Many companies have adopted party plan selling programs in an attempt to increase the income-earning opportunities of the reps. Other companies have expanded their product lines to provide their direct sales reps with more commission

Exhibit 3   Highlights for Children, Inc.: Annual Gross Sales by Source, 1976–1985 ($000)

	Reps	Telephone	Mail
1976	$ 11,400	$ 860	$10,700
1977	11,800	1,500	11,300
1978	12,100	2,300	12,100
1979	10,300	3,300	14,400
1980	10,400	6,400	16,300
1981	11,100	8,400	16,400
1982	12,400	9,000	21,400
1983	12,300	13,400	28,000
1984	10,800	20,400	36,000
1985	10,200	23,800	46,000

Exhibit 4   Sales Opportunity Fact Sheet

Highlights for Children is an educational magazine for children ages 2 through 12. There are 11 issues published each year, and the December issue includes an annual Resource Index, which turns that year's books into a home reference library for the whole family.

Highlights is available by enrollment only. It is not sold on any newsstand, contains no advertising, and is created primarily for family use. The vast majority of its subscribers are parents. *Highlights* contains a wide range of fiction, nonfiction, thinking and reasoning features, contributions from readers, and things to make and do. The high interest articles include humor, mystery, sports, folk tales, science, history, arts, animal stories, crafts, quizzes, recipes, action rhymes, poems, and riddles.

Dr. Garry Cleveland Myers and Caroline Clark Myers founded *Highlights for Children* in 1946 as the outcome of years of professional work in child psychology, family life, education, and publishing for children. *Highlights* has grown from a first issue circulation of 22,000 to over 1,500,000 in 1982 and is the world's most honored book for children.

Noted educator, psychologist, and author, Dr. Walter B. Barbe, is the editor-in-chief of *Highlights.* Dr. Barbe's books and professional publications have made him nationally renowned in education and in demand as an international speaker. The ongoing production of each issue is coordinated by a talented staff of educators, most of whom are parents. The editorial offices are located in Honesdale, Pennsylvania. The marketing arm for *Highlights for Children* is Parent and Child Resource Center, Inc., and the administrative offices are centered in Columbus, Ohio, where a dedicated representative sales staff plans and directs the business of selling and delivering *Highlights* all around the world.

Highlights for Children is sold nationally by authorized independent representatives directly to families, teachers, preschools, daycare centers, doctors' offices, and to any other person or place interested in welfare and development of children. This is a direct, person-to-person sales opportunity.

As an independent contractor selling *Highlights*'s products, you are free to work the hours you want and earn as much commission as possible. You are in business for yourself with exclusive leads and virtually no product competition. There is no investment required, and you are provided with the information and instruction you need to grow in skill, experience, and earnings. Your business will grow in proportion to the time, skill, and resourcefulness you use in presenting the values of *Highlights* to families, individuals, groups in your community. Your job is to visit with prospective customers, show them how *Highlights* will benefit their children, and write up the order. Statistics show that one out of three contacts will enroll.

You find that selling *Highlights*'s products is enjoyable, pleasant, and profitable. The only qualifications necessary are that you enjoy meeting people and have a sincere interest in children.

There is no limit to your earnings. Every home with children aged 2 through 12 is a potential customer. You retain a liberal commission on every enrollment at the time of the sale, plus additional commissions as your sales record grows. You receive bonuses for the quantity of sales you report, bonuses for the quality of the sale you make, and bonuses for recommending others as representatives. Your sales can also make you eligible to win incentive contests with cash and/or merchandise prizes.

If you are interested in a sales career, complete the enclosed Confidential Information form and mail it today!

Exhibit 5   Fact Sheet

Summary: 1985 Direct Selling Industry Survey

Total Retail Sales: $8,360,000

Percent of Sales by Major Product Group:

Personal care products	34.8%
Home/family care products	50.0
Leisure/educational products	9.4
Services/other	5.8

Sales Approach (method used to generate sales reported as a percent of sales dollars):

One-on-one contact	81.0%
Groups sales/party plan	19.0
In the home	77.0
In a workplace	11.8
At a public event*	2.5
Over the phone	6.9
Other	1.8

Total Salespeople: 2,967,887

Demographics of Salespeople:

Independent	97.9%
Employed	2.1
Full-time (30+ hours per week)	11.7
Part-time	88.3
Male	22.0
Female	78.0

*Such as a fair, exhibition shopping mall, theme park, etc.

Source: Direct Selling Association, Washington, DC.

opportunities. Exhibit 5, a fact sheet published by the Direct Selling Association, provides a summary of the 1985 direct selling industry.

Meider, on the other hand, thinks that despite these trends, the direct sales reps are not working as hard as they should and are not following prescribed and proven methods of selling. Reps are supposed to ask customers who have ordered a subscription to *Highlights for Children* for the names of others who might be interested in subscribing. Since the reps knew they could secure company-generated leads free, there was no financial incentive for them to ask for referrals. This referral process has been the mainstay method of direct selling not only for *Highlights for Children* but other direct-selling companies as well. Reps are expected to engage in local prospecting, which involves locating residential areas occupied by parents of young children. These activities have been neglected, and reps today rely solely on company-generated leads.

Sales reps continually ask for more leads than they can process, resulting in lost opportunities. By the time the leads are sent back to Columbus, they are of limited value. Meider was particularly distressed to learn that several reps had established their own telemarketing operations to enhance their earnings opportunities. As a result of this practice, Highlights was paying the reps a commission that was twice the amount normally paid for telemarketing sales. A report prepared by Marilyn Fisk, vice president of business information services, added further to Meider's concern. Her report contained the following points:

- Telemarketing sales in general are for the magazine only; sales of other products are very limited.

- Telemarketing sales do not involve a down payment; hence, there are more cancellations.

- Recruiting of additional direct sales reps has declined, especially in those situations where the reps, with the assistance or blessing of their managers, have started their own telemarketing operations.

Meider's reaction to Fisk's report further solidified his decision that changes are needed. He could understand why the managers would favor telemarketing conducted by their direct reps. Each subscription netted a $4 override for the manager regardless of how it was secured, although suggestions had been made that the $4 override was not adequate. And the direct reps received their usual commission. He had previously attempted to persuade the former national sales manager to do something about this practice only to be told the direct reps were independent and would view this as interference. Besides, as the national sales manager indicated, "The reps view the annual Christmas mailing as a direct threat and want the program to be eliminated or at least share in the commissions on sales from their territories."

Some time later, the national sales manager left Highlights for Children, Inc., due to a reorganization that eliminated the position. Meider hired two regional sales managers who work in the field and can provide closer supervision of the direct sales reps and their managers. Meider divided the United States into two regions: east and west. This move greatly reduced the span of control problems experienced by the former national sales manager.

Meider discussed these problems with Garry Myers III and asked for his reactions. Myers noted that it should not be surprising that reps rely totally on company-generated leads. As Myers stated, "Our reps want to make the most sales, and the best avenue is to call on people who have taken the effort to complete a card and mail it in to Highlights. Reps know that these leads are more likely to produce sales than what they are likely to obtain using the referral process." Myers likened the referral process to "cold-call selling" and company-generated leads as "warm-call selling." Regardless, Highlights for Children is losing profits as a result of these practices, and Myers hoped Meider's report would be available soon.

Meider indicated his initial report would contain a series of alternative recommendations that would be used to generate discussion. For example, Meider suggested that one alternative would be to eliminate company-generated leads. Another possibility, suggested by Meider, would limit the number of company-generated leads a rep could receive each month. The number received might be a function of previous referral sales or some other factor. Meider also suggested charging the managers and/or the reps for each company-generated lead. To offset these additional charges, one likely countersuggestion would be to increase commissions paid to the reps. The Fisk report prompted another option: reducing the commission paid to reps for orders received without a down payment. This might curtail the use of telemarketing by the reps, a practice Meider wanted to stop. Finally, one manager suggested the school reps be charged a small fee for all of the sample copies that are left at schools for K–4 distribution. The manager said, "If the regular reps are wasteful of the excessive leads that they receive, then the school reps may be just as guilty when they give away too many free samples."

Eliminating the independent reps is one alternative, as is increasing the number of reps. Meider did not agree with Bell that more reps was the best solution, although he did think it was an alternative to consider. Expanding the product line to give the reps more items to sell and more commission opportunities was another alternative suggested to Meider. Currently, a three-year subscription at $49.95 produces a commission of $24.97.

Meider knew no one would suggest replacing the direct sales force with a company sales force. Such a move would increase overhead expenses by at least 15 percent to cover fringe benefits costs plus staff additions needed for purposes of governmental reporting. Eliminating the direct selling arm would be a better solution than creating a company sales force.

Myers thought Meider's suggestions would produce much discussion among his management team. At this juncture, he believed Meider should narrow the alternatives to a final set of recommendations.

Case 3–7

Wentworth Industrial Cleaning Supplies*

Wentworth Industrial Cleaning Supplies (WICS), located in Lincoln, Nebraska, is experiencing a slowdown in growth; sales of all WICS products have leveled off far below the volume expected by management. Although total sales volume has increased for the industry, WICS's share of this growth has not kept pace. J. Randall Griffith, vice president of marketing, has been directed to determine what factors are stunting growth and to institute a program that will facilitate further expansion.

Company and Industry Background

WICS is a division of Wentworth International, competing in the janitorial maintenance chemical market. According to trade association estimates, the total market is roughly $2.5 billion in 1998. Exhibit 1 shows the nature of this market. Four segments comprise the institutional maintenance chemical market, which consists of approximately 2,000 manufacturers providing both national and private labels.

Total industry sales volume in dollars of janitorial supplies is approximately $1.3 billion. Exhibit 2 shows the breakdown by product type for the janitorial market. WICS addresses 75 percent of the market's product needs with a line of high-quality products. The composition of WICS's product line is as follows:

Special purpose cleaners	46%
Air fresheners	9
General purpose cleaners	16
Disinfectants	15
Other	14

The janitorial maintenance chemical market is highly fragmented; no one firm, including WICS, has more than 10 percent market share. Agate and Marshfield Chemical sell directly to the end-user, while Lynx, Lexington Labs, and WICS utilize a distributor network. Most of WICS's competitors utilize only one channel of distribution; only Organic Labs and Swanson sell both ways. Most private-label products move through distributors. Sanitary supply distributors (SSDs) deliver 65 percent of end-user dollars, while direct-to-end-user dollar sales are 35 percent (Exhibit 3).[1] The following (page 636) shows the sales breakdown by target market by type of distribution:

---

*Joan Russler and Jeffrey Forbes, MBAs–Marketing, University of Wisconsin–Madison, assisted in the preparation of this case. Copyright © 1998 Neil M. Ford.

[1]Includes paper supply distributors that carry janitorial supplies.

Exhibit I   Institutional Maintenance Chemical Market

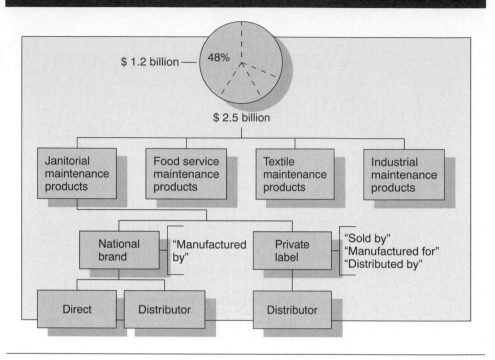

Distributor Sales

Retail	20%
Industrial	18
Health care	18
Schools	11
Building supply contractors	10
Restaurants	3
Hotels	3
Other	17

Direct Sales

Retail	47%
Building supply contractors	35
Health care	15
Hotels	2
Restaurants	1

Trade association data plus information from other sources estimate the number of SSDs to be between 5,000 and 6,000. The following shows the sales volume breakdown for the SSDs based on an average of 5,500:

Size in Sales Volume

Less than $100,000	1,210
$100,000–$499,999	2,475
$500,000–$1,000,000	1,375
More than $1,000,000	400
Total	5,500

According to a recent analysis of end-users, WICS provides cleaning supplies for approximately 20,000 customers. WICS's sales force is expected to call on these accounts

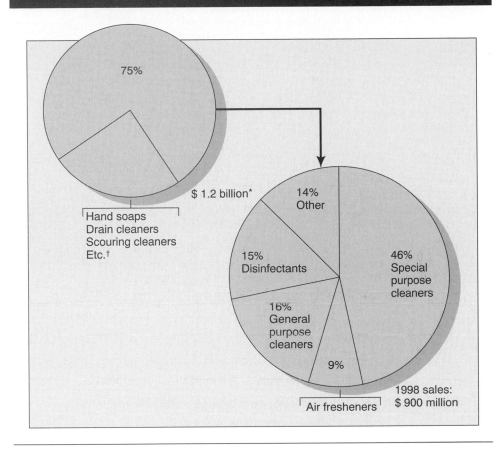

Exhibit 2   WICS "Served" Portion of the Janitorial Maintenance Chemical Market

75%

$ 1.2 billion*

Hand soaps
Drain cleaners
Scouring cleaners
Etc.†

14%
Other

15%
Disinfectants

46%
Special
purpose
cleaners

16%
General
purpose
cleaners

9%

Air fresheners

1998 sales:
$ 900 million

*End-user dollars.

†Includes some general purpose cleaners and air fresheners that WICS does not manufacture.

as well as prospect for new business. These 20,000 end-users receive product from the SSDs who supply cleaning supplies manufactured by WICS and others as well. About one-third of the average SSD's total sales is accounted for by WICS's products. An exception is the paper supply distributor, where WICS's products account for an average of 10 percent of sales.

The typical SSD carries other related items. In fact, according to a survey conducted by an independent firm, SSDs almost always carry a private-label line of cleaning supplies plus one to two additional branded products besides the WICS line. This survey revealed that 60 percent of the SSDs carry a private-label line along with WICS and a private label. The private label may be a regional label or the SSD's own label.

WICS places almost total reliance on selling through the SSDs, although a small amount of sales (less than 10 percent) are made direct. WICS sells its janitorial maintenance products through roughly 400 distributors, who in turn "see" 65 percent of the end-user dollar market. Thus 65 percent of sales in the total janitorial maintenance market are made through SSDs (35 percent are direct sales); and the 400 SSDs used by WICS pro-

Exhibit 3   Janitorial Maintenance Chemical Market (end-user dollars)

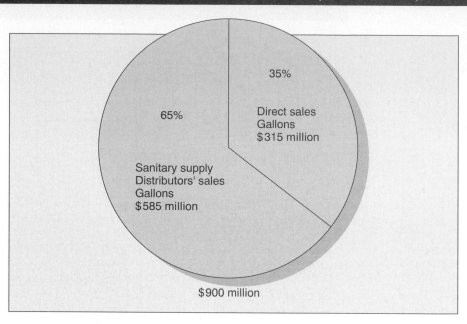

vided 65 percent coverage. The market seen by each distributor, referred to as his or her *window* on the market, is a function of the following:

Product lines carried (paper versus chemical).

Customer base (type and size).

Nature of business (specialization by market versus specialization by sales function).

The combination of these factors produces end-user market coverage of 42 percent (65 percent distributor sales × 65 percent coverage). WICS has very limited direct sales.

To reach its market, WICS uses a sales force of 135 area managers, 21 territory managers, and 4 regional managers (Exhibit 4). Regional managers are located in San Francisco, Denver, Chicago, and Boston. Although WICS is viewed as a giant in the industry, it does not produce a complete line of janitorial chemicals. Janitorial chemicals are rated based on their performance. WICS produces products that have average to premium performance ratings; WICS has no products in the economy class. Moreover, due to various factors, WICS's coverage in the average and premium classes is not complete. The emphasis on premium and average products results in providing only 75 percent of the market's product needs.

To provide high distributor margins and extensive sales support, WICS charges premium prices. Recent estimates reveal that only 40 percent of the served market is willing to pay these premium prices. The impact of WICS's limited product line coupled with its premium prices is evident in Exhibit 5.

An overall description of WICS's marketing program shows that it has focused on market development. Distributors receive high margins (30 to 40 percent) and sales costs are high (10 to 15 percent) due to emphasis on selling technical benefits, demonstrations,

Exhibit 4   WICS's Access to the Market

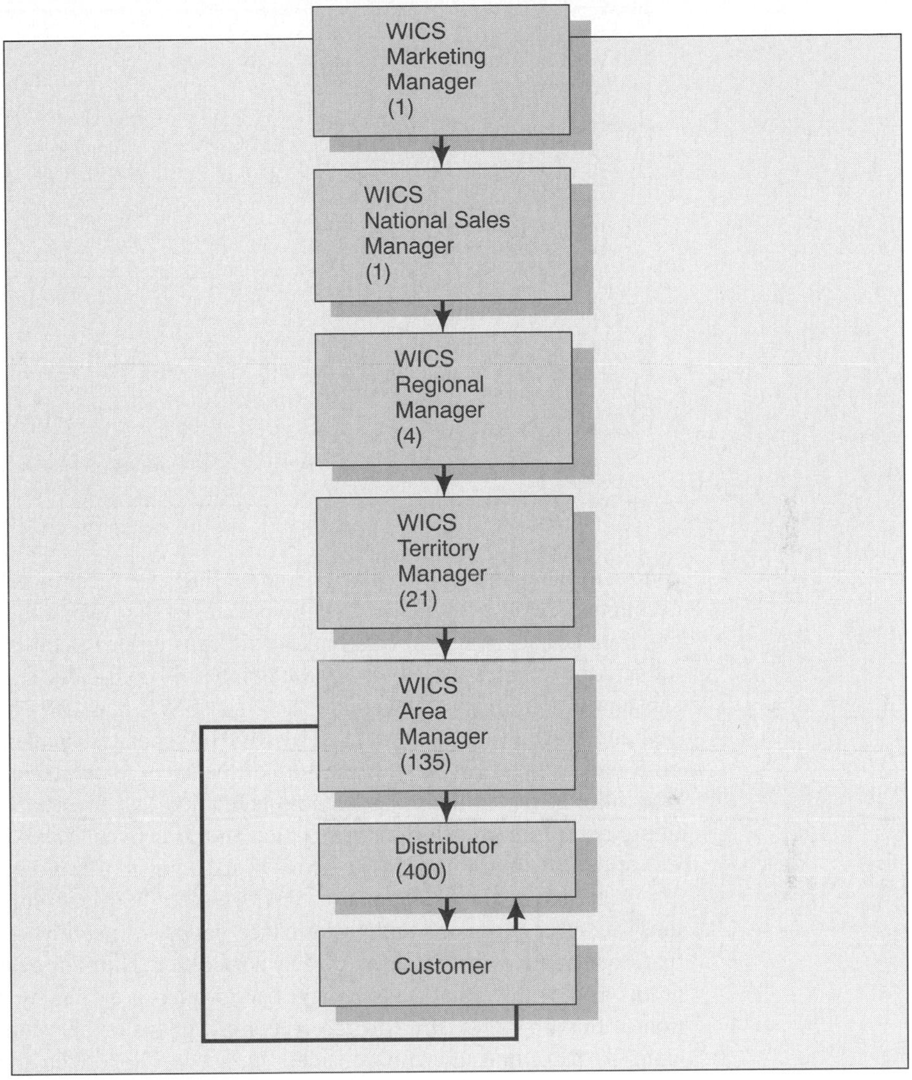

and cold calls. Area managers call on prospective end-users to develop the market for the SSD. By comparison, WICS's competitors offer SSDs low margins (15 to 20 percent) and incur low sales costs (5 to 8 percent).

Griffith recently received a memo from Steve Shenken, WICS's national sales manager, reporting on a study of the effectiveness of SSDs. Territory managers evaluated each SSD in their respective regions on a basis of reach (advertising and promotional programs) and frequency of sales calls. The composite report indicated distributors as a whole were doing an excellent job servicing present accounts. In other words, 400 SSDs provide WICS with a sizable share of the market.

Area managers (AMs) represent WICS in distributor relations. The AMs' "prime focus is to sell and service existing key end-user accounts and selected new target ac-

Exhibit 5 End-User Product Coverage

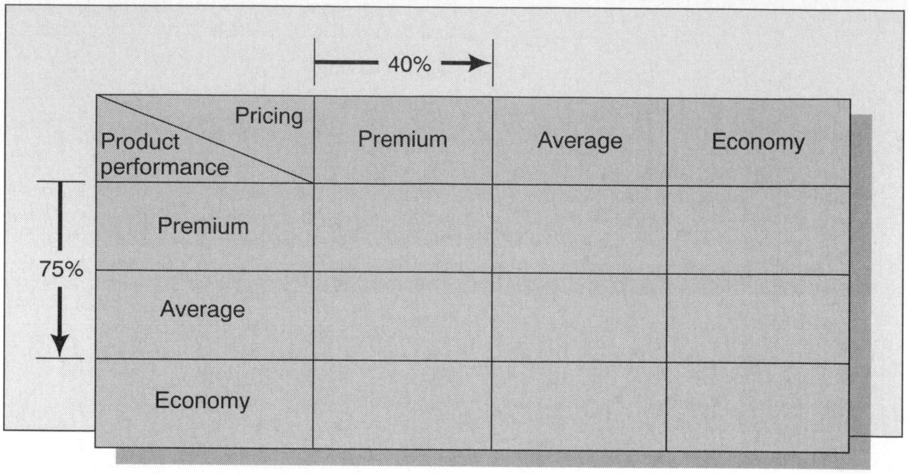

counts in their assigned territories." According to a recent study, maintenance of current accounts comprises approximately 80 percent of the AMs' time (Exhibit 6). In addition to handling old accounts, the AM makes cold calls on prospective distributors as directed by the territory managers. However, the number of cold calls made monthly has decreased substantially in the past year since the major SSDs now carry WICS products. A study of AM and SSD attitudes, conducted by MGH Associates, management consultants, is presented in Appendixes A and B. Some of the sales management staff question the use of AM time; however, there has been no indication that formal changes will be made in the future regarding sales force organization and directives. The AM job description has seen few revisions, if any, during the firm's past 10 years of rapid growth (Exhibit 7).

Area managers are compensated with a straight salary, enhanced periodically by various incentive programs and performance bonuses. Incentive programs generally require that AMs attain a certain sales level by a specified date. For example, the "Christmas Program" necessitated that AMs achieve fourth-quarter quotas by November 15; on completion of this objective, the AM received a gift of his or her choice, such as a color television. To date, management considers the Zone Glory Cup the most effective incentive program. The Glory Cup is an annual competition among areas within territories, which entails meeting or exceeding sales objectives by a specified date. An all-expense-paid vacation at a plush resort for area, territory, and region managers and their "legal" spouses is the prize for the winning team. However, management at WICS believes that prestige is the prime motivator in this competition and the underlying reason for the program's success.

In a recent meeting, Terry Luther, executive vice president of the WICS division of Wentworth International, expressed his concern to Griffith about WICS's mediocre performance. Luther indicated corporate cash flow expectations from WICS were not being met and that a plan was needed from Griffith concerning how WICS could improve its overall operating performance. Griffith was quite aware that Wentworth International would make personnel changes to meet corporate objectives and that selling off divisions not able to meet corporate expectations was not unlikely. Griffith informed Luther that an action plan would be developed and be on his desk within 30 days.

Exhibit 6   Allocation of Area Manager Duties*

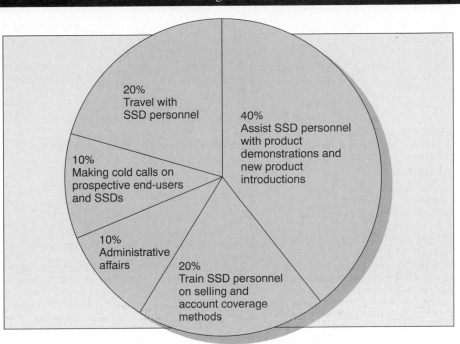

20%
Travel with
SSD personnel

40%
Assist SSD personnel
with product
demonstrations and
new product
introductions

10%
Making cold calls on
prospective end-users
and SSDs

10%
Administrative
affairs

20%
Train SSD personnel
on selling and
account coverage
methods

*Based on an analysis of call reports.

Griffith's first step was to approve an earlier request made by Mike Toner, sales and distributor relations manager, for a study of sales force and distributor attitudes and opinions (Appendixes A and B). Next, the memo in Exhibit 8 was sent, discussing Griffith's assignment from Luther:

Staff reaction to Griffith's memo (on page 644) was one of frustration and anger. Several managers thought they had already complied with Griffith's request. One person commented, "I've told Randy numerous times what we need to do to turn the division around, and all he does is nod his head. Why go through this 'wheel-spinning' exercise again?" Another said, "The only time old J. R. listens to us is when the top brass leans on him for results." Despite staff reaction, the meeting would be held, and everybody would have suggestions for consideration.

To provide adequate time, Griffith scheduled an all-day meeting to be held at Wentworth's nearby lodge, located on Lake Woebegone. Griffith started the meeting by reviewing past performance. Next, he asked each manager to outline his or her proposal. First to speak was Steve Shenken, who indicated that Mike Toner would present a proposal combining both of their ideas. Shenken also said he would listen to all sales force proposals and try to combine the best parts into an overall plan.

Mike Toner's proposal

Toner's proposal was rather basic. If improving market was WICS's objective, then more SSDs are needed in all territories. According to Toner:

Exhibit 7   Wentworth Industrial Cleaning Supplies Position Description

Date: January 1, 1986

Approved by: (1) ——————
            (2) ——————
            (3) ——————

Position: Area Manager, Maint. Prods.

Incumbent: 135 Positions Nationally

Division: Janitorial Maintenance
                         Products Division

Reports to: Territory Manager,
                         Janitorial Maintenance
                         Products Division

POSITION PURPOSE:

To sell and service user accounts and authorized distributors in an assigned territory to assure that territory sales objectives are attained or exceeded.

DIMENSIONS:

Annual sales:	$300 M	(average)
Number of distributors:	4	(average)
Number of distributor salesmen:	12	(average)
Annual expense budget:	$4.2 M	(average)
Company assets controlled or affected:	$8 M	(average)

NATURE AND SCOPE

This position reports to a territory manager, janitorial maintenance products. Each district is subdivided into sales territories that are either assigned to an individual member of the district or to a team effort, based on market and/or manpower requirements.

The janitorial maintenance products division is responsible for developing and marketing a broad line of chemical products for building maintenance purposes.

The incumbent's prime focus is to sell and service existing key-user accounts and selected new target accounts in his assigned territory. He multiples his personal sales results by spending a major portion of his time working with distributor sales personnel, selling WICS maintenance products and systems to key accounts such as commercial, industrial, institutional, governmental accounts, and contract cleaners. When working alone, he sells key-user accounts through an authorized distributor as specified by the user customer.

The incumbent plans, schedules, and manages his selling time for maximum sales productivity. He interviews decision makers and/or people who influence the buying decision. He identifies and evaluates customer needs through careful observation, listening and questioning techniques to assure proper recommendations. He plans sales strategy to include long-term/quick-sell objectives and develops personalized user presentations to meet individual sales situations, utilizing product literature, manuals, spot demonstrations, and sales aids to reinforce presentations. This position sells systems of maintenance to major volume user accounts through the use of surveys and proposals, test programs, and other advanced sales techniques. He develops effective closing techniques for maximum sales effectiveness. This position trains custodial personnel in product usage techniques through the use of product demonstrations and/or audiovisual training to assure customer satisfaction. He follows up promptly on customer leads and inquiries. He services customer and distributor complaints or problems and provides technical support as required. On a predetermined frequency basis, he surveys and sells assigned local accounts currently being sold on national contract. He represents the division in local custodial clinics and trade shows as required. He maintains an adequate current supply of literature, forms, and samples and maintains assigned equipment and sales tools in a businesslike condition.

The incumbent is responsible for training, developing, and motivating distributor sales personnel. This is accomplished by frequent on-the-job training in areas of product knowledge, selling skills, and demonstration techniques. He sells distributor management and assists distributors to maintain an adequate and balanced inventory of the full product line. He introduces marketing plans and sells new products and sales promotions to distributor management. He participates in distributor sales meetings to launch new products or sales promotions, or for training and motivational purposes. He keeps abreast of pertinent competitive activities, product performance, new maintenance techniques, and other problems and opportunities in the territory. Periodically, he communicates Wentworth growth objectives versus distributor progress to distributor management (i.e., sales coverage, volume and product sales, etc.). He assists the distributor to maintain a current and adequate supply of product literature, price lists, and sales aids.

The incumbent prepares daily sales reports, weekly reports, travel schedules, weekly expense reports, and the like, and maintains territory and customer records. He maintains close communication with his immediate supervisor concerning products, sales, distributor and shipping problems.

(continued)

Exhibit 7   (concluded)

He controls travel and business expenses with economy and sound judgment. He handles and maintains assigned company equipment and territory records in a businesslike manner.

Major challenges to this position include maintaining established major users, selling prospective new target accounts, and strengthening distribution and sales coverage to attain or exceed sales objectives.

The incumbent operates within divisional policies, procedures, and objectives. He consults with his immediate supervisor for recommendations and/or approval concerning distributor additions or terminations, exceptions to approved selling procedures, and selling the headquarters level of national or regional accounts.

Internally, he consults with the editing office concerning distributor shipments, credit, and so forth. Externally, he works closely with distributor personnel to increase sales and sales coverage and with user accounts to sell new or additional products.

The effectiveness of this position is measured by the ability of the incumbent to attain or exceed territory sales objectives.

This position requires an incumbent with an in-depth and professional knowledge of user account selling techniques, product line, and janitorial maintenance products distributors, and a minimum of supervision.

PRINCIPAL ACCOUNTABILITIES

1. Sell and service key-user accounts to assure attainment of territory sales objectives.
2. Sell, train, develop, and motivate assigned distributors to assure attainment of product sales, distribution, and sales coverage objectives.
3. Plan, schedule, and manage personal selling efforts to assure maximum sales productivity.
4. Plan and develop professional sales techniques to assure maximum effectiveness.
5. Train custodial personnel in the use of Wentworth products and systems to assure customer satisfaction.
6. Maintain a close awareness of territory and market activities to keep the immediate supervisor abreast of problems and opportunities.
7. Perform administrative responsibilities to conduct an efficient territory operation.
8. Control travel and selling expenses to contribute toward profitable territory operation.

Each area manager serves, on the average, four SSDs. Since we can only get so much business out of an SSD, then to increase sales we need more SSDs. I suggest that each area manager add two more distributors. Of course, this move will require that we either add more area managers or that we hire and train a special group to call on new and end-users and new distributors. It's difficult to attract new SSDs unless we show them a group of prospective end-users who are ready to buy WICS's products. Now, I have not made any estimates of how many more people are needed, but we do know that present AMs do not have enough time to adequately seek new business.

After Toner presented this proposal, Griffith asked if the existing AMs could not be motivated to apply more effort toward securing new business. Calla Hart thought the AMs could do more and that her proposal, if adopted, would alleviate the need for expansion of the AMs and SSDs.

Calla Hart's proposal

As expected, Hart's proposal revolved around her extensive experience with WICS's incentive programs. This satisfactory experience led Calla to suggest the following:

If I thought that the AMs and the SSDs were working at full capacity, I would not propose more incentive programs. But they are not! We can motivate the AMs to secure more new business, and we can get more new business from our distributors. We all know that the SSDs are content to sit back and wait for the AMs to hand them new business. Well, let's make it worthwhile to the SSDs by including them in our incentive programs. For the AMs I suggest that we provide quarterly incentives much like our Christmas Program. AMs who achieve their quotas by the 15th of the second month of the quarter would receive a gift.

In addition, we need to develop a program for recognizing new end-user sales. Paying bonuses for obtaining new end-user accounts would be one approach. For example, let's

> **Exhibit 8   Griffith's Memo**
>
> Intra-Office Memorandum
>
> To: Steve Shenken, National Sales Manager
>   Caitlin Smith, Manager—Sales Analysis
>   Ryan Michaels, Manager—Sales Training
>   Calla Hart, Manager—Special Sales Program
>   Charlotte Webber, Senior Product Manager
>   Mike Toner, Sales and Distributor Relations Manager
>
> From: Randall Griffith, Vice President—Marketing
>
> Subject: WICS Performance Review
>
> As you all know, our performance has not met corporate expectations. To rectify this situation, before we all lose our jobs, we need to meet to discuss ways for improving our market performance.
>
> At our next meeting, I want each of you to develop proposals for your areas of responsibility. These proposals need not be detailed at this time. For the moment, I am seeking ideas, not final solutions.

reward the AM from each territory who secures the highest percentage increase in new end-user accounts. At the same time, we need to reward the distributor from each territory who achieves the highest percentage increase in new end-user sales dollars. And let's recognize these top producers each quarter and at year end as well. Our incentive programs work. We know that, so let's expand their application to new sales.

Finally, on a different note, I support establishing quotas for our distributors. We have quotas for our sales force, and we enforce them. AMs who do not make quotas do not stay around very long. Why not the same procedures for some of our SSDs? We all know that there are some distributors who need to be replaced. Likewise, I have not made any cost estimates but feel that we are just searching for new ideas.

Griffith thanked Hart for her comments. He wondered whether applying more pressure to the distributors was the most suitable approach. He agreed with Hart that WICS's incentive programs seemed to be very popular but questioned if other techniques might not work. Griffith then asked Ryan Michaels for his comments.

Ryan Michaels's proposal

During his short time with WICS, Michaels has gained respect as being very thorough and analytical. He is not willing to accept as evidence such comments as "We know it works" as a reason for doing something. Determining the value of sales training, Michaels's area of assignment, has caused him considerable concern. He knows it is useful, but how useful is the question he is trying to answer. According to Michaels, WICS needs to examine the basic selling duties of the area managers:

Before we recruit more AMs and SSDs, or try to motivate them to obtain more new business with incentive programs, we need to examine their job activities. I favor doing a job analysis of the area manager. Some evidence that I have seen indicates that job descriptions are outmoded. AMs do not perform the activities detailed in the job descriptions. For example, most AMs spend very little time calling on prospective end-users. Accompanying distributor sales reps on daily calls does not lead to new end-user business. Possibly the AMs could better spend their time doing new account development work. But before we make any decisions concerning time allocation, we need to conduct a job analysis. And, while we are collecting data, let's ask the AMs what rewards are important to them. How do they value promotions, pay increases, recognition, and so forth? Maybe the AMs do not want more contests.

Griffith agreed that the job descriptions were out of date. He also contended this is typical and nothing to be concerned about in the short run. The idea of finding out what rewards AMs value intrigued Griffith. Next, Griffith asked Charlotte Webber for her reactions to WICS's market share problem.

Charlotte Webber's proposal

Webber's proposal was more strategic in nature than the previous suggestions. Her experience as a product manager led her to consider product-oriented solutions and to suggest the following:

> I think we can increase market share and sales volume through the expansion of current lines and the addition of a full line of economy-based products. We can expand our present premium and average lines to cover 100 percent of the product class by adding air fresheners and general purpose cleaners. In addition we must introduce the economy-based products to counter competition.
>
> The proposed plan would not be costly because we could use our existing distributor network. If additional SSDs are necessary, we can select those in the $500,000 to $1,000,000 sales volume range. I feel that through these extensions and an increased number of SSDs we can address 75 percent of the SSD end-user dollars.

Griffith agreed that line extensions were a viable means of achieving some corporate goals. He expressed concern over entry into the low-quality segment of the market due to WICS's present customer perceptions of the company as a high-quality producer. Griffith turned to Caitlin Smith for additional suggestions on how to increase market share.

Caitlin Smith's proposal

Smith's proposal came as no surprise to those attending the meeting. Her position in sales analysis made her critically aware of WICS's high cost of sales. It was only recently, however, that she developed a plan incorporating market share and cost of sales. Her views were accurate, but often given little weight due to her inexperience. According to Smith:

> Our costs of sales are currently running at 10 to 15 percent, while our competitors' costs average 5 to 8 percent. As many of you know I am in favor of changing the job description of the area manager and the sales presentation. These changes are necessary due to our products' stage in the life cycle and customer service level preferences. Recently I have become convinced that there is another means of reducing sales costs. By reducing prices we could increase sales volume and reduce the cost of sales. This strategy would also increase penetration and market share.

Griffith conceded that price reductions were a possibility but expressed concern over the possibility of weakening consumer perceptions of WICS as a high-quality manufacturer. He also questioned Smith's assumption that the industrial cleaning supplies industry was presently in the mature stage of the product life cycle.

Following these comments, Griffith thanked the participants for their input and adjourned the meeting. On retiring to his room, he reflected on the suggestions presented during the meeting and his own beliefs. He knew he must begin to formulate an action plan immediately since the 30-day deadline was drawing near.

Appendix A

CONCLUSIONS OF STUDY OF AREA MANAGER ATTITUDES

MGH Associates, management consultants, was retained by WICS to investigate attitudes and opinions of field personnel and sanitary supply distributors. Initially, MGH conducted lengthy interviews with selected individuals, followed by the administration of a comprehensive questionnaire. The results below identify role expectations and attitudes toward their reasonableness.

Territory Manager's Role Expectations

MGH Associates's interviews included territory managers because the territory manager is really the only management level contact the distributor has.

The territory manager interprets his or her role to be that of an overseer, to assure that WICS objectives are achieved and that quotas are met.

The territory manager interprets his or her role to include:

- Training the area managers to
  Sell WICS products.
- Training and motivating the distributor sales force.
- Coordinating area manager activities with headquarters in Lincoln.
- Hiring and firing area managers.
- Striving for new product commitments from the distributors.
- Acting as "referee" for competition between distributors.
- "Building the book" for the adding or deleting of distributors.
- Submitting the "study" to the regional manager, who writes a proposal based on the territory manager's "study." It is submitted to corporate management, where the final decision is made.

Area Manager's Role Expectations

The following is the area manager's view of the role he or she believes WICS management expects to be performed:

- Multiply sales effort through distributor's sales force (listed first because it was consistently mentioned first).
- Teach and motivate the distributor's sales force to sell WICS products.
- Introduce new products to the market through
  Direct calls on end-users.
  Distributors.
- Keep margins high to keep distributors happy. If they are happy, they will push WICS.
- Follow through on direct sales responsibilities.
- Collect information for management.
- Fulfill responsibilities relating to incentives:
  New gallon sales.
  Repeat gallon sales.
  Demonstrations.
  30, 35, 40? calls/week.
  Major account calls.
  Cold calls—"to develop business the distributor is reluctant to go after."

Area Manager's Role Problems

The area manager's perception of what management expects does not imply that the area manager feels that management's approach is working. In general, the sales force appears frustrated by a sales role they see as ineffective:

- A sales role that stresses:
  New gallon sales.
  Cold calls on end-users.
  Product demonstrations.
  New product introduction.
- "Checking the boxes" rather than being "creatively productive."
  15 demos.

10 cold calls.

5 distributor training sessions.

- Incentives stress selling techniques that may not be the most productive ways to sell.

  Emphasis is on new gallon sales over repeat gallon sales. Incentives weight new gallons over repeat gallons (two to one).

  Emphasis to "demonstrate as often as possible" for the points. Demonstrate to show you are a "regular guy" who gets his or her hands dirty, not necessarily to show product benefits.

- Bonus incentives appear to be a "carrot" only for those who don't regularly make bonus, that is, "hit 106 for maximum bonus and minimum quota increase."

- The sales role gives the area manager little ability to impact his or her own success to

  Change distribution.

  Move distributor outside his or her window.

- The area manager describes his or her role as:

  A "lackey."

  A "chauffeur."

  A "caretaker of old business."

Area Manager's Role: Making Cold Calls

One of the causes of area manager frustration is the general ineffectiveness of their cold calls sales role:

- The area manager makes cold calls on end-users not presently sold by the WICS distributor, with the difficult objective of moving these accounts to the WICS distributor.

- If the area manager succeeds in moving this account over to WICS products, chances are small that the distributor will keep the business.

  Without a major portion of the account's total purchases, the distributor cannot afford to continue to call on the account.

  Distributor sales rep is on commission.

  After five calls, will stop calling if purchases have not begun to increase.

- The distributor that lost the account will try extremely hard to get back the business. This may mean giving the product away to keep control of the account—maintain majority of the account's purchases. Past experience indicates it is very difficult to move distributors outside their "window."

Appendix

B

CONCLUSIONS OF STUDY OF WICS SANITARY SUPPLY DISTRIBUTOR ATTITUDES

WICS Distributor's Role Expectations

The following is the WICS distributor's role as outlined by WICS management and sales force.

- Act as an extension of the WICS sales force.

- Push and promote WICS product line in a *specified area*.

  Sell WICS over other brands.

Always sell the premium benefits of WICS products to the end-user, instead of distributor's private label.

Be aware that the WICS line could be lost if private label sales grow too large.

- Actively market new WICS products.

Distributor's Role Problems

Distributors have been angered by WICS's attempt to run their businesses ("WICS is trying to tell me what to do").

- WICS makes demands—"uses pressure tactics."

  Distributors say they are told "our way or no way."

  Distributors feel they are forced to carry products they don't want.

     High minimum buy-ins.

     "Won't see area manager if we don't carry the new product."

  Distributors say WICS management doesn't "realize we make our living selling all our products—not just WICS."

- Communication is poor with WICS management.

  One way—"Our opinions never reach Lincoln."

- "WICS uses the distributor as a testing ground for new products."

  Distributor is not told what to expect.

  After 14-week blitz, "You never hear about the product again."

  The distributor sales force is not trained to sell to, and cannot afford to call on, certain segments of the market.

- Growth takes the distributor into new geographical market areas, and WICS may elect not to go/grow with the distributor.

  New branch in different city.

  Growth may take distributor sales personnel out of area manager's district.

     Receives no support from WICS.

Worst case—distributor sales rep's territory is completely outside district.

     No WICS representative at any accounts.

     Prefer to sell other than WICS.

- WICS does not realize that a distributor's total business extends beyond "its own backyard" in many markets.

Distributor's Role Selling Costs

Distributors have shown concern over the high cost of selling WICS products. Sales costs are approximately 45 percent of the total operating costs.

- "WICS products are basically no better than anyone else's."

- Yet WICS asks distributors to switch competitor's accounts over to WICS products.

  Price advantage is very rare.

  A problem must exist.

  A demonstration is required.

- All these make the "problem-solving" sale time-consuming and costly.

- Result: When WICS product is sold, it is easy for competitive WICS distributors to cut price to try to get the business.

  They have very low sales costs.

- Required action: Original distributor must cut margin to keep the business.

  This frustrates distributor salespeople.

  Causes them to sell private label.

Case 3–8

Olympic Electronics Corporation*

The corporate planning process for Olympic Electronics Corporation had just concluded, and Martha Hampton, president of Marketing, was reviewing the corporate goals for 1998. Even though Hampton had participated in the deliberations and the drafting of the final document, she was impressed with the ambitious goals. For example, the corporate plan established a sales goal of $37 million for 1998, when sales volume for 1997 was estimated to be $27 million.

During the planning process, a number of other executives had voiced concern over whether the distribution approach used by Olympic Electronics was appropriate for the expanded sales goal. Hampton felt that their concerns had merit and should be given careful consideration. Though she had considerable latitude in devising the distribution strategy, the final choice would have to be consistent with the overall marketing program for the company in 1998. A recommendation and supporting documentation had to be prepared in a relatively short time to permit an integrated marketing program introduction in January 1998.

The Company

Olympic Electronics Corporation was formed in 1961 by Karl Hampton, who had a Ph.D. in electrical engineering. The company introduced a stereo radio unit in 1964 and a line of television sets in 1966. By the early 1980s, the company had expanded its product line to include a full line of *home entertainment* equipment.

Olympic Electronics is an assembler rather than a manufacturer of home entertainment equipment. As an assembler, the company purchases components under contract from large (usually foreign) manufacturers. These components are then identified as Olympic Electronics Corporation products and placed in consoles or other packages for sale under the **Olympia** brand name.

Olympic Electronics distributes its products directly to 425 independent specialty home entertainment dealers and 50 exclusive dealers which are of standard industry size in terms of selling space. Combined, these 475 dealers service 150 markets in 11 western and Rocky Mountain states. According to Hampton, this disparity in market coverage occurred as a result of the company's early difficulty in gaining adequate distribution.[1]

---

*This case was prepared by Professor Roger A. Kerin, of the Edwin L. Cox School of Business, Southern Methodist University, Dallas, TX. Copyright © by Roger A. Kerin. No part of this case may be reproduced without written permission of the copyright holder.

[1]Exclusive dealerships had chosen to operate in this manner. This was not the policy of Olympic Electronics Corporation. However, Olympic Electronics did not pursue additional dealers in these markets for the purpose of carrying company products.

The independent dealers typically carry 10 or more brands of home entertainment equipment products, whereas the exclusive dealerships carry only Olympic Electronics products and noncompetitive complementary products. Dealerships are located in market areas with populations of approximately 100,000 or fewer. In contrast, major competitors tend to be national in scope. Partially as a result of that—and partially because of economics of scale in advertising and distribution—these firms had been selling an increasing proportion of their products through mass merchandisers such as chain and discount stores. The overwhelming majority of these stores were located in retail trading areas with 1 million or more inhabitants.

The company employs 10 sales representatives, each responsible for a territory that is generally delineated by state borders. These representatives deal primarily with the independent dealers and call on them twice a month on average.

The Home Entertainment Industry

The home entertainment industry grew considerably in the 1980s with the rise in consumer disposable income, changes in lifestyles, and product innovation. Estimates of the actual dollar volume of the industry are extremely vague, partly because of the rapidly changing product mix encompassed by the general term *home entertainment* and constant product innovation.

Despite the difficulty in estimating market size, it is generally accepted that Thomson (GE and RCA brands), Zenith, Matsushita (Panasonic and Quasar brands), Sony, and North American Philips (Magnavox, Sylvania, and Philco brands) account for the bulk of total dollar volume. Private brands, produced by several of these firms and many others, are also important in the industry. The total market was estimated to be growing at a rate of 6 percent annually.

Though it is difficult to define specifically the product mix in the industry at any one time, eight general product categories exist: television, compact disc players, video cassette recorders, radios, phonographs, tape recorders, tape decks, and high-fidelity stereo system components. Product categories vary dramatically in terms of saturation. For example, 99 percent of the households in the United States have a television set, 65 percent have a video cassette recorder, and 48 percent have a portable radio or tape player. By comparison, 14 percent of households in the United States have a compact disc player and only 6 percent have a portable compact disc player. Exhibit 1 shows the incidence of first purchase and replacement purchases for selected home entertainment products.

In 1994 the company commissioned a study on the socioeconomic characteristics and purchase behavior of buyers of home entertainment products. Exhibit 2 shows selected demographic characteristics of buyers of selected home entertainment products. The study reported that these purchasers had median household incomes above the median household income of the U.S. population as a whole. The research also revealed the following:

1. In-store demonstration, friend or relative recommendation, dealer or salesperson presentation, and advertising are dominant influences when buyers decide what brand of home entertainment products to purchase.

2. The median number of shopping trips made before purchasing home entertainment products was 2.4.

3. The most frequently shopped outlets for home entertainment products were radio/TV stores.

The vast majority of home entertainment products are distributed through five types of retail outlets: (1) home furnishings/furniture stores, (2) housewares/hardware stores, (3)

Exhibit 1   First Purchase and Replacement Purchases for Selected Home Entertainment Products

	Percentage of Households Buying			
	For First Time	As Replacement	In Addition to One Now Owned	Total Market
Color console TV	37	49	14	100
Color portable TV	41	30	29	100
Color table-model TV	44	31	25	100
Stereo receiver/amplifier	58	23	19	100
Stereo speakers	55	21	24	100
Tape deck	71	14	15	100
Tape recorder	61	15	24	100
Video cassette recorder	85	10	5	100

Source: Company records.

auto supply stores, (4) department stores/mass merchandisers (such as Circuit City), and (5) radio/TV stores. The volume of home entertainment merchandise sold by these outlets is unknown because of the variety of merchandise offered. However, selected data on the radio/TV store group with a more homogeneous product mix are available (see Exhibit 3). These types of dealers represent all of Olympic Electronics's accounts and operate with a gross margin of 27.5 percent.

Olympic Electronics Corporate Policy for 1998

The following is an excerpted version of the company's statement of policy.

General corporate objective

Our customer is the discriminating purchaser of home entertainment products who makes the purchase decision in a deliberate manner. To this customer we will provide, under the **Olympia** brand, quality home entertainment products in the higher-priced brackets that require specialty selling. These products will be retailed through reputable electronics specialists who provide good service.

Marketing objectives and strategy

The company's marketing objective is to serve the discriminating purchaser of home entertainment products who approaches a purchase in a deliberate manner with heavy consideration of long-term benefits. We will emphasize home entertainment products with superior performance, style, reliability, and value that require representative display, professional selling, trained service, and brand acceptance—retailed through reputable electronics specialists to those consumers whom the company can most effectively service. This will be accomplished by:

1. A focused marketing effort to serve the customer who approaches the purchase of a home entertainment product as an investment.

2. Concentration on our areas of differential advantage: high-technology television, audio, and related home entertainment products with innovative features, superior re-

Exhibit 2	Demographic Characteristics of Heads of Households Buying Selected Types of Home Entertainment Products		

	For First Time	As Replacement	In Addition to One Now Owned
Color console TV:			
Median age	38	50	42
Median number of household members	3.3	3.3	4.3
College graduate	21.3%	15.4%	30.6%
Color table-model TV:			
Median age	36	45	46
Median number of household members	3.4	3.2	4.3
College graduate	44.0%	22.5%	30.8%
Color portable TV:			
Median age	41	43	43
Median number of household members	3.1	2.9	3.8
College graduate	24.2%	32.2%	33.9%
Stereo receiver/amplifier:			
Median age	39	40	46
Median number of household members	3.6	3.3	4.3
College graduate	32.1%	43.8%	46.8%
Stereo speakers:			
Median age	37	34	41
Median number of household members	3.5	3.0	4.1
College graduate	34.7%	38.8%	38.7%
Video cassette recorder:			
Median age	39	39	NA
Median number of household members	3.2	3.4	NA
College graduate	42.1%	20.1%	NA
Tape recorder:			
Median age	43	44	43
Median number of household members	3.7	4.2	3.9
College graduate	28.1%	39.4%	39.1%
Tape deck:			
Median age	40	34	49
Median number of household members	3.9	3.5	4.2
College graduate	27.5%	20.5%	29.6%

Source: Company records.

liability, and high performance levels—products that generally sell for more than $600 at retail.

3. Emphasis on products requiring display, demonstration, and product education, which must be delivered to and serviced in the home, to be sold through reputable merchants that specialize in home entertainment products and provide good service.

4. Concentration on distribution in existing markets, and general exclusion of large core cities with populations of 1 million or more.

5. Developing brand acceptance by obtaining in every market served a market position of at least $6.50 sales per capita, which our research indicates is possible.

Olympic Electronics's 1998 policy statement and marketing strategy represented a significant departure from the company's previous marketing posture. For many years the

Exhibit 3   Number of Retail Sales of Radio/TV Stores in the Western and Rocky Mountain States

State	Number	Sales (thousands of dollars)
Arizona	289	$ 164,870
California	2,375	1,581,046
Colorado	331	180,119
Idaho	86	30,029
Montana	81	38,408
Nevada	88	55,397
New Mexico	113	42,749
Oregon	286	132,726
Utah	124	57,204
Washington	457	182,993
Wyoming	59	20,252
11-state total	4,289	2,485,793

Source: Census of Retail Trade and Olympic Electronics Corporation estimate.

company had manufactured and marketed good-quality, medium- and promotionally priced home entertainment products. In the last few years, however, the company had begun to emphasize more expensive and more luxurious home entertainment equipment.

Although this was not stated in the overall marketing strategy, the company had also become more aggressive in its advertising. The advertising budget for 1998 included television advertising, which the company had previously eschewed in favor of local newspaper advertising on a cooperative basis with dealers. In 1998, television advertising would be allotted $3 million and would be directed at the 100 highest-potential markets, 50 markets served by exclusive dealers and 50 other current markets that had the next-highest potential.

The overall direction of the marketing program had been reaffirmed in the recent corporate planning sessions. The sales target of $37 million was viewed as both ambitious and necessary. Olympic Electronics's senior managers were of the firm belief that the company had to attain a larger, critical mass of sales volume to preserve its buying position with component suppliers, particularly with respect to component prices and discounts.

Even though there was agreement on the marketing effort and the need to expand sales volume, different viewpoints were raised concerning the capacity of present dealers to deliver $37 million in sales. This matter had consumed much of Hampton's time recently.

The Distribution Strategy Issue

Hampton was well aware of the value that Olympic Electronics placed on its dealers and the importance of developing a close linkage between the company and the dealers. The company had long emphasized that dealers are an asset that must be consistently supported.

Hampton saw his charge as determining the characteristics, the number, and the locations of the dealers Olympic Electronics would need to meet its sales goal of $37 million in 1998. Initially this would involve identifying the types of dealers that would satisfy the needs of the kind of customer the company sought and that would work closely with the company in meeting corporate objectives.

A number of different viewpoints had been voiced by Hampton's fellow executives. One viewpoint favored increasing the number of dealers in the markets currently served by the company. The reasoning behind this position was that it would be difficult for existing dealers to attain the $37 million sales goal specified in the corporate plan. Executives expressing this view noted that even with a 6 percent increase in sales following the industry trend, it would be necessary to add at least another 100 dealers. They said these dealers would likely be independent (nonexclusive) dealers located in the 100 markets not served by exclusive dealerships. Hampton believed that adding another 100 dealers over the next year would not be easy and would require increasing the sales force that serviced nonexclusive dealers. Executives acknowledged that this plan had more merit in the long run of, say, three to four years. However, their idea had merit as a long-term distribution policy, they thought. The incremental direct cost of adding a sales representative was $50,000 per year.

A second viewpoint favored the development of an exclusive franchise program, since 27 nonexclusive dealers had posed such a possibility in the last year. Each of these dealers represented a different market and each of these markets was considered to have high potential and be a candidate for the new advertising program. These dealers were prepared to sell off competing lines. They would sell Olympic Electronics home entertainment products exclusively in their market for a specified franchise fee. In exchange for the dealer's contractual obligation to promote, merchandise, and service Olympic Electronics products in a specified manner consistent with corporate objectives, Olympic Electronics would drop present dealers in their markets and not add new dealers. Further, these dealers noted, the company's current contractual arrangements with its independent dealers allowed for cancellation by either party, without cause, with 90 days' advance notification. Thus, the program could be implemented during the traditionally slow first quarter of the upcoming year. If it was adopted, Olympic Electronics executives believed the franchise program in these 27 markets could be served by the television advertising program. The other 50 markets served by exclusive dealers would be unaffected, since this advertising program was already being applied. The remaining 73 markets would also be unaffected, except for increased advertising in 23 high-potential markets.

A third viewpoint called for a general reduction in the number of dealerships without granting any exclusive franchises. Executives supporting this approach cited a number of factors favoring it. First, analysis of dealers' sales indicated that 10.5 percent of Olympic Electronics dealers (all exclusive dealers) produced 80 percent of company sales. Second, an improvement in sales force effort and possibly increased sales might result if more time were given to fewer dealers. Third, committing Olympic Electronics to an exclusive franchise program would limit its flexibility in the future. Although a number had not been set, some consideration had been given to the idea of reducing the number of dealers in the 150 markets served by the company from 475 to 250. This would mean that the 50 exclusive dealers would be retained and 200 nonexclusive dealers would operate in the remaining 100 markets, of which the top 50 would benefit from the television advertising program.

A fourth viewpoint voiced by several executives was not to change either the distribution strategy or the dealers. Rather, they believed that the company should do a better job with the current distribution system. It was their opinion that additional sales personnel and the expanded television advertising budget should be sufficient. Moreover, they argued that because of a recessionary environment, the late 1990s was not the time for major changes in distribution policy and practices.

Case 3–9

ISG Technologies Inc.*

Mike Hopkinson, Director of North American Sales for ISG Technologies Inc. (ISG) of Mississauga, Ontario, paced his office and considered what he should do about the deteriorating relationship between ISG and its North American distributor, Precision Medical Instruments Ltd. (Precision).[1] ISG was a Canadian company that sold medical imaging computers in North America and Europe; 1991 sales had been $11.4 million.

It was January 1992 and Hopkinson was furious after receiving a telephone message from Precision's sales manager telling Hopkinson that Precision had set a new sales record in December with orders for 40 magnetic resonance imaging systems. Although Hopkinson would have expected sales of 10 to 15 of ISG's add-on imaging computer systems with that many orders, Precision had sold only one. Most of ISG's U.S. sales were being made either through ISG's own efforts or from a contact with Philips Medical Systems Nederland B.V. to supply a similar computer workstation product that was sold under the Philips brand name.

Despite recent overtures from Precision offering to rebuild the increasingly strained relationship with ISG and Precision's promises of better sales performance in the months ahead, Hopkinson felt that the time had come to consider other alternatives. He knew that any recommendation he made would be critically important to ISG since 90 percent of its sales were in the United States. Hopkinson had to make a decision soon as his recommendation could affect planned product launches and negotiations with other distributors in Europe and the Far East.

ISG's Products

Radiologists used computed tomography (CT or CAT) scanners and magnetic resonance imaging (MRI or MR) scanners to examine the internal anatomy of patients. CT and MRI scanners were essentially X-ray machines capable of producing a cross-sectional image through a patient's anatomy. CT scanners were used to examine bony structures and MRI scanners were used to create similar images of soft tissues. MRI images were very effective in detecting cancer such as brain tumors that would otherwise be difficult, if not impossible, to detect.

Both of these imaging systems gave radiologists and surgeons a series of images, each a "slice" through the patient's anatomy. A single examination might yield as many as 150

IVEY

[1]Disguised name.

individual "slices" through the relevant anatomy. The surgeons and radiologists then had to visualize a three-dimensional picture of the patient's anatomy based on these individual frames.

ISG designed products that took these individual images and combined them in a computer to build a two-dimensional or three-dimensional model of the anatomy. The surgeon or radiologist could then view the model on a computer screen, rotate it, remove portions of it, make it transparent, color code tissue types, or perform a multitude of other manipulations. For example, a surgeon could examine the interior of someone's brain to locate a tumor. They could then determine its exact position relative to other tissues, measure its volume and plan a surgical approach. The hospital could realize significant time savings in the operating room because of less time taken in exploration. In the radiology department, these images were a great aid in diagnosis.

Allegro

The Allegro was ISG's primary product. It comprised a computer workstation and a software package for data processing and image manipulation. A radiologist transferred scanner data on computer tape to the Allegro where it is processed into a two-dimensional or three-dimensional model. A radiologist or surgeon could then manipulate the image on the workstation screen and then save it or print it out. (See Exhibit 1 for a photograph of the Allegro and Exhibit 2 for an example of the Allegro's output.)

ISG modified off-the-shelf workstations[2] by adding proprietary graphics accelerators.[3] The Allegro was a stand-alone device that competed with several other similar products and with workstations sold by original equipment manufacturers (OEMs) with CT and MRI scanners. It had several advantages over both of these competing product groups. Unlike many other third-party workstations, the Allegro was compatible with several major scanners. Also, unlike most other third-party manufacturers, ISG was aggressive in upgrading the Allegro to avoid obsolescence as new ISG software or scanning capabilities became available. The Allegro had much more power and flexibility than workstations provided by manufacturers of scanning equipment. Additionally, while other manufacturers' workstations were being used for image manipulation, the scanner in some cases had to remain idle. Because the Allegro was not directly connected to the scanner, it decoupled image manipulation from the scanning process, allowing institutions to obtain greater capacity utilization from their expensive scanning equipment.

The Allegro was priced at $140,000 to $200,000 depending upon options requested. Despite being more expensive (competitive products were priced from $70,000 to $300,000) than most of its competitors, the Allegro sold well because radiologists considered it superior in terms of image quality. The Allegro had faster hardware and more sophisticated software that resulted in better, more usable images. Between the Allegro and Gyroview (see below) products, ISG held 45 percent of the independent medical imaging market in 1991. From early 1988 until December 1991, ISG had sold 106 Allegros, and Mike Hopkinson was forecasting sales of 80 units in calendar year 1992.

ISG was, at that time, developing several Allegro spin-off products called Plan View Stations. Surgeons and other specialists would use these workstations to view and further manipulate images previously processed by the Allegro. Because a Plan View Station would not have to process scanner input, it would require less computing capacity and would be lower priced than the Allegro.

---

[2] A workstation is the industry term for a very fast microcomputer.

[3] Graphics accelerators were add-on circuit boards that greatly increased a computer's speed in processing complex graphic images. Such accelerators were widely used in computer aided design applications, for example.

Exhibit 1   The Allegro: Technical Specifications

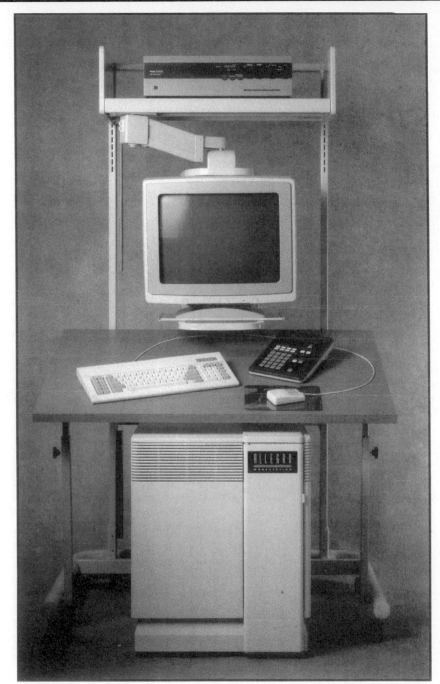

Data Input

1600 bpi magnetic tape drive
(800 and 6250 bpi optional)
8" floppy disk drive (optional)
5¼" optical disk (optional)
Direct connections to scanner
    (optional)

Hardcopy Interfaces

Laser images (optional)
Analog cameras (optional)
Video recorders (optional)
Color thermal printers (optional)

Monitor

Color 19"
1280 × 1024 60 Hz
Non-interlaced

User Input

Optical mouse
Keyboard
Trackball (optional)

Image Processors

8 TMS320C25 DSPs operating at 10
    MHz (additional 8 DSPs optional)

Processing Power

80 MIPS (160 MIPS optional)

Image Memory

32 Mbyte (64 or 128 Mbytes optional)

Image Display

Dual 1024×1024×8 frame buffers

User Interface Display

1280×1024×4 frame buffers

Color Display

256 colors from palette of 16.7 million

Host Computer

Selection includes SGI and Sun

Host Memory

8 Mbytes. Additional memory available

Host Storage

1000 Mbytes
Additional storage available

Operating System

Unix

Software

2D viewing with background printing
Interactive 2D melt-thru reformats
Highspeed 3D reconstruction
Interactive 3D display
2D/3D correlation
2D/3D measurements

Optional Software

MR Angiography
Dental/Knee Application Package
Cardiac Application Package
Spine Application Package

Modem

2400 baud

Workstation Viewing Desk

Ergonomic viewing desk with
    peripherals cabinet (optional)

Exhibit 2   An Example of Allegro Output

Clinical Applications of the Allegro Imaging Workstation

Cutplanes and Wedges

Simulate the surgeon's cuts to reveal interior detail and hidden anatomy

Variable Translucency

Allows the physician to see through overlying structures to better understand anatomical relationships

2-D/3-D Cross-Reference Display

Provides a simultaneous presentation of related 2-D and 3-D images to help the physician correlate the two

Cutplanes and Wedges

Variable Translucency

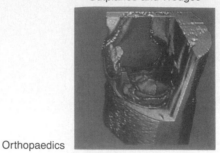

Orthopaedics

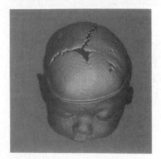

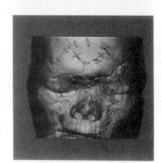

Neurosurgery

Craniofacial Reconstructive Surgery

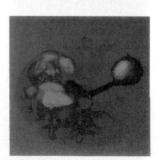

Oncology

Allegro, Physician's ReviewStation, and Viewing Wand are unregistered trademarks of the Company. UNIX is a registered trademark of AT&T.

Gyroview

This product was similar to an Allegro workstation but sold under the Philips brand name as an add-on to Philips MRI scanners. Philips shipped their own workstations to ISG, who then installed graphics accelerators and software that had been developed exclusively for Philips, but functioned in a similar manner to the Allegro's software. ISG had recently finished a new software package that allowed the Gyroview to operate with Philips CT scanners as well. The agreement between Philips and ISG required that ISG ensure that the software used to run the Gyroview remained exclusive to the Philips product and that Philips would pay a fixed unit price. By December 1991, 141 Gyroview workstations had been sold, an average of one Gyroview for every two Philips MRI sales. ISG's contract with Philips had expired in October 1991 and had been extended for successive one-month periods since. The parties were negotiating a new, more flexible contract during the winter of 1992. Because Philips provided the hardware, ISG charged a much lower price than it did to retail customers of the Allegro. The usual invoice price on a Gyroview unit was $46,000, which provided a 66 percent gross margin for ISG.

Viewing Wand

The Viewing Wand was an articulated arm which connected to a modified Allegro workstation. It had several joints and culminated in a thin metal probe about 6 inches long. When the patient's anatomy was displayed in an image on the screen, the surgeon could, during an operation, place the probe into an incision in the patient's head, for example, and an image of the probe would appear on the screen in the image of the interior structures of the patient's head. The image on the monitor could be rotated, sliced, sectioned, or manipulated in different ways. The surgeon was then able to know exactly where he or she was at that stage in relation to the interior structures of the brain, thus potentially reducing the size of the skull incision, the amount of collateral damage to sensitive brain tissue, and the total surgery time. Clinical trials had indicated that the average time spent establishing tumor location was reduced from hours to minutes with use of the Wand. This product represented the first successful attempt to bring computer-based real-time three-dimensional imaging into the operating room and was believed to have the potential to expand ISG's potential market dramatically.

Although it was still in clinical trials and awaiting regulatory approval in the United States, the Wand had generated significant interest among neurosurgeons. ISG expected to expand its application to other medical specialties soon after introduction. The Wand and its accompanying workstation were to be priced at around $200,000.

Other products

ISG also marketed several other products. There was a series of add-on software packages designed for specific medical applications such as knee surgery. These products were collectively called Clinical Application Packages (CAP). ISG also licensed their basic software architecture to GE, who used it as a base for the software sold with GE workstations. ISG was hoping that this software architecture (called IAP) would become an industry standard and would generate significant license fees. ISG also gained revenue from service contracts and from providing hardware and software upgrades to existing customers. For the last six months of 1991, the breakdown of sales by product was: Allegro—46 percent, Gyroview—37 percent, Viewing Wand—4 percent, CAP—4 percent, upgrades—4 percent, IAP—3 percent, service—2 percent.

The Medical Imaging Market

The customers

CT and MR scanners were in different phases of product life cycle. CT scanners had been available since the early 1970s and there were approximately 5,000 in operation in the United States, with sales estimated at 600 per year and prices ranging from $0.5 million to $1.0 million. CT scanners were nearing the saturation level. The rate of sales growth was flat and the price had been dropping steadily. MR scanners, on the other hand, were newer and more sophisticated. This market was in a growth phase with sales of 400 units per year with unit prices ranging from $1.0 million to $2.0 million. By 1991, approximately 2,500 MR scanners had been installed in the United States. Sales in Canada were forecast to total 40–50 units in 1992 for both types of scanner. Patients usually were sent through a CT scan first and then sent to the MR scanner only if additional information was needed. Some managers at ISG maintained that MR scanners would eventually entirely replace CT scanners as the price came down. If true, ISG would benefit greatly as the management believed that their products were superior to all others in the interpretation of MR images.

There were two kinds of institutional customers for medical imaging systems: (1) hospitals, which accounted for 70 percent of ISG sales, and (2) imaging centers, which accounted for 30 percent. In the United States, there were about 1,000 free-standing imaging centers. These were private companies that owned and operated expensive imaging equipment and functioned much like private labs doing medical tests. Centers such as these obtained reimbursement from private and public medical insurers for the procedures performed. In early 1992, however, the future status of these centers was in question. Many were owned or partly owned by physicians. Activists and medical insurers had uncovered evidence of physicians prescribing self-referred tests that had been carried out at clinics in which they had financial interests. As a result of these charges, several politicians had introduced legislation that would force massive divestitures by physicians. The actual implications of the legislation were still unclear and confusion reigned about the status of many of these clinics. As a result, few clinics were prepared to make major equipment purchases and sales to this segment had almost stopped.

The other major segment was hospitals, of which there were about 6,000 in the United States and 600 in Canada. The key hospital decision maker was typically the director of Radiology. The Radiology department usually encompassed most kinds of imaging used by the hospital including ultrasound, nuclear medicine, X-rays, and scanning. Their services were provided to different physicians such as general practitioners, cardiologists, surgeons, and other specialists.

The director of Radiology controlled a large personnel and equipment budget and made decisions about how that money should be spent. These directors were subject to pressure for equipment acquisitions from several different divisions within Radiology. For example, the chief of Nuclear Medicine might make a case to replace outdated equipment, while the head of Ultrasound might argue that extra capacity was needed in her area. Surgeons and other physicians, through the kind of procedures they requested, also had an influence upon equipment purchases. This was because surgeons were responsible for bringing patients into the hospitals, thereby creating revenue.

A director would decide that a certain piece of equipment was needed on medical grounds and initiate the first phase of product investigation. The chief radiology technician would research product offerings, invite bids, and structure alternatives. If the purchase was routine, the director would make a decision and pass it on to the administration for a "rubber stamp" approval. If the purchase was outside the normal budget or was in some way risky, the director might form a committee of two or three qualified persons, from within and beyond the hospital, to examine the options and make recommendations. Large purchase recommendations were often reviewed by the hospital board of directors. In past years, administrators had traditionally stayed clear of involvement in the evaluation of equipment acquisition decisions. However, by the early 1990s, hospital administrators had become more involved in the decision process in response to the funding crisis that was overtaking many institutions.

The economics of medical technology markets were driven by health insurance. Hospital and imaging center revenues were derived from reimbursement by public and private medical insurers. A case for a new piece of equipment and the resulting new procedure could be made on the grounds of a medical case, a business case, or both. As medical insurance costs were under constant review by these insurers, it was always possible that reimbursement for these procedures could be reduced or eliminated. There were two schools of thought about how the realities of rising health care costs might affect ISG. The first opinion held that expensive imaging tests might someday be eliminated or restricted by insurers that needed to drastically cut reimbursements. The second held that products like ISG's that improved efficiency were unlikely to suffer from future cost reductions.

The competitive environment

The medical imaging market was highly competitive and characterized by rapid technological advances. For a manufacturer, success depended on technological superiority, price and performance measures, and equipment upgrades that kept installed equipment current with the increasingly sophisticated needs of medical practitioners. Additionally, product reliability, effective service, and customer support played significant roles in developing and maintaining customer preferences.

ISG currently had four independent workstation competitors who shared roughly equal market shares. Some of these competitors had links to important major scanner manufacturers. Independently manufactured workstations accounted for 30 percent of the overall image processing market. While these products were integral to the scanner systems they interpreted, all were either more expensive and/or inferior in performance to the Allegro. (See Exhibits 3 and 4 for scanner market share.) The major X-ray manufacturers dominated the imaging workstation market with a combined total of 75 percent of all workstation sales. The independent manufacturers accounted for the rest. ISG was the most important of these with an overall market share of 11.25 percent. ISG's four other third-party competitors had roughly equal market shares of approximately 3.5 percent each.

ISG managers worried little about the independent competition. Competing products were not as sophisticated in either software or hardware as those of ISG. These third-party manufacturers had sales forces of three to five people. The major scanner manufacturers were a different matter. Despite similar product shortfalls, they had a competitive edge when it came to making sales. The scanner salespeople argued that the hospital and clinics should not risk the problems that might come from trying to add an independently manufactured workstation to their expensive new scanner. It would be much safer, they suggested, to stay with the workstation provided by the company that made the scanner in the first place. The scanner companies could also offer deep discounts on workstations that were, to them, relatively low cost add-ons to the more lucrative scanner sales. The major manufacturers' sales force totaled over 500 persons in the United States.

The regulatory environment

Governmental agencies regulated the marketing and sale of ISG's products in most jurisdictions. In the United States, the products were regulated under two different acts, both

Exhibit 3

North American Overall Workstation Imaging Market Share 1990

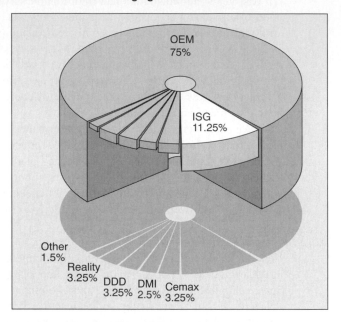

North American Independent Workstation Imaging Market Share 1990

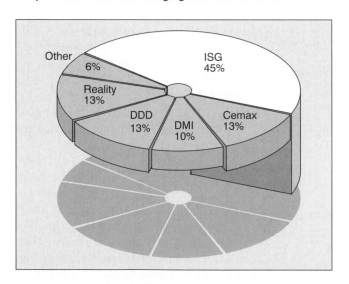

Exhibit 4

North American Magnetic Resonance Imaging (MRI) Market Share 1990

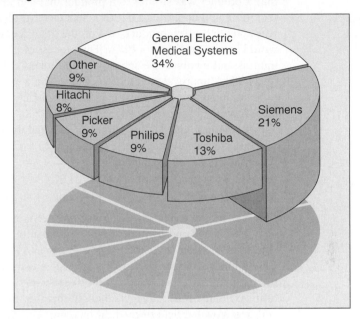

North American Computed Tomography (CT) Market Share 1990

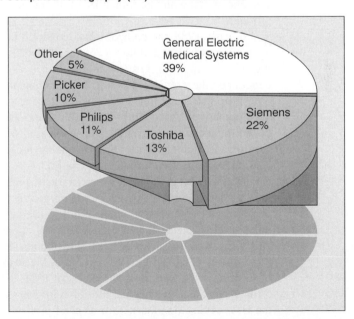

administered by the Food and Drug Administration (FDA). The FDA had required all medical devices introduced into the market to obtain either (1) a Premarket Notification Clearance, known as a 510(K), or (2) a Premarket Approval (PMA). If the FDA accepted that a product was similar to a product that had already been approved, then the manufacturer could apply for a 510(K) clearance. If, on the other hand, the FDA felt that this was an entirely new product, or a product that required special scrutiny, the manufacturer would have to apply for a PMA. The process of obtaining a 510(K) typically took several months and involved the submission of limited clinical data and supporting information, while PMA approval usually took more than a year and required the submission of significant quantities of clinical data and manufacturing information. All of ISG's previous clearances had taken place through the 510(K) process. In requesting clearance for its Viewing Wand, ISG had argued that it was merely a new application of the previously approved Allegro and should, therefore, qualify for the 510(K) process. In January 1992, the FDA had yet to rule on this request.

ISG History

ISG was founded in 1982 as an imaging technology contract research and development firm. The company's initial success had been the "Tour of the Universe," a space flight simulator installed at Toronto's CN Tower in 1986. Thereafter, ISG concentrated on the development of imaging products for the aerospace industry but found little success due to an "unpolished" product and the skepticism of potential customers about ISG's capabilities. Some of the managers thought that they might adapt ISG's technology to the new and less crowded field of medical imaging. The company hired Dr. Michael Greenberg, a Toronto neurosurgeon, as a consultant to examine the possibility. Dr. Greenberg's study was encouraging and he joined ISG full time in 1987 to help develop a medical imaging product.

In early 1988, the company had expanded the funds raised in earlier years and, with a negative cash flow and no successful products, was experiencing great difficulty in raising more capital. Dr. Greenberg, however, was able to arrange new venture capital financing on the strength of the medical imaging product's market potential. Conditions imposed by the new financiers included concentration of company resources on the development of a medical product and the elevation of Dr. Greenberg to president. Some of the founders of the firm became displeased with their resulting demotions and loss of control, and within a year of the refinancing, most of the original employees had departed, leaving Dr. Greenberg in effective control.

Dr. Greenberg proved to be an energetic president. The company vigorously pursued product development and constructed a prototype. Key improvements were made in image quality and MRI scanner compatibility. Marketing plans were developed and implemented. Dr. Greenberg had established a relationship with a U.S. distributor (Precision) and was personally involved in the sale of units to the more important and prestigious customers like Johns Hopkins of Baltimore, Maryland; Yale University; and The University of California–Los Angeles. During fiscal 1991, ISG had turned a small profit (see Exhibit 5 for financial statements and Exhibit 6 for sales data) and achieved a 10 percent share in the U.S. workstation market for its chief product, the Allegro workstation.

ISG's Marketing Strategy

ISG's overall plan was straightforward. It sought to translate high R&D expenditures into innovative, leading-edge products supported by superior customer service. The Viewing Wand was an example of this strategy; ISG had developed from the R&D on the Allegro an entirely new product for an as-yet-untapped market, real-time three-dimensional computer imaging for the operating room.

Sales efforts were concentrated on directors of Radiology and the physicians who might generate demand for procedures the Allegro could provide. ISG, in concert with Precision, used several sales tools. They commissioned peer-reviewed medical research papers from physicians using their system to make a medical case to others. Videos, brochures, and other sales material were generated for the Precision sales force, and salespeople used customized profit analyses to make the business case for the Allegro (see Exhibit 7 for a typical business case). ISG also participated in trade shows to build brand awareness and preference. The premier sales tool, however, was the "roadshow," staged by ISG for qualified prospects.[4]

Exhibit 5   ISG Financial Statements

ISG TECHNOLOGIES INC.

Consolidated Balance Sheets

June 30,

	1990	1991	December 31, 1991
			(Unaudited)
Assets			
Current assets:			
Accounts receivable (note 2)	$ 2,109,307	$ 5,975,249	$ 8,402,449
Inventory (note 3)	1,145,413	1,489,488	1,175,394
Prepaid expenses	168,884	160,497	256,404
	3,423,604	7,625,234	9,834,247
Fixed assets (note 4)	511,907	569,623	670,240
Other assets (note 5)	50,000	129,766	1,014,954
	$ 3,985,511	$ 8,324,623	$ 11,519,441
Liabilities and Shareholders' Equity			
Current liabilities:			
Bank indebtedness (note 6)	$ 569,905	$ 1,611,390	$ 1,086,555
Accounts payable and accrued liabilities (note 7)	1,974,060	2,999,424	2,719,109
Current portion of capital lease payments	27,182	43,774	38,718
Convertible debenture (note 8)	—	1,100,001	—
	2,571,147	5,754,589	3,844,382
Long-term debt:			
Capitalized leases (note 9)	49,078	56,539	39,847
Shareholders' equity:			
Capital stock (note 10)	14,146,952	15,295,366	21,151,156
Deficit	(12,781,666)	(12,781,871)	(13,515,944)
	1,365,286	2,513,495	7,635,212
Contingency (note 11)			
Subsequent events (note 16)			
	$ 3,985,511	$ 8,324,623	$ 11,519,441

On behalf of the Board:

(SIGNED) MICHAEL M. GREENBERG   (SIGNED) RICHARD L. LOCKIE
            DIRECTOR   DIRECTOR

(continued)

---

[4]A qualified prospect was one that (a) had the budget, (b) was planning a decision within 90 days, and (c) had a champion in the prospect's organization who would drum up interest in the roadshow.

Exhibit 5 *(concluded)*

ISG TECHNOLOGIES INC.

Consolidated Statement of Income

	Years ended June 30,					Six months ended December 31, (unaudited)	
	1987	1988	1989	1990	1991	1990	1991
Sales	$ —	$ 862,427	$ 1,784,240	$ 6,338,678	$11,394,952	$ 4,745,532	$ 6,265,398
Cost of goods sold	—	358,000	862,960	2,926,712	4,738,535	2,091,754	3,032,069
Gross profit	—	504,427	921,280	3,411,966	6,656,417	2,653,778	3,233,329
Other income:							
Contract revenue	56,447	172,494	212,692	278,480	924,111	345,753	624,091
Service and other revenue	82,635	60,902	62,266	116,819	57,922	116,751	444,308
	139,082	233,396	274,958	395,299	982,033	462,504	1,068,399
	139,082	737,823	1,196,238	3,807,265	7,638,450	3,116,282	4,301,728
Expenses:							
Research and development	1,114,000	997,000	1,535,520	1,903,104	2,368,169	1,074,573	1,511,186
Marketing	671,942	1,882,131	1,426,606	2,098,615	2,415,933	1,015,046	1,850,699
Sales commissions	—	—	134,299	1,043,733	1,242,044	546,234	386,549
General and administrative	402,752	767,914	1,564,405	1,555,572	1,710,957	818,127	1,053,138
Interest:							
Long-term (note 8)	—	90,555	35,258	13,647	78,143	11,412	(45,443)
Other	24,474	38,749	111,460	36,609	105,953	44,138	110,409
Depreciation	206,337	309,959	189,659	224,438	281,848	135,728	176,209
	2,419,505	4,086,308	4,997,207	6,875,718	8,203,047	3,645,258	5,042,747
Less expenditures recovered (note 2)	141,597	—	361,288	570,069	580,466	336,022	92,097
	2,277,908	4,086,308	4,635,919	6,305,649	7,622,581	3,309,236	4,950,650
Income (loss) before extraordinary item	(2,138,826)	(3,348,485)	(3,439,681)	(2,498,384)	15,869	(192,954)	(648,922)
Extraordinary item—write-off of note receivable net of deferred taxes of $2,082,500 (note 12)	(2,417,500)	—	—	—	—	—	—
Net income (loss)	$ (4,556,326)	$ (3,348,485)	$ (3,439,681)	$ (2,498,384)	$ 15,869	$ (192,954)	$ (648,922)
Earnings (loss) per share before extraordinary item	$ (1.16)	$ (1.81)	$ (1.00)	$ (.44)	$ 0.00	$ (0.03)	$ (0.10)
Earnings (loss) per share after extraordinary item	$ (2.46)	$ (1.81)	$ (1.00)	$ (.44)	$ 0.00	$ (0.03)	$ (0.10)

Exhibit 6   ISG Sales Data

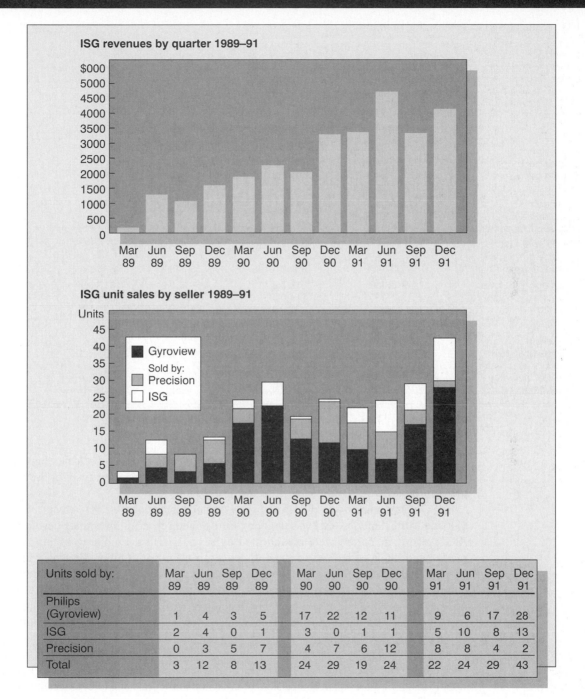

ISG revenues by quarter 1989–91

ISG unit sales by seller 1989–91

Units sold by:	Mar 89	Jun 89	Sep 89	Dec 89	Mar 90	Jun 90	Sep 90	Dec 90	Mar 91	Jun 91	Sep 91	Dec 91
Philips (Gyroview)	1	4	3	5	17	22	12	11	9	6	17	28
ISG	2	4	0	1	3	0	1	1	5	10	8	13
Precision	0	3	5	7	4	7	6	12	8	8	4	2
Total	3	12	8	13	24	29	19	24	22	24	29	43

Exhibit 7   Typical ISG-Supplied Business Case

ISG Technologies Inc. Profitability Analysis

Lessee:
Equipment: Allegro
Price: $175,000
Lease Term: 60 mos.
Lease Rate Factor: 0.0254
Monthly Payment: $4,445

	Year 1	Year 2	Year 3	Year 4	Year 5
Studies per day	2	3	4	5	6
Studies per month	40	60	80	100	120
Studies per year	480	720	960	1200	1440
Charges per study	$350	$364	$379	$394	$409
Revenue	$168,000	$262,080	$363,418	$472,443	$589,609
Less bad debt	20%	20%	20%	20%	20%
Less supplies per study	$15	$15	$15	$15	$15
Net revenue	$127,200	$209,664	$290,734	$377,394	$471,687
Expenses:					
Lease payment	$53,340	$53,340	$53,340	$53,340	$53,340
Personnel (½ time)	$15,000	$15,750	$16,538	$17,364	$18,233
Maintenance/service	$0	$14,000	$14,700	$15,435	$16,207
Rent/overhead	$1,000	$1,050	$1,103	$1,158	$1,216
Operating profit	$57,860	$125,524	$205,054	$290,657	$382,692
Breakeven:					
Studies per day	1.1	1.3	1.2	1.2	1.2
Studies per month	22	25	25	24	24
Studies per year	262	305	298	291	285
Charge per study	$265	$276	$288	$300	$313

A salesperson and a technician would visit the customer's premises with an Allegro workstation and process the customer's own clinical data. By applying the technology to the physician's own cases, ISG found that it could make a more persuasive case for the product to be purchased.

ISG's key market was the United States, which accounted for 90 percent of sales.[5] Outside North America, ISG was targeting Europe and Japan for immediate development. ISG's efforts in Europe were complicated by several factors. Europe was Philips' main market and ISG's policy was to avoid direct competition with Philips whenever possible. In early 1992, ISG had a two-person direct sales force based in the United Kingdom. The company had inherited these salespeople from its former European distributor, who had gone bankrupt. ISG had a month-to-month contract with these salespeople. This arrangement gave ISG some European coverage while allowing time to develop an overall strategy for the European market.

Europe was an agglomeration of many totally distinct national markets, each with its own ethnic, cultural, economic, and political characteristics. For example, the British National Health Service had been in a state of crisis for some years due to health care cutbacks by the Thatcher government. Germany was preoccupied with raising the former East Germany's health care standards to western levels. ISG recognized that it would have to develop a strategy for each of these distinct markets, or find someone who could do it for them.

---

[5]ISG's sales were divided between the United States (90 percent), Canada (2 percent), and Europe (8 percent).

Japan, on the other hand, was a relatively homogeneous market, similar to Canada and other countries where medical expenditures were centralized in government health ministries. Japanese doctors were more technically oriented than those in other countries and liked to know the technical details of products they used. The Japanese manufactured their own scanners, so that the price was comparatively low and they were in wide use. ISG's main problem was in developing the sort of cultural understanding and personal ties needed to do business in an environment where it was difficult for non-Japanese products to develop credibility. In the winter of 1992, ISG was actively seeking allies who would be able to help overcome these barriers. Despite its negative experience with Precision, it had considered establishing a dealer relationship in Japan.

History of relationship with Precision

When Greenberg took over the company in the spring of 1988, ISG found itself with only one salesperson to cover 5,000 hospitals in the United States. With Dr. Greenberg and some of the engineering staff working part-time on sales, ISG was able to field four salespeople. This sales team was too small to provide the company with the kind of growth desired by ISG's management. The management team realized that with a 1988 loss of $3 million on revenues of $1 million, ISG could ill afford the expense of hiring its own sales force. To build an effective team, ISG thought that it would have to train new salespeople for six months, and support them with the resources needed to compete with the salespeople fielded by major manufacturers and independent suppliers.

Because of the difficulty of financing such a strategy, ISG sought a distributor for North America. Although many distributors were considered, few had the industry experience that ISG sought and most were regionally, rather than nationally, focused. After several months, ISG opened negotiations with Precision, a large nationwide distributor of medical imaging equipment with sales of $70 million. Precision had a sales force of 25 persons across North America and an effective service and support organization.

Precision's corporate strategy and the key to their success had been the aggressive selling of products less expensive than those available from the big U.S.-based scanning companies. Precision marketed Hitachi MRI scanners which sold for 30 percent less than a similar machine from GE, for example. Their market focus was exclusively on the radiology departments to which they sold CT and MRI scanners, specialized cameras, ultrasound equipment, and other products. Both ISG and Precision reasoned that when Precision found a buyer for a scanner, they could promote an ISG workstation along with it, with little extra selling effort.

A one-year contract between ISG and Precision was signed on June 1, 1989. It stated that Precision would be the exclusive agent for the sale of ISG's CAMRA S2000 (the predecessor of the Allegro) throughout Canada and the continental United States. Certain clients with whom ISG preferred to deal directly were exempted.[6] ISG agreed to train all Precision sales personnel, provide sales kits and promotional material, engage in customer

---

[6]ISG reserved the area surrounding New York City and a number of "house accounts" which ISG had previously established for the purpose of new product testing and collaborative research. These accounts were:

Sunnybrook Hospital, Toronto, Ontario, Canada

The Toronto General Hospital, Toronto, Ontario, Canada

Buffalo Children's Hospital, Buffalo, NY, USA

Johns Hopkins Memorial Hospital, Baltimore, Maryland, USA

Boston Children's Hospital, Boston, Massachusetts, USA

Massachusetts General Hospital, Boston, Massachusetts, USA

training, and promote the product at industry trade shows. Precision promised to pursue sales leads, achieve stated quarterly quotas, participate in trade shows and roadshows in conjunction with ISG, and participate in monthly sales meetings at ISG's head office. Termination of the contract could be accomplished with 30 days' notice in writing by either party if they felt that the other had violated or failed to comply with any of the terms of the agreement. The contract could be extended by mutual agreement.

ISG projected sales of 60 CAMRA S2000 in North America for the first year of the agreement and expected Precision to sell 54 of these systems, with ISG selling the remainder. No formal quotas were set, however, for complete workstation systems, spare parts, or accessories. Instead, Precision sales forecasts were used as informal quotas. The chronology of a typical sale was as follows: (1) Precision salespeople would identify potential leads through client visits for scanner or related equipment sales. (2) Precision would make an initial sales pitch. (3) Likely leads would be qualified by Precision and ISG. (4) Precision would arrange a "roadshow" for qualified prospects; ISG personnel would participate. (5) Precision would close the sale with help from ISG representatives. (6) ISG would install the unit and train the client personnel. (7) Precision would invoice ISG for the commission. (8) ISG would receive payment from the client and pay the Precision invoice.

ISG determined commissions by using a complicated schedule that plotted the list price of the product against the actual sale price. Under this system, commissions varied from 23 percent to 27 percent of the actual customer-paid price for products discounted 0 percent to 12 percent. This meant that commissions usually ranged from $20,000 to $35,000 on a $150,000 workstation.

ISG began training the Precision sales force in Toronto immediately following the verbal agreement in March 1989. The newly trained sales force began selling in April 1989. Despite Precision's sale of three systems compared to a target of six in the first full quarter, ISG thought the results promising in light of the dramatic increase in sales prospects turned up by the Precision sales force. By March 1990, however, orders began to decline. When asked by ISG, Precision was vague about the causes. Despite Precision's contention that it was not quite the end of the quarter and that sales were still forthcoming, there was no improvement in April or May.

In June, an ISG technician who had been on a field installation was told that Precision was in the process of changing its sales strategy and completely reorganizing its sales organization. Precision confirmed this and informed ISG that its current structure was ill-suited to the quickly changing marketplace and unable to compete effectively. Precision told ISG that the salespeople often found that it took more time to sell the workstation than it did to sell the scanner. Precision promised ISG a new, dedicated sales force. To ISG's chagrin, the new sales force was to be comprised of approximately 20 new college graduates with little or no previous sales experience. In addition to the Allegro (which had replaced the CAMRA S2000), this sales force would also be responsible for a new Hitachi cardiac ultrasound product.

ISG stockholders became restive in the next six months as sales languished while the new sales team was trained. By January 1991, however, the new sales force was showing progress and it appeared that sales would reach a level satisfactory to ISG. Unfortunately, it soon became apparent that one of the tools Precision was using to drive sales was deep discounting. Large discounts seriously eroded ISG's profits as well as Precision's salespersons' commissions. Discounting in the form of including extra options at no extra charge had always been a tactic that both companies had agreed with in the past. ISG now began to question the practice, thinking that a lower list price might make more sense. In response to a request made by Precision, ISG set minimum commissions of $25,000 for orders not exceeding a total discount of $60,000 and a minimum of $20,000 for orders that did exceed a $60,000 total discount. This plan was put in place for February and March. ISG considered setting these minimums even lower to discourage the practice of deep discounting.[7]

In March, sales started to slip again, but because of reporting lags, ISG did not become aware of this until June. Pressed by ISG, Precision explained that the problem stemmed from another realignment of sales force responsibilities. Sales of the Hitachi cardiac ultrasound product were booming and Precision had transferred sales staff previously dedicated to ISG back to the original Hitachi MRI sales force. This was the same sales force that Precision had taken the Allegro away from the year before. This sales force would then theoretically represent ISG products with 20 representatives. ISG management had doubts about how effective that representation would be.

Managers at ISG were extremely upset with these developments. They felt that ISG was losing control of sales, and that Precision might never develop ISG products to their full market potential. Serious consideration was given to forming a dedicated ISG sales organization. The company already had three technical sales managers[8] who could form the nucleus of a direct sales organization. Before a firm decision was made, however, the vice president–Sales, Marketing, and Service left the company.

The decision

Mike Hopkinson joined ISG as director of North American Sales in October 1991. He had 20 years of experience in the computerized medical imaging equipment sales field and had previously been national sales manager at Dornier Medical Systems (Canada) of Toronto and North American sales manager at Quantified Signal Imaging Inc., also of Toronto.

Hopkinson felt that there were several options open to ISG. First, stay with Precision, re-educate the new sales force, and specify minimum quotas in the contract. Second, change direction and develop relationships with other major scanner companies, similar to the Philips arrangement, while dropping direct sales altogether. Third, focus on a single exclusive alliance with a major scanner company. Fourth, develop an ISG direct sales force.

Several issues would affect Hopkinson's choice. One outside analyst projected total ISG sales for 1992 at almost $17 million in North America. (See Exhibit 8 for geographic breakdown of ISG sales.) Half of this revenue was expected to come from sales of the Allegro, 40 percent from Gyroview, 7 percent from sales of the Viewing Wand, and the rest from licensing proprietary software to GE. Hopkinson thought that this goal could be met by the Precision sales force if they made sales of ISG products a high priority. He was uncertain whether an ISG sales force, which would have to be trained for six months, could meet these goals within the fiscal reporting period.

Preliminary investigations showed that a salesperson would cost ISG about $60,000 per annum in salary, $5,000 per month in travel and administration expenses, and $5,000 in commissions per sale. This would be offset by the elimination of the commissions now being paid to Precision. The other marketing expenses, amounting to $2.4 million in 1991, would remain unchanged whether the products were sold by ISG or by Precision. If he

---

[7]On an average sale of $150,000 US, ISG made a gross profit of $84,000–$85,000 before commissions. The accounting system did not assign any fixed cost on a per-unit basis, but costs such as R&D and other overheads were allocated on a product-by-product basis at the end of the fiscal year. During the six months ending on December 31, 1991, ISG paid sales commissions to Precision of $330,000 and commissions of $54,000 to ISG personnel.

[8]The technical sales managers provided technical and sales support to Precision.

Exhibit 8   Geographic Breakdown of ISG Sales

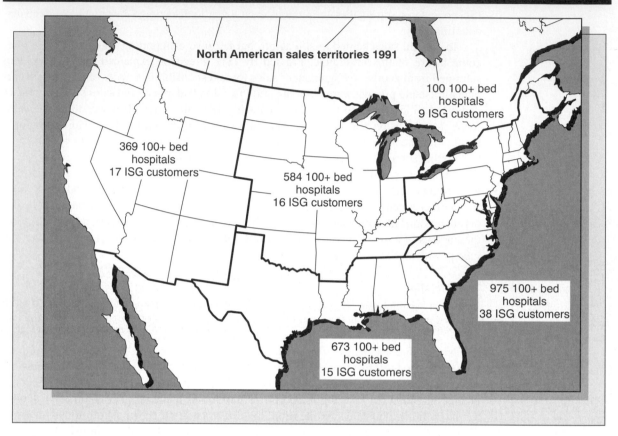

chose any other option besides staying with Precision, Hopkinson would need to consider the best time to break the contract, how much preparation should be done before it was broken, and what impact such a move would have on ISG's revenues.

Hopkinson also knew that his decision about Precision would have an effect upon ISG's negotiations with other distributors in Europe and Japan. With the imminent introduction of the Viewing Wand and the year-end in sight, Hopkinson had to make a speedy decision.

Case 3–10

Dendrite International*

In July 1993, John Bailye, president of Dendrite International, was considering changes affecting Dendrite's customer base. Bailye commented:

> Dendrite is currently a leading sales automation supplier to pharmaceutical firms. We have been unique in this marketplace, offering a global product that is customized to local market needs and backed up with in-depth customer service. But in the United States, 80% of pharmaceutical sales reps are supported by automation systems of one kind or another. Other developments may reduce the size of pharmaceutical sales forces in the United States, Europe, and Japan.

Among the issues raised by these developments were the best means of ensuring Dendrite's future growth and possible changes in account management procedures.

Company and Industry Background

John Bailye had been a partner of Foresearch, an Australian company that provided market research services to pharmaceutical firms operating in Australia and southeast Asia. During the early 1980s, government regulations in many of these countries affected drug pricing and physicians' incomes. Bailye recalled: "Doctors had less time to see sales reps but reps continued to be measured on the number of calls they made, which is still standard practice in the industry. Meanwhile, the introduction of laptop computers offered a vehicle for improving sales productivity." Bailye established a division called Dendrite,[1] which in 1985 developed software to assist with call planning and reporting tasks. After a one-year pilot with an Australian firm, financial support for Dendrite was provided by a chemical company.

In 1987, Bailye and 12 employees moved their families and Dendrite headquarters from Sydney, Australia to Warren, New Jersey. Bailye recalled:

> In trying to sell our product to major pharmaceutical firms, we soon found that they wanted a visible commitment in the United States, the single biggest market in the industry. We chose New Jersey because many pharmaceutical firms are headquartered there and because the Unix system we use on our main computer was developed at AT&T's Bell Labs, which is also in New Jersey. We therefore felt this area would provide well-trained technicians.

*Professor Frank V. Cespedes and Research Associate Marie Bell prepared this case as the basis for class discussion rather than to illustrate either effective or ineffective handling of an administrative situation. Certain company data, while useful for discussion purposes, have been disguised.

[1] A dendrite conducts impulses from a nerve cell to central nerve fiber.

But we knew little else about what we were getting into. It probably is hard for most Americans to realize how complex and different this country is. Our early days were tough: we had no credit background, little cash, and our families were adjusting to new ways of doing things. We also learned that, in the United States, it is not the product alone that matters. You must present a credible total organization to be given a real business opportunity.

In the United States, Dendrite was the ninth vendor supplying sales automation software to pharmaceutical firms. "All of these firms were of similar size and financial standing," Bailye noted, "so competition was fierce but relatively even." In 1988, however, Dun & Bradstreet (a $4 billion firm operating in a variety of information services markets) acquired a competitor, Sales Technologies, Inc. (STI), which soon dropped product prices and promoted itself as the only viable long-term option for corporate customers. "Customers started to compare this new 'giant' with other 'start-up' vendors and new business moved to STI," Bailye explained. "Dendrite was too new in the market to have credibility, despite the fact that our technology was better and, unlike STI, focused on the sales tasks of pharmaceutical reps. We also lacked the financial resources to wage a price war. Change was necessary and eventually involved all elements of organizational structure, market positioning, and technology applications."

Management first reassessed its primary target market. It decided that pharmaceutical firms were still the best market for Dendrite. "These firms are large, profitable, driven by sales productivity requirements, and among the earliest to adopt sales automation," noted Bailye. "The industry also comprised the core of our applications knowledge and working relationships." To distinguish itself, Dendrite decided to become a global supplier of both software and service to pharmaceutical firms. Martha Cleary, vice president of Planning, commented:

> This was an audacious decision for a small firm. In this industry, sales automation software had been supplied on a "turn-key" basis, leaving the customer to operate the system after its installation. We decided to introduce and enhance the concept of outsourcing, whereby Dendrite provided continuous support to maintain and operate the technology and service the needs of client sales reps through help line, training, and facilities management services. This strategy required that we provide full-service facilities in countries which, together, represent 75% of pharmaceutical salespeople.
>
> We had to make many changes simultaneously: redesign the software for multinational application; refinance the company to allow for expansion; restructure marketing programs to emphasize recurring service income, which was necessary to attract capital; and adopt new costing methods, since a key issue in running a service business is managing many unpredictable costs.

Management raised funds from venture capital firms and, by 1991, had established subsidiaries in Belgium, England, France, Germany, Italy, Japan, and Spain in addition to its offices in Australia, New Zealand, and the United States. This expansion was aided by Dendrite's product development strategy. About 80% of the programming code was "core code" which Dendrite then customized to local market needs and company specifications. One executive emphasized:

> Developing this core code took four years and over $5 million in funds from a cash-constrained company. But it's the generic engine which allows us to move into new markets more quickly and cost effectively than competitors. For example, we were able to enter Europe with 300,000 lines of core code which meant that we had to write an additional 100,000 lines for each local market. Competitors must start from scratch and each line is a potential "bug."

Dendrite's sales, less than $250,000 in 1987, were more than $23 million in 1992 (Exhibit 1), about 60% from software licensing and product customization fees and 40% from service, maintenance, and facilities management agreements. Projected sales for 1993 were $33 million. In 1993, more than 15,000 sales reps at 40 companies in 11 countries used Dendrite systems. Commenting on the company's growth, Bailye remarked:

> A number of big pharmaceutical firms found that the risks associated with installing sales productivity tools are reduced with a single vendor as opposed to different vendors in each country. And the risks for customers are considerable: when 3,000 reps can't or won't use a system installed at a total cost of $15 million or more, that bends careers in Sales and IS at these firms. We were fortunate that, during this period, our major competition sold standardized systems installed without comprehensive service, and so many of these systems weren't utilized.

Product and pricing

Vendors providing electronic territory management (ETM) and other sales automation systems multiplied in the 1980s. Productivity gains from such systems varied widely. The biggest impact generally resulted from a reallocation of time from administrative to selling tasks (an average 25% decrease in administrative tasks, according to Dendrite client studies) and from better targeting and territory management (2%–9% sales gains, according to Dendrite client studies). Bailye described "an evolution in field automation during the past decade":

> Product development among vendors has begun to take two distinct paths. Some firms focus on more intensive tools for sales efficiencies, while others seek diversity of functionality—i.e., to provide the means for improving information linkages between Sales and other functions in client companies.

Dendrite's product was a mix of software and services which, in a typical application (see Exhibit 2), could be briefly described as follows. Sales reps carried a laptop or notebook computer (purchased by the client company), which contained a database of a given rep's territory data (physician profiles, call histories, etc.). Each night, reps phoned the host computer and communicated their activities for reporting purposes. In turn, the system allowed reps to:

- Access a database concerning current and potential customers including physicians, hospitals, pharmacies, HMOs, etc. Information included basic data such as names and phone numbers as well as data about drug prescribing patterns which was collected by third parties, processed by Dendrite on its host computer, and "downloaded" through phone lines to the rep's laptop.

- Develop targeted lists of high-potential customers, and integrate these lists into a call plan that could be discussed with field managers.

- Record most sales-related activities such as number and type of sales calls, time spent in training or district meetings, and vacation or sick days.

- Send and receive messages via electronic mail with anyone else on the system, and also produce personalized letters and administrative documents.

- Use programs that provide quantitative tools useful in analyzing customer data and tracking progress against quarterly or annual objectives.

Sales managers received reports (weekly or monthly, depending on client preference) from Dendrite about the data continuously collected by the host computer. Field managers could also query the host database directly and produce their own reports. "They can com-

Exhibit 1   Consolidated Statements of Operations for Year Ended December 31, 1992 and Period September 1, 1991 (Date of Reorganization) to December 31, 1991 ($'000s)

	1992	1991
Operating revenues	$23,300	$4,853
Cost and expenses	20,953	5,647
Operating profit (loss)	2,347	(794)
Other income (expense):	(8)	(35)
Interest expense	71	7
Other	63	(28)
Income taxes:		
Reduction of income taxes from net operating		
loss carryforwards	286	—
Net income (loss)	$ 1,161	(822)

Consolidated Balance Sheets, December 31, 1992 and 1991 ($'000s)

Assets

Current Assets:		
Cash and cash equivalents	600	874
Trade accounts receivable	5,063	1,762
Prepaid expenses and other current assets	669	479
Deferred tax assets	80	—
Total Current Assets	6,412	3,115
Fixed assets, net of accumulated depreciation	1,699	1,448
Intangible assets, net of accumulated amortization	2,106	2,688
Organization costs, net of accumulated amortization	2,106	2,688
Capitalized software development costs	895	30
	$11,204	$7,398

Liabilities and Stockholders' Equity

Current Liabilities:		
Trade accounts payable and other current liabilities	$2,825	$1,464
Current installments of lease obligations	65	26
Current portion of deferred revenues	2,050	120
Current income taxes payable	270	—
Total Current Liabilities	5,210	2,710
Obligations under capital leases	41	31
Deferred revenues, excluding current portion	110	146
Deferred tax liabilities	435	—
Total Liabilities	5,796	2,887
Stockholders' Equity:		
Common stock, no par value	3	3
Retained earnings (accumulated deficit)	339	(822)
Equity adjustment for foreign currency translation	(445)	(94)
Less consideration to former stockholder of acquired		
business in excess of his basis in net assets sold	(1,364)	(1,364)
Total Stockholders' Equity	5,408	4,511
	$11,204	$7,398

Exhibit 2

SaleStar™ is a turn-key system of user-friendly softwware, hardware and support services that enables you to turn information management into increased productivity. Developed by Dendrite International, Inc., SaleStar™ is backed by the same focus on client service and support that has made Dendrite the leader in state-of-the-art electronic territory management systems for the global pharmaceutical industry.

FEATURES	BENEFITS
Call Planning	Enables sales representatives to improve productivity and performance by providing strategy to the call planning process.
Customer Profiles	Enables sales representatives to increase the productivity of every call by providing easy access to vital information (e.g., demographics, call history, pre- and post-call analysis, prescribing profile) on all their accounts.
Call Reporting	Enables sales representatives to easily and effectively track and communicate information from each sales call.
Customer Targeting	Easy manipulation of customer information enables sales representatives to target customers strategically based on a variety of criteria (e.g., best times to call, hospital department, affiliation, rating, call frequency, etc.)
Sample Tracking	Enables the home office to assess current and future sample needs, adjust marketing plans, determine how well a product is being received, and meet regulatory requirements.
Report Viewing	Provides sales representatives and managers easy and timely access to internal and third-party information such as product pricing, sales data and comprehensive management reports.
Third-Party Information	Provides sales representatives with up-to-date micromarketing data on customer and industry profiles. (Information may be gained from several sources, including Scriptrac, AMA, SMG, and others.)
Expense Forms/ WeeklyAttendance	Enables sales representatives to spend more time on sales by making administrative reporting faster and easier.
Meeting Planning & Recording	Enables sales representatives to easily and effectively plan, record and review information gained from peer programs, focus groups, or multiple customer presentations.
Electronic Mail	Provides managers and sales representatives with daily access to a reliable communication tool that doesn't depend on memos or telephone calls.

CUSTOMER SUPPORT SERVICES — SALESTAR™ SERVICES

Field User/Manager Support — HelpLine ✔, "How to" Instructions ✔, Log-in Advice ✔, Dendrite Log-in Reports ✔, System Disk Request ✔, System Utilities ✔, Profile Q & A ✔, Profile Addition/Deletion/Move ✔, Correct Entry Error ✔, E-mail Support ✔, Rep. Tracking ✔, Call Tracking ✔

Home Office Support — Reports QC/QA ✔, Reports Distribution ✔, Help Desk ✔, Field Support-Home Office ✔, Realignment Support ✔, Client Meetings ✔

Hardware Services ✔ — Field Hardware Support ✔, Hardware Diagnosis ✔, Hardware Replacement Request ✔, Hardware Tracking ✔

TECHNICAL SUPPORT SERVICES ✔ — SALESTAR™ SERVICES

System Administration–Hardware ✔ — Daily, Weekly, Monthly Back-ups ✔, Communications Support ✔, Off-Site Storage ✔, System Security ✔, Laptop Support ✔

System Administration–Software ✔ — Transaction Processing ✔, File Structure/Source Code Maintenance ✔, E-mail Administration ✔, Software Defect Resolution ✔

Help/Screen File Updates ✔

Processing/Dist. of Suite of Reports ✔

Customer Support Services ✔ — Error Correction ✔, Date Issues ✔

Sales and Marketing Support ✔ — Territory Realignments ✔, Third Party Data Updates ✔, Data Extracts ✔, Reports Generation, Processing & Dist. ✔

pare the calling activities of different reps," a Dendrite manager noted, "or telemarket to all physicians to whom presentations on a particular drug were made the day or week before. We find that the capability spurs new marketing ideas at clients." Headquarters managers also received reports and could query the database. "Corporate sales managers," explained a Dendrite executive, "often use the data for redeployment purposes or to cross-reference their data with third-party information."

Dendrite's software was sold in two parts: the Base system (which provided the fundamentals required to manage call reporting) and various Added Value Modules (for advanced applications where territory-planning and optimization models were provided). Service involved a dedicated client team composed of customer service personnel at Help Centers (located in Dendrite offices) as well as technical service personnel who assisted clients in customizing, implementing, and maintaining the system.

Depending upon the configuration purchased, pricing involved a license fee, maintenance and support agreement, and service contract (see Exhibit 3 for examples). The initial license fee was a one-time charge, ranging from $250,000 to over $1 million for the use of Dendrite's software. Maintenance and support agreements involved annual fees to maintain and customize the software, and provide a predetermined number of enhance-

Exhibit 3   Project Pricing and Costs: Examples (in thousands, for twelve months ended December 1992)

"Small" = client with < 400 users; "Large" = client with 1,500+ users

	Small	Large
Sales:	—	—
One-time license fees[a]	—	—
Service fees	—	—
Customization	—	—
Implementation	—	—
Software maintenance	—	—
Hardware support	—	—
In-house publishing	—	—
Other	—	—
Total Revenue	$891.6	$3,244.0
Cost of Sales	$489.5	$1,753.2
Gross Margin	$402.1	$1,490.8
Gross Margin (%)	45.1%	46.0%
Operating Expenses:	—	—
Repair/Maintenance	—	—
Travel	—	—
Entertainment	—	—
Supplies/Computer supplies	—	—
Personnel	—	—
Hardware support	—	—
In-house publishing	—	—
Overhead allocation	—	—
Total Expenses	$370.9	$ 962.6
Project Trading Profit	$ 31.2	$ 528.2
Headcount (Dendrite Client Team)	7.00	20.30

[a]These examples represent established clients. In year one of these projects, software license fees were 50%–60% of revenues.

ments. Service contracts covered ongoing facilities management and other services provided by Dendrite's client teams. In the United States and Japan, Dendrite's service pricing was based on the number of system users, and ranged from $300 to $2,000 per user annually; in Europe, where pharmaceutical sales forces were smaller, service contracts were often quoted as a fixed annual fee.

Customers incurred other costs for ETM projects, including the purchase or upgrade of computers for salespeople and communications linkages between the host computer and corporate systems. Typical total costs for implementing an ETM project in a large pharmaceutical firm in 1993 might be $8 million, of which 35% was for Dendrite products and services and 65% for other products and services required to operate the system.

Competition

Including the hardware, forecasts indicated a worldwide $900 million market for ETM by 1995. In 1993, the majority of ETM sales were from hundreds of vendors offering generic, stand-alone software packages which retailed for $100–$400 per unit. These systems allowed a diligent user to collect and maintain information on customers, but were not designed for any specific industry or for integration with other parts of a firm's management system.

The latter capability was available from vendors who offered integrated systems that sold for $1 million or more. Some of these vendors (like Dendrite) specialized in an industry or vertical segment, and others sold across industry segments. In 1993, most were serving 5,000 to 10,000 representatives on their systems. In the pharmaceutical industry, Dendrite's major competitors in this category were STI, Walsh International, PharmaSystems, and Cornet. Dendrite's management believed that key success factors in integrated systems were service support and product flexibility (i.e., the ability to modify database structures to accommodate specific client requirements and subsequent ability to integrate with other client information systems). Management believed that Dendrite offered much higher levels of service than its competitors and, with the exception of Cornet, greater product flexibility. In addition, Dendrite was currently the only supplier with an ETM product developed for the Japanese Kanji language.

STI had estimated 1992 sales of $48 million from ETM systems used in industries including consumer packaged goods and petrochemicals. In pharmaceuticals it held a 40% share of installed reps in the United States. D&B also owned IMS, a supplier of market data to the pharmaceutical industry. In 1992 in Europe, STI began offering IMS data on its ETM system. However, STI had encountered lengthy delays in product development and implementation of its systems, some service problems, and had lost two major clients during the past 18 months. In late 1992 a number of top executives at STI were removed by D&B.

Walsh International, based in the United Kingdom, had sales of about $100 million, mainly derived from paper-based call reporting and data services for pharmaceutical firms. In 1990, Walsh launched an ETM system called PRECISE and by 1993 had automated about 5% of pharmaceutical reps worldwide. A Dendrite executive commented that "Walsh grew in the 1980s by acquiring call reporting companies in Europe and Canada, but they also have an office in Japan and claim to be producing a Japanese ETM product. Their main business is the sale and analysis of industry data, and they are a major competitor for IMS. They're in the process of converting their paper-based clients to PRECISE and often position the product as a 'give away' for clients buying their data. However, their ETM system is fairly rigid and does not currently lend itself well to integration with established client communication procedures and systems."

Pharma Systems (PS), based in the United Kingdom, was a newer company with a focus on ETM and management reporting systems. PS had entered the U.S. market in 1991 with venture backing from the British Coal Board. To date, PS had less than $1 million in sales and only one major client. But other firms had expressed interest in the PS system because it was compatible with a database called Express, which was also used in a market information system utilized by many pharmaceutical firms.

Cornet, based in the United States, had an installed base of about 13% of pharmaceutical reps worldwide, mainly derived from two large firms who licensed Cornet's software code for in-house development and customization. A Dendrite executive noted that "strategically, outright sale of code can get your foot in the door; we did that with a large firm in 1988. But there is no recurring income and the cost of keeping the code current is high. Cornet will need to develop a product-service package in order to remain a player."

Phoenix, based in the United States, had an installed base of about 8% of pharmaceutical reps. The firm also offered direct mail, sample fulfillment, telemarketing, and market research services to pharmaceutical firms. In ETM, Phoenix offered a low-end product which sold for about $1,500 per year per user (including the handheld hardware unit), but had little potential for integration with other client information systems.

Dendrite also faced indirect competition from information services firms such as Andersen Consulting and Electronic Data Systems. These firms managed the design and installation of hardware and software systems, and had recently managed projects that affected sales and marketing information systems at some pharmaceutical companies. Further, some pharmaceutical firms developed their own ETM systems via in-house MIS departments.

Customers

Worldwide in 1993, there were about 200,000 pharmaceutical salespeople (and an additional 20,000 sales managers), 80% of whom sold in the United States, Western Europe, and Japan (Exhibit 4). In nearly all countries, pharmaceutical salespeople did not take orders; their primary task was to persuade doctors to choose their firm's product over that of a competitor.

The selling cycle for Dendrite usually required 18 months or more, during which time Dendrite's salesperson typically maintained daily telephone contact in addition to weekly on-site visits. "Ideally," a Dendrite salesperson noted, "we begin with the V.P. of Sales, who recognizes a productivity problem and delegates the issue to a direct report, usually the head of Sales Administration (responsible for sales reporting systems at the firm). The

---

Exhibit 4   Estimated ETM Market Size (1992)

	United States	Western Europe[a]	Japan	Rest of World	Total
Number of reps	44,000	70,000	42,000	44,000	200,000
Number of reps automated	35,331	5,683	2,760	N/A	43,774
Percent automated	80.3%	8.1%	6.6%	N/A	21.9%
Number automated by Dendrite	7,893	2,467	2,305	0	12,665
Number automated by other firms and internal sources	27,438	3,216	455	N/A	31,109

[a]Western Europe includes England, France, Germany, Italy, Spain, and the Benelux countries.

decision-making unit quickly expands from there, and often includes various users and commentators from Sales, Marketing, and IS." Another salesperson noted: "User groups help to define the business needs to be addressed by the system, while IS translates those needs into technical specs and possible connections with other aspects of the company's information infrastructure."

Following preliminary discussions with a prospect, Dendrite's salesperson arranged for a software demonstration and sought to have key decision makers attend full-day orientations about the system at Dendrite headquarters. The goal was to familiarize the prospect about Dendrite's support capabilities and, as one salesperson commented, "to build necessary trust and credibility":

> Eighty-five percent of my time is spent face-to-face with client personnel, ranging from sales reps to VPs of Sales and IS. They're investing millions in hardware and software that is very visible in their organizations. They want to know whom they're dealing with. I have been a pharmaceutical sales rep and field manager, and know what information the client's sales force wants. I also bring client personnel to meet our technical people, business managers, and customer service reps, and have them talk to the people that staff our Help lines.

Clients usually ranked vendors on the basis of ease of use, functionality, connectivity with other company systems, financial strength, and commitment to product development since an installed system involved continual maintenance and new technology applications. The "short list" of potential vendors generally included at least three firms. Also, while most pharmaceutical firms were interested in ETM systems, their goals often varied by geographical market.

In the *United States* (about 30% of worldwide pharmaceutical sales and 60% of Dendrite sales in 1992), pharmaceutical sales forces were among the largest in the world, ranging from 500 to more than 3,000 reps per firm. Sales reps called on medical personnel every four to six weeks to leave product samples and literature, perform service tasks, and (especially in private office segments) build relationships with prescribing physicians. A Dendrite manager explained, "U.S. managers are concerned with customer profile data such as prescribing patterns, medical specializations, and patient volume. In evaluating field productivity, they tend to focus on call frequency as well as sales in the rep's territory for higher-margin products."

In *Western Europe* (32% of pharmaceutical sales), sales forces were generally 100 to 200 reps in size, with the largest being 700. Government funding of health care and large, managed-care organizations were common. Most of these organizations had established "formularies" (lists of approved drugs from which their employee physicians could choose) and also restricted the activities of pharmaceutical reps with prescribing physicians. "In Europe," a Dendrite manager noted, "pharmaceutical reps generally see a given doctor once per year, always by appointment, and can only leave one sample. This places more marketing emphasis on advertising, direct mail, medical meetings and conferences, and on the information flows relevant to linking all people in the vendor organization who have contacts with managed care personnel." Bruce Savage, Dendrite's VP for Europe, commented:

> Europe requires more product customization due to language and regulatory differences by country. Also, European clients are more price sensitive. It's often easier for a U.S. pharmaceutical executive to justify a budget request for a 2000-person sales force than it is for the European executive to do this for a 200-person sales force. Postsale, we require about $1,300 per user to cover the personnel costs on our client support teams, and smaller sales forces mean fewer economies of scope in ongoing maintenance and service tasks.

In *Japan* (18% of pharmaceutical sales), sales force sizes were like those in the United States and, with fewer doctors, there was one pharmaceutical salesperson in Japan for every six physicians. Twenty U.S. pharmaceutical firms employed about 63,000 reps in Japan.

In the United States and Europe, physicians prescribed but did not dispense (or sell) drugs to patients. In Japan, physicians had historically combined prescribing and dispensing functions. Sales reps typically negotiated prices with individual physicians, who often received fees from pharmaceutical firms based on the number of prescriptions written. Many Japanese physicians also derived income from using free samples with patients and then submitting the prescription record to the government for reimbursement. Hence, abundant samples (often provided through allied wholesalers) were an accepted part of the selling process. In addition, most Japanese doctors worked in clinics or hospitals which required sales reps to wait outside to see the doctor. One result, a Dendrite executive explained, is that "social selling is very important in Japan. Reps develop face time with doctors by washing their cars, entertaining them, and running all sorts of errands. In turn, tracking these expenses is a key task for Japanese pharmaceutical firms. Daily call reports involve detailed information about the hospital, doctor, samples distributed, and any gifts or other expense-item tasks performed." Bill Magee, Dendrite's VP for Asia, added:

> In the United States and Europe, our ratio of support staff to client sales reps is 1:200, but 1:100 in Japan due to the emphasis on personal service. We generally don't make money with a Japanese client until the second or third year. Also, while we're the only vendor with a fully operational Kanji system, there's a bias here toward doing business with Japanese-owned firms.

Market developments

In 1992, spending on prescription drugs in the United States was about $50 billion and, as a portion of medical spending, had declined from 16% in the 1960s to 7% by 1990. However, U.S. health care costs had grown to over $900 billion by 1992, more than 14% of GNP. President Clinton had made health care a key issue in his campaign and had appointed a task force to draft legislation. The task force had singled out drugs for attention and, in mid-1993, was reviewing various options. While the eventual outcome of any government action was unclear, most observers believed that more managed-care facilities was a likely outcome in the United States.

Managed care referred to institutions such as HMOs that limited a patient's choice of doctor and hospital(s), used centralized buying and formularies to lower product acquisition costs, and eschewed traditional fee-for-service physician compensation in favor of cost controls aimed at diagnosing and treating ailments with fewer tests and visits. By 1993, 56% of Americans in group health plans were enrolled in managed-care networks, up from 29% in 1988. Forecasts indicated that by 1995, 20% of prescription sales in the United States would be from pharmacies in managed-care facilities and another 35% via contracts between retail pharmacies and managed-care institutions that employ hundreds of staff physicians. One observer commented:

> Admission to the formulary will depend on physicians' input, but will be heavily influenced by administrators interested in price, cost-in-use, and added value services in addition to product safety and efficacy. Also, the many doctors practicing in both managed care and private-office settings are unlikely to sustain different prescribing habits for their patients. So a firm with products on the formulary also has access to another large market.

> Many managed-care firms are also developing information systems to track pre-

scribing practices for each patient and physician and to develop therapy guidelines. Physicians who continually prescribe outside the guidelines will be questioned and may suffer economic penalties. Conversely, pharmaceutical firms will face greater demands for comparative data and cost-benefit information as a prerequisite for formulary admission.

In this environment, pharmaceutical sales forces in the United States will be downsized. After R&D, the Sales organization represents the largest fixed asset investment of a pharmaceutical company. The targets for their activities will drop from 250,000–300,000 individual physicians to about 35,000 committees. The optimum size of the field force for a major pharmaceutical firm operating in the United States may be 400 to 700 reps, rather than 1,500 or more.

In Europe, managed care was already more common than in the United States, but pharmaceutical spending was a bigger portion of health care costs than in the United States. In response, many European countries were imposing price controls and other regulations. In early 1993, Germany imposed reimbursement regulations that resulted in a 27% reduction in prescriptions in the first month and a 32% reduction in the second. In the United Kingdom, there was a trend toward more centralized buying of health care products, including drugs. In response, noted one observer, "pharmaceutical firms in Europe may move toward even smaller, more specialized sales forces focused on a given product or therapeutic area."

In Japan in 1992, fixed-invoice pricing for pharmaceuticals was mandated and wholesaler rebating abolished. Under the previous system, wholesalers were reimbursed by manufacturers for supplying products to customers at prices below manufacturers' list price. Under the new system, manufacturers were barred from intervening in wholesaler/customer price negotiations. Japan also instituted caps on health care reimbursement, including drugs, and was moving toward the separation of prescribing and dispensing for pharmaceuticals. One observer commented:

> Sales reps can no longer discuss product price and discounts with physicians, and more attention must be paid to wholesalers. They must place more emphasis on the therapeutic qualities of their companies' products. Reimbursement caps make Japanese clinics and hospitals more price sensitive, and the separation of dispensing and prescribing by doctors would alter pharmaceutical sales tasks. Samples become a less effective device for building relationships; product and market information becomes more pertinent; and pharmaceutical firms would also need to develop and coordinate distribution to more pharmacies and other drug suppliers. That may mean more reps.

Worldwide, there were fewer "blockbuster" drugs in the product pipelines of many firms. Of the 30 biggest selling drugs in the United States, for instance, 14 would be off-patent by the end of 1996, leaving billions in annual sales vulnerable to lower-priced generic competition. A Dendrite executive commented: "Pharmaceutical sales forces expanded in the 1980s, fueled by patented products whose margins made increased selling resources possible and desirable. But companies without such products are less likely to add to their already sizable distribution costs."

Organization

Exhibit 5 outlines Dendrite's organization in 1993. Reporting to John Bailye were vice presidents for each geographical area as well as controller, planning, and technical services (responsible for new product development and support and maintenance of core code). Client teams in each country reported to their area vice president.

Exhibit 5

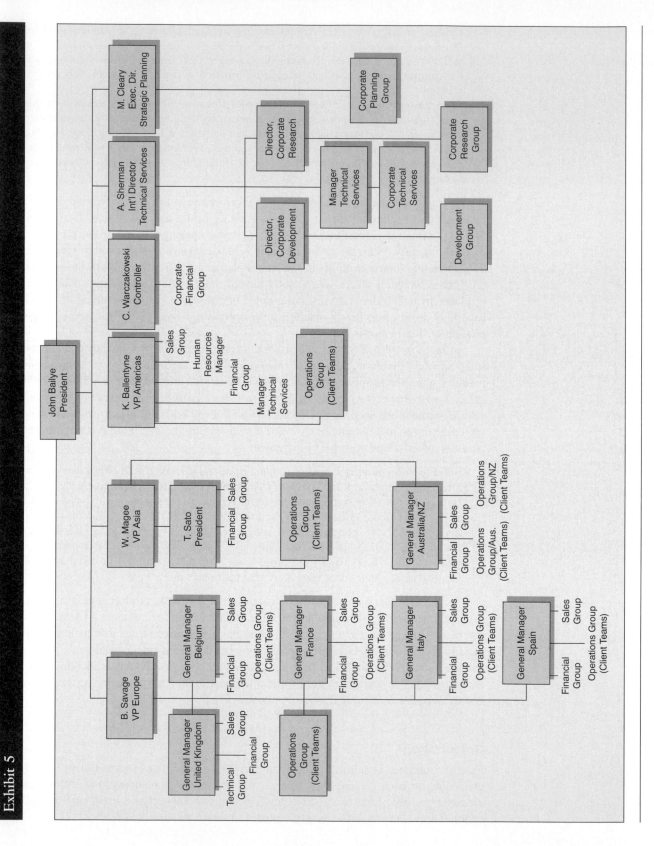

Sales

"We have two types of sales activities," noted one executive, "initial sales to clients and follow-on sales to existing accounts." Initial sales were handled by salespeople, all of whom had previous experience in the pharmaceutical industry, supplemented by the area vice presidents. Salesperson compensation involved a base salary, and a commission based on both the dollar volume of the contract and account profitability; sales commissions were paid only after the annual budget for that client team had been achieved, not when the contract was signed. Incentive compensation in 1992 averaged about 30% of the salesperson's total compensation. One salesperson commented:

> In a customized software business, no two client situations are identical. Hence, we must be flexible in pricing, delivery dates, and the array of services and support we offer to clients in order to close a sale. This is especially true for a global supplier. Many corporate pharmaceutical executives want to negotiate pricing on a global basis. And for us, multiyear contracts in several countries are attractive. But their country managers are usually very protective of their autonomy. That means many changes in our system for each country at the same client. So, while we in Sales may negotiate a price that assumes standardized reports across a client's countries, postsale margins may suffer as many changes are required to get and keep the system in a country organization.
>
> I ultimately can't control client demands, and this is a very competitive business where we tend to be the high-service/premium-priced suppliers. Also, the selling process involves working across Sales, IS, and other client functions for a major capital expense which attracts board of director attention. I don't want to see a multimillion dollar agreement killed because of a quarrel about an additional $50,000 worth of applications or support service.

As well as managing client teams, Business Managers (BMs) were responsible for business development at existing accounts. Incremental sales were made by adding users to the system and/or application modules (priced on a per-user basis) as user feedback revealed additional client needs. A Dendrite executive noted: "Facilities management allows us to collect information about clients' changing business demands. The BM's task is to provide, from our range of modules, the applications most pertinent to their evolving concerns. They are in an ideal position to identify ongoing sales-enhancement tools."

Dendrite had 20 BMs in 1993. Most had a technical background and experience in operations or IS project management, usually outside the pharmaceutical industry. Their compensation involved a base salary and a bonus based on achieving financial and customer satisfaction goals (based on quarterly surveys of customers). Each client team was a profit center, and BMs were responsible for managing expenses. One BM noted:

> Postsale, my major contacts are with the client's IS managers. I soon know more about their user needs than they do. For example, the field data we collect is very relevant to their Product Management and Market Research functions, and can also help Finance and Procurement manage supplies and other expenses. These areas often don't realize that Dendrite is a data and communications source. IS is very leery about vendor personnel approaching other functions and acts as a strong gatekeeper. A BM must be a good technical analyst in order to identify applications opportunities and then an accomplished diplomat in order to sell any opportunity to and beyond IS.
>
> Meanwhile, my primary job is managing services for clients and account profitability for Dendrite. I'm usually brought in after price negotiations with the client and so "inherit" what Sales has negotiated. In an increasingly cost-conscious environment, Sales often agrees to provide applications, services, and delivery dates with less attention than I'd like to the costs, headcount, and deadlines involved. Most of my postsales time is absorbed by the efforts required to deliver on these agreements and still break even on the project.

Client teams

Upon an agreement with a client, Dendrite formed a dedicated team responsible for customized applications, hardware connections, pilot testing, rollout, and then ongoing maintenance and management of the account (Exhibit 6). Team size was related to the number of users and ranged from 3 to 50 members, with an average of 22 people. Each team was headed by a BM and included Customer Support (CS) and Technical Support (TS) managers. Annual fully burdened costs for the BM, one TS rep, and one CS rep were more than $250,000, with additional costs for additional technical and service personnel dedicated to the account.

In the project phase, IS managers defined, customized, and installed the system on the client's hardware and computer network. TS also helped clients in purchasing equipment from vendors and managed Dendrite's leased-equipment program. After rollout, TS managers focused on system maintenance which involved system backups, communications support, data security, ongoing software enhancements, and 24-hour service for any hardware or system problems. In the project phase, CS managers developed system documentation, company-specific training materials and service manuals, and user training programs at client sites. One CS manager noted:

> The field reception of an ETM system is a function of how the client's corporate headquarters has "sold" the system, and we're there to help in this process. When it's been sold well, reps see the system as a tool that can help them, not a big-brother device to micromanage their activities. Also, it takes about one month for a rep to use the system efficiently, and our role is to accelerate this learning curve.

After rollout, CS managers focused on the telephone Help lines dedicated to that client. Help lines were available to users from 8:00 to 5:00 P.M. daily (in each time zone) and in the United States averaged 400 calls per month per client. A CS rep explained that "Help line calls range from questions about software or malfunctioning power cords to requests for data. We receive training about the client's product line and, during rollout, quickly become familiar to the client's field reps. They will call to discuss marketing ideas, suggestions about reformatting a report, or other matters." In general, there was one CS rep and one TS rep for every 200 system users at clients.

Exhibit 7 outlines BM responsibilites. Before rollout, BMs worked closely with client IS and Sales Administration managers on system design, installation, and training. After rollout, BMs worked on ongoing customization, new or add-on modules to be incorporated in the system, and (with client IS managers) on evaluating the reception and effectiveness of the system.

One BM noted that "Clients basically want two things from the BM: that you really listen and care; and that you do everything else yesterday." Another noted that "As a rule of thumb, a cost-effective client team needs a minimum of 400 users. That makes European clients especially challenging from a P&L point of view. We have shared client teams, but that limits the levels and types of service you can provide." A third BM commented that "An ongoing issue in account management is guarding against 'service creep': most contracts negotiated with clients stipulate a flat fee per user, and clients have a tendency to ask for more and more services under this flat fee arrangement. If BMs were involved earlier in the sales process, we could identify this and try to price service more appropriately." A Dendrite executive commented:

> There's a shift in the BM's role from consultant during project development and installation, to service provider and account manager after rollout. The service role tends to be focused on daily firefighting tasks across a client's many field locations. These concerns make IS the key contact for BMs; and IS tends to focus on minimizing software bugs and

Exhibit 6   Project Life Cycle

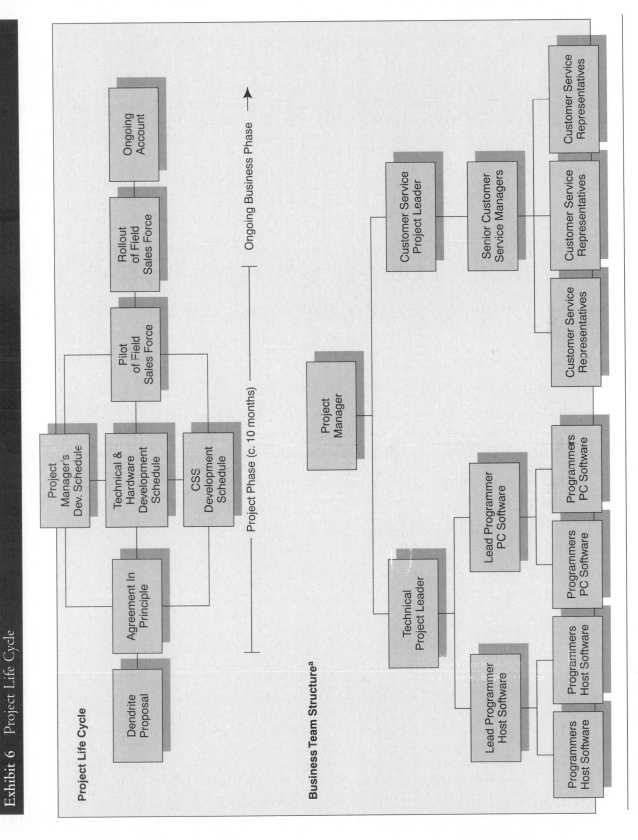

Project Life Cycle

Business Team Structure[a]

[a]Typical U.S. team = 22–30 people.

Exhibit 7 Business Managers' Project Responsibilities

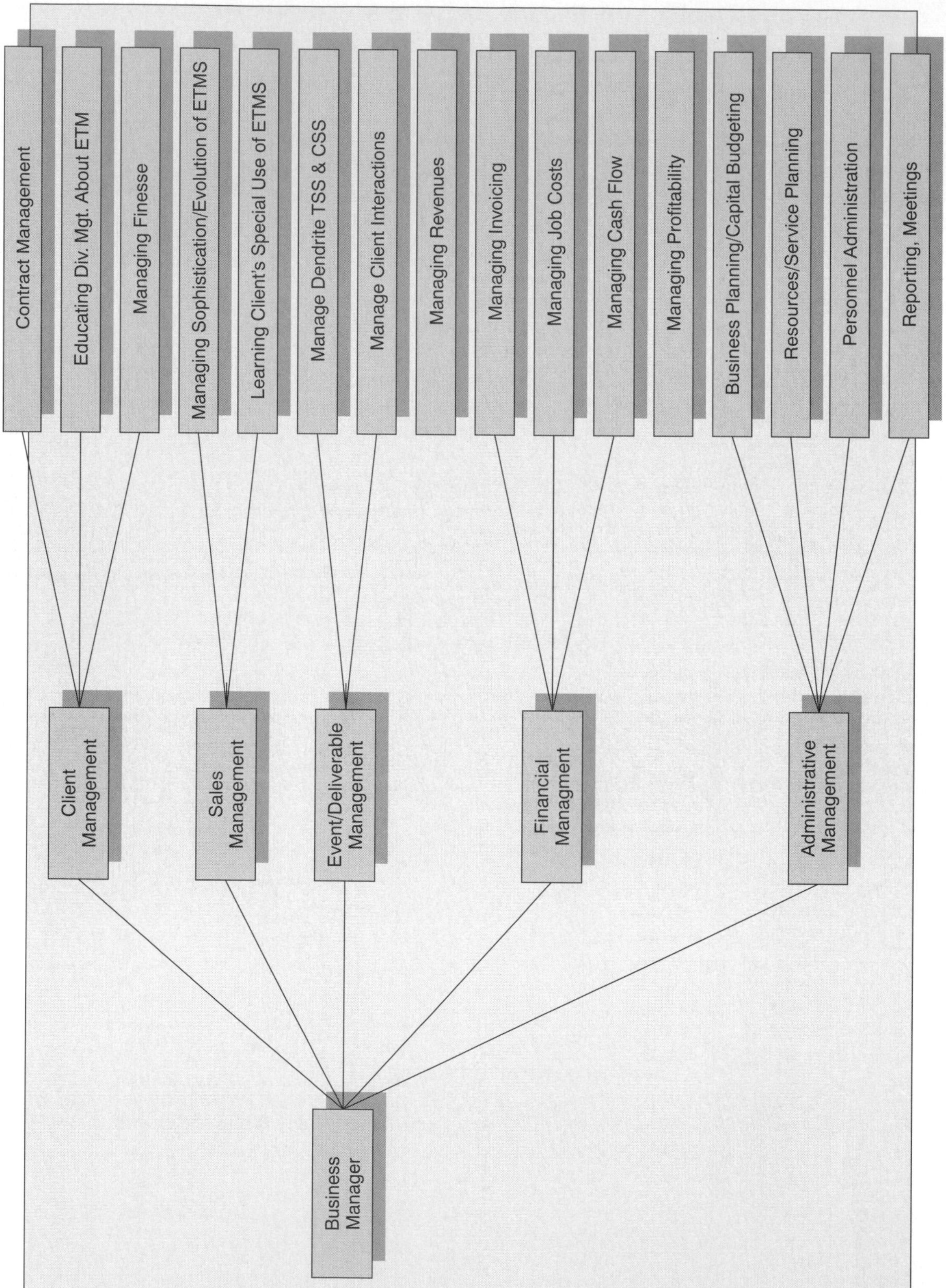

Contract Management

Educating Div. Mgt. About ETM

Managing Finesse

Managing Sophistication/Evolution of ETMS

Learning Client's Special Use of ETMS

Manage Dendrite TSS & CSS

Manage Client Interactions

Managing Revenues

Managing Invoicing

Managing Job Costs

Managing Cash Flow

Managing Profitability

Business Planning/Capital Budgeting

Resources/Service Planning

Personnel Administration

Reporting, Meetings

Client Management

Sales Management

Event/Deliverable Management

Financial Managment

Administrative Management

Business Manager

Note: TSS = Technical Support Services
CSS = Customer Support Services

hassles, not on business goals. Their measure of success is our product's technical performance, not productivity improvements or enhancements. In fact, for IS, enhancements run the risk of generating problems (for which they are blamed) and not just more sales calls or revenues (for which Sales or Marketing gets credit). That's one reason IS managers don't like BMs talking to other departments.

Current Issues

Commenting on Dendrite in mid-1993, Bailye said: "Technology and customer concerns are dynamic. New programming tools make it possible for six computer jockeys in a garage to reverse-engineer basic software and sell it more cheaply. The pharmaceutical industry is poised for a shift in many countries. Meanwhile, what we can do with our own product-service offering has also changed, and that raises fundamental strategic choices." Bailye was considering several alternative routes of potential company growth: into other markets besides pharmaceuticals, into other functional areas within pharmaceutical clients, or "deeper" into sales and marketing applications in the current target market.

Most sales automation vendors targeted multiple markets besides pharmaceuticals, including insurance consumer package goods, and other industries that relied on large field forces to sell products. Some managers believed that Dendrite should also expand into other vertical markets. "We have both offensive and defensive reasons to do this," noted one manager. "On the one hand, our software remains among the best for sales reporting and data dissemination, and specific formats can be customized for various industries. On the other hand, with fewer large pharmaceutical field forces available, the economics of our current market are changing. Also, the entry point for new vendors is typically smaller field forces, and we should expect increasingly heavy competition for pharmaceutical clients."

Estimates indicated that $10 million would be required to adapt core code and facilities management services to another industry's selling tasks, implying some time before a market entry would break even for Dendrite. This investment could be reduced substantially if development focused on stand-alone software with little or no support services provided by Dendrite.

Another possibility was to expand into other functional areas within pharmaceutical firms. One manager noted that "We are now the link between our clients' sales reps and their IS and sales administration managers. But the data we collect and disseminate has enormous cross-functional value for clients, and we can be the link between other departments and ongoing field sales and customer activity data. As sales force sizes decrease, we must evolve from a sales planning to a management information tool for clients." Another manager emphasized:

> Both technological and customer developments support this strategy. Network technologies, which allow computers to share data, are spreading throughout industry, making cross-functional linkages more accessible. And, for pharmaceutical firms in particular, selling to big managed-care organizations will require better information links between field sales, national account groups, product marketing, finance, and distribution. We are now experts about a critical node in these evolving networks and should capitalize on our position.

Dendrite had under development a managed-care module for its current system, and estimated additional core-code development costs of $2–$5 million depending upon the number of areas covered by a cross-functional approach. However, other managers wondered about the selling and service requirements inherent in this approach, and noted that competition would include multinational information consulting firms that were much larger than Dendrite and already had long-standing relationships beyond IS and Sales departments in clients.

A third option was to continue concentrating on sales applications and product enhancements that increased Dendrite's value to pharmaceutical clients. One manager noted:

> The United States may be a mature market for sales automation, but not Europe or Japan. Also, some competitors are beginning to link with industry data providers, and we must continue to add value to our system through module applications and support. Pharmaceutical firms are very protective of their databases and there's a limit to how far they will let any vendor into their organization. To be successful, we must link our initiatives to sales automation because that's our base and identity in these firms.

Dendrite could develop many product extensions, including computer-based training modules, additional analysis and performance evaluation systems, multimedia applications that allowed for individualized sales presentations tied to on-line data sources, and use of current software for palm-sized computers expected to be introduced in coming years. Development costs for these enhancements were generally $1 million and often shared with current clients interested in expanding sales force applications.

Another issue facing the company was the coordination of Dendrite's sales and service efforts and possible changes in the role of the Business Manager. Many believed that the current arrangement immersed BMs in daily operations with little time to develop business opportunities. They proposed the addition of an Operations Manager to client teams, responsible for day-to-day technical and customer support issues. Costs of such a position would be comparable to those for the BM position. One executive commented:

> Growing an account requires a strategic rather than tactical focus, and contacts beyond IS and sales administration. Ideally, we would want two project teams: one for development/installation phases and one for on-going support. Now, however, the installation phase identifies the BM as the tactician who handles all the details and ties that person closely to IS, who doesn't want the BM "wasting" time with other functional areas. The Operations Manager position would free BMs from daily firefighting and allow them to sell to other areas at the client. It would also create a career path for CS and TS managers to become Operations Managers and subsequently grow into a BM role.

Others were uncertain about the impact of this proposal on service provision during the various phases from initial proposal to installation and ongoing operations. They argued for involving BMs earlier in the process, before contracts are signed. "If involved during the first draft of an agreement," said one manager, "a BM can impact the product configuration and deliverables, recognize the true costs of postsale service, and establish relationships with the other client personnel who get involved before a contract is signed but who tend not to interact with our client teams after the contract is signed." Still others questioned whether BMs had the skills or temperament required for selling new business. One manager commented: "People should do what they do best. BMs' strengths are in project management and fixing problems. Even with sales training, they will remain operations managers. And, given developments in our customer base, they will need to manage ongoing service and support costs even more tightly."

Reflecting on these options, John Bailye commented:

> We are financing the business from ongoing operations and our venture backers will eventually look to reap returns on their investments via an IPO. Hence, growth remains important even as we face an environment where there are lots of forecasts but no certain-

ties. Should we grow within the sales function across geographics, into other departments at global clients, or into new vertical markets? What are the implications for BMs and the organization of our account management activities? And how do possible changes at pharmaceutical firms affect current and future strategy? I want Dendrite working on those areas that will yield the best return over the long haul.

Notes

Chapter 1

1. Barton A. Weitz, Stephen B. Castleberry, and John F. Tanner, Jr., *Selling: Building Partnerships,* 3d ed. (New York: Irwin/McGraw–Hill), pp. 6-8.

2. Betsy Spethman, "Working for Peanuts," *PROMO* (May 1998), pp. 46–50.

3. Some of the early works include Gilbert A. Churchill, Jr., Neil M. Ford, and Orville C. Walker, Jr., "Organizational Climate and Job Satisfaction in the Salesforce," *Journal of Marketing Research* (November 1976), pp. 323–32; and Alan J. Dubinsky, "Perceptions of the Sales Job: How Students Compare with Industrial Salespeople," *Journal of the Academy of Marketing Science* (Fall 1918), pp. 352–67. It is interesting to note that these findings seem to be equally true for both male and female sales representatives and haven't changed much over time. See Darrell D. Muehling and William A. Weeks, "Women's Perceptions of Personal Selling: Some Positive Results," *Journal of Personal Selling and Sales Management* (May 1988), pp. 11–20; and Judy A. Siguaw and Earl D. Honeycutt, Jr., "An Examination of Gender Differences in Selling Behaviors and Job Attitudes," *Industrial Marketing Management* 24 (1995), pp. 45–52.

4. Weitz, Castleberry, and Tanner, chapter 1.

5. "Rebirth of a Salesman: Willy Loman Goes Electronic," *Business Week* (February 27, 1984), p. 104. See also Jaclyn Fierman, "The Death and Rebirth of the Salesman," *Fortune,* (July 25, 1994), pp. 80–91; and David W. Cravens, "The Changing Role of the Sales Force," *Marketing Management* (Fall 1995), pp. 49–57.

6. Neil M. Ford, Orville C. Walker, Jr., and Gilbert A. Churchill, Jr., "Differences in the Attractiveness of Alternative Rewards among Industrial Salespeople: Additional Evidence," *Journal of Business Research* (April 1985), pp. 123–38.

7. Thayer C. Taylor, "Going Mobile," *Sales & Marketing Management* (May 1994), pp. 94–101.

8. "Marketing Newsletter," *Sales & Marketing Management* (February 1987), p. 27.

9. "By the Numbers," *Sales & Marketing Management* (June 1998), p. 14.

10. William Keenan, Jr., "Facing Extinction: The End of the Sales Manager," *Sales & Marketing Management* (October 1994), pp. 67–74.

Chapter 2

1. The interested reader might turn to a number of sources for more information about the strategic planning process and its impact on marketing and sales management. These include Orville C. Walker, Jr., Harper W. Boyd, Jr., and Jean-Claude Larréché, *Marketing Strategy: Planning and Implementation,* 2d ed. (Burr Ridge, IL: Richard D. Irwin, 1996); and David A. Aaker, *Strategic Market Management,* 3d ed. (New York: John Wiley & Sons, 1992).

2. This section is based on Robert Dwyer and John F. Tanner, Jr., *Business Marketing: Connecting Strategy, Relationships, and Learning* (New York: Irwin/McGraw–Hill, 1999).

3. George Huber, "Organizational Learning: The Contributing Processes and the Literatures," *Organizational Science* 2 (February 1991), pp. 88–115.

4. Theodore Levitt, "Marketing Myopia," *Harvard Business Review* (September–October, 1975), pp. 26–44.

5. Gary Hamel and C.K. Prahalad, "Corporate Imagination and Expeditionary Marketing," *Harvard Business Review* 69 (July/August 1991), pp. 81–92.

6. Edwin A. Locke and Vinod K. Jain, "Organizational Learning and Continuous Improvement," *International Journal of Organizational Analysis* 3 (January 1995), pp. 45–68.

7. P.J. Schoemaker, "Multiple Scenario Development: Its Conceptual and Behavior Foundation," *Strategic Management Journal* 14 (1993), pp. 193–213.

8. John Humble, David Jackson, and Alan Thomson, "The Strategic Power of Corporate Values," *Long Range Planning* 24 no. 6 (1994), pp. 28–42.

9. George S. Day, "The Capabilities of Market-Driven Organizations," *Journal of Marketing* 58 (October 1994), pp. 37–52.

10. Rohit Deshpande, John Farley, and Frederick Webster, "Corporate Culture, Customer Orientation, and Innovativeness in Japanese Firms: A Quadrad Analysis," *Journal of Marketing* 57 (January 1993), pp. 23–37; Bernard Jaworski and Ajay Kohli, "Market Orientation: Antecedents and Consequences," *Journal of Marketing* 57 (July 1993), pp. 53–70; John C. Narver and Stanley Slater, "The Effects of a Marketing Orientation on Business Profitability," *Journal of Marketing* 54 (October 1990), pp. 20–35.

11. Daniel G. Simpson, "Why Most Strategic Planning Is a Waste of Time and What You Can Do About It," *Long Range Planning* 31, no. 3 (1998), pp. 476–80.

12. Michael E. Porter, *Competitive Strategy* (New York: The Free Press, 1980), chapter 2.

13. Raymond E. Miles and Charles C. Snow, *Organizational Strategy, Structure and Process* (New York: McGraw–Hill, 1978). Miles and Snow also identified a fourth category of businesses, which they called "reactors." However, because reactors are businesses with no clearly defined or consistent competitive strategy, we will ignore this group.

14. For a more detailed discussion of how a business's competitive strategy influences its marketing and sales strategies and programs, see Orville C. Walker, Jr., and Robert W. Ruekert, "Marketing's Role in the Implementation of Business Strategies: A Critical Review and Conceptual Framework,"

Journal of Marketing (July 1987), pp. 15–33. See also Walker, Boyd, and Larréché, *Marketing Strategy,* chapter 3.

15. Allison Lucas, "Portrait of a Salesperson," *Sales & Marketing Management* (June 1995), p. 13.

16. For example, see David A. Aaker, *Managing Brand Equity* (New York: The Free Press, 1991); Linda M. Keefe, "Corporate Voice in Relation to Product Brands," *Design Management Journal* 6 (1995), pp. 45–49.

17. David A. Andelman, "Betting on the Net," *Sales & Marketing Management* (June 1995), pp. 47–59.

18. For a more detailed discussion of the role of personal selling and other promotional tools in building long-term relationships with resellers, see James A. Narus and James C. Anderson, "Turn Your Industrial Distributors into Partners," *Harvard Business Review* (March–April 1986), pp. 66–71; F. Robert Dwyer, Paul H. Schurr, and Sejo Oh, "Developing Buyer–Seller Relationships," *Journal of Marketing* (April 1987), pp. 11–27; Jan Heide and George John, "Do Norms Matter in Marketing Relationships?" *Journal of Marketing* (April 1992), pp. 32–44.

19. Bill Saporito, "Behind the Tumult at P&G," *Fortune* (March 7, 1994), pp. 74–82. For other examples involving industrial goods, see Joseph B. Fuller, James O'Conor, and Richard Rawlinson, "Tailored Logistics: The Next Advantage," *Harvard Business Review* (May–June 1993), pp. 87–98; W. David Gibson, "Holy Alliances," *Sales & Marketing Management* (July 1993), pp. 85–87.

20. Frederick F. Reichheld, "Loyalty and the Renaissance of Marketing," *Marketing Management* 2, 1994, pp. 10–21. Also see Rahul Jacob, "Why Some Customers Are More Equal than Others," *Fortune* (September 19, 1994), pp. 215–24.

21. Reichheld, "Loyalty and the Renaissance of Marketing."

Chapter 3

1. For more comprehensive reviews of the literature concerning organizational buying behavior for goods and services, see Wesley J. Johnston and Jeffrey E. Lewin, "Organizational Buying Behavior: Toward an Integrative Framework," *Journal of Business Research* 35 (1996), pp. 1–15.

2. A classic article regarding buying influence is Thomas V. Bonoma's "Major Sales: Who Really Does the Buying?" *Harvard Business Review* (May–June 1982), pp. 111–19. Also see Susan Lynn, "Identifying Buying Influences for a Professional Service: Implications for Marketing Efforts," *Industrial Marketing Management* (May 1987), pp. 119–30, and, more recently, John F. Tanner, Jr., and Stephen B. Castleberry, "The Participation Model: Factors Related to Buying Decision Participation," *Journal of Business-to-Business Marketing* 1, no. 3 (1993), pp. 35–61.

3. For a comprehensive review of buying center research, see Richard G. Jennings and Richard E. Plank, "When the Purchasing Agent Is a Committee: Implications for Industrial Marketing," *Industrial Marketing Management* 24 (November 1995), pp. 411–19.

4. However, evidence suggests that under some circumstances even a straight rebuy can involve a large number of buying center participants. See Robert D. McWilliams, Earl Naumann, and Stan Scott, "Determining Buying Center Size," *Industrial Marketing Management* 21 (February 1992), pp. 43–50.

Regarding the issue of risk, see Tony L. Henthorne, Michael S. LaTour, and Alvin J. Williams, "How Organizational Buyers Reduce Risk," *Industrial Marketing Management* 22 (1993), pp. 41–48, and V.W. Mitchell, "Buy-Phase and Buy-Class Effects on Organizational Risk Perceptions and Reduction in Purchasing Professional Services," *Journal of Business and Industrial Marketing* 13 (1998), pp. 461–71.

5. Joseph A. Bellizzi, "Organizational Size and Buying Influences," *Industrial Marketing Management* 10 (1981), pp. 17–21.

6. Jerome M. Katrichis, "Exploring Departmental Level Interaction Patterns in Organizational Purchasing Decisions," *Industrial Marketing Management* 27 (1998), pp. 135–46.

7. Jennings and Plank, "When the Purchasing Agent Is a Committee."

8. Patrick J. Robinson, Charles W. Faris, and Yoram Wind, *Industrial Buying and Creative Marketing* (Boston: Allyn & Bacon, 1967). See also Gary L. Lilien and M. Anthony Wong, "An Exploratory Investigation of the Structure of the Buying Center in the Metalworking Industry," *Journal of Marketing Research* (February 1984), pp. 1–11.

9. Anita M. Kennedy, "The Complex Decision to Select a Supplier: A Case Study," *Industrial Marketing Management* 2 (1983), pp. 45–56. Also see Morry Ghingold, "Testing the 'Buygrid' Buying Process Model," *Journal of Purchasing and Materials Management* (Winter 1986), pp. 30–36; and Erin Anderson, Wujin Chu, and Barton Weitz, "Industrial Buying: An Empirical Exploration of the Buyclass Framework," *Journal of Marketing* (July 1987), pp. 71–86.

10. Guy R. Banville and Ronald J. Dornoff, "Industrial Source Selection Behavior—An Industry Study," *Industrial Marketing Management* (June 1973); and Geoff Gordon, Roger Calantone, and C.A. diBenedetto, "How Electrical Contractors Choose Distributors," *Industrial Marketing Management* 20 (February 1991), pp. 29–42. See also Christopher P. Puto, Wesley E. Patton III, and Ronald H. King, "Risk Handling Strategies in Industrial Vendor Selection Decisions," *Journal of Marketing* (Winter 1985), pp. 89–98; and I. Fredrick Trawick, John E. Swan, Gail W. McGee, and David R. Rink, "Influence of Buyer Ethics and Salesperson Behavior on Intention to Choose a Supplier," *Journal of the Academy of Marketing Science* 19 (1991), pp. 17–23.

11. Elizabeth J. Wilson, "The Relative Importance of Supplier Selection Criteria: A Review and Update," *International Journal of Purchasing and Materials Management* 30 (Summer 1994), pp. 35–41.

12. William C. Moncrief III, "Selling Activity and Sales Position Taxonomies for Industrial Salesforces," *Journal of Marketing Research* (August 1986), pp. 261–70.

13. William A. O'Connell and William Keenan, Jr., "The Shape of Things to Come," *Sales & Marketing Management* (January 1990), pp. 36–41.

14. Allison Lucas, "Portrait of a Salesperson," *Sales & Marketing Management* (June 1995), p. 13.

15. O'Connell and Keenan, "The Shape of Things," p. 38.

16. For a brief summary of some of these classification schemes, see Alan J. Dubinsky and P.J. O'Connor, "A Multidimensional

Analysis of Preferences for Sales Positions," *Journal of Personal Selling and Sales Management* (November 1983), pp. 31–41.

17. Derek A. Newton, *Sales Force Performance and Turnover* (Cambridge, MA: Marketing Science Institute, 1973), p. 3.

18. For example, see Barton A. Weitz, Stephen B. Castleberry, and John F. Tanner, Jr., *Selling: Building Partnerships,* 3d ed. (New York: Irwin/McGraw–Hill, 1999).

19. David A. Andelman, "Betting on the 'Net," *Sales & Marketing Management* (June 1995), pp. 47–59.

20. Benson P. Shapiro, *Sales Program Management: Formulation and Implementation* (New York: McGraw–Hill, 1977), p. 160.

21. Milt Grassell, "What Purchasing Managers Like in a Salesperson . . . and What Drives Them up the Wall," *Business Marketing* (June 1986), pp. 72–77. See also Edith Cohen, "The View from the Other Side," *Sales & Marketing Management* (June 1990), pp. 108–10; and "Ten Ways to Lose a Sale," *Sales & Marketing Management* (December 1992), p. 35.

22. Grassell, "What Purchasing Managers Like," p. 75. Also see Barry Farber and Joyce Wycoff, "Customer Service: Evolution and Revolution," *Sales & Marketing Management* (May 1991), pp. 44–51.

23. Frederick F. Reichheld, "Loyalty and the Renaissance of Marketing," *Marketing Management* 2 (1994), pp. 10–21.

24. John F. Tanner, Jr., "Users' Role in the Purchase: Their Influence, Satisfaction, and Desire to Participate in the Next Purchase," *Journal of Business and Industrial Marketing* 13, no. 6 (1998), pp. 479–91.

25. James P. Morgan and Shirley Cayer, "Working with World-Class Suppliers: True Believers," *Purchasing* (August 13, 1992), pp. 50–52.

26. See Thomas Wotruba, "The Evolution of Personal Selling," *Journal of Personal Selling and Sales Management* (Summer 1991), pp. 1–12; Robert Krapfel, Deborah Salmond, and Robert Spekman, "A Strategic Approach to Managing Buyer–Seller Relationships," *European Journal of Marketing* 25 (1991), pp. 22–37.

27. Roy Chitwood, *World Class Selling* (Minneapolis, MN: Best Sellers Publishing, 1996).

28. Dan T. Dunn and Claude A. Thomas, "Partnering with Customers," *Journal of Business and Industrial Marketing* (1994), pp. 34–46.

Chapter 4

1. Lawrence B. Chonko, John F. Tanner, Jr., and Ellen Reid Smith, "The Sales Force's Role in International Marketing Research and Marketing Information Systems," *Journal of Personal Selling and Sales Management* 11 (Winter 1991), pp. 69–79.

2. Andy Cohen, "The Misuse of Competitive Intelligence," *Sales & Marketing Management* (March 1998), p. 13.

3. Robert A. Cooke, *Ethics in Business: A Perspective* (Chicago: Arthur Anderson & Co., 1988).

4. I. Fredrick Trawick, John E. Swan, Gail W. McGee, and David R. Rink, "Influence of Buyer Ethics and Salesperson Behavior on Intention to Choose a Supplier," *Journal of the Academy of Marketing Science* 19 (1991), pp. 17–23.

5. For example, see F. Robert Dwyer, Paul H. Schurr, and Sejo Oh, "Developing Buyer–Seller Relationships," *Journal of Marketing* (April 1987), pp. 11–27; Shay Sayre, Mary L. Joyce, and David R. Lambert, "The Relevance of Ethical Salesperson Behavior on Relationship Quality: The Pharmaceutical Industry," *Journal of Personal Selling and Sales Management* (Fall 1991), pp. 39–48; and Jan Heide and George John, "Do Norms Matter in Marketing Relationships?" *Journal of Marketing* (1992), pp. 32–34.

6. "White Collar Crime Cost Increases," *USA Today,* January 8, 1987, p. A1. See also Dawn Bryan, "Using Gifts to Make the Sale," *Sales & Marketing Management* (September 1989), pp. 48–53; Thomas R. Wotruba, "A Comprehensive Framework for the Analysis of Ethical Behavior, with a Focus on Sales Organizations," *Journal of Personal Selling and Sales Management* (Spring 1990), pp. 29–42; and Ralph W. Clark and Alice Darnell Lattal, "The Ethics of Sales: Finding an Appropriate Balance," *Business Horizons* (July–August 1993), pp. 66–69.

7. Betsy Weisendanger, "Doing the Right Thing," *Sales & Marketing Management* (January 1991), pp. 82–83.

8. Ibid., p. 83.

9. Ibid., p. 82.

10. William Rudelius and Rogene A. Buchholz, "Ethical Problems of Purchasing Managers," *Harvard Business Review* (March–April 1979), p. 8. See also Alan J. Dubinsky, "Studying Field Salespeoples' Ethical Problems: An Approach for Designing Company Policies," in *Marketing Ethics: Guidelines for Managers,* ed. Gene R. Laczniak and Patrick E. Murphy (Lexington, MA: Lexington Books, 1985); Michael R. Hyman, Robert Skipper, and Richard Tansey, "Ethical Codes Are Not Enough," *Business Horizons* (March–April 1990), pp. 15–22; K. Douglas Hoffman, Vince Howe, and Donald W. Hardigree, "Ethical Dilemmas Faced in the Selling of Complex Services: Significant Others and Competitive Pressures," *Journal of Personal Selling and Sales Management* (Fall 1991), pp. 13–26; and Kenneth Labich, "The New Crisis in Business Ethics," *Fortune* (April 20, 1992), pp. 167–76.

11. Terry W. Loe and John F. Tanner, Jr., "Federal Sentencing Guidelines: Implications for Teaching Sales Management," National Sales Conference 1999.

12. For a discussion of the accelerating pace of new product development, the advantages of being a new product pioneer, and some marketing strategies for new products, see Walker, Boyd, and Larréché, *Marketing Strategy,* chapter 8.

13. David W. Cravens, "The Changing Role of the Sales Force," *Marketing Management* (Fall 1995), pp. 48–57.

14. Ibid., p. 51.

15. Liam Fahey, William R. King, and Vadake K. Narayanan, "Environmental Scanning and Forecasting in Strategic Planning—The State of the Art," *Long-Range Planning* (February 1981), pp. 32–39. However, some evidence suggests that the kind and amount of environmental scanning that firms do also depend on the volatility of their environments. See Richard L. Daft, Juhani Sormunen, and Don Parks, "Chief Executive Scanning, Environmental Characteristics, and Company Performance: An Empirical Study," *Strategic Management Journal* 9 (1988), pp. 123–29.

16. Joel E. Ross and Ronnie Silverblatt, "Developing the Strategic Plan," *Industrial Marketing Management* 16 (1987), pp. 103–8.

17. William Keenan, Jr., "What's Sales Got to Do with It?" *Sales & Marketing Management* (March 1994), pp. 66–73.

18. Alfred P. Sloan. *My Years with General Motors* (Garden City, NY: Doubleday, 1964), p. 140.

Chapter 5

1. For examples, see Patricia Sellers, "How to Remake Your Sales Force," *Fortune* 5/4 (1992), pp. 96–102.

2. Martin Everett, "When There's More than One Route to the Customer," *Sales & Marketing Management* (August 1990), pp. 48–56.

3. Jerome A. Colletti and Gary S. Tubridy, eds., *Reinventing the Sales Organization* (Scottsdale, AZ: The Alexander Group, Inc., 1993).

4. Louis W. Stern and Adel I. El-Ansary, *Marketing Channels,* 3d ed. (Englewood Cliffs, NJ: Prentice Hall, 1988), chapter 3. See also Edwin E. Bobrow, "The Question of Reps," *Sales & Marketing Management* (June 1991), pp. 33–35.

5. Jayashree Mahajan, G.A. Churchill, Jr., N.M. Ford, and O.C. Walker, Jr., "A Comparison of the Impact of Organizational Climate on the Job Satisfaction of Manufacturers' Agents and Company Salespeople: An Exploratory Study," *Journal of Personal Selling and Sales Management* (May 1984), pp. 1–10.

6. Allen M. Weiss and Erin Anderson, "Converting from Independent to Employee Salesforces: The Role of Perceived Switching Costs," *Journal of Marketing Research* (February 1992), pp. 101–15.

7. Bernard J. Jaworski, "Toward a Theory of Marketing Control: Environmental Context, Control Types, and Consequences," *Journal of Marketing* (July 1988), pp. 23–39.

8. Transaction cost analysis was first developed in Oliver E. Williamson, *Markets and Hierarchies: Analysis and Antitrust Implications* (New York: The Free Press, 1975). For empirical evidence that largely supports TCA's predictions about the conditions under which firms will employ independent agents versus company salespeople, see Erin Anderson, "The Salesperson as Outside Agent or Employee: A Transaction Cost Analysis," *Marketing Science* 4 (1985), pp. 234–54; Erin Anderson and Barton Weitz, "Make or Buy Decisions: Vertical Integration and Marketing Productivity," *Sloan Management Review* (Spring 1986), pp. 1–19; and Jan B. Heide and George John, "The Role of Dependence Balancing in Safeguarding Transaction-Specific Assets in Conventional Channels," *Journal of Marketing* (January 1988), pp. 20–35.

9. For example, see James C. Anderson and James A. Narus, "A Model of Distributor Firm and Manufacturer Firm Working Partnerships," *Journal of Marketing* (January 1990), pp. 42–58; Jan B. Heide and George John, "Do Norms Matter in Marketing Relationships?" *Journal of Marketing* (April 1992), pp. 32–44; and Erin Anderson and Barton Weitz, "The Use of Pledges to Build and Sustain Commitment in Distribution Channels," *Journal of Marketing Research* (February 1992), pp. 18–34.

10. Robert W. Ruekert, Orville C. Walker, Jr., and Kenneth J. Roering, "The Organization of Marketing Activities: A Contingency Theory of Structure and Performance," *Journal of*

Marketing (Winter 1985), pp. 13–25; and Melissa Campanelli, "Agents of Change," *Sales and Marketing Management* (February 1995), pp. 71–75.

11. Daniel S. Levine, "Justice Served," *Sales & Marketing Management* (May 1995), pp. 53–61. For additional examples see Sellers, "How to Remake Your Sales Force."

12. For a more detailed discussion of the variety of objectives and activities that telemarketing can accomplish, see Denise Herman, "Telemarketing Success: A Tough Act to Follow," *Telemarketing* (March 1987), pp. 25–28; and Francy Blackwood, "Did You Sell $5 Million Last Year?" *Selling* (October 1995), pp. 44–53.

13. "Rebirth of a Salesman: Willy Loman Goes Electronic," *Business Week* (February 27, 1984), p. 104.

14. Programs that coordinate the efforts of outside salespeople with the use of telemarketing, direct mail, and other promotional efforts are often referred to as "integrated direct marketing" programs. See Ernan Roman, "Integrated Direct Marketing: Managing the Mix," *Sales & Marketing Management* (May 1991), pp. 83–87; and David A. Andelman, "Betting on the 'Net," *Sales & Marketing Management* (June 1995), pp. 47–59.

15. For a more detailed discussion of the sales management problems involved in administering effective telemarketing programs, see William C. Moncrief, Charles W. Lamb, Jr., and Terry Dielman, "Developing Telemarketing Support Systems," *Journal of Personal Selling and Sales Management* (August 1986), pp. 43–49; and Blackwood, "Did You Sell $5 Million Last Year?"

16. Robert J. Hershock, "Notes from the Revolution," in *Reinventing the Sales Organization* (New York: The Conference Board, 1995), pp. 10–13.

17. William A. O'Connell and William Keenan, Jr., "The Shape of Things to Come," *Sales & Marketing Management* (January 1990), p. 36.

18. O.E. McDaniel, "The New Name of the Game: Global Account Marketing," *National Account Marketing Association Journal* (Fall 1990), pp. 1–5.

19. For a more detailed discussion of the emerging relationship between suppliers and their customers, see Arun Sharma, "Who Prefers Key Account Management Programs? An Investigation of Business Buying Behavior and Buying Firm Characteristics," *The Journal of Personal Selling and Sales Management* (Fall 1997), pp. 27–39; and Catherine Pardo, "Key Account Management in the Business to Business Field: The Key Account's Point of View," *The Journal of Personal Selling and Sales Management* (Fall 1997), pp. 17–26.

20. Frederick F. Reichheld, "Loyalty and the Renaissance of Marketing," *Marketing Management* 2 (1994), pp. 10–21. Also see Rahul Jacob, "Why Some Customers Are More Equal than Others," *Fortune* (September 19, 1994), pp. 215–24. And finally Sangit Sungupta, Robert E. Krapfel, and Michael Pusateri, "Switching Costs in Key Account Relationships," *The Journal of Personal Selling and Sales Management* (Fall 1997), pp. 9–16.

21. Benson P. Shapiro and Rowland T. Moriarity, *Organizing the National Account Force* (Cambridge, MA: The Marketing Science Institute, 1984), pp. 1–37. See also Jerome A. Colletti and Gary S. Tubridy, "Effective Major Account Sales

Management," *Journal of Personal Selling and Sales Management* (August 1987), pp. 1–10.

22. Mark A. Moon and Susan Forquer Gupta, "Examining the Formation of Selling Centers: A Conceptual Framework," *The Journal of Personal Selling and Sales Management* (Spring 1997), pp. 31–42.

23. Andy Cohen, "Top of the Charts—Lear Corporation," *Sales and Marketing Management* (July 1998), p. 40.

24. Joseph Conlin, "Teaming Up," *Sales & Marketing Management* (October 1993), pp. 98–104.

25. Ibid., p. 99.

26. Dan T. Dunne, Jr., and Claude A. Thomas, "Strategy for Systems Sellers: A Team Approach," *Journal of Personal Selling and Sales Management* (August 1986), pp. 1–10. See also Cynthia R. Cauthern, "Moving Technical Support into the Sales Loop," *Sales & Marketing Management* (August 1990), pp. 58–61.

27. Conlin, "Teaming Up," p. 100. See also Louis Bucklin and Sanjit Singupta, "Organizing Successful Co-Marketing Alliances," *Journal of Marketing* (April 1993), pp. 32–46.

28. Cohen, Andy, "Top of the Charts—Pfizer," *Sales and Marketing Management* (July 1998), p. 41.

29. For examples, see Tom Murray, "Just-in-Time Isn't Just for Show—It Sells," *Sales & Marketing Management* (May 1990), pp. 62–67; and Joseph B. Fuller, James O'Conor, and Richard Rawlinson, "Tailored Logistics: The Next Advantage," *Harvard Business Review* (May–June 1993), pp. 87–98.

30. Peter Petre, "How to Keep Customers Happy Captives," *Fortune* (September 2, 1985), pp. 42–46; and Sang-Lin Han, David T. Wilson, and Shirish P. Dant, "Buyer–Supplier Relationships Today," *Industrial Marketing Management* 22 (1993), pp. 331–38.

31. John S. Hill and Richard R. Still, "Organizing the Overseas Sales Force: How Multinationals Do It," *Journal of Personal Selling and Sales Management* (Spring 1990), pp. 57–66. See also John S. Hill and Arthur Allaway, "How U.S.-Based Companies Manage Sales in Foreign Countries," *Industrial Marketing Management* 27 (1993), pp. 7–16.

32. Chad, Kaydo. "Top of the Charts—FedEx," *Sales & Marketing Management* (July 1998), pp. 46, 48.

33. Donald S. Tull, Bruce E. Cooley, Mark R. Phillips, Jr., and Harry S. Watkins, "The Organization of Marketing Activities of American Manufacturers," Report #91–126 (Cambridge, MA: The Marketing Science Institute, October 1991).

34. Barry Farber and Joyce Wycoff, "Customer Service: Evolution and Revolution," *Sales & Marketing Management* (May 1991), pp. 44–51.

35. For a more general discussion of the advantages of outsourcing and other actions for improving the efficiency of marketing and sales activities, see Jagdish N. Sheth and Rajendra S. Sisodia, "Feeling the Heat," *Marketing Management* (Fall 1995), pp. 9–23.

Chapter 6

1. Kyle Pope, "Compaq Can't Cope with Demand for ProLinea PCs," *The Wall Street Journal* (July 10, 1992), p. B1; Bart Ziegler, "IBM's O'Malley Resigns Post at PC Division," *The Wall Street Journal* (February 7, 1995), p. B14.

2. William J. Stanton and Richard H. Buskirk, *Management of the Sales Force,* 6th ed. (Homewood, IL: Richard D. Irwin, 1983), p. 412.

3. For a discussion of some other, less common forecasting techniques, see one of the many books on the subject, such as George J. Kress and John Snyder, *Forecasting and Market Analysis Techniques* (Westport, CT: Quorum Books, 1994); Spyros G. Makridakis, *Forecasting, Planning, and Strategy for the 21st Century* (London: Collier MacMillan, 1990); Spyros Makridakis and Steven C. Wheelwright, *Forecasting: Methods and Applications* (New York: John Wiley & Sons, 1978); Douglas Wood and Robert Fildes, *Forecasting for Business: Methods and Applications* (New York: Longment Group Limited, 1976); Spyros Makridakis, *Handbook of Forecasting: A Manager's Guide,* 2d ed. (New York: John Wiley & Sons, 1987); Steven C. Wheelwright and Spyros G. Makridakis, *Forecasting Methods for Management,* 5th ed. (New York: John Wiley & Sons, 1989).

4. See also David M. Georgoff and Robert Murdick, "Manager's Guide to Forecasting," *Harvard Business Review* 64 (January–February 1986), pp. 110–20, which contains a chart in which 20 forecasting techniques are rated on 16 evaluative dimensions.

5. Brian Silverman, "Get Em While They're Hot," *Sales & Marketing Management* (February 1997), pp. 47–52.

6. "Sales Forecasts: Getting There from Here," *Business Marketing* 73 (October 1988), pp. 36–37. For a more complete discussion of the advantages and disadvantages of intention to purchase as a measure of expectations, see Manohar U. Kalwani and Alvin J. Silk, "On the Reliability and Predictive Validity of Purchase Intention Measures," *Marketing Science* 1 (Summer 1982), pp. 243 86. Those organizations that collect purchase intentions data regularly often adjust the data based on their past experience as to how much bias intention data might contain. For discussion of some popular adjustment procedures, see Linda F. Jamieson and Frank M. Bass, "Adjusting Stated Intention Measures to Predict Trial Purchase of New Products: A Comparison of Models and Methods," *Journal of Marketing Research* 26 (August 1989), pp. 336–45; Vicki G. Morwitz and David Schmittlein, "Using Segmentation to Improve Sales Forecasts Based on Purchase Intent: Which 'Intenders' Actually Buy?" *Journal of Marketing Research* 29 (November 1992), pp. 391–405.

7. David Hurwood, Elliott S. Grossman, and Earl L. Bailey, *Sales Forecasting* (New York: The Conference Board, 1978). The empirical evidence indicates about 50 percent of the consumer goods companies and 70 percent of the industrial goods companies among the Fortune 500 firms used the sales force composite to forecast sales. See Robin T. Peterson, "Sales Force Composite Forecasting—an Exploratory Analysis," *Journal of Business Forecasting* 8 (Spring 1989), pp. 23–27. For specific examples of other companies that use the sales force composite method, see William Keenan, Jr., "Numbers Racket," *Sales & Marketing Management* 147 (May 1995), pp. 64–76.

8. Richard B. Barrett and David J. Kitska, "Forecasting System at Rubbermaid," *Journal of Business Forecasting* 6 (Spring 1987), pp. 7–9.

9. The technique was originally devised at the Rand Corporation to assist in forecasting the likely state of technology in the

future. See Norman C. Dalkey, *The Delphi Method: An Experimental Study of Group Opinion* (Santa Monica, CA: The Rand Corporation, 1969). The method has been adopted for sales forecasting. See C.L. Jain, "Delphi-Forecast with Experts' Opinion," *The Journal of Business Forecasting* 4 (Winter 1985–86), pp. 22–23.

10. Jeffrey L. Johnson, "A Ten-Year Delphi Forecast in the Electronics Industry," *Industrial Marketing Management* 5 (March 1976), pp. 45–55.

11. Hurwood, Grossman, and Bailey, *Sales Forecasting*, pp. 16–17.

12. Those who wish a more comprehensive coverage of forecasting with time series should see one of the books specifically devoted to forecasting methods in general, such as Wheelwright and Makridakis, *Forecasting Methods for Management*, or time series forecasting methods in particular, such as Peter J. Brockwell and Richard A. Davis, *Time Series: Theory and Methods* (New York: Springer–Verlag, 1991).

13. For examples of the use of exponential smoothing, see Pauline Sheldon, "Forecasting Tourism: Expenditures versus Arrivals," *Journal of Travel Research* 32 (Summer 1993), pp. 13–20; Robert J. Thomas, "Method and Situational Factors in Sales Forecast Accuracy," *Journal of Forecasting* 12 (January 1993), pp. 69–77.

14. The entire process is illustrated in Wheelwright and Makridakis, *Forecasting Methods for Management*. The best-known decomposition method is the technique developed by Julius Shiskin, "Electronic Computers and Business Indicators," National Bureau of Economic Research, Occasional Paper 57, which is used in forecasting many national statistics. It is also possible to adjust for trading day effects or sales patterns with heavier volumes on certain days, such as weekends, using similar procedures. See Arthur J. Adams, "Using the Calendar to Improve Sales Forecasts," *Journal of the Academy of Marketing Science* 12 (Summer 1984), pp. 103–12.

15. Dick Berry, "Inside the Art of Regression-Based Sales Forecasting," *Business Marketing* 69 (June 1984), pp. 100–11. For other examples of statistical demand analysis, see Sue L. Chang, "The Role of Marketing Research in Forecasting at Lennox Industries," *Journal of Business Forecasting* 12 (Summer 1993), pp. 23–24; George F. Meyer, "Marketing Research and Sales Forecasting at Schlegel Corporation," *Journal of Business Forecasting* 12 (Summer 1993), pp. 22–23.

16. Stanley J. PoKempner and Earl L. Bailey, *Sales Forecasting Practices: An Appraisal* (New York: National Industrial Conference Board, 1970). See also J. Scott Armstrong, Roderick J. Brodie, and Shelby H. McIntyre, "Forecasting Methods for Marketing: Review of Empirical Research," *International Journal of Forecasting* 3, nos. 3–4, pp. 355–76; Robin T. Peterson, "Forecasting Practices in Retail Industry," *Journal of Business Forecasting* 12 (Spring 1993), pp. 11–14.

17. PoKempner and Bailey, *Sales Forecasting Practices*, p. 32.

18. Ibid.

19. Spyros Makridakis et al., "The Accuracy of Extrapolation (Times-Series) Methods: Results of a Forecasting Competition," *Journal of Forecasting* 1 (April–June 1982), pp. 111–53. See also Spyros Makridakis et al., *The Forecasting Accuracy of Major Time Series Methods* (New York: John Wiley & Sons, 1984).

20. Spyros Makridakis and Michele Hibon, "Accuracy of Forecasting: An Empirical Investigation," *Journal of the Royal Statistical Society* 142, pt. 2 (1979), pp. 97–145; R.M. Hogarth and Spyros Makridakis, "Forecasting and Planning: An Evaluation," *Management Science* 27 (February 1981), pp. 115–38.

21. Mark M. Moriarity and Arthur J. Adams, "Management Judgment Forecasts, Composite Forecasting Models, and Conditional Efficiency," *Journal of Marketing Research* 21 (August 1984), pp. 239–50.

22. Steven P. Schnaars, "Situational Factors Affecting Forecast Accuracy," *Journal of Marketing Research* 21 (August 1984), pp. 290–97; Steven W. Hartley and William Rudelius, "How Data Format and Problem Structure Affect Judgmental Sales Forecasts: An Experiment," in *AMA Educator's Conference Proceedings*, Terrence A. Shimp et al. (Chicago: American Marketing Association, 1986), pp. 297–302; Douglas J. Dalrymple, "Sales Forecasting Practices: Results from a United States Survey," *International Journal of Forecasting* 3 (November 1987), pp. 379–91.

23. See, for example, J. Holton Wilson and Deborah Allison-Koerber, "Combining Subjective and Objective Forecasts Improves Results," *Journal of Business Forecasting* 11 (Fall 1992), pp. 3–8. For reviews of the literature on combining forecasts, see Robert Clemens, "Combining Forecasts: A Review and Annotated Bibliography," *International Journal of Forecasting* 5, no. 4 (1989), pp. 559–88; C.W.J. Granger, "Invited Review: Combining Forecasts—Twenty Years Later," *Journal of Forecasting* 8 (July–September 1989), pp. 167–73.

24. Pierre Wack, "Scenarios: Unchartered Waters Ahead," *Harvard Business Review* 63 (September–October 1985), p. 73.

25. Pierre Wack, "Scenarios: Shooting the Rapids," *Harvard Business Review* 63 (November–December 1985), p. 146. See also Peter W. Beck, "Debate over Alternate Scenarios Replaces Forecasts at Shell U.K.," *Journal of Business Forecasting* 3 (Spring 1984), pp. 2–6.

26. Thomas Moore, "Different Folks, Different Strokes," *Fortune* 112 (September 16, 1985), p. 68. This article describes what several companies are doing to take advantage of regional variations in demand.

27. The buying power index (BPI) discussed below provides an example of a market index-based allocation of total estimated demand to a territory.

28. See Richard D. Rosenberg, "Forecasting Derived Product Demand in Commercial Construction," *Industrial Marketing Management* 11 (February 1982), pp. 39–46, for details regarding the development and use of the indexes. Similarly, the Building Products Division of Schlegel Corporation (a leading supplier of weatherstripping, hardware, thresholds, and related window and door components) uses housing starts and remodeling activity in an area to estimate territory demand for its products. See Fred Meyer, "Building Products Sales Forecasting at Schlegel," *Journal of Business Forecasting* 10 (Winter 1991–92), pp. 23–24.

29. For an overview of useful secondary data published by the Bureau of the Census and other public and private agencies, see Churchill, *Marketing Research*, pp. 318–35.

30. Thomas R. Wotruba, *Sales Management: Planning,*

Accomplishment, and Evaluation (New York: Holt, Rinehart & Winston, 1971), p. 195. See also Thomas R. Wotruba and Edwin K. Simpson, *Sales Management: Text and Cases,* 2d ed. (Belmont, CA: Wadsworth Publishing Co., 1992).

31. William J. Stanton and Richard H. Buskirk, *Management of the Sales Force,* 7th ed. (Homewood, IL: Richard D. Irwin, 1987), p. 535.

32. We will have more to say about how sales quotas pinpoint potential marketing strategy deficiencies in the chapter on sales analysis.

33. Julia Flynn, "Did Sears Take Other Customers for a Ride," *Business Week* (August 3, 1992), pp. 24–25; Judy Quinn, "Employee Motivation: Repair Job," *Incentive* 166 (October 1992), pp. 40–46.

34. Jeffrey Rothfeder and Stephen Phillips, "Damage Control at Dun and Bradstreet," *Business Week* (November 27, 1989), pp. 187–90; Johnnie L. Roberts, "Dun's Credit Reports, Vital Tool of Business, Can Be off the Mark," *The Wall Street Journal* (October 5, 1989), pp. A1, A10.

35. Thayer C. Taylor, "Ramtek Sharpens Its Marketing Picture," *Sales & Marketing Management* 131 (September 12, 1983), pp. 45–48. Ramtek's strategy is consistent with the empirical evidence that suggests that as quota levels are increased for most people, effort increases only up to a point, after which increases in the level of the quota may actually decrease effort. See Jhinuk Chowdhury, "The Motivational Impact of Sales Quota on Effort," *Journal of Marketing Research* 30 (February 1993), pp. 28–42.

36. Benjamin G. Ammons, "Get Greater Commitment by Letting Salespeople Help Set the Quotas," *Sales & Marketing Management* 124 (April 7, 1980), p. 90. See also Vincent Alonzo, "Beyond Sales Quotas," *Incentive* 168 (February 1994), pp. 32–34.

37. Exhibit 6.17 and much of the surrounding discussion are adapted from Wotruba, *Sales Management,* pp. 201–23, which provides an excellent discussion of the subject.

38. Alan J. Dubinsky and Thomas E. Barry, "A Survey of Sales Management Practices," *Industrial Marketing Management* 11 (April 1982), pp. 133–41.

39. Richard R. Still, Edward W. Cundiff, and Normal A.P. Govoni, *Sales Management Decisions, Strategies, and Cases,* 4th ed. (Englewood Cliffs, NJ: Prentice Hall, 1981), p. 598. Reprinted by permission.

40. Barton A. Weitz, Stephen B. Castleberry, and John F. Tanner, Jr. *Selling: Building Partnerships* (Burr Ridge, IL: Richard D. Irwin, 1992), p. 445.

41. Richard I. Levin, "Who's on First?" *Sales Management: The Marketing Magazine,* no. 93 (July 17, 1964), p. 56.

42. "Haworth Pegs Quotas to Local Markets," *Sales & Marketing Management* 135 (December 9, 1985), pp. 68, 70.

43. See Jacob Gonik, "Tie Salesmen's Bonuses to Their Forecasts," *Harvard Business Review* 56 (May–June 1978), pp. 119–20, for a more detailed explanation of the system, which has also been used by the St. Regis Paper Company, which tied salespeople's compensation to potential quota differences. See "Managing by- and with-Objectives," *Studies in Personnel Policy,* no. 212 (New York: The National Industrial Conference Board, 1968),

pp. 43–45. See also Murali K. Mantrala and Kalyan Raman, "Analysis of a Sales Force Incentive Plan for Accurate Sales Forecasting and Performance," *International Journal of Research in Marketing* 7 (December 1990), pp. 189–202.

Chapter 7

1. Betsy D. Gelb and Basckeer M. Khumawala, "Reconfiguration of an Insurance Company's Sales Regions," *Interfaces* 14 (November–December 1984), pp. 87–94. See also Melissa Campanelli, "Reshuffling the Deck," *Sales & Marketing Management* 146 (June 1994), pp. 83–90.

2. Karsten Hellebust, "Bindicator Finds a Fair Measure for Sales Territory Performance," *Sales & Marketing Management* 135 (November 11, 1985), pp. 45–48.

3. The average number of calls per day is somewhat lower for salespeople selling industrial goods than it is for salespeople selling consumer goods or services, where the averages are 4.5 and 6 calls per day, respectively. See "1991 Sales Manager Budget Planning," *Sales & Marketing Management* 143 (June 17, 1991), p. 6.

4. This percentage has remained relatively constant over time. See *Allocating Field Sales Resources, Experiences in Marketing Management* (New York: National Industrial Conference Board, 1970), p. 92; and Richard Clucas, "Powering Up Your Sales Force," *Personal Computing* 8 (May 1984), pp. 98–99, 101, 103, 105. The insurance industry estimates the average salesperson is actually selling only 1 1/2 hours a day; the rest of the time is spent in preparation and travel. See "Training Agency Salespeople #2: How to Make Every Sales Minute Count," *Agency Sales Magazine* 19 (May 1989), pp. 42–45.

5. Raymond W. LaForge, David W. Cravens, and Clifford E. Young, "Improving Salesforce Productivity," *Business Horizons* 28 (September–October 1985), p. 50. For an empirical examination of the relationship between use of time and performance, see William A. Weeks and Lynn R. Kahle, "Salespeople's Time Use and Performance," *Journal of Personal Selling and Sales Management* 8 (August 1988), pp. 9–20.

6. Several of the computer models that try to treat simultaneously the complex interactions that arise between the decisions of sales force size and sales territory design incorporate other variables as well, such as the allocation of selling effort to customers or products. For an overview of the thrust of the various sales territory computer decision models, see David W. Cravens, "Salesforce Decision Models: A Comparative Assessment," in *Sales Management: New Developments from Behavioral and Decision Model Research,* ed. Richard P. Bagozzi (Cambridge, MA: Marketing Science Institute, 1979), pp. 310–24; Raymond W. La Forge, David W. Cravens, and Clifford E. Young, "Using Contingency Analysis to Select Selling Effort Allocation Methods," *Journal of Personal Selling and Sales Management* 6 (August 1986), pp. 19–28.

7. The method was first proposed by Walter J. Talley, Jr., "How to Design Sales Territories," *Journal of Marketing* 25 (January 1961), pp. 7–13.

8. Porter Henry, "The Important Few—The Unimportant Many," *1980 Portfolio of Sales and Marketing Plans* (New York: Sales and Marketing Management, 1980), pp. 34–37.

9. For these examples, see Jeffrey H. Wecker, "An Approach to

Higher Profits with Reduced Selling Costs," *Industrial Marketing* 62 (December 1977), pp. 57–58. For a general discussion on how to identify attractive accounts, see John Morton, "How to Spot the Really Important Prospects," *Business Marketing* 75 (January 1990), pp. 62–67.

10. It is possible to calculate the net present value of an account by considering these and other factors. See Donald L. Brady, "Determining the Value of an Industrial Prospect: A Prospect Preference Index Model," *Journal of Personal Selling and Sales Management* 7 (August 1987), pp. 27–32.

11. The method was first proposed by Semlow, although Weinberg and Lucas subsequently demonstrated there was a flaw in Semlow's procedure for operationalizing the notion. See Walter J. Semlow, "How Many Salesmen Do You Need," *Harvard Business Review* 37 (May–June 1959), pp. 126–32; Charles B. Weinberg and Henry C. Lucas, Jr., "Semlow's Results Are Based on a Spurious Relationship," *Journal of Marketing* 41 (April 1977), pp. 146–47.

12. Zarrell Lambert and Fred W. Kniffen, "Response Functions and Their Applications in Sales Force Management," *Southern Journal of Business* 5 (January 1970), pp. 1–9.

13. The Office of Management and Budget adopted the new designation and new standards for defining MSAs in 1980, although the changes did not go into effect until June 30, 1983. See "OMB Revises Metropolitan Statistical Area Definitions," *Data User News* 18 (April 1983), p. 3. While the definitions of SMSAs and MSAs were determined strictly on the basis of statistical data through the early 1980s, political considerations now seem to play a role. See Eugene Carlson, "What's a Metropolitan Area? Whatever Congress Says It Is," *The Wall Street Journal* (September 22, 1987), p. 37. For discussion of the advantages that can accrue from MSA status, see David Shribman, "Census '90 Indicates a New Megalopolis," *The Wall Street Journal* (February 6, 1991), pp. B1, B6.

14. See, for example, Jenny Thom and Linda Wolters, "A Map for Marketing," *Sales & Marketing Management* 144 (July 1992), pp. 102–4; Thayer C. Taylor, "Mapping Out a Strategy," *Sales & Marketing Management* 146 (February 1994), pp. 51–56.

15. A. Parasuraman, "An Approach for Allocating Sales Call Effort," *Industrial Marketing Management* 11 (1982), pp. 75–79; Renato Fiocca, "Account Portfolio Analysis for Strategy Development," *Industrial Marketing Management* 11 (1982), pp. 53–62. For an empirical assessment of the factors that affect the call frequency of a sample of salespeople representing 34 different firms, see Rosann L. Spiro and William D. Perreault, Jr., "Factors Influencing Sales Call Frequency of Industrial Salespersons," *Journal of Business Research* 6 (January 1978), pp. 1–15.

16. Fiocca, "Account Portfolio Analysis." La Forge and Cravens argue similarly that it is useful to classify all PCUs (planning and control units, in this case, accounts) according to two criteria: (1) PCU opportunity reflecting the potential available to all firms from the PCU, and (2) sales organization strength or the ability of the sales organization to take advantage of the opportunity. See Raymond La Forge and David W. Cravens, "Steps in Selling Effort Deployment," *Industrial Marketing Management* 11 (1982), pp. 183–94; or David W. Cravens and Raymond W. La Forge, "Salesforce Deployment Analysis," *Industrial*

Marketing Management 12 (July 1983), pp. 179–92. Dubinsky and Ingram suggest the cells of the matrix should be defined using the criteria of present profit (high/low) and profit potential (low/high). See Alan J. Dubinsky and Thomas N. Ingram, "A Portfolio Approach to Account Profitability," *Industrial Marketing Management* 13 (February 1984), pp. 33–41.

17. Parasuraman, "An Approach for Allocating."

18. The empirical evidence suggests the two approaches yield similar guidelines regarding the amount of effort that should be allocated to accounts. See Raymond W. La Forge and David W. Cravens, "Empirical and Judgment-Based Sales-Force Decision Models: A Comparative Assessment," *Decision Sciences* 16 (Spring 1985), pp. 177–95.

19. The evidence seems to suggest these functions are relatively stable over time. See Adrian B. Ryans and Charles B. Weinberg, "Territory Sales Response Models: Stability over Time," *Journal of Marketing Research* 24 (May 1987), pp. 229–33.

20. Leonard M. Lodish, "CALLPLAN: An Interactive Salesman's Call Planning System," *Management Science* 18 (December 1971), pp. 25–40.

21. William K. Fudge and Leonard M. Lodish, "Evaluation of the Effectiveness of a Model Based Salesman's Planning System by Field Experimentation," *Interfaces* 8 (November 1977), p. 104. See also Erin Anderson, Leonard M. Lodish, and Barton A. Weitz, "Resource Allocation Behavior in Conventional Channels," *Journal of Marketing Research* 24 (February 1987), pp. 85–97.

22. There are computer programs that formally incorporate the time it takes to service each account by considering distances as well as natural obstacles like mountains and rivers. See Andres Zoltners and Prabhakant Sinha, "Sales Territory Alignment: A Review and Model," *Management Science* 29 (November 1983), pp. 1,237–56; Probha Sinha and Andres Zoltners, "Matching Manpower and Markets," *Business Marketing* 73 (September 1988), pp. 95–98; Leon A. Wortman, "STARmanager Makes Big Promises: Does It Deliver?" *Business Marketing* 76 (April 1991), p. 59.

23. William P. Hall, "Improving Sales Force Productivity," *Business Horizons* 18 (August 1975), pp. 32–42.

24. Some of the computer call allocation models allow for product and customer mix considerations. They determine the optimal number of sales territories, which salespeople should cover which customers, and which products salespeople should emphasize, in addition to determining how often and for how long each account should be called on. For a review of the models as to their basic differences, see R.S. Howick and M. Pidd, "Sales Force Deployment Models," *European Journal of Operational Research* 48 (October 1990), pp. 295–310.

Chapter 8

1. This chapter borrows heavily from the following articles: Orville C. Walker, Jr., Gilbert A. Churchill, Jr., and Neil M. Ford, "Motivation and Performance in Industrial Selling: Present Knowledge and Needed Research," *Journal of Marketing Research* 14 (May 1977), pp. 156–68; Orville C. Walker, Jr., Gilbert A. Churchill, Jr., and Neil M. Ford, "Where Do We Go from Here? Selected Conceptual and Empirical Issues Concerning the Motivation and Performance of the

Industrial Salesforce," in *Critical Issues in Sales Management: State of the Art and Future Research Needs,* ed. Gerald Albaum and Gilbert A. Churchill, Jr. (Eugene: University of Oregon, 1979), pp. 10–75. See also Richard E. Plank and David A. Reid, "The Mediating Role of Sales Behaviors: An Alternative Perspective of Sales Performance and Effectiveness," *Journal of Personal Selling and Sales Management* 14 (Summer 1994), pp. 43–56; and Steven P. Brown, William Cron, and John W. Slocum, Jr., "Effects of Goal Directed Emotions on Salesperson Volitions, Behavior, and Performance: A Longitudinal Study," *Journal of Marketing* (January 1997), pp. 39–50.

2. For studies of how role perceptions can affect salespeople's job satisfaction and performance, see Douglas N. Behrman, William B. Bigoness, and William D. Perreault, Jr., "Sources of Job Related Ambiguity and Their Consequences upon Salesperson's Job Satisfaction and Performance," *Management Science* 27 (November 1981), pp. 1,246–60; Douglas N. Behrman and William D. Perreault, Jr., "A Role Stress Model of the Performance and Satisfaction of Industrial Salespeople," *Journal of Marketing* 48 (Fall 1984), pp. 9–21; Alan J. Dubinsky and Steven W. Hartley, "A Path-Analytic Study of a Model of Salesperson Performance," *Journal of the Academy of Marketing Science* 14 (Spring 1986), pp. 36–46; Linda S. Hartenian, Farrand J. Hadaway, and Gordon J. Badovick, "Antecedents and Consequences of Role Perceptions: A Path Analytic Approach," *Journal of Applied Business Research* 10 (Spring 1994), pp. 40–50.

3. R. Kenneth Teas, "Supervisory Behavior, Role Stress, and the Job Satisfaction of Industrial Salespeople," *Journal of Marketing Research* 20 (February 1983), pp. 84–91; Ajay K. Kohli, "Some Unexplored Supervisory Behaviors and Their Influence on Salespeople's Role Clarity, Specific Job Esteem, Job Satisfaction, and Motivation," *Journal of Marketing Research* 22 (November 1985), pp. 424–33; Rosemary R. Lagace, Stephen B. Castleberry, and Rick E. Ridnour, "An Exploratory Salesforce Study of Relationship between Leader–Member Exchange and Motivation, Role Stress, and Manager Evaluation," *Journal of Applied Business Research* 9 (Fall 1993), pp. 110–19. See also Goutam N. Challagalla and Tasaddug A. Servani, "Dimensions and Types of Supervisory Control Effects of Salesperson Performance and Satisfaction," *Journal of Marketing* (January 1996), pp. 89–105, and Thomas E. DeCarlo, R. Kenneth Teas, and James C. McElroy, "Salesperson Performance Attributions Process and the Formulation of Expectancy Estimates," *The Journal of Personal Selling and Sales Management* (Summer 1997), pp. 1–17.

4. For summaries of the results of these studies, see Edwin E. Ghiselli, *The Validity of Occupational Aptitude Tests* (New York: John Wiley & Sons, 1966), pp. 41–43; Barton A. Weitz, "A Critical Review of Personal Selling Research: The Need for Contingency Approaches," in *Critical Issues in Sales Management,* ed. Albaum and Churchill, Jr., pp. 76–126; and Neil M. Ford et al., "Selecting Successful Salespeople: A Meta-Analysis of Biographical and Psychological Selection Criteria," in *Review of Marketing 1987,* ed. Michael J. Houston (Chicago: American Marketing Association, 1987), pp. 90–131. For an example, see Lawrence M. Lamont and William J. Lundstrom, "Identifying Successful Industrial Salesmen by Personality and Personal Characteristics," *Journal of Marketing Research* 14 (November 1977), pp. 517–29.

5. Siew Meng Leong, Paul S. Busch, and Deborah Roedder John, "Knowledge Bases and Salesperson Effectiveness: A Script-Theoretic Analysis," *Journal of Marketing Research* 26 (May 1990), pp. 164–78.

6. R. Kenneth Teas, "An Empirical Test of Models of Salespersons' Job Expectancy and Instrumentality Perceptions," *Journal of Marketing Research* 18 (May 1981), pp. 209–26; Thomas L. Quick, "The Best-Kept Secret for Increasing Productivity," *Sales & Marketing Management* 141 (July 1989), pp. 34–38. For empirical evidence regarding the things that motivate salespeople in the United States versus salespeople in other countries, see Alan J. Dubinsky, Masaaki Kotabe, Chae Un Lim, and Ronald E. Michaels, "Differences in Motivational Perceptions among U.S., Japanese, and Korean Sales Personnel," *Journal of Business Research* 30 (June 1994), pp. 175–85.

7. Gilbert A. Churchill, Jr., Neil M. Ford, and Orville C. Walker, Jr., "Motivating the Industrial Salesforce: The Attractiveness of Alternative Rewards," *Journal of Business Research* 7 (1979), pp. 25–50; William L. Cron and John W. Slocum, Jr., "The Influence of Career Stages on Salespeople's Job Attitudes, Work Perceptions, and Performance," *Journal of Marketing Research* 23 (May 1986), pp. 119–29; Pradeep K. Tyagi, "Organizational Climate, Inequities, and Attractiveness of Salesperson Rewards," *Journal of Personal Selling and Sales Management* 5 (November 1985), pp. 31–37; Lawrence B. Chonko, John F. Tanner, and William A. Weeks, "Selling and Sales Management in Action: Reward Preferences of Salespeople," *Journal of Personal Selling and Sales Management* 12 (Summer 1992), pp. 67–75.

8. See Gilbert A. Churchill, Jr., Neil M. Ford, and Orville C. Walker, Jr., "Measuring the Job Satisfaction of Industrial Salesmen," *Journal of Marketing Research* 11 (August 1974), pp. 254–60, for a description of the procedures used to construct the scale. See also Rosemary R. Lagace, Jerry R. Goolsby, and Jule B. Gassenheimer, "Scaling and Measurement: A Quasi-Replicative Assessment of a Revised Version of Indsales," *Journal of Personal Selling and Sales Management* 13 (Winter 1993), pp. 65–72.

9. Steven P. Brown and Robert A. Peterson, "Antecedents and Consequences of Salesperson Job Satisfaction: Meta-Analysis and Assessment of Causal Effects," *Journal of Marketing Research* 30 (February 1993), pp. 63–77.

10. The definition of the salesperson's role is a continuous process. The definition process begins when the individual is first socialized into the organization and continues through the person's employment with the company. See Alan J. Dubinsky et al., "Salesforce Socialization," *Journal of Marketing* 50 (October 1986), pp. 192-207, for discussion of the socialization process.

11. Robert L. Kahn et al., *Organizational Stress* (New York: John Wiley & Sons, 1964), pp. 57–71. For reviews of this literature, see Mary Van Sell, Arthur P. Brief, and Randall S. Schuler, "Role Conflict and Role Ambiguity: Integration of the Literature and Directions for Future Research," *Human Relations* 34 (January 1981), pp. 43–71; Cynthia D. Fisher and Richard Gitelson, "A Meta-Analysis of the Correlates of Role Conflict and Ambiguity," *Journal of Applied Psychology* 68 (May 1983), pp. 320–33. See also Rosemary Ramsey Lagace, "Role Stress Differences between Salesmen and Saleswomen:

Effect on Job Satisfaction and Performance," *Psychological Reports* 62 (June 1988), pp. 815–25; Jagdip Singh, "Boundary Role Ambiguity: Facets, Determinants, and Impacts," *Journal of Marketing* 57 (April 1993), pp. 11–31.

12. Product design is only one of the areas where there is often conflict between marketing and engineering departments with respect to how best to serve customers' needs. See J. Donald Weinrauch and Richard Anderson, "Conflicts between Engineering and Marketing Units," *Industrial Marketing Management* 11 (October 1982), pp. 291–301. Product managers also serve as boundary spanners, which creates role conflict for them. See Steven Lysonski and Arch G. Woodside, "Boundary Role Spanning Behavior, Conflicts and Performance of Industrial Product Managers," *Journal of Product Innovation Management* 6 (September 1989), pp. 169–84.

13. Weinrauch and Anderson, "Conflicts between Engineering and Marketing Units," pp. 291–301.

14. Ibid., p. 292.

15. Neil M. Ford, Orville C. Walker, Jr., and Gilbert A. Churchill, Jr., "Expectation-Specific Measures of the Intersender Conflict and Role Ambiguity Experienced by Industrial Salesmen," *Journal of Business Research* 3 (April 1975), pp. 95–112; Raghu Tadepalli, "Perceptions of Role Stress by Boundary Role Persons: An Empirical Investigation," *Journal of Applied Behavioral Science* 27 (December 1991), pp. 490–514.

16. Neil M. Ford, Orville C. Walker, Jr., and Gilbert A. Churchill, Jr., "The Psychological Consequences of Role Conflict and Ambiguity in the Industrial Salesforce," in *Marketing: 1776–1976 and Beyond,* ed. Kenneth L. Bernhardt (Chicago: American Marketing Association, 1976), pp. 403–8; Douglas N. Behrman and William D. Perrault, Jr., "A Role Stress Model of the Performance and Satisfaction of Industrial Salespeople," *Journal of Marketing* 48 (Fall 1984), pp. 9–21; R. Kenneth Teas, "Supervisory Behavior, Role Stress, and the Job Satisfaction of Industrial Salespeople," *Journal of Marketing Research* 20 (February 1983), pp. 84–91.

17. Kahn et al., *Organizational Stress,* pp. 72–95; Ajay K. Kohli, "Some Unexplored Supervisory Behaviors and Their Influence on Salespeople's Role Clarity, Specific Self-Esteem, Job Satisfaction and Motivation," *Journal of Marketing Research* 22 (November 1985), pp. 424–33; Louis W. Fry, Charles M. Futrell, A. Parasuraman, and Margaret Chmielewski, "An Analysis of Alternate Causal Models of Salesperson Role Perceptions and Work Related Attitudes," *Journal of Marketing Research* 23 (May 1986), pp. 153–63; Jeffrey Sager, "A Structural Model Depicting Salespeople's Job Stress," *Journal of the Academy of Marketing Science* 22 (Winter 1994), pp. 74–84.

18. James H. Donnelly, Jr., and John M. Ivancevich, "Role Clarity and the Salesman," *Journal of Marketing* 39 (January 1975), pp. 71–74; R. Kenneth Teas, John G. Wacker, and R. Eugene Hughes, "A Path Analysis of Causes and Consequences of Salespeople's Perceptions of Role Clarity," *Journal of Marketing Research* 16 (August 1979), pp. 355–69; Richard P. Bagozzi, "The Nature and Causes of Self-Esteem, Performance, and Satisfaction in the Sales Force: A Structural Equation Approach," *Journal of Business* 53 (1980), pp. 315–31; Gary K. Rhoads, Jagdip Singh, and Phillips W. Goodell, "The Multiple Dimensions of Role Ambiguity and Their Impact upon

Psychological and Behavioral Outcomes of Industrial Salespeople," *Journal of Personal Selling and Sales Management* 14 (Summer 1994), pp. 1–24.

19. Charles M. Futrell and A. Parasuraman, "The Relationship of Satisfaction and Performance to Salesforce Turnover," *Journal of Marketing* 48 (Fall 1984), pp. 33–40; George H. Lucas, Jr., et al., "An Empirical Study of Salesforce Turnover," *Journal of Marketing* 51 (July 1987), pp. 34–59.

20. Richard P. Bagozzi, "Salesforce Performance and Satisfaction as a Function of Individual Difference, Interpersonal, and Situational Factors," *Journal of Marketing Research* 15 (November 1978), pp. 517–31; Douglas N. Behrman, William J. Bigoness, and William D. Perreault, Jr., "Sources of Job-Related Ambiguity and Their Consequences upon Salesperson Job Satisfaction and Performance," *Management Science* 27 (November 1981), pp. 1,246–60.

21. Lawrence B. Chonko, Roy D. Howell, and Danny N. Bellenger, "Consequence in Sales Force Evaluation: Relation to Sales Force Perceptions of Conflict and Ambiguity," *Journal of Personal Selling and Sales Management* 6 (May 1986), pp. 35–48.

22. Orville C. Walker, Jr., Gilbert A. Churchill, Jr., and Neil M. Ford, "Organizational Determinants of the Role Conflict and Ambiguity Experienced by Industrial Salesmen," *Journal of Marketing* 39 (January 1975), pp. 32–39.

23. Ibid., Kohli, "Some Unexplored Supervisory Behaviors."

24. Lawrence B. Chonko, "The Relationship of Span of Control to Sales Representatives, Experienced Role Conflict and Role Ambiguity," *Academy of Management Journal* 25 (June 1982), pp. 452–56; Linda S. Hartenian, Farrand J. Hadaway, and Gordon J. Badovick, "Antecedents and Consequences of Role Perceptions: A Path Analytic Approach," *Journal of Applied Business Research* 10 (Spring 1994), pp. 40–50.

25. Paul Busch, "The Sales Manager's Bases of Social Power and Influence upon the Sales Force," *Journal of Marketing* 44 (Summer 1980), pp. 91–101; and Ronald E. Michaels, William L. Cron, Alan J. Dubinsky, and Erich A. Joachimsthaler, "Influence of Formalization on the Organizational Commitment and Work Alienation of Salespeople and Industrial Buyers," *Journal of Marketing Research* 25 (November 1988), pp. 376–83.

26. Role ambiguity and role conflict can also influence a salesperson's motivation to work. See Pradeep K. Tyagi, "The Effects of Stressful Organizational Conditions on Salesperson Work Motivation," *Journal of the Academy of Marketing Science* 13 (Winter/Spring 1985), pp. 290–309; Susan M. Keaveney and James E. Nelson, "Coping with Organizational Role Stress: Intrinsic Motivational Orientation, Perceived Role Benefits and Psychological Withdrawal," *Journal of the Academy of Marketing Science* 21 (Spring 1993), pp. 113–24.

27. For studies investigating the frequency with which salespeople engage in various activities and the importance of these activities to their success, see William C. Moncrief, "Selling Activity and Sales Position Taxonomies for Industrial Salesforces," *Journal of Marketing Research* 23 (August 1986), pp. 261–70; William C. Moncrief, "Ten Key Activities of Industrial Salespeople," *Industrial Marketing Management* 15 (November 1986), pp. 309–17; Robert E. Hite and Joseph A. Bellizzi,

"Differences in the Importance of Selling Techniques between Consumer and Industrial Salespeople," *Journal of Personal Selling and Sales Management* 5 (November 1985), pp. 19–30.

28. Terry Deutscher, Judith Marshall, and David Burgoyne, "The Process of Obtaining New Accounts," *Industrial Marketing Management* 11 (July 1982), pp. 173–81. See also Douglas M. Lambert, Howard Marmorstein, and Arun Sharma, "The Accuracy of Salespersons' Perceptions of Their Customers: Conceptual Examination and an Empirical Study," *Journal of Personal Selling and Sales Management* 10 (Winter 1990), pp. 1–9.

29. Deutscher et al., "The Process of Obtaining New Accounts," p. 175.

Chapter 9

1. John P. Campbell and Robert D. Pritchard, "Motivation Theory in Industrial and Organizational Psychology," in *Handbook of Industrial and Organizational Psychology,* ed. Marvin D. Dunnette (Chicago: Rand McNally, 1976), p. 65.

2. Theories of motivation can be classified into two groups: content theories and process theories. Major content theories include Maslow's need hierarchy, Alderfer's ERG theory, Herzberg's Hygiene–Motivation theory, and McClelland's theory of learned needs. Many of these content theories are briefly discussed in a later section of this chapter. In addition to expectancy theory, other process theories of motivation include equity theory, attribution theory, and reinforcement theory. For a discussion of both sets of theories and their interrelationships, see James L. Gibson, John M. Ivancevich, and James H. Donnelly, Jr., *Organizations: Behavior, Structure, Processes,* 7th ed. (Homewood, IL: Richard D. Irwin, 1991).

3. Barton A. Weitz, Harish Sujan, and Mita Sujan, "Knowledge, Motivation, and Adaptive Behavior: A Framework for Improving Selling Effectiveness," *Journal of Marketing* (October 1986), pp. 174–91. See also Harish Sujan, "Smarter versus Harder: An Exploratory Attributional Analysis of Salespeople's Motivation," *Journal of Marketing Research* (February 1986), pp. 41–49.

4. The argument is often advanced, for example, that salespeople should be given pricing flexibility in that they are closest to the customers and have the best perspective on the price that will be needed to make the sales. Interestingly, one study that investigated the admonition found that among a sample of 108 firms, those firms that gave salespeople the highest degree of pricing authority generated the lowest sales and profit performance. See P. Ronald Stephenson, William L. Cron, and Gary L. Frazier, "Delegating Pricing Authority in the Sales Force: The Effects on Sales and Profit Performance," *Journal of Marketing* (Spring 1979), pp. 21–28. See also Richard Kern, "Letting Your Salespeople Set Prices (Sort of)," *Sales and Marketing Management* (August 1989), pp. 44–49.

5. Abraham K. Korma, "Expectanices as Determinants of Performance," *Journal of Applied Psychology* 55 (1971), pp. 218–22. Edward E. Lawler III, "Job Attitudes and Employee Motivation: Theory, Research and Practice," *Personnel Psychology* 23 (1970), pp. 223–37; Roy D. Howell, Danny N. Bellenger, and James B. Wilcox, "Self-Esteem, Role Stress, and Job Satisfaction among Marketing Managers," *Journal of Business Research* (February 1987), pp. 71–84. See also Jeffrey

Sager, Junsub Yi, and Charles M. Futrell, "A Model of Depicting Salesperson's Perceptions," *Journal of Personal Selling and Sales Management* (Summer 1998), pp. 1–22.

6. Rosemary Lagace, Stephen B. Castleberry, and Rick Ridnour, "An Exploratory Salesforce Study of the Relationship between Lead–Member Exchange and Motivation, Role Stress, and Manager Evaluation," *Journal of Applied Business Research* (Fall 1993), pp. 110–19.

7. Edward E. Lawler III, *Pay and Organizational Effectiveness: A Psychological View* (New York: McGraw–Hill, 1971).

8. Alfie Kohn, *Punished by Rewards* (New York: Houghton-Mifflin, 1993). Also see William Keenan, Jr., "Breaking with Tradition," *Sales & Marketing Management* (June 1994), pp. 94–99.

9. For example, see Thomas N. Ingram and Danny N. Bellenger, "Personal and Organizational Variables: Their Relative Effect on Reward Valences of Industrial Salespeople," *Journal of Marketing Research* (May 1983), pp. 198–205; Neil M. Ford, Orville C. Walker, Jr., and Gilbert A. Churchill, Jr., "Differences in the Attractiveness of Alternative Rewards among Industrial Salespeople: Additional Evidence," *Journal of Business Research* (April 1985), pp. 123–38; and Lawrence B. Chonko, John F. Tanner, Jr., and William A. Weeks, "Reward Preferences of Salespeople," *Journal of Personal Selling and Sales Management* (Summer 1992), pp. 67–76; Thomas E. DeCarlo, R. Kenneth Teas, and James C. McElroy, "Salesperson Performance Attribution and Processes and Formation of Expectancy Estimates," *Journal of Personal Selling and Sales Management* (Summer 1997), pp. 1–17. For an interesting cross-cultural comparison of reward valences—as well as expectancy and instrumentality perceptions—across salespeople in the United States, Korea, and Japan, see Alan J. Dubinsky, Masaaki Kotabe, Chae Un Lim, and Ronald E. Michaels, "Differences in Motivational Perceptions among U.S., Japanese, and Korean Sales Personnel," *Journal of Business Research* 30 (1994), pp. 175–85.

10. Gilbert A. Churchill, Jr., Neil M. Ford, and Orville C. Walker, Jr., *Motivating the Industrial Salesforce: The Attractiveness of Alternvative Rewards,* Report #76-115 (Cambridge, MA: The Marketing Science Institute, 1976).

11. For a detailed discussion of a large number of such studies, see Campbell and Pritchard, "Motivation Theory," pp. 63–130. For a study that tests the model with a sample of salespeople, see Gilbert A. Churchill, Jr., Neil M. Ford, and Orville C. Walker, Jr., "Predicting a Salesperson's Job Effort and Performance: Theoretical, Empirical, and Methodological Considerations," in *Sales Management: New Developments from Behavioral and Decision Model Research,* ed. Richard P. Bagozzi (Cambridge, MA: Marketing Science Institute, 1979), pp. 3–39.

12. Campbell and Pritchard, "Motivation Theory." For a study focused on industrial salespeople, see Richard L. Oliver, "Expectancy Theory Predictions of Salesmen's Performance," *Journal of Marketing Research* (August 1974), pp. 243–53.

13. Abraham H. Maslow, *Motivation and Personality,* 2d ed. (New York: Harper & Row, 1970).

14. Frederick Herzberg, Bernard Mauser, and Barbara Snyderman, *The Motivation to Work,* 2d ed. (New York: John Wiley & Sons, 1959). See also Robert Berl, Terry Powell, and Nicholas C.

Williamson, "Industrial Salesforce Satisfaction and Performance with Herzberg's Theory," *Industrial Marketing Management* (February 1984), pp. 11–19; and David D. Shipley and Julia A. Kiely, "Industrial Salesforce Motivation and Herzberg's Dual Factor Theory: A U.K. Perspective," *Journal of Personal Selling and Sales Management* (May 1986), pp. 9–16.

15. Clayton P. Alderfer, "An Empirical Test of a New Theory of Human Needs," *Organizational Behavior and Human Performance* 4 (1969), pp. 142–75.

16. Gilbert A. Churchill, Jr., Neil M. Ford, and Orville C. Walker, Jr., "Personal Characteristics of Salespeople and the Attractiveness of Alternative Rewards," *Journal of Business Research* (1979), pp. 25–50; Ford, Walker, and Churchill, "Differences in the Attractiveness of Alternative Rewards"; Ingram and Bellenger, "Personal and Organizational Variables"; and Robert L. Berl, Nicholas C. Williamson, and Terry Powell, "Industrial Salesforce Motivation: A Critique and Test of Maslow's Hierarchy of Needs," *Journal of Personal Selling and Sales Management* (May 1984), pp. 33–39.

17. See Lawler, *Pay and Organizational Effectiveness,* especially pp. 46–59, and the same references as in note 13.

18. Wesley J. Johnson and Keysuk Kim, "Performance, Attribution, and Expectancy Linkages in Personal Selling," *Journal of Marketing* (October 1994), pp. 68–81.

19. David C. McClelland, John W. Atkinson, Russell A. Clark, and Edgar L. Lowell, *The Achievement Motive* (New York: Appleton–Century–Crofts, 1953); and John W. Atkinson, *An Introduction to Motivation* (Princeton, NJ: Van Nostrand, 1964).

20. See, for example, E.E. Lawler III, "Job Attitudes and Employee Motivation: Theory, Research, and Practice," *Personnel Psychology* 23 (1970), pp. 223–37; or Julian B. Rotter, "Generalized Expectancies for Internal versus External Control of Reinforcement," *Psychological Monographs: General and Applied* 80 (1966).

21. Ibid.

22. Abraham K. Korman, "Expectancies as Determinants of Performance," *Journal of Applied Psychology* 55 (1971), pp. 218–22; and Lawler, "Job Attitudes," pp. 223–37.

23. Ingram and Bellenger, "Personal and Organizational Variables," pp. 203–4.

24. R. Kenneth Teas and James C. McElroy, "Causal Attributions and Expectancy Estimates: A Framework for Understanding the Dynamics of Salesforce Motivation," *Journal of Marketing* (January 1986), pp. 75–86; and Johnson and Kim, "Performance, Attribution, and Expectancy Linkages," pp. 68–81.

25. See also Harish Sujan, "Smarter versus Harder," pp. 41–49.

26. The following discussion is largely based on material found in William L. Cron, "Industrial Salesperson Development: A Career Stages Perspective," *Journal of Marketing* (Fall 1984), pp. 41–52; William L. Cron and John W. Slocum, Jr., "The Influence of Career Stages on Salespeople's Job Attitudes, Work Perceptions, and Performance," *Journal of Marketing Research* (May 1986), pp. 119–29; William L. Cron, Alan J. Dubinsky, and Ronald E. Michaels, "The Influence of Career Stages on Components of Salesperson Motivation," *Journal of Marketing* (January 1988), pp. 78–92; and William L. Cron,

Ellen F. Jackofsky, and John W. Slocum, Jr., "Job Performance and Attitudes of Disengagement Stage Salespeople Who Are about to Retire," *Journal of Personal Selling and Sales Management* (Spring 1993), pp. 1–13.

27. Robin T. Peterson, "Beyond the Plateau," *Sales & Marketing Management* (July 1993), pp. 78–82. Also see William Keenan, Jr., "The Nagging Problem of the Plateaued Salesperson," *Sales & Marketing Management* (March 1989), pp. 36–41.

28. Robert House, "A Path–Goal Theory of Leadership Effectiveness," *Administrative Science Quarterly* (1971), pp. 321–39.

29. Bill Kelley, "How Much Help Does a Salesperson Need?" *Sales & Marketing Management* (May 1989), pp. 32–34.

30. Gilbert A. Churchill, Jr., Neil M. Ford, and Orville C. Walker, Jr., "Organizational Climate and Job Satisfaction in the Sales Force," *Journal of Marketing Research* (November 1976), pp. 323–32; and Pradeep K. Tyagi, "Relative Importance of Key Job Dimensions and Leadership Behaviors in Motivating Salesperson Work Performance," *Journal of Marketing* (Summer 1985), pp. 76–86. See also Susan K. DelVecchio, "The Quality of Salesperson–Manager Relationship: The Effect of Latitude, Loyalty and Competence," *Journal of Personal Selling and Sales Management* (Winter 1998), pp. 31–48.

31. Ingram and Bellenger, "Personal and Organizational Variables."

Chapter 10

1. Arthur Bragg, "Are Good Salespeople Born or Made?" *Sales & Marketing Management* (September 1988), pp. 74–78.

2. Ibid., p. 74.

3. Gilbert A. Churchill, Jr., Neil M. Ford, Steven W. Hartley, and Orville C. Walker, Jr., "The Determinants of Salesperson Performance: A Meta-Analysis," *Journal of Marketing Research* (May 1985), pp. 103–18. See also Neil M. Ford, Orville C. Walker, Jr., and Gilbert A. Churchill, Jr., "Selecting Successful Salespeople: A Meta-Analysis of Biographical and Psychological Selection Criteria," in *Review of Marketing,* ed. Michael J. Houston (Chicago: American Marketing Association, 1988), pp. 90–131. See also Goutam Challagalla and Tasaddug A. Shervani, "Dimensions and Types of Supervisory Control: Effects on Sales Performance and Satisfaction," *Journal of Marketing* (January 1996), pp. 47–60.

4. Christen P. Heide, *Dartnell's 28th Sales Force Compensation Survey 1994–95* (Chicago: The Dartnell Corporation, 1994), p. 189.

5. Jeffrey K. Sager, "Recruiting and Retaining Committed Salespeople," *Industrial Marketing Management* (May 1991), pp. 99–103.

6. Heide, *Dartnell's 28th Sales Force Compensation Survey 1994–95,* p. 143.

7. Bragg, "Are Good Salespeople Born or Made?" pp. 74–78.

8. Stan Moss, "What Sales Executives Look for in New Salespeople," *Sales & Marketing Management* (March 1978), pp. 43–48; Thomas Rollins, "How to Tell Competent Salespeople from the Other Kind," *Sales & Marketing Management* (September 1990), pp. 116–17, 145–46; and Bristol Voss, "Six Steps to Better Hires," *Sales & Marketing Management* (June 1993), pp. 44–48.

9. Ford et al., "Selecting Successful Salespeople," pp. 90–131.

10. For a description of the various tests and techniques commonly used to measure such variables, see ibid. Also see Seymour Adler, "Personality Tests for Salesforce Selection: Worth a Fresh Look," *Review of Business* (Summer 1994), pp. 27–31.

11. Eleanore Swartz, "Women in Sales: Will the Walls Come Tumbling Down?" *Sales Management* (August 15, 1969), pp. 39–40.

12. For a detailed review of such issues, see C. David Shepherd and James C. Heartfield, "Discrimination Issues in the Selection of Salespeople: A Review and Managerial Suggestions," *Journal of Personal Selling and Sales Management* (Fall 1991), pp. 67–75.

13. Bobbi Linkemer, "Women in Sales: What Do They Really Want?" *Sales & Marketing Management* (January 1989), pp. 61–65.

14. John E. Swan, David R. Rink, G.E. Kiser, and Warren S. Martin, "Industrial Buyer Image of the Saleswomen," *Journal of Marketing* (Winter 1984), pp. 110–16. See also Myron Gable and B.J. Reed, "The Current Status of Women in Professional Selling," *Journal of Personal Selling and Sales Management* (May 1987), pp. 33–39; Bill Kelley, "Selling in a Man's World," *Sales & Marketing Management* (January 1991), pp. 28–35; and Nancy Arnott, "It's a Woman's World," *Sales & Marketing Management* (March 1995), pp 54–59; and Lucette B. Comer, J.A.F. Nicholls, and Leslie J. Vermillion, "Diversity in the Sales Force: Problems and Challenges," *Journal of Personal Selling and Sales Management* (Fall 1998), pp. 1–20.

15. Lucette B. Comer and Marvin A. Jolson, "Perceptions of Gender Stereotypic Behavior: An Exploratory Study of Women in Selling," *Journal of Personal Selling and Sales Management* (Winter 1991), pp. 43–59. See also Judy A. Siguaw and Earl D. Honeycutt, Jr., "An Examination of Gender Differences in Selling Behaviors and Job Attitudes," *Industrial Marketing Management* 24 (1995), pp. 45–52.

16. Franklin Evans, "Selling as a Dyadic Relationship—A New Approach," *American Behavioral Scientist* (May 1963), pp. 76–79.

17. Gilbert A. Churchill, Jr., Robert H. Collins, and William A. Strang, "Should Retail Salespersons Be Similar to Their Customers?" *Journal of Retailing* (Fall 1975), pp. 29–42. See also Barton A. Weitz, "Effectiveness in Sales Interactions: A Contingency Framework," *Journal of Marketing* (Winter 1981), pp. 85–103.

18. Rene Y. Darmon, "Where Do the Best Sales Force Profit Producers Come From?" *Journal of Personal Selling and Sales Management* (Summer 1993), pp. 17–29.

19. Adler, "Personality Tests for Salesforce Selection."

20. While another study examines job-specific abilities, it focuses on only one type of sales job—missionary selling. See Dan C. Weilbaker, "The Identification of Selling Abilities Needed for Missionary Type Sales," *Journal of Personal Selling and Sales Management* (Summer 1990), pp. 45–58.

21. Derek A. Newton, "Get the Most out of Your Salesforce," *Harvard Business Review* (September–October 1969), pp. 130–43. See also Weilbaker, "The Identification of Selling Abilities."

Chapter 11

1. Thomas Rollins, "How to Tell Competent Salespeople from the Other Kind," *Sales & Marketing Management* (September 1990), pp. 116–18, 145–46.

2. Ibid. See also Timothy J. Trow, "The Secret of a Good Hire: Profiling," *Sales & Marketing Management* (May 1990), pp. 44–55.

3. For a detailed discussion of critical job dimensions, see Phil Faris, "No More Winging It," *Sales & Marketing Management* (August 1986), pp. 88–91.

4. Rene Y. Darmon and S.J. Shapiro, "Sales Recruiting—A Major Area of Underinvestment," *Industrial Marketing Management* 9 (1980), pp. 47–51; and Julia Lawlor, "Highly Classified," *Sales & Marketing Management* (March 1995), pp. 75–85; and Barry Farber, "Start at the Beginning," *Sales & Marketing Management* (March 1996), pp. 24–25.

5. George J. Avlonitis, Kevin A. Boyle, and A.G. Kouremenos, "Matching Salesmen to the Selling Job," *Industrial Marketing Management* 15 (1986), pp. 45–54. See also Lawlor, "Highly Classified," p. 84.

6. Marianne Matthews, "If Your Ads Aren't Pulling Top Sales Talent . . . ," *Sales & Marketing Management* (February 1990), pp. 73–79.

7. Ibid.

8. Arthur Bragg, "Shell-Shocked on the Battlefield of Selling," *Sales & Marketing Management* (July 1990), pp. 52–58; and "Postcards from the Class of '95," *Sales & Marketing Management* (June 1995), pp. 73–77.

9. For a detailed review of these—as well as some less commonly used selection tools, see E. James Randall and Cindy H. Randall, "Review of Salesperson Selection Techniques and Criteria: A Managerial Approach," *International Journal of Research in Marketing* 7 (1990), pp. 81–95.

10. John E. Hunter and R.F. Hunter, "Validity and Utility of Alternative Predictors of Job Performance," *Psychological Bulletin* 96 (1984), pp. 72–98. For a discussion of the validity of different selection procedures as applied to the evaluation of salespeople, see Neil M. Ford, Orville C. Walker, Jr., and Gilbert A. Churchill, Jr., "Selecting Successful Salespeople: A Meta-Analysis of Biographical and Psychological Selection Criteria," in *Review of Marketing,* ed. Michael J. Houston (Chicago: American Marketing Association, 1988), pp. 90–131.

11. Myron Gable, Charles Hollon, and Frank Dangello, "Increasing the Utility of the Application Blank: Relationship between Job Application Information and Subsequent Performance and Turnover of Salespeople," *Journal of Personal Selling and Sales Management* (Summer 1992), pp. 39–55.

12. For a discussion of how an interviewer can obtain more detailed information through probing questions, see John H. Rose, *How to Recruit, Interview, and Select Prospective Sales Representatives* (Orlando, FL: National Society of Sales Training Executives, 1981); and Lawlor, "Highly Classified."

13. "How Fredrick's McElveen Finds Super Salesmen," *Sales Management* (August 5, 1974), p. 4. Also see William Keenan, Jr., "Who Has the Right Stuff?" *Sales & Marketing Management* (August 1993), pp. 28–29.

14. Arthur Bragg, "Checking References," *Sales & Marketing Management* (November 1990), pp. 68–71.

15. C. David Shepherd and James C. Heartfield, "Discrimination Issues in the Selection of Salespeople: A Review and Managerial Suggestions," *Journal of Personal Selling and Sales Management* (Fall 1991), p. 71. See also Allison Lucas, "Race Matters," *Sales and Marketing Management* (September 1996), pp. 50–62.

16. Seymour Adler, "Personality Tests for Salesforce Selection: Worth a Fresh Look," *Review of Business* (Summer 1994), pp. 27–31.

17. Richard Kern, "IQ Tests for Salesmen Make a Comeback," *Sales & Marketing Management* (April 1988), pp. 42–46; and Richard Nelson, "Maybe It's Time to Take Another Look at Tests as a Selection Tool," *Journal of Personal Selling and Sales Management* (August 1987), pp. 33–38.

18. Leon E. Wynter, "Would Rights Bill Boost Volume of Job Suits?" *The Wall Street Journal* (August 22, 1991), p. B1.

19. For a detailed discussion of the procedures required to validate employment tests, see *Principles for the Validation and Use of Personnel Selection Procedures* (College Park, MD: Society for Industrial and Organizational Psychology, Inc., 1987).

Chapter 12

1. Frank Cespedes, *Organizing and Implementing the Marketing Effort: Text and Cases* (Reading, MA: Addison–Wesley, 1991), pp. 87–88.

2. Willian Keenan, Jr., "American's Best Sales Managers," *Sales & Marketing Management* (August 1995), pp. 35–44.

3. Jack Falvey, "Compare Football to Selling? Nonsense," *Sales & Marketing Management* (January 1989), pp. 15, 17.

4. Keenan, "America's Best Sales Managers," p. 40.

5. "Keep on Trucking," *Sales & Marketing Management* (June 1995), pp. 17–19.

6. "What's the Problem with Sales Training?" *Training Today* (March 1990), p. 16.

7. James F. Evered, "Measuring Sales Training Effectiveness," *Sales & Marketing Management* (February 1988), pp. 9–12, 16–18. See also Alan J. Dubinsky "Sales Training and Education: Some Assumptions about the Effectiveness of Sales Training," *Journal of Personal Selling and Sales Management* (Summer 1996), pp. 67–76.

8. The following discussion is based to a large extent on Gene Hahne, "Creating Credibility for Your Sales Training," *Training and Development Journal* (November 1981), pp. 34–38.

9. Ibid., p. 38.

10. *Dartnell's 30th Sales Force Compensation Survey: 1998–1999* (Chicago: Dartnell Corp., 1999), p. 142.

11. Ibid., p. 144.

12. William Keenan, Jr., "Are You Overspending on Training?" *Sales & Marketing Management* (January 1990), pp 36–40.

13. H. Robert Dodge, *Field Sales Management* (Dallas: Business Publications, Inc., 1973), p. 226.

14. The following discussion is based to a large extent on "Study Reveals Sales Training Needs of Business Markets," *Marketing News* (March 13, 1989), p. 6.

15. Greg Burns, "Life Insurance: Bogus Bait to Make You Switch," *Business Week* (November 27, 1995), p. 136.

16. Minda Zetlin, "Kicking the Discount Habit: Teach Your Salespeople to Stop Leaving Money on the Table," *Sales & Marketing Management* (May 1994), pp. 102–6.

17. Edward Roberts, "Training Trade Show Salespeople How Caterpillar Does It," *Business Marketing* (June 1988), pp. 70, 72–73.

18. Priscilla Donovan, "Selling Right and Left," *Sales & Marketing Management* (June 3, 1985), pp. 62–63.

19. Alan J. Zaremba, "Beyond Body Language," *Business Marketing* (March 1987), pp. 133–34.

20. *Dartnell's 30th Sales Force Compensation Survey: 1998–1999,* p. 140.

21. Jack Falvey, "Forget the Sharks: Swim with Your Salespeople," *Sales & Marketing Management* (November 1990), p. 8.

22. Ibid.

23. Garry J. DeRose and Janet McLaughlin, "Outsourcing through Partnerships," *Training & Development* (October 1995), pp. 51–55.

24. Jack Falvey, "Myths of Sales Training," *Sales & Marketing Management* (June 1978), p. 80.

25. Ibid., p. 78.

26. Ibid., p. 64.

27. Al Urbanski, "Electronic Training May Be in Your Future," *Sales & Marketing Management* (March 1988), pp. 46, 48.

28. Patricia Sellers, "How IBM Teaches Techies to Sell," *Fortune* (June 6, 1988), pp. 141–42, 146.

29. For an excellent discussion of expert systems, see Arlyn R. Rubash, Rawlie R. Sullivan, and Paul H. Herzog, "Microcomputer Applications: Accelerating the Salesperson Learning Curve," *Journal of Personal Selling and Sales Management* (November 1988), pp. 77–82.

30. Urbanski, "Electronic Training May Be in Your Future," p. 46.

31. Diane Lynn Kastiel, "Psyching Out Buyers with AI," *Business Marketing* (March 1987), pp. 72–74.

32. Barton A. Weitz, Harish Sujan, and Mita Sujan, "Knowledge, Motivation, and Adaptive Behavior: A Framework for Improving Selling Effectiveness," *Journal of Marketing* (October 1986), pp. 174–91.

33. The following discussion is based to a large extent on Thomas W. Leigh and Patrick McGraw, "Mapping the Procedureal Knowledge of Industrial Sales Personnel: A Script-Theoretic Investigation," *Journal of Marketing* (January 1989), pp. 16–34.

34. David M. Szymanski, "Explaining Differences in Selling Effectiveness: A Knowledge Structure Approach to Examining the Ability of Sales Personnel to Prospect for Clients," unpublished doctoral dissertation, School of Business, University of Wisconsin–Madison, 1987.

35. David M. Szymanski, "Determinants of Selling Effectiveness: The Imporance of Declarative Knowledge to the Personal Selling Concept," *Journal of Marketing* (January 1988), pp. 64–77.

36. Robert C. Erffmeyer, K. Randall Russ, and Joseph F. Hair, Jr., "Needs Assessment and Evaluation in Sales-Training

Programs," *Journal of Personal Selling & Sales Management* 11 (Winter 1991), pp. 17–31.

37. Earl D. Honeycutt and Thomas H. Stevenson, "Evaluating Sales Training Programs," *Industrial Marketing Management* (August 1989), pp. 215–22.

38. Beverly Geber, "Does Training Make a Difference? Prove It!" *Training* (March 1995), pp. 27–34.

39. Rick Mendoza, "There's a Payoff?" *Sales & Marketing Management* (June 1995), pp. 64–71.

40. Ibid., p. 69.

Chapter 13

1. David M. Gardner and Kenneth M. Rowland, "A Self-Tailored Approach to Incentives," *Personnel Journal* (November 1979), pp 907–12; and Todd J. Englander, "Let Salespeople Design Your Incentive Plan," *Sales & Marketing Management* (September 1991), pp. 155–56.

2. Ron Donoho, "Pay Plans Get Low Marks," *Sales & Marketing Management* (December 1994), pp. 11–12.

3. For example, see Regina Eisman, "Justifying Your Incentive Program," *Sales & Marketing Management* (April 1993), pp. 43–52.

4. Andy Cohen, "Right on Target," *Sales & Marketing Management* (December 1994), pp. 59–63.

5. Arun Sharma and Dan Sarel, "The Impact of Customer Satisfaction Based Incentive Systems on Salespeople's Customer Service Response: An Empirical Study," *Journal of Personal Selling and Sales Management* (Summer 1995), pp. 17–29.

6. Jerome A. Colletti and Linda J. Mahoney, "Should You Pay Your Sales Force for Customer Satisfaction?" *Perspectives in Total Compensation* 2, no. 11 (Scottsdale, AZ: American Compensation Association, November 1991); Alan M. Johnson, "The Incentive Program's Contribution to Quality," *Sales & Marketing Management* (April 1991), pp. 91–93; Barry Farber and Joyce Wycoff, "Customer Service: Evolution and Revolution," *Sales & Marketing Management* (May 1991), pp. 44–51; and Cohen, "Right on Target."

7. Englander, "Let Salespeople Design Your Incentive Plan."

8. Rene Y. Darmon, "Setting Sales Quotas with Conjoint Analysis," *Journal of Marketing Research* (February 1979), pp. 133–40.

9. Gregg Cebrzynski, "Sales Compensation Survey Shows Some 'Dramatic' Findings," *Marketing News* (November 7, 1986), p. 32.

10. "What Happens When a Salesperson Earns More than His Manager?" *Sales & Marketing Management* (May 1990), pp. 32–34.

11. Rene Y. Darmon, "Salesmen's Responses to Financial Incentives," *Journal of Marketing Research* (July 1974), pp. 39–46.

12. William A. O'Connell and William Keenan, Jr., "The Shape of Things to Come," *Sales & Marketing Management* (January 1990), pp. 36–41.

13. William Keenan, Jr., "What Salespeople Are Paid," *Sales & Marketing Management* (February 1995), pp. 30–32.

14. Amiya K. Basu, Rajiv Lal, V. Srinivasan, and Richard Staelin,

"Sales Compensation Plans: An Agency Theoretic Perspective," *Marketing Science* (Fall 1985), pp. 267–91; George John and Barton Weitz, "Salesforce Compensation: An Empirical Investigation of Factors Related to the Use of Salary versus Incentive Compensation," *Journal of Marketing Research* (February 1989), pp. 1–14; and Richard L. Oliver and Barton Weitz, "The Effects of Risk Preference, Uncertainty, and Incentive Compensation on Salesperson Motivation," Report Number 91–104 (Cambridge, MA: Marketing Science Institute, 1991). For a more detailed review of agency theory propositions and research concerning the appropriate conditions for the use of salary versus incentive compensation, see Mark Bergen, Shantanu Dutta, and Orville C. Walker, Jr., "Agency Relationships in Marketing: A Review of the Applications and Implications of Agency and Related Theories," *Journal of Marketing* (July 1992), pp. 1–24.

15. For a more detailed discussion of this and other potential problems with drawing accounts, see Rick Dogen, "Don't Be Too Quick on the Draw," *Sales & Marketing Management* (September 1988), pp. 59–62; and Joanne Dahm, "Using Draws Wisely in Your Sales Compensation Plan," *Sales & Marketing Management* (August 1990), pp. 92–93. See also Leslie M. Fine and Janice R. Franke, "Legal Aspects of Salesperson Commission Payments: Implications for the Implementation of Commission Sales Programs," *Journal of Personal Selling and Sales Management* (Winter 1995), pp. 53–68.

16. Richard C. Smyth and Matthew J. Murphy, *Compensating and Motivating Salesmen* (New York: American Management Association, 1969), p. 58.

17. Jerry McAdams, "Rewarding Sales and Marketing Performance," *Management Review* (April 1987), pp. 33–38.

18. Charles A. Peck, *Compensating Field Sales Representatives*, Report No. 828 (New York: The Conference Board, 1982), p. 14.

19. Lesley Barnes, "Finding the Best Sales Compensation Plan," *Sales & Marketing Management* (August 1986), pp. 46–49; and William Keenan, Jr., "Is Your Pay Plan Putting the Squeeze on Top Performers?" *Sales & Marketing Management* (January 1990), pp. 74–75.

20. Donoho, "Pay Plans Get Low Marks."

21. Arun Sharma, "Customer Satisfaction-Based Incentive Systems: Some Managerial and Salesperson Considerations," *Journal of Personal Selling and Sales Management* (Spring 1997), pp. 61–70.

22. Christen P. Heide, *Dartnell's 28th Sales Force Compensation Survey* (Chicago: The Dartnell Corporation, 1994), p. 165.

23. Michelle Marchetti, "Are Your Salespeople Green with Envy?," *Sales & Marketing Management* (March 1998), p. 89.

24. *Current Practices in Sales Incentives* (New York: The Alexander Group, Inc., 1988), p. 21.

25. Sally Scanlon, "A New Role for Incentives," *Sales & Marketing Management* (April 7, 1975), p. 43. See also Jack Falvey, "Make 'Em All Winners," *Sales & Marketing Management* (June 1991), pp. 8–11.

26. For a more detailed discussion of some of the pros and cons of sales contests and how management might evaluate the effectiveness of such contests, see Albert R. Wildt, James D. Parker, and Clyde E. Harris, Jr., "Assessing the Impact of Sales Force

Contests: An Application," *Journal of Business Research* 15 (1987), pp. 145–55; Richard F. Beltramini and Kenneth R. Evans, "Salesperson Motivation to Perform and Job Satisfaction: A Sales Contest Participant Perspective," *Journal of Personal Selling and Sales Management* (August 1988), pp. 35–42; and William C. Moncrief, Sandra H. Hart, and Dan H. Robertson, "Sales Contests: A New Look at an Old Management Tool," *Journal of Personal Selling and Sales Management* (November 1988), pp. 55–61.

27. *Current Practices in Sales Incentives,* p. 23.

28. Benson P. Shapiro, *Sales Program Management: Formulation and Implementation* (New York: McGraw–Hill, 1977), p. 309.

29. In addition to the discussion of career stages and valence for promotion in Chapter 14, see William L. Cron, Alan J. Dubinsky, and Ronald E. Michaels, "The Influence of Career Stages on Components of Salesperson Motivation," *Journal of Marketing* (January 1988), pp. 78–92.

30. Bill Kelley, "Recognition Reaps Rewards," *Sales & Marketing Management* (June 1986), pp. 102–5; and Jeanne Greenberg and Herb Greenberg, "Money Isn't Everything," *Sales & Marketing Management* (May 1991), pp. 10–12.

31. Heide, *Dartnell's 28th Sales Force Compensation Survey,* p. 119.

32. Alan J. Dubinsky and Thomas E. Barry, "A Survey of Sales Management Practices," *Industrial Marketing Management* 11 (1982), p. 137.

33. Thomas R. Mott and Tom Peiffer, "Should Sales Compensation Be Based on Where Your Salespeople Live?" *Sales & Marketing Management* (December 1990), pp. 116–17.

Chapter 14

1. For discussion of the concept and conduct of a sales manage-ment audit, see Alan J. Dubinsky and Richard W. Hansen, "The Sales Force Management Audit," *California Management Review* 24 (Winter 1984), pp. 86–95; Jim Cook, "Conducting an Audit of the Sales Organization," in *Sales Manager's Handbook,* ed. Edwin E. Bobrow and Larry Wizenberg (Homewood, IL: Dow Jones–Irwin, 1983), pp. 467–76. For dis-cussion of the issues that arise in a marketing audit, see D. T. Brownlie, "The Marketing Audit: A Metrology and Explanation," *Marketing Intelligence and Planning,* no. 1 (1993), pp. 4–12.

2. John F. Tanner, Jr., and Earl D. Honeycutt, "Reengineering the Sales Force Using the Theory of Constraints," *Industrial Marketing Management* 25 (1996), pp. 1–9.

3. Carolyn Milhiser, "Welded Tube Redirects Business to Distributors," *Metal Center News* 34 (January 1994), pp. 44–49.

4. Meg Cox, "Marketing & Media: Bantam Doubleday Sales Operations Are Restructured," *The Wall Street Journal* (May 9, 1991), p. B6. The role matrix is useful for addressing organiza-tional issues in an audit. See Peter Spillard, Matthew Moriarty, and John Woodthorpe, "The Role Matrix: A Diagnostic Test of Marketing Health," *European Journal of Marketing* 28, no. 7 (1994), pp. 55–76.

5. *Sales Analysis, Studies in Business Policy,* no. 13 (New York: National Industrial Conference Board, 1965), p. 3. This early classic is still one of the best sources on the conduct of a sales analysis.

6. See, for example, E. Jerome McCarthy and William D. Perreault, Jr., *Basic Marketing: A Global–Managerial Approach,* 12th ed. (Burr Ridge, IL: Richard D. Irwin, 1996), p. 635; Charles H. Sevin, *Marketing Productivity Analysis* (New York: McGraw–Hill, 1965), pp. 7–8, another classic; Robert Dwyer and John F. Tanner, Jr., *Business Marketing: Connecting Strategy, Relationships, and Learning* (New York: McGraw–Hill, 1999), chapter 16.

7. Harry D. Wolfe and Gerald Albaum, "Inequality in Products, Orders, Customers, Salesmen, and Sales Territories," *Journal of Business* 35 (July 1962), pp. 298–301. For discussion of how specific firms are increasing profits by attempting to systemati-cally alter the 80:20 principle, see Alan J. Dubinsky and Richard W. Hansen, "Improving Marketing Productivity: The 80/20 Principle Revisited," *California Management Review* 25 (Fall 1982), pp. 96–105; Richard T. Hise and Stanley H. Kratchman, "Developing and Managing a 20/80 Program," *Business Horizons* 30 (September–October 1987), pp. 66–73. For discussion of how to estimate the level of concentration, see David C. Schmittlein, Lee G. Cooper, and Donald G. Morrison, "Truth in Concentration in the Land of (80/20) Laws," *Marketing Science* 12 (Spring 1993), pp. 167–83.

8. Sevin, *Marketing Productivity Analysis,* pp. 7–8.

9. Jon G. Udell and Gene R. Laczniak, *Marketing in an Age of Change* (New York: John Wiley & Sons, 1981), p. 154.

10. Adopted from *Sales Analysis,* p. 68.

11. BPI percentages in Exhibit 14.9 were taken from *Sales & Marketing Management*'s "Survey of Buying Power," which is published each July.

Chapter 15

1. Robert Dwyer and John F. Tanner, Jr., *Business Marketing: Connecting Strategy, Relationships, and Learning* (New York: McGraw–Hill, 1999).

2. See, for example, David Jobber, Graham J. Hooley, and David Shipley, "Organizational Size and Salesforce Evaluation Practices," *Journal of Personal Selling & Sales Management* 13 (Spring 1993), pp. 37–48.

3. For a review of the controversy, as well as a historical perspec-tive on why it exists, see John J. Wheatley, "The Allocation Controversy in Marketing Cost Analysis," *University of Washington Business Review* (Summer 1971), pp. 61–70.

4. Sanford R. Simon, *Managing Marketing Profitability* (New York: American Management Association, 1969), p. 37. All serious students of marketing cost analysis are urged to read this classic book on marketing profitability analysis. It illus-trates the process that should be followed in carrying out a mar-keting cost analysis and the insights gained from doing so with detailed examples. Much of this and the following section rely heavily on this excellent book. See also Robin Cooper and Robert S. Kaplan, "Profit Priorities from Activity-Based Costing," *Harvard Business Review* 69 (May–June 1991), pp. 130–35.

5. Simon, *Managing Marketing profitability,* pp. 37–38.

6. Gayle Rayburn, "Accounting Tools in the Analysis and Control of Marketing Performance," *Industrial Marketing Management* 6 (1977), pp. 175–82.

7. The early "classics" on marketing cost analysis emphasized the

full-cost approach. See J.B. Heckert and R.B. Miner, *Distribution Costs* (New York: Ronald Press, 1953); and D.R. Longman and M. Schiff, *Practical Distribution Cost Analysis* (Homewood, IL: Richard D. Irwin, 1955).

8. See, for example, Simon, *Managing Marketing Profitability;* Charles H. Sevin, *Marketing Productivity Analysis* (New York: McGraw-Hill, 1965); L. Gayle Rayburn, *Financial Tools for Effective Marketing Administration* (New York: American Management Association, 1976); Robin Cooperand Robert S. Kaplan, "Measure Costs Right: Make the Right Decision," *Harvard Business Review* 66 (September–October 1988), pp. 96–103.

9. See Donald W. Jackson and Lonnie L. Ostrom, "Grouping Segments for Profitability Analysis," *MSU Business Topics* 28 (1980), pp. 39–44, for a discussion of the segments that are typically used in a marketing cost analysis. See also Robin Cooper and Robert S. Kaplan, "Activity-Based Systems: Measuring the Cost of Resource Usage," *Accounting Horizons* 6 (September 1992), pp. 1–13. For another method of dividing revenue (customers) into segments, see the discussion on decile analysis in Dwyer and Tanner, chapter 5.

10. Edmund D. McCarry, "Some Functions of Marketing Reconsidered," in *Theory in Marketing,* ed. Reavis Cox and Wroc Anderson (Homewood, IL: Richard D. Irwin, 1950), p. 267.

11. It is, in fact, the most frequently used basis. See Douglas M. Lambert and Jay U. Sterling, "What Types of Profitability Reports Do Marketing Managers Receive?" *Industrial Marketing Management* 16 (November 1987), pp. 295–304.

12. Charles R. Horngren, *Cost Accounting: A Managerial Emphasis,* 2d ed. (Englewood Cliffs, NJ: Prentice Hall, 1967), p. 381. See also Fred Selnes, "Analyzing Marketing Profitability: Sales Are a Dangerous Cost-Driver," *European Journal of Marketing* 26, no. 2 (1992), pp. 15–26.

13. The example is purposely hypothetical to throw the basic process into more bold relief, while at the same time illustrating some common features of such situations. For actual examples, which at times can get quite complex, see Simon, *Managing Marketing Profitability;* Sevin, *Marketing Productivity Analysis;* J.S. Schiff and M. Schiff, *Strategic Management of the Sales Territory* (New York: New York Sales Marketing Executives, 1980); Robert A. Howell and Stephen R. Soucy, "Customer Profitability—As Critical as Product Profitability," *Management Accounting* 72 (October 1990), pp. 43–47.

14. In addition to the references previously cited, see Dana Smith Morgan and Fred W. Morgan, "Marketing Cost Controls: A Survey of Industry Practices," *Industrial Marketing Management* 9 (July 1980), pp. 217–21; Thomas M. Petro, "Profitability: The Fifth 'P' of Marketing," *Basic Marketing* 22 (September 1990), pp. 48–52.

15. The current business literature suggests that firms are attempting to minimize the amount of working capital dedicated to accounts receivable and inventories so as to increase the return to shareholders. See, for example, Shawn Tully, "The Real Key to Creating Wealth," *Fortune* (September 20, 1993), pp. 38–50; Shawn Tully, "Raiding a Company's Hidden Cash," *Fortune* (August 22, 1994), pp. 82–87.

16. J.S. Schiff and Michael Schiff, "New Sales Management Tool: ROAM," *Harvard Business Review* 45 (July–August 1967), pp. 59–66. For the application of ROAM to evaluating sales territories, see J.S. Schiff, "Evaluating the Sales Force as a Business," *Industrial Marketing Management* 12 (April 1983), pp. 131–37. One problem with the return on assets managed measure for evaluating segment performance is that it neglects the firm's opportunity costs for the capital invested in the assets. Residual income analysis is a preferred alternative on these grounds for evaluating the profitability of the personal selling effort. See William L. Cron and Michael Levy, "Sales Management Performance Evaluation: A Residual Income Perspective," *Journal of Personal Selling and Sales Management* 7 (August 1987), pp. 57–66.

17. Alfred P. Sloan, *My Years with General Motors* (Garden City, NY: Doubleday, 1964), p. 140.

Chapter 16

1. This section borrows heavily from the paper by Orville C. Walker, Jr., Gilbert A. Churchill, Jr., and Neil M. Ford, "Where Do We Go from Here: Selected Conceptual and Empirical Issues concerning the Motivation and Performance of the Industrial Sales Force," in *Critical Issues in Sales Management: State-of-the-Art and Future Research Needs,* ed. Gerald Albaum and Gilbert A. Churchill, Jr. (Eugene: College of Business Administration, University of Oregon, 1979), pp. 10–75. See also Ramon A. Avila, Edward F. Fern, and O. Karl Mann, "Unraveling Criteria for Assessing the Performance of Salespeople: A Causal Analysis," *Journal of Personal Selling and Sales Management* 8 (May 1988), pp. 45–54; Richard E. Plank and David A. Reid, "The Mediating Role of Sales Behaviors: An Alternative Perspective of Sales Performance and Effectiveness," *Journal of Personal Selling and Sales Management* 14 (Summer 1994), pp. 43–56.

2. G.P. Latham and K.N. Wexley, *Increasing Productivity through Performance Appraisal* (Reading, MA: Addison-Wesley, 1981); Donald A. Tavers, James B. Hunt, and Ken Bass, "Behavioral Self-Management as a Supplement to External Sales Force Controls," *Journal of Personal Selling and Sales Management* 10 (Summer 1990), pp. 17–28.

3. Bernard Jaworksi, Vlasis Stathakopoulos, and Shanker Krishan, "Control Combinations in Marketing: Conceptual Framework and Empirical Evidence," *Journal of Marketing* 57 (January 1993), pp. 57–69; John S. Hill and Arthur W. Allaway, "How U.S.–Based Companies Manage Sales in Foreign Countries," *Industrial Marketing Management* 22 (February 1993), pp. 7–16.

4. For a discussion of the steps in the selling process, see Barton S. Weitz, Stephen B. Castleberry, and John F. Tanner, *Selling: Building Partnerships,* 3d ed. (New York: Irwin/McGraw–Hill, 1998).

5. The distinction between outcomes and desirable behaviors is an important one. Many performance appraisal systems emphasize the former rather than the latter—a condition that has been labeled the "Achilles heel of the personnel profession." In outcome-based systems, salespeople are held accountable for their results but not for how they achieve the results. However, behavior-based systems address the process of selling rather than simply the outcomes. Behavior-based systems involve much more monitoring and directing of salespeople's activities.

See Erin Anderson and Richard L. Oliver, "Perspectives on Behavior-Based versus Outcome-Based Salesforce Control Systems," *Journal of Marketing* 51 (October 1987), pp. 76–88, for a discussion of the differences in philosophy between the systems and what these philosophical differences imply for managing salespeople. See also David W. Cravens, Thomas N. Ingram, Raymond W. LaForge, and Clifford E. Young, "Behavior-Based and Outcome-Based Salesforce Control Systems," *Journal of Marketing* 57 (October 1993), pp. 47–59.

6. Because of their finite stock, some people hold that standards for acceptable sales calls should be established, and each call should be measured against these standards. See, for example, Stewart Washburn, "Measuring Sales Effectiveness and Productivity," in *Sales Manager's Handbook,* ed. Edwin E. Bobrow and Larry Wizenberg (Homewood, IL: Dow Jones–Irwin, 1983), pp. 233–63; Henry P. Polly, "Sales Call Reports—A Necessary Tool for Marketing?" *Secured Lender* 45 (May–June 1989), pp. 22–24. Weitz, Castleberry, and Tanner discuss the value of sales calls on pp. 473–74, noting that a salesperson has to earn $434 per hour of face-to-face selling time in order to earn $40,000 per year.

7. Dan H. Robertson, "Sales Force Feedback on Competitive Activities," *Journal of Marketing* 38 (April 1974), pp. 69–72. See also Douglas M. Lambert, Howard Marmorstein, and Arun Sharma, "Industrial Salespeople as a Source of Market Information," *Industrial Marketing Management* 19 (May 1990), pp. 141–48; and Lawrence B. Chonko, John F. Tanner, Jr., and Ellen Reid Smith, "The Sales Force's Role in International Marketing Research and Marketing Information Systems," *Journal of Personal Selling and Sales Management* XI, no. 1 (Winter 1991), pp. 69–79.

8. For general tips on working with ratios, see Charles A. Krueger, "How to Work with Ratios," *1986–87 Personal Planning Guide for Management Development* (Madison, WI: Management Institute, University of Wisconsin, 1986). For discussion of the use of ratios to analyze salesperson peformance specifically, see Dick Berry, "A Method to Portray and Analyze Sales Performance," *Industrial Marketing Management* 16 (May 1987), pp. 131–44; Alan Test, "Selling Is Still a Numbers Game," *American Salesmen* 38 (June 1993), pp. 10–14; and Pete Frye, *The Complete Selling System* (Dover, NH: Upstart Publishing Co., 1992).

9. W.E. Patton III and Ronald H. King, "The Use of Human Judgment Models in Evaluating Sales Force Performance," *Journal of Personal Selling and Sales Management* 5 (May 1985), pp. 1–14; David Jobber, Graham J. Hooley, and David Shipley, "Organizational Size and Salesforce Evaluation Practices," *Journal of Personal Selling and Sales Management* 13 (Spring 1993), pp. 37–48.

10. Benton Cocanougher and John M. Ivancevich, " 'BARS' Performance Rating for Sales Force Personnel," *Journal of Marketing* 42 (July 1978), pp. 87–95; Mark R. Edwards, W. Theodore Cummings, and John L. Schlacter, "The Paris–Peoria Solution: Innovations in Appraising Regional and International Sales Personnel," *Journal of Personal Selling and Sales Management* 4 (November 1984), pp. 26–38.

11. For examples of the many studies that have attempted to assess the relationship between personality factors and salespeople's performance, see Lyndon E. Dawson, Jr., Barlow Soper, and

Charles E. Pettijohn, "The Effects of Empathy on Salesperson Effectiveness," *Psychology and Marketing* 9 (July–August 1992), pp. 297–310. For a summary of the results of these kinds of studies, see Neil M. Ford, Orville C. Walker, Jr., Gilbert A. Churchill, Jr., and Steven W. Hartley, "Selecting Successful Salespeople: A Meta-Analysis of Biographical and Psychological Selection Criteria," in *Annual Review of Marketing,* ed. Michael J. Houston (Chicago: American Marketing Association, 1987), pp. 90–131.

12. William D. Perreault, Jr., and Frederick A. Russell, "Comparing Multiattribute Evaluation Process Models," *Behavioral Science* 22 (November 1977), pp. 423–31. See also William A. Weeks, Lawrence B. Chonko, and Lynn R. Kahle, "Performance Congruence and Value Congruence Impact on Sales Force Annual Sales," *Journal of the Academy of Marketing Science* 17 (Fall 1989), pp. 345–51; Scott B. MacKenzie, Philip M. Podsakoff, and Richard Fetter, "The Impact of Organizational Citizenship Behavior on Evaluations of Salesperson Performance," *Journal of Marketing* 57 (January 1993), pp. 70–80. See also Cravens, Ingram, LaForge, and Young, "Behavior–Based."

13. Cocanougher and Ivancevich, " 'BARS' Performance Rating," p. 89. For some suggestions on how ratings of employees can be made more comparable, see Mark R. Edwards, Michael Wolfe, and J. Ruth Sproull, "Improving Comparability in Performance Appraisal," *Business Horizons* 26 (September–October 1983), pp. 75–83; Jan P. Muczyk and Myron Gable, "Managing Sales Performance through a Comprehensive Performance Appraisal System," *Journal of Personal Selling and Sales Management* 7 (May 1987), pp. 41–52.

14. *Measuring Salesmen's Performance,* Business Policy Study No. 114 (New York: National Industrial Conference Board), 1965, p. 8. Despite such admonitions, there is evidence that there is an attribution bias in sales managers' ratings of salespeople. For example, sales managers sometimes consider and sometimes do not consider contextual factors like territory differences when evaluating salespeople's performance. See John C. Mowen, Janet E. Keith, Stephen W. Brown, and Donald W. Jackson, Jr., "Utilizing Effort and Task Difficulty Information in Evaluating Salespeople," *Journal of Marketing Research* 22 (May 1985), pp. 185–91; Greg W. Marshall, John C. Mowen, and Keith J. Fabes, "The Impact of Territory Difficulty and Self versus Other Ratings on Managerial Evaluations of Sales Personnel," *Journal of Personal Selling and Sales Management* 12 (Fall 1992), pp. 35–47.

15. John Franco, "Managing Sales Success," *Business Marketing* 69 (December 1984), pp. 48–57. Neil Rackham reports results from such a study in his book *SPIN Selling* (New York: McGraw–Hill, 1988). Look also at Brian Tracy, "Stop Talking . . . and Start Asking Questions," *Sales & Marketing Management* (February 1995), pp 79–87.

16. Cocanougher and Ivancevich, " 'BARS' Performance Rating," pp. 90–99. For a detailed example illustrating the process, see Robert P. Bush, Alan J. Bush, David J. Ortinau, and Joseph F. Hair, Jr., "Developing a Behavior–Based Scale to Assess Retail Salesperson Performance," *Journal of Retailing* 66 (Spring 1990), pp. 119–36.

17. For sales-related application of the critical incident techique, see Mary Jo Bitner, Bernard H. Booms, and Mary Stanfield Tetreault, "The Service Encounter: Diagnosing Favorable and Unfavorable Incidents," *Journal of Marketing* 54 (January 1990), pp. 71–84.

18. For discussion of some of the limitations of BARS that have restricted its use, see Roger J. Placky, "Appraisal Scales That Measure Performance Outcomes and Job Results," *Personnel* 60 (May–June 1983), pp. 57–65.

Case Index

Name Index

Subject Index

NOTES

~

~

~